Contemporary Intellectual Property

The University of Law
133 Great Hampton Street
Birmingham B18 6AQ
Telephone: 01483 216041
Email: library-birmingham@law.ac.uk

This book must be returned on or before the last date recorded below.

Contemporary Intellectual Property

Law and Policy

Fifth edition

Abbe Brown

Smita Kheria

Jane Cornwell

Marta Iljadica

OXFORD
UNIVERSITY PRESS

OXFORD
UNIVERSITY PRESS

Great Clarendon Street, Oxford, OX2 6DP,
United Kingdom

Oxford University Press is a department of the University of Oxford.
It furthers the University's objective of excellence in research, scholarship,
and education by publishing worldwide. Oxford is a registered trade mark of
Oxford University Press in the UK and in certain other countries

Second Edition 2010
Third Edition 2013
Fourth Edition 2016

Impression: 1

Published in the United States of America by Oxford University Press
198 Madison Avenue, New York, NY 10016, United States of America

British Library Cataloguing in Publication Data
Data available

Library of Congress Control Number: 2019939544

ISBN 978–0–19–879980–1

Printed in Great Britain by
Bell & Bain Ltd., Glasgow

Acknowledgement

We are delighted to acknowledge the invaluable contributions made by Professor Charlotte Waelde, Professor Graeme Laurie, and Professor Hector MacQueen to this textbook over previous editions.

Towards a diverse and equal community: in intellectual property and in general

Preface

Starting this preface in a darkening afternoon as the winter break looms, it seems no time since we last wrote a preface for *Contemporary Intellectual Property*. Since then, the world has continued to turn and bring opportunities and challenges, including for intellectual property. New technologies are developing, societal attitudes evolve (to an extent) and the tensions between power and sharing continue. Further, as this book is finalised, uncertainty exists regarding the prospect of the UK leaving the European Union and the basis on which it may do so.

This fifth edition remains broadly similar in structure to previous editions, although we have moved the 'Intellectual property and international private law' chapter to the online resources, along with other material which we hope readers will find useful. Within the overall structure we have reordered and slightly reorganised the chapters in the copyright, patents, and trade mark sections—not least because some issues which were 'contemporary' and in chapters under that name are now long established (if not entirely resolved).

In the time since the fourth edition, IP law has continued to be a stimulating, enjoyable, and at times frustrating area in which to teach and research. We have updated the text to include developments up to 31 August 2018, and in some cases, we have been able to include developments after that. For example, on copyright, we can now explore in this edition CJEU case law on communication to the public (*Land Nordrhein-Westfalen v Dirk Renckhoff; Stichting Brein v Ziggo; Stichting Brein v Jack Frederik Wullems; GS Media v Sanoma*), developments in relation to the proposed and controversial EU Directive on Copyright in the Digital Single Market, and case law from jurisdictions in the UK regarding the subsistence of copyright in TV formats (*Banner v Endemol*), fair dealing for the purpose of reporting current events (*England and Wales Cricket Board v Tixdaq*), and subsistence of database right (*Technomed v BlueCrest*). On designs, we cover the recent flurry of CJEU decisions in *Nintendo v BigBen*, *Doceram*, and *Acacia*, among other developments. We have updated the trade mark chapters to incorporate all changes to the UK Trade Marks Act 1994 that came into effect up to January 2019, plus the latest versions of the Trade Marks Directive 2015 and EU Trade Mark Regulation 2017, bringing together the changes to trade mark law, introduced by the EU's 2015 trade mark reform package, which were mentioned as forthcoming in the fourth edition. There is a shorter list but an important one in respect of patents: the decisions of the UK Supreme Court in *Eli Lilly v Actavis* regarding patent interpretation and construction and in *Warner Lambert v Generics* regarding medical use claims and plausibility, and the rocky progress of the Unified Patent. And for remedies, key new issues are the latest case law from the CJEU on the IP Enforcement Directive and the UK Supreme Court on blocking injunctions in *Cartier v BSkyB*. Key developments since 31 August 2018 which we have not addressed, but which we should introduce here, are the decision of the Supreme Court in obviousness in *Actavis v ICOS*, the EU Directive on Copyright in the Digital Single Market (entering into force 7 June 2019 with member states having two years to implement it in national law) and the decision of the Outer House of the Court of Session in *BC v Chief Constable Police Service of Scotland* finding that there is a right of privacy in Scots common law.

Once again, we must offer thanks to the team at Oxford University Press, in particular to Carol Barbersmith, Guy Jackson, Fiona Barry, Hayley Buckley, and Emily Cunningham, and to our research assistant Lynne Chave.

In this edition, we said farewell, with friendship and respect, to Professor Charlotte Waelde as she continues her exciting research on dance at Coventry University. We are delighted to welcome Marta Iljadica of the University of Glasgow as an author, and are pleased that as a team we now cross three leading Scottish universities.

By chance, this book again has an all-female team. We have had interesting discussions about the extent to which, if any, we have experienced gender issues in our careers in IP and in IP in the academy. More widely, evidence suggests that challenges relating to gender, race, and disability continue in IP, in the academy, and in wider society. We are pleased, therefore, to make a contribution to addressing this. In our dedication, we encourage all with an interest in IP, whatever their background and characteristics, to see that IP is and should be a welcoming and challenging place. Join us.

Abbe Brown
Smita Kheria
Jane Cornwell
Marta Iljadica
December 2018

New to this edition

- Engagement with Brexit in the introduction and throughout relevant chapters
- Coverage of important recent CJEU case law on communication to the public (*Land Nordrhein-Westfalen v Dirk Renckhoff; Stichting Brein v Ziggo; Stichting Brein v Jack Frederik Wullems; GS Media v Sanoma*), and developments in relation to the EU Directive on Copyright in the Digital Single Market
- Discussion of recent UK case law on subsistence of copyright in TV formats (*Banner v Endemol*), fair dealing for the purpose of reporting current events (*England and Wales Cricket Board v Tixdaq*), and subsistence of database right (*Technomed v BlueCrest*)
- Coverage of recent CJEU design case law on technical functionality (Doceram), defences (*Nintendo v BigBen*), and spare parts (*Acacia v Audi and Porsche*)
- Fully updated to incorporate all changes to the UK Trade Marks Act 1994, plus the latest versions of the Trade Marks Directive 2015 and EU Trade Mark Regulation 2017, bringing together the changes to trade mark law introduced by the EU's 2015 trade mark reform package
- Discussion of EU Trade Secrets Directive and accompanying developments
- Coverage of new Supreme Court decisions on patent interpretation and construction (*Eli Lilly v Actavis*) and medical use claims and plausibility (*Warner Lambert v Generics*)
- The latest updates on remedies, including recent case law from the CJEU on the IP Enforcement Directive, and the UK Supreme Court on blocking injunctions in *Cartier v BSkyB*
- The chapters on copyright, trade marks, and patents have been restructured

Table of contents

Detailed table of contents

Walk-through guide to the educational features of this book

This book is full of features that are designed to help students engage with the subject matter, to acquire and refine critical and reflective skills, and to remain up to date with the fast-paced developments that typify intellectual property law. This guide is a step-by-step walk through these features and you should pay close attention to ensure that you get the most out of the book.

Parts

The book is divided into parts, each of which deals with a discrete area of intellectual property law. The beginning of each part contains an overview of what will be covered and an account of the key sources of law. Internet links to the actual text of these instruments are also provided.

Part II

Copyright

Introduction

This Part of the book explains and discusses the law of copyright. It has six chapters. The first considers the scope of copyright in the UK against the background of international and EU law on the subject, and its historical

Learning objectives

Each chapter gives an account of the learning objectives that you should be able to meet once you have worked through the chapter. For example, the first learning objective in Chapter 2 states: 'By the end of this chapter you should be able to describe and explain the development of copyright, and its rationale.' If you cannot meet the objectives, then you need to work through the chapter again!

and entertainment to their users. As such, the chapter outlines the technological dev have brought copyright reform to the forefront in recent times and looks at difficultie environment presents for copyright, the rules of which were mostly created in a world came to users in the form of single copies or performances put on the market by intermed or another, such as publishers, broadcasters, and film and sound recording producers. policy context in general will assist in understanding how specific aspects of the copyright developed and the challenges posed in adapting the framework.

Learning objectives

By the end of this chapter you should be able to describe and explain:

- the development of copyright, and its rationale;
- the policy and reform context for copyright law;
- the significance of the digital environment, and other related concerns for copyright

The rest of the chapter looks like this:

- Early history (2.4–2.7)

Key points

Every chapter uses key points to highlight essential features of the chapter or area of law that you need to know. These help to focus your study and serve as valuable milestones as you move through the different parts of the book.

Key points on modern developments

- Copyright internationalised from the late 19th century onwards—today there is bo and a European dimension to law-making, meaning that scope for purely national limited. An appreciation of the European developments as well as the internationa therefore vital to fully understand the present law in the UK.
- Copyright extended further, to photographs, films, sound recordings, broadcasts, a technology (software and databases).
- There is a division apparent in most legal systems between the copyright treatment works' (covered by the Berne Convention) and 'neighbouring' or 'media works' (co Rome Convention)—see further para 3.39.

Copyright framework in the UK—European an

Key extracts from cases and materials

Every legal case tells a story, and we have designed the format of the book to ensure that crucial extracts and legal points are clearly communicated to the reader.

■ *Lucasfilm Ltd v Ainsworth* [2008] EWHC 1878 (Ch); [2009] FSR 2

For the facts of this case (the 'Star Wars' case), see also paras 3.62 and 3.71. It illustrates v between classic and inverse passing off. L. relied on the goodwill and reputation gen asserting that this extended to the business of licensing toys, models, and other goods re the film, including the fictional characters in the film and their costumes. L's claim in pu primarily from publicity on A's website, which stressed the authenticity of his products (

Andrew Ainsworth and Shepperton Design Studios created the original helmets and arm sci-fi fantasy film of all time. Now, almost 30 years on and for the FIRST time ever, YOU can collectible replica of the original movie helmets. **Made by the original prop-maker from the o** emboldening is in the original.] Produced and endorsed by Andrew Ainsworth at Shepper these unique props offer collectors a rare opportunity of owning some of the most iconic cinema. These unique collectibles are the ONLY helmets ever produced from the original m the screen-used helmets . . . .

L. argued that this would mislead members of the public into thinking that it had lice approved the manufacture and sale of the helmets and armour. Furthermore, it was clai of the public would be misled into thinking that A was the creator or designer of the armour. Finally, L. alleged that A's claims amounted to inverse passing off because he

Important websites

We highlight systematically important web pages where you can check out the most up-to-date developments in your chosen area of study. Website addresses themselves will be updated in the book's online resources at **www.oup.com/uk/brown5e**.

Questions

We ask questions throughout each chapter to help you assess your developing knowledge. These will usually be factual questions or 'reminder' questions and the answer can normally be found within the text itself.

Discussion points

These points are designed to encourage you to think more widely about particular ideas and legal issues raised in a chapter. Guidance on answering discussion points will appear in the online resources at **www.oup.com/uk/brown5e**.

Exercises

Exercises can be used to help you with coursework and assignments that require you to undertake further research and read more widely about particular topics.

Brexit

Throughout the book we consider the possible impact of the UK's withdrawal from the European Union on different areas of intellectual property law.

Further reading

Every chapter ends with suggestions for additional reading which are specially selected to highlight key areas of the chapter and to help you to take your learning further.

Guide to the online resources

www.oup.com/uk/brown5e

This book is accompanied by online resources, which are designed to enhance your learning experience and which include the following features:

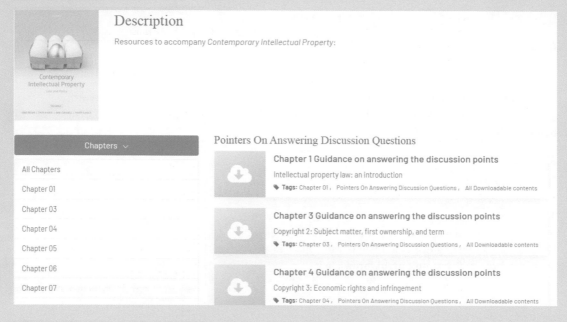

Guidance

Guidance on addressing each of the discussion points in the book will be provided in the online resources to aid your understanding of the subject matter and help to refine your analytical skills.

Bonus material

Two short chapters from the author team provide historical context to the areas of registered and unregistered design protection in the UK, while a third chapter explores the topic of intellectual property and international private law.

Updates

These document recent developments, changes in law and policy, and other information relevant to your study of intellectual property law.

Further reading and web links

Recently published sources for further reading will be added to the online resources to help you in your research. New and updated web links will be provided, together with links to images which can help your understanding of the law.

Table of cases

Table of statutory instruments

Table of EU legislation
Treaties and conventions

Regulations

List of figures

Abbreviations

General

ACTA	Anti Counterfeiting Trade Agreement
ADNDRC	Asian Domain Name Dispute Resolution
aff'd	affirmed
ALCS	Authors' Licensing and Collecting Society
APIG	All Party Parliamentary Internet Group
APPSI	Advisory Panel on Public Sector Information
BAILII	British and Irish Legal Information Institute
BECS	British Equity Collecting Society
CAD	computer-aided design
CBD	Convention on Biological Diversity
CC	Creative Commons
ccTLD	Country code Top Level Domain
CCTV	closed circuit television
CD	compact disc
CDPA 1988	Copyright, Designs and Patents Act 1988
CDR	Community Design Regulation
CEWG	Consultative Expert Working Group on Research and Development
CFI	Court of First Instance (now General Court of the CJEU)
CHI	cultural heritage institution
CIPIH	Commission on Intellectual Property Rights, Innovation and Public Health
CISAC	International Confederation of Societies of Authors and Composers
CJ	Court of Justice (higher tier of the CJEU)
CJEU	Court of Justice of the European Union
CLA	Copyright Licensing Authority
CLIP	(European Max Planck Group on) Conflict of Laws in Intellectual Property
Cm	Command Number
CPC	Community Patent Convention
CSS	Content scramble system
CT	Copyright Tribunal
CTM	Community Trade Mark
CTMR	Community Trade Mark Regulation
DACS	Design and Artists Copyright Society
DD EU	Directive on Legal Protection of Designs
DO	Designation of Origin
DRM	Digital rights management
DSB	Dispute Settlement Body (WTO)
DSM	Digital Single Market
DSU	Dispute Settlement Understanding (WTO)
DVD	digital versatile disk
EBA	Enlarged Board of Appeal (EPO)
EC	European Community

ECHR	European Convention on Human Rights
ECJ	European Court of Justice (now Court of Justice of the European Union)
ECtHR	European Court of Human Rights
EEA	European Economic Area
EEC	European Economic Community
EFTA	European Free Trade Association
EGE	European Group on Ethics in Science and New Technologies
EPC	European Patent Convention
EPO	European Patent Office
EPO	erythropoietin
eRes	eResolution
ESTs	Expressed Sequence Tags
EUIPO	European Union Intellectual Property Office
EUTMR	EU Trade Mark Regulation 2017
EUWA	UK European Union (Withdrawal) Act 2018
FACT	Federation Against Copyright Theft
FAST	Federation Against Software Theft
FRAND	fair, reasonable, and non-discriminatory
GATT	General Agreement on Tariffs and Trade
GC	General Court (lower tier of the CJEU)
GI	geographical indication
gTLD	generic Top Level Domain
GUI	Graphical user interface
HCA	High Court of Australia
HMRC	Her Majesty's Commissioners of Revenue and Customs
HRA 1998	Human Rights Act 1998
ICANN	Internet Corporation for Assigned Names and Numbers
ICSID	International Centre for Settlement of Investment Disputes
IDN	Internationalised Domain Name
IFPI	International Federation of Phonographic Industry
IGC	Intergovernmental Committee on Intellectual Property and Genetic Resources, Traditional Knowledge and Folklore
IGWG	Intergovernmental Working Group
InfoSoc Directive	Copyright in the Information Society Directive
IP	Intellectual property
IPED	Intellectual Property Enforcement Directive
IPL	International Private Law
IPO	Intellectual Property Office
IPRs	intellectual property rights
ISP	Internet Service Provider
LDCs	Least Developed Countries
MCPS	Mechanical Copyright Protection Society
MMC	Monopoly and Mergers Commission
MPEP	Manual of Patent Examining Procedure
MR	Master of the Rolls
NAF	National Arbitration Forum
NICE	National Institute for Health and Clinical Excellence
NZCA	New Zealand Court of Appeal

OD	Opposition Division (EPO)
OECD	Organisation for Economic Co-operation and Development
OEM	original equipment manufacturer
OFT	Office of Fair Trading
OHIM	Office for Harmonisation in the Internal Market
OPSI	Office of Public Sector Information
OQT	Optional Quality Terms
OUP	Oxford University Press
P2P	peer-to-peer
PACT	Producers Alliance for Cinema and Television
PCC	Patents County Court
PCT	Patent Cooperation Treaty
PDO	Protected Designations of Origin
PGI	Protected Geographical Indication
PPL	Phonographic Performance Limited
PRS	Performing Right Society
PSB	public sector body
R&D	research and development
RDA 1949	Registered Designs Act 1949
rev'd	reversed
RMI	Rights management information system
SABIP	Strategic Advisory Board for Intellectual Property Policy
SC	Supreme Court
SI	Statutory Instrument
SNPs	Single Nucleotide Polymorphisms
SPC	Supplementary Protection Certificate
STM	science, technical, and medical
TFEU	Treaty on the Functioning of the European Union
TLD	top level domain
TLT	Trade Mark Law Treaty
TM	trade mark
TMA 1994	Trade Marks Act 1994
TMD	Trade Mark Directive 2015
TNA	The National Archives
TPM	technical protection measure
TRIPS (Agreement on)	Trade-Related Aspects of Intellectual Property Rights
TSG	Traditional Specialty Guaranteed
TTBE	Technology Transfer Block Exemption
TTBER	Technology Transfer Block Exemption Regulation
UCITA	Uniform Computer Information Transaction Act (USA)
UDR	Unregistered Design Right
UDRP (ICANN)	Uniform Domain Name Dispute Resolution Policy
UIP	Utilization Implementation Project
UK IPO	United Kingdom Intellectual Property Office
UPCA	Unified Patent Court Agreement
UPOV	International Union for the Protection of New Varieties of Plants
USC	United States Code
USPTO	US Patent and Trademark Office

VAT	value-added tax
VBER	Vertical Agreement Block Exemption Regulation
V-C	Vice-Chancellor
WCT	WIPO Copyright Treaty 1996
WHO	World Health Organization
WIPO	World Intellectual Property Organization
WPPT	WIPO Performances and Phonograms Treaty 1996
WTO	World Trade Organization

Law reports, journals etc

AC	Law Reports, Third Series, Appeal Cases
AIPLA QJ	American Intellectual Property Law Association Quarterly Journal
All ER	All England Law Reports
ALR	Adelaide Law Review
ALR	Aden Law Reports
ALR	Argus Law Reports (Aust)
ALR	Australian Law Reports
App Cas	Appeal Cases
BCLC	Butterworths Company Law Cases
Beav	Beavan
BPIR	Bankruptcy and Personal Insolvency Reports
Bro PC	Brown's Chancery Reports
Bus LR	Business Law Review
Ch	Law Reports, Third Series, Chancery Division
Ch D	Law Reports, Second Series, Chancery Division
CIPAJ	Chartered Institute of Patent Agents Journal
CLJ	Cambridge Law Journal
CLR	Canada Law Reports
CLR	Common Law Reports
CLR	Commonwealth Law Reports (Aust)
CLSR	Computer Law and Security Report
CML Rev	Common Market Law Review
CMLR	Common Market Law Reports
COM	European Commission Document
CP Rep	Civil Procedure Reports
CPR	Canadian Patent Reporter
Cr App Rep	Criminal Appeal Reports
Crim LR	Criminal Law Review
CSIH	Court of Session (Inner House)
CSOH	Court of Session (Outer House)
CTLR	Computer and Telecommunications Law Review
D	Session Cases, 2nd Series [Dunlop] (Sc)
De G & Sm	De Gex and Smale's Chancery Reports
EBL Rev	European Business Law Review
ECC	European Commercial Cases
ECDR	European Copyright and Design Reports
ECL&P	E-Commerce Law & Policy
ECLR	European Competition Law Review

ECR	European Court Reports
EHRLR	European Human Rights Law Review
EHRR	European Human Rights Reports
EIPR	European Intellectual Property Review
EL Rev	European Law Review
EMLR	Entertainment and Media Law Reports
EntLR	Entertainment Law Review
EPOR	European Patent Office Reports
ER	English Reports
ETMR	European Trade Mark Reports
EWCA	Crim Media neutral citation from the Court of Appeal (Criminal Division)
EWHC	Media neutral citation from the High Court
EWPCC	Media neutral citation from the Patent County Court Ex Exchequer Reports
Ex CR	Exchequer Court Reports
F	Session Cases, 5th Series [Fraser] (Sc)
F 2d	Federal Reporter, Second Series (USA)
F 3d	Federal Reporter, Third Series (USA)
F Supp	Federal Supplement (USA)
FC	Federal Court
FCA	Federal Court of Australia
FILJ	Fordham International Law Journal
FSR	Fleet Street Reports
GRUR	Gewerblicher Rechtsschutz und Urheberrecht
GWD	Green's Weekly Digest (Sc)
Harv LR	Harvard Law Review
HC	House of Commons
HL	Law Reports, First Series, English and Irish Appeals
HL	House of Lords
HMSO	Her Majesty's Stationery Office
HR	House of Representatives (USA)
IIC	International Review of Industrial Property and Copyright Law
IJL & IT	International Journal of Law and Information Technology
ILR	International Law Reports
Int TLR	International Trade Law and Regulation
IPQ	Intellectual Property Quarterly
IPR	Intellectual Property Reports
JBL	Journal of Business Law
JCLE	Journal of Competition Law and Economics
JIEL	Journal of International Economic Law
JILT	Journal of Information, Law and Technology
JIPLP	Journal of Intellectual Property Law & Practice
JML	Journal of Media Law
JR	Juridical Review
K & J	Kay & Johnson's Vice Chancellor's Reports
KB	Law Reports, Third Series, King's Bench
LJPC	Law Journal Reports, Privy Council

LMCLQ	Lloyd's Maritime and Commercial Law Quarterly
LQR	Law Quarterly Review
LR (QB)	Law Reports, Queens Bench
LSG	Law Society Gazette
LT	Law Times Reports
M	Session Cases, 3rd Series [Macpherson] (Sc)
Mac & G	Macnaghten and Gordon's Chancery Reports
MCC	Macgillivray's Copyright Cases
Med LR	Medical Law Reports
MLR	Modern Law Review
Mor	Morison's Dictionary of Decisions of the Court of Session
NZLR	New Zealand Law Reports
OJ	Official Journal of the European Communities
OJEPO	Official Journal of the European Patent Office
OJLS	Oxford Journal of Legal Studies
PC	Privy Council
PD	Law Reports, Second Series, Probate Division
QB	Queen's Bench
QBD	Law Reports, Second Series, Queen's Bench Division
R	Session Cases, 4th Series [Rettie] (Sc)
RPC	Reports of Patent Design and Trade Mark Cases
S	Senate
S	Session Cases [Shaw] (Sc)
S Ct	Supreme Court Reporter (USA)
SALR	South African Law Reports
SC	Session Cases (Sc)
SCLR	Scottish Civil Law Reports
SCR	Supreme Court Reports, Canada
SEC	(European) Commission Staff Working Document
SGCA	Singapore Court of Appeal
SLT	Scots Law Times
TLR	Times Law Reports
TMR	Trade Mark Reports
TW	Trademark World
UKHL	Media neutral citation from the House of Lords
US	United States Supreme Court Reports
USPQ	United States Patent Quarterly
VR	Victorian Reports (Aust)
WIPR	World Intellectual Property Reports
WL	Westlaw
WLR	Weekly Law Reports
WN	Weekly Notes

Part I

Introduction

Intellectual property law: an introduction

Introduction

Scope and overview of chapter

1.1 This chapter is an introduction to the discipline of intellectual property (IP) law. You will examine the nature of IP as well as the aims and content of IP law. A brief overview will be given of the main rights and actions which make up IP law, together with an analysis of the various themes which underpin this area of law. The importance of the European and international dimensions to IP law will be emphasised, although throughout the starting point for discussion will be the jurisdictions of the United Kingdom (UK). Here we lay the groundwork for the rest of this book, and you should use this chapter as a platform for further in-depth study.

1.2
> **Learning objectives**
>
> By the end of this chapter you should be able to:
>
> - define IP and the broad church that is IP law;
>
> - articulate the aims and objectives of IP law and place it in its wider commercial setting;
>
> - give a brief account of the range and type of intellectual property rights (IPRs) which exist;
>
> - appreciate the relationships between different levels of IP law—that is, (a) national, (b) European, and (c) international; and
>
> - understand the various influences on the formation, justifications for, and development of IP law, as well as the tensions that arise when the law seeks to protect IP.

1.3 The rest of the chapter looks like this:

- What is intellectual property law? (1.4–1.16)
- What is intellectual property? (1.17–1.44)
- Developing intellectual property law (1.45–1.74)

> **Exercise**
>
> Before reading this chapter, ask yourself, 'What is 'intellectual property?' Do you think that it should receive legal protection? What form should that legal protection take? Try to justify your responses and then compare your views with what we say later.

What is intellectual property law?

1.4   This is a book about the law that protects IP. Let us begin, then, with a very brief overview of the various elements of this area of law, which at first will seem disconnected. We will then go on to explore the themes that tie these elements together, and to consider the influences that shape and form modern IP law.

1.5   IP law comprises a wide range of forms of protection for IP. It encompasses statutory and common law arrangements and has aspects which are shaped by international, European, and national considerations. Under the umbrella of IP, a significant number of IPRs exist; each is tailored to protect a particular example of IP.

The statutory rights

1.6   There are four principal forms of IP, and in the UK, these are protected by statute. They are as follows.

Patents: Patents Act 1977

1.7   Patent law protects *inventions*, which can be described as technical solutions to technical problems. An invention can be a product or a process. An invention is the paradigmatic example of 'industrial property'—a concept which we will explore in detail later. The Intellectual Property Office (UK IPO) in Newport, Gwent is responsible for the grant of patents in the UK.[1] The European Patent Office in Munich (which is distinct from the European Union (EU)), is responsible for the grant of 'European' patents.[2] There is no such thing as a world patent.[3] Patents require to be registered.

Copyright: Copyright, Designs and Patents Act 1988

1.8   Copyright law is designed to protect aesthetic and artistic creations such as literary, musical, dramatic, and artistic works, known as *original works*, together with *derivative works* such as films, sound recordings, cable programmes, broadcasts, and the typographical arrangement of a published work (ie the way the material is laid out). Copyright was expanded considerably throughout the course of the twentieth century to protect new and emerging forms of IP such as computer software and databases. Copyright protection arises on the creation of a protectable work. There is no need to register the right (cf patents).

Designs: Registered Designs Act 1949 and Copyright, Designs and Patents Act 1988

1.9   Design law protects the way a product or article 'looks'. In the UK, designs can either be protected by registration or automatically, through unregistered design protection, on the creation of a design document or an article embodying the design. The two forms of protection are not mutually exclusive. There is potential for overlap between copyright protection for artistic works and design protection, and in the UK this is a complex interaction. The UK Intellectual Property Office (IPO) is responsible for the grant of UK registered designs and for maintaining the Design Register. Unregistered and registered Community design rights have also been available since 2002 and 2003 respectively, governed by Regulation 6/2002/EC on Community designs. Oversight of this system and the registration process is handled by the Office for Harmonisation in the Internal Market (OHIM), now the European Union Intellectual Property Office (EUIPO) in Alicante, Spain.[4]

Trade marks: Trade Marks Act 1994

1.10   Trade marks operate to distinguish the goods and services of one enterprise from those of another. They exist as badges of origin and help the consumer to avoid confusion between goods or services of variable

---

[1] www.ipo.gov.uk/pro-home.htm.
[2] www.european-patent-office.org.
[3] Other important patent offices are the US Patent and Trademark Office at www.uspto.gov and the Japanese Patent Office at www.jpo.go.jp.
[4] http://oami.europa.eu/ows/rw/pages/index.en.do.

quality. Trade marks can assist greatly in bolstering protection for goods already protected by another form of IP law. For example, patent-protected drugs will invariably carry their own trade mark: for instance, 'Viagra' is the trade mark for the drug sildenafil citrate, the patent on which expired in 2013. The advantage of trade marks on patented products is that the trade mark can continue long after the patent has expired. Trade mark protection is awarded by registration. In the UK, this is handled by the Trade Mark Registry, once again, at the UK IPO in Newport. An EU trade mark (formerly Community trade mark) is also available, awarded by the what is now the EUIPO, formerly known as OHIM.

Common law actions

1.11   Beyond these statutory rights a number of common law actions are also considered to make up the body of IP law in the UK. We examine these in full depth in Chapters 16, 17, and 18. For now, it is only important that you understand the ambit of the two main actions.

Passing off

1.12   Passing off protects the 'goodwill' of traders in respect of their product 'get-up', name, or trading style. The action becomes relevant when traders copy a rival's 'get-up' and when this leads to, or is likely to lead to, public confusion between the competing products. There is much scope for overlap between trade mark protection and passing off. Often both actions are brought in the same dispute.

Breach of confidence

1.13   The common law action of breach of confidence is often included in the definition of IP law.[5] The action can provide ancillary support in the protection of the interests of IP producers, especially when information about IP that is going to eventually be registered must be kept out of the public domain prior to registration, for example patents and registered designs. Registrable IPRs do require full public disclosure in the course of the application process. By its protection of trade secrets, breach of confidence provides an alternative means of protecting valuable knowledge if a decision is made (to try to) keep it permanently outside the public domain. In 2016 the EU passed a Directive on trade secrets.[6] It will be interesting to see how this develops and what changes, if any, will need to be made to the position in the UK jurisdictions, which is considered in Chapter 17.

Sui generis rights

1.14   Over the past few decades, a series of new IPRs have been introduced. This has usually been because of the success of arguments that existing forms of protection are inadequate to accommodate emerging technologies, and/or because political agendas have desired a novel and unique form of protection. Some key examples include the following, and some of these are considered in more detail later in this book:

Plant breeders' rights: Plant Varieties Act 1997

1.15   New varieties of plants and seeds can be protected by a right of protection under UK legislation which complies with a European Community Regulation from 1994.[7] Moreover, protection of the rights in

---

[5]   The meaning of 'intellectual property' was considered by the Supreme Court (*Phillips v News Group Newspapers* [2012] UKSC 28) in the context of a legislative privilege against self-incrimination (section 72 Senior Courts Act 1981). The Supreme Court held that, for these purposes only, all technical or commercial information which is confidential would be treated as intellectual property.

[6]   Directive 2016/943 on the protection of undisclosed know how and business information against their unlawful acquisition, use and disclosure.

[7]   Council Regulation (EC) No. 2100/94 of 27 July 1994 on Community plant variety rights (as amended).

question is required by the International Union for the Protection of New Varieties of Plants (UPOV) Convention of 1961, as amended in 1991.[8]

Database rights: Copyright and Rights in Databases Regulations 1997 (SI 1997/3032), now incorporated into Copyright, Designs, Patents Act 1988

1.16 Compilations of data can receive protection in Europe as a *database* in two separate ways. First, if the structure of the compilation is original, then the structure is protected by copyright. If it is not original, then the underlying material can be protected through a 'database right' if sufficient investment has been made in its compilation. 'Investment' is broadly defined and includes investment of both time and money. The database right entitles the 'maker' of the database to prevent another from extracting the whole or a significant part of the database without permission. This is a *sui generis* form of protection which is not required under international obligations. It will therefore only be accorded to foreign nationals whose country accords similar degrees of protection. Copyright protection in the contents of the database is not precluded by the existence of the new right. Database rights are considered in more detail in Chapter 7.

Question

What could possibly unite the disparate areas of protection which have been considered so far? Can you see any common themes that might link them together?

What is intellectual property?

1.17 In this section we will attempt to make sense of this seemingly disparate collection of legal rights. Let us begin by asking, 'What really is "intellectual property"'?

1.18 IP is frequently referred to as 'the novel products of human intellectual endeavour'. Yet, the use of the term 'property' to describe intellectual products implies the existence of rights and, perhaps more importantly, remedies in respect of the property and any unwarranted interference with it. A property paradigm, in turn, implies a system of control to be exercised by the right holder over the subject matter of their property right. What makes a book *your* book in legal terms is the fact that no one can take, use, or otherwise interfere with your property without your permission. At this level, IP protection operates in a similar fashion to that afforded to other forms of property. IP is concerned with identifying and controlling permissible and impermissible dealings with intellectual products, usually by reference to the consent of the right holder, at least in the first instance. However, in many other respects an analogy with tangible property rights—that is, property rights over physical entities—does not help us to understand what we mean by *intellectual* property. For example, your book will not stop being your book at midnight tonight, yet in most cases IPRs eventually expire, leaving the subject matter without an owner and so free to be used or exploited by anyone. Similarly, no one can require you to lend your book to others so that they might benefit from it, whereas with certain forms of IP compulsory licences can be granted to third parties to exploit the property in question. Finally, for all forms of IP to exist, stringent criteria must be met, with these varying with the kind of IP protection that is sought. This is not true of other forms of property, which assume the quality of *property* by sheer dint of their existence.

1.19 In order to understand how and why IP is treated in this way we must first appreciate that at the broadest level of abstraction IP is concerned with protection of information. Eminen's songs, Margaret Atwood's latest poem, the website that supports this textbook, Louis Vuitton's designer labels, OUP's electronic

---

[8] UPOV Convention for the Protection of New Varieties of Plants 1961, 1991.

databases of authors, the chemical formulae for new cancer drugs, and the shape of Volvic's newest mineral water bottle, are all protectable as IP; but equally they are all simply classes of information. Thus, unlike many forms of property, IPRs protect intangibles. This gives rise to considerable problems over the control of the property and its protection. If I borrow your book you are automatically precluded from using it, but if I copy your process for refining sugar this in no way precludes you from using the process for your own ends, or indeed, from passing it to others. This makes protection and exploitation potentially problematic. It is largely for this reason that rights and remedies are not available for intellectual products in the abstract. Protectable IP does not exist, therefore, in unspecific and ill-defined ideas alone. Such ideas must be reduced to some tangible embodiment before rights and remedies will accrue.[9]

1.20   But this does not explain why IPRs expire, nor why the scope of these rights can be limited in certain circumstances. To understand these features of IP protection we must ask:

 Question

Which interests are furthered, or compromised, by the protection of IP? Revisit your thoughts after you have considered the rest of this chapter.

A wide range of arguments can be put forward to justify IP. These will now be explored—and as will be seen, they are not necessarily consistent with each other.

Moral interests

1.21   A wise and now long-dead Scottish lawyer once wrote: 'Of all things, the produce of a man's intellectual labour is most peculiarly distinguishable as his own.'[10] This neatly sums up the moral argument as to why IP is protected. Intellectual products are produced by the efforts of people who have contributed from within themselves to the creation of the new entity, and so it is thought that IP reflects a moral connection between the property and its creator. Thus, in theory at least, to protect the property is also to protect certain crucial personal interests. Such interests can be compromised, for example when control is relinquished to a third party and the property is subjected to some form of derogatory treatment. And, while a creator might happily renounce their economic stake in their property, for example by selling it, this does not mean that their moral interests are also abandoned. This sort of reasoning is directly reflected in the law of copyright, as we discuss in Chapters 4 and 6.

1.22   Another common moral reason to protect IP is because it would be unjust for others to benefit from a creator's time, labour, and expenditure if it were possible simply to copy new intellectual products without fear of reprisal. The standard example is the experience of the pharmaceutical company. It is estimated that it costs upwards of $2.5 billion to bring a new drug to market.[11] Most of this is spent in research and development and in gaining regulatory approval for the drug's safety and efficacy. However, once a drug is available it is incredibly easy to copy at a tiny fraction of this original cost. Would it be fair if rival companies were allowed to do so? Moreover, in that situation would any company go to the bother and expense of being the first to develop and market a new drug? These arguments focus, of course, on the investors or employers in respect of the innovation, rather than the individual innovator. It can also be argued that IP

---

[9] A possible variation on this occurs with the protection of confidential information, which need not be in written form to be protected but must nevertheless be sufficiently identifiable to merit protection. See Chapter 17.

[10] Bell, *Commentaries*, I, 103.

[11] R Mullin, 'Cost to develop new pharmaceutical drug now exceeds $2.5B' (24 November 2014) www.scientificamerican.com/article/cost-to-develop-new-pharmaceutical-drug-now-exceeds-2-5b.

can lead to inefficient work to avoid existing rights, and can slow down the future innovation of others. Further, it could be said, at least in some sectors (software being a notable example), that there would be innovation without IP, and that even in pharmaceuticals there are other means, such as prizes, which would support innovation without the need for IP. Discussion about this is very much alive, for example in the UK's Industrial Strategy White Paper of 2017.[12] This brings us to the all-important issue of social interests which can be met, and hindered, by IP.

Social interests

1.23 Considerable social benefit can arise from IP. Indeed, it is precisely this argument that is advanced by pharmaceutical companies: 'give us protection for our drugs and we will have an incentive to produce them: deprive us of that protection and the incentive is gone'. This may be true, but it is also important to appreciate that social interests can be significantly compromised if IP is protected too strongly. An inventor might choose to suppress a significant technological development or refuse to license it to third parties, thereby compromising social interests which could benefit from access to the technology. Indeed, these arguments help to explain why limits are placed on IPRs, and we explore them further below.

1.24 In addition, the granting of IPRs over certain novel creations can give rise to social consternation about the morality of certain acts of creation and the legal protection of them. This has been most notable in recent years in the context of the patentability of the outputs of the biotechnology industry. Patents have been granted for the creation of genetically engineered human gene fragments and the development of transgenic animals which contain genetic material from foreign species, including humans. Many voices have been raised in Europe in objection to this as a fundamentally immoral practice. We explore this debate and its outcome in Chapter 11. It should be noted, however, that questions of morality in the granting of IPRs have also impinged on all of the statutory forms of IP,[13] as IPRs are granted at the behest of the state. It is noteworthy that courts have been seen to be unwilling to treat iniquitous information as 'confidential' for the purposes of the common law.[14]

Economic interests

1.25 The economic interests of the producer of IP *and* their competitors *and* their customers will be affected when that property is exploited in the marketplace. The degree to which this occurs depends on the rights and remedies which are accorded to the property in question. It is here that we find one of the most serious areas of tension in IP protection. When IP is introduced into a market (as part of a product or through a licence to another person to make a product), it can have profound effects on the market's overall economic balance and on economic well-being. There is, therefore, considerable room for dispute between the legitimate boundaries of IP protection and the encouragement of a free market economy. This is most acutely felt within the confines of the EU, where the commitment of member states to a single market in which goods can circulate freely between states is threatened by the exercise of IPRs, which, by their nature, potentially erect barriers to such free trade. We discuss this later in further detail, particularly in Chapter 19.

1.26 Considering all of these interests, it should be clear that what is required is a balance that seeks to ensure that no one interest or group of interests dominates, while at the same time ensuring a fair and just degree of protection for any IP that has been produced. It is the overarching role and aim of IP law to achieve such a balance.

---

[12] See HM Government, 'Industrial strategy. Building a Britain fit for the future' (2017) www.gov.uk/government/uploads/system/uploads/attachment_data/file/662508/industrial-strategy-white-paper.pdf.

[13] See, eg, *Re Masterman's Application* [1991] RPC 89 (registered designs); *Re Hack's Application* (1941) 58 RPC 91 (trade marks).

[14] See *Coco v AN Clark (Engineers) Ltd* [1969] RPC 41, and *Attorney General v Guardian Newspapers (No 2)* [1990] 1 AC 109. Note also *Glyn v Weston Feature Films* [1916] 1 Ch 261 (copyright).

Policies and tensions in intellectual property

1.27   Consistent with the range of justifications for IP, the ongoing protection of IP is also driven by a number of important, and at times competing, policies. The outcome of any tussle between these policies ultimately shapes the nature and scope of IPRs and determines the future direction of IP law. Let us consider in more depth the various interests and policies at stake.

The protection of private interests through property rights

1.28   Property rights generally support and promote private interests, paramount among which is the interest of the owner to enjoy their property. Thus, and as noted above, these rights usually include exclusive control of the property and the right to exclude others from unauthorised use. Only in rare circumstances are the private rights of an owner curtailed to further a public interest, for example through the compulsory acquisition of land. The enjoyment of one's property is guaranteed as a matter of individual human right,[15] and it is a fundamental tenet of EU law that national systems of property law should not be influenced by European measures.[16]

Reconciling public and private interests

1.29   The mere existence of IP can, however, significantly influence a number of public interests, as we have seen previously. All forms of IP contribute something new to the sum total of human knowledge, and this can occur across every conceivable realm of human experience; from the development of new pharmaceuticals to treat cancer and AIDS to the design of more comfortable office chairs; from the creation of beautiful (and not so beautiful) works of art, literature, music, or dance to the introduction of distinctive packaging to assist consumers in distinguishing between the ever-burgeoning range of soft drinks on offer; from the splicing of genetic material to create a new strain of rose to the rights over the collections of data and algorithms in respect of them, on which we increasingly rely. All of these innovations can be the subject of IPRs, and their introduction to the public realm can surely only enrich the human condition.

1.30   It should be self-evident, then, that innovations such as these are to be encouraged, and the so-called *reward theory* of IP (see Figure 1.1) seeks to promote this by engendering a cyclical pattern of social interaction whereby those who innovate are rewarded by the grant of property rights, which in turn act as an incentive to others to innovate, who are rewarded in their turn, and so on.

Figure 1.1 The cyclical pattern of intellectual property production and protection

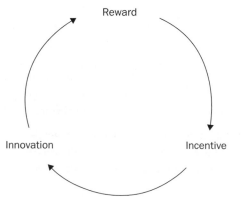

---

[15] European Convention for the Protection of Human Rights and Fundamental Freedoms (1950) Protocol 1, Art 1: 'Every natural person is entitled to the peaceful enjoyment of his possessions. No one shall be deprived of his possessions except in the public interest and subject to the conditions provided for by law and by the general principles of international law.'

[16] Article 345 TFEU states: 'The Treaties shall in no way prejudice the rules in Member States governing the system of property ownership.' See also Art 17 EU Charter.

1.31   This model only serves its purpose, however, if the intellectual products find their way into the public domain, and it is one of the paradoxes of the IP regime that it seeks to promote public interests by granting private rights which imply exclusive control over the subject matter. The public interest can, therefore, be jeopardised if private rights are exercised in a way that means that the property in question is not used or exploited in a public setting.

1.32   A further paradox arises from the particular type of property right that is granted. The IP holder can exclude others from a variety of activities; for example, direct copying of their property by rivals or importation of samples of the property from a country where the price is lower, thereby stopping the importer from undercutting their prices. Not only might various technological, scientific, artistic, or consumer ends be thwarted, but overzealous use of these rights can lead to a distortion in competition, which in turn impacts on wider economic interests, including those of the individual consumer, who might have to pay higher prices to obtain new products, and those of competitors, who must find another way to compete.

1.33   This is not to say that the existence of exclusive rights necessarily leads to these outcomes. Indeed, economists and others argue endlessly about whether exclusive rights hinder or promote competition, in that the rights can also serve as an incentive to others to engage in their own innovation and go on to obtain their own exclusive rights. What can be said with certainty, however, is that some exercise of power can have adverse outcomes. We see this most obviously in the context of Articles 101 and 102 of the Treaty on the Functioning of the European Union (TFEU), which respectively prohibit practices amounting to anti-competitive agreements (cartels) or abuses of a dominant market position, where these are likely to affect trade between member states. Each of these prohibitions has a potential direct bearing on the ways in which IP owners can exercise their rights, and the relationship between IP and competition has been receiving increasing attention from courts, regulators, and academics. We revisit these provisions later, as well as in more detail in Chapter 20.

1.34   In other contexts the matter distils, once again, into a question of striking a balance between the potentially competing public and private interests. It is in this respect that IPRs differ most significantly from traditional property rights. Consider, for example, the following features that are found in the domain of IPRs:

- In some contexts, an IP owner cannot simply refuse to exploit, or prevent others from exploiting, their property once they have received protection for it. The technological developments would not actually be used during the IPR term and further innovation would be stifled under the threat of a law suit for infringement of IPRs. Thus, in the context of patents and UK unregistered design law, compulsory licences can be granted to third parties who apply to the relevant authority[17] if the right holder does not exploit their property within a certain period of time (three years from the date of grant, as in the case of patents),[18] or when the IPR is nearing the end of its term (the last five years of protection in the case of UK unregistered design right).[19] The IPR owners are compensated to the extent that the third parties' entitlements are akin to those that would have been granted under a reasonable licence agreement, with a 'just' licence fee to be paid to the owner of the IP. A variation on this theme is the right of a government department to engage in otherwise infringing acts in relation to a patented invention or a registered design without the consent of the proprietor when they are 'for services of the Crown'.[20] Here too compensation is payable to the IP owner (or an exclusive licensee) for any loss resulting from them not being awarded a contract to supply the products which are the subject of the IPRs.[21]

---

[17]   This is the UK IPO Office in the UK.
[18]   Patents Act 1977, s 48.
[19]   Copyright, Designs and Patents Act 1988, s 237.
[20]   Patents Act 1977, ss 55–58; Registered Designs Act 1949, s 12 and Sch 1.
[21]   Patents Act 1977, s 57A; Registered Designs Act 1949, Sch 1 para 2A.

- In other contexts, an IP owner may not be able to prevent certain uses of their property by others when these uses serve another valuable public interest. For example, copyright is not infringed when a third party engages in 'permitted acts' with respect to the work. These acts include copying done for the purposes of research or private study,[22] dealings with the work for the purposes of criticism, review or news reporting,[23] and things done for the purposes of instruction, examination, or education.[24] A continuous theme across these is that the activity is fair dealing with the work, in that it serves independent and worthwhile interests without unduly compromising the individual (economic) interests of the copyright holder. The question of what is 'fair' is a matter of endless dispute, as we discuss in Chapter 5. Similarly, a trade mark owner cannot prevent the use of its trade mark by a rival who simply engages in comparative advertising—that is, compares its goods or services with those of the trade mark owner—if this is done in an accurate and honest manner.[25] This latter practice is thought to encourage competition by raising consumer awareness about the range and quality of products available on the market. This is discussed in Chapter 15.

- In all cases, as has been noted, for intellectual products to qualify for protection they must satisfy certain predetermined criteria in order to assume the quality of *property*. The stringency of the qualification criteria for each IPR will be seen to be aligned to the strength and length of the exclusive right that might ultimately be granted or obtained.

1.35   The balance which the law strikes between all these competing interests and ideas is endlessly controversial, with the result that proposals for reform, and actual reforms, are continuously occurring. For example, in the UK a review of IP and growth was undertaken by Ian Hargreaves and published in 2011.[26] Many of these conclusions, recommendations, and steps which were subsequently taken, as well as ongoing consultations,[27] will be discussed later in this book. Further, as society evolves, questions can arise regarding the legitimacy of IP (eg, should all information be open to all for no charge, even if there is a relevant IP right?). Questions can also accompany the development of new technologies which might seem to clash with IP—for example, new opportunities raised by the internet, or 3D printing. These issues will also be considered throughout this book.

 Exercise

Compare and contrast the following forms of IP.

1.36   *Patents* protect inventions which must display *novelty*, that is, the invention must never previously have been made available to the public by any means anywhere in the world. This is the strictest requirement of its kind in IP law. It can also be difficult to establish, and this can lead to arguments that some patents involve established knowledge, including that of indigenous groups in developing areas (traditional knowledge). If novelty and the other patentability criteria are met, the reward—the patent—is the strongest type of IP right available. This confers the right for the holder to prevent every unauthorised use of their invention in the marketplace. Thus, rivals cannot make and sell copies of the protected invention, nor import any such copies, nor indeed sell the invention in a kit form without fear of an infringement action.[28] There is no requirement of 'copying'—the patent owner has the power to control any use of the invention, howsoever that arises. Thus, even if Abraham has no idea that Jacob already holds a patent for a vacuum cleaner that

---

[22] Copyright, Designs and Patents Act 1988, s 29.

[23] Copyright, Designs and Patents Act 1988, s 30.

[24] Copyright, Designs and Patents Act 1988, ss 32–36.

[25] Trade Marks Act 1994, s 10(6), although note decision of the Court of Appeal in *O2 Holdings Ltd v Hutchison 3G Ltd* [2006] EWCA Civ 1656; [2006] ETMR 55 regarding this provision.

[26] See www.gov.uk/government/uploads/system/uploads/attachment_data/file/32563/ipreview-finalreport.pdf.

[27] See www.gov.uk/government/publications?departments%5B%5D=intellectual-property-office&publication_filter_option=consultations.

[28] Patents Act 1977, s 60.

employs cyclone technology, and even when there is no suggestion whatsoever of any copying, Abraham can be prevented from entering the public arena with his independently created version of the machine if it effectively embodies the kernel of Jacob's invention.

1.37   *Copyright* protects works that demonstrate *originality*. Here, originality simply means that there must be some evidence of independent skill or intellectual endeavour on the part of the creator, and that the work is not simply copied from an existing work. Thus, if we take our class on an outing to Princes Street Gardens in Edinburgh and every member of the class sketches Edinburgh Castle, each and every sketch will attract copyright protection from the moment that it is created. It does not matter that the subject is the same because the drawings themselves are original works deserving legal protection. Moreover, if half of the class also takes a photograph of the castle, each photograph will also be protected by copyright. The originality requirement is met by the simple act of holding the camera at a certain angle and the independent exercise of judgement by each person as to when they release the shutter. In the realm of copyright, it does not matter that millions of photographs have already been taken of Edinburgh Castle: *originality* does not mean *novelty* in the same sense we find in patent law. There is a good reason why different terminology is used because the threshold to qualify for protection is set at a very different level. Furthermore, none of the people who have previously photographed or sketched the castle can prevent our students from doing so. The right received in copyright law is, as the name suggests, merely a right to prevent unauthorised copying or interference with one's own work. It is not a right to control all use of the underlying subject matter. As we explain in Chapter 3, copyright relates to the particular *expression* that the IP creator gives to their work. This is just as well, for were it otherwise the power of copyright could significantly hinder the production of works in the fields of literature and the arts. Human beings are not very imaginative creatures. We always explore the same basic themes through our stories: birth, death, love, betrayal, revenge, hate, reconciliation, and salvation. Copyright does not prevent anyone writing about these subjects; it merely protects the ways in which particular stories are told.

1.38   We can see, then, that the rights conferred by a copyright are much weaker than those conferred by a patent. Not only does this affect the nature and scope of the private rights of the property owner, but it also means that each of these IPRs will have a very different impact on the public sphere where it is exercised. Differential time limits are employed to minimise these effects. For example, a patent will initially only be granted for four years, although it can be renewed in successive years on the payment of a steadily increasing renewal fee,[29] up to a maximum of 20 years.[30] Compare this with copyright protection which, in the context of original works, lasts for the life of the author plus 70 years after their death. The compromise that is achieved balances, on the one hand, short and strong protection with, on the other, longer and weaker protection. In all cases when an IPR expires, however, the property enters the public sphere unconditionally, where it is free to be used by anyone.

1.39   Registration of IP is a common, although not universal, feature of protection regimes. Patents, trade marks, and some design rights must be registered. In contrast, copyright protection arises whenever a work which satisfies the qualification criteria is created and UK unregistered design right exists whenever a design document is produced,[31] or an article is made to the design. Registration serves a number of functions, including identification of the subject matter to be protected, and a means to test whether the putative property is indeed 'new' (since a search of the relevant register can be carried out to determine if a similar or identical piece of property is already protected). Registers are public documents and provide a single point of reference for third parties to consider the current state of play in a particular field of innovation.

---

[29] Patents (Fees) Rules 2007 (SI 2007/3292).

[30] A notable exception to this is the Supplementary Protection Certificate (SPC). These certificates can be granted in respect of 'medical products' and 'plant protection products' to extend legal protection for a further five years at the end of the initial 20-year period of patent protection. The market lead-in time for such products is often prolonged because of the requirement to subject them to regulatory and safety controls in the public interest. This results in a net reduction in the effectiveness of any patent that is granted, and the SPC addresses this. Both forms of SPC operate under European Regulations (Regulation 469/2009 (medicinal products) 1992 OJ L182/1; Regulation 1610/96 (plant protection products) 1996 OJ L198/30).

[31] Defined in Copyright, Designs and Patents Act 1988, s 263(1).

Discussion point   For answer guidance visit **www.oup.com/uk/brown5e**.

Look at Figure 1.2 below. Why do each of patents, copyright, and design rights ultimately expire whereas a trade mark can be protected for all time as long as it is renewed every ten years?

1.40   When a right must be registered it is important to bear in mind that, as has been noted, the qualification criteria can be fairly stringent, and can call for no prior disclosure of the creation. The classic example of this is patent law, which requires that an invention must never have been made available to the public prior to the filing of an application for patent protection.

What protection do intellectual products receive prior to registration?

1.41   Here, as noted, the importance of common law protection through the action of breach of confidence can become important. As we discuss in Chapter 17, the law of confidence protects confidential information, that is, information which is not part of the public domain. The action provides a remedy against those who disclose confidential information into that domain or are likely to do so. Thus, the threat of an action of breach of confidence can assist considerably in protecting the interests of IP producers in the period between the initial conception of their idea for a new creation and the time when they file for registration.

1.42   However, in order to receive any protection at all, you must be able to express your idea with a sufficient degree of specificity to make it realisable as a final product.[32] This does not necessarily mean that you should write it down, although you would be wise to do so, but it does require that you can give sufficient substance to the information for which you wish to claim protection. Above all, you must keep the information secret and only disclose it to those persons upon whom you can impose a duty of confidence.

Figure 1.2 Core features of the statutory intellectual property rights

	Qualification criterion	Length of protection period	Strength of monopoly
Patents	Novelty	20 years max	Absolute monopoly
Copyright	Originality	Life of the author + 70 years for original works	Monopoly only over the expression of one's own creation
Registered designs	Novelty and with individual character	25 years max (five 5-year renewal periods)	Absolute monopoly
UK unregistered designs	Originality and not commonplace in the design field	15 years max (more limited if design exploited)	Monopoly against copying of design
Trade marks	Capacity to distinguish goods or services of right holder from those of another trader + No conflict with 'earlier trade mark'	10-year periods in perpetuity (with re-registration) Loss of right if no use for five consecutive years	Monopoly over use of mark in respect of goods or services for which it is registered If mark has a reputation right holder can prevent use on 'dissimilar' goods

---

[32] *De Maudsley v Palumbo and Others* [1996] FSR 447.

Summary of common themes

1.43   A series of common themes and elements run through many, and sometimes all, forms of IP protection:

- **Qualification for protection:** *newness*

  All forms of IP must be 'new' in order to receive the protection of the law. However, the degree to which a creation must be new varies with each form of IP right.

- **Procedure for protection:** *registration*

  Many of the statutory IPRs require registration. This assists in the identification of the property to be protected and administration of the rights to be granted.

- **Form of protection:** *control*

  IP owners can control how their property is used and exploited by others. Different rights are conferred by the different IPRs. Note, however, that a common feature is that they only give a negative right of exclusion from the marketplace. That is, there is no positive entitlement to privilege or success in the market and so no real monopoly. The IPRs are rights to be exercised against those who would compete with the IP holder in a public forum. IP constraints rarely reach into the private sphere. Thus, as will be seen in Chapter 12, a patent is not infringed by acts done privately and for purposes which are not commercial.

- **Duration of protection:** *time limits*

  One feature of the need to strike a balance in the provision of IP protection can be seen in the imposition of time limits on the duration of many IPRs. Often, this is inversely related to the strength of the right which is offered.

- **Implementation of protection:** *remedies*

The remedies which are available for infringement of IPRs are, in the main, uniform. These are:

Injunction (interdict)	An action requiring a third party to desist from unlawful conduct, or to prevent them engaging therein. For example, an injunction might be granted to prevent a trader from selling infringing copies of your latest book—or perhaps a product made using a 3D printer.
Delivery up	But what is to stop the rogue trader from selling the 10,000 infringing copies anyway? This remedy ensures that the infringer must hand over all infringing copies for destruction.
Damages or account of profits	*Damages* will be assessed by the Court to reflect what, in its opinion, you have lost as a result of an infringer's activities. An *account of profits* requires that the infringer's profits made from their illegal activities be handed over to you. Note that these two remedies have generally been regarded as mutually exclusive, that is, you must opt for one or the other—you cannot ask for both.

Summary of common expressions and notices

1.44   Here are some common expressions and notices that you will find attached to works that claim IP protection:

- **Notices of protection**

Patent pending	This term is used once a patent has been applied for but before it is granted. Inventors attach this to their inventions to put rivals on notice that an application is being considered. Once an application is filed, marketing of the invention can go ahead without any risk of prejudice to the patent application.
©	Copyright protection arises automatically whenever a qualifying work is created. However, in order to gain international recognition and reciprocity of that protection under the Universal Copyright Convention (1971), this symbol should appear on the work, together with the name of the author and the date when the work was first made publicly available.

®	This symbol indicates that a trade mark is registered. Only formally registered marks are entitled to appear with this symbol. It is an offence falsely to represent that a mark is a registered trade mark.[33]
TM	Intellectual property producers sometimes attach this symbol to signs, names, or logos in an attempt to put third parties on notice that they regard their signs as trade marks. In Europe, this symbol has no legal effect whatsoever.
Ⓓ	This notice may appear on registered designs which seek recognition under The Hague Agreement concerning the International Registration of Industrial Designs (1960). Under the 1960 agreement, the encircled D is to be accompanied by the year of the deposit, the name of the depositor, and the number of the international deposit.
Ⓟ	This symbol puts others on notice that rights of producers of phonograms or performers are being claimed under the Convention for the Protection of Performers, Producers of Phonograms and Broadcasting Organisations (1961). As previously, name and date must also appear.

Developing intellectual property law

1.45   IP law is more in demand now than it has ever been. Businesses are increasingly seeing IP as important for their survival, and as a consequence increased pressure has been brought to bear on IP law to provide adequate protection for new and emerging technologies. Two forms of development have been possible:[34]

- *Accretion* occurs when an existing right is extended to protect a new activity, for example the extension of copyright protection to computer software and databases.

- *Emulation* occurs when a new right is created to protect a new activity. This was used to protect the content of databases.

A paradox in development?

1.46   At the time of writing, IPRs remain creatures of national territorial effect only, with a few notable exceptions. National IP laws have been, however, under supranational influences for centuries, and indeed the drivers of modern IP development come almost exclusively from the international sphere. IP law is truly an international subject, and one cannot acquire a true understanding of the discipline by looking only at national rights.

The Map of Intellectual Property Law

National law

MOST IPRs ARE CREATURES
OF TERRITORIAL EFFECT ONLY

European Union law influences on IP law

(a) Programme of harmonisation and approximation of laws
(b) EU-wide IPRs
(Community trade marks and designs)

---

[33] Trade Marks Act 1994, s 95.
[34] See WR Cornish, 'The international relations of intellectual property' (1993) 52 CLJ 46.

(c) Treaty on the Functioning of the European Union
Free movement of goods and services
(Arts 345, 34, and 36)
Anti-restrictive and monopolistic practices
(Arts 101 and 102)

International agreements, conventions, protocols etc

Common features:
(1) Access to protection and 'national treatment' for foreigners
(2) Minimum (harmonised) standards of protection to be offered by national laws

National law

1.47   You will see later that many international instruments and EU initiatives now shape and direct IP law. Despite this, there are very few IPRs which have an effect beyond the particular country jurisdiction in which they are granted. For the IPRs that must be registered, this means that IP producers must register their rights in each jurisdiction where they seek protection. This cumbersome process is eased in some cases by international agreements that permit one application to be lodged and then considered for a number of specified countries. For example, the Patent Cooperation Treaty (1970) provides such a mechanism for patents, the Madrid Agreement concerning the International Registration of Marks (1891) and the Madrid Protocol (1989) offer an equivalent system for trade marks, and The Hague Agreement concerning the Deposit of Industrial Designs (1925) allows for the deposit of a single design application which will be recognised throughout all countries that are signatories to the agreement. In each case, however, it is national rights which are obtained ultimately, and infringement and enforcement procedures can only be invoked in the domestic courts of individual states.

1.48   In the context of copyright, signatory countries to the Berne Convention for the Protection of Literary and Artistic Works (1886) and the Universal Copyright Convention (1952) guarantee mutual recognition of copyright to nationals of fellow signatory states.

 Exercise

To which of the previously mentioned international agreements is the UK a signatory? (Hint: each of these measures is administered by the World Intellectual Property Organization (WIPO) based in Geneva.)

A tension between legislative onslaught and judicial reticence

1.49   One outcome of this rather curious mix of national and international dimensions to IP law is that we can see the discipline being pulled in different directions depending on who is holding the reins at any given time. For example, there is a very significant push to maintain international legislative initiatives designed to extend IP protection in the economic interests of IP producers. At the same time, it will be seen throughout this book that domestic courts, especially in the jurisdictions in the UK, are often seeking to restrict the scope and influence of IPRs through the interpretations that they give to IP legislation, as regards both itself and in relation to other principles such as competition and human rights. This affects IP law in a number of different ways. For one thing, it means that there may be considerable disharmony between different countries in terms of the actual rights that IP holders enjoy. Thus, even if the substantive legal provisions are the same, as they have been agreed internationally and incorporated into the letter of domestic law, the effect given to those provisions through interpretation by the national courts can result in fairly wide variations in practice.

 Exercise

Consider whether this is an accurate statement of a phenomenon in modern IP law as you read through this book. Why might the courts approach IP questions in a manner which is different from that taken by policymakers? What are the wider implications of this disparity of approach? Which faction is likely to win out in the end? Will this be the right result?

The European Union dimension

1.50   It is precisely because IPRs have traditionally only been effective in individual states that the EU has taken such an interest in this area of law. Primarily, this is because of the prospect that the exercise of IPRs within the European single market will have the effect of partitioning that market and thereby thwart one of the fundamental guiding principles of the Union, namely, that goods should be allowed to circulate freely within the single market. A moment's reflection should reveal how this can happen. If A has a patent only in France, the invention will only be protected in that country. They cannot, therefore, prevent the making or use of the invention elsewhere in the EU, nor can they control what happens to versions of the invention which they have produced once they leave French soil. However, the French patent should, in principle at least, allow them to prevent any imports into France, both of infringing goods that they have not authorised, and also of products comprising the invention which they might have sold elsewhere. While the first of these rights is thought to be permissible, the second has been severely curtailed in the name of protection of the single market. Other problems can arise when IPRs are protected unevenly within the single market's territory. For example, if copyright is protected for the life of the author plus 50 years in the UK (as used to be so), but subsists for the life of the author plus 70 years in Germany, material will fall out of copyright in the former earlier than the latter allowing it to be copied by anyone and to circulate freely except in Germany, where it retains an additional 20 years of protection. Once again, this can lead to a division of the single market along private property lines.[35]

1.51   The Union has launched a three-pronged offensive on IPRs as a result of these concerns in an attempt to minimise their adverse effects.

Harmonisation and approximation of laws

1.52   The Union has been engaged in a robust programme of harmonisation (also sometimes 'approximation') of certain crucial areas of IP law over several decades. There is more potential for such action since the Lisbon Treaty came into effect in 2009. Article 118 TFEU provides for the promulgation of 'measures for the creation of European intellectual property rights to provide uniform protection of intellectual property rights throughout the Union and for the setting up of centralised Union-wide authorisation, coordination and supervision arrangements'.[36] Harmonisation has several advantages beyond ensuring that each member state applies the same legal provisions to IP protection. Perhaps most importantly, it brings the interpretation of IP law within the rubric of the Court of Justice of the European Union (CJEU). This is one way of addressing the potential for residual unevenness around the Union in the way in which IPRs are given effect by domestic courts.

---

[35] The term of copyright protection was made uniform by Council Directive 93/98/EEC of 29 October 1993 harmonising the term of protection of copyright and certain related rights.

[36] Treaty of Lisbon 2007/C OJ 306 17 December 2007, Art 84 inserts a new Art 97A into the Treaty on European Union, which became Art 118. For discussion as to the possible impact of this, see W Kingston, 'Intellectual property in the Lisbon Treaty' (2008) 30(11) EIPR 439–43.

1.53 Already a number of projects have been completed or are in progress. Other initiatives also exist. Here are some key and more recent examples, some of which have already been addressed:

- *Trade mark approximation* (UK law) Trade Marks Act 1994.[37] Establishment of the Community trade mark (now the EU trade mark), administered by the OHIM (now the EUIPO), in Alicante, Spain.[38]

- Harmonisation of the *legal protection of databases*, now embodied in the UK under the Copyright and Rights in Databases Regulations 1997 (SI 1997/3032), as incorporated into the Copyright, Designs and Patents Act 1988.[39]

- Harmonisation of *legal protection of biotechnological* inventions. Parliament and Council Directive of July 1998, incorporated into domestic UK law in the Patents Regulations 2000 (SI 2000/2037).[40]

- Harmonisation of *design law*. The UK complied through amending the Registered Designs Act 1949 by the Registered Designs Regulations 2001 (SI 2001/3949).[41] Establishment of Community registered and unregistered design rights, administered through the OHIM, now EUIPO.[42]

- Harmonisation of the *period of duration of rights in copyright* (now life of the author plus 70 years for original works, following the German model). See Duration of Copyright and Rights in Performances Regulations 1995 (SI 1995/3297).[43]

- Extended term protection for performers rights in sound recordings from 50 years to 70 years, in the context of a controversial public consultation in which many stakeholders argued against such a move. See Directive 2011/77/EU, adopted on 12 September 2011, which came into effect in the UK on 1 November 2013 (Copyright and duration of rights in performances Regulations (SI 2013/1782)).

- *Patent law harmonisation* (European Patent Convention (EPC) (1973 and 2000)), establishing the European Patent Office in Munich, Germany (1978). Note that this is *not* part of the European Union framework. UK law was brought into line via the Patents Act 1977.[44]

Web link

EU internal market IP website:

https://ec.europa.eu/growth/industry/intellectual-property_en

---

EU rights

1.54 You should note from the list in paragraph 1.53 that in two instances the European Union (formerly Community) has instituted Union-wide IPRs, which have been mentioned earlier in this chapter. The first of these was the Community trade mark, established by means of a Council Regulation in 1996.[45] It is administered through the OHIM.[46] The Council subsequently adopted the Community Design Regulation,

---

[37] Council Directive 89/104/EEC of 21 December 1988 to approximate the laws of the member states relating to trade marks as codified in Directive 2008/95/EC of 22 October 2008, recast in Directive (EU) 2015/2436.

[38] Council Regulation (EC) No 40/94 of 20 December 1993 on the Community trade mark, and Council Regulation (EC) No 207/2009 of 26 February 2009 on the Community trade mark (codified version) and amended by Regulation (EU) 2015/2424 then codified in Regulation (EU) 2017/1001.

[39] Directive 96/9/EC of the European Parliament and of the Council of 11 March 1996 on the legal protection of databases.

[40] Directive 98/44/EC of the European Parliament and of the Council of 6 July 1998 on the legal protection of biotechnological inventions.

[41] Directive 98/71/EC of the European Parliament and of the Council of 13 October 1998 on the legal protection of designs.

[42] Council Regulation (EC) No 6/2002 of 12 December 2001 on Community designs.

[43] Council Directive 93/98/EEC of 29 October 1993 harmonising the term of protection of copyright and certain related rights, which was replaced by Directive 2006/116/E, a consolidated version, which has now been amended by Directive 2011/77/EU.

[44] There are currently 38 signatories to the EPC, including the 28 member states of the EU (as at late 2018—see lists at www.epo.org/about-us/organisation/member-states.html).

[45] See n 42. [46] See n 4.

which introduced both registered and unregistered design rights with effect throughout the Union, and which is also administered by the OHIM.[47] Neither of these measures supplants the existing frameworks for domestic protection.

Discussion point   For answer guidance visit www.oup.com/uk/brown5e.

How is it possible for the Union (and formerly the Community) to legislate on property matters when Article 345 TFEU states: 'This Treaty shall in no way prejudice the rules in Member States governing the system of property ownership'? Will the existence of a single right render national rights redundant?

1.55   Union-wide rights are the best means to resolve the tension between territorial IPRs and the aims of the single market, for reasons which should be self-evident. There can be no partitioning of the market if only a unitary right can subsist throughout its territory. Moreover, the creation of new legal provisions means that mechanisms can be incorporated *ab initio* to prevent some particular uses of the IPRs which have just been discussed. We explore the details and the functioning of the EU IPRs in Chapters 8, 9, and 13.

1.56   These EU successes have not been easy to bring about. Often there is difficulty in getting consensus on the terms of protection, the languages to be used for registration purposes, and the scope of the eventual rights to be granted. In particular, disputes about the extent of protection of spare parts held up the Community Design Regulation for a number of years. Longer still in the making have been proposals for an EU patent (formerly called the Community patent). This has been on the cards since the mid-1970s, but sufficient agreement has never been reached to bring an international instrument into force.[48] This is distinct from the EPC discussed in paragraph 1.53. The EU patent emerged as a viable option with a proposal for a Council Regulation in 2000,[49] although there was little progress until 2007, when the Commission adopted a Communication on 'Enhancing the patent system'. This became a draft Agreement to establish a unified patent litigation system, but this was found by the CJEU to be beyond the legislative capacities set out in the EU Treaties.[50] The Commission quickly turned to a proposal for unitary patent courts, which led in late 2012 to the European Parliament approving a unitary package patent, which addresses both the application and enforcement process.[51] The same problems have re-emerged at each stage, including the very thorny issue of language: if patent law requires that an inventor describe in intricate detail the workings of his invention, and there are 23 official languages of the EU, the question of in which language or languages this description must appear invariably arises. Translations into all official languages would make patenting prohibitively expensive, but if we do not require all, then which? And where would any central court or courts be located? It will be interesting to note how the unitary patent package develops. We discuss this further in Chapter 10.

Question

Can you think of a reasonable compromise? Is it the same as that in the unitary patent package?

Free movement of goods and restrictions on anti-competitive practices

1.57   Another important influence of European law comes from certain key provisions in the TFEU. Because of the potential for IPRs to interfere with the aims and smooth operation of the single market, the European

---

[47] See n 4.
[48] Convention for the European Patent for the Common Market (Community Patent Convention) (Luxembourg, 1975, revised 1989).
[49] Commission Proposal for a Council Regulation on the Community Patent, COM(200) 412 final.
[50] [2011] 3 CMLR 4.
[51] See details on http://ec.europa.eu/growth/industry/intellectual-property/patents/unitary-patent/index_en.htm.

Court of Justice (ECJ) as it was then had taken it upon itself to rule on the extent to which the exercise of IPRs conflicts with European law, and to temper the scope of those rights as a result. Attention has focused on the interpretation of what are now Articles 34, 36, and 345 TFEU. Article 345 specifically reserves property law matters to the member states, including IP laws, but the Court has interpreted this to mean that only the *existence* of such rights enjoys unfettered national protection. The *exercise* of those rights may be curtailed if it represents an unjustified interference with free trading practices. Articles 34 and 36 operate to prohibit unjustified restrictions upon what can be imported and exported between member states. And, while Article 36 allows restrictions upon imports if they are justified to protect 'industrial or commercial property', it will not do so if the restriction which is imposed amounts to 'arbitrary discrimination' or 'disguised restriction' on trade which is otherwise legitimate.

1.58   A common example of how the Court has taken all of these interpretations and applied them to the exercise of IPRs is found in the context of parallel imports. While it is acceptable for an IP right holder to exercise their right within a particular member state, they will be deemed to have 'exhausted' their right if they permit export to one or more member states, or exercise the right there itself or allow the right to be exercised with their (free) consent. If, then, a third party who has legitimate possession of protected goods in member state X wishes to re-import the goods into the IP right holder's country (undoubtedly at a lower price than they are being sold by the right holder), the latter cannot prevent the former from doing so, as it would represent an unfair fetter on free trade. The right holder is said to have *exhausted* their rights in this regard, and can no longer impose any restrictions on the free circulation of those goods within the single market. Thus, in one sense the scope of the IP right is modified, in that 'the right to first market' now forms part of the right but also operates as a limitation on it. In all other senses, however, IPRs operate normally. Note, too, that these restrictions only apply when the intellectual products have been first marketed by the right holder themselves or with their 'consent', and this has led in turn to debate about the legal meaning of consent, requiring further rulings by the ECJ (now CJEU).[52] This is considered in more detail in Chapter 19.

International exhaustion

1.59   All of this is done in the name of protecting the integrity of the single market, that is, in regulating what happens *within* that market. But what is the position of the right holder who wants to exercise his rights to prevent goods entering the single market from outside its borders? Well, the ECJ has ruled that the principle of 'international exhaustion' does not apply to IPRs protected within the European Economic Area (EEA) (the European Union plus the members of the European Free Trade Association, namely Iceland, Liechtenstein, and Norway). Thus, when S, the manufacturer of designer sunglasses, sold his previous year's stock to a trader in Bulgaria—at that time outside the EU—it was nonetheless able to use its trade mark right in respect of the sunglasses (*Silhouette*) to prevent an Austrian retailer from buying the glasses cheaply and importing them back into the EEA to compete with the right holder.[53] This has been a very controversial decision, not least because it is seen to favour the interests of manufacturers and IP holders over the interests of consumers, by keeping lower cost, quality products out of the EU marketplace. Further, neither the product nor the mark is being held out as anything other than that which it is, namely, the goods and mark of the IP holder. Thus, in strict terms, has the trade mark right not served its function, which is to act as a mark of quality and a badge of origin, albeit that there is conduct which is covered by the exclusive rights conferred on the national trade mark owner? Again, we explore this, and other, controversial issues in this realm in Chapter 19.

Anti-competitive practices

1.60   Articles 101 and 102 TFEU operate to ensure that free trade is not compromised by unacceptable, restrictive or monopolistic practices. Article 101 prohibits, inter alia, the establishment and operation of cartels

---

[52] See, eg, Joined Cases C-414/99, C-415/99, and C-416/99 *Zino Davidoff SA v A & G Imports Ltd and Levi Strauss & Co and Others v Tesco Stores Ltd and Others*, Judgment of the Court, 20 November 2001.

[53] See *Silhouette International Schmied GmbH & Co KG v Hartlauer Handelsgesellschaft mbH* [1998] ECR I-4799.

between enterprises which have as their object or effect the distortion or prevention of competition in the single market. Article 102 concerns the abuse of a dominant position within a particular market by any particular commercial enterprise, to the extent that it affects trade *between* member states. This Article offers examples of how such an abuse might be affected; namely: (a) directly or indirectly imposing unfair purchase or selling prices or other unfair trading conditions; (b) limiting production, markets, or technical development to the prejudice of consumers; (c) applying dissimilar conditions to equivalent transactions with other trading parties, thereby placing them at a competitive disadvantage; (d) making the conclusion of contracts subject to acceptance by the other parties of supplementary obligations which, by their nature or according to commercial usage, have no connection with the subject of the contracts. Any agreements which contravene Article 101 or 102 are void.

1.61   These provisions are policed by the European Commission, which can offer guidance on the fine line between acceptable and unacceptable practices, as it has done, inter alia, by issuing 'block exemptions' for certain types of agreement or terms in agreements.[54] By the same token, the Commission is also empowered to fine any undertaking which contravenes the terms of Articles 101 and 102.

1.62   The relevance of these provisions for IP right holders is seen most acutely in the context of licensing. IP can be exploited through licences, which are simply agreements between the right holder and third parties to determine how, when, where, and for how much the third party can exploit the IP of the owner. Ordinarily, these licences are subject to domestic contract law, with the proviso that they must also accord with Articles 101 and 102. Thus, the terms of these agreements are liable to scrutiny by the Commission, although the granting of block exemptions has made it clearer as to which provisions may or may not be included. Moreover, a refusal to enter an agreement with a third party to exploit IP is not automatically a contravention of the TFEU, even though this might leave the right holder with exclusive control of its IP in the market.[55] In some rare circumstances, however, it may be abuse of a dominant position to refuse to license.[56] We discuss the margins of permissible and impermissible conduct in Chapter 20.

Implications of the UK withdrawal from the European Union

As has been seen so far, there are strong links between UK IP law and EU law, from the existence of unitary pan-European rights to harmonising Directives. At the time of writing in late 2018 and production in 2019, the UK has triggered the process for it to leave the EU. If this process is completed, it will inevitably have an impact on the issues explored in this book.

First, some background. An advisory referendum on EU membership was held in the UK in 2016, in which the majority of those who voted, chose 'leave'.[57] The UK government then chose, in March 2017, to activate the process in Article 50 TFEU, pursuant to which the UK would leave after two years—making the leave date 29 March 2019. A withdrawal agreement was negotiated between the EU and UK to deliver 'an orderly withdrawal' and a transition period to 31 December 2020.[58] At the time

---

[54]   The current block exemption most relevant to intellectual property is Commission Regulation (EU) No 316/2014 of 21 March 2014 on the application of Article 101(3) of the Treaty on the Functioning of the European Union to categories of technology transfer agreements text with EEA relevance OJ L 93/17 of 23 March 2014.

[55]   *AB Volvo v Erik Veng (UK) Ltd* [1988] ECR 6211.

[56]   The first landmark case is *Radio Telefis Eireann v EC Commission* [1991] ECR II-485.

[57]   For a contemporaneous analysis of the reasons for the holding of the referendum, see *Financial Times*, 'What is Brexit and why is the referendum being held' (22 February 2016) www.ft.com/content/a23ce766-d0ed-11e5-831d-09f7778e7377.

[58]   Agreement on the withdrawal of the United Kingdom of Great Britain and Northern Ireland from the European Union and the European Atomic Energy Community, as endorsed by leaders at a special meeting of the European Council on 25 November 2018 at https://assets.publishing.service.gov.uk/government/uploads/system/uploads/attachment_data/file/759019/25_November_Agreement_on_the_with-drawal_of_the_United_Kingdom_of_Great_Britain_and_Northern_Ireland_from_the_European_Union_and_the_European_Atomic_Energy_Community.pdf ('Withdrawal Agreement'), see Preamble para 5, 2 and Art 126.

of final writing, there is resistance as to whether this agreement will be acceptable to the UK Parliament (it has been rejected three times by April 2019) and an extension has been granted to the leave date to 31 October 2019.[59] These developments are intertwined with arguments by some that the UK should revoke its notice under Article 50 and remain in the EU,[60] and by others that the UK should leave the EU without any further agreement being reached regarding the withdrawal process.[61] There is also an agreed draft Political Declaration,[62] which accompanies the withdrawal agreement. This sets out the framework on which a new relationship between the UK and the EU, likely through a new trade agreement, is to be negotiated.

Secondly, there is the question of the impact of 'Brexit' on IP and related issues. There are two elements to this: what will happen internally to UK law; and what will happen externally.

Internally within the UK, the UK European Union (Withdrawal) Act 2018 (EUWA) provides that the European Communities Act 1972, which has provided the legislative mechanism through which EU law takes effect in the UK, will be repealed on the UK's 'Exit Day'.[63] EU-derived domestic legislation (say, the provisions of the Registered Designs Act 1949 (as amended) which were implemented to give effect to the EU Designs Directive) will continue in domestic law.[64] Direct EU legislation (such as Regulations) will also continue to be part of domestic law.[65] However, this will be of no assistance in relation to EU IP rights such as EU trade marks or Community designs, as they are defined in the relevant EU Regulations as covering the territory of the EU—of which the UK will no longer be part. The EUWA confers power on the UK government to pass primary and secondary legislation to make changes to retained laws—and this is likely to be an area for future debate.[66] The EWCA provides that the principle of supremacy of EU law continues so far as relevant to any enactment or rule of law passed before Exit Day, but not thereafter.[67] The Charter of Fundamental Rights will also not be part of domestic law on or after Exit Day.[68] The Supreme Court is not bound by retained EU case law.[69] Courts in the UK are not bound by decisions of the CJEU on or after Exit Day and cannot make new references to the CJEU; however, courts can have regard to anything done by the CJEU or the EU in so far as relevant to a matter before it.[70]

Externally, if the draft withdrawal agreement is accepted by the UK Parliament (which again is by no means certain) the starting point is the proposed transition period the UK and EU negotiate their future relationship. The draft withdrawal agreement provides that EU law (legislation and the provisions of EU treaties—so including competition law and free movement) will be applicable in the UK

---

[59]   For a useful summary of the processes and the issues, see K Ziegler, 'Brexit: what has to happen in UK and EU parliaments to ratify withdrawal and future trade agreements' (19 November 2018) http://theconversation.com/brexit-what-has-to-happen-in-uk-and-eu-parliaments-to-ratify-withdrawal-and-future-trade-agreements-107127. See also Conclusions of Special Meeting of the European Council (Art 50) (10 April 2019) EUCO XT 20015/19.

[60]   *Wightman and Others v Secretary of State for Existing the European Union* C- 621/18 finding that the Article 50 notice could be unilaterally revoked by the UK.

[61]   For reflection on this and possible consequences, see I Glinavos and A Shipman, 'No-deal Brexit: experts on what the UK government's advice means' (24 August 2018) https://theconversation.com/no-deal-brexit-experts-on-what-the-uk-governments-advice-means-102074.

[62]   Draft political declaration setting out the framework for the future relationship between the United Kingdom and the European Union (22 November 2018) www.gov.uk/government/publications/draft-political-declaration-setting-out-the-framework-for-the-future-relationship-between-the-european-union-and-the-united-kingdom-agreed-at-negotia ('Political Declaration').

[63]   EUWA 2018, s1.

[64]   7(1) EUWA 2018, s2(1), 7(1).

[65]   EUWA 2018, s3(1).

[66]   EUWA 2018, s7(2), (3), 8, Sch 8 in particular para 3.

[67]   EUWA 2018, s5(1) and (2).

[68]   EUWA 2018, s5(4).

[69]   EUWA 2018, s6(4).

[70]   EUWA 2018, s6(1), (2).

during the transition period.[71] The draft withdrawal agreement also engages specifically[72] with IP and makes some key points.[73]

- The holders of EU trade marks, Community registered designs, and Community plant variety rights at the end of the transition period are to become holders of comparable registered and enforceable national rights in the UK.

- Owners of unregistered Community design rights are to be entitled to the same level of protection in the UK.

- Database rights will continue to have the same level of protection under UK law as they do at present.

- IP rights which were exhausted (through the free movement/IP interface) before the end of the transition period will be exhausted in the EU and also in the UK.

The draft political declaration refers to IP; parties should protect and enforce IP to stimulate innovation, creativity, and economic activity going beyond TRIPS (the Agreement on trade-related aspects of intellectual property rights, 1994) and the WIPO conventions where relevant, and parties are to maintain the freedom to establish their own regimes for exhaustion of IP rights. The parties are also to have autonomy to regulate economic activity to achieve legitimate public policy objectives, with reference made inter alia to public health, climate change, privacy and data protection, and cultural diversity, and to ensuring a level playing field for open and fair competition.[74]

The draft withdrawal agreement and the draft political declaration do not refer to the Unified Patent Court, although this had been a main focus of UK post Brexit proposals, notwithstanding the Court's reliance on the supremacy of EU law.[75]

Brexit issues will be addressed in more depth as appropriate in the relevant sections of this book, again in specially headed textboxes. It is likely that during the currency of this book there will be further developments—of whatever nature. For now, one can only echo the comments of the EU:[76]

The withdrawal of the United Kingdom from the European Union will create uncertainty for UK and EU27 stakeholders alike in relation to the scope of protection in the United Kingdom of certain intellectual property rights; to the treatment of applications for certain rights and to the exhaustion of rights conferred by intellectual property rights. This uncertainty will significantly affect the con-

---

[71] Withdrawal Agreement, Art 127.

[72] Withdrawal Agreement, Titles IV and VII.

[73] Of possible interest might be the documents released by the EU and the UK on IP. From the UK, HM Government, 'The Future Relationship between the United Kingdom and the European Union' Cm 9593 (July 2018) https://assets.publishing.service.gov.uk/government/uploads/system/uploads/attachment_data/file/725288/The_future_relationship_between_the_United_Kingdom_and_the_European_Union.pdf, see 42 para 128(h) and 46–7 paras 149–152; UK, 'Trade marks and designs if there's no Brexit deal' (17 January 2019) www.gov.uk/government/publications/trade-marks-and-designs-if-theres-no-brexit-deal (24 September 2018); UK, 'Patents if there's no Brexit deal' (24 September 2018) www.gov.uk/government/publications/patents-if-theres-no-brexit-deal; UK, 'Exhaustion of intellectual property rights if there's no Brexit deal' (24 September 2018) www.gov.uk/government/publications/exhaustion-of-intellectual-property-rights-if-theres-no-brexit-deal/exhaustion-of-intellectual-property-rights-if-theres-no-brexit-deal; and UK, 'Copyright if there's no Brexit deal' (24 September 2018) www.gov.uk/government/publications/copyright-if-theres-no-brexit-deal/copyright-if-theres-no-brexit-deal.
  From the EU, see Position paper transmitted to EU27 on Intellectual property rights (including geographical indications) (6 September 2017) https://ec.europa.eu/commission/publications/position-paper-transmitted-eu27-intellectual-property-rights-including-geographical-indications_en and Position paper TF50(2017)11/2 Commission to the UK (20 September 2017); TF50 (2018) 33 Commission to EU 27 (28 February 2018), see Title IV 30–35 Arts 50–57.

[74] Political Declaration, paras 8–10, 17–18, Parts II, VII, and XIV.

[75] HM Government, 'The Future Relationship between the United Kingdom and the European Union' Cm 9593 (July 2018) https://assets.publishing.service.gov.uk/government/uploads/system/uploads/attachment_data/file/725288/The_future_relationship_between_the_United_Kingdom_and_the_European_Union.pdf, see 42 para 128(h) and 46–7 paras 150–151; UK, 'Patents if there's no Brexit deal' (24 September 2018) www.gov.uk/government/publications/patents-if-theres-no-brexit-deal; and HM Government, 'The Future Relationship between the United Kingdom and the European Union' CM 9593 para 128(h), 150–152. See also House of Lords European Union Committee, 'Brexit: the Withdrawal Agreement and Political Declaration', HL Paper 245 (4 December 2018) para 231.

[76] Position paper TF50 (2017) 11/2 Commission to the UK (20 September 2017) 2.

ditions under which goods that are placed on the market in the Union before the withdrawal date could continue to circulate between the EU27 and the UK.

To this, add the potential for divergence between decisions of the CJEU and courts in jurisdictions in the UK. In future editions of this book, the content of the EU-related sections may be in a different form. But they will continue to be an important part of the legal and practical landscape for innovators and creators.

International obligations

1.63   The EU has its own particular agenda for interfering with the exercise of IPRs and guiding their future development. However, beyond this particularised regional influence, other agendas have operated for well over a century, and today a large number of internationally imposed obligations mould the nature and content of IPRs and ultimately determine the direction of IP law.

1.64   Although it has been the tradition of IP law to protect rights first and foremost at the national level, the international possibilities for the exploitation of IP have long been appreciated. Markets do not recognise territorial boundaries, and IP producers will always gravitate towards a potential market. And, as international trade became a more realistic possibility with the advent of the industrial revolution in the nineteenth century, so too industrialised nations realised that disparities between markets in terms of IP protection could have an adverse impact on the rights of their IP producers and, in turn, on their own economic interests. In a spirit of economic reciprocity, then, a number of countries sought to establish multilateral treaties to minimise these adverse effects. The first instruments to emerge were the Paris Convention for the Protection of Industrial Property (1883), and the Berne Convention for the Protection of Literary and Artistic Works (1886).

Paris Convention for the Protection of Industrial Property (1883, as revised)

The protection of 'industrial property' has as its objects patents, utility models, industrial designs, trade marks, service marks, trade names, indications of source or appellations of origin and the repression of unfair competition.

Berne Convention for the Protection of Literary and Artistic Works (1886, as revised)

The expression 'literary and artistic works' shall include every production in the literary, scientific and artistic domain, whatever may be the mode or form of its expression, such as books, pamphlets and other writings; lectures, addresses, sermons and other words of the same nature; dramatic or dramatico-musical works; choreographic works and entertainments in dumb show; musical compositions with or without words; cinematographic works to which are assimilated works expressed by a process analogous to cinematography; works of drawing, painting, architecture, sculpture, engraving and lithography; photographic works to which are assimilated works expressed by a process analogous to photography; works of applied art; illustrations, maps, plans, sketches and three-dimensional works related to geography, topography, architecture or science.

 Question

Why two conventions and not one? What differentiates 'industrial property' under the Paris Convention from the entities protected under the Berne Convention? Does this remain a meaningful distinction in the modern age?

1.65   Signatory countries to these conventions undertook to provide two key elements of protection. The first is *national treatment* of foreigners, which, as the name suggests, means that any entity seeking protection in a signatory country beyond their own shores must be dealt with on the same terms as if they were a national of that country. Secondly, these instruments sought to establish certain baselines of protection, as the previous definitions indicate, to ensure that the same kinds of 'property' were protected in the various party states. The obligation to provide this level of protection is, however, very broadly drafted. For example, the UK does not have a specific law to guard against unfair competition, yet the argument is made that the UK nonetheless complies with its international obligations under the Paris Convention in a piecemeal fashion, inter alia, because of the existence of common law actions such as passing off and breach of confidence considered in Chapters 16 and 17.

Discussion point   For answer **guidance** visit **www.oup.com/uk/brown5e**.

What does protection against unfair competition mean? Do you think that the UK maintains a defensible position in this regard? Would it be preferable to institute a specific law in this area? Reconsider the question after you have read Chapter 16.

1.66   In summary, two main themes typify international agreements on IP protection: (1) access to protection and 'national treatment' for foreigners; and (2) minimum (harmonised) standards of protection to be offered by national laws.

1.67   The Paris and Berne Conventions, and indeed many other instruments, are administered by WIPO in Geneva.[77] Disputes and compliance measures may be dealt with through the International Court of Justice.

TRIPS Agreement (Agreement on trade-related aspects of intellectual property rights, 1994)

1.68   The TRIPS Agreement was included in the Accord which finalised the Uruguay Round of the General Agreement on Tariffs and Trade, establishing the World Trade Organization (WTO) in 1994. TRIPS touches all the major forms of IPR and is administered by the World Trade Organization, also based in Geneva. Importantly, states which do not comply with the provisions of TRIPS may face proceedings before the WTO dispute settlement system. A variable timescale for implementing TRIPS continues to operate to ensure that developing and least developed countries have a transitional period in which to bring their laws into compliance with the Agreement.

1.69   TRIPS is similar to the Paris and Berne Conventions in that it provides for national treatment and seeks to harmonise basic IP provisions. However, in other respects it goes far beyond its nineteenth-century counterparts. For example, TRIPS puts more flesh on the bones of the elements of protection required of signatory countries, as we shall see in each of the chapters to come that deal with the substantive law. Moreover, TRIPS ties these countries into many of the essential terms of the Paris and Berne Conventions, even if they are not signatories to them, thereby considerably extending the reach of these instruments.[78]

1.70   The motivation for the implementation of TRIPS is almost entirely economic. It was driven by the concerns of Western industrialised countries, and most notably the United States, which could not countenance the multi-billion-dollar trade in unauthorised IP that had developed over the years, despite the existence of the Paris and Berne Conventions. One of the problems was that these Conventions had not attracted universal support, and in particular many of the countries where illicit trading was taking place were not signatories

---

[77]   For more information on international treaties and agreements, see the WIPO website at www.wipo.org.
[78]   TRIPS (1994), Arts 2 and 9.

to them, and so were not subject to their terms. How then to implement a regime that could bring offending states under its influence? The answer was trade. By linking TRIPS to trade, and so thereby bringing all signatory states under the auspices of the WTO, the relevant politicians and governments in control have been able to establish a system which is almost impossible to resist. No state in the modern world can develop without international trade; and so tight is the hold on that regime through the WTO, that no state can fail to sign up, and thereby become obliged to comply with TRIPS. The real stroke of economic genius has been to link non-compliance with TRIPS to the withdrawal of WTO privileges and the prospect of trade sanctions in the event of an adverse ruling by the WTO—which could potentially cripple a state's entire economy.[79] And if there is a potential clash between TRIPS and the priorities of other regimes which have less effective enforcement measures, this may lead to countries choosing to follow the TRIPS requirements—or indeed, how some large countries which host IP owners would prefer these requirements to be interpreted.

1.71   Finally, despite the power available for IP owners as a result of TRIPS, there has also been an increase in bilateral and regional trade agreements which require that states provide other parties with higher levels of protection than is required or enabled by TRIPS. Given the national treatment requirement this can lead to higher levels of protection in a state's IP laws as a whole.[80] This is known as the phenomenon of TRIPS-plus. Similar themes were seen when several developed countries led secret negotiations of the Anti-Counterfeiting Trade Agreement (ACTA). Activist groups, with a focus on access to knowledge and innovation, led strong challenges to this,[81] and its content became more moderate; ultimately, several countries, including the EU, refused to ratify ACTA.[82] Undeterred, IP has also formed part of (further) secret trade agreements, for example the Trans-Pacific Partnership, which was agreed in October 2015.[83] Another issue receiving significant attention and objection is agreements including investor state dispute settlement chapters, enabling IP owners to challenge directly state action.[84] The relationship between IP, trade, and investment is constantly evolving. In 2018 the Comprehensive Trans-Pacific Partnership[85] (largely superseding the Trans-Pacific Partnership which did not come into force) and the Comprehensive Economic and Trade Agreement[86] have more measured approaches to IP and also to investor state dispute settlement. Assuming Brexit comes about, these types of agreements will be particularly important to the UK in its future international dealings.

Other international instruments

1.72   This has clearly not been an exhaustive account of the international measures which impact on IP law. It is not intended to be. Rather, this overview should give a good idea of the influences which international measures have on the discipline. Bear these in mind as you proceed through this book. For the sake of completeness, however, note too that there are many other international instruments which exist in this realm. We will consider them where this is relevant in the forthcoming chapters.

---

[79]   For further discussion, see F Ravida, 'Influence of WTO decisions on international intellectual property' (2008) 3(5) JIPLP 314–26 and D Gervais, *The TRIPs Agreement: Drafting History and Analysis* (4th edn, 2012).

[80]   D Vivas Eugui and J von Braun, 'Beyond FTA negotiations: implementing the new generation of intellectual property obligations' at 113 and P Drahos, 'Doing deals with Al Capone: paying protection money for intellectual property in the global knowledge economy' at 141 in P Yu (ed), *Intellectual Property and Information Wealth: Issues and Practices in the Digital Age. Volume 4: International Intellectual Property Law and Policy* (2007).

[81]   PK Yu, 'Six secret (and now open) fears of ACTA' (2011) 64 SMU Law Rev 975; discussion on ACTA FFII Blog at http://acta.ffii. org/?p=633; see also www.ustr.gov/acta (including text).

[82]   European Parliament News, 'Everything you need to know about ACTA' (18 July 2012) www.europarl.europa.eu/sides/getDoc. do?type=IM-PRESS&reference=20120220FCS38611&format=XML&language=EN.

[83]   For criticism of this, see www.eff.org/issues/tpp (which compares the agreement to ACTA) and for a supportive approach, see www. ustr.gov/tpp.

[84]   See consideration in IP Watch, 'Inside views: how the leaked TPP ISDS chapter threatens intellectual property limitations and exceptions' (26 March 2015) www.ip-watch.org/2015/03/26/how-the-leaked-tpp-isds-chapter-threatens-intellectual-property-limitations-and-exceptions.

[85]   www.mfat.govt.nz/en/trade/free-trade-agreements/free-trade-agreements-in-force/cptpp.

[86]   See http://ec.europa.eu/trade/policy/in-focus/ceta/index_en.htm.

- *Patents*
  - Patent Cooperation Treaty, Washington 1970
  - Budapest Treaty on the International Recognition of the Deposit of Microorganisms for the Purposes of Patent Procedure, 1977
- *Copyright*
  - WIPO Copyright Treaty, 1996, and associated Agreed Statements
  - Marrakech Treaty to Facilitate Access to Published Works for Persons with Visual Impairment (2013)
- *Designs*
  - Hague Agreement concerning the International Registration of Industrial Designs, 1925, as revised
- *Trade marks*
  - Trade Mark Law Treaty, Geneva 1994
- *Appellations of origin*
  - Lisbon Agreement for the Protection of Appellations of Origin and their International Registration (1958, as revised)
- *Performers' rights*
  - WIPO Performances and Phonograms Treaty, 1996, and Agreed Statements
  - Rome Convention for the Protection of Performers, Producers of Phonograms and Broadcasting Organizations (1961)
  - The Beijing Treaty on Audiovisual Performances 2012 (adopted June 2012, not yet in force)
  - Geneva Convention for the Protection of Producers of Phonograms against Unauthorized Duplication of their Phonograms, 1971
- *Integrated circuits*
  - Treaty on Intellectual Property in Respect of Integrated Circuits, 1989

Intellectual property and human rights

1.73   A final influence on the possible development of IP law comes once again from the international plane, although this time the forces at work may be pulling in different directions. The European Convention for the Protection of Human Rights and Fundamental Freedoms (1950) was a post-war initiative by the Council of Europe designed to prevent a repeat of the atrocities of the era that had gone immediately before. Its general approach was to establish fundamental, and largely negative, rights for individuals against the state: rights of non-interference. Over the years a rich and complex jurisprudence has grown around the Articles of the Convention through the work of the European Court of Human Rights in Strasbourg, but for the most part its rulings have only touched the lives of UK citizens indirectly, because successive governments had refused to make the terms of the Convention part of domestic law. The Human Rights Act 1998 came into full force in October 2000 heralding an explosion in speculation and litigation about the possible impact of human rights in every conceivable area of law, including IP law.[87] The place of human rights within the discussion of IP was strengthened further (although again with uncertain impact)[88] through the Lisbon Treaty, which includes the Charter of Fundamental Rights. Article 17(2) provides that 'Intellectual property shall be protected', in addition to potentially conflicting provisions, such as in respect of freedom of expression. Further, negotiations are ongoing for the EU to become a party to the Convention.[89] In

---

[87] *Ashdown v Telegraph Newspapers* [2001] 4 All ER 666. See also for a theoretical exploration of human rights in the context of copyright, STM Newman, 'Human rights and copyrights: a look at practical jurisprudence with reference to authors' rights' (2009) 31(2) EIPR 88.

[88] See N MacCormick, 'Human rights and competition law: possible impact of the proposed EU Constitution' (2005) 2(4) SCRIPTed 444 (https://script-ed.org/wp-content/uploads/2016/07/2-4-MacCormick.pdf) and C Geiger, 'Intellectual property shall be protected!? Article 17(2) of the Charter of Fundamental Rights of the European Union: a mysterious provision with an unclear scope' (2009) 31(3) EIPR 113.

[89] See, eg, existing presumptions of compliance, C Banner and A Thomson, 'Human rights review of state acts performed in compliance with EC law—*Bosphorus Airways v Ireland*' (2005) 6 EHRLR 649.

December 2014, however, the CJEU held that the agreement as drafted was incompatible with EU law.[90] The next step remains to be seen.[91]

1.74   The existence of IP, its infringement, business, and societal impact (in particular in complex areas such as health, communications, and the environment), the interaction between IP and other interests, and the conflicts between IP owners, access seekers, and activists, will be explored in more detail in the following chapters.

Further reading

Books

WR Cornish, *Intellectual Property: Omnipresent, Distracting, Irrelevant?* (2004)

GB Dinwoodie and RC Dreyfuss, *A Neofederalist Vision of TRIPS* (2012)

P Drahos, *A Philosophy of Intellectual Property* (1996)

P Drahos with J Braithwaite, *Information Feudalism: Who Owns the Knowledge Economy?* (2003)

P Drahos and R Mayne, *Global Intellectual Property Rights: Knowledge, Access and Development* (2002)

G Ghidini, *Intellectual Property, Competition and Consumer Welfare in Intellectual Property Law* (2010)

HR Howe and J Griffiths, *Concepts of Property in Intellectual Property Law* (2013)

D Llewelyn and T Aplin, *Cornish, Llewelyn and Aplin Intellectual Property: Patents, Copyright, Trade Marks and Allied Rights* (9th edn, 2019)

MR Pugatch, *The Intellectual Property Debate: Perspectives from Law, Economics and Political Economy* (2006)

B Sherman and L Bently, *The Making of Modern Intellectual Property* (1999)

B Sherman, L Bently, and D Gangjee, P Johnson *Intellectual Property* (5th edn, 2018)

U Suthersanen, G Dutfield, and KB Chow (eds), *Innovation Without Patents: Harnessing the Creative Spirit in a Diverse World* (2007)

Reports

Report of UK Commission on Intellectual Property Rights (2002) www.iprcommission.org

Articles and lectures

E Cameron and J Berger, 'Patents and public health: principle, politics and paradox', Inaugural British Academy Law Lecture, https://script-ed.org/wp-content/uploads/2016/07/1-4-Cameron.pdf

E Derclaye, 'Should patent law help cool the planet? An inquiry from the point of view of environmental law', Part 1: (2009) 31(3) EIPR 168 and Part 2: (2009) 31(5) EIPR 227

C Geiger, 'Fundamental rights—a safeguard for the coherence of intellectual property law' (2004) 35 IIC 268

EC Hettinger, 'Justifying intellectual property' (1989) 19 Philosophy and Public Affairs 31

R Jacob, 'Is intellectual property the grit in the wheels of industry?' (2012) 2 UCL JL and J 1(2) 1–14

A Kur, 'A new framework for intellectual property rights—horizontal issues' (2004) 35 IIC 1

Sir H Laddie, 'National IP rights: a moribund anachronism in a federal Europe?' (2001) 23(9) EIPR 402

M Lemley, 'Ex ante versus ex post justifications for intellectual property' (2004) 71 University of Chicago Law Review 129 http://papers.ssrn.com/sol3/papers.cfm?abstract_id=494424

---

[90] Opinion 2/13 [2015] 2 CMLR 21: key points were the impact on autonomy, coordination between the ECHR and the EU Charter, and the level of external control which would be involved.

[91] See sources at www.europarl.europa.eu/legislative-train/theme-area-of-justice-and-fundamental-rights/file-completion-of-eu-accession-to-the-echr.

K Maskus and J Reichman, 'The globalisation of private knowledge goods and the privatization of global public goods' (2004) 7 JIEL 279–320

C Oguamanam, 'IP in global governance: a venture in critical reflection' (2011) WIPOJ 2(2) 196–216

D Vaver, 'Intellectual property: still a "bargain"?' (Editorial) (2012) 34(9) EIPR 579–86

K Weatherall, 'Intellectual property in the TPP: not "The New TRIPS"' (2016) 17(2) Melbourne J Int Law 1–29.

PK Yu, 'Currents and crosscurrents in the international intellectual property regime' (2004) 38 Loyola of Los Angeles Law Rev 323

Radio

Clive Anderson, 'Unreliable Evidence' www.bbc.co.uk/programmes/b00zsjzf

Ongoing updates

The IPKat blog at http://ipkitten.blogspot.com (also Twitter feed)

IPWatch at www.ip-watch.org (also Twitter feed)

WIPO consideration of protection of Traditional Knowledge at www.wipo.int/tk/en/tk

Part II

Copyright

Introduction

This Part of the book explains and discusses the law of copyright. It has six chapters. The first considers the scope of copyright in the UK against the background of international and EU law on the subject, and its historical development. This also throws light on the rationales or justifications for copyright, as well as the recent policy context within which copyright law has developed. The second chapter discusses the subject matter of copyright, that is to say, those things—or works—which come under its protection. It goes on to explain which persons can claim the benefits of copyright and the length of time for which the protection endures. The next chapter explains what constitutes infringement of copyright, and is followed by a chapter discussing the exceptions to copyright. The fifth of the copyright chapters examines rights granted exclusively to authors—moral rights and artist's resale right. A crucial point is that the forms of infringement of economic rights—or restricted acts—also define how copyright may be exploited to obtain financial returns for its owner. Other persons who wish to do one or more of these acts will have to obtain the copyright owner's permission—or licence—to do so and usually that permission will come at a price, unless an exception applies. This chapter also discusses fundamental rules on such exploitation and use of copyright. The final chapter examines rights that are very similar to, but different from, copyright— the *sui generis* database right and performers' rights. Throughout the six chapters, some of the most important contemporary issues affecting the development of copyright law—including the internet, the concept of the public domain, and the impact of human rights law—are highlighted.

Sources of the law: key websites

- Copyright, Designs and Patents Act 1988 as amended
  www.legislation.gov.uk/ukpga/1988/48/contents

- Decisions of the courts in the various jurisdictions of the UK, for which see the British and Irish Legal Information Institute (BAILII)
  www.bailii.org

- EU Copyright Directives, for which see the Commission's Internal Market Directorate General's website
  https://ec.europa.eu/digital-single-market/en/eu-copyright-legislation

- Berne Convention for the Protection of Literary and Artistic Works, for which see the World Intellectual Property Organization (WIPO) website
  www.wipo.int/treaties/en/ip/berne/trtdocs_wo001.html

- Rome Convention for the Protection of Performers, Producers of Phonograms and Broadcasting Organizations, for which see the WIPO website
  www.wipo.int/treaties/en/ip/rome/index.html

- The UK Intellectual Property Organization (IPO) website has a useful section devoted to copyright
  www.gov.uk/topic/intellectual-property/copyright

- UK government guidance on Copyright and Brexit
  www.gov.uk/government/publications/changes-to-copyright-law-in-the-event-of-no-deal/changes-to-copyright-law-in-the-event-of-no-deal
  www.gov.uk/government/publications/copyright-if-theres-no-brexit-deal

Copyright 1: history, rationale, and policy context

Introduction

Scope and overview of chapter

2.1 This chapter considers the evolution of modern copyright law against a background of its historical development in the UK and the international and European frameworks within which UK copyright law has been set since the 19th century. It examines the rationale and justifications for copyright, and also identifies and examines the general policy context within which law and policy has developed in the UK and the European Union (EU). What holds many of these developments and initiatives together is the development of digital, mobile, and interactive technology as the means of delivering ideas, information, and entertainment to their users. As such, the chapter outlines the technological developments which have brought copyright reform to the forefront in recent times and looks at difficulties which this new environment presents for copyright, the rules of which were mostly created in a world where material came to users in the form of single copies or performances put on the market by intermediaries of one kind or another, such as publishers, broadcasters, and film and sound recording producers. This survey of the policy context in general will assist in understanding how specific aspects of the copyright framework have developed and the challenges posed in adapting the framework.

2.2 **Learning objectives**

By the end of this chapter you should be able to describe and explain:

- the development of copyright, and its rationale;
- the policy and reform context for copyright law;
- the significance of the digital environment, and other related concerns for copyright law.

2.3 The rest of the chapter looks like this:

- Early history (2.4–2.7)
- International developments (2.8–2.13)
- European developments (2.14–2.15)
- Copyright framework in the UK (2.16–2.20)

- Rationale of copyright (2.21–2.25)
- Policy context (2.26–2.39).

Early history

2.4   In most European countries the origins of copyright law lie in the efforts of government to regulate and control the output of printers once the technology of printing had been invented and become established in the 15th and 16th centuries. Whereas before printing a writing, once created, could only be physically multiplied by the highly laborious and error-prone process of manual copying out, printing made it possible to have as many exact copies of a work as there were persons who wanted and could afford to buy them. This meant much more rapid and widespread circulation of ideas and information. While the state and church thought this was to be encouraged in many aspects (eg dissemination of material such as Bibles and government information), it also meant that undesirable content—dissent and criticism of government and established religion, for example—could circulate too quickly for their comfort. So, all over Europe, government established controls over printing, by requiring printers to have official licences to be in business and produce books. These licences typically gave the printer the exclusive right to print particular works for a fixed period of years, enabling him to prevent others from doing so during that period. Although the official licences could only grant rights to print in the territory of the state that had granted them, and therefore could not prevent printing of the same works in other territories, they did usually prohibit the import of such foreign printings into the territory where the licence had been granted. In England, the printers (then termed 'stationers') formed a collective organisation, known as the Stationers' Company, which in the 16th century was given the power to require the entry in its register of all lawfully printed books. Further, only members of the Company could enter books in the register. As a result, the Company achieved a dominant position over publishing in 17th-century England. But there was no equivalent in contemporary Scotland or Ireland.[1] However, in 1694 the English Parliament deprived the Stationers' Company of its powers of control, creating uncertainty about regulation of the printing industry at a critical juncture in British history.[2]

 Question

How was the printing of books regulated in England before 1707?[3]

2.5   In 1707 the Parliaments of England and Scotland were united in a single body as the result of the Anglo–Scottish Union finally agreed that year, after much debate. The new Parliament was enjoined to respect the separate identities of the English and Scottish legal systems, but was enabled to change the laws of both countries as part of an overall project that today might be described as the creation of a single market in the UK. An important early piece of legislation to this end was the Copyright Act of 1709,[4] which created a single regime for application in both England and Scotland. The Act marks an important shift of emphasis in the law, because it gave the 'sole right and liberty of printing books', not to printers, but to the authors of the books. This is the first formal legal recognition that a reason for conferring exclusive or property rights

---

[1]   On the pre-history of copyright in Scotland, see AJ Mann, 'Scottish copyright before the Statute of 1710' [2000] JR 11; also the same author's *The Scottish Book Trade 1500–1720* (2000), Ch 4 and App 1; and 'Some property is theft: copyright law and illegal activity in early modern Scotland' in R Myers, M Harris, and G Mandelbrote (eds), *Against the Law: Crime, Sharp Practice and the Control of Print* (2004).

[2]   See in general M Rose, *Authors and Owners* (1993); J Greene, *The Trouble with Ownership: Literary Property and Authorial Liability in England, 1660–1730* (2005).

[3]   See 'Primary Sources on Copyright (1450–1900)' at www.copyrighthistory.org, a digital collection of primary sources from the UK and beyond and related commentary.

[4]   Often known to copyright lawyers as 'the Statute or Act of Anne', after Queen Anne, who reigned 1702–1714. The Act entered into force in 1710 and is sometimes given that date rather than 1709.

in this area was the work of its creator or originator. It may reflect the theories of contemporary philosophers such as John Locke, who held that rights of property flowed first from the labour of the person who created the thing to be owned. But the 1709 Act also enabled the author to transfer his rights to 'assigns', who would typically be the printer, without whom the author would be unable to disseminate and profit from his creation. Further, a precondition of the right was registration of the work at Stationers' Hall; something of a disadvantage for Scottish and Irish printers, since the Hall was in London. The right lasted for 14 years from first publication and if at the end of that time the author was still alive, it was renewed for another 14 years.[5]

 Question

When was the first copyright statute passed? What changes did it make to the previous regime described in para 2.4?

2.6   The next critical stage in the early history of British copyright came from the 1730s on, as the first copyrights created under the 1709 Act began to expire. Did those who had held statutory rights to prevent unauthorised copies also have an underlying right at common law which now revived to enable them to continue to control printing and publication of their work? There was intense controversy and much litigation in both England and Scotland on this question.[6] Matters were not resolved until the great cases of *Hinton v Donaldson*[7] in Scotland in 1773 and *Donaldson v Beckett*[8] in England in 1774. In these decisions, the Court of Session and the House of Lords respectively held that there was no copyright at common law in works which had been published and enjoyed copyright under the 1709 Act. While the common law of both England and Scotland went on to develop with regard to *unpublished* works (only the author or his licensee could authorise publication), the development of copyright would henceforth be principally through statute. The common law copyright in unpublished work remained significant until the beginning of the 20th century, however, because unlike the statutory copyrights, it had no specific time limit, and lasted until lawful publication (ie it could go on forever if publication never occurred).

 Question

What was the effect of the decisions in *Donaldson v Beckett* and *Hinton v Donaldson*?

2.7   The primary development of copyright after *Donaldson v Beckett* was by statute. Engravings had been given copyright by statutes in 1734 and 1766, and further Acts for this subject matter were passed in 1777 and 1836;[9] sculptures joined books as copyright subject matter in 1798;[10] and paintings, drawings, and photographs (the last a form of art recently made possible by technological development) were added by the Fine Arts Copyright Act 1862. Plays were protected against unauthorised public performance as well as printing by the

---

[5]   See further R Deazley, *On the Origin of the Right to Copy—Charting the Movement of Copyright Law in Eighteenth Century Britain (1695–1775)* (2004); JC Ginsburg, '"Un chose publique?" The author's domain and the public domain in early British, French and US copyright law' (2006) 16 CLJ 636.

[6]   In addition to works already cited, see WR Cornish, 'The author's surrogate: the genesis of British copyright' in K O'Donovan and GR Rubin (eds), *Human Rights and Legal History: Essays in Honour of Brian Simpson* (2000); W St Clair, *The Reading Nation in the Romantic Period* (2004); W McDougall, 'Copyright litigation in the Court of Session, 1738–1749, and the rise of the Scottish book trade' (1987) 5 Edinburgh Bibliographical Soc Trans 2–31; HL MacQueen, 'Intellectual property and the common law in Scotland c1700–c1850' in L Bently, C Ng, and G D'Agostino (eds), *The Common Law of Intellectual Property: Essays in Honour of David Vaver* (2010).

[7]   1773 Mor 8307. Full text of the judicial opinions in the case can be found in J Boswell, *The Decisions of the Court of Session upon the Question of Literary Property in the Cause of John Hinton of London, Bookseller, against Alexander Donaldson and John Wood, Booksellers in Edinburgh, and James Meurose, Bookseller in Kilmarnock* (1774). See further MacQueen, 'Intellectual property and the common law', note 6, 33–38.

[8]   (1774) 2 Bro PC 129. See further R Deazley, *Rethinking Copyright: History, Theory, Language* (2006).

[9]   Engraving Copyright Acts 1734, 1766, 1777, and 1836.

[10]   Sculpture Copyright Act 1798; replaced by the Sculpture Copyright Act 1814.

Dramatic Copyright Act 1833, and public lectures were given limited protection by the Lectures Copyright Act 1835. The length of the copyright term began to increase, moved by ideas that, if the basis of copyright was the recognition and encouragement of authorship, its duration should be extended for the benefit of family and descendants who might otherwise suffer for their relative's art.[11] In 1814 the term for books became the longer of 28 years or the author's lifetime, while in 1842 there was a further extension, inspired by the lawyer-playwright Thomas Talfourd, to the longer of 42 years or the author's lifetime plus seven years. These extensions of copyright did not have an easy passage through Parliament: for example, the debates on the 1842 Act include TB Macaulay's famous criticism that copyright was 'a tax on readers for the purpose of giving a bounty to authors'.[12] In general, however, it was accepted that if authorship in literature, drama, music, and art was to be rewarded, then the protection of copyright was essential.[13]

Key points on the early history

- Modern copyright begins in the 18th century, mainly for printed books.
- It is decided that copyright is primarily a statutory right, which endures only for the period laid down by the statute.
- Unpublished works have a common law copyright which lasts for as long as the work is unpublished.
- In the 19th century, copyright is extended to works of art and drama, and the period of protection gets longer.

International developments

Berne Convention 1886

2.8   The major problem which domestic legislation alone could not solve was unauthorised activity outside the UK. Copyright remained, like the old licensing systems from which it sprang, entirely limited to the territory in which it was granted, leaving authors and publishers unprotected beyond their home shores. As international markets for creative output began to take off in the course of the 19th century, so states began to enter into negotiations for the mutual recognition and enforcement of foreigners' copyrights. This culminated in 1886 in the multinational arrangement known as the *Berne Convention*, although the treaty also underwent important revisions at Paris in 1896, Berlin in 1908, Rome in 1928, Brussels in 1948, Stockholm in 1967, and Paris in 1971.[14] The Convention relates to literary and artistic works, amongst which are included films, and requires its member states to provide protection for every production in the literary, scientific, and artistic domain.

 Question

When did the Berne Convention come into being, and how often has it been revised? What is the policy objective of the Convention?

---

[11]   Particularly significant writers in this regard were William Wordsworth and Sir Walter Scott.

[12]   See for a very full account of the genesis of the 1842 Act, C Seville, *Literary Copyright Reform in Early Victorian England* (1999).

[13]   On the 19th-century 'crystallisation' of copyright in the UK, see B Sherman and L Bently, *The Making of Modern Intellectual Property* (1999), 111–28, 137–40.

[14]   See in general S Ricketson and J Ginsburg, *International Copyright and Neighbouring Rights: The Berne Convention and Beyond* (2006); C Seville, *The Internationalisation of Copyright Law: Books, Buccaneers and the Black Flag in the Nineteenth Century* (2006).

The other main features of the Berne Convention which have emerged from the international activity of the last 120 years are:

- The principle of *national treatment*: each member state of the Convention would give citizens of other member states the same rights of copyright that it gave to its own citizens (Arts 3–5).

- *Minimum standards for national copyright legislation*—each member state agreed to certain basic rules which their national laws must contain, although it could, if it wished, increase the amount of protection given to right holders. One of these minimum rules was that copyright should arise with the creation of a work and not depend upon any formality such as a system of public registration (Art 5(2)). This entailed the end of the British system of registration at Stationers' Hall when the UK finally implemented the Berne Convention in the Copyright Act 1911. Another important Berne rule, also implemented in the 1911 Act, was that the term of copyright was to be a minimum of the author's lifetime plus 50 years.

- *A focus on the author* as the key figure in copyright law: apart from the prohibition of registration requirements and the extension of the copyright term, the Berne Convention emphasised in other ways the centrality of authorship in copyright. Its purpose was 'the protection of the rights of authors in their literary and artistic works' (Art 1), not the protection of publishers and other actors in the process of disseminating works to their public. In the 1928 revision the concept of moral rights was introduced (Art 6*bis*), giving authors the right to be identified as such and to object to derogatory treatment of their works. These rights, unlike those which have become known as the economic rights to prevent reproduction, public performance and, in due course, broadcasting, could not be transferred to others.

- The possibility of *exceptions to copyright*, enabling the reproduction of literary and artistic works without the right holder's prior permission. The precise nature of these exceptions was for national legislation: the guiding principle stated that such exceptions were permitted 'in certain special cases, provided that such reproduction does not conflict with a normal exploitation of the work and does not unreasonably prejudice the legitimate interests of the author' (Art 9). Free use of works was expressly permitted in the cases of quotation from lawfully published works, illustration for teaching purposes, and news reporting (Art 10).

2.9   The importance of the Berne Convention cannot be overstated. It remains the basis for international copyright relations and domestic copyright law. Originally a mainly European instrument, it now extends to most of the world, including since 1989 the United States. Under the Trade-Related Aspects of Intellectual Property Rights Agreement of 1994 (TRIPS; see para 2.10), states wishing to participate in international trade must join and comply with the Berne Convention. In 1961, a Berne-like treaty, the Rome Convention on the Protection of Performers, Producers of Phonograms and Broadcasting Organizations (Rome Convention 1961), was created to provide the international basis for the protection of performers, phonograph producers, and broadcasters.

 Question

What are the differences in subject matter of the Berne and Rome Conventions?

Further international developments

2.10   There were important developments in the international protection of copyright in the 1990s. The TRIPS Agreement 1994 contains a number of provisions on copyright, compliance with which is required of states wishing to be members of the World Trade Organization (WTO). They have to:

- sign up to the Berne Convention, apart from its provisions on moral rights (Art 9(1));
- protect computer programs and databases (Art 10);

- provide for rental rights in at least computer programs and films (Art 11);
- where the duration of copyright is calculated other than by reference to the life of a natural person, give a minimum term of 50 years calculated from, as the case may be, the date of authorised publication or of the work being made (Art 12).

Further, TRIPS makes explicit what had previously been an underlying principle of copyright law, namely, that it protects expression rather than ideas.[15] The agreement also states that member states must 'confine' limitations or exceptions to copyright to 'certain special cases which do not conflict with a normal exploitation of the work and do not unreasonably prejudice the legitimate interests of the right holder'.[16] The verb 'confine', not found in this context in the Berne Convention, is significant, hinting as it does at a hostile attitude towards copyright exceptions and limitations. Finally, there is provision for the protection of performers, producers of sound recordings, and broadcasting organisations.[17]

 Question

What does TRIPS add to the Berne and Rome Conventions?

2.11   In 1996 two further treaties supplementing the Berne Convention were agreed at the World Intellectual Property Organization (WIPO). The WIPO Copyright Treaty (WCT) followed TRIPS in:

- providing that copyright protected only the form in which a work was expressed and not its underlying ideas (Art 2);
- requiring copyright protection for computer programs and databases (Arts 4 and 5);
- recognising rental right in relation to computer programs and films, and extending it to sound recordings (Art 7);
- adopting the language of 'confining' copyright exceptions and limitations (Art 10 WCT).

2.12   But where TRIPS was driven by concerns about international trade, the WCT was primarily concerned to respond to the problems created by the rise of the internet, and hence it added rights to deal with distribution and public communication of works and to support the use of technological measures in the protection from unauthorised use of works recorded digitally.[18] The other treaty concluded in 1996, WIPO Performances and Phonograms Treaty (WPPT), was for the further protection of performers and producers of sound recordings, significantly supplementing the provisions of the Rome Convention 1961 (see para 2.9) in this regard.

 Question

What did WCT 1996 add to previous international agreements on copyright? What was its main policy goal?

2.13   In June 2013, the WIPO-administered Marrakesh Treaty to Facilitate Access to Published Works for Persons Who Are Blind, Visually Impaired or Otherwise Print Disabled (Marrakesh Treaty) was adopted. Aimed at improving access to copyright-protected materials for those with visual disabilities, it introduces limitations and exceptions to copyright to facilitate reproduction, distribution, and making available of works in accessible formats. The UK is not yet a contracting party to it. However, the EU is, and the treaty has been implemented in the EU and the UK (paras 5.11 and 5.47).

---

[15] TRIPS, Art 9(2).   [16] TRIPS, Art 13.   [17] TRIPS, Art 14.   [18] WCT, Arts 6, 8, 11, and 12.

Exercise

Look at the Marrakesh Treaty and find out more about the negotiations up to the adoption of the treaty. Was the main policy goal of the treaty easy to achieve? Were any compromises made?

European developments

2.14   In the 1980s the EU[19] began to become more interested in copyright as an element in the creation of a single market. In 1991 there began a programme of Directives on copyright, designed to harmonise the national laws of the member states in certain key areas (computer programs[20] and databases[21]) and to reduce the potential for differences to cause unjustified obstacles to the free movement of goods and services (rental rights,[22] satellite broadcasting,[23] copyright duration,[24] resale rights in works of art[25]).[26] The international activity in the 1990s had further significant effects upon harmonisation of copyright law in the EU.[27] In particular, the WCT led to the introduction in 1997 of the first draft of what eventually became, after much debate and controversy, the Information Society (InfoSoc) Directive 2001.[28] This collection of significant directives focused on approximating laws in specific areas of copyright and led to piecemeal partial harmonisation of copyright in the EU. The Commission's piecemeal harmonisation has continued thereafter, in the form of more specific initiatives such as directives on the term of copyright in sound recordings, collective rights management and multi-territorial licensing of rights in musical works for online uses, and certain permitted uses of orphan works.[29] In addition to implementation of these EU directives, references for preliminary rulings on the interpretation of these Directives on copyright have also been regularly made by member states to the Court of Justice of the European Union (CJEU).

Question

What topics have been dealt with in the EU's copyright Directives?

ACTA

The Anti-Counterfeiting Trade Agreement (ACTA), a controversial plurilateral agreement, was aimed at creating effective common enforcement standards to combat global proliferation of counterfeiting through enhanced international cooperation. The agreement was signed by a number of countries including the US, the UK, and the EU between 2011 and 2012 and contained, amongst others, general provisions on civil

---

[19]   At the time called the European Community.

[20]   Directive 91/250/EEC on the legal protection of computer programs, repealed and replaced by Directive 2009/24/EC.

[21]   Directive 96/9/EC on the legal protection of databases.

[22]   Directive 92/100/EEC on rental right and lending right, repealed and replaced by Directive 2006/115/EEC.

[23]   Directive 93/83/EEC on satellite broadcasting and cable retransmission.

[24]   Directive 93/98/EEC harmonising the term of protection, repealed and replaced by Directive 2006/116/EC, amended by Directive 2011/77/EU.

[25]   Directive 2001/84/EC on the resale right for the benefit of the author of an original work of art.

[26]   For all EU Directives and Regulations in the area of copyright, see European Commission, 'The EU copyright legislation' at https://ec.europa.eu/digital-single-market/en/eu-copyright-legislation.

[27]   WCT and WPPT were signed by the EU in December 1996 and ratified in December 2009.

[28]   Directive 2001/29/EC on the harmonisation of certain aspects of copyright and related rights in the information society.

[29]   Term Directive 2011 (see paras 7.43–7.44); Directive 2012/28/EU of the European Parliament and of the Council of 25 October 2012 on certain permitted uses of orphan works; Directive 2014/26/EU of the European Parliament and of the Council of 26 February 2014 on collective management of copyright and related rights and multi-territorial licensing of rights in musical works for online use in the internal market.

and criminal enforcement, especially for copyright infringement on a commercial scale, and intellectual property (IP) enforcement in the digital environment. ACTA was met with strong opposition, in particular due to mistrust developed as a result of the agreement being negotiated outside the traditional international forums on IP as well as concerns about its effect on freedom of expression and privacy. The CJEU was asked to review the compatibility of the agreement with fundamental rights. In July 2012, the European Parliament resoundingly rejected the agreement.

A Digital Single Market

2.15   At the same time as CJEU's attempts to harmonise aspects of the copyright framework, the European Commission has continued with its harmonisation programme and evaluated further initiatives. In May 2015, the Commission issued its Communication on a Digital Single Market (DSM) Strategy for Europe, with the aim of creating legislative steps to modernise 'copyright rules in the light of the digital revolution and changed consumer behaviour'.[30] In December 2015, delivering on its DSM strategy, the Commission outlined its vision of a modern EU copyright framework and issued an action plan to modernise EU copyright rules.[31] It then released three key legislative proposals. First, on making content portable across borders, as part of the DSM strategy, it introduced the Portability Regulation,[32] which allows consumers to access their online content services (eg video streaming) when they travel to another EU member state, as if they are at home. Second, the EU adopted a directive and a regulation for the implementation of the Marrakesh treaty in the EU.[33] Third, in September 2016, the Commission released its plans to modernise the EU copyright framework through a Proposal for a Directive on Copyright in the Digital Single Market (Draft Copyright Directive 2016).[34] This includes significant reforms in the area of copyright exceptions and limitations, provisions for fair remuneration in the copyright contracts of authors and performers, use of out-of-commerce works by cultural heritage institutions, a new right for press publications in relation to their digital uses (press publishers' right), and an obligation on online services in relation to certain uses of copyright-protected content (value gap). In undergoing the EU legislative process, the draft directive has proved to be particularly controversial in relation to its provisions on the value gap and press publishers' right.[35] Various amendments have been proposed, as reflected in the positions adopted by the European Council and the European Parliament,[36] and after a successful vote on the directive in the European Parliament on 12 September 2018, trilogue negotiations are now underway (three-way negotiations between the Parliament, Council, and the Commission) with a final vote on the text due in 2019. At the time of submission of this manuscript, the legislative process is not complete and references to the draft directive will be made, where relevant.

---

[30] COM(2015) 192 final; see generally http://ec.europa.eu/priorities/digital-single-market_en.

[31] http://europa.eu/rapid/press-release_IP-15-6261_en.htm; see 'Towards a modern, more European copyright framework', COM(2015) 626 final.

[32] Regulation (EU) 2017/1128 of the European Parliament and of the Council of 14 June 2017 on cross-border portability of online content services in the internal market.

[33] Directive (EU) 2017/1564 on certain permitted uses of certain works and other subject matter protected by copyright and related rights for the benefit of persons who are blind, visually impaired or otherwise print-disabled; Regulation (EU) 2017/1563 on the cross-border exchange between the Union and third countries of accessible format copies of certain works and other subject matter protected by copyright and related rights for the benefit of persons who are blind, visually impaired or otherwise print-disabled.

[34] Proposal for a Directive on Copyright in the Digital Single Market, 14 September 2016, COM(2016) 593 final.

[35] B Farrand, 'Towards a modern, more European copyright framework, or, how to rebrand the same old approach?' [2019] EIPR 65.

[36] See amendments adopted by the European Parliament on 12 September 2018 at www.europarl.europa.eu/sides/getDoc.do?pubRef=-//EP//TEXT+TA+P8-TA-2018-0337+0+DOC+XML+V0//EN; see also, the European Council's position as adopted on 25 May 2018 at https://eur-lex.europa.eu/legal-content/EN/TXT/PDF/?uri=CONSIL:ST_9134_2018_INIT&from=EN.

Exercise

Find out whether the EU legislative process for the Draft Copyright Directive 2016 is complete. If it has resulted in the adoption of a new directive, then find out the time period for its implementation by EU member states.

Key points on modern developments

- Copyright internationalised from the late 19th century onwards—today there is both a global and a European dimension to law-making, meaning that scope for purely national initiatives is limited. An appreciation of the European developments as well as the international background is therefore vital to fully understand the present law in the UK.

- Copyright extended further, to photographs, films, sound recordings, broadcasts, and computer technology (software and databases).

- There is a division apparent in most legal systems between the copyright treatment of 'author works' (covered by the Berne Convention) and 'neighbouring' or 'media works' (covered by the Rome Convention)—see further para 3.39.

Copyright framework in the UK—European and international influences

Copyright Acts 1911–1988

2.16   As already noted, the UK implemented the Berne Convention in the Copyright Act 1911, which came into force on 1 July 1912. The Act swept away all the particular copyrights which had grown up over the 19th century (see para 2.7), and replaced them with a much more general approach. It also abolished the common law copyright in unpublished works, replacing that with a statutory scheme for such material. The Act also responded to technological development by conferring a copyright on a new subject matter not mentioned in Berne, namely sound recordings. Yet more new technology underlay the 1911 Act's replacement with the Copyright Act 1956, which came into force on 1 June 1957, and extended protection to films and broadcasts, and also to the typographical arrangements of published editions of works. Between them the two statutes brought under the umbrella of copyright works which, apart from films, were seen in Continental European systems as belonging to a distinct category of their own. They were not author works, but rather technological media works, by which entrepreneurs brought such works to new audiences in a different form. While they deserved copyright-like protection, the substance of the protection did not need to be as great as with author works. The Continental European systems thus developed systems for the protection of what were termed 'neighbouring rights' quite distinct from those for author works. The approach was reinforced by the Rome Convention's provision on neighbouring rights. But in the UK the 1956 Act followed the distinction between author and media works only in a modified form: one part of the Act gave copyright to literary, dramatic, musical, and artistic works, while a second part gave a somewhat modified form of what was still called copyright to sound recordings, films, broadcasts, and published editions.

CDPA 1988

2.17   The current legislative framework for copyright and related rights in the UK is the Copyright, Designs and Patents Act 1988 (CDPA 1988), which came into force on 1 August 1989. It sets out, in Part I, the subject matter, ownership, and duration of copyright protection, the bundle of economic rights given to copyright owners which allows them to use and exploit copyright-protected works and also prevent infringement, and the acts which are permitted in relation to use of copyright-protected works. It also sets out moral rights provided to authors. CDPA 1988 was also a response to technological development. Again, new ways of creating and disseminating works—for example, computer programs or software, and cable and satellite broadcasting—were recognised. But even more important in giving rise to the replacement of the 1956 Act were expansions in the ways by which copies might be made of works, notably photocopying, re-recording sound recordings on audio cassettes, and videoing broadcasts. Advances in copying technology meant that not only could individuals make copies for their personal or business use, but so too could so-called 'pirates', that is, persons who made copies in great quantities for commercial resale at prices significantly lower than those of the copyright owner. The Act continued to apply the concept of copyright generally to both author and media works, but it also moved towards the Continental European model by recognising moral rights for authors in literary, dramatic, musical, and artistic works and films.

 Question

List and date the three UK copyright statutes of the 20th century, and give the dates when each of the Acts came into force.

2.18   The implementation in the UK of WCT and WPPT and several EU Directives (para 2.14) led to significant amendment of CDPA 1988, generally by way of amending regulations. In addition to the implementation of EU directives, references to the CJEU for preliminary rulings on the interpretation of these directives have also played an important role because the CDPA 1988 has to be interpreted in conformity with them. In fact, recent judgments of the CJEU on copyright matters have attempted to indirectly, and arguably in depth, harmonise some fundamental copyright concepts, which were previously believed to have remained unharmonised by the piecemeal framework of copyright directives (see paras 3.13, 3.19, 3.25–3.28, 5.41) and as such received criticism for having 'deepened the harmonisation of copyright well beyond that which had been agreed politically'.[37] The full impact of such judgments on UK copyright law remains an important concern.

2.19   There have been notable domestic copyright reform initiatives in the UK in the 21st century. Copyright featured prominently among the issues addressed by two major UK independent reviews of intellectual property. The remit of the *Gowers Review of Intellectual Property* published in 2006[38] included, in particular, whether the 'infringement framework reflects the digital environment'; whether 'fair use' (sic) provisions for citizens are reasonable; and what the term of protection for sound recordings should be. This followed the Labour Party manifesto commitment with which it entered and won the 2005 general election: 'Copyright in a digital age: We will modernise copyright and other forms of protection of intellectual property rights so that they are appropriate for the digital age.'

2.20   The *Hargreaves Review of Intellectual Property and Growth* was published in 2011, commissioned by the Conservative Party-led government. Prime Minister David Cameron, when launching the review, stated: 'I can announce today that we are reviewing our IP laws, to see if we can make them fit for the internet age . . . [the review will] focus on how the IP system can be improved to help the new business models arising from the digital age.'[39] The Hargreaves Review made significant recommendations for reform in the area of copyright exceptions (it rejected a US-style 'fair use' defence but considered exemptions for format-shifting, parody, non-commercial research, library archiving) and copyright licensing (enabling licensing

---

[37] L Bently, 'The return of industrial copyright?' [2012] EIPR 654 at 671; see also S Vousden, 'Infopaq and the Europeanisation of copyright law' [2010] WIPO J 197 and E Rosati, 'Towards an EU-wide copyright? (Judicial) pride and (legislative) prejudice' [2013] IPQ 47.

[38] *Gowers Review of Intellectual Property* (HM Treasury 2006).

[39] I Hargreaves, *Digital Opportunity: A Review of Intellectual Property and Growth* (IPO 2011).

of orphan works).[40] It also recommended the introduction of a 'Digital Copyright Exchange', which would provide a common platform for cross-sectoral licensing transactions and provide a marketplace where such licences can be bought and sold. The government appointed Richard Hooper to lead an independent review of this proposal. The second phase of this review recommended the creation of a 'Copyright Hub' in the UK and in March 2013, the government announced it would give £150,000 funding to kick-start the Copyright Hub.[41] The Copyright Hub's aim is 'to help copyright work the way the internet works by making the process of giving and getting permission—the basic building block of the copyright process—fit for purpose in the age of the Internet'.[42]

Brexit

The UK has recently triggered the process for it to leave the EU (para 1.62). As noted in Chapter 1, at the time of writing it is not clear whether the draft Withdrawal Agreement will be concluded or, if the UK will exit the EU without concluding any form of withdrawal agreement at all ie a 'no deal' Brexit. A 'no deal' Brexit will affect creators, right owners, and users, in relation to cross-border mechanisms provided under EU law, and will inevitably have an impact on the current framework of copyright and related rights in the UK as well as initiatives for copyright reform. While copyright remains a national right, the EU has harmonised a number of key aspects of copyright (notably several exclusive rights, duration of copyright, exceptions and limitations) and a substantial part of UK copyright law now derives from, or is framed in light of, such EU law. However, two things are important to note here. First, such EU law and its implementation in the UK will be preserved as retained EU law under the powers in the European Union (Withdrawal) Act 2018. Second, much of this EU law, although not all, builds on and implements international treaties to which both the UK and other EU member states are party. Under such treaties, member countries provide copyright protection for works originating in or made by nationals of other countries under the 'national treatment' rule (see para 2.8). Consequently, in a 'no-deal' scenario, the UK government's view is that 'the UK's continued membership of the main international treaties on copyright will ensure that the scope of protection for copyright works in the UK and for UK works abroad will remain largely unchanged'.[43] The harmonised aspects of copyright to which there is likely to be little impact will be flagged up in subsequent chapters.

There is also a body of EU law on copyright and related rights that goes beyond the provisions of the international treaties and in particular provides for several cross-border copyright mechanisms unique to the EU through which reciprocal protections and benefits between EU member states are established (eg certain permitted uses of orphan works, artist's resale right, *sui generis* database right). Because many such cross-border initiatives extend only to member states of the EU or EEA, in a 'no-deal' scenario the UK will be treated as a third country. Consequently, the reciprocal element of these mechanisms will cease to apply to the UK. Specific examples in this regard, where relevant, will be flagged up in subsequent chapters.

Finally, in the past few decades, there has been an understanding that any significant reform in the area of copyright would stem from the EU or even more widely based international institutions (although

---

[40] A number of the recommended changes were implemented in 2014 and are discussed in Chapter 5.
[41] www.gov.uk/government/news/government-gives-150-000-funding-to-kick-start-copyright-hub.
[42] www.copyrighthub.org.
[43] UK Government, 'Copyright if there's no Brexit deal' (September 2018) www.gov.uk/government/publications/copyright-if-theres-no-brexit-deal; although some changes to such retained UK copyright law in the CDPA 1988 will be necessary in a 'no-deal' scenario. The UK government has indicated that it will implement such changes through amending regulations. For instance, one change necessary will be removal of references to the EU and EEA member states. See further UK Government, 'Changes to copyright law in the event of no deal' (26 October 2018) www.gov.uk/government/publications/changes-to-copyright-law-in-the-event-of-no-deal/changes-to-copyright-law-in-the-event-of-no-deal.

reform at this level is even slower), and any major solutions are likely to be Europe-wide rather than in a merely UK context.[44] However, a 'no-deal' Brexit would significantly change this understanding. First, the UK might have no obligation to implement any changes that may eventually emerge from current EU reforms proposed in the Draft Copyright Directive 2016. This would depend on when a final directive is adopted by the EU, and whether the UK has exited the EU before the end of the period for the implementation of such directive. Second, the UK may also choose not to continue to adapt to CJEU jurisprudence as it will not be bound by it. Finally, there will be scope in the future, to substantially diverge from EU law and introduce domestic copyright reform in specific areas, albeit while complying with relevant international frameworks. These possibilities, where relevant, will be highlighted in subsequent chapters.

Rationale of copyright

2.21   Copyright first developed in the early modern period as a response to the growth of the printing technology that facilitated the rapid multiplication and distribution of copies of written works. As shown by the history described in the early part of the chapter, change in the law has continued to be driven by technological advance in the means by which works can be presented to the public at large, and protection has been extended and adapted to cover photography, cinematography, sound recording, broadcasting, cable transmissions, computer programs, and, most recently, the internet. The practical benefit of developing protections within the copyright mould is the applicability of the international regime under the Berne Convention and other treaties which ensure potentially worldwide protection for right holders.

2.22   Despite the harmonising effects of the Berne Convention and other more recent international instruments, two distinct major conceptualisations of the functions of copyright can still be identified in the world's legal systems.[45] The Anglo–American or common law tradition emphasises the *economic role of copyright*. Protection of copyright subject matter against unauthorised acts of exploitation enables right holders either to go to market themselves with a product based on the material, or to grant others, by outright transfer or, more typically, by licence, the right to do so for whatever seems an appropriate price. In the absence of copyright, which would enable free-riding by would-be users, it is unlikely that producers of the material would earn any return for their work, and without that incentive production would dry up or slacken significantly. Copyright is thus essentially a response to market failure, a means by which socially beneficial activities can be made financially worthwhile for those engaging in them. It rests ultimately upon the general or public interest in having works containing ideas, information, instruction, and entertainment made available, and in rewarding those—publishers as well as the creators of the works—who perform this function in society in accordance with the public demand for their efforts.[46] In contrast, the Continental European or civil law tradition sees copyright as springing from the *personality rights of the individual creator* of the subject matter. This perception is reflected in the name 'author-law' given to the topic by the various Continental systems—*droit d'auteur, urheberrecht*, and so on. Protection is given out of respect for the individual's creative act of production, and extends beyond the merely economic to the so-called 'moral rights': the right to be identified as the creator of a work, the right to have the integrity of a work preserved,

---

[44]   See further E Derclaye (ed), *Research Handbook on the Future of EU Copyright* (2009); M van Eechoud et al, *Harmonizing European Copyright Law: The Challenges of Better Lawmaking* (2009).

[45]   For a comparative overview, see G Davies, *Copyright and the Public Interest* (2nd edn, 2003), especially Chs 5–7. See also B Sherman and A Strowel (eds), *Of Authors and Origins: Essays on Copyright Law* (1994).

[46]   The economics of copyright are explored in, eg, W Landes and R Posner, *The Economic Structure of Intellectual Property Law* (2003), Chs 2–6, 8–10; R Towse (ed), *Copyright and the Cultural Industries* (2002); MA Einhorn, *Media, Technology and Copyright: Integrating Law and Economics* (2004). Many classic earlier studies are reprinted in R Towse and R Holzhauer (eds), *The Economics of Intellectual Property* (2002), vol 1 (Introduction and Copyright).

and others. Copyright is thus rooted in protection of the individual personality and interests of the author as expressed in his work. Companies and organisations as such cannot be creators.

2.23   The distinction between the two conceptualisations is sometimes summarised by saying that the Anglo–American tradition is centred on the entrepreneur, the Continental one on the author. It is reflected in various rules. For example:

- where the Anglo–American tradition gives copyright protection to media works such as sound recordings and broadcasts, the Continental tradition uses a separate group of 'neighbouring rights' for these non-author works;

- where the Anglo–American tradition vests first ownership of copyright in the employer of an author making a work in the course of employment, the Continental tradition gives it to the author;

- where the Anglo–American tradition operates a relatively low threshold of 'originality' for works to enjoy copyright, based mainly upon the author's effort in not copying previous work, the Continental tradition tends to require a higher level of creativity before works will be protected.

 Question

Explain with illustrative examples the differences between the Anglo–American and Continental European conceptions of what copyright is for.

2.24   A further significant aspect of the distinctness of the two traditions is their stances in relation to the *copyright limitations and exceptions* allowed under the Berne Convention (see para 2.8); that is, those activities in which members of the public may engage with regard to copyright works without any authorisation from the right holders concerned. The Anglo–American tradition has traditionally allowed 'fair dealing' or 'fair use' for free in areas where it is thought that the public interest in the dissemination of information and ideas outweighs the interest of the right holder in earning reward from the exploitation of the work and the public interest in encouraging the author's activities. In contrast, although the Continental traditions typically permit private copying, the author still receives remuneration by way of levies imposed upon the sale of the equipment that enables the copying to take place. There is generally a less expansive approach to exceptions and limitations based upon wider interests than those of the author and the publisher.

2.25   The significance of such distinctions should not be overemphasised. Continental copyright laws are also a basis for market operations with regard to ideas, information, and entertainment, while, as we shall see (paras 3.82–3.112), the author plays a fundamental role in Anglo–American copyright laws, where moral rights are now also available (paras 6.4–6.22). Membership of the Berne Convention has embraced countries from both traditions for most of its history and since 1989 has included the United States. The convergence promoted by the Convention's minimum standards has been further advanced by TRIPS and the WIPO Treaties of 1996, as well as the copyright Directives of the EU. Nonetheless the deep-seated differences in basic concepts have an effect upon international discussions, the outcomes of which occasionally reflect a somewhat uneasy compromise between the competing schools of thought.

Key points on rationales

- Copyright has an economic function, enabling the production of information, ideas, and entertainment to be rewarding for their authors and publishers.

- Copyright also has a non-economic function, related in some legal systems to the idea of recognising creativity as an aspect of individual personality.

> • Copyright rewards individuals for their contributions; but this is offset by recognition of the interests—if not the rights—of the wider public in the free dissemination of material in certain circumstances.
>
> • Different legal systems give different emphases to these functions, making it sometimes difficult to achieve European or global harmonisation.

Policy context

2.26   The Director General of WIPO, Francis Gurry, noted in 2011 that copyright laws and rights holder business models should more appropriately suit the digital age:[47]

> I am firmly of the view that a passive and reactive approach to copyright and the digital revolution entails the major risk that policy outcomes will be determined by a Darwinian process of the survival of the fittest business model. The fittest business model may turn out to be the one that achieves or respects the right social balances in cultural policy. It may also, however, turn out not to respect those balances. The balances should not, in other words, be left to the chances of technological possibility and business evolution. They should, rather, be established through a conscious policy response.

The President of the European Union, Jean-Claude Juncker, noted in 2016, the same day as the European Commission set out its proposals on the modernisation of copyright for the digital single market:[48]

> I want journalists, publishers and authors to be paid fairly for their work, whether it is made in studios or living rooms, whether it is disseminated offline or online, whether it is published via a copying machine or commercially hyperlinked on the web.

The approach taken in this short section is to consider the general background of recent technological development (the 'digital environment') as the policy context within which the initiatives at international, European, and domestic level described above have developed. The importance of doing this is to understand why reform of copyright has been, and continues to be, such an important question in light of rapid development of new technologies; and to understand how such challenges in relation to reform are ultimately related to the purpose(s) of copyright. This also enables one to come to grips with the policy and law reform issues with which copyright law has to deal, recognising the sometimes sharply opposed views that exist on these matters. At the best of times, law reform is a slow process. This and the subsequent chapters show how difficult it is in relation to copyright.

New technologies

2.27   A huge range of areas of activity are affected by copyright: government, entertainment, education, creativity, technology, and international development, to name but a few. Much of the current debate on copyright, which has brought copyright reform to the fore in the UK and Europe, has arisen in the context of the ever-expanding scope and possibilities of using digital, wireless, and mobile technologies for the creation, dissemination, and reproduction of ideas, information, and entertainment. The context for policy thinking in the areas traditionally covered by copyright has been transformed by the ability to make material available so that it is potentially always accessible to users at times and places chosen by them; especially when it has gone along with expanding possibilities of, and demand for, interactivity between suppliers and users who,

---

[47] See his comments at the February 2011 Blue Sky Conference in Queensland Australia at www.wipo.int/about-wipo/en/dgo/speeches/dg_blueskyconf_11.html.

[48] http://europa.eu/rapid/press-release_IP-16-3010_en.htm.

starting on the basis of what already exists, may themselves become creators, developers, and suppliers of further material. It is also clear that increasing amounts of material from both the digital and pre-digital era is becoming available electronically: not only sound recordings, films, and broadcasts, but also works of art and literature of all kinds and all periods. The idea of the digital environment as a cultural jukebox, always on and available for use, shifts the traditional relationships between users and consumers, on the one hand, and creators and repositories such as libraries, archives, museums and galleries, and publishers and broadcasters, on the other. Further, because the digital environment does not know jurisdictional and national frontiers, the law's approach has to be an international one, moving beyond the traditional international approach of setting minimum standards of copyright protection (which does not entail the law and rights being the same everywhere), and according to foreigners whatever protection the national law affords its own nationals (see para 2.8).

Exercise

Can you give some specific examples of copyright policy issues arising from attempts to create, disseminate, and reproduce ideas, information, and entertainment in the digital environment?

2.28   Debate is sparked, however, by varying visions of what the internet and, following it, the 'information superhighway' through wireless and mobile communication systems should be about. For *government and commercial interests*, it is primarily a means of *economic development*. For instance, the DSM strategy (see para 2.15), aimed at adapting the EU's single market to changes in the internet and digital technologies, is made up of three 'pillars' or policy areas: better access for consumers and businesses to digital goods and services across Europe; creating the right conditions and a level playing field for digital networks and innovative services to flourish; and maximising the growth potential of the digital economy.[49] Technology now provides an information, marketing, and selling device capable of reaching an ever-widening number of citizens, consumers, and buyers. All kinds of producers can in effect set up electronic shops and information resources. Some simply sell goods and services that are already available (but usually more expensively) through traditional outlets. Good examples are Amazon (the online store) offering books, music, and films and easyJet, offering airline services; and each contracting with customers principally by way of electronic communication across the web. eBay, the online auction site, is a slightly different example of the same thing, electronically putting sellers in contact with potential buyers of whatever they have to sell. But digital technology also creates the possibility of new types of purely electronic products and services that can be traded primarily through communication systems. Computer programs and games were the most familiar type of digital product before the internet took off; these could now be made available on the internet for downloading directly to computers and mobile devices from the relevant website. Familiar also by the end of the 1980s were the digital CD-ROMs, which were largely replacing analogue cassettes and the still-surviving vinyl record as the primary means of disseminating recorded musical performances. The internet opened up the possibility, soon realised by Napster and others, of the global jukebox from which music enthusiasts could at any time download to a local computer, a mobile telephone, or other device (eg an iPod) whatever took their fancy at the time. From music it was but a short step to films, aided by the arrival of broadband. Broadcasting has also moved into the digital era via 'podcasting', 'webcasting', and 'streaming', so that viewers and listeners can increasingly choose where and when to watch and hear programmes, and interrupt, pause, and replay them to suit their own rather than the broadcaster's convenience (eg on-demand services like Netflix and Spotify). Digitisation also enabled the rapid development of the

49   https://ec.europa.eu/digital-single-market/en/policies/shaping-digital-single-market.

multimedia product, combining writing, sounds, and images still and moving. Finally, the most obviously new kind of service made both necessary and possible in the digital environment was the search engine provided by such organisations as Google and Yahoo!, through which users of the internet could find their way most speedily to the material they wanted.

2.29   The key point in all this for copyright is that, by contrast with the analogue world in which, although copying was easy, the copy was invariably less good than the original, the digital work will always copy perfectly. The downloader gets as good a version as the master copy on the original site—and gets it increasingly easily and quickly as the technology moves on. Nor does the user necessarily have to have, keep, or find space for the products involved: access by way of streaming, webcasting, and cloud-based computing may soon replace acquisition of anything other than the devices which provide the means of access. The internet and subsequent developments in mobile communications systems thus provide a tremendous new way to reach consumers of information and entertainment products in the comfort of their own homes and social patterns. But the difficulty also facing those minded to exploit these opportunities is precisely the ease and speed of digital reproduction and transmission. How can consumers be made to pay for the material they download or receive in this way? How can pirates, those making copies and providing access for their own commercial gain without the authority of the originator, be stopped from exploiting the technology and thereby undercutting the latter's market? Piracy—the unlicensed mass reproduction of copyright material such as sound recordings, films, and computer games for free or for resale at prices far undercutting those of the copyright owner—has continued to be a serious issue for the affected industries, as it was also for most of the second half of the 20th century.

2.30   A further question is raised, however, from the perspective of those who see the new technology as raising other exciting possibilities of ever greater and wider access to, and expression and circulation of, ideas and information. In this perspective, the ease and speed of digital communication and reproduction is an opportunity rather than a problem; a real step forward in allowing the realisation of both individual and societal goals. This is the perspective which lies behind the idea of 'open source', in which material is made freely available to others—'free' here meaning, as it has famously been put, 'free' as in 'free expression' rather than as in 'free beer'. By their very nature, information and ideas want to be free in the same sense as a prisoner or a caged wild animal might want. As economists point out, information and ideas are 'public goods', meaning that their availability is not diminished no matter how many people have enjoyed or employed them. Insofar as copyright is a barrier to the free flow of information and ideas, it is misused. Some go as far as to say that copyright is always such a barrier; the purpose of others, such as Creative Commons, however, is to recognise the value possessed by copyright, provided that it is not used simply to obstruct otherwise beneficial further activity and creativity. There are also widespread perceptions of copyright as complex, inaccessible, productive of difficulty and uncertainty in relation to otherwise lawful activities, and sometimes absurd.

2.31   File-sharing (paras 4.73–4.79) provides a good example for argument about the different perspectives. The music industry has viewed the transfer of music recordings from user to user without charge as the main reason, apart from piracy, behind a significant decline in the sale of music CDs since 2000 (the year in which the Napster operation first took off). The industry argues that without profit its investment in new talent will necessarily decline, with the end result being less opportunity for, and so overall less, new recorded music. Those supporting a more 'open' approach argue that the music industry failed to move quickly enough to meet the potential of the internet as a means of distributing music, and that users of the unlicensed file-sharing services actually did continue to buy CDs, turning to the services only for hard-to-obtain or actually unavailable material. The industry had only itself to blame for its financial woes, having been exposed by others more innovative and better attuned to the ways in which consumers wished to acquire and use their music in the digital environment, and who made that pay in different ways (eg by selling advertising space on their services). More recently, the industry appears to have embraced legal offerings of content through streaming services such as Netflix, Spotify, and Apple Music, but continues to see piracy as an ongoing problem.

2.32   In the pre-digital world, an author and a person wishing to use the author's work would have very little opportunity or incentive to meet and negotiate the terms and conditions of the latter's use; hence, the need for copyright law to set down some general social bargain, as it were, and also for intermediaries such as publishers to enable works to find their markets and audiences. But in the digital environment it is potentially much easier for author and audience to find each other directly, and for them to use technology to conclude their own bespoke bargain about terms and conditions of use of the author's work. The use of DRM (digital rights management)—*technical protection measures* (TPMs) and *rights management information systems* (RMIs)—built into CDs, databases, websites, and games consoles, can prevent access to and use of a work unless and until such contractual conditions as the producer imposes are met by the would-be user. Such technologies are intensely controversial, and usually seen by critics hostile to current legal developments in the field as the manifestation of the worst of current copyright rules, since the law protects them against circumvention by third parties even though their use can enable not only the prevention of activities falling within the exceptions to copyright, but, indeed, the protection of works no longer or never in copyright. The position of the right owner thus appears to be considerably strengthened at the expense of the user, since money can be made even from a work without copyright, as long as it is technologically protectable. Right owners can also use DRM to enable consumers to make further uses of their products (eg making additional copies to store on additional devices), particularly if different consumers might be prepared to pay variable prices for different packages of permissions made available through DRM.

2.33   Contracts between the author/producer and the exploiter of copyright works also assume importance in the digital world. While such contracts promote economic efficiency in relation to exploitation of protected works, they may also require policing against the potential for abuse and lack of fairness. Although there are some provisions in copyright legislation that regulate copyright contracts, and the common law on restraint of trade and undue influence have also been deployed in such contracts, an important issue is whether anything more is required to balance the position of authors and exploiters in copyright contracts. Should copyright contracts be more closely vetted for general unconscionability or should compulsory equitable remuneration provisions, such as already exist in relation to performers' rights (see paras 7.39–7.40) be extended to all copyright contracts? It may be noted that, while users of copyright products can often be at least analogised with consumers, authors are often persons whose work is being consumed by their publishers; in a sense, therefore, their claim to protection from market forces is more like that of the employee in labour law than the consumer. Further, however, and like the employee who is a member of a trade union or professional association, the author has some possibility of self-protection through collective action by way of copyright management societies, trade unions, professional organisations, and pressure groups. In the digital environment, it becomes particularly important to separately understand the interests of authors from the exploiters, in relation to reform initiatives and their impact.

2.34   Contracts, such as the forms provided by Creative Commons, can also help facilitate dissemination of and access to protected works as an author can indicate in advance, as it were, those uses of the work by others which, although within the scope of copyright protection, are nonetheless permitted; further, the author can require those using this permission to apply those terms and conditions to further downstream sub-users. So, in this context contracts and technology can operate in support of widespread use and later creativity with existing works. However, there are limits to what can be achieved through this means of promoting access to protected works, and reform initiatives such as those introduced for orphan works, or proposed for out of commerce works, remain of much significance in the digital environment.

2.35   An obvious tricky point is that it is copyright, for the most part, which, at least initially, creates the subject matter around which contracting parties can subsequently bargain. In the absence of copyright at the point of creation, there might be no room for bargaining at all. In particular, the individual author/creator without access to the means of sophisticated technological protection, dissemination, and online payment methods (and such persons will continue to exist for a long time, even in the digital environment) would be at a serious disadvantage without copyright in dealing with the entrepreneur who will convert the work into a marketable product. One could, of course, try to create some sort of 'fair contract' or 'minimum terms' regime for such authors, but that instrument would either assume the existence of copyright, or alternatively the 'minimum contract' that would have to be created in the absence of copyright might end up looking remarkably similar to copyright!

2.36   Further, the economic interests protected by copyright are not limited to those of the author/creator of the work and the entrepreneur who first takes it to market. Since the economic rights protected by copyright are freely transferable to third parties, the person who at any given moment owns the copyright and reaps the economic returns it gives may well be someone who had no hand in the original production of the work or the product flowing from it. How far such investors in works may deserve the same level of protection as the originators of the work is a nice question: after all, they are risk-takers to a greater extent than those from whom they bought the rights, and they have helped to ensure that the author/creator/first producer does, indeed, earn reward from their work.

Adelphi Charter

The Adelphi Charter on creativity, innovation, and intellectual property was published in October 2005, calling upon governments to maintain a balance between public domain and private right, and between competition and monopoly, with regard to intellectual property rights in general; to ensure in particular that the copyright term is limited in time and does not extend beyond what is proportionate and necessary; and to facilitate a wide range of policies to stimulate access and innovation, including non-proprietary models such as open-source software licensing and open access to scientific literature.

Purpose of copyright in the digital environment

2.37   A fundamental question in thinking about these challenges arising from the digital environment is the purpose, or purposes, of copyright. Only with clear ideas of what we are trying to achieve will clear, coherent, and principled law emerge. We have already discussed at some length many of copyright's underlying ideas:

- The *economic role* (para 2.22)—incentivising and rewarding, in accordance with market demand, those involved in the creation and publication of certain kinds of work. Economic interests therefore include not only creators, but also entrepreneurs who convert what is created into products for the marketplace. Copyright is a response to market failure; without it, the *expression* of ideas and information, creativity, and innovation would be available to all, without reward for those who invested in the creation and dissemination of the works thereby produced, either personally or financially. With copyright, the way is open for the reward of creative individuals and those who convert their creative work into products that the public will buy or otherwise spend money on.

- Protection of the *creative individual's personality rights* (para 2.22), most evident in the moral rights, and their recognition of inalienable, non-economic interests that an author (but no one else) may continue to exercise in respect of a work, even though no longer owner of the copyright or of the physical form in which the work was first created and recorded. This recognition of copyright is also apparent in the copyright terms, much longer than a strict economic analysis would suggest is necessary for the fulfilment of the economic goal. There may also be a link between moral rights and the fundamental human rights that underlie many personality rights in general. Human rights to dignity and respect seem particularly apt to support the right to be identified in connection with one's work and to have that work treated appropriately by others. Copyright can also protect the individual's interest in *privacy.* There is no obligation to publish or make available one's work, and copyright serves to protect that position should that be the author's wish.

- The *rights of users, or the public domain* (para 5.4). By placing various limitations upon what it protects on the producer side, copyright also protects, directly or indirectly, non-producer interests. Thus:
  - freedom of expression and information are protected by the limitation of copyright to forms of expression, as distinct from the ideas and information which are expressed;
  - works which fall below the threshold requirement of 'originality' do not have copyright, even if in other respects they come within one of the categories of protected work (eg being written, they are literary);
  - works which do not fit into the expressed categories of the law do not receive copyright protection;
  - copyright exceptions, for example fair dealing for a number of specified purposes, reflect a recognition that certain non-producer interests outweigh producer ones in at least some circumstances; or at any rate the impracticability of certain kinds of copyright enforcement; and
  - the *product* embodying the protected work can generally be dealt with freely by the first and subsequent purchasers apart from integrity/commercial rental/lending/public communication rights.

We might also take note of a further dimension:

- The *cultural purposes* of copyright: this dimension is apparent in the nature of what copyright protects—literary, dramatic, musical, and artistic works, films, sound recordings, and broadcasts—and also in the length of time for which it gives that protection.

2.38   The digital environment puts these purposes into sharp conflict with each other. Should the economic interests of the author and entrepreneur, and also the interests of society, require the strengthening of economic rights and their enforcement, because protected material is easier to copy and the business models on which the creative sectors have been built are under threat over the last two decades? Or should the rights of users, as well as economic and cultural interests of the society, require the weakening of economic rights to allow for wider access to protected works? What is the role of powerful and disruptive technological companies in this debate? It is worth keeping these contestations in mind in understanding specific aspects of the copyright and related rights framework in Chapters 3–7.

2.39   It is not suggested here that current UK law does anything other than reflect a mixture of the various purposes set out above, which attempts to provide a *balance* between the different interests involved. Nor is it suggested that the present balance is satisfactory, or that it was at any time in the past. The interests inevitably come into conflict, especially those related to economic and personality interests in works, on the one hand, and those reflecting the public domain dimension, on the other. All that law-makers can do is be sensitive to all the interests involved, make choices between options from time to time, and be prepared to act should it become apparent that a solution, old or new, is not working as it should, or has become inappropriate in changing circumstances.

Further reading

Books

L Bently, B Sherman, D Gangjee, and P Johnson, *Intellectual Property Law* (5th edn, 2018), Ch 2

A Brown and C Waelde (eds), *Research Handbook on Intellectual Property and Creative Industries* (2018)

N Caddick, G Davies, and G Harbottle (eds), *Copinger & Skone James on Copyright* (17th edn, 2019), Ch 1

WR Cornish, *Intellectual Property: Omnipresent, Distracting, Irrelevant?* (2004), Ch 2

R Deazley, *On the Origin of the Right to Copy* (2004)

MA Einhorn, *Media, Technology and Copyright: Integrating Law and Economics* (2004)

S Frankel and D Gervais, *The Evolution and Equilibrium of Copyright in the Digital Age* (2014)

PB Hugenholtz (ed), *The Future of Copyright in a Digital Environment* (1996)

W Landes and R Posner, *The Economic Structure of Intellectual Property Law* (2003), Chs 2–6, 8–10

J Litman, *Digital Copyright* (2001)

D Llewelyn and T Aplin, *Cornish, Llewelyn and Aplin Intellectual Property: Patents, Copyright, Trade Marks and Allied Rights* (9th edn, 2019), Ch 10

G Mazziotti, *EU Digital Copyright Law and the End-User* (2008)

C Seville, *Literary Copyright Reform in Early Victorian England* (1999)

C Seville, *The Internationalisation of Copyright Law: Books, Buccaneers and the Black Flag in the Nineteenth Century* (2006)

B Sherman and L Bently, *The Making of Modern Intellectual Property* (1999)

R Towse (ed), *Copyright and the Cultural Industries* (2002)

R Towse and R Holzhauer (eds), *The Economics of Intellectual Property* (2002), vol 1 (Introduction and Copyright)

G Westkamp, *Digital Copyright Laws in Europe* (2011)

Articles

R Arnold, 'The need for a new Copyright Act: a case study in law reform' (2015) 5(2) Queen Mary Journal of Intellectual Property 110

T Cook and E Derclaye, 'An EU copyright code: what and how, if ever?' [2011] IPQ 259

C Geiger et al, 'The resolution of the European Parliament of July 9, 2015: paving the way (finally) for a copyright reform in the European Union?' [2015] EIPR 683

B Farrand, 'Towards a modern, more European copyright framework, or, how to rebrand the same old approach?' [2019] EIPR 65

A Rahmatian, 'The Hargreaves Review on copyright licensing and exceptions: a missed moment of opportunity' [2011] Ent LR 219

E Rosati, 'The Hargreaves report and copyright licensing: can national initiatives work per se?' [2011] EIPR 67

3

Copyright 2: subject matter, first ownership, and term

Introduction

Scope and overview of chapter

3.1 This chapter initially examines the subject matter in which copyright subsists. This centres on the concept of the 'protected work', and makes use of a distinction between what are sometimes known as 'author works' (literary, dramatic, musical, artistic, and film works) and 'media works' (typographical arrangements, sound recordings, and broadcasts). It then considers the identification of the first owner of the copyright when it comes into existence. Normally this is the author of the work, subject to certain exceptions, but this concept is not so easily applied to media works. This involves further analysis of the legal notion of authorship and how it helps establish first ownership of copyright, and of the difference between 'author' and 'media' copyright works. Copyright is generally a right of limited duration, however, and the final section of the chapter expounds the various periods of time for which it lasts.

3.2 **Learning objectives**

By the end of this chapter you should be able to describe and explain:

- the subject matter that copyright protects, and the different categories of work used by the law;
- who is the first owner of copyright in a protected work (usually the author or equivalent);
- how long the protection of copyright lasts in relation to each of the categories of its subject matter.

3.3 Copyright is a form of property which comes into existence with the creation of its subject matter (no registration process is required, unlike patents, trade marks, or designs), so it is important to consider in detail the subsistence of copyright and the subject matter which the law protects. There are some important rules to identify the first owner of the right thus created. This is usually the author with author works, and an equivalent in the case of media works. Finally, copyright protection lasts for a specified period of time, the duration varying according to the subject matter protected. In sum, the chapter explains the subject matter of copyright protection, who is the first to benefit from the protection of copyright, and for how long the protection lasts. So, the rest of the chapter looks like this:

- Subject matter (3.4–3.41)
- Author works (3.42–3.74)
- Media works (3.75–3.81)
- First ownership (3.82–3.112)
- Duration of copyright (3.113–3.129).

Subject matter

3.4   Under the Copyright, Designs and Patents Act (CDPA) 1988, as now several times amended, the following subject matter is protected by copyright:[1]

- original literary, dramatic, musical, and artistic works (literary work including computer programs, databases, and compilations other than databases);
- films;
- sound recordings;
- broadcasts;
- the typographical arrangement of published editions of literary, dramatic, or musical works.

The Act is seen to meet the requirements of the Berne Convention (protection for literary and artistic works—see para 2.8), the Rome Convention as supplemented in 1996 (protection for sound recordings and broadcasts—see para 2.17), and the World Intellectual Property Organization Copyright Treaty (WCT) (computer programs and databases—see para 2.11). In order for copyright to subsist in the above categories of works, there are some key requirements for protection: all categories of works must meet the qualification requirements set out in the Act;[2] literary, dramatic, and musical works must be recorded in writing or otherwise; and, literary, dramatic, musical, and artistic works must be original. A number of general points in this regard follow, before turning to the detailed law of each category of work.

Products may have more than one copyright

3.5   A very important point is that any product in the domain of the subject matter listed in the previous paragraph (para 3.4) is quite likely to have more than one copyright in it. Thus, a book will have copyright as a literary work, but there will also be a copyright in its typographical arrangement, as would also be the case with printed dramatic scripts and musical scores. A database has copyright in the selection and arrangement of its contents,[3] but this does not affect any copyright those items of content may have in their own right. A sound recording of a piece of music will involve subsistence of copyright, not only in the sound recording as such, but also, separately, one in the music. And if the work recorded is a song, there will be a further copyright in the song lyrics.[4] A broadcast of a film or sound recording will have copyright as a broadcast, but this will leave unaffected the respective copyright in the film or sound recording. While the sound track accompanying a film is treated as part of the film for copyright purposes, a copyright may also subsist in the sound track as a sound recording.[5] With the advent of digital technology, the multimedia product (eg a computer game, a film on a DVD, the BBC website), which consists of digitised material

---

[1] CDPA 1988, ss 1–8.   [2] CDPA 1988, s 153.   [3] CDPA 1988, s 3A.

[4] Note how CDPA 1988, s 3(1) defines 'musical work' as excluding any words intended to be spoken or sung with the music.

[5] CDPA 1988, s 5B(2), (5).

combining audio, video, text, and images still and moving played through a computer, and with which the user may interact, has become commonplace, raising difficult questions about the mixture of copyrights which such a product may have.[6]

Question

Explain what it means to say that a product may have more than one copyright, and give some examples.

Need for a work

3.6   Copyright protects works. Section 1 of the 1988 Act states the following:

> (1) Copyright is a property right which subsists in accordance with this Part in the following
>
> descriptions of work—
>
> . . .
>
> (2) . . . "copyright work" means a work of any of those descriptions in which copyright subsists.

While the concept of 'work' clearly refers to the subject matter protected by copyright, the concept is itself not further elaborated upon. To paraphrase the Agreement on Trade-Related Aspects of Intellectual Property Rights (TRIPS) and the WCT (see paras 2.10–2.12), the concern in relation to the concept of a 'work' here is, not with ideas as such, but with their expression.[7] There can be difficult issues, however, in knowing when an expression, in whatever medium, reaches the level of a work capable of copyright protection. In a case about the copyright in law reports, Canadian judges argued that a work is something which generally is whole, complete, or able to stand on its own, and that:[8]

> if a production is dependent upon surrounding materials such that it is rendered meaningless or its utility largely disappears when taken apart from the context in which it is disseminated, then that component will instead be merely a part of a work.

With this approach, they were nonetheless able to conclude that component parts of a law report, such as its key words and headnote, were, like the full report itself, works that attracted copyright. The idea that, when an expression is 'able to stand on its own', there is a work, presumably covers the many well-known examples of incomplete productions such as Schubert's Unfinished Symphony and Samuel Taylor Coleridge's poem 'Kubla Khan', the composition of which was famously interrupted by a person on business from Porlock, with the consequence that the poet's inspiration was lost and the work never completed.

■ *Sweeney v Macmillan Publishers Ltd* [2002] RPC 35

This complex case concerned the copyright in James Joyce's novel *Ulysses*, first published in 1922, and the publication of a new edition of that work in 1997, edited by DR. The novel was written over a long period, and considerably revised and rewritten in the process. Joyce's manuscripts and other preparatory material, such as corrected and amended typescripts and proofs, continued to exist. As originally published, the book contained many typographical errors. Some of these were corrected in later editions, which, however,

---

[6] See I Stamatoudi, *Copyright and Multimedia Works: A Comparative Analysis* (2002); T Aplin, *Copyright Law in the Digital Society* (2005).

[7] The classic discussion of this distinction is in the US case of *Baker v Selden* 101 US 99 (1879). See also *University of London Press v University Tutorial Press* [1916] 2 Ch 601 and J Pila, 'An intentional view of the copyright work' (2008) 71 MLR 535.

[8] *CCH Canadian Ltd v Law Society of Upper Canada* [2002] 4 FC 213 (CA) at 260 per Linden JA at para 66. See also at 308 per Rothstein JA at paras 197–199. The court's conclusion was upheld by the Supreme Court of Canada, which did not find it necessary, however, to dwell on the meaning of 'work' in this context: see *Law Society of Upper Canada v CCH Canadian Ltd* [2004] 1 SCR 339.

also introduced new ones. Facsimiles of the Joyce manuscripts and other materials were published from 1975 onwards. The 1997 edition was based on a collation of all this material with the published editions, and sought the publication of the text intended by Joyce. The Joyce estate, which owned the copyright in *Ulysses* and the preparatory material, claimed infringement of copyright by the new edition. It was held that copyright subsisted in each chapter and perhaps each page or even sentence of *Ulysses* as it was written; but as each passage was incorporated into the larger work, copyright should be regarded as residing in that rather than in its constituent parts.[9] Copyright thus subsisted in Joyce's fair copy manuscript. Copyright also subsisted in earlier drafts of the work and in successive typescripts and proofs. DR had copied parts of this material, and its copyright had been infringed.

3.7   Nor is there a requirement of minimum length or substance to constitute a work: for example, musical copyright was found to exist in the four notes constituting the Channel 4 television theme.[10] More recently, newspaper headlines have been found to be independent literary works.[11] On the other hand, single words, titles, the catchphrases of a TV personality, headings on computer menus, and individual command names in a computer program[12] have been held to be too insubstantial to be literary works.

Discussion point   For answer guidance visit **www.oup.com/uk/brown5e**.

Can '4 Minutes 33 Seconds', by the composer John Cage, be held to be a work? In this composition, an orchestra is on stage at the outset, but does not start to play any of its instruments. Instead, the members of the orchestra silently sit on the platform for a period of just over four-and-a-half minutes. If it is a work, does the fact that its author is generally regarded as a composer of music make the work musical? Are there any other possibilities? See further Cheng Lim Saw, 'Protecting the sound of silence in 4'33"—a timely revisit of basic principles in copyright law' [2005] EIPR 467.

3.8   While the general principle, that copyright protects the expression of a work rather than its ideas is central, it is also important not to be misled as to its scope. In considering the concept, bear in mind what constitutes infringement of copyright, for example see paras 4.9ff. Analysis of this part of the law shows it to be misleading to say that copyright protects no more than the form of expression. Otherwise it would not be possible for the author of a book to be able to control the exploitation of his work in other media such as film and broadcasting. Such adaptations will almost certainly adopt a distinct mode of expression, yet must be authorised by the author to be legitimate.[13] The author of a two-dimensional artistic work may challenge a three-dimensional reproduction, and vice versa.[14] Editors of anthologies and collections of material produced by others have a copyright, not so much in the words gathered together by them, as in the arrangement and ordering of the material.[15] Of course this is a form of expression, but it shows that we should not take 'form of expression' in any narrow sense coloured by the idea that copyright prevents only slavish imitation. Thus a particular interpretation of historical events has been held capable of copyright protection.[16] The best view seems to be that there is no copyright in ideas while they remain just that,

[9]   Contrast *Robin Ray v Classic FM plc* [1998] FSR 622, where a catalogue was subsumed into a database, but Lightman J rejected an argument that as a result the copyright of the first work was also subsumed into that of the second.
[10]   *Lawton v Lord David Dundas*, *The Times*, 13 June 1985. Another example might be the Intel Inside theme.
[11]   *Newspaper Licensing Agency Ltd v Meltwater Holding BV* [2010] EWHC 3099 (Ch); affirmed in [2011] EWCA Civ 890 (CA).
[12]   *Navitaire Inc v EasyJet Airline Co Ltd* [2006] RPC 3.
[13]   CDPA 1988, ss 16(1)(e) and 21.   [14]   CDPA 1988, s 17(3). See further para 4.26.
[15]   *Macmillan v Suresh Chunder Deb* (1890) ILR 17 Calc 951; *Macmillan v Cooper* (1923) 93 LJPC 113. Note also Berne Convention, Art 2(5): 'Collections of literary or artistic works such as encyclopaedias and anthologies which, by reason of the selection and arrangement of their contents, constitute intellectual creations shall be protected as such, without prejudice to the copyright in each of the works forming part of such collections.'
[16]   *Harman Pictures NV v Osborne* [1967] 1 WLR 723 (Charge of the Light Brigade); see further para 4.31.

but that once the ideas have been expressed in some form it would be wrong to assume that a different expression of the same ideas must necessarily be a new work with its own copyright, or cannot be an infringement of the earlier work.

 Question

Give some examples to illustrate the difference between protectable expression and unprotectable ideas.

3.9   Lord Hoffmann said the following on this topic in *Designers Guild Ltd v Russell Williams (Textiles) Ltd*:[17]

> Plainly there can be no copyright in an idea which is merely in the head, which has not been expressed in copyrightable form, as a literary, dramatic, musical or artistic work, but the distinction between ideas and expression cannot mean anything so trivial as that. On the other hand, every element in the expression of an artistic work (unless it got there by accident or compulsion) is the expression of an idea on the part of the author. It represents her choice to paint stripes rather than polka dots, flowers rather than tadpoles, use one colour and brush technique rather than another, and so on. The expression of these ideas is protected, both as a cumulative whole and also to the extent to which they form a 'substantial part' of the work. (para 24) . . . My Lords, if one examines the cases in which the distinction between ideas and the expression of ideas has been given effect, I think it will be found that they support two quite distinct propositions. The first is that a copyright work may express certain ideas which are not protected because they have no connection with the literary, dramatic, musical or artistic nature of the work. It is on this ground that, for example, a literary work which describes a system or invention does not entitle the author to claim protection for his system or invention as such. The same is true of an inventive concept expressed in an artistic work. However striking or original it may be, others are (in the absence of patent protection) free to express it in works of their own: see *Kleeneze Ltd v DRG (UK) Ltd* [1984] FSR 399. The other proposition is that certain ideas expressed by a copyright work may not be protected because, although they are ideas of a literary, dramatic or artistic nature they are not original, or so commonplace as not to form a substantial part of the work. *Kenrick & Co v Lawrence & Co* (1890) 25 QBD 99 is a well-known example. It is on this ground that the mere notion of combining stripes and flowers would not have amounted to a substantial part of the plaintiff's work. At that level of abstraction, the idea, though expressed in the design, would not have represented sufficient of the author's skill and labour as to attract copyright protection (para 25).

3.10   Lord Hoffmann here connects the translation of unprotectable idea into copyright expression with the degree of originality, ie skill, labour, and judgment, shown by the author, and more will be said of that later (para 3.22).[18] Clearly, each case will turn on its own facts in this area, although it can perhaps be said that the higher the level of generality, or abstraction, of the idea of a work, the less likely it is to be protected as such.[19] Lord Hoffmann also connects the expression of ideas with the nature of the work. A celebrated dictum in this regard is: 'You do not infringe copyright in a recipe by making a cake.'[20] Similarly, a literary work consisting of instructions is not infringed by making a fabric according to it.[21]

■ *Interlego AG v Tyco Industries Inc* [1989] AC 217 (PC)

Artistic copyright was claimed in engineering drawings modifying an earlier design by the same author (the Lego company). The visual impression from the two sets of drawings was much the same; the distinction lay mainly in the technical information as to dimensions and tolerances. It was held that the later drawings were

---

[17] [2001] FSR 11, paras 24 and 25.

[18] See further M Spence and T Endicott, 'Vagueness in the scope of copyright' (2005) 121 LQR 657.

[19] *Plix Products v Winstone* [1986] FSR 63 per Prichard J at 92–94 (aff'd [1986] FSR 608); *Nova Productions Ltd v Mazooma Games Ltd* [2007] RPC 25 (CA), paras 31–55 (Jacob LJ).

[20] *J & S Davis (Holdings) Ltd v Wright Health Group* [1988] RPC 403 per Whitford J at 414.

[21] *Abraham Moon & Sons Ltd v Thornber and Others* [2012] EWPCC 37, where a fabric 'ticket stamp'—ie instructions to produce a design— was held to be both a literary and artistic work, but only the artistic work was infringed by a plaid design fabric.

not new works for the purposes of artistic copyright: the new ideas in the second drawings were not artistic, but literary. 'Nobody draws a tolerance, nor can it be reproduced three-dimensionally' (per Lord Oliver at 258). This was important because literary copyright knows no equivalent to artistic copyright's concept of three-dimensional infringement.

3.11   While the European Union (EU) directives use the concept of a 'work' in relation to the rights accorded to copyright owners, and also exceptions and limitations to the rights,[22] they do not define the concept of a work, nor has the concept been harmonised so far through the Court of Justice of the European Union (CJEU) jurisprudence. However, in *Levola v Hengelo* a recent reference for a preliminary ruling, the Court of Justice has been asked whether EU law, under the InfoSoc Directive 2001, precludes the taste of a food product from being granted copyright protection.[23] AG Wathelet noted that the concept of work under Articles 2–4 of the InfoSc Directive is not defined by the Directive, nor do those provisions make any reference to national law in this regard, and consequently, it must be regarded as an autonomous concept of EU law and interpreted uniformly through the EU; and, in order to be eligible for copyright protection the subject matter must be a work, in addition to being original.[24] Confirming that copyright protection extends to original expressions and not to ideas, he took the view that 'original expressions should be identifiable with sufficient precision and objectivity' and since 'taste themselves are ephemeral, volatile and unstable', they cannot be identified precisely and objectively and do no constitute a work.[25] A judgment is pending at the time of writing and the implications of this important reference on the concept of work remains to be seen.

Work of a relevant kind

3.12   There must be a work of a relevant kind—literary, dramatic, musical, artistic, film, sound recording, broadcast, or published edition—that is, a work which does not fit into these expressed eight categories under the law does not receive copyright protection or causes uncertainty about the category to which it belongs.[26] The CDPA 1988 provides fairly short definitions of the different categories of works but case law has elaborated on the nature, scope, and limits of such categories (see paras 3.39ff). However, the categorisation of works into eight exhaustive categories (not to mention the sub-categorisation within that of artistic works) can be problematic, creating the possibility of a single work being protected in more than one category, or causing uncertainty about the category to which it belongs. Categorisation is not required under the Berne Convention: only protection of 'literary and artistic work', which includes 'every production in the literary, scientific and artistic domain, whatever may be the mode or form of its expression'. The Convention provides an illustrative list of works, while elsewhere, and only so to speak incidentally, it refers to dramatic, musical, and cinematographic works. French law speaks of 'works of the mind whatever their kind, form of expression, merit or purpose' and gives thereafter an illustrative list. This approach reduces the need to struggle with categories, albeit it may carry its own obvious uncertainties. But these uncertainties also have the attractive feature of being perhaps more flexible than narrower categories in meeting the emergence of new kinds of work. It also limits the possibility of giving the categories unnecessary or cumbersome substantive content: that is, having rules making it matter whether a work is literary or artistic, musical or dramatic. A question of policy is therefore whether the requirement that a work falls into one of the relevant categories should continue to remain; or should there be a change in the law to make the categories illustrative only.

3.13   The closed list of categories of works protected under the 1988 Act may also be contrary to EU law. The UK system of providing an exhaustive list of subject matter, and its protected categories, appears to be at odds with recent CJEU jurisprudence which suggests that provided a work is original in the sense of being the author's own intellectual creation (for its meaning, see paras 3.25–3.28), it is capable of protection, at least

---

[22]   See, eg, Arts 2–5, Information Society (InfoSoc) Directive 2001.   [23]   Case C-310/17 *Levola Hengelo BV v Smilde Foods BV*.
[24]   ibid, Opinion, paras 37–40 and 44.   [25]   ibid, Opinion, paras 55–56 and 60–61.   [26]   CDPA 1988, s 1(1), (2).

with respect to the harmonised rights, whether or not the existing categories of work accommodate it. In recent references, the Court of Justice has noted that a GUI (graphic user interface of a computer program),[27] and a video game (in its entirety consisting of computer program, graphic, and sound elements),[28] as a work, can be protected under the ordinary law of copyright by virtue of the InfoSoc Directive 2001, if they are the author's own intellectual creation. Does this mean that the only requirement for copyright protection is originality in the sense of being an author's own intellectual creation? AG Opinion in *Levola v Hengelo* (para 3.11 above) appears to suggest not, in that both the presence of a work, and originality is required.[29] But this case law does challenge the UK's scheme of closed categories and suggests that new kinds of subject matter or unconventional subject matter which may not fit the categorisation in the 1988 Act can still be protected if they are a work, and an author's own intellectual creation. Consequently, it may no longer be possible to object that copyright does not subsist in a subject matter which is a work, and original, but is 'not one of the kinds of work listed in section 1(1)(a)' of the 1988 Act, so long as it is 'a literary or artistic work within the meaning of Article 2(1) of the Berne Convention'.[30] Whether these EU developments will force a change in the way the UK courts view works capable of copyright protection or the way they interpret existing categories of works remains to be seen. In the meantime, categories continue to be relevant for assessing whether a work receives protection in the UK and the nature of such protection. Each category protected in the UK will be discussed in detail later in this chapter.

Key points so far on subject matter

- Copyright protects works which constitute expressions rather than ideas and information as such.

- There must be a *work* of a relevant kind: literary, dramatic, musical, artistic, film, sound recording, broadcast, published edition.

Fixation

3.14   One way of establishing whether or not there is a work is to find a recording, or fixation, of the expression which constitutes the work.

The *Berne Convention* says that copyright subsists in literary and artistic works 'whatever may be the mode or form of its expression' (Art 2(1)), but then allows national law 'to prescribe that works in general or any specified categories of works shall not be protected unless they have been fixed in some material form' (Art 2(2)). Note that this means that member states have a choice as to whether to require fixation.

In the UK, the *CDPA 1988* provides that copyright does not subsist in a literary, dramatic, or musical work unless and until it is recorded in writing or otherwise (s 3(2)). 'Writing' includes any form of notation or code, whether by hand or otherwise, and regardless of the method by which, or medium in or on which, it is recorded (s 178). There is no definition of 'otherwise'!

---

[27] Case C-393/09 *Bezpečnostní softwarová asociace v Ministerstvo kultury* [2011] ECDR 3 (CJ), paras 44–47; see further, C Handig, 'Infopaq International A/S v Danske Dagblades Forening (C-5/08): is the term "work" of the CDPA 1988 in line with the European Directives?' [2010] EIPR 53.

[28] C-355/12 *Nintendo v PC Box* [2014] ECDR 6 (CJ), paras 21–23.

[29] Case C-310/17 *Levola Hengelo BV v Smilde Foods BV* AG Opinion, para 44. At para 46 AG Wathelet specifically notes that the concepts of work and originality are distinct and should not be combined or amalgamanted.

[30] *SAS Institute v World Programming* [2013] EWHC 69 (Ch) at para 27.

3.15   The UK thus opts for an explicit requirement of fixation before any literary, dramatic, or musical work may enjoy copyright protection. The main form of fixation mentioned in the 1988 Act is writing; but the definition previously quoted is very broad and obviously capable of covering, for example, the use of shorthand.[31] In any event, writing is not the only possible method of recording literary, dramatic, and musical works, nor does the 1988 Act so limit its requirement. The electronic storage of work in digital form on discs and in computer memories is well known. Literary work means work which is spoken and sung as well as written,[32] while music and drama can be created in improvised performances as well as based upon scores and scripts. So far as concerns speech, singing, and music, the tape and cassette recorder have been familiar ways of making recordings for a long time, and film, video, and digital recording, including voice recognition software, can now be added to the list of methods of fixation sufficient to confer copyright on the work recorded. A further possibility might arise through lip-reading what a speaker is saying on a film without a sound track, as for example with closed-circuit TV (CCTV) cameras.

3.16   The requirement of fixation still means, however, that there is no copyright in the unrecorded spoken word, ad lib stage performance, or aleatory musical composition. Since the copyright does not come into existence unless and until the recording is made, copyright confers no right on a speaker to stop people making recordings of what is said. If there is any right at all to prevent recording of one's words, it must be sought in other branches of the law.[33] However, the 1988 Act expressly provides that, for the purposes of conferring copyright on a work by recording it, it is immaterial whether the work is recorded by or with the permission of the author, that is, the speaker.[34] Thus, while I may eavesdrop on and record other people's telephone conversations without infringing copyright in what they say, as soon as the recording is made, the words have copyright and the subsequent reproduction and publication of these words elsewhere may be controlled by the speaker.[35]

Question

What will constitute fixation of a work so that it can enjoy copyright?

■ *Norowzian v Arks Ltd (No 2)* [1999] FSR 79; aff'd [2000] FSR 363

N produced a film called 'Joy'. It showed a man dancing to music. Use of the editing technique known as 'jump cutting' made it appear that the man was making sudden changes of position not possible as successive movements in reality. An issue in the case was whether the film was a recording of a dramatic work. Rattee J held not, in the following passage later approved by the Court of Appeal:[36]

'Joy', unlike some films, is not a recording of a dramatic work, because, as a result of the drastic editing process adopted by Mr Norowzian, it is not a recording of anything that was, or could be, performed or danced by anyone . . . It may well be, in the case of 'Joy', that the original unedited film of the actor's performance, what I believe are called 'the rushes', was a recording of a dramatic work, but Mr Norowzian's claim is not in respect of copyright in them or their subject-matter. His claim is in respect of the finished film ([1999] FSR at 87–88, approved [2000] FSR at 367).

---

[31] See *Pitman v Hine* (1884) 1 TLR 82.   [32] CDPA 1988, s 3(1).
[33] See, eg, the Regulation of Investigatory Powers Act 2000 or breach of confidence.   [34] CDPA 1988, s 3(3).
[35] See, for further discussion, HL MacQueen, '"My tongue is mine ain": copyright, the spoken word and privacy' (2005) 68 MLR 349.
[36] See further on the *Norowzian* case, A Barron, 'The legal properties of film' (2004) 67 MLR 177.

Discussion point   For answer guidance, visit **www.oup.com/uk/brown5e**.

How exact or good must a recording be to confer copyright on unscripted speech (eg a lecture), drama, or music? Do a student's non-verbatim lecture notes make the lecturer's extempore words protectable? Or a bootlegger's poor-quality and unauthorised recording of a live 'jamming' session by a musician?

3.17 There is no explicit requirement of fixation in the 1988 Act with regard to artistic works, but it seems clear from the definitions within the category (see further at paras 3.54–3.71) that copyright will not exist until the work is recorded in either tangible or visible form. Similarly, films and sound recordings must both be 'recordings' on some medium from which sounds or moving images, as the case may be, can be reproduced.[37] Broadcasts, however, are electronic transmissions of visual images, sounds, or other information which need only be visible and/or audible to their intended audience.

 Question 1

What is the significance of having an explicit fixation requirement for literary, dramatic, and musical works, but not for the other categories of copyright works?

Question 2

Is it possible to have copyright works which have not been 'fixed' in the sense just discussed?

3.18 As noted above, the Berne Convention allows national law 'to prescribe that works in general or any specified categories of works shall not be protected unless they have been fixed in some material form'. The UK in general requires fixation of a work before copyright can come into existence, leading to some peculiar, even absurd, rules, the effect of which is that while unauthorised recording of my ad lib speech or aleatory musical creation cannot be prevented by copyright, I can nonetheless control the subsequent reproduction and publication of the recording which has made those words or music the subject of copyright. Other legal systems within the Berne Union exercise their discretion to avoid the imposition of any requirement of fixation. In the UK, the requirement in relation to literary, dramatic, and musical works appears intended to serve a mainly evidential purpose, but to be cast in a right-constituting form. A question of policy therefore is whether the requirement of fixation in UK law should be dropped, and the question of the existence of a literary, dramatic, or musical work be left as a matter of evidence (in which the existence of a recorded form is always likely to be the best kind of evidence).

Originality

3.19 Another important test of whether or not a work protected by copyright has been created is the requirement of originality. The 1988 Act says that to have copyright, literary, dramatic, musical, and artistic works must all be original.[38] There is no statutory definition of originality, except for databases which are a sub-category of literary works (see further para 3.26).[39] However, the concept has been developed through UK case law, which suggests that for a work to be original, it should originate from the author and must not be a copy of a

---

[37] CDPA 1988, s 5A and 5B.   [38] CDPA 1988, s 1(1)(a).   [39] CDPA 1988, s 3A(2).

preceding work. In addition, a common theme found in case law is the test of the *skill, labour, and judgment* which the author has invested in the work. Where this test is satisfied, there is likely to be a copyright in the result. But the production of a copy of a work may involve considerable labour and no little skill; yet in that case there will be no originality and no copyright (see all these themes developed further at paras 3.20–3.24). In contrast, the EU directives, through the language therein, or their interpretation, refer to originality in the sense of being the 'author's own intellectual creation'. This standard for originality has been harmonised throughout the Union after the decision in *Infopaq* (see paras 3.27–3.28). As such, the British case law that has been developed over the years will be discussed first and then the EU developments and implications will be discussed. There is no express requirement of originality as such in relation to films, sound recordings, broadcasts, and typographical arrangements of published editions,[40] but copyright does not subsist in a sound recording or film or typographical arrangement of a published edition which is, or to the extent that it is, respectively, a copy taken from a previous sound recording or film, or reproduces the typographical arrangement of a previous edition.[41]

Question

Which kinds of work must be 'original' to enjoy copyright protection?

Originality in the UK: a combination of factors

3.20   In order to be original, a work must not be a copy of a preceding work and should originate from the author. The underlying idea is still best expressed in the classic words of Peterson J:[42]

> The word 'original' does not in this connection mean that the work must be the expression of original or inventive thought. Copyright Acts are not concerned with the originality of ideas, but with the expression of thought. . . . The originality which is required relates to the expression of the thought. But the Act does not require that the expression must be in an original or novel form, but that the work must not be copied from another work—that it should originate from the author.

Originality, in other words, is not a high standard for entry into copyright protection. It imposes no requirement of aesthetic or intellectual quality: even the most mundane of works, rehearsing old ideas and information, has copyright if expressed in the author's own way. This is reinforced by other provisions of the copyright legislation: for example, that certain artistic works are protected 'irrespective of artistic quality', or that tables and compilations are to be counted as literary works.[43] Another theme found in discussions of originality is the test of the skill, labour, and judgment which the author has invested in the work. Where this test is satisfied, there is likely to be a copyright in the result. Finally, there is the point succinctly made by Peterson J himself: 'What is worth copying is worth protecting.'[44] This is not in itself a test of the originality of the work that has been copied, but if someone has copied another's work, that tends to suggest the value of the latter and its possible need for copyright protection to ensure that the return goes to its author.

All these themes require some qualification, however. While what is worth copying is worth protecting, it is not always clear that copyright is the appropriate form of protection. With regard to ideas, 'as the late Professor Joad used to observe, it all depends on what you mean by ideas'.[45] Although copyright may not specify intellectual or aesthetic qualities as essential for its protection, nonetheless courts do assess

---

[40] CDPA 1988, s 1(1)(b), (c).   [41] CDPA 1988, ss 5A(2), 5B(4), and 8(2). For broadcasts, see para 3.33.
[42] *University of London Press v University Tutorial Press* [1916] 2 Ch 601 at 608.   [43] CDPA 1988, ss 3(1)(a) and 4(1)(a).
[44] *University of London Press v University Tutorial Press* [1916] 2 Ch 601 at 610.
[45] Lord Hailsham in *LB (Plastics) Ltd v Swish Products Ltd* [1979] RPC 551 at 629. Professor Cyril Joad (1891–1953) was a professor of philosophy at Birkbeck College London, who became famous through appearances on a BBC show, The Brains Trust, and the catchphrase with which he prefaced the answer to any question, 'Well, it depends what you mean by . . .'. This is also quite a useful phrase for a lawyer's conversational armoury.

the fitness of works to the designated categories under the legislation, such as literary or dramatic, the identification of which may involve assessment of just such qualities. Similarly, the mere expenditure of skill and labour may not be sufficient to give rise to copyright if the end result is not a work of a 'literary nature' or likewise. The appropriate general conclusion seems to be that originality is not definable in terms of a single, simple test, but should rather be considered as a combination of factors, the relative importance of which may vary according to the nature of the case and the type of work in question.[46]

 Question

What are the main elements of originality in British case law for copyright purposes?

No requirement of quality or merit

3.21 It is easy to misunderstand the absence of any requirement that a work should possess intellectual or aesthetic merit. What is clear is that, in determining whether or not a work has copyright, the Court is not called upon to judge the work on standards of good or bad in its field. This would be much too subjective to be acceptable. On the other hand, the Court evaluates whether a work falls into one or other of the categories found in the copyright legislation, and this is bound to involve some effort to judge what objective qualities constitute a work of this kind.

■ *George Hensher Ltd v Restawile Upholstery (Lancashire) Ltd* [1976] AC 64

An example is the difficulty in which the House of Lords found itself in this case where it had to determine whether a rough prototype for a suite of furniture was a work of artistic craftsmanship (see further at paras 3.68–3.70). This required an understanding of how such a work might be identified—how to distinguish it from a sculpture, for example—which called for some sort of aesthetic judgment. It was held that the prototype was not a work of artistic craftsmanship.

■ *Green v Broadcasting Corp of New Zealand* [1989] 2 All ER 1056 (PC)

Similarly, in this case (see further para 3.51) the Privy Council had to grapple with the question of whether a few catchphrases used constantly by the host of a television talent show (*Opportunity Knocks*) constituted a dramatic work. The phrases included: 'For [competitor's name], opportunity knocks!'; 'This is your show, folks, and I do mean you'; and 'Make up your mind time'. The show also used a device called the 'clapometer' to measure the levels of applause attracted by each act. It was held that this did not amount to a dramatic work.

In both these cases, the works in question were excluded from copyright, not on the ground of lack of merit, but on the ground that they lacked the intellectual qualities of the categories under which copyright was claimed. Here there is some overlap with the requirement that skill, labour, and judgment should be employed by the author to gain copyright: is the work one which needed such qualities to be brought into existence?

Skill, labour, and judgment

3.22 The expenditure of independent skill, labour, and judgment by the author is often seen as the essence of originality in the field of copyright. The amount of skill, labour, and judgment required should be sufficient and more than minimal or negligible[47] but cannot be defined in 'precise terms' as it depends on the facts

---

[46] For a discussion of the standards of originality for copyright protection, and whether all protected works have elements in common or are different in nature, see A Waisman, 'Revisiting originality' [2009] EIPR 370.

[47] *Ladbroke v William Hill* [1964] 1 WLR 273 (HL); *Express Newspapers plc v News (UK) Ltd* [1990] FSR 359.

of the case and is a question of degree.[48] Use of the skill, labour, and judgment test can be seen in cases of copyright in a compilation, particularly where it is of information or material which was available before the publication of the work. In such cases, it is the skill and labour of the compiler in arranging the material which receives protection.[49] If this has occurred, it is unlikely that the resulting work will be merely derivative. In *Cramp v Smythson*,[50] on the other hand, it was held that tables and information printed on part of a pocket diary had no copyright because their selection and arrangement had not required the exercise of any judgment or taste by the compiler. Behind all this lies the idea that simple copying does not involve the requisite degree of activity to justify the award of copyright. This is so even though copying may require at least labour, and often skill and judgment as well, as Lord Oliver pointed out in *Interlego AG v Tyco Industries Inc*:

> Originality in the context of literary copyright has been said in several well known cases to depend upon the degree of skill, labour and judgment involved in preparing a compilation . . . that the amount of skill, judgment or labour is likely to be decisive in the case of compilations. To apply that, however, as a universal test of originality in all copyright cases is not only unwarranted by the context in which the observations were made but palpably erroneous. Take the simplest case of artistic copyright, a painting or a photograph. It takes great skill, judgment and labour to produce a good copy by painting or to produce an enlarged photograph from a positive print, but no one would reasonably contend that the copy painting or enlargement was an 'original' artistic work in which the copier is entitled to claim copyright. Skill, labour or judgment merely in the process of copying cannot confer originality . . . A well-executed tracing is the result of much labour and skill but remains what it is, a tracing.[51]

3.23   In the *Interlego* case the subject of the copyright claim was the design of Lego bricks, which included modifications of some technical importance in relation to earlier designs but where the visual impression was much the same. Skill and labour had been expended on the technical changes, but these did not change the artistic or visual character of the drawings. Accordingly, the later drawings were not original. Another case in which it was accepted that much effort, skill, labour, and investment of money had gone into the creation of the work in question, yet its author was not entitled to a copyright, is *Exxon Corporation v Exxon Insurance*.[52] The claim was to literary copyright in the single word 'Exxon'. Here the failure was to achieve a literary work,[53] rather than originality as such, but the point to be stressed in the context of the present discussion is that *effort, skill, labour, and judgment by itself is not necessarily enough for the result to have copyright*. It would seem that, while the presence of skill, labour, and judgment will often be very important, it has not been adopted as a universal test of originality, and that it is also necessary to consider exactly what type of skill, labour, and judgment has been involved in relation to the nature of the copyright claimed.[54]

 Question

Why are skill, labour, and judgment not *necessarily* enough for originality?

Independent but similar works

3.24   As indicated by the dictum of Peterson J quoted at the outset of this section (para 3.20), 'the Act does not require that the expression must be in an original or novel form, but that the work must not be copied from another work'.[55] Thus, if two works are similar, it does not follow that one cannot be original in the sense of copyright law. Unless there is derivation of one from another, a link between them beyond the similarity,

---

[48] *Macmillan & Co Ltd v K & J Cooper* (1923) 93 LJPC 113.   [49] ibid.

[50] [1944] AC 329. Compare the decision of the US Supreme Court in *Feist Publications Inc v Rural Telephone Service Co Inc* 499 US 340 (1991), where it was held that there was no copyright in a telephone directory organised by alphabetical listing of surnames. But see further paras 3.34–3.38.

[51] [1989] AC 217 (PC) at 262–63.   [52] [1982] Ch 119 (CA).

[53] See further paras 3.43ff.   [54] *Interlego AG v Tyco Industries Inc* [1989] AC 217 at 262.

[55] *University of London Press v University Tutorial Press* [1916] 2 Ch 601 at 608.

the question cannot arise. The point is perhaps most significant in the field of artistic works, particularly paintings and photographs, where certain subjects and themes (eg representations of well-known scenes, landmarks, and buildings) are or become well worn. Probably there is often some indirect derivation—influence may be a better word—in relation to earlier works in such cases, but it may well be difficult, if not impossible, to establish the absolute originality of a particular view, even in the limited copyright sense of the originator as the person who first gave expression to it.

Question

List again all the elements to be considered in dealing with issues about originality. Which do you consider the most significant?

Author's own intellectual creation

3.25   The UK has been seen to have a different tradition to Continental Europe with regard to originality. Speaking very generally, Continental systems require works to manifest 'intellectual creation' and the UK test of 'skill, labour, and judgment' is generally taken to be less demanding in comparison. However, it is the 'intellectual creation' standard which has so far been applied in those EU Directives referring to originality. The Software Directive 1991 declared in Article 1(3) that 'a computer program shall be protected if it is original in the sense that it is the author's own intellectual creation'. The UK took no action to implement the formula in its resultant legislation. The Commission noted that the UK's implementation was lacking a specific clause and whether this would lead to over-extensive protection of computer programs remained to be seen.[56] However, it took no action to suggest that this failure involved non-compliance with the Directive. The Term Directive 1993 also provided in Article 6 that 'photographs which are original in the sense that they are the author's own intellectual creation shall be protected' in accordance with the term specified in the Directive but member states were also free to provide for the protection of other photographs. As such, this resulted in no changes in the CDPA 1998 with regards to originality.

3.26   A different result occurred, however, in the implementation of the Database Directive 1996, which again used the phrase *'the author's own intellectual creation'* in defining the object of protection. This time the UK took action to implement it, and section 3A of the CDPA 1988 provided that a database is to be considered original 'only if, by reason of the selection or arrangement of the contents of the database the database constitutes the author's own intellectual creation'. This meant that the test of originality *for databases* in the UK was no more the same as for other literary works. As a result, many databases which would have been protected by copyright before s 3A was introduced were no longer protected. This is why the *sui generis* database right was created, establishing a special new and additional form of protection for databases, even if they did not attract copyright under the more rigorous originality test (see para 7.4). The aim was clearly to provide an alternative for those who would have had copyright in places such as the UK before the Directive. Therefore, the UK test for originality remained 'skill, labour, and judgment' for all works, except for databases, which required 'author's own intellectual creation'.

3.27   These developments raised concerns at least about the lack of express implementation of the higher standard of originality with regard to computer programs, and perhaps photographs, but also whether there should be an EU-wide and comprehensive test of originality for all copyright works. A Commission Consultation Paper in 2004[57] suggested that the 'intellectual creation' standard adopted in the Directives was necessary to

---

[56] European Commission Report on the implementation and effects of Directive 91/250/EEC, COM(2000) 199 final.

[57] European Commission Staff Working Paper on the review of the EC legal framework in the field of copyright and related rights, SEC(2004) 995.

take account of the special features or the special technical nature of software, photographs, and databases and that apart from these categories of works, member states remained free to determine the standard of originality. It also concluded that the lack of harmonisation of the concept of originality for other categories of works was not creating a problem for the functioning of the internal market and therefore there was no need for legislative action at the time.

However, in *Infopaq v Danske Dagblades Forening*,[58] a reference made to the European Court of Justice (ECJ) on infringement of the reproduction right and exceptions to copyright (both of which had been harmonised under the InfoSoc Directive 2001), the ECJ, in providing guidance on such matters, also clarified the meaning of originality. It held that copyright protection under the InfoSoc Directive only applies if a work is original in the sense of 'author's own intellectual creation'. Even though the Directive does not provide for originality, and as such was not seen to be harmonising the concept, the Court reasoned as follows:

34 It is, moreover, apparent from the general scheme of the Berne Convention, in particular arts 2(5) and (8), that the protection of certain subject-matters as artistic or literary works presupposes that they are intellectual creations.

35 Similarly, under arts 1(3) of Directive 91/250, 3(1) of Directive 96/9 and 6 of Directive 2006/116, works such as computer programs, databases or photographs are protected by copyright only if they are original in the sense that they are their author's own intellectual creation.

36 In establishing a harmonised legal framework for copyright, Directive 2001/29 is based on the same principle, as evidenced by recitals 4, 9–11 and 20 in the preamble thereto.

37 In those circumstances, copyright within the meaning of art. 2(a) of Directive 2001/29 is liable to apply only in relation to a subject-matter which is original in the sense that it is its author's own intellectual creation.

Subsequent rulings of the CJEU have followed *Infopaq* to indicate that the test for originality has now been *de facto* harmonised for all works.[59] They have also provided guidance on the meaning of 'author's own intellectual creation' in relation to computer programs, photographs, and databases (see paras 3.46, 3.60, and 3.48–3.50),[60] in which the author's ability to exercise free and creative choices and to express personal creativity, or stamp a personal touch, appear to be key.

3.28   Consequently, UK law must be interpreted in light of the standard of 'author's intellectual creation'. However, an important question is whether the UK test of 'skill, labour, and judgment' is no longer relevant. This question is based on the assumption that 'author's intellectual creation' is different to and distinct from 'skill, labour, and judgment'.[61] In the case of *Newspaper Licensing Agency Ltd v Meltwater Holding BV*, the UK courts had an opportunity to address this issue. In the High Court, Proudman J while applying *Infopaq*, noted that it 'may sit awkwardly with some provisions of English law, that many questions remain unanswered by the ECJ and that the full implications of the decision have not yet been worked out'.[62] The Court of Appeal noted that the use of the term 'intellectual creation' in the *Infopaq* decision related to the question of origin of a work and not its novelty or merit, and as such, it has not qualified the long-standing test of originality, in that the work originates from the author, established by UK case law.[63] Some recent decisions have adopted the language of 'author's own intellectual creation' interchangeably with 'skill,

---

[58] Case C-5/08 *Infopaq International A/S v Danske Dagblades Forening* [2009] ECDR 16 (ECJ).

[59] See Case C-393/09 *Bezpečnostni Softwarová Asociace—Svaz Softwarove Ochrany v Ministerstvo Kultury* [2011] ECDR 3 (CJ), para 45; Cases C-403/08 and C429/08 *Football Association Premier League Ltd v QC Leisure, Murphy v Media Protection Services Ltd* [2012] 1 CMLR 29 (CJ), para 97; Case C-145/10 *Painer v Standard Verlags GmbH* [2012] ECDR 6 (CJ), para 87; *Nintendo v PC Box* C-355/12 [2014] ECDR 6 (CJ), para 21; see also, E Rosati, 'Originality in a work, or a work of originality: the effects of the Infopaq decision' [2011] EIPR 746.

[60] Case C-393/09 *Bezpečnostni Softwarová Asociace—Svaz Softwarove Ochrany v Ministerstvo Kultury* [2011] ECDR 3 (CJ); Case C-145/10 *Painer v Standard Verlags GmbH* [2012] ECDR 6 (CJ); Case C-604/10 *Football Dataco v Yahoo* [2012] ECDR 10 (CJ); Case C-406/10 *SAS Institute Inc v World Programming Ltd* [2012] ECDR 22 (CJ).

[61] See E Derclaye, 'Infopaq International A/S v Danske Dagblades-Forening (C-5/08): wonderful or worrisome? The impact of the ECJ ruling in Infopaq on UK copyright law' [2010] EIPR 247.

[62] *Newspaper Licensing Agency Ltd v Meltwater Holding BV* [2010] EWHC 3099 (Ch) at para 81.

[63] *Newspaper Licensing Agency Ltd v Meltwater Holding BV* [2011] EWCA Civ 890 (CA) at para 20.

labour, and judgment'.[64] Others have used both the language of 'author's own intellectual creation' and the guidance given by CJEU in applying it.[65] Even if 'skill, labour, and judgment' and 'author's own intellectual creation' are different, the latter might still be a low hurdle,[66] and the result as to originality might be the same in most instances.[67] While the full impact on the UK's test of 'skill, labour, and judgment' remains to be seen, it can be concluded that in the meantime, the language of 'author's own intellectual creation' and any CJEU guidance on it requires due consideration in assessing originality under UK law, and previous UK case law on originality will also continue to be relevant.[68]

Key points on originality

- Literary, dramatic, musical, and artistic works must be *'original'* to attract copyright.

- Originality is not a high standard, or a requirement of quality/merit/novelty.

- Although individual facts and circumstances are always significant, the following factors are often cumulatively of use in assessing originality under UK case law: work not copied; work is a product of author's own skill, labour, and judgment.

- The test for originality has now been *de facto* harmonised in the EU for all works to the author's intellectual creation standard, and UK law must be interpreted in light of this standard.

Originality and derivative works

3.29   Derivative works, which draw on, even copy from, other works (whether or not such underlying works are protected or unprotected by copyright) can have their own copyright if they meet the requirement of originality.[69] The obvious examples in the material already discussed in this section are compilations and anthologies. Other straightforward instances in the literary world would be books and articles quoting or summarising source material, as for example in a legal textbook. Originality is not simply a matter of not copying, therefore. In all the examples given, it is clear that while the author is copying, he is also exercising independent skill and labour, or expressing intellectual creativity, both in the selection of sources and quotations, and in the choice of words in which to express the material, so that the work is not entirely derivative. Less straightforward may be the cases where a new edition of a text, or a new version of a drawing, is produced. If a new copyright is to be created, the alterations must be extensive and substantial.[70] If a text is printed unaltered from a previous edition and the editorial matter consists of annotations or appendices, then again, as long as these have independent value, there will be a new copyright, independent of that of the text, if any.[71]

■ *Black v Murray* (1870) 9 M 341

B had published an edition of the poetry of Sir Walter Scott which had gone out of copyright. B published a second edition of the texts together with amendments, alterations, and editorial notes. M published what purported to be a reprint of B's first edition, but which included material taken from the second edition as well. It was held

---

[64] See, eg, tables and compilations: *Forensic Telecommunications Services Ltd v Chief Constable of West Yorkshire* [2011] EWHC 2892 (Ch); photographs: *Temple Island Collections Ltd v New English Teas Ltd* [2012] FSR 9; film script *Martin v Kogan* [2017] EWHC 2927 (IPEC); see also A Rahmatian, 'Temple Island Collections v New English Teas: an incorrect decision based on the right law?' [2012] EIPR 796.

[65] See *SAS Institute v World Programming* [2013] EWHC69 (Ch).

[66] *Technomed Ltd v Bluecrest Health Screening Ltd* [2017] EWHC 2142 (Ch), paras 89, 96, 122, and 134.

[67] See D Rose and N O'Sullivan, 'Football Dataco v Yahoo! Implications of the ECJ judgment' (2012) JIPLP 792; see also *John Kaldor Fabricmaker v Lee Ann Fashions* [2014] EWHC 3779 (IPEC) at para 21.

[68] For a detailed discussion, see L Bently et al, *Intellectual Property Law* (5th edn, 2018), Ch 3.

[69] It is worth noting that a derivative work, while being original, may also be infringing. One doesn't exclude the other.

[70] cf *Technomed Ltd v Bluecrest Health Screening Ltd* [2017] EWHC 2142 (Ch), paras 131–134, where small visual and literary changes made to a stock image to create two drawings of a heart were held to be sufficient to create a new original work.

[71] *Black v Murray* (1870) 9 M 341 (editorial material in the works of Sir Walter Scott).

that the changes made in B's second edition had their own copyright, but that M's takings were substantial, and infringed copyright, only in relation to the editorial notes.

3.30   Translations, adaptations, and dramatisations will attract their own copyright, even though manifestly derivative, as do arrangements, orchestrations, and transcriptions of musical works.[72] In the computer world, many programs are developed from existing ones, either by the creators themselves or by competitors engaging in 'reverse engineering', but it seems to be accepted that even when the end result is very close to the original work a new copyright has come into existence.

■ *Walter v Lane* [1900] AC 539

The House of Lords allowed *The Times* newspaper copyright in its reporter's verbatim transcript of a speech by Lord Rosebery, a leading politician of the day. Clearly, the reporter's work was derivative, but its creation had involved the expenditure of individual skill and effort. Since the case was decided before originality became a statutory requirement, it has been questioned whether the copyright would be accepted now, as otherwise an audio typist would acquire rights in dictated material.[73] However, the current judicial view appears to favour the reporter's copyright established in *Walter v Lane*.[74]

Question

Is there a relevant difference between a typist taking dictation or typing from material recorded on a Dictaphone, on the one hand, and a transcriber such as the journalist in *Walter v Lane*?

■ *Eisenman v Qimron* (2000) 54(3) PD 817, [2001] ECDR 6 (Supreme Court of Israel)

Q deciphered and put together a text from 67 fragments of an ancient Dead Sea scroll known as 4QMMT. Publication was planned but not yet accomplished when S published in the archaeology journal he edited a copy of the text as edited by Q. S had been critical of the long delays in publishing the Dead Sea scrolls, and this publication formed part of his campaign. Q sued for infringement of his copyright. The defendant contended that Q's editorial labours amounted to no more than an attempt to reproduce as faithfully as possible what had been originated by the scribe who wrote 4QMMT, and therefore lacked the originality required for copyright. It was held that Q's work had copyright and that S had infringed. Q's work was original in the sense that he 'used his knowledge, expertise and imagination, exercised judgment and chose between different alternatives'.[75]

■ *Sawkins v Hyperion Records Ltd* [2005] RPC 32 (CA)

S edited the work of a late 17th/early 18th-century composer, L. The editing involved the insertion of notes missing or inaccurately recorded in L's original scores, the addition or correction of flourishes, and other performing indications and the supply of figuring which, in relation to the bass line of baroque works, was the foundation of the work. The expert evidence was that without this last the works could not have been

---

[72]   See also Berne Convention, Art 2(3): 'Translations, adaptations, arrangements of music and other alterations of a literary or artistic work shall be protected as original works without prejudice to the copyright in the original work.' And see the UNESCO Nairobi Recommendation: the Translator's Charter (1994), available at www.fit-ift.org.

[73]   *Roberton v Lewis* [1976] RPC 169 per Cross J at 174–75.

[74]   See *Express Newspapers plc v News (UK) Ltd* [1990] FSR 359 per Sir Nicolas Browne-Wilkinson V-C at 365–66, preferring the views expressed in *Sands McDougall Pty Ltd v Robinson* (1917) 23 CLR 49 to those of Cross J. See further HL MacQueen, '"My tongue is mine ain". copyright, the spoken word, and privacy' (2005) 68 MLR 349 at 369–73.

[75]   For an English translation of the judgments in this case and discussion of its content, see TH Lim, HL MacQueen, and CM Carmichael (eds), *On Scrolls, Artefacts and Intellectual Property* (2001). The extensive discussion of this case is critically reviewed in HL MacQueen, 'The legal definition of authorship and the scrolls' in JJ Collins and TH Lim (eds), *Oxford Handbook of the Dead Sea Scrolls* (2010).

performed in a modern recording session using the original sources. HR produced CDs of the music using S's editions but without a licence. It was held that HR had infringed S's copyright in the work. S's work was original, involving skill and labour over a considerable period of time, going beyond mere transcription.

Discussion point   For answer guidance visit **www.oup.com/uk/brown5e.**

Consider whether *Walter v Lane*, *Interlego v Tyco*, and *Sawkins v Hyperion Records* are correctly decided on the originality point. See further J Pila, 'An intentional view of the copyright work' (2008) 71 MLR 535 and NP Gravells, 'Authorship and originality: the persistent influence of *Walter v Lane*' [2007] IPQ 267.

3.31   In the *Interlego* case, Lord Oliver recognised that a derivative artistic work might be original where there was *'some element of material alteration or embellishment'* in it by comparison with the previous work.[76]

■ *Baumann v Fussell* **[1978] RPC 485 (CA)**

A photograph of two cocks fighting each other was used as the basis of a painting. The composition of the subject matter was followed closely but the painter employed different colouring to heighten the dramatic effect of the representation. It was held that there was no infringement. It seems likely, therefore, that the painting would have been held to be original and so qualified for its own copyright.

Contrast the New York case of:

■ *Bridgeman Art Library Ltd v Corel Corp* **25 F Supp 421 (1999)**

Kaplan J found that he was obliged to apply UK law in a case where the question was whether photographs of public domain works of art were the subject of copyright so that their unauthorised digitisation and inclusion in the defendants' CD-ROMs was infringement. It was held that, since the photographs aspired to create as accurate as possible a copy of the subject of the photograph, their work lacked originality under UK law and could not be protected (see further para 3.60).

Discussion point   For answer guidance visit **www.oup.com/uk/5e.**

Is this decision a correct application of the concept of originality? Compare with *Eisenman v Qimron*, described previously (para 3.30). See further K Garnett, 'Copyright in photographs' [2000] EIPR 229; R Deazley, 'Photographing paintings in the public domain: a response to Garnett' [2001] EIPR 229; S Stokes, 'Photographing paintings in the public domain: a response to Garnett' [2001] EIPR 354; and R Arnold, 'Copyright in photographs: a case for reform' [2005] EIPR 303.

Consider further:

■ *Antiquesportfolio.com plc v Rodney Fitch & Co Ltd* **[2001] FSR 345**

It was held that a photograph of a single static item was an original artistic work, because it could be said that the positioning of the object, the angle at which it was taken, the lighting, and the focus were all matters of personal judgment, albeit in many cases at a very basic level.

[76] [1989] AC 217 at 263.

Discussion point   For answer guidance visit **www.oup.com/uk/brown5e**.

Do the auto-focus, portrait, landscape, and action shot functions in a digital camera mean that there is insufficient input from the user of the camera to make his or her photographs with the camera original for copyright purposes?

Originality in sound recordings, films, and published editions

3.32   With regard to sound recordings, films, and the typographical arrangements of published editions, there is no express requirement of originality; but no copyright arises in such a work to the extent that it reproduces another work in the same category. This is regardless of whether or not the earlier work had, or is still in, copyright. Thus a photographic reprint of an out-of-copyright book does not preclude others from making another edition of the same work using the same technique, although any additional editorial matter in the first work would have its own copyright in accordance with *Black v Murray*.[77] The matter is becoming ever more important in the film and recording industries, where digital technology has made it possible to re-record old material with greatly enhanced quality of sound and visual reproduction, with the possibility of embellishments such as colourisation of black-and-white films, or the stripping out of production effects in the original which are no longer wanted.[78] Although such re-recordings are derivative works, it may well be that the further technological input will be enough to mean that the new version is not merely a copy of the old but gains a new copyright.

 Exercise

Through use of a 'sampler', a digital recorder converts small samples of sound from other records into digits and stores them in microchips. These samples are then capable of electronic manipulation—for example, by slowing down or speeding up—and the results are then mixed to produce a new record. In effect, it is equivalent to a compilation of extracts from previous records. Quite apart from the question of the extent to which such activities infringe the copyrights in the original recordings, is the collection of samples itself a subject of copyright? (See further L Bently, 'Sampling and copyright: is the law on the right track?' [1989] JBL 113 and 405.)

Broadcasts

3.33   The position of broadcasts with regard to requirements of originality is different from that of sound recordings, films, and typographical arrangements. The CDPA 1988 provides that copyright does not subsist in a broadcast which infringes, or to the extent that it infringes, the copyright in another broadcast.[79] The background to this is that merely broadcasting a programme which has already been put out has the effect of creating a new copyright. This is clear from the provisions of what is now section 14(5) of the 1988 Act, which states that 'copyright in a repeat broadcast expires at the same time as the copyright in the original broadcast'. As the subsection goes on to say, however, 'accordingly no copyright arises in respect of

---

[77] (1870) 9 M 341 (discussed at para 3.29).

[78] See, eg, the colourisation of John Huston's film, 'The Maltese Falcon' and, the removal from a 2003 re-release of The Beatles' final album, 'Let It Be', of effects added in the original by the producer Phil Spector.

[79] CDPA 1988, s 6(6).

a repeat broadcast which is broadcast after the expiry of the copyright in the original broadcast'. It is also clear from this that only unauthorised repeats infringe the original copyright and are therefore unable to claim copyright themselves. This seems obvious, but it makes an important contrast with the forms of work discussed in the previous paragraph (para 3.32), where no copy, authorised or unauthorised, can bring a new copyright into existence.

The 'originality' threshold

3.34 In relation to the originality test, there have been relevant developments in the common law world outside England, seeming to elevate 'skill' over 'labour' in the traditional test of originality. In the United States, the standard of 'originality' was raised by the Supreme Court in 1991, in *Feist v Rural Telephone Service Company Inc*[80], a case concerned with whether a telephone directory enjoyed copyright. In answering the question negatively, *Feist* recast the originality requirement in US law, from a 'sweat-of-the-brow' test to one of 'spark of creativity'. But *Feist* must be seen in the context of its own facts, namely, once again, the protection of a compilation or database. In this context, what copyright protects is, in the language of the Berne Convention, the 'selection and arrangement' of the contents of the work, and since all subscribers were included in the directory, and alphabetical listing was the only possible usable way of presenting the results, the originality of the selection and arrangement was indeed negligible.

3.35 The decision equivalent to *Feist* in Canada is *Tele-Direct (Publications) Inc v American Business Information*.[81] The case concerned the yellow pages section of a telephone directory, and again it was held that there was insufficient originality for copyright. But a later court confined *Tele-Direct* to the compilation/database area, saying that difficulties arose there 'because such works are not likely to exhibit, on their face, indicia of the author's personal style or manner of expression'.[82] *Tele-Direct* has also been the subject of criticism by the Federal Court of Appeal in *CCH Canadian Ltd v Law Society of Upper Canada*,[83] a case about the copyright in law reports rather than databases. On appeal in that case, the Supreme Court took up a mid-position, emphasising that originality lay, not in either labour and 'sweat of the brow' or 'sparks of creativity', but in the author's exercise of skill and judgment.

3.36 Adoption of a higher-threshold criterion of originality (or equivalent) might remove from the ambit of copyright some of the relatively trivial and ephemeral material that has been within the scope of copyright. The disadvantage would be that someone (ultimately the courts) would have to take the decision as to which side of the line any given work fell. The possibility of seeming absurdity would be replaced by perhaps dangerous uncertainty.

3.37 An alternative approach would be to drop any threshold test whatsoever. Possibly this might sit best in a world where copyright had been displaced by contract, with the material which its producer did not want disseminated to a wider world being protected by laws of confidentiality and privacy (for which see Chapters 17–18). The protection afforded by contract would be relevant for any item for which a buyer was prepared to pay; that of confidentiality and privacy for material which was indeed confidential or private and which the producer was not prepared to sell or give away.

3.38 The policy issue here is the desirability of threshold tests for 'originality' such as 'skill, labour and judgment', or 'intellectual creation', in particular in the digital environment, and what the consequences would be if there was a higher or lower threshold, or indeed no threshold test at all.

---

[80] 499 US 340 (1991).   [81] [1998] 2 FCR 22 (CA (Can)).   [82] *Hager v ECW Press* [1999] 2 FC 311.
[83] *Law Society of Upper Canada v CCH Canadian* [2004] 1 SCR 339.

Subject matter of copyright and Brexit

Although the current UK copyright framework in relation to certain subject matter is framed in light of EU directives (Database Directive, Software Directive) and CJEU jurisprudence (author's intellectual creation standard for originality), the implementation of such directives will be preserved in UK law as retained EU law under the powers in the EU Withdrawal Act 2018. Both the UK and EU member states are party to the main international treaties which are applicable to the current underlying framework of copyright-protected subject matter and under which the main obligations in this area arise (eg Berne Convention, WCT, TRIPS). Consequently, in a 'no-deal' scenario, the relationship between the UK and EU member states will be governed through the principles of such treaties (see para 2.20). The UK government 'no-deal' guidance notes that as a result, 'the scope of protection for copyright works in the UK and for UK works abroad will remain largely unchanged'.[84]

However, in a 'no-deal' scenario, there could be scope in the future for the UK to substantially diverge from EU law on some specific issues, albeit while complying with relevant international frameworks. One example is the standard required for assessment of originality. One of the major issues in harmonising copyright in Europe has been the different traditions of the UK ('skill, labour, and judgment' standard) and the Continent ('author's own intellectual creation' standard) with regard to originality. The question of how to choose between the two standards in developing a copyright law suitable for the digital environment seems so far to have been resolved in favour of the Continental approach, especially in the light of recent CJEU jurisprudence. However, what a genuinely Europe-wide and comprehensive test of originality should be has remained an unresolved question. Brexit offers an opportunity for stronger harmonisation, and future codification in the EU, of the Continental tradition. On the other hand, in a 'no-deal' scenario, the UK may simply revert to the 'skill, labour, and judgment' standard, instead of trying half-heartedly (as it has done so far) to embrace the author's own intellectual creation standard. Another example is the concept of work and the limits imposed by the categories in the UK. The UK courts have yet to fully consider adapting to the interpretation offered in recent CJEU decisions on the matter. Again, they may choose to not do so, since the UK will not be bound by CJEU decisions in a 'no-deal' Brexit.

Author works and media works

3.39   Where Continental countries have a strong tradition of distinguishing between authors' rights and neighbouring rights in substance as well as form, the UK awards copyright to both authors and entrepreneurial producers of works, albeit with differentiated content of rights—for example, clearly distinct copyright terms (see paras 3.113–3.126). For convenience, in the remainder of this chapter, literary, dramatic, musical, and artistic works and films will be collectively referred to as *'author works'*, and the other categories will be grouped as *'media works'*. The distinction is reflected in international conventions, and has already been discussed insofar as it can be derived from the international structure of copyright: the Berne Convention for literary and artistic productions, broadly conceived (see para 2.8) and the Rome Convention for sound recordings and broadcasts (see para 2.9). The distinction rests on a number of points, of which the most important conceptually is the idea that the second group relies essentially on the operation of machinery and technology, where the first depends upon one or more individuals as creator.

---

[84]   UK Government, 'Copyright if there's no Brexit deal' (24 September 2018) www.gov.uk/government/publications/copyright-if-theres-no-brexit-deal.

The nature of authorship, as understood in the law of copyright, is dealt with in further detail later (paras 3.82–3.112). Another element may be that in author works *content* is protected, whereas with media works it is the *medium* itself, or the *signal*, that is protected, rather than the material embodied within it. So, a song or music have author copyright, while the sound recording and broadcast containing them are purely media ones. Note also that the distinction has some difficulties in dealing with photographs and films, although in the law and in this book, both are included in the author rather than the media work category. The point here is that anyone can get a result by wielding a camera, but does that make the person an author with protection for the content of the result?[85]

3.40   The distinction between author and media works has practical consequences in differences in the rules applying to the two groups. The first owner of the copyright in an author work is generally the author,[86] whereas in the media work it is the person by whose investment (to be conceived more widely than the kind of investment that is authorship or composition) the work was produced. Only author works need be original to be protected,[87] meaning that they must be the author's own intellectual creation.[88] Author works alone attract moral rights.[89] Author work copyright lasts significantly longer than media work copyright: with the former, it normally lasts for the lifetime of the author plus 70 years, while for broadcasts it is 50 years from the year in which the broadcast is made.[90]

3.41   The distinction between author and media works raises several policy questions. For instance, the proliferation in use of digital technologies for production and dissemination of creative content challenges the relevance of the distinction. If increasingly all kinds of work are carried out and fixed (insofar as they are ever fixed) in digital media, is the distinction between authorship and medium increasingly obsolescent? Further, in the post-modern world of culture generally, authors and artists are rejecting past understandings of their respective disciplines and consequent self-imposed limitations to seek more and more to cross boundaries and use the huge flexibility of digital technology to convey their message, whatever it may be, to the world. It seems most likely, however, that for the time being the basic distinction between author and other works will continue to be drawn, if only because it also underlies some of the basic international infrastructure, which will not be easily shifted. But, nonetheless, there may still be questions about the way in which UK law gives effect to the distinction. Only in the 1990s, for example, were films brought into author rather than media work protection in the UK, as a result of the Term Directive 1993 (Art 2). Also, there are major differences in substantive content between author and media works, as will be explained in detail later in the chapter.

Key points on author and media works

- The distinction between *author* and *media* work, rests in principle on the degree of individual, as opposed to technological creativity involved.
- The difference in rules applying to each of the groups is explained in detail later.

---

[85] For an interesting discussion of this point, see R Arnold, 'Copyright in photographs: a case for reform' [2005] EIPR 303.

[86] In the case of films in the UK, joint authorship is attributed to the principal director and the producer (CDPA 1988, s 9(2)(ab)). Note also (1) the British concept of a computer-generated work where there is no human author (CDPA 1988, ss 9(3) and 178); and (2) that copyright in a work produced in the course of employment falls to the employer unless otherwise agreed (CDPA 1988, s 11(2)). Employment should be distinguished from a commission, where the copyright would remain with the author unless otherwise agreed.

[87] But note that there is no express requirement that a film be original (see CDPA 1988, s 1(1)(b), and para 3.32).

[88] See further paras 3.25–3.28.

[89] Apart from computer programs (CDPA 1988, s 79(2)(a)); see further para 6.11.

[90] See further paras 3.113–3.126 for copyright terms.

Author works

3.42   The following are the categories of author works:

- literary;
- dramatic;
- musical;
- artistic;
- films.

The distinctions between these groups of author works are not without importance, but in a number of recent cases the English courts have held that a work may belong to more than one of the categories. So, for example, circuit diagrams have been held to be both literary and artistic works,[91] while a film has been held to be also a dramatic work.[92] As Laddie J has pointed out, this is a different point from the one made earlier in this chapter (para 3.5), that one product may embody several copyrights:[93]

> although different copyrights can protect simultaneously a particular product and an author can produce more than one copyright work during the course of a single episode of creative effort, for example a competent musician may write the words and the music for a song at the same time, it is quite another thing to say that a single piece of work by an author gives rise to two or more copyrights in respect of the same creative effort. In some cases the borderline between one category of copyright work and another may be difficult to define, but that does not justify giving to the author protection in both categories. The categories of copyright work are, to some extent, arbitrarily defined. In the case of a borderline work, I think there are compelling arguments that the author must be confined to one or other of the possible categories. The proper category is that which most nearly suits the characteristics of the work in issue.

From a taxonomic point of view there must be much to be said for the approach of Laddie J; what, after all, is the point of having categories if they are not mutually exclusive? And if they are not mutually exclusive, or fail to capture particular types of work adequately, should the categorisation not be abandoned or re-thought? The principle of Occam's razor might usefully be applied:[94] categories are not to be multiplied unnecessarily in copyright law, and perhaps the present UK statute is guilty of that offence (see further on this theme, paras 3.5, 3.12).[95]

 Exercise

Explain clearly the difference between copyright in a work and the several copyrights which may coexist in a product such as a CD. Why does this distinction matter? Consider in particular the multimedia product (eg the BBC website, a computer game), which consists of digitised material combining audio, video, text, and images still and moving played through a computer, and with which the user may interact.

---

[91] *Anacon Corp Ltd v Environmental Research Technology Ltd* [1994] FSR 659; *Electronic Techniques (Anglia) Ltd v Critchley Components Ltd* [1997] FSR 401; *Sandman v Panasonic UK Ltd* [1998] FSR 651.

[92] *Norowzian v Arks Ltd (No 2)* [2000] FSR 363; *Abraham Moon & Sons Ltd v Thornber and Others* [2012] EWPCC 37, where a fabric 'ticket stamp'—ie instructions to produce a design—was held to be both a literary and artistic work.

[93] *Electronic Techniques (Anglia) Ltd v Critchley Components Ltd* [1997] FSR 401 at 413.

[94] For Occam's razor, see http://en.wikipedia.org/wiki/Occam's_Razor, or for a more reliable source, see J W Shavlik and T G Dietterich, *Readings in Machine Learning* (1990) 201–04.

[95] See further, A Christie, 'A proposal for simplifying UK copyright law' [2001] EIPR 26; I Stamatoudi, *Copyright and Multimedia Works: A Comparative Analysis* (2002); T Aplin, *Copyright Law in the Digital Society* (2005), Ch 6; B Bandey, 'Over-categorisation in copyright law: computer and internet programming perspectives' [2007] EIPR 461.

Literary works

3.43   The 1988 Act defines 'literary work' as follows in s 3(1):

> any work other than a dramatic or musical work which is written, spoken or sung, and accordingly includes a table or compilation other than a database, a computer program, preparatory design material for a computer program, and a database.

This statutory definition is not exhaustive and there are a number of cases in which the courts have had to give an opinion one way or the other as a matter of impression. Standard examples of literary works protected by copyright would include novels, short stories, poetry, song lyrics, non-fiction books, and periodical articles. But, as already noted in the discussion of originality (para 3.21), the law does not require works to possess, or even to aspire to possess, aesthetic merit before they can be the subject of copyright as literary works. Trade catalogues,[96] examination papers,[97] a grid containing 25 letters and two separate rows of five letters each,[98] and the critical apparatus or annotations attached to an edition of another work[99] may all be literary works. Moreover, while the work must have some meaning,[100] it is not necessary for it to be expressed in a conventional way, so that a work written in shorthand or in code may be a literary work.[101] A knitting guide consisting of 'various words and numerals . . . which constitute detailed instructions intelligible to anyone who understands the production of knitwear'[102] would presumably be a literary work.

Single words and phrases

3.44   On the other hand, the courts usually had great difficulty in according copyright to single words and phrases as literary works.[103]

■ *Exxon Corporation v Exxon Insurance Consultants* [1982] Ch 119

Copyright was claimed in the invented single word 'Exxon', which had been developed as a new company name with great expenditure of time and money by the company in question. The Court held that a literary work must be 'intended to afford either information and instruction or pleasure in the form of literary enjoyment',[104] and that this could not be the case with a single word, even though research and effort had been involved in its creation.

Similarly it has been said that in general the title of a work by itself does not have copyright,[105] while advertising slogans consisting of stock phrases or a few commonplace sentences have also been denied copyright as literary works.[106] It has been held in a number of cases that there is no copyright in the names of computer program commands, since they are merely 'triggers' for a set of instructions to be given effect by the computer.[107]

3.45   But there are also recent departures from the generally negative view of short works of this kind, which demonstrate a renewed willingness on the part of the courts to recognise copyright in phrases.[108]

---

[96] *Harpers v Barry Henry & Co* (1892) 20 R 133.   [97] *University of London Press v University Tutorial Press* [1916] 2 Ch 601.

[98] *Express Newspapers plc v Liverpool Daily Post & Echo plc* [1985] FSR 306.   [99] *Black v Murray* (1870) 9 M 341.

[100] *Fournet v Pearson* (1897) 14 TLR 82.   [101] *Pitman v Hine* (1884) 1 TLR 82; *Anderson & Co v Lieber Code Co* [1917] 2 KB 469.

[102] *Brigid Foley Ltd v Ellott* [1982] RPC 433 per Sir Robert Megarry V-C at 434; see also *Abraham Moon & Sons Ltd v Thornber and Others* [2012] EWPCC 37.

[103] Although single words and phrases can be accorded protection through other IP rights, see Chapters 13–16.

[104] Phrasing derived from *Hollinrake v Truswell* [1894] 3 Ch 420.

[105] *Francis Day & Hunter Ltd v Twentieth Century Fox Corp Ltd* [1940] AC 112 (PC) per Lord Wright at 123; *Rose v Information Services Ltd* [1987] FSR 254; cf *Dicks v Yates* (1881) 18 Ch D 76 per Jessel MR at 89.

[106] *Kirk v J & R Fleming* [1928–35] MCC 44; *Sinanide v La Maison Kosmeo* (1928) 139 LT 365 (CA).

[107] *Powerflex Services Pty Ltd v Data Access Corporation* (1996) 137 ALR 498 (Fed Ct Aus); aff'd (1999) 202 CLR 1 (HCA); *Navitaire Inc v EasyJet Airline Co Ltd* [2006] RPC 3 (Pumfrey J).

[108] See also P Sumpter, 'Copyright in slogans: another bald spot exposed' [2009] EIPR 287.

■ *Shetland Times v Wills* [1997] FSR 604

The *Shetland Times* home page used its newspaper headlines as links to the material deeper within the site. The headline texts were used by the *Shetland News* website to act as the deep links on to the relative *Times* stories. But, in a prima facie view granting interim interdict, Lord Hamilton held that the headline texts had copyright, so that the actions of the *News* in copying them for reproduction on its own website was infringement. In defence of Lord Hamilton's view, the creation of a headline does involve skill and labour, in that the reader's attention has to be attracted, information about the relevant item conveyed, and (at least in the case of the tabloid press, which much favours punning and jokey headlines) entertainment provided.

■ Case C-5/08 *Infopaq International A/S v Danske Dagblades Forening* [2009] ECDR 16 (ECJ)

For the facts of this case, which related to an electronic news-cuttings service, see para 4.19. The ECJ stated that 'words, considered in isolation, are not as such an intellectual creation of the author who employs them' (para 45); but

> the possibility may not be ruled out that certain isolated sentences, or even certain parts of sentences . . . may be suitable for conveying to the reader the originality of a publication such as a newspaper article, by communicating to that reader an element which is, in itself, the expression of the intellectual creation of the author of that article (para 47).

■ *Newspaper Licensing Agency Ltd v Meltwater Holding BV* [2010] EWHC 3099 (Ch); [2011] EWCA Civ 890 (CA)

For the facts of this case, which related to a media-monitoring service, see para 4.19. A question for determination was whether headlines in newspapers could be literary works which would attract copyright independently of the substantive article. In the High Court, Proudman J applied *Infopaq* and held that 'headlines are capable of being literary works, whether independently or as part of the articles to which they relate. Some of the headlines . . . with which I have been provided are certainly independent literary works within the Infopaq test' (para 71). It was also concluded that 'a mere 11 word extract may now be sufficient in quantity provided it includes an expression of the intellectual creation of the author' (para 77). Both these conclusions were affirmed by the Court of Appeal, which rejected the argument that 'a 256 character extract would be too short and factual to give a reader more than an idea of what the article is about but with no sense of the author's intellectual creation' (paras 27–28).

These cases reinforce that sentences in the form of headlines or extracts from newspaper articles can be independent literary works and protected if there is sufficient originality. It also means that slightly more elaborate texts, such as notes on what will be found through using a link, or material on help menus and 'frequently asked questions' facilities could also be protected.

Question

What is needed for there to be a literary work?

Computer programs as literary works

3.46   The CDPA 1988 states that a computer program[109] and its preparatory design material are literary works.[110] The Act does not otherwise define the meaning of computer program. Jacob LJ has pointed out that the Software Directive implemented by the 1988 Act envisages one rather than two separate copyrights in

---

[109]   See generally, D Bainbridge, *Legal Protection of Computer Software* (2008); S Gordon, 'The very idea! Why copyright law is an inappropriate way to protect computer programs' [1998] EIPR 10.

[110]   CDPA 1988, s 3(1)(b), (c). Note also the possibility of software patents, discussed at paras 11.114ff.

the program *and* its preparatory material.[111] In general a computer program is a set of instructions to a computer to perform certain tasks. The production of a program is a complex process involving first the expression of an analysis of the functions to be performed as a set of algorithms (often most simply represented by means of a flow chart or some other logical flow diagram); secondly, its restatement (usually by a programmer, but also often by a computer) in a computer language (the source code); and, finally, the translation by a computer running under a compiler program of the source code into a machine-readable language (the object code).

■ **Case C-406/10 *SAS Institute Inc v World Programming Ltd* [2012] ECDR 22 (CJ)**

This reference involved questions on copyright protection available to computer programs under the Software Directive.[112] The CJ held that the object of the protection is the expression in any form of a computer program which permits reproduction in different computer languages (para 35). As such, source code and object code are clearly protectable forms of expressions. Protection includes expression in the preparatory design material for a computer program which must be such that a computer program can result from it at some stage (para 36).[113] Such matter as the logic, algorithms, and programming languages lying behind the source code comprise unprotectable ideas and principles.[114] The functionality of a computer program, as well as programming language and format of data files used in a computer program, do not constitute a form of expression of that program (para 39). The Court also noted that 'keywords, syntax, commands and combinations of commands, options, defaults and iterations consist of words, figures or mathematical concepts which, considered in isolation, are not, as such, an intellectual creation of the author of the computer program' and 'it is only through the choice, sequence and combination of those words, figures or mathematical concepts that the author may express his creativity in an original manner and achieve a result, namely the user manual for the computer program, which is an intellectual creation' (paras 66–67).

The lack of a definition of a computer program is to avoid failure to cover advances in the technology.[115] Some examples of computer programs that have been protected are: a 'hardware lock' enabling a computer program to run (Australia);[116] codes embedded in microchips within the computer (United States);[117] and a video game simulating a game of pool (UK).[118] It has been held that a GUI, which enables communication between the computer program and the user, is not a form of expression of a computer program because it 'does not enable the reproduction of that computer program, but merely constitutes one element of that program by means of which users make use of the features of that program'.[119]

 Question

What is the difference between source code and object code?

[111] *Nova Productions Ltd v Mazooma Games Ltd* [2007] RPC 25 (CA), para 28.
[112] See further D Gervais and E Derclaye, 'The scope of computer program protection after SAS: are we closer to answers?' [2012] EIPR 565.
[113] See Case C-393/09 *Bezpečnostní softwarová asociace v Ministerstvo kultury* [2011] ECDR 3 (CJ) at paras 34–37.
[114] Software Directive 1991, recitals 7, 13, 14, and 15 (note this is now consolidated into Directive 2009/24/EC); see *Navitaire Inc v EasyJet Airline Co Ltd* [2006] RPC 3 (Pumfrey J), for an example of denial of copyright to programming languages comprised by defined user command interfaces (despite its ad hoc character) and a collection of commands; see also *SAS Institute v World Programming* [2010] ECDR 15 (Arnold J) at para 217; [2013] EWHC 69 (Ch).
[115] This argument succeeded in the Australian case of *Apple Computer Inc v Computer Edge Pty Ltd* [1986] FSR 537.
[116] *Autodesk Inc v Dyason and Kelly* [1992] RPC 575 (HCA); criticised in *Cantor Fitzgerald v Tradition UK* [2000] RPC 95.
[117] *NEC Corp v Intel Corp 835 F 2d 1546* (1988). See also recital 7 of the Software Directive 1991.
[118] *Nova Productions Ltd v Mazooma Games Ltd* [2006] RPC 14 (Kitchin J); aff'd [2007] RPC 25 (CA).
[119] Case C-393/09 *Bezpečnostní softwarová asociace v Ministerstvo kultury* [2011] ECDR 3 (CJ) at para 41.

Tables and compilations

3.47   Tables and compilations may be literary works. Thus import and export lists,[120] railway timetables,[121] television programme schedules,[122] and football fixture lists[123] have been held to be literary works, as have poetry anthologies[124] and football pools coupons.[125] Character-based screen displays used for online booking of tickets on a 'ticketless' airline, providing a static framework within which the dynamic data supplied by customers caused the booking software to operate were also held to be copyright tables, but in the same case a collection of computer programs was held not to be a compilation, since there was no overall design underlying the collection, simply an accretion of material over time.[126] Similarly, a list of 33 pairs of electronic addresses allowing police to recover deleted data from mobile phones was held not to be a compilation because it was not planned, lacked overall design, and was simply an accretion of data acquired by happenstance over time.[127] The component parts of a compilation may be out of copyright, but the compilation will still enjoy copyright as such.[128] But such material has always to be subjected to the test of originality before copyright can be claimed.

 Question

What is it that copyright protects in relation to tables and compilations?

Databases

3.48   Until 1 January 1998, databases[129] were thought to be protected under UK law as 'compilations'; but from that date the position was changed as a result of the implementation of the EU's Database Directive 1996.[130] 'Compilation' now expressly does not include databases.[131] A database is defined as:[132]

> a collection of independent works, data or other materials arranged in a systematic or methodical way and individually accessible by electronic or other means.

This definition means that, unlike traditional compilations, database protection is not confined to collections the basic form of which is written, as distinct from other forms of expression (eg graphic). As per this definition, three specific elements are required for a work to be categorised as a database: (1) independence of the constituent elements; (2) systematic or methodical arrangement of the elements; and, (3) individual accessibility of the elements. The meaning of each of these elements can be understood from the rulings of the CJEU and guidance from the Opinions of the Advocate General, and is set out in more detail in Chapter 7 (paras 7.6–7.8).

Databases include:[133]

> literary, artistic, musical or other collections of works or collections of other materials such as texts, sounds, images, numbers, facts, and data.

[120] *Walford v Johnston* (1846) 20 D 1160; *Maclean v Moody* (1858) 20 D 1154.   [121] *Leslie v Young* (1894) 21 R (HL) 57.

[122] *Independent Television Publications Ltd v Time Out Ltd* [1984] FSR 64.

[123] *Football League v Littlewoods Pools* [1959] Ch 637.   [124] *Macmillan v Suresh Chunder Deb* (1890) ILR 17 Calc 951.

[125] *Ladbroke (Football) Ltd v William Hill (Football) Ltd* [1964] 1 WLR 273 (HL).

[126] *Navitaire Inc v EasyJet Airline Co Ltd* [2006] RPC 3 (Pumfrey J).

[127] *Forensic Telecommunications Services Ltd v Chief Constable of West Yorkshire Police* [2011] EWHC 2892 (Ch).

[128] *Ashmore v Douglas Home* [1987] FSR 553.

[129] See generally, E Derclaye, *The Legal Protection of Databases* (2008); T Aplin, *Copyright Law in the Digital Society: The Challenges of Multimedia* (2005), 41–73.

[130] Directive 96/9/EC on the legal protection of databases, Art 3(1), implemented in the UK by the Copyright and Rights in Databases Regulations 1997 (SI 1997/3032).

[131] CDPA 1988, s 3(1)(a).   [132] CDPA 1988, s 3A(1).   [133] Database Directive 1996, recital 17.

That is, they can be *multimedia works*. So, the elements of a database may be works in their own right, or simply items of information in textual, visual, or audio form. Many websites are database-driven, for example, particularly where they are interactive. But databases are not merely electronic compilations or collections; they can also be created in non-electronic media. The CJEU has indicated that the term 'database' is intended to have wide scope.[134] The term is capable of including football fixture lists, telephone directories, trade directories, news websites, topographic maps, and pdf documents.[135] However, a database does not include computer programs used in the making or operation of databases accessible by electronic means.[136]

 Question

What is protected by the copyright (if any) in a database? What is the difference between a database and a compilation?

3.49   The CDPA 1988 expressly provides for the level of originality that a database must show:

> if, and only if, by reason of the selection or *arrangement of the contents* of the database the database constitutes the *author's own intellectual creation* (s 3A(2); emphasis added).

This provision, introduced as a result of the Database Directive 1996 is generally taken to require a higher level of originality than the traditional 'skill, labour, and judgment' test used in the UK (see paras 3.22–3.23). One result of this provision was that many databases which would previously have been protected by copyright in the UK were no longer protected. For this reason, the Database Directive also introduced a special, or *sui generis*, database right for the protection of databases not covered by copyright. An account of this special right is given in paras 7.4–7.25. Another consequence of the special definition of originality is to make clear that database copyright covers not the contents of the database but their *selection or arrangement*—that is, the way in which the contents are structured.[137] It is this structure that must be the *author's own intellectual creation* (see further para 3.25).

3.50   As such for copyright protection to subsist, the subject matter must be a database, and must be the author's own intellectual creation by reason of the selection or arrangement of its contents.[138] The protection is offered to the selection and arrangement of the database, rather than to its contents as such, although the latter may attract copyright—or several copyrights—in their own right. It is irrelevant whether the collection is made up of materials from a source or sources other than the person making up the collection, materials created by that person, or a combination of the two.[139] The Database Directive says that, as a rule (ie normally), the compilation of several recordings of musical performances on a CD does not attract copyright protection as a database (see para 7.12).[140]

---

[134] Case C-444/02 *Fixtures Marketing Ltd v OPAP* [2005] ECDR 3 (ECJ), paras 20–24.
[135] See Case C-444/02 *Fixtures Marketing Ltd v OPAP* [2005] ECDR 3 (ECJ); Unauthorised reproduction of telephone directories on CDROM [2002] ECDR 3; *Société Tigest SARL v Société Reed Expositions France* [2002] ECC 29; *SA Prline v SA Communication and Sales and Sarl News Invest* [2002] ECDR 2 (Trib de Comm); *Danske Dagblades Forening v Newsbooster* [2003] ECDR 5; Case C-490/14 *Freistaat Bayern v Verlag Esterbauer GmbH* [2016] ECDR 6 (CJ); *Technomed Ltd v Bluecrest Health Screening Ltd* [2017] EWHC 2142 (Ch).
[136] Database Directive, Art 1(3). Computer programs have copyright as such (see para 3.46).
[137] Case C-604/10 *Football Dataco Ltd v Yahoo! UK Ltd* [2012] ECDR 10 (CJ).
[138] CDPA 1988, s 3A. See also for use of this formulation Council Directive on the legal protection of computer programs 91/250/EEC (now consolidated in Software Directive 2009), Art 1(3); but in the implementation of this Directive the UK did not see fit to use the phrase. See paras 3.25 and 3.26.
[139] Case C-444/02 *Fixtures Marketing Ltd v OPAP* [2004] ECR I-10549 (ECJ), para 25.
[140] Database Directive 1996, recital 19.

■ Case C-604/10 *Football Dataco Ltd v Yahoo! UK Ltd* [2012] ECDR 10 (CJ)

It was claimed that fixtures lists of English and Scottish football leagues were protected by copyright in databases and the Court of Appeal referred questions on the interpretation of the Database Directive.[141] The Court of Justice held that national legislation is precluded from granting database copyright under conditions which are different than that of originality as laid down in the Directive. It then provided guidance on the meaning of 'author's own intellectual creation'. Copyright protection of database concerns the structure of the database; it does not concern the contents of the database or the elements constituting its contents, and does not extend to the data itself. As such, intellectual effort and skill expended on creating data is not relevant for assessment of database copyright (paras 30–33). The originality requirement for databases is satisfied when 'through the selection or arrangement of the data which it contains, its author expresses his creative ability in an original manner by making free and creative choices . . . and thus stamps his "personal touch"' (para 38). In contrast, it is not satisfied 'when the setting up of the database is dictated by technical considerations, rules or constraints which leave no room for creative freedom' (para 39). There is no need for the author to 'add important significance' to the data through the selection or arrangement (para 41). The fact that the author had used significant labour and skill in setting up the database may be irrelevant if the labour and skill does not express originality in the selection or arrangement of the data; this is a matter for the national court to assess (para 42). As to whether the fixtures lists are original, the Court of Justice's guidance on 'intellectual creation' seems particularly likely to *exclude* alphabetical or chronological ordering.

The lack of intellectual creation does not mean that the collection fails to be a database, however. Rather, the database does not have copyright; but it may still be protected by the *sui generis* database right, for which see further paras 7.4–7.25.

 Question

Are the following databases: (1) newspapers; (2) websites; (3) multimedia works? If so, how far is the database covered as such by copyright?

 Discussion point   For answer guidance visit **www.oup.com/uk/brown5e**.

Imagine a compilation which is not a database for legal purposes, that is, is not a collection of independent works or items of information, systematically arranged and individually accessible. Would the work you have thus imagined be protectable by copyright?

Dramatic works

3.51   The 1988 Act indicates that a 'dramatic work' includes a work of dance or mime but does not provide further details.[142] In *Norowzian v Arks Ltd (No 2)*, Nourse LJ noted that a dramatic work must be given its natural and ordinary meaning, and defined it as 'a work of action, with or without words or music, which is capable of being performed before an audience'.[143] A scene created to be part of the cover for a forthcoming album by the pop group Oasis was held not to be a dramatic work, since it involved no action.[144] The Privy Council has stated that a dramatic work must have 'sufficient unity' to be capable of performance, leading to a

---

[141]   On the effects of this ruling, see D Rose and N O'Sullivan, 'Football Dataco v Yahoo! Implications of the ECJ judgment' (2012) JIPLP 792.
[142]   CDPA 1988, s 3(1).   [143]   [2000] FSR 363 (CA) per Nourse LJ at 366–67.
[144]   *Creation Records Ltd v News Group Newspapers Ltd* [1997] EMLR 444.

decision that the stock phrases and other aspects of the format of a television talent show did not constitute a dramatic work in themselves, being merely accessories to the show.[145] The sequence of images produced by a computer video game was held not to be a dramatic work, because it varied too much each time the game was played and lacked the unity for it to be a work capable of performance.[146] In *Banner v Endemol*, a claim for subsistence of copyright in a TV gameshow format called *Minute Winner* was dismissed because the show's features were commonplace and indistinguishable from other game shows.[147] However, Snowden J took the view that 'it is at least arguable, as a matter of concept' for the format of a television game show or quiz show to be the subject of protection as a dramatic work, even though these types of shows 'will contain elements of spontaneity and events that change from episode to episode'; and, protection will not subsist unless, as a minimum, two requirements are met:[148]

(i) there are a number of clearly identified features which, taken together, distinguish the show in question from others of a similar type; and (ii) that those distinguishing features are connected with each other in a coherent framework which can be repeatedly applied so as to enable the show to be reproduced in recognisable form.

Question

How may a dramatic work be defined for copyright purposes?

3.52   The 1988 Act omits from its definition of dramatic work some words which appeared in the 1956 Act, that the phrase does not include a cinematograph film as distinct from a scenario or script for a cinematograph film.[149] Did this change mean that films, which retain their own copyright under the CDPA 1988,[150] can now also be protected as dramatic works? In *Norowzian v Arks Ltd (No 2)*,[151] the Court of Appeal concluded that a film which was a work of action and which could be performed before an audience could as a result also be a dramatic work. A film might be both a recording of a dramatic work and a dramatic work in itself; sometimes it might not be a recording of a dramatic work but would nonetheless itself be a dramatic work. The questions arising from overlapping categories are reduced inasmuch as films and dramatic works both attract moral rights, have more or less the same duration of copyright,[152] and enjoy the same categories of restricted acts.

Discussion point 1   For answer guidance visit www.oup.com/uk/brown5e.

Is a television commercial a dramatic work?

Discussion point 2

How should works which contain a musical element but are intended for stage performance or to be made as a film—for example, an opera, a ballet, or the type of entertainment known as a 'musical'—be characterised for the purposes of copyright?

---

[145]   *Green v Broadcasting Corp of New Zealand* [1989] 2 All ER 1056 per Lord Bridge of Harwich at 1058.

[146]   *Nova Productions Ltd v Mazooma Games Ltd* [2006] RPC 14 (Kitchin J); point not discussed in the Court of Appeal ([2007] RPC 25).

[147]   [2017] EWHC 2600 at para 46. See also *The Ukulele Orchestra of Great Britain v Clausen* [2015] EWHC 1772 (IPEC), para 104; *Meakin v BBC* [2010] EWHC 2065, para 30.

[148]   *Banner v Endemol* [2017] EWHC 2600 at paras 43–44.

[149]   1956 Act, s 48(1).   [150]   CDPA 1988, s 1(1)(b).

[151]   [2001] FSR 363 (CA); see para 3.16. See further A Barron, 'The legal property of film' (2004) 67 MLR 177; I Stamatoudi, 'Joy for the claimant: can a film also be protected as a dramatic work?' [2000] IPQ 117; R Arnold, 'Joy: a reply' [2001] IPQ 10.

[152]   Note, however, that the only relevant author for duration of copyright in a dramatic work is the dramatist, whereas for a film it is not only the screenplay writer and dialogue author but also the principal director and the composer of any special music, and the duration of the copyright is determined by the death of the last of these to die. A film may thus enjoy copyright for longer as such than it does as a dramatic work. See para 3.121.

Musical works

3.53   A musical work[153] is a work consisting of music, exclusive of any words or action intended to be sung, spoken, or performed with the music.[154] Words written to be sung to music thus do not form part of any musical work but have their own literary or dramatic copyright. Music, it might be thought, consists of sounds other than words, recorded in writing or otherwise. At the same time, the limits of the definition of music are unclear. It seems to go beyond the notes on a score to include the combination of melodies and harmonies, the figuring of the bass, ornamentation, and performance directions.[155] Music also covers the sampling and scratching of tracks by DJs of works composed by other artists which create a new work. Another problem is the example of John Cage's '4 Minutes 33 Seconds', which has already been mentioned on the question of what constitutes a work (para 3.7): is a deliberately created silence in a concert hall, lasting for a fixed period, a musical work?[156] Most other gaps in the definition can probably be filled by the categories of literary, dramatic, and artistic work, or by sound recording copyright. Cage's work might be regarded as a dramatic one, for example inasmuch as it involves a performance before an audience.

 Question

What is the definition of a musical work? Can you define music?

Artistic works

3.54   An artistic work[157] is defined[158] as:

- a graphic work, photograph, sculpture, or collage, irrespective of artistic quality;
- a work of architecture, being either a building or a model for a building;
- a work of artistic craftsmanship.

Note the use of the word 'means' in s 4(1) CDPA 1988 indicating that this list of artistic works is exhaustive.

Graphic work, photograph, sculpture, or collage

3.55   The CDPA 1988 defines most, but not all, of these works:[159]

- Graphic work includes any painting, drawing, diagram, map, chart, or plan, and any engraving, etching, lithograph, woodcut, print, or similar work.
- Photograph means a recording of light or other radiation on any medium on which an image is produced or from which an image may by any means be produced, and which is not part of a film.
- Sculpture includes any cast or model made for the purposes of sculpture.

Graphic works

3.56   The first point to note is that the definition of graphic work is non-exclusive, so that it may catch works other than those listed. Thus, the screen layouts of websites have been held to be graphic works, even though only recorded as such in digital code. The same case found that icons used in the displays were also graphic

---

[153] See generally, S Frith and L Marshall, *Music and Copyright* (2nd edn, 2004); A Rahmatian, 'Music and creativity as perceived by copyright law' [2005] IPQ 267.

[154] CDPA 1988, s 3(1).   [155] See *Sawkins v Hyperion Records Ltd* [2005] RPC 32 (CA).

[156] See Cheng Lim Saw, 'Protecting the sound of silence in 4'33"—a timely revisit of basic principles in copyright law' [2005] EIPR 467.

[157] See generally, P Kearns, *The Legal Concept of Art* (1998); D McClean and K Schubert (eds), *Dear Images: Art, Culture and Copyright* (2002); S Stokes, *Art and Copyright* (2012); A Barron, 'Copyright law and the claims of art' [2002] IPQ 369; D Booton, 'Framing pictures: defining art in UK copyright law' [2003] IPQ 38; W Landes and R Posner, *Economic Structure of Intellectual Property Law* (2004), Ch 9 ('The legal protection of postmodern art').

[158] CDPA 1988, s 4(1). See further T Rychlicki, 'Legal questions about illegal art' (2008) 3 JIPLP 393.   [159] CDPA 1988, s 4(2).

works, but as drawings.[160] But the Court of Appeal has held that a common feature of graphic works as defined in the CDPA 1988 is their static and non-moving character. So, video games are not graphic works, while a series of drawings is a series of graphic works, not a single one.[161]

Paintings

3.57   The word 'painting' is not defined by the Act. There has been a judicial attempt to do so:

■ *Merchandising Corporation of America v Harpbond* [1983] FSR 32

It was held that a painting required a surface before it could be a protected work. Paint without a surface is not a painting. From this premise it was concluded that a flamboyant style of facial make-up forming part of the distinctive image of Adam Ant, a well-known popular musician, could not be a painting for copyright purposes.[162] Works of graffiti could, under this definition, fall within the purview of artistic works for the purposes of copyright protection.[163]

 Question

Does the fact that the surface in question in the Adam Ant case was a person's face take the work out of the judge's definition of a painting?

Drawings

3.58   The most significant of the categories of artistic work in terms of reported litigation is that of drawings. Examples of works held to be drawings include architects' plans,[164] sketches of garments,[165] engineering and machine part drawings,[166] cartoon characters,[167] and trade mark and label designs.[168] The rudimentary nature of a drawing is no objection to copyright subsistence; thus, for example, a drawing of three concentric rings has been held to have artistic copyright.[169] Many of the cases concerning design drawings should now be read with caution, however. While such drawings retain copyright under the CDPA 1988, the scope of infringement has been severely restricted in relation to them, and the principal mode of protection is likely to be under design right. (See further Part III of this book.)

Diagrams, maps, charts, and plans

3.59   The special feature of all these kinds of work is that, while they have a strong visual dimension, at the very least literary matter also found on the work (words and numbers) is necessary for its full meaning to be comprehended or utilised. Indeed, between the 1911 and the 1956 Acts they were treated as literary works, and the appearance of the phrase 'irrespective of artistic quality' in the provision about graphic works (see para 3.66) is to be explained by the inclusion of this then new subject matter in the category of artistic works. One important effect of the change, in particular with regard to plans, is that as artistic works these two-dimensional works can be infringed by three-dimensional reproductions, which would not be so if they were literary works.[170] This rule then had rather disastrous knock-on effects with regard to the protection of

---

[160]   *Navitaire Inc v EasyJet Airline Co Ltd* [2006] RPC 3 (Pumfrey J).

[161]   *Nova Productions Ltd v Mazooma Games Ltd* [2007] RPC 25 (CA).

[162]   For more about Adam Ant, see www.bbc.co.uk/music/artists/e188a520-9cb7-4f73-a3d7-2f70c6538e92.

[163]   T Rychlicki, 'Legal questions about illegal art' (2008) 3 JIPLP 393 at 396. See also M Iljadica, *Copyright Beyond Law: Regulating Creativity in the Graffiti Subculture* (2016) Ch 4.

[164]   See, eg, *Robert Allan & Partners v Scottish Ideal Homes* 1972 SLT (Sh Ct) 32.

[165]   See, eg, *Howard Clark v David Allan & Co Ltd* 1987 SLT 271.

[166]   See, eg, *British Leyland v Armstrong Patents* [1986] AC 577.

[167]   *King Features Syndicate Inc v OM Kleeman Ltd* [1941] AC 417 (Popeye the Sailorman).

[168]   KARO STEP Trade Mark [1977] RPC 255.

[169]   *Solar Thomson Engineering v Barton* [1977] RPC 537. For the drawing see 540.   [170]   See para 4.26.

industrial designs (see the online resources), and the scope of copyright infringement by three-dimensional reproductions in this context is now carefully restricted (see paras 9.79–9.93). But the rule remains in full effect outside industrial design protection.

Photographs

3.60   With regard to photographs,[171] the 1988 Act's definition (see para 3.55) is clearly intended to cover continuing development in the technology of photography. The replacement of film by digital recording as the ordinary mode of photography well demonstrates the need for definitional flexibility of this kind. Photographs of antiques have been protected where they were taken with a view to exhibiting particular qualities such as colour, features, and other details because some degree of skill is involved in the lighting, angling, and judging of positioning in these circumstances.[172]

■ **Case C-145/10** *Painer v Standard Verlags GmbH* [2012] ECDR 6 (CJ)

The Court of Justice held that a portrait photograph could be protected by copyright if the photograph is an intellectual creation of the author in that it reflects the author's personality, that is, the author expresses his creative abilities by making free and creative choices in the production of the photograph and stamps his 'personal touch'. Such choices can be made in several ways:

> In the preparation phase, the photographer can choose the background, the subject's pose and the lighting. When taking a portrait photograph, he can choose the framing, the angle of view and the atmosphere created. Finally, when selecting the snapshot, the photographer may choose from a variety of developing techniques the one he wishes to adopt or, where appropriate, use computer software (para 91).

The protection of the photograph is not inferior to any other work protected by copyright.

■ *Temple Island Collections Ltd v New English Teas Ltd* [2012] FSR 9 (PCC)

This case concerned two similar photos, by F and H, showing a London bus in red in the foreground in front of a black-and-white image of iconic London landmarks. Both photos had been altered using a computer program. Judge Birss QC referred to the decisions in *Infopaq* and *Painer* to state that copyright may subsist in a photograph if it is the author's own intellectual creation. The judge held that:

> A photograph of an object found in nature or for that matter a building, which although not natural is something found by the creator and not created by him, can have the character of an artistic work in terms of copyright law if the task of taking the photograph leaves ample room for an individual arrangement. What is decisive are the arrangements (motif, visual angle, illumination, etc.) selected by the photographer himself or herself (para 20).

The judge viewed F's image as not a mere photograph ('an image which is nothing more than the result of happening to click his camera in the right place at the right time') but as a photographic work (where the 'appearance is the product of deliberate choices and also deliberate manipulations by the author' such as choosing where to stand, when to click, as well as changes wrought after the basic image had been recorded), and noted that, 'the image may look like just another photograph in that location but its appearance derives from more than that' (para 66).

---

[171] See generally, Y Gendreau, *Copyright and Photographs: An International Survey* (1999); C Mihalos, *The Law of Photography and Digital Images* (2004); K Garnett, 'Copyright in photographs' [2000] EIPR 229; R Deazley, 'Photographing paintings in the public domain: a response to Garnett' [2001] EIPR 229; S Stokes, 'Photographing paintings in the public domain: a response to Garnett' [2001] EIPR 354; and R Arnold, 'Copyright in photographs: a case for reform' [2005] EIPR 303.

[172] *Antiquesportfolio.com plc v Rodney Fitch & Co Ltd* [2001] FSR 345.

Discussion point   For answer guidance visit **www.oup.com/uk/brown5e**.

Does the definition of a photograph cover the case whereby the camera records the image digitally and the photographer then adjusts the result electronically, for example to insert other images, as by putting the head of the prime minister on what is otherwise an image of a footballer; or merely editing out unwanted parts of the image captured? Is there still a photograph where the image has been digitally enhanced, for example by sharpening contrasts, or heightening/lowering colours?

Sculptures

3.61   Sculptures are plainly three-dimensional works and must be distinguished from works of archi-tecture and of artistic craftsmanship. Casts and models for the purposes of sculpture are included in the category.[173] The vagueness of the statutory definition has been used by those seeking copyright protection for industrial designs.

■ *Wham-O Manufacturing Co v Lincoln Industries Ltd* [1985] RPC 127

In this case[174] it was held that wooden model prototypes for the Frisbee toy were sculptures.[175] The New Zealand Court held that sculpture could no longer be confined to the process of carving and modelling representations using natural materials, but should simply be thought of as the three-dimensional expression of an idea of its creator. The model fitted this conception, but not, the Court held, the Frisbee itself. A plastic injection process for mass production could not give rise to a sculpture.

3.62   Similar arguments were rejected in English cases, which have generally construed 'sculpture' narrowly, in accordance with its ordinary dictionary meaning. These authorities were reviewed in a powerful judgment by Mann J in the 'Star Wars' case, subsequently approved in the Court of Appeal and the Supreme Court:

■ *Lucasfilm Ltd v Ainsworth* [2009] FSR 2 (Ch D); [2009] EWCA Civ 1328 (CA); [2012] 1 AC 208 (SC)

A established a website in 2004 selling replica helmets and body armour used in the *Star Wars* films. Working from general designs prepared by L, A had previously created the moulds used to create the various pieces of armour used in the original 1977 film for the Imperial stormtroopers and other characters. These included white helmets, as well as armour referred to as the 'cheesegrater', 'jawbone', 'X-wing fighter pilot', 'rebel troop', 'TIE fighter' helmets, and a 'chest box' worn by the TIE fighter pilots. L's claim of copyright infringement against A was met with a counterclaim to enforce A's alleged copyright in the helmets and armour as sculptures. It was held that the Imperial Stormtrooper helmet was not a sculpture within the meaning of the Act. It was a mixture of costume and prop, but its primary function was utilitarian. Mann J, at the first instance, indicated that 'while it has an interest as an object, and while it was intended to express an idea, it was not conceived, or created, with the intention that it should do so other than as part of character portrayal in the film' (para 121). Furthermore, he opined that it was not that it lacked artistic merit, but that it lacked artistic purpose. The same reasoning applied to the armour.

---

[173]   CDPA 1988, s 4(2).
[174]   See also *Plix Products v Winstone* [1985] 1 NZLR 376.
[175]   For more on the Frisbee, see http://en.wikipedia.org/wiki/Frisbee.

Toy models marketed by L after the film became successful were also not deemed to be sculptures for the reason that their primary purpose was for play. The *Wham-O* decision was disapproved for similar reasons: the purpose of the model for the Frisbee was not artistic. The Supreme Court held that:

> it would not accord with the normal use of language to apply the term 'sculpture' to a 20th-century military helmet used in the making of a film, whether it was the real thing or a replica made in different material, however great its contribution to the artistic effect of the finished film . . . it was the Star Wars film that was the work of art . . . The helmet was utilitarian in the sense that it was an element in the process of production of the film (para 44).

Mann J provided the following multi-factorial approach on the meaning of sculpture:

(1) Regard was to be had to the normal use of the word.

(2) Nevertheless, the concept could be applicable to things going beyond what would normally be expected to be art in the sense of the sort of things expected to be found in art galleries.

(3) It was inappropriate to stray too far from what would normally be regarded as sculpture.

(4) No judgment was to be made about artistic worth.

(5) Not every three-dimensional representation of a concept could be regarded as a sculpture, otherwise every three-dimensional construction or fabrication would be a sculpture.

(6) It was of the essence of a sculpture that it should have, as part of its purpose, a visual appeal in the sense that it might be enjoyed for that purpose alone, whether or not it might have another purpose as well. The purpose was that of the creator and it was this underlying purpose that was important.

(7) The fact that the object had some other use did not necessarily disqualify it from being a sculpture, but it still had to have the intrinsic quality of being intended to be enjoyed as a visual thing.

(8) The process of fabrication was relevant but not decisive. There was no reason why a purely functional item, not intended to be at all decorative, should be treated as a sculpture simply because it had been (for example) carved out of wood or stone.

The Court of Appeal approved the judge's reasoning and held that he had correctly applied his 'multi-factorial approach' (para 77) finding that 'Neither the armour nor the helmet are sculpture' (para 80). With regard to the toy stormtroopers it noted: 'We are not dealing here with highly crafted models designed to appeal to the collector but which might be played with by his children. These are mass produced plastic toys. They are no more works of sculpture than the helmet and the armour which they reproduce' (para 82). The Supreme Court, while affirming the multi-factorial approach, rejected the 'elephant test' proposed by the Court of Appeal. It stated that:

> Any zoologist has no difficulty in recognising an elephant on sight, and most could no doubt also give a clear and accurate description of its essential identifying features. By contrast a judge, even one very experienced in intellectual property matters, does not have some special power of divination which leads instantly to an infallible conclusion, and no judge would claim to have such a power. The judge reads and hears the evidence (often including expert evidence), reads and listens to the advocates' submissions, and takes what the Court of Appeal rightly called a multi-factorial approach. Moreover the judge has to give reasons to explain his or her conclusions (para 47).

In the light of this decision,[176] earlier cases denying protection to moulds for making functional cartridges[177] and prototypes of plastic dental impression trays[178] were correct, unlike the protection given to scallop-shaped ones for use in toasted sandwich-makers.[179]

---

[176] See further, S Clark, 'Lucasfilm Ltd and Others v Ainsworth and Another: the force of copyright protection for three-dimensional designs as sculptures or works of artistic craftsmanship' [2009] EIPR 384; A Hobson, 'Imperial stormtroopers, art works, and copyright defences' (2009) 4 JIPLP 16; J Pila, 'The "Star Wars" copyright claim: an ambivalent view of the Empire' (2012) 128 LQR 15.

[177] *Metix v Maughan* [1997] FSR 718.   [178] *J & S Davis (Holdings) Ltd v Wright Health Group* [1988] RPC 403.

[179] *Breville Europe v Thorn EMI* [1995] FSR 77.

Discussion point 1   For answer guidance visit **www.oup.com/uk/5e**.

Should ice sculptures be protected as sculptures? Is the snowman you make during a white Christmas so protected?

Discussion point 2

Kinetic sculptures are sculptures with moving parts, or in which motion is incorporated as part of the design, so that the form or colour of the work may change continuously or from time to time. Does mobility or motion within the sculpture take it out of the dictionary definition of 'sculpture'? See also the case of *Komesaroff v Mickle* [1988] RPC 204, discussed later (para 3.70) for a similar issue with works of artistic craftsmanship.

Engravings

3.63   The *Wham-O* case (para 3.61)[180] is also an authority on engravings, which the New Zealand Court held the markings on the surface of the Frisbee to be, along with the plastic injection mould. Engraving is first a process of cutting or incising images into material such as wood or metal, and then using the result for the purpose of producing prints of the image.[181] In the 1956 Act it was defined to include etchings, lithographs, woodcuts, and prints, but photographs were expressly excluded.[182] Using this, it was held that an engraving included both the original engraved plate and the resulting print, and further that, given the apparent need to exclude the process of producing prints known as photography, engraving was not confined to processes involving cutting into material to produce the plate.[183] This approach enabled the Court in *Wham-O* to hold that the mould was a plate and the Frisbee disc a 'print' thereof.[184]

 Exercise

Compare the *Wham-O* case with *George Hensher Ltd v Restawile Upholstery (Lancs) Ltd* [1976] AC 64, discussed at paras 3.68ff. What, if any, policy reasons justify the different results reached in these cases with regard to the protection of models to be used in the mass production of consumer objects?

3.64   As already noted, however, the CDPA 1988 differs somewhat from the 1956 Act in respect of engravings. In particular, the word 'print' no longer appears either in juxtaposition (as with etchings, lithographs, and woodcuts) or in any definition. Nor is photography mentioned.[185] It is not clear whether this excludes the reasoning of the *Wham-O* decision, given that mere changes of expression in the 1988 Act do not necessarily entail departure from the previous law.[186] But considering the Act's overall policy of excluding copyright from the field of industrial design, it is suggested that the result in *Wham-O* should now be treated with caution, although its general discussion of both engravings and sculptures remains helpful. With regard to both categories of work, the case may be an example of a court anxious to protect the skill and labour of the plaintiff from piracy and forcing the facts rather uneasily into unsuitable concepts. Design rights probably

---

[180] [1985] RPC 127.   [181] For an example, see *Martin v Polyplas* [1969] NZLR 1046.   [182] 1956 Act, s 48(1).
[183] *James Arnold & Co v Miafern Ltd* [1980] RPC 397 esp at 403–04: rubber stereos for printing designs on ties held to be engravings.
[184] [1985] RPC 127.
[185] CDPA 1988, s 4(2).   [186] CDPA 1988, s 172(2).

offer more satisfactory solutions to such problems now.[187] In *Greenfield Products Pty Ltd v Rover-Scott Bonnar Ltd*,[188] an argument that a mould of a lawnmower engine was an engraving was rejected. Pincus J said:[189]

> It is not all cutting which is engraving . . . The term does not cover shaping a piece of metal or wood on a lathe, but has to do with marking, cutting or working the surface—typically the flat surface—of an object . . .

Collages

3.65   The last item specifically mentioned is the collage. A collage is an artistic equivalent to the literary compilation. The creator assembles diverse fragments of material, some of which may be extracts from other copyright or formerly copyright works, artistic and others, some of which may be incapable of copyright at all (eg a piece of string), and places them either on a single surface or in some other form of juxtaposition, often with incongruous effect. Without this specific reference in the CDPA 1988, there is an obvious danger that such works may fail to attract copyright on the ground of lack of originality or the inherent nature of the material used. Collage has been held not to be constituted by ephemeral collocation, whether or not with artistic intent, of random, unrelated, and unfixed elements.[190]

Artistic quality of graphic works, etc

3.66   An artistic work in any of the categories just discussed need not have aesthetic appeal or be a work of fine art in the ordinary sense, for it is provided that the copyright subsists 'irrespective of its artistic quality'.[191] The phrase 'artistic work' is rather to be taken as an indication of the methods by which the work must be produced. Some recent decisions suggest that it may be necessary to show that the work is intended to be permanent, insofar as anything can be, or at least not transient in form.[192] On the other hand, with a very simple drawing, it may be difficult to show infringement of the copyright.[193] As a consequence, however, there can be difficult questions of definition where there is some overlap with other forms of work. Although it is clear that plain lettering cannot be the subject of artistic copyright,[194] fancy lettering, for example in a greetings card, a label, or a trade mark, may well be a drawing. In relation in particular to maps, charts, diagrams, and plans, lettering, words, and figures may form an integral part of the representation and would fall to be protected by artistic rather than literary copyright; but where a drawing is merely an explanatory adjunct to written material, the latter has literary copyright.[195]

Works of architecture

3.67   Works of architecture[196] are either buildings or models for buildings and do not include architects' plans, which are dealt with as drawings for copyright purposes.[197] A building includes any fixed structure,[198] and it would appear from the use of the word 'any' that no consideration need be given to the question of artistic quality in determining whether or not a work of architecture has copyright, a view supported by an *obiter* dictum of Lord Reid.[199] The meaning of 'structure' has not been judicially discussed since the passage of the 1956 Act, but in an earlier case it had been held that a garden layout including stone walls, steps, and ponds

---

[187]   For design rights, see Part III (see Chapters 8 and 9).   [188]   (1990) 95 ALR 275.

[189]   ibid at 285. See also *Talk of the Town v Hagstrom* (1991) 19 IPR 649 at 655.

[190]   *Creation Records Ltd v News Group Newspapers Ltd* [1997] EMLR 444. See further at para 3.71.

[191]   CDPA 1988, s 4(1)(a).

[192]   *Merchandising Corp of America v Harpbond* [1983] FSR 32; also *Komesaroff v Mickle* [1988] RPC 204. Note that there is no explicit requirement of fixation with artistic works, unlike literary, dramatic, and musical works (see paras 3.14–3.18).

[193]   *Kenrick v Lawrence* (1890) 25 QBD 99.

[194]   *Miller and Lang Ltd v Macniven & Cameron Ltd* (1908) 16 SLT 56.

[195]   *Duriron Co Inc v Hugh Jennings & Co Ltd* [1984] FSR 1; *British Leyland v Armstrong Patents* [1986] RPC 279 per Oliver LJ at 289–96; *Interlego AG v Tyco Industries Inc* [1989] AC 217 per Lord Oliver at 264–65.

[196]   See further A Adrian, 'Architecture and copyright: a quick survey of the law' (2008) 3 JIPLP 524.

[197]   CDPA 1988, s 4(1)(b).   [198]   CDPA 1988, s 4(2).   [199]   *Hensher v Restawile* [1976] AC 64 per Lord Reid at 78.

had copyright as a structure;[200] department store buildings[201] and semi-detached villas[202] have also been accorded copyright. It may be suggested that a building is an artificial structure attached to land, but difficult questions of definition can be seen by examining some of the leading cases on fixtures.[203]

Exercise

Consider, for example, the Scottish case of *Christie v Smith's Executrix* 1949 SC 572, which raised the question whether a summerhouse which rested on specially laid foundations on land by virtue of its considerable weight was sufficiently attached to the land to be a fixture (answer: yes). Was the summerhouse also a work of architecture for copyright purposes?

Works of artistic craftsmanship

3.68 The phrase 'artistic craftsmanship' is not defined in the CDPA 1988 and no single clear meaning has emerged from the cases on the subject.[204] Considering the phrase in the context of the section on artistic works as a whole, it would appear to cover works in three dimensions which are not sculptures or buildings; since the decision of the House of Lords in *George Hensher Ltd v Restawile Upholstery (Lancs) Ltd*,[205] it has also been accepted that for a work to be one of artistic craftsmanship it must be of a quality making it capable of being described as artistic. The problem which is fully but inconclusively discussed in *Hensher* is how the Court may test the issue of artistic quality without becoming involved in subjective discussion of the merits of a work.

■ *George Hensher Ltd v Restawile Upholstery (Lancs) Ltd* [1976] AC 64

H produced popular suites of furniture deploying a boat-shaped theme. Expert witnesses described the shape as 'flashy', 'horrible', 'middle of the road', 'mediocre', and 'slightly vulgar', although obviously quite a good commercial design, and a 'winner' in terms of its appeal to the market.[206] R, competitors of H, produced similar-looking suites, and H sued for infringement of copyright, relying not on any right in the finished articles but in the original three-dimensional prototype of the design made before the furniture went into production. Their claim was that the prototype was a work of craftsmanship, artistic quality was not necessary for protection, and therefore the adjective 'artistic' added nothing to the legal meaning of the subject matter to be protected; accordingly, the prototype fell within the scope of copyright. All the judges in the House of Lords agreed with those of the Court of Appeal that the prototype was not a work of artistic craftsmanship, but there was considerable disagreement as to the reasons why this should be so.

3.69 In *Hensher* the House of Lords rejected the view expressed by the Court of Appeal in the case, that the test was whether the work would be purchased for its aesthetic appeal rather than for its utility, but their Lordships differed among themselves about what the test should be and about whether it was a test of fact depending on the evidence or a test of law for the Court. One view was that the intention of the author of the work to produce a work of art was the critical factor, and this is supported in other earlier cases.[207] A second view was to ask whether a substantial part of the public would regard the work as artistic, this being distinct from the question of whether or not the primary reason for purchasing it was its aesthetic appeal. But the most cogent speech in *Hensher* is that of Lord Simon of Glaisdale, who argued that works of

---

[200] *Vincent v Universal Housing Co* [1928–35] MCC 275.   [201] *Meikle v Maufe* [1941] 3 All ER 144.

[202] *Blake v Warren* [1928–35] MCC 268.

[203] For the English and Scots law of fixtures, see *Halsbury's Laws of England*, and *Laws of Scotland: Stair Memorial Encyclopaedia*.

[204] See also M Rushton, 'An economic approach to copyright in works of artistic craftsmanship' [2003] IPQ 255.   [205] [1976] AC 64.

[206] Three slightly fuzzy black-and-white photographs of the plaintiff's suites are available in [1975] RPC 31 at 33–34.

[207] *Burke v Spicers Dress Design* [1936] Ch 400 per Clauson J at 407–08; *Cuisenaire v Reed* [1963] VR 719 per Pape J at 730; *Cuisenaire v South West Imports* [1968] 1 Ex CR 493 per Niel J at 574.

artistic craftsmanship first came to be copyright subjects under the Copyright Act 1911 as a consequence of the influence of the Arts and Crafts movement of the 19th century, which emphasised the necessary connection between form and function. The phrase 'artistic craftsmanship' should therefore be construed as a whole rather than by separate examination of its constituent words. So, the question to be asked of a work in which copyright was claimed under this heading is: is this the work of one who was in this respect an artist–craftsman? The artistic merit of the work was thus not an issue to be considered. The question was to be answered on the evidence, and the best evidence was likely to be that of acknowledged artist–craftsmen or those concerned with training artist–craftsmen.[208]

3.70   The test of the creator's intention seemed to gain ground in decisions holding that a baby's raincape and a plastic dental impression tray were not works of artistic craftsmanship.[209] But it remains far from clear exactly what works will come under this head of artistic copyright. If Lord Simon's historical analysis in *Hensher* is correct, then we should begin with articles which have some function to perform, for example furniture, crockery, cutlery, and clothing, and it should not necessarily be an objection that the article is the subject of industrial production, or that its function is industrial, or indeed merely decorative.

■ *Komesaroff v Mickle* [1988] RPC 204 (Sup Ct of Victoria)

K developed and marketed a product named 'moving sand pictures', which was made by enclosing inside glass panels a mixture of liquid, coloured sands, and a layer of air bubbles. Miniature sand landscapes were brought about when the sands trickled through the bubbles under the influence of gravity. The process could be repeated by shaking the product. M copied and commenced marketing an identical product. It was held that K's product was not a work of artistic craftsmanship because her activity did not directly bring about the sand landscapes which resulted from shaking the product, and there was no craftsmanship in what she had done.

■ *Burge v Swarbrick* [2007] FSR 27 (HCA)

The question in this case was whether a model known as a 'plug' from which a mould for a yacht hull could be derived was a work of artistic craftsmanship. Following Lord Simon in *Hensher*, the Court held that artistic craftsmanship is not limited to artistic handicraft and so can include machine production items and indeed prototypes such as the 'plug'. There was no antithesis between utility and beauty. A conclusion on the question of the 'plug's' character was not controlled by the creator's intentions, but was one for objective determination by the Court. Matters of visual and aesthetic appeal were but one element in the design, and were subordinated to the achievement of the purely functional aspects of the design. The determination of artistic craftsmanship turns on assessing the extent to which the work's artistic expression is unconstrained by functional considerations. The more substantial the latter, the less the scope for real or substantial artistic effort. The evidence in this case was that the designer had been constrained to such an extent that his work was not that of an artist–craftsman.

3.71   A difficult question is whether there must be an individual artist–craftsman whose concept the work is; it has been suggested that where the idea and the execution are separated there can be no work of artistic craftsmanship.[210] But this may be too restrictive, as has been held in the New Zealand case of *Bonz Group v Cooke*,[211] which involved the production of hand-knitted woollen sweaters where the designer and the hand-knitters were different persons. *Bonz Group* was applied in the English case of *Vermaat and Powell v Boncrest Ltd*,[212] which was concerned with sample patchwork bedspreads and matching cushion covers made by seamstresses to a design produced by another. It was finally held, however, that while the work of the seamstresses might have involved craftsmanship, the result was not a work of artistic craftsmanship.

---

[208] Lord Simon's approach was preferred by the Federal Court of Australia in *Coogi Australia v Hysport International* (1999) 157 ALR 247 and by the High Court of Australia in *Burge v Swarbrick* [2007] FSR 27.

[209] *Merlet v Mothercare* [1986] RPC 115; *J & S Davis (Holdings) Ltd v Wright Health Group* [1988] RPC 403.

[210] *Burke v Spicers Dress Design* [1936] Ch 400.   [211] [1994] 3 NZLR 216.   [212] [2001] FSR 5.

■ *Lucasfilm Ltd v Ainsworth* [2009] FSR 2

See also para 3.62 for the facts of this case. Mann J held that the intention of the creator was relevant in determining whether a work was one of artistic craftsmanship. *Bonz Group (Pty) Ltd v Cooke* was approved and applied, with the judge stating that the artist and the craftsman did not have to be the same person but there had to be a proper nexus between them. The producer of the helmets in this case was a craftsman producing high-quality products with justifiable pride in his work. However, his works could not be described as works of artistic craftsmanship. They did not have the purpose of being aesthetically appealing. Instead, they were used to provide an impression in a film. Unlike a work of artistic craftsmanship, they were not intended to sustain close scrutiny.[213]

Discussion point 1   For answer guidance visit **www.oup.com/uk/brown5e.**

Are the designer and the hand-knitters in the *Bonz Group* case joint authors? See paras 3.85–3.92.

Discussion point 2

Could and should a recipe constitute a work of artistic craftsmanship? See TSL Cheng, 'Copyright protection of haute cuisine: recipe for disaster?' [2008] EIPR 93.

Exercise

Consider the two following cases and how, if at all, they may be reconciled (or distinguished).

■ *Shelley Films Ltd v Rex Features Ltd* [1994] EMLR 134

SF was making a film called *Mary Shelley's Frankenstein*. RF took an unauthorised photograph of a scene from the film as it was being shot. The picture was later published in *The People* newspaper. SF claimed infringement of copyright in the actors' costumes and the set as works of artistic craftsmanship, and in the latex prostheses being worn by the star of the film (Robert de Niro), as either a sculpture or a work of artistic craftsmanship. In preliminary proceedings, all the claims of copyright were held to be arguable and an injunction was granted against RF.

■ *Creation Records Ltd v News Group Newspapers Ltd* [1997] EMLR 444

CR devised a scene (a white Rolls Royce in a swimming pool with various other props, none of them made for the purpose) to be the background for a photograph of a pop group (Oasis) to appear on the cover of their forthcoming album. An unauthorised photograph of the scene was taken and published in *The Sun* newspaper, which also intended to market the picture as a poster. CR claimed copyright in the scene as a sculpture or work of artistic craftsmanship. It was held that the scene was not a sculpture, since its making involved no carving, modelling, or other techniques of sculpture. Nor was such an assemblage of *objets trouvés* a work of artistic craftsmanship, since neither subject nor result involved craftsmanship.

Films

3.72   A film[214] is:[215]

> a recording in any medium from which a moving image may by any means be reproduced.

---

[213] There was no appeal on this point: [2009] EWCA Civ 1328 (CA); and nor was it argued before the Supreme Court: [2012] 1 AC 208 (SC).
[214] See generally, P Kamina, *Film Copyright in the EU* (2002); I Stamatoudi, *Copyright in Multimedia Products: A Comparative Analysis* (2002).
[215] CPDA 1988, s 5B(1).

Again, there is apparent in this broad definition the effort of the CDPA 1988 to retain the ability to offer copyright protection whatever technical changes may occur in the film industry. Thus, the recording embodied in a video, a CD-ROM, or a DVD, or captured by a CCTV camera, has copyright just as much as if it were recorded on traditional translucent film. The sound track accompanying a film is part of the work for copyright purposes, although it may also have an independent copyright as a sound recording.[216] Computer games can be protected as films,[217] but it is very doubtful whether images consisting purely of written text and/or still pictures can ever be treated as film, even if the reader is able to move the material around on her screen by use of scroll bars, cursors, and other control mechanisms.[218]

3.73   Questions of overlap with other copyright works and subject matter may sometimes arise with films. It has already been noted that a film may be a dramatic work.[219] The definition of a photograph excludes any part of a film,[220] so that there is no possibility of a film claiming copyright as a set of photographs; but modern still cameras may include motor drive units which enable photographs to be taken in very rapid sequence. If these are capable of being shown as moving images then there may be a film for copyright purposes. The converse case is the camera which is fixed on one place, for example part of the sky or the ground, and captures images at intervals; which when played in sequence at normal speed show speeded-up and striking images of cloud movement or plant growth.

3.74   For the purposes of infringement, a photograph may be a copy of a film.[221] It would seem to follow from this, and the exclusion of parts of a film from the definition of a photograph, that a publicity poster using an image from the film would not have a copyright in that image as such. The protection would be that of a film, and it would be achieved through the concept of indirect copying (see para 4.21). It has also been suggested that a completed set of drawings intended for use in a cartoon film will by itself be a film because it is capable of being shown as a moving picture.

Question

What is a film for copyright purposes? Is there an overlap with other categories of copyright work?

Media works

Sound recordings

3.75   A sound recording is defined as:[222]

> . . . either
> (a) a recording of sounds, from which the sounds may be reproduced, or
> (b) a recording of the whole or any part of a literary, dramatic or musical work, from which sounds reproducing the work or part may be reproduced.

---

[216] CPDA 1988, s 5B(2), (5).

[217] See *Sega Enterprises Ltd v Galaxy Electronics Pty Ltd* (1997) 145 ALR 21 (Fed Ct of Australia); *Golden China TV Game Centre v Nintendo Co Ltd* 1997 (1) SA 405 (A); *Nova Productions Ltd v Mazooma Games Ltd* [2007] RPC 25 (CA). The computer program incorporated in the game will also have its own copyright as a literary work.

[218] cf *WGN Continental Broadcasting Co v United Video Inc* 693 F 2d 622 (7th Cir, 1982), where teletext accompanying a TV programme but broadcast from a different channel was held to be an audiovisual work.

[219] See *Norowzian v Arks Ltd (No 2)* [2000] FSR 363; and see para 3.52.   [220] CDPA 1988, s 4(2).   [221] CDPA 1988, s 17(4).

[222] CDPA 1988, s 5A(1).

Sounds in category (a) might include, for example, bird-song or sound effects for use in a dramatic production, while category (b) includes readings as well as, most importantly from a commercial point of view, music. The Act seeks to retain coverage against technical development in sound recording by providing that there will be copyright regardless of the medium on which the recording is made or the method by which the sounds are reproduced or produced.[223] Copyright subsists in every sound recording that is not a copy taken from a previous sound recording.[224] Accordingly, copyright will not subsist in the records, cassettes, and CDs as such as sold to the public, since these are merely copies of the producer's master recording. But to copy from such copies will still be infringement of the master recording's copyright.[225]

 Question

Looking at the statutory definition of a sound recording given previously, what in essence is protected by the copyright in this subject matter?

Broadcasts

3.76 This embraces both television and radio. There is no significant difference in the technology involved in radio and television broadcasting, merely in the end result, television embracing visual images as well as sound. Under the law until 2003, a distinction was drawn between the wireless technology of broadcasting and the supply of programme services by cable, but this has been dropped as a result of the implementation of the InfoSoc Directive 2001. A broadcast is now defined as:[226]

an electronic transmission of visual images, sounds, or other information, either

(a) transmitted for simultaneous reception by members of the public and is capable of being lawfully received by them; or

(b) transmitted at a time determined solely by the person making the transmission for presentation to members of the public.

The purpose of distinguishing between (a) and (b) is to accommodate the phenomenon of satellite alongside more traditional terrestrial wireless and cable broadcasting. The latter are covered by (a); (b) requires some explanation of satellite technology in broadcasting.

Satellite broadcasting

3.77 There are two main forms of satellite broadcasting:

(1) point-to-point or fixed satellite broadcasts; and

(2) direct broadcasting by satellite.

The former involves the transmission of signals to a satellite by one broadcaster, which are then transmitted to another broadcaster, who includes the signals in his own transmissions. Familiar examples of this include the broadcasting by the BBC and ITV of sports events taking place in other countries, where the initial signal is sent by a broadcaster in the other country. With direct broadcasting by satellite, the signal of the originating broadcaster is transmitted through the satellite direct to the receivers of the public. These receivers may require special equipment to receive the signal, for example satellite dishes, and to decode it for the purposes of viewing. Signals broadcast from satellites may be encrypted or scrambled in order to ensure that only those so equipped—that is, subscribers to the service—can receive the signal in intelligible form. Sky Television provides an example of this technology currently familiar in the UK.

---

[223] CDPA 1988, s 5A(1).   [224] CDPA 1988, s 5A(2).   [225] See further at para 4.21.   [226] CDPA 1988, s 6(1).

3.78   This simplified account of broadcasting technology helps in understanding some of the problems underlying the provisions in the CDPA 1988 defining broadcasting. Doubts as to whether a signal directed initially only to a satellite (the 'up-leg') could be a broadcast are removed, because it is an electronic transmission of visual images and sounds made at a time determined solely by the person making the transmission for presentation to members of the public. The purpose of the transmission is such a presentation, although as such the signal is not capable of lawful reception by the public. There were similar doubts as to whether the signal from the satellite (the 'down-leg') could be a broadcast if it was encrypted. The 1988 Act provides that an encrypted transmission shall be regarded as capable of being lawfully received by members of the public (and therefore a broadcast) only if decoding equipment has been made available to the public by or with the authority of the person making the transmission or the person providing the contents of the transmission.[227]

Teletext and internet transmissions

3.79   The definition of broadcasting makes clear that broadcasting is not restricted to the transmission of sounds and visual images, but can include other material such as teletext information services.[228] Internet transmissions are in general not to be treated as broadcasts,[229] since in general they are neither transmitted simultaneously to their audience nor does the transmitter decide the time of transmission (the recipient generally does that). However, an internet transmission can fall within the definition of a broadcast if:[230]

(1)   the transmission takes place simultaneously on the internet and by other means, such as conventional TV or radio ('streaming');

(2)   it is a concurrent transmission of a live event; or

(3)   it is a transmission of recorded moving images or sounds forming part of a programme service offered by the person responsible for making the transmission, being a service in which programmes are transmitted at scheduled times determined by that person.

Discussion point 1   For answer guidance visit **www.oup.com/uk/brown5e**.

Consider 'podcasting', a method of distributing audio or audiovisual material on the internet, for playback on personal computers or mobile devices at a time chosen by the user. This technique is increasingly being used by broadcasting companies to allow viewers/listeners to see/hear programmes or other material at a time convenient to them.

Is a 'podcast' a broadcast for copyright purposes?

Discussion point 2

Consider also the possibility increasingly deployed in digital broadcasting, where the viewer may 'pause and record' a programme as it is transmitted, thereby allowing him to answer the doorbell or telephone without missing any part of the programme. What are the implications for the distinction between broadcasts and other forms of transmission?

Repeats

3.80   Many broadcasts on television and radio are repeated once or more. Such repeats have a copyright separate from or additional to that of the original broadcast,[231] unless it infringes the copyright in another broadcast or in a cable programme.[232]

---

[227] CDPA 1988, s 6(2); and see s 6(1)(b) and 6(4).   [228] CDPA 1988, s 6(1).

[229] So, the decision in *Shetland Times v Wills* [1997] FSR 604 that a website was a cable programme service could not now be reached. None of the exceptions to the general rule would have applied either.

[230] CDPA 1988, s 6(1A); see also *ITV v TVCatchup* [2015] EWCA Civ 2014, para 69.

[231] See CDPA 1988, s 14(2), (5) (note duration of copyright in a repeat cannot exceed that of the original transmission).

[232] CDPA 1988, s 6(6).

Published editions of literary, dramatic, and musical works

3.81   Copyright subsists in the typographical arrangement of every published edition of a literary, dramatic, or musical work.[233] A new edition is not a reprint of the work reproducing the typographical arrangement of a previous edition, but some new mode of presenting the work. The concept of 'edition' used here should be distinguished from the use of the word in describing versions of, say, a textbook, where each successive edition involves a change, not only in the typographical arrangement but also in the content of the text thus presented. The same text may be published several times, but as long as each publication adopts a different typographical arrangement, there will be separate copyrights for the publishers.[234] Equally, the text itself may be out of copyright, but there will be a copyright in the typographical arrangement of any edition which is not a reproduction, in whole or in part, of a previous typographical arrangement.[235]

■ *Newspaper Licensing Agency Ltd v Marks and Spencer plc* [2003] 1 AC 551

M&S subscribed to a press-cutting service which provided a daily supply of photocopies of items of interest appearing in national and daily newspapers. The press-cutting service had a licence from the newspapers' collecting society, the NLA. M&S copied the photocopies for distribution to individuals within its organisation, but had no licence for this. The NLA sued for infringement of a copyright in the typographical arrangement of the published editions of the newspapers. The issue was whether the copyright subsisted only in the whole newspaper, or separately in each article within the newspaper. Giving the main speech, Lord Hoffmann said: 'In my opinion, the frame of reference for the term 'published edition' is the language of the publishing trade. The edition is the product, generally between covers, which the publisher offers to the public' (para 14). While the articles each had literary copyright in their own right, this did not mean that each article as printed was a separate published edition, and a newspaper a collection of such editions. Lord Hoffmann added:

> In the case of a modern newspaper, I think that the skill and labour devoted to typographical arrangement is principally expressed in the overall design. It is not the choice of a particular typeface, the precise number or width of the columns, the breadth of margins and the relationship of headlines and straplines to the other text, the number of articles on a page and the distribution of photographs and advertisements but the combination of all of these into pages which give the newspaper as a whole its distinctive appearance . . . I find it difficult to think of the skill and labour which has gone into the typographical arrangement of a newspaper being expressed in anything less than a full page. The particular fonts, columns, margins and so forth are only, so to speak, the typographical vocabulary in which the arrangement is expressed (para 23).

First ownership

Introduction

3.82   It is necessary to consider ownership of copyright in two parts:

(1)   the *initial ownership* of the copyright, which in general pertains to the *author or creator* of the work in question;

(2)   given that copyright is an item of property, ownership of which may be transferred and which may also endure beyond the author's lifetime, the *transfer of copyright and consequent rights*.

This section considers only the first of these issues. The second issue is covered in the chapter on exploitation of copyright (see Chapter 6).

---

[233] CDPA 1988, ss 1(1)(c) and 8(1).

[234] See further discussion of this point by Lord Hoffmann in *Newspaper Licensing Agency Ltd v Marks and Spencer plc* [2003] 1 AC 551 at paras 11 and 16.

[235] CDPA 1988, s 8(2).

3.83   The *author* of a work is usually the *first owner* of the copyright in the work (CDPA 1988, s 11(1)). There is no *requirement of registration*, in contrast with most other forms of intellectual property, and *copyright will arise automatically with the creation of the work*. An *author is the person who creates the work* (s 9(1)), a concept readily applicable to most literary, dramatic, musical, and artistic works. However, the CDPA 1988 gives explicit definitions of who is to be taken as the author of sound recordings, films, broadcasts, and computer-generated works. Further, an important exception to first ownership following authorship is that the *employer will be the first owner of copyright in any literary, dramatic, musical, or artistic work or film authored by an employee in the course of employment unless there is an agreement to the contrary* (s 11(2)). In these provisions can be most clearly seen the UK's attribution of ownership and control of the work to the entrepreneur as distinct from the creator. Finally, there are *special rules relating to Crown and parliamentary copyright*, and copyright vested in certain international organisations.

Author of literary, dramatic, musical, or artistic work

3.84   With literary, dramatic, musical, and artistic works which are not computer-generated (for which see para 3.100), the author is the person who creates the work.[236] There is a statutory presumption that, where a name purporting to be that of the author appears on copies of a literary, dramatic, musical, or artistic work when published, or when made, the person whose name so appears is the author of the work, and that the work was made in circumstances not involving that person's course of employment, Crown or parliamentary copyright, or the copyright vested in certain international organisations. Like any presumption, this may be rebutted by contrary proof.[237] In general, the author is the person by whose 'skill and labour' (see para 3.22–3.23), or by whose 'intellectual creativity' (post *Infopaq*, see paras 3.25–3.28), the work took on its final material form and achieved the *originality* required for copyright protection. The broad principle that copyright subsists, not in ideas but in the way in which ideas are expressed (see paras 3.6–3.11) should also be borne in mind here. Copyright law has thus not taken up the post-modern deconstructionist critique, which rejects what it calls 'the Romantic concept of the author', and argues that works are not so much the expression of an individual as of the whole society and culture in which they are made.[238] Such analysis can be taken to undermine the individual author's claim to ownership of rights in the work and to highlight instead the claims that society as a whole is entitled to make. The foundation of copyright law remains, however, its recognition of the author's contribution against anyone or anything else.

Question

Who may be treated as the author of a literary, dramatic, musical, or artistic work?

Joint authorship

3.85   However, the law does recognise that a work may have more than one author. There may be joint authorship of a work where it is:[239]

> a work produced by the collaboration of two or more authors in which the contribution of each author is not distinct from that of the other author or authors.

---

[236] CDPA 1988, s 9(1).   [237] CDPA 1988, s 104(2).

[238] The classic analyses are: M Foucault, 'Qu'est ce qu'un auteur?' (1969) 64 Bulletin de la Société française de Philosophie 73 (translated as 'What is an author?' in JV Harris (ed), *Textual Strategies: Perspectives in Post-Structuralist Criticism* (1979)); R Barthes, 'The death of the author' in *Image Music Text* (1977); and J Derrida, 'Limited Inc a b c' in *Limited Inc* (1988). The literature in English is immense: see, eg, L Zemer, *The Idea of Authorship in Copyright* (2007). See too JC Ginsburg, 'The concept of authorship in comparative copyright law' (2003) 52 De Paul LR 1063; J Pila, 'An intentional view of the copyright work' (2008) 71 MLR 535; J Phillips, 'Authorship, ownership, wikiship: copyright in the twenty-first century' (2008) 3 JIPLP 788; WR Cornish, 'Conserving culture and copyright: a partial history' (2009) 13 Edinburgh Law Review 8; HL MacQueen, 'The legal definition of authorship and the scrolls' in JJ Collins and TH Lim (eds), *Oxford Handbook of the Dead Sea Scrolls* (2010).

[239] CDPA 1988, s 10(1).

Works of joint authorship are usually readily identifiable as such because the names of all authors appear on the work and no effort is made to separate their contributions. The presumption of authorship in favour of those whose names appear on copies of literary, dramatic, musical, or artistic works[240] applies also to works of joint authorship. Complexities may arise where there is no express attribution to joint authors.[241] However, the essence of joint authorship is collaboration between the authors in the execution of the work; lack of *separation* between the *contribution* of authors; and a *sufficient contribution* by each author towards originality of the work, ie contribution of a significant part of the skill and labour, or intellectual creativity, protected by the copyright.[242]

3.86 Collaboration suggests a process of cooperation between the authors in the furtherance of a common design to produce a work and even if one carries out a larger share of work than the other, each author is required to make a 'significant contribution'.[243] However, the authors' contributions should not be separate or distinct.[244] Does collaboration require a joint intention to create a joint work? In an old case the test of joint authorship was said to be whether the authors had a 'pre-concerted joint design' so that one who improved or touched up the work of another was not a joint author of the eventual production.[245] In *Beckingham v Hodgens*,[246] however, the Court of Appeal held that the existence of a common intention to produce a joint work was not a requirement for a work of joint authorship.

3.87 The decision as to whether or not there is joint authorship will turn on the nature of each of the contributions, linked to the fundamental concept of copyright pertaining to the form of expression rather than to ideas and information. Did one person supply only ideas and material which were translated into a work by the other, or did the former's contribution amount to a part in formulating the expression, that is, authorship?

■ *Brown v Mcasso Music* [2005] FSR 40

M had drafted lyrics for a rap song to be used in a TV commercial. B had then amended the lyrics to give them greater authenticity as a rap song, changing idiomatically incorrect language, using appropriate Jamaican English to match word rhythm to the music and adding extempore exclamations. It was held that B was a joint author of the song. His contribution to the writing was an active one, involving skill and judgment to obtain the authentic feel of rap. Although he made use of standard elements of rap culture, his work satisfied originality in the copyright sense.[247]

 Question

When may a person be identified as a joint author?

In cases where clearly one person supplies ideas and information, and another one puts these into literary or artistic form, the latter is author and owner of the copyright. So a person who supplied the ideas for the plot of a play,[248] a director who added ideas during the rehearsals and development of a play's script,[249] and a person who had had the idea of using an outline drawing of a human hand as an indicator on a ballot paper,[250] were all held not entitled to the copyright in the resultant works, while in *Donoghue v Allied Newspapers*[251] the ghostwriter of a jockey's memoirs was held to be the owner of the copyright therein as the person responsible for the language in which the work was cast. General instructions to the photographer

---

[240] CDPA 1988, s 104(2), (3).
[241] See generally L Zemer, 'Contribution and collaboration in joint authorship: too many misconceptions' (2006) 1 JIPLP 283.
[242] See a helpful summary of the law on joint authorship in *Martin v Kogan* [2017] EWHC 2927 (IPEC).
[243] *Levy v Rutley* (1871) LR 6 CP 523; *Cala Homes (South) v Alfred McAlpine Homes East* [1995] FSR 818 at 834–35.
[244] *Beckingham v Hodgens* [2002] EMLR 45 (Ch D).   [245] *Bagge v Miller* [1917–23] MCC 179; see also *Levy v Rutley* (1871) LR 6 CP 523.
[246] [2003] EMLR 18.   [247] Leave to appeal was refused by the Court of Appeal: [2006] FSR 24.
[248] *Tate v Thomas* [1921] 1 Ch 503; also *Wiseman v Weidenfeld & Nicolson* [1985] FSR 525.   [249] *Brighton v Jones* [2005] FSR 288.
[250] *Kenrick & Co v Lawrence & Co* (1890) 25 QBD 99.   [251] [1938] Ch 106; also *Evans v Hulton & Co* (1924) 131 LT 534.

as to the type of photographs, along with a general acceptance that a photo shoot was a team effort, was held not to be enough to result in joint authorship, if the photographer was the only person with sufficient control over taking the photograph.[252]

■ *Robin Ray v Classic FM plc* [1998] FSR 622

RR, an individual with wide knowledge of classical music, entered a consultancy arrangement with Classic FM under which he provided a catalogue of 50,000 items to be in the radio station's music library, categorised in a way which would enable it to be used to establish the station's playlists. A database incorporating RR's work was established by Classic FM, which then sought to license its use by overseas radio stations without RR's consent. RR claimed copyright in the catalogue and its categorisation, and argued that Classic FM were infringing. Classic FM replied that they were joint authors. It was held that RR was the sole author of the catalogue; Classic FM had supplied ideas, suggestions and materials for RR's use, but he alone composed the catalogue.

Some particular examples of joint authorship issues

3.88   There have been a number of difficult cases where parties were working together in the production of new software.

■ *Fylde Microsystems Ltd v Key Radio Systems Ltd* [1998] FSR 449

The parties were cooperating (without a contract) in the development of radios. FM wrote software for installation in KRS's radios, which the latter then sold. The parties fell into dispute over ownership of the copyright in the software. KRS admitted that FM was the writer but argued that it was a joint author by setting the specification for the software, reporting errors and bugs, making suggestions as to the cause of faults, and providing technical information about the hardware in which the software had to operate. It was held that although KRS's activities involved much skill and labour, it was not of the nature of authorship, and the parties were not joint authors.

■ *Cyprotex Discovery Ltd v University of Sheffield* [2004] RPC 4

In this case[253] the university and a company (C) were engaged together under a contract in the development for practical application of software initially created by the university. The relationship broke down and an issue emerged as to whether the parties were joint authors of the software which had been developed under the contract. It was held that the university's contribution to the new software—provision of background information about the initial software, assistance in compilation of the technical specifications of what the new software should contain, and vetting the suggestions of third-party sponsors of the work—was not that of an author but of a client wishing to ensure the functionality of the new software when completed. It therefore had no claim to the copyright in the new software.

 Exercise

Consider the case of two sets of solicitors negotiating and drafting written contracts on behalf of their respective clients. Is the contractual document which results a work of joint authorship or not? See David Vaver, 'Copyright in legal documents' (1993) 31 Osgoode Hall LJ 661.

3.89   Another quite common situation is the development of musical work by a group working together but developing the ideas by playing them on their instruments rather than writing them down.[254] Contrast the two following cases, where there were different results on the particular facts:

---

[252] *Celebrity Pictures v B Hannah* [2012] EWPCC 32.   [253] On appeal the decision was affirmed on other grounds: [2004] RPC 44 (CA).
[254] In addition to the cases cited in the following text, see *Beckingham v Hodgens* [2003] EMLR 18 (music of the Bluebells' 'Young at heart' a work of joint authorship); *Fisher v Brooker* [2007] FSR 12 (music of Procol Harum's 'A Whiter Shade of Pale' also a work of joint authorship); aff'd on this point [2008] FSR 26 (CA). The issue of joint authorship was not discussed when the case reached the House of Lords; *Fisher v Brooker*

■ *Stuart v Barrett* [1994] EMLR 448

The case concerned the output of a pop group called Keep it Dark. S was the drummer and, after his expulsion from the group, he claimed joint authorship in the music of the band's songs. The music resulted from 'jamming' sessions at which, after one member of the group began with an opening phrase or series of notes, the group then played together, improvising and composing by ear; no one wrote down any notes. Thomas Morison QC held that the music was the result of joint authorship, although emphasising that there was no general rule for such group compositions. With regard to S's contribution, the judge said:

> I also have no doubt that in principle a drummer may claim copyright in a piece of music if, as here, he had collaborated with the other members of the group to produce an original piece of music. Whilst the player of tuned percussion might be more readily recognisable as a contributor to a musical composition than a drummer, in my judgment it would be a misinterpretation of the drummer's contribution to composition in contemporary music, whether pop or otherwise, to reject his contribution in principle. I listened to some of the tapes produced in Court and I am in no doubt about the significance of the drum part to the whole of the work. The work is given shape and drive by the drummer and a good drummer, as I accept the plaintiff is, can significantly influence the whole composition (at 460).

■ *Hadley v Kemp* [1999] EMLR 589

This case originated in the break-up of the 1980s pop-rock band Spandau Ballet. The band's music was generally attributed to Gary Kemp (GK), one of its five members; three of the others claimed joint authorship on the basis that, although GK initiated the compositions, he did not write them down but presented them aurally to the other band members, from whence the material was developed by further performance. It was held on the evidence that the compositions remained those of GK and that the contribution of the other band members to the final product were matters of performance and was not in the nature of composition (authorship).

 Question

What is the distinction between the previous two cases?

3.90   Even where a person is not the originator of the whole of a work, he may still be the sole author for copyright purposes: it is 'not a question which . . . can be determined by counting' the material produced by the respective parties but 'has to be regarded as a matter of substance'.[255] The person who improves or amends another's work—as, for example, the editor of a new and updated edition of a legal textbook originally composed by someone else—would most likely have a separate copyright in his contribution to the result rather than a joint one, provided there was sufficient independent skill and labour.[256]

 Discussion point 1   For answer guidance visit www.oup.com/uk/brown5e.

Is this book a work of joint authorship? What do you need to know to answer this question?

Discussion point 2

The novel *Swan*, published in 1994, is said on its dust jacket and title page to be by the supermodel, Naomi Campbell. However, on the catalogue page it is said to be 'Copyright© Naomi Campbell and Caroline Upcher: The Author and the Writer have asserted their moral rights.' Who would have been the first owner of the copyright in the text of *Swan*? Who has the moral right to be identified as the author of the novel? See further at para 3.91, *Najma Heptulla v Orient Longman Ltd* [1989] 1 FSR 598.

[2009] FSR 25 (HL). See on this latter case in the Court of Appeal, N Elsborg, 'Skip the light fandango, turning cartwheels "cross the court"' (2008) 3 JIPLP 626. For a recent application of the concept to a musical work, see *Minder Music v Sharples* [2015] EWHC 1454 (IPEC). See generally on authorship in musical works, R Arnold, 'Reflections on "The Triumph of Music": copyrights and performers' rights in music' [2010] IPQ 153.

[255] *Samuelson v Producers Distributing Co* (1931) 48 RPC 580 per Romer LJ at 593.

[256] See, eg, the cases on editorial work at para 3.30: *Sawkins v Hyperion Records* [2005] RPC 32 (CA).

Problems in the spiritual world

■ *Cummins v Bond* [1927] 1 Ch 167

The plaintiff produced a literary work called *The Chronicle of Cleophas*, which was written at high speed while she was participating in seances and which all parties to the litigation believed to be a communication from 'some being no longer inhabiting this world, and who has been out of it for a length of time sufficient to justify the hope that he has no reasons for wishing to return to it' (per Eve J at 172). The defendant (who was present at the seances), transcribed, punctuated, and arranged the work, and argued that he had also contributed to the work by the silent transfer of ideas to the plaintiff during the seances. It was held that copyright belonged to the plaintiff only and was not owned jointly with the defendant. The defendant also argued that the work had no copyright as neither he nor the plaintiff was its originator. Eve J said:

> The conclusion which the defendant invites me to come to in this submission involves the expression of an opinion I am not prepared to make, that the authorship and copyright rest with some one already domiciled on the other side of the inevitable river. That is a matter I must leave for solution by others more competent to decide it than I am. I can only look upon the matter as a terrestrial one, of the earth earthy, and I propose to deal with it on that footing (at 175).

■ *Leah v Two Worlds Publishing Ltd* [1951] Ch 393

An artist produced pictures of the dead by means, as he claimed, of extrasensory perception activated by contact with living persons who wished to have the representation made. Here it was accepted that the artist was the author of the resultant work even though 'inspired by influences of which perhaps no easy explanation can be given' (per Vaisey J at 398).

3.91   There may, however, be exceptional cases where the contribution of the person supplying material to the person actually executing the work is sufficient to allow a claim of copyright as either sole or joint author: that is to say, it goes beyond giving ideas to giving directions or instructions as to the mode of expression or execution. A straightforward example would be where someone is dictating to an amanuensis, in which case he is plainly the sole author. It also appears certain that a builder cannot claim copyright in a work of architecture, where the architect is regarded as the author.[257]

■ *Najma Heptulla v Orient Longman Ltd* [1989] 1 FSR 598 (High Court, India)

MA, a leader of the Indian independence movement, dictated his memoirs to HK, with whom he also discussed the content. MA was not confident writing in English (the language of the memoirs) and this was why he worked with HK. MA read the whole manuscript, made many corrections, and ordered a deletion. It was held that HK was not the sole author of the book. In a literary work both language and subject matter are important. Joint authorship arose where there was an intellectual contribution by two or more persons in pursuit of a pre-concerted joint design.

Nature of joint ownership: common property

3.92   In cases of joint authorship, all the authors own the copyright in the work.[258] The main consequence of joint authorship for a work is that there is only one copyright in the whole work, the duration of which is tied to the death of the last-surviving author alone.[259] The copyright is usually held by the authors as common property, subject to any circumstances or agreement to the contrary, each having a title to his own share which he can alienate and which passes to his estate on death.[260] It would also follow that each co-owner is

---

[257] *Meikle v Maufe* [1941] 3 All ER 144.   [258] CDPA 1988, ss 10(3) and 11(1).   [259] CDPA 1988, s 12(8); and see para 3.117.
[260] See *Lauri v Renad* (1892) 3 Ch 402; *Slater v Wimmer* [2012] EWPCC 7 (PCC) at para 89. The point is not entirely free from doubt and it still might be open, at least to a Scottish court, to hold that this was a case of joint property, in which case all the rights would ultimately accresce in the estate of the last-surviving author. Possibly, however, this would be unfair. On joint and common property, see generally *Halsbury's Laws of England*; *Laws of Scotland: Stair Memorial Encyclopaedia*.

entitled to share in the management of the common property, meaning in this case that the consent of all must be obtained before any licence is granted.[261] In any event, it is provided that where copyright is owned jointly any requirement of the licence of the copyright owner requires the licence of all the owners.[262] It has been held, however, that a co-author may sue for infringement of copyright without the other authors.[263]

Key points on joint authorship

- This arises where more than one person *collaborates* in the *execution* of a work (ie in formulating the expression) and the contributions are indistinguishable in the final work.
- Supply of ideas/information is insufficient to make one a joint author.
- Improvement/amendment/editing of another's work is not enough to make one a joint author.
- Giving another directions/instructions as to the mode of expression may lead to one becoming at least a joint author.
- Dictation makes one the sole author
- Ownership is usually common, not joint: that is, there is one copyright, each party owning a share of the whole which passes to his estate on death; each may share in management, or sell the share.

Co-authorship

3.93   The definition of joint authorship makes it possible to distinguish what may be called works of co-authorship, that is, works produced by some collaboration but where the contributions of the collaborators are separate from each other.[264] A song in which the words were written by one person and the music by another, where they were created to be used together, is specifically set out in the statute as a work of co-authorship.[265] No other works are classified as works of co-authorship in the CDPA 1988. In a co-authored work each contributor has a separate copyright as the author of his part of the work.

Discussion point   For answer guidance visit **www.oup.com/uk/brown5e**.

What is the position where a work is produced as apparently one of joint authorship within the meaning of the CDPA 1988, but the authors indicate, perhaps in a prefatory statement, that responsibility has in fact been divided along certain lines?

Compilations and authorship

3.94   Compilations must also be distinguished from both works of co-authorship and works of joint authorship: compilations have copyright and the compiler is an author even though there may be several different works by other authors represented in the compilation. The borderline can be unclear: thus, *Who's Who*, which is compiled from returns completed by the subjects of each entry, has been held to be a compilation rather than a collection of autobiographies, with the subjects each having copyright in their own contributions.[266]

---

[261] *Powell v Head* (1879) 12 Ch D 686; *Mail Newspapers v Express Newspapers* [1987] FSR 90.   [262] CDPA 1988, s 173(2).

[263] *Waterlow Publishers v Rose, The Times*, 8 December 1989 (CA).

[264] Note that CDPA 1988, s 178 unhelpfully defines 'collective work' to include works of joint authorship as well as a work in which there are distinct contributions, eg the category of work discussed in this paragraph.

[265] CDPA 1988, s 10A added by Copyright and Duration of Rights in Performances Regulations 2013/1782. See also *Redwood Music Ltd v Feldman & Co Ltd* [1979] RPC 385 esp at 400–03 (a decision on the 1911 Act).

[266] *A & C Black Ltd v Claude Stacey Ltd* [1929] 1 Ch 177.

Authors of films

3.95   The authors of a film are its producer and principal director,[267] and the film will be treated as a work of joint authorship unless these two are the same person.[268]

Sound recordings

3.96   The first copyright in a sound recording is owned by the producer.[269]

Broadcasts

3.97   The first copyright in every broadcast is owned by the person making the broadcast or, in the case of a broadcast which relays another broadcast by reception and immediate re-transmission, the person making that other broadcast.[270] The person making the broadcast is the person transmitting the programme, if he has any responsibility for its contents, or any person providing the programme who makes with the person transmitting it the arrangements necessary for its transmission; a programme is any item included in a broadcast.[271] An example of a situation where the transmitter has no responsibility for the contents is when he is simply transmitting a signal received from a satellite.

Published editions

3.98   The copyright in a published edition of a literary, dramatic, or musical work belongs to its publisher.[272]

Joint authorship and the media copyrights

3.99   There is no restriction of the concept of joint authorship to literary, dramatic, musical, and artistic works. As already noted, joint authorship arises with films; and there is express provision for joint authorship in broadcasts when a person provides a programme having made arrangements with the person actually transmitting it which are necessary for the programme's transmission.[273] Joint authorship might also arise with sound recordings produced by joint ventures or other collaborations over arrangements needed to make the record.

Using computers: computer-generated works

3.100   Problems may arise with computers. It is obvious that a person composing a computer program is the author and (subject to the rules of employment discussed at paras 3.103–3.109) first owner of the copyright in the work. When a work is produced by a computer program, the computer can be seen as a tool or as an aid, meaning that the copyright in the work belongs to the person who employed the computer as a tool to enable this function.[274] If a computer program, such as a word-processing package, is used in the production of another work, the appropriate analogy would appear to be with a person using a pen,

---

[267] CDPA 1988, s 9(2)(ab). Note that this provision resulted from implementation of EU Directives and the Court of Justice, in Case C-277/10 *Martin Luksan v Petrus van der Let* (9 February 2012), has confirmed that under EU law, member states must allocate initial rights in films to the principal director and cannot exclusively grant them to the producer, although they have the option of laying down a rebuttable presumption of transfer of rights in favour of the producer.

[268] CDPA 1988, s 10(1A). For a discussion of the terms 'producer' and 'principal director', see *Slater v Wimmer* [2012] EWPCC 7 (PCC). On joint authorship, see paras 3.85–3.92.

[269] CDPA 1988, ss 9(2)(aa) and 11(1). For a discussion of the term 'producer' in this context, see *Henry Hadaway Organisation Ltd v Pickwick Group Ltd* [2015] EWHC 3407 (IPEC).

[270] CDPA 1988, ss 9(2)(b) and 11(1).   [271] For all this see CDPA 1988, s 6(3).   [272] CDPA 1988, ss 9(2)(d) and 11(1).

[273] CDPA 1988, ss 10(2) and 6(3).   [274] *Express Newspapers v Liverpool Daily Post and Echo* [1985] FSR 306.

typewriter, or paintbrush to create something, where the copyright would plainly be in the user of the tool rather than in its maker. The CDPA 1988 introduces a further complication into this difficult area, the *computer-generated work*. This means that the work is generated by computer in circumstances such that there is no human author of the work.[275] In such circumstances, the author is taken to be the person by whom the arrangements necessary for the creation of the work are undertaken.[276] It seems that a distinction now requires to be made between works thus *generated* and those which are computer-*aided*. A work seems likely to be treated as computer-generated when the machine is merely provided with data by its operators, which it analyses and converts into output. Where the operator has some role in the formulation of the output beyond the supply of data, then the work is more likely to be computer-aided only. The sequence of images generated in playing a computer video game has been held to be a computer- rather than player-generated work; the person playing the game was merely a player, not an author.[277] Recent developments in relation to 'Big data analytics' and Artificial Intelligence (AI) lead to several issues, as for example whether material obtained from a database[278] by means of a user's questioning (an example of this would be a search on a particular topic in a library catalogue or in Lexis[279]) is computer- or user-generated; or who owns works generated by AI.[280] The question of whose skill and labour, or intellectual creativity, is also relevant in such cases. The importance of the point is that the user in such cases may well be distinct from the person by whom the arrangements necessary for the creation of the work were undertaken. With computers, relevant factors may include ownership or possession of the machine, control of access, and degree of input in terms of programming and data.

> **Question**
>
> What is a computer-generated work? Who owns copyright in works created by AI? Should copyright subsist in such works?

Anonymous and pseudonymous works

3.101   A literary, dramatic, musical, or artistic work may be composed in such circumstances that it is not possible to identify any author. The work is thus *anonymous*. Alternatively, authors may choose to use names or badges of identity other than their true names in connection with their works. The works will then be *pseudonymous*. Both are what the CDPA 1988 terms 'works of unknown authorship'.[281] In both cases, copyright in the work remains with the author, whoever that may be, because where the identity is ascertainable by reasonable inquiry (eg where the identity of an author can be identified despite of the use of a pseudonym)[282] the term of copyright is determined by reference to the date of that person's death.[283] But there is a statutory presumption that, where no name purporting to be that of an author appears upon a published literary, dramatic, musical, or artistic work, and a name purporting to be that of the publisher does appear on copies of the work as first published, the person whose name appeared is presumed, until the contrary is proved, to have been the owner of the copyright at the time of publication.[284] The presumption operates even in cases where the publisher is not a party.

---

[275] CDPA 1988, s 178.   [276] CDPA 1988, s 9(3).   [277] *Nova Productions Ltd v Mazooma Games Ltd* [2006] RPC 14 (Kitchin J).

[278] Which may have its own copyright or relate to a *sui generis* database right.

[279] Especially where the user can obtain a printout of the results of the search.

[280] See M Perry and T Margoni, 'From music tracks to Google maps: who owns computer-generated works?' (2010) 26 CLSR 621; J Dickenson et al, 'Creative machines: ownership of copyright in content created by artificial intelligence applications' [2017] EIPR 457.

[281] CDPA 1988, s 9(4).   [282] CDPA 1988, s 9(5).   [283] CDPA 1988, s 12(2). Otherwise, the term is determined under s 12(3).

[284] CDPA 1988, s 104(4). For an example, see *Waterlow Publishers v Rose*, *The Times*, 8 December 1989 (CA). Note here the author's moral right to be identified as such (paras 6.8–6.11), and a person's right not to have a work falsely attributed to him (para 6.17).

■ *Warwick Film Productions v Eisinger* [1969] 1 Ch 508

WFP claimed that the executor of the author of an anonymous book had assigned its copyright to them. It was held that, as WFP had not rebutted the presumption that the publisher owned the copyright, their case on this point failed. Plowman J also said that it would not have helped WFP to prove who the author was; the presumption could only be rebutted by evidence that the publishers did not own the copyright. This seems to go too far: the basic position under the statute is that the author is the first owner of copyright and, in the case of published anonymous and pseudonymous works, if his identity can be established his date of death determines the term of the copyright. Viewed in this context, the presumption that the publisher owns the copyright must be rebuttable by evidence of who the author was.

3.102   The presumption does not deal with either the unpublished work or the work where the name that appears as author is a pseudonym, and the identity of the author is not reasonably discoverable in either case. Ownership may then hang in something of a void in both cases; but the effects of this are mitigated by the provision that where it is reasonable to assume that copyright has expired or that the author died 70 years or more before the beginning of the current calendar year, then no act can constitute infringement of copyright.[285]

 Discussion point   For answer guidance visit **www.oup.com/uk/brown5e**.

What advice would you give to someone who wished to include in an anthology of verse a poem published in a student magazine in 1900 under the name 'John Smith', but who had no idea who John Smith was?

Employment

3.103   In general, where a literary, dramatic, musical, or artistic work, or a film, is made in the course of the author's employment by another person, the employer is entitled to the copyright in the work.[286] The converse is, of course, that unless any contract under which a literary, dramatic, musical, or artistic work, or a film, is made is one of employment, the author will always be the first owner of the copyright.[287] An important issue as such is to determine whether the author is an employee at the time of creation of the work and whether there is a contract of employment. The CDPA 1988 in s 178 provides that the words 'employed', 'employee', 'employer', and 'employment' refer to employment under a contract of service or of apprenticeship.[288] Consequently, in determining ownership of copyright, it must be asked whether the author is under a contract *of service* or of apprenticeship, as opposed to a contract *for services*.[289]

3.104   The 1988 Act's general provisions on the effect of employment on copyright are subject to any agreement to the contrary, and it is worth noting that there are no formal requirements with respect to such agreements.[290] Agreements can be implied from actions, as for example where universities have generally not claimed

---

[285] CDPA 1988, s 57(1).

[286] CDPA 1988, s 11(2). The 1988 Act also removed any claim by an employee-journalist to copyright in his work. See 1956 Act, s 4(2), which was not replaced in CDPA 1988.

[287] For the meaning of employment, see *Halsbury's Laws of England*; *Laws of Scotland: Stair Memorial Encyclopaedia*.

[288] See *Chadwick v Lypiatt Studio Ltd* [2018] EWHC 1986 (Ch), where the court applied general principles on whether a contract is one of employment, including those set out in *Chitty on Contracts*. See generally Ch 3 in D Cabrelli, *Employment Law in Practice* (2018).

[289] For the difference between these two types of contracts, see *Beloff v Pressdram Ltd* [1973] FSR 33 at 36-43; *Stephenson Jordan and Harrison v Macdonald and Evans* (1952) 69 RPC 10 at 22.

[290] CDPA 1988, s 11(2).

copyright in their academic employees' works, even though the production of such works might be said to be in the course of employment.[291]

Question

When is an employer entitled to the copyright in an employee's work?

■ *Noah v Shuba* [1991] FSR 14 (Mummery J)

N was employed as an epidemiologist at the Public Health Laboratory Scheme (PHLS). He wrote a book entitled *A Guide to Hygienic Skin Piercing*. In accordance with the usual practice of the PHLS, under which employees retained copyright in works written by them, the book showed N as the author and copyright owner. In an action for copyright infringement which N brought against third parties, Mummery J stated *obiter* that the long-standing practice of PHLS with regard to employees' copyright works meant that N's contract contained an implied term against the application of the employment rule in the 1988 Act.

In the course of employment

3.105   Before the employer can claim any copyright in his employee's literary, dramatic, musical, or artistic work, it must be shown to have been made in the course of the author's employment.[292]

■ *Stephenson Jordan and Harrison v Macdonald and Evans* (1952) 69 RPC 10

A former employee of the plaintiffs had published a book made up of the texts of public lectures composed and delivered by him before various audiences, and also of a report prepared by him for a client of the plaintiffs. Both parts had been written during the period of his employment. It was held that copyright in the report belonged to the employers, because the author wrote it as part of what he was employed to do; but with regard to the text of the lectures, even though the employers had encouraged the author to give the lectures and had met his resultant expenses, it was held that the employers had no copyright. An analogy was drawn between the employee and a university lecturer, and it was said to be 'both just and commonsense' (per Lord Evershed at 18) that the latter rather than his university, had copyright in his lectures. The grounds for this view do not clearly appear in the case but it has been suggested that the employee was only employed to deliver and not to write the lectures. However, this appears inconsistent with the observation of Morris LJ that it had not been shown that the employee could have been ordered either to write or to deliver the lectures (at 24).

■ *Byrne v Statist Co* [1914] 1 KB 622

A member of the editorial staff of a newspaper made a translation into English of a speech reported in a foreign language for publication in the paper. The work was commissioned and paid for by his employers, but he carried it out in his own time and independently of his normal duties. It was held that he was the owner of the copyright, not having made the translation in the course of his employment.

---

[291] See further on universities and copyright ownership, J Pila, 'Who owns the intellectual property rights in academic work?' [2010] EIPR 609; A Monotti with S Ricketson, *Universities and Intellectual Property: Ownership and Exploitation* (2003); C McSherry, *Who Owns Academic Work? Battling for Control of Intellectual Property* (2001); and D Bok, *Universities in the Marketplace: The Commercialisation of Higher Education* (2003) Chs 4, 5, 8, 9.

[292] CDPA 1988, s 11(2).

■ *Mei Fields Designs Ltd v Saffron Cards and Gifts Ltd* [2018] EWHC 1332 (IPEC)

M, was employed as a design director by MWL but was held to have designed greeting cards outside the course of employment. The Court noted that there is no single test for whether an act is carried out in the course of employment, this being a multifactorial assessment. The relevant factors, with no single factor being determinative, and the list not being exhaustive, may include:

> (a) the terms of the contract of employment; (b) where the work was created; (c) whether the work was created during normal office hours; (d) who provided the materials for the work to be create; (e) the level of direction provided to the author; (f) whether the author can refuse to create the work/s; and (g) whether the work is "integral" to the business' (para 42).

■ *King v The South African Weather Service* [2009] FSR 6 (Supreme Court of Appeal, Republic of South Africa)

An employee created a computer program working both from home and in the office, over which he asserted his own copyright. His employer, a weather-forecasting service, argued that the program was created 'in the course of employment' and so the copyright belonged to it. This was despite the fact that the employee's duties as a meteorologist did not include computer programming. The program assisted him in his duties to collect, collate, and transmit weather data. The Court held that the creation of the program, which fitted into the service's automated weather system, had been to the advantage of the employer. The employment had been the *causa causans* of the programs. A format for the program had been prescribed by the employer which also had to approve the program prior to its installation on the system. Furthermore, the appellant's job description was initially not intended to be comprehensive and was later amended to state that work outside the terms of the contract could still be created 'in the course of employment'. The scope of the employment could change either explicitly or implicitly.[293]

Discussion point   For answer guidance visit **www.oup.com/uk/brown5e**.

Discuss whether a schoolteacher who writes and publishes a text for use in schools would have the copyright in it. Is there any difference in the position of the university lecturer who writes a book or articles? What about the composition of a database or a computer program by the same lecturer?

Presumption against employer

3.106   Where the name of a person purporting to be that of the author appears on a published copy of a literary, dramatic, musical, or artistic work, or on a work when it is made, it is presumed that he is the author and that he did not make that work in the course of his employment. The contrary must therefore be proved.[294]

Should employees be rewarded further?

3.107   Under UK (but not Continental) laws, where an employee creates a work in the course of employment, the employer gets first ownership of the resulting copyright. Given that the employer is an investor who is backing the production of copyright works, his gaining the copyright (at least in its economic aspects) and the return therefrom does not seem so dreadful as is sometimes suggested by those from systems more focused on copyright as reflecting more of personality rights than economic interests. The Software Directive

---

[293] See further L Tong, 'South African Supreme Court of Appeal interprets "course of employment" for copyright' (2009) 4 JIPLP 323.

[294] CDPA 1988, s 104(2). For an example where the presumption was not displaced by the employer, see *Mei Fields Designs Ltd v Saffron Cards and Gifts Ltd* [2018] EWHC 1332 (IPEC).

in Article 2(3) laid down that the economic rights in a computer program should go to the employer unless otherwise provided by contract, thus pointing Europeanisation for the digital environment in a UK or Anglo-American direction; but there has been no similar provision in any subsequent Directive.

3.108   The UK model of giving an employer the first copyright in an employee's work, raises questions as to whether employees should be rewarded further, and if so, how to compensate them for the loss of the right that would otherwise (eg work created outside the course of employment) have fallen to them. Patent law provides a possible example: the employer is entitled to patent inventions by employees working in the course of their employment, but the employee has a right to participate in the economic benefit which the work brings to the employer. However, that scheme does not appear to have been regularly used and is not easy to apply. But this may also be because well-advised employers put in place suitable or satisfactory schemes of their own devising as part of the contract of employment. Another model of possible relevance is the artist's resale right, introduced into UK law on 14 February 2006 (see paras 6.23–6.26). The right guarantees the original artist a share of the returns being earned from sales of the original art work, regardless of whether the artist still owns the copyright in the work in question.

3.109   Were an employee reward scheme along this or similar lines to be introduced into copyright, the question of whether it should be a default scheme subject to contract would have to be addressed.

Commissioned works

3.110   Employment should be distinguished from a *commission*.[295] In the CDPA 1988, there are no express provisions on commissions as such, and so general principles will apply. The general principle is that the author will be the first owner of copyright unless otherwise agreed, for instance through a contract. This is particularly important because this is an area where the 1988 Act departed from its predecessor's position. Under the 1956 Act, the commissioner was the first owner of copyright in respect of a limited class of artistic works; now in every case an assignation from the author will be needed to achieve this result.[296] If the parties agree that the commissioner is to have the copyright in the commissioned work, the agreement will have to take the form of an assignation by the author, which the 1988 Act requires to be in writing.[297] In the absence of any terms in the contract regarding ownership of copyright in a commissioned work, the Court will apply the usual contractual principles and may imply a term by taking a minimalist approach: 'an implication may only be made if this is necessary, and then only of what is necessary and no more'.[298] In implying a term in favour of the commissioner (eg an assignment, or a licence for the particular use for which the work is commissioned), no greater incursion into the rights of the copyright owner should be made than is necessary.[299]

Crown copyright

3.111   The monarch is entitled to copyright[300] in every work made in the copyright area by the monarch or an officer or servant of the Crown in the course of his duties.[301] It seems that, for the most part, the position of the Crown is little different from that of any other employer, apart from the much longer duration of the copyright. It may

---

[295] Note that a whether a relationship is one of employment or commission depends on the *true relationship* between the parties, and not simply the label chosen to describe the relationship. *Sprint Electric Ltd v Buyer's Dream Ltd* [2018] EWHC 1924 (Ch).

[296] 1956 Act, s 4(3). See CDPA 1988, Sch 1, para 11 for transitional provisions. For an example of the copyright in a commissioned work vesting in the author, see *Oilfield Publications Ltd v MacLachlan* 1989 GWD 26-1128.

[297] CDPA 1988, s 90(3).

[298] *Griggs v Evans* [2005] FSR 31 (CA) at para 13, confirming the general principles set out by Lightman J in *Robin Ray v Classic FM plc* [1998] FSR 622 on the respective rights of the commissioner and author.

[299] *Celebrity Pictures v B Hannah* [2012] EWPCC 32 at para 18.

[300] See further the website of the Information Management section of the National Archives, which administers Crown copyright at www.nationalarchives.gov.uk/information-management/re-using-public-sector-information/copyright-and-re-use/crown-copyright.

[301] CDPA 1988, s 163(1).

have some unusual rights in respect of the works of former intelligence officers where these breach the lifelong duty of confidentiality owed to the Crown by such persons. According to some of the judges in *Attorney General v Guardian Newspapers Ltd (No 2)*,[302] copyright in such works may vest in the Crown even though their creation occurs after the employment has ceased and cannot in any event be said to be in the course of the author's employment. The monarch is also entitled to copyright in every Act of Parliament, Act of the Scottish Parliament, Act of the Welsh and Northern Ireland Assemblies, or Measure of the General Synod of the Church of England.[303] Finally, the monarch has copyright in works made in his private capacity. This is presumably affected by the special provisions as to the term of Crown copyrights, on the basis that such works are made by the monarch in terms of the section. Members of the royal family who make copyright works have the usual rights[304] and are not affected by any aspect of Crown copyright, since their works are not made by the monarch.[305]

Parliamentary copyright

3.112   The first ownership of copyright in works made by or under the direction or control of the House of Commons or the House of Lords[306] falls to the relevant House, or, if it is made by or under the direction and control of both Houses, jointly to the two Houses.[307] The CDPA 1988 also provides that the copyright of every Bill introduced into the UK Parliament is vested in one or both of the Houses.[308] Copyright in a public Bill belongs in the first instance to the House in which the Bill is introduced, and after the Bill has been carried to the second House to both Houses jointly.[309] Copyright in a private Bill belongs to both Houses jointly.[310] Copyright in a personal Bill belongs in the first instance to the House of Lords, and after the Bill has been carried to the House of Commons to both Houses jointly.[311] Copyright in a Bill ceases when it receives Royal Assent (in which case it becomes an Act and subject to Crown copyright) or on the withdrawal or rejection of the Bill.[312] There are similar provisions for the Bills of the Scottish Parliament (first copyright belongs to the Scottish Parliamentary Corporate Body) and the Welsh and Northern Ireland Assemblies (first owner the Welsh and Northern Ireland Assembly Commissions, respectively).[313]

 Question

Why was there no provision for Welsh Assembly copyright before the coming into force of the Government of Wales Act 2006, Sch 10, para 28?

Duration of copyright

Introduction

3.113   The rights conferred by copyright generally endure for a limited period of time only. The Berne Convention provides for a *minimum* period of the author's lifetime plus 50 years for the works to which it applies (Art 7), while the Rome Convention lays down another minimum of at least 20 years for sound recordings and

---

[302] [1988] 3 All ER 545 per Scott J at 567, per Dillon LJ at 621 (CA), and per Lords Keith and Griffiths at 645 and 654 (HL). The argument is dependent on notions of equitable ownership which it would be impossible to apply in the Scottish context.

[303] CDPA 1988, s 164(1); Scotland Act 1998, s 92(3). For the Bill stage, see para 3.112.

[304] *Prince Albert v Strange* (1848) 2 De G & Sm 652 (64 ER 293); aff'd (1849) 1 Mac & G 25 (41 ER 1171); *HRH The Prince of Wales v Associated Newspapers Ltd (No 3)* [2006] EWHC 522 (Ch) (Blackburne J).

[305] For a valuable discussion of the development and contemporary significance of Crown copyright, see S Saxby, 'Crown copyright regulation in the UK—is the debate still alive?' (2005) 13(3) IJL & IT 299.

[306] See generally the website of the Information Management service of the National Archives at www.nationalarchives.gov.uk and N Cox, 'Copyright in statutes, regulations and judicial decisions in common law jurisdictions: public ownership or commercial enterprise?' (2006) 27(3) Statute Law Review 185.

[307] CDPA 1988, s 165(1).   [308] CDPA 1988, s 166(1).   [309] CDPA 1988, s 166(2).   [310] CDPA 1988, s 166(3).

[311] CDPA 1988, s 166(4).   [312] CDPA 1988, s 166(5). For the Crown copyright in an Act, see para 3.111.

[313] CDPA 1988, ss 166A, 166B, 166C, and 166D.

broadcasts (Art 14). Various formulae are used in the UK legislation, generally involving a period of either 70 or 50 years from the end of the calendar year in which a given event occurred. The present position is the result of EU Directives, with the first one enacted in 1993 and implemented in the UK in 1995.[314] In the following paragraphs, references to the 70- or 50-year periods should be understood as references to these formulae. The use of 'the end of the calendar year' as part of the formula is to avoid disputes as to precisely when the event in question occurred. With literary, dramatic, musical, and artistic works, the copyright period is tied first to the lifetime of the author, with the 70-year period added on after his death (*post mortem auctoris*). This reflects recognition of the author's 'natural' right of property in his work, but it continues to be the period even where the copyright in the work is in other hands.[315] The extension of copyright beyond the author's lifetime was initially conceived as a form of protection for his family and descendants, but again the period applies even when the copyright has been transferred to others. With the media copyrights, there are shorter periods, such as a 50-year period, not tied to any particular lifetime, but rather to the making or publication of the work; reflecting views that works of this kind involve a lesser creative endeavour on the part of the individuals concerned; that the first owner will usually be a company, making it impossible to calculate the term by reference to a human life; and that the protection is essentially to support investment rather than creativity. The UK position parallels the rest of the EU, since the rules on copyright terms were harmonised by the 1993 Directive but, outside the Union, different copyright terms may apply in other jurisdictions. This can have the effect that a work which is in copyright in the EU may not have it in other countries, and vice versa. This can create problems for the international flow of copyright products.

Economic rights in literary, dramatic, musical, and artistic works

3.114   All literary, dramatic, musical, and artistic works, published or unpublished, enjoy the economic rights conferred by copyright—that is, the rights of reproduction, distribution, rental and lending, public performance, communication to the public, and adaptation (see further para 4.9)—until the end of the 70-year period after the author's death (see Figure 3.1).[316]

Figure 3.1 Author copyright table

70 years
Creation - Author's death—year end - - - - - - - - - - - - - - - - - - Copyright expires

Under the pre-1988 Act law, unpublished works could enjoy copyright for as long as they remained unpublished, which might mean in perpetuity. But under the 1988 Act there is now no possibility of a new perpetual copyright coming into existence. The perpetual copyrights which existed under pre-1988 legislation have had dates of expiry placed upon them (generally the end of the 50-year period from the end of the year when the 1988 Act came into force, meaning that there could be a sort of copyright bonanza on 1 January 2040).[317] There is one exception to this, found in provisions added at a very late stage of the parliamentary progress of the 1988 Act, giving the Hospital for Sick Children, Great Ormond Street, London, a right without limit of time to a royalty in respect of public performances, commercial publications, broadcasting or use in a cable programme service of JM Barrie's Peter Pan, notwithstanding that the copyright therein expired on 31 December 1987. Although the 1988 Act does not preserve the work's copyright in so many words, the effect is much as though it had.[318]

---

[314] Directive 93/98/EEC of 29 October 1993 harmonising the term of protection for copyright and certain related rights implemented by the Duration of Copyright and Rights in Performances Regulations 1995 (SI 1995/3297). The Directive was replaced by a consolidated version, European Parliament and Council Directive 2006/116/EC, which was amended by Directive 2011/77/EU.

[315] On economic justifications for the copyright terms, see W Landes and R Posner, *Economic Structure of Intellectual Property Law* (2004), Ch 8. See also the still thought-provoking K Puri, 'The term of copyright protection: is it too long in the wake of new technologies?' [1990] EIPR 12.

[316] CDPA 1988, s 12(1), (2).   [317] CDPA 1988, Sch 1, para 12.   [318] CDPA 1988, s 301 and Sch 6.

Question

If the author of a book published in 2010 was born in June 1956, when will the copyright in the book expire?

Computer-generated works

3.115   Where a literary, dramatic, musical, or artistic work is computer-generated (see para 3.100), the copyright expires at the end of the period of 50 years from the end of the calendar year in which the work was made,[319] as there is no reason to attach the work to the lifetime of any particular person.

Anonymous and pseudonymous works

3.116   Anonymity and pseudonymity (see paras 3.101–3.102) affect only the period for which the copyright endures. The copyright continues until the end of the 70-year period following the end of the calendar year in which either (1) the work was made; or (2) the work was first made available to the public.[320] But if the identity of the author becomes known before the end of those periods, then the usual period of that person's lifetime plus 70 years applies.[321] Literary, dramatic, and musical works are made available to the public by performance in public or by being communicated to the public, although this definition does not exhaust the possible ways in which such works are made available to the public.[322] In the case of an artistic work, making available to the public includes exhibition in public, showing in public a film including the work, and communication to the public.[323] No account is taken, however, of any unauthorised act.[324]

 Discussion point   For answer guidance visit **www.oup.com/uk/brown5e**.

A person is copying and collecting with a view to publication the verses engraved on tombstones in local churchyards, most of which appear to have been erected in the 19th or early 20th centuries. The verses are otherwise unpublished and of unknown authorship. What steps should the collector take to avoid any danger of being sued for copyright infringement?

Works of joint authorship and co-authorship

3.117   The term of copyright for a work of joint authorship (see paras 3.85–3.92) is determined by reference, where appropriate, to the date of death of the author who died last.[325] Copyright in the jointly authored work will therefore expire 70 years from the end of the calendar year in which there occurred the death of the author who died last of the group of joint authors. Where the identity of one or more of the authors is known, and the identity of one or more is not, copyright expires 70 years from the end of the calendar year in which died the last of the authors whose identity is known.[326] Songs which are set out as 'co-authored works' in the statute (para 3.93) are treated in the same way as a work of joint authorship for the purposes of duration.[327]

 Question

When will the copyright in this book expire? How do the relevant rules affect moral rights?

---

[319] CDPA 1988, s 12(7).   [320] CDPA 1988, s 12(3).   [321] CDPA 1988, s 12(4).   [322] CDPA 1988, s 12(5)(a).
[323] CDPA 1988, s 12(5)(b).   [324] CDPA 1988, s 12(5) proviso.   [325] CDPA 1988, s 12(8)(a)(i).
[326] CDPA 1988, s 12(8)(a)(ii).   [327] CDPA 1988, s 12(8).

Term of Crown copyright in literary, dramatic, musical, and artistic works

3.118   Where the monarch is entitled to the copyright in a literary, dramatic, musical, or artistic work, it subsists until the end of the period of 125 years from the end of the calendar year in which the work was made or, if the work is published commercially before the end of the period of 75 years from the end of the calendar year in which it was made, until the end of the period of 50 years from the end of the calendar year in which it was first so published.[328] The 125-year period is therefore a maximum which may be shortened by commercial publication during the first 75 years after the work is made. Commercial publication consists in issuing copies of the work to the public at a time when copies made in advance of the receipt of orders are generally available to the public, or when the work is made available to the public by means of an electronic retrieval system.[329] Crown copyright in sound recordings and films is of the same duration as for other owners.

 Discussion point   For answer guidance visit **www.oup.com/uk/brown5e**.

Why is Crown copyright in literary, dramatic, musical, and artistic works not subject to the usual rules on duration?

Crown copyright in Acts and Measures

3.119   The Crown copyright in Acts of Parliament, the Scottish Parliament, and the Welsh and Northern Ireland Assemblies, and Measures of the General Synod of the Church of England subsists until the end of the period of 50 years from the end of the calendar year in which Royal Assent or approval by Her Majesty in Council was given.[330]

Term of parliamentary copyright

3.120   Copyright in literary, dramatic, musical, or artistic works made by or under the direction or control of the Houses of Parliament subsists until the end of the period of 50 years from the end of the calendar year in which the work was made.[331] Where copyright has subsisted in a parliamentary Bill, it ceases when the Bill receives the Royal Assent or is withdrawn or rejected or at the end of the parliamentary session.[332] There are similar provisions for Bills of the Scottish Parliament and the Northern Ireland and Welsh Assemblies.[333] If a Bill is rejected by the House of Lords but may be presented for Royal Assent by virtue of the Parliament Acts 1911 and 1949, copyright will continue to subsist in it notwithstanding the Lords' rejection.[334]

Films

3.121   Film copyright expires at the end of the period of 70 years from the end of the calendar year in which the death occurs of the last to die of (1) the principal director; (2) the screenplay author; (3) the dialogue author; or (4) the composer of music specially created for and used in the film.

If the identity of one or more of these persons is unknown, but the identity of another is not, the relevant death date is that of the last whose identity is known. If the identity of none of these persons is known, the film copyright subsists as follows:[335]

(1)   until the end of the 70-year period from the end of the calendar year in which the work is first made; or

(2)   if, during period (1) it is made available to the public by being shown in or communicated to the public, 70 years from the end of the calendar year in which it is first so made available.

---

[328] CDPA 1988, s 163(3).   [329] CDPA 1988, s 175(2).   [330] CDPA 1988, s 164(2).   [331] CDPA 1988, s 165(3).
[332] CDPA 1988, s 166(5).   [333] CDPA 1988, ss 166A(2), 166B(2), 166C(2), and 166D(2).   [334] CDPA 1988, s 166(5) proviso.
[335] CDPA 1988, s 13B(2)–(4).

In determining whether a film has been made available to the public, no account is taken of any unauthorised act.[336] Finally, if there is no principal director, screenplay or dialogue author, or composer of music specially for the film, copyright expires at the end of 50 years from the end of the calendar year in which the film was made.[337]

> **? Question**
>
> Remind yourself of who is to be treated as the author of a film (para 3.95). Are there any anomalies when you compare these rules with the rules about the duration of film copyright?

Sound recordings

3.122   The copyright in a sound recording subsists as follows:[338]

(1)   until the end of the 50-year period from the end of the calendar year in which the work is first made; or

(2)   if it is published before the end of period (1), 70 years from the end of the calendar year in which it is first published; or

(3)   if, during period (1) it is not published but is made available to the public by being played in or communicated to the public, 70 years from the end of the calendar year in which it is first so made available.

See Figure 3.2.

Figure 3.2 Sound recordings table

In determining whether a sound recording has been published, played in, or communicated to the public, no account is taken of any unauthorised act.[339]

3.123   The current term of copyright in sound recordings is the result of a recent and rather controversial term extension in the EU. In July 2008 the European Commission published a proposal for a Directive to extend the term for sound recordings from 50 to 95 years.[340] The primary incentive behind this proposal was to improve the position of performers (see paras 7.43–7.44). However, it faced strong opposition from academics, who questioned the potential for benefit to performers.[341] Although the UK was originally

---

[336] CDPA 1988, s 13B(6) proviso.   [337] CDPA 1988, s 13B(9).

[338] CDPA 1988, s 13A(2) as amended by Reg 8 Copyright and Duration of Rights in Performances Regulations 2013/1782.

[339] CDPA 1988, s 13A(2) proviso.

[340] The proposal is accessible at http://eur-lex.europa.eu/LexUriServ/LexUriServ.do?uri=COM:2008:0464:FIN:EN:PDF.

[341] Centre for Intellectual Property Policy and Management, Centre for Intellectual Property and Information Law, Institute for Information Law and Max Planck Institute for Intellectual Property, Competition and Tax Law, 'The Proposed Directive for a Copyright Term Extension—A Backward-Looking Package', Letter to the Commission (27 October 2008).

against any term extension,[342] it later became a strong supporter.[343] The proposal led to a Directive which extended the term of protection for sound recordings from 50 years to 70 years,[344] and was implemented in the UK on 1 November 2013.[345]

Broadcasts

3.124   Copyright in a broadcast expires 50 years from the end of the year in which the broadcast is made.[346] Copyright in a repeat broadcast expires at the same time as the copyright in the original broadcast.[347]

Published editions

3.125   The publisher's copyright in the typographical arrangement of published editions of literary, dramatic, and musical works expires 25 years from the end of the calendar year in which the edition was first published.[348]

Discussion point   For answer guidance visit **www.oup.com/uk/brown5e**.

Why is the publisher's copyright in its typographical arrangement so much shorter than other copyrights?

Expiry of copyright term in a single product

3.126   One issue relating to the term of copyright is whether when a multiplicity of copyrights exists in a single product (eg the basic media right, depending on which medium the product is using, and the right or rights which subsist in the author work or works embodied in the product) they should all expire together, at least as regards reproduction of similar products. This issue results from the categorisation of works (see para 3.5) in that many products in the copyright domain are likely to enjoy more than one copyright (eg a sound recording). Each one of these rights may then have a different owner (see paras 3.82–3.112) and consequently, a different term of protection. The resulting variability in the term of protection in different elements of a single product can mean that while one element of the product is in the public domain, another is not. Several undesirable effects are possible: damage to the remaining copyright interest in the work in question; inhibition of perfectly lawful and appropriate free use of the product; or simply confused people. A question of policy may therefore be whether, when a product enjoys multiple copyrights, these ought to stand and fall together, at least in relation to products of the kind in question; and this, whatever the duration of the rights may finally be.

Optimal duration of copyright

3.127   As seen above, copyright is not unlimited in duration, and works which fall out of copyright at the end of their term are available to all for any purpose. However, one ongoing issue is what is the optimal duration of copyright. It is clear from economic studies that the precise duration of copyright is not governed by the

---

[342] See *Gower's Review of Intellectual Property* (2006), at paras 4.20–4.47 therein and the government's reply to the Committee in Media Culture and Sport Report (Cmnd 718).

[343] Speech by Andy Burnham at Creator's Conference, 11 December 2008 (http://webarchive.nationalarchives.gov.uk/+/http://www.culture.gov.uk/reference_library/minister_Speeches/5685.aspx).

[344] Directive 2011/77/EU.   [345] Copyright and Duration of Rights in Performances Regulations 2013/1782.

[346] CDPA 1988, s 14(2).   [347] CDPA 1988, s 14(5). See para 3.80 for copyright in repeats.   [348] CDPA 1988, s 15.

need to incentivise production with the promise of a long-lasting reward should the product be successful. Production is generally governed by other incentives from the point of view of creative authors, and by much shorter-term calculations of likely return by copyright entrepreneurs. On the other hand, the length of copyright enables the author and the entrepreneur to take benefit from the development of new markets through changing technology (eg the emergence of the home video and DVD markets for films) and so encourages (and enables) them to take greater investment risks with new works only a very few of which will become such long-term winners. This is also true of the income generated by successful products over the lifetime of a successful product, whether or not there is relevant technological change. Empirical and economic analysis of the effects of the copyright term on entrepreneurial behaviour over time could be helpful in the formation of policy in this area.

3.128   On the basis of the economic literature to date, however, it seems quite likely that such a study would show the impact of the copyright term on economic behaviour and initial decision-making about creation and publication to be negligible, whatever the length of time involved, as long as it extends beyond the period needed to ensure 'lead time' (ie the benefit of being first to market with a particular product), and consequent opportunity to earn a profit on the investment made. Much more difficult would be the question of how to measure and assess the effects of works falling out of copyright at the expiry of term. This question would be raised in particular if it was decided, for example, to create a copyright of indefinite duration to support a world in which copyright owners contracted directly and online with would-be users for access to and use of works.

3.129   What then is the value, economically, socially, and intellectually, of works entering the public domain because they no longer enjoy copyright? One imagines that for the great majority of works it is nil or negligible; is there a point of time at which the enduring value of a relatively small number of works should be taken out of the ordinary interplay of market and social conditions (by giving them a long-enduring copyright) which otherwise produces a price for them as between supplier and customer? How far can copyright be analogised with, say, the antiques, paintings, or books markets, where some (but not many) very old works can command extremely high prices despite the absence of any particular legal protection of their exclusivity? Or do old works derive their value in these markets from uniqueness or rarity, and/or associations (eg famous former owners), whereas in the digital environment it is increasingly unlikely that any manifestation of a work will have that quality of uniqueness or rarity?

 Copyright and Brexit

Although the current UK copyright framework in relation to certain elements of authorship (eg film), and the scheme of duration of rights (Term Directive), is framed in light of EU directives and CJEU jurisprudence, the implementation of such directives will be preserved in UK law as retained EU law under the powers in the EU Withdrawal Act 2018. Both the UK and EU member states are party to the main international treaties which are applicable to the current underlying framework and under which the main obligations in this area arise (eg Berne Convention, WCT, TRIPS). Consequently, in a 'no-deal' scenario, the relationship between the UK and EU member states will be governed through the principles of such treaties (see para 2.20). The UK government 'no-deal' guidance notes that as a

---

[349] UK Government, 'Copyright if there's no Brexit deal' (24 September 2018) www.gov.uk/government/publications/copyright-if-theres-no-brexit-deal.

[350] UK Government, 'Changes to copyright law in the event of no deal' (26 October 2018) www.gov.uk/government/publications/changes-to-copyright-law-in-the-event-of-no-deal.

result, 'the scope of protection for copyright works in the UK and for UK works abroad will remain largely unchanged'.[349] However, in case of a 'no-deal' Brexit, 'UK legislation will be amended to remove preferential treatment of EEA works and apply the same general rule on duration as for non-EEA works' but 'this will not have any immediate impact on copyright duration offered in the UK for UK, EEA, and third country works'.[350]

Further reading

Books

L Bently, B Sherman, D Gangjee and P Johnson, *Intellectual Property Law* (5th edn, 2018), Chs 3–5, 7

N Caddick et al (eds), *Copinger & Skone James on Copyright* (17th edn, 2019), Chs 3, 4, 6

D Llewelyn and T Aplin, *Cornish, Llewelyn and Aplin Intellectual Property:patents, Copyright, Trade Marks and Allied Rights* (9th edn, 2019), Chs 11, 20.1

E Rosati, *Originality in EU Copyright: Full Harmonization through Case Law* (2013)

Multimedia

T Aplin, *Copyright Law in the Digital Society: The Challenges of Multimedia* (2005)

I Stamatoudi, *Copyright and Multimedia Products: A Comparative Analysis* (2002)

Musical works

S Frith and L Marshall, *Music and Copyright* (2nd edn, 2004)

Artistic works

Y Gendreau, *Copyright and Photographs: An International Survey* (1999)

C Mihalos, *The Law of Photography and Digital Images* (2004)

S Stokes, *Art and Copyright* (2012)

Authorship

M van Eechoud, *The Work of Authorship* (2014)

L Zemer, *The Idea of Authorship in Copyright* (2007)

Employment and universities

A Monotti with S Ricketson, *Universities and Intellectual Property: Ownership and Exploitation* (2003)

Articles

Works

J Pila, 'An intentional view of the copyright work' (2008) 71 MLR 535

Originality

HL MacQueen, 'The legal definition of authorship and the scrolls' in JJ Collins and TH Lim (eds), *Oxford Handbook of the Dead Sea Scrolls* (2010)

E Rosati, 'Originality in a work, or a work of originality: the effects of the Infopaq decision' [2011] EIPR 746

A Waisman, 'Revisiting originality' [2009] EIPR 370

Musical works

A Rahmatian, 'Music and creativity as perceived by copyright law' [2005] IPQ 267

Artistic works

J Pila, 'The "Star Wars" copyright claim: an ambivalent view of the Empire' (2012) 128 LQR 15

M Rushton, 'An economic approach to copyright in works of artistic craftsmanship' [2003] IPQ 255

T Rychlicki, 'Legal questions about illegal art' (2008) 3 JIPLP 393

Authorship and ownership

R Arnold, 'Reflections on "The Triumph of Music": copyrights and performers' rights in music' [2010] IPQ 153

WR Cornish, 'Conserving culture and copyright: a partial history' (2009) 13 Edinburgh Law Review 8

J Dickenson et al, 'Creative machines: ownership of copyright in content created by artificial intelligence applications' [2017] EIPR 457

J Phillips, 'Authorship, ownership, wikiship: copyright in the twenty-first century' (2008) 3 JIPLP 788

J Pila, 'Who owns the intellectual property rights in academic work?' [2010] EIPR 609

Crown copyright

S Saxby, 'Crown copyright regulation in the UK—is the debate still alive?' (2005) 13(3) IJL & IT 299

Parliamentary copyright

N Cox, 'Copyright in statutes, regulations and judicial decisions in common law jurisdictions: public ownership or commercial enterprise?' (2006) 27(3) Statute Law Review 185

Term

C Angelopoulos, 'The myth of European term harmonisation—27 public domains for 27 Member States' [2012] IIC 567

N Helberger et al, 'Never forever: why extending the term of protection for sound recordings is a bad idea' [2008] EIPR 174

Copyright 3: economic rights and infringement

Introduction

Scope and overview of chapter

4.1 This chapter considers the rights which the owner of copyright enjoys while the copyright endures, apart from the moral rights of authors discussed in Chapter 6. The rights to be considered here are usually known as *'economic rights'*, because, unlike authors' moral rights, they may be exploited by transferring them to others or licensing others to use them for a price (paras 6.27–6.54). The basic scheme of the Copyright, Designs and Patents Act 1988 (CDPA 1988) is to define a group of what it calls *'acts restricted by copyright'*. This concept has two functions:

- one is to define those acts by others in relation to the copyright work which the right holder can challenge and stop by *court action*;

- the other is to tell persons who wish to use works the copyright in which is owned by another whether or not that use requires the permission of the right holder. In other words, the restricted acts define the ground on which right holder and would-be user will *negotiate the terms and conditions* on which the use will be permitted.

An important point of which we need to remind ourselves constantly is that in practical terms copyright is useless to its owner unless others want to perform the various restricted acts, whereupon it becomes the basis upon which a bargain may be struck between the two sides. It may be that the owner has no wish to bargain, and expressly or impliedly gives carte blanche to users. On the other hand, the owner who does not wish to bargain may simply want to prevent anyone else from disseminating the work, in which case the would-be user's remedy, if any, lies in competition law (for which, see Chapter 20).

4.2

> ### Learning objectives
>
> By the end of this chapter you should be able to describe and explain:
>
> - the general nature of the economic rights conferred by copyright upon its owners;
>
> - the infringement of economic rights;
>
> - the specific economic rights (to make copies, issue copies to the public; rent or lend to the public; perform, show, or play in public; communication to the public; make adaptations).

4.3   The chapter opens with a general discussion of the rights flowing from ownership of copyright and the international framework which underpins them, noting in particular the influence upon UK law of a number of European Union (EU) Directives. It next elaborates upon the nature of economic rights, and the general principles pertaining to infringement, before turning to the detailed rules on each economic right in the CDPA 1988. It discusses authorisation of infringement (accessory liability) in relation to these economic rights, and finally considers secondary infringement of copyright. So, the rest of the chapter looks like this:

- International and European developments (4.4–4.8)
- Economic rights in general (4.9–4.11)
- Economic rights and primary infringements: general principles (4.12–4.22)
- Restricted acts and primary infringement: detail (4.23–4.69)
- Authorisation of infringement (4.70–4.79)
- Secondary infringement of copyright (4.80–4.82).

International and European developments

Berne Convention

4.4   In addition to the non-transferable moral rights that are discussed in Chapter 6 (paras 6.4–6.22), the Berne Convention 1886 recognises *transferable economic rights* enabling copyright owners to control the following activities in relation to their works:

- translation (Art 8);
- reproduction (Arts 9, 14);
- public performance and communication (Arts 11, 11*ter*, 14);
- broadcasting (Art 11*bis*);
- adaptation (Art 12).

Economic rights are so known because it is essentially through these rights that copyright can become a source of income for its owner, by selling them or licensing others to perform the acts restricted by the rights. Moral rights, on the other hand, cannot be transferred to persons other than the author of the work, and are essentially linked to the author's interests in the work as an expression of an individual's personality.

    Question

How may economic and moral rights be distinguished? How would you characterise resale right in relation to these two (see further Chapter 6)?

TRIPS and WCT

4.5   Modern international activity has, unsurprisingly, focused almost entirely on economic rights, and the Trade-Related Aspects of Intellectual Property Rights (TRIPS) Agreement of 1994 expressly states that its members have no rights or obligations under Article 6*bis* of Berne,[1] that is, the moral rights Article. TRIPS did require members to provide commercial rental rights in respect of 'at least' computer programs and

---

[1] TRIPS, Art 9(1).

films,[2] and this was also laid down in the World Intellectual Property Organization (WIPO) Copyright Treaty of 1996 (WCT).[3] The Treaty further provided for a *distribution, or first sale, right*[4] and a *public communication right*. This was to be without prejudice to the relevant provisions of Berne.[5]

Rome Convention, TRIPS, and WPPT

4.6   Economic rights in neighbouring or media works were initially dealt with in the Rome Convention 1961, which enables producers of phonograms (sound recordings) to authorise or prohibit direct or indirect reproduction of their products.[6] Broadcasters have likewise the right to authorise or prohibit re-broadcasting, fixation, reproduction of fixations in certain circumstances, and public communication, again in certain circumstances, of broadcasts.[7] TRIPS and the WIPO Performances and Phonograms Treaty 1996 (WPPT) restated these minimum rights for phonogram producers,[8] while the WPPT added distribution, commercial rental, and 'making available to the public' rights.[9]

EU Directives

4.7   The following EU Directives contain provisions relevant to copyright ownership and economic rights:

- Software Directive 2009 (Art 4);[10]
- Rental and Lending Right Directive 2006;[11]
- Satellite Broadcasting Directive 1993;
- Database Directive 1996 (Art 5);
- Information Society (InfoSoc) Directive 2001 (Arts 2–4).

Essentially these implement in Europe the policies also apparent in the development of the international instruments described in the previous two paragraphs (paras 4.5–4.6), requiring member states to have distribution, rental, and public communication rights. All made necessary significant changes to the UK CDPA 1988, as will emerge from the account of UK law from para 4.9 onwards.

4.8   A specifically European initiative is the inclusion of temporary or transient reproduction as an act restricted by copyright, which as yet has not been agreed at the global level. Attempts to include a provision of this kind in the WCT 1996 failed. First introduced in the EU in respect of software, so that copyright owners could regulate the use of programs in computers,[12] it was extended next to databases,[13] and now covers all author works, phonograms, films, and broadcasts.[14] But the UK did not have to make any change here, as the concept of infringement by transient copying had already been introduced in the 1988 Act.[15] See further at para 4.35.

Key points on international and European developments

- The Berne Convention recognises two groups of rights:
  - the economic (basis on which copyright can be used to make money);
  - the moral (recognition of author's personality claims).

---

[2] TRIPS, Art 11.   [3] WCT, Art 7.   [4] WCT, Art 6.

[5] WCT, Art 8, referring to Berne Convention, Arts 11, 11*ter*, and 14—see para 4.4.   [6] Rome Convention 1961, Art 10.

[7] Rome Convention, Art 13. See also TRIPS, Art 14(3).   [8] TRIPS, Art 14(2); WPPT, Art 11.   [9] WPPT, Arts 12–14.

[10] Directive 2009/24/EC amended and consolidated Directive 91/250/EEC. Unless stated otherwise, all references will be to the 2009 directive.

[11] Directive 2006/115/EC consolidated and replaced Directive 92/100/EEC. Unless stated otherwise, all references will be to the 2006 directive.

[12] Software Directive 2009, Art 4(1).   [13] Database Directive 1996, Art 5(a).   [14] InfoSoc Directive 2001, Art 2.

[15] CDPA 1988, s 17(6).

- The Berne Convention has been supplemented with respect to media works by the Rome Convention.

- The economic rights have been the subject of most international activity in modern times, through TRIPS, the WCT, and the WPPT.

- Much of this more recent international activity has been concerned with new technology subject matter such as computer programs and databases, and new rights such as the rental right.

- Within the EU, the developing global framework has been reflected and sometimes led by initiatives embodied in Directives aimed at harmonising the laws of the member states.

Economic rights in general

Primary restricted acts

4.9 There are six exclusive economic rights arising from ownership of the copyright in a protected work. The restricted acts for which a licence must be sought if they are to be lawfully carried out by a person other than the copyright owner may be listed as follows:[16]

- copying (reproduction right);

- issuing copies of the work to the public (first sale or distribution right);

- renting or lending the work to the public (rental/lending right);

- performing, showing or playing the work in public (public performance right);

- communicating the work to the public (public communication right);

- making an adaptation of the work (adaptation right).

4.10 The restricted acts may be described as *methods of reproducing the work*. Defining their scope is important for the copyright owner in two main ways: first, in determining the areas in which generally his licence must be sought by others wishing to use the work; and, secondly, in deciding when action may be taken in respect of infringement of copyright. In addition, a person who without right to do so authorises another to do any of the restricted acts is himself an infringer as well.[17]

 Question

List the ways in which copyright in a work may be infringed.

 Restricted acts and Brexit

Although the current copyright framework in relation to restricted acts is framed in light of EU directives and Court of Justice of the European Union (CJEU) jurisprudence (with most exclusive rights having been harmonised), the implementation of such directives will be preserved in UK law as retained EU law under the powers in the EU Withdrawal Act 2018. Both the UK and EU member states are party to the main international treaties which are applicable to the current underlying framework

[16] CDPA 1988, s 16(1).   [17] CDPA 1988, s 16(2).

of economic rights, and under which the main obligations in the area arise (eg Berne Convention, WCT, TRIPS). Consequently, in a 'no-deal' scenario, the relationship between the UK and EU member states will be governed through the principles of such treaties (see para 2.20). The UK government 'no-deal' guidance notes that as a result, 'the scope of protection for copyright works in the UK and for UK works abroad will remain largely unchanged'. [18]

However, in a 'no-deal' scenario, there could be scope in the future for the UK to substantially diverge from EU law on some specific issues, albeit while complying with relevant international frameworks. One example is in the assessment of infringement of economic rights, the test for substantial part using the author's own intellectual creation standard, where the UK courts have only just begun to adapt the interpretation offered in recent CJEU decisions (paras 4.13–4.20). They may choose not to continue to do so, since the UK will not be bound by CJEU decisions in a 'no-deal' Brexit.

Secondary infringement

4.11   In addition, *dealing in infringing copies* of a work—for example, selling, importing, or exporting copies made without the licence of the copyright owner—may also be an infringement of copyright. This type of infringement is termed *secondary infringement*, the contrast being with the *primary infringements* constituted by the six restricted acts listed previously.[19] It is unlikely that a copyright owner will grant licences to deal in infringing copies, and the nature of secondary infringement is distinct in various other ways, in particular in requiring that the infringer should know or have reason to believe that he was dealing in infringing copies. There is nothing comparable in respect of the primary infringements, as unauthorised performances of the restricted acts will henceforth be called. With these, liability is strict and not dependent on the knowledge or fault of the infringer.

 Question

What is the difference between primary and secondary infringement of copyright?

Economic rights and primary infringements: general principles

4.12   In this section the economic rights as defined by UK law are discussed in more detail. The principal focus is on the six restricted acts and infringing authorisation thereof, with secondary infringement given relatively brief treatment after that. The restricted acts will be considered mainly in the context of infringement of copyright (ie the primary infringements), leaving the question of exploitation by transfer and, in particular, licensing to Chapter 6. The six restricted acts each attract their own law, which will be set out in detail later. But there are some concepts which are applicable to each of them, and which need to be discussed first.

General principles: (1) taking of the whole or a substantial part

4.13   In general and subject to some exceptions, it is not necessary that the whole of the copyright work should be taken by the infringer. Infringement may be constituted as much by the doing of an act in relation to a substantial part of a work as by the doing of such acts in relation to the whole of the work.[20] It is also

---

[18] UK Government, 'Copyright if there's no Brexit deal' (24 September 2018) www.gov.uk/government/publications/copyright-if-theres-no-brexit-deal.

[19] See CDPA 1988, ss 22–26, headed 'Secondary infringement of copyright'.   [20] CDPA 1988, s 16(3)(a).

specifically provided that copying in relation to a film or broadcast includes making a photograph of the whole or any substantial part of any image forming part of the work.[21] It follows that if what is done is in relation to an insubstantial part of a work there is no infringement.[22] In *Nova Productions Ltd v Mazooma Games Ltd*, Jacob LJ emphasised that a finding that there had been some copying of an earlier work was 'a starting point for a finding of infringement, not the end point'. If the copying is of 'small, unimportant details', rather than of a substantial part of the earlier work, there is no infringement.[23] The EU Directives, in several provisions, also restrict reproduction of works 'in whole or in part'[24] and in this respect, the CJEU case law has harmonised that 'parts of the work' are protected as being original in the sense of the 'author's own intellectual creation' (for the harmonised standard for originality after the decision in *Infopaq*, see paras 3.27–3.28). As such, the British case law that has been developed over the years is discussed first and then the EU developments and implications.

Substantial part: quality of what is copied

4.14   British case law has suggested a number of, not always consistent, approaches to the question of what constitutes a substantial part that are not always consistent. For instance, what constitutes a substantial part of a work 'depends much more on the quality than on the quantity of what he has taken';[25] hence, an extract of some 28 bars lasting about 50 seconds from a musical work which took about four minutes to play was held to be a substantial part because it constituted that section which would ensure recognition of the work by the public.[26] But to be a substantial part the section taken does not have to be a copyright work in its own right: in arguments about infringement, the issue is not whether the component taken would have copyright in its own right, but rather whether that component is a substantial part of a larger, copyright, work.[27]

4.15   The emphasis on quality rather than quantity of taking does not mean that the latter has always been irrelevant, however.[28] There is some authority to the effect that separate acts of copying of what are in themselves insubstantial parts may be taken as a whole to constitute substantial taking, either as acts in relation to a serial work, such as a newspaper treated as a single copyright work, or as simply a single act spread over time.[29] Substantiality has also been tested by looking at what was the matter of consequence to users of the original work.[30]

■ *Ludlow Music Inc v Robbie Williams* [2001] FSR 19

In 1961 Woody Guthrie composed a song called 'New York Town', containing the line, 'Every good man gets a little hard luck sometimes'. LM owned the copyright in this work. In 1973 Loudon Wainwright III composed a parody of Guthrie's song, entitled 'I Am the Way (New York Town)', obtaining LM's permission to do so and later assigning the copyright in the parody to LM. The fourth verse of the parody consisted of the line 'Every Son of God gets a little hard luck sometime', repeated three times and followed by 'Especially when

---

[21] CDPA 1988, s 17(4); see *Spelling Goldberg v BPC Publishing* [1981] RPC 283 (CA).

[22] *Warwick Film Productions Ltd v Eisinger* [1969] 1 Ch 508.

[23] *Nova Productions Ltd v Mazooma Games Ltd* [2007] RPC 25 (CA) at para 26 for both points.

[24] See, eg, InfoSoc Directive 2001, Art 2; Software Directive 2009, Art 4(1)(a).

[25] *Ladbroke (Football) Ltd v William Hill (Football) Ltd* [1964] 1 WLR 273 per Lord Reid at 276.

[26] *Hawkes & Son Ltd v Paramount Film Services* [1934] Ch 593 (CA).

[27] *Ladbroke (Football) Ltd v William Hill (Football) Ltd* [1964] 1 WLR 273 per Lord Reid at 276; to like effect, Lord Hodson at 285, Lord Devlin at 290, and Lord Pearce at 293. The context is the component parts of a football pools coupon. See also *Law Society of Upper Canada v CCH Canadian Ltd* [2004] 1 SCR 339.

[28] *Sillitoe v McGraw Hill Book Co* [1983] FSR 545.

[29] *Cate v Devon and Exeter Constitutional Newspaper Co* (1889) 40 Ch D 500; *Electronic Techniques (Anglia) Ltd v Critchley Components Ltd* [1997] FSR 401. See also the provisions for such infringement of the *sui generis* database right (paras 7.19–7.20).

[30] *Express Newspapers v Liverpool Daily Post and Echo* [1985] FSR 306 per Whitford J at 311.

he goes around saying he's the way'. In 1998 RW composed and recorded a song entitled 'Jesus in a Camper Van', containing the lines 'I suppose even the Son of God/Gets it hard sometimes/Especially when he goes round/Saying I am the way'. This was repeated, then the first two lines were repeated twice. The Wainwright parody was brought to RW's attention, but copyright negotiations between him and RW were unsuccessful.

LM sued RW for infringement. It was held that 'Jesus in a Camper Van' took its central idea, that the Son of God attracted bad luck by going around saying 'I am the way', from 'I Am the Way (New York Town)', and embodied it in virtually identical words. This was sufficiently substantial copying to be infringement.

Discussion point   For answer guidance visit **www.oup.com/uk/brown5e**.

Does this case go too far in its use of the concept of 'copying of a substantial part' towards protecting the idea rather than the expression of a work?

4.16   On the other hand, where the taking is only of the idea rather than the substance of the work, there is no infringement.[31] Similarly there is no protection for what is merely the style or technique with which a work is created.

■ *Norowzian v Arks Ltd (No 2)* [1999] FSR 79 (Rattee J) ChD; [2000] FSR 363 (CA)

A film entitled *Joy* showed a man dancing to music and produced its principal effects through the technique of 'jump cutting', 'whereby the editor excises pieces of the original film within a sequence of movements by the actor, with the result that on the edited version of the film he appears to have performed successively, without an interval, two movements that in reality could not have immediately succeeded each other . . . This gives the finished film . . . a surreal effect' (per Rattee J at 81). The allegedly infringing film was an advertisement for Guinness called *Anticipation* which used the same technique in showing a man dancing while waiting for his newly poured pint of Guinness to settle. It was held that *Anticipation* did not infringe *Joy*. Although there was a striking similarity of style and technique, no copyright subsisted in these elements. A choreographer also gave evidence that there was no particular similarity in the dance movements of the two films.[32]

Substantial part: quality that gives the copied part its originality

4.17   More recent case law from the UK has suggested that originality of the copied part is the main test to be applied. The House of Lords has held that generally the role played by the component in the allegedly infringing work is irrelevant, and that substantiality is related to the qualities that give the copied work its originality, or to the skill and labour involved.

■ *Designers Guild Ltd v Russell Williams (Textiles) Ltd* [2001] FSR 11 (HL)

DGL sued RWT for infringement of the copyright in its *Ixia* fabric design by the latter's *Marguerite* design.[33] The trial judge found that *Marguerite* had been copied from *Ixia*, and that the copying had been of a substantial part. The Court of Appeal, although unable to overturn the judge's finding of fact that there had been copying, reversed his decision on the basis that there had been no copying of a substantial part: the designs were not similar enough. The House of Lords agreed that the approach of the Court of Appeal had been wrong, and that in general the question of substantiality had to be tested only in relation to the

---

[31]   *Williamson Music Ltd v Pearson Partnership Ltd* [1987] FSR 97.

[32]   See further A Barron, 'The legal properties of film' (2004) 67 MLR 177.

[33]   The competing designs in the case are illustrated in colour at [2000] FSR 121 at 136 and 137.

copyright work, not the allegedly infringing work. The similarity or otherwise of the two designs, while relevant to the basic question of copying, was irrelevant to substantiality. Lord Hoffmann said:[34]

> Generally speaking, in cases of artistic copyright, the more abstract and simple the copied idea, the less likely it is to constitute a substantial part. Originality, in the sense of the contribution of the author's skill and labour, tends to lie in the detail with which the basic idea is presented. Copyright law protects foxes better than hedgehogs (para 26).

Lord Scott of Foscote distinguished between cases where an identifiable part of the whole of a work, but not the whole, had been copied, and those of what he called 'altered copying', where the copying relates to the whole of a work but has not been exact but rather with modifications. He proposed that in such cases, of which the present was one, the test of substantiality should be whether the infringer had incorporated a substantial part of the independent skill and labour contributed by the original author in creating the copyright work, and that for these purposes a comparison between the two designs was legitimate, albeit that once there had been found to be copying in such cases, it was almost inevitable that it would be found to be of a substantial part as well. Lord Millett criticised Lord Scott's distinction and emphasised the irrelevance of the copied design to the issue of substantiality. Lords Bingham of Cornhill and Hope of Craighead expressed no view other than that the Court of Appeal had illegitimately taken to itself the role of the trial judge in re-deciding the issue of substantiality.[35]

Discussion point   For answer guidance visit **www.oup.com/uk/brown5e**.

What does the *Designers Guild* case tell us about the meaning of substantiality in relation to infringement? What else may be learned from the cases described in the next two paragraphs?

4.18   The House of Lords also appeared to accept the relevance of the copyright owner's skill and labour to substantiality in the later case of:

■ *Newspaper Licensing Agency Ltd v Marks and Spencer plc* [2003] 1 AC 551

For the facts, see para 3.81. The question was, given that the typographical arrangement copyright in a newspaper applied only to the whole newspaper, and not to individual articles within the newspaper, whether the copying of an article from the newspaper was copying of a substantial part of the newspaper's typographical arrangement. The House of Lords held that it was not. In general, the quality relevant for the purposes of substantiality was the originality of, or skill and labour in, what had been copied. In typographical arrangement copyright as applied to newspapers, what mattered was the overall appearance of the newspaper, and Lord Hoffmann, giving the only reasoned speech, found it 'difficult to think of the skill and labour which has gone into the typographical arrangement of a newspaper being expressed in anything less than a full page' (para 23).

Substantial part: originality as in the 'author's own intellectual creation'

4.19   The provision on 'substantial part' in section 16(3) of the CDPA 1988 must be construed in conformity with the Information Society (InfoSoc) Directive 2001. The Directive in Article 2, titled 'reproduction right', does not mention 'substantial part' but prohibits reproduction 'in whole or in part' and must be interpreted in the same way throughout the EU.[36] The meaning of 'reproduction in part' has been considered by the CJEU.

---

[34] 'The fox knows many things, but the hedgehog knows one big thing' (Archilochus, 7th-century BCE Greek poet). See also Isaiah Berlin, *The Hedgehog and the Fox: An Essay on Tolstoy's View of History* (1953). See further *L Woolley Jewellers Ltd v A & A Jewellery Ltd* [2003] FSR 15 per Arden LJ at 259–60.

[35] For discussion of the issues raised by this case, see M Spence and T Endicott, 'Vagueness in the scope of copyright' (2005) 121 LQR 657.

[36] Case C-5/08 *Infopaq International A/S v Danske Dagblades Forening* [2009] ECDR 16, paras 27–29; Cases C-403/08 and C-429/08 *Football Association Premier League Ltd v QC Leisure, Murphy v Media Protection Services Ltd* [2012] 1 CMLR 29, para 154; C-355/12 *Nintendo v PC Box* [2014] ECDR 6, para 22.

■ **Case C-5/08** *Infopaq International A/S v Danske Dagblades Forening* **[2009] ECDR 16**

The case concerned an electronic newspaper cuttings firm which undertook a complex process of searching, scanning, and printing for the material which it then distributed to its customers. The European Court of Justice (ECJ) held that this data capture process, consisting in the particular case of storing an extract of a copyrighted work amounting to 11 words and subsequently printing it, amounted to 'reproduction in part' if the elements reproduced were an expression of the intellectual creation of their author. The Court emphasised that Article 2 had to be given a broad interpretation and stated:

> As regards the parts of a work, it should be borne in mind that there is nothing in Directive 2001/29 or any other relevant Directive indicating that those parts are to be treated any differently from the work as a whole. It follows that they are protected by copyright since, as such, they share the originality of the whole work . . . the various parts of a work thus enjoy protection under Art.2(a) of Directive 2001/29, provided that they contain elements which are the expression of the intellectual creation of the author of the work (paras 38–39).

The UK courts, in a number of cases, have considered the implications of this judgment on the assessment of 'substantial part'. In *SAS Institute Inc v World Programming Ltd*[37] Arnold J noted that the ECJ's approach in *Infopaq* is the same as that mentioned in the House of Lords' decision in *Newspaper Licensing Agency Ltd v Marks and Spencer plc* and stated:

> when considering whether a substantial part has been reproduced, it is necessary to focus upon what has been reproduced and to consider whether it expresses the author's own intellectual creation. To that extent, some dissection is not merely permissible, but required. On the other hand, the Court of Justice also held . . . that it is necessary to consider the cumulative effect of what has been reproduced (para 243).

This approach was confirmed by the Court of Appeal, with Lord Justice Lewison stating:[38]

> It has long been the position in domestic law that what is substantial is a question to be answered qualitatively rather than quantitatively. In *Infopaq* the court said that parts of a work are entitled to the same protection as the work as a whole. But the parts in question must 'contain elements which are the expression of the intellectual creation of the author of the work': [39]. This is now the test for determining whether a restricted act has been done in relation to a substantial part of a work (para 38).

■ *Newspaper Licensing Agency Ltd v Meltwater Holding BV* **[2010] EWHC 3099 (Ch); [2011] EWCA Civ 890 (CA)**

M, a commercial online media monitoring service, monitored publishers' websites using software which 'scraped' content, and recorded the position of every word in every article in an index. It then provided a monitoring report, based on the customer's search terms, of content comprising article headline, opening text and an extract from the article. N, who represented a number of newspapers, claimed infringement and argued that M required an end-user licence for its customers to use its services. Proudman J, with whom the Court of Appeal agreed, found that the extracts constituted a substantial part of the article and the receiving and using of monitoring reports by users was infringing. In following *Infopaq*, Proudman J stated:

> It therefore seems that the ECJ is saying that no distinction is to be made between the part and the whole, provided that the part contains 'elements which are the expression of the intellectual creation of the author'. There is no reference to 'substantial part' in art.2; the ECJ makes it clear that *originality rather than substantiality is the test to be applied to the part extracted*. As a matter of principle this is now the only real test (para 69).

> It seems to me wrong in principle to suggest that the court must conduct some sort of assessment of whether the extract is itself novel or artistically worthwhile. That would be tantamount to determining whether the extract is itself a literary work . . . (para 80).

> In my judgment the test of quality has been re-stated but for present purposes not significantly altered by *Infopaq* . . . The effect of the *Infopaq* case . . . is that *even a very small part of the original* may be protected

[37]   *SAS Institute Inc v World Programming Ltd* [2010] ECDR 15.
[38]   *SAS Institute Inc v World Programming Limited* [2013] EWCA Civ 1482 (CA).

by copyright if it demonstrates the stamp of individuality reflective of the creation of the author or authors of the article. Whether it does so remains a question of fact and degree in each case. It is often a matter of impression whether use has been made of those features of the article which, by reason of the skill and labour employed in its production, constitute it an original copyright work (paras 81–83; emphasis added).

From the above cases, it is clear that the originality of the copied part is the main test to be applied in this regard. While originality is to be understood in the sense of 'author's intellectual creation' (see paras 3.25–3.28), as confirmed by the Court of Appeal in *SAS*, the full impact, especially in practical terms, of this in the decision-making by the British courts remains to be seen.[39] The main implication of this shift appears to be an expansion in the scope of protection offered under copyright.

4.20   The provision on 'substantial part' in section 16(3) applies to both works that must be 'original' (literary, dramatic, musical, and artistic works) to attract copyright, as well as those works that do not not require originality (sound recordings, films, published editions, and broadcasts) for copyright subsistence (see paras 3.32–3.33). Should 'substantial part' in relation to the latter works be judged as per the 'author's own intellectual creation' standard or some other standard?

▪ *England and Wales Cricket Board v Tixdaq* [2016] EWHC 575 (Ch)

E owned copyright in TV broadcasts, and in films incorporated within such broadcasts, of certain cricket matches. T operated an app, amongst others, to which T's employees, contractors, and users uploaded clips of broadcasts of cricket matches lasting up to eight seconds. In assessing whether such clips were infringing, Arnold J considered the correct test for the assessment of what amounts to a substantial part of films and broadcasts. He noted that copyright in films and broadcasts being 'signal rights and not content rights', they are essentially 'entrepreneurial rights which protect the investment of the broadcaster and film producer respectively' (paras 58–62). They do not protect the creativity of an author, and that is why the 1988 Act does not require them to be original. The *Infopaq* test of author's own intellectual creation is inapplicable to films and broadcasts, which fall under Articles 2(d) and (e), because the test only applied to works in Article 2(a) of the InfoSoc Directive 2001. However, an approach similar to *Infopaq* should be applied, and this should reflect the rationale for protecting enterpreneurial rights, ie the investment made by the broadcaster or producer. He held that 'the correct test of substantiality is to consider the degree of reproduction both quantitatively and qualitatively, having regard to the extent to which the reproduction exploits the investment made by the broadcaster or producer.' (para 66) He proceeded on the basis that the works of broadcasts and films comprised 'each session of play' lasting around two hours or more, of which, quantitatively, eight seconds is not a large proportion. However, qualitatively, the clips constituted highlights of the matches (wickets taken, appeals refused, centuries scored) and replays of highlights, and showed something of interest and value. Consequently, they substantially exploited E's investment in producing the relevant broadcast and films.

General principles: (2) doing a restricted act directly or indirectly

4.21   The doing of a restricted act is infringement whether carried out directly or indirectly.[40] In other words, it is no answer to a claim of infringement to say that the restricted act was carried out, not in relation to the original work, but to some other work which was derived from it.

▪ *King Features Syndicate Inc v Kleeman Ltd* [1941] AC 417

Copyright in drawings of Popeye the Sailor Man was held to be infringed, although the defendant had copied not the drawings, but the plaintiffs' licensed dolls and brooches based on these drawings.

---

[39] See, eg, *John Kaldor Fabricmaker UK Limited v Lee Ann Fashions Limited* [2014] EWHC 3779 (IPEC), paras 12–22.
[40] CDPA 1988, s 16(3)(b).

■ *Sony Music v Easyinternetcafé Ltd* [2003] FSR 48

Internet cafés operated by E provided a CD-burning service for customers, which could include sound recordings downloaded from the internet by the customers. Fees were payable for this service. The owners of the copyright in sound recordings sued E for copyright infringement. It was held that E was guilty of indirect infringement by copying the copies which its customers had made. It was not an involuntary copier like an internet service provider or the recipient of a fax. It was irrelevant that the customer might be going on to use the CD for private and domestic purposes; E was in business for commercial gain.

Reverse engineering

4.22   *'Reverse engineering'* can thus be an infringement of copyright. This involves a party working back from a finished product to the copyright work which underlies it, and then evolving a work of his own. Formerly of greatest significance in the field of industrial design (see Part III), it also raises problems for the software industry, where competitive development is commonly achieved by such endeavours in relation to the embodiment of the program in a disk.[41] Often 'reverse engineering' will be carried out through a process of *'redesign'* or *'clean-room' procedure*, where the analysis of the original product and the briefing of the designers of the new one are kept rigorously apart within the organisation carrying out the work. It has been held that a defender cannot escape liability by showing that the copy was made by a third party if the third party acted in accordance with the defender's instructions;[42] but there have been successful arguments that redesign is not copying.[43] In considering whether a restricted act has been carried out indirectly, it is immaterial whether any intervening acts themselves infringe copyright, as for example might be the case in the preparation of a redesign brief.

Question

What is the difference between direct and indirect infringement? Give an example of each form of infringement.

Key points on general principles applicable to all restricted acts

- The restrictions apply whether the act in question relates to the whole of the copyright work or only part of it.

- Where the act relates to only part of the copyright work, it must be a substantial part of the work to be an infringement of the copyright.

- Substantiality depends on whether the part taken is original in the sense of the author's own intellectual creation; or in the case of entrepreneurial works, on whether the reproduction exploits the investment made.

- A restricted act may infringe copyright whether performed directly or indirectly, via some intermediate work.

---

[41]   See, eg, *Autodesk Inc v Dyason and Kelly* (1990) 96 ALR 57. Note, however, that 'decompilation' of a computer program in low-level language (ie the object code) is not infringement if certain conditions are met: CDPA 1988, s 50B; discussed further at para 5.54.

[42]   *Solar Thomson Engineering Co Ltd v Barton* [1977] RPC 537; *Howard Clark v David Allan & Co Ltd* 1987 SLT 271.

[43]   *Merlet v Mothercare* [1986] RPC 115 (CA); *Rose Plastics GmbH v Wm Beckett & Co* [1989] FSR 113.

Restricted acts and primary infringement: detail

4.23   We now turn to detailed discussion of each of the restricted acts, viewed primarily through the lens of infringement actions.

(1) Copying (reproduction)

4.24   Two basics need to be established in any action for infringement based on a claim of copying:

- *similarity* of the alleged infringing work with that of the copyright owner;
- that *the similarity is caused by copying* the copyright owner's work.

When are two works similar?

4.25   The starting point is the similarity of two works. In many instances of infringement, this is not a problem. The development of modern copying technology has made the production of *exact copies* in the fields of reprography, software and other digital works, and audiovisual works, increasingly easy, and this is one of the major policy issues which copyright law has to confront. From a conceptual rather than a policy point of view, however, identifying the use of such technology as potentially infringing copying is not difficult.

Works similar but not the same

4.26   Generally, problems begin to arise when *works are similar but not the same*. It is clear from the law on substantial copying (paras 4.13–4.20) that the later work need not be identical to the earlier work in order to infringe the latter's copyright, although the limits of this, given the basic principle that copyright subsists in modes of expression rather than ideas, are uncertain. The issue is perhaps most acute where it is alleged that a work has been reproduced in a different medium from the original. Copying in relation to a literary, dramatic, musical, or artistic work means reproducing the work in any material form, including storing the work in any medium by electronic means.[44] This certainly includes reproduction in the form of a record or a film,[45] as well as reproduction in a broadcast or in a computer, computer disk, or on the internet. In the case of an artistic work, a version produced by representing a two-dimensional work in three dimensions is a reproduction, as is a version produced by the reverse process.[46] An example illustrating the second instance might be a photograph of a work of artistic craftsmanship.[47] Not being exhaustive, these statutory definitions are but particular instances showing the general principle that the reproduction need not be in the same form as the original to be an infringement. Other examples might include a painting of a photograph.[48] However, there may be a difficulty where a literary work is translated into an artistic or quasi-artistic form: for example, the conversion of statistical data into drawings and graphs. Arguably, in the absence of express provision, reproducing the literary work is confined to reproductions which have some literary form in the sense of using words.

■ *Cuisenaire v Reed* [1963] VR 719

It was held here that coloured rods used for arithmetical calculations did not reproduce a literary work describing such rods.

---

[44] CDPA 1988, s 17(2).   [45] As was specifically provided in s 48 of the 1956 Act.   [46] CDPA 1988, s 17(3).
[47] If not situated in a public place—see CDPA 1988, s 62 (para 5.51).
[48] See *Bauman v Fussell* [1978] RPC 485.

■ *Brigid Foley v Ellott* [1982] RPC 433

It was held here that garments did not reproduce the words and numerals constituting a knitting guide. A reproduction of a literary work must be, according to Sir Robert Megarry V-C, 'some copy of or representation of the original' (at 434).[49]

■ *Anacon Corporation Ltd v Environmental Research Technology Ltd* [1994] FSR 659

ACL were held to have both literary and artistic copyright in electronic circuit diagrams relating to an electronic dust meter. ERTL produced circuit boards using information derived from ACL's boards, involving the creation of a 'net list' of all the components in ACL's circuits, and the connections between them; by feeding such lists into a computer, a new circuit diagram could be produced, and a scheme for producing a printed circuit board. It was held, with regard to the artistic copyright, that ACL's claim of infringement failed, because the alleged infringement did not look like the copyright work. With regard to the literary copyright, however, the claim succeeded so far as the net lists reproduced the information which was the literary work contained in the diagram. Jacob J preferred not to decide whether the ERTL circuits themselves, 'because in relation to each of the components there is also a written or coded indication of what it is' (at 663), were also infringements.

■ *Electronic Techniques (Anglia) Ltd v Critchley Components Ltd* [1997] FSR 401

This was another case about infringement of copyright electronic circuit diagrams in which Laddie J too held that they were literary works but that the defendant's taking might be insufficiently substantial to be infringement.

■ *Sandman v Panasonic UK Ltd* [1998] FSR 651

This was also a case on whether the copyright in electronic circuit diagrams was infringed by electronic circuits. It was held that the diagrams had both artistic and literary copyright. The artistic copyright would only be infringed if the circuit reproduced from a circuit diagram was visually similar to the latter, at least when laid out on the circuit. With regard to the literary copyright, there was no equivalent to the artistic infringement of two-dimensional by three-dimensional works, but it was possible for a circuit itself to contain the content of the literary aspects of the circuit diagram.

 Discussion point   For answer guidance visit **www.oup.com/uk/brown5e**.

How may the copyright in electronic circuit diagrams be infringed?

Causal connection between two works

4.27   It is necessary to show the causal connection of copying between two works, since there may be many other explanations for a similarity between them which do not involve infringement of the right holder's copyright: for example, mere chance, a common source, the nature of the subject matter, or that the claimant copied the other party's work.[50]

■ *Purefoy v Sykes Boxall* (1955) 72 RPC 89

P produced a trade catalogue containing illustrations of its products. SB's products copied P's. SB produced a catalogue of its imitative products, and P sued for infringement of the copyright in the catalogue. It was

---

[49] See also *Interlego AG v Tyco Industries Inc* [1989] AC 217 per Lord Oliver at 265 (PC); also *J & S Davis (Holdings) Ltd v Wright Health Group* [1988] RPC 403 per Whitford J at 414.

[50] *Corelli v Gray* (1913) 29 TLR 570 per Sargent J at 570 (Ch D).

held that these facts by themselves were not enough to establish that SB's catalogue was a copy, direct or indirect, of P's catalogue. SB's copying of the products was not indirect copying of P's catalogue. However, other evidence showed that SB had copied certain advertisements and tables in P's catalogues; there was also indirect copying, since SB had copied certain tables from sheets prepared with P's consent by its customer, H, who had supplied them to SB.

4.28   In general, it may be said that if two works are strikingly alike, if the claimant's work predates that of the defendant, and if the latter had access to it, then the Court will be ready to infer that copying took place.[51] '[I]n most copyright cases . . . infringement can only be established by inference because there is no evidence of anyone being present and looking over the defendants' shoulder.'[52] But before proceeding to make that inference, the Court must consider when it can be displaced by other evidence.[53] However, the more strikingly similar the two works are, the more likely the proposition that there has been copying, and as such more cogent evidence is required for a rebuttal than where the similarities are less striking, this being a matter of weighing up the evidence.[54] This is not a matter of the copyright owner shifting the evidential burden to the alleged infringer but rather of making 'a prima facie case for [him] to answer'.[55]

 Question

When will a court infer that copying has taken place?

Relevance of knowledge

4.29   So far as the issue of whether or not there has been infringement is concerned, it is irrelevant that the defendant did not know or was unaware of the existence of the original work (as might be the case, for example, where he was copying from a copy of it) or of the fact that the original work had copyright. All that matters is the causal chain between the original and the derivative work, and that chain may have several links. Even where the defender produces a work apparently independently it has been said that he may be liable if subconscious copying can be established by the usual tests of similarity, dating, and access.[56] However, the inference that subconscious copying has taken place is one to be considered on the evidence as a whole and if subconscious copying is a proper inference to be drawn in the light of all the circumstances, then it is not a presumption to be rebutted, but is a conclusion of copying.[57]

■ *Francis Day & Hunter Ltd v Bron* [1963] Ch 587 (CA)

FDH owned the copyright in a musical work 'In a Little Spanish Town' (published in 1926 and performed in a 1955 recording by Bing Crosby), and claimed that it was infringed by the conscious or unconscious taking of its first eight bars in another work, 'Why', published by B in 1959. There was considerable similarity, but the composer (Peter de Angelis) gave evidence, accepted by the judge (Wilberforce J), that he had not consciously copied, or indeed heard 'In a Little Spanish Town', and that his main musical influences were Puccini, Ravel, and Debussy; if he had heard 'In a Little Spanish Town', this had probably occurred when he was young. It was held that there was no infringement, although subconscious copying was a possibility, which might amount to infringement. But, 'if subconscious copying is to be found, there must be proof (or

---

[51] See *Designers Guild Ltd v Russell Williams (Textiles) Ltd* [2001] FSR 11 (HL).
[52] *Sifam Electrical Instrument Co Ltd v Sangamo Weston Ltd* [1971] 2 All ER 1074 per Graham J at 1076.
[53] *LB (Plastics) Ltd v Swish Products Ltd* [1979] RPC 551 per Lord Wilberforce at 621.
[54] *Mitchell v BBC* [2011] EWPCC 42, para 25.
[55] *Francis Day & Hunter Ltd v Bron* [1963] Ch 587 per Willmer LJ at 612. See also *Abraham Moon & Sons Ltd v Thornber and Others* [2012] EWPCC 37 at para 25.
[56] *Francis Day & Hunter Ltd v Bron* [1963] Ch 587. See also *Industrial Furnaces Ltd v Reaves* [1970] RPC 605 per Graham J at 623–624.
[57] *Mitchell v BBC* [2011] EWPCC 42, para 39.

at least a strong inference) of de facto familiarity with the work alleged to be copied. In the present case, on the findings of Wilberforce J, this element is conspicuously lacking' (per Willmer LJ at 613).

■ *Jones v Tower Hamlets London Borough* [2001] RPC 23

J, an architect, was instructed by ADL, a property development company, to produce plans for a housing development commissioned by THLB and to be carried out by ADL. After starting work, ADL was dismissed by THLB, which continued the development but developing its own plans. J had not been paid his fees of £219,000 by ADL and remained unpaid when ADL went into liquidation. In an action against THLB, J claimed that the 'footprint' of the houses as built on the site and some interior floor plans infringed the copyright in his plans. The claim was largely rejected save in respect of a 'wrap around' bathroom partition. Although the THLB official concerned could not remember seeing J's plan for this, it was so striking that the only possible inference was that there had been copying, J's plans having possibly remained subconsciously in the official's mind.

■ *John Kaldor Fabricmaker UK Ltd v Lee Ann Fashions Ltd* [2014] EWHC 3779 (IPEC)

J, a fabric designer, claimed that a dress manufactured by L had used one of its fabric designs. In relation to indirect and subconscious copying, the Court noted that the first stage was to consider whether J had established a prima facie inference of copying by reason of the similarities between the works, and the stronger that case, the more compelling the defendant's evidence would have to be to rebut that inference (para 11). The similarities between the designs, and the evidence offered, was ultimately not sufficient to infer copying.

Question

What is the relevance of knowledge in a question about copying?

Copying and adaptation

4.30   Adaptation of a work is a form of infringement distinct from copying, applying only to literary, dramatic, and musical works.[58] Adaptation is given a restricted meaning—it covers dramatisations and translations, for example—and it is specifically provided that no inference as to what does or does not amount to copying a work should be drawn from the definition of adaptation.[59] There may well be overlap, but copying is wider in scope. However, the dividing line between what amounts to a reproduction of a work and what amounts to an adaptation of a work can be unclear.[60]

■ *Hodgson v Isaac* [2010] EWPCC 37 (PCC)

H wrote an autobiography and entered into an agreement with I to make a film based on the book. Permission to use the book was later withdrawn and H claimed infringement by adaptation, but the claim also referred to reproduction. I claimed that he did not need permission, as the film script was not an adaptation of the book but rather based on I's own creative input. The similar elements in the two works were 'the main characters, many of the settings and contexts in which the events take place and a good number of the incidents themselves' (para 77). Birss J noted that adaptation was a more apt description of the facts here; while these elements were not quantitatively the majority of the book and there was much more in the book than the script, this was due to the different nature of the works; nature of film scripts meant they will often have fewer incidents as the scriptwriter's skill involves distilling down the essence of a story in a book to a suitable film. The judge held that the elements reproduced were not generic but a recognisable part of the story, including incidents and their interpretations, which were a key part of what made the book an original work. The fact that such elements

---

[58] See CDPA 1988, s 21 and generally paras 4.68–4.69.   [59] CDPA 1988, s 21(5).   [60] *Hodgson v Isaac* [2010] EWPCC 37, para 21.

are presented as factual rather than fictional did not make a difference and producing an autobiography is an intellectual effort of creation. Such elements together amounted to a substantial part of the book.

Ideas and impressions

4.31   Even where both works are in the same medium or form of expression, it can be difficult to determine whether one reproduces another. Reproduction must be substantial rather than exact or complete,[61] and so the substance of a work must be determined in order to judge the scope of the copyright owner's rights. In some cases, this has extended well beyond expression in the simple sense of words used, to touch on the ways in which information and ideas have been arranged by the author, for example historical incidents.

■ *Harman Pictures NV v Osborne* [1967] 1 WLR 723

It was held here that similarities of incidents and situations suggested that a film screenplay by John Osborne infringed the copyright in a historical book (*The Reason Why* by Mrs Cecil Woodham Smith), even though there were also many dissimilarities between the two works and both were based upon historical events (the 'Charge of the Light Brigade' in the Crimean War).

Several other cases demonstrate that where the question is whether or not one dramatic or musical or artistic work reproduces another of the same kind, account may be taken of factors other than the similarity of the respective modes of expression. With dramatic works, the essence of the copyright may be not so much in the words used as in the characterisation and sequence of incidents and events and where that is taken there is infringement of copyright.[62] With musical works, 'infringement of copyright . . . is not a question of note for note comparison', but falls to be determined 'by the ear as well as by the eye'.[63]

4.32   But there are limits to how far this approach can be taken, since it can make unacceptable inroads upon the basic principle that copyright does not protect ideas and information, which are available for all to use in their own work.

■ *Bauman v Fussell* [1978] RPC 485

A photograph of two cocks fighting each other was used as the basis of a painting. The composition of the subject matter was followed closely but the painter employed different colouring to heighten the dramatic effect of the representation. It was held that it was appropriate to consider the different effects of each work on the viewer in assessing whether there had been an infringement of artistic copyright (answer in this case, no).

■ *Baigent v Random House Group Ltd* [2006] EMLR 16 (Peter Smith J); aff'd [2007] FSR 24 (CA)

This case was based on a claim that the best-selling novel, *The Da Vinci Code* (DVC) by Dan Brown, infringed copyright in an earlier, non-fictional work called *The Holy Blood and the Holy Grail* (HBHG), written by B and others. The claimants relied on *Ravenscroft v Herbert*, arguing that Dan Brown had used the central theme and argument of HBHG in constructing the plot of DVC, and so infringed their copyright. The evidence showed that Dan Brown had used HBHG while working on DVC, and there was some limited textual copying. It was held that DVC did not infringe any copyright in HBHG. The central theme or argument claimed for HBHG was not made out in the book itself, but was an artificial creation put together for the purposes of raising the claim. DVC did not copy any central theme of HBHG, and the textual copying was insubstantial. While the way in which facts, themes, or ideas were put together could

[61]   CDPA 1988, s 16(3)(a).
[62]   *Rees v Melville* [1911–16] MCC 168.
[63]   *Austin v Columbia Gramophone Co Ltd* [1917–23] MCC 398 at 409 and 415, quoted with approval by Willmer LJ in *Francis Day & Hunter Ltd v Bron* [1963] Ch 587 at 608.

be protected by copyright, because this was the result of the skill and labour of the author, the facts, themes, and ideas in themselves were open to anyone else.

■ *Allen v Bloomsbury Publishing plc* [2010] EWHC 2560 (Ch)

A alleged that B's *Harry Potter and the Goblet of Fire* infringed an earlier work, *Willy the Wizard*, because of the similarities in plot elements in the two works: the main characters are wizards and compete in a contest; they have to work out the nature of their main task; they work this out covertly in a bathroom; they complete it using information from helpers; it involves rescuing human hostages from half-human, half-animal creatures. B sought summary judgment arguing that any similarities were of a general nature and arose purely by chance. Kitchin J noted that the similarities seemed to constitute ideas which are relatively simple and abstract and was inclined to view them as ideas rather than expressions due to their high level of generality. However, the judge refused summary judgment because while A's claim had an improbable chance of success, it was not so bad as to be described as fanciful. The merits of the case were not tested further as the case was struck out after a failure to abide by an aspect of court procedure.[64]

■ *Temple Island Collections Ltd v New English Teas Ltd* [2012] FSR 9 (PCC)

This case concerned two similar photos, by F and H, showing a London Routemaster bus in red in the foreground, on a black-and-white background of Westminster Bridge and the Houses of Parliament. Both photos had been altered using a computer program.[65] The defendants had settled a previous case of infringement based on an earlier photograph. Birss J stated that photographs, as one species of artistic work, are not to be treated differently from other artistic works and, as such, infringement is not limited only to facsimile reproductions of a photograph and in an appropriate case infringement can take place by recreating a scene which was photographed (para 31). The defendant argued that the place of the picture was where many tourists stand and it was altered using a 'bog-standard bit of software'. The judge noted that:

> What falls to be considered, in order to decide if a substantial part of an artistic work has been reproduced, are elements of the work which have visual significance. What is visually significant in an artistic work is not the skill and labour (or intellectual creative effort) which led up to the work, it is the product of that activity. The fact that the artist may have used commonplace techniques to produce his work is not the issue. What is important is that he or she has used them under the guidance of their own aesthetic sense to create the visual effect in question (para 34).

The defendant also argued that their expression of the same idea was very different, in almost every respect, to the claimant's. The judge noted that:

> I have not found this to be an easy question but I have decided that the defendants' work does reproduce a substantial part of the claimant's artistic work. In the end the issue turns on a qualitative assessment of the reproduced elements. The elements which have been reproduced are a substantial part of the claimant's work because, despite the absence of some important compositional elements, they still include the key combination of what I have called the visual contrast features with the basic composition of the scene itself. It is that combination which makes . . . [the claimant's] . . . image visually interesting. It is not just another photograph of clichéd London icons (para 63).

The judge found that while images of London landmarks are free to be used, the defendant went to elaborate lengths to produce an image in which they sought lawfully to produce an image which bore some resemblance to the claimant's image but would not infringe the copyright of the claimant. The decision is seen as an unsatisfactory application of the basic principle that copyright does not protect ideas and information.[66]

---

[64] *Allen v Bloomsbury Publishing plc* [2011] EWCA Civ 943.

[65] The competing images in the case are reproduced in colour at the end of the judgment.

[66] A Rahmatian, 'Temple Island Collections v New English Teas: an incorrect decision based on the right law?' [2012] EIPR 796.

> **? Question**
>
> How useful is the distinction between idea and expression? How does it work in relation to, say, poetry, music, or art?

Computer programs and infringement

4.33   Particular problems have arisen with copyright in computer programs. It is clearly infringement to make an exact copy of a program.[67] More complex, however, is the situation often arising as a result of 'reverse engineering',[68] where the aim of the second party is to produce a program which can perform the same functions on the same machines as the first program (ie compatibility or interoperability). This functional similarity can be achieved with quite distinct underlying codes. Thus, the reverse engineer's product may not be an exact or literal copy of the original program, and the question which arises is how far the first programmer's copyright may be pressed in challenging such non-literal copies as infringements of a substantial part of his work. As already noted (paras 4.31–4.32), copyright protection is not confined to literal copying, and can extend to sequences of ideas and effects. But the Software Directive 2009 provides that ideas and principles which underlie any element of a computer program, including those which underlie its interfaces, are not to be protected.[69]

The scope of infringement of software copyright by non-literal copying has been addressed by the courts.

■ *Navitaire Inc v EasyJet Airline Co Inc* [2006] RPC 3 (Pumfrey J)

EJ had taken a licence from N to use their 'OpenRes' copyright software for an online 'ticketless' airline booking system and another program ('TakeFlight') for the web user interface accompanying it. EJ moved on to another web interface and B wrote for them the code for a new booking system ('eRes'). N alleged that its 'OpenRes' copyright was infringed by 'eRes'. There was no dispute that the underlying software was different, that EJ had wanted a new system substantially indistinguishable from 'OpenRes' in respect of its user interface, and that 'eRes' acted upon identical or very similar inputs and produced very similar results. N argued that there was non-textual copying, akin to that involved in copying the plot of a book, or copying of the 'business logic' of the program. It was held that there was no infringement by non-textual copying. The analogy with infringement of the copyright in a plot was inapt because a computer program did not have a theme, events, or narrative flow, but was rather a series of pre-defined operations to produce a result in response to a user's requests or commands. 'Business logic' fell within the scope of unprotectable ideas and principles.

■ *SAS Institute Inc v World Programming Ltd* [2010] ECDR 15 (Arnold J); Case C-406/10 [2012] ECDR 22 (CJ); [2013] EWHC 69 (Ch); [2013] EWCA Civ 1482 (CA)

S developed analytical software (SAS), which consisted of an integrated set of programs and its core component (Base SAS) allowed users to write and run application programs which were written in the SAS language. W studied the SAS manuals and functioning of SAS to create competing software (WPS), which emulated much of the functionality of SAS; that is, the same inputs would generate the same outputs as SAS. There was no suggestion that W had copied the source code of SAS. S argued that the Court's decision in *Navitaire*, that it is not infringement of copyright in a computer program for a competitor to engineer a program that emulates the functionality of the first, was incorrect. In addition, S claimed that W had infringed the copyright within manuals for the program, and had breached the contract of use of a learning

---

[67]   Note, however, CDPA 1988, s 50A, providing that the making of a back-up copy of a computer program necessary for the purposes of lawful use is not infringement, and may not be prevented by contract (para 5.54).

[68]   For this phrase, see para 4.22.   [69]   Art 1(2).

edition. Arnold J reiterated the decision in *Navitaire* and was not persuaded that it was incorrect. The judge concluded that W had not infringed components of SAS but the resolution of the case depended on a number of issues of interpretation of the Software Directive 1991 (now consolidated in Software Directive 2009). As such, several questions were referred to the Court of Justice (CJ) to clarify whether copyright in computer programs protected programming language, interfaces, and functions.

The CJ held that the source code and the object code are forms of expression which can be protected by copyright but the ideas and principles which underlie a computer program are not protected by copyright. The Court found that neither the functionality nor the programming language and the format of data files used in a computer program constitutes a form of expression of that program and are not protected under the Directive. The Court noted that: 'to accept that the functionality of a computer program can be protected by copyright would amount to making it possible to monopolise ideas, to the detriment of technological progress and industrial development' (para 40). This interpretation is generally consistent with the approach taken in UK case law.

The Court held that a lawful user of a program could, without further authorisation, observe, study or test the functionality of a program to determine underlying ideas and principles, where he is carrying out acts covered by the licence. However, the Court also held that reproduction, in a computer program or a user manual for that program, of certain elements described in the user manual for another computer program is capable of constituting an infringement if the reproduction constitutes the expression of the intellectual creation of the author of the user manual for the computer program protected by copyright (see also para 3.46).

In applying this interpretation to the facts of the case, the High Court noted that the CJ had in effect endorsed Pumfrey J's judgment in *Navitaire Inc*: 'In short, copyright in a computer program does not protect either the programming language in which it is written or its interfaces (specifically, its data file formats) or its functionality from being copied' (para 16). This is because, as the Court of Appeal noted, 'the nature of the skill and judgment expended in devising the functionality of a computer program (which will inevitably involve making choices) still falls on the ideas side of the line' (para 46). The Court of Appeal did, however, go on to hold that copyright in the SAS manuals, as a literary work in itself rather than the program it related to, had been infringed to an extent. It emphasised that the question was whether there had been reproduction of the intellectual creation of the author of the manual; the intellectual creation of the author of the computer program it related to was not relevant (para 63).

4.34 Even where the form of expression in computer language is distinct from the first version, there may still be infringement by adaptation.[70] With regard to screen displays, a problem may be the idea that a literary work (which includes a computer program) cannot be infringed by a visual representation.[71] On the other hand, the display may have an independent artistic copyright of its own, which would be infringed by substantially similar displays.

Transient copies: computer programs, databases, and the internet

4.35 Copying in relation to any description of work includes the making of copies which are transient or are incidental to some other use of the work.[72] This again has particular significance in relation to computer programs. When a program is loaded into a computer, it is generally copied from the source into the computer's random-access memory and central processing unit. This may well be transient or incidental, but is nonetheless infringement unless authorised. Similarly, in browsing the internet, a user who calls up a webpage on his computer screen would be making a copy of the materials. It applies to 'data scraping', the use of programs to copy data from a website or database. The concept of transient reproduction also embraces activities such as proxy server caching where, by deploying appropriate software technology internet service providers, librarians, archivists, and others make and store on their own servers temporary and regularly

---

[70] See CDPA 1988, s 21(3)(a)(i) and (4), discussed later.   [71] See para 4.26.   [72] CDPA 1988, s 17(6).

updated copies of materials contained on other servers with the purpose of making the information more readily available to their own clients by avoiding congestion at the 'live' site. Such operations may also amount to the infringing act of storage by electronic means.[73]

On creation of small transient fragments of a work, such as those in the memory of a satellite decoder or in the buffers of a streaming service, an important question for assessing reproduction is whether it is appropriate to consider the fragments on a cumulative or rolling basis. It has been held that the rolling basis is not to be applied 'where the copies relied upon are successively destroyed as an inherent part of the process'; this is because what is restricted is a 'a transient copy of a substantial part of the work' and as such 'the substantial part must be embodied in the transient copy, not a series of different transient copies which are stored one after the other in the decoder box'.[74]

■ Cases C-403/08 and C429/08 *Football Association Premier League Ltd v QC Leisure, Murphy v Media Protection Services Ltd* [2012] 1 CMLR 29 (CJ)

This case concerned the reception of Premier League matches, in a pub, through foreign decoders, which included the Premier League anthem, pre-recorded films showing highlights of recent matches, and various graphics (for the facts, see para 20.26). As part of the reception, transient sequential fragments of works are created within the memory of a satellite decoder and on a television screen which are immediately effaced and replaced by the next fragments. The Court of Justice was asked whether the reproduction right extends to these fragments of works (para 153).

The Court began by emphasising that the concept of 'reproduction' is to be given an autonomous and uniform interpretation throughout the EU, and various parts of a work enjoy protection provided they contain elements which are the expression of the intellectual creation of the author (see discussion on *Infopaq* at para 4.19). The Court confirmed that reproduction extends to transient fragments of works within the memory of a satellite decoder and on a television screen, if those fragments contain elements which are the author's own intellectual creation. The Court also noted that:

> the unit composed of the fragments reproduced simultaneously—and therefore existing at a given moment—should be examined in order to determine whether it contains such elements. If it does, it must be classified as partial reproduction . . . it is not relevant whether a work is reproduced by means of linear fragments which may have an ephemeral existence because they are immediately effaced in the course of a technical process (para 157).

In *ITV Broadcasting Ltd v TVCatchup Ltd*,[75] which concerned reproduction of films in memory buffers of a streaming service and on TV screens, Floyd J noted that the *FAPL* decision by the Court of Justice had clarified that the rolling approach is incorrect and, as such, it should not be applied to either films or broadcasts. The judge concluded that there was reproduction of a substantial part of the films in the memory buffers but not on the TV screens. It is important to note here that copying of such transient fragments can be allowed as a permitted act where it is an integral and essential part of a technological process, the sole purpose of which is to enable a transmission of the work in a network between third parties by an intermediary or a lawful use of the work and the temporary copy has no independent economic significance.[76] Otherwise, the remarkable result would be that the technical basis of the operation of the internet itself is illegal. In fact, this exception was seen as applicable in both the *FAPL* and *ITV* decisions, as well as to temporary copies generated during browsing by the users of a media monitoring service (see further at para 5.19).[77]

---

[73] CDPA 1988, s 17(2).
[74] *Football Association Premier League Ltd v QC Leisure (No 2)* [2008] EWHC 1411 (Ch) at para 227.
[75] *ITV Broadcasting Ltd v TVCatchup Ltd* [2011] EWHC 2977 (Pat).
[76] CDPA 1988, s 28A, inserted after the InfoSoc Directive 2001, Art 5(1).
[77] C-360/13 *Newspaper Licensing Agency Ltd v Meltwater Holding BV* [2014] AC 1438 (CJ).

Common source material; admittedly derivative work

4.36 Difficult questions can also arise with compilations where the same generally available information or material is conveyed in a different way; but if it is shown that in fact the second work was based on the first then it will be held to infringe copyright.

■ *Alexander v Mackenzie* (1847) 9 D 748

A, a solicitor, published a work entitled *An Analysis of the Heritable Securities and Infeftment Acts with an Appendix, containing Practical Forms of the Writs and Instruments thereby introduced*. The Acts, which had been passed in 1845, were aimed at the simplification of conveyancing, and gave general directions and descriptions of the styles to be used henceforth by conveyancers. A used industry and his knowledge as a conveyancer to produce 19 new styles. A committee of the Society of Writers to the Signet (a society of solicitors in Edinburgh) prepared and circulated amongst its membership reports on the two statutes, which also had an appendix containing a number of forms. The forms were largely based on those in A's work; A, who was a member of the committee, objected to this way of proceeding. It was held that the styles, being the creation of industry and knowledge rather than a mere reproduction of what was in the statutes, were copyright subject matter; the committee's alterations in its forms were of a trivial and unimportant nature; the committee styles were presented in the same order as A's; actual copying was acknowledged; and A's copyright was infringed.

■ *Elanco Products Ltd v Mandops (Agrochemical Specialists) Ltd* [1980] RPC 213 (CA)

EP invented, patented, and marketed a weed killer. The product was accompanied by an instruction leaflet. The information contained in this leaflet was also available by way of scientific journals. When the patent expired, M brought out a competing version of the product accompanied by an instruction leaflet very similar to that of EP. When EP challenged M, the latter produced new versions of the leaflet embodying the information but which was not so similar to EP's leaflet. EP sought an interlocutory injunction and it was held that EP had an arguable case. It appeared on the evidence that M had begun by making a simple and unauthorised copy, which M had then revised. This was not sufficient to cure the copyright infringement. It would have been different if M had researched all the other available information as well as EP's leaflet before writing their leaflet; then, even if the results had been extremely similar, there would have been no infringement.

4.37 But, on the other hand, it may be admitted that the allegedly infringing work was based upon the pursuer's work, yet, because the defender put in sufficient independent skill and labour, the result was not an infringement but a new and independent work. See, for example, the case of *Bauman v Fussell* [1978] RPC 485, described at para 4.32. Again, there may be issues about whether a product emanates from the claimant's work or from a wider source upon which both products ultimately depend.

■ *JHP Ltd v BBC Worldwide Ltd* [2008] FSR 29 (Ch D)

JHP sought an injunction to prevent further publication of *The Daleks Survival Guide*, which the BBC published in 2002 as a 'secret dossier on this deadly breed of embossed exterminators'. The book was said to be in breach of the copyright in previous books, published in the 1960s, in which JHP now claimed the rights. Though the judge found that JHP did not hold the rights claimed, he went on to consider the issue of copying and substantiality had they held the rights. Any similarities between the new book and the three original ones were held to arise from the texts all referring to material in the TV series, which existed as a published artistic concept separate from the books. In any case, even if there had been copying, the quantity was insignificant.

Parodies as reproductions

4.38 A parody of another work may or may not be an infringement of its copyright, depending on whether a substantial part is copied or not. Prior to October 2014, a 'parody' was neither necessarily an infringement of copyright,[78] nor an independent, substantive defence to a charge of infringement.[79] However, as a result of the Hargreaves Review, fair dealing with a work for the purposes of caricature, parody, or pastiche is now a defence to infringement. As such, a parody of another work may now be an infringement of its copyright only if it is a reproduction of a substantial part thereof, and also doesn't fall within the remit of the new exception (see paras 5.39–5.41).

Abridgements as reproductions

4.39   Abridgements have received favourable treatment in England in being held not to infringe copyright, as long as the abridger does not make excessive use of the original's mode of expression.[80] It was held that an abridgement infringed copyright, however, in a Scottish case on the subject.[81] Again, therefore, it is apparent that the question of whether or not an abridgement is an infringement depends on the normal principles of copyright: how much and in what way has use been made of the original work and its mode of expression?

Copying of sound recordings, films, and broadcasts

4.40   The copyright in a sound recording, film, or broadcast is infringed by copying the work.[82] This can include the copying of a substantial part of the work (para 4.20) as well as the whole,[83] and so in relation to a film or broadcast making a photograph of the whole or any substantial part of any image forming part of the work is an infringement.[84] This would cover, for example, the enlargement of one section of an image from a film or broadcast. However, film copyright may be infringed only by 'copying of the particular recording of the film'.[85] Perhaps the most important general point to note here is that 'home copying' of such works by private individuals is infringement, without any general exception being made for private use.[86] Similarly, downloading from unlicensed music or film sites on the internet is infringement of the copyright in the sound recordings or films in question.[87] On the other hand, in practical terms, it is expensive as well as exceptionally difficult to enforce this right against individual infringers.

Copying in relation to the typographical arrangement of a published edition

4.41   Copying in relation to the typographical arrangement of a published edition means making a facsimile copy of the arrangement.[88] The most important example of this is photocopying or reprography, which is therefore prima facie infringement of the publisher's right, as well as that of the author of the text.[89] The scope of the publisher's protection is, however, restricted to a certain extent by provisions on the permitted acts and on licensing.[90]

---

[78] See *Joy Music Ltd v Sunday Pictorial Newspapers* [1960] 2 QB 60; *Schweppes v Wellingtons* [1984] FSR 210.

[79] It could have been defended then on the basis that it was 'fair dealing . . . for purposes of criticism'. See CDPA 1988, s 30(1); M Spence, 'Intellectual property and the problem of parody' (1998) 114 LQR 594.

[80] See *Sillitoe v McGraw Hill* [1983] FSR 545.   [81] *Murray v McFarquhar* (1785) Mor 8309.   [82] CDPA 1988, s 17(1).

[83] CDPA 1988, s 16(3)(a).   [84] CDPA 1988, s 17(4).

[85] *Norowzian v Arks Ltd (No 1)* [1998] FSR 394. See also para 63 in *Dramatico* (note 87).

[86] Note, however, the provision for 'time-shifting' in CDPA 1988, s 70, discussed at para 5.55; and note that a private copying exception was introduced in 2014 and repealed in 2015, for full details of which see para 5.56.

[87] *Dramatico Entertainment Ltd and Others v BSkyB and Others* [2012] ECDR 14 (Ch). See further paras 4.65 and 4.75.

[88] CDPA 1988, s 17(5).

[89] See for discussion of copying in relation to typographical arrangements, *Newspaper Licensing Agency Ltd v Marks & Spencer plc* [2003] 1 AC 551, discussed at para 4.18.

[90] See, eg, paras 5.25–5.28 and 5.42–5.44.

> ### Key points on copying
>
> - Copying means that there must be a causal link between two works in that one is derived from the other.
> - Copying does not have to be intentional to be infringement.
> - The copying does not have to be exact ('literal').
> - The copy may be transient or temporary (this is especially important for computer programs, databases, and the internet).

(2) Infringement by issuing to the public copies of the work

4.42   The issue to the public of the original work or of copies of the work without the authority of the copyright owner is an infringement of the copyright.[91] *Issuing to the public* means:[92]

> putting into circulation in the United Kingdom copies not previously put into circulation in the European Economic Area (EEA) by or with the consent of the copyright owner.

Specifically excluded from the definition is any *subsequent* distribution, sale, hiring, or loan of copies previously put into circulation.[93] In other words, the owner has the right to be *first* to produce copies of the copyright work to be available to the public, whether in the form of books, posters, records, videos, or whatever. The right is therefore sometimes described as the right of *first sale* or of *distribution*. Only the copyright owner or his licensee can put a new reproduction of the work on the market. The right exists only as far as, or is *exhausted* by, the initial issue of copies in the EEA, however. So, the second-hand bookseller of books legitimately put into circulation does not require copyright licences in order to carry on business.[94] Generally, of course, the author will exercise the right by the grant of a licence to a commercial publisher, because it is the latter's business to put material into public circulation. Once the publisher has put copies of the work on the market, these may be dealt with freely, and no subsequent sale or other dealing with those copies can be an infringement of copyright.

Issuing

4.43   The issue must take place in the copyright territory, that is, the area to which the CDPA applies. But what does 'issuing' mean? And at what point does infringement occur? In *Independiente Ltd v Music Trading On-line (HK) Ltd*[95] (the 'CD-WOW case'), where a parallel importer posted infringing copies of CDs from Hong Kong to customers in the UK, who made orders by way of the supplier's website, it was held that infringement by issuing to the public took place when the goods were delivered to the customer through the post. The case was strengthened by the fact that the CD-WOW website was clearly intended to attract customers in the UK. Issuing must also be understood in accordance with the EU notion of 'distribution to the public' (under InfoSoc Directive 2001, Art 4).

---

[91]   CDPA 1988, s 18(1), (4). Corresponding provisions can be found in Software Directive 2009, Art 4; Rental and Lending Right Directive 2006, Art 9; InfoSoc Directive 2001, Art 4.

[92]   CDPA 1988, s 18(2), as amended by Copyright and Related Rights (Marrakesh Treaty etc.) (Amendment) Regulations 2018 (SI 2018/995).

[93]   CDPA 1988, s 18(3), as amended by Copyright and Related Rights (Marrakesh Treaty etc.) (Amendment) Regulations 2018 (SI 2018/995). But note the proviso to the subsection, about rental and lending rights (on which see further paras 4.46–4.49).

[94]   For corresponding provisions on exhaustion in EU Directives, see Software Directive 2009, Art 4(2) and InfoSoc Directive 2001, Art 4(2). On the application of exhaustion to tangible and digital copies of copyright works, see paras 19.66–19.74. For parallel importing in the EEA, see Chapter 19.

[95]   [2007] FSR 21 (Ch).

■ Case C-5/11 *Criminal proceedings against Titus Alexander Jochen Donner* [2015] ECDR 22 (June 2012)

The Court of Justice noted that distribution is 'characterised by a series of acts going, at the very least, from the conclusion of a contract of sale to the performance thereof by delivery to a member of the public' and, in a cross-border sale, distribution may take place in a number of member states. As such, the right may be infringed in a number of member states (para 26).[96] The Court noted that:

> a trader who directs his advertising at members of the public residing in a given member state and creates or makes available to them a specific delivery system and payment method, or allows a third party to do so, thereby enabling those members of the public to receive delivery of copies of works protected by copyright in that same Member State, makes, in the member state where the delivery takes place, a 'distribution to the public' (para 30).

In these circumstances, the trader not only bears responsibility for any act carried out by him or on his behalf but acts carried out by third parties, such as freight forwarders, may also be attributed to him, where he specifically targeted the public of the destination and was aware of the actions of the third party.

■ Case C-516/13 *Dimensione Direct Sales Srl v Knoll International SpA* [2015] ECDR 12 (May 2015)

The Court of Justice held that the right of distribution includes advertisement for sale of protected works. The judgment in *Donner* (above) did not exclude 'acts or steps preceding the conclusion of a contract of sale' from the concept of distribution because the Court used the term 'at the very least' (para 26). As such, the right owner can prevent an offer for sale, or an advertisement in the press or by direct mail for sale, of the original or a copy of the work, whereby the consumers of the member state of the protected work are invited to purchase it. It is irrelevant that the advertisement does not result in a purchase or transfer of ownership. The Court of Justice justified this interpretation in light of the objectives of the InfoSoc Directive to provide rigorous, effective, and a high-level of protection to right owners. In strengthening the position of the right owners, the Court has expanded the notion of distribution.

■ Case C-419/13 *Art & Allposters International v Stichting Pictoright* [2015] ECDR 8 (January 2015)

S had licensed protected images for use to produce posters. A transferred images from the paper posters to canvasses by means of a chemical process, during which the image disappears from the poster. The CJ was asked whether S's Article 4 right was exhausted on distribution of the images incorporated into the tangible posters (for an answer to which see para 19.73). The Court noted that the replacement of the tangible medium, from the poster to the canvas, resulted in the creation of a new object. Such alteration of the protected work constitutes a new copy of work for the purposes of the distribution right and requires the right holder's authorisation (para 43).

 Discussion point   For answer guidance visit **www.oup.com/uk/brown5e**.

A similar factual situation to *Allposters* arose in an earlier Canadian case, *Galerie d'Art du Petit Champlain inc v Théberge*,[97] where T, a well-known painter, sued art galleries for purchasing licensed cards and posters with images owned by T and transferring them to canvas, leaving the originals blank. By a majority of 4:3, the Supreme Court of Canada held that there was no infringement. Find out the majority and minority views in the case. Which do you prefer, and why? How do you think it compares to the decision in *Allposters*?

---

[96] See also Case C-98/13 *Martin Blomqvist v Rolex SA* [2014] ECDR 10, where the CJ held that distribution to the public is proven where a contract of sale and dispatch has been concluded.
[97] [2002] 2 SCR 336; see further S Stokes, 'Copyright and the reproduction of artistic works' [2003] EIPR 486.

Issuing to the public and publication

4.44   Issue of copies to the public should be kept distinct from publication, which is important for other aspects of copyright such as term and qualification for protection in the UK, and receives an independent definition.[98] A key element in the constitution of publication is that it does not include publication which is merely colourable and not intended to satisfy the reasonable requirements of the public.[99] This would not apply to the right of the owner to be the first to issue copies of his work, and so private publication for limited circulation might exhaust that right, although it might not constitute publication for other purposes. Nevertheless, it is probably true to say that most acts constituting publication under the 1988 Act will also constitute issuing copies to the public.

 Question

What is the difference between 'issuing to the public' and 'publication'?

The public

4.45   The question—*who are the public for these purposes?*—is one on which there is no direct authority, and it may be that it should be answered in the same way as it has been in the cases concerning infringement by performing the work in public.[100] However, issue to the public should be kept distinct from the other forms of infringement, in particular performance and public communication. Issuing a substantial part of a work to the public will constitute infringement of the copyright where copies of the work have not previously been put into circulation.[101]

> **Key points about issuing to the public**
>
> - The right is to be the first to sell or otherwise distribute copies of a work to the public.
> - A typical example is when an author licenses a publisher to publish his book.
> - The right does not reach second or subsequent sales: it is *exhausted* by the first transaction.

4.46   (3) Rental or lending of a work to the public

The copyright owner's right to be the first to issue copies of his work to the public (paras 4.42–4.45) generally does not preclude subsequent dealing with those copies so as to make them available to the public, for example through a public library. But since the 1988 Act and its subsequent amendment as a result of the Rental Right Directive of 1992,[102] certain forms of subsequent dealing are within the scope of the restricted acts by virtue of an express provision stating that in relation to most forms of copyright work, *rental or lending of copies to the public* is an act restricted by the copyright in the work.[103] The works to which rental and lending right do *not* apply are works of architecture in the form of a building or a model for a building, works of applied art, and broadcasts.[104]

---

[98] CDPA 1988, s 175.   [99] CDPA 1988, s 175(5).   [100] See paras 4.50–4.56.   [101] CDPA 1988, s 16(3)(a).
[102] Council Directive 92/100/EEC, now in a consolidated version, Directive 2006/115/EC.   [103] CDPA 1988, s 18A(1).
[104] CDPA 1988, s 18A(1)(b)(i), (ii). For works of applied art, see para 8.5 and Berne Convention, Arts 2(7) and 7(4).

Discussion point   For answer guidance visit **www.oup.com/uk/brown5e**.

Why do rental and lending rights not apply to works of architecture in the form of buildings or models for buildings, works of applied art, and broadcasts?

4.47   *Rental* is:[105]

> making a copy of a work available for use, on terms that it will or may be returned, for direct or indirect economic or commercial advantage.

The typical scenario where the right applies is that of a business or other organisation which has purchased authorised copies of the works in question; in order to engage in the business of rental of these copies to customers, a licence from the copyright owner is required. Licences permit control of rental outlets and libraries, while royalties to the copyright owner provide some sort of compensation for the supposedly illicit copying carried out by the outlet's customers.

 Question

How does 'rental' differ from 'issuing to the public'?

4.48   *Lending* right, an innovation of the Directive, is defined similarly to rental (para 4.47), save that the restricted act is one performed *otherwise* than for direct or indirect economic or commercial advantage, *and* is carried out through an establishment which is accessible to the public.[106] Thus, a public library's lending activities require a copyright licence.[107] But if you lend a book or DVD to a friend there is no copyright infringement, since you are not an establishment accessible to the public. The Court of Justice has clarified that lending includes e-lending of the 'one copy, one user' type, ie:[108]

> the lending of a digital copy of a book, where that lending was carried out by placing that copy on the server of a public library and allowing a user to reproduce that copy by downloading it onto his own computer, bearing in mind that only one copy may be downloaded during the lending period and that, after that period had expired, the downloaded copy could no longer be used by that user.

 Question

How does 'lending' differ from rental?

4.49   Neither rental nor lending covers making copies available for the purpose of performance, showing, playing, or exhibiting in public, or communication to the public (activities subject to their own regime of rights—see further at paras 4.50 ff), or for the purpose of on-the-spot reference use, as for example in a reference library or in the reference section of a university or college library.[109]

 Question

How do the provisions on lending right affect your university or college library?

---

[105] CDPA 1988, s 18A(2)(a).   [106] CDPA 1988, s 18A(2)(b).
[107] However, see CDPA 1988, ss 40A and 36A (paras 5.44–46).
[108] Case C-174/15 *Vereniging Openbare Bibliotheken v Stichting Leenrecht* [2017] ECDR 3, para 54.   [109] CDPA 1988, s 18A(3).

> **Key points on rental and lending**
>
> - Both are about the right to issue products to the public, on condition that the product will or may be returned to the issuer.
> - Rental involves an economic return to the party issuing the product, while lending involves no economic return.
> - The issuer will typically be someone who has a licence to do so from the copyright owner, rather than the copyright owner itself.

(4) Public performance, showing, and playing

4.50   Public performance of a literary, dramatic, or musical work in public infringes its copyright.[110] *Performance* includes:[111]

> delivery, in relation to lectures, addresses, speeches and sermons; it also includes any mode of visual or acoustic presentation, including presentation by means of a sound recording, film, or broadcast of the work.

Since this definition only 'includes', other things than the activities mentioned may amount to performance. It has sbeen suggested that the meaning of performance should be confined to performing in the sense of entertaining or instructing; otherwise it might be possible to argue, for example, that the copyright in a concert programme was infringed by the performance of the items there listed.[112] The performance need only be of a substantial part of the copyright work to infringe.[113] *Playing or showing* a sound recording, film, or broadcast in public is also an infringement of copyright.[114]

 Discussion point   For answer guidance visit **www.oup.com/uk/brown5e**.

Can an artistic work be performed, played, or shown in public? Why are artistic works excluded from protection under this head?

When is a performance in public?

4.51   Public performance is a 'direct representation or performance', encompassing interpretation of the works before the public that is in direct physical contact with the actor or performer of those work[115] and is different from 'communication to the public'[116] (see para 4.59). Most of the UK case law on this topic has been concerned with when a performance is in public. It is clear that the performance must be addressed to an audience before any question of infringement can arise and that it is the nature of the audience which

---

[110] CDPA 1988, s 19(1).   [111] CDPA 1988, s 19(2).

[112] See *British Broadcasting Co v Wireless League Gazette Publishing Co* [1926] Ch 433 per Astbury J at 442 for the example.

[113] CDPA 1988, s 16(3)(a).   [114] CDPA 1988, s 19(3).

[115] Such as a live presentation or performance of a work; the public performance right has not been harmonised, see Case C-283/10 *Circ & Variete Globus Bucureşti v Uniunea Compozitorilor şi Muzicologilor din România—Asociaţia pentru Drepturi de Autor—UCMR—ADA* (24 November 2011), para 40.

[116] Cases C-403/08 and C429/08 *Football Association Premier League Ltd v QC Leisure, Murphy v Media Protection Services Ltd* [2012] 1 CMLR 29, para 201. There may, however, be overlap between CDPA 1988, s 19 and s 20 in that certain activities may fall under both, *FAPL v QC Leisure* [2012] EWHC 108 (Ch) at para 63.

determines whether it is in public. It is not necessary that the performance be one which the public at large may attend. The test has been well put in a Scottish case:

■ *Performing Right Society v Rangers FC Supporters Club* 1974 SC 49

At one end of the spectrum there is what has been described as the domestic situation. At the other end is the situation where the promoter invites the public to attend the performance on payment of an entrance fee. In between there is a wide range of varying situations. 'Domestic' has been extended to include 'semi-domestic'. What is the underlying reasoning behind the exclusion of domestic or quasi-domestic performances? It is to be found in the relationship between the audience and the owner of the copyright. In a situation where a person organises a private party in his own home, or in what might reasonably be deemed to be an extension of his own home, then it seems reasonable to assume that the unauthorised publication or use of the copyright work is not rebounding to the financial disadvantage of the owner of the copyright, since the selected audience is not enjoying the work under conditions in which they would normally pay for the privilege in one form or another. A performance of the work in such circumstances would ordinarily be regarded as being in private (per Lord Justice-Clerk Wheatley at 59).

Discussion point   For answer guidance visit **www.oup.com/uk/brown5e**.

If there is no charge to attend a performance, does that make it private? See also para 4.56.

4.52   The test is the relationship between the audience and the copyright owner. The courts have held that performances in the following places were in public:

- members' clubs (*Harms (Incorporated) Ltd v Martans Club Ltd* [1926] Ch 870; *PRS v Rangers FC Supporters Club* 1974 SC 49);

- the lounge of a hotel (*PRS v Hawthorns Hotel (Bournemouth) Ltd* [1933] Ch 855);

- a factory during working hours (*Ernest Turner Electrical Instruments v PRS* [1943] Ch 167 (CA));

- a meeting of a women's rural institute (*Jennings v Stephens* [1936] Ch 469);

- performance of musical works in a record shop by playing records over a loudspeaker system (*PRS v Harlequin Record Shops* [1979] 1 WLR 851);

- a butcher's shop (*South African Music Rights Organisation Ltd v Trust Butchers (Pty) Ltd* [1978] 1 SALR 1052).

4.53   In most of these cases, attendance at the performance was restricted to certain categories of the public only. It is also apparent that it is not relevant to consider either the size of the audience or the return, if any, received by the performer. But if the audience is unrestricted and the performer is acting for profit, the performance is clearly an infringement. It has been said that 'a performance given to any audience consisting of the persons present in a shop which the public at large are permitted, and indeed encouraged, to enter without payment or invitation, with a view to increasing the shopowner's profit, can only properly be described as a performance "in public"'.[117] The nature of the retailer's business is unimportant in deciding whether or not performances of this type are in public.[118]

---

[117] *PRS v Harlequin Record Shops* [1979] 1 WLR 851 at 858.
[118] *South African Music Rights Organisation Ltd v Trust Butchers (Pty) Ltd* [1978] 1 SALR 1052.

■ *Brown v Mcasso Music Ltd* [2005] FSR 40

B and M were joint authors of a rap song (see para 3.87), which was used in a TV commercial for two months. Subsequently M made the work available on its website for nine months, in order to advertise M's services to prospective clients. After that, the work was archived on a part of the website not intended to be accessible to the public. M had only paid B for the two months' transmission in the TV commercial. It was held that the initial nine months' use of the song on the website infringed B's joint copyright, and damages of £180 were awarded (challenged on appeal). *Obiter*, however, Fysh J noted that the website archiving was not an infringing public performance.

An audience of one, or of several, but at different times?

4.54 A gathering of the audience together in one place is not a necessary condition for performance in public. It has been held in Australia that playing recorded music 'on hold' to users of mobile telephones was 'in public' even though the distribution of the material was not necessarily, or even very often, simultaneous for each member of the audience.[119] The fact that the members of the audience would be quite unaware of each other, and joining and leaving the audience at various times, would not seem to be relevant. Nor would the fact that the audience might consist of only one person at any given moment. Many such cases may now be dealt with by the public communication right (paras 4.57–4.67).

Exercise

I book a venue at the Edinburgh Festival Fringe at which I advertise that I will be giving readings from my favourite 20th-century poets, most of whose work is still in copyright. But I do not seek any copyright licences. Tickets for my show cost £10 each, but none are sold and no one comes to any of my performances, which I nonetheless resolutely give in an otherwise empty room. Have I infringed the various poets' copyrights by public performance? Would it make any difference to your answer if:

(1) one night a newspaper critic came on a complimentary ticket, but did not publish any review of the show; or

(2) the venue provided a couple of staff to man the public entrance and operate the lighting and sound systems for the show?

Performing for one's own benefit but in public places; education

4.55 It is arguable that there is no performance in public in situations where the performer is acting essentially for personal benefit or pleasure and incidentally members of the public constitute an audience which watches or listens: for example, the members' sing-song in a club[120] or labourers playing music on a radio at a building site.[121] The same would seem to apply to playing a sound recording on a personal stereo which can be overheard by persons close to the wearer of the equipment. Note that performance of a literary, dramatic, or musical work in the course of the activities of an educational establishment (school, college, university) before an audience of teachers, pupils, and other persons directly connected with the establishment's activities[122] is not in public if the performers are teachers or pupils or if the performance is for the purpose

---

[119] *Telstra Corporation Ltd v Australasian Performing Right Association Ltd* (1997) 191 CLR 140 (HCA).

[120] See *PRS v Rangers FC Supporters Club* 1974 SC 49 per Lord Stott at 55.

[121] See, however, *PRS v Kwik-Fit Group Ltd* [2008] ECDR 2, where it was held arguable that employees using personal radios at their place of work in such a way that members of the public and customers of the employer could hear the music being played might be guilty of infringing public performances.

[122] A parent of a pupil is not as such directly connected (CDPA 1988, s 34(3)).

of instruction.[123] The rule is the same for playing or showing a sound recording, film, or broadcast to such an audience in the course of instruction at an educational establishment.[124]

Use of apparatus for receiving visual images or sounds conveyed by electronic means

4.56   One of the most important ways of performing, playing, or showing a work may be through a television screen or radio set situated in a public place, on which a literary, dramatic, or musical work may be being performed, or a sound recording, film, or broadcast played or shown. It is provided that in such cases the person by whom the images or sounds are sent is not an infringer and, in the case of a performance, nor is any performer;[125] but there is nothing to define who is the primary infringer in such cases; or, to put it another way, who should be seeking the licence for the performance in question. The 1956 Act provided that the occupier of the premises where the apparatus was situated would be taken as giving the performance, playing, or showing if he also provided the apparatus itself.[126] This may still be the most useful guide. It should be noted, however, that an occupier of premises who gave permission for the apparatus to be brought on to the premises can be liable as a secondary infringer.[127] There is also a narrow exception on free public showing or playing of broadcast.[128]

Key points on public performance

Whether a performance, playing, or showing of a work is in public depends on a number of factors:

- Is the audience paying, in some form or another, to attend the performance?
- Is the person responsible for the performance engaged in a profit-making activity?
- The audience must consist of members of the public, but restrictions on who may attend do not prevent the performance being in public.
- The performance need not be simultaneous for each member of the audience.

---

(5) Public communication right

4.57   The communication to the public of the work is an act restricted by the copyright in literary, dramatic, musical, and artistic works, sound recordings, films, and broadcasts.[129] This right was introduced in implementation of the InfoSoc Directive 2001, which in turn implemented for the EU the WCT 1996.[130] Article 3 of the InfoSoc Directive requires member states to provide for 'the exclusive right to authorise or prohibit any communication to the public . . . including the making available to the public'. Article 3(1) provides the right to authors. Article 3(2) provides the right to producers of sound recordings and films and to broadcasters for fixations of broadcasts only.[131] The concept of 'making available to the public' here forms part of the wider 'communication to the public', but 'making available to the public', refers to 'interactive

---

[123]   CDPA 1988, s 34(1).   [124]   CDPA 1988, s 34(2).   [125]   CDPA 1988, s 19(4).

[126]   1956 Act, s 48(6). See also *Phonographic Performance Ltd v Lion Breweries* [1980] FSR 1 (NZ).

[127]   CDPA 1988, s 26(3); and see further at paras 4.80–4.82.

[128]   CDPA 1988, s 72. This exception was amended by The Copyright (Free Public Showing or Playing) (Amendment) Regulations 2016 following decisions which found the provision incompatible with InfoSoc Directive 2001. The Intellectual Property Office ran a consultation to seek views on its proposals to clarify and narrow the scope of s 72; see IPO, 'A consultation on changes to Section 72 of the Copyright, Designs and Patents Act 1988' (2015). See also para 4.81.

[129]   CDPA 1988, s 20(1). See further J Ginsburg, 'The (new?) right of making available to the public' in D Vaver and L Bently (eds), *Intellectual Property in the New Millennium* (2004).

[130]   See paras 4.5–4.8. Note also that the concept of communication to the public is now the same for related rights, eg equitable remuneration right for performers (see further at para 7.40).

[131]   The right is also given to performers for fixations of their performances (para 7.31).

on-demand transmissions' for which an act, must cumulatively, meet both conditions: members of the public may access the work from a place *and* at a time individually chosen by them.[132] Live TV broadcasts on the internet cannot be classified as 'making available' under Article 3(2); however, national legislation can give more protection to broadcasting organisations by giving a 'communication to the public' right to cover acts of transmissions of live broadcasts on the internet, provided that such an extension does not undermine copyright protection.[133] Section 20(1) CDPA does exactly this and does grant a communication to the public right in broadcasts beyond what is required by the InfoSoc Directive.[134]

Public communication for these purposes means electronic transmission (CDPA 1988, s 20(2)).

It includes:

(1) **broadcasting** the work (CDPA 1988, s 20(2)(a)).
electronic transmission of visual images, sounds, or other information,
transmitted for simultaneous reception by members of the public
capable of being lawfully received by members of the public
transmitted at a time determined solely by the person in question for presentation to members of the public
(CDPA 1988, s 6(1) and see paras 3.76–3.79).

Public communication also includes:

(2) **making available** to the public of the work by electronic transmission in such a way that members of the public may access it from a place and at a time individually chosen by them (s 20(2)(b)).

 Question

What are the differences between 'broadcasting' and 'making available' in these definitions?

4.58   Although the definition of public communication in the CDPA 1988 uses the term 'include' to refer to the two particular cases, it is not limited to those cases alone and the term is technologically neutral.[135] *Internet transmission* is public communication under the 'making available' head, and only the copyright owner or its licensee may so transmit a work. Accordingly, those who make copyright material such as sound recordings or films available for internet transmission without authorisation will infringe copyright under this category of restricted act. This is the chief purpose of the new right. Uploaders in peer-to-peer networks or on bulletin boards would be examples of such infringers. In the case of broadcasting, the infringer will be the person transmitting the programme, if he has responsibility to any extent for its contents, or the person providing the programme who made with the person transmitting it the arrangements necessary for its transmission.[136] There used to be an important limitation on this form of infringement under section 73 of the Act, which applied where a wireless broadcast was included in a cable programme service by reception and immediate retransmission, but it has been recently repealed.[137]

---

[132]   C-279/13 C *More Entertainment AB v Sandberg Case* [2015] ECDR 15 paras 24–26.

[133]   C-279/13 C *More Entertainment AB v Sandberg Case* [2015] ECDR 15, paras 27, 36.

[134]   See *ITV Broadcasting Ltd v TVCatchup Ltd* [2011] FSR 40; see also, A Ross, 'Linking to live: C More Entertainment AB v Linus Sandberg' [2015] Ent LR 203.

[135]   *ITV Broadcasting Ltd v TVCatchup Ltd* [2011] FSR 40, paras 45, 81.

[136]   CDPA 1988, s 6(3).

[137]   CDPA 1988, s 73 was repealed in July 2017 by the Digital Economy Act 2017. See also the consultation on repealing the provision, Department for Digital, Culture, Media and Sport (DCMS), 'The balance of payments between television platforms and public service broadcasters: options for deregulation' (March 2015); and the government response, DCMS, 'The balance of payments between television platforms and public service broadcasters consultation report' (July 2016).

> **Key points on public communication right**
> - The right is concerned with electronic transmission of works to the public.
> - The right includes broadcasting and internet transmissions of works.
> - The right covers both transmissions where the transmitter decides when the transmission takes place and those where the recipient decides.

4.59   The meaning and scope of the concept of 'communication to the public' has been the subject of much CJEU jurisprudence through which some key principles have emerged. Since the concept has not been defined by the InfoSoc Directive, its meaning and scope must be determined in light of the objectives pursued by the Directive, and in the context in which the provision being interpreted is set.[138] The term must be given an autonomous and uniform interpretation throughout the EU and interpreted broadly to achieve the principal objective of establishing a high level of protection to authors.[139] The term must also be interpreted in a manner that is consistent with international law, in particular taking account of the Berne Convention, Rome Convention, TRIPS, WPT, and WPPT.[140] The concept of 'communication to the public' includes two cumulative criteria: there must be 'an act of communication' of a work, and the communication of that work must be to a 'public'.[141]

4.60   An 'act of communication' refers to any transmission of the protected works, irrespective of the technical means or process used;[142] and, every transmission or retransmission of a work which uses a specific technical means must, as a rule, be individually authorised.[143] For the existence of an 'act of communication', it is sufficient that a work is made available to a public in such a way that the persons forming that public *may* access it, irrespective of whether or not they avail themselves of that opportunity.[144] The concept of 'public' refers to an 'indeterminate' number of potential recipients and implies 'a fairly large number of persons'.[145] This can be understood as follows: the 'indeterminate' nature means making a work perceptible in any appropriate manner to 'persons in general', and not restricted to specific individuals belonging to a private group;[146] a fairly large number of people indicates that 'public' has a 'certain de minimis threshold' so it does not include groups which are too small or insignificant;[147] in determining the size of the audience, the cumulative effects of making works available to potential audiences must be taken account of, ie how many persons have access to the same work at the same time and how many of them have access to it in succession.[148]

---

[138] Case C-161/17 *Land Nordrhein-Westfalen v Dirk Renckhoff* [2018] ECDR 21, para 17; Case C-610/15 *Stichting Brein v Ziggo* [2017] ECDR 19, para 21.

[139] Case C-306/05 *SGAE v Rafael Hoteles SL* [2006] ECR I-11519, paras 31 and 36; Case C-607/11 *ITV Broadcasting Ltd v TVCatchup Ltd* [2013] ECDR 9, para 20.

[140] Case C-306/05 *SGAE v Rafael Hoteles SL* [2006] ECR I-11519, para 35; Case C-135/10 *Società Consortile Fonografici (SCF) v Del Corso* [2012] ECDR 16, para 56; Cases C-403/08 and C-429/08 *Football Association Premier League Ltd v QC Leisure, Murphy v Media Protection Services Ltd* [2012] 1 CMLR 29, para 189.

[141] Case C-325/14 *SBS Belgium* [2016] ECDR 3, para 15; Case C-117/15 *Reha Training v GEMA* [2016] 3 CMLR 40, para 37; Case C-527/15 *Stichting Brein v Jack Frederik Wullems* [2017] ECDR 14, para 29; Case C-161/17 *Land Nordrhein-Westfalen v Dirk Renckhoff* [2018] ECDR 21, para 19.

[142] Cases C-403/08 and C-429/08 *Football Association Premier League Ltd v QC Leisure, Murphy v Media Protection Services Ltd* [2012] 1 CMLR 29, para 193; Case C-325/14 *SBS Belgium* [2016] ECDR 3, para 16; Case C-117/15 *Reha Training v GEMA* [2016] 3 CMLR 40, para 38.

[143] Case C-325/14 *SBS Belgium* [2016] ECDR 3, para 17.

[144] C-466/12 *Svensson v Retriever Sverige AB* [2014] ECDR 9, para 19; Case C-610/15 *Stichting Brein v Ziggo* [2017] ECDR 19, para 31; Case C-161/17 *Land Nordrhein-Westfalen v Dirk Renckhoff* [2018] ECDR 21, para 20.

[145] C-466/12 *Svensson v Retriever Sverige AB* [2014] ECDR 9, para 21; Case C-161/17 *Land Nordrhein-Westfalen v Dirk Renckhoff* [2018] ECDR 21, para 22.

[146] Case C-117/15 *Reha Training v GEMA* [2016] 3 CMLR 40, para 42; Case C-135/10 *Società Consortile Fonografici (SCF) v Del Corso* [2012] ECDR 16, para 85.

[147] Case C-117/15 *Reha Training v GEMA* [2016] 3 CMLR 40, para 43; Case C-135/10 *Società Consortile Fonografici (SCF) v Del Corso* [2012] ECDR 16, para 86.

[148] Case C-117/15 *Reha Training v GEMA* [2016] 3 CMLR 40, para 44; Case C-306/05 *SGAE v Rafael Hoteles SL* [2006] ECR I-11519, para 39; Case C-162/10 *Phonographic Performance (Ireland) Ltd v Ireland* [2012] ECDR 15, para 35.

4.61   Specific challenges arise when there is a retransmission, especially in an online context, of works which have already been communicated to the public with the consent of the right owner, for example a work has been initially communicated by the right owner on a website, but it is then retransmitted by a third party through a hyperlink. In such cases, in order to be a communication to the public,[149]

> the protected work must be communicated using specific technical means, different from those previously used or, failing that, to a 'new public', that is to say, to a public that was not already taken into account by the copyright holders when they authorised the initial communication to the public of their work.

Essentially, either a different technical means must be present,[150] in which case 'new public' is not required,[151] or, more often in the case of hyperlinking, the technical means is not different, so a 'new public' is required.[152] The Court has also indicated that the concept of 'communication to the public' requires an 'individual assessment'.[153] For the purpose of such assessment account has to be taken 'of several complementary criteria, which are not autonomous and are interdependent'; such criteria 'may, in different situations, be present to widely varying degrees' so 'they must be applied both individually and in their interaction with one another'.[154] Such criteria include the role played by the user who transmits the work and the deliberate nature of their intervention, as well as the profit-making nature of the communication.[155]

4.62   The CJEU has developed this meaning of 'communication to the public', not always consistently, by considering the right in a range of contexts.

■ **Case C-306/05 *SGAE v Rafael Hoteles SL* [2006] ECR I-11519 (December 2006)**

S, a collecting society, claimed that provision of television sets with broadcast signals within hotel rooms owned by R required copyright licences as public communications. The ECJ held that the distribution of a signal by means of a TV to different customers in individual hotel bedrooms amounted to communication even though the mere provision of physical facilities did not.[156] The hotel was intervening and transmitting the broadcasts to a new public consisting of a rapid turnover of guests who could decide whether to watch the TVs. In the absence of such intervention, the guests would not be able to enjoy the broadcast work, although physically within that area. The Court identified hotel customers as 'a public' distinct from other 'publics', when holding that the copyright author's licence to the TV broadcasters to communicate its work to the public covered only 'direct' users of the broadcasts, that is, 'owners of reception equipment who, either personally or within their own private or family circles, receive the programme' (para 41). This did not extend to occupants of hotel bedrooms receiving the work by way of a further transmission process inside the hotel, who were a new and different public for the work; a further licence was needed before the material could be communicated to them. In determining the relevant numbers of the public, it is relevant to consider 'the fact that, usually, hotel customers quickly succeed each other' (para 38), that is, it is not a matter of 'freezing' the audience at any particular moment in time.

---

[149]   Case C-161/17 *Land Nordrhein-Westfalen v Dirk Renckhoff* [2018] ECDR 21, para 24. See also, C-466/12 *Svensson v Retriever Sverige AB* [2014] ECDR 9, para 24.

[150]   For example, streaming is a different technical means to cable or satellite broadcasts, *UEFA v BT* [2017] EWHC 3414 (Ch), para 9; *FAPL v BT* [2017] EWHC 480 (Ch), para 36.

[151]   See also Case C-265/16 *VCAST Ltd v RTI SpA* [2018] ECDR 5, paras 48–50; Case C-607/11 *ITV Broadcasting Ltd v TVCatchup Ltd* [2013] ECDR 9, para 39.

[152]   The 'new public' requirement has been subject to criticism and considered by some to be erroneous. See S Karapapa, 'The requirement for a 'new public' in EU copyright law' [2017] E L Rev 63.

[153]   Case C-160/15 *GS Media v Sanoma* [2016] ECDR 25, para 33.

[154]   Case C-117/15 *Reha Training v GEMA* [2016] 3 CMLR 40, para 35; Case C-160/15 *GS Media v Sanoma* [2016] ECDR 25, para 34.

[155]   Case C-160/15 *GS Media v Sanoma* [2016] ECDR 25, paras 35 and 38.

[156]   In Case C-351/12 *OSA v Léčebné* [2014] ECDR 25, a spa was held to be similar to a hotel, in that distribution of a signal by TV or radio sets in patients' rooms in the spa had been communication to the public.

Moreover, whether or not customers switch on the TVs is unimportant; or, putting the point more generally, whether or not members of the public actually access the communication. The ECJ noted that the seemingly very wide potential liability is somewhat restricted by a statement in the InfoSoc Directive recitals: 'the mere provision of physical facilities for enabling or making a communication does not in itself amount to communication within the meaning of this Directive'.[157] Thus, according to the Court, merely installing TV sets in the bedrooms would not be enough for liability, whereas transmitting signals to be picked up by those TVs would complete the infringement. Just as it did not matter there whether or not customers switched on the TVs, whether or not they received the same communications by way of the transmission or whether they were received simultaneously or at different times was also unimportant. But the Court noted that it is not necessary that the unlicensed communicator had to make a profit or receive some other benefit from the activity to be liable for it, but held that the hotel clearly did do so in the case before it, since it affected both the hotel's standing and the price of its rooms (para 44).[158] The view of the Court in relation to profit is also borne out by the absence of any reference to such a requirement in the Directive, but subsequent cases have differed in this regard. The Court observed that the public or private nature of the place where the communication took place was immaterial. The essence of 'making available' was the recipient's ability to choose the place and time of the communication, and this would be rendered meaningless if her choice of a private place made a difference.

■ Cases C-403/08 and C-429/08 *Football Association Premier League Ltd v QC Leisure, Murphy v Media Protection Services Ltd* [2012] 1 CMLR 29 (October 2011)

For the facts in brief, see para 4.35. The Court of Justice held that communication to the public covers transmission of broadcasts, such as showing of football matches on a television to customers in a pub.[159] The customers present in the pub are a new public and the publican intervenes by giving the customers access to the broadcast, without which the customers cannot enjoy them. The profit-making nature of the communication in a pub, in that it attracts an increased number of interested customers, is not irrelevant. The Court noted that communication to the public requires that the work broadcast must be transmitted to a 'public not present at the place where the communication originates' per Article 23 of InfoSoc Directive (paras 200–203).[160] As such, it does not cover any activity which does not involve a 'transmission' or a 'retransmission' of a work.[161]

■ *ITV Broadcasting Ltd v TVCatchup Ltd* [2011] EWHC 2977 (Pat); Case C-607/11 [2013] ECDR 9 (CJ) (March 2013); [2015] EWCA Civ 204 (CA)

ITV, and other commercial television broadcasters, contended that TVC's internet-based broadcasting service permitting its users to receive live streams of free-to-air television broadcasts amounted to acts of communication to the public of ITV's copyright in the films and broadcasts. TVC ensured that its users located in the UK could only watch what they were entitled by virtue of holding a valid TV licence for the free-to-air broadcasts. Floyd J was not persuaded that the principle of law was clear and made a referral to the CJEU. The CJ held that 'each transmission or retransmission of a work which uses a specific technical means' must be individually authorised by the right owner. Since retransmission of a terrestrial TV broadcast over the internet requires a specific technical means, different from that used for the original transmission, it is a 'communication' and requires authorisation when communicated to the public. It was irrelevant that the original transmission could already be lawfully accessed by the user by other means.

---

[157] InfoSoc Directive 2001, recital 27; Case C-306/05 *SGAE v Rafael Hoteles SL* [2006] ECR I-11519, paras 45–47.

[158] AG Sharpston had felt it not necessary to decide this particular point (paras 56–57 of her Opinion).

[159] Kitchin J applied this and held that defendants had infringed the public communication right: *FAPL v QC Leisure* [2012] EWHC 108 (Ch).

[160] This differentiates it from direct representation or live performance of a work, which is covered by the right of public performance (see paras 4.50–4.56).

[161] Case C-283/10 *Circ & Variete Globus București v Uniunea Compozitorilor și Muzicologilor din România—Asociația pentru Drepturi de Autor—UCMR—ADA* (24 November 2011) at para 40.

The profit-making and competitive nature of TVC did not influence the outcome. Floyd J then applied this to the case in October 2013, holding that TVC infringed ITV's copyright in films and broadcasts.[162]

■ C-466/12 *Svensson v Retriever Sverige AB* [2014] ECDR 9 (February 2014)

S were authors of articles in a Swedish Newspaper which were freely available on the newspaper's website. R operated a website that provided its clients with hyperlinks to S' articles. The CJ found that provisions of hyperlinks to protected works, published on the original site without access restrictions, gives users direct access to the works and is 'making available' the linked work, and as such, an act of communication. However, R's website was not communicating to a 'new public' because the newspaper's website did not have any restrictive measures to prevent access and as such, the public targeted by it were all internet users who could freely access them. Therefore, the public using the hyperlinks on R's website were already a 'public' taken into account by the newspaper's website and there was no 'new public'. As such, 'provision on a website of clickable links to works freely available on another website does not constitute an act of communication to the public' (para 32). It is not relevant that when users click on the link, it gives an impression of appearing on the second site rather than the original site. The Court did, however, suggest that if a hyperlink is used to circumvent restrictions placed by the original site to restrict access to the protected works to its subscribers only, hence allowing users who would not otherwise be able to access the work on the original site, then this would be 'communication to the public', the reasoning being this would be communicating to a 'new public' which was not taken into account by the copyright holders when they authorised communication of the protected works on the original site (para 31).

This idea of a 'new public' being necessary in order for a hyperlink to constitute a communication to the public was reiterateds by the CJ in the German reference *BestWater v Mebes*,[163] which involved the framing of B's YouTube video on M's website, ie frame links or embedded links.

■ Case C-117/15 *Reha Training v GEMA* [2016] 3 CMLR 40 (May 2016)

The Court of Justice held that installation of television sets and showing of programmes in a rehabilitation centre constituted communication to the public. It noted that although broadcasting of television programmes is intended to create a diversion for the patients during treatment or in the waiting time, it does constitute an additional service, which does not have medical benefit but has an impact on the establishment's standing and attractiveness and gives it a competitive advantage (para 63). As such, the broadcasting of programmes has a profit-making nature, which is capable of being taken into account to determine the remuneration due.

■ Case C-160/15 *GS Media v Sanoma* [2016] ECDR 25 (September 2016)

S, publisher of *Playboy* magazine, had exclusive rights in photographs from a photoshoot. GS operated a website that provided hyperlinks to such photographs, which had been published without restrictions on another website by a third party without the consent of S. The Court of Justice reiterated that the concept of communication to the public requires an individual assessment, for which several complementary criteria, which are not autonomous and are interdependent, must be taken into account (paras 33–34). Such criteria include 'the indispensable role played by the user and the deliberate nature of its intervention' and the relevance of a communication being of a profit-making nature (paras 35 and 38). The Court also noted the importance of the internet to freedom of expression and of information, and the role of hyperlinking in the sound operation of the internet. It also acknowledged a practical challenge that 'it may be difficult, in particular for individuals who wish to post such links, to ascertain whether a website to which those links are expected to lead, provides access to works which are protected and, if necessary, whether the copyright

---

[162] Floyd J accepted that TVC had a defence for its online streams (but not mobile streams) which fell within the meaning of retransmission by cable under section 73 of the CDPA. The section has been repealed since (see para 4.58).

[163]   Case C-348/13 (October 2014).

holders of those works have consented to their posting on the internet' (para 46). Consequently, if the hyperlinks are being provided by a person who in doing so, does not pursue financial gain and who does not know or could not reasonably have known the illegal nature of the initial publication, then there is no communication to the public; in such a situation, the person providing hyperlinks 'does not, as a general rule, intervene in full knowledge of the consequences of his conduct in order to give customers access to a work illegally posted on the internet' (paras 47–48). On the contrary, if a person knew or ought to have known the illegal nature of the initial publication (eg he was notified of this by the copyright holders) then there is communication to the public (para 49). Equally, if the hyperlinks are provided for profit, then such knowledge must be presumed; due to the profit-making nature of the communication, 'it can be expected that the person who posted such a link carries out the necessary checks to ensure that the work concerned is not illegally published on the website to which those hyperlinks lead' (para 51).

■ Case C-527/15 *Stichting Brein v Jack Frederik Wullems* [2017] ECDR 14 (April 2017)

W sold *Filmspeler*, a multi-media player, in which he pre-installed add-ons with hyperlinks to websites providing protected works without the consent of copyright holders. The Court of Justice applied the *Svensson* and *GS media* decisions. It held that there was an act of communication, as the multimedia player afforded purchasers of the player direct access to protected works available freely on the internet, just as hyperlinks did. The multi-media player was not a 'mere' provision of physical facilities for enabling or making a communication because W pre-installs and markets the add-ons, with such 'intervention enabling a direct link to be established between websites broadcasting counterfeit works and purchasers of the multimedia player, without which the purchasers would find it difficult to benefit from those protected works' (para 41). The multimedia players were supplied for profit-making, and the main attraction for purchasers was the pre-installed add-ons providing access to works published illegally on the internet. They were also sold with full knowledge that pre-installed add-ons containing hyperlinks gave access to works published illegally, as specifically stated on the advertising for the player. Consequently, the sale of the multimedia player constitutes a communication to the public.

■ Case C-610/15 *Stichting Brein v Ziggo* [2017] ECDR 19 (June 2017)

Z and others were internet access providers whose subscribers were using an online file-sharing platform, The Pirate Bay (TPB), which indexes BitTorrent files.[164] In this reference from the Supreme Court of the Netherlands, the question was whether The Pirate Bay communicates works to the public even though it doesn't host them. The Court of Justice, inferred from previous case law that 'as a rule, any act by which a user, with full knowledge of the relevant facts, provides its clients with access to protected works is liable to constitute an "act of communication"' (para 34). TPB platform operators play an essential role in making works available, as they 'intervene, with full knowledge of the consequences of their conduct, to provide access to protected works, by indexing on that platform torrent files which allow users of the platform to locate those works and to share them within the context of a peer-to-peer network' without which the works could not be shared by the users, or sharing would be more complex (para 36). TBP operators do not merely provide physical facilities because the 'platform indexes torrent files in such a way that the works to which the torrent files refer may be easily located and downloaded by the users' and the platform offers a search engine as well as 'an index classifying the works under different categories, based on the type of the works, their genre or their popularity, within which the works made available are divided, with the platform's operators checking to ensure that a work has been placed in the appropriate category' and deleting obsolete or faulty files and actively filtering some content (para 38). The TPB was run for profit-making by generating advertising revenues and its operators were aware that the platform provided access to works published illegally as they were informed of this, and they themselves expressed this to be their purpose. As such, there was communication to a 'new public' (paras 45–46). The Court held that making available and managing an online sharing platform like TPB constitutes a communication to the public.

---

[164] For an explanation of how file-sharing through BitTorrent works, see paras 9–12 of this decision.

■ **Case C-161/17** *Land Nordrhein-Westfalen v Dirk Renckhoff* **[2018] ECDR 21 (August 2018)**

DR, a photographer, gave the right of use in a photograph exclusively to the operators of an online travel portal. The photograph was available on the travel website without any restrictions on downloading. A pupil of a school (a school under the responsibity of L) downloaded the photo and used it to illustrate a school presentation. The presentation was uploaded to the school website, from which the photograph was available for anyone to download. The Court of Justice noted that both the the the initial communication of the work by the travel portal and its subsequent communication by the school website were made with the same technical means, so the issue was whether the photograph had been communicated to a 'new public' (paras 25–26). The Court held that 'the public taken into account by the copyright holder when he consented to the communication of his work on the website on which it was originally published is composed solely of users of that site and not of users of the website on which the work was subsequently published without the consent of the rightholder, or other internet users' (para 35). It was irrelevant that 'the copyright holder did not limit the ways in which internet users could use the photograph' (para 36). Consequently, there was communication to a 'new public'. The Court gave three reasons: first, authors' right to communication is preventative in nature and it would be deprived of its effectiveness if reposting of materials without consent was not a communication to a new public; second, to hold that reposting of materials without consent does not constitute a communication to a new public would amount to applying an exhaustion rule to the right of communication and this would be contrary to InfoSoc Directive Article 3(3); third, to hold so would also deprive the copyright holder of the opportunity to claim an appropriate reward for the use of his work (paras 30–34).

L had argued that the *Svensson* case must be applied because there should be no difference between hyperlinking to a material posted on one website, and reposting such material by uploading it to another website. The Court of Justice did not agree and distinguished previous case law on hyperlinking. It noted that first, hyperlinks contribute to the sound operation of the internet by enabling the dissemination of large amount of works online but the reposting of a work previously uploaded on another website does not contribute, to the same extent, to such objective. Secondly, in the case of hyperlinking, the author has control if he no longer wishes to communicate the work, ie the author can remove the original upload, rendering any hyperlinks to it by third parties obsolete. However, in the case of reposting, the author loses control and the new upload is independent of the original upload and may remain available online. Thirdly, unlike hyperlinking, the user downloading and then reposting the work on the latter website plays 'a decisive role' in communicating the work to a new public.

4.63 Although recent CJEU jurisprudence has helpfully clarified the broad scope of 'communication to the public', some ambiguities in relation to its application to online services remain. For instance, when users upload infringing works on online platforms (eg YouTube, Vimeo) which host content, as opposed to operating as a peer to peer network or hyperlinking, then are such platforms communicating the work to the public? The Court of Justice has not yet directly addressed this. However, the European Commission has identified a problem, and proposed reforms in this area under the Draft Copyright Directive 2016, which notes in Recital 37:[165]

> Over the last years, the functioning of the online content marketplace has gained in complexity. Online services providing access to copyright protected content uploaded by their users without the involvement of right holders have flourished and have become main sources of access to content online. This affects rightholders' possibilities to determine whether, and under which conditions, their work and other subject-matter are used as well as their possibilities to get an appropriate remuneration for it.

---

[165] Proposal for a Directive on Copyright in the Digital Single Market, 14 September 2016, COM(2016) 593 final. See also, M Leistner and A Metzger, 'The EU copyright package: a way out of the dilemma in two stages' [2017] IIC 381; M Senftleben et al, 'The recommendation on measures to safeguard fundamental rights and the open internet in the framework of the EU copyright reform' [2018] EIPR 149.

One consequence of this is a 'value gap', ie the gap between the revenues of online platforms from user generated content and the revenues received by right holders. To address this lack of transfer of value from platforms to right holders, Article 13 proposes an obligation on online platforms which store and give access to large amounts of works uploaded by their users. They must take measures, in cooperation with rightholders, to ensure the functioning of agreements concluded with rightholders for the use of their works, or to prevent the availability on their services of infringing works identified by rightholders, through measures such as deploying content recognition technologies. This provision has been the most controversial aspect of the reforms proposed under the Directive, and generated significant academic commentary and media attention, as well as intense lobbying on the part of both the creative industries and the tech giants. At the time of writing, the EU legislative process is not complete (see para 2.15).

 Value gap and Brexit

In a 'no-deal' scenario resulting from the withdrawal of the UK from the EU, the UK may not have any obligation (see further para 2.20) to implement any changes in relation to value gap that may eventually emerge from Article 13 of the Draft Copyright Directive.

 Question

Find out whether the EU legislative process for the Draft Copyright Directive 2016 is complete and if so, what provisions on the so-called 'value gap' have been adopted in the final text.

4.64   The application of 'communication to the public' to different types of file-sharing, and other unauthorised activity on the internet has also received much attention in the UK (primarily in relation to the grant of s 97A injunctions, see para 4.78). The issue of whether operators of file-sharing websites can be liable themselves for 'making available' infringing material even though that material is placed upon its servers by others[166] arose in the UK much earlier than it did in CJEU jurisprudence (see the *Ziggo* decision at para 4.62). In *Twentieth Century Fox v Newzbin*[167] (for facts see para 4.74), the claimants contended that N made their films available to the public under section 20(2)(b) of the CDPA 1988, while N argued that its service was passive and it acted as an intermediary providing links to the sites for the films. Kitchin J held that N had intervened in a highly material way to make the films available to a new audience, being its premium subscription-paying members. Although N did not store the films, it had intervened 'by providing a sophisticated technical and editorial system which allows its premium members to download all the component messages of the film of their choice upon pressing a button, and so avoid days of (potentially futile) effort in seeking to gather those messages together for themselves' (para 125). Similarly, operators of several BitTorrent indexing websites (eg KAT, H33T, and Fenopy) have also been held to infringe rights owners' copyright by communication to the public.[168] It has also become possible to access infringing content through set-top boxes, media players (eg Amazon Fire TV Stick) and mobile device apps which connect directly to streaming servers via their IP addresses, and do not rely on connecting to specific websites. It has been held that operators of such streaming servers, which provide live footage of Premier league football matches, infringe copyright by communication to the public.[169]

---

[166] The operators may, however, have available the defences discussed at para 4.77.

[167] [2010] ECDR 8 (Ch).

[168] *EMI Records Ltd v British Sky Broadcasting Ltd* [2013] ECDR 8 (Ch), paras 44–51; *1967 Ltd v British Sky Broadcasting Ltd* [2014] EWHC 3444 (Ch), paras 18–21. This cause of action was not pursued against the operators of The Pirate Bay in the UK case of *Dramatico Entertainment Ltd and Others v BSkyB and Others* (see para 4.75).

[169] *FAPL v BT* [2017] EWHC 480 (Ch). Notably, in this case, Arnold J applied the decisions in *Svensson* and *GS Media* to reach this conclusion regarding communication to the public by the operators.

4.65   Another issue has been whether the users of file-sharing websites, who upload material, can be liable for 'making available'. In *Dramatico v BSkyB*,[170] the claimant contended that users of The Pirate Bay website communicated their copyright works to the public. Arnold J held that users of The Pirate Bay do make the works available under section 20(2)(b) of the CDPA 1988 and as such infringe claimant's copyright. They communicate them to users, who have not purchased the works from an authorised source who are the new public, being 'a public which was not taken into account by the right holders when authorising the distribution of the recordings' (para 70). This approach has been followed to hold that uploading of copyright protected files by users of several other BitTorrent indexing websites is communication to the public.[171]

4.66   Another issue has been whether operators and users of websites that provide hyperlinks to copyright protected works in a categorised and searchable form can be liable for public communication, even though the protected works themselves are hosted on third-party sites. In *Paramount v British Sky Broadcasting Ltd*,[172] decided before the decisions in *Svensson* and *BestWater*, Arnold J held that while a mere provision of a hyperlink may not amount to communication to the public, it becomes so where the provider of hyperlinks also intervenes in a highly material way to make the copyright works available to a new audience. In this case, without the hyperlinks on SolarMovie and TubePlus websites it would be very difficult for the public to access much of the works directly from third-party host sites. Even where works could be accessed directly from host sites, the hyperlinks made it much easier to access such works. As such, the operators of these websites communicated the works to the public. The judge noted that if he is wrong on this point, then the operators were jointly liable with host sites who clearly communicated the works to the public (paras 34–35). It was also held that the users providing hyperlinks was communication to the public as a result of the combined effect of providing links and also uploading works to the host sites (para 37). In *Paramount v British Sky Broadcasting Ltd*,[173] Henderson J followed the decision by Arnold J above and held operators of similar websites providing hyperlinks to third-party hosted content were communicating to the public. The judge distinguished the decision in *Svensson* (para 4.62) on its facts.[174]

4.67   An interesting question was raised in *Twentieth Century Fox v Sky UK*,[175] where 'Popcorn Time-type' websites allowed users to download an application to their computer, which then allowed access to indexed and catalogued copyright works using BitTorrent protocol directly from host sites. The Court noted that it was the application itself, running on the user's computer, which provided access to indexed catalogues of protected works, and once downloaded the application never re-connected to the website from which it originated. For these reasons the operators of the Popcorn Time-type websites were not communicating works to the public, as there is no transmission or re-transmission of the works at all, and all they provided was a tool, in the form of the application (para 38).[176]

(6) Infringement by adaptation

4.68   Making any adaptation of a literary, dramatic, or musical work infringes its copyright (see also para 4.30).[177] An adaptation is made when it is recorded in writing or otherwise.[178] Copying such an adaptation in any material form, issuing it to the public for the first time, performing it in public, broadcasting it,

---

[170] [2012] ECDR 14 (Ch).

[171] *EMI Records Ltd v British Sky Broadcasting Ltd* [2013] ECDR 8 (Ch), paras 44–51. *1967 Ltd v British Sky Broadcasting Ltd* [2014] EWHC 3444 (Ch), paras 15–17; importantly, it was noted in this case at para 16 that the CJ judgment in *Svensson* did not detract from the reasoning adopted in earlier UK cases on infringement by users.

[172] [2013] EWHC 3479 (Ch) (November 2013).   [173] [2014] EWHC 937 (Ch) (February 2014).   [174] ibid, paras 31–33.

[175] [2015] EWHC 1082 (Ch).

[176] However, operators of host sites were communicating to the public and operators of Popcorn Time-type websites were jointly liable with them, ibid, para 55; see also, S Baggs et al, 'Curtains down on Popcorn Time: s.97A takes centre stage' [2016] EIPR 56.

[177] CDPA 1988, s 21(1).   [178] CDPA 1988, s 21(1).

communicating it to the public, or further adapting it, also infringes the copyright in the original work.[179] In relation to *literary works other than computer programs or databases*, or to dramatic works, adaptation means any of the following things:[180]

- a *translation* of the work (eg from French into English);

- in the case of a dramatic work, conversion into a non-dramatic work or, in the case of a non-dramatic work, a *dramatisation*;

- a *version* of the work in which the story or action is conveyed wholly or mainly by means *of pictures* in a form suitable for reproduction in a book or in a newspaper, magazine or similar periodical.

4.69   In relation to *computer programs and databases*, adaptation means an arrangement or altered version, or a translation.[181] Translation is given a particular meaning in relation to computer programs, where it is to include a version of the program in which it is converted into or out of a computer language or code or into a different computer language or code.[182] This is of particular importance in respect of 'reverse engineering' activities, which may well be caught by this provision if not by the prohibition on copying.[183]

Discussion point   For answer guidance visit **www.oup.com/uk/brown5e**.

What does 'adaptation' add to the concept of 'copying' (paras 4.24–4.41)? Is there adaptation or copying when a book is made into a film, or when a film is made into (1) a book; or (2) a play?

Key point on adaptation

- Adaptation deals with specific cases not clearly within the concept of 'copying'.

Authorisation of infringement

4.70   The copyright in a work is infringed by:[184]

> any person who, without the licence of the copyright owner, authorises another person to do any of the restricted acts.

The 1988 Act provides for both primary liability (person who 'does' without the licence of the copyright owner any of the restricted acts) as well as accessory liability (person who 'authorises another person to do' without the licence of the copyright owner any of the restricted acts). There cannot be infringement by authorisation unless there has been an infringement, ie someone 'does' the restricted acts. To authorise an infringement is to 'sanction, approve, or countenance' it,[185] a formulation capable of a very wide meaning, especially when conjoined with the apparent willingness of the courts to treat indifference as capable of being authorisation.[186] However, the concept has previously been applied in a relatively restricted way, by employing a test of the degree of authority, or control, which the defender had over those who actually carried out the infringement.

---

[179] CDPA 1988, s 21(2).   [180] CDPA 1988, s 21(3)(a).   [181] CDPA 1988, s 21(3)(ab), (ac).   [182] CDPA 1988, s 21(4).
[183] See para 4.22 for reverse engineering.   [184] CDPA 1988, s 16(2).
[185] This definition of 'authorise' was first stated in *Monckton v Pathe Freres Pathephone Ltd* [1914] 1 KB 395 and *Evans v Hulton & Co Ltd* [1924] WN 130.
[186] *PRS v Ciryl Theatrical Syndicate* [1924] 1 KB 1; *Moorhouse v University of New South Wales* [1976] RPC 151 (HCA); *CBS v Ames Record & Tapes* [1982] Ch 91; *PRS v Kwik-Fit Group Ltd* [2008] ECDR 2.

■ *CBS v Ames Records and Tapes* [1982] Ch 91

The defendants owned a chain of record shops and began to operate record lending libraries in them. This facilitated infringing copying of records by borrowers from the libraries and the plaintiffs argued that this was 'countenancing' infringement in such a way as to authorise it. Whitford J refused to grant an injunction: 'an authorisation can only come from somebody having or purporting to have authority . . . an act is not authorised by somebody who merely enables or possibly assists or even encourages another to do that act, but does not purport to have any authority which he can grant to justify the doing of the act' (at 105).

■ *RCA Corp v John Fairfax & Sons Ltd* [1982] RPC 91 (NSW Supreme Court)

Publishing a newspaper article or advertisement referring to the possibility of tape-recording records by use of machinery does not authorise infringement because the authors cannot control what individuals do with the machinery once they have bought it.

■ *Vigneux v Canadian PRS* [1945] AC 108 (PC)

A company which rented a juke box to restaurateurs was held not to authorise infringement of the copyright in musical works by performance because it 'had no control over the use of the machine [and] . . . no voice as to whether at any particular time it was to be available to the restaurant customers or not' (per Lord Russell of Killowen at 123).

■ *CBS Songs Ltd v Amstrad Consumer Electronics plc* [1988] 1 AC 1013

The manufacture, distribution and supply of machines capable of use by buyers for copying copyright works at high speed cannot be by themselves authorisations of infringement since, again, the manufacturer lacks control over the uses to which the machine is put, and it is also capable of legitimate use.

Discussion point   For answer guidance visit **www.oup.com/uk/brown5e**.

Find out what happened in the leading case on the US copyright law equivalent of infringement by authorisation—contributory infringement: *Sony Corp of America v Universal City Studios Inc* 464 US 417 (1984) (US Supreme Court). Would a UK court have reached the same decision?

Cases finding authorisation to have taken place

4.71   The decisions just discussed may be compared with those where there has been held to be authorisation. Supply of a film of a play for exhibition at a cinema was held to authorise infringement of the copyright in the play in *Falcon v Famous Players Film Co*.[187] Ordering spare parts from a manufacturer authorised him to infringe the copyright in drawings of those spare parts.[188] The prior approval by a local authority of the list of musical works to be played on a public bandstand was held to be an authorisation of infringement.[189] A restaurant owner allowing DJs to play in his restaurant was held to be authorisation of infringement, because the authorisation of the playing of music in public is the relevant act in such circumstances, and it is not the authorisation of specific songs which infringe the copyright.[190] In all these cases there was a direct and immediate link between the act of the defendant and the infringement which followed. They differ, too,

---

[187] [1926] 2 KB 474.   [188] *Standen Engineering v Spalding & Sons* [1984] FSR 554.
[189] *PRS v Bray UDC* [1930] AC 377 (PC).
[190] *PPL Ltd v Abimbola Balgun t/a Mama Africa* [2018] EWHC 1327 (Ch), paras 27–28.

from most of the cases cited in the previous paragraph where what was really being complained of was the fact that the defendant had created an opportunity for others to infringe which had probably, even certainly, been taken up, but specific instances of this were not brought to the Court's attention.[191] However, where the complaint is about the provision to others of the opportunity to infringe and it can be coupled with the necessary degree of control over those others and specific instances of infringement, then there may be liability for authorisation.

■ *Moorhouse v University of New South Wales* [1976] RPC 151 (HCA)

The High Court of Australia held that a university had authorised infringement by students (and, presumably, staff) by providing photocopying facilities in the university library without adequate supervision of what was copied. A notice near the photocopiers warning against copyright infringement was insufficient to avoid liability. Specific incidents of infringing copying were established and the Court stressed that authorisation might be implied from indifference to infringement where it was likely that such infringement would occur. Here the university also had power to control the access of students to photocopying facilities, either by not providing them or by ensuring through supervision that no infringing copying was done and accordingly it was liable.[192]

> In a complaint, the Advertising Standards Authority in the UK, an independent regulator for advertising, had to unusually consider the potential for copyright infringement (ASA Adjudication on 3GA Ltd, Complaint 140713). The adjudication concerned an advert which read:
>
> 'The Brennan JB7 is a CD player with a hard disk that stores up to 5,000 CDs . . . It saves space and clutter and delivers near immediate access to an entire music collection . . . The Brennan also records from vinyl and cassette so you can enjoy your entire music collection but keep it out of the way in another room or retire it to the attic . . . What's the point in owning hundreds of CDs worth thousands of pounds if you never listen to them? . . . CDs are great but they are also inconvenient, inaccessible and a bit of a chore . . . Load CDs in about four minutes . . . One touch record from vinyl, cassette or radio.'
>
> The complaint was upheld as the advertisement was misleading because it made references to the product being able to copy music and encouraged customers to do so but did not make it clear that copying was illegal without permission from the copyright owner, and so it incited customers to break the law.

Notices and statements as defences against claims of authorisation

4.72   A further significant point in the *Moorhouse* case concerned the use of notices as a defence to a claim of authorisation. The university issued guides for library users which made incomplete reference to the provisions of the copyright legislation on copying and stated that a copy of the Act was available in the photocopying room. It was held that these were insufficient to rebut authorisation, but that an invitation to use copying facilities might be so restricted as to avoid liability.[193] But even the fullest possible notices will be inadequate if, despite their existence, infringing copying continues and the person able to control its occurrence remains indifferent to this.[194] The placing of copyright warning notices in the premises and on

---

[191] See in particular the discussion of the problem of 'home copying', which was the real issue in *CBS Songs Ltd v Amstrad Consumer Electronics plc* [1988] 1 AC 1013.

[192] Compare *CBS v Ames Records & Tapes* [1982] Ch 91, where no copying machines were provided. Under the CDPA 1988, the Moorhouse situation would be avoided through the limited scope of the permitted acts (eg, see CDPA 1988, ss 29 and 36) and reprography licensing (ss 130 and 136–141). The Copyright Licensing Agency plays a significant role here. See further at www.cla.co.uk/education.

[193] *Moorhouse v University of New South Wales* [1976] RPC 151 (HCA).

[194] *Moorhouse v University of New South Wales* [1976] RPC 151 per Jacobs J at 166.

the copies of records lent was an important (but not the sole) factor in the *Ames Records & Tapes* case, where it was held that there had been no authorisation.[195] Contrast with:

■ *Law Society of Upper Canada v CCH* [2004] 1 SCR 339 (Supreme Court of Canada)

The Law Society of Upper Canada maintained its Great Library at Osgoode Hall in Toronto. The library was for reference and research and had one of the largest collections of legal material in Canada. A self-service photocopier was located in the library for the use of patrons (Law Society members, the judiciary, and other authorised researchers), alongside a notice warning that the library would not be responsible for any copies made in infringement of copyright. Law publishers challenged these practices as authorisation of infringement. It was held that the Law Society did not authorise copyright infringement. Authorisation could be inferred from indirect acts and omissions, but the authorisation of use of equipment which could be used to infringe copyright was not enough. Posting a notice warning against infringement was not an express acknowledgement that the machines would be used in an illegal manner. Authorisations should be presumed to be given to lawful acts only, this being rebuttable if a relationship or degree of control existed between the authoriser and persons who infringed copyright. This was not the case here, and there was no evidence of actual infringements. *Moorhouse* was criticised as shifting the balance in copyright too far in favour of the owner's rights, unnecessarily interfering with the proper use of copyrighted works for the good of society as a whole.

Discussion point For answer guidance visit **www.oup.com/uk/brown5e**.

Is the criticism of *Moorhouse* in this case justified? Consider the implications for internet service provider liability, discussed in paras 4.73–4.78.

Key points on authorisation

- Authorisation of infringement is sanctioning, countenancing, or approving another person's primary infringement where one has authority or control over a primary infringer.

- Creating opportunities for others to infringe, for example by means of machinery, is not by itself authorisation, especially where legitimate activities are also made possible by the action.

- Notices warning against infringement may be a factor in preventing authorisation, but are not usually enough by themselves.

Authorisation and infringement on the internet

4.73 Liability by authorisation has obvious importance for infringement on the internet against various service providers such as the operators of unlicensed file-sharing networks or website operators but also broadband providers, universities, and other bodies which enable access to the internet for customers, students, and others by means of which infringing internet activity can take place, whether by way of copying or the public communication right. Can such bodies be liable for authorising such infringing use? Operators of early unlicensed 'file-sharing' on peer-to-peer (P2P) networks such as Napster, Grokster, and Kazaa, had been held liable in an important body of case law in the US[196] (under the equivalent of authorisation,

---

[195] *CBS v Ames Record & Tapes* [1982] Ch 91.

[196] *A&M Records v Napster* 239 F 3d 1004 (2001); *Metro-Goldwyn-Mayer Studios Inc v Grokster Ltd* 380 F 3d 1154 (9th Cir, 2004); 545 US 913 (2005) (US Supreme Court).

the concept of contributory infringement) and Australia[197] in the 2000s. During this period, there was uncertainty as to whether similar service providers may be liable for authorisation of infringement in the UK. The *Amstrad* and *Ames Records & Tapes* cases had held the providers of facilities not liable despite the fact that their services and products rendered infringement easy and probable;[198] the crucial factors being that lawful activity is possible with the facilities provided and that the defendants had given express warnings to customers against use for infringing copying. This may have seemed encouraging for those whose facilities enable others to make use of the internet: the facilities are capable of many lawful as well as infringing uses, and the providers generally give warnings to users against unlawful activity with the service.

 Discussion point   For answer guidance visit **www.oup.com/uk/brown5e**.

Find out how the US and Australian equivalent of authorisation of infringement was applied to early file-sharing services like Napster, Grokster, and Kazaa in the cases referred to in nn 196–197.

4.74   However, in an important judgment in 2010, it was made clear that service providers and site operators on the internet may nonetheless be liable for authorisation of infringement.

■ *Twentieth Century Fox and Others v Newzbin* [2010] ECDR 8

Usenet, a worldwide internet discussion system, allowed users to post content such as films, which could be split into lots of smaller-sized components, and could be retrieved by downloading and reassembling all of the components. N operated a website, which allowed its premium members to search and locate the content on Usenet and allowed them to download an NZB file for each content, which when run on a computer would reassemble the content from its component parts and make an infringing copy. The claimants, makers, and distributors of films contended that N had authorised infringement by its members. N claimed that its website was just a search engine and content-agnostic. Kitchin J first reviewed earlier case law on authorisation and noted that:

> it is clear . . . that 'authorise' means the grant or purported grant of the right to do the act complained of. It does not extend to mere enablement, assistance or even encouragement. The grant or purported grant to do the relevant act may be express or implied from all the relevant circumstances. In a case which involves an allegation of authorisation by supply, these circumstances may include the nature of the relationship between the alleged authoriser and the primary infringer, whether the equipment or other material supplied constitutes the means used to infringe, whether it is inevitable it will be used to infringe, the degree of control which the supplier retains and whether he has taken any steps to prevent infringement. These are matters to be taken into account and may or may not be determinative depending upon all the other circumstances (para 90).

The judge held that N had actively encouraged, guided, and rewarded its editors to make reports on films; provided a facility which went beyond indexing and categorisation, and instead identified components of a content and saved its members the 'the very substantial task of manually locating and identifying each of them separately'; provided useful information in relation to the content; created and controlled the NZB facility which was the means of infringement; and had failed to install any filtering system.[199]

---

[197]   *Universal Music Australia Pty Ltd v Sharman License Holdings Ltd* (2005) 220 ALR 1 (FCA).
[198]   *CBS Inc v Ames Records & Tapes Ltd* [1982] Ch 91; *CBS Songs Ltd v Amstrad Consumer Electronics plc* [1988] 1 AC 1013.
[199]   Bear in mind also that unauthorised file-sharing might also involve infringement of the public communication right by the operators themselves (para 4.64).

4.75   In *Dramatico Entertainment Ltd and Others v BSkyB and Others*,[200] Arnold J followed the four factors suggested in *Newzbin* and held that operators of The Pirate Bay website authorised its users' infringing acts of copying and communication to the public.[201] The judge noted that The Pirate Bay provides a sophisticated and user-friendly facility and goes well beyond enabling infringement to sanctioning and approving it. Authorisation of infringement has since been routinely argued as a basis for liability against a range of site operators on the internet.[202]

Tackling infringement on the internet—an ongoing challenge with no 'perfect' solution

4.76   The music and other entertainment industries have claimed that unauthorised file-sharing, link sharing, and streaming activity of their protected content has had, and is having, a significant impact upon the 'legitimate' market for their products. Although it is possible to make individual file-sharers, both downloaders and uploaders of infringing content, liable for infringing copyright (paras 4.40 and 4.65), this is generally seen as an expensive option with little deterrent effect. So how can online infringement be prevented? The two major developments since the phenomenon first became prominent through the Napster case in the United States in 2000–01 (see para 4.73) have been the growth of licensed downloading and streaming sites, as well as several Court decisions around the world, including the UK, against the operators (eg by authorisation) and users of unlicensed file-sharing sites as infringers of copyright. The latter in particular, has paved the way for injunctions to be obtained against internet access providers to block access to infringing websites.

Internet service providers: 'safe harbours' and injunctions

4.77   The Directive on electronic commerce in the EU[203] sets out an exemption from liability for intermediaries where they play a wholly passive role as mere conduits of information from third parties.[204] It also limits service providers' liability for other activities such as the storage of information provided by recipients of the service and at their request (hosting), as long as the provider does not know of the illegal activity, is unaware of the facts and circumstances from which illegal activity is apparent, and acts expeditiously to remove or disable access upon learning or becoming aware of the activity.[205] There is explicitly no obligation actively to screen or monitor third-party content.[206] In the United States, the Digital Millennium Copyright Act 1998 exempts the service provider from liability where it has no knowledge or information about the infringing material in its system, acts expeditiously to remove or block access to material when knowledge or information comes to hand, does not receive any financial benefit directly attributable to the infringing material, and complies with certain 'notice and take-down' provisions of the Act enabling copyright owners to require the service provider to remove or block access to infringing material.

4.78   The EU safe harbour provisions exempt liability, but they do not preclude injunctive relief. Under section 97A of the CDPA 1988,[207] the High Court can grant an injunction against a service provider where that

---

[200] [2012] ECDR 14 (Ch).

[201] Note that, in contrast, the Court of Justice in *Ziggo* (para 4.62) held that the operators of TPB themselves communicated the works to the public, as the Court did not differentiate between primary liability and accessory liability. See further, A Ross, 'Communication to the public–Court of Justice gives the Pirate Bay no quarter' [2017] Ent LR 248; N Cordell and B Potts, 'Communication to the public or accessory liability? Is the CJEU using communication to the public to harmonise accessory liability across the EU?' [2018] EIPR 289.

[202] See, eg, BitTorrent indexing websites KAT, H33T, and Fenopy in *EMI Records Ltd v British Sky Broadcasting Ltd* [2013] ECDR 8 (Ch); SolarMovie and TubePlus websites providing hyperlinks to third-party hosted content in *Paramount Home Entertainment v BSkyB* [2013] EWHC 3479 (Ch); cf Popcorn Time-type websites providing an application in *Twentieth Century Fox v Sky UK* [2015] EWHC 1082 (Ch) (see para 4.67). See also R Arnold & P S Davies, 'Accessory liability for intellectual property infringement: the case of authorisation' [2017] LQR 442.

[203] European Parliament and Council Directive 2000/31/EC on certain legal aspects of Information Society services, in particular electronic commerce, in the Internal Market (E-Commerce Directive), implemented in the Electronic Commerce (EC Directive) Regulations 2002 (SI 2002/2013).

[204] E-Commerce Directive, Art 12; Electronic Commerce Regulations, reg 17.

[205] See E-Commerce Directive, Art 14; Electronic Commerce Regulations, reg 19 (hosting). See also Case C-236/08 *Google France Sarl v Louis Vuitton Malletier SA* [2010] RPC 19; Case C-324/09 *L'Oréal SA v eBay International AG* [2011] RPC 27.

[206] E-Commerce Directive 2000, Art 15.

[207] Implementing Art 8(3) of the InfoSoc Directive 2001. See also Enforcement Directive 2004/48/EC, Art 11; R Arnold, 'Website-blocking injunctions: the question of legislative basis' [2015] EIPR 623; see further paras 21.79–21.80.

service provider has actual knowledge of another person (eg users and operators of websites) using its service to infringe copyright. Rights owners have been successful in obtaining a series of injunctions against providers of broadband internet access, whose services were used by one or more subscribers to receive infringing copies of works, to block access to a range of websites including Newzbin2 and The Pirate Bay,[208] and recently, WatchOnlineSeries.[209] More recently, the High Court has also granted such injunctions requiring 'live blocking' of streaming servers which are used to stream Premier League and Champions League football matches.[210] Such injunctions have been held not to be in contravention of the safe harbour provisions above.[211] Although these injunctions have proved to be quite popular in the UK, the policy question is whether they are the best mechanism to tackle the problem of online infringement.

Graduated response mechanism

4.79   Other solutions such as a 'graduated response' mechanism for tackling online infringement have also been considered in the UK.[212] The Digital Economy Act 2010, was enacted to allow for imposition of obligations on internet access providers to make them assist, cooperate, and participate in reducing unlawful file-sharing. The provisions in sections 3–18 aim to reduce illegal file-sharing through a system of cooperation between such internet service providers (ISPs) and right owners, whereby they work together to prevent and act upon copyright infringement on the ISP's network. It provides for imposition of certain obligations on ISPs requiring them to: notify subscribers of reported infringements once they receive a copyright infringement report from a right owner who suspects that his right has been infringed by a particular IP address, which is a subscriber of the ISP; to provide infringement lists to copyright owners on request, being a list of infringement reports made relating to a subscriber without identifying them[213] (together known as 'initial obligations'); and to take technical measures to limit internet access of subscribers should initial obligations be ineffective and infringement continues (known as 'technical obligations').[214] A further provision, section 17, requiring ISPs to block websites, was dropped by the government, although rights owners have successfully achieved the same result through injunctions under section 97A (para 4.78). The Act is an example of a graduated response mechanism for reducing infringement from persistent infringers but also a mechanism to provide education and information about legitimate services for accessing copyright content online. However, it has also been controversial, partly due to strong objections to its contents by users, rights groups, and ISPs,[215] but also due to the rush to enact it in the parliamentary wash-up period. These provisions were not implemented and the UK government shelved the regime.[216] One policy issue, however, is whether statutorily approved graduated response mechanisms or voluntary industry-led education, enforcement, or alert, schemes are a step in the right direction to reduce unlawful file-sharing.

---

[208] *Twentieth Century Fox Film Corporation and Others v BT* [2011] RPC 28, [2011] EWHC 2714 (Ch); *Dramatico Entertainment Ltd and Others v BSkyB and Others* [2012] ECDR 24 (Ch). See A Shaw, '"Newz-binned": High Court grants first copyright infringement blocking order against a UK ISP': Twentieth Century Fox Film Corporation & others v British Telecommunications PLC' (2012) 18(4) CTLR 105.

[209] *Twentieth Century Fox v Sky UK* [2015] EWHC 1082 (Ch).

[210] *FAPL v BT* [2017] EWHC 480 (Ch); *UEFA v BT* [2017] EWHC 3414 (Ch); *FAPL v BT* [2018] EWHC 1828 (Ch).

[211] *Twentieth Century Fox Film Corporation and Others v BT* [2011] RPC 28, [2011] EWHC 2714 (Ch).

[212] See generally A Barron, 'Graduated response' à l'anglaise: online copyright infringement and the Digital Economy Act (U.K.) 2010' [2011] 3(2) J Media Law 305; R Giblin, 'Evaluating graduated response' (2014) 37(2) Columbia J Law & Arts 147.

[213] To ensure compliance with data protection, right owners can apply for a court order should they want the infringer to be named.

[214] The Digital Economy Act provides for insertion of relevant provisions in the Communications Act 2003. These obligations are to be governed and implemented by regulatory codes to be prepared by the telecoms regulator Ofcom and approved by Parliament. Ofcom published a draft 'Initial Obligations Code' in June 2012.

[215] It also faced opposition through an attempted judicial review by UK ISPs TalkTalk and BT, on the basis that its provisions are not compatible with EU law. The Court of Appeal held that it was compatible with a number of EU Directives, including the E-Commerce Directive 2000 and the Data Protection Directive 1995. See *R (on the application of British Telecommunications plc) v Secretary of State for Business, Innovation and Skills* [2012] 2 CMLR 23.

[216] www.out-law.com/en/articles/2014/july/digital-economy-act-copyright-regime-shelved-by-uk-government .

Secondary infringement of copyright

4.80   'Secondary' infringements[217] of copyright are distinguished from 'primary' infringements because the defender is not liable unless he knew or had reason to believe that he was handling infringing copies, or that the performances would infringe copyright.[218] The following acts in relation to infringing copies of works constitute 'secondary' infringements of copyright:

- importing otherwise than for the importer's private and domestic use;
- possessing in the course of a business;
- selling or hiring or offering or exposing for sale or hire;
- exhibiting or distributing in the course of a business;
- distribution otherwise in the course of a business to such an extent as to affect prejudicially the copyright owner.

Discussion point   For answer guidance visit **www.oup.com/uk/brown5e**.

What is the common feature of this list of secondary infringements?

4.81   Also categorised as secondary infringements are:

- providing the means for making infringing copies;
- permitting the use of premises for infringing performances;
- provision of apparatus for infringing performances.

Where no charge is made for admission to the premises, however, there is no infringement of any copyright in a broadcast, or any sound recording included in it, by showing or playing in public a broadcast.[219] An audience has paid for admission to premises if (1) it has to pay for admission to *part* only of the premises; (2) it pays prices for goods or services on the premises either (a) *substantially* attributable to the facilities afforded for hearing or seeing the broadcast, or (b) exceeding those usually paid there and *partly* attributable to the facilities.[220]

Discussion point   For answer guidance visit **www.oup.com/uk/brown5e**.

How do these rules interact with those on public performance, showing, or playing as a primary infringement (paras 4.50–4.56)?

---

[217] See the headings to the relevant sections of the CDPA 1988, ss 22–26.   [218] See ss 22, 23, 24, 25(1), and 26(2)–(4).
[219] CDPA 1988, s 72(1) amended by The Copyright (Free Public Showing or Playing) (Amendment) Regulations 2016. See further, para 4.56.
[220] CDPA 1988, s 72(2). On this test, the employer was probably not guilty of secondary infringement under this head in *PRS v Kwik-Fit Group Ltd* [2008] ECDR 2 (allowed employees to play personal radios at work so that music could be heard by customers of the employer).

Importance of secondary infringement

4.82   Claims of secondary infringement are of great importance in preventing commercial piracy, in particular the circulation of infringing sound recordings, videos, CDs, and DVDs, where it is not possible to identify or take action against the person actually making the copies. The question of the degree and amount of knowledge required to make someone liable as a secondary infringer is one on which there is little clear authority. The 1988 Act requires that only 'reason to believe' need be shown to impose the liability.[221] The case law suggests that this is an objective test, requiring knowledge of facts from which a reasonable person would, after the passage of a reasonable amount of time, arrive at the relevant belief; facts giving rise only to suspicion would not be enough.[222] In practice, the safest approach where a possible infringement is discovered will be to send the defendant a warning letter as a first step; this will fix him with actual knowledge sufficient to justify action should the activities continue. The copyright owner should allow a reasonable time after receipt of the letter to enable the defender to consider his position, before further action is taken.[223]

> **Key points on secondary infringements**
>
> - Secondary infringements are essentially those of dealing commercially in products the making of which was a primary infringement of copyright, or which enable such products to be made.
> - The infringer must know or have reason to believe that infringing copies were being handled.

Further reading

Books

General

L Bently, B Sherman, D Gangjee, and P Johnson, *Intellectual Property Law* (5th edn, 2018), Chs 6, 8

N Caddick, G Davies, and G Harbottle (eds), *Copinger & Skone James on Copyright* (17th edn, 2019), Chs 7, 8

D Llewelyn and T Aplin, *Cornish, Llewelyn and Aplin Intellectual Property: Patents, Copyright, Trade Marks and Allied Rights* (9th edn, 2019), Chs 12.1–2, 12.5

I Stamatoudi and P Torremans (eds), *EU Copyright Law: A Commentary* (2014)

A Strowel (ed), *Peer-to-Peer File Sharing and Secondary Liability in Copyright Law* (2009)

G Westkamp, *Digital Copyright Laws in Europe: Regulating Information Access* (2011)

Articles

R Arnold, 'Website-blocking injunctions: the question of legislative basis' [2015] EIPR 623

R Arnold and P S Davies, 'Accessory liability for intellectual property infringement: the case of authorisation' [2017] LQR 442

---

[221]   See ss 22, 23, 24, 25(1), and 26(2)–(4).
[222]   *ZYX Music GmbH v King* [1997] 2 All ER 129 (CA); *Pensher Security Door Co Ltd v Sunderland City Council* [2000] RPC 249 (CA); *Vermaat and Powell v Boncrest (No 2)* [2002] FSR 21; *Whitby v Yorkshire* [2014] EWHC 4242 (Pat).
[223]   *Van Dusen v Kritz* [1936] 2 KB 176; *Vermaat and Powell v Boncrest (No 2)* [2002] FSR 21.

N Cordell and B Potts, 'Communication to the public or accessory liability? Is the CJEU using communication to the public to harmonise accessory liability across the EU?' [2018] EIPR 289

J Ginsburg, 'The (new?) right of making available to the public' in D Vaver and L Bently (eds), *Intellectual Property in the New Millennium* (2004)

R Hoy, 'Internet blocking injunctions are alive and well in the post Svensson world' [2015] Ent LR 44

S Karapapa, 'The requirement for a 'new public' in EU copyright law' [2017] E L Rev 63

D Liu, 'Test of infringement: what is it now?' [2014] EIPR 588

A Ross, 'Communication to the public–Court of Justice gives the Pirate Bay no quarter' [2017] Ent LR 248

A Ross and C Livingstone, 'Communication to the public: Part 1' [2012] Ent LR 169 and 'Communication to the public: Part 2' [2012] Ent LR 209

5

Copyright 4: exceptions and limitations

Introduction

Scope and overview of chapter

5.1 This chapter considers exceptions and limitations to the rights of the copyright owner described in Chapter 4. Copyright law establishes many such exceptions and limitations, listed in the Copyright, Designs and Patents Act 1988 (CDPA 1988) as what it calls the *'permitted acts'*, 'acts which may be done in relation to copyright works notwithstanding the subsistence of copyright' (CDPA 1988, s 28). These are acts which can be carried out in relation to the copyright work *without* the owner's permission or, in some cases, which can be performed subject to terms and conditions specified by the statute rather than by the copyright owner.

5.2 **Learning objectives**

By the end of this chapter you should be able to describe and explain:

- the general nature of exceptions and limitations to the rights conferred by copyright;
- specific copyright exceptions in the United Kingdom.

5.3 The chapter analyses the 'permitted acts' under CDPA 1988 and the freedoms afforded through them to the users, and also, briefly, how far they may be set aside by contractual provision. So, the rest of the chapter looks like this:

- The public domain and copyright exceptions in general (5.4–5.7)
- International and European developments (5.8–5.14)
- Copyright exceptions in the UK (5.15–5.59)
- Other limitations on copyright (5.60–5.62)
- Contracting out of the exceptions (5.63–5.66).

The public domain and copyright exceptions in general

5.4 This chapter deals with what people may do with works without the authorisation or permission of the copyright owner.[1] Some material, of course, is never in copyright—for example, a single word because it is not a literary work,[2] or an unoriginal artistic work.[3] Some material which once was in copyright is no longer because the term of copyright has expired. In both cases, people are free to do all the things which in other cases copyright would restrict: that is, copy the work; issue copies to the public whether for sale, rental, or commercial lending; perform the work in public; communicate it to the public; or adapt it. Some uses of copyright works do not fall within the scope of the restricted acts and may be freely carried out: for example, reselling a book of which you were the first purchaser or performing a work of music in private. This copyright-free zone is sometimes known as the *public domain*.[4] It has been argued that there is a 'virtuous circle' between copyright and the public domain, with the latter feeding the creation of new copyright works which in turn fall bit by bit into the public domain, the process becoming complete when the copyright expires.[5]

 Question

How may the 'public domain' be defined in relation to copyright?

5.5 Further, and most importantly for the purposes of this section of the chapter, people may do certain things with copyright material without the licence of the copyright owner which *would* otherwise fall within the scope of the restricted acts, for example make a copy for private study and research, record a film on TV to watch it at a more convenient time, or quote a work for purposes such as criticising it or reporting the news. This is because British copyright law contains extensive and detailed provisions by which various carefully specified acts which would otherwise be infringements of copyright are made lawful. They are described in the CDPA 1988 under the general heading, 'Acts Permitted in Relation to Copyright Works'.[6] Such acts do not require any licence from the copyright owner and may be freely performed by others.

5.6 The contents of the list of permitted acts reflect a legislative perception that certain interests in certain circumstances outweigh the interest in conferring and enforcing copyright. Some of the items on the list of permitted acts are grouped together as 'fair dealing', but there is no general principle that 'fair dealing' beyond the listed acts or for other than the listed purposes is allowed. (Note, however, the rather uncertain principle that copyright may be limited by what is known as the defence of 'public interest', discussed further at para 5.60.)

5.7 In this avoidance of a general principle and concentration upon a specific list of permitted acts, there is a contrast with US law, which provides a general 'fair use' defence covering purposes 'such as' criticism, comment, teaching, scholarship and research, and indicating that factors to be taken into account 'include' such matters as whether the use is of a commercial nature or for non-profit educational purposes, the amount and substantiality of the portion used in relation to the whole work, and the effect of the use upon the market or value of the copyright work.[7] The argument against such a general approach is that it creates

---

[1] See in general G Davies, *Copyright and the Public Interest* (2nd edn, 2003); LMCR Guibault, *Copyright Limitations and Contracts: An Analysis of the Contractual Overridability of Limitations on Copyright* (2002); R Burrell and A Coleman, *Copyright Exceptions: The Digital Impact* (2005); RL Okediji (ed), *Copyright Law in an Age of Limitations and Exceptions* (2017).

[2] See *Exxon Corp v Exxon Insurance* [1982] Ch 119.   [3] CDPA 1988, s1(1)(a). See also para 3.4.

[4] See generally C Waelde and HL MacQueen (eds), *The Many Faces of the Public Domain* (2007), and references therein.

[5] W Davies and K Withers, *Public Innovation: Intellectual Property in a Digital Age* (Institute of Public Policy Research, 2006); see also MD de Rosnay and JC de Martin (eds), *The Digital Public Domain: Foundations for an Open Culture* (2012).

[6] CDPA 1988, ss 28–76. See also, ss 44B and 76A dealing with Orphan Works (paras 6.46–6.50).

[7] US Copyright Act 1976, s 107.

uncertainty by contrast with the more specific approach in the UK;[8] on the other hand, the flexibility of a general approach may enable the law to deal better with changing ways of producing and exploiting copyright works. There is also a different contrast between the UK and many of the Continental laws, which tend to exclude private non-commercial copying from the scope of copyright, although a concomitant in many of these systems is levies on blank devices and storage media that facilitate copying (eg audio cassettes, CDs, and DVDs), the proceeds from which are routed back ultimately to copyright owners via their collecting societies.[9] Thus, the permitted use is nonetheless one for which the copyright owner ultimately receives remuneration, whether paid directly or indirectly by the user. The UK, on the other hand, has resisted both a general exemption for private use and the correlative deployment of levies on materials and machinery used for copying purposes.[10]

 Question

What contrasts exist between UK, US, and Continental European approaches to permitted acts?

Key points on permitted acts (introduction)

- Works never in copyright, or the copyright in which has expired, are often said to be 'in the public domain'.

- The permitted acts are ones which would be infringements of copyright but are made lawful by specific statutory provision.

- UK law takes a specific rather than a general 'fair use' or 'private use' approach to this subject.

International and European developments

Berne Convention ('three-step test'), TRIPS, and WCT

5.8   Under Article 9(2) of the Berne Convention members of the Union may:

> permit the reproduction of such [literary and artistic] works in certain special cases, provided that such reproduction does not conflict with a normal exploitation of the work and does not unreasonably prejudice the legitimate interests of the author.

Article 10, under the heading 'Certain Free Uses of Works', goes on to permit quotation from work lawfully made available to the public, provided that this is 'compatible with fair practice' and is not in excess of what is 'justified by the purpose'. The Article also allows members of the Union to permit 'utilisation, to the extent justified by the purpose' of literary and artistic works by way of illustration for teaching, provided that this is 'compatible with fair practice'. In both cases, the source and the name of the author must be identified. Article 10*bis* of the Convention adds 'Further Possible Free Uses of Works' for the reporting of current events. The Trade-Related Aspects of Intellectual Property Rights (TRIPS) Agreement of 1994 notes that

---

[8] For a recent discussion on whether the UK should adopt 'fair use', see I Hargreaves, *Digital Opportunity: A Review of Intellectual Property and Growth* (2011) available at www.gov.uk/government/uploads/system/uploads/attachment_data/file/32563/ipreview-finalreport.pdf (Hargreaves Review). See also paras 5.16 and 5.59.

[9] See, eg, the French Intellectual Property Code of 1 July 1992, L122–5, L211–3, L212–10, and L311; and German Copyright Act (Urheberrechtsgesetz) 1965, as last amended in 2017, ss 53, 54, and 54a–h.

[10] See paras 5.56–5.57 for further details.

limitations or exceptions to copyright are to be 'confined' to 'certain special cases which do not conflict with a normal exploitation of the work and do not unreasonably prejudice the legitimate interests of the right holder'.[11] For some reason, Article 10 of the World Intellectual Property Organization (WIPO) Copyright Treaty (WCT) 1996 repeats this formula no less than twice but, like TRIPS, where the Berne Convention talks of 'permitting' such acts, the WCT Article speaks of 'confining' them. In 2000 a Dispute Panel of the World Trade Organization (WTO) issued an opinion on the scope of the three-step test, holding that section 110(5) of the US Copyright Act 1976 violated the test by allowing public performance of works received from broadcasts. All three steps had to be complied with in any copyright exception. While minor or *de minimis* departures from the test were permissible, section 110(5) did not fall into that category.[12]

Question

The Berne Convention regulation of exceptions to copyright is sometimes known as the 'three-step test'. What are these three steps?

Discussion point   For answer guidance visit www.oup.com/uk/brown5e.

Why do TRIPS and the WCT 1996 want to 'confine' exceptions to copyright?

European Union

5.9   The Information Society (InfoSoc) Directive 2001, the European Union's implementation of the WCT 1996, provides for 'Exceptions and Limitations' to copyright. The exhaustive list of exceptions under Article 5 are applicable to the exclusive rights that the Directive regulates, thus limiting the ability of individual member states to provide further exceptions in respect of those rights.[13] However, only one of the exceptions listed in Article 5 is mandatory, and the rest are permissive—that is, the member states may (and therefore need not) introduce them. The result is that an unharmonised scheme of exceptions and limitations continues to exist in the European Union (EU). It should also be noted that the Software and Database Directives made provision for exceptions to the rights which they conferred,[14] and that these are largely unaffected by the InfoSoc Directive 2001.

5.10   The UK system has differed from at least some Continental ones regarding the way in which exceptions or limitations operate, with the former taking them to be rather a limit on the grant of property whilst, by contrast, the latter perceive them rather as an exception to the property right granted. Equally, there are differences in approach with the way in which they operate in domestic law, with the UK favouring relatively broadly drawn fair dealing provisions for several statutory purposes (eg criticism, news reporting), but the Continental systems focusing rather on specific, narrow categories. How should the two approaches be reconciled? This question was still too difficult to be answered in the InfoSoc Directive of 2001, which set out a long list of possible exceptions, but gave member states the option to enact some, all, or none,

---

[11] TRIPS, Art 13.

[12] Report of the WTO Panel dated 15 June 2000, WT/DS160/R. See further C Geiger, J Griffiths, and RM Hilty, 'Towards a balanced interpretation of the "three-step test" in copyright law' [2008] EIPR 489. C Geiger et al, 'The three-step-test revisited: How to use the test's flexibility in national copyright law' (2014) 29(3) American University Int Law Rev 581.

[13] See recital 32 and Art 5(3)(o), the latter of which permits member states to provide for 'use in certain other cases of minor importance where exceptions already exist under national law, provided *that they only concern analogue uses* and do not affect the free circulation of goods and services within the Community (now Union; emphasis added)'.

[14] Software Directive 2009 (Software Directive 1991 was consolidated into Directive 2009/24/EC and unless stated otherwise, all references will be to the latter directive), Arts 5, 6; Database Directive 1996, Arts 6, 9.

and thus failed to achieve any sort of harmonisation on the matter. Indeed, the lack of true harmonisation of exceptions continues to be a concern and the European Parliament's Resolution of July 2015 called on the Commission to consider and examine a number of issues in this regard. In September 2016, when the European Commission released its plans to modernise the EU copyright framework in the Draft Copyright Directive 2016 (see para 2.15), this included reforms to exceptions and limitations in order to adapt them to the digital and cross-border environment.[15] The Draft Copyright Directive proposes to introduce mandatory exceptions in three areas: digital education, text and data mining, and cultural heritage. Unlike the optional scheme in the InfoSoc Directive 2001, the mandatory nature of these exceptions is a welcome step towards harmonisation and achieving the Digital Single Market, but the proposal does not go far enough: the InfoSoc exceptions remain optional and there remains scope for further reforms in the form of additional exceptions as well as changes to current scheme.[16] At the time of writing, the directive is going through the EU legislative process and proving particularly controversial, albeit not as much for its provisions on copyright exceptions.

5.11   EU directives have also made provision for exceptions in two specific areas. In 2012, the EU adopted a Directive on orphan works, allowing certain cultural organisations to digitise such works and make them available across the EEA (see paras 6.46–6.50).[17] In September 2017, the EU agreed upon the implementation of the Marrakesh Treaty to Facilitate Access to Published Works for Persons Who Are Blind, Visually Impaired or Otherwise Print Disabled (2013) (see further para 2.13) through two instruments. The Marrakesh Treaty Directive harmonised and established a mandatory exception for the benefit of those who are blind, visually impaired, or otherwise print disabled (para 5.48).[18] Also, the Marrakesh Treaty Regulation,[19] entered into force in the member states on 12 October 2018, allowing the import and export of accessible format copies made in accordance with the Marrakesh Treaty Directive.

5.12   EU Directives (InfoSoc, Database, and Marrakesh, as well as the Draft Copyright Directive) refer to the 'three-step test' in that the exceptions and limitations thereunder are to be applied:[20]

  (1)   only in certain special cases;

  (2)   not conflicting with normal exploitation; and

  (3)   not unreasonably prejudicing the legitimate interests of the copyright owner.

It is unclear whether the three-step test is an additional requirement for the member states' legislature when they frame their national laws on exceptions, or whether it is also relevant for the national courts, as a guide, when they interpret and apply the exceptions under the Directives in individual cases.[21]

 Discussion point   For answer guidance visit **www.oup/com/uk/brown5e.**

Find out whether there were any controversies during the prolonged gestation of the InfoSoc Directive 2001, and why.

---

[15] Proposal for a Directive on Copyright in the Digital Single Market, 14 September 2016, COM(2016) 593 final, Arts 3–6.

[16] C Geiger, G Frosio, and O Bulayenko, 'The EU Commission's proposal to reform copyright limitations: a good but far too timid step in the right direction' [2018] EIPR 4.

[17] Directive 2012/28/EU on certain permitted uses of orphan works.

[18] Directive (EU) 2017/1564 on certain permitted uses of certain works and other subject matter protected by copyright and related rights for the benefit of persons who are blind, visually impaired or otherwise print-disabled.

[19] Regulation (EU) 2017/1563 on the cross-border exchange between the Union and third countries of accessible format copies of certain works and other subject matter protected by copyright and related rights for the benefit of persons who are blind, visually impaired or otherwise print-disabled.

[20] Database Directive 1996, Art 6(3); InfoSoc Directive 2001, Art 5(5); Marrakesh Treaty Directive 2017, Art 3(3); Draft Copyright Directive 2016, Art 6. See also, Software Directive 2009 Art 6(3); Orphan Works Directive 2012, Recital 20.

[21] *England and Wales Cricket Board v Tixdaq* [2016] EWHC 575 (Ch) para 72.

5.13   A generally restrictive approach to the exceptions is visible in the InfoSoc Directive:

> the provision of . . . exceptions [to copyright] . . . should . . . duly reflect the increased economic impact that such exceptions . . . may have in the context of the new electronic environment. Therefore, the scope of certain exceptions may have to be even more limited when it comes to certain new uses of copyright works . . . (recital 44).

Court of Justice of the European Union (CJEU) decisions, in interpreting provisions of the Directive, suggest a preference for a strict, and consequently, narrower interpretation of the exceptions (since they are derogations from the general principles established thereunder) but also indicate that interpretations should be purposive: to enable them to be effective and for their purpose to be observed.[22] The Court of Justice (CJ) has held that an independent and uniform interpretation must be given to terms which make no express reference to national law for determining its meaning and scope and such uniform interpretation is not invalidated by the optional nature of the exceptions. It has also emphasised the need to achieve a 'fair balance', as stated in recital 31, between the rights and interests of authors and those of the users, and it is a matter for the national courts to determine, in light of all circumstances, if such balance is preserved in the application of an exception.[23]

5.14   Article 9 of the InfoSoc Directive 2001 indicates that its provisions are without prejudice to, amongst others, the law of contract, applicable in the member states. This seems to suggest that in at least some circumstances contractual provision may eliminate copyright exceptions. The Software Directive notably lays down that most of the exceptions to copyright in computer programs—in particular, making back-up copies, decompilation and observation, studying, and testing—cannot be overcome by contractual agreement (paras 5.63–5.66).[24] The Draft Copyright Directive 2016 also indicates that any contractual provision contrary to the mandatory exception on text and data mining shall be unenforceable.[25]

Exercise

Why have copyright exceptions 'increased economic impact' in the electronic environment? Should contract prevail over exceptions in that electronic environment?

Copyright exceptions in the UK

5.15   The UK implemented the InfoSoc Directive provisions on copyright exceptions and limitations with effect from 31 October 2003.[26] In negotiating and implementing the Directive, the UK government's policy was to maintain as far as possible the previously existing regime, adjusting it as necessary. No new exceptions allowed under the Directive were introduced at the time; but none of the existing exceptions that were permitted by the Directive were eliminated, although some were narrowed significantly in scope.

5.16   Copyright exceptions then featured prominently among the issues addressed by two major UK independent reviews of intellectual property: the Gowers Review 2006 and the Hargreaves Review 2011. Questions had certainly arisen previously about whether exceptions are actually necessary in the digital environment (with which Gowers was also specifically concerned) and can be adapted to the digital environment (with

---

[22] *England and Wales Cricket Board v Tixdaq* [2016] EWHC 575 (Ch) para 71; see also, J Griffiths et al, 'The European Copyright Society's Opinion on the judgment of the CJEU in Case C-201/13 Deckmyn' [2015] EIPR 127.

[23] See C-201/13 *Deckmyn v Vandersteen* [2014] ECDR 21, paras 15–16 and 27–28 for these points. See also *England and Wales Cricket Board v Tixdaq* [2016] EWHC 575 (Ch) para 73.

[24] Software Directive 2009, Arts 5(2), (3), 6(1), and 8. See CDPA 1988, ss 50A(3), 50B(4), 50BA(2), and 296A. See also Database Directive 1996, Arts 6(1), 15, and CDPA 1988, ss 50D(2) and 296B.

[25] Draft Copyright Directive 2016, Art 3(2).   [26] Copyright and Related Rights Regulations 2003 (SI 2003/2498).

which Hargreaves was concerned). It can be argued that copyright exceptions and limitations were created because they related to areas of activity in which the creation of an efficient market in which producers and users could bargain about prices for access to and use of works seemed impossible, or at least far too costly; but if that was so, one question was whether the internet solved the market's failure by providing an environment in which transaction costs are hugely reduced by the automation of the contracting process between supplier and consumer. The Gowers Review of intellectual property published in 2006[27] asked whether 'fair use' (sic) provisions for citizens are reasonable. Many of the issues about exceptions raised by the Gowers Review 2006 were taken up in a UK Intellectual Property Office (IPO) consultation published in January 2008. However, despite the then government's acceptance of Gower's recommendations, it failed to adopt those exceptions. The Hargreaves Review termed this as 'a clear demonstration of the failure of the copyright framework to adapt'.[28] While it rejected a US-style 'fair use' defence, it recommended several significant changes. This time, the government broadly accepted the recommendations in its response.[29]

5.17   In 2014, major reforms to copyright exceptions came into force. These reforms followed from the Hargreaves Review, which had indicated that the UK could benefit by taking up exceptions already permitted under the InfoSoc Directive and had recommended a number of changes for the purposes of, inter alia, format shifting, parody, non-commercial research, and library archiving, in order to update the copyright exceptions framework for the digital age.[30] The following account is based upon the law as amended by the '2014 reforms'[31] and will make use of authorities from the pre-Directive law and pre-2014 reforms, to the extent relevant.[32] It also deals with the implementation of the Software and Database Directives' provisions on exceptions and limitations, where relevant, as well as the Marrakesh Treaty Directive (see Figure 5.1).

 Copyright exceptions and Brexit

Although the current UK framework of copyright exceptions is framed in light of EU Directives and CJEU jurisprudence, the implementation of such Directives will be largely preserved in UK law as retained EU law under the powers in the EU Withdrawal Act 2018. Both the UK and EU member states are party to the main international treaties which are applicable to this current framework of copyright exceptions, and under which the main obligations in the area arise (eg the Berne Convention, WCT, TRIPS). Consequently, in a 'no-deal' scenario, the relationship between the UK and EU member states will be governed through the principles of such treaties (see para 2.20). The UK government 'no-deal' guidance notes that as a result, 'the scope of protection for copyright works in the UK and for UK works abroad will remain largely unchanged'.[33]

However, there is specific EU law on exceptions where reciprocal arrangements between EU member states are provided for and will be affected in a 'no-deal' scenario; eg the Marrakesh Treaty Regulation

---

[27] *Gowers Review of Intellectual Property* (HM Treasury, 2006) 4.   [28] Hargreaves Review, 50.

[29] IPO, 'The Government Response to the Hargreaves Review of Intellectual Property and Growth', August 2011.

[30] Hargreaves Review. The government, in its response to the review, broadly accepted the recommendations. See IPO, 'The Government Response to the Hargreaves Review of Intellectual Property and Growth', August 2011. It then launched a consultation to seek views on its proposals to widen copyright exceptions, see IPO, 'Consultation on Copyright', December 2011; and then outlined its plans for policy reform—see IPO, 'Modernising Copyright: A Modern, Robust and Flexible Framework' (2012). The government then published draft legislation on changes to UK copyright exceptions in 2013 and undertook a technical review of the draft exceptions; see IPO, 'Technical Review of Draft Legislation on Copyright Exceptions: Government Response' (2014).

[31] Copyright and Rights in Performances (Research, Education, Libraries and Archives) Regulations (SI 2014/1372); Copyright and Rights in Performances (Disability) Regulations (SI 2014/1384); Copyright (Public Administration) Regulations (SI 2014/1385); Copyright and Rights in Performances (Quotation and Parody) Regulations (SI 2014/2356).

[32] In *England and Wales Cricket Board v Tixdaq* [2016] EWHC 575 (Ch) para 74, Arnold J indicated that pre-Directive authorities should be treated with a degree of caution as they were decided before the CJEU jurisprudence on exceptions and lack consideration of the three-step test.

[33] UK Government, 'Copyright if there's no Brexit deal' (24 September 2018), www.gov.uk/government/publications/copyright-if-theres-no-brexit-deal.

has resulted in cross-border mechanisms which are unique to the EU. Also, the UK is not yet a party (outside its membership of the EU) to the Marrakesh Treaty. Although the EU Withdrawal Act 2018 will preserve the UK's implementation of such EU law, and resulting obligations, the EU member states will have no obligation to continue to recognise rights of UK nationals. Implications in this regard are noted in paras 5.47–5.48. See also paras 6.46–6.50 on orphan works.

In a 'no-deal' scenario, the UK may not have any obligation to implement any changes to copyright exceptions that may eventually emerge from Articles 3–6 of the Draft Copyright Directive 2016 (see para 2.15).

Finally, in a 'no-deal' scenario, there could be scope in the future for the UK to substantially diverge from EU law in the area of exceptions, albeit while complying with relevant international frameworks (eg Berne Convention Art 9(2), 10; TRIPS Art 13). On some specific issues, the UK courts have only just begun to adapt to recent CJEU decisions, and they may choose to not continue to do so, since the UK will not be bound by them in a 'no-deal' Brexit. The UK may also choose to introduce new exceptions or amend existing ones in a way that the current exhaustive list of exceptions under the InfoSoc Directive 2001 or CJEU jurisprudence requiring uniform interpretation does not permit.

Figure 5.1 Exceptions to copyright

Exceptions	Subject matter to which applicable	Exceptions	Subject matter to which applicable
Fair dealing: Non-commercial research	All	Disability	All
Fair dealing: Private Study	All	Public Administration	All
Fair dealing: Criticism or review	All	Incidental inclusion	All
Fair dealing: Quotation	All	Text and data analysis for non-commercial research	All
Fair dealing: Reporting current events	All, except photographs	Time-shifting	Broadcasts
Fair dealing: Caricature, parody or pastiche	All	Temporary reproduction (general)	All, apart from computer programs and databases
Fair dealing: Illustration for instruction	All	Temporary reproduction (special)	Computer programs and databases
Educational Establishments	All - varies according to individual provisions	Back up; decompilation; observe, study, test; adapt for lawful use/error correction	Computer programs
Libraries and archives	All	Certain permitted uses of orphan works by a relevant body	All

Making temporary copies

5.18   As noted earlier (para 4.35), copying in relation to any description of work includes the making of copies which are transient or incidental to some other use of the work.[34] Major examples of what may therefore be infringement of copyright without the licence of the copyright owner are loading a computer program into a computer's RAM, or accessing an online database or website, where again copies are made in the RAM of the machine being used for the purpose. Indeed, the actual operation of the internet, which involves the transmission of data in small packets from computer to computer across a network, also involves the making of temporary copies in each of the computers through which the packages are forwarded on their way. The technology only works by the making of these copies, and its only purpose is to play a role in the transmission of the information from a website to the person accessing it. As such, Article 5(1) of the InfoSoc Directive 2001 provides for the important exception which prevents such temporary copying being infringement in certain, carefully defined circumstances, and stops copyright from becoming an impediment to perfectly reasonable, indeed often necessary, activities. This is the only mandatory exception under the Directive. Recital 33 of the Directive states that 'this exception should include acts which enable browsing as well as acts of caching to take place, including those which enable transmission systems to function effectively'.

Temporary reproduction exception

5.19   Copyright in author works (apart from computer programs and databases) and in typographical arrangements of a published edition, sound recordings, or films is not infringed by the making of a temporary copy which is transient or incidental, as long as:[35]

(1)   the making is an *integral and essential part of a technological process*,

and

(2)   the *sole purpose* is to enable *either—*

   (a)   a *transmission of the work in a network* between third parties by an intermediary;

   or

   (b)   a *lawful use* of the work *and*

(3)   the temporary copy has no *independent economic significance*.

Recent rulings by the CJEU have provided some guidance on the interpretation of this exception.

■ Case C-5/08 *Infopaq International A/S v Danske Dagblades Forening (Infopaq I)* [2009] ECDR 16 (ECJ)

For the facts of this case see para 4.19. The European Court of Justice (ECJ) found that the acts of *printing* 11-word extracts from electronic news articles, carried out during the data capture process of an electronic 'cuttings' service by an agency, were not 'transient' copies. As a derogation from general principle (ie reproduction is infringement), the exception was to be interpreted restrictively and for the exception to apply, five cumulative conditions must be fulfilled (paras 54–71):

(1)   the act must be temporary;

(2)   it must be transient or incidental;

(3)   it must be an integral and essential part of the technological process;

---

[34] CDPA 1988, s 17(6).   [35] CDPA 1988, s 28A implementing Art 5(1) of the InfoSoc Directive 2001.

(4) the sole purpose of the process must be to enable a transmission network between third parties by an intermediary or the lawful use of the work or protected subject matter; and,

(5) the act must have no independent economic significance.

The Court also noted that the storage and deletion of the copy must be automatic and not dependent on discretionary human intervention, particularly by the user and, the duration of the process must not exceed what is necessary for the proper completion of that technological process (paras 62 and 64).

■ **Case C-302/10** *Infopaq International A/S v Danske Dagblades Forening* (*Infopaq II*) (17 January 2012) (CJ)

The Court of Justice found that acts of temporary reproduction carried out during the *data capture process* of an electronic 'cuttings' service by an agency met requirements (3)–(5) of the exception as laid out above in *Infopaq I*. The Court re-emphasised that the exemption must be interpreted strictly. The exception aims to make access to the protected works and their use possible. As such, temporary copying should take place in the context of the implementation of the technological process (in this case data capturing) and not outside it, and the technological process would not function correctly and efficiently without the temporary copying. Technological process involving human intervention is not precluded, including being activated manually (paras 29–39). Recital 33 indicates that a use is lawful either where it is authorised by the right holder or where it is not restricted by the applicable legislation. The technological process of copying was to enable drafting of summaries of news articles and such activity, while not permitted by the rights holders, is not restricted by EU legislation, and as such is not unlawful (paras 42–46). Acts of reproduction do not have independent economic significance if the implementation of those acts does not enable the generation of additional profit going beyond that derived from the lawful use of the work, and the temporary reproduction does not modify the work in any way (paras 47–54).[36] The Court also said that if the activity meets all the criteria set down in Article 5(1) of the InfoSoc Directive 2001, then it must be regarded as fulfilling the requirements of Article 5(5) (paras 55–57).

■ *Newspaper Licensing Agency Ltd v Meltwater Holding BV* [2010] EWHC 3099 (Ch); [2011] EWCA Civ 890 (CA); [2013] UKSC 18 (SC); C-360/13 [2014] AC 1438 (CJ)

For the facts of this case see para 4.19. The UK courts considered this exception in the context of a media-monitoring service. The High Court, with which the Court of Appeal agreed, found that the users of the service needed an end-user licence from N, for both receiving the monitoring reports by email, and browsing the report on M's website. Section 28A of the CDPA 1988 did not exempt the users from liability for making on-screen and cached copies of headlines and extracts of newspaper articles while browsing the monitoring reports because: the making of copies was generated by the user's own volition, through his voluntary decision to access the webpage and as such, was not part of the technological process; such copies were not an essential or integral part of the technological process but the end which the process was designed to achieve; and, viewing the copies did not constitute 'lawful use' because the copies were not authorised by the copyright owner. On appeal to the Supreme Court (SC), confined to the issue of whether the users required a licence for browsing the report on M's website, Lord Sumption began by noting that: 'This appeal raises an important question about the application of copyright law to the technical processes involved in viewing copyright material on the internet' (para 1). He explained that the five requirements of Article 5(1) are overlapping and repetitive, and must be read together to achieve the combined purpose of them all and usefully reviewed the effect of

---

[36] See also Case C-429/08 *Football Association Premier League Ltd v QC Leisure, Murphy v Media Protection Services Ltd* (FAPL) [2012] 1 CMLR 29, paras 174–178 where the reproduction taking place in the memory of a satellite decoder and its visual display were found to fulfil the conditions of Art 5(5) and in particular, was found to have no independent economic significance beyond the advantage derived from mere reception of the broadcasts at issue and to have the sole purpose of enabling a lawful use. See also *ITV Broadcasting Ltd v TVCatchup* [2011] EWHC 2977 (Pat), paras 28–31 for reproduction taking place in the server memory of a streaming service.

the relevant CJEU decisions (paras 11 and 26). He explained that the exception applied to copies generated during browsing by the user and the High Court and Court of Appeal could not have arrived at their decision 'if they had had the benefit of the judgments' in *FAPL* and *Infopaq II*, where the CJEU had given a 'far broader meaning' to the concept of 'lawful use' (paras 26 and 37). Nonetheless, the SC requested a preliminary ruling from the CJ as it found, that 'the issue has a transnational dimension and that the application of copyright law to internet use has important implications for many millions of people across the European Union making use of what has become a basic technical facility' (para 38). The CJ found that copies made by an end-user, on the user's computer screen and in the internet cache of that computer's hard disk, in the course of viewing a website, satisfied Article 5(1) requirements and did not require authorisation of the copyright holders (para 63). In addition, and unlike *Infopaq II*, the Court also analysed the conditions of Article 5(5), containing the three-step test, and held that: on-screen copies and cached copies constituted a special case because they are created only for the purpose of viewing websites; the legitimate interests of the copyright holders are properly safeguarded because publishers are still required to obtain authorisation from copyright holders even though the copies allow users to access works on websites without authorisation from them; since the viewing of websites represents a normal exploitation of the works, and the creation of on-screen and cached copies forms part of such viewing, it doesn't conflict with the normal exploitation of the works (paras 54–62).

■ **Case C-527/15** *Stichting Brein v Jack Frederik Wullems* **[2017] ECDR 14 (CJ)**

For the facts of this case, see the *Filmspeler* decision at para 4.62. In assessing whether the temporary reproduction applied to the end user's streaming of copyright protected content from the multimedia player, the Court of Justice noted that the five requirements as elaborated in *Infopaq I* and *Infopaq II* 'are cumulative in the sense that non-compliance with any one of them will lead to the act of reproduction not being exempted' (para 61), and focussed on the fourth requirement. Since the referring court had indicated that the end users' acts were not to enable a transmission, the key issue was whether the end user's acts had the sole purpose of enabling a lawful use of the work. In assessing this, the issue was whether the end user's acts were not restricted by the applicable legislation, since their use was not authorised by right holders. The Court in holding the end user's acts were not to enable a lawful use, emphasised the advertising of the multimedia players and the main attraction of the players for potential purchasers (ie users) being the pre-installed add-ons. It held that the purchasers 'deliberately and in full knowledge of the circumstances' access 'a free and unauthorised offer of protected works' (para 69). It also held that temporary acts of reproduction on the type of multimedia players in question (which allow streaming of unauthorised content from third-party websites) 'adversely affect the normal exploitation of relevant works and causes unreasonable prejudice to the legitimate interests of the right holder', because such 'practice would usually result in a diminution of lawful transactions relating to the protected works, which would cause unreasonable prejudice to copyright holders' (para 70). This conclusion is unsurprising but quite significant, as the Court of Justice has clarified that in the case of unauthorised streaming end users cannot benefit from the temporary reproduction exception.

 Question

Under what conditions is temporary reproduction a permitted act rather than an infringement? Give some illustrative examples.

Temporary reproduction of databases and computer programs

5.20   The Database Directive[37] and, following it, section 50D of the 1988 Act provide in effect that temporary reproduction of a database which is necessary for the purpose of access to and normal use of the contents of

---

[37]   Database Directive 1996, reading Art 6(1) in conjunction with Art 5(a).

a database, or part thereof, by a person with a right to use the database, does not require the authorisation of the author of the database. A person will have a right to use through licence, express or implied, or by way of the generally permitted acts as far as they apply to databases. Any term or condition of an agreement purporting to prohibit an act permitted under this provision of the 1988 Act is void.[38] The Software Directive[39] and, following it, section 50C of the 1988 Act also provide in effect that temporary reproduction or adaptation of a computer program necessary for a lawful user's lawful use of the program is permitted. But, in an example of contract prevailing over exceptions (unlike the position with databases just described), a term of any contract regulating the circumstances in which the user's use is lawful, and prohibiting the copying or adaptation in question, will make those acts infringements. There are, however, a number of other acts in relation to computer programs which may be undertaken by a lawful user thereof, and which cannot be overridden by contract—making a back-up copy of the program, decompilation in terms of section 50B(2), and observing, studying, or testing the functioning of the program in accordance with section 50BA(2).[40] And for the owner of copyright in a computer program to put it on the market without granting a licence, express or implied, to enable the purchaser to load it into a computer's RAM and run it (thereby making the purchaser a lawful user) would seem an absurd scenario.

> ### Key points on exceptions for temporary reproduction
>
> - The general exception, which does not apply to computer programs and databases, is for copying as an integral part of a technological process enabling either a network transmission or a lawful use of the work, and having no independent economic significance.
> - This is intended to allow 'browsing' on the internet and 'caching'.
> - There are special exceptions for computer programs and databases, most of which cannot be contractually overridden.

Fair dealing exceptions

5.21   Fair dealing with a work will not constitute infringement of the copyright in the work if it is carried out for one of the permitted statutory purposes in CDPA 1988, and satisfies related requirements. The question whether the use by an infringer was 'for the purpose' set out in the Act is to be judged objectively: 'it is not necessary for the court to put itself in the shoes of the infringer of the copyright in order to decide whether the offending piece was published' for the statutory purpose, and the notion that all that is required is for the user to have the sincere belief, however misguided, that they are using the work for the statutory purpose should not be encouraged.[41] Fair dealing for any other purpose, or dealing which is only fair in general, is not permitted as such, and if there is not to be liability for infringement of copyright the activity will have to be shown to fall within some other category of permitted act. But dealing for one of the statutory purposes

---

[38] CDPA 1988, ss 50D(2) and 296B. For an example of a clause being held void under s 50D, see *Navitaire Inc v EasyJet Airline Co Inc* [2006] RPC 3.

[39] Software Directive 2009, reading Art 5(1) in conjunction with Art 4(a).

[40] See C-406/10 *SAS Institute Inc v World Programming Ltd* [2012] ECDR 22 and *SAS Institute Inc v World Programming Ltd* [2013] EWCA Civ 1482, discussed at para 4.33.

[41] *England and Wales Cricket Board v Tixdaq* [2016] EWHC 575 (Ch) para 75, citing *Pro Sieben Media AG v Carlton UK Television Ltd* [1999] FSR 610 (CA) at 620.

and, at the same time, also for some other purpose may still be fair dealing.[42] The permitted statutory purposes requiring 'fair dealing' and applicable to all types of works are:

- *research for a non-commercial* purpose (CDPA 1988, s 29(1));
- *private study* (CDPA 1988, s 29(1C));
- *criticism or review* (CDPA 1988, s 30(1));
- *quotation* (CDPA 1988, s 30(1ZA));
- *reporting current events* (CDPA 1988, s 30(2);[43]
- *caricature, parody or pastiche* (CDPA 1988 s 30A(1));
- *illustration for instruction* (CDPA 1988, s 32(1)).

Before the 2014 reforms, the exceptions for non-commercial research and private study were limited to literary, dramatic, musical, or artistic works and the typographical arrangement of a published edition. They did not extend to films, sound recordings, and broadcasts. As a result of recommendations by the Hargreaves Review, the exceptions were extended to cover *all* types of works.[44] Sufficient acknowledgement is required for the above permitted purposes, except private study and caricature, parody, or pastiche. This section discusses the meaning of 'fair dealing' and 'sufficient acknowledgement' first, before addressing each of the statutory purposes requiring 'fair dealing' in more detail.[45] It then discusses other exceptions available to a range of bodies (eg educational establishments, libraries, archives, and museums) or for specific purposes (eg text and data analysis, public administration).

 Question

In the 2014 reforms, why was fair dealing for the purposes of non-commercial research or private study extended to cover films, sound recordings, and broadcasts?

Fair dealing and the 'three-step test'

5.22   The dealing with the copyright work, for all the above permitted statutory purposes, must be fair; but the Act, both before and after the 2003 and 2014 amendments, contains no elaboration of what is or is not fair. Fair dealing is seen to be a question of degree and matter of impression.[46] Contrast the list of factors to be taken into account under the fair use provisions of the US Copyright Act, which 'include' such matters as whether the use is of a commercial nature or for non-profit educational purposes, the amount and substantiality of the portion used in relation to the whole work, and the effect of the use upon the market or value of the copyright work (see para 5.7). Some of these (eg commercial use) are built into the structure of the specific exceptions in the UK, and others have emerged in the case law, as will appear from the following account. But the question of fairness is still, to at least some extent, at large. However, the first important element is the express reference to the Berne 'three-step test' (para 5.8), not in the amended text of the 1988 Act, but in the underlying Software, Database, and InfoSoc Directives (para 5.12), which may require consideration of essentially the same factors as fair dealing.[47] The second element is the notion of 'fair balance' in the InfoSoc Directive 2001 and recent CJEU jurisprudence (para 5.13).

---

[42] *Sillitoe v McGraw-Hill Book Co Ltd* [1983] FSR 545.

[43] Note that photographs are not included under the exception for reporting current events.

[44] Copyright and Rights in Performances (Research, Education, Libraries and Archives) Regulations 2014, reg 3(1)(a), (b).

[45] Note that the illustration for instruction exception is not discussed separately as a 'fair dealing' exception, but within the broader context of exceptions for educational establishments.

[46] *Hubbard v Vosper* [1972] 2 QB 84.   [47] *England and Wales Cricket Board v Tixdaq* [2016] EWHC 575 (Ch), paras 88–89.

Fairness

5.23   Even if the dealing is shown to be for the statutory purposes, and appropriate acknowledgement has been made, the test of *fairness* remains to be satisfied. The British courts have taken a number of factors into account, according to the nature of the permitted purpose. For example, the quantity of material quoted and reproduced is relevant: to take large extracts from a work and criticise only some of them may be unfair and make the dealing an infringement rather than a permitted act for the purposes of criticism.[48] Similarly, the impact of the infringer's activity upon the market for the right holder's work, if any, can be a relevant factor in assessing the fairness of that activity: even if the infringer's activity involves criticism of someone else's work, comparative advertising is nonetheless not fair dealing because its primary purpose is to advance the critic's own work.[49] The Court of Appeal (CA) in one case on reporting current events, noted that in assessing fair dealing, 'it is appropriate to take into account the motives of the alleged infringer, the extent and purpose of the use, and whether that extent was necessary for the purpose of reporting the current events in question' and also, 'if the work had not been published or circulated to the public'.[50] Fairness must be judged by 'the objective standard of whether a fair minded and honest person would have dealt with the copyright work in the manner' that the defendant did for the purpose of reporting the current events.[51] In another case, it considered the three important factors for fair dealing to be commercial competition, prior publication, and the amount and importance of the work taken.[52]

Sufficient acknowledgement

5.24   A *sufficient acknowledgement* is an identification of the work in question by its title or other description and, unless the work is published anonymously or the identity of the author cannot be ascertained by reasonable inquiry, also identifying the author.[53] It is not sufficient for it to be merely possible to identify the original work and author in the activity said to be fair dealing; the acknowledgement must be such as to suggest recognition of the position or claim of the author in respect of the original work. Thus study aids on the work of well-known authors, aimed at school pupils, did not sufficiently acknowledge their position or claim even though the merest glance at the study aids revealed the works and authors in question.[54] Similarly, a brief reference in a newspaper story to the fact that quoted words had been given in answer to another newspaper's questions did not constitute sufficient acknowledgement of its authorship as distinct from its copyright.[55]

Fair dealing: (a) research for non-commercial purposes

5.25   Fair dealing with any kind of copyright-protected work, for the purposes of research for a non-commercial purpose, is a permitted act.[56] A contractual term that purports to prevent or restrict this permitted act is unenforceable.[57] Research is required to be accompanied by a sufficient acknowledgement, unless such acknowledgement is impossible for reasons of practicality or otherwise.[58]

Meaning of research

5.26   The meaning of the word 'research' appears never to have been judicially considered in the UK. Prior to the 2003 amendments it was linked to 'private study' but the two have now been severed, so they must each have a separate rather than a cumulative meaning. The *Oxford English Dictionary* defines research as

---

[48] *Hubbard v Vosper* [1972] 2 QB 84; *Sillitoe v McGraw-Hill Book Co (UK) Ltd* [1983] FSR 545.
[49] *IPC Media Ltd v News Group Newspapers Ltd* [2005] FSR (35) 752.
[50] *Hyde Park v Yelland* [2000] RPC 604 (CA) per Aldous LJ at para 37.   [51] ibid, para 38.
[52] *Ashdown v Telegraph Group Ltd* [2002] ECC 19 (CA).   [53] CDPA 1988, s 178.
[54] *Sillitoe v McGraw-Hill Book Co (UK) Ltd* [1983] FSR 545.
[55] *Express Newspapers plc v News (UK) Ltd* [1990] FSR 359.
[56] CDPA 1988, s 29(1). Note s 29(4) and (4A) in relation to computer programs.   [57] CDPA 1988, s 29(4B).
[58] CDPA 1988, s 29(1) and (1B).

a process of search or investigation undertaken to discover facts and reach new conclusions by the critical study of a subject or by a course of scientific inquiry; or as a systematic investigation into and study of materials, sources, and so on, to establish facts or collate information. Study, on the other hand, is more about the application of the mind to the acquisition of knowledge, or reading a book or text with close attention.[59] Research may therefore be thought of as having some end product in view, a contribution to knowledge and understanding; while study is more about acquiring knowledge and understanding that already exists. But on these definitions, it must also be admitted that research is hardly conceivable without study, and that any distinction between the two is difficult to maintain. In the university context, research would be the characteristic activity of the PhD student and study that of the first-year undergraduate; but between the two levels there is a wide spectrum, indeed a progression, of activity partaking of both study and research. Thus, the undergraduate will study for exams and research for essays or dissertations, while the postgraduate will have studied for an undergraduate degree and to establish the base from which the subject of the doctoral research can be identified. The professor or lecturer, on the other hand, will research to write learned articles in scholarly journals, perhaps merely study in order to give lectures and tutorials, and be somewhere in between in writing a student textbook. It is not clear whether the professor merely keeping up to date in his field—for example reading and making copies of new publications and filing them for possible future use—can be said to be carrying out research: on these definitions, probably not, but perhaps it amounts to private study. While photocopying and scanning for the purpose of research would clearly be covered by this exception, it is not clear, however, how much of the material can be copied on this basis; the dealing does have to be fair, and the publisher's loss of a sale, for example, might be seen as unfair in at least some contexts. Whether research includes the publication of research results (ie quotation from research materials in the resulting publication) is perhaps a moot point. But it is difficult to see how one accompanies research carried out in one's own office, or in a library, archive, or gallery, with the 'sufficient acknowledgement' required by the statute. The use of that phrase with regard to the research exception (but not that for private study) at least suggests that the former *does* cover quotation from research materials (with appropriate citation) in the publication of the researcher's results.[60] Nevertheless, quotation is now specifically permitted under the new s 30(1ZA) (see para 5.34). The InfoSoc Directive talks of 'scientific research', but this does not mean that only research in what would generally be thought of as science (as opposed to arts, humanities, or social sciences) is covered; rather, it means research directed to the development of knowledge and understanding (*scientia*) in whatever discipline.

Non-commercial purpose

5.27   The really crucial change to UK law which was made by the InfoSoc Directive and the 2003 Regulations was the restriction of the exception or permission for research to research carried out for a *non-commercial purpose*. This restriction was not seen as satisfactory, and the meaning and scope of 'non-commercial' causes much concern in university and professional research circles. In its 2003 report on 'Keeping Science Open', the Royal Society stated: 'We believe that the limitation of fair dealing to non-commercial purposes gives rise to uncertainty, is not useful and is complex to operate, and we recommend that it be renegotiated when the Copyright [InfoSoc] Directive 2001 is reviewed in 2005.'[61] The British Academy stated in its 2006 review of copyright and research in the humanities and social sciences: 'we believe that statutory clarification will be necessary to protect scholarship and the public interest in research'.[62]

[59] For these definitions see the *Oxford English Dictionary*; note also the Australian and New Zealand cases of *De Garis v Neville Jeffress Pidler* (1990) 18 IPR 292 (Fed Ct Aus); *Television New Zealand v Newsmonitor Services* [1994] 2 NZLR 91 (High Ct NZ); and *Copyright Licensing v University of Auckland* (2002) 53 IPR 618 (NZ).

[60] R Burrell and A Coleman, *Copyright Exceptions: The Digital Impact* (2005), 117, argue the opposite view, supporting it by reference to CDPA 1988, s 29(3)(b). Guidance had been promulgated by the British Academy and the Publishers Association in April 2008, entitled 'Joint Guidelines on Copyright and Academic Research', available at www.britac.ac.uk/policy/joint-copyright-guide.cfm.

[61] The Royal Society, 'Keeping Science Open: The Effects of Intellectual Property Policy on the Conduct of Science' (2003), para 4.19.

[62] The British Academy, 'Copyright and Research in the Humanities and Social Sciences' (2006), para 29.

5.28   What does 'non-commercial' mean in this context? For example, the copying which might have been involved in a lawyer carrying out legal research on behalf of a client requires authorisation from—and probably the payment of a fee to—the copyright owner.[63] On the other hand, the research carried out by an undergraduate writing an essay for assessment is clearly for a non-commercial purpose, as would be that carried out by a civil servant while preparing an internal report for a government minister. Unfortunately, however, there is a large amount of ambiguity in the distinction between commercial and non-commercial research. To pursue the university context as an example: what is the position of the professor writing a learned monograph which will be published by a commercial publisher, and from which the professor will earn royalties?[64] Is it different if the product is for a professional journal or conference for which the professor will receive a fee? Or for research, which is initially published in an academic journal, for no fee, but which subsequently becomes the basis for the development of a commercial product? The language of the statute seems to suggest that the purpose of the research is to be tested at the time it is carried out, and that it is sufficient if there is 'a' non-commercial purpose.[65] However, if at the time of the research, the 'end use' is contemplated to be for a purpose with some commercial value, then this exception does not provide a defence.

■ *Controller HMSO and Ordnance Survey v Green Amps* [2007] EWHC 2755 (Ch)

HMSO provided map data for a database service available to universities and the research community in the UK. Green Amps Ltd (GAL), a private company, gained unlicensed access to that service but argued that it came within the non-commercial research provision because it had used the data for a mapping tool facility in development, and their use thus had research and development status. The Court held that, even if use of the mapping data by GAL, a commercial company, had at that point only been for research, the intended end use, and as such, the research was for commercial purposes. Further, GAL's actions could not be described as fair dealing considering the extent and covert manner of its copying.[66]

 Discussion point   For answer guidance visit **www.oup.com/uk/brown5e**.

Does the InfoSoc Directive 2001 require the exclusion of all commercial research from the benefit of the exception for research?

 Exercise

The government commissions a private research consultancy company to investigate and report back on a social issue upon which it is proposed there should be legislation. The company will receive a substantial fee for its work. Is the company's research for government non-commercial? Would your answer be any different if the research was to be carried out by a charity active in the area where the social issue arises? Or by a law firm with expertise on it?

---

[63]   So the comment in *Law Society of Upper Canada v CCH Canadian* [2004] 1 SCR 339, para 51 ('Lawyers carrying on the business of law for profit are conducting research') may be literally true, but that would probably not enjoy the benefit of the exception in the UK.

[64]   Contrary to popular belief amongst students, academic authors do earn royalties!

[65]   Note that Database Directive 1996, Art 6(2)(b) and InfoSoc Directive 2001, Art 5(3)(a) say that the 'sole purpose' must be scientific research.

[66]   See further E Derclaye, 'Of maps, Crown copyright, research and the environment' [2008] EIPR 162.

> **Key points on the exception for non-commercial research**
>
> - Research, a process of search and investigation, must be distinguished from private study.
> - Research for a commercial purpose is not within the exception. It is enough that there is 'a' commercial purpose; the presence of other non-commercial purposes will probably not bring the research within the exception.
> - The purpose is tested at the time the research is carried out, but the contemplated end use at the time should not be commercial.
> - This exception applies to all copyright works.
> - Sufficient acknowledgement is required.

Fair dealing: (b) private study

5.29   Fair dealing with any kind of copyright-protected work for the purpose of private study is a permitted act.[67] A contractual term that purports to prevent or restrict this permitted act is unenforceable.[68] Private study doesn't have a 'sufficient acknowledgement' requirement. We have already defined 'study' as the application of the mind to the acquisition of knowledge (para 5.26). 'Private study' does not include any study which is directly or indirectly for a commercial purpose.[69] It must be the private study of the person dealing with the work. The fact that some third party may use the secondary work for purposes of private study does not protect the copier from a claim of infringement of copyright. Thus, the reprinting of examination papers as a collection for sale to students was not fair dealing with the examination papers,[70] nor was the publication of study aids on well-known literary works for the use of school pupils.[71] This principle is reinforced by statutory provision to the effect that copying by a person other than the student himself is not fair dealing in two cases. First is the provision of copies by librarians outside the special provisions for them found elsewhere in the 1988 Act.[72] Second is the person who makes the copy, knowing or having reason to believe that it will result in copies of substantially the same material being provided to more than one person at substantially the same time and for substantially the same purpose.[73] This seems to ensure that the production of multiple copies cannot be justified under the heading of private study. It would also seem that study carried out for another person—an employer, for example—cannot be private study. Private must mean that the study is for one's own personal purposes.

Private study and students in schools, colleges, and universities

5.30   The exception for private study is of particular importance to students undertaking education in schools, colleges, and universities.[74] There is extensive provision in the 1988 Act restricting reprography (ie photocopying, digital scanning) *by educational establishments*, which sets out what can be freely done by and on behalf of an educational establishment for the purposes of providing instruction (paras 5.42–5.44), but *not* what can be done *by the individual receiving instruction* or, indeed, carrying out research, where the fair dealing exceptions may be relevant. An institution making and distributing photocopies or printouts to a class as a course pack can be distinguished from students copying parts of or complete works for their own study.

---

[67] CDPA 1988, s 29(1C). Note s 29(4) and (4A) in relation to computer programs.   [68] CDPA 1988, s 29(4B).
[69] CDPA 1988, s 178.   [70] *University of London Press Ltd v University Tutorial Press Ltd* [1916] 2 Ch 601.
[71] *Sillitoe v McGraw-Hill Book Co Ltd* [1983] FSR 545.   [72] CDPA 1988, s 29(3)(a); and see further para 5.45.
[73] CDPA 1988, s 29(3)(b).
[74] See generally *Universities UK v Copyright Licensing Agency* [2002] RPC 36 (Copyright Tribunal), paras 31–40. For educational establishments, see CDPA 1988, s 174 and Copyright (Educational Establishments) Order 2005 (SI 2005/223). See also para 6.44.

Such copying does not fall within the scope of any of the other exceptions for educational reprography or copying by librarians, but this does not mean that the defence of fair dealing for private study is unavailable.[75]

Exercise

Find out what the policies of your educational establishment are with regard to the making and distribution of copies of material for study purposes. Who, if anyone, pays for the making of these copies?

Key points on the exception for private study

- Study, the application of the mind to the acquisition of knowledge, is distinct from research.
- 'Private' means that the study is for the student's personal purposes.
- Copying or issuing material to the public for the purpose of others' private study is not within the exception.
- There are a number of special exceptions for educational establishments and libraries to enable them to provide copies for others' private study.
- The exception applies to all copyright works.

Fair dealing: (c) criticism or review

Criticism or review

5.31 Fair dealing with any kind of copyright-protected work, for purposes of *criticism and review* of that, or of another, work or of a performance of a work, is also a permitted act if accompanied by a *sufficient acknowledgement*, and provided that the work has been made available to the public.[76] *Review* requires, as a minimum, some dealing with an original copyrighted work other than condensing that work into a summary. *Criticism*, on the other hand, is not solely focused on the style of a copyrighted work but can also extend to the ideas or theories that work contains. Sufficient acknowledgement is required unless this would be impossible for reasons of practicality or otherwise.[77]

5.32 A typical example of an activity coming within the exception would be a review of a book with quotations in illustration of critical points, or a film review on a TV programme containing extracts from the film in question. Another instance would be comments upon a book in another book or article, with the use of quotations to point the criticism. The criticism need not be hostile. But how much of the original work can be used for such purposes? Lengthy extracts from the original work have been permitted where the purpose was purely to enable criticism to be made,[78] but where the purpose is not so much to provide criticism but the same information as the original work and to compete with it, the activity cannot be allowed.[79] Further, the criticism or review must be directed to the original or another work, not at the author or against the person whose activities are the subject of the original work.[80] The original or other work criticised must be a work of the kind protected by copyright, although it need not be in copyright at the time.[81]

---

[75] See CDPA 1988, s 28(4).   [76] CDPA 1988, s 30(1).

[77] CDPA 1988, s 30(1), as amended by Copyright and Rights in Performances (Quotation and Parody) Regulations 2014, reg 3(3).

[78] *Hubbard v Vosper* [1972] 2 QB 84; cf *Sillitoe v McGraw-Hill Book Co Ltd* [1983] FSR 545.

[79] *Independent Television Publications Ltd v Time Out Ltd* [1984] FSR 64.

[80] *Ashdown v Telegraph Group Ltd* [2002] ECC 19 (CA).   [81] *Fraser-Woodward Ltd v BBC and another* [2005] FSR (36) 762.

■ *Hubbard v Vosper* [1972] 2 QB 84 (CA)

This case involved the unauthorised publication (although in a traditional rather than an electronic medium) of the works of L Ron Hubbard, founder of the Church of Scientology, together with critical commentary thereupon. The Court of Appeal found that the criticism was sufficient to make the taking of substantial extracts of the copyright material fair dealing.[82]

■ *Pro Sieben Media AG v Carlton UK Television Ltd* [1999] FSR 610 (CA)

The case concerned a German TV programme in which Mandy Allwood, then pregnant with eight foetuses as a result of fertility treatment, was interviewed with her boyfriend, both having been paid for their participation. Carlton TV used unauthorised extracts from the German programme in another documentary attacking 'chequebook' journalism. It was held that their use was fair dealing as criticism and review rather than copying to take the right holder's market. The Court of Appeal said that the extent of use was relevant in considering fair dealing, but that relevance would depend on the circumstances of each case. Most important was the degree of competition, if any, between the two works in question. The mental element of the user was of little importance, so that a sincere belief that one was being critical in one's handling of the previous work would not be enough to make out the defence. However, the Court emphasised that the phrase 'criticism or review' was of wide and indefinite scope, and should be interpreted liberally.

■ *Fraser-Woodward Ltd v BBC and Another* [2005] FSR 36

Photographs of a well-known footballer (David Beckham) and his family were published under licence in tabloid newspapers. The defendants used images of the newspaper pages with the photographs in a BBC TV programme, to criticise their coverage of the doings of celebrities. The copyright owner sued for infringement of the copyright in the photographs. It was held that the defendants' use was for the purposes of criticism and review of the newspapers rather than the photographs themselves. But since under section 30(1) a work could be used to criticise 'another work', the defendants' activity fell within the scope of the permitted act. The other work had to be a work itself capable of copyright protection, but it did not have to be still in copyright. The *Pro Sieben* case also showed that the ideas or philosophy underlying a certain style of journalism could be the subject of criticism within the scope of section 30(1).

■ *IPC Media Ltd v News Group Newspapers Ltd* [2005] FSR 35

The *Sun* newspaper advertised its new magazine with illustrations of the front covers of two other magazines with which it was to compete. The owners of the rival magazines sued for copyright infringement, to which the owners of the *Sun* responded with a claim of fair dealing for purposes of criticism or review. It was held that the criticism/review in this case was directed not at the claimant's *work*, but at their product. Comparative advertising was intended to advance the *Sun*'s work at the expense of the other works, and this was not fair dealing.

Discussion point 1   For answer guidance visit **www.oup.com/uk/brown5e**.

Do you agree with the decision of the Court of Appeal in *Hubbard v Vosper*?

Discussion point 2

Why is a 'wide, liberal' approach needed for the exemption for criticism and review? How does this compare to the CJEU's approach to exceptions?

---

[82] cf the US case of *Religious Technology Center v Lerma*, 1996 WL 633131 (ED Va). See also *Religious Technology Center v Netcom On-Line Communication Service* 907 F Supp 1361 (ND Cal, 1995).

Public availability of work being criticised and reviewed

5.33   *Only* criticism and review of a work which has been made available to the public is fair dealing.[83] The work may have been made available by any means—by issue of copies to the public, by making work available through an electronic retrieval system, by way of public rental, lending, performance, exhibition, showing, or playing, or through public communication. However, no account is to be taken in this regard of any unauthorised act.[84] Thus, it would seem that criticism or review of unpublished material involving quotation thereof, or where the material has been obtained surreptitiously or by breach of confidence, cannot claim to be fair dealing as criticism or review.[85]

 Discussion point   For answer guidance visit **www.oup.com/uk/brown5e.**

The 2003 regulations implemented the requirement of the InfoSoc Directive 2001 for the copyright work to have already been lawfully made available to the public for the purposes of criticism and review. Find out what was the position under the law before 31 October 2003.

■ *Beloff v Pressdram* [1973] RPC 765

B, a political journalist for the *Observer*, sent an internal memorandum to colleagues revealing the view of a serving Cabinet minister that another minister was the natural successor to the then Prime Minister. A copy of this memorandum was obtained surreptitiously by *Private Eye*, which published and commented on the memorandum as part of an attack on the serving Cabinet minister and on the journalist, who had previously criticised the magazine's campaign against the second minister. It was held that *Private Eye*'s actions were not fair dealing for purposes of criticism and review, although it was not the law (then) that unpublished works were outside the fair dealing defences.

 Question

How would this case be decided today? See further the following case.

■ *HRH The Prince of Wales v Associated Newspapers Ltd (No 3)* [2008] Ch 57 (CA)

Extracts from unpublished journals of the Prince of Wales recording his impressions from his official visit to Hong Kong were published in the *Mail on Sunday* in 2005, without the Prince's consent. It was held that since the journals were unpublished, the exception for criticism and review was inapplicable. The fact that much of the *information* contained in the journals was already in the public domain made no difference.

Key points on exception for criticism and review

- This exception applies to all forms of copyright work.
- The work criticised/reviewed must be one that is publicly available.
- The exception should be given a wide and liberal interpretation.
- Use of a copyright work in the criticism or review of another work, even one that is not in copyright, may be justified under the exception.

---

[83] CDPA 1988, s 30(1), as amended by 2003 Regulations.   [84] For all this see CDPA 1988, s 30(1A), added by 2003 Regulations.
[85] In appropriate cases, however, it might be fair dealing for the purpose of reporting current events: see further paras 5.37–5.38.

- But the exception does not allow one freely to criticise the author of the work as distinct from the work itself, or the person whose activities are the subject of the work's content.
- Sufficient acknowledgement is required.

Fair dealing: (d) quotation

5.34   Before the 2014 reforms, the law allowed users to quote from copyright works if the purpose of that quotation was criticism or review. However, the Berne Convention 1886 does not limit the exception for quotation by any purpose and, the corresponding provision in the InfoSoc Directive 2001 is also broader as it refers to 'quotations for purposes *such as* criticism *or* review' (emphasis added).[86] In response to criticism of the narrow scope of this exception, the UK government introduced a new exception allowing quotation from a work, whether for the purpose of criticism or review or otherwise.[87] The exception was envisaged to remove unnecessary restrictions to freedom of expression and improve the alignment of UK law with international copyright standards.[88]

5.35   Quotation is not defined in the statutory provision. Most requirements are similar to that of the criticism and review exception (paras 5.31–5.33): the work is available to the public; the use of the quotation is fair dealing with the work; and the quotation is accompanied by sufficient acknowledgement, unless this would be impossible for reasons of practicality or otherwise. The only additional requirement is that the extent of the quotation is no more than is required by the specific purpose for which it is used.[89] A contractual term that purports to prevent or restrict this permitted act is unenforceable.[90]

5.36   The exception appears to allow for quotations, from any form of copyright work, such as films or photographs and not just literary works, and for any purpose, so long as the extent of the quotation is no more than is required to achieve such purpose. However, the exception was envisaged to only permit 'minor uses' such as quotations in academic papers, internet blogs, and tweets and, seen as 'highly unlikely' to allow for unauthorised uses of commercially available clips from news agencies and film archives because the fairness requirement would not be met where such use conflicted with the normal exploitation of the work or harm the rights holders unreasonably.[91] It remains to be seen if the courts will use the 'fairness' requirement to curtail the scope of the exception by assessing whether certain purposes are justified or not, and whether the form of work is important.

Key points on exception for quotation

- This exception applies to all forms of copyright work.
- The work quoted from must be one that is publicly available.
- The quotation can be used for criticism or review or any other purpose.
- The extent of the quotation should be no more than is required by the specific purpose for which it is used.
- Sufficient acknowledgement is required.

---

[86] Article 10(1) of the Berne Convention 1886 and Art 5(3)(d) of the InfoSoc Directive 2001. See Case C-145/10 *Painer v Standard Verlags GmbH* [2012] ECDR 6, paras 133–137; see also the pending reference to the CJEU in Case C-476/17 *Pelham v Hütter*.

[87] CDPA 1988, s 30(1ZA), added by Copyright and Rights in Performances (Quotation and Parody) Regulations 2014, reg 3(4).

[88] IPO, 'Modernising Copyright: A Modern, Robust and Flexible Framework' (2012), 26.

[89] CDPA 1988, s30(1ZA)(c). Article 5(3)(d) of the InfoSoc Directive 2001 requires the use to be 'in accordance with fair practice, and to the extent required by the specific purpose'.

[90] CDPA 1988, s 30(4).   [91] IPO, 'Modernising Copyright: A Modern, Robust and Flexible Framework' (2012), 4 and 27.

Fair dealing: (e) reporting current events

5.37 Fair dealing with any work *other than a photograph* for the purpose of reporting current events does not infringe copyright, provided that it is accompanied by a sufficient acknowledgement. However, no acknowledgement is required when current events are being reported by means of a sound recording, film, or broadcast, where this would be impossible for reasons of practicality or otherwise.[92] The underlying idea here is clearly to support the circulation of news, the purpose being 'to provide an exception to, or limit upon, copyright protection in the public interest, namely freedom of expression'.[93] There is no requirement like that for the criticism/review exception, that the work being reported is available to the public, although in the modern case law unauthorised takings of material subsequently quoted in news reports has been a factor in holding the publication not fair dealing.[94] Photographs are exempted altogether from the fair dealing provisions on news reporting.[95] Since news reporting is a major use of photographs in all media, the availability of a fair dealing exception in respect of these works was felt to undermine the market position of the photographer too much.

5.38 The event reported must be *current*, the copied material must be used for *reporting* the current event, and the dealing must be fair. The defence is not limited to general news programmes and was upheld in *BBC v BSB Ltd*,[96] where extracts from BBC sports broadcasts lasting from 14 to 37 seconds and made with acknowledgement to the BBC were included without permission in BSB sports news programmes. In *Newspaper Licensing Agency v Meltwater* (for the facts of this case, see para 4.19),[97] it was held that scraped extracts from articles in media monitoring reports provided by M, were not intended for public consumption and not made for the purpose of reporting current events; their purpose was to enable the end-user to see when, where, and in what context the search terms were used. The Court of Appeal in *Pro Sieben Media AG v Carlton UK Television*[98] indicated that, like 'criticism or review', 'reporting current events' is an expression of wide scope and is to be interpreted liberally.

■ *Hyde Park Residence Ltd v Yelland* [1999] RPC 655 (Jacob J); [2000] RPC 604 (CA)

This case was concerned with the unauthorised publication by the *Sun* in September 1998 of CCTV photographs of Princess Diana and Dodi al-Fayed, taken before their deaths on 31 August 1997 at the former mansion of the Duchess of Windsor. Jacob J held that the one-year gap in time did not prevent these events continuing to be 'current', given the continuing publicity about the visit arising from statements made two days before the publication in question by Mohammed al-Fayed, tenant of the mansion and, through a security company which he controlled, owner of the copyright in the photographs. This 'liberal' approach to the definition of current events was accepted by the Court of Appeal, even though the *Sun's* actual use of the photographs was held not to be fair dealing, because the falsity of Mr al-Fayed's statements was already public knowledge, and the spread given to material itself dishonestly obtained and hitherto unpublished was excessive.

■ *Ashdown v Telegraph Group Ltd* [2002] ECC 19 (CA)

The 'liberal' approach to the currency of events was again applied by the Court of Appeal in this case. The *Sunday Telegraph* newspaper had published unlicensed extracts from the diaries of Paddy Ashdown, the

---

[92] CDPA 1988, s 30(2) & (3). See also s 45(2) in relation to reporting parliamentary and judicial proceedings.
[93] *England and Wales Cricket Board v Tixdaq* [2016] EWHC 575 (Ch) para 112.
[94] See *Hyde Park Residence Ltd v Yelland* [2000] RPC 604 (CA); *Ashdown v Telegraph Group Ltd* [2002] ECC 19 (CA); and further J Griffiths, 'Copyright law after *Ashdown*: time to deal fairly with the public' [2002] IPQ 240.
[95] CDPA 1988, s 30(2).   [96] [1992] Ch 141.
[97] [2010] EWHC 3099 (Ch); [2011] EWCA Civ 890 (CA). See also *Newspaper Licensing Agency v Marks and Spencer plc* [2001] Ch 257 (CA).
[98] [1999] FSR 610 (CA).

former Liberal Democrat leader, shortly before they were due to be published by him as a book. The copying in question occurred in November 1999 but related to events over two years earlier. These were nonetheless arguably current events:

> The defence provided by section 30(2) is clearly intended to protect the role of the media in informing the public about matters of current concern to the public . . . In a democratic society, information about a meeting between the Prime Minister and an opposition party leader during the then current Parliament to discuss possible close co-operation between those parties is very likely to be of legitimate and continuing public interest. It might impinge upon the way in which the public would vote at the next general election (para 64).

But in the end the Telegraph Group's dealings were unfair: the publication destroyed part of the commercial value of Ashdown's diary, which he intended to publish himself;[99] much of the material covered was already in the public domain at the time of publication, although the diary was previously unpublished; the material had been obtained in breach of confidence; and a substantial portion was copied, adding significant commercial value for the newspaper.

■ *HRH The Prince of Wales v Associated Newspapers Ltd (No 3)* [2008] Ch 57 (CA)

For the facts of this case, see para 5.33. It was held that the exception for reporting current events was inapplicable. The events in question—the UK's return of Hong Kong to the People's Republic of China in 1997—were no longer current in 2005, when the extracts were published. While there was some faint light on the recent conduct of the heir to the throne and his approach to his position, the overall impression of the article was of a selection of 'choice passages' from the journal, with the revelation of the contents of the journal itself the event of interest.

Discussion point   For answer guidance visit **www.oup.com/uk/brown5e**.

Is the death of Princess Diana in August 1997 still a current event? Or the events in New York on 11 September 2001? Or the fall of the Berlin Wall in 1989?

■ *England and Wales Cricket Board v Tixdaq* [2016] EWHC 575 (Ch)

For the facts of this case, see para 4.20. In considering whether the clips uploaded to the app could benefit from the exception for reporting current events, Arnold J noted that the exception must be construed in accordance with Article 5(3)(c) of the InfoSoc Directive 2001 and an important consideration in the assessment of 'fair dealing' here is 'whether the extent of the use is justified by the informatory purpose' (paras 68–70). He confirmed that a contemporaneous sporting event, such as a cricket match, qualifies as a current event (para 106) and it is necessary to construe the term 'reporting' purposively, according to the context (para 112). Consequently, reporting current events is not restricted to traditional media, and citizen journalism can qualify for it too. He noted that:

> If a member of the public captures images and/or sound of a newsworthy event using their mobile phone and uploads it to a social media site like Twitter, then that may well qualify as reporting current events even if it is accompanied by relatively little in the way of commentary (para 114).

However, he held that the clips had not been used by T 'to inform the audience about a current event, but presented for consumption because of their intrinsic interest and value', and its use was 'purely commercial rather than genuinely informatory' (para 129). He also held that even if T's use did qualify as reporting current events, it was not fair dealing because it was commercially damaging to the claimants and conflicted with the normal exploitation of the underlying copyright works (para 147).

---

[99] And, in fact did, in November 2000: *The Ashdown Diaries, vol 1: 1988–1997* (2000).

> **Key points on the exception for reporting current events**
>
> - The exception applies to all copyright works except photographs.
> - There must be sufficient acknowledgement of the source.
> - The exception is to receive wide scope and a liberal interpretation.
> - Events may remain 'current' for some time after their occurrence, but not indefinitely.

Fair dealing: (f) caricature, parody, or pastiche

5.39   Before the 2014 reforms, creating a 'parody' of another work was neither necessarily an infringement of copyright, nor an independent, substantive defence to a charge of infringement. Whether a parody of another work had infringed its copyright depended on whether a substantial part was copied or not; the infringement not being dependent on it being a parody (see para 4.38). Equally, there was no defence based solely on the fact that work was a parody; instead a user would have had to demonstrate that their parody fell within one of the permitted acts available at the time, such as fair dealing for criticism or review. This arrangement was far from satisfactory for a number of reasons. A parody may require copying of more than an insubstantial part of a work. The criticism and review exception could only indirectly, if at all, cover the nature of a parody: it requires criticism of a 'work' or 'ideas or philosophy underlying a work' so parodies of wider social practices would not fit; it requires sufficient acknowledgement while a parody would usually seek to evoke another work without expressly identifying the work or its author.[100]

5.40   Article 5(3)(k) of the InfoSoc Directive 2001 permits an exception for caricature, parody or pastiche but the UK government, in transposing the Directive, had chosen not to implement it.[101] The Gowers Review in 2006 had recommended that an exception be expressly introduced in the UK. The Hargreaves Review also recommended use of the parody exception allowed in the EU as it has both economic and cultural consequences in the digital environment. As a result, in October 2014, the UK government introduced a new exception allowing fair dealing with a work for the purposes of caricature, parody, or pastiche.[102] There is no requirement for sufficient acknowledgement. A contractual term that purports to prevent or restrict this permitted act is unenforceable.[103]

5.41   The statutory provision lacks detail as to when a use is a caricature, parody, or pastiche[104] and what may amount to fair dealing. However, there is some guidance by the CJEU on the meaning of parody.[105]

■ **C-201/13** *Deckmyn v Vandersteen* **[2014] ECDR 21 (CJ)**

D, a member of a Belgian political party, reproduced a drawing resembling the cover of a *Suske en Wiske* comic book, authored by V. In the original drawing, one of the book's main characters, wearing a white tunic, is throwing coins to people, who are trying to pick them up. D had replaced the character with 'the Mayor of the City of Ghent and the people picking up the coins' with 'people wearing veils and people of colour'.

---

[100]   See further R Deazley, 'Copyright and parody: taking backward the Gowers Review?' (2010) 73(5) MLR 785.

[101]   Several other EU member states have allowed a parody exception. See, eg, French Intellectual Property Code L.122–5(4) ('La parodie, le pastiche et la caricature, compte tenu des lois du genre'). Also, outside the EU, the United States has allowed 'parody' as fair use, although it is a creation of the courts rather than something spelled out in the legislation.

[102]   CDPA 1988, s 30A, added by Copyright and Rights in Performances (Quotation and Parody) Regulations 2014, reg 5(1).

[103]   CDPA 1988, s 30A(2).

[104]   E Hudson, 'The pastiche exception in copyright law: a case of mashed-up drafting?' [2017] IPQ 346.

[105]   See further, D Jongsma, 'Parody after Deckmyn—a comparative overview of the approach to parody under copyright law in Belgium, France, Germany and the Netherlands' [2017] IIC 652.

The Brussels Court of First Instance held D's drawing to be infringing but on appeal, the drawing was argued to fall with the parody exception and the Court referred it to CJ, seeking guidance on the meaning of parody. CJ held that despite the optional nature of the parody exception in the InfoSoc Directive, 'parody' must be regarded as an autonomous concept of EU law and interpreted uniformly through the EU (paras 15–16). The meaning and scope of 'parody' must be determined by considering its usual meaning in everyday language and with regard to such meaning there are two essential characteristics of a parody: it evokes an existing work, while being noticeably different from it; and, it constitutes an expression of humour or mockery. The concept of parody is *not* required to fulfil other conditions such as the following: that it should display an original character of its own, other than that of displaying noticeable differences with respect to the original parodied work; or, it could reasonably be attributed to a person other than the author of the original work itself; or it should relate to the original work itself or mention the source of the parodied work (paras 19–21). It is for the national courts to determine, in light of all circumstances, whether a 'fair balance' is preserved in the application of the exception, between the rights and interests of right owners and the freedom of expression of the user of the copyright work (paras 26–28). The fairness test in the UK will be key to achieving this balancing exercise, and factors used in relation to other fair dealing exceptions are likely to be relevant. CJ also noted that the national court must have regard to the copyright holder's legitimate interest in the protected work not being associated with a discriminatory message conflicting with the principle of equal treatment between persons irrespective of race, colour, or ethnic origin (paras 29–31). This is seen to be a problematic aspect of the ruling because copyright may not be the most appropriate mechanism for regulating discriminatory messages and while moral rights might be more suitable for the purpose, they are outside the scope of InfoSoc Directive 2001.[106]

Key points on exception for caricature, parody, or pastiche

- This exception applies to all forms of copyright work.
- The work can be used for the purposes of caricature, parody, or pastiche.
- Parody should evoke an existing work, while being noticeably different, and constitute an expression of humour or mockery.
- Sufficient acknowledgement is not required.

 Exercise

Consider the case of a database protected by copyright (as distinct from *sui generis* database right, see paras 3.48–3.50). Do the fair dealing exceptions discussed previously apply to such databases? Has the UK properly implemented Article 6 of the Database Directive?

Educational establishments

5.42   There are a number of exceptions in favour of educational establishments (schools, further education colleges, and universities).[107] In the 2014 reforms, several changes were made to these exceptions in order to allow educational establishments increased use of materials in conjunction with educational licensing schemes, and teachers to deliver multi-media teaching without infringement. Two examples are the exceptions for illustration for instruction and copying and use of extracts by educational establishments.

---

[106] J Griffiths et al, 'The European Copyright Society's Opinion on the judgment of the CJEU in Case C-201/13 Deckmyn' [2015] EIPR 127.
[107] CDPA 1988, ss 32–36A; s 174 (meaning of educational establishment); Copyright (Educational Establishments) Order 2005 (SI 2005/223). See generally IPO, 'Exceptions to Copyright: Education and Teaching' (October 2014).

5.43 Fair dealing with *any* copyright-protected work for the sole purpose of illustration for instruction is not infringement provided that the dealing is done by the person giving or receiving instruction or in preparation for the same, is for a non-commercial purpose, and is accompanied by a sufficient acknowledgement unless practically or otherwise impossible.[108] The purpose of instruction includes setting, communicating, and answering examination questions and a contractual term that purports to prevent or restrict this permitted act is unenforceable.[109] Copying of extracts of a work by educational establishments, and communicating to its pupils and staff, is also permitted.[110] However, there are several prescribed conditions: the copy made should be for the purposes of instruction for a non-commercial purpose and accompanied by sufficient acknowledgement; a broadcast, and an artistic work not incorporated into another work, are excluded; copying of more than 5 per cent of any work in any 12-month period is prohibited; and acts allowed under this provision are not permitted if licences for such copying are available[111] and the educational establishment knew or ought to have known of that fact.[112] Online distance learning is now accommodated by permitting communication of a copy of an extract outside the premises of the establishment, only if made by means of a secure electronic network that is accessible only by the establishment's pupils and staff.[113]

Question

What steps, if any, should be taken by a school teacher wishing to distribute copies of a copyright-protected poem for discussion in her class?

5.44 Other exemptions for educational establishments include:

- inclusion in educational anthologies of short extracts from published literary and dramatic works;[114]
- performing, playing, or showing works in the course of educational activities;[115]
- recording broadcasts for educational purposes;[116]
- lending of copies.[117]

Education is clearly an area of activity for which dissemination of material amongst teachers and students is important, and the 2014 reforms have significantly increased the subject matter, nature, and scope of uses permitted under the provisions above. However, the permissions continue to restrict what can be freely done by and on behalf of an educational establishment for the purposes of providing instruction, and are really aimed at providing a basis upon which the real needs of the educational establishment can only be met by obtaining and paying for a licence from collecting societies acting on behalf of authors and publishers. Reforms are forthcoming in this area as part of the European Commission's Draft Copyright Directive 2016. Article 4 proposes a mandatory exception to allow for the digital use of works for the sole purpose of illustration for teaching, to the extent it is justified by the non-commercial purpose. Such use is required to take place on the premises of an educational establishment or through a secure electronic

---

[108] CDPA 1988, s 32(1) as amended by Copyright and Rights in Performances (Research, Education, Libraries and Archives) Regulations 2014, reg 4(1).

[109] CDPA 1988, s 32(2) & (3).

[110] CDPA 1988, s 36, as amended by Copyright and Rights in Performances (Research, Education, Libraries and Archives) Regulations 2014, reg 4(3).

[111] As they commonly will be, from the Copyright Licensing Agency: see *Universities UK v Copyright Licensing Agency* [2002] RPC 36 (para 6.44), and see further U Suthersanen, 'Copyright and educational policies: a stakeholder analysis' (2003) 23 OJLS 585.

[112] CDPA 1988, s 36(1)&(4)–(6).

[113] CDPA 1988, s 36(3). See also s 40B permitting making work available through dedicated terminals (para 5.45).

[114] CDPA 1988, s 33.   [115] CDPA 1988, s 34; and see paras 4.50–4.56.

[116] CDPA 1988, s 35 as amended by Copyright and Rights in Performances (Research, Education, Libraries and Archives) Regulations 2014, reg 4(2).

[117] CDPA 1988 s 36A. See further para 5.45.

network accessible only by the establishment's students and teaching staff. It also contains options for the member states to provide fair compensation for the harm caused to right holders and make the exception subject to availability of licences. The text adopted by the European Parliament[118] now includes minor amendments to broaden the scope of the exception, and also a new sub-section as per which contractual provision contrary to the exception shall be unenforceable. At the time of writing, the EU legislative process is not complete (see para 2.15).

 Question

Do the provisions in the UK for educational establishments go as far as Article 5(3)(a) of the InfoSoc Directive, which allows exceptions for 'use for the sole purpose of illustration for teaching . . . to the extent justified by the non-commercial purpose to be achieved'?

Libraries, archives, and museums

5.45   There are a number of exceptions for libraries, archives, and museums in the CDPA 1988.[119] The 2014 reforms simplified and extended these exceptions to make them more suitable for the digital environment.[120] A public library does not infringe copyright in a work of any description by lending books, audiobooks, or e-books within the Public Lending Right scheme,[121] while libraries and archives other than public libraries, not conducted for profit, likewise do not infringe copyright by lending copies of the work.[122] Librarians, of libraries not conduced for profit, are permitted to make and supply readers with a single copy of published works for the purposes of private study or non-commercial research, subject to prescribed conditions.[123] Further, libraries, archives, museums, and educational establishments, are also permitted to communicate or make available to the public works by means of a dedicated terminal on its premises, for the purposes of private study or non-commercial research, subject to prescribed conditions.[124] This new exemption is geared to enabling access to digital copies of books, sound recordings, and images through cultural institutions. Libraries, archives, and museums are also permitted to make replacement copies of works from their permanent collection subject to prescribed conditions,[125] enabling them to preserve their collections. They can also supply single copies of works to other libraries.[126] Article 5 of the European Commission's Draft Copyright Directive 2016 proposes a mandatory exception to permit cultural heritage institutions to make copies of works from their permanent collection for the sole purpose of the preservation. The text adopted by the European Parliament[127] further restricts contractual override of this exception and also prevents copyright subsistence in faithful copies of public domain materials produced for the purpose of preservation. At the time of writing, the EU legislative process is not complete (see para 2.15).

---

[118]   See amendments adopted by the European Parliament on 12 September 2018 at www.europarl.europa.eu/sides/getDoc.do?pubRef=-// EP//TEXT+TA+P8-TA-2018-0337+0+DOC+XML+V0//EN; see also, the European Council's position as adopted on 25 May 2018 at https://eur-lex.europa.eu/legal-content/EN/TXT/PDF/?uri=CONSIL:ST_9134_2018_INIT&from=EN.

[119]   CDPA 1988, ss 40A–44A.

[120]   Copyright and Rights in Performances (Research, Education, Libraries and Archives) Regulations 2014; see generally, IPO, 'Exceptions to Copyright: Libraries, Archives and Museums' (October 2014).

[121]   CDPA 1988 s 40A(1). See also sub-sections 1ZA and 1A. See further the Public Lending Right Act 1979.

[122]   CDPA 1988, s 40A(2).   [123]   CDPA 1988, s 42A; see s 43 for unpublished works.

[124]   CDPA 1988, s 40B; a corresponding provision can be found in InfoSoc Directive 2001, Art 5(3)(n), for the scope of which see Case C-117/13 *TU Darmstadt v Ulmer* [2014] ECDR 23.

[125]   CDPA 1988, s 42; see also ss 44B and 76A permitting digitisation and use of orphan works (paras 6.46–6.50).

[126]   CDPA 1988, s 41 permitting institutional sharing.

[127]   See amendments adopted by the European Parliament on 12 September 2018 at www.europarl.europa.eu/sides/getDoc.do?pubRef=-// EP//TEXT+TA+P8-TA-2018-0337+0+DOC+XML+V0//EN; see also, the European Council's position as adopted on 25 May 2018 at https://eur-lex.europa.eu/legal-content/EN/TXT/PDF/?uri=CONSIL:ST_9134_2018_INIT&from=EN.

Deposit libraries

5.46   The Legal Deposit Libraries Act 2003 is the current provision under which those who publish print material in the UK can be required to deposit a copy of the publication with each of the following libraries: the British Library, the National Libraries of Scotland and Wales, the Bodleian Library, Oxford, the Cambridge University Library, and the Library of Trinity College Dublin. The deposit rights have existed since the 18th century; the purpose of the 2003 Act was to extend the deposit obligation beyond print, and in particular to non-print works published on the internet. In order to facilitate the capture of internet material for the deposit libraries, the Act introduced an exception allowing them to make copies of such material for the purpose.[128]

Key points on libraries, archives, and museums

- Libraries receive some special exemptions in relation to their lending activities.

- Libraries, archives, and museums are also enabled to provide access to works to readers for their private study or non-commercial research, under specified conditions.

- There are six 'copyright libraries', each entitled to receive a copy of every copyright work printed in the UK, and a framework for collecting non print works is also in operation.

Provisions for disability

5.47   The InfoSoc Directive 2001 allows 'uses for the benefit of people with a disability, which are directly related to the disability and of a non-commercial nature, to the extent required by the specific disability'.[129] As originally passed in 1988, the CDPA contained provisions enabling designated bodies to make copies of broadcasts and issue them to the public with subtitles for the deaf and hard of hearing, or otherwise modified for the special needs of those physically or mentally handicapped in other ways.[130] The 1988 Act was supplemented in 2002, and again simplified and supplemented by the 2014 reforms, which broadened the provisions.[131] In May 2018, the UK government launched a public consultation for implementation of the Marrakesh Directive (see para 5.11).[132] It indicated the government's intended approach to not discriminate between people with different types of disability, and its intention to apply changes in general to the provisions in the 1988 Act, even though the Directive's focus is narrower. The Directive was implemented in the UK in October 2018,[133] broadening the existing provisions even further; eg previously the exceptions did not apply if a commercial accessible format copy of a work was available, but the commercial availability provisions have now been deleted. The consultation had also sought views on whether, and if so how, the UK should implement a form of compensation scheme for right holders, an option in the Directive. However, the government decided not to implement a compensation scheme due to lack of robust evidence of harm to rightholders and the government's desire for fair outcomes for authorised bodies, ie to not subject UK-based bodies to a compensation scheme when those based outside the UK are not subject to the same obligations.[134]

---

[128]   CDPA 1988, s 44A; the 2003 Act came into force on 1 February 2004 (Legal Deposit Libraries Act 2003 (Commencement) Order 2004 (SI 2004/130)), but Regulations bringing the internet provisions came into operation on 6 April 2013 (The Legal Deposit Libraries (non-print works) Regulations 2013 (SI 2013/777)).

[129]   Art 5(3)(b).   [130]   CDPA 1988, s 74, repealed in 2014.

[131]   Copyright (Visually Impaired Persons) Act 2002; Copyright and Rights in Performances (Disability) Regulations 2014; see generally IPO, 'Exceptions to Copyright: Accessible Formats for disabled people' (October 2014).

[132]   IPO, 'Consultation on UK's Implementation of the Marrakesh Treaty' (May 2018).

[133]   Copyright and Related Rights (Marrakesh Treaty etc) (Amendment) Regulations 2018 (SI 2018/995).

[134]   IPO, 'Government response to Marrakesh Consultation' (Sep 2018).

5.48   There are two types of exceptions.[135] A disabled person, or a person acting on their behalf, is permitted to make accessible copies of a work for the personal use of a disabled person, provided that the disabled person has lawful access to a copy of the work, and the person's disability prevents them from enjoying the work to substantially the same degree as a person who does not have that disability.[136] Further, authorised bodies that have lawful access to a published work may make, communicate, distribute, or lend, accessible copies of the work on a non-profit basis for the personal use of disabled persons.[137] Authorised body means an educational establishment, or a body that is not conducted for profit.[138] Disability includes both physical and mental impairments which prevent the person from enjoying a work to substantially the same degree as a person who does not have that impairment.[139]

 The Marrakesh Treaty and Brexit

The Marrakesh Treaty Directive and Regulation have entered into force in the UK. Both the Regulation and the UK's implementation of the Directive will be preserved in UK law. However, the UK's obligation under the Marrakesh Treaty arises out of its membership of the EU. In the event of a 'no-deal' Brexit, the UK will have to ratify the Marrakesh Treaty in its own name to benefit from cross-border exchange of accessible format copies of copyright works.[140] The UK government's 'no-deal' guidance indicates an intention to do so, and remain party to the Treaty following EU exit.[141] Consequently, it notes that the implication will be that 'between exit and the point of ratification, businesses, organisations or individuals transferring accessible format copies between the EU and UK may not be able to rely on the EU Regulation'.[142]

Public administration

5.49   Copyright is not infringed by a number of actions which are grouped under the heading of public administration.[143] Again, this is permitted under the InfoSoc Directive 2001,[144] as use for the purpose of 'public security'[145] or to ensure the proper performance or reporting of administrative, parliamentary, or judicial proceedings. Only one example, perhaps of particular pertinence to law students and lawyers, will be given here. Anything done for the purpose of reporting parliamentary or judicial proceedings does not infringe copyright; but this does not authorise the copying of a work which is itself a published report of the proceedings (eg Hansard, a law report).[146]

Incidental inclusion

5.50   Copyright in a work is not infringed by its incidental inclusion in an artistic work, sound recording, film, or broadcast:[147] for example, the inclusion in the background of an informal photographic portrait of a painting or sculpture, or its appearance in the background of a television broadcast. Copyright is not infringed by the issue to the public of copies (eg videos of the broadcast), or the playing, showing, or broadcasting or

---

[135] See in general CDPA 1988, s 31A–31F.   [136] CDPA 1988, s 31A.

[137] CDPA 1988, s 31B. See also s 31BA permitting making of intermediate copies.   [138] CDPA 1988, s 31F.

[139] CDPA 1988, s 31F.

[140] UK Government, 'Changes to copyright law in the event of no deal' (26 October 2018), www.gov.uk/government/publications/changes-to-copyright-law-in-the-event-of-no-deal/changes-to-copyright-law-in-the-event-of-no-deal.

[141] UK Government, 'Copyright if there's no Brexit deal' (24 September 2018) www.gov.uk/government/publications/copyright-if-theres-no-brexit-deal.

[142] ibid.   [143] CDPA 1988, ss 45–50.   [144] Article 5(3)(e).

[145] On the use of public security, see Case C-145/10 *Painer v Standard Verlags GmbH* [2012] ECDR 6.

[146] CDPA 1988, s 45(2). For successful uses of s 45, see *Ebden v News International Ltd* [2011] EWHC 4082 (Ch); *BBC, Petitioners (in the case of HM Advocate v Hainey)* [2012] SLT 476.

[147] CDPA 1988, s 31(1). See generally R Burrell and A Coleman, *Copyright Exceptions: The Digital Impact* (2005), 64–66.

communication to the public of such a work.[148] A musical work, words spoken or sung with music, or so much of a sound recording, or broadcast as includes a musical work or such words, is not to be regarded as incidentally included in another work if it is deliberately included[149]—for example, as part of background noise in a film or television production; thus, copyright permission will be required.

■ *FA Premier League v Panini* [2004] FSR 1 (CA)

P distributed an unofficial football sticker album and a sticker collection of pictures of players from Premier League clubs wearing team strips showing the Premier League logo or the logo of a Premier League club. FAPL, acting on behalf of the clubs, had granted exclusive rights to T, to use and reproduce the official team logos in stickers and albums. It was held at first instance that there was infringement. The use of the logos was not incidental, meaning casual or of secondary importance, but integral to showing the footballer in his current strip. An appeal was dismissed. 'Incidental' did not mean only unintentional or non-deliberate inclusion, and the question had to be answered by considering the circumstances in which the relevant artistic work was created. There was no necessary dichotomy between 'incidental' and 'integral'. Where a copyright-protected artistic work appeared in a photograph because it was part of the setting in which the photographer found his subject, it could properly be said to be an integral part of that photograph. In order to test whether the use of one work in another was incidental, it was proper to ask why it had been included in the other, considering both commercial and aesthetic reasons. Applying that test, it was evident that the use of the team and Premier League logos in the stickers was not incidental. Further, the defence would probably not apply to the albums since they were arguably literary works.

 Question

What does 'incidental' mean in this context?

Representation of certain artistic works on public display

5.51   Alongside the rule of incidental exclusion exception should be considered the exception permitting certain acts in respect of buildings, sculptures, models for buildings, and works of artistic craftsmanship (three-dimensional works) which are situated permanently in a public place or in premises open to the public: they may be made the subject of a graphic work, a photograph or film, or included in a broadcast as a visual image without their copyright being infringed thereby.[150] Copyright is not infringed by the issue to the public of copies (eg videos of the broadcast), or the communication to the public of such a work.[151] Although EU reform in this area was recently considered, it did not go ahead.[152]

 Discussion point 1   For answer guidance visit **www.oup.com/uk/brown5e**.

Is 'incidental inclusion' really an exception to copyright? Or does it just follow from the definitions of copyright and infringement thereof?

Discussion point 2

If I take a photograph of my family against the background of a statue in a city square in order to create a striking overall image, is the sculptor's copyright infringed? Is it any different from taking a picture of a well-known actor against the background of a sculpture in his home because I think the statue symbolises something of the actor's personality?

---

[148] CDPA 1988, ss 31(2).   [149] CDPA 1988, s 31(3).   [150] CDPA 1988, s 62.   [151] CDPA 1988, s 62(3).
[152] See further A Lorrain and J Reda, 'Freedom of panorama: a political selfie in Brussels' [2015] EIPR 753.

Text and data analysis

5.52   The Hargreaves Review noted that copyright can inhibit use of valuable new technologies like text and data mining which requires copying of large amount of data, in order to computationally find patterns and associations that would assist researchers (eg text analysis, through a computer software, of a large number of research articles describing malaria in different communities, could identify useful relationships and provide significant insights for prevention of malaria today). It recommended extension of exceptions to enable use of analytics for non-commercial use. The 2014 reforms introduced a new exception which permits the making of a copy of a work by a person who has lawful access to the work provided that the copy is made for the person to carry out a computational analysis of anything recorded in the work for the sole purpose of research for a non-commercial purpose.[153] The copy should be accompanied by sufficient acknowledgement unless this would be impossible for reasons of practicality or otherwise. Transfer of the copy to any other person, or use of the copy for any other purpose, is infringement unless authorised by the copyright owner. The person must have lawful access to the work, for instance, through a sale or licence. A contractual term that purports to prevent or restrict this permitted act is unenforceable. There is no fairness requirement for the exception to apply.

 Question

Although the Hargreaves Review led to the introduction of this exception 'for a non-commercial purpose', it also recommended the government to press at EU level for such an exception for commercial use (at para 5.26). Should research and text and data analysis be permitted for commercial purposes in the UK?

5.53   Forthcoming reforms in this area are part of the European Commission's Draft Copyright Directive 2016. Article 3 proposes a mandatory exception 'for reproductions and extractions made by research organisations in order to carry out text and data mining of works or other subject-matter to which they have lawful access for the purposes of scientific research'. Unlike the UK provision, this restricts the exception to the nature of the user (research organisations) but does not restrict the purpose to non-commercial (scientific research). However, the text adopted by the European Parliament on 12 September 2018,[154] includes amendments requiring storage, in a secure manner, of reproductions and extractions made for text and data mining, and allowing member States to continue to provide text and data mining exceptions in accordance with Article 5(3)(a) of the InfoSoc Directive 2001. It also contains a new and broader optional exception in Article 3a for text and data mining that would be applicable to all entities, but this, like the scheme in the InfoSoc Directive, poses a challenge in achieving harmonization across the member states. At the time of writing, the EU legislative process is not complete (see para 2.15).

 Question

Find out whether the EU legislative process for the Draft Copyright Directive 2016 is complete and if so, what provisions on exceptions and limitations have been adopted in the final text.

---

[153] CDPA 1988, s 29A. For ambiguities in the scope of the new exception see S Kheria, C Waelde, and N Levin, 'Digital transformations in the Arts and Humanities: Negotiating the copyright landscape in the United Kingdom', in R Hobbs (ed), *The Routledge Companion to Media Education, Copyright, and Fair Use* (2018).

[154] See amendments adopted by the European Parliament on 12 September 2018 at www.europarl.europa.eu/sides/getDoc.do?pubRef=-//EP//TEXT+TA+P8-TA-2018-0337+0+DOC+XML+V0//EN; see also, the European Council's position as adopted on 25 May 2018 at https://eur-lex.europa.eu/legal-content/EN/TXT/PDF/?uri=CONSIL:ST_9134_2018_INIT&from=EN.

Lawful uses of computer programs

5.54 A lawful user of a computer program (meaning someone who has a right to use it, whether under a licence or otherwise, eg under a fair dealing exception) who does the following things with the program is not infringing copyright:

- makes a *back up* copy necessary for his lawful use (CDPA 1988, s 50A);

- *decompiles* the program (ie converts it from a low-level language (object code) to a high-level one, incidentally copying it in the process), for the sole purpose of obtaining the information necessary to enable the creation of another program which will be interoperable with the original one (CDPA 1988, s 50B);

- *observes, studies, or tests* the functioning of the program to determine its underlying ideas and principles, while loading, displaying, running, transmitting, or storing the program as entitled to do (CDPA 1988, s 50BA);

- *copies or adapts as necessary for lawful use*, and so far as not contractually prohibited, in particular for the purpose of *error correction* (CDPA 1988, s 50C).

Only the last of these is subject to any overriding contractual clause; in the other three cases, such clauses are void.[155]

Discussion point   For answer guidance visit **www.oup.com/uk/brown5e**.

To what extent may the exceptions for lawful use of computer programs be compared with fair dealing for purposes of private study and non-commercial research?

Time-shifting

5.55 The development of the video recorder as a consumer item made it normal for individuals to be able to make copies of television programmes which can be viewed later at a more convenient time than that scheduled by the broadcasting authority. This is commonly known as 'time-shifting'. Such activities do not constitute infringement of copyright either in the broadcast or in any work included in it—for example, a film—as long as carried out in domestic premises for private and domestic use.[156] The provision also applies to audio-taping of a radio broadcast. Similarly, the making for private and domestic use of a photograph of the whole or any part of an image forming part of a television broadcast, or a copy of such a photograph, does not infringe any copyright in the broadcast or in any film included in it.[157] Selling or otherwise dealing with a copy made under these provisions will become an infringement of copyright.[158]

Further issues for reform

Private copying

5.56 Historically, there has been no exception in favour of 'place-shifting' in the UK for private and domestic use in relation to copyright works, akin to that already in existence for 'time-shifting' for broadcasts, ie allowing the owner of a lawful copy of a sound recording or film to make copies usable on other machinery; for example copy a CD held in the house to obtain a copy to keep in the car, or in a portable playing device. A private copying exception, provided that fair compensation is paid to the rights holder, is allowed within

---

[155] CDPA 1988, s 296A.   [156] CDPA 1988, s 70.   [157] CDPA 1988, s 71.   [158] CDPA 1988, ss 70(2), (3) and 71(2), (3).

the EU framework (InfoSoc Directive, Art 5(2)(b)) although its exact nature and scope remains unclear.[159] The requirement for fair compensation has meant that in many of the EU states where this exception has been introduced, it has been done so alongside a levy system. The idea being that levies are imposed on equipment used for private copying, for example on blank CDs, the proceeds of which are then fed back to the right holder to compensate for the exception to their right. The Gowers Review 2006 recommended the non-retrospective introduction of a limited private copying exception for this purpose, confined to 'format-shifting' such as transferring a CD to an MP3 player or a video cassette to a DVD. Noting that in many other member states of the EU such exceptions were funded by levies on the sale prices of the relevant equipment, from which copyright owners were then remunerated, the Review argued that owners themselves could set sale prices at levels reflecting the additional use conferred by the new exception. The Hargreaves Review 2011 also recommended the introduction of a limited private copying exception to allow making of copies by individuals for their own and immediate family's use on different media. The government consulted on the impact of a potential exception and concluded that if it introduced a narrow exception limited to personal use, rather than use by friends and family, there would be no harm to the right holder and hence no need for a levy, the main argument being that the sellers had already priced in to the initial sale price any loss made from an infringing private copy.

5.57   In October 2014, a new private use exception was introduced in the UK[160] without a compensation scheme but it was subsequently repealed, and was only in force for a short period. The exception required several conditions to be met: first, the person must be an individual, not a corporate entity. Secondly, it must be 'the individual's own copy of the work' and they must have acquired the copy lawfully.[161] Thirdly, they must hold that copy on a permanent basis, rather than it being loaned by a friend, for example.[162] Finally, the copy could only be made for the user's private use and not have a commercial end.[163] Moreover, any contract which seeks to restrict or override the exception would be unenforceable.[164] The decision to not implement a levy scheme, however, proved controversial. In November 2014 several representatives of various authors and right owners applied for judicial review of the new section 28B, claiming it was incompatible with Article 5(2)(b) as it did not provide fair compensation.[165] They argued that the evidence the government had relied on to decide that no harm would come to right holders, and hence no compensation was necessary, was inadequate. The Court agreed with the claimants, on the basis that the conclusions and inferences drawn from the evidence were not justified and the decision to introduce section 28B without a compensation mechanism was unlawful. In a further judgment, on 17 July 2015, the Court ordered for section 28B to be quashed with prospective effect.[166] While an exception for private copying corresponds to what consumers are already doing, such acts became unlawful again in the UK after the repeal of section 28B. A policy issue then is whether the government should try again to introduce new proposals to legalise private copying in the UK, and whether this should be with a levy system.

 Discussion point   For answer guidance visit **www.oup.com/uk/brown5e**.

Is 'place-shifting' as legitimate as 'time-shifting'? Ought there to be such an exception to copyright?

---

[159] The provision has given rise to a number of decisions by the Court of Justice.

[160] Copyright and Rights in Performances (Personal Copies for Private Use) Regulations 2014 (SI 2014/2361) inserted s 28B in the CDPA 1988. It was repealed on 17 July 2015.

[161] CDPA 1988, s 28B(2).   [162] CDPA 1988, s 28B(2) and (4).   [163] CDPA 1988, s 28B(1) and (5).   [164] CDPA 1988, s 28B(10).

[165] *R (on the application of British Academy of Songwriters, Composers and Authors) v Secretary of State for Business, Innovation and Skills* [2015] EWHC 1723 (Admin).

[166] *R (on the application of British Academy of Songwriters, Composers and Authors) v Secretary of State for Business, Innovation and Skills* [2015] EWHC 2041 (Admin).

Specific or open-ended exceptions

5.58   A significant amount of copyright reform in the UK in the past two decades has been aimed at broadening the nature and scope of exceptions and limitations. A policy issue as such is whether further exceptions are necessary in the digital context. The Gowers Review 2006 had boldly recommended an exception for creative, transformative, or derivative works within the Berne three-step test, to legitimise clearly the reworking of existing material for a new purpose or to give it a new meaning, and to align the law with that of the United States. The transformative use would have to be such as not to prejudice the market or the artistic integrity of the work so used. The InfoSoc Directive 2001 does not permit such an exception. But should the UK leave the EU with a 'no-deal' Brexit, it could consider introducing further specific exceptions such as the one recommended by the Gowers review, to improve access to works for creative and transformative uses and to reflect the realities and practice of appropriation and remixing in the digital environment.

5.59   Unlike the UK approach of permitting a range of specific exceptions, the approach of the US copyright statute is to provide a general 'fair use' defence covering purposes 'such as' criticism, comment, teaching, scholarship, and research, and indicating that factors to be taken into account 'include' such matters as whether the use is of a commercial nature or for non-profit educational purposes, the amount and substantiality of the portion used in relation to the whole work, and the effect of the use upon the market or value of the copyright work. The very openness of the defence makes it vulnerable to the charge that it creates uncertainty. A proposal for such a general fair use exception to be included in the InfoSoc Directive was rejected during its negotiation. In the UK, both Gowers and Hargreaves were asked to consider whether fair use would be beneficial in the UK. The Hargreaves Review 2011 rejected this because there were genuine legal doubts about viability of transposing fair use into the UK legal framework which is based in a European context. Instead, it recommended the use of all copyright exceptions at national level which are allowed in the EU by the InfoSoc Directive. However, a policy issue is whether the approach of carving out an ever-growing list of specific exceptions is ill-suited for dealing with very rapid technological and societal changes, and whether the UK should re-consider a broad, fair-use style exception, should it leave the EU with a 'no-deal' Brexit.

Exercise

Consider the current range of exceptions in the UK, in light of the Europeanisation of the law, and also the need to create a copyright law appropriate to the digital environment. What do you think remain important challenges for users of copyright works, what would your solutions be, and how would you justify them?

Other limitations on copyright

Public interest and public policy

5.60   The 1988 Act saves various rights and privileges in general terms as unaffected by its provisions.[167] For instance, it is provided that nothing in the Act affects the law on breach of trust or confidence,[168] or any rule preventing or restricting the enforcement of copyright on grounds of public interest or otherwise.[169] The *public policy* concept is that certain types of work—pornography or material published in breach of a lifelong obligation of secrecy, for example—are undeserving of the protection of copyright because it would be against public policy to protect them and the Court can refuse to enforce copyright on public policy

---

[167] CDPA 1988, s 171.   [168] CDPA 1988, s 171(1)(e).   [169] CDPA 1988, s 171(3).

grounds.[170] A second limitation is one which allows otherwise infringing acts—or enables dissemination—on the ground that they are in the *public interest*.[171] In a pre-CDPA case, it was held that a public interest defence, which had been well established in the law of confidential information, also extended to copyright.[172] However, the existence of this defence since then has been contested and its scope remains uncertain.[173]

■ *Hyde Park Residence Ltd v Yelland* [1999] RPC 655 (Jacob J); [2000] RPC 604 (CA)

Jacob J held that a public interest defence existed and was applicable against a private individual (Mohammed al-Fayed), enabling the defendant to counter misleading public statements about how much time Princess Diana and Dodi al-Fayed had spent at the 'House of Windsor' in Paris on the day of their deaths. He formulated the test as being one of reasonable certainty that no right-thinking member of society would quarrel with the result.[174] But this was overturned by the CA, the majority (Aldous and Stuart-Smith LJJ) holding that (1) the Act does not give the Court a general power to enable an infringer to use another's copyright in the public interest, but the courts have 'an inherent jurisdiction to refuse to allow their process to be used in certain circumstances' and this inherent jurisdiction is preserved by s 171(3) (paras 43–44); (2) the circumstances in which copyright would not be enforced, because it be against the policy of the law, must derive from the work itself (ie its immoral character or deleterious effects) rather than from the conduct of the owner of copyright; and (3) the considerations arising in breach of confidence cases, where the courts balanced the public interest in maintaining confidentiality against the public interest in knowledge of the truth and freedom of expression, were different from copyright ones, where property rights were involved and the legislation already provided fair dealing defences in the public interest. It should not be possible for public interest to uphold as legitimate an act that had been found, as in this case, not to be fair dealing (see para 5.38).[175] While generally agreeing with this approach, the third member of the Court, Mance LJ, indicated that there might be cases where a public interest dimension did arise from the ownership of the work, although this was not such a case.[176]

■ *Ashdown v Telegraph Group Ltd* [2002] ECC 19 (CA)

The approach of Mance LJ was preferred by a subsequent Court of Appeal in this case (see para 5.38). The Court held that section 171(3) of the CDPA permitted a defence of public interest to be raised, noting that:

> We do not consider that this conclusion will lead to a flood of cases where freedom of expression is invoked as a defence to a claim for breach of copyright. It will be very rare for the public interest to justify the copying of the form of a work to which copyright attaches (paras 58–59).

The Court emphasised in particular the public interest in freedom of expression under Article 10 of the European Convention on Human Rights, albeit on the facts of the case it was held that the defence was not made out, since the newspaper had extracted from Mr Ashdown's diaries 'colourful passages . . . likely to add flavour to the article and thus to appeal to the readership of the newspaper . . . for reasons that were essentially journalistic in furtherance of the commercial interests of the Telegraph Group' (para 82) rather than in the public interest.

In *HRH The Prince of Wales v Associated Newspapers Ltd (No 3)*,[177] it was held that the unauthorised publication in a newspaper of extracts from the Prince's unpublished journals was not justified by any public

---

[170] See, eg, *Glyn v Weston Feature Film Co* [1916] 1 Ch 261; *Attorney General v Guardian Newspapers Ltd (No 2)* [1990] 1 AC 109; *ZYX Music v King* [1995] FSR 566. See also A Sims, 'The denial of copyright on public policy grounds' [2008] EIPR 189.

[171] *Beloff v Pressdram* [1973] RPC 765. See generally G Davies, *Copyright and the Public Interest* (2nd edn, 2003); R Burrell and A Coleman, *Copyright Exceptions: The Digital Impact* (2005), 80–112.

[172] *Lions Laboratories v Evans* [1985] QB 526 (CA).

[173] A Sims, 'The public interest defence in copyright law: myth or reality?' [2006] EIPR 335. See also J Griffiths, 'Pre-empting conflict—a re-examination of the public interest defence in UK copyright law' [2014] 34(1) Legal Studies 76.

[174] See also Jacob J in *Mars UK Ltd v Teknowledge Ltd* [2000] FSR 138.

[175] See paras 55, 58, 64–67.   [176] See paras 79–83.   [177] [2008] Ch 57 (CA), see paras 5.33 and 5.38.

interest defence, such as making more widely known the political views of the heir to the throne in relation to an important foreign power (the People's Republic of China). The Court of Appeal noted that it would be rare for a case on public interest to succeed where the fair dealing defences had been found inapplicable. Public interest also rarely justified copying content rather than simply referring to the information therein. Two recent cases appear to confirm that a defence of public interest exists, but it will only be in very rare instances where public interest will 'trump' the right of the copyright owner.[178]

Exercise 1

Explain the distinction between 'public policy' and 'public interest', if any. What difference does it make?

Exercise 2

Should pornography be unprotected by copyright? Does this encourage or discourage freedom of expression?

Human rights and exceptions to copyright

5.61 How do human rights interact with exceptions to copyright?[179] In *Ashdown v Telegraph Group*,[180] the Court of Appeal held that exceptions to copyright must be read in the light of the European Convention on Human Rights. The *Sunday Telegraph* newspaper had published unlicensed extracts from the diaries of Paddy Ashdown, the former Liberal Democrat leader. The issue concerned the impact of the Article 10 right to freedom of expression upon the fair dealing defences to claims of infringement under the CDPA 1988. At first instance Sir Andrew Morritt V-C held that the fair dealing provisions of the statute in themselves satisfied the requirements of Article 10 and that there was no need to bring into play section 3 of the Human Rights Act 1998 (which requires statutes to be interpreted as far as possible in consistency with Convention rights):[181]

> the balance between the rights of the owner of the copyright and those of the public has been struck by the legislative organ of the democratic state itself in the legislation it has enacted. There is no room for any further defences outside the code which establishes the particular species of intellectual property in question.

The Court of Appeal concluded, however, that:[182]

> rare circumstances can arise where the right of freedom of expression will come into conflict with the protection afforded by the Copyright Act, notwithstanding the express exceptions to be found in the Act. In these circumstances, we consider that the court is bound, insofar as it is able, to apply the Act in a manner that accommodates the right of freedom of expression.

This view must be correct under section 3 of the Human Rights Act 1998. The Court went on to observe that, at least in this case, the approach required could be fulfilled, not so much through examination of the statutory language as such, as by way of the remedies granted to enforce the legislation: in the particular case, by withholding the discretionary relief of an injunction and leaving the copyright owner to a damages claim or an account of profits.[183] Further, while the statutory defences and the judicial precedents elaborating

---

[178] See *BBC, Petitioners (in the case of HM Advocate v Hainey)* [2012] SLT 476; *Ames v Spamhaus Project Ltd* [2015] EWHC 127 (QB).

[179] See generally P Torremans (ed), *Intellectual Property and Human Rights* (2015), Part II; PB Hugenholtz, 'Copyright and freedom of expression in Europe' in RC Dreyfuss, DL Zimmerman, and H First (eds), *Expanding the Boundaries of Intellectual Property* (2001), 343–64. On the relationship between copyright exceptions in the EU and fundamental rights, see also the pending reference in cases C-516/17 *Spiegel Online GmbH v Volker Beck*, and C-469/17 *Funke Medien NRW GmbH v Federal Republic of Germany*.

[180] [2001] ECDR 21 (Morritt V-C); rev'd [2002] ECC 19 (CA). [181] [2001] ECDR 21, para 20.

[182] [2002] ECC 19, para 45. [183] ibid, paras 46 and 59.

upon their application fell to be reconsidered in the light of Article 10, this did not require the defendant to be able to profit from the use of another's copyright material without paying compensation. The political interest of the matters discussed and freedom of expression under Article 10 of the European Convention on Human Rights did not justify deliberate filleting of and selection of the most colourful passages from the Ashdown diary.

■ *BBC, Petitioners (in the case of HM Advocate v Hainey)* [2012] SLT 476

B sought to engage the right of freedom of expression to access photos lodged as Crown productions in H's trial for the murder of H's son. H objected on the basis of ownership of copyright in the photos. B was successful in gaining access to photos of the son only. The Court suggested that the permitted act provisions in the CDPA 1988, particularly fair dealing provisions, usually provide a defence where there is a potential conflict between Article 10 rights and the rights of the copyright owner; but there are 'exceptional and rare' cases where this is not the case, even if the CDPA 1988 is given a generous interpretation to accommodate the right (para 24).[184] The Court also stated *obiter* that 'were it necessary to do so, the public interest in the proper and full reporting of this case is sufficient to "trump" any right of the copyright owner' (para 26).

■ *Ames v Spamhaus Project Ltd* [2015] EWHC 127 (QB)

C, owner of S claimed copyright infringement against A, for placing a photograph of him on a website and naming him on a list of the world's worst spammers. A argued the publication of the photograph was in the public interest. The Court considered the competing Article 8 right of C with A's right to freedom of expression, but refused to strike out the claim and observed that it is clear law that a defence of public interest exists, but it will be rare for it to justify copying, although 'the implications of the Human Rights Act 1998 must always be considered when an injunction is sought' (para 57).

  Exercise

What other ECHR rights apart from freedom of expression (Art 10) might be relevant to copyright exceptions?

No derogation from grant

5.62   In *British Leyland v Armstrong Patents*,[185] the House of Lords declared that a copyright owner could be deprived of his rights where their exercise was in 'derogation from grant'. The context was the manufacture and supply to consumers of spare parts for cars, to which the car manufacturers took objection by means of copyright. The House found that car owners had a right to repair their vehicles, and that the car manufacturers could not exercise their copyright so as to prevent third parties enabling the owners to exercise their own separate and pre-existing rights as cheaply as possible. This was founded on the general legal principle of 'no derogation from grant', established in the context of leases, sales of goodwill, and easements or servitudes. It had never been previously applied to copyright, and the reasoning of the House on the point is unsatisfactory. The Privy Council has since indicated that the principle should be interpreted very narrowly in copyright law, and that it is really based on public policy.[186] The defence was also unsuccessful in a case

---

[184] Citing with approval *Copinger and Skone James on Copyright* at para 3-308.
[185] [1986] AC 577 gives the House of Lords' speeches only.
[186] *Canon Kabushiki Kaisha v Green Cartridge Co (Hong Kong) Ltd* [1997] AC 728.

concerning reverse engineering of computer programs and databases.[187] Although there is nothing in the 1988 Act that affects this defence, it is understood to be of less importance now.[188]

User rights

There has been little discussion in the UK to compare with a US and Canadian debate as to whether the rules on permitted acts merely provide defences to claims of infringement or are free-standing user or public rights.[189] The difference is important because, if the permitted acts are substantive 'user rights', then the copyright owner should not be able to prevent actions designed to exercise them. But if the permitted acts are merely defences, then they can be invoked only when the copyright owner sues for infringement. The 1988 Act does say that its provisions on permitted acts: 'relate only to the question of infringement of copyright and do not affect any other right or obligation restricting the doing of any of the specified acts'.[190]

This is clearly against the notion that the permissions are to be seen as user rights. Further, the UK approach, of laying down carefully specified, extensive, and detailed exceptions is also not really consistent with the idea that such permitted acts are 'user rights' (see paras 5.5–5.7). However, recent CJEU jurisprudence on exceptions and limitations uses the language of rights of users, in noting that the exceptions set out in Article 5 of the InfoSoc Directive 2001 'seek to achieve a "fair balance" between, in particular, the rights and interests of authors on the one hand, and the rights of users of protected subject-matter on the other'.[191]

 Discussion point 1   For answer guidance visit **www.oup.com/uk/brown5e**.

Is there a real difference between acts which are not within the scope of copyright at all and acts which are permitted as exceptions to copyright? Is this important in the context of the idea of 'user rights'?

Discussion point 2

Can you distinguish between 'fair dealing' and 'public interest' exceptions to copyright?

Contracting out of the exceptions?

5.63   An important issue for protection of users' interests is whether exceptions and limitations prevail over contrary contractual provision, contained, for example, in a copyright licence. To put it another way, can one contract out of exceptions?[192] The unargued assumption in the UK had been that exceptions prevail over contract but this assumption was ill-founded, at least as a generalisation. The Hargreaves Review

---

[187] *Mars UK Ltd v Teknowledge Ltd* [2000] FSR 138 (Jacob J).

[188] N Caddick, G Davies, and G Harbottle (eds), *Copinger & Skone James on Copyright* (2019), para 5.246.

[189] The language of 'user rights' features strongly in *Law Society of Upper Canada v CCH Canadian Ltd* [2004] 1 SCR 339. For a different perspective, see H Cohen Jehoram, 'Restrictions on copyright and their abuse' [2005] EIPR 359.

[190] CDPA 1988, s 28(1).

[191] C-201/13 *Deckmyn v Vandersteen* [2014] ECDR 21, para 26. See further C Geiger et al, 'Limitations and exceptions as key elements of the legal framework for copyright in the European Union: opinion of the European Copyright Society on the CJEU ruling in Case C-201/13 Deckmyn' [2015] IIC 93.

[192] See LMCR Guibault, *Copyright Limitations and Contracts: An Analysis of the Contractual Overridability of Limitations on Copyright* (2002); R Burrell and A Coleman, *Copyright Exceptions: The Digital Impact* (2005), 67–70, 269–70, 306–10.

in 2011 noted that 'at present it is possible for rights holders licensing rights to insist, through licensing contracts, that the exceptions established by law cannot be exercised in practice' and recommended that the government should make exceptions mandatory and legislate to make it clear that contract cannot override copyright exceptions.[193] It cited a study by the British Library that had demonstrated that contracts often overrode copyright exceptions in practice. Consequently, the 2014 reforms introduced several provisions to this effect (see para 5.65).

5.64   The current framework of exceptions in the UK contains two types of provisions. On the one hand, there are provisions that suggest that copyright licensing and contractual terms prevail over exceptions and limitations in certain circumstances. For example, the exception enabling educational establishments to make a limited quantity of copies of works for purposes of instruction does not apply if a licence for such activity is available (para 5.43).[194] There is also an introductory provision on exceptions, which might be read as meaning that beyond the permitted acts may lie, unaffected, other rights or obligations restricting the doing of any of the specified acts.[195] Another example of contract prevailing over exceptions relates to the permitted act of temporary reproduction or adaptation of a computer program necessary for a lawful user's lawful use of the program: a term of any contract regulating the circumstances in which the user's use is lawful, and prohibiting the copying or adaptation in question will make those acts infringements (para 5.20).[196]

5.65   On the other hand, there are several provisions emphasising that contract does *not* prevail over exceptions and limitations in certain circumstances. For instance, any term or condition of an agreement purporting to prohibit the permitted act of temporary reproduction of a database necessary for the purpose of access to and normal use of the database contents by a person with a right to use the database is void.[197] A number of other acts in relation to computer programs which are permitted to a lawful user thereof cannot be overridden by contract: that is, making a back-up copy of the program;[198] decompilation;[199] and observing, studying, or testing the functioning of the program.[200] As a result of 2014 reforms, any contractual term that purports to prevent or restrict the permitted acts of research for non-commercial purpose, private study, quotation, parody, caricature and pastiche, text and data analysis, and illustration for instruction, is unenforceable.[201]

5.66   Overall, this seems to reflect the view of Burrell and Coleman that it is:[202]

> generally possible to contract out of the permitted acts. There is, however, a growing list of circumstances in which it is not possible to contract out of the permitted acts, Parliament and the European legislator having recognised that it ought not to be possible to exclude the exceptions in certain circumstances.

They argue that such a piecemeal approach is preferable to the inflexibility which would arise from a blanket prohibition on contractual exclusion of the permitted acts.[203] It would be better, in their view, to distinguish types of use, those excludable by contract and those not.[204]

 Question

As a result of reforms in 2014, any contract that purports to prevent or restrict the permitted acts of research for non-commercial purpose, private study, quotation, parody, caricature and pastiche, text and data analysis, and illustration for instruction, is unenforceable. However, similar provisions were

---

[193] Hargreaves Review, 51.   [194] CDPA 1988, s 36(6).   [195] CDPA 1988, s 28(1).
[196] CDPA 1988, s 50C. See also Art 5(1) in conjunction with Art 4(a) of Software Directive 2009.
[197] CDPA 1988, ss 50D(2) and 296B.   [198] CDPA 1988, s 50A(3).   [199] CDPA 1988, s 50B(4).   [200] CDPA 1988, s 50BA(2).
[201] CDPA 1988, ss 29(4B), 30(4), 30A(2), 29A(5), and 32(3).
[202] R Burrell and A Coleman, *Copyright Exceptions: The Digital Impact* (2005), 69.   [203] ibid, 70.   [204] ibid, 269–70, 306–10.

not introduced with respect to, arguably important, fair dealing exceptions for criticism and review or current events. Should this anomaly in the current law be rectified? Is it symptomatic of a wider problem of lack of codification of copyright law in the UK (resulting from the CDPA being amended numerous times in a piecemeal fashion)?

Further reading

Books

General

L Bently, B Sherman, D Gangjee, and P Johnson *Intellectual Property Law* (5th edn, 2018), Ch 9

N Caddick, G Davies, and G Harbottle (eds), *Copinger & Skone James on Copyright* (17th edn, 2019), Ch 9

D Llewelyn and T Aplin, *Cornish, Llewelyn and Aplin Intellectual Property: Patents, Copyright, Trade Marks and Allied Rights* (9th edn, 2019), Chs 12.3, 12.4, 14.1, 14.2

R L Okediji (ed) *Copyright Law in an Age of Limitations and Exceptions* (2017)

Copyright exceptions and public interest

R Burrell and A Coleman, *Copyright Exceptions: The Digital Impact* (2005)

G Davies, *Copyright and the Public Interest* (2nd edn, 2003)

LMCR Guibault, *Copyright Limitations and Contracts: An Analysis of the Contractual Overridability of Limitations on Copyright* (2002)

G Mazziotti, *EU Digital Copyright Law and the End-User* (2008)

M Senftleben, *Copyright Limitations and the Three-Step Test: An Analysis of the Three-Step Test in International and EC Copyright Law* (2004)

C Waelde and HL MacQueen (eds), *The Many Faces of the Public Domain* (2007)

Exceptions and human rights

C Geiger (ed), *Research Handbook on Human Rights and Intellectual Property* (2015)

J Griffiths and U Suthersanen (eds), *Copyright and Free Speech* (2005)

P Torremans (ed), *Intellectual Property and Human Rights* (2015)

Articles

General

H Cohen Jehoram, 'Is there a hidden agenda behind the general non-implementation of the EU three-step test?' [2009] EIPR 408

C Geiger, G Frosio, and O Bulayenko, 'The EU Commission's proposal to reform copyright limitations: a good but far too timid step in the right direction' [2018] EIPR 4

C Geiger, D J Gervais, and M Senftleben, 'The three-step-test revisited: How to use the test's flexibility in national copyright law' (2014) 29(3) American University Int Law Rev 581.

A W Dnes, 'Should the UK move to a fair-use copyright exception?' [2013] IIC 418

E Hudson, 'The pastiche exception in copyright law: a case of mashed-up drafting?' [2017] IPQ 346

D Jongsma, 'Parody after Deckmyn—a comparative overview of the approach to parody under copyright law in Belgium, France, Germany and the Netherlands' [2017] IIC 652

A Sims, 'Strangling their creation: the courts' treatment of fair dealing in copyright law since 1911' [2010] IPQ 192

6

Copyright 5: authors' rights, and exploitation of copyright

Introduction

Scope and overview of chapter

6.1 This chapter begins by considering authors' rights, dealing first with 'moral rights', that is, the right to be identified as the author of the protected work, and to have that work's integrity respected by others, and then with the artist's resale right. The second half of the chapter discusses exploitation and use of copyright. It discusses a range of rules relevant to exploitation of copyright, and also highlights some contemporary issues.

6.2 **Learning objectives**

By the end of this chapter you should be able to describe and explain:

- the moral rights of the author to be identified and to have the work's integrity respected;
- the artist's resale right;
- the basic rules on assignment and licensing of copyright;
- contemporary issues relating to exploitation of copyright, including the regulatory controls on exploitation, contractual practices, orphan works, and the legal protection of technical protection measures.

6.3 The author's moral rights to be identified and to have the integrity of a work respected are discussed first, along with the right to prevent false attribution, and the special right of privacy in relation to certain commissioned photographs. Unlike moral rights, the artist's resale right enables authors to take a share of the profit made by others from sales of their original art works and are highly economic in nature. Commercial exploitation of copyright by a right owner takes place within the context of the general framework of laws in any particular country (eg contract, commercial, and employment laws). Specific rules govern dealings with rights in copyright-protected works, such as assignment and licensing. Specific challenges arise due to the weak bargaining position of authors in contractual relationships. There are also specific features of copyright exploitation, for example collective licensing, and also specific challenges faced in the exploitation and use of copyright works, for example orphan works. Finally, during the exploitation of copyright, right owners may also use technological protection measures (TPMs) to prevent unauthorised use of or access to works. This chapter addresses all these issues and looks like this:

- Author's moral rights (6.4– 6.22)
- Artist's resale right (6.23–6.26)
- Exploitation of copyright (6.27–6.32)
- Copyright contract practices (6.33-6.41)
- Collective licensing (6.42–6.44)
- Further licensing issues (6.45–6.54)
- Technical protection measures and rights management information systems (6.55–6.66).

Author's moral rights

International background

6.4   As noted in its historical introduction (para 2.8), the Berne Convention 1886 developed the concept of *non-transferable (inalienable) moral rights* (to claim authorship and to object to derogatory treatment of the work prejudicial to the author's honour or reputation (Art 6*bis*)).[1] Moral rights thus recognise certain non-economic interests which an author (but no one else) may continue to exercise in respect of a work even though no longer owner of the copyright or of the physical form in which the work was first created and recorded, this last being particularly important in respect of artistic works. The rights are reinforced by their recognition in the 1948 Universal Declaration of Human Rights: 'everyone has the right to the protection of the moral and material interests resulting from any scientific, literary or artistic production of which he is the author' (Art 27(2)).[2]

6.5   As also noted in para 2.22, moral rights first developed in Continental European legal systems, and were not recognised in UK law until introduced by the Copyright, Designs and Patents Act 1988 (CDPA 1988). In the Continental traditions, moral rights are plainly seen as an important aspect of copyright, protecting significant interests of authors. Yet, European Union (EU) Directives have nothing substantive to say about moral rights.[3] The Commission Copyright Paper 2004, consistent with the emphasis it generally placed on the economic rights in European reforms, saw 'no apparent need to harmonise moral rights protection at this stage'.[4]

The law in the UK

6.6   The two principal moral rights introduced in the UK[5] by the CDPA 1988 are:

> **Paternity:** *the right to be identified as author* of a literary, dramatic, musical, or artistic work, or as director of a film (CDPA 1988, s 77).
>
> **Integrity:** *the right* of such *authors and directors to prevent derogatory treatment of their work* (CDPA 1988, s 80).

[1] See in general E Adeney, *The Moral Rights of Authors and Performers: An International and Comparative Analysis* (2006), Chs 5–7.

[2] Note also the International Covenant on Economic, Social and Cultural Rights 1966, Art 15(1): 'the States Parties to the present covenant recognize the right of everyone . . . to benefit from the protection of the moral and material interests resulting from any scientific, literary or artistic production of which he is the author'.

[3] See InfoSoc Directive 2001, recital 19. See also the Database Directive 1996, recital 28: 'whereas the moral rights of the natural person who created the database belong to the author and should be exercised according to the legislation of the Member States and the provisions of the Berne Convention for the Protection of Literary and Artistic Works; whereas such moral rights remain outside the scope of this Directive'.

[4] Commission Staff Working Paper on the review of the EC legal framework in the field of copyright and related right SEC(2004) 995, 16.

[5] See E Adeney, *The Moral Rights of Authors and Performers: An International and Comparative Analysis* (2006), Chs 13, 14; S Kheria, 'An exploration of the dissonance between protection of moral rights in the UK and creative practitioners' perspectives' in A Favreau (ed), *La propriété intellectuelle en dehors de ses frontières* (2019).

Moral rights of paternity and integrity are accorded to authors of a range of copyright-protected works (literary, dramatic, musical, and artistic works) and directors of copyright-protected films. Under the heading of 'moral rights', the 1988 Act also deals with *prevention of false attributions* to one of literary, dramatic, musical, or artistic works and films,[6] and a *right of privacy in certain photographs and films*.[7] It should be noted, however, that these are not usually seen as moral rights in other legal systems, or under the Berne Convention.

 Question

What moral rights are recognised in the UK?

Characteristics of moral rights

6.7   Moral rights last as long as the other rights conferred by copyright: in the UK, the rights of paternity and integrity subsist as long as copyright in the works in question.[8] This contrasts with the position in some Continental European countries, where the moral rights are of indefinite duration.[9] Being conceived as highly personal to the author, moral rights are not assignable[10]—that is, transferable to third parties—but they can be waived by an instrument in writing signed by the person giving up the right.[11] It is also not an infringement of the moral rights to do anything to which the person entitled to the right has consented.[12] In these ways, UK moral rights are significantly weaker than their Continental counterparts. Infringements of the rights are treated as breaches of statutory duty, giving rise to remedies such as injunction and damages.[13]

 Question

May the owner of moral rights choose not to enforce them?

Key points about moral rights in general

- The main moral rights are the rights of paternity and integrity.
- These moral rights last for the same length of time as the economic rights (see paras 3.113 ff).
- The rights are inalienable, but can be waived, while the holder may also consent to acts which would otherwise be infringements.

Paternity right

6.8   The precise extent of the right to be identified as the author of a copyright work varies according to the nature of the work. When it is required, the identification must be clear and reasonably prominent so as

---

[6] CDPA 1988, s 84.   [7] CDPA 1988, s 85.   [8] CDPA 1988, s 86(1).

[9] For example, France (E Adeney, *The Moral Rights of Authors and Performers: An International and Comparative Analysis* (2006), Ch 8); cf Ch 9 (Germany). Compare Canada, the United States, and Australia, also discussed in ibid, Chs 12, 16, 18.

[10] CDPA 1988, s 94.   [11] CDPA 1988, s 87(2)–(4).   [12] CDPA 1988, s 87(1).

[13] CDPA 1988, s 103. Note that an injunction may prohibit the doing of any act infringing the right of integrity unless a disclaimer is made dissociating the author or director from the treatment of the work (s 103(2)). For a discussion on measuring damages for breach of moral rights, see *Walmsley v Education* 2014 WL2194626 at 13.

to bring the identity of the author or director to the attention of the public.[14] The right applies to the whole or any substantial part of a work.[15] Identification is required in the following circumstances:

Literary and dramatic works (excluding song lyrics)

Whenever the work is published commercially, performed in public, or communicated to the public, or whenever copies of a film or sound recording including the work are issued to the public, or when any of these events occur in relation to an adaptation of the work.

Musical works and song lyrics

Whenever there is commercial publication or copies of a sound recording are issued to the public, or where it is the soundtrack of a film available to the public, or when any of these events occur in relation to an adaptation.

Artistic works

Whenever there is commercial publication or public exhibition, or when a visual image is communicated to the public, or included in a film available to the public. In the case of three-dimensional artistic works, the author must be identified when copies of graphic works representing them or photographs of them are issued to the public. The author of a work of architecture in the form of a building has the right to be identified on the building as constructed, by appropriate means visible to persons entering or approaching the building.

Films

Whenever the film is shown in public, communicated to the public, or copies of the film are issued to the public.

 Question

When must the author of a work be identified?

Paternity must be 'asserted'

6.9   There is no infringement of the right of paternity unless it has been previously asserted by the author.[16] Assertion is by *statement in writing* to that effect, either in any assignation of copyright in the work or in any other instrument in writing signed by the author (eg in a licence or in a warning letter to an infringer, actual or potential).[17] The requirement may well offend against the Berne Convention provision that the enjoyment and exercise of rights under the Convention (which include moral rights) shall not be subject to any formality.[18] The assertion may be general or in relation to any specified act or acts. A statement that the right has been asserted will commonly be found in the prelim pages of books, usually saying something like, 'The right of XYZ to be identified as the author of this work has been asserted in accordance with the Copyright, Designs and Patents Act 1988.' The Act contains *no requirement that paternity be asserted before the publication of a work*; but any delay in asserting the right is to be taken into account by a court in deciding whether or not to grant a remedy for breach of the right.[19]

---

[14] CDPA 1988, s 77(2)–(7).   [15] CDPA 1988, s 89(1).   [16] CDPA 1988, s 78(1).   [17] CDPA 1988, s 78(2).
[18] Berne Convention 1886, Art 5(2).   [19] CDPA 1988, s 78(5).

■ *Sawkins v Hyperion Records* [2005] RPC 32 (CA)

For the facts, see para 3.30. Hyperion issued a CD of Lalande's music with the statement 'With thanks to Dr Lionel Sawkins for his preparation of performance materials for this recording'. Since this did not identify Sawkins as the author of a copyright work, the attribution right was held infringed. Sawkins had previously asserted his right with a letter during pre-recording negotiations with Hyperion in which he stated that the CD sleeve notes should bear the legend '© Copyright 2002 by Lionel Sawkins'.

■ *Walmsley v Education Ltd* 2014 WL 2194626

W was accepted to have asserted his moral rights in two photographs through: asserting copyright and his status as author in the copyright rubric in the book where they were used as illustrations; and, through a watermark stating '(c) John Walmsley 1969 all rights reserved' on many copies of the photos appearing on the internet. It was noted that while an assertion is necessary at some point in time, it is not required continuously or every single time the copyright work is used.

Question

How and when must 'paternity' be asserted to be effective?

Exercise

Have the authors of this book asserted their rights of paternity? If not, why not?

Public exhibition of artistic works

6.10   There are some special provisions in respect of the *public exhibition of artistic works*. If the author affixes his name to the original or a copy when he or the first owner parts with possession of it, he has asserted the moral right to be identified as its author against any subsequent possessors, whether or not the original identification is still present or visible on the work.[20] Further, where the author licenses the making of copies, the author's moral to be identified in the event of the public exhibition of a copy made in pursuance of the licence, may be asserted through a statement in the licence.[21] This affects the licensee and anyone into whose hands a copy made in pursuance of the licence comes, regardless of whether or not he has notice of the assertion.[22]

Exercise

A city council commissions a large, bronze statue of a phoenix to stand in the city's main square, symbolising its post-industrial renaissance. The sculpture is erected and becomes a popular success. However, no information is provided at the site about the identity of the sculptor, although it is publicised in newspapers at the time of the commission and again at the unveiling ceremony. The sculptor also identifies herself as the creator on her website, and her name is mentioned in official tourist and business guides. The commissioning contract contained no provisions about identification of the sculptor at the site, but it did give the council merchandising rights such as the reproduction and sale of miniatures of the sculpture, and the marketing of T-shirts bearing its image. Now the sculptor has approached the council, requesting that she be identified at the site of the sculpture and on merchandising material. Must the council comply with this request?

---

[20] CDPA 1988, s 78(3)(a) and (4)(c).   [21] CDPA 1988, s 78(3)(b).   [22] CDPa 1988, s 78(4)(d).

Limits on the right to be identified as author or director

6.11   The right to be identified as author does not exist in respect of computer programs, the design of typefaces, or computer-generated works.[23] Where copyright first vested in an employer, nothing done or authorised by him infringes the author's right to be identified.[24] Certain acts permitted in respect of the copyright in a work—fair dealing for certain purposes, for example—are not to be taken as infringements of the moral right to be identified as author.[25] The right does not apply to works in which Crown or parliamentary copyright subsists, unless the author or director has previously been identified as such on or in published copies of the work.[26] Nor does it apply to publications in newspapers, magazines, or similar periodicals, or in an encyclopaedia, dictionary, yearbook, or other collective works of reference where the work was made for the purposes of such publication.[27]

Discussion point   For answer guidance visit **www.oup.com/uk/brown5e**.

What is the reason for these limitations on the right of paternity?

Key points about the moral right of paternity

- Paternity is the right to be identified as the author of a work.
- It applies in varying ways to literary, dramatic, musical, and artistic works and films, but not to computer programs.
- The right must be asserted by a statement in writing.
- An employer who owns the copyright in a work cannot infringe the employee-author's moral rights.

Right of integrity

6.12   The author of a work or director of a film has the right to object to *derogatory treatment* of his work. This moral right does not need to be asserted in any formal way. The right applies to the treatment of the whole or any part (without a requirement that it be a substantial part) of the work.[28] Derogatory treatment will occur when there is:[29]

> *addition* to, *deletion* from or *alteration* to or *adaptation* of a work which *amounts to distortion or mutilation* of the work or is otherwise *prejudicial to the honour or reputation* of the author or director.

There must be a *treatment* of the work (in the form of addition, deletion, alteration, or adaptation) and such treatment must be *derogatory* (a distortion or mutilation that must also be prejudicial to the author's honour or reputation).[30] But a translation of a literary or dramatic work will not amount to derogatory treatment, nor will an arrangement or transcription of a musical work involving no more than a change of key or register.[31] The right affects those who:

- publish commercially, perform in public or communicate to the public, or issue to the public copies of a film or sound recording of, or including, a literary, dramatic, or musical work (CDPA 1988, s 80(3));
- publish commercially, exhibit in public, communicate to the public, show or issue to the public copies of a film including images of, an artistic work (CDPA 1988, s 80(4)(a), (b));

---

[23] CDPA 1988, s 79(2).   [24] CDPA 1988, s 79(3).   [25] CDPA 1988, s 79(4), (4A), (5).   [26] CDPA 1988, s 79(7).
[27] CDPA 1988, s 79(6).   [28] CDPA 1988, s 89(2).   [29] CDPA 1988, s 80(2).
[30] *Pasterfield v Denham* [1999] FSR 168; *Confetti Records v Warner Music UK Ltd* [2003] EMLR 35.   [31] CDPA 1988, s 80(2)(a).

- issue to the public copies of a graphic work or photograph of works of architecture in the form of models, sculptures, or works of artistic craftsmanship (CDPA 1988, s 80(4)(c)). Note that the author of a building has only the right to require that his identification be removed from it in the event of derogatory treatment (s 80(5));

- show in public, communicate to the public, or issue to the public copies of, a film (CDPA 1988, s 80(6)).

If any of these activities includes a derogatory treatment of a work to which the right pertains, the right of integrity has been infringed.[32] Further, dealing in an article which infringes this right will also attract a secondary infringement liability.[33]

 Question

Identify the common features of the various situations in which the moral right of integrity may be infringed.

 Discussion point   For answer guidance visit **www.oup.com/uk/brown5e**.

How far may the right of integrity be compared to one of private censorship?

6.13   The potentially wide scope of this right can be illustrated with well-known decisions from other jurisdictions: for example, the French decision that the moral rights of the film director John Huston were infringed by the colourisation of his black-and-white film 'The Asphalt Jungle', even although the colouriser had a contractual right to do so and there was no right of integrity in Huston's home territory of the United States;[34] in a Canadian case it was held that the integrity of a sculpture in a public place was infringed by festooning it with Christmas decorations.[35]

6.14   There have been few cases to date in the UK courts about the right of integrity, and they exhibit a cautious approach.

■ *Morrison Leahy Music Ltd v Lightbond Ltd* [1993] EMLR 144

L produced a sound recording entitled 'Bad Boys Megamix' which took bits of the music and words from five George Michael compositions (the copyright of which MLM owned) and put them together in snatches lasting from ten to 65 seconds, where the works from which they were taken lasted from three minutes, 22 seconds to six minutes, 45 seconds. It was held that it was plainly arguable that such relatively short snatches did alter the character of the original works by removing them from their original context and creating a new one.

■ *Tidy v Natural History Museum Trustees* (1995) 39 IPR 501

T, a cartoonist, produced large-scale dinosaur cartoons to hang in the museum. It was held that the right of integrity did not entitle T to prevent the re-publication of the cartoons on a much smaller scale in a book being published by the museum trustees.

■ *Pasterfield v Denham* [1999] FSR 168

P was commissioned by Plymouth City Council in 1988 to design promotional leaflets for the Plymouth Dome, a tourist attraction. The leaflet used devices of a satellite, a German bomber formation, and a detailed

---

[32] CDPA 1988, s 80(1).   [33] CDPA 1988, s 83.   [34] *Huston v Turner Entertainment Inc* (1992) 23 IIC 702.

[35] *Snow v Eaton Centre Ltd* (1982) 70 CPR (2d) 105 (Ont).

cut-away drawing of the Dome's interior. In 1994, the council commissioned D to produce a new leaflet for the Dome: this included copies of the satellite and bomber formation, along with a smaller and altered version of the cut-away drawing. The alterations included the omission of features on the edge of the original drawing and a variation in colouring. It was held that these differences were so trivial that they could only be seen by close inspection, and so could not amount to derogatory treatment. Such treatment had also to be prejudicial to the author's honour or reputation as an artist; it was not enough that the artist felt aggrieved.

■ *Confetti Records v Warner Music UK Ltd* [2003] EMLR 35

The composer of a musical work called 'Burnin' sued for derogatory treatment by way of mixing it on a compilation album with rap material referring to violence and drugs. It was held that merely distorting or mutilating a work did not infringe the right of integrity; prejudice to the author's honour and reputation was also required. In giving evidence the composer made no complaint about the treatment of 'Burnin', and the Court should not infer prejudice for him. The words of the rap were for practical purposes in a foreign language the content of which was not proved, and they were anyway hard to decipher. All this went against any conclusion that the treatment infringed the right of integrity.

■ *Harrison v Harrison* [2010] ECDR 12

JP had written the first edition of a book and its second edition was edited and published by JD. JP claimed that the second edition was prejudicial to his honour or reputation. Fysh J noted that 'treatment' is a broad general concept implying a spectrum of possible acts, 'from the addition of, say, a single word to a poem to the destruction of the entire work' (para 60). The generality of the term 'treatment' is limited by the requirement of prejudice to the honour or reputation of the author to arise from such treatment. It was held that there was no infringement of the integrity right because it is not enough for the author to point to a 'miscellany of arguable trivia' to substantiate a case for derogatory treatment (para 66).

■ *Delves-Broughton v House of Harlot Ltd* [2012] EWPCC 29

D took a photograph depicting a model in a forest wearing clothes supplied by H which H included in its website after cropping it, reversing the image, and removing the background. On D's claim for infringement of integrity right, it was found that considerable time and effort had been spent in the composition of the photograph for which D considered the forest to be particularly important. The judge held that the changes to the photograph amounted to distortion, that such treatment of the work was therefore derogatory and awarded £50 for it. Surprisingly, the judge noted that the changes were not prejudicial to D's honour or reputation. The approach and outcome in this case is inconsistent with earlier cases, which suggest that mere distortion/mutilation is not sufficient unless such distortion/mutilation also prejudices the author's honour or reputation.

 Exercise

> A local authority commissions a new concert hall and paintings to be hung in its entrance hall. The paintings are unpopular and much criticised in the local media for their abstract character. Following an election leading to a change of party in control of the authority, and amidst much publicity, the council orders the removal of the paintings to storage, and their replacement with cartoons humorously depicting aspects of local life. Can either the architect of the hall or the painter object to the council's action on the basis of their rights of integrity? You may find it helpful in thinking about this problem to consider the Indian case of *Sehgal v Union of India* [2005] FSR 39.

Limits on the right of integrity

6.15   The limits on the kinds of work affected by the right of integrity are similar to those operative in the right of paternity:[36] for example, computer programs, computer-generated works,[37] publications in collective works,[38] and works where the employer, Crown, or Parliament has the first copyright.[39] There are some important further limits on the integrity right, however. It does not apply in relation to any work made for the purpose of reporting current events, since otherwise the traditional sub-editing process could be severely hampered.[40] In the case of anonymous and pseudonymous works where it is reasonable to suppose that copyright has expired,[41] no act will infringe the right of integrity if it would not infringe copyright.[42] The right is not infringed by anything done for the purpose of avoiding the commission of an offence, or complying with a duty imposed by or under an enactment.[43] Finally, anything done by the BBC for the purpose of avoiding the inclusion in a programme of anything which offends against good taste or decency or which is likely to encourage or incite crime or lead to disorder or to be offensive to public feeling will not infringe the right of integrity.[44]

Exercise 1

Before the 1988 Act came into force, the author of a play about the Falklands War to be broadcast on the BBC strenuously objected to the Corporation's cutting of passages that presented the Prime Minister Mrs Thatcher in an unfavourable light.[45] Would that author now be able to make a claim under the right of integrity, and would the BBC be able to plead its privileged position (described previously) in its defence?

Exercise 2

Would Elinor Glyn have been able to argue that the film satire 'Pimple's Three Weeks (without the option)' infringed the moral rights in her novel *Three Weeks* (see *Glyn v Weston Feature Film Co* [1916] 1 Ch 261)?

Exercise 3

To what extent are authors able to use the right to control the way in which their works are presented to the world—for example, through distasteful association, packaging, or advertising, or through adaptations in other media which travesty their work (at least in their view)?

Exercise 4

Consider the case of *Galerie d'Art du Petit Champlain inc v Théberge* [2002] 2 SCR 336 (Supreme Court of Canada), discussed at para 4.43. Was the artist's right of integrity infringed in that case?

Exercise 5

Could an author who had become dissatisfied with the quality of his work demand its withdrawal from public circulation, on the basis that its continued availability would damage his honour and reputation?[46] Consider in this connection the old Scottish case of *Davis v Miller* (1855) 17 D 1166.

---

[36] See generally CDPA 1988, ss 81 and 82, and para 6.11.
[37] CDPA 1988, s 81(2). But there is a right of integrity in a typeface.   [38] CDPA 1988, s 81(4).   [39] CDPA 1988, s 82.
[40] CDPA 1988, s 81(3).   [41] CDPA 1988, ss 57 and 66A; also see paras 3.101–3.102 and 3.116.
[42] CDPA 1988, s 81(5).   [43] CDPA 1988, s 81(6)(a), (b).
[44] CDPA 1988, s 81(6)(c). There is no specific exemption for commercial broadcasters, which will therefore have to rely on the general exemption in respect of avoiding the commission of offences or breach of a statutory duty (see n 43).
[45] cf *Frisby v British Broadcasting Corporation* [1967] Ch 932, where a similar complaint was dealt with as a matter of interpreting the author's contract.
[46] The example is drawn from the well-known French case of *Eden v Whistler* DP 1900, I 497, where the famous artist was allowed to refuse to deliver a portrait to its commissioner, despite previously exhibiting it himself. The permission was conditional on Whistler repaying his fee and undertaking not to exhibit the painting again. On honour, see E Adeney, 'The moral right of integrity: the past and future of "honour"' [2005] IPQ 111.

> **Exercise 6**
>
> Consider the case of *Hugo v SA Plon* [2007] ECDR 9 (Cour de Cassation, France) in which the moral right of Victor Hugo (1802–85) in his famous novel *Les Misérables* (published 1862 and out of copyright) was held not infringed by the publication in 2001 of two works purporting to be sequels to the novel and using characters from it. French law requires respect for the author's name, title, and work. Apart from the questions of location, term, and assertion, would it have been possible to sue on these facts for infringement of the UK moral rights of paternity or integrity?

Meaning of publishing commercially

6.16   Both the rights of paternity and integrity arise, inter alia, when a work is published commercially. Commercial publication means issuing copies of the work to the public at a time when copies made in advance of the receipt of orders are generally available to the public (eg through a retail outlet), or making the work available to the public by means of an electronic retrieval system.[47]

> **Key points on the moral right of integrity**
>
> - The right is to prevent derogatory treatment of copyright works when they are published or otherwise put before the public.
> - Derogatory treatment is distortion or mutilation of a work or treatment which is otherwise prejudicial to the honour or reputation of the author.
> - The UK courts have not given the right expansive scope in their decisions on the matter.

False attribution of authorship

6.17   A person has a right not to have a work falsely attributed to him as author or director.[48] This is the counterpart of the right to be identified as the author. There is a potential secondary liability for dealers in copies which infringe this right.[49] The right applies to the whole or any part (without any requirement of substantiality) of the work.[50] The right subsists until 20 years after a person's death.[51] This creates the curious possibility of false attribution being lawful 20 years and one day after the death of the person.

■ ***Clark v Associated Newspapers Ltd* [1998] 1 All ER 959**

In this case[52] the London Evening Standard published a series of articles entitled 'Alan Clark's Secret Election Diary' or 'Alan Clark's Secret Political Diaries' set beside a photograph of Clark, a prominent Conservative politician and an author well known for the publication of his personal diaries, which were 'malicious, lecherous and self-pitying, and . . . enormous fun'. The Standard articles sought to parody or spoof the real diaries, and contained a statement that 'Peter Bradshaw . . . imagines what a new diary might contain'. The statement was in a font bigger than that of the main text but much smaller than the heading and title. It was held that there had been a false attribution. The statement of attribution had to have a clear single meaning, but the law did not require proof of damage, nor was there a cure for the attribution in the 'counter-messages' about Bradshaw's contribution. If 'counter-messages' are to be effective, they have to be as bold, precise, and compelling as the false statement.

---

[47] CDPA 1988, s 175(2).   [48] CDPA 1988, s 84.   [49] CDPA 1988, s 84(3)–(7).   [50] CDPA 1988, s 89(2).
[51] CDPA 1988, s 86(2).   [52] See also on the passing-off aspects of this case in Chapter 16.

■ *Harrison v Harrison* [2010] ECDR 12

JP had written the first edition of a book and its second edition was edited and published by JD. JP claimed that the promotion of the second edition, through testimonials on the back cover of the second edition which referred to the first edition, created the impression that both editions were, contrary to fact, written by the same author. The Court held that there was false attribution of authorship because the single message to the reader from the back cover was praise for the author responsible for the creation of the first edition, not the publisher, who would usually produce a number of books on different subjects and, without any indication to the contrary, the reader would assume that the author of the title had not changed (para 55).

Right of privacy of certain photographs and films

6.18   A person who for private and domestic purposes commissions the taking of a photograph or the making of a film has, where copyright subsists in the resulting work, the right not to have copies of the work issued to the public, the work exhibited or shown in public, or the work communicated to the public.[53] The statutory right applies in relation to the whole or any substantial part of the photograph or film.[54] Any person doing or authorising one of these acts is liable as an infringer. An example would be the display of wedding photographs in the photographer's shop window where that was not authorised contractually or otherwise.[55] The right is not infringed where the act occurs in the context of certain specified acts which would not infringe copyright in the work (eg incidental inclusion).[56]

Moral rights reform

6.19   The subject of moral rights is otherwise and in general underplayed in recent international, European, and domestic negotiations, discussions, and instruments. One policy issue in relation to moral rights is whether they should be stronger. In the UK, moral rights cannot be alienated, but it simply means that these rights cannot be the subject of commerce in themselves; they may be waived, albeit this requires writing. Further, the paternity right must be 'asserted' before it can apply, and it is not generally available to authors whose works are created in the course of employment. In all these respects, the British moral rights are weaker than the systems found, for example, in some other EU member states.

6.20   That a strong moral rights regime is nonetheless in the public interest has been argued, on the following grounds:

- a trade mark-like function of assuring the public as to the origin and quality of the work;
- social reward (prestige, status, recognition) going to where it belongs;
- cultural preservation, helping to maintain the record of the country's culture;
- author empowerment in connection with the exploitation of their work.

The rights may also be considered particularly significant in an online digital world, where works can be speedily and endlessly transmitted and retransmitted, readily modified and reshaped, and integrated, in whole or in part, in other works. Even if economic interests in the digital environment can be as effectively defended by way of contract as by copyright, it is much less clear that this is so with the moral rights, since it will not necessarily be the author who is making the product available to the public (contractually or otherwise). Many of the functions of moral rights identified previously could also be of great importance in a world of open access journal publishing, to ensure author recognition. After much debate, the rights are recognised in

---

[53] CDPA 1988, s 85(1).   [54] CDPA 1988, s 89(1).

[55] See also *McCosh v Crow & Co* (1903) 5 F 670 and *Pollard v Photographic Co* (1889) 40 Ch D 345; *Carina Trimingham v Associated Newspapers* [2012] EWHC 1296 (QB).

[56] CDPA 1988, s 85(2).

the Creative Commons licences (paras 6.52–6.53) for England and Wales, and Scotland. The right of integrity caused particular concern because it might seem to hamper the rights of users to rework existing material in their own works. The answer to this concern is that such reuse will only infringe the integrity right if it is derogatory to the earlier work, which ought not to happen very often with genuinely creative reuse.

6.21   If the arguments in favour of a stronger moral rights regime are accepted, then questions follow about the present UK position, in particular the position with regard to:

- the exclusion of employees from the paternity right in their work (para 6.11);

- the need to assert paternity right (para 6.9);

- whether waivers of moral rights should be allowed (para 6.7);

- regulation of waivers for unconscionability;

- duration (paras 6.7 and 6.17)—it is not clear, especially in the light of some of the underlying policies referred to previously, why there should be a time limitation on any of the moral rights; on the other hand, moral rights which endure beyond an author's lifetime may be an undue limitation of the public domain, putting powers capable of amounting to censorship in the hands of people other than the person in whose interest the rights were created;

- the name of the rights, at least in the UK, where 'moral' in the context of rights tends to suggest, at least to the uninformed, 'not legal', and so to devalue their significance; 'author's personality rights', while cumbersome, might better convey what the law seeks to protect here.

6.22   In the context of the EU, another issue has been whether the rights should have been harmonised, especially in light of the digital environment. It is possible to imagine situations where export of a lawful product from a weak moral rights member state could be blocked in one with stronger rights. In the Continental traditions, moral rights are plainly seen as an important aspect of copyright, protecting significant interests, and these were therefore unlikely to be much watered down in a Europe-wide regulation. Consequently, any codification or reform process of moral rights would have required compromise between the Continental and British approaches. The Commission has made no attempt to harmonise or reform moral rights. In the 2004 Copyright paper, it took the view that the lack of harmonisation or reform of moral rights did not affect the functioning of the internal market, noting that 'no evidence exists in the digital environment either that the current state of affairs does affect the good functioning of the Internal Market'.[57] However, the good functioning of the internal market should not have been the only relevant consideration in the harmonisation and reform of authors' rights in Europe.

 Exercise

Take each of the points previously listed, and consider how, if at all, the present UK rules on moral rights should be reformed.

 Author's moral rights and Brexit

Author's moral rights exemplify an area that has been untouched by EU harmonisation. The UK provides this protection under the international framework and will continue to do so post-Brexit. However, in a post-Brexit policy-making environment, without the barrier of accommodating a weaker British moral rights regime, and a cautious Anglo-American approach to moral rights, the EU might find it easier to harmonise these rights in the future, should it choose to.

---

[57] Commission Staff Working Paper on the review of the EC legal framework in the field of copyright and related right SEC (2004) 995, 16.

Artist's resale right

International background

6.23   The Berne Convention 1886 provides (Art 14*ter*) for an author's inalienable resale right (*droit de suite*) in works of art and original manuscripts, giving him a right to a share of the proceeds of any sale of the work after the first transfer by the author. This right is, however, optional for Berne states. Although the EU has chosen to not harmonise authors' moral rights (para 6.22), in a significant move, in 2001, the Resale Right Directive was enacted, to be implemented in the member states for the benefit of living artists by 2006 and for those who had died before then by 2012 at the latest.[58] It applies only to works of art and not to literary or musical manuscripts, thus taking partial advantage of the option of resale rights under Art 14*ter* of the Berne Convention. The Directive gives the artist a right to a share of the proceeds of any resale of the original of his work after the sale by the artist to a first purchaser. While the Directive's objective is primarily economic, its content also owes much to moral right ideas, notably the resale right's inalienability from the author of the work to which they attach (see further at para 6.7). However, it is worth noting that this authors' right is not a moral right, as a result of its highly economic character. The Directive was enacted against British opposition, but the majority of the then EU member states already had such a system in place and perceived distortion in the European art market resulting from the variability of the national laws, as well as an injustice to the artist, who gained no benefit from the value others came to place on the original of his work.

The law in the UK

6.24   The artist's resale right was introduced in the UK on 14 February 2006, in implementation of the EU Resale Right Directive 2001.[59] The author of a work of graphic or plastic art in which copyright subsists has a right to a royalty on any sale of a work that is a resale subsequent to the first transfer of ownership by the author.[60] The right subsists as long as the copyright subsists,[61] one effect of this being that 'only the originals of works of modern and contemporary art ... fall within the scope of the resale right'.[62] In general, and in the fashion of a moral right, this right cannot be assigned,[63] waived,[64] or shared[65] by the author, although it can be transmitted on death, whether by will or the rules of intestate succession,[66] and the right may be transferred to a charity.[67] But the right can be exercised *only* through a collecting society.[68] The holder of the right can choose which such collecting society to mandate for this purpose,[69] but in the absence of such a transfer of management, the collecting society managing copyright on behalf of artists (eg the Design and Artists' Copyright Society (DACS))[70] is deemed mandated to manage the right[71]—that is, collect the resale royalty

---

[58]   EC Directive 2001/84/EC on the resale right for the benefit of the author of an original work of art (Resale Right Directive 2001).

[59]   Resale Right Directive 2001 was implemented by the Artist's Resale Right Regulations 2006 (SI 2006/346), amended by Artist's Resale Right (Amendment) Regulations 2009 (SI 2009/2792) and 2011 (SI 2011/2873). See generally S Stokes, 'Droit de suite: an artistic stroke of genius? A critical exploration of the European Directive and its resultant effects' [2012] EIPR 305.

[60]   Artist's Resale Right Regulations 2006, regs 3(1) and 4. A sale is a transfer of ownership of the work from seller to buyer under a contract in exchange for a money consideration called the price (Sale of Goods Act 1979, s 2 and reg 2 (definition of 'sale')). The author is the person who creates the work (reg 2, definition of 'author'). For a presumption that the author is the person whose name appears on the work as such, see reg 6.

[61]   Artist's Resale Right Regulations 2006, reg 3(2).   [62]   Resale Right Directive 2001, recital 17.

[63]   Artist's Resale Right Regulations 2006, reg 7(1). Any charge on a resale right is void (reg 7(2)).

[64]   Artist's Resale Right Regulations 2006, reg 8(1).

[65]   Artist's Resale Right Regulations 2006, reg 8(2). Note, however, the provisions for cases of joint authorship, where resale right is owned in common unless otherwise agreed in writing (reg 5).

[66]   Artist's Resale Right Regulations 2006, reg 9. The person into whose hands the right is transmitted may likewise transmit it. The Court of Justice, in Case C-518/08 *Fundacion Gala-Salvador Dali v ADAGP* [2010] ECDR 13, ruled that national law provisions reserving the benefit of the right to artist's heirs at law alone, to the exclusion of testamentary legatees, is not precluded by the Directive.

[67]   Artist's Resale Right Regulations 2006, Reg 7(3)–(5).   [68]   Artist's Resale Right Regulations 2006, reg 14(1).

[69]   Artist's Resale Right Regulations 2006, reg 14(3).   [70]   See the DACS website at www.dacs.org.uk.

[71]   Artist's Resale Right Regulations 2006, reg 14(2).

in return for a fixed percentage or fee of the money so ingathered.[72] The amount of the royalty is calculated in relation to the resale price,[73] the resale price being taken to be the price obtained for the sale net of any tax payable on the transaction and converted into euros at the European Central Bank reference rate prevailing at the contract date.[74] The (not especially generous) royalty rates[75] are shown in Figure 6.1.

Figure 6.1 Royalty rates table

Portion of the sale price	Percentage amount
From 0 to 50,000 euro	4%
From 50,000.01 to 200,000 euro	3%
From 200,000.01 to 350,000 euro	1%
From 350,000.01 to 500,000 euro	0.5%
Exceeding 500,000 euro	0.25%

A resale becomes liable to the royalty where the buyer or the seller or the agent of either is acting in the course of a business of dealing in works of art, and the sale price is not less than €1,000.[76] The persons liable to pay the royalty are the seller *and*, if acting in the course of a business of dealing in works of art, the seller's agent, the buyer's agent if there is no seller's agent, and, where there are no such agents, the buyer.[77] The liability of these parties is joint and several.[78] The liability to make the payment arises on completion of the resale.[79]

6.25   A number of other points should be made about the artist's resale right:

- The royalty is only payable on the *resale of works of graphic or plastic art* in which copyright subsists. Works of graphic or plastic art include, for example, a picture, collage, painting, drawing, engraving, print, lithograph, sculpture, tapestry, ceramic, glassware item, or photograph.[80] The work sold must be the one which the artist created. The resale of a *copy* of a work of art is not subject to the royalty right unless it is one of a limited number made by the author or under his authority.[81]

- The royalty is only payable on a resale *after* the *first transfer of ownership of the work of art by the author*. While the author's first transfer of ownership will typically be a sale to another person, the transaction need not be for any consideration,[82] and so might be a gift. Transfer also includes transmission on death by will or by intestate succession, and disposal of the work by the author's personal representatives for estate administration purposes, as well as disposal by the administrator of the author's insolvent estate.[83]

- Where the seller previously acquired the work directly from the author less than three years before the resale *and* the sale price now does not exceed €10,000, there is no liability to a resale royalty.[84]

- There are complex *transitional* provisions. Resale royalties are not payable in respect of contracts concluded before 14 February 2006, but the right does otherwise apply to works made before that date.[85] Where the artist died before 14 February 2006, rules for determination of artist's successors are provided.[86]

[72] Artist's Resale Right Regulations 2006, reg 14(5)(b).   [73] Artist's Resale Right Regulations 2006, reg 3(3).
[74] Artist's Resale Right Regulations 2006, reg 3(4).   [75] Artist's Resale Right Regulations 2006, schedule 1.
[76] Artist's Resale Right Regulations 2006, reg 12(2), (3).
[77] Artist's Resale Right Regulations 2006, reg 13(1), (2). See also Case C-41/14 *Christie's France SNC v Syndicat national des antiquaries* [2015] ECDR14 on who can bear the cost of resale royalty.
[78] Artist's Resale Right Regulations 2006, reg 13(1).
[79] Artist's Resale Right Regulations 2006, reg 13(3). The liable person may withhold payment until evidence of entitlement to be paid the royalty is produced (reg 13(3)).
[80] Artist's Resale Right Regulations 2006, reg 4(1).   [81] Artist's Resale Right Regulations 2006, reg 4(2).
[82] Artist's Resale Right Regulations 2006, reg 12(1).   [83] Artist's Resale Right Regulations 2006, reg 3(5).
[84] Artist's Resale Right Regulations 2006, reg 12(4).   [85] Artist's Resale Right Regulations 2006, reg 16(1).
[86] Artist's Resale Right Regulations 2006, reg 16(2).

- The right initially applied only to living artists. The UK took advantage of a provision in the Directive intended to enable the economic operators in those member states which did not, at the time of the adoption of the Directive, apply a resale right to adapt gradually to the right whilst maintaining their economic viability.[87] As such, resale rights transmitted on the death of the artist (as per reg 16(2) or actually transmitted on or after 14 February 2006), were not exercisable in respect of any sale where the contract date preceded 1 January 2010.[88] The UK government chose to extend this derogation until 1 January 2012.[89] The derogation has since expired, meaning the right is now applicable to deceased artists, and the Secretary of State is required to review the regulations periodically.[90]

6.26   The purpose of an artist's resale right is succinctly summarised in one of the recitals to the Resale Right Directive:[91]

> to ensure that authors of graphic and plastic works of art share in the economic success of their original works of art . . . to redress the balance between the economic situation of authors of graphic and plastic works of art and that of other creators who benefit from successive exploitations of their works.

Crudely, the model is one of the impecunious artist forced to sell his creations, only to see others later earning riches from dealings in those creations. As already noted, the right did not exist in the UK before 14 February 2006, but it was found in the majority of other EU member states, albeit with variable rules. The harmonisation under the Directive was thus intended to eliminate the differences found in the EU, in order to remove an obstacle to the operation of a single European market in this field. The Directive was highly contested, because the resale right is not widely found outside Europe, and there was significant concern that what is effectively a form of tax on dealings in art would drive business away from Europe to other centres such as the United States (in particular New York).[92] The UK was particularly concerned because the success of its international art market could be attributed, some thought, to the absence of artist's resale right. More fundamentally, it can be argued against the right that those who make successful businesses through dealing in art are not necessarily merely enriching themselves on the back of the artist, but play a significant independent role in ensuring that art works generate wealth.[93] On the other hand, DACS argues that the right 'enables artists to have a share in the increasing value of their work and allows artists' estates to continue to care for an artist's legacy' noting in its White paper, reviewing ten years of the artist's resale right in the UK, that there has been no evidence to support any negative impact on the UK art market or diversion of sales to non-artist's resale right markets.[94]

 Discussion point   For answer guidance visit **www.oup.com/uk/brown5e**.

Why should resale right be limited to works of art? Why are there no equivalent rights for authors of literary, dramatic, and musical works in relation to their manuscripts, as provided in the Berne Convention, Article 14*ter* (para 6.23)? (Note recital 19 of the Resale Right Directive: 'the harmonisation brought about by this Directive does not apply to original manuscripts of writers and composers').

---

[87] Resale Right Directive 2001, recital 17 and Art 8(2), (3).

[88] See reg 17 as originally enacted in Artist's Resale Right Regulations 2006 (SI 2006/346).

[89] See reg 17 as amended by Artist's Resale Right (Amendment) Regulations 2009 (SI 2009/2792); in 2008 the UK IPO undertook a consultation proposing that the UK exemption be extended for a further two years and 90 per cent of respondents stated that the derogation should not be extended (https://webarchive.nationalarchives.gov.uk/20140603152113/http://www.ipo.gov.uk/response-artist.pdf).

[90] Reg 17 as amended by Artist's Resale Right (Amendment) Regulations 2011 (SI 2011/2873).

[91] Resale Right Directive 2001, recital 3.

[92] For a discussion of the impact of the resale right in the UK, see S Blakeney, 'The great debate—using artistic licence to resist the artist's resale right' [2011] Ent LR 22; S Stokes, 'Artist's resale right—good intentions, bad law' [2013] Ent LR 35.

[93] J Merryman, 'The proposed generalization of the droit de suite in the European Communities' [1997] IPQ 16.

[94] DACS, 'Ten Years of the Artist's Resale Right: Giving artists their fair share' (2016) 2 and 8, at www.dacs.org.uk/DACSO/media/DACSDocs/reports-and-submissions/Ten-Years-of-the-Artist-s-Resale-Right-Giving-artists-their-fair-share-DACS-Feb-16.pdf.

> **Key points about artist's resale right**
>
> - The aim of the right is to enable artists to take a share of the profit made by others from sales of their original art works.
> - The right lasts for the same period as the copyright in the work.
> - The right is inalienable, although it transmits on death.

 Artist's resale right and Brexit

Although the artist's resale right is an option under the Berne Convention, it was enacted in the UK because of EU membership, and the obligations under the EU Resale Right Directive. The Political Declaration on the future relationship with the EU indicates an intention to preserve the artist's resale right in the UK.[95] Notably, under the Directive, EU member states recognise resale rights of nationals of all EU member states and, significantly, also third countries that provide resale rights. In a 'no-deal' scenario, the UK intends to keep the resale right as currently enacted. Consequently, the UK government guidance notes the following implication: 'Nationals of the UK and countries that recognise the resale rights of UK nationals will continue to receive resale rights in the UK after we leave the EU, in accordance with the Berne Convention. No changes are being made to the calculation of royalty payments.'[96]

Exploitation of copyright

6.27   Copyright is a property right.[97] It is primarily a negative right of exclusion, similar to other IPRs, providing no positive entitlement to privilege or success in the market (see para 1.43). However, in practical terms, copyright has both an external and internal aspect in how it benefits the right owner: the external aspect enables the right owner to exclude others from the market by enforcing the rights granted exclusively to them (see Ch 4 for infringement and Ch 21 for enforcement procedures and remedies available to the right owner); the internal aspect enables the right owner to exploit and use the rights exclusively granted to them through contractual arrangements, usually for financial return.[98] This section considers only the second aspect: the exploitation and use of copyright. Contracts play a crucial role in the exploitation of copyright. The acts restricted by copyright (see para 4.9) can be transferred by assignment, by testamentary disposition, or by operation of law, as personal or moveable property, and they can also be licensed,[99] all of which can endure beyond the author's lifetime. Key issues in relation to contractual exploitation, including those regulated by the 1988 Act,[100] and contemporary issues are discussed below.

---

[95]   UK Government, Draft political declaration setting out the framework for the future relationship between the United Kingdom and the European Union (22 November 2018), para 45 at www.gov.uk/government/publications/draft-political-declaration-setting-out-the-framework-for-the-future-relationship-between-the-european-union-and-the-united-kingdom-agreed-at-negotia.

[96]   UK Government, 'Changes to copyright law in the event of no deal' (26 October 2018) www.gov.uk/government/publications/changes-to-copyright-law-in-the-event-of-no-deal/changes-to-copyright-law-in-the-event-of-no-deal.

[97]   CDPA 1988 s 1(1). Contrast ss 94–95, whereby moral rights cannot be assigned but are transmissible on death.

[98]   S Kheria, 'Visual Arts: artists' voices from the field' in A Brown and C Waelde (eds), *Research Handbook on Intellectual Property and Creative Industries* (2018).

[99]   CDPA 1988, ss 90(1), 92. See also s 93 for copyright to pass under a will in case of an unpublished work.

[100]   CDPA 1988, Chapters V, VII, and VIII.

Assignment

6.28   The owner of copyright may choose to assign that right to a third party. An assignment (known as assignation in Scotland) is the transfer of ownership of copyright from one party to another. When copyright is assigned, the assignee stands in the shoes of the assignor and can deal with the right as they wish. An assignment of copyright can be partial in terms of the manner of exploitation and time.[101] A prospective copyright owner can also assign future copyright, that is 'copyright which will or may come into existence in respect of a future work or class of works or on the occurrence of a future event'.[102] To be effective, an assignment must be in writing, and signed by, or on behalf of, the assignor.[103] 'Writing' is broadly defined to include 'any form of notation or code, whether by hand or otherwise and regardless of the method by which, or medium in or on which, it is recorded'.[104] There is no requirement for the assignment to be registered. However, without a signed document the requirements of a legal assignment are not fulfilled.[105]

> **Question**
>
> Find out whether, and to what extent, the rules on assignations are different for other IPRs?

Licensing

6.29   Licensing is a central feature of exploitation and use of copyright. An author may be the first owner of copyright, but may not have the resources or the expertise to exploit their works protected by copyright. For instance, a music band may need the help of a record label to produce and market a song. Literary authors may need the assistance of a collecting society to enable them to monitor some uses of a work (eg photocopying of literary works) and to receive a return from exploitation. If the author does not assign the copyright in her work, then she will need to enter into a licence to permit such exploitation and management of the bundle of rights that copyright provides. When copyright is owned by more than one person jointly, then a licence by all the owners is required.[106]

6.30   Copyright licences can be exclusive, non-exclusive, or sole. An exclusive licence means a licence in writing, signed by or on behalf of the copyright owner, by which the owner licenses a third party to carry out some or all of the restricted acts to the exclusion of all others including the owner.[107] A sole licence permits the owner of the IPR to exploit the right as well as the person to whom she has licensed the work. A non-exclusive licence permits the owner to exploit the right and also to license as many other people as she wishes to carry out the same act. The 1988 Act sets out no formalities for a non-exclusive licence. Licences for copyright can carve up an author's exclusive rights in many ways in order to maximise the opportunities for financial return to them.[108] So they could cover some but not all of the rights pertaining to a particular work. For example, the author of a book might license the right to one publisher to publish the book in hardback, but another publisher may be granted the serial rights. Or one publisher may be given permission to publish the book in English, but another the translation rights. One director might be given permission to turn a work into a play, another to turn the work into a film. Licences also tend to be limited in terms of duration and territory and include terms of financial return (eg royalty calculation, costs to be deducted).

---

[101] CDPA 1988, s 90(2).   [102] CDPA 1988, ss 91(1) and 91(2). See also, *PRS v B4U Network* [2014] FSR 17 (CA).

[103] CDPA 1988, ss 90(3), 91(1).   [104] CDPA 1988, s 178.

[105] Although there could be an equitable assignment; see, eg, *Fresh Trading v Deepend Fresh Recovery* [2015] EWHC 52 (Ch).

[106] CDPA 1988, s 173(2).   [107] CDPA 1988, s 92(1).

[108] Whether such exploitation of copyright *in fact* leads to financial return for authors and benefits them is a separate issue, for an exploration of which see S Kheria, 'Copyright in the everyday practice of writers' in J Jefferies and S Kember (eds), *Whose Book Is It Anyway? A View from Elsewhere on Publishing, Copyright and Creativity* (2019).

Exercise

Imagine scenarios where these different types of copyright licence might be used and consider why it might be appropriate to use one type of licence rather than another in any given set of circumstances. Consider the interests that require to be met when making a choice.

Assignment or licence?

6.31   Sometimes a question can arise as to whether a document is an assignment or a licence. In a case involving rights to the song 'A Whiter Shade of Pale', the House of Lords stated that in order for there to be an implied assignment:[109]

> (a) it would have been obvious to Mr Fisher [the assignor] (as well as Essex [the record company]) that his interest in the musical copyright was being, or had to be, assigned to Essex [the record company], or, which may amount to the same thing, (b) the commercial relationship between the parties could not sensibly have functioned without such an assignment.

The House of Lords ruled that there was no implied assignment and that the recording contract merely granted the record company the right to exploit the original recording.[110] The general principles applicable to construction of contracts also apply to the determination of whether a copyright contract is an assignment or a licence.[111]

6.32   If a reverter clause is present in an agreement, a question may arise as to whether the agreement is a licence or an assignation. In *JHP Ltd v BBC Worldwide Ltd*[112] it was held to be an exclusive licence rather than an assignation. The Court reviewed the relevant authorities. In *Chaplin v Frewin*[113] an agreement in a publishers' contract whereby the publishers should, during the legal term of the copyright, have the exclusive right of producing, publishing, and selling a work in volume form in any language throughout the world was held to be an assignment of copyright. In *Messager v BBC*[114] the composers and authors of an opera granted to the proprietor of the theatre the sole and exclusive right of representing a play, in which it was provided that the copyright in the music of the play should remain the property of the composer and in certain events the right of representation should 'revert to and become again the absolute property of [the composer and the authors]'. The Court in that case said that there had been use of 'inept language in which to describe the mere cessation of a licence and ... much more apt to describe the reversion to the licensors of rights which had been assigned'. The Court in *JHP* came to the conclusion that:[115]

> the concept of reverter (rather than of termination or cessation) is strongly suggestive of the assignment or a transfer of a property right that does not depend for its existence on the very agreement which contains the reverter provision itself. But ... there is no general principle that a reverter clause automatically indicates an assignment.

Copyright contract practices: authors' weak bargaining position

6.33   In UK law there are few statutory controls on contracts negotiated between individual authors and exploiters in the field of copyright and related rights. As seen above, these controls are largely concerned with formalities of execution (eg assignment, exclusive licence) and flexibilities in terms of what can be transferred (eg partial

---

[109]   *Fisher v Brooker and Another* [2009] UKHL 41; [2009] 1 WLR 1764, para 50.   [110]   ibid, paras 57 and 58.

[111]   For a recent summary of relevant principles, see *Mei Fields Designs Ltd v Saffron Cards and Gifts Ltd* [2018] EWHC 1332 (IPEC) para 83.

[112]   [2008] EWHC 757 (Ch).   [113]   [1966] Ch 71.   [114]   [1929] AC 151.

[115]   *JHP Ltd v BBC Worldwide Ltd* [2008] EWHC 757 (Ch) para 14. See also *Crosstown Music Co 1 LLC v Rive Droite Music Ltd* [2010] EWCA Civ 1222. A provision in an assignment of copyright allowing automatic reversion of the rights to the assignor on a future event, namely an unremedied material breach of contract by the assignee, was a valid partial assignment within the CDPA 1988, s 90(2).

assignment, assignment of future copyright). They do not regulate the substantive terms on which a work may be exploited. However, in practice, an author may have a weak bargaining position when entering contractual relationships, and several difficulties may be encountered due to the inequality of bargaining power as between the author and the exploiter. For instance, contracts between authors and exploiters might be non-negotiable and provided to authors on a 'take it or leave it' basis, or they may contain terms which are one-sided and overwhelmingly in favour of the exploiters. In such situations, general principles of contract law have sometimes been called upon to give relief to the author, albeit with limited success. In other instances, specific statutory provisions have been created to ensure that authors benefit from exploitation of their works in certain situations. In practical terms, collecting societies (para 6.42), trade unions, and professional organisations representing authors also play a role in representing authors' interests and strengthening their bargaining position to some extent. EU reform is also under way to improve the bargaining position of authors in contractual relationships. These issues are discussed below.

Copyright contract practices: the music company and the musician

6.34   Perhaps the most well-known examples of contractual controls on copyright licences as between the author and exploiter arise in the entertainment field, most particularly in the music sector. Recording companies have long argued that their business model is predicated on the success of a minority of musicians. The financial return that the companies receive from this minority enables them in turn to engage other musicians. To ensure that the record company can profit from the future success of the few, it is in the interests of the record company to enter into a relationship with a musician for as long as possible. Equally, the record company will not want to be bound to the unsuccessful musician, and in particular it does not want to be under any obligation to publish and distribute music that may not have found favour in the market. This has caused some problems where record companies have signed musicians in the early stages of their career, and where the musicians have not had the benefit of independent advice in relation to the contract into which they entered. A few examples where general principles of contract law have been called upon to give relief to the musician are now discussed.

Restraint of trade

6.35   In *Schroeder Music Publishing v Macaulay*,[116] Macaulay entered into a standard form agreement with Schroeder Music Publishing in which he agreed to assign the copyright in his works to the publisher for five years and, if the royalties exceeded £5,000, for a further five-year period. However, Schroeder was not required to exploit the works. The House of Lords held that this agreement was invalid as it was in restraint of trade. Lord Reid was particularly concerned as to the one-sided nature of the contract, which assigned the copyright in the work to the publisher, but which did not require the publisher to exploit that work:[117]

> it appears to me to be an unreasonable restraint to tie the composer for this period of years so that his work will be sterilised and he can earn nothing from his abilities as a composer if the publisher chooses not to publish. If there had been . . . any provision entitling the composer to terminate the agreement in such an event the case might have had a very different appearance. But as the agreement stands not only is the composer tied but he cannot recover the copyright of work which the publisher refuses to publish.

6.36   The doctrine is, however, not without its limits. Georgios Panayiotou (aka George Michael) challenged his contract with Sony Music Entertainment,[118] from which he wanted to resile on the ground that it

---

[116] [1974] 1 WLR 1308. See also *Elton John v James* (1983) [1991] FSR 397.

[117] [1974] 1 WLR 1308 at 1313–14. For another example of restraint of trade, see *Proactive Sports Management Ltd v Rooney* [2011] EWCA Civ 1444, which concerned footballer Wayne Rooney and a contract dealing with exploitation of his image rights.

[118] *Panayiotou and Others v Sony Music Entertainment* [1994] EMLR 229.

was in restraint of trade. The history between the parties was complex, and a number of changes to their contractual relationship had occurred during the 1980s, the last of which was in 1988. The High Court refused to set aside the agreement, largely because it was considered that to do so would be contrary to public policy.

Undue influence

6.37   In *O'Sullivan and Another v Management Agency*[119] Gilbert O'Sullivan had entered into various contracts with a management agency and publishing company without receiving any independent advice. The Court of Appeal held that the onus was on those asserting that the agreements were valid to show that they had been entered into with full information as to the nature of the transaction—which was not so in this case.[120]

> **Question**
>
> Despite these examples, there have been few other cases in which the contractual arrangement between a musician and a record company has been challenged in court. Why do you think this is the case? When considering this question, you might like to browse the Musicians' Union website at www.musiciansunion.org.uk. What activities does the Musicians' Union undertake on behalf of its members? Does it assist its members regarding the contractual relationships they might enter into? If so, how?

6.38   It is not only in the music industry that difficulties may be encountered due to the inequality of bargaining power as between the author and the exploiter. To assist, a number of different societies representing the interests of the author have developed best practice guidelines as well as specimen agreements that an author can use in negotiations. Further, the Writers' Guild has negotiated a raft of minimum terms agreements applicable as between their members and organisations such as the BBC, ITV, and the Producers Alliance for Cinema and Television (PACT); Equity does the same for performers' rights (see Ch7) with respect to the exploitation of performances in, for example, cinema and on television.[121]

> **Question**
>
> Do other authors' organisations (eg Society of Authors, Scottish Artists' Union, Association of Illustrators) assist their members in relation to copyright contracts, and if so, how?

Copyright contracts and equitable remuneration

6.39   Although there are few statutory controls on copyright contracts negotiated between individual authors and exploiters, one exception is in relation to the rental right in a film or sound recording belonging to the author. When the right is voluntarily, or is presumed to be, transferred to a producer, the author retains a right to equitable remuneration for the rental.[122] This right cannot be transferred or waived, although it can be assigned to a collecting society or may transfer by testamentary disposition or operation of law. The level of remuneration is to be determined by agreement or, failing agreement, by the copyright tribunal.

---

[119] [1985] QB 428.

[120] The doctrines of restraint of trade and undue influence may be subject to acquiescence: *Zang Tumb Tuum Records Ltd v Johnson* [1993] EMLR 61.

[121] A number of the Writers' Guild agreements can be found at www.writersguild.org.uk and the Equity agreements at www.equity.org.uk.

[122] CDPA 1988, ss 93A and 93B. Relevant authors pertaining to a sound recording or film are set out in s 93B(1).

Consequently, the author has an unwaivable right to benefit from successful exploitation of the work, albeit in this relatively narrow area.[123]

6.40   In contrast to the position of authors, performers not only benefit from similar provisions in relation to the rental right, there are also further statutory controls in place for them (paras 7.39–7.40).[124] A policy question then is whether a right to equitable remuneration should be extended in the area of copyright. For instance, if a literary work becomes a best-seller, should the author, who might have assigned or licensed exclusive rights to the publisher, be entitled through a statutory mechanism to benefit from the financial success of the work? In some jurisdictions, measures can be found within copyright and related rights legislation which are protective of the author. For example, the copyright framework in Germany provides that an author is entitled to equitable or adequate remuneration for the exploitation of a work, to be judged by the standard of the prevailing levels in the industry.[125]

6.41   The European Commission's Draft Copyright Directive 2016 (see para 2.15) specifically acknowledges the weak bargaining position of authors in contractual relationships and proposes reforms in this area. Chapter 3, entitled 'Fair remuneration in contracts of authors and performers' is aimed at benefitting authors (and also performers, see Ch 7) once their works have been exploited through a contractual relationship, but it does not address the formation of contracts. Article 15 sets out an obligation on member states to provide for a contract adjustment mechanism, whereby authors and performers are entitled to request additional, appropriate remuneration from the exploiter when the remuneration originally agreed is disproportionately low compared to the subsequent revenues and benefits derived from the exploitation of the work concerned. The Draft Directive also provides for transparency obligations under Article 14 to ensure that authors receive adequate and sufficient information on the exploitation of their works from their exploiter, parricularly in relation to modes of exploitation, revenues generated, and remuneration due. In undergoing the EU legislative process, several amendments have been proposed to these provisions. For instance, the text adopted by the European Parliament in September 2018 includes the following changes:[126] it restricts the mechanism in Article 15 to situations where there are no collective bargaining agreements providing for a comparable mechanism; it introduces the term 'fair' in relation to additional, appropriate remuneration; and it also broadens the scope of the mechanism by changing the entitlement from 'request' to 'claim'; it extends the entitlement to organisations acting on behalf of an author, thus strengthening the position of authors; and it also includes a new Article 16a with a right of revocation for the author. At the time of writing, the EU legislative process is not complete (see para 2.15).

Copyright contracts and Brexit

The majority of statutory provisions in the UK on dealings with rights in copyright-protected works do not derive from EU law. The exceptions pertain to the rights of authors (and performers) to equitable remuneration for their rental rights, and their implementation in the UK will be preserved as retained EU law under the powers in the EU Withdrawal Act 2018. In a 'no-deal' scenario, the UK may not have any obligation to implement any benefits accruing to authors that may eventually emerge from the provisions in Articles 14–16 of the Draft Copyright Directive 2016 (para 2.20).

---

[123] The only other statutory mechanism through which an author has an entitlement to benefit from the exploitation of her work is under the resale right (para 6.23).

[124] Musical performers also have a right to equitable remuneration where a commercially published sound recording is played in public or otherwise communicated to the public (see para 7.39). They also benefit from additional protective measures such as the 'use it or lose it' mechanism and the '20% fund' (see para 7.44). Such benefits attempt to address the weak bargaining position in which performers involved in the production of sound recordings may find themselves.

[125] German Copyright Act (Urheberrechtsgesetz) 1965, as last amended in 2017, ss 11 and 32. See further, European Parliament Legal Affairs Committee Study, 'Contractual Arrangements Applicable to Creators: Law and Practice of Selected Member States' (2014).

[126] See amendments adopted by the European Parliament on 12 September 2018 at www.europarl.europa.eu/sides/getDoc.do?pubRef=-//EP//TEXT+TA+P8-TA-2018-0337+0+DOC+XML+V0//EN; see also, the European Council's position as adopted on 25 May 2018 at https://eur-lex.europa.eu/legal-content/EN/TXT/PDF/?uri=CONSIL:ST_9134_2018_INIT&from=EN.

Exercise

Should the UK introduce provisions similar to those in Articles 14–16 of the Draft Copyright Directive 2016 to ensure that authors benefit from the financial success of their works? Should the UK go further and introduce a general fairness requirement in copyright contracts, limiting the freedom to contract, to protect authors?[127] Find out whether the EU legislative process for the Draft Copyright Directive 2016 is complete and if so, what provisions have been adopted in the final text on authors' contractual relationships.

Key points on dealings with rights in copyright-protected works

- Copyright is a property right and the rights restricted by copyright can be transferred by assignment, by testamentary disposition, or by operation of law, as personal or moveable property, and can also be licensed,

- Both an assignment and an exclusive licence are required to be in writing, signed by or on behalf of the copyright owner.

- The doctrines of restraint of trade and undue influence can sometimes control copyright contractual practices.

- Equitable remuneration is available for authors who transfer the rental right in a sound recording or film.

Collective licensing

6.42 Exploiting works protected by copyright can cause practical problems for both the copyright owner (whether an author, or an exploiter) and the prospective licensee. A copyright owner can find it difficult to keep track of third parties who wish to exploit those works in one form or another. Similarly, a licensee may wish to incorporate a large number of works protected by copyright into their repertoire, but have difficulty in tracing the copyright owners to obtain permission. For example, educational establishments and businesses often make copies of published literary works which do not fall under the fair dealing provisions in the copyright legislation[128] and broadcasters frequently use musical works which are protected by copyright. In order to facilitate the management of these rights, collecting societies were introduced.[129] Authors of works protected by copyright are able to assign or license their rights to the collecting societies (or the collecting society will act as agent on their behalf), which then manage the rights on behalf of their members. Thus, the authors are saved from having to spend a lot of time on administration, and those who wish to exploit the works have one place from which they can seek permission to use them.

6.43 Examples of collecting societies currently operating in the UK include the Copyright Licensing Agency (CLA) and the PRS for Music (formerly the Performing Rights Society (PRS) and the Mechanical Copyright

---

[127] See further, European Parliament Legal and Parliamentary Affairs Committee Study, 'Strengthening the Position of Press Publishers and Authors and Performers in the Copyright Directive' (2017); Study for the European Commission, 'Remuneration of Authors and Performers for the Use of Their Works and the Fixations of Their Performances' (2015); European Parliament Legal Affairs Committee Study, 'Contractual Arrangements Applicable to Creators: Law and Practice of Selected Member States' (2014); WR Cornish, 'The author as risk-sharer' (2003) 26(1) Columbia J Law and the Arts 1.

[128] See Chapter 5.

[129] See generally D Gervais, *Collective Management of Copyright and Related Rights* (2015); see UK government guidance at www.gov.uk/guidance/licensing-bodies-and-collective-management-organisations.

Protection Society (MCPS)). Different societies operate in different ways. PRS for Music, which represents composers, authors, and publishers of music, has copyright assigned to it and administers licences and enforces copyright as the owner of the copyright. Royalties are distributed to the members in proportion to the use made of a particular work.[130] In contrast, the MCPS was authorised by the composer, author, or publisher of a work to license the recording of the work on his behalf—there was no assignment of the copyright. In addition, there is also provision in the CDPA 1988 for statutory extended collective licensing, under which a licensing body such as a collecting society can be authorized by the Secretary of State to grant licenses not just on behalf of its rightholder members, but also on behalf of non-member rightholders.[131]

 Question

Have a look at the websites of the Authors' Licensing Collecting Society (ALCS) **www.alcs.co.uk**, PRS for Music **www.prsformusic.com**, Phonographic Performance Limited (PPL) **www.ppluk.com**, and DACS **www.dacs.org.uk**. Find out who these organisations represent, what rights they manage on behalf of their members, and how they administer such rights? Can you find any similar organisations in other jurisdictions?

6.44   Collecting societies occupy a powerful role, both in relation to the authors of the works, and in relation to users: they can control a very large repertoire of works, set terms for membership and administration of rights in relation to authors, and also the terms (including royalty rates) on which works are licensed, or not licensed, to individuals and groups. Consequently, some oversight of their activities has been found to be essential. The 1988 Act sets out the regulatory framework for oversight of copyright licensing schemes and the activities of collecting societies. It defines both licensing schemes and licensing bodies, and gives the Copyright Tribunal broad powers to monitor the licensing schemes of collecting societies.[132] Thus, for instance, those parties who wish to take a licence from the collecting society but who feel that the terms are unfair or where the society might have refused to grant them a licence, may take a complaint and have it heard by the Tribunal.[133]

■ *Universities UK v The Copyright Licensing Agency* [2002] RPC 36

In this case, universities in the UK asked the Copyright Tribunal to rule on the terms of the Higher Education Copying Accord promulgated by the CLA and which allows, inter alia, students in higher education institutions to make copies, up to a certain amount, of published works during the currency of their educational courses. Negotiations had broken down on matters concerning both the scope of and the fee for the licence. The Copyright Tribunal made an order referring to both of these matters: the course pack provision (which had required separate negotiation each time a 'course pack' was provided to a class of students), so disliked in education, was to be abolished, artistic works were to be included in the licence, and the fee was to be set at £4.00 per full-time enrolled student.

---

[130] PRS uses the following methods, in order of preference, for distribution: census, sample and analogy. See www.prsformusic.com/royalties/royalty-payment-dates/prs-distribution-policy.

[131] CDPA 1988, s 116B, and Copyright and Rights in Performances (Extended Collective Licensing) Regulations 2014 (SI 2014/2588). See UK government guidance at www.gov.uk/government/publications/extended-collective-licensing. See also Draft Copyright Directive 2016, Art 7.

[132] See CDPA 1988, ss 116, 117–123. For example, in *BPI v MCPS* [2008] EMLR 5, the Copyright Tribunal confirmed that songwriters, composers, and publishers should receive 8 per cent of gross revenues from online music service providers for on-demand services including downloads and subscription streaming services, 6.5 per cent of revenues for interactive webcasting services, and 5.75 per cent for non-interactive webcasting.

[133] See *In Respect of the Appeal of Phonographic Performance Ltd v The Appeal of the British Hospitality Association and Other Interested Parties* [2008] EWHC 2715 (Ch); also *CSC Media Group Ltd v Video Performance Ltd* [2011] EWCA Civ 650 (CA); *PPL v British Hospitality Association* [2010] EWHC 209 (Ch); CT 127/14 *ITV Network Ltd v Performing Right Society Ltd* [2016] 6 WLUK 631 affirmed in [2017] EWHC 234 (Ch).

> **Exercise**
>
> Have a look at the final decision of the Copyright Tribunal. What do you think of the outcome of the hearing? What price do you think should be paid to authors and publishers for photocopying materials for educational purposes?

The 1988 Act also contains powers exercisable by the Secretary of State or the Competition and Markets Authority in relation to collecting societies and anti-competetive practices (see also paras 20.83–20.92).[134] In addition, the Collective Management of Copyright Regulations 2016[135] set out a range of obligations of collecting societies, particularly towards their rightholder members. These obligations were introduced as a result of the 2014 EU Directive on collective management which aimed to set down a high standard of governance, financial management, transparency and reporting on collecting societies,[136] and also facilitate multi-territorial licensing, for which see para 20.92.

Further licensing issues

Compulsory licences

6.45   International obligations under the Berne and Rome Conventions mean that compulsory licences will be granted in respect of the exploitation of copyright in only limited circumstances under UK law. The Berne Convention 1886 allows for the grant of compulsory licences for jukeboxes, and mechanical licences for musical works, both subject to conditions. However, the UK does not take advantage of either of these relaxations.[137] Under the Rome Convention 1961 compulsory licences may only be granted as regards broadcasting or communication to the public of phonograms.[138]

Orphan works

6.46   If a user wishes to use a substantial part of an existing protected work in a new work, then permission must be obtained from the owner of the copyright. Since copyright is an unregistered right and copyright in author works extends well after the death of the author (and the date of that event may be difficult to ascertain), would-be users and re-publishers of works who wish to comply with the law frequently find it impracticable or impossible to take the necessary steps to do what they want to do lawfully, that is, find out whether a work is still in copyright and, if so, who is now the owner. Tracing copyright owners can be a complex, costly, and time-consuming activity, particularly where a work may be out of print, the copyright may have devolved amongst countless heirs, or the work may simply have been forgotten about. Where an owner cannot be located after reasonable inquiry, some term the work an 'orphan work'. Orphan works have been the subject of intense discussion at international, European, and national policy-making levels in recent years.[139]

6.47   The problem of orphan works was summarised in a UK Government Policy Statement:[140]

> it benefits no-one to have a wealth of copyright works be entirely unusable under any circumstances because the owner of one or more rights in the work cannot be contacted. This is not simply a cultural issue; it is also a very real economic issue that potentially valuable intangible assets are not being used, and an issue of respect for copyright if they are being used unlawfully.

---

[134]   CDPA 1988, s 144.   [135]   SI 2016/221.

[136]   Directive 2014/26/EU of the European Parliament and of the Council of 26 February 2014 on collective management of copyright and related rights and multi-territorial licensing of rights in musical works for online use in the internal market, recital 9.

[137]   The jukebox licence: Berne Convention 1886, Art 11*bis* (2), and the mechanical licence: Berne Convention, Art 13.

[138]   Rome Convention 1961, Art 12.

[139]   One of the earliest investigations took the form of an inquiry by the US Copyright Office. See http://copyright.gov/orphan.

[140]   IPO, 'Government Policy Statement: Consultation on Modernising Copyright,' (July 2012), 7.

Despite the obvious difficulty such orphan works may create, it took a number of years for there to be a legislative solution. The Hargreaves Review 2011 proposed establishing licensing and clearance procedures for orphan works—a suggestion subsequently investigated further in the Hooper Report.[141] The EU also took the initiative to partially alleviate the problem of orphan works by adopting the Orphan Works Directive in 2012,[142] allowing certain cultural organisations to digitise orphan works for non-commercial use throughout the EU. Consequently, in October 2014, UK copyright law was changed in two main ways.[143]

6.48   First, a statutory licensing scheme for orphan works, administered through the Intellectual Property Office (IPO), was introduced.[144] The licensing scheme enables an applicant to apply for a licence to use an orphan work having carried out a 'diligent search' for the right holder and met other formalities.[145] An application fee is payable, and if successful, a fee is also payable for the licence to use the work. The IPO may grant a licence for non-exclusive use of the work in the UK for no more than seven years. The use can be commercial or non-commercial, and the licence acts as if it was granted by the right owner of the work. The IPO may refuse to grant a licence if a diligent search has been inadequate or if the proposed use by the applicant is not appropriate. The IPO also maintains an orphan works register of works for which applications have been made, and works for which licences have been granted. Consequently, any right owner whose work has been licensed can contact the IPO to claim the licence fee paid; or a right owner whose work is the subject of an application can ask the IPO to the stop the application.

 Exercise

Explore the UK Orphan works register at www.orphanworkslicensing.service.gov.uk/view-register. Find out the number of applications made, and the number of licences granted, and the types of works for which applications are made and licences granted. Do you think the UK licensing scheme for orphan works is functioning effectively?

6.49   Secondly, a new permitted act was also introduced as a result of which cultural heritage institutions (eg a publicly accessible library, an educational establishment, museum, or an archive) could copy certain types of orphan works in their collections and make them available to the public without the permission of the right owner.[146] Under this exception, the use must be non-commercial (eg relate to the institution's public interest mission) and the institutions are required to carry out a diligent search. The institutions are also required to register such orphan works used under the exception on a database maintained by the EU Intellectual Property Office (EUIPO).[147]

6.50   A key challenge in allowing use of orphan works without authorisation of the right owner is ensuring an adequate balance between interests of rights owners and users (eg addressing the right owners' concerns about abuse of such permitted use while allowing sufficient uses, and an easy and efficient mechanism for the users). Whether the recent changes in the UK will achieve such balance remains to be seen. A completely different solution to the problem of orphan works would be a copyright registration system, but that would presumably be a radical step too far, since it is inconsistent with the Berne Convention.

---

[141] R Hooper and R Lynch, 'Copyright Works: Streamlining Copyright Licensing for the Digital Age' independent report (IPO, 2012). The *Gowers Review of Intellectual Property* in 2006 had recommended that a proposal should be put to the European Commission to introduce a provision on orphan works in the form of a Directive.

[142] Directive 2012/28/EU on certain permitted uses of orphan works.

[143] Copyright and Rights in Performances (certain permitted use of orphan works) Regulations 2014 (SI 2014/2861), transposing the relevant parts of the Orphan Works Directive 2012; and the Copyright and the Rights in Performances (Licensing of Orphan Works) Regulations 2014 (SI 2014/2863) resulting from Hargreaves' recommendations.

[144] CDPA 1988, s 116A.

[145] See www.gov.uk/guidance/copyright-orphan-works.

[146] CDPA 1988, ss 44B, 76A, and schedule ZA1.

[147] https://euipo.europa.eu/ohimportal/en/web/observatory/orphan-works-db

Orphan works and Brexit

The orphan works exception was created in the UK as a result of the EU Orphan Works Directive 2012. In the event of a 'no-deal' Brexit scenario, the UK exception will be repealed and consequently, UK cultural heritage institutions (CHIs) will not be able to rely on the EU exception, and may face claims of copyright infringement for works placed online prior to and post exit. The UK government 'no-deal' advice is that:[148] 'CHIs that wish to digitise and make available online orphan works in their collections will not be able to do so in the UK under an exception to copyright. Works that UK CHIs have previously placed online will need to be removed to avoid infringing the copyright in those works. CHIs that wish to maintain their online collections within the UK may be able to do so via the UK's orphan works licensing scheme.'

Individual online licensing schemes

6.51   The digital environment has opened up opportunities for authors for self-publishing and for making creative works available over the Internet themselves. As such, the onus falls upon authors to choose and use an appropriate licence (although there is no obligation to do so) when disseminating works online. In some such instances, authors may wish to use restrictive licences such as those that keep all rights reserved to the author, or which only permit very limited use. In other instances, authors may wish to provide a more permissive licence, enabling wide dissemination and re-use of their works, rather than a restrictive licence. A number of individual online licensing schemes that facilitate the dissemination and re-use of creative work have proliferated. These initiatives are interesting in that they operate within the existing copyright framework but are designed to meet the challenges imposed by what many perceive to be the opaque boundaries of the law on re-use of works protected by copyright.

Creative Commons

6.52   Perhaps the best known of these is Creative Commons (CC). Its aim is to offer a range of licences that can be used by authors and artists. Started in the United States, it has now become international, with licences offered in many jurisdictions. Creative Commons was inspired originally by the 'open source' movement which began in connection with computer software and was conceived in opposition to the existence of copyright in such material. The credo was that software should be made available in such a way that others might use and build upon it, especially in developing new software, as this was the best way to facilitate further such innovation. This does not necessarily mean that the software must be made available free of charge, but rather that copyright should not be used to block further development of what already exists. However, in order to grant an effective licence removing any restrictions of use, or granting wide use, copyright must subsist.[149] There is a certain irony in the fact that copyleft needs copyright in order to function.

6.53   Creative Commons UK was established (building on a US model), with the aim of developing forms of licence under which copyright is retained but users are given advance permission to copy and distribute the work for their own purposes, as long as due credit is given to the original work and similar conditions

[148] UK Government, 'Changes to copyright law in the event of no deal' (26 October 2018) www.gov.uk/government/publications/changes-to-copyright-law-in-the-event-of-no-deal/changes-to-copyright-law-in-the-event-of-no-deal.

[149] See, eg, J Boyle, 'A manifesto on WIPO and the future of intellectual property' (2004) 9 Duke Law & Tech Rev 1; A Guadamuz, 'Viral contracts or unenforceable documents? Contractual validity of copyleft licenses' [2004] EIPR 331.

are imposed upon any further sub-users; this being, it is argued, the most appropriate way to support and encourage creativity and innovation in the online and digital environments. The licensor can indicate those types of use which remain restricted; but the starting point is that use is free and restrictions on use have to be stated, whereas the underpinning assumption of traditional licences is that no use is allowed unless expressly permitted. In the UK, licences are available for England and Wales and for Scotland.

Creative Commons offers several licences enabling authors (or other right holders) to select which rights they wish to reserve and which they wish to offer.[150]

> Six different licences are available:[151]
>
> CC BY Attribution: lets others distribute remix, tweak, and build upon the work, including for commercial purposes, as long as the author is attributed.
>
> CC BY-SA Attribution-ShareAlike: lets others remix, tweak, and build upon a work, including for commercial purposes, as long as the author is attributed and the new creation is licensed under identical terms.
>
> CC BY-ND Attribution—NoDerivs: allows for commercial and non-commercial redistribution as long as the author is attributed and the work is passed on unchanged.
>
> CC BY-NC Attribution–NonCommercial: lets others remix, tweak, and build on the work for non-commercial purposes, as long as the author is attributed.
>
> CC BY-NC-SA Attribution—NonCommercial—ShareAlike: lets others remix, tweak, and build on for non-commercial purposes as long as the author is attributed and the new work is licensed on identical terms.
>
> CC BY-NC-ND Attribution—NonCommercial-NoDerivs: allows download and unchanged non-commercial sharing of the work as long as attributed.

Other schemes

6.54   Other licensing schemes, some of which have been trialled and some of which were established to meet similar ends, include AE ShareNet[152] run by a non-profit company in Australia to streamline the licensing of IP within the education sector; the Creative Archive[153] licence which was used by the BBC to make available programmes from its archive (the pilot ended in 2006); and BC Commons[154] (offered by the BC (British Columbia) Campus organisation in Canada) for post-secondary institutions developing online content.

Each of these was conceived of and developed in response to the complexities which arise when licensing digital content online. Each aimed to make the process of licensing works simple and efficient and, importantly, to set out clearly the parameters on re-use.

The CC licence scheme is undoubtedly the largest and the one that has outlasted the others.

   Exercise

Go to the Creative Commons webpage and have a browse around it. How many works licensed under a CC licence do you think are available today? Can you find cases where the courts have upheld the licence or addressed an aspect of the licence?

---

[150] For a critique of Creative Commons, see N Elkin-Koren, 'What contracts cannot do: the limits of private ordering in facilitating a Creative Commons' (2006) 74 Fordham L Rev 375.

[151] For full details, see http://creativecommons.org/licenses.

[152] See J Gilding and C Fripp, 'AEShareNet: Reflections on an innovative venture to move copyright licensing into the digital age' 52 (2003) The Australian Library Journal 5.

[153] www.bbc.co.uk/creativearchive.   [154] https://solr.bccampus.ca/wp/summary-of-bc-commons-license-version-2-0/.

> **Key points on copyright licensing**
>
> - Collective licensing is a notable feature in copyright exploitation.
> - Collecting societies are subject to regulatory oversight.
> - Compulsory licences may be granted in respect of copyright in only very limited circumstances laid down in the Berne and Rome Conventions.
> - The UK has a statutory licensing scheme for orphan works and also an exception permitting certain uses in relation to orphan works by relevant prescribed bodies.
> - Several licensing schemes have emerged in recent years to facilitate individual licensing of digital works protected by copyright, the most well known of which is Creative Commons.

Technical protection measures and rights management information systems

6.55   In the process of exploiting copyright works, producers and exploiters of digital works wish to deploy digital rights management systems to restrict unauthorised access to and use of the works. Digital rights management systems (DRMs)—the generic term for collectively referring to technical protection measures (TPMs) and rights management information systems (RMIs) together—allows right holders to do so, and were of critical importance to the creation of markets using the new forms of distribution made possible by the internet and digitisation. Therefore, DRMs themselves received specific legal protection at both the international and EU level.

Historical background

6.56   The Software Directive 1991 provided that there should be appropriate remedies in national legislation against a person putting into circulation, or possessing for commercial purposes, any means the sole intended purpose of which was to facilitate the unauthorised removal or circumvention of any technical device applied to protect a computer program.[155] The aim of this legislation was to support the pragmatic answer to the problems of protecting electronic or digital works deployed to ensure that users and consumers paid for their access and use. That answer had been provided by the technology itself: products could be locked behind technological barriers (or 'walls' or 'fences'), for example, encryption, passwords, activation codes, and so on, requiring payment and/or authorisation by electronic means before they could be opened up or set aside. Other examples operate through interaction between software and hardware: the former is encrypted and will only operate if the latter contains a device or key with which decryption is possible. Such devices protecting against unauthorised access are commonly known as *technical protection measures* (TPMs).[156]

6.57   The New York case of *Universal Studios Inc v Corley*[157] provides an explanation of one well-known such TPM, the 'content scramble system' (CSS) protecting DVDs:

> CSS is an encryption scheme that employs an algorithm configured by a set of 'keys' to encrypt a DVD's contents. The algorithm is a type of mathematical formula for transforming the contents of the movie file into gibberish; the 'keys' are in actuality strings of 0's and 1's that serve as values for the mathematical formula.

---

[155]   Software Directive 2009 (Software Directive 1991 was consolidated into Directive 2009/24/EC and unless stated otherwise, all references will be to the latter directive), Art 7(1)(c).

[156]   See further G Davies, 'Technical devices as a solution to private copying' in IA Stamatoudi and PLC Torremans (eds), *Copyright in the New Digital Environment* (2000); 'Digital Rights Management', Report of an Inquiry by the All Party Internet Group (June 2006). For an international perspective, see P Akester, *A Practical Guide to Digital Copyright* (2008), Ch 6.

[157]   273 F 3d 429 (2nd Cir, 2001).

Decryption in the case of CSS requires a set of 'player keys' contained in compliant DVD players, as well as an understanding of the CSS encryption algorithm. Without the player keys and the algorithm, a DVD player cannot access the contents of a DVD. With the player keys and the algorithm, a DVD player can display the movie on a television or a computer screen, but does not give a viewer the ability to use the copy function of the computer to copy the movie or to manipulate the digital content of the DVD (at paras 436–437).

From 1989, making and supplying devices to enable such TPMs to be evaded was made equivalent to infringement of copyright itself and, in the UK, also invited criminal penalties. In the early days, the primary kind of protected work was the computer program; but databases, CDs, commercial websites on the internet, and DVDs quickly joined the ranks of works technologically protected against unauthorised copying.

6.58   The WCT 1996 and the InfoSoc Directive 2001 contained further provisions designed to support and strengthen the rules against circumvention devices and their use, and also extended protection to 'electronic rights management information systems' (RMIs). The latter are electronic tags or fingerprints included in copies of digital products, enabling them to be traced and identified electronically wherever they may be in use, lawfully or otherwise. The systems typically identify the software, the copyright owner, and the rights held by that party and the users of the work, respectively. The information in the system may well often appear on the computer screen when the work is installed or run. Such systems are of particular importance in the internet context, through which most tracing and identification activity is likely to be conducted.[158] As a result of the InfoSoc Directive, UK law on the protection of DRMs was substantially amended and added to, and it is to the present position that we now turn.

 Question

Explain the difference between technological protection measures and electronic rights management systems.

Law in the UK

6.59   There are specific provisions for TPMs in relation to computer programs, since the Software Directive was not superseded on this point by the InfoSoc Directive.[159] Any technical device applied to a computer program that is intended to prevent or restrict acts unauthorised by the copyright owner *and* restricted by copyright is protected. Making, dealing in, or possessing for commercial purposes a circumvention device while knowing or having reason to believe that it will be used to make infringing copies makes the person in question liable as an infringer of copyright in his own right.

6.60   The rules for TPMs are similar in respect of copyright works that are not computer programs (eg broadcasts, databases, sound recording CDs, film DVDs, websites), but wider in scope.[160] Here there is a provision that the person who circumvents an effective technological measure, knowing or having reasonable grounds to know that he is pursuing that objective, is to be treated as a copyright infringer.[161] So now we are dealing with actual circumvention, and not just the manufacture of, dealing in, or commercial possession of a circumvention device. The rules apply to protect not just technical devices, but any effective technological measures applied to the work. This covers any technology, device, or component designed in the normal

---

[158]   See further P and R Akester, 'Digital rights management in the 21st century' [2006] EIPR 159; 'Digital Rights Management', Report of an Inquiry by the All Party Internet Group (June 2006).
[159]   CDPA 1988, s 296.
[160]   Section 296ZA–ZF, implementing Art 6 of the InfoSoc Directive 2001; s296ZA provides civil remedies while s296ZB provides criminal sanctions.
[161]   CDPA 1988, s 296ZA.

course of its operation to protect a copyright work, that is, to prevent or restrict acts unauthorised by the copyright owner *and* restricted by copyright.[162] These measures are 'effective' if use of the work within the scope of the acts restricted by copyright is controlled by the copyright owner through either (1) an *access control* or protection process such as encryption, scrambling, or other transformation of the work; *or* (2) a *copy control* mechanism.[163]

 Question

What are the differences between the protection of technical protection measures for computer programs and the protection of those for other kinds of copyright work?

6.61   In *Nintendo Co Ltd v Playables Ltd and Another*,[164] Floyd J held that both section 296 and section 296ZD were infringed by the defendants who imported and sold mod-chips which allowed users to play pirated games on Nintendo's consoles. Technical devices had been applied to the copyright computer programs in the games console and game cards and the sole purpose of mod-chips was to circumvent them. On the question of knowledge, the Court held that since it was well known that mod-chips were used for piracy and given the minor proportion of the market represented by lawful use and the large numbers sold, the defendants did not have a realistic prospect of asserting lack of knowledge of unlawful uses.

Technical protection systems being developed by the entertainment industries include ones built into the hardware used to access and copy digital works, such as DVD players and games consoles. For instance, an encryption code in the work that prohibits access is more effective if the work has to be run through a chip embedded in a computer which decrypts the work, rather than simply relying on the code itself. Are systems so constructed in the hardware subject to the protection for 'effective technological measures'? What falls within the concept of an effective technological measure? Are there any limitations to the scope of protection offered?[165]

■ *Sony v Ball* [2005] FSR 9

This was another case about the territorially based protection of Sony's *PlayStation 2*. B produced mod-chips to fit the console and trick it into believing that unauthorised or foreign DVDs being played had the necessary embedded code. It was held that summary judgment could be granted to prevent sales of B's chips in the UK (but not elsewhere). It did not matter that Sony's protection system was partly in the hardware (the console) and only partly in the software (the games DVD).[166]

■ C-355/12 *Nintendo Co Ltd v PC Box Srl* [2014] ECDR 6 (CJ)

This reference to the CJ by the Milan District Court concerned Nintendo games and consoles, which were manufactured such that they had to recognise each other in order for the game to work. The aim was to ensure that only games produced under a licence by Nintendo could be played. P manufactured devices which would allow other games, not produced or authorised by Nintendo, to be played on the console. The CJ found that Article 6 of InfoSoc Directive 2001 required a member state to provide adequate legal protection against circumvention of any 'effective technological measure' which must be understood to include a protection

---

[162] CDPA 1988, s 296ZF(1), (3).   [163] CDPA 1988, s 296ZF(2).

[164] [2010] FSR 36.

[165] In the context of s 296ZB, see *R v Higgs (Neil Stanley)* [2008] FSR 34 (CA); see also *R v Gilham* [2009] EWCA Crim 2293 (CA); *Nintendo Co Ltd and Another v Playables Ltd and Another* [2010] FSR 36 (Ch). See generally D Booton and A Macculloch, 'Liability for the circumvention of technological protection measures applied to videogames: lessons from the United Kingdom's experience' (2012) Journal of Business Law 165.

[166] See A Macculloch, 'Game over: the "region lock" in video games' [2005] EIPR 176.

system that was incorporated both in the hardware (the console) as well as the DVD (housing the copyright protected video game itself, see para 3.13) where the aim of the required interaction between the two was to prevent or to limit acts adversely affecting rights of the copyright holder. The Court also confirmed that legal protection is granted 'only with regard to technological measures which pursue the objective of preventing or eliminating, as regards works, acts not authorised by the rightholder of copyright referred' and 'those measures must be suitable for achieving that objective and must not go beyond what is necessary for this purpose' (para 31). This makes it necessary to examine whether other measures could have caused less interference with the activities of third parties, while still providing comparable protection to rightholder's rights (para 31). It is for the national court to determine this. In doing so, it is relevant to take account of: the relative costs of different types of technical measures; their technological and practical aspects; their effectiveness in protecting right holders, although the effectiveness doesn't have to be absolute; and, the purpose of circumvention devices. Evidence of actual use of circumvention devices will be relevant, in particular, how often they are in fact used to disregard copyright and how often they are used for non-infringing purposes.

Rights management information systems

6.62 The approach to the protection of rights management systems is likewise to make it akin to infringement of copyright knowingly and without authority to remove or alter digital rights management information associated with a copy of a copyright work or which appears in connection with a communication of the work to the public.[167] Also caught is the person who knowingly and without authority distributes, imports for distribution, or communicates to the public copies of a copyright work from which the RMI has been removed or altered.[168] In both cases the person so acting must know, or have reason to believe, that the action induces, enables, facilitates, or conceals an infringement of copyright.

Persons enjoying the anti-circumvention rights

6.63 The people who can sue under any of the anti-circumvention rights are:

- those who have issued copies of the protected work, or communicated it, to the public;
- the copyright owner or his exclusive licensee.[169]

In addition, with regard to devices protecting computer programs, the owner/exclusive licensee of any intellectual property right in the protection device itself may take action.[170]

Dealing in apparatus for unauthorised reception of transmissions

6.64 A person who makes charges for the reception of broadcasts provided from a place in the UK, or who sends encrypted transmissions of any other description from a place in the UK, has the same rights and remedies as a copyright owner in respect of infringement against a person dealing in any apparatus or device designed or adapted to enable or assist persons to receive the programmes or other transmissions when they are not entitled to do so, or publishing information calculated so as to enable or assist them.[171] The provisions may also be applied in relation to services provided from outside the UK.[172] There are criminal law sanctions against manufacturing, dealing in or with, or installing, maintaining, or replacing unauthorised decoders (counterfeit or stolen viewing cards, or illicit devices); punishments include imprisonment and/or fines.[173]

---

[167] CDPA 1988, s 296ZG(1), (3).   [168] CDPA 1988, s 296ZG(2).
[169] CDPA 1988, s 296(2), 296ZA(3), and 296ZG(3), (4).   [170] CDPa 1988, s 296(2)(c).
[171] CDPA 1988, s 298(1), (2).
[172] CDPA 1988, s 299(1)(b). See SI 1989/2003. Note that s 299(2) was repealed by the Broadcasting Act 1990, s 179(2).
[173] CDPA 1988, s 297A.

Controlling TPMs and RMIs

6.65   Arguably TPMs are also capable of preventing use permitted under the copyright exceptions (Chapter 5) and, indeed, when a work has fallen out of copyright altogether (eg at the expiry of its term) or when the work never had copyright. Yet copyright law gives protection to TPMs, which makes their circumvention illegal as long as the protected work is made available by way of contractual terms. Thus, technology has the potential to create protection akin to copyright for works which have never had, or have ceased to have, copyright, as well as to extend protection beyond the scope of copyright where that exists.[174] Consequently, TPMs can set up a world in which right holders and would-be users *contract* for the use of the copyright work, raising complex questions about the interrelationship between exceptions to copyright, TPMs, and contract rights.

6.66   The InfoSoc Directive, in the fourth paragraph of Article 6(4), appears to give pre-eminence to contractual terms over copyright exceptions, where works are made available in such a way that they may be accessed from places and at times individually chosen by users. This reinforces the position of the right holder barring access in order to create an opportunity to establish a contractual nexus under which the user pays for his use; and it is really only against the right holder who wishes to deny access in order to be paid for the privilege that exceptions and limitations giving access regardless of the right holder's wishes are of any significance. Concerns that the legal protection of TPMs had the potential to deprive copyright exceptions of their content and value are also addressed in Article 6(4) of the Directive by a provision which requires member states to take:

> appropriate measures to ensure that right-holders make available to the beneficiary of an exception or limitation provided for in national law [in accordance with the Directive] the means of benefiting from that exception or limitation, to the extent necessary to benefit from that exception or limitation and where that beneficiary has legal access to the protected work or subject-matter concerned.

The UK has implemented Article 6(4) in the following rather complex fashion.[175] Where the application of any effective technological measure to a copyright work other than a computer program prevents a person from carrying out a permitted act in relation to that work, then that person (or a person who is a representative of a class of persons prevented from carrying out a permitted act) may complain to the Secretary of State (ie the relevant government minister). The Secretary of State may thereupon issue written directions to the copyright holder, with which the latter must comply. The complainant must be someone who has lawful access to the protected copyright work. This provision only applies to certain (and not all) permitted acts.[176] It includes, for example, research and private study, as well as making a copy available for a disabled person. It is noteworthy, however, that it does not apply to criticism, review, and news reporting, despite the particular importance which the courts have attributed to these exceptions in the interests of freedom of speech and expression (see Ch 5).[177] None of this is applicable, however, where the copyright work in question has been 'made available to the public on agreed contractual terms in such a way that members of the public may access them from a place and at a time individually chosen by them'.[178] So, for example, there can be no complaint about TPMs and RMIs attached to music files downloaded from the iTunes service.[179] This would seem to suggest that the only complaint likely to be successful is one where access is completely blocked.

---

[174] N Braun, 'The interface between the protection of technological measures and the exercise of exceptions to copyright and related rights: comparing the situation in the US and the EU' [2003] EIPR 496; W Davies and K Withers, *Public Innovation: Intellectual Property in a Digital Age* (Institute of Public Policy Research, 2006), 46–48, 84–87.

[175] CDPA 1988, s 296ZE, as amended by Copyright and Related Rights (Marrakesh Treaty etc.) (Amendment) Regulations 2018.

[176] CDPA 1988, Sch 5A, Part 1, as amended by the 2014 reforms to copyright exceptions (see Ch5).

[177] P Akester, 'Technological Accommodation of Conflicts between Freedom of Expression and DRM: The First Empirical Assessment' (2009) at https://ssrn.com/abstract=1469412.

[178] CDPA 1988, s 296ZE(9).

[179] Example suggested in W Davies and K Withers, *Public Innovation: Intellectual Property in a Digital Age* (Institute of Public Policy Research, 2006), 23.

Question 1

Who may apply to the Secretary of State that the application of a TPM is preventing the exercise of an exception to copyright?

Question 2

What kinds of order may the Secretary of State make?

Question 3

What must be shown before the Secretary of State will issue an order?

Key points on TPM and RMI protection

- During exploitation of copyright works, TPMs and RMIs, generically known as digital rights management (DRM) systems, enable right owners to prevent unauthorised access to and use of them.

- TPMs are any technological means within a copyright product designed to prevent acts restricted by copyright unless the authorisation of the copyright owner is obtained, usually by electronic means provided within the system.

- RMIs are electronic systems built into digital products which record information about the identity and use of the product, thus enabling their tracing and the pursuit of unauthorised uses.

- Copyright legislation prohibits circumvention of TPMs and removal or alteration of RMIs, treating these as infringements of copyright if carried out with knowledge, or reasonable grounds to know. The law is more limited with regard to computer programs.

- The legislation also treats as a form of infringement manufacturing or dealing in devices designed to circumvent TPMs or in products whose RMIs have been removed or altered.

- Concerns arise about the scope of TPMs, especially when they can prevent use permitted under copyright exceptions.

Further reading

Books

General

L Bently, B Sherman, D Gangjee, and P Johnson, *Intellectual Property Law* (5th edn, 2018), Chs 10–13.

N Caddick, G Davies, and G Harbottle (eds), *Copinger & Skone James on Copyright* (17th edn, 2019), Chs 11, 15, 20, 26, and 27.

Moral rights

E Adeney, *The Moral Rights of Authors and Performers: An International and Comparative Analysis* (2006)

FW Grosheide, 'Moral rights' in E Derclaye (ed), *Research Handbook on the Future of EU Copyright* (2009), Ch 10

MT Sundara Rajan, *Moral Rights: Principles, Practice and New Technology* (2011)

Artist's resale right

S Stokes, *Artist's Resale Right UK Law and Practice* (2nd edn, 2012)

Licensing

L Guibault, 'Relationship between copyright and contract law', Chapter 20, in E Derclaye (ed), *Research Handbook on the Future of EU Copyright* (2009)

L Guibault and C Angelopoulos, *Open Content Licensing: From Theory to Practice* (2011)

Technological protection measures and rights management information

P Akester, *A Practical Guide to Digital Copyright* (2008), Ch 6

Articles and reports

Licensing

M Kretschmer, 'Copyright and Contract Law: Regulating Creator Contracts: The State of the Art and a Research Agenda' (2010) 18(1) J Intell Prop L 141

M Kretschmer, 'Access and reward in the information society: regulating the collective management of copyright' (2005) http://eprints.bournemouth.ac.uk/3695/1/CollSoc07.pdf

G Grassie, 'A UK digital copyright exchange: will the pipe dream ever become a reality?' (2012) 7(1) JIPLP 23

European Parliament Legal and Parliamentary Affairs Committee Study, 'Strengthening the Position of Press Publishers and Authors and Performers in the Copyright Directive' (2017)

European Parliament Legal Affairs Committee Study, 'Contractual Arrangements Applicable to Creators: Law and Practice of Selected Member States' (2014)

Orphan works

A Ross, 'Orphan works—the law's in place; now here's the process' [2015] Ent LR 40

Technical protection measures and rights management information systems

P Akester, 'The new challenges of striking the right balance between copyright protection and access to knowledge, information and culture' [2010] EIPR 372

P and R Akester, 'Digital rights management in the 21st century' [2006] EIPR 159

M Favale, 'Death and resurrection of copyright between law and technology' 23 (2014) Information & Communications Technology Law 117

Websites

Intellectual Property Office, Guidance on orphan works: www.gov.uk/guidance/copyright-orphan-works

EU Intellectual Property Office, Orphan Works Database: https://euipo.europa.eu/ohimportal/en/web/observatory/orphan-works-db

Rights akin to copyright: database right and performers' rights

Introduction

Scope and overview of chapter

7.1　This chapter considers two rights closely akin to copyright in many ways, in terms of both subject matter and the substantive contents of the rights. Both rights have also been relatively recently introduced into the armoury of intellectual property law. The rights in question are (1) the special or *sui generis* database right, which operates alongside the copyright in databases (for which see paras 3.48–3.50); and (2) performers' rights. The chapter gives an account of each of these rights, comparing them with copyright, but also underlining the differences between the regimes, and the reasons behind these differences.

7.2　**Learning objectives**

By the end of this chapter you should be able to describe and explain:

- the special or *sui generis* database right;
- performers' rights;
- the ways in which each of these rights compares with copyright;
- the reasons why these rights have been created and are distinct from copyright.

7.3　The chapter first explores the *sui generis* database right, explaining the reasons for its introduction by the Database Directive 1996 and considering in detail its exposition by the jurisprudence of the Court of Justice of the European Union (CJEU). The chapter then turns to performers' rights, again providing an introduction to the rights in their present form, and considering also developments now in prospect. So, the rest of the chapter looks like this:

- *Sui generis* database right (7.4–7.25)
- Performers' rights (7.26–7.46)

Sui generis database right

Reasons for introduction of the *sui generis* right

7.4   The Database Directive 1996[1] not only harmonised the copyright protection of databases in the EU, but also introduced an additional, special (*sui generis*) database right to protect those commercially valuable and expensively created databases henceforth believed to be excluded from copyright in some member states (notably the UK) by the higher originality requirement now imposed under the Directive (see paras 3.49–3.50).[2] The UK implemented the Directive in the Database Regulations 1997.[3]

Criteria for protection to arise

Definition of a database

7.5   The definition of database applying for copyright purposes (para 3.48) also applies for the *sui generis* right: (1) independence of the constituent elements; (2) systematic or methodical arrangement of the elements; and (3) individual accessibility of the elements.[4] However, there is no requirement of originality in the sense of 'intellectual creation' for the database right to subsist; that is, the database contents must still be organised in a systematic or methodical way but the system or method need not be a personal intellectual creation.[5] A database can consist of copyright-protected elements and, a collection of data contained within a copyright-protected work like a novel can also be a qualifying database for the *sui generis* right.[6]

Defining databases: (1) independence of the constituent elements

7.6   The constituent materials must be separable without their informative, literary, artistic, musical, or other value being affected.[7] So films as such are not databases, because there *is* interaction between script, music, sound recordings, and the moving images.[8] But an entry in a telephone directory can be understood standing alone, and so the directory is a database. Sports fixtures, the subject of several CJEU references, provide more complex examples. Is the fixture information, 'X v Y', an item which can be understood on its own? Is it separate from the date information without which 'X v Y' is probably meaningless? Or is 'X v Y, 1 January 2010' the single item of information which can be understood on its own and which therefore renders the whole collection of such items a potentially qualifying database? Data relating to sporting activity is not precluded from recognition as a database[9] and the combination of the date and time of, and the identity of two teams playing in, both home and away matches are covered by the concept of independent materials with autonomous informative value.[10] As such, not only an individual piece of information, but also a combination of pieces of information can constitute independent materials, following which geographical information on an analog topographical map such as tracks appropriate for cyclists, mountain bikers, and inline skaters, is not precluded from being independent material provided their extraction does not affect

---

[1]   Directive 96/9/EC of the European Parliament and of the Council of 11 March 1996 on the legal protection of databases.

[2]   Database Directive 1996, recitals 1–12, 38–39. On the purpose of the right see also *Football Dataco v Sportradar* [2013] ECC 12, paras 60 and 66.

[3]   Copyright and Rights in Databases Regulations 1997 (SI 1997/3032) and amended since by the Copyright and Rights in Databases (Amendment) Regulations 2003/2501. See generally E Derclaye, *The Legal Protection of Databases: A Comparative Analysis* (2008); T Aplin, *Copyright Law in the Digital Society: The Challenges of Multimedia* (2005), 41–73.

[4]   Database Regulations 1997, regs 6 and 12(1). See reg 18 for qualification requirement of the database maker.

[5]   So, eg, an arrangement of surnames in alphabetical order would attract database right provided the other criteria for protection are met.

[6]   *Football Dataco v Sportradar* [2013] ECC 12, paras 24–29.

[7]   Case C-444/02 *Fixtures Marketing Ltd v OPAP* [2004] ECR I-10549 (ECJ), para 29.

[8]   See also Database Directive 1996, recital 17: 'a recording or an audio visual cinematographic, literary or musical work as such does not fall within the scope of this Directive'.

[9]   Case C-444/02 *Fixtures Marketing Ltd v OPAP* [2004] ECR I-10549 (ECJ), paras 23 and 32–35.

[10]   Case C-604/10 *Football Dataco Ltd v Yahoo! UK Ltd* [2012] ECDR 10 (CJ), para 26.

the value of their informative content.[11] Further, merely because there is a decline in the informative value of material once extracted from a collection, such as a church on a map, it can still be 'independent material' if it retains autonomous informative value; but the autonomous informative value of such material must be assessed from the perspective of each third party interested in extracting the material, instead of the perspective of the typical user of the collection concerned.[12]

Defining databases: (2) systematic or methodical arrangement of the elements

7.7   The purpose of this requirement is 'to exclude random accumulations of data and ensure that only planned collections of data are covered, that is to say, data organised to specific criteria'.[13] The arrangement required here need not be a physical one,[14] but the European Court of Justice (ECJ) has stated that the condition implies that the collection should be contained in a fixed base of some kind; such a base may be technical (eg electronic, electro-magnetic, or electro-optical processes), or something else (eg an index, table of contents, or a particular plan or method of classification), to allow retrieval of any independent material contained within it.[15] Thus, the arrangement involved is *conceptual*, that is to say, it is about the way in which the contents are presented to and retrievable by the user of the database. Alphabetical, chronological, or subject arrangements will be enough to meet this element of the definition of a database.[16]

Defining databases: (3) individual accessibility of the elements

7.8   This requirement may seem ambiguous at first glance. Does it mean that the works or items comprising the database must be separately retrievable by the user and, if so, how must that access work? The ECJ has stated that a means of retrieving each of a database's constituent materials, technical or otherwise (as described in para 7.7), was what made it possible to distinguish a protected database from a mere collection.[17] Nevertheless, this and the previous requirement do not appear to be difficult to satisfy. A table consisting of 33 electronic addresses was held to be systematically arranged and individually accessible by virtue of its arrangement into columns and rows.[18] A pdf document was held to have individual accessibility because the contents can be accessed 'through electronic conversion, through digital character recognition, or old-fashioned reading or re-typing'.[19]

 Exercise

Take a printed telephone directory or sports fixture list. When you access an item of information therein (eg a person's telephone number you want to call, a match you want to attend), is it 'individually accessible by electronic or other means' simply because you can read it and ignore the rest of what is visible on the printed page? Or is it accessible only alongside the other information on the page, and therefore not individually or separately retrievable? Compare what happens if you search an electronic telephone directory for a particular person, or a fixtures database for the match on a particular date, or for the date your team plays its local 'derby' game on its home ground. Should there be a different result according to whether the information is collected in print or electronic form?

---

[11]   Case C-490/14 *Freistaat Bayern v Verlag Esterbauer GmbH* [2016] ECDR 6 (CJ), paras 20–21.   [12] ibid, paras 24 and 27.
[13]   Case C-444/02 *Fixtures Marketing Ltd v OPAP* [2004] ECR I-10549 (AG), para 40.   [14] Database Directive 1996, recital 21.
[15]   Case C-444/02 *Fixtures Marketing Ltd v OPAP* [2004] ECR I-10549 (ECJ), para 30.
[16]   Although note that for copyright protection to subsist in a database, there is the additional requirement of originality in that the selection and arrangement must be an 'intellectual creation', for which see further para 3.49.
[17]   Case C-444/02 *Fixtures Marketing Ltd v OPAP* [2004] ECR I-10549 (ECJ), paras 31–32.
[18]   *Forensic Telecommunications Services Ltd v Chief Constable of West Yorkshire Police* [2011] EWHC 2892 (Ch).
[19]   *Technomed Ltd v Bluecrest Health Screening Ltd* [2017] EWHC 2142 (Ch), para 69.

Database right and copyright in a database

7.9 A database enjoying copyright protection is not precluded from also enjoying database right. The relevance of this is that database right confers protection against extraction and re-utilisation of the contents of the database where it amounts to a substantial part (see further paras 7.16–7.20) rather than the copyright protection for the selection and arrangement of the contents. The database right protects the database itself, and no copyright is created in the underlying data.[20] The principal substantive ground for database right protection is the creator's substantial investment in obtaining, verifying, or presenting the contents of the database, and it is immaterial whether or not the database is also a copyright work; that is, is an intellectual creation of the compiler in its selection or arrangement.[21]

Question

Can a copyright-protected database also be protected by the *sui generis* right? Will a database protected by the *sui generis* right also have copyright?

Obtaining, verifying, or presenting the contents of the database

7.10 Database right arises where there has been substantial investment in 'obtaining, verifying or presenting the contents of the database'.[22] The first question to which this has given rise is whether, if the investment is in *creating* rather than *obtaining* data, database right is excluded. In other words, must the data exist before the investment is made? The ECJ's answer to this question, in the leading cases decided in 2004, surprised many.

■ *British Horseracing Board v William Hill Organization Ltd* [2001] RPC 31 (Laddie J); [2002] ECDR 4 (CA); Case C-203/02 [2005] RPC 13 (ECJ); [2005] RPC 35 (CA)

The British Horseracing Board (BHB) administered British horse-racing, creating the fixture lists each year, and distributing information about races to subscribers.[23] WHO were subscribers who used the BHB data in relation to their betting services. An issue arose between the parties about whether WHO's unauthorised use of the BHB data in its new internet betting service infringed BHB's database right. The Court of Appeal referred the question of whether 'obtaining' covered 'creating' as well as 'compiling' to the ECJ. The ECJ held that merely creating data did *not* amount to obtaining it, or to its verification or presentation. Investment in 'obtaining' involved the seeking out and collecting of existing independent materials in a database, not the investment in creation of such independent materials (paras 29–34). The Court of Appeal then applied this interpretation of the law to deny the existence of database right in BHB's database, since BHB created the data rather than collecting it from existing independent sources. The decision appears to restrict considerably the scope of protection given by the *sui generis* right.[24]

Discussion point   For answer guidance visit www.oup.com/uk/brown5e.

Explain why the exclusion of creation from obtaining limits the scope of *sui generis* database right.

---

[20] *Football Dataco v Sportradar* [2013] ECC 12, para 24.   [21] Database Regulations 1997, reg 13.   [22] ibid.

[23] For a useful analysis of the legal outcomes of the whole litigation, see J Jenkins, 'Database rights' subsistence: under starter's orders' (2006) 1 JIPLP 467.

[24] See MJ Davison and PB Hugenholtz, 'Football fixtures, horseraces and spin offs: the ECJ domesticates the database right' [2005] EIPR 113; T Aplin, 'The ECJ elucidates the database right' [2005] IPQ 204.

The difficult distinction between creating data and obtaining pre-existent data can be understood through decisions regarding databases containing information about football matches in England and Scotland. The ECJ provided the same reasoning as the horse-racing case in a group of cases concerned with football fixture lists (the *Fixtures* cases),[25] meaning that organisation of football leagues by deploying sources for determining dates, times, and team pairings for home and away matches involves creating data. Subsequently, fixture lists have been denied database protection in the UK.[26]

■ *Football Dataco Ltd v Sportradar* [2012] ECC 26 (ChD) (Floyd J); [2013] ECC 12 (CA)

F was a provider of Football Live database containing live data from football matches, such as goals and their times, scorers, assists, type of shot, etc. Such data would be provided by a football analyst, paid by F to be present at match grounds, to a sports information processor, as a running commentary, and entered into F's systems. F estimated the operation to cost £600,000 per season and exploited the database by licensing it to various customers. At first instance, Floyd J distinguished 'fixtures data' (eg team pairings), which are created by event organisers, from 'match data' (eg goals), which are created by the footballers, with the organisers only providing the environment for them to be scored. He held that 'factual data which is collected and recorded at a live event' relating to 'events outside the control of the person doing the collection and recording is not created by that person, but is obtained by him' (para 60). Collecting and recording data falls within the ordinary meaning of 'obtaining' but 'creating' suggests creation of new information.[27] The recording of existing facts, such as the fact of a goal which is created when the ball hits the back of the net, is not the same as creating new information (para 61). The Court of Appeal affirmed that F's database qualified for protection (paras 31–69). The court rejected the argument that the act of recording a fact amounts to creation of data, or that data that has not been previously recorded (eg a goal) cannot be collected. Instead, it was noted that 'a scientist who takes a measurement would be astonished to be told that she was creating data. She would say she is creating a record of pre-existing fact, recording data, not creating it' (para 39). The requirement of seeking out 'existing independent materials' did not preclude 'measuring a temperature or recording an event' (para 49). Although 'Football Live' contained a mixture of data, both objective (eg goals and scorers) and subjective (eg man of the match), collected by one indivisible process, the objective elements were generated on the field and not as a result of F's resources (which were not used to create those elements but merely to collect the data that was generated). The court held that it would be absurd for the database to lose protection because it included some subjective elements and the purpose of database right protection would be lost. However, the extraction of such subjective elements would not be protected by the database right (paras 61–68).

7.11   'Obtaining' data is only one of three alternative ways in which an investment may be rewarded with database right. There may still be protection by way of 'verification' and 'presentation' for the creator of data *later* put into a database. Verification involves checking the accuracy, completeness, and reliability of the data *once in the database*, while presentation is about giving the database its function of processing information; that is, the resources used for the systematic or methodical arrangement of the data and the organisation of their individual accessibility.[28] So the concept includes materials necessary for the operation or consultation of the database by users such as thesaurus and indexation systems, as well as the structuring of the contents (the conceptual as distinct from the external format of the database). What is crucial is that, to be relevant for the establishment of *sui generis* protection, investment in verification and presentation must be subsequent to and not part of the process of creation of the data.

---

[25] Cases C-338/02 *Fixtures Marketing Ltd v Svenska Spel AB* [2005] ECDR 4 (ECJ), paras 24–31; C-444/02 *Fixtures Marketing Ltd v OPAP* [2004] ECR I-10549 (ECJ), paras 40–47; and C-46/02 *Fixtures Marketing Ltd v Oy Veikkaus Ab* [2005] ECDR 2 (ECJ), paras 34–42.

[26] *Football Dataco Ltd v Brittens Pools Ltd* [2010] RPC 17 (ChD), para 92; *Football Dataco Ltd v Brittens Pools Ltd* [2011] ECDR 9 (CA), paras 10–12.

[27] See also *British Sky Broadcasting Group plc v Digital Satellite Warranty Cover Ltd (In Liquidation)* [2012] FSR 14 (Ch D), paras 19–21.

[28] Cases C-338/02 *Fixtures Marketing Ltd v Svenska Spel AB* [2005] ECDR 4 (ECJ), para 27; C-444/02 *Fixtures Marketing Ltd v OPAP* [2004] ECR I-10549 (ECJ), para 43; C-46/02 *Fixtures Marketing Ltd v Oy Veikkaus Ab* [2005] ECDR 2 (ECJ), para 37; and C-203/02 *British Horseracing Board Ltd v William Hill Organization Ltd* [2005] RPC 13 (ECJ), paras 34–41. See also recital 20 of the Database Directive 1996.

Discussion point   For answer guidance visit **www.oup.com/uk/brown5e**.

Consider the derivation of data from naturally occurring phenomena such as the weather or the genetic sequences of living creatures. Is that derivation an act of creation or obtaining for the purposes
of *sui generis* database right? Read the Court of Appeal decision in *Football Dataco Ltd v Sportradar*
[2013] ECC 12 at paras 31–69 and the sources mentioned therein.

Substantial investment

7.12   The investment necessary for the existence of database right need not be merely financial, but can include
human, technical, and professional resources, as well as the expenditure of time, effort, and energy.[29] The
substantiality of an investment may be measured qualitatively and/or quantitatively.[30] In her Opinion in
Fixtures Marketing v Svenska, the Advocate General said that the substantiality of an investment is to be
assessed 'first in relation to costs and their redemption and secondly in relation to the scale, nature and
contents of the database and the sector to which it belongs'. But she added that substantiality is not only
a relative matter: 'the Directive requires an absolute lower threshold for investments worthy of protection
as a sort of de minimis rule'.[31] This was justified by reference to recital 19 of the Directive, which states
that, as a rule (ie usually), the compilation of several recordings of musical performances on a CD does
not represent a substantial enough investment to be eligible for the *sui generis* right.[32] The difficulty is in
using this rather specific example as a basis for determining what is the minimum threshold making an
investment substantial, or indeed that there is such a requirement. The ECJ did not comment on this aspect
of the Advocate General's Opinion.

'Spin-off' databases

7.13   Are 'spin-off' databases—databases created as a by-product or a sort of side effect of activity and investment
of resources which had other aims primarily in mind—excluded from database right protection? For
example, investing in the creation of sports fixture lists or a horse-racing calendar is not done just to build a
database, but to organise and structure the season of the sport in question and provide advance information
for participants, the media, and potential spectators. The Advocate General took the view in the *Fixtures*
cases that the Directive imposes no requirement as to the purpose for which the database is created and,
in principle, spin-off databases could be protected.[33] The Court of Appeal has noted that the ECJ in *British
Horseracing Board v William Hill Organization* had rejected the spin-off theory as the basis of excluding
protection and essentially indicated that 'spin-off' databases can be protected by the *sui generis* right if there
is additional substantial investment directed specifically at the creation of the database, above and beyond,
and independent of, the investment in data creation, most probably in the verification or presentation of
the data contained within it.[34]

[29]   Database Regulations 1997, reg 12(1); Cases C-338/02 *Fixtures Marketing Ltd v Svenska Spel AB* [2005] ECDR 4 (ECJ), para 28; C-444/02
Fixtures Marketing Ltd v OPAP [2004] ECR I-10549 (ECJ), para 44; and C-46/02 *Fixtures Marketing Ltd v Oy Veikkaus Ab* [2005] ECDR 2
(ECJ), para 38.
[30]   Database Regulations 1997, reg 12(1); Cases C-338/02 *Fixtures Marketing Ltd v Svenska Spel AB* [2005] ECDR 4 (ECJ), para 28; C-444/02
Fixtures Marketing Ltd v OPAP [2004] ECR I-10549 (ECJ), para 44; and C-46/02 *Fixtures Marketing Ltd v Oy Veikkaus Ab* [2005] ECDR 2
(ECJ), para 38.
[31]   C-338/02 *Fixtures Marketing Ltd v Svenska Spel AB* [2004] ECR I-10497, paras 38–39 (AG) (for both quotations).
[32]   Database Directive 1996, recital 19.
[33]   C-338/02 *Fixtures Marketing Ltd v Svenska Spel AB* [2004] ECR I-10497, paras 41–45, 57 (AG).
[34]   *Football Dataco v Sportradar* [2013] ECC 12 (CA), paras 53–54. See also, Cases C-338/02 *Fixtures Marketing Ltd v Svenska Spel AB*
[2005] ECDR 4 (ECJ), paras 23–29; C-444/02 *Fixtures Marketing Ltd v OPAP* [2004] ECR I-10549 (ECJ), paras 39–45; and C-46/02 *Fixtures
Marketing Ltd v Oy Veikkaus Ab* [2005] ECDR 2 (ECJ), paras 33–39.

> **Key points on *sui generis* database right**
>
> - The right covers databases (collections of independent data, arranged systematically, individually accessible).
> - Selection and arrangement need not be original (contrast copyright protection).
> - There needs to be substantial investment (financial/human/technical/professional; qualitative and/or quantitative) in:
>   - obtaining (*not* creating—horse-racing and football fixtures cases)
>   - verifying
>   - presenting
>
>   the contents of the database.

First ownership

7.14   The maker of a database is the first owner of the *sui generis* database right in it.[35] There is a presumption that a name appearing on copies of a database as its maker is the maker unless the contrary is proved.[36] The maker is the person taking the initiative in obtaining, verifying, or presenting the database contents and assuming the risk of investing in those activities.[37] If, however, a database is anonymous, in the sense that it is not possible by reasonable inquiry to ascertain its maker's identity, and it is reasonable to assume that database right has expired, then extraction and re-utilisation of the database contents is not infringement.[38] There may be joint makers if two or more parties collaborate in taking the initiative and assuming the risk.[39] Where an employee makes a database in the course of employment, the employer is to be regarded as the maker in the absence of any agreement to the contrary.[40] There is also provision for Crown and parliamentary database right.[41]

Duration

7.15   The *sui generis* database right has its own special period of duration which, on the face of it, is much shorter than any of the main copyright terms.[42] The right lasts for 15 years from the end of the year in which the making of the database was completed, or in which it was first made available to the public if that event occurs before the end of the first period.

Figure 7.1 Duration of database right

---

[35] Database Regulations 1997, reg 15.   [36] Database Regulations 1997, reg 22.   [37] Database Regulations 1997, reg 14(1).
[38] Database Regulations 1997, reg 21.   [39] Database Regulations 1997, reg 14(5).
[40] Database Regulations 1997, reg 14(2); cf *Cureton v Mark Insulations Ltd* [2006] EWHC 2279, where an issue was ownership of a database in an agency relationship, and Bean J held that a sales agent was the first owner of a customer database prepared on behalf of and paid for by its principal.
[41] Database Regulations 1997, reg 14(3)–(4A).
[42] Database Regulations 1997, reg 17 (see also reg 30).

However, the right can last much longer than either of these 15-year periods, because any substantial change to the contents of a database (eg, arising from additions, deletions, or alterations to its content) which would result in the database being considered a substantial new investment will qualify the database resulting from that investment for its own new 15-year period of protection. The same result might follow from a substantial investment in verification of the contents of the database.[43] A dynamic database could therefore end up with a rolling series of 15-year protections which will keep the right alive as long as the owner thinks it worthwhile to continue investment in it.[44]

Figure 7.2 Duration of database right after substantial investment

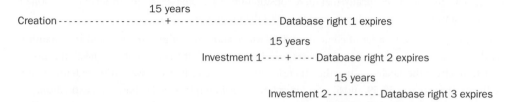

Creation - - - - - - - - - - - - - - - - - - - + - - - - - - - - - - - - - - - - - - - Database right 1 expires

Investment 1 - - - - + - - - - Database right 2 expires

Investment 2 - - - - - - - - - Database right 3 expires

Infringement

7.16   The *sui generis* database right has its own infringement regime distinct from that of copyright.[45] *Unauthorised extraction from or re-utilisation of all or a substantial part of the database* is prohibited.

> Extraction means 'in relation to any contents of a database, . . . the permanent or temporary transfer of those contents to another medium by any means or in any form' (Database Regulations 1997, reg 12(1)). Re-utilisation means 'in relation to any contents of a database, . . . making these contents available to the public by any means' (Database Regulations 1997, reg 12(1)).

Rental or lending of a database otherwise than for direct or indirect economic or commercial advantage through an establishment accessible to the public is not extraction or re-utilisation for these purposes;[46] but this does not apply to making available for on-the-spot reference use.[47] Payment which does no more than cover the establishment's costs gives rise to no direct or indirect economic or commercial advantage.[48] The rights are exhausted after the *first sale* of the database in the European Economic Area (EEA), as long as that sale was with the consent of the owner of the database right.[49]

Extraction and re-utilisation of a substantial part

7.17   The meaning of the infringement provisions of the Database Directive was considered in detail by the ECJ in the *British Horseracing Board* case[50] (for facts of the case, see para 7.10). The following points emerge from the Court's judgment:

- The terms 'extraction' and 're-utilisation' must be interpreted in the light of the objective pursued by the *sui generis* right (para 45). The concepts of extraction and re-utilisation are intended to have a wide definition, cannot be exhaustively defined, and must be 'interpreted as referring to any act of

---

[43] Database Regulations 1997, reg 17(3). Database Directive 1996, recital 55.

[44] See the Opinion of the Advocate General in Case C-203/02 *British Horseracing Board Ltd v William Hill Organization Ltd* [2005] RPC 13, paras 143–154.

[45] Database Regulations 1997, reg 16.

[46] Database Regulations 1997, reg 12(2).   [47] Database Regulations 1997, reg 12(4).   [48] Database Regulations 1997, reg 12(3).

[49] Database Regulations 1997, reg 12(5).   [50] [2005] RPC 13.

appropriating and making available to the public, without the consent of the maker of the database, the results of his investment, thus depriving him of revenue which should have enabled him to redeem the cost of the investment' (paras 51–52). The purpose of extraction and re-utilisation, whether for creating another database or a commercial or non-commercial purpose, is irrelevant (paras 47–48).

- Extraction and re-utilisation can be either direct or indirect; that is, either from the database itself, or from a copy of the database (paras 52–53). The context is provided by the facts of the case, where the defendants had obtained the data, not from BHB's database, but from one of BHB's licensed distributors. Since temporary transfer of database contents is specifically included in relation to extraction, it would appear that any unauthorised access to a database would be extraction. However, the ECJ said specifically, albeit delphically, that mere consultation of a database was not an act of extraction or re-utilisation, but gave no further guidance on this distinction (para 54).

- Extraction meant the transfer of contents of database to another medium and covered any unauthorised act of appropriation. It does imply transfer in the sense that the contents in question must be transferred from the database altogether; there is extraction even when afterwards the contents remain on the database (paras 58, 59, and 67). So, for example, a printout from a database is an extraction.[51]

- Re-utilisation is making available to the public the database contents and covers any unauthorised distribution to the public. It therefore embraces both online transmission and distribution or rental/lending of the database, and is not limited to a right to first publication of the contents (paras 58, 59, and 67). Exhaustion only arises in relation to the sale of physical copies of the database (eg on CD and DVD).[52]

- Substantiality of the part of the database extracted or re-utilised can be assessed both quantitatively and qualitatively. A quantitative measure is the volume of data extracted compared to the volume of the contents of the whole database; while a qualitative measure is the scale of the investment required in relation to the material extracted or re-utilised. The intrinsic value of the data, as distinct from the cost of the investment, is not a relevant consideration for the qualitative measurement of the substantiality of a part (paras 70–72). Finally, 'it must be held', said the Court, 'that any part which does not fulfil the definition of a substantial part, evaluated both quantitatively and qualitatively, falls within the definition of an insubstantial part of the contents of a database' (para 73).

While the ECJ only gives guidance to national courts on the interpretation of Union law, it did make the following comment on how, in the light of its opinion, summarised in the previous points, on the meaning of the infringement provisions of the Database Directive, this case should be decided. Thus, as far as concerned the quantitative measure of whether a substantial part of the database had been extracted or re-utilised:

> the materials displayed on William Hill's internet sites, which derive from the BHB database, represent only a very small proportion of . . . that database . . . It must therefore be held that those materials do not constitute a substantial part, evaluated quantitatively, of the contents of that database (para 74).

With regard to qualitative measurement:[53]

> The intrinsic value of the data affected . . . does not constitute a relevant criterion for assessing whether the part in question is substantial, evaluated qualitatively. The fact that the data extracted and re-utilised by WH are vital to the organisation of the [BHB] horse races . . . is thus irrelevant to the assessment . . . [of] substantial part (para 78).

7.18   Several recent decisions provide guidance on the interpretation of extraction, re-utilisation, and substantial part, as well as proof and place of infringement.

---

[51] See also para 100 (AG); [2001] RPC 31, para 57.   [52] See also para 109 (AG).

[53] This and the preceding issue were not considered when the case returned to the Court of Appeal, since there it was decided that the database in question was not protected by the *sui generis* right ([2005] RPC 35).

■ Case C-304/07 *Directmedia Publishing GmbH v Albert-Ludwigs-Universitat Freiburg* [2008] ECR I-7565 (ECJ)

This case concerned alleged infringement of a university's *sui generis* database right in a list of poetry titles. D used the database as a guide to the creation of its CD-ROM entitled *1,000 poems everyone should have*, omitting certain poems, adding others and critically examining each selection made by the professor who created the original database. Despite D taking the texts of each poem from its own resources, the ECJ held that the concept of 'extraction' covered the transfer of material from a protected database to another database following an on-screen consultation of the first database and an individual assessment of the extracted contents. The Court noted that the objective of the Directive is to guarantee the maker of a database, created through substantial human, financial, or technical resource investment, a return on the investment involved without unauthorised appropriation of the results at a fraction of the cost needed to design it independently. As such, extraction is to be given a wide meaning (paras 33–34). The concept is 'not dependent on the nature and form of the mode of operation used' and covers an act of transfer of 'all or part of the contents of the database concerned to another medium, whether of the same nature as the medium of that database or of a different nature' (paras 35–36). Therefore, extraction is not limited to physical taking, and also includes taking that is preceded by the taker's critical evaluation of the material. The information 'extracted' from the database could be transferred in any way to another medium, such as manual recopying, photocopying, or downloading. It was irrelevant that the copied information was adapted into a different format. The objective pursued in the act of transfer was also immaterial.

■ Case C-545/07 *Apis-Hristovich EOOD v Lakorda AD* [2009] 3 CMLR 3 (ECJ)

A, which operated a legal database, claimed that L, which had been set up by two ex-employees of A, infringed its database rights by extracting without A's consent substantial parts of two modules of the database. These extracted elements, it was argued, were used by the defendants to develop a similar system. L argued that it had invested significant independent time and money in the new database. Any similarities to the two modules were argued to be due to the fact that the legal sources relied upon were publicly available. The Court held that protection could be claimed in database sub-groups provided that each sub-group qualified as a protected database. If they did, the level of extraction was compared against the amount of data in the sub-group. If they did not, the level of extraction was measured against the entire database, rather than its constituent parts. While 'extraction' should be given a broad definition, the purpose of extraction was irrelevant, as was the unique feature of the new database. Furthermore, the Court noted that the public availability of materials did not preclude protection as long as there had been qualitative and/or quantitative substantial investment when obtaining, verifying, or presenting the contents of the database. Additionally, the use of hyperlinks or other such similar features in both databases could be indicative, though not determinative, of extraction, as could such materials not available to the public.

■ Case C-173/11 *Football Dataco v Sportradar* [2013] FSR 4 (CJ); [2013] ECC 12 (CA)

For the facts of this case, see para 7.10. F claimed database right infringement against S, a German company and its Swiss parent company which provided live football statistics via the internet through its service *Sport Live Data*. S held its data in a member state outside the UK but the public in the UK could access the service. The Court of Justice (CJ) noted that the database right protection, although harmonised, is provided by the national law of a member state and as such acts of infringement must take place in that member state. It held that re-utilisation covers the act of sending data, previously extracted from a protected database, by means of a web server in member state A, to another person's computer in member state B, at their request, for the purpose of storage in that computer's memory and display on its screen. Such re-utilisation takes place, at least, in member state B, if there is evidence from which it may be concluded that the act discloses an intention on the part of the sender to target members of the public in member state B (para 47). The Court of Appeal held S liable for infringement.

■ *Beechwood House Publishing Ltd v Guardian Products Ltd* [2011] EWHC 22 (PCC)

B, a publisher of a database consisting of details of individuals associated with GP practices, put seeds—dummy or fictitious entries not belonging to real people but to addresses of its staff—in its database which led them to find out that G, a direct marketing information provider, was using information from its database for printed mail outs. Judge Birss QC held that 6,000 practice nurse records which were extracted by G for a mailing exercise, representing about 14 per cent of the database, was a quantitatively substantial part, even if it was at the lower end of what could be regarded as such. Alternatively, it was a qualitatively substantial part as the scale of human and financial investment they represented was significant.[54]

Repeated and systematic extraction/re-utilisation of insubstantial parts

7.19   Repeated and systematic extraction/re-utilisation of *insubstantial* parts of database contents may amount to the extraction/re-utilisation of a substantial part of those contents.[55] In the *British Horseracing Board* case,[56] Laddie J held that the defendant's daily use of the BHB database was caught by this provision, but the issue of its meaning was referred to the ECJ by the Court of Appeal. The Advocate General made clear that repetition and system are cumulative rather than alternative requirements, and imply acts at regular intervals such as weekly or monthly. The ECJ noted that the purpose of the rule was to prevent circumvention of the basic exclusive right conferred by the Directive by a series of insubstantial acts which would cumulatively cause serious prejudice to the investment of the maker of the database. It went on to hold that the prohibition affected repeated and systematic acts leading to the reconstitution of the whole database or a substantial part of it, whether or not the acts were carried out to create such a database. Third parties were also prevented from repeated and systematic making available to the public of insubstantial parts of the database.

7.20   The Directive says that the repeated and systematic acts must either (1) conflict with normal exploitation of the database; or (2) unreasonably prejudice the legitimate interests of its maker.[57] The ECJ held that this refers to serious prejudice to the database maker's investment by unauthorised acts the cumulative effect of which is (a) the reconstitution; or (b) making available to the public, of the whole or a substantial part of the contents of a protected database.[58] The Court concluded that the defendant's acts in this case would not result in the reconstitution of the BHB database, or in making it available to the public, so the prohibition did not apply. However, in *Innoweb v Wegener*, the CJ held that an operator of a meta search engine re-utilises a database when it provides the user with the same search facility as the database, translates user queries by searching all the information on that database's search engine, and presents results in an order comparable to the database's engine.[59]

> ### Key points on infringement of *sui generis* database right
>
> - The right is infringed by unauthorised extraction or re-utilisation of all or a substantial part of the database.
>
> - Extraction is transfer of database contents to another medium (but removal is not needed).
>
> - Re-utilisation is making database contents available to the public by any form of distribution.

---

[54] For another example of a successful case of database infringement, see *Forensic Telecommunications Services Ltd v Chief Constable of West Yorkshire* [2011] EWHC 2892 (Ch).

[55] Database Regulations 1997, reg 16(2).   [56] [2001] RPC 31 (Laddie J); [2002] ECDR 4 (CA); Case C-203/02 [2005] RPC 13 (ECJ).

[57] Database Directive 1996, Art 7(5); not transposed as such in the 1997 Regulations.   [58] [2005] RPC 13, para 89.

[59] Case C-202/12 [2014] Bus LR 308 (CJ).

- Extraction/re-utilisation are to be given a wide meaning and may be direct or indirect.

- Substantiality is measured both quantitatively and qualitatively, but the intrinsic value of the data is not a factor in this assessment.

- Repeated and systematic extraction/re-utilisation of insubstantial parts may cumulatively amount to extraction/re-utilisation of a substantial part.

Exceptions

7.21   The Database Regulations 1997 provides for exceptions for non-commercial research and teaching and also a deposit library exception.[60] Unlike copyright, there are no exceptions for the purposes of criticism, review, and reporting current events. The Database Regulations do, however, make it clear that a lawful user of a database which has been made available to the public in any manner shall be entitled to extract or re-utilise an *insubstantial* part of the contents of the database for any purpose,[61] and that any term in an agreement purporting to limit this entitlement shall be void.[62] This illustrates that contract provisions may not be used to extend the scope of the *sui generis* right itself; it is infringed only by taking of a *substantial* part of the database contents (see paras 7.16–7.20). However, such a mandatory right for the 'lawful user' of a protected database is not available to users of unprotected databases (those that are not protected by either copyright or *sui generis* right), authors of which are not precluded from laying down contractual limitations to prevent its use by third parties.[63]

7.22   There is an exception, like copyright, permitting extraction for non-commercial research purposes from a database protected by the *sui generis* database right.[64] The database must have been made available to the public, and the person making the extraction must already be a lawful user apart from the exception. The source must be acknowledged. The exception covers only extraction of a substantial part of the database, so presumably extraction of an insubstantial part, not being infringement, requires no exception. It is worth noting that the ECJ has said in the *British Horseracing Board* case that mere consultation of a database is not extraction of the database.[65] No similar exception exists for the other act restricted by database right, re-utilisation.

7.23   There is also an exception to allow extraction (but, again, not re-utilisation) from a database made available to the public, by one already a lawful user of the database, for the purpose of illustration for teaching and not for any commercial purpose, as long as the source is indicated.[66]

 Discussion point   For answer guidance visit **www.oup.com/uk/brown5e**.

Why do the non-commercial research and teaching exceptions apply only to extraction of content from a database and not to its re-utilisation?

---

[60]   Database Regulations 1997, regs 20 and 20A. See also reg 20B and Sch1.   [61]Database Regulations 1997, reg 19(1).

[62]   Database Regulations 1997, reg 19(2). Note there is no equivalent provision preventing contractual override in regs 20 and 20A.

[63]   Case C-30/14 *Ryanair v PR Aviation* [2015] ECDR 13 (CJ). The decision has been criticised for giving stronger contractual protection to unprotected databases, especially sole-source databases, as a result of which both user access and the functioning of the internal market is hindered; see M Borghi and S Karapapa, 'Contractual restrictions on lawful use of information: sole-source databases protected by the back door?' [2015] EIPR 505.

[64]   Database Regulations 1997, reg 20; cf the equivalent copyright exception, discussed at para 5.25.

[65]   [2005] RPC 13, para 54.   [66]   Database Regulations 1997, reg 20.

Exercise

Compare the exceptions to *sui generis* database right with the exceptions to copyright in a database (see para 5.15 ff). Are the two systems compatible? Is it possible to exclude exceptions to *sui generis* database right by contractual agreement between the rightholder and user?

Key points on exceptions to *sui generis* database right

- The principal exceptions are for non-commercial research and teaching.
- These exceptions are only in relation to extraction and not to re-utilisation.

Commission's evaluation of database right

7.24   The *sui generis* database right has met with mixed results,[67] and there remain fundamental concerns about the necessity and relevance of the *sui generis* right. The first evaluation of the right by the European Commission noted that decisions of the ECJ had substantially curtailed the right.[68] The Commission's research also suggested that the *sui generis* right had anyway failed to achieve its objective of boosting the global competitiveness of the European database industry. Abolition of the right was accordingly one of the options in the first evaluation, along with amendment of the Directive to reverse the effects of the Court decisions, repeal of the whole Directive, or doing nothing, simply awaiting further judicial decisions. The last always looked the likeliest outcome, and the cases that have emerged since have shown a broader view being taken of the right's scope. However, a recent decision has, arguably, given stronger contractual protection to unprotected databases, and consequently, made database protection far less attractive (para 7.21).

7.25   The Commission published a second evaluation in 2018 where it noted that the conclusions of the 2005 evaluation remain applicable and there was no evidence to show that the database right 'has been fully effective in stimulating investment in the European database industry, nor in creating a fully functioning access regime for stakeholders'.[69] However, it concluded that the benefits of the right, albeit moderate, are higher than the costs, and keeping the current status quo would be a good option, as reforming the right would be largely disproportionate at this stage. Despite this conclusion, several concerns, some of which were raised in the second evaluation, remain applicable. Since the right protects against extraction and re-utilisation of the contents of the database, and not merely the selection and arrangement thereof, does it preclude access to that which in the past has circulated freely amongst would-be users? An example which has been much discussed is scientific information, now commonly held on databases. Another example is public-sector datasets. The policy issues that remain here, as such, are fundamental: are the exceptions to the *sui generis* database right too narrow? What is the social cost of database right protection? Does the right serve any useful purpose, and should it be amended in any particular way?

 Exercise

Read the second evaluation of the Database Right Directive 1996 published in 2018. What advantages and disadvantages of the *sui generis* database right are raised by relevant stakeholders in the evaluation? Do you agree with the Commission's conclusions?

---

[67] See E Derclaye, *The Legal Protection of Databases: A Comparative Analysis* (2008).

[68] See European Commission Working Paper, First Evaluation of Directive 96/9/EC (2005).

[69] European Commission, Staff Working Document, Evaluation of Directive 96/9/EC (2018), p.46. The evaluation was supported by an external study. See https://ec.europa.eu/digital-single-market/en/protection-databases.

Database right and Brexit

The *sui generis* database right subsists because of the EU Database Directive 1996. This is an example of EU law that goes beyond the provisions of the international treaties, and provides for rights unique to the EU: ie database rights are available to the nationals, residents, and businesses of all the EEA member states (Database Regulations 1997, reg 18) but not non-EEA nationals, residents, and businesses. The Political Declaration on the future relationship with the EU indicates an intention to preserve the database right in the UK.[70] In a 'no-deal' scenario, the UK government plans to retain the database right domestically and has indicated that 'database rights that exist in the UK prior to exit (whether held by UK or EEA persons or businesses) will continue to exist in the UK' and 'UK legislation will be amended so that only UK citizens, residents, and businesses are eligible for new database rights after exit.'[71] However, in these circumstances, the reciprocity under cross-border protection in this area will not be available. As such, the government's 'no-deal' guidance indicates that 'there will be no obligation for EEA states to provide database rights to UK nationals, residents, and businesses' and that 'UK owners may want to consider relying on other forms of protection (e.g. restrictive licensing agreements or copyright where applicable) for their databases.'[72]

Performers' rights

Introduction

7.26   Performers[73] were, historically, not well protected in the UK and the UK acts appeared to give rise to only criminal liability.[74] The Rome Convention for the Protection of Performers, Producers of Phonograms and Broadcasting Organizations 1961 provided the international basis for performers' protection. But it only gives performers the possibility of 'preventing' a list of acts, rather than a right to authorise and prohibit them in advance.[75] Thus, it was argued that the approach through the criminal law could continue.[76] However, in 1977 the Whitford Committee[77] recommended that performers should be given a civil right of action for injunctions and damages, but that this should not amount to copyright. The Copyright, Designs and Patents Act 1988 (CDPA 1988) introduced two distinct kinds of civil rights in performances: non-property rights (personal and non-assignable) and property rights (assignable).[78] In addition, performers now also have moral rights and remuneration rights.

Discussion point   For answer guidance visit **www.oup.com/uk/brown5e**.

Look up the historical background to protection of performers' rights. Why was such protection weak?

---

[70] UK Government Draft political declaration setting out the framework for the future relationship between the United Kingdom and the European Union (22 November 2018), para 45 www.gov.uk/government/publications/draft-political-declaration-setting-out-the-framework-for-the-future-relationship-between-the-european-union-and-the-united-kingdom-agreed-at-negotia.

[71] UK Government, 'Changes to copyright law in the event of no deal' (26 October 2018) www.gov.uk/government/publications/changes-to-copyright-law-in-the-event-of-no-deal/changes-to-copyright-law-in-the-event-of-no-deal.

[72] UK Government, 'Copyright if there's no Brexit deal' (24 September 2018) www.gov.uk/government/publications/copyright-if-theres-no-brexit-deal.

[73] See generally R Arnold, *Performers' Rights* (5th edn, 2015).

[74] See Dramatic and Musical Performers' Protection Act 1925; *Rickless v United Artists Corp* [1988] QB 40.

[75] Article 7; cf Articles 10 and 13.

[76] D Llewelyn and T Aplin, *Cornish, Llewelyn and Aplin Intellectual Property: Patents, Copyright, Trade Marks and Allied Rights* (9th edn, 2019), para 14.030.

[77] Cmnd 6732.   [78] See CDPA 1988, ss 191A and 192A.

7.27   A number of EU Directives further changed the position for performers. Measures affecting the position of performers are to be found in the following:

- Rental Right Directive;[79]
- Satellite and Cable Directive[80] (which applies these requirements to satellite broadcasting);
- Term Directive;[81] and
- InfoSoc Directive.[82]

Each of these resulted in significant amendments to the CDPA 1988.[83]

Current law on performers' rights

7.28   A performer is not defined in the Act, but a performance means a dramatic performance (including dance or mime), a musical one, a reading or recitation of a literary work, or a performance of a variety act or any similar presentation.[84] The term 'variety act' is not defined. It can include performances by magicians, clowns, jugglers, acrobats (all involving human performers).[85] It can also include an animal act where a human and animal are working together, with each playing 'a necessary part', particularly where their presentation has been rehearsed.[86] There is no requirement for a performance to be in public and in any performance given by more than one person, each performer would be entitled to rights in their own part.[87] Performers' rights arise in respect of qualifying performances: a performance given by a qualifying individual or one that takes place in a qualifying country.[88]

 Question

The Edinburgh Festivals, which take place every year in the summer, see a plethora of interesting, diverse, and ingenious individuals engaged in all manner of behaviour. Under the statutory definition of a performance, would the following meet the requirements:

- an individual dressed as a Greek Goddess standing stock still on an upturned bucket in the middle of the Royal Mile;
- a group of individuals attentively engaged in drawing collaborative pictures on the pavement;

---

[79] Originally Council Directive 92/100/EEC on rental right and lending right and on certain rights related to copyright in the field of intellectual property; now in a consolidated version, European Parliament and Council Directive 2006/115/EC. For a challenge to the UK implementation of the Rental Right Directive, see *Phonographic Performance Limited v Department of Trade and Industry and Another* [2004] 3 CMLR 31 (ChD).

[80] Council Directive 93/83/EEC on the coordination of certain rules concerning copyright and rights related to copyright applicable to satellite broadcasting and cable retransmission.

[81] Originally Council Directive 93/98/EEC harmonising the term of protection of copyright and certain related rights; it was replaced by a consolidated version, European Parliament and Council Directive 2006/116/EC; amended then by Directive 2011/77/EU (see paras 7.43–7.44).

[82] Directive 2001/29/EC of the European Parliament and of the Council on the harmonisation of certain aspects of copyright and related rights in the information society.

[83] The current law is to be found in the CDPA 1988, Part II, as amended. For a case about the legislation's application to pre-Act performances, see *Experience Hendrix LLC v Purple Haze Records Ltd and Others* [2007] FSR 31 (CA). The European Commission has proposed reforms aimed at benefitting performers (and authors) in the Draft Copyright Directive 2016 (para 6.41).

[84] CDPA 1988, s 180(2); on definition of a performance see D Liu, 'Performers' rights: muddled or mangled? Bungled or boggled?' [2012] EIPR 374.

[85] *Heythrop Zoological Gardens Ltd v Captive Animals Protection Society* [2016] EWHC 1370 (IPEC), paras 32–33, where Birss J cites with approval R Arnold, *Performers' Rights* (5th edn, 2015) paras 2.15–2.17.

[86] *Heythrop Zoological Gardens Ltd v Captive Animals Protection Society* [2016] EWHC 1370 (IPEC), paras 36 and 40.

[87] In *Bamgboye v Reed* [2002] EWHC 2922 (QB) it was held that a performance can be one that is made in a recording studio as there is no need for an audience.

[88] CDPA 1988, s 181.

- a group of individuals in Princes Street Gardens intently following instructions given by a keep-fit expert, the purpose of which is to teach the elderly to keep fit;

- an individual juggling with balls of fire whilst on top of a monocycle;

- a fortune teller seated in a gypsy caravan gazing into a crystal ball;

- a group of models parading around Edinburgh Castle showing off the latest collections by up-and-coming Scottish designers;

- a heated debate between Professor Alexander McCall Smith and an audience over whether the latest course of action taken by Precious Ramotswe was morally justifiable.

Categories of performers' rights

7.29   Figure 7.3 shows performers' rights by reference to the CDPA 1988.

Figure 7.3 Categories of performers' rights

Property rights in recordings of performances	Non-property rights against 'bootlegging'	Remuneration right	Moral rights
reproduction (182A)	fixation and live broadcasting (182)	on any public playing or broadcasting of commercially published sound recording (182D)	right to be identified (205C) right to object to derogatory treatment (205F)
distribution (182B)	public performance and communication to the public of recording made without consent (183)		
rental (182C)	dealings in illicit recordings (184)		
lending (182C)			
making available (182CA)			

Performers' property and non-property rights

7.30   The majority of performers' rights are divided into two main categories:

- performers' non-property rights: rights against bootlegging (recordings of live performances made without performers' consent);

- performers' property rights: rights in authorised copies of performances.

The main distinctions between the non-property and property rights are:

- non-property rights cannot be assigned, although they are transmissible on death, whereas the property rights are capable of transfer and assignation;

- infringements of non-property rights are actionable only as breach of statutory duty, whereas infringement of property rights are actionable in the same way as other property rights, including copyright.

Performers' property rights

7.31   A performer's property rights are infringed by the following (compare with the economic rights conferred by copyright: see paras 4.9–4.11):

- **Reproduction**

By a person who, without consent, either directly or indirectly makes a copy of a recording of the whole or any substantial part of a qualifying performance.[89]

- **Distribution**

By a person who, without consent, issues to the public copies of a recording of the whole or any substantial part of a qualifying performance. The rights are exhausted once copies are placed into circulation within the EEA by or with the consent of the performer (but note consent is still required for rental or lending).[90]

- **Rental and lending**

By a person who, without consent, rents or lends to the public copies of a recording of the whole or any substantial part of a qualifying performance.[91] *Rental* means the making of a copy of a recording available for use, on terms that it will or may be returned for direct or indirect economic or commercial advantage, and *lending* means making a copy of a recording available for use on terms that it will or may be returned otherwise than for direct or indirect economic or commercial advantage through an establishment which is accessible to the public.[92]

- **Making available**

By a person who, without consent, makes available to the public a recording of the whole or any substantial part of a qualifying performance by electronic transmission in such a way that members of the public may access the recording from a place and at a time individually chosen by them.[93]

 Discussion point   For answer guidance visit **www.oup.com/uk/brown5e**.

Which of the economic rights conferred by copyright (para 4.9) is not to be found in the previous list? Why not?

Performers' non-property rights

7.32   A performer's non-property rights are infringed by the following (again, compare with the economic rights conferred by copyright: see para 4.9):

- **Fixation; live broadcasting**

By a person who, without consent:

(1)   makes a recording of the whole or any substantial part of a qualifying performance directly from the live performance;

---

[89] CDPA 1988, s 182A.   [90] CDPA 1988, s 182B.   [91] CDPA 1988, s 182C.

[92] CDPA 1988, s 182C(2)(a), (b). There are other definitions in this section; eg the terms 'rental' and 'lending' do not include making available for the purpose of public performance, playing, or showing in public or broadcasting. In addition, the expression 'lending' does not include making available between establishments which are accessible to the public (CDPA 1988, s 182C(3), (4)).

[93] CDPA 1988, s 182CA.

(2)   broadcasts live, the whole or any part of a qualifying performance;

(3)   makes a recording of the whole or any substantial part of a qualifying performance directly from a broadcast of the live performance.[94]

No damages will be awarded against a defendant who shows that at the time of the recording he believed on reasonable grounds that consent had been given.[95]

- **Public performance; communication to the public**

Where a person, without consent, shows or plays in public the whole or any substantial part of a qualifying performance, or communicates to the public the whole or any substantial part of a qualifying performance where the person knows or has reason to believe the recording was made without the performer's consent.[96]

- **Dealings in illicit recordings**

Where a person, imports into the UK otherwise than for private or domestic use, or in the course of business possesses, sells or lets for hire, or exposes for sale or hire, or distributes, an illicit recording of a qualifying performance.[97]

Non-property rights and exclusive recording contracts

7.33   Where a performer enters into an exclusive recording contract with another person under which that person is entitled to the exclusion of all other persons (including the performer) to make a recording of one or more of his performances with a view to their commercial exploitation,[98] consent of *both* the person having exclusive recording rights and the performer is necessary for:

- recording of the whole or any substantial part of the performance;[99]

- showing or playing in public the whole or any substantial part of the performance;

- communicating to the public the whole or any substantial part of the performance;[100] and

- importing it into the UK otherwise than for private or domestic use, or selling or letting for hire the performance in the course of a business.[101]

 Exercise

Why are performers' rights classified into property and non-property rights? Are there coherent policy objectives underlying this aspect of the law? What would you do to reform the law in this area and what would be your underlying objectives in suggesting such reform?

Restrictions on the scope of performers' property and non-property rights

7.34   The CDPA 1988 details various permitted acts in relation to performers' property and non-property rights.[102] These may be compared with the exceptions to copyright (see Chapter 5). The permitted acts relate to the question of infringement of the rights. They include such matters as things done for purposes of

---

[94] CDPA 1988, s 182(1).   [95] CDPA 1988, s 182(3).   [96] CDPA 1988, s 183(a), (b).
[97] CDPA 1988, s 184(1).   [98] CDPA 1988, s 185(1).   [99] CDPA 1988, s 186(1).
[100] CDPA 1988, s 187(1)(a), (b).   [101] CDPA 1988, s 188(1)(a), (b).   [102] CDPA 1988, s 189.

non-commercial research and private study;[103] text and data analysis;[104] criticism, review, quotation, or news reporting;[105] caricature, parody, or pastiche;[106] copies for disabled persons;[107] illustration for instruction;[108] certain uses by educational establishments and libraries;[109] recording of folksongs;[110] recording for time-shifting;[111] and certain permitted uses of orphan works.[112] The exceptions largely cover the same ground as those to be found in the 1988 Act as defences to an action of infringement of copyright.[113]

Moral rights

7.35   It was only with the adoption of the WIPO Performances and Phonograms Treaty 1996 (WPPT) that the question of moral rights arose for performers in the UK. Article 5 of the WPPT states:

Moral Rights of Performers

(1) Independently of a performer's economic rights, and even after the transfer of those rights, the performer shall, as regards his live aural performances or performances fixed in phonograms have the right to claim to be identified as the performer of his performances, except where omission is dictated by the manner of the use of the performance, and to object to any distortion, mutilation or other modification of his performances that would be prejudicial to his reputation.

The UK Patent Office (now the Intellectual Property Office (IPO)) carried out an extensive consultation exercise on the implementation of these rights,[114] asking also whether the provisions should be extended to audio-visual performers (ie those whose performances are captured in television broadcasts, films, DVDs, and the like), who are not included within the WPPT. Predictably, the responses fell into two broad camps:

- performers, authors, and film directors favoured a broad implementation of the rights and an extension to audio-visual performers;
- film and television producers, film distributors, cinema exhibitors, broadcasters, record producers, and theatres argued for narrow implementation restricted to the obligations under the WPPT, with no extension to audio-visual performers.

The UK Regulations[115] came into force on 1 February 2006 and extend only as far as required under the WPPT, in some respects giving weaker protection to performers than might have been the case.

Right to be identified

7.36   A performer will be given the right to be identified as performer whenever a person:[116]

- produces or puts on a qualifying performance that is given in public;
- broadcasts live a qualifying performance;
- communicates to the public a sound recording of a qualifying performance; or
- issues to the public copies of such a recording.

---

[103] CDPA 1988, Sch 2, para 1C.   [104] CDPA 1988, Sch 2, para 1D.

[105] CDPA 1988, Sch 2, para 2. See also *Heythrop Zoological Gardens Ltd v Captive Animals Protection Society* [2016] EWHC 1370 (IPEC), paras 42–44.

[106] CDPA 1988, Sch 2, para 2A.   [107] CDPA 1988, Sch 2, para 3A–3E.   [108] CDPA 1988, Sch 2, para 4.

[109] CDPA 1988, Sch 2, paras 5–6H.   [110] CDPA 1988, Sch 2, para 14.   [111] CDPA 1988, Sch 2, para 17A.

[112] CDPA 1988, Sch 2, para 6I. See also para 6.49.   [113] See corresponding permitted uses in Chapter 5.

[114] See UK Patent Office, 'Moral Rights for Performers: A Consultation Paper on Implementation in the UK of the WIPO Performances and Phonograms Treaty Obligations on Performers' Moral Rights and on Further Developments in WIPO on Performers' Moral Rights' (1999).

[115] Performances (Moral Rights, etc) Regulations 2006 (SI 2006/18), amending CDPA 1988 (to which following references are made).

[116] CDPA 1988, s 205C(1).

The right to be identified is one:[117]

- in the case of a performance that is given in public, to be identified in any programme accompanying the performance or in some other manner likely to bring his identity to the notice of a person seeing or hearing the performance;
- in the case of a performance that is broadcast, to be identified in a manner likely to bring his identity to the notice of a person seeing or hearing the broadcast;
- in the case of a sound recording that is communicated to the public, to be identified in a manner likely to bring his identity to the notice of a person hearing the communication;
- in the case of a sound recording that is issued to the public, to be identified in or on each copy or, if that is not appropriate, in some other manner likely to bring his identity to the notice of a person acquiring a copy.

However, the right to be identified will not be infringed unless it has first been asserted,[118] and is also hedged with a number of exceptions including:[119]

- where it is not reasonably practicable to identify the performer (or, where identification of a group is permitted);
- in relation to any performance given for the purposes of reporting current events;
- in relation to any performance given for the purposes of advertising any goods or services.

In addition, the right will not be infringed by an act which is covered by provisions relating to inter alia:[120]

- news reporting;
- incidental inclusion of a performance or recording;
- things done for the purposes of examination.

Right to object to derogatory treatment

7.37   A performer has a right to object where a performance:[121]

- is broadcast live, or
- by means of a sound recording the performance is played in public or communicated to the public,

with any distortion, mutilation, or other modification that is prejudicial to the reputation of the performer. Again, this right is subject to a number of exceptions. Thus, it does not apply or is not infringed:

- in relation to any performance given for the purposes of reporting current events;[122]
- by modifications made to a performance which are consistent with normal editorial or production practice.[123]

A performer may also waive the rights to be identified and to object to derogatory treatment.[124]

 Exercise

Compare and contrast a performer's rights of attribution and to object to derogatory treatment with those conferred on authors under sections 77–82 of the CDPA 1988 (see paras 6.4–6.22). Has the UK successfully implemented its obligations under the WPPT with respect to the moral rights of performers?

---

[117] CDPA 1988, s 205C(2).   [118] CDPA 1988, s 205D(1).   [119] CDPA 1988, s 205E.
[120] CDPA 1988, s 205E(5).   [121] CDPA 1988, s 205F(1).   [122] CDPA 1988, s 205G(2).
[123] CDPA 1988, s 205G(3).   [124] CDPA 1988, s 205J.

> **Key points on performers' moral rights**
>
> Moral rights exist for performers only in respect of their live aural performance and performances fixed in phonograms. Audio-visual performers do not have moral rights.
>
> The moral rights conferred are:
>
> - the right to be identified;
> - the right to prevent derogatory treatment of one's performance.

Audio-visual performers

7.38   As indicated in para 7.35, the provisions in the WPPT concerning moral rights cover only performers in respect of their live aural performance and performances fixed in phonograms. This engendered a debate concerning moral rights for audio-visual performers (ie those appearing in films and TV broadcasts). WIPO convened a diplomatic conference in December 2000 to discuss the protection of audio-visual performances.[125] After nearly 12 years, in June 2012, it adopted a new international treaty, the Beijing Treaty on Audiovisual Performances,[126] which will provide for moral rights of attribution and integrity to audio-visual performers. Article 5(1) of the Treaty states:

> Independently of a performer's economic rights, and even after the transfer of those rights, the performer shall, as regards his live performances or performances fixed in audiovisual fixations, have the right:
>
> (i) to claim to be identified as the performer of his performances, except where omission is dictated by the manner of the use of the performance; and
> (ii) to object to any distortion, mutilation or other modification of his performances that would be prejudicial to his reputation, taking due account of the nature of audiovisual fixations.

An agreed statement in the Treaty in relation to Article 5 states:

> For the purposes of this Treaty and without prejudice to any other treaty, it is understood that, considering the nature of audiovisual fixations and their production and distribution, modifications of a performance that are made in the normal course of exploitation of the performance, such as editing, compression, dubbing, or formatting, in existing or new media or formats, and that are made in the course of a use authorized by the performer, would not in themselves amount to modifications within the meaning of Article 5(1)(ii). Rights under Article 5(1)(ii) are concerned only with changes that are objectively prejudicial to the performer's reputation in a substantial way. It is also understood that the mere use of new or changed technology or media, as such, does not amount to modification within the meaning of Article 5(1)(ii).

Ever since the 2000 conference, WIPO's member states, particularly the producer countries, have had concerns over the extent to which moral rights of audio-visual performers might hinder the exploitation of collective works. Hence, the agreed statement in relation to Article 5 allowing modifications consistent with the normal exploitation of a performance.

---

[125] For a full discussion, see S von Lewinski, 'The WIPO Diplomatic Conference on Audiovisual Performances: a first resumé' [2001] EIPR 333.

[126] It was signed on 26 June 2012 after attendance by 156 member states, six intergovernmental organisations, and 45 non-governmental organisations, the highest level of participation to date at a WIPO diplomatic conference. The treaty will enter into force once 30 eligible parties have ratified it: www.wipo.int/treaties/en/ip/beijing.

Performers' remuneration rights

7.39   An aspect of performers' rights which appears to be distinctive is the right to equitable remuneration. Two such rights are available to performers, introduced as a result of the Rental Right Directive (para 7.27):

- A performer can claim equitable remuneration from the owner of the copyright in the sound recording[127] where a commercially published sound recording of a qualifying performance (but not a film) is played in public or communicated to the public otherwise than under the 'making available to the public' right.[128] The right may not be assigned except to a collecting society for the purpose of enabling it to enforce the right on the performer's behalf.[129] The amount payable is as agreed by the parties[130] or, failing agreement, application may be made to the Copyright Tribunal to determine the amount payable.[131] Any agreement purporting to exclude or restrict the right to equitable remuneration, or purporting to prevent a person questioning the amount of equitable remuneration or to restrict the powers of the Copyright Tribunal, is of no effect.[132]

- A performer retains a right to equitable remuneration where she transfers (or is presumed to transfer) her rental right in a film or sound recording to the producer.[133] Any agreement purporting to exclude or restrict the right to equitable remuneration is of no effect.[134] The right may not be assigned by the performer except to a collecting society for the purpose of enabling it to enforce the right on her behalf.[135] The Copyright Tribunal has jurisdiction to determine the amount payable failing agreement.[136]

7.40   In *Phonographic Performance (Ireland) Ltd v Ireland*,[137] the Court of Justice held that a hotel was liable to pay equitable remuneration for the communication to the public of a sound recording, in addition to that paid by the broadcaster, when it provides televisions or radios in the guest bedrooms to which it distributes a broadcast signal. In contrast, in *Società Consortile Fonografici (SCF) v Del Corso*,[138] the Court of Justice held that a dentist who played a radio in his surgery whilst patients were present was not liable to pay equitable remuneration. The use of the concept of 'communication to the public' appearing in the Rental Right Directive and the InfoSoc Directive (para 7.27) is different in contexts, and pursues similar but divergent objectives: in the former, performers are only given a right to equitable remuneration, while in the latter authors are given exclusive rights. However, it has been recently held that the concept should be given the same meaning in relation to the rights provided under both the directives, since there is 'no evidence' that the EU legislature wished to confer on the word a different meaning in the respective contexts.[139] Consequently, the criteria and case law discussed at paras 4.57–4.62 are of relevance here.

---

[127] CDPA 1988, s 182D.   [128] CDPA 1988, s 182CA(1).   [129] CDPA 1988, s 182D(2).

[130] CDPA 1988, s 182D(3).

[131] CDPA 1988, s 182D(5). The Tribunal may order any method of calculation and payment of equitable remuneration it may determine to be reasonable in the circumstances, taking into account the importance of the contribution of the performer to the sound recording (CDPA 1988, s 182D(6)).

[132] CDPA 1988, s 182D(7).   [133] CDPA 1988, s 191F–191H.   [134] CDPA 1988, s 191G(5).

[135] CDPA 1988, s 191G(2). The collecting society must be an organisation which has as its main object, or one of its main objects, the exercise of the right to equitable remuneration on behalf of more than one performer, CDPA 1988, s 191G(6).

[136] Remuneration shall not be considered inequitable merely because it was paid by way of a single payment or at the time of the transfer of the rental right (CDPA 1988, s 191H(4)).

[137] Case C-162/10 *Phonographic Performance (Ireland) Ltd v Ireland* [2012] ECDR 15 (CJ).

[138] Case C-135/10 *Società Consortile Fonografici (SCF) v Del Corso* [2012] ECDR 16 (CJ).

[139] Case C-117/15 *Reha Training v GEMA* [2016] 3 CMLR 40 (CJ), paras 29–34.

> **Key points on equitable remuneration right**
>
> - A performer can claim equitable remuneration from the copyright owner in a commercially published sound recording of a performance (but not a film) when it is played in public or communicated to the public.
> - A performer retains a right to equitable remuneration where she transfers (or is presumed to transfer) her rental right in a film or sound recording to the producer.
> - These rights cannot be excluded by contract.
> - The rights are not assignable except to a collecting society.

 Exercise

What other areas of copyright and related rights contain provisions for equitable remuneration? Should such schemes be extended more generally across the area of copyright and related rights? Why do we not move from the 'property' system we have at present to one which is merely a right to remuneration for exploitation?

Duration of rights

7.41　The rights conferred in relation to a performance expire at the end of the period of 50 years from the end of the calendar year in which the performance takes place.[140] If a recording of a performance, other than a sound recording, is released during that period, the rights expire 50 years from the end of the calendar year in which it is released.[141] If a sound recording of a performance, is released during that period, the rights expire 70 years from the end of the calendar year in which it is released.[142]

7.42　A recording is released when it is first published, played, or shown in public or communicated to the public.[143] Where a performer is not a national of an EEA state, the duration of rights is that to which the performer is entitled in the country of which he is a national, provided this does not extend the period to which he would be entitled if he were an EEA national.[144] Moral rights of performers endure for the same period as the performers' economic rights.[145]

 Discussion point　For answer guidance visit **www.oup.com/uk/brown5e.**

Why are all performers not given rights lasting for the same duration as authors of works protected by copyright? Should they be?

7.43　The current duration of performers' rights in sound recordings resulted from the implementation of the Term Directive 2011 in the UK,[146] which extended the duration of performers' rights in sound recordings to 70 years (see para 7.41 above).[147] The initial proposal for the Directive appeared to be primarily motivated

---

[140]　CDPA 1988, s 191(2)(a)　　[141]　CDPA 1988, s 191(2)(b).　　[142]　CDPA 1988, s 191(2)(c).

[143]　No account is to be taken of any unauthorised act (CDPA 1988, s 191(3)).　　[144]　CDPA 1988, s 191(4).

[145]　CDPA 1988, s 205I.

[146]　Directive 2011/77/EU was implemented through the Copyright and Duration of Rights in Performances Regulations 2013 (SI 2013/1782).

[147]　The rights of performers in other performances did not change. While the extension applied to performances which were still protected at the time, it did not revive any rights which had expired, see Term Directive 2011, Art 1(2).

by the following: many of the most popular sound recordings made in the 1950s and 1960s started falling into the public domain; the belief that session musicians are outliving the current 50-year term and are left without income when their rights expire;[148] such musicians only have the protection of performers' rights as their contribution to the musical work is insufficient to attract copyright. The preamble to the Directive also states that 'the socially recognised importance of the creative contribution of performers should be reflected in a level of protection that acknowledges their creative and artistic contribution'. However, the term extension proposal was widely criticised by many academics, primarily on the ground that the main benefit of the extension will fall to the record labels.[149] It was also argued that given the inherent inequality of bargaining position in the relationship between the labels and the performers, it is unlikely that performers will see any increase in revenue. While the Commission clearly sought to address these concerns in the additional rights created in the Directive (see para 7.44 below), whether the legal changes have actually improved the position of performers remains to be seen. Although economic analysis may not support the term extension, it is arguable that the natural rights justifications for copyright do not support a distinction between performers and authors.[150]

Additional benefits for performers

7.44   The implementation of the Term Directive 2011 (see paras 7.27 and 7.43) introduced a number of additional benefits for musical performers:[151]

- A 'use-it-or-lose-it' provision: where the performer has assigned the rights in the sound recording of a performance to the producer (eg a record company), the performer will be able to terminate the agreement at the end of 50-year period, provided certain conditions are met. The conditions are: the producer fails to issue to the public copies of the recording in sufficient quantities or make it available on demand by electronic transmission. While this provision may allow the performer to terminate the agreement if the recording is not being exploited, the conditions above make it difficult to do so in practice.

- A 20 per cent fund: the producer must pay 20 per cent of gross revenue earned during the extended 20 years of protection to a collecting society, which will be used to pay an annual supplementary remuneration to the performers who had assigned their rights for a one-off payment (an arrangement common for non-featured 'session musicians'). This is to ensure that such performers receive some benefit from the term extension.

- The producer must pay the full agreed royalties from the revenue earned during the extended 20 years of protection to the performers who had assigned their rights for recurring payments (an arrangement common for 'featured musicians') and cannot withhold or deduct sums that may be allowed under the assignment agreement (eg deductions of any initial advance paid from the royalties due). This is to ensure that it is the performers that fully benefit from the term extension and not the producers alone.

---

[148] See the opinion of the then European Commissioner, Charlie McCreevy at http://europa.eu/rapid/press-release_IP-08-240_en.htm?locale=en.

[149] Criticism of the extension can be found in B Farrand, 'Too much is never enough? The 2011 Copyright in Sound Recordings Extension Directive' [2012] EIPR 297; *Gowers Review of Intellectual Property* (HM Treasury 2006), para 4.33; Centre for Intellectual Property Policy & Management, Centre for Intellectual Property and Information Law, Institute for Information Law, and Max Planck Institute for Intellectual Property, Competition and Tax Law, 'The Proposed Directive for a Copyright Term Extension—A Backward-Looking Package', Letter to the Commission (27 October 2008), 8; N Helberger et al, 'Never forever: why extending the term of protection for sound recordings is a bad idea' [2008] EIPR 174.

[150] See, eg, R Arnold, *Performers' Rights* (5th edn, 2015).

[151] CDPA 1988, s 191HA and 191HB.

Question

Do you agree with the European Commissioner Michel Barnier's statement, made on the adoption of the Term Directive 2011, that the term extension introduced therein will 'make a real difference for performers'?[152] See 'Implementation of the Directive 2011/77/EU: copyright term of protection', a study requested by the JURI Committee of the European Parliament (2018).[153]

The nature of performers' rights

7.45   As will be evident from the preceding summary, the characterisation of performers' rights within the UK statutory regime is far from clear. One opinion is that performers' rights should not be considered as falling under the head of copyright,[154] while admitting that, since the inclusion of performers' property rights in the legislation, those rights have now 'inched . . . close to copyright'.[155] Others have said that although the performers' property rights granted by the 1988 Act were not described as copyright, 'in effect new copyrights were conferred on performers'.[156]

7.46   Nor is it easy to classify performers' rights as neighbouring or media rights as traditionally understood in the UK. Although UK legislation does not formally distinguish between authorial and other works, that distinction still underlies a good part of the assumptions on which the legal framework is built. In this context, authors' rights are understood to refer to the works created by authors such as books, plays, music, and art. By contrast, neighbouring or entrepreneurial or media rights are derivative, and in general it is the investment in technical and organisational skill that is being protected, rather than the creative effort. Perhaps in response to this conundrum, performers' non-property rights which are personal and non-assignable rights have been described as 'a form of neighbouring right to copyright'.[157] The Act makes clear that the rights conferred in relation to performers are independent of any copyright in, or moral rights relating to, any work performed or any film or sound recording of, or broadcast including the performance.[158] For these reasons some have referred to performers' rights as 'rights associated with copyright',[159] or as 'related rights'[160] which is perhaps the most suitable terminology to use. Yet performers appear rather closer to authors as figures with a claim to the law's protection, and the introduction of moral rights for the former as well as the latter makes the analogy even closer.[161]

 Question

How should performers' rights be characterised in relation to copyright?

---

[152]   M Barnier, 'Copyright: extension of the term of protection for performers' (12 September 2011) http://ec.europa.eu/archives/commission_2010-2014/barnier/headlines/news/2011/09/20110912_en.html.

[153]   www.europarl.europa.eu/thinktank/en/document.html?reference=IPOL_STU(2018)604957.

[154]   D Llewelyn and T Aplin, *Cornish, Llewelyn and Aplin Intellectual Property: Patents, Copyright, Trade Marks and Allied Rights* (9th edn, 2019), para 11.002.

[155]   ibid, para 14.36.

[156]   N Caddick, G Davies, and G Harbottle (eds), *Copinger & Skone James on Copyright* (17th edn, 2019), para 12.06.

[157]   D Llewelyn and T Aplin, *Cornish, Llewelyn and Aplin Intellectual Property: Patents, Copyright, Trade Marks and Allied Rights* (9th edn, 2019), para 14.032.

[158]   CDPA 1988, s 180(4)(a).

[159]   L Bently et al, *Intellectual Property Law* (5th edn, 2018), Ch 13.

[160]   N Caddick, G Davies, and G Harbottle (eds), *Copinger & Skone James on Copyright* (17th edn, 2019), para 1.05.

[161]   The distinction between joint author and performer was considered in the case of *Fisher v Brooker* [2009] 1 WLR 1764 (HL); see also L McDonagh, 'Rearranging the roles of the performer and the composer in the music industry: the potential significance of Fisher v. Brooker' [2012] IPQ 64.

Performers' rights and Brexit

Although the current UK framework of performers' rights is framed in light of several EU directives and CJEU jurisprudence, the implementation of such directives will be preserved in UK law as retained EU law under the powers in the EU Withdrawal Act 2018. Both the UK and EU member states are party to the main international treaties which are applicable to the current framework of performers' rights, and under which the main obligations in area arise (eg Rome Convention, WPPT). Consequently, in a 'no deal' scenario, the relationship between the UK and EU member states will be governed through the principles of such treaties (para 2.20). The UK government 'no deal' guidance does not specifically mention performers' rights but similar to the protection of copyright, the scope of performers' rights will remain largely unchanged.[162] However, some specific areas will be affected, for example the exception for certain permitted uses of orphan works which currently applies to both performers' rights (para 7.34) and copyright (see para 6.49); reciprocal protections under the Satellite and Cable Directive.[163] Also, the UK may not have any obligation to implement any benefits accruing to performers (and authors) that may eventually emerge from Articles 14–16 of the Draft Copyright Directive 2016 (see para 6.41)

Further reading

Books

General

R Arnold, *Performers' Rights* (5th edn, 2015)

L Bently, B Sherman, D Gangjee, and P Johnson *Intellectual Property Law* (5th edn, 2018), Ch 13

N Caddick, G Davies, and G Harbottle (eds), *Copinger & Skone James on Copyright* (17th edn, 2019), Chs 12, 18

E Derclaye, *The Legal Protection of Databases: A Comparative Analysis* (2008)

D Llewelyn and T Aplin, *Cornish, Llewelyn and Aplin Intellectual Property: Patents, Copyright, Trade Marks and Allied Rights* (9th edn, 2019), Chs 14.4, 20.2

Articles

R Arnold, 'Reflections on "The Triumph of Music": copyrights and performers' rights in music' [2010] IPQ 153

S Atkinson, 'Sir Cliff Richard's victory: an extra 20 years for copyright protection in sound recordings and performers' rights where a sound recording of the performance is released' [2014] EIPR 75

D Liu, 'The Beijing Treaty on Audiovisual Performances and its impact on the future of performers' rights under English law' [2015] EIPR 81

J Thomson, 'The Database Directive: a clean bill of health?' [2019] EIPR 228

Websites

Diplomatic Conference on the Protection of Audiovisual Performances: www.wipo.int/dc2012/en

Beijing Treaty on Audiovisual Performances: www.wipo.int/treaties/en/ip/beijing

European Commission, Protection of Databases: https://ec.europa.eu/digital-single-market/en/protection-databases

---

[162] UK Government, 'Copyright if there's no Brexit deal' (24 September 2018) www.gov.uk/government/publications/copyright-if-theres-no-brexit-deal.

[163] UK Government, 'Changes to copyright law in the event of no deal' (26 October 2018) www.gov.uk/government/publications/changes-to-copyright-law-in-the-event-of-no-deal/changes-to-copyright-law-in-the-event-of-no-deal.

Part III

Design protection

Introduction

In this Part of the book, our focus will shift to design law.

Design law is a complicated area of intellectual property (IP). It has a complex history, driven by changing and difficult policy concerns. Views have evolved over time about the extent to which design law should protect functional designs, or should impose some requirement of aesthetic interest or ornamentation. There have also been continuing issues in deciding on the extent to which copyright should continue to play a role in protecting designs. However, with the importance of good design and of the creative economy increasingly recognised by policymakers and with the European design regime beginning to show its muscle in high-profile disputes such as the *Samsung v Apple* litigation discussed in Chapter 8, there is no doubt that design protection is undergoing something of a renaissance in terms of both legal and policy interest.

Material on the history and development of design law in the UK can be found in this book's online resources. With its connections to all of copyright, trade mark, and patent law, there can be difficulties in terms of positioning design law intellectually within the overall scheme of IP protection. Matters are complicated by the multiplicity of coexisting different regimes for design protection in the UK. These different regimes currently include registered and unregistered design protection at national and EU level. There is also a limited residual role for copyright.

Chapter 8 deals with the regime governing protection of designs by way of registration. It looks at the protection which arises from registration of a design in the UK and at a pan-EU level in the form of the Community registered design. The EU has effected a harmonisation of national registered design laws and has created new unitary Community design protection. These steps were achieved by way of Designs Directive 98/71/EC and Community Design Regulation 6/2002/EC. The regime for design protection in the EU introduced by the Directive and Regulation was novel and posed a number of interpretative challenges for the courts which are being worked out in the case law. Brexit will have a significant impact, particularly for Community registered designs—the implications will be outlined in Chapter 8.

Chapter 9 considers unregistered design protection. Unlike UK *registered* design protection, UK *unregistered* design protection has been unaffected by the EU initiatives in this area and UK unregistered design right remains very different to other forms of design protection. At the same time, there is at present also the potential for EU-level unregistered design protection through the Community unregistered design—although, again, Brexit will have an impact, as outlined further in Chapter 9. Chapter 9 also looks further at copyright protection for designs, insofar as copyright has a continuing role in this field in the UK.

Sources of the law: key websites

- UK Intellectual Property Office (UK IPO) designs pages: www.gov.uk/topic/intellectual-property/designs
- European Union Intellectual Property Office (EUIPO) Community design pages: https://euipo.europa.eu/ohimportal/en/designs

Registered designs

Introduction

Scope and overview of chapter

8.1 This chapter deals with registered designs. It considers which designs may be validly registered and the nature and extent of the rights conferred. Because of European Union (EU) legislation, the rules on these matters are currently the same in the UK and at EU level. We can therefore consider the substantive law pertaining to UK registered designs and Community registered designs together. It is, however, also important to highlight the implications of Brexit for registered design law going forward, particularly in relation to the Community registered design.

8.2 ### Learning objectives

By the end of this chapter you should be able to describe and explain:

- the international treaty context for design law, development of UK and EU law, and likely implications of Brexit;
- the criteria designs must meet to be validly registered in the UK and as a Community registered design, and the exclusions from protection;
- the special rules dealing with the designs of component parts of complex products and spare parts;
- the rules on ownership of, and dealings in, UK and Community registered designs;
- on what grounds a design registration may be invalidated;
- the rights given as a result of a valid registration, including the scope of protection against infringement and defences; and
- the interaction between registered design protection and other intellectual property (IP) rights, in particular copyright.

8.3 The chapter begins by outlining the international treaty context. It also reviews the development of UK and EU law, and looks briefly at the possible consequences of Brexit. The chapter then looks at the substantive law of registered designs: what designs may be validly registered and what is excluded from protection (including the difficult problems of 'complex products' and spare parts); ownership of and dealings in UK and Community registered designs; challenging the validity of a registration; the rights conferred by a valid registration; and the defences to infringement. It also looks briefly at the interaction between registered design protection and other IP rights, in particular copyright (a topic considered further in Chapter 9). The rest of the chapter looks like this:

- The international background (8.4–8.10)
- Development of UK and EU law, including Brexit (8.11–8.19)
- Designs that can be validly protected by registration (8.20–8.90)
- Complex products (8.91–8.97)
- Spare parts (8.98–8.105)
- Ownership of and dealings in UK and Community registered designs (8.106–8.109)
- Invalidation (8.110–8.116)
- Rights given by registration, infringement, defences, and duration of rights (8.117–8.129)
- Interaction with other IP rights (8.130–8.134)

The international background

8.4   Unlike for copyright, there is no international treaty stipulating detailed substantive requirements for protection of designs. Of all the principal IP rights, designs are the least harmonised at international treaty level.

8.5   The revision of the Berne Convention in 1948 opened up the possibility of copyright protection for industrial designs, including 'works of applied art' within the definition of protected 'literary and artistic works' (Art 2(1)). The expression 'works of applied art' is, however, not defined. The Berne Convention gave its members freedom to determine the extent of the application (or not) of their copyright laws to 'works of applied art' and 'industrial designs and models', the conditions under which they were to be protected (Art 2(7)), and the term of protection for 'works of applied art in so far as they are protected as artistic works', subject to a minimum of 25 years from the making of such a work (Art 7(4)). Berne adds the following, however, ensuring that a distinction is drawn between copyright on the one hand and design protection on the other, where systems for the latter exist:

> Works protected in the country of origin solely as designs and models shall be entitled in another country of the Union only to such special protection as is granted in that country to designs and models; however, if no such special protection is granted in that country, such works shall be protected as artistic works (Art 2(7)).

Thus, the Berne Convention allows copyright protection for industrial designs, but tends to exclude it in favour of design laws (if available) for designs originating in countries where special non-copyright protection for designs exists.

8.6   Designs are also only briefly addressed in the Paris Convention. The Paris Convention provides that: 'Industrial designs shall be protected in all the countries of the Union' (Art 5 *quinquies*) but leaves open how that protection is to be given. Thus, designs may be protected through a registration system, an unregistered system, or a combination of the two. Consistently with its general approach to industrial property protection based on registration (national treatment for non-nationals—Art 2, and see para 1.65), the Paris Convention also requires its members to allow foreigners access to national design registration systems, with an application in one Paris Convention country giving a right of priority in the others (Art 4A(1)). A registrant can thereby have the validity of his later filings for a particular design assessed as at the date of his first filing for that design in a Paris Convention country, provided his later filings are made within the prescribed priority period, currently set at six months for designs—Article 4C(1).

Question

In what ways do the Berne and Paris Conventions allow designs to be protected?

8.7 The Hague Agreement Concerning the International Registration of Industrial Designs ('Hague Agreement') enables international design applications but, in effect, simply provides a means whereby a central deposit at the World Intellectual Property Organization (WIPO) can give rise to filings in the Agreement's member states. It contains no substantive provisions governing design protection. In 1968 the Locarno Agreement Establishing an International Classification for Industrial Designs (the 'Locarno Agreement') was also concluded. The Locarno Classification (at the time of writing, in its eleventh edition) consists of a series of classes and sub-classes providing indications as to the sector of goods incorporating the relevant design. Design registries of the contracting states must include the numbers of the relevant classes and sub-classes in the official documents for the deposit or registration of designs, and, if they are officially published, in corresponding publications. However, the Locarno Agreement explicitly describes classification as an administrative matter, leaving it to national laws to address the scope of protection of designs (Art 2(1)).

 Question

What are the Hague and Locarno Agreements and what is their effect?

8.8 The Agreement on Trade-Related Aspects of Intellectual Property Rights (TRIPS) contains two Articles on design protection (Arts 25 and 26). These deal with substantive matters of design law in some more detail than previous treaties; however, much is still left to the discretion of TRIPS member states. In terms of requirements for protection, the only mandatory requirement is that members shall provide for the protection of 'independently created industrial designs that are new or original' (Art 25(1)). None of these expressions are defined. Members *may* provide that designs are not new or original 'if they do not significantly differ from known designs or combinations of known design features' (Art 25(1)). Members are also given discretion as to whether to extend protection to 'designs dictated essentially by technical or functional considerations' (Art 25(1)). In terms of infringement, the only mandatory requirement is that the owner of a protected industrial design must have the right to prevent unauthorised third parties from making, selling, or importing articles bearing or embodying a design which is a copy, or substantially a copy, of the protected design, when such acts are undertaken for commercial purposes (Art 26(1)). There may be limited exceptions to design rights, as long as they do not unreasonably conflict with normal exploitation of protected industrial designs and do not unreasonably prejudice the legitimate interests of the owner, taking into account the legitimate interests of third parties (Art 26(2)). Finally, the protection must last for at least ten years (Art 26(3)).

> **Key points on the international framework for design law**
>
> - Individual states have considerable discretion as to how to protect industrial designs.
> - Protection may be by means of copyright or through a special system for the protection of designs.
> - There is no need for any special system for protection of designs to be one of registration, but where a registration system exists non-nationals must be given access to it.
> - TRIPS has increased the international harmonisation on the minimum content of design protection, but without limiting the options as to how it is achieved.

8.9   The essence of the minimum content as found in TRIPS can be put like this:

- Independently created and new or original designs are to be protected.

- Designs dictated by technical or functional considerations do not have to be protected.

- The minimum scope of the exclusive right is to prevent third parties commercially manufacturing/selling/importing articles bearing or embodying a design which is a copy, or substantially a copy, of the protected design.

- Exceptions to design protection are allowed if they are consistent with normal exploitation and do not prejudice the owner's legitimate interests, taking into account the legitimate interests of third parties.

- Duration of protection must be at least ten years (note also previously the Berne Convention minimum of 25 years for works of applied art insofar as protected as artistic works).

8.10   The low demands made of states by international law in the field of design protection has led to very variable national protection. However, the minimum standards set down in TRIPS may be the first step towards a more harmonised global picture.

Development of UK and EU law

The Designs Directive and Community Design Regulation

8.11   An account of the development of registered design law in the UK may be found in this book's online resources. The UK has had a registration process for the legal protection of product designs since the 18th century. For most of the 20th century before the EU intervention in the field, UK legislation sought to exclude purely functional designs from registration. What constituted a registrable 'design' under the old UK law was very different to the present position and included a requirement of so-called 'eye appeal', now abolished. As we shall see, much has now changed as a result of the EU's legislative activity.

8.12   In the late 1980s the EU began to take a serious interest in design law as part of its efforts to ensure that national IP laws did not pose barriers to the creation of a single market in Europe. The European Court of Justice (ECJ) had held that a design registration system (in this case, the Benelux system) was 'industrial and commercial property' the rights in which might be exercised in derogation from the free movement of goods within the European Community, provided that the goods in question had not already been put on the market in the exporting member state by or with the consent of the right holder.[1] Thus a national design right could be used to prevent the import of goods lawfully produced in one member state into another member state. However, national design laws varied very considerably and a party who had rights in a design in one member state might not have had equivalent rights in another member state. There was, therefore, significant potential for divergent national design laws to impede the free movement of goods within the single market.

 Question

Consider the recitals to Designs Directive 98/71/EC and Community Design Regulation 6/2002/EC. What were the main objectives of the EU design legislation?

---

[1] Case 144/81 *Keurkoop BV v Nancy Kean Gifts BV* [1983] FSR 381.

8.13   Although it took over a decade, the EU finally settled on two steps with regard to the protection of designs:

(1)   harmonisation of the national registered design laws of member states by Directive 98/71/EC on the legal protection of designs (referred to in this chapter as the 'Designs Directive' or 'DD'); and

(2)   creation of two new Community design rights, both unitary rights covering the whole of the EU. This took effect by way of Regulation 6/2002/EC on Community designs (referred to here as the 'Community Design Regulation' or 'CDR'). This created the Community registered design (discussed in this chapter) and the Community unregistered design (discussed in Chapter 9), both of which are together referred to as 'Community designs'.

In the UK, the Designs Directive necessitated very substantial amendment of the Registered Designs Act 1949 ('RDA 1949'), effected by way of the Registered Design Regulations 2001 (SI 2001/3949), which came into force on 9 December 2001.[2] UK registered designs are granted and administered by the UK IPO. The Community Design Regulation took direct effect in all member states without any need for transposition into national laws; applications for Community registered designs were accepted at what was called the Office for Harmonisation in the Internal Market (OHIM) and is now called the EU Intellectual Property Office (EUIPO) in Alicante, Spain, and at various national offices, effective from 1 April 2003.

8.14   Community designs, registered and unregistered, are unitary rights, meaning that they consist of one single right which has equal effect throughout all EU member states and can only be registered, transferred, surrendered, or found invalid in respect of the whole of the EU (CDR, Art 1(3)). Applying for a Community registered design carries considerable benefits in terms of cost and ease of administration compared to applying for national design registrations in all EU member states. Another very important advantage of Community design protection is the ability of the right holder, in certain circumstances, to apply to one court in one jurisdiction to obtain an injunction stopping infringement and granting other relief effective across the whole of the EU.[3] This brings considerable cost savings at the enforcement stage as well.

8.15   For the purposes of the present chapter, two important points emerge about the Designs Directive and Community Design Regulation. First, they introduced a number of key new concepts which have required consideration and elucidation by the courts. Secondly, they created a basically unified substantive law of registered designs in the EU. The rules on the definition of protectable designs, requirements for and exclusions from protection, challenges to validity, infringement, and defences are the same for UK national design registrations and Community registered designs, meaning that they can be treated together in this chapter. Within the Community Design Regulation, subject to certain matters discussed further in Chapter 9, the substantive rules on these matters are in large part also the same between Community registered designs and Community unregistered designs, with the result that case law on national registered designs, Community registered designs, and Community unregistered designs is all relevant when considering their common substantive concepts and requirements. Given this, decisions emanating from the EUIPO, the EU General Court, and the Court of Justice of the European Union (CJEU) are all relevant, as well as UK case law and judgments from the courts of other member states.

---

[2] The amended law applies to all UK design registrations resulting from an application filed on or after 9 December 2001. Infringement of earlier-filed designs will also be governed by the new law. However, the validity of earlier-filed designs will continue to be determined on the basis of the old pre-harmonisation version of the RDA 1949.

[3] See CDR, Arts 80–83.

> **Key points on the Designs Directive and Community Design Regulation**
>
> - The intervention of the EU in design law came about to prevent differences in national design laws creating an obstacle to the single European market by preventing the free movement of goods.
> - There are two major EU instruments:
>   - Directive 98/71/EC, harmonising the national registered design laws of EU member states;
>   - Regulation 6/2002/EC, creating the pan-EU unitary Community design, registered and unregistered.
> - The result is that there are EU-level and national systems of registered designs running in parallel which employ the same substantive legal rules on the definition of protectable designs, requirements for and exclusions from protection, challenges to validity, infringement, and defences.

Brexit—what are the implications for registered designs?

8.16   Having looked at the Designs Directive and Community Design Regulation, and their impact on UK law, we also need to ask ourselves what the consequences of Brexit are likely to be for registered design law going forward.

8.17   The IP implications of Brexit have been outlined generally in Chapter 1. When Brexit takes effect, the most immediate and serious consequence for registered design law will be that, because the UK will cease to be a member of the EU, the territorial scope of the Community registered design will no longer cover the UK. Because this is a potentially very significant adverse consequence for all Community design rightholders, there are provisions dealing with this issue in the draft Withdrawal Agreement negotiated between the EU and UK discussed in Chapter 1. The most recent version of the Withdrawal Agreement at the time of writing (issued 14 November 2018) provides at draft Article 54 that, after the Brexit transition period it is hoped will be put in place:[4]

> The holder of any of the following intellectual property rights which have been registered or granted before the end of the transition period shall, without any re-examination, become the holder of a comparable registered and enforceable intellectual property right in the United Kingdom under the law of the United Kingdom.

Article 54(1)(b) specifically adds for Community registered designs:

> the holder of a Community design registered . . . in accordance with Council Regulation (EC) No 6/2002 shall become the holder of a registered design right in the United Kingdom for the same design.

Article 54(6) provides that the term of protection conferred on this newly created UK right is to be at least equal to the remaining period of protection due for the corresponding Community registered design, and that the new UK right is also to inherit the same filing and priority dates as the original Community registered design. According to Article 55(1), the registration of the new UK right is to be carried out free of charge by the relevant entities in the UK, using the data available from the EUIPO design register. According to draft Article 59(1), owners of pending Community design applications as at the date of Brexit can reapply in the UK. If done within nine months of Brexit, applicants will be able to claim the same filing and priority dates as for the original Community design application.

8.18   As noted in Chapter 1, at the time of writing it is not clear whether the draft Withdrawal Agreement will be concluded in this form or, indeed, if there will be a withdrawal agreement between the EU and the UK at all. If there is 'no deal' (that is, if the UK exits the EU without concluding any form of withdrawal agreement or

---

[4]   See https://assets.publishing.service.gov.uk/government/uploads/system/uploads/attachment_data/file/756374/14_November_Draft_Agreement_on_the_Withdrawal_of_the_United_Kingdom_of_Great_Britain_and_Northern_Ireland_from_the_European_Union.pdf.

other agreement on a transition period), the UK has indicated its intention to carry out, of its own accord, a similar exercise of 'cloning' rights from the EUIPO designs register onto the designs register in the UK.[5] This will be done, it is said, with 'minimal administrative burden'; owners of Community designs who do not wish to receive a parallel UK right will have the ability to opt out.

8.19   Either way (whether or not there is a 'no-deal' Brexit) post-Brexit UK registered design law may ultimately follow a different direction to the developing European jurisprudence. As explained at Chapter 1, after Brexit preliminary references to the CJEU will no longer be possible from the UK courts. According to the European Union (Withdrawal) Act 2018, existing decisions of the CJEU will effectively have the same status as decisions of the UK Supreme Court: it will therefore necessitate an appeal to the Supreme Court to reverse principles derived from existing CJEU designs case law. However, under section 6(2) of the 2018 Act, the UK courts have a discretion as to whether they 'have regard to anything done on or after exit day by the European Court, another EU entity or the EU so far as it is relevant to any matter before the court or tribunal'. Post-Brexit, it will therefore be possible for UK courts to follow or not follow future CJEU designs decisions, as they see fit.

 Registered designs and Brexit

When the UK leaves the EU, the UK will no longer fall within the territorial scope of the Community registered design.

According to the current draft of the EU–UK Withdrawal Agreement (as at the time of writing), Community design registrations existing at the end of the withdrawal transition period will be cloned onto the UK design register in order to provide continuity of protection in the UK. This will be free and the cloned UK right will inherit the same filing and priority dates as the Community design registration from which it is derived. The holders of pending Community design applications as at the end of the transition period will be able to refile in the UK within nine months to claim the same filing and priority dates as the original Community design application.

In the event of a 'no-deal' Brexit, the UK has indicated its intentions to carry out a broadly similar cloning exercise. Either way, although existing CJEU registered design decisions will, in effect, need an appeal to the UK Supreme Court to be reversed, the UK courts will be free to follow or not follow future CJEU design decisions when interpreting and applying the RDA 1949 (as amended).

Designs that can be validly protected by registration

8.20   This chapter will generally cite relevant provisions from the RDA 1949 (as amended), supported by reference to the Designs Directive and the Community Design Regulation.[6] In terms of case law, the chapter focuses on key developments before the General Court and the Court of Justice together with the leading UK cases. In an attempt to step away from the two dominant but markedly different approaches to design protection which had previously existed in member states' national laws (the so-called 'copyright approach' and the so-called 'patent approach'), the Designs Directive and Community Design Regulation adopted a new 'design approach'. This new 'design approach' was intended to reflect that 'the importance of design in modern societies is at least to a large extent due to the fact that it constitutes a marketing instrument' and a focus, in particular, on the 'communication relationship established between the design and the public'.[7] As we will see, this is reflected in a number of aspects of the Designs Directive and Community Design Regulation discussed in this chapter.

---

[5] UK Government, 'Trade marks and designs if there's no Brexit deal', 24 September 2018, www.gov.uk/government/publications/trade-marks-and-designs-if-theres-no-brexit-deal/trade-marks-and-designs-if-theres-no-brexit-deal.

[6] The RDA 1949 does not always transpose the provisions of the Designs Directive into UK law *verbatim*. This chapter will generally quote the relevant provisions from the RDA 1949 and give details of the corresponding Articles from the Designs Directive and Community Design Regulation, but readers should always check the precise terms of the DD and CDR.

[7] A Kur, 'The Green Paper's "Design Approach"—what's wrong with it?' [1993] EIPR 374–78 at 376–77.

8.21 For a design to be validly registered, it must:

- fall within the definition of 'design' given by the legislation (paras 8.23–8.40);
- be 'new' and have 'individual character' (paras 8.41–8.78); and
- not fall within any of the exclusions from protection (paras 8.79–8.90).

The first two bullet points may be described as *positive* requirements—characteristics that a design must have to be validly registered—while the exclusions are *negative* in character—either the design should be refused registration or should not have been registered or, if a registered design consists in part of such features, the right conferred by registration does not extend to those features.

8.22 Unlike copyright and the unregistered forms of design protection discussed in Chapter 9, protection as a registered design does not arise automatically. An application must be filed and accepted by the relevant registry. However, for designs this is much more of a formality than for other registered IP rights such as trade marks and patents. Neither the UK IPO (for UK registered designs) nor the EUIPO (for registered Community designs) will examine a design application for novelty or individual character. There is also no third-party opposition procedure. As a result, a design may be registered but may well not actually meet the requirements for protection. The novelty and individual character of a UK or Community registered design will only be tested if challenged by a third party.

Definition of 'design'

8.23 'Design' means:[8]

> the appearance of the whole or a part of a product resulting from the features of, in particular, the lines, contours, colours, shape, texture or materials of the product or its ornamentation.

The essence of this definition is that a 'design' is constituted by 'the *appearance* of the whole or part of a *product* . . .'. However, it is the *design* in itself which is protected, not its application to, or embodiment in, a specific product as such.[9] As we shall see later (see para 8.122), this means that the protection conferred by the design registration encompasses use of the design for any product, whether or not the same as the product of the design right holder.

8.24 The features of appearance which may constitute a protectable design can be three-dimensional (eg contours or shape) or two-dimensional (eg colours). The lawyer is at once led to two further questions:

(1) What is a 'product'?

(2) What is meant by the 'appearance' of a product?

Product

8.25 'Product' is defined as:[10]

> any industrial or handicraft item other than a computer program; and, in particular, includes packaging, get-up, graphic symbols, typographic typefaces and parts intended to be assembled into a complex product.

We will return to the issues relating to 'complex products' later (see paras 8.91–8.97).

8.26 An immediately striking feature of the definition of 'product' is its inclusion of 'handicraft items' as well as industrial items, so that the design of artisan items, including sculptures and works of artistic craftsmanship, may be protectable as well as the results of mass production processes. The reference to '*a* product' (emphasis

---

[8] RDA 1949, s 1(2); DD, Art 1(a); CDR, Art 3(a).

[9] For Community registered designs, the application must include an indication of the products in which the design is to be incorporated or to which it is intended to be applied. However, this does not affect the scope of protection of the design: CDR, Arts 36(2) and (6).

[10] RDA 1949, s 1(3); DD, Art 1(b); CDR, Art 3(b).

added) in the definition of 'design' means that the subject matter of a design must consist of a single 'unitary object'; a group of articles may only constitute 'a product' if they are 'linked by aesthetic and functional complementarity' and are 'usually marketed as a unitary product'—for example a cutlery set (consisting of knife, fork, and spoon) or a set consisting of chess board and pieces.[11]

8.27   The inclusion of matter such as graphic symbols within the definition of 'product' represents a change, from a UK perspective, in the way in which this subject is approached. In pre-Directive UK law, these might at most have been seen as designs applied to an article.[12] But now they are to be seen as products in and of themselves. In other words, products (as well as the protectable features of their appearance) may be two-dimensional. Typefaces are also expressly included in the definition of 'product'.

Question

Explain how we can tell from the legislation that two-dimensional designs are now protectable by registration.

8.28   The new law's inclusion of two-dimensional items in the definition of 'product' raises issues about overlap with other IP rights, particularly trade marks and copyright. There is, for example, no reason in principle why a logo which might primarily be thought of as a trade mark cannot also be protected as a registered design—the logo being the *design* for a two-dimensional *product* in the form of a *graphic symbol*.[13] A design could also include an artistic work painted or drawn onto a canvas or paper. The old UK law used to avoid overlaps with copyright in such circumstances by denying registration to printed items of a primarily literary or artistic character and in cases where the article was no more than a carrier for the design.[14] This is no longer the case in the EU design regime, which explicitly envisages cumulation of protection with other IP rights, including trade marks and copyright, as we shall see further at paras 8.130–8.134.

8.29   There are a number of further points of interest arising in relation to the definition of what constitutes a 'product'. It appears, for example, that products do not need to have a physically tangible form. The word 'item' which appears in the definition of 'product' is not defined but does not in itself appear to limit the concept to goods or corporeal moveables. This ties into the notion that designs for, for example, computer screen icons are registrable as designs for two-dimensional *intangible* products. On a different note, there may be questions about how far the word 'item' can be taken to include matter such as buildings and works of architecture. Old UK law did allow registration of designs for structures such as poultry and animal sheds which were prefabricated and portable in that they were delivered to purchasers as a whole.[15] Separately, in a case involving an application to register a heart-shaped strawberry as a design, the EUIPO Third Board of Appeal rejected the notion that living organisms can be considered 'products', on the basis that they are not industrial or handicraft items.[16]

Discussion point   For answer guidance visit **www.oup.com/uk/brown5e**.

To what extent does the definition of 'product' mean that there are overlaps between registered design and copyright subject matter?

---

[11]   Case T-9/15 *Ball Beverage Packaging Europe Ltd v EUIPO* [2018] ECDR 8, paras 41 and 60.

[12]   See, eg, *Apple Computer Inc v Design Registry* [2002] FSR 38 considering the registrability of computer screen icons under the old RDA 1949. Icons appearing on a computer into which they were inherently built (because they were built into the software included in the machine) were treated as designs applied to the computer, the computer being an 'article' for the purposes of the old UK RDA 1949.

[13]   On the overlap with trade marks, see further A Kur, 'No logo!?' (2004) 35(2) IIC 184–86 and A Carboni, 'The overlap between registered Community designs and Community trade marks' (2006) 1(4) JIPLP 256–65.

[14]   Registered Design Rules 1989 (SI 1989/1105), rule 26 (now repealed); *Re Littlewoods Pools Application* (1949) 66 RPC 309.

[15]   Although an air-raid shelter cast in reinforced concrete on site was denied registration under the old RDA 1949: see *Concrete Ltd's Application* (1940) 57 RPC 121.

[16]   Third Board of Appeal, Case R 595/2012–13 *ACJ Ammerlaan*, 18 February 2013.

> **Key points on the meaning of 'product'**
>
> - 'Product' encompasses two- as well as three-dimensional items, and even intangible items such as computer screen icons.
> - 'Product' also includes handicraft items as well as industrial items.
> - The definition of 'product' increases the potential overlap between registered designs and matter which may be the subject of copyright or trade mark protection.

Appearance

8.30   *Appearance* is the second essential element in the definition of design. 'Appearance' is not defined but is said to 'result from':[17]

> the features of, in particular, the lines, contours, colours, shape, texture or materials of the product or its ornamentation.

It is important to note that the expression 'appearance', and thus the definition of 'design', contains no requirement of 'eye appeal' or aesthetic quality. Instead, the expressions 'appearance' and 'design' are neutral in terms of protecting both aesthetic and functional design features. Although difficulties may arise for some functional designs in terms of the exclusions from protection (see paras 8.79–8.86), in itself the definition of 'design' is capable of encompassing purely aesthetic and purely functional designs, as well as designs which are a mixture of both. This was a major departure from the approach taken under old national laws and is one of the most significant features of the 'design approach' adopted in the new EU design regime.[18]

8.31   An interesting question is what, if anything, is intended by the reference to 'texture and materials' in the definition of 'design'. Does this mean that how a product 'feels' as well as how it 'looks' is protectable? Or does the concept of 'appearance' imply that protection is only for design features that can be perceived visually?

8.32   Although there was some suggestion in the Commission's 1991 Green Paper on designs that the concept of design should include aspects of design perceived by the various human senses such as touch as well as sight,[19] the argument that the concept of 'appearance' in the legislation as finally enacted concentrates only on what can be seen is supported by various aspects of the Designs Directive and Community Design Regulation, including:

- the ordinary meaning of the word 'appearance', not only in English but also in the versions found in the other language versions of the Designs Directive and Community Design Regulation;
- the reference in recital 11 of the Designs Directive to registration conferring protection upon design features shown *visibly* in an application; and
- the reference in recital 13 DD and recital 14 CDR, on the assessment of a design's individual character, to 'the overall impression produced on an informed user *viewing* the design'.

As a practical matter, texture and material are also at least to some extent discernible to the eye. In any event, it has now been emphasised by the General Court and the Advocate General that registered design protection under the Designs Directive and Community Design Regulation is concerned with *visual* appearance only. In his Opinion in *PepsiCo, Inc v Grupo Promer Mon Graphic SA*, the Advocate General stated that:[20]

> the protection of designs under the Regulation takes into account only the *visual* impression which the designs produce on the informed user.

---

[17]   RDA 1949, s 1(2); DD, Art 1(a); CDR, Art 3(a).

[18]   See further A Kur, 'The Green Paper's "Design Approach"—what's wrong with it?' [1993] EIPR 374–78 and G Dinwoodie, 'Federalized Functionalism: The Future of Design Protection in the European Union' (1996) 24 AIPLA QJ 611.

[19]   Green Paper on the legal protection of industrial design, European Commission, June 1991, III/F/5131/91-EN, paras 5.4.7.1 and 5.4.7.2.

[20]   Case C-281/10 P *PepsiCo, Inc v Grupo Promer Mon Graphic SA*, Opinion of Advocate General Mengozzi, [2012] FSR 5, para AG73 (emphasis in original).

In his view, this reading of the Regulation had been 'convincingly demonstrated' by the General Court in its decision in the *Grupo Promer* case.[21] The UK courts have taken the same view. In *Gimex International Groupe Import Export v Chill Bag Co Ltd and Others* (Patents County Court, England & Wales), Judge Birss QC considered the reference to 'materials' in the definition of 'design' at Article 3(a) CDR. He noted:[22]

> it bears emphasising that Community design law is concerned with the *visual* appearance of products. The materials can only be relevant insofar as they influence the appearance of a product (emphasis added).

 Exercise

Are there any policy arguments which you can think of to counter the view that, as a matter of principle, design laws should be solely concerned with what can be seen? Can you think of any examples where 'feel' might be an important element in product design, particularly for the user of the relevant product?

8.33   In general, the interpretation of 'appearance' as being about what can be seen does not mean that the features in question must at all times be visible to the customer or user. Thus, to take an example from the old UK law, computer screen icons only visible when the related software is running on the computer should continue to be capable of being registered as they were under the old UK law.[23] What will be important is that the designs have an 'appearance' in that they are capable of being seen.[24] In *Biscuits Poult*, the General Court held that protection is only conferred on 'the visible parts' of a product, meaning in that case that a Community registration for the design of a chocolate cookie could not include, as part of the protected 'design', an element of chocolate filling visible only if the cookie was broken open.[25] This decision has been criticised for its undue focus on only the *externally* visible elements of the design,[26] and may be confusing the special rules applied to 'complex products' which were not applicable in the case. It would, it is suggested, have been more correct to accept the internal elements of the cookie as constituting part of the 'design' since those internal elements do have an appearance which is visually perceptible.

Interpreting design representations

8.34   For registered designs, the design features forming the protected 'design' must be depicted in a representation, or series of representations showing the design from different perspectives. The representations must be filed as part of the design application and will be used to identify what constitutes the 'design' for which protection is sought.[27] The importance of getting the design representations right is illustrated by the Court of Justice decision in the *Jägermeister* case.[28] In that case, there was a dispute over whether the design applicant had provided sufficiently clear representations in two Community design filings. The difficulty was that, while the applicant claimed that its designs only related to drinking beakers, the representations

---

[21] ibid, Opinion of Advocate General Mengozzi, para AG73. See further General Court, Case T-9/07 *Grupo Promer Mon Graphic SA v Office for Harmonisation in the Internal Market (Trade Marks and Designs) (OHIM) with PepsiCo Inc (Intervener)* [2010] ECDR 7, para 50. This aspect of the General Court's decision was not appealed to the Court of Justice in the *Grupo Promer* case: see further para 8.49.

[22] [2012] ECDR 25, para 25; see also para 58.

[23] *Apple Computer Inc v Design Registry* [2002] FSR 38.

[24] Note, however, the special rules on visibility in normal use, novelty, and individual character for component parts of complex products in RDA 1949, s 1B(8)–(9), DD, Art 3(3)–(4), and CDR, Art 4(2)–(3) (see paras 8.91–8.97).

[25] Case T-494/12 *Biscuits Poult SAS v Office for Harmonisation in the Internal Market (Trade Marks and Designs) (OHIM), Banketbakkkerij Merba BV* (intervener), General Court, 9 September 2014 (currently unreported).

[26] M Howe, *Russell-Clarke and Howe on Industrial Designs* (9th edn, 2016), para 2-026; D Stone, *European Union Design Law: A Practitioner's Guide* (2nd edn, 2016), paras 4.41–4.42.

[27] For UK designs, the application may also include a written description: rule 4(5) of the Registered Designs Rules 2006. For Community registered designs, an application may optionally contain a description explaining the representations, but it is explicitly provided in the CDR that this shall not affect the scope of protection of the design: Arts 36(3)(a) and 36(6) CDR. The General Court has confirmed that a description has no impact on the scope of protection for or in the assessment of novelty and individual character of a Community registered design: Case T-9/15 *Ball Beverage Packaging Europe Ltd v EUIPO* [2018] ECDR 8, paras 66 and 67.

[28] Case C-217/17 P *Mast-Jägermeister SE v EUIPO* [2018] ECDR 20.

which it had filed showed beakers and drinks bottles. It was therefore uncertain precisely what was claimed. The applicant was offered the opportunity to amend its representations, but did not take this up. The Court of Justice upheld the refusal of the disputed applications, on the basis that the applicant's design representations did not enable what was claimed as the design to be clearly identified.

8.35   Design representations are critical in determining what constitutes the protected registered design. An applicant may choose to represent his design using a range of means including line drawings, computer-aided design (CAD) drawings, or photographs.[29] Some of these will be more effective—and some more limiting—than others. The *Magmatic* dispute concerning the 'Trunki' ride-on children's suitcase (see further para 8.66) provides a salutary lesson in the care with which the applicant must decide how to represent his design. Various points of dispute arose over the interpretation of the greyscale CAD drawings used in the contested design registration (see Figure 8.11). One of those related to the differences in tonal shading between, on the one hand, the body of the case and horns which were shown in grey and, on the other, the wheels and strap, which were shown in black. At first instance, Arnold J treated the design as claiming just the shape of the suitcase. However, both the Court of Appeal and Supreme Court attached significance to these tonal differences. Giving the judgment of the Supreme Court, Lord Neuberger described the design as claiming 'not merely a specific shape, but a shape in two contrasting colours'.[30] The fact that the allegedly infringing cases did not have this colour contrast was a factor supporting the finding that they did not infringe.

8.36   Picking the right form of design representation has proved to be a particular issue when it comes to distinguishing between, on the one hand, designs for 'shape only'—that is, designs which are intended to consist of the shape of a product without specification or limitation as to any surface decoration or colour—and, on the other hand, designs for 'unadorned shape'—that is, designs consisting of a shape which is specifically intended to be unadorned. 'Shape only' designs can be infringed by products which are decorated in different ways—a 'like for like' comparison in the infringement analysis should compare only the shapes of the protected design and alleged infringement, without taking into account their respective (and possibly very different) surface decorations. In contrast, in the case of a design for an 'unadorned shape', any kind of decoration or adornment on the alleged infringement could take it outside the scope of protection of the design.

8.37   The conventional understanding has generally been that representations showing a design with no surface ornamentation should result in protection for the depicted design against infringements both with and without added surface decoration or ornamentation. This understanding has, however, been challenged by UK case law. In *Samsung* (para 8.64), a dispute over a Community registered design belonging to Apple for a design of a tablet computer, breaking with the generally accepted convention, Apple claimed an absence of ornamentation as a specific feature of its Community design.[31] The issue also arose in *Magmatic*. While the judge at first instance treated the design representations as claiming only the shape of the Magmatic suitcase without specification or limitation as to surface decoration, the Court of Appeal specifically took into account the absence of any surface decoration or ornamentation in Magmatic's CAD drawings as a positive feature of the Magmatic 'design'.[32] This led to the Court of Appeal overturning the first instance judgment and finding that there was no infringement of the Magmatic designs, because of the different overall impressions created by the combined shape and surface decoration of the alleged infringements compared to the (unadorned) Magmatic registration. The Supreme Court upheld the Court of Appeal's approach. Unhelpfully, however, the Supreme Court also declined to provide authoritative guidance on how a design applicant is supposed to be able to identify, in his design representations, whether his design is for 'shape only' or 'unadorned shape'. Lord Neuberger indicated that a line drawing would be 'much more likely' to be interpreted as claiming 'shape only' than a CAD image.[33] However,

---

[29] The EUIPO currently also accepts 3D computer-animated files, although only in addition to conventional static views.
[30] *PMS International Group Plc v Magmatic Ltd* [2016] ECDR 15, para 53.
[31] On that basis, the presence of a trade mark on the front and rear of Samsung's products could constitute a difference, even if only a slight one, when compared to the registered design: *Samsung Electronics (UK) Ltd v Apple Inc* [2013] ECDR 2, paras 15–20.
[32] *Magmatic Ltd v PMS International Ltd* [2014] ECDR 20, para 41.
[33] *PMS International Group Plc v Magmatic Ltd* [2016] ECDR 15, para 46.

after considering arguments pointing either way in relation to the Magmatic design, he preferred to 'leave . . . open' the question of whether absence of ornamentation was or was not a feature of the disputed design in that case.[34] The Supreme Court also declined to refer the matter to the CJEU. This ruling has been much criticised for its lack of clarity and for the state of uncertainty in which it leaves designers and practitioners in the UK. On a practical level, commentators have speculated whether Magmatic's case would have been better served if a set of line drawings for the shape of the 'Trunki' case had been used rather than a CAD image. In the meantime, it is generally thought that black-and-white line drawings will confer the broadest scope of protection.[35]

8.38   A further challenge arises when an applicant only wants to claim design protection for the appearance of *part* of a product. For Community registered designs,[36] there is no option for the design applicant to provide a written statement which can be used determinatively to identify the part of the product for which protection is claimed, or to disclaim elements which are not part of the claimed design. How then can the applicant indicate visually, in the design representations themselves, the particular part of the product for which he wishes to claim protection?

8.39   A common drafting convention is the use of dotted or broken lines to denote parts of the depicted product in which protection is not claimed. The dotted lines serve as a form of visual disclaimer, indicating that the dotted elements are not intended to form part of the protected 'design'. In *Sphere Time*, a validity dispute concerning a Community design for a lanyard with attached watch, the General Court recognised this drafting convention, also noted in the EUIPO's examination guidelines, and held that the elements shown in dotted lines in the contested design (see Figure 8.1) did not form part of the protected design.

Figure 8.1 *Sphere Time* design representation

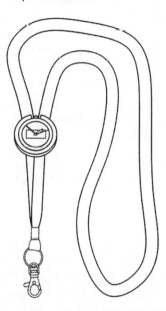

8.40   The English courts have, however, adopted a different approach. The practice in the UK has been to construe each design representation on its own merits. This has led to varying interpretations of dotted lines. For example, in *Samsung* (para 8.64), while some elements shown in dotted lines in Apple's design representations (socket connectors) were held not to form part of the contested design, another element

[34]   ibid, para 50.

[35]   See, eg, J Stobbs, G Weller, and Y Zhou, 'Overview of United Kingdom trade marks and design decisions 2016' (2017) 48(2) IIC 195–207; B Trimmer and G Parsons, 'Trunki's crazy (registered design) ride: PMS International Group Plc v Magmatic Ltd' (2016) 38(7) EIPR 451–58.

[36]   Disclaimers are permitted for UK registered designs: rule 6 Registered Designs Rules 2006.

shown in dotted lines (the border around the screen under the glass surface of the tablet) was treated as a visible part of the Apple 'design'.[37] Similarly, in *Kohler Mira Ltd v Bristan Group Ltd*, a dispute concerning designs for shower control panels, while for one design registration dashed lines around the front face of the shower control unit were held to indicate that the face was transparent or translucent, in the other design registration dashed lines around the shower control knobs (see Figure 8.2) were held to indicate that no protection was sought for the knobs.[38] Conversely, in *Pulseon OY v Garmin (Europe) Limited*, a case concerning designs for wrist heart rate monitoring devices, the High Court was prepared to accept that the design protected by the claimant's registered Community designs did not include certain screws, which were shown in the design representations holding the bar where the wrist strap for the device would be fastened. This was despite the fact that the screws were not shown in dotted lines—so, according to the usual conventions, would have been understood to form part of the claimed design.[39]

Figure 8.2 *Kohler Mira* design representation

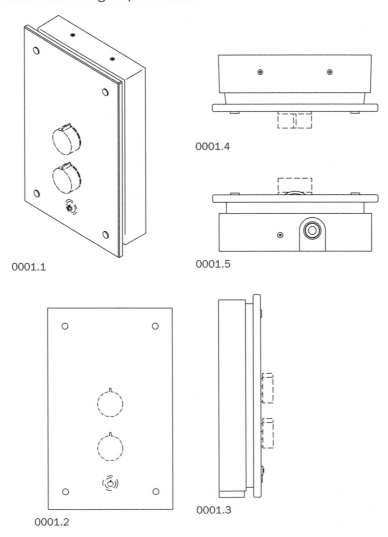

0001.1

0001.4

0001.5

0001.2

0001.3

---

[37] *Samsung Electronics (UK) Ltd v Apple Inc* (High Court, 9 July 2012) [2013] ECDR 1, paras 9–11; *Samsung Electronics (UK) Ltd v Apple Inc* (Court of Appeal, 18 October 2012) [2013] ECDR 2, paras 21–24.

[38] *Kohler Mira Ltd v Bristan Group Ltd* (Patents County Court, 23 January 2013) [2014] FSR 1, para 52.

[39] *Pulseon OY v Garmin (Europe) Limited* [2018] EWHC 47 (Ch), paras 44–45.

The difference in approach between the practices of, on the one hand, the EUIPO and the General Court and, on the other, the English courts creates uncertainties for design applicants in deciding how best to represent their designs, and for third parties consulting the designs register in understanding whether dotted or dashed elements in design representations are or are not part of the protected 'design'.

> **Key points about appearance**
>
> - Appearance is concerned with what can be *seen* in a product and not, despite the legislation's reference to 'texture or materials', with what can be perceived by other human senses.
>
> - This does not mean that the design feature in question has to be visible all the time, but it must relate to a visible part of the product.
>
> - There are no requirements that the appearance must be aesthetic or have 'eye-appeal' and the definition of 'design' does not in itself distinguish between functional or aesthetic design features.

The requirements of novelty and individual character

8.41   In order to be validly registered, a design must be 'new' and have 'individual character'.[40] These are separate and cumulative requirements. The determination of whether a design is new (sometimes also referred to as 'novel') and has individual character is made by way of a comparison with other designs that have been made available to the public before the 'relevant date'. This body of existing designs is sometimes referred to as the 'prior art'. For registered designs, the relevant date is the date on which the application for the registration of the design was made or the priority date of that application, where priority is claimed (see para 8.6). As will be seen, the requirements of novelty and individual character impose a higher threshold for designs to meet in order to be protected than the requirement of originality in copyright law. However, the nature of the protection conferred by a registered design is also stronger than the rights conferred by copyright, justifying a more demanding regime.

Novelty

8.42   A design is 'new':[41]

> if no identical design or no design whose features differ only in immaterial details has been made available to the public before the relevant date.

8.43   To be 'new', therefore, a design must differ from previous designs, at least in material details. However, what constitutes an 'immaterial' detail is not defined. The General Court has taken this to refer to 'details that are not immediately perceptible'.[42] In practice, the requirement of novelty is likely to be of relatively limited importance, since a design which is novel must nonetheless go on to meet the more demanding requirement of 'individual character'.

8.44   As well as the question of what constitutes a material or immaterial design detail, there are also as yet unresolved issues over how to assess novelty—for example, should this be done through the eyes of the 'informed user' as in the assessment of 'individual character' (see below) or on some other basis and, if so, what? The English courts have suggested that the perspective of the 'informed user' is not relevant to the assessment of novelty.[43]

---

[40] RDA 1949, s 1B(1); DD, Art 3(2); CDR, Art 4(1).   [41] RDA 1949, s 1B(2); DD, Art 4; CDR, Art 5.

[42] Case T-68/11 *Erich Kastenholz v Office for Harmonisation in the Internal Market (Trade Marks and Designs) (OHIM), Qwatchme A/S (intervener)*, General Court (unreported), para 37.

[43] *Green Lane Products Ltd v PMS International Group Ltd* [2008] FSR 28 (CA), para 41.

Discussion point   For answer guidance visit **www.oup.com/uk/brown5e**.

In what circumstances is the test of novelty likely to dispose of an invalidity challenge? Why is the test of individual character likely to be more important in practice?

Key points on novelty

- To be validly registered, a design must be 'new'.
- A design is 'new' if it is not identical to any previous design and differs from such designs in more than immaterial details.

Individual character

8.45   A design will have 'individual character' if:[44]

> the overall impression it produces on the informed user differs from the overall impression produced on such a user by any design which has been made available to the public before the relevant date.

In assessing the extent to which a design has individual character:[45]

> the degree of freedom of the author in creating the design shall be taken into consideration.

The recitals to the Designs Directive and Community Design Regulation add:[46]

> The assessment as to whether a design has individual character should be based on whether the overall impression produced on an informed user viewing the design clearly differs from that produced on him by the existing design corpus, taking into consideration the nature of the product to which the design is applied or in which it is incorporated, and in particular the industrial sector to which it belongs and the degree of freedom of the designer in developing the design.

Question

What factors must be considered according to the legislation in assessing the 'individual character' of a design?

8.46   Assessing individual character is more complex than assessing novelty. The concepts of 'individual character', 'overall impression', the 'informed user', and 'design freedom' were all new to the Designs Directive and Community Design Regulation and are a key part of the new 'design approach' underlying the EU legislation. These expressions are, however, not defined. Unsurprisingly given the key importance of the requirement of individual character in the overall process of determining validity, the interpretation and application of these concepts have received much more by way of judicial attention from the General Court, Court of Justice, and higher courts in the UK.

8.47   It should be noted that the scope of protection against infringement conferred upon a design by the European regime is also dependent on the concept of 'overall impression': a protected design will be infringed by any design which does not produce on the informed user a different overall impression (see para 8.117).[47]

---

[44] RDA 1949, s 1B(3); DD, Art 5(1); CDR, Art 6(1).

[45] RDA 1949, s 1B(4); DD, Art 5(2); CDR, Art 6(2). RDA 1949, s 1B(4) uses the expression 'author' as this is the term used in the RDA 1949 in relation to first ownership (see RDA 1949, s 2; see also para 8.106). However, the DD and CDR both refer to the 'degree of freedom of the *designer*' (DD, Art 5(2); CDR, Art 6(2)). This terminology, referring to the 'degree of freedom of the designer', is more widely used, including in UK case law, and will be used in this chapter.

[46] DD, recital 13; CDR, recital 14.   [47] RDA 1949, s 7(1); DD, Art 9(1); CDR, Art 10(1).

The degree of freedom of the designer in developing the design is also to be taken into consideration in assessing the scope of protection against infringement.[48] The assessment of whether a design produces the same or a different 'overall impression' on the 'informed user' should be the same in the context of both validity and infringement. This adds to the critical importance of the concept of 'overall impression' within the EU design regime. It is also possible to draw from validity case law in infringement cases and vice versa when dealing with 'overall impression' and related concepts, and we shall do so in this section of the chapter.

8.48   The interpretation and application of the concepts of 'individual character', 'overall impression', the 'informed user', and 'design freedom' have been addressed in validity decisions by the General Court and Court of Justice and (in particular) in four major UK infringement cases which have reached the English Court of Appeal and, in one instance, the UK Supreme Court.[49] As noted previously, the principles developed in relation to the assessment of overall impression should be equally applicable to infringement and validity cases; so, although these were infringement disputes, these cases are of considerable importance to this discussion of individual character and will be discussed here. This section will look at each of the key concepts in turn.

The 'informed user'

8.49   Whether a design has individual character depends on whether it produces a different overall impression upon the 'informed user' compared to earlier designs. The 'informed user' is the first of a number of notional legal persons which we will encounter during the course of this book, others being the 'average consumer' of registered trade mark law (see para 15.49) and the 'skilled person' of patent law (see paras 11.53–11.55). It is necessary to adopt the perspective of the 'informed user' when assessing the overall impression produced by a design. However, the concept of the 'informed user' is not defined in the Designs Directive or Community Design Regulation. The leading authorities at an EU level can be found in two judgments of the General Court and a judgment in one of those cases, *Grupo Promer*, from the Court of Justice:

■ **Case T-9/07 *PepsiCo, Inc v Grupo Promer Mon Graphic SA*, General Court [2010] ECDR 7; Case C-281/10 P Court of Justice [2012] FSR 5**

This case concerned an invalidity challenge to a registered Community design for products described by the registrant as 'promotional items for games'. These were small, round discs, more commonly known as 'pogs', 'rappers', or 'tazos'. These are often distributed as free gifts for children inside the packaging of other products. The EUIPO Third Board of Appeal had dismissed the challenge to validity based on conflict with an earlier design belonging to the challenger, Grupo Promer (see Figures 8.3 and 8.4). The General Court found that the registered Community design was invalid for lack of individual character. The case was appealed to the Court of Justice, which upheld the General Court's ruling.

Figure 8.3 PepsiCo Community registered design no 74463–0001

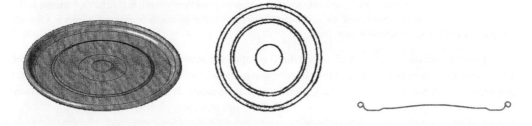

---

[48]   RDA 1949, s 7(3); DD, Art 9(2); CDR, Art 10(2). The English courts have also looked to DD, recital 13 and CDR, recital 14 for guidance in the context of infringement case law. Eg: *Procter & Gamble Co v Reckitt Benckiser (UK) Ltd* (CA) [2008] FSR 8, paras 15–19; *Dyson Ltd v Vax Ltd* (HC) [2010] ECDR 18, paras 39 and 44–45 and (CA) [2012] FSR 4, para 34; *Samsung Electronics (UK) Ltd v Apple, Inc* (HC) [2013] ECDR 1, para 48.

[49]   The General Court has also considered and applied the test of individual character/overall impression in a number of further appeals from the Boards of Appeal; there are also now numerous further first instance UK designs decisions.

Figure 8.4 Grupo Promer Community registered design no 53186–0001

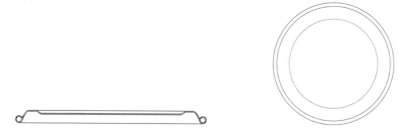

■ Case T-153/08 *Shenzhen Taiden Industrial Co Ltd v Office for Harmonisation in the Internal Market (Trade Marks and Designs) (OHIM), Bosch Security Systems BV,* General Court, 22 June 2010 (currently unreported)

This dispute concerned a registered Community design for units to be used by speakers at conferences.[50] The design was challenged for lack of individual character in the light of an earlier registered design and documentary evidence of the advertisement for sale of units made to that design. The designs in question had a similar overall shape and a number of similar features including speakers, microphone on a stem, control buttons, and screen. This judgment of the General Court post-dates its own earlier decision in *Grupo Promer* but predates the decision of the Court of Justice in the *Grupo Promer* case. In *Shenzhen*, the registered Community design was found by the General Court to be invalid for lack of individual character.

8.50   In *Grupo Promer*, the General Court held that the informed user is 'neither a manufacturer nor a seller' of the relevant products, and that he/she is 'particularly observant and has some awareness of the state of the prior art'.[51] This was upheld and expanded on by the Court of Justice. The Court of Justice held that the 'informed user' was a concept which must be understood as:[52]

> lying somewhere between that of the average consumer, applicable in trade mark matters, who need not have any specific knowledge and who, as a rule, makes no direct comparison between the trade marks in conflict, and the sectoral expert, who is an expert with detailed technical expertise. Thus, the concept of the informed user may be understood as referring, not to a user of average attention, but to a particularly observant one, either because of his personal experience or his extensive knowledge of the sector in question.

The Court of Justice went on to say that:[53]

> as regards the informed user's level of attention, it should be noted that, although the informed user is not the well-informed and reasonably observant and circumspect average consumer who normally perceives a design as a whole and does not proceed to analyse its various details . . ., he is also not an expert or specialist capable of observing in detail the minimal differences that may exist between the designs in conflict. Thus, the qualifier 'informed' suggests that, without being a designer or a technical expert, the user knows the various designs which exist in the sector concerned, possesses a certain degree of knowledge with regard to the features which those designs normally include, and, as a result of his interest in the products concerned, shows a relatively high degree of attention when he uses them.

8.51   Where possible, the informed user will make a direct comparison between the designs in dispute; however, such a comparison may be impracticable or uncommon in the sector concerned, in which case an indirect comparison of the designs in suit based on recollection may be valid.[54] It is possible for the 'informed user'

---

[50] A copy of the decision of the General Court, including images of the contested registered Community design and evidence of prior designs relied upon is available at http://curia.europa.eu/juris/document/document.jsf?text=&docid=81091&pageIndex=0&doclang=en&mode=lst&dir=&occ=first&part=1&cid=831028.

[51] Case T-9/07 *Grupo Promer Mon Graphic SA v Office for Harmonisation in the Internal Market (Trade Marks and Designs) (OHIM) with PepsiCo Inc (Intervener)*, General Court [2010] ECDR 7, para 62.

[52] Case C-281/10 P *PepsiCo, Inc v Grupo Promer Mon Graphic SA*, Court of Justice, [2012] FSR 5, para 53.

[53] ibid, para 59.   [54] ibid, paras 55–57.

to have more than one embodiment and the Court of Justice approved the finding of the General Court that, on the facts of the *Grupo Promer* case, the informed user was capable of being both a child in the approximate age range of five to ten or a marketing manager in a company that made goods promoted by giving away 'pogs', 'rappers', or 'tazos'.[55]

8.52 In *Shenzhen*, the General Court also elaborated upon the level of technical expertise of the informed user. The General Court emphasised that 'the status of "user" implies that the person concerned uses the product in which the design is incorporated, in accordance with the purpose for which that product is intended'.[56] The General Court added that although the qualifier 'informed' suggests that the user knows the various designs which exist in the sector concerned, possesses a certain degree of knowledge with regard to their normal features, and shows a relatively high degree of attention when using them:[57]

> that factor does not imply that the informed user is able to distinguish, beyond the experience gained by using the product concerned, the aspects of the appearance of the product which are dictated by the product's technical function from those which are arbitrary.

On the facts of *Shenzhen*, the General Court agreed with the Board of Appeal's characterisation of the informed user as 'anyone who regularly attends conferences or formal meetings at which the various participants have a conference unit with a microphone on the table in front of them'.[58]

8.53 The decisions of the General Court and Court of Justice in *Grupo Promer* and *Shenzhen* have been extensively cited and applied by the English courts on the issue of the 'informed user'. The principles are usefully summarised in the *Samsung* first instance decision.[59] In *Dyson* (para 8.57), a dispute concerning bagless cyclonic vacuum cleaners, the 'informed user' was held to be a 'knowledgeable user of domestic vacuum cleaners'.[60] In *Samsung* (para 8.64), the dispute concerning tablet computers, it was held that the informed user was a 'user of handheld (tablet) computers'.[61] In *Magmatic* (para 8.66), the dispute concerning the 'Trunki' ride-on suitcase, the 'informed user' was agreed between the parties to be both a three-to-six-year-old child and a parent, carer, or relative of such a child.[62]

The degree of freedom of the designer
8.54 This was discussed at some length by the General Court in the *Grupo Promer* case.[63] The General Court explained that:[64]

> the designer's degree of freedom in developing his design is established, *inter alia*, by the constraints of the features imposed by the technical function of the product or an element thereof, or by statutory requirements applicable to the product. Those constraints result in a standardisation of certain features, which will thus be common to the designs applied to the product concerned.

[55] ibid, para 54. Several further General Court cases have confirmed that there may be more than one informed user—for example: *Sphere Time v OHIM, Punch SAS* (Case T-68/10) [2011] ECDR 20; *El Hogar Perfecto del Siglio XXI, SL v OHIM, Wenf International Advisers Ltd (intervening)* [2014] ECDR 1. In *Sphere Time*, the General Court held that, in cases in which there may be multiple embodiments of the informed user, it is sufficient for a finding of lack of individual character that only one of the relevant categories of informed user perceives the designs in suit as producing the same overall impression: para 56.
[56] Case T-153/08 *Shenzhen Taiden Industrial Co Ltd v Office for Harmonisation in the Internal Market (Trade Marks and Designs) (OHIM), Bosch Security Systems BV* (22 June 2010, currently unreported), para 46.
[57] ibid, paras 48–49.   [58] ibid, paras 49–50.
[59] *Samsung Electronics (UK) Ltd v Apple, Inc* (HC) [2013] ECDR 1, paras 33–35, cited subsequently in *Whitby Specialist Vehicles Ltd v Yorkshire Specialist Vehicles Ltd and Others* [2015] ECDR 11, para 20; *Pulseon OY v Garmin (Europe) Limited* [2018] EWHC 47 (Ch), para 19; *L'Oréal Société Anonyme v RN Ventures Ltd* [2018] ECDR 14, para 145.
[60] *Dyson Ltd v Vax Ltd* (HC) [2010] ECDR 18, para 50.   [61] *Samsung Electronics (UK) Ltd v Apple, Inc* (HC) [2013] ECDR 1, para 66.
[62] *Magmatic Ltd v PMS International Ltd* (High Court) [2013] ECC 29, para 55, although Arnold J had some doubt about whether a child should be regarded as an informed user for a product which, unlike the 'pogs' in *Grupo Promer*, were not something which the child might purchase with his or her pocket money.
[63] This aspect of the General Court's decision was unaffected by the appeal to the Court of Justice. See Case C-281/10 P *PepsiCo, Inc v Grupo Promer Mon Graphic SA*, Court of Justice, [2012] FSR 5, paras 39–46.
[64] Case T-9/07 *Grupo Promer Mon Graphic SA v Office for Harmonisation in the Internal Market (Trade Marks and Designs) (OHIM) with PepsiCo Inc (Intervener)*, General Court [2010] ECDR 7, para 67.

On the facts of the case, the designer's design freedom was 'severely constrained' by the need for the product to fit the paradigm of a small, flat, or nearly flat disc made of plastic or metal, often slightly curved towards the centre so that it made a noise if the centre of the disc was pressed by a child, a design not possessing these characteristics being unlikely to be accepted by the marketplace; design freedom was also constrained by the need for the product to be inexpensive, safe for children, and fit to be added to the products which it promoted.[65] Although not explicitly commented upon, these factual findings on design freedom seem to widen the scope of relevant constraints further from just the technical and statutory matters explicitly identified as relevant by the Court in the passage quoted immediately above. This was not addressed by the Court of Justice in the *Grupo Promer* appeal.[66]

8.55   In *Grupo Promer*, the General Court also explained how to take design freedom into account as part of the assessment of overall impression. It held that:[67]

> in so far as similarities between the designs at issue relate to common features such as those described . . . above, those similarities will have only minor importance in the overall impression produced by those designs on the informed user. In addition, the more the designer's freedom in developing the design is restricted, the more likely minor differences between the designs at issue will be sufficient to produce a different overall impression on the informed user.

In other words, similarities between designs which relate to common features dictated by design constraints will have only minor importance in the overall impression produced by the designs on the informed user, the informed user being more affected by those aspects of the designs which are not subject to design constraints. As the Advocate General explained in the *Grupo Promer* appeal to the Court of Justice:[68]

> The need to take account of the designer's creative freedom arises because some features of the product to which the design relates are, so to speak, 'compulsory': as a result, the designer is not free to change them and the fact that they bear similarities to the features of another design cannot be regarded as significant.

However, the greater the restrictions on the designer's freedom in developing the contested design, the more it is likely that minor differences in the unconstrained aspects of the design will be enough to produce a different overall impression on the informed user.

8.56   Design freedom was also considered by the General Court in *Shenzhen*. In that case, the General Court accepted that design freedom was restricted insofar as certain features, such as a speaker and microphone, control buttons, and screen, were necessary in a conference unit, but held that that only concerned the presence of such features in the unit and did not have a significant impact on how those features were actually configured or on the specific form or appearance of the unit itself.[69] Evidence of design freedom could be found in the evidence of varying designs in the existing design corpus.[70] On the facts, the Court found that the degree of design freedom for conference units was relatively wide.[71] General trends in design were not relevant.[72]

8.57   The issue of design freedom has also been considered in UK case law, with the English courts addressing some further points of principle.

---

[65] ibid, paras 68–70.

[66] The Advocate General in *Grupo Promer* expressed the view that design freedom should only be impacted by constraints of a strictly functional nature: Case C-281/10 P *PepsiCo, Inc v Grupo Promer Mon Graphic SA*, Court of Justice, [2012] FSR 5, para AG31. Subsequent General Court decisions have reiterated the focus on constraints arising from technical function or statutory requirements: Case T-525/13 *H&M Hennes & Mauritz BV & Co KG* [2015] ECDR 20, para 28; Case T-90/16 *Thomas Murphy v EUIPO* [2018] ECDR 9, para 36.

[67] Case T-9/07 *Grupo Promer Mon Graphic SA v Office for Harmonisation in the Internal Market (Trade Marks and Designs) (OHIM) with PepsiCo Inc (Intervener)*, General Court [2010] ECDR 7, para 72.

[68] Case C-281/10 P *PepsiCo, Inc v Grupo Promer Mon Graphic SA*, Opinion of Advocate General Mengozzi, [2012] FSR 5, para AG29. See further paras AG28–32.

[69] Case T-153/08 *Shenzhen Taiden Industrial Co Ltd v Office for Harmonisation in the Internal Market (Trade Marks and Designs) (OHIM), Bosch Security Systems BV* (22 June 2010, currently unreported), paras 53–54.

[70] ibid, para 55.   [71] ibid, para 62.

[72] ibid, para 58; see also Case T-357/12 *Sachi Premium-Outdoor Furniture v OHIM* (unreported), para 23. Followed in the UK in *Cantel Medical (UK) Limited and Another v ARC Medical Design Limited* [2018] EWHC 345 (Pat), para 176.

■ *Procter & Gamble Co v Reckitt Benckiser (UK) Ltd* [2008] FSR 8 (CA)

The competing designs were for air freshener spray canisters. Images of the registered Community design and the alleged infringement, said by the claimant to produce the same overall impression, are shown at Figures 8.5 and 8.6.

Figure 8.5 Images from Procter & Gamble Community registered design no 000097969–0001

Figure 8.6 Images of the alleged infringement in *Procter & Gamble Co v Reckitt Benckiser (UK) Ltd* [2008] FSR 8

At first instance, Lewison J had found that the designs did produce the same overall impression on the informed user. However, on appeal the Court of Appeal disagreed. The Court of Appeal's comments on the informed user and overall impression test did not have the benefit of the guidance from the General Court and Court of Justice discussed previously and should, therefore, be read subject to these more recent developments and other, more recent UK case law. However, the Court of Appeal did nonetheless identify some helpful points of principle on design freedom which, it is suggested, remain correct and relevant. Jacob LJ observed, in particular, that:

- the 'degree of freedom of the designer' to be taken into account in assessing overall impression is an objective concept, not defined by the actual constraints specifically acting upon any particular party (para 31);

- a registered design which marks a large departure from the existing design corpus is indicative of a wide degree of design freedom (para 57).

■ *Dyson Ltd v Vax Ltd* [2010] ECDR 18 (HC); [2012] FSR 4 (CA)

Dyson was proprietor of a UK registered design for a bagless cyclonic vacuum cleaner. Vax was alleged to have infringed Dyson's registration by selling its own bagless cyclonic vacuum called the 'Mach Zen'. Although Dyson's registration predated the Designs Directive, the claim fell to be decided under the new regime and the key question was, therefore, whether the 'Mach Zen' produced the same overall impression on the informed user. Images from Dyson's UK design registration and corresponding views of the 'Mach Zen' are shown at Figures 8.7 and 8.8.

By the time of the first instance decision in *Dyson* the General Court had given judgment in *Grupo Promer* and *Shenzhen* and Arnold J adopted the key aspects of these decisions in dealing with the *Dyson* case.[73] Arnold J held that evidence of design freedom could come not only from the earlier design corpus, but also from designs produced after the registered design if, for example, they showed a wide variety of different designs.[74] However, in this case there were various constraints on design freedom which he accepted could be relevant to the assessment of overall impression, including matters of technical functionality, the need to incorporate features common to the relevant products, economic considerations (eg price), and technical specification (eg whether the designs were for higher or lower performance products).[75] Moreover, whereas a design which was markedly different from what had gone before should normally have a wider scope of protection (as held in *Procter & Gamble*), that would not be the case where the striking elements of the design were, in fact, ones where there was little design freedom because of technical constraints—this might be the case, for example, where a new design reflected new technology which also carried with it new technical requirements that had not been relevant to earlier designs.[76]

In comparing the registered design and the alleged infringement, the judge considered a number of different design features, including: their transparent bins; the angle at which the bins were inclined; the oversized design of the rear wheels and their spacing; and the wheel arches, operational buttons,

Figure 8.7 Images from Dyson's UK design registration no 2,043,779

---

[73] The Court of Justice had not given its judgment in *Grupo Promer* at the time.
[74] *Dyson Ltd v Vax Ltd* (HC) [2010] ECDR 18, para 37.   [75] ibid, paras 33–34 and 61–62.   [76] ibid, paras 40–41.

Figure 8.8 Images of the alleged infringement in *Dyson Ltd v Vax Ltd* [2012] FSR 4

and pedals. Although there were similarities between the designs, the judge concluded that many of these features were subject to design constraints and that the informed user would not therefore consider the similarities to be particularly significant. There were also a number of visual differences between Dyson's design and the Mach Zen. The judge held that, 'standing back from the details' (para 92), Dyson's registered design and the Mach Zen produced different overall impressions. He noted also that:

> The overall impression produced by the Registered Design is smooth, curving and elegant. The overall impression produced by the Mach Zen is rugged, angular and industrial, even somewhat brutal (para 93).

Other than in relation to one point on design freedom,[77] the Court of Appeal agreed with this assessment and upheld the finding that the two designs produced different overall impressions.[78]

8.58 In *Samsung* (para 8.64), the first instance judge endorsed Arnold J's ruling on the potential limiting effect of design constraints on the overall impression produced by otherwise strikingly new designs, although in *Samsung* there also was some disagreement (not resolved) between the parties as to whether relevant constraints on design freedom should encompass factors other than technical ones as had been held in *Dyson*.[79] That disagreement persists into more recent English case law.[80]

Overall impression

8.59 As emphasised by the General Court in *Shenzhen*, the individual character of a design is not assessed by looking at an amalgam of selected features of a number of different earlier designs. Instead, the comparison must be conducted on a design-by-design basis, comparing the overall impression produced by the registered design against the overall impression produced, in turn, by each individual earlier design relied on in support of the allegation of invalidity.[81] This has been confirmed by the Court of Justice in *Karen Millen*.[82]

---

[77] *Dyson Ltd v Vax Ltd* (CA) [2012] FSR 4. The Court of Appeal held that the assessment of design freedom should have related only to features of the registered design, not features of the 'Mach Zen' as had been the approach of the judge at first instance. However, as Arnold J's approach had had no bearing on the actual outcome of the case, this point did not affect his overall judgment: paras 18–20. It remains to be seen how the UK courts will approach this issue in cases where the alleged infringement takes the form of a completely different product which is subject to entirely different constraints.

[78] ibid, paras 21–33.

[79] On the facts in *Samsung*, Judge Birss QC held that it was not necessary to decide this issue: *Samsung Electronics (UK) Ltd v Apple, Inc* (HC) [2013] ECDR 1, paras 40–41. On scope of protection and design freedom, see also paras 48–49.

[80] *Whitby Specialist Vehicles Ltd v Yorkshire Specialist Vehicles Ltd and Others* [2015] ECDR 11, para 24; *Scomadi Ltd v RA Engineering Co Ltd* [2018] FSR 14, para 80.

[81] Case T-153/08 *Shenzhen Taiden Industrial Co Ltd v Office for Harmonisation in the Internal Market (Trade Marks and Designs) (OHIM), Bosch Security Systems BV* (22 June 2010, currently unreported), paras 23–24.

[82] Case C-345/13 *Karen Millen Fashions Ltd v Dunnes Stores* (Court of Justice) [2014] Bus LR 756, para 35.

8.60   The General Court's assessment of overall impression in the *Grupo Promer* case illustrates how this exercise involves a process of evaluating the visual significance to be attached to the different features of the designs in suit and assessing the relative significance of those features to form a view of the overall impression produced on the informed user. In *Grupo Promer*, the General Court examined the similarities and differences between the designs in suit. The General Court held that the fact that both designs were for small, almost flat, discs and had a rounded edge would not attract the informed user's attention because of design constraints; however, the inner concentric circle present in both designs, the raising of the rounded edges of both discs in relation to the intermediate area of the disc between the edge and the raised central area, and the common respective dimensions of the central and intermediate parts of both discs were not dictated by design constraints and would attract the attention of the informed user.[83] The General Court concluded that any differences in the two designs were insufficient for the registered Community design to produce a different overall impression and that the registered Community design in dispute was invalid for lack of individual character.[84]

8.61   A similar approach to analysing overall impression was taken in *Shenzhen*, although that decision is perhaps questionable for the extent of the emphasis put by the General Court on how the informed user would view the relevant product when in use. In *Shenzhen*, the General Court said that overall impression 'must necessarily be determined . . . in the light of the manner in which the product at issue is used, in particular on the basis of the handling to which it is normally subject on that occasion'.[85] Features outside 'the user's immediate field of vision' during use played a less important or no role at all in assessment of the overall impression produced by the designs.[86] However, more recent cases have taken a broader approach, working on the basis that the assessment of overall impression should include all perspectives on the design that the informed user will realistically adopt,[87] not just looking narrowly at the user's perspective on the design only when in use.

8.62   The General Court has also held that the assessment of overall impression may be affected by proof of the 'saturation' of the state of the art—that is, by proof that the relevant design field was, at the time of filing, a crowded one with many closely similar designs. Saturation of the state of the art can make the informed user 'more attentive to . . . differences of detail' between conflicting designs, meaning that smaller design differences may be more likely to create a different overall impression (and thereby confer individual character) than might otherwise be the case.[88] Relevant evidence would include catalogues showing the products marketed by a large number of competitors, statements from sectoral experts or representatives of manufacturer or consumer associations, and surveys or other forms of sectoral study.[89]

---

[83] Case T-9/07 *Grupo Promer Mon Graphic SA v Office for Harmonisation in the Internal Market (Trade Marks and Designs) (OHIM) with PepsiCo Inc (Intervener)*, General Court [2010] ECDR 7, paras 76–82.

[84] ibid, paras 83–85. The General Court's findings on this issue were unaffected by the appeal to the Court of Justice: Case C-281/10 P *PepsiCo, Inc v Grupo Promer Mon Graphic SA*, [2012] FSR 5, paras 76–82.

[85] Case T-153/08 *Shenzhen Taiden Industrial Co Ltd v Office for Harmonisation in the Internal Market (Trade Marks and Designs) (OHIM), Bosch Security Systems BV* (22 June 2010, currently unreported), para 66.

[86] ibid, para 65. The Court concluded that the disputed and earlier designs produced the same overall impression on the informed user: paras 63–75.

[87] Joined Cases T-22/13 and T-23/13 *Senz Technologies BV v OHIM and Impliva BV (intervener)* (unreported), para 97, cited in *Scomadi Ltd v RA Engineering Co. Ltd* [2018] FSR 14, para 79.

[88] Joined Cases T-83/11 and T-84/11 *Antrax v OHIM* (unreported), paras 96–97; Case T-666/11 *Danuta Budziewska v OHIM, Puma SE (intervener)* (unreported), para 31; Joined Cases T-828/14 and 829/14 *Antrax It Srl v EUIPO* [2018] ECDR 7, paras 54–55.

[89] Joined Cases 828/14 and 829/14 *Antrax It Srl v EUIPO* [2018] ECDR 7, paras 63 and 69.

8.63 In the UK, the Court of Appeal's decision on overall impression in *Proctor & Gamble* (para 8.57) has been criticised in a number of respects, not least for its apparent reliance on matters such as how the two devices would feel when being held by the informed user.[90]

However, as a matter of principle the Court of Appeal rightly held that protection for a strikingly novel product will be greater than for a product which is only incrementally different from the prior art; its overall impression will be 'more significant', leading to a greater potential for differences in other designs still to result in the same overall impression (para 35(iii)). Although the CJEU has cast some doubt (wrongly, it is suggested here) on this proposition,[91] this aspect of Court of Appeal's ruling in *Proctor & Gamble* has continued to be applied in subsequent English cases.[92]

8.64 The more recent case of *Samsung Electronics (UK) Ltd v Apple Inc* shows development in terms of the sophistication and complexity of analysis of overall impression engaged in by the UK courts:

■ *Samsung Electronics (UK) Ltd v Apple, Inc* [2013] ECDR 1 (HC); [2013] ECDR 2 (CA)

This was the first full trial decision arising from a number of infringement claims brought by Apple in jurisdictions across Europe in relation to the design of various Samsung tablet devices. Apple argued that these devices produced the same overall impression as one of its registered Community designs. Images from Apple's registered design and of one of the contested Samsung devices are at Figures 8.9 and 8.10.

Figure 8.9 Image from the Apple design registration, from Annex A to *Samsung Electronics (UK) Ltd v Apple Inc* [2012] EWHC 1882 (Pat)

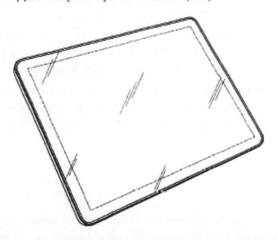

[90] See A Carboni, 'Design validity and infringement: feel the difference' [2008] EIPR 111–17 and D Stone, 'Some clarity, some confusion: 12 *P&G v Reckitt Benckiser* decisions help explain Community designs' (2008) 3(6) JIPLP 376–85.

[91] In Case C-538/17 P *Thomas Murphy v EUIPO* [2018] ECDR 12, the CJEU cited with approval comments by the Advocate General which appeared to reject the proposition that an earlier design which constitutes a significant advance should benefit from more extensive protection. It is not clear whether the CJEU saw these comments as applying only to the assessment of overall impression for registrability purposes, or also to infringement cases.

[92] *Whitby Specialist Vehicles Ltd v Yorkshire Specialist Vehicles Ltd and Others* [2015] ECDR 11, para 28; *L'Oréal Société Anonyme v RN Ventures Ltd* [2018] ECDR 14, para 153; *Cantel Medical (UK) Limited and Another v ARC Medical Design Limited* [2018] EWHC 345 (Pat), para 169.

Figure 8.10 Image of one of the contested Samsung products, from Annex B to *Samsung Electronics (UK) Ltd v Apple Inc* [2012] EWHC 1882 (Pat)

The judge explained that, once the informed user and existing design corpus had been identified, although the case turned on 'overall impression', as a practical matter the design should be broken down into features. Each feature needed to be considered in order to give it appropriate significance or weight. Features dictated solely by technical function should be disregarded. The remaining features should then be considered against the design corpus and from the point of view of design freedom. Differences between the design and the alleged infringement also needed to be addressed and weighted. The aim of this exercise is to assess the significance of these matters to the informed user, so as to allow the court to decide whether the registered design and alleged infringement produce the same overall impression.[93] Judge Birss QC also commented as follows:[94]

> How similar does the alleged infringement have to be to infringe? Community design rights are not simply concerned with anti-counterfeiting. One could imagine a design registration system which was intended only to allow for protection against counterfeits. In that system only identical or nearly identical products would infringe. The test of 'different overall impression' is clearly wider than that. The scope of protection of a Community registered design clearly can include products which can be distinguished to some degree from the registration. On the other hand the fact that the informed user is particularly observant and the fact that designs will often be considered side by side are both clearly intended to narrow the scope of design protection. Although no doubt minute scrutiny by the informed user is not the right approach, attention to detail matters.

Specific features of Apple's registered Community design and the alleged infringements which were compared included: their overall form as rectangular biaxially symmetrical slabs, with four evenly and slightly rounded corners; flat unornamented transparent front surfaces; very thin rim; rectangular display screens; rear surfaces; thin profiles; and overall 'extreme simplicity' of design without features which specified orientation (paras 92–175). Ultimately, although the view of the front of Samsung's devices was 'very, very similar' to the Apple design (para 184), the judge held that the significance of that similarity was reduced in the eyes of the informed user because of a body of prior designs which appeared to form a

[93] *Samsung* (HC) [2013] ECDR 1, paras 53–56.

[94] ibid, para 58. In several cases, the General Court has framed the assessment of overall impression in terms of whether the contested and earlier designs produce the same 'déjà vu' (Case T-666/11 *Danuta Budziewska v OHIM, Puma SE (intervener)* (unreported), para 29; Joined Cases T-828/14 and 829/14 *Antrax It Srl v EUIPO*, [2018] ECDR 7, para 53; Case T-9/15 *Ball Beverage Packaging Europe Ltd v EUIPO* [2018] ECDR 8, para 78; Case T-306/16 *Gamet SA v EUIPO* (unreported), para 38), but this seems an over-broad and unhappy choice of terminology in this context.

'family' of which both the Apple design and Samsung devices were part (para 189). As a result, the overall significance of that similarity was 'much reduced' and the informed user's attention to differences at the back and sides of the designs 'enhanced considerably' (para 189). The different degrees of thinness of the devices and the differences in detailing present on the back of the designs were 'major differences' (paras 185 and 190). It was held that there was no infringement, the judge concluding that Samsung's products:

> do not have the same understated and extreme simplicity which is possessed by the Apple design. They are not as cool. The overall impression produced is different (para 190).

This conclusion was upheld on appeal.[95]

8.65   The *Samsung* case highlights the importance of conducting the comparison of overall impression in context in the light of the full existing design corpus. On the facts of the case, the relevant design corpus included a range of different designs, including designs for products which were not computers (such as a child's 'Etch-A-Sketch' toy) and which had never been marketed as such (such as a display device from the film *2001: A Space Odyssey*). The judge at first instance emphasised that, while having initially been struck by how similar the Apple and Samsung designs were, those similarities did not stand out 'to anything like the same extent' after having examined the prior art and placed himself in the shoes of the informed user.[96] As part of this exercise, the judge had heard detailed evidence from experts on both sides. The English courts have tended to stress that, in designs cases, 'what really matters is what the court can see with its own eyes'.[97] In *Procter & Gamble Co v Reckitt Benckiser (UK) Ltd* Jacob LJ had said of designs cases that the:[98]

> place for evidence is very limited indeed. By and large it should be possible to decide a registered design case in a few hours . . . The evidence of experts, particularly about consumer products, is unlikely to be of much assistance: anyone can point out similarities and differences, though an educated eye can sometimes help a bit. Sometimes there may be a piece of technical evidence which is relevant—eg that design freedom is limited by certain constraints. But even so, that is usually more or less self-evident and certainly unlikely to be controversial to the point of a need for cross-examination, still less substantial cross-examination.

While this may remain the case for disputes involving simple designs for basic consumer goods, whether post-*Samsung* this can still be said to be the way in which all designs cases will be resolved remains to be seen.[99]

8.66   The most recent leading UK case is *Magmatic*, the 'Trunki' ride-on suitcase dispute:

■ *Magmatic Ltd v PMS International Ltd* [2013] ECC 29 (HC); [2014] ECDR 20 (CA); [2016] ECDR 15 (UKSC)

Magmatic was the owner of a Community registered design for a design relating to the award-winning 'Trunki' ride-on suitcase. 'Trunki' suitcases were sold in various versions, decorated with different animal and insect depictions. PMS imported into the UK and sold a competing 'ride-on' suitcase, called the 'Kiddee case'. Images from the Magmatic Community design registration (shown in the first column) and corresponding views of two versions of the 'Kiddee case' (shown in the second and third columns) are at Figure 8.11. At first instance, Arnold J held that Magmatic's design represented a substantial departure from the prior design corpus, which consisted of adults' clamshell suitcases. Given this, together with a considerable degree of design freedom, the first instance judge held that Magmatic's design was entitled to a broad scope of protection. Working on the basis that Magmatic's design was for the shape of the case, without specification or limitation as to surface decoration, Arnold J concluded that the PMS cases produced the same overall impression and infringed Magmatic's Community registered design.

[95] *Samsung* (CA) [2013] ECDR 2, paras 7–54.   [96] *Samsung* (HC) [2013] ECDR 1, para 189.
[97] ibid, para 31, referring to the observations of Sir Robin Jacob in *Dyson Ltd v Vax Ltd* (CA) [2012] FSR 4, paras 8–9 and in *Procter & Gamble* (CA), paras 3–4 (see para 8.57).
[98] *Procter & Gamble Co v Reckitt Benckiser (UK) Ltd* [2008] FSR 8 (CA), para 4 (see para 8.57).
[99] See further D Smyth, '*Samsung v Apple*: how does the judge become an "informed user"?' (2012) 7(11) JIPLP 776–78.

Figure 8.11 Images of the Magmatic design registration and contested PMS products from the Annex to *Magmatic Ltd v PMS International Ltd* [2014] EWCA Civ 181

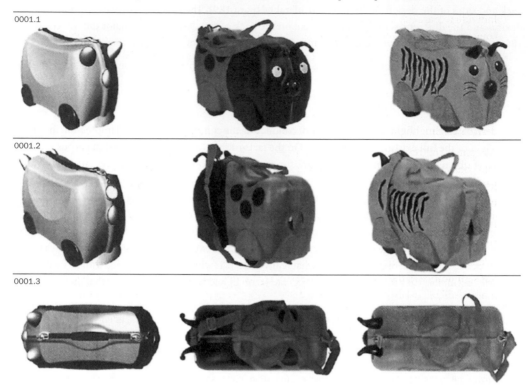

This conclusion was, however, reversed on appeal. Critical to this was the different conclusion reached by the Court of Appeal on what was depicted in the representations of Magmatic's design (para 8.35). Treating Magmatic's design as being the shape of the case unadorned with imagery, the Court of Appeal held that the Magmatic case 'looks like a horned animal with a nose and a tail' (para 41). The features on the front and sides of the 'Kiddee case' created a different impression: the two-tone body and spots on the insect version of the 'Kiddee case' made the case look like a ladybird and the handles on its front like antennae; the stripes on the flanks and whiskers on the nose of the animal version of the 'Kiddee case' made that case look like a tiger (para 47). These were 'very different' overall impressions to the 'horned animal' impression created by Magmatic's design. The Court of Appeal also concluded that Arnold J had been wrong to ignore the different tonal shading between the body and wheels of Magmatic's design, a feature which the Court of Appeal regarded as 'fairly striking' but which was not present in the 'Kiddee case' (para 48). The Court of Appeal reversed the first instance decision and held that there was no infringement. The Supreme Court agreed. As well as the points on colour contrast and the CAD drawings used by Magmatic in their design representations discussed above (see para 8.35), the Supreme Court concurred with the view of the Court of Appeal that the judge at first instance had failed to take into account that the overall impression given by the Community registered design was that of a 'horned animal'.[100] The Supreme Court's decision has met with criticism, including for its approach on the 'horned animal point' upon which, it is arguable, the judge had taken into account the factors highlighted by the Supreme Court—just without the same degree of explicit emphasis.[101]

[100] *PMS International Group Plc v Magmatic Ltd* [2016] ECDR 15, paras 37–39.
[101] D Stone, 'Trunki—how did things go so wrong?' (2016) 11(9) JIPLP 662–81.

Key points about 'individual character'

- Individual character is assessed by establishing the overall impression produced by the design compared to that produced by any design made available to the public before the relevant date.

- The comparison must be against a specific earlier design, not an amalgam of different design features taken from multiple different designs.

- The relevant overall impression in question is that produced on the informed user.

- The informed user is more sophisticated than the 'average consumer' of trade mark law, but is not a designer, technical expert, or specialist.

- Assessment of the overall impression produced by a design on the informed user must take into consideration the nature of the product to which the design is applied or in which it is incorporated, the industrial sector to which it belongs, and the degree of freedom of the designer in developing the design. 'Saturation' of the art may also be relevant.

- In assessing design freedom, relevant constraints include the technical function of the product and statutory requirements, and may include other objectively applicable factors.

- In assessing overall impression, design features which are subject to design constraints will have less significance in the eyes of the informed user; the more design freedom is constrained, the more readily small differences between designs will produce a different overall impression.

- The assessment of the significance to the informed user of similarities in overall impression between two designs will also involve comparison of those similarities against the existing design corpus.

Discussion point   For answer guidance visit **www.oup.com/uk/brown5e.**

Now that you have considered the leading case law as well as the legislative wording, what factors do you think are to be taken into account in assessing a design's 'individual character'?

What designs are 'available to the public'?

8.67   Assessing novelty and individual character is about comparing the design with designs already available to the public before the relevant date (the application date or priority date, as appropriate). Designs have been made available to the public before the relevant date if they have been:

- published (following registration or otherwise);
- exhibited;
- used in trade (eg the design has already been applied to a product which is available in the marketplace);
- otherwise disclosed before the relevant date (see for all this RDA 1949, s 1B(5); DD, Art 6(1); CDR, Art 7(1)).

This is very broad and will essentially capture any placing of the earlier design into the public domain. There is no requirement that the earlier design must have enjoyed any form of legal protection: any design which has come into the public domain will count. The evidence which may be considered on this matter can be widely varied: the EUIPO Invalidity Division has accepted material found as a result of a Google search, for example.[102] But it is important that the evidence be dateable: in some cases material discovered on the internet, the posting of which could not be dated, has been dismissed as irrelevant.[103]

 Question

Why is the dating of designs important in considering 'availability to the public'?

8.68   In *Gimex International Groupe Import Export v Chill Bag Co Ltd and Others* (Patents County Court, England & Wales),[104] the court considered the question of whether the prior art designs against which novelty and individual character are to be assessed can include designs for products used for different purposes to the registered design. This is one of the many complexities arising from the fact that the Designs Directive and Community Design Regulation protect the design as such, without tying or limiting the protected right to any specific product; as a result, just as the scope of protection conferred by registration encompasses the use of the design on any product (see para 8.122), so too the relevant prior art can also include designs for any kind of product from any sector.

8.69   Building on the English Court of Appeal's analysis of Article 7 of the Community Design Regulation in *Green Lane v PMS* (see para 8.73), in *Gimex* Judge Birss QC confirmed that designs for products used for different purposes to the registered design are relevant prior art which must be taken into account. He held that:[105]

> All prior designs for anything are capable of being relevant.

The judge emphasised that, for a design to be valid, it must be new and have individual character over the whole of the prior art.[106] It makes no difference whether the earlier design against which it is being compared would or would not have been known to the informed user. The informed user is the user of the registered design. If the earlier design was used for a different product/purpose than the registered design, the earlier design may not form part of the informed user's general 'design awareness', but all earlier designs must nonetheless be taken into account as prior designs and assessed by the informed user for the purposes of determining novelty and individual character.[107]

8.70   An earlier disclosure will not count as part of the prior art, meaning that the design for which registration is sought could still be novel or have individual character even if conflicting with the earlier design, if the earlier disclosure:[108]

(1) Could not reasonably have become known in the normal course of business to the circles specialising in the sector concerned operating within the Community

8.71   This 'safeguard clause' means that novelty and individual character are assessed by comparison with designs the disclosure of which was or could reasonably have become known in the normal course of business to circles specialised in the sector concerned within the Community; thus, for example, a disclosure in another part of the world might not affect novelty or individual character in the European context. This carve-out from the scope of the relevant prior art was introduced into the Designs Directive and Community Design Regulation as a result of lobbying by the textile industry.[109] It marks a significant difference to how the 'prior art' is defined in patent law, where there is no such carve-out and even obscure overseas disclosures are relevant (see para 11.37).

---

[102] See, eg, *Leng d'Or SA v Crown Confectionery Co Ltd*, Invalidity Division (ICD 000000388), 20 September 2005.

[103] See, eg, *Dryson AB v Birger Olsson*, Invalidity Division (ICD 0000000982), 17 March 2006 and *Holding C Vlemmix BV v E van Hellenberg Hubar*, Invalidity Division (ICD 000001303), 23 March 2006.

[104] [2012] ECDR 25.   [105] ibid, para 42; see also para 72.   [106] ibid, para 45.   [107] ibid, para 45.

[108] For what follows see RDA 1949, s 1B(6); DD, Art 6; CDR, Art 7.

[109] *Green Lane Products Ltd v PMS International Group Ltd* [2008] FSR 28, paras 64–74.

Discussion point   For answer guidance visit **www.oup.com/il/brown5e**.

Who is being 'safeguarded' by this rule?

8.72   In *Gautzsch Großhandel*, the Court of Justice was asked whether a design could be considered to have been made available to the public within the Community in a way which could reasonably have become known to the circles specialised in the sector concerned for the purpose of Article 7(1) CDR if disclosed in an event occurring outside the EU or disclosed only to a single entity. The CJ confirmed that this could amount to sufficient disclosure depending on the facts, which were for the national court to determine.[110] There have been some instructive failed attempts to rely on this 'safeguard clause', both in relation to activities conducted in other parts of the world and in relation to the range and nature of industry information within the Community which those specialising in the circles concerned may be expected to know about:

■ **Case R 9/2008-3 *Crocs Inc v Holey Soles Holdings Ltd with Partenaire Hospitalier International* (Third Board of Appeal) [2010] ECDR 11**

In this case, the EUIPO Third Board of Appeal ruled that a Community registered design for the 'Crocs' shoe lacked novelty in the light of prior sales by Crocs of 10,000 shoes in the United States, display of the 'Crocs' shoe at the Fort Lauderdale International Boat Show, and disclosure of the design on the www.crocs.com website. The Board of Appeal held that the argument that these activities could not reasonably have become known in the normal course of business to the circles specialising in the sector concerned operating within the Community was 'not persuasive', commenting that:[111]

Exhibiting a new product at a fair, uploading it on the Internet and selling it on the marketplace—these activities having been furthermore carried out over a period of several months— are precisely the sort of activities that may become known 'in the course of business' to anybody active in the same field.

In further invalidity proceedings relating to the same design, the General Court emphasised that, under Article 7 CDR, a design is deemed to have been made available to the public once the events constituting disclosure have been proven. The onus is then on the design rightholder to establish that the circumstances of the case are such that the disclosure could not have become known in the normal course of business to the circles specialised in the sector concerned.[112]

■ **Joined Cases T-22/13 and T-23/13 *Senz Technologies BV v OHIM and Impliva BV (intervener)* (General Court) 21 May 2015 (currently unreported)**

This case concerned two registered Community designs for asymmetric, highly wind-resistant umbrellas. The two Community designs were challenged for lack of individual character. The earlier designs relied upon included a published US patent which contained various drawings and schematics for an asymmetric wind-resistant umbrella. The Community design owner argued that the US patent was not a disclosure which could reasonably have become known in the normal course of business to circles specialised in the sector concerned in the Community and could not, therefore, be taken into account in the validity challenge. This argument was rejected by the General Court. Given that wind-resistant umbrellas needed to meet technical as well as aesthetic requirements, it was reasonable that such a product might have been patented. It was also reasonable that a search might be undertaken in the US patent register, given the commercial importance of the United States as a market. The General Court upheld the decision of the Board of Appeal that the US patent had been made available within the meaning of Art 7(1) CDR.

---

[110]   Case C-479/12 *H Gautzsch Großhandel GmbH & Co KG v Münchener Boulevard Möbel Joseph Duna GmbH* [2014] ECDR 14, para 36.
[111]   [2010] ECDR 11, para 60.
[112]   Case T-651/16 *Crocs, Inc v EUIPO and Gifi Diffusion* (unreported), paras 47 and 54 in particular. At the time of writing, this decision has been appealed to the CJEU.

8.73   One of the most difficult questions in interpreting and applying this 'safeguard clause' relates to the scenario in which the relevant prior art comes from within the Community (that is to say, is not 'obscure' on geographic grounds) but stems from an industry sector unrelated to that of the registered design. This scenario has been addressed by the English Court of Appeal in *Green Lane Products Ltd v PMS International Group Ltd* and by the CJEU in *Easy Sanitary Solutions*:

■ *Green Lane Products Ltd v PMS International Group Ltd* [2008] FSR 28 (CA)

The products in issue in this case were spiky plastic balls. PMS had imported such balls from China and sold them extensively as massage balls in the EU from 2002. Green Lane sold such balls for use in tumble driers. In August 2004, Green Lane had registered four Community designs for such balls, describing the class of products to which the designs were to be applied as 'flatirons and washing, cleaning and drying equipment'. In 2006, PMS proposed to market their products for other uses as well as massage balls, including as laundry dryer balls. Green Lane argued that PMS would infringe its Community registered designs by use of their balls for anything other than massage balls. PMS contended that Green Lane's registrations were invalid for lack of novelty in the light of PMS's earlier sales of the balls as massage balls. Green Lane responded by arguing that the prior uses by PMS 'could not reasonably have become known in the normal course of business to the circles specialised in the sector concerned' and that the 'sector concerned' means the sector for which the design was registered (ie those specialising in tumble drier balls). At first instance, Green Lane's arguments were rejected and it was held that the relevant 'sector concerned' was that consisting of or including the sector of the alleged prior art. This was upheld by the Court of Appeal. Jacob LJ said: 'the right gives a monopoly over any kind of goods according to the design. It makes complete sense that the prior art available for attacking novelty should also extend to all kinds of goods, subject only to the limited exception of prior art obscure even in the sector from which it comes' (para 79). This interpretation reduces the potential application of the 'safeguard clause' carve-out from the prior art very considerably.

■ Joined Cases C-361/15 P and C-405/15 P *Easy Sanitary Solutions BV and EUIPO v Group Nivelles NV* [2018] ECDR 4

This case arose from EUIPO invalidation proceedings against a Community registered design for a shower drain. One of the issues in the case was the scope of the relevant prior art. The design rightholder argued that Article 7 CDR only covered prior art products that belonged to the same sector or were of the same nature and intended for the same use as the contested design. The Court of Justice rejected this argument. The Court said: 'The fact that the protection granted to a design is not limited only to the products in which it is intended to be incorporated or to which it is intended to be applied must . . . mean that the assessment of the novelty of a design must also not be limited to those products alone.'[113] Looking at the legislative history of the CDR, the Court emphasised that the purpose of the 'safeguard' carve-out in Article 7(1) CDR related to disclosures which are difficult to verify and which occur in a third country; its purpose was not to make distinctions between different business sectors within the EU.[114] There was also nothing in Article 7(1) CDR limiting the prior art to that which was known to the informed user of the contested design.[115] The Court of Justice's decision (which overturns a much-criticised decision of the General Court) is to be welcomed and *Easy Sanitary Solutions* has been cited with approval in subsequent English case law.[116]

 Question

How does the 'safeguard provision' in the Designs Directive and the Community Design Regulation compare to how we define the relevant prior art in patent law? Consider the points made by Jacob LJ about the differences between design and patent laws on this issue in *Green Lane* [2008] FSR 28. What are the pros and cons of the two different approaches?

---

[113]   Joined Cases C-361/15 P and C-405/15 P *Easy Sanitary Solutions BV and EUIPO v Group Nivelles NV* [2018] ECDR 4, para 96.
[114]   ibid, para 102.   [115]   ibid, para 131.   [116]   *L'Oréal Société Anonyme v RN Ventures Ltd* [2018] ECDR 14, paras 146–152.

(2) Was made to a person other than the designer, or any successor in title of his, under explicit or implicit conditions of confidentiality

8.74 For example, a designer may create a design for a product and show it under conditions of confidentiality to potential manufacturers, potential commercial partners, or for the purposes of research and development; this will not affect the possibility of later registration of the design by the designer.

(3) Was made by the designer, any successor in title of his, or a third person as a result of information provided or action taken by the designer or any successor in title of his during the period of 12 months immediately preceding the relevant date

8.75 The purpose of this 'grace period' is to enable exhibition or market-testing, on an open and non-confidential basis, of a design before undertaking the costs and process of registration.[117] It will also include accidental public disclosures, where made by the designer or his successor in title in the 12-month period.

8.76 This also gives the proprietor of the design a 12-month window to register his design in cases such as where the designer authorises another party to manufacture a product according to the design and that third party places the design in the public domain in some way.

(4) Was made during the period of 12 months immediately preceding the relevant date as a consequence of an abuse in relation to the designer or any successor in title

8.77 This might apply, for example, if a third party obtains the design by way of industrial espionage or someone to whom the design has been disclosed in confidence breaks that confidence and publishes the design.

8.78 The 12-month *grace periods* are extremely important. They cover the designer's own non-confidential disclosure by way of publication, exhibition, trade use, or other disclosure and also third-party disclosures, where effected as a result of information or action from the design right holder or as an abuse. However, there are also some important caveats. Even if the disclosure is an abuse of the designer's interests by the third party, the designer still has only 12 months within which to file his application for registration. It is also not clear whether the grace period can be relied upon, in any circumstances, if the designer makes any changes (even if only minor) to his design after disclosure but before filing, as he might quite reasonably want to do after (say) market testing. It is also essential to remember that these grace periods only save the proprietor's design from being invalidated on the basis of the particular act of disclosure referred to in each subsection. The grace period does *not* give a general protection against other relevant disclosures in the 12-month period. So, if a competing design is placed in the public domain in that 12-month period in circumstances not covered by the provisions set out previously, that will be problematic in terms of novelty or individual character.

Key points on designs 'available to the public'

- Relevant earlier designs will be those made available to the public in any way prior to the relevant date (the filing or priority date of the registered design in question).
- This will exclude disclosures which could not reasonably have become known in the normal course of business to circles specialised in the sector concerned operating within the Community.
- It will also exclude confidential disclosures and certain public disclosures in the 12-month period before the relevant date, for example if made by the designer or his successor in title or in breach of an obligation of confidentiality.

---

[117] Case T-68/10 *Sphere Time v OHIM, Punch SAS* [2011] ECDR 20, paras 24–25.

Discussion point   For answer guidance visit **www.oup.com/uk/brown5e.**

Once a design has been disclosed, whether with or without the consent of the designer, what advice would you give the designer with regard to the registration of that design?

Exclusions: functionality

8.79   Rights in registered designs do *not* subsist in:[118]

> features of appearance of a product which are solely dictated by the product's technical function.

Recital 14 DD and recital 10 CDR explain:

> Technological innovation should not be hampered by granting design protection to features dictated solely by a technical function.

The recitals also make clear, however, that this does not require a design to have an aesthetic quality. At the same time, a competing underlying policy objective is that purely technological or technical innovation should be protected by patents, with the innovation required to meet the relatively high standards of patent-law novelty and inventiveness in order to qualify for protection, rather than the lower standards of novelty and individual character required of a design.

8.80   This exclusion from protection is separate and different to the exercise of evaluating design freedom in the context of the assessment of individual character. There, design constraints are considered in a relatively flexible way to ascribe more or less weight to particular design features. Here, we are concerned with the binary question of whether relevant design features are dictated by function or not. If a design feature is dictated by function, under this exclusion there will be no protection at all for that feature.[119] The extent to which this exclusion removes all entitlement to protection for a particular design will depend on whether, once the features dictated by technical function are discounted, the remainder of the design is still entitled to protection because that remainder meets the requirements of novelty, individual character, and so on. So, it may or may not act as a total bar to protection: whether this is the case will depend on the design in question.

Question

Why are functional designs excluded from protection by registration?

8.81   The functionality exclusion continues what had been a well-established characteristic of previous registered design law in the UK. The old UK law had led, however, to some complex litigation around the meaning of the phrase 'solely dictated'. Two ways of construing this phrase had been considered in pre-harmonisation UK case law. The first way of construing this expression, sometimes called the 'multiplicity-of-forms' approach, provided that even purely functional designs were not excluded from protection as long as that particular design was not the *only* way of achieving the relevant function. The second way of construing this phrase, sometimes called the 'causality theory' (or, in the UK, the '*Amp* approach' after the House of Lords' pre-harmonisation decision in *Amp Incorporated v Utilux Proprietary Ltd* [1972] RPC 103), looked not at the question of whether alternative designs could achieve the same function, but instead turned on whether the design features in question were there for the purpose of function alone. The two approaches are very

---

[118]   RDA 1949, s 1C(1); DD, Art 7(1); CDR, Art 8(1).
[119]   *Cantel Medical (UK) Limited and Another v ARC Medical Design Limited* [2018] EWHC 345 (Pat), para 168.

Exclusions: 'must fit' elements

8.87   The exclusion for design features 'solely dictated by . . . technical function' is supplemented by a 'must fit'-
style exclusion, which is expressed in the following terms:[137]

> A right in a registered design shall not subsist in features of appearance of a product which must necessarily be
> reproduced in their exact form and dimensions so as to permit the product in which the design is incorporated
> or to which it is applied to be mechanically connected to, or placed in, around or against, another product so
> that either product may perform its function.

Question

What are the key elements in this exclusion? How similar is it to the 'must fit' exclusion in UK
unregistered design right discussed in Chapter 9?

8.88   Recital 14 DD and recital 10 CDR explain that 'the interoperability of products of different makes should
not be hindered by extending protection to the design of mechanical fittings'. A simple example of when
this exclusion might operate is the exhaust pipe of a car. An exhaust pipe for a given model of car is a product
which must, in large part, be of certain exact dimensions and form to take its place in that model of car—
that is, to be mechanically connected to, placed in, around, or against the car. This is needed for either to
perform its function: the car cannot run without the exhaust pipe, and the exhaust pipe cannot discharge
fumes unless connected to the car. This exclusion would operate to deny protection to those features of the
design of the exhaust which necessarily had to take the exact form and dimensions required in order for the
exhaust pipe to be mechanically connected to, placed in, around, or against the car.

8.89   However, this 'must fit' exclusion from protection does not prevent a right in a registered design subsisting in a
design serving the purpose of allowing multiple assembly or connection of mutually interchangeable products
within a modular system.[138] Recital 15 DD and recital 11 CDR offer the explanation that 'the mechanical fittings
of modular products may nevertheless constitute an important element of the innovative characteristics of
modular products and present a major marketing asset, and therefore should be eligible for protection'. The
legislative background clarifies the provision somewhat. During the negotiations and lobbying leading up to
the enactment of the Designs Directive, Denmark was anxious to protect the position of the Lego company
with regard to its toy bricks, a key feature of which is the interconnecting elements. Other toy manufacturers
were supportive, and the provision entered European designs law. Its scope remains unclear.

Key points on the 'must fit' exclusion

- Design protection will not subsist in features of the appearance of a product which must
  necessarily be reproduced in their exact form and dimensions so as to permit the product in which
  the design is incorporated or to which it is applied to be mechanically connected to, or placed in,
  around, or against, another product so that either product may perform its function.

- Only those design features which are there for this purpose are excluded under this rule—other
  parts of the design may be validly registrable if they otherwise meet the criteria of registrability.

- This exclusion is subject to an 'exclusion-from-the-exclusion' for designs serving the purpose of
  allowing multiple assembly or connection of mutually interchangeable products within a modular
  system, which are capable of registration, although the scope of this provision remains unclear.

---

[137] RDA 1949, s 1C(2); DD, Art 7(2); CDR, Art 8(2).   [138] RDA 1949, s 1C(3); DD, Art 7(3); CDR, Art 8(3).

Exclusions: public policy and morality

8.90   Rights in a registered design also do not subsist in a:[139]

> design which is contrary to public policy or to accepted principles of morality.

What may be contrary to public policy or accepted principles of morality is not spelled out in the legislation, and recital 16 DD is careful to say that 'this Directive does not constitute a harmonisation of national concepts of public policy or accepted principles of morality'. Thus, each member state is free to bring to bear its own approach to this exclusion. The pre-Directive law of the UK also contained an exclusion of designs which, in the opinion of the Registrar, would be contrary to law or morality.[140] The limited case law on this provision probably continues to be relevant in the UK:

■ *Masterman's Design* [1991] RPC 89 (HC)

This case concerned an application to register the design of a furry doll representing a Highlander-like figure wearing a sporran, the lifting of which revealed his genitalia. An objection on the grounds of immorality was refused, and registration allowed. The test was not whether some section of the public would be offended, but whether the design was of such a nature that its use would offend moral principles of right-thinking members of the public such that it would be wrong for the law to protect it.

Discussion point   For answer guidance visit **www.oup.com/uk/brown5e**.

Can you think of any immoral designs, or designs contrary to public policy?

Complex products

8.91   As a result of the European legislation, the RDA 1949 (as amended) now contains a rather complicated series of provisions dealing with what are called 'complex products'. A *complex product* is a *product* (see paras 8.25–8.26) which is:[141]

> composed of at least two replaceable component parts permitting disassembly and reassembly of the product.

There are special rules for such complex products with regard to novelty, individual character, and visibility in normal use.

Question

What are the key elements of the definition of a 'complex product'?

8.92   It may be helpful to understanding what follows to have in mind an example of a complex product. A good one is a car. The vehicle's body will be made up of a number of parts—the chassis and shell, the wings, the doors, the lids of the bonnet and boot. There will also be the engine, probably a complex product in its own right, as well as necessary attachments such as the fuel and exhaust pipes. There will be fittings—external ones, such as wheels, lights, bumpers and wing mirrors, and internal ones, such as the steering wheel, seats, and dashboard. The process of building a car is a process of assembling all the parts, and most, if not all of these are replaceable; indeed, whole industries thrive on the business of manufacturing and supplying

---

[139] RDA 1949, s 1D; DD, Art 8; CDR, Art 9.   [140] Old version of the RDA 1949, s 43(1).

[141] RDA 1949, s 1(3); DD, Art 1(c); CDR, Art 3(c).

replacement parts for cars. At the same time, *component parts* can be distinguished from *accessories*. For example, a car roof box or roof rack is an accessory rather than a component part: it is best viewed as an 'extra' to the car, rather than part of the car itself. So, while the component parts of the car would be subject to the special rules described here, a roof box or roof rack would not.

Discussion point   For answer guidance visit **www.oup.com/uk/brown5e**.

Can you give any other examples of complex products?

8.93   A design applied to or incorporated in a product which constitutes a component part of a complex product can only be validly registered if two conditions *over and above* those already stated generally (see para 8.21) are both met:[142]

- Once incorporated in the complex product, the *component part must remain visible* while the complex product is *in normal use*.

- These *visible parts* of the component part *must in themselves be new and have individual character*.

'Normal use' means use by the end user; but this does not include any maintenance, servicing, or repair work.[143]

> **Key points on the special requirements for component parts of complex products**
>
> - Only features of the component part that are visible during normal use of the complex product can be protected through registration, and then only if these visible features have novelty and individual character.
>
> - This rule applies *only* to designs for component parts of complex products; the requirement of visibility in normal use does *not* apply to designs generally.

8.94   If we take our example of a car, let us consider the position with regard to an exhaust pipe again. We have discussed previously how the 'must fit' exclusion might affect the ability to protect an exhaust pipe through design registration (see para 8.88). The special requirements for component parts of complex products will further impact upon the registrability of an exhaust pipe design. The exhaust pipe is clearly a component part of a complex product. When the complex product—the car—is in normal use (ie being driven along, idling in traffic queues, parked, or being unloaded), only a very small part of the exhaust pipe as a component part is visible. The fact that much of the pipe could be seen if its owner or a mechanic went underneath the car to inspect it (whether by lying down on the ground beneath the car, raising it on a lift, or parking it over a service pit) would be irrelevant, because that kind of maintenance or servicing activity is excluded from normal use. Likewise, if the exhaust pipe had to be replaced: repair is not normal use either, and the fact that a pipe could be seen in full once removed or that the replacement was also wholly visible during the process would be irrelevant. Only the normally visible parts of the exhaust pipe are capable of entitlement to protection by registered design rights, and it is to these visible parts of the exhaust pipe that the tests of novelty and individual character have to be applied. Probably the average visible part of an exhaust pipe does

---

[142] RDA 1949, s 1B(8); DD, Art 3(3); CDR, Art 4(2).   [143] RDA 1949, s 1B(9); DD, Art 3(4); CDR, Art 4(3).

not qualify as novel or having individual character, but there are some more extravagant examples on the road—the exhaust pipes of some long-distance trucks, for instance—which might come within the scope of protection.

8.95   An example of this sort of analysis in action can be found in a case before the General Court considering the design of internal combustion engines for lawnmowers. In Case T-10/08 *Kwang Yang Motor Co, Ltd v OHIM and Honda Giken Kogyo Kabushiki Kaisha*, the General Court held that the engine was a component part of the lawnmower as the overall 'complex product' into which the engine was incorporated. It was the design of the upper side of the engine only which was visible in normal use and thus only that upper side which was capable of protection, if the requirements of novelty and individual character were met:[144]

> During the normal use of a lawnmower, it is placed on the ground and the user stands behind the lawnmower. Thus, the user, standing behind the lawnmower sees the engine from the top and therefore sees principally the upper side of the engine. It follows that the upper side of the engine determines the overall impression produced by the engine.

8.96   In a different context, there is also debate about how far *consumables*—for example, printer ink cartridges— should be considered to be 'component parts' for these purposes. A printer is a complex product and an element such as an ink cartridge is both replaceable and not visible in normal use. On that analysis, an ink cartridge could not be protected as a design under the 'complex product' rules. On the other hand, however, it would be hard to argue that the printer is somehow 'broken' or 'incomplete' as a product if there is no ink cartridge present. There is yet to be any high-level case law on this issue, but the issue is a significant one with important practical ramifications: if ink cartridges (or similar consumables) are considered to be component parts of the printer as a complex product, then it will not be possible to rely on design protection to stop sale of (cheaper) third party substitutes.

8.97   Complications may also arise where the design is for a component part which can be used in multiple different products and may be visible in some, but not all, of those different products.[145] Neither the DD nor the CDR indicate how this should be dealt with. In *AIC v ACV*, the General Court took quite a hard-line approach, excluding from protection a design for a component part (a heat exchanger) on the basis that it was not visible in at least one of the different complex products in which it could be used (in this instance, a domestic boiler).[146] Issues may also arise in relation to component parts which are visible some—but not all—of the time in normal use of the complex product. On this, the position seems to be more generous to design right holders. The issue was considered by the EUIPO Third Board of Appeal in Case R 690/2007/3 *Lindner Recyclingtech GmbH v Franssons Verkstäder AB*. The Third Board of Appeal held that Article 4(2) (a) of the Community Design Regulation:[147]

> does not require a component part to be clearly visible in its entirety at every moment of use. It is sufficient if the whole of the component can be seen some of the time in such a way that all of its essential features can be apprehended.

In that case, the rotor element of a shredding machine was considered to remain sufficiently visible in normal use even though the rotor was spinning and largely covered by the material to be shredded: the registrant adduced sufficient evidence that the rotor would, at least to a limited degree, be visible in normal use as it was necessary for it to remain capable of observation during the shredding process.[148]

---

[144] [2012] ECDR 2, para 22.

[145] See further D Musker, 'Hidden meaning? UK perspectives on invisible in use designs' [2003] EIPR 450–56.

[146] Case T-615/13 *AIC SA v OHIM, ACV Manufacturing (intervening)* (20 January 2015, unreported), paras 23–31.

[147] [2010] ECDR 1, para 21.

[148] Case R 690/2007–3 *Lindner Recyclingtech GmbH v Franssons Verkstäder AB* (Third Board of Appeal) [2010] ECDR 1, para 19.

Exercise

Discuss how far the following items may be protected as simple products in their own right, or whether they are to be seen as component parts of complex products:

- car roof rack bars;
- car head rests;
- car mud flaps;
- spoilers fitted to a car by an owner rather than as part of the original manufacturing and assembly process.

Spare parts

8.98 Taking them together and looking at the issues under debate at the time of the introduction of the Designs Directive and the Community Design Regulation, what are the 'complex product' and 'must fit' rules trying to achieve? The essential issue was about replacement or spare parts—components in complex products which could be replaced, either because they needed repair (eg an exhaust pipe with a hole in it) or the owner of the product wished to do so (eg replacing a conventional steering wheel with a racing one). There was clearly a significant secondary market in such components, both for repair and otherwise for customisation. Should that secondary market be subject to the control of the manufacturers of the complex products, who could use their rights in the designs of the original components to tie in customers if the customer wanted to source a replacement or spare part? Or should design protection not be available for such replacements and spares, potentially allowing third-party providers to provide the same products at a lower price to the consumer?

The response to these issues produced in the European design legislation is not a simple one. Complex products have produced complex law.

Key points on how the rules on component parts and the 'must fit' exception apply to spare and replacement parts

- In essence, the law denies protection to:
  - those features of component parts of complex products that are not visible in normal use; and
  - the 'must fit' elements of products that must necessarily be reproduced in their exact form and dimensions so as to permit the product in which the design is incorporated or to which it is applied to be mechanically connected to, or placed in, around or against, another product so that either product may perform its function.
- But this does not mean that spare or replacement parts are beyond protection through the registration process.
- Design features which are visible in normal use and which are not subject to the 'must fit' exclusion can be validly registered if they meet the requirements of novelty and individual character.

8.99 A further element in the debate about spare parts leading up to the Designs Directive and the Community Designs Regulation was a proposed exclusion from protection for what were, at least in the UK, called '*must match*' designs. The name came from the UK legislation on UK unregistered design right, to be discussed in detail in Chapter 9. For present purposes, it suffices to note that UK unregistered design right does not subsist in:[149]

> features of shape or configuration of an article which . . . are dependent upon the appearance of another article of which the article is intended by the designer to form an integral part.

This exception focuses on aesthetic aspects of design. It was designed to ensure that car body parts would not enjoy UK unregistered design rights, and followed competition investigations in the 1980s by both the UK and the European Community, the subject of which was the Ford Motor Company's refusal to grant licences to third parties to enable them to compete in the market for replacement body parts. A replacement car wing or door must match the remainder of the car in aesthetic terms and a refusal by a car manufacturer to license potential competitors would leave them free to control the market and set prices for such replacement parts. The denial of UK unregistered design rights for such parts in the UK was therefore part of an attempt to open up this market to competition for the benefit of consumers. The CDPA 1988 also extended this 'must match' exception into the then (but now repealed) UK registered designs law.

8.100   Although the same concerns were raised during the drafting of the European design legislation (and despite the time now elapsed since the Directive and Regulation were enacted), the issues have still not yet been fully resolved. The legislative history on this issue has been usefully summarised by Arnold J in *Bayerische Motoren Werke Aktiengesellschaft v Round & Metal Ltd*.[150] The original idea in the Commission's proposals for the Designs Directive and the Community Design Regulation was that, three years after the first putting on the market of a product incorporating a protected design or to which such a design had been applied, the rights conferred by a registered Community design or national registered design could not be exercised to stop use of the design by third parties where the product incorporating the design or to which it was applied was part of a complex product upon whose appearance the protected design was dependent and the purpose of the third party's use was to permit the repair of the complex product so as to restore its original appearance.[151] During the debate on these proposals, the European Parliament proposed that the right holder should receive remuneration for any repair use. However, there was no agreement from the European Council.

8.101   Ultimately, following a conciliation procedure, the so-called 'freeze plus' compromise was adopted. The recitals to the Designs Directive state that, although 'the rapid adoption of this Directive has become a matter of urgency' for a number of industrial sectors:

> full-scale approximation of the laws of the Member States on the use of protected designs for the purpose of permitting the repair of a complex product so as to restore its original appearance . . . cannot be introduced at the present stage.

The Designs Directive also contains Articles providing for future action which have become known as the '*freeze or standstill plus*' solution to the problem of 'must match' designs. Article 14, which is the 'freeze' or 'standstill' element, states:

> Until such time as amendments to this Directive are adopted on a proposal from the Commission in accordance with the provisions of Article 18, Member States shall maintain in force their existing legal provisions relating to the use of the design of a component part used for the purpose of the repair of a complex product so as to restore its original appearance and shall introduce changes to those provisions only if the purpose is to liberalise the market for such parts.

8.102   In the UK this was taken to require the repeal of the former 'must match' exception introduced into registered design law by the 1988 Act. However, a new defence to claims of infringement of a UK registered design was

---

[149] CDPA 1988, s 213(3)(b)(ii).   [150] [2012] ECC 28 (English HC), paras 18–46.

[151] Proposal for a European Parliament and Council Directive on the legal protection of designs, COM(93) 344 final-COD 464, 3 December 1993, Art 14 of the proposed Directive; and Proposal for a European Parliament and Council Regulation on the Community Design, COM(93) 342 final-COD 463, 3 December 1993, Art 23 of the draft Regulation. Both also proposed a requirement that the public should not be misled as to the origin of the product used for the repair.

introduced, providing that the right in a UK registered design of a component part is not infringed by any use of the design for the purpose of the repair of the complex product so as to restore its original appearance.[152]

8.103 Article 18 of the Directive provided the 'plus' element of the compromise. It required the Commission to submit, by three years after the deadline for member states to implement the reforms brought about by the Directive, 'an analysis of the consequences of the provisions of this Directive for Community industry, in particular the industrial sectors which are most affected, particularly manufacturers of complex products and component parts, for consumers, for competition and for the functioning of the internal market'. Within one further year any necessary changes to the Directive to complete the internal market in relation to component parts were to be proposed. Recital 19 mentioned possibilities such as a remuneration system and a limited term of exclusivity. In 2004, the Commission issued a liberalising proposal for an amendment to the Directive.[153] However, after making no legislative progress, this was withdrawn in 2014. The position at the national level remains unharmonised as a result.

8.104 In the meantime, the position is different in relation to the Community Design Regulation. The Regulation also takes up the 'freeze plus' position, recital 13 stating that it would not be appropriate to confer protection as a Community design on a design for a component part of a complex product upon whose appearance the design is dependent and which is used for the purpose of repairing the complex product so as to restore its original appearance, until the Council has decided on its policy in the light of the Commission's proposals. Article 110(1) of the Regulation therefore provides that, until such time as the Community Design Regulation is amended, protection as a Community design will not exist for a design constituting a component part of a complex product used for the purpose of the repair of that complex product so as to restore its original appearance—effectively the same solution as that adopted in UK registered design law (see para 8.102).

8.105 The wording of Article 110(1) CDR is, however, not entirely clear and it has given rise to some issues of interpretation. The CJEU has confirmed in the *Ford v Wheeltrims* case that it does not allow the manufacturer of permitted spare parts to reproduce the trade marks of the original equipment manufacturer on the relevant parts—whether and, if so, when that might be permitted is a matter for trade mark law.[154] Beyond this, the interpretation of Article 110(1) of the Community Designs Regulation was also considered by the English High Court in *Bayerische Motoren Werke Aktiengesellschaft v Round & Metal Ltd*.[155] In that case, Arnold J gave his view that Article 110(1) operates as a defence to an infringement claim (rather than an exclusion from protection for designs for component parts of complex products) and applies only where the component part is used for the purpose of repair of the complex product (rather than, say, sale of the component part as part of the complex product).[156] Reading Article 110(1) in line with recital 13 CDR, it was also Arnold J's view that Article 110(1) was restricted to component parts which are dependent on the appearance of the complex product—that is, 'must-match spares'.[157] Arnold J declined, however, to refer these matters to the Court of Justice for clarification.[158] In hindsight, this was perhaps unfortunate: more recently, in joined cases *Acacia v Audi* and *Acacia v Porsche* the Court of Justice has now issued a very different ruling on the scope and application of Article 110(1):

■ Joined Cases C-397/16 and C-435/16 *Acacia Srl v Pneusgarda Srl, Audi AG; Acacia Srl, Rolando D'Amato v Dr Ing hcF Porsche AG* [2018] Bus LR 927

Acacia manufactured and sold alloy wheel rims which corresponded to registered Community designs belonging to Audi and Porsche. Acacia argued that these were covered by the spare parts defence at Article 110(1) CDR. Audi and Porsche contested this, referring to recital 13 CDR (above, para 8.104) and arguing

---

[152] RDA 1949, s 7A(5).

[153] COM(2004) 582 final, http://eur-lex.europa.eu/LexUriServ/LexUriServ.do?uri=COM:2004:0582:FIN:EN:PDF.

[154] Case C-500/14 *Ford Motor Company v Wheeltrims srl* [2016] ECDR 14.   [155] [2012] ECC 28.   [156] ibid, para 51.

[157] ibid, para 57.   [158] ibid, para 76.

that Article 110(1) only applied to component parts the design of which was *dependent* on the appearance of the complex product of which they formed part. Because purchasers of a car can choose between different styles, this would not cover wheel rims: the design of the wheel rims cannot be said to be dependent on the appearance of the car as a whole.

Taking the opposite line to Arnold J in *Bayerische Motoren Werke Aktiengesellschaft v Round & Metal*, the Court of Justice dismissed the right holder's arguments. The Court held that Article 110(1) is *not* limited in its scope just to component parts the design of which is dependent on the appearance of the overall complex product.[159] Article 110(1) covers any component parts which can be replaced permitting disassembly and assembly of the complex product and without which the complex product cannot be subject to normal use.[160] However, the replacement of a part for aesthetic purposes or customization does not constitute 'repair' within the meaning of Article 110(1); Article 110(1) can additionally only apply to replacement parts which are visually identical to the original parts.[161] Third-party manufacturers and sellers are under a three-part 'duty of diligence' to ensure that downstream users use their component parts only for repair, in compliance with Article 110(1).[162] They must inform users 'through a clear and visible indication' on the product, its packaging, or in other documentation that the component part incorporates a design belonging to another party and is intended exclusively for repair to restore original appearance. They must also ensure 'through appropriate means, in particular contractual means' that downstream users do not intend to use the parts inconsistently with Article 110(1). Finally, they must also refrain from selling a component part where they know or 'in the light of all the relevant circumstances, ought reasonably to know' that the part will not be used in accordance with Article 110(1).[163] The decision of the Court of Justice has been criticised for its reading of Article 110(1).[164] The new 'duty of diligence' introduced in *Acacia* also seems ripe to generate further disputes and, potentially, references to the CJEU.

> ### Key points on 'must match'/repair exceptions to registered designs
>
> - There is currently no exclusion in registered design law like the 'must match' exception found in UK unregistered design law (see Chapter 9).
> - There is also no harmonised position in the Designs Directive on the use of designs for component parts for repair of complex products so as to restore their original appearance.
> - However, the UK RDA 1949 (as amended) and the Community Design Regulation do permit use of design for a component part of a complex product for the purpose of the repair of that complex product so as to restore its original appearance.

Ownership of and dealings in UK and Community registered designs

8.106   Ownership is one of the few substantive aspects of national registered design protection which was not harmonised by the Designs Directive. As a result, member states were free to keep their own rules on ownership. The UK rules on ownership of UK national registered designs were initially different from those relating to Community designs on the issue of commissioned designs. This was an important issue to be aware of in practice, with the risk that UK and Community protection in a commissioned design

---

[159] Joined Cases C-397/16 and C-435/16 *Acacia Srl v Pneusgarda Srl, Audi AG; Acacia Srl, Rolando D'Amato v Dr Ing hcF Porsche AG* [2018] Bus LR 927, para 53.
[160] ibid, paras 65 and 66.   [161] ibid, paras 69–70 and 74–75.   [162] ibid, para 85.   [163] ibid, paras 86–88.
[164] J Cornwell, '*Nintendo v BigBen and Acacia v Audi; Acacia v Porsche*: design exceptions at the CJEU' (2019) 14(1) JIPLP 51–61.

could vest in different people unless addressed by contractual arrangement between the designer and the commissioning party. However, the provisions in the RDA 1949 on ownership of UK registered designs have now been amended to bring them in line with the corresponding provisions in the Community Design Regulation. The right to a UK registered design or to a Community design vests in the designer or his successor in title, unless a design is developed by an employee in the execution of his duties or following the instructions given by his employer, in which case the rights vest in the employer unless (for Community designs only) otherwise agreed or specified in national law.[165] In *Fundación Española para la Innovación de la Artesanía (FEIA) v Cul de Sac Espacio Creativo SL*, the Court of Justice confirmed that these rules do not apply to Community designs produced as a result of a contract for commission.[166] The owner of a commissioned design will be the designer, not the commissioning party. As discussed in further detail later, it is a ground for invalidation for UK and Community registered designs that the registered proprietor is not the actual proprietor of the design (see para 8.111). There is also provision in the RDA 1949 and the Community Designs Regulation for the true proprietor to apply for the register to be rectified so that he becomes the registered proprietor of the design.[167]

8.107 A UK registered design or an application for a UK registered design is personal property (or, in Scotland, incorporeal moveable property).[168] A UK registered design or an application for a UK registered design can be assigned or transferred by testamentary disposition or operation of law, licensed, or made the subject of legal security, all subject to certain formalities set out in the RDA 1949.[169] An assignment of a registered design does not require to be recorded on the register to be effective. However, it is policy to encourage recordal of assignments of registered IPRs and, when a registered design is assigned, or otherwise transferred or licensed, the person taking an interest in the design should apply for the registration of his interest on the UK register of designs. The principal benefit of this is that third parties are deemed to have notice of these interests via the register of designs: any transmission of a UK registered design or an application is subject to any rights vested in another person of which notice has been entered on the register.[170] If no entry has been made on the design register, then any document recording an assignation may not be admitted as evidence of title unless the court otherwise directs.[171]

8.108 The provisions relating to dealing in Community designs face potential complexities arising out of the fact that Community designs cover, and are effective in, all EU member states, all of which have their own systems of property law. Addressing this issue, Article 27 CDR states that, unless otherwise provided in the Regulation, a Community design as an object of property:

> shall be dealt with in its entirety, and for the whole area of the Community

as a national design right of the member state in which, on the relevant date, the holder has his seat or domicile or, if this is not applicable, an establishment.[172] However, a Community design may be licensed for whole or part of the Community.[173]

8.109 Transfers of a Community registered design must, at the request of one of the parties (ie either side of the transaction), be entered in the register and published, before which time the new owner may not invoke the rights under the Community registered design.[174] A registered Community design may also be granted in security and all Community designs may be licensed, and those transactions must likewise be registered where they relate to registered Community designs.[175] The effects of such transactions as regards third

---

[165] RDA 1949, s 2(1) and 2(1B); CDR, Art 14.   [166] Case C-32/08, Court of Justice, [2010] RPC 13.
[167] RDA 1949, s 20, in particular s 20(1)(c); CDR, Art 15.   [168] RDA 1949, s 15A.
[169] RDA 1949, s 15B. An assignment must be in writing signed by the assignor: RDA 1949, s 15B(3).
[170] RDA 1949, ss 15B(2) and 19.   [171] RDA 1949, s 19(5).
[172] CDR, Art 27(1). Article 27(3) and (4) goes on to address the position in relation to jointly owned designs or where none of these provisions apply.
[173] CDR, Art 32(1).   [174] CDR, Art 28.   [175] CDR, Arts 29 and 32(5).

parties are governed by the law of the member state determined according to Article 27. However, transfers, grants in security, and licences can only have effect in relation to third parties in all member states after their entry in the register,[176] although a transaction can have effect before registration in relation to a third party who acquires rights after its date (ie in a further, later transaction) but who at the time of acquiring the rights knows of the earlier transaction.[177]

Invalidation

8.110   As noted earlier, the UK IPO and EUIPO do not engage in detailed examination of applications to test their compliance with the requirements of registrability discussed in this chapter. There is also no provision for third-party opposition. Save in exceptional cases, the application is likely to go through to registration. However, registered designs may be subject to subsequent challenge on the basis that, although accepted for registration, they do not meet the requirements for registrability laid down by the law. The challenge may come from a defendant when the right holder is seeking to enforce the design in court, but it is also possible (and common) for challenges to be raised directly by application to the EUIPO or the UK IPO as appropriate.[178]

8.111   The grounds for invalidation of a registered design are essentially the same for UK registered designs and Community designs.[179] UK registered designs and Community designs may be declared invalid on the grounds that:[180]

- the matter registered does not fall within the definition of 'design';[181]

- the design does not otherwise meet the requirements of registrability (ie that it lacks novelty or individual character or is subject to one of the exclusions from protection such as being dictated by technical function or being contrary to public policy or morality);[182]

- the design is not new or possessed of an individual character in comparison with a design made available to the public on or after the contested application for registration *but* which has priority over the contested design by virtue of earlier registration or application for registration under the RDA 1949, Community Design Regulation, or in an international registration designating the Community;[183]

- the registered proprietor is not the proprietor of the design;[184]

- the design involves the use of an earlier distinctive sign which provides the right to prohibit the use of that sign;[185] and

- the design constitutes an unauthorised use of a work protected by copyright.[186]

---

[176]   CDR, Art 33(2).

[177]   CDR, Art 33(2). This rule does not apply where a Community registered design or right concerning the Community registered design is acquired by way of the transfer of the whole of a company's undertaking (eg in a takeover) or by any other universal succession (eg transmission of a whole estate on death) (Art 33(3)).

[178]   For invalidity applications to the UK IPO in relation to UK registered designs, see RDA 1949, s 11ZB; for invalidity applications to the EUIPO in relation to Community registered designs, see CDR, Arts 24 and 52.

[179]   Although they are worded slightly differently.

[180]   There are also additional grounds for invalidation in the UK relating essentially to the protection of Royal emblems, Olympic symbols, and certain other insignia protected by the Paris Convention: RDA 1949, s 11ZA(1)(c). For similar provisions relating to Community designs, see CDR, Art 25(1)(g). See also DD, Art 11(2)(c).

[181]   RDA 1949, s 11ZA(1)(a); DD, Art 11(1)(a); CDR, Art 25(1)(a).   [182]   RDA 1949, s 11ZA(1)(b); DD, Art 11(1)(b); CDR, Art 25(1)(b).

[183]   RDA 1949, s 11ZA(1A); DD, Art 11(1)(d); CDR, Art 25(1)(d).

[184]   RDA 1949, s 11ZA(2); DD, Art 11(1)(c); CDR, Art 25(1)(c). Article 25(1)(c) CDR is worded slightly differently to the broadly equivalent provision in the RDA 1949 and introduces a requirement of a court decision on ownership ('if, by virtue of a court decision, the right holder is not entitled to the Community design under Article 14').

[185]   RDA 1949, s 11ZA(3); DD, Art 11(2)(a); CDR, Art 25(1)(e).   [186]   RDA 1949, s 11ZA(4); DD, Art 11(2)(b); CDR, Art 25(1)(f).

8.112   An invalidation challenge based on the grounds outlined at the first two bullet points may be brought by any interested person.[187] Otherwise, the challenge must be brought by the owner of the earlier right relied upon or, if it is claimed that the registered proprietor is not the proprietor of the design, by the person claiming to be the true proprietor of the design.[188] If a ground of invalidity is made out, there will be a declaration of invalidity, which can be whole or partial, with an option for the proprietor to modify and maintain his design registration in amended form in certain circumstances.[189]

 Question

Who may bring an invalidity challenge and on what grounds may a design registration be declared invalid?

8.113   The General Court in *Grupo Promer Mon Graphic SA v OHIM and PepsiCo Inc* confirmed that the grounds of invalidity set out in Article 25 CDR are exhaustive: it is therefore not possible to apply for invalidation of a registered design on grounds not mentioned in the Directive or Regulation, such as bad faith.[190] It follows that the grounds of invalidity set out in the Directive, and transposed into national law, are also exhaustive. Three further particular grounds for invalidation merit noting:

Earlier unpublished designs

8.114   Earlier unpublished design applications or registrations are the focus of Article 11(1)(d) DD/Article 25(1)(d) CDR. Because they are unpublished, such applications or registrations cannot be taken to form part of the prior art for the purposes of assessing novelty and individual character. However, the scheme of the Designs Directive and the Community Design Regulation is that they should nonetheless be able to trump a later design application or registration if the later design is too close. According to the Designs Directive and the Community Design Regulation, a later design will be invalid if it is 'in conflict with' an earlier unpublished design. The expression 'in conflict with' is not defined. In *Grupo Promer*, the General Court confirmed that a design is 'in conflict with' a prior design for these purposes when, taking into consideration the freedom of the designer in developing the design, that design does not produce on the informed user a different overall impression from that produced by the prior design relied upon.[191] The upshot is that the test is essentially the same as for individual character.

Earlier trade marks

8.115   According to Article 11(2)(a) DD/Article 25(1)(e) CDR there are grounds for invalidation 'if a distinctive sign is used in a subsequent design, and Community law or the law of the Member State governing that sign confers on the right holder of the sign the right to prohibit such use'. Neither the DD nor the CDR

---

[187] RDA 1949, s 11ZB(1).

[188] RDA 1949, s 11ZA(2), (3) and (4) and s 11ZB(5); DD, Art 11(3) and (4); CDR, Art 25(2) and (3).

[189] RDA 1949, s 11ZC and 11ZD; DD, Art 11(7); CDR, Art 25(6).

[190] Case T-9/07 *Grupo Promer Mon Graphic SA v Office for Harmonisation in the Internal Market (Trade Marks and Designs) (OHIM) with PepsiCo Inc (Intervener)* [2010] ECDR 7, para 30 (not appealed to the Court of Justice on this point).

[191] ibid, para 52 (not appealed to the Court of Justice on this point). Note that the transposing provision in the RDA 1949 does not use the wording 'in conflict with' but is intended to cover the same situation.

define what is meant by saying that a distinctive sign is 'used' in a subsequent design. In Case T-148/08 *Beifa Group Co Ltd v OHIM and Schwan-Stabilo Schwanhäußer GmbH & Co KG*, a case involving a challenge to a Community registered design on the basis of an earlier trade mark registration, the General Court confirmed that there may be grounds for invalidation where the registered design is not only the same as, but also similar to, the earlier distinctive sign. The issue is whether the owner of the earlier distinctive sign has the right to prohibit the use of its sign in the later design pursuant to the relevant law governing protection of that distinctive sign.[192]

■ **Case T-695/15 *BMB sp zoo v EU IPO and Ferrero SpA* (General Court) [2018] ETMR 2**

This case provides a good example of this ground for invalidation in action. BMB owned a Community design registration, filed in 2007, for the design shown in Figure 8.12. Ferrero owned an international trade mark registration, registered in 1974 and effective in various countries including France, for the three-dimensional mark shown at Figure 8.13. It was found by the EUIPO Cancellation Division and Third Board of Appeal that BMB's Community design was invalid under Article 25(1)(e) CDR. The General Court upheld this conclusion, applying the relevant provision of the French Intellectual Property Code to determine whether Ferrero had the right to prohibit use of the contested BMB design on the basis of its prior trade mark rights. The General Court concluded that, as a matter of relevant trade mark law, there was a likelihood of confusion between Ferrero's earlier registered mark and the later BMB design.[193]

Figure 8.12 BMB Community registered design in *BMB sp zoo v EU IPO and Ferrero SpA* (General Court, Case T-695/15) [2018] ETMR 2

---

[192] [2010] ETMR 42, paras 50–59 and 63.
[193] At the time of writing, the General Court's decision is on appeal to the Court of Justice, pending as Case C-693/17.

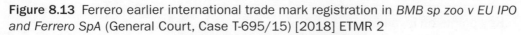

Figure 8.13 Ferrero earlier international trade mark registration in *BMB sp zoo v EU IPO and Ferrero SpA* (General Court, Case T-695/15) [2018] ETMR 2

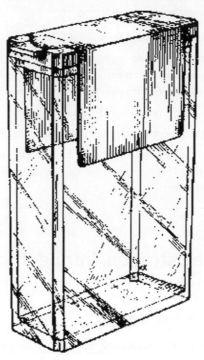

Earlier rights in copyright

8.116   According to Article 11(2)(b) DD/Article 25(1)(f) CDR, a design will be invalid if it 'constitutes an unauthorised use of a work protected under the copyright law of a Member State'. This ground for invalidation was relied upon before the General Court in the case *Viejo Valle*.[194] That case concerned a design for items of crockery. The validity of the design was challenged on the basis that it used a pattern of surface ornamentation (consisting of fine concentric grooves) previously used on the crockery of the applicant for invalidity and which was protected in copyright under French law. According to the General Court, it was not appropriate to compare the design as a whole with the crockery of the applicant for invalidity. Instead, the question was simply whether the challenged design 'used' the earlier copyright work, which related to surface decoration only. The General Court held that the pattern on the contested design 'greatly resemble[d]' the decoration of the crockery of the applicant for invalidity, 'both as concerns the identical nature of the covered surfaces and as concerns the concentric nature, regularity and narrowness of the grooves' (para 101). Although the design right holder claimed that the grooves on the challenged design were thicker and more pronounced, the General Court held that this was not sufficient to obscure this similarity. The challenged design was held to be invalid. Curiously, this outcome was reached despite the design right holder producing two French court judgments in which it had been held that the applicant for invalidity did not have any copyright protection in the particular pattern of surface decoration relied upon.

---

[194]   Joined Cases T-566/11 and T-567/11 *Viejo Valle SA v Office for Harmonisation in the Internal Market (Trade Marks and Designs) (OHIM) and Etablissements Coquet (intervener)* (23 October 2013, unreported).

> **Key points on invalidity**
>
> A registration may be challenged on the grounds that:
>
> - the design does not meet the requirements for registration;
> - the design is in conflict with an earlier design protected under the RDA 1949, Community Designs Regulation, or by an international registration designating the Community which had not been published as at the relevant date but which does have an earlier priority date;
> - the registered proprietor is not the proprietor of the design;
> - the use of the design could be prevented by earlier rights in copyright or trade marks;
> - a challenge based on the ground that the design does not meet the requirements for registration can be brought by any interested person; otherwise, challenges are limited to the true owner of the design or the owner of any earlier right relied upon.

Rights given by registration, infringement, defences, and duration of rights

Exclusive right to use the design

8.117   The right conferred by registration is the 'exclusive right' to 'use' the design and:[195]

> any design which does not produce on the informed user a different overall impression.

It is thus a right, not only to the registered design itself, but to any other design which produces the same overall impression on the informed user. The crucial point for present purposes—considering the scope of the rights conferred—is that *protection extends beyond the exact design registered.* 'Overall impression' and the 'informed user' are concepts we have already encountered when discussing the requirement of individual character (see paras 8.45ff). In assessing the scope of protection, as for assessment of individual character, the degree of freedom of the designer in developing his design is also to be taken into account.[196] It is now clear that the assessment of 'overall impression' is the same for validity and infringement purposes, the suggestion that this might be otherwise by the English Court of Appeal in *Procter & Gamble Co v Reckitt Benckiser (UK) Ltd* (see para 8.57) having been explicitly reversed by the English Court of Appeal in its more recent decision in *Dyson Ltd v Vax Ltd* (see para 8.57).[197] As the assessment of 'overall impression' is the same for validity and infringement, the reader is referred to the discussion of individual character/'overall impression' at paras 8.45ff for the key case law and principles.

 Question

What exclusive right is conferred upon the owner of a registered design?

---

[195]   RDA 1949, s 7(1); DD, Arts 9(1) and 12(1); CDR, Arts 10(1) and 19(1).

[196]   RDA, s 7(3); DD, Art 9(2); CDR, Art 10(2).

[197]   In *Procter & Gamble Co v Reckitt Benckiser (UK) Ltd* [2008] FSR 8 (CA) (see para 8.57), Jacob LJ held that, for validity purposes, a design needed to produce a 'clearly different' overall impression compared to earlier designs to have individual character but that, for infringement purposes, a design needed only to produce a 'different' overall impression to fall outside the scope of the design relied upon: paras 18–19. The English Court of Appeal in *Dyson* has, however, now explicitly stated that its ruling in *Procter & Gamble* to the effect that these tests were different was incorrect: *Dyson Ltd v Vax Ltd* [2012] FSR 4 (CA), para 34.

8.118 As the Designs Directive and the Community Design Regulation put it, the exclusive right conferred by registration confers on the proprietor:[198]

> the exclusive right to use [the design] and to prevent any third party not having his consent from using it.

So, the exclusive right is a basis for challenging—in court if necessary—unauthorised use of the design by others.[199] The converse of that, of course, is that the right holder can authorise others to use the design by way of licences. But the right holder can decide not to do so, and to exploit the exclusive right himself.

8.119 A further, fundamentally important, point is that the right to prevent third-party 'use' is a very different concept from the right to prevent 'copying', which is characteristic of the scope of protection conferred by copyright. 'Copying' involves reproduction of an earlier work and a causal connection between the earlier and later works (see para 4.27). The right to prevent other parties from 'using' a design is not limited in this way and will entitle the holder of a UK registered design and Community registered design to stop 'use' of an infringing design even where that design has been developed wholly independently by the infringer, without any knowledge of the UK registered design or Community registered design relied upon. Because of this, the very strong protection conferred by a UK registered design and Community registered design— sometimes called a 'full monopoly right'—can be equated more closely to the rights conferred by a patent than those arising in copyright.

8.120 The broad nature of this exclusive right is linked, in part, to the operation of the design registration system. In principle, a person who proposes to use a design can check the register to see if the same or a similar design has been registered; if it has, the person is then in a position to know that the proposed use is illegitimate. It is accordingly fair to grant a 'full monopoly' right to registered designs to prevent any use of an infringing design, whether copied or not. If, however, a design is unregistered, the only way a person can know whether someone else has already produced the same or a similar design is by finding it already in use in the market place; so, as we will see in Chapter 9 on unregistered design rights, it is only fair that such a person can only be liable to the existing user if he has copied the latter's design.

8.121 The concept of 'use' includes in particular but is not limited to:[200]

> the making, offering, putting on the market, importing, exporting or using of a product in which the design is incorporated or to which it is applied, or stocking such a product for those purposes.

Much of this will typically be *commercial or trading activity*—manufacture, sale, import, export, stocking— but infringement is not limited to the commercial context. However, when we turn to the defences (see paras 8.123–8.127), we find that the right in a registered design is not infringed by an act which is done privately and for purposes which are not commercial.[201]

8.122 Finally, it is critically important to note that there is no need for an infringer's product(s) to be the same as the product(s) marketed by the right holder or mentioned in the product statements included in the

---

[198] DD, Art 12(1); CDR, Art 19(1).

[199] The references in the DD and CDR to 'the exclusive right to use [the design]' should not be understood as conferring an absolute positive right on the proprietor to use his design. In Case C-488/10 *Celaya Emparanza y Galdos Internacional SA v Proyectos Integrales de Balizamientos SL* [2012] ECDR 17, the Court of Justice confirmed that, in a dispute relating to infringement of a registered Community design, the right to prevent use by third parties of a design which does not produce a different overall impression extends to all third parties, including the holder of a later registered Community design. The holder of a later-registered Community design which produces the same overall impression as an earlier-registered Community design can be sued for infringement without a need to invalidate the later registration, and will have to defend his position by proving that the earlier design does not meet the conditions for registration by seeking declaration of invalidity (paras 32–52). Infringements may be actionable by a licensee of the design in certain circumstances: see Arts 32(3) and (4) CDR, considered by the CJEU in Case C-419/15 *Thomas Phipps GmbH & Co KG v Grüne Welle Vertriebs GmbH* (unreported). For UK registered designs, see s24F RDA 1949 on the rights and remedies of exclusive licensees.

[200] RDA 1949, s 7(2); DD, Art 12(1); CDR, Art 19(1).

[201] RDA 1949, s 7A(2)(a); DD, Art 13(1)(a); CDR, Art 20(1)(a).

UK or Community design application forms. This was confirmed by the English Court of Appeal in *Green Lane Products Ltd v PMS International Group Ltd*, in which Jacob LJ emphasised:[202]

> It is particularly important to realise that the scope of protection covers any use of the design for article, whatever its intended purpose. The scope provision . . . does not limit infringement to 'articles for which the design is registered' or anything like that. So if you register a design for a car you can stop use of the design for a brooch or a cake or a toy, or if you register a textile design you can stop its use on wallpaper, a shirt or a plate.

Any use of the design, or one producing the same overall impression on the informed user, will constitute infringement whatever the product to which it is applied or in which it is incorporated. However, it remains to be fully explored in case law how far, in cases where the alleged infringement is a different product, that difference in product may impact upon the overall impressions produced by the alleged infringement and thus the question of whether the infringement produces the same overall impression as the registered design.

Key points on the exclusive right conferred by a registered design

- The scope of protection conferred by a registered design includes the registered design and any design which does not produce a different overall impression on the informed user.

- The assessment of overall impression for infringement purposes is the same as for validity purposes and, as a result, the key cases and principles relating to 'overall impression' are common across infringement and validity.

- The holder of a registered design can stop anyone else using the design for a product, regardless of whether or not that use is the result of copying and regardless of whether that use relates to the same product(s) as those of the holder of the registered design.

Defences

8.123   The principal defences to infringement of a UK registered design and Community design cover:

- acts done privately and for non-commercial purposes;[203]

- acts done for experimental purposes;[204] and

- acts of reproduction for the purposes of making citations or of teaching, provided that such acts 'are compatible with fair trade practice' and 'do not unduly prejudice the normal exploitation of the design', and that mention is made of the source.[205]

Article 22 CDR also preserves limited rights of prior use for third parties who had, before the relevant date, in good faith commenced use of a design included within the scope of a registered Community design or made serious and effective preparations to that end. Although not originally included in UK law, the RDA 1949 has now been amended so as also to include an equivalent defence to infringement of a UK registered design.[206] There are also defences for equipment on ships and aircraft which are registered in another country when these temporarily enter the relevant territory, the importation into the relevant territory of spare parts and accessories for the purpose of repairing such craft, and the execution of repairs on such craft.[207]

---

[202] [2008] FSR 28, para 27.
[203] RDA 1949 s 7A(2)(a); DD Art 13(1)(a); CDR Art 20(1)(a).   [204] RDA 1949 s 7A(2)(b); DD Art 13(1)(b); CDR Art 20(1)(b).
[205] RDA 1949, s 7A(2)(c) and (3); DD, Art 13(1)(c); CDR, Art 20(1)(c).   [206] RDA 1949, s 7B.
[207] RDA 1949, s 7A(2)(d)–(f); DD, Art 13(2); CDR, Art 20(2).

8.124 Looking in more detail at the principal defences, as regards the private and non-commercial use defence there is a similarly worded exception in patent law. However, that patent law exception has caused some difficulties of interpretation.[208] The acts must be both private *and* non-commercial; so, a private act which was commercial would be infringement, as would a non-commercial act which was public. The difficulties in defining private and non-commercial are not inconsiderable.

8.125 As for the exception for acts done for experimental purposes, there is also a similarly worded exception in patent law; and once more its interpretation is open to debate.[209] In the context of design law, experiments may occur with a view to determining the best design by which particular functions of a product may be achieved, but one can also imagine experiments being conducted to find designs which were most attractive to consumers. What sort of 'experimental purposes' are covered by the defence as compared to those, say, to test market acceptability is yet to be clarified.

8.126 The exception for acts of reproduction for the purposes of making citations or of teaching has been the subject of recent controversial Court of Justice case law. On its face, this defence seems closer to some of those familiar from copyright law. Its reference to 'teaching' certainly facilitates activities in relation to design instruction in schools, art and design colleges, and universities; however, this is not explicitly confined to activities of educational institutions and so might potentially be capable of application in an industrial or commercial context as well. The reference to citation appears to cover the use of designs in publications such as books of instruction for designers and, it is suggested, textbooks for intellectual property lawyers and students. This would seem perfectly compatible with fair trade practice and not unduly to prejudice the normal exploitation of the design—indeed, not to do so at all. The source of the design has to be given in both teaching and citation activities if they are to enjoy the benefit of the defence. Going beyond this, however, in *Nintendo v BigBen* the Court of Justice has controversially interpreted the reference to 'citation' in Article 20(1)(c) CDR as extending to cover certain forms of marketing activity:

■ Joined Cases C-24/16 and C-25/16 *Nintendo Co Ltd v BigBen Interactive GmbH*; *BigBen Interactive SA* [2018] ECDR 3

BigBen manufactured and sold accessories compatible with the Nintendo Wii games console. BigBen sought to rely on the defence at Article 20(1)(c) CDR to allow it to use on its product packaging and website various images of Nintendo products. Those images corresponded to Nintendo registered Community designs. BigBen argued that this constituted 'making citations' within the meaning of Article 20(1)(c) CDR and, somewhat unexpectedly, the Court of Justice agreed. The Court held that, where a party lawfully sells goods which are intended to be used with specific goods corresponding to a Community design, 'making citations' can include reproducing the protected design 'in order to explain or demonstrate the joint use' of the third party's and right holder's goods.[210] As regards the three sub-conditions at Article 20(1)(c) CDR, trade mark case law on 'honest practices in industrial and commercial matters' (see paras 15.96–15.98) was to apply *mutatis mutandis* to the condition that the defendant's acts be 'compatible with fair trade practice'.[211] The sub condition requiring the relevant acts not unduly prejudice the normal exploitation of the design was aimed 'inter alia to prevent the act of reproduction … from negatively affecting the economic interests that the holder of the rights … may derive from a normal exploitation of those designs'.[212] Mention of the source needed to be such as to enable 'a reasonably well-informed and reasonably observant and circumspect consumer easily to identify the commercial origin of the product corresponding to the Community design'.[213] It remains to be seen how these requirements are interpreted and applied in practice by national courts.

---

[208] Patents Act 1977, s 60(5)(a); see para 12.88.   [209] Patents Act 1977, s 60(5)(b); see para 12.89–12.94.
[210] Joined Cases C-24/16 and C-25/16 *Nintendo Co Ltd v BigBen Interactive GmbH*; *BigBen Interactive SA* (Court of Justice) [2018] ECDR 3, para 77.
[211] ibid, paras 79–80.   [212] ibid, para 82.   [213] ibid, para 84.

8.127   Rights in registered designs are also not infringed by an act relating to a product in which a registered design is incorporated or to which it has been applied if the product has been put on the market in the European Economic Area (EEA) by the registered proprietor or with his consent (see further the discussion of exhaustion of rights at Chapter 19).[214] In addition, although not part of the harmonised regime enacted by the Designs Directive, for both UK registered designs and Community designs it is also not an infringement to use the registered design for a component part for the purpose of repair of a complex product so as to restore its original appearance (the 'must match' defence) (see paras 8.102 and 8.104).[215]

Key points on defences

- UK registered designs and Community designs are not infringed by:
  - acts done privately and for non-commercial purposes;
  - acts done for experimental purposes;
  - acts of reproduction for the purposes of making citations or of teaching, provided that such acts 'are compatible with fair trade practice' and 'do not unduly prejudice the normal exploitation of the design', and that mention is made of the source.
- Although not part of the harmonised regime enacted by the Designs Directive, it is also not an infringement of UK registered designs and Community designs to use the registered design for a component part for the purpose of repair of a complex product so as to restore its original appearance.

Duration of rights

8.128   Once granted, design registrations are protected from the date of filing. The rights in a registered design last initially for five years from the filing date.[216] The right can be renewed for up to four more periods of five years, up to a maximum of 25 years in total.[217] Failure to renew leads to the right ceasing to have effect,[218] but a renewal can be made within six months of a renewal deadline subject to certain consequences.[219] It may also be possible thereafter to restore a lapsed right in a registered design in certain circumstances.[220] The renewal fees which are payable at the five-year renewal deadlines grow more expensive at each stage.

8.129   The registered proprietor of a UK registered design and a Community design can effectively abandon his registration at any time by notifying the relevant registry.[221]

Interaction with other IP rights

8.130   As discussed previously, there is clear potential for overlap between entitlement to protection under the European designs regime and under other IP rights. The harmonisation effected by the Designs Directive is limited only to national registered design protection. Article 16 DD states:

> The provisions of this Directive shall be without prejudice to any provisions of Community law or the law of the member state concerned relating to unregistered design rights, trade marks or other distinctive signs, patents and utility models, typefaces, civil liability or unfair competition (see also recital 7).

---

[214] RDA 1949, s 7A(4); DD, Art 15; CDR, Art 21.   [215] RDA 1949, s 7A(5); CDR, Art 110(1).
[216] RDA 1949, s 8(1); DD, Art 10; CDR, Art 12.   [217] RDA 1949, s 8(2); DD, Art 10; CDR, Art 12.   [218] RDA 1949, s 8(3).
[219] RDA 1949, s 8(4); CDR, Art 13(3).   [220] RDA 1949, s 8A; CDR, Art 67.
[221] RDA 1949, s 11; CDR, Art 51.

There is equivalent provision in the CDR (Art 96(1) and recital 31). These provisions leave open the potential for cumulation of protection for a particular design as a registered design and under such other rights, if such other protection is available.

8.131   The Designs Directive and the Community Design Regulation also envisage cumulation of protection with copyright. Article 17 DD states:

> A design protected by a design right registered in or in respect of a Member State in accordance with this Directive shall also be eligible for protection under the law of copyright of that State as from the date on which the design was created or fixed in any form. The extent to which, and the conditions under which, such protection is conferred, including the level of originality required, shall be determined by each Member State (see also recital 8).

Again, there is equivalent provision in Article 96(2) and recital 32 CDR.

8.132   Article 17 DD has been considered by the Court of Justice in *Flos SpA v Semeraro Casa e Famiglia SpA*.[222] In this preliminary reference from the Italian courts, the Court of Justice considered a number of complex issues arising from the Italian legislation transposing the Designs Directive into Italian law. Much of the detail is particular to the Italian legislation, but some points of more general significance were made in the Court of Justice's decision. The Court stressed the importance of the principle of cumulation with copyright highlighted at recital 8 of the Directive. Article 17 DD relates only to designs registered in accordance with the Directive. Although the first sentence of Article 17 provides that such designs are eligible for copyright protection, the second sentence of Article 17 allows member states to determine the extent to which, and conditions under which, such copyright protection is conferred, including the level of originality required. However, the second sentence of Article 17 does not give member states a choice as to whether or not to confer copyright protection for a registered design if the design meets the conditions in that member state under which copyright protection is conferred. Controversially, the Court went on to say that it is clear from Article 17 DD that copyright protection *must* be conferred on all designs protected by a design right registered in or in respect of the member state concerned. It also held that the entitlement to determine the extent of copyright protection and conditions under which it is conferred does *not* include freedom to decide term of protection, as that has been harmonised at the EU level by the Term Directive.[223] The *Flos* ruling has been criticised, with concerns expressed about the potential reintroduction of 'industrial copyright' in designs (as to which see further Chapter 9) as a result of the Court's interpretation of the relevant legislation as *requiring* designs to be protected by copyright rather than, as has been argued to be the underlying legislative intention of Article 17 DD, simply making it impermissible to deny copyright protection to a design merely because it was registered as a design.[224]

8.133   According to the Designs Directive and the Community Design Regulation, there is therefore considerable scope for a design to be protected as a registered design and in copyright at the same time. In the UK, however, the scope for infringing the copyright subsisting in such a design is significantly restricted by the effect of section 51 of the CDPA 1988. Section 51 was introduced in UK law a number of years before the Designs Directive and Community Design Regulation were enacted and, as will be discussed in greater detail in Chapter 9 (see paras 9.81–9.88), forms a key part of the provisions in the CDPA 1988 regulating the relationship between copyright, UK unregistered design right, and the extent to which copyright claims based on design drawings can be enforced in relation to industrial designs. Because section 51 of the CDPA 1988 will apply to restrict the ability to make a copyright claim based on any design drawing which falls within its scope, as a matter of UK law the copyright in many design drawings, which would otherwise have been allowed to coexist with design protection under the Designs Directive and the Community Design

---

[222] Case C-168/09, 27 January 2011, [2011] ECDR 8.
[223] ibid, paras 32–39 in particular.
[224] See further L Bently, 'The return of industrial copyright?' [2012] EIPR 654–72.

Regulation, will not in fact be enforceable in the UK. Other copyright claims would in the past also have been affected by section 52 of the CDPA 1988, which was enacted to cut the period of enforceability in certain copyright artistic works down to 25 years in certain circumstances—however, section 52 has now been repealed (see paras 9.89–9.93). These are all domestic matters particular to the UK. For more detail, the reader is referred to Chapter 9.

8.134   In the meantime, where UK registered design protection and copyright coexist in a design which is also an artistic work, copyright is not infringed by anything done in pursuance of an assignment or licence of the registered design granted by the person recorded on the register as its proprietor in good faith reliance on the registration, even when the person registered as the proprietor of the design was not the proprietor for the purposes of the RDA 1949.[225]

Key points on interaction with other IP rights

- The Designs Directive and the Community Design Regulation do not affect other IP rights which may coexist in a design and leave open the potential for cumulation between such other rights and the protection available for that design under the Designs Directive and the Community Designs Regulation.

- The Designs Directive and the Community Design Regulation also provide that a protected design is eligible for copyright protection as from the date on which the design was created or fixed in any form, although the extent to which, and the conditions under which, such protection is conferred, including the level of originality required, shall be determined by each member state.

- In the UK, the potential for cumulation of design protection and protection in copyright is significantly curtailed by the CDPA 1988, discussed further in Chapter 9.

Further reading

Books

G. Hasselblatt (ed) *Community Design Regulation (EC) No 6/2002—A Commentary* (2015)

M Howe, *Russell-Clarke and Howe on Industrial Designs* (9th edn, 2016)

D Stone, *European Union Design Law: A Practitioner's Guide* (2nd edn, 2016)

U Suthersanen, *Design Law: European Union and United States of America* (2nd edn, 2010)

Edited collections

A. Kur, M. Levin, and J. Schovsbo (eds), *The EU Design Approach—A Global Appraisal* (2018)

History

B Sherman and L Bently, *The Making of Intellectual Property Law* (1999), Chs 3, 4

Studies

European Commission, 'Legal review on industrial design protection in Europe', June 2016, https://ec.europa.eu/growth/content/legal-review-industrial-design-protection-europe-0_en.

Articles

S Ashby, 'The UK Supreme Court and the Trunki case: missed opportunities, mysteries and misunderstood' (2016) 38(9) EIPR 527–32

---

[225] CDPA 1988, s 53.

L Bently, 'The return of industrial copyright?' [2012] EIPR 654–72

L Brancusi, 'Designs determined by the product's technical function: arguments for an autonomous test' [2016] EIPR 23–30

J Cornwell, 'Dyson and Samsung compared: functionality and aesthetics in the design infringement analysis' [2013] EIPR 273–86

J Cornwell, 'Under-referred, under-reasoned, under-resourced? Re-examining EU design law before the Court of Justice and General Court' (2016) 4 IPQ 318–51

J Cornwell, 'Nintendo v BigBen and Acacia v Audi; Acacia v Porsche: design exceptions at the CJEU' (2019) 14(1) JIPLP 51–61

G Dinwoodie, 'Federalized Functionalism: The Future of Design Protection in the European Union' (1996) 24 AIPLA QJ 611

J Drexl, RM Hilty, and A Kur, 'Design protection for spare parts and the Commission's proposal for a repairs clause' (2005) 36(4) IIC 448–57

J Du Mont and M Janis 'Functionality in US Design Patent & Community Design Law', Indiana Legal Studies Research Paper No 342, https://ssrn.com/abstract=2773070

A Gerdau de Borja, 'Exceptions to design rights: the potential impact of Article 26(2) TRIPS' [2008] EIPR 500–08

PGFA Geerts, 'The informed user in design law: what should he compare and how should he make the comparison?' [2014] EIPR 181–85

H Hartwig, 'Spare parts under European design and trade mark law' (2016) 11(2) JIPLP 121–29

N Kapyrina, 'Limitations in the field of designs' (2018) 49(1) IIC 41–62

A Kingsbury, 'International harmonisation of designs law: the case for diversity' [2010] EIPR 382–95

A Kur, 'The Green Paper's "Design Approach"—what's wrong with it?' [1993] EIPR 374–78

D Musker, 'Hidden meaning? UK perspectives on invisible in use designs' [2003] EIPR 450–56

D Musker, '"Making citations"—mystery or mistranslation? The Opinion of Advocate General Bot in Nintendo v BigBen' (2017) 12(10) JIPLP 834–36

B Trimmer and G Parsons, 'Trunki's crazy (registered design) ride: PMS International Group Plc v Magmatic Ltd' [2016] EIPR 451–58

D Smyth, 'Samsung v Apple: how does the judge become an "informed user"?' (2012) 7(11) JIPLP 776–78

D Smyth, 'How is the scope of protection of a registered Community design to be determined?' (2013) 8(4) JIPLP 270–72

D Stone, 'Transparency over the use of dotted lines?' (2013) 8(6) JIPLP 437–40

D Stone, 'Trunki—how did things go so wrong?' (2016) 11(9) JIPLP 662–81

D Stone, 'Design law misplayed in Nintendo AG Opinion' [2017] 12(7) JIPLP 558–64

J Straus, 'Design protection for spare parts gone in Europe? Proposed changes to the EC Directive: the Commission's mandate and its doubtful execution' [2005] EIPR 391–404

Unregistered designs

Introduction

Scope and overview of chapter

9.1 This chapter deals with unregistered design protection. There are two main forms of protection: the unregistered design right established for the UK by Part III of the Copyright, Designs and Patents Act 1988 (hereafter referred to as 'UK UDR'), and the Community unregistered design right more recently created by Community Design Regulation 6/2002/EC (hereafter referred to as 'Community UDR'). In contrast to registered design protection, both of these forms of protection arise automatically if the relevant requirements are met. The chapter looks at each of these unregistered rights in turn, also considering the implications of Brexit for Community UDR. Building on the brief discussion at the end of Chapter 8, this chapter also considers in more detail the role still enjoyed by copyright in relation to the protection of designs in the UK.

9.2 **Learning objectives**

By the end of this chapter you should be able to describe and explain:

- the legal protection conferred upon unregistered designs in UK law and as Community unregistered designs, the differences between these two systems, and the implications of Brexit for Community UDR protection;

- the key differences between unregistered and registered design protection;

- the interaction between unregistered design rights, registered designs, and copyright.

9.3 The chapter begins by setting unregistered design protection in its international context, as described in more detail in Chapter 8. There then follows a detailed account and analysis of UK UDR. Thereafter, there is an assessment of the interaction with copyright in the UK. The chapter concludes by examining Community UDR, including the implications of Brexit. The rest of the chapter looks like this:

- International context (9.4–9.7)

- Historical background to UK UDR (9.8–9.12)

- UK UDR: what is a 'design'? (9.13–9.32)

- Exclusions from protection in UK UDR (9.33–9.49)

- Original and not 'commonplace' (9.50–9.57)

- Duration (9.58–9.66)

- Rights in UK UDR (9.67–9.78)

- Interaction with copyright (9.79–9.93)

- Community UDR, including Brexit (9.94–9.105)

International context

9.4 In Chapter 8 (see paras 8.4–8.10) we saw how the international treaty framework for the protection of designs did not require protection to be given through a registration system, and even allowed states to choose to protect designs through copyright law. The general permissiveness of the international framework extends to enabling states to use more than one form of protection for designs. The creation of unregistered forms of design protection alongside registered designs and copyright systems by, first, the UK, and then by the European Union (EU) is therefore perfectly consistent with international requirements.

9.5 We also saw in Chapter 8 that, if there was a registration system, the Paris Convention obliged its member states to give foreigners access to that system; and, of course, the Berne Convention requires member states to provide protection under their national law for persons and works from other Berne countries (see para 2.8). However, there is no equivalent international requirement for any system of unregistered design right protection separate from copyright.

9.6 This gap was used by the UK when it created UK UDR in the late 1980s. UK UDR uses a system of *'reciprocity'*. Foreign nationals were only to enjoy UK UDR under the rules governing 'qualification' for UK UDR protection (Copyright, Designs and Patents Act 1988 (CDPA 1988), ss 213(5) and 217–221) where their own legal system provided equivalent protection for UK nationals. The effect of this was to be that UK companies were able to copy foreign products entering the UK without fear of litigation on the basis of UK UDR ensuing, unless they came from countries with equivalents to UK UDR. The EU countries were recognised as granting an equivalent protection to the designs of UK nationals, but not the United States and Japan.[1]

 Question

How does 'reciprocity' differ from the usual international principle of 'national treatment'?

9.7 The US Semiconductor Chip Protection Act 1984 was the first piece of legislation to use this technique of 'reciprocity' to gain international compliance with a system of intellectual property (IP) rights created to protect national rights. In this it was very successful. When the UK introduced UK UDR in 1988, it followed the US model. The qualification requirements are complex and depend, variously, upon the identity of the designer, the identity of the designer's employer if relevant, or upon the first marketing of articles made to the design.[2] The qualification rules have been simplified to some degree by the Intellectual Property Act 2014 so that, for all designs created from 1 October 2014 onwards, a 'qualifying person' (designer, employer etc) can be of any nationality provided that (for individuals) they are habitually resident in a qualifying country or (for legal persons) they are either formed under the law of a qualifying country or have a place of business there at which substantial business activity is carried on (CDPA, s 217(1)).

There is no requirement of 'reciprocity' or equivalent limitation of access to Community UDR.

---

[1] CDPA 1988, s 217(3); the Design Right (Reciprocal Protection) (No 2) Order (SI 1989/1294).
[2] See CDPA 1988, ss 217–221 and 255–256.

> **Key points on international context**
>
> • Unregistered design rights are allowed under the international IP treaties.
>
> • There may also be more than one form of protection at a time for designs.
>
> • Under the Paris Convention, there is no requirement of national treatment outside any design registration system. Because of the UK rules on 'reciprocity', foreigners may only access UK UDR if their national laws give equivalent protection in their countries to UK nationals. There are no such restrictions on access to Community UDR.

Historical background to UK UDR

9.8   To understand UK UDR, it is necessary to find out why in the past some businesses thought copyright protection was more useful than registration of designs and why policymakers thought that this use of copyright protection was not desirable.

9.9   Since the 19th century, legislation in the UK continually tried to prevent copyright protection for designs operating alongside the registration system. However, the form of the UK copyright legislation between 1956 and 1988 unintentionally allowed the courts to conclude that unregistered and unregistrable designs could be protected by copyright. This had particular importance in the car replacement parts industry.

9.10   Copyright subsists in original artistic works. Artistic works include graphic works, irrespective of artistic quality, and a graphic work includes any drawing, diagram, map, chart, or plan (see para 3.55). In relation to an artistic work, the restricted acts of copying include reproduction in any material form and the making of a copy in three dimensions of a two-dimensional work (see para 4.26). It was therefore possible to claim copyright infringement in relation to three-dimensional articles which represented indirect copies of their underlying design drawings, however simple those drawings had been. Laddie J explained the problem thus:[3]

> In the twenty years prior to the passing of the 1988 Act, copyright lawyers found a new area in which to enforce copyright. The copyright in production drawings was argued to be infringed by the manufacture of three dimensional articles copied, directly or indirectly, from them. The era of industrial copyright had arrived. Litigation proliferated as manufacturers of mundane industrial articles and parts used the copyright in their production drawings to prevent competitors from copying their finished products derived from those drawings. Even if the copyright work consisted of no more than a drawing of two concentric circles on a piece of paper and the alleged infringement consisted of a washer made indirectly from it, copyright could be invoked to take the competing product off the market. It is hardly surprising that not everyone was persuaded that this was the proper place for copyright or that it was of benefit to industry.

Ultimately, to stop this practice the House of Lords held in *British Leyland Motor Corporation Ltd v Armstrong Patents Co Ltd*[4] in 1986 that the copyright in the design drawing for a replacement part (in the case, a car exhaust pipe) could not be exercised 'in derogation from grant' to prevent repair using parts sourced from elsewhere, thereby accepting the existence of the copyright and the infringement claim based on indirect copying, but denying it any practical effect.

9.11   The problem of car spare parts as manifested by, for example, the *British Leyland* case, had made apparent the need to remove impediments to a competitive market. The new law in the CDPA 1988, in effect, severely limited protection in UK law for spare parts for cars. But this has not been achieved by legislating specifically for car spare parts, but instead by the use of general provisions capable of covering many other situations.

---

[3] *Ocular Sciences Ltd v Aspect Vision Care Ltd* [1997] RPC 289 at 421.
[4] [1986] AC 577. See para 5.62.

Question

What was the underlying policy of the 1988 Act with regard to unregistered design protection?

9.12   For present purposes, the 1988 Act dealt with the problem in two key ways:

- first, by severely limiting when the copyright subsisting in certain designs and design drawings may be enforced; and
- secondly, by creating a new unregistered design right, UK UDR, of more limited effect and duration than either copyright or registered design protection.

The intention was that, as a result of the new provisions in the 1988 Act, copyright should cease to be of major significance for industrial designs. The spare parts defence propounded by the House of Lords in *British Leyland* (ie no derogation from grant) was not removed in so many words and indeed section 171(3) of the CDPA 1988 provides that nothing in the Act affects any rule of law preventing or restricting the enforcement of copyright on grounds of public interest or otherwise. However, although the defence was used after the entry into force of the 1988 Act, its death sentence was pronounced in an appeal to the Privy Council in 1997.[5]

A fuller account of the development of unregistered design law may be found in this book's online resources. As a wholly UK-created right, UK UDR will be unaffected by Brexit.

UK UDR: what is a 'design'?

9.13   UK UDR is dealt with in Part III of the CDPA 1988. We begin our analysis by considering the designs which may be protected by UK UDR, and noting how this differs from the definition of design already encountered in our discussion of registered designs. As noted previously (see paras 9.6 and 9.7), a design also must meet the rules on qualification for UK UDR protection.

9.14   As we will see in more detail, UK UDR concentrates on the shape and configuration of the whole or part of an article. Surface decoration is not protected. There is, however, no requirement that the design should have any aesthetic qualities.[6] Indeed, it is clear that wholly functional designs can be protected in UK UDR.[7] So there are a number of contrasts with registered design law.

9.15   The definition of what constitutes a protectable 'design' for UK UDR purposes is set out in section 213 of the CDPA 1988, of which Jacob LJ has memorably observed:[8]

It has the merit of being short. It has no other . . . It is not just a question of drafting (though words and phrases such as 'commonplace', 'dependent', 'aspect of shape or configuration of part of an article' and 'design field in question' are full of uncertainty in themselves and pose near impossible factual questions). The problem is deeper: neither the language used nor the context of the legislation give any clear idea of what was intended. Time and time again one struggles but fails to ascertain a precise meaning, a meaning which men of business can reasonably use to guide their conduct.

The definition of 'design' has recently been amended by the Intellectual Property Act 2014 as discussed further below, although the impact of this amendment still remains to be seen.

---

[5] *Canon Kabushiki Kaisha v Green Cartridge Co (Hong Kong) Ltd* [1997] AC 728 (PC, appeal from Hong Kong). See para 5.62.

[6] Contrast the former requirement of 'eye-appeal' in the pre-harmonisation RDA 1949, discussed in the historical outline of the subject accessible in the 'Bonus material' in this book's online resources.

[7] *Landor & Hawa International Ltd v Azure Designs Ltd* [2007] FSR 9, paras 10 and 16. See also D Wilkinson, 'Case closed: functional designs protected by design right' [2007] EIPR 118–22.

[8] *Dyson Ltd v Qualtex (UK) Ltd* [2006] RPC 31, para 14.

Definition of 'design'

9.16   For the purposes of UK UDR, the current definition of a 'design' (incorporating the changes made by the Intellectual Property Act 2014) is:[9]

> the design of the shape or configuration (whether internal or external) of the whole or part of an article.

Before the 2014 amendment, the definition referred to the design of 'any aspect of' the shape or configuration of the whole or part of an article. We will discuss the impact of the deletion of the words 'any aspect of' below.

9.17   Before turning to explain the different elements in this definition, we should also take note of section 213(6) which states that:

> Design right does not subsist unless and until the design has been recorded in a design document or an article has been made to the design.

So, like copyright, the mere idea of a design is not protected; it must be expressed in some tangible form.[10]

9.18   *Design document* is defined as:[11]

> any record of a design, whether in the form of a drawing, a written description, a photograph, data stored in a computer or otherwise.

The scope of this definition is wide and, importantly, is not limited to 'documents' as such.

Data stored in a computer is capable of constituting a design document. Section 214(2) of the CDPA 1988 also refers to computer-generated designs.

Key points on design document

- There must be a design document before UK UDR can subsist.
- A design document is any record of the design and can include the article itself as well as drawings, written descriptions, or data stored in a computer.

9.19   We now take each part of the definition of 'design' in turn, although not in the order in which they appear in the statutory wording.

Design of the whole or part of an 'article'

9.20   Despite the importance of component or spare parts in the history lying behind UK UDR, UK UDR is not limited to that kind of product. UK UDR applies to 'articles' of all kinds. UK UDR therefore helps the manufacturers of many different kinds of products. UK UDR has been held to subsist in agricultural machinery, contact lenses, jeans, sandwich cartons, and even the design of an ice cream van, so the reach of the right is varied and extensive.

9.21   There is no statutory definition of the meaning of the word 'article' for the purposes of UK UDR. However, there was case law on the meaning of the word 'article' for the purposes of UK registered design law under the old Registered Designs Act 1949 (RDA 1949) as it stood before its amendment to implement the harmonised European registered design regime discussed in Chapter 8:

---

[9] CDPA 1988, s 213(2).
[10] *Rolawn Ltd v Turfmech Machinery Ltd* [2008] ECDR 13 per Mann J at paras 79–83. See also *Virgin Atlantic Airways Ltd v Premium Aircraft Interiors Group Ltd* [2009] ECDR 11, paras 24–25.   [11] CDPA 1988, s 263(1).

■ *R v Registered Designs Appeal Tribunal, ex p Ford Motor Co* [1995] 1 WLR 18 (HL)

As it stood at the time of this dispute, the RDA 1949 defined 'article' for the purposes of registered design protection as 'any article of manufacture [including] any part of an article if that part is made and sold separately'. The House of Lords held that there was an essential difference between an item designed for incorporation in a larger article, whether as an original component or a spare part, which would not fall within this definition, and an item designed for general use, albeit aimed principally at use with the manufacturer's own artefacts, which would fall within this definition. In order to constitute an 'article' under the then RDA 1949, an item had to have 'an independent life as an article of commerce' and could not be 'merely an adjunct of some larger article of which it forms part' (per Lord Mustill at 26).

9.22 Adopting a similar approach, there might be an argument that the expression 'article' in section 213(2) of the CDPA 1988 means that UK UDR is intended to arise for the overall design of products complete in themselves. However, it is clear from the 'must fit' and 'must match' exceptions that an 'article' which is entitled to protection in its own right in UK UDR can also be part of a larger 'article'; it has also been noted in commentary that there is no reason to import considerations from the old RDA 1949 case law into the definition of 'article' for UK UDR purposes.[12] In *Dyson Ltd v Qualtex (UK) Ltd*,[13] Mann J and the Court of Appeal had no difficulty in holding that parts for vacuum cleaners attracted UK UDR in their own right and not simply as part of the overall design of the cleaners as a whole. Similarly, in *Farmers Build Ltd v Carier Bulk Materials Handling Ltd*, it was held:[14]

> the individual parts, combinations of parts and the parts made up into a whole machine are all 'articles' with a shape and a configuration.

So in principle component parts, including spare parts, can attract UK UDR; however, this is subject to the 'must fit' and 'must match' exceptions, which are intended to exclude such articles from protection to at least some extent (see further paras 9.37ff).

2014 amendment: 'any aspect of' shape or configuration

9.23 Before the amendment to the definition of 'design' at section 213(2) of the CDPA 1988 by the Intellectual Property Act 2014, UK UDR protection could subsist in 'any aspect of' the shape or configuration of the whole or part of an article. This included aspects of detail.[15] It had been held that this meant any 'discernible' or 'recognisable' element of the shape or configuration,[16] although the design feature did not need not be visually significant.[17] For example:

■ *Ocular Sciences Ltd v Aspect Vision Care Ltd* [1997] RPC 289 (Laddie J)

The products in this case were contact lenses. The designs in which UK UDR was claimed related to the front surface dimensions of the lens, the rear surface dimensions, and the edge characteristics. The lenses differed from each other only in fine dimensional details, but the plaintiffs argued that these dimensions defined the shape or configuration of the lenses. It was held that, although these differences of dimension were indistinguishable by the human eye, that did not mean that they were excluded from protection on the grounds that they were not designs.

---

[12] M Howe, *Russell-Clarke and Howe on Industrial Designs* (9th edn, 2016), para 4-010.

[13] [2005] RPC 19 (Mann J); aff'd [2006] RPC 31 (CA). For commentary on the significance of this case, see A Michaels, 'The end of the road for "pattern spare" parts? *Dyson Ltd v Qualtex (UK) Ltd*' [2006] EIPR 396–98 and J Sykes, 'Designs: the unregistered design right: interpretation and practical application of the must match exemption' (2006) 1(7) JIPLP 442–46.

[14] *Farmers Build Ltd v Carier Bulk Materials Handling Ltd* [1999] RPC 461 at 475. Note that it is not correct to say, as Mummery LJ did in *Farmers Build*, that 'the purpose of introducing the design right was . . . in the case of spare parts, to remove protection from copying completely' (at 480).

[15] *Dyson Ltd v Qualtex (UK) Ltd* [2006] RPC 31 (CA), para 26.

[16] *A Fulton v Totes Isotoner (UK) Ltd* [2004] RPC 16, para 31; *Dyson Ltd v Qualtex (UK) Ltd* (CA) [2006] RPC 31, paras 22–23.

[17] *Virgin Atlantic Airways Ltd v Premium Aircraft Interiors Group Ltd* [2009] ECDR 11, para 26.

9.24   The result of the old definition of 'design' at section 213(2) of the CDPA 1988 was that UK UDR could subsist in many different 'aspects' of the shape or configuration of an article, with many different 'designs', separate or overlapping in different permutations, existing in relation to the same article—as observed by Jacob LJ in *Dyson Ltd v Qualtex (UK) Ltd*, 'as many "aspects" of the whole or part of the article as can be'.[18]

9.25   This had important tactical implications. As noted by the UK courts, the right holder could tailor his definition of what he said constituted his 'design' by reference to the particular aspects of shape or configuration of his article which he said had been copied:[19]

> The proprietor can choose to assert design right in the whole or *any* part of his product. If the right is said to reside in the design of a teapot, this can mean that it resides in design of the whole pot, or in a part such as the spout, the handle or the lid, or, indeed, in a part of the lid. This means that the proprietor can trim his design right claim to most closely match what he believes the defendant to have taken. The defendant will not know in what the alleged monopoly resides until the letter before action or, more usually, the service of the statement of claim.

It had been observed that there was a danger that the ability of the claimant to focus on parts of his design which were small in comparison to the overall article could give rise to 'a distorted impression of what the defendant has done which comes close to reversing the burden of proof'.[20]

9.26   These concerns led to the decision, in the Intellectual Property Act 2014, to delete the words 'any aspect of' from the definition of 'design'. What effect does this amendment have? The Explanatory Notes accompanying the 2014 Act indicated that the intention was to restrict the availability of UK UDR protection for 'trivial features' of designs and to reduce tendencies towards overstating the breadth of UK UDR protection and the related uncertainty this caused in litigation.[21] It is, however, still possible for UK UDR to be claimed in respect of 'part of' an article. There is no explicit limitation on what may constitute such a 'part'. Given this, just how much difference will the deletion of the words 'any aspect of' actually make? Although not ultimately relevant on the facts, in *DKH Retail* the judge at first instance rejected the argument that, because it is still possible to claim UK UDR in part of an article, the deletion has no effect: in his view, the amendment must limit the scope of UK UDR in some respect.[22] Considerable uncertainty remains, however, as to exactly what is the impact of this amendment. More recent case law has suggested that some pre-2014 cases entailed the claiming of designs which only ever consisted 'in the abstract', going beyond the actual article in question through the claiming of different abstract combinations of different features. It is this kind of of 'abstract' UK UDR claim which recent case law suggests has now been ruled out.[23] However, highly-regarded commentary on UK UDR rejects as a 'heresy' the notion that such 'abstract' claiming was ever possible.[24] Either way, it has been noted that in many cases the amendment will make no difference to the outcome.[25] It has been held that the amendment is not fully retrospective in effect: it does not extinguish claims arising under the old law for infringements committed before 1 October 2014.[26]

---

[18]   *Dyson Ltd v Qualtex (UK) Ltd* [2006] RPC 31 (CA), para 22.

[19]   *Ocular Sciences Ltd v Aspect Vision Care Ltd* [1997] RPC 289 at 422.

[20]   *Virgin Atlantic Airways Ltd v Premium Aircraft Interiors Group Ltd* [2009] ECDR 11, para 29.

[21]   *Explanatory Notes*, www.legislation.gov.uk/ukpga/2014/18/notes/contents, para 10.

[22]   *DKH Retail Ltd v H Young (Operations) Ltd* [2014] EWHC 4034 (IPEC), para 14.

[23]   *Action Storage Systems Ltd v G-Force Europe.com Ltd* [2017] FSR 18 (IPEC), paras 13–16, noted in *Cantel Medical (UK) Ltd v Arc Medical Design Ltd* [2018] EWHC 345 (Pat), para 221. See also *Neptune (Europe) Ltd v Devol Kitchens Ltd* [2017] ECDR 25, para 44 (differentiating between 'aspects' of a design in the sense of 'disembodied features which are merely recognisable or discernable' and 'parts' of a design covering 'concrete parts which can be identified as such').

[24]   M Howe, *Russell-Clarke and Howe on Industrial Designs* (9th edn, 2016), para 4-007, footnote 22. Howe emphasises at para 4-015 that UK UDR:

   subsists in the actual shape or configuration (whether of the whole or part of an article), not in an abstraction or a set of features of the kind seen in a patent claim. That would in effect be according design right to a range or class of different shapes or configurations, not to one specific design .

[25]   *DKH Retail Ltd v H Young (Operations) Ltd* [2014] EWHC 4034 (IPEC); *Whitby Specialist Vehicles Limited v Yorkshire Specialist Vehicles Limited and Others* [2014] EWHC 4242 (Pat), para 41.

[26]   *Neptune (Europe) Ltd v Devol Kitchens Ltd* [2017] ECDR 25, paras 29–42. Earlier cases had expressed some uncertainty on the issue.

'Whether internal or external': visibility

9.27   UK UDR is expressly not limited to what is visible when the article in question is in use. The design could be one which spends its entire operative life concealed within or beneath another article, as with a terminal in a washing machine, or an exhaust pipe in a car; or it could be the internal parts of a product which also has external parts, such as the shape and configuration of the inside of a car roof box. For example, in *Farmers Build Ltd v Carier Bulk Materials Handling Ltd*,[27] the designs in question included internal component parts of the disputed slurry separators.

'Shape or configuration'

9.28   At the time of the enactment of the CDPA 1988, 'shape' and 'configuration' were concepts already familiar from UK registered design law where, until the reforms to UK registered design law triggered by Designs Directive 98/71/EC, they were usually taken as referring to the three-dimensional aspects of a product, as distinct from two-dimensional pattern or ornamentation applied to the surface of the article. Thus, a feature of UK UDR which appeared distinctive in 1988 was that it did *not* apply to two-dimensional 'pattern and ornamentation'. This seemed also to be underlined by the exclusion of 'surface decoration' of an article from the scope of UK UDR. However, the UK UDR case law has blurred the distinction between the three- and the two-dimensional.

9.29   The basis for this has been the legislation's apparent distinction between 'shape' *or* 'configuration'. While shape certainly refers to three-dimensional features, it has been suggested that configuration may cover at least some two- as well as three-dimensional designs. So electronic circuit diagrams[28] have been held covered by UK UDR as 'configurations'.

■ *Mackie Designs Inc v Behringer Specialised Studio Equipment (UK) Ltd* [1999] RPC 717 (Pumfrey J)

It was held that electronic circuit diagrams were covered by UK UDR, as 'configuration' rather than shape; 'configuration' should be broadly construed to cover 'the relative arrangement of parts or elements'.

9.30   The limits of this broad approach to 'configuration' are not clear, although the case has potential analogies with mechanical engineering designs, such as pneumatic and hydraulic circuits, and chemical or process flow diagrams. Design right applies to semiconductor topographies, although these are essentially patterns fixed or etched upon semiconductor material, rather than shapes or configurations. The availability of the protection is, however, the result of express legislation, the Design Right (Semiconductor Topographies) Regulations 1989,[29] which apply the design right provisions of the 1988 Act to this subject matter.

9.31   The broad approach suggested in *Mackie* has been criticised: a merely schematic diagram[30] of something, which does not convey the physical actuality of that which is represented, cannot be the design of an article, since it could be represented by any one of several different articles. Contrast this earlier case (not discussed in *Mackie Designs*):

■ *Baby Dan AS v Brevi Srl and Another* [1999] FSR 377 (HC)

BD manufactured and sold child safety barriers in the UK, and BS distributed them in Italy. The barrier consisted of various component parts. When the distributorship ceased, BS started to manufacture child

---

[27]   [1999] RPC 461.

[28]   On the nature of electronic circuit diagrams in copyright law, see para 3.42. See also, for analysis before the cases began to come before the courts, J Reynolds and P Brownlow, 'Increased legal protection for schematic designs in the United Kingdom' [1994] EIPR 398–400.

[29]   SI 1989/1100 (as amended).

[30]   A well-known example of a schematic diagram, discussed in *Lambretta Clothing Co Ltd v Teddy Smith (UK) Ltd* [2005] RPC 6 (CA) at para 27, is the map of the London Underground, from which it is not possible to determine the actual geographical position of the stations or of the exact routes followed by the tunnels, although one can tell what the relative positions are and the connections between them. Jacob LJ in *Lambretta* noted that 'there may well be force' in the criticism of *Mackie*: para 27.

safety barriers in Italy, and the second defendant imported and sold these barriers in the UK. BD claimed that there was copying by BS and infringement by both defendants. It was held that the *relative locations* of interrelated functional parts of BD's safety barrier were not aspects of its configuration.

Although there remains considerable criticism of the approach taken in *Mackie*, when invited more recently to hold that *Mackie* was wrong, Arnold J in *CliniSupplies Ltd v Park* concluded that the matter should be taken as settled law unless and until considered by the Court of Appeal.[31]

 Discussion point   For answer guidance visit **www.oup.com/uk/brown5e**.

Refer to the discussion above about electronic circuit diagrams, then consider how such diagrams differ from the designs of child safety barriers as revealed in the *Baby Dan* case. Why are the relative locations of the component parts of the latter not 'configuration' when electronic circuit diagrams apparently are? Can this outcome be justified?

9.32   The courts have rejected arguments that seek to reduce down the definition of what constitutes 'configuration' simply to a question of whether the design is two- or three-dimensional:

■ *Lambretta Clothing Co Ltd v Teddy Smith (UK) Ltd* [2005] RPC 6 (CA)

The article in question was L's track top, the shape of which was old (or 'retro'). The new feature was the choice of colours ('colourways')—blue for the body, red for the arms, white for the zip. L claimed T was copying and selling these tops. L claimed that the colourways were protected as configuration of the garment. It was held that UK UDR did not subsist in L's top. Giving the main judgment, Jacob LJ ruled that, even with a wide interpretation of the word 'configuration', UK UDR does not subsist in the arrangement of colours or in patterns, such as that of a patchwork quilt. Suggesting that it was 'a peripheral dead-end' to seek to analyse the issue by reference to whether the design was two- or three-dimensional (para 23), Jacob LJ remarked:[32]

> I do not think that a debate about dimensions assists. All articles (even thin flat ones) are 3 dimensional (using the practical Euclidean view of the world—not that of modern physics). There is no reason why a 'design' should not subsist in what people would ordinarily call a 'flat' or '2-dimensional' thing—for instance a new design of doily would have a new 'shape' and could in principle have UK UDR in it.

■ *A Fulton Co Ltd v Grant Barnett & Co Ltd* [2001] RPC 16 (Park J)

Outward-facing stitched seams on the edges of a rectangular box-shaped case for a compact umbrella accentuated the rectangular (rather than the more usual cylindrical) character of the product. It was held that the seams were protected as significant aspects of the shape or configuration of the case (and not excluded as surface decoration), even though only marginally three-dimensional. This was described as a 'value judgment for the court to make'.[33]

Key points on the definition of 'design'

- UK UDR can apply to 'articles' of all kinds, including component and spare parts.
- UK UDR will subsist in the shape or configuration, internal or external, of the whole or part of an article; the relevant feature need not be visible in ordinary use. It is not yet fully clear what will be the impact of the deletion of the words 'any aspect of' from the definition of UK UDR 'design'.

---

[31] *CliniSupplies Ltd v Park* [2013] FSR 27, para 53.
[32] [2005] RPC 6, para 24.   [33] [2001] RPC 257, para 79.

- The words 'shape or configuration' suggest that UK UDR protects the design of three- rather than two-dimensional design features, but the concept of 'configuration' has proved controversial and difficult to define, with courts reluctant to simplify the issue to a three- vs two-dimensional analysis.

- Purely functional designs are not excluded from UK UDR (but note 'must fit/must match' exclusions discussed at paras 9.37ff).

Exclusions from protection in UK UDR

Surface decoration

9.33 Section 213(3)(c) of the CDPA 1988 excludes 'surface decoration' from the scope of UK UDR. This exclusion is justified on the basis that generally such surface decoration will be the subject of copyright and so does not need the additional protection of UK UDR.[34] At first sight, the exclusion seems simply to reaffirm the primary concern of UK UDR with the three-dimensional rather than the two-dimensional. However, the case law shows that the position is somewhat more complex, since the exclusion has been held to affect three-dimensional features of a design in some instances:

■ *Mark Wilkinson Furniture Ltd v Woodcraft Designs (Radcliffe) Ltd* [1998] FSR 63 (HC)

This case concerned fitted kitchens. The plaintiff's kitchen units had a number of features including a painted surface, curved quadrant corners between the front and side panels, cornicing, shallow v-grooves, cockbeading, and recessed panels. It was held that surface decoration included both decoration lying on the surface of the article (such as a painted finish) and decorative features of the surface itself (such as beading or engraving), and was not restricted to features that were essentially two-dimensional. Applying this test, the painted finish, v-grooves, and cockbeading were excluded from protection as surface decoration. But the cornice, quadrant corners, and recessed panels were not excluded from UK UDR.

■ *A Fulton Co Ltd v Grant Barnett & Co Ltd* [2001] RPC 16 (HC)

It was argued that the stitched seams of the umbrella case were excluded as surface decoration. This argument was rejected. The judge emphasised that it did not follow that, because the seams existed only very slightly in three dimensions, they must be surface decoration. In the court's view, the seams were 'significant aspects' of shape or configuration and not excluded as surface decoration (para 78).

■ *Lambretta Clothing Co Ltd v Teddy Smith (UK) Ltd* [2005] RPC 6 (CA)

See previously para 9.32. T claimed that the colourways of the retro track tops were surface decoration; L responded that the colours ran right through the garment, not just its surface. This argument was rejected and it was held that UK UDR did not subsist in L's top, Jacob LJ commenting:

> It is true that the parts of the garment are dyed right through, but any realistic and practical construction of the words 'surface decoration' must cover both the case where a surface is covered with a thin layer and where the decoration, like that in Brighton rock, runs throughout the article. To hold otherwise would mean that whether or not UDR could subsist in two different articles, having exactly the same outward appearance, depended on how deep the colours went. Parliament cannot have intended anything so capricious (para 30).

---

[34] *Dyson Ltd v Qualtex (UK) Ltd* [2006] RPC 31 per Jacob LJ at para 76.

The court affirmed the approach of the judge in *Mark Wilkinson* (above) that surface decoration could be more than essentially flat, and could be three-dimensional.

■ *Dyson Ltd v Qualtex (UK) Ltd* [2006] RPC 31 (CA)

It was argued that ribbing on the handle and tool adaptor of a design of the Dyson vacuum cleaner was excluded from protection in UK UDR because it was surface decoration. Jacob LJ held that the exclusion should be limited 'to that which can fairly be described as a decorated surface' (para 81). Surface features which had 'significant function' were not surface decoration (para 83). In this case, the ribbing had a functional purpose of providing a grip and was not excluded. This was, furthermore, consistent with the perception of the reasonable consumer or designer, who would not have regarded the ribbing as merely a decorated surface.[35]

9.34   In *Dyson Ltd v Qualtex (UK) Ltd*,[36] Jacob LJ held that whether matter on a surface constituted surface decoration was 'a question of degree'. The judge at first instance in this case had described this as potentially a 'matter of fact and impression, or a value judgment'.[37] The judge in *Fulton v Grant Barnett* (see para 9.32) also described this as a 'value judgment'.[38] It is clear from these cases that determining whether a particular design feature is 'surface decoration' cannot be resolved simply by asking whether the feature is two- or three-dimensional; instead, this will be a qualitative and fact-dependent exercise to be assessed in the individual context of each case. As the recent case of *Neptune v Devol* illustrates, this approach is perhaps not entirely helpful in terms of certainty for designers or practitioners. Like the *Mark Wilkinson* case (above, para 9.33) *Neptune v Devol* concerned the design of kitchen units. However, taking quite the opposite approach to the judge in *Wilkinson*, in *Neptune v Devol* the judge concluded on the facts that cockbeading and moulding on the doors of the claimant's kitchen units were important design features which were not mere 'surface decoration' in the context of those specific designs and which were accordingly protected under UK UDR.[39]

 Discussion point   For answer guidance visit **www.oup.com/uk/brown5e**.

What is the difference between 'shape or configuration' and 'surface decoration'?

Key points on the surface decoration exclusion

- Surface decoration is not limited to two-dimensional ornamentation of the article but can extend to three-dimensional features.

- It can include features which run right through an article from its surface (eg colourways on a garment).

- If the feature has a significant functional purpose, it is unlikely to be excluded from UK UDR protection as mere surface decoration.

---

[35] [2006] RPC 31 (CA), paras 73–84.   [36] ibid, para 81.

[37] *Dyson Ltd v Qualtex (UK) Ltd* [2005] RPC 19 (Mann J), para 38.   [38] [2001] RPC 257, para 79.

[39] *Neptune (Europe) Ltd v Devol Kitchens Ltd* [2017] ECDR 25, paras 26–28.

Methods or principles of construction

9.35 Methods and principles of construction are excluded from UK UDR by section 213(3)(a) of the CDPA 1988. This excludes from protection the process or operation by which a shape is produced, rather than the resulting shape itself:

■ *A Fulton Co Ltd v Grant Barnett & Co Ltd* [2001] RPC 16 (HC)

In this case, the outward-facing stitched seams and box-shape of the compact umbrella case were challenged as constituting 'methods or principles of construction'. This challenge was rejected. It was held:

> It is certainly true that there are methods of construction involved in the creation of the Miniflat case . . . However, the design of the case is the shape or configuration produced by those methods of construction, not the methods by which that shape or configuration is produced. The fact that a special method or principle of construction may have to be used in order to create an article with a particular shape or configuration does not mean that there is no design right in the shape or configuration. The law of design right will not prevent competitors using that method or principle of construction to create competing designs . . . as long as the competing designs do not have the same shape or configuration as the design right owner's design has.[40]

■ *Bailey (t/a Elite Angling Products) v Haynes (t/a RAGS)* [2007] FSR 10

This case concerned a design for a woven micro-mesh used to form bait bags used in fishing. It was claimed that the design of the weave was protected by UK UDR. This was countered by the alleged infringers with the argument that the design was excluded from protection because it was for a 'method or principle of construction'. They argued that the weave for which UK UDR was claimed was inevitably generated by use of a particular knitting technique. The judge agreed and held that the exclusion applied.

9.36 This exclusion does not exclude a design from protection because it has a functional purpose:

■ *Landor & Hawa International Ltd v Azure Designs Ltd* [2007] FSR 9 (CA)

The arrangement of zippers and piping for the expander section of a suitcase design was held *not* to be a principle or method of construction. Upholding the judge at first instance, Neuberger LJ emphasised that section 213(3)(a) does not exclude a design merely because it has a functional purpose or because every element of the design was intended to perform a functional purpose. While section 213(3)(a) might apply if the design in suit was the only way of achieving the functional purpose of the design, such that the UK UDR protection for the shape of the design in effect also granted protection for the method of its construction and would thereby stop others from using that method, that was not the case on the facts.[41]

'Must fit, must match'

9.37 The so-called '*must fit*' and '*must match*' exclusions reflect some of the problem areas relating to spare parts, particularly automobile spare parts, which developed as a result of the availability of copyright protection before the CDPA 1988. These exclusions are, however, not limited to spare parts but will apply to any design falling within their terms. Although commonly referred to as the 'must fit' and 'must match' exclusions, when interpreting and applying these provisions the Court of Appeal has cautioned that 'one must go by the actual language and not by the epithet or even the notion behind the epithet'.[42]

---

[40] [2001] RPC 16, para 70.   [41] [2007] FSR 9 (CA), paras 8–29.
[42] *Dyson Ltd v Qualtex (UK) Ltd* [2006] RPC 31 (CA), para 27.

9.38   The 'must fit' exclusion removes from protection in UK UDR features of shape or configuration of an article which:[43]

> enable the article to be connected to or placed in, around or against another article so that either article may perform its function.

9.39   The 'must match' exclusion removes from UK UDR features of shape or configuration of an article which:[44]

> are dependent upon the appearance of another article of which the article is intended by the designer to form an integral part.

 Question

What are the key elements in these definitions of 'must fit' and 'must match' designs?

9.40   Despite the legislative background, the Court of Appeal has held that it is not possible to discern any clear purposive intent in terms of whether these provisions are pro- or anti-spare parts:[45]

> I do not think it is possible to approach the provisions with any clear purposive intent in mind. Given the White Paper and the extremely complex economic arguments involved it is not possible to give a purposive construction—you need a reasonably clear idea of purpose before you can do that. . . . Here on the one hand Parliament refused to create a general spare parts exception, and on the other hand clearly did not intend that OEMs [original equipment manufacturers] should have absolute control over the manufacture of spares. A compromise (some might say fudge) in the form of the language actually chosen in the Act was what was done. We must construe it as it would be read by a reasonable reader. Here that means taking the language as it stands.

 Question

What was the main objective of the 'must fit' and 'must match' exceptions to UK UDR?

9.41   What, then, is the scope of the exceptions? The case law now allows us to say quite a bit more about both exceptions.

'Must fit'

9.42   A good example of the 'must-fit' exclusion in operation is the *Ocular Sciences* case:

■ *Ocular Sciences Ltd v Aspect Vision Care Ltd* [1997] RPC 289 (Laddie J)

The defendants argued that a number of the features of the lenses in which UK UDR was claimed were present to enable the lens to fit another article—the wearer's eyeball—and to correct the wearer's vision, that is, perform its function. The plaintiffs responded that the eyeball, as a part of the human body, was not an 'article' to which the lens was to be fitted. It was held (*obiter*)[46] that any design feature falling within the criteria at section 213(3)(b)(i) was excluded from protection by the 'must fit' exception, even if it performed another function (eg if it was attractive). There was no requirement that the design feature be the only way of achieving the desired interface. There is also no requirement that the designer's intention be for the

---

[43] CDPA 1988, s 213(3)(b)(i).   [44] CDPA 1988, s 213(3)(b)(ii).
[45] *Dyson Ltd v Qualtex (UK) Ltd* [2006] RPC 31 (CA), para 11.
[46] Because it was held that in any event there was no copying and thus no infringement.

articles to fit: it is sufficient if they in fact do. In addition, the word 'article' did not have a restricted meaning, and could apply to living and formerly living things as well as inanimate objects. The back radius, diameter, 'CN bevel', and parallel peripheral carrier of the contact lenses in suit enabled them to fit against the eyeball and to perform their function of correcting vision while remaining stable in the eye. These features were excluded from UK UDR under the 'must fit' exception.

9.43   There is nothing in the statutory language that requires a feature to be the only way to achieve an interface between two products for it to fall within the exclusion. If a number of 'fits' are possible, the feature is still 'must fit': see *Ocular Sciences*.[47] There does, however, need to be 'a degree of precision' in the interrelationship between the articles in question.[48]

Discussion point   For answer guidance visit **www.oup.com/uk/brown5e.**

What if any parts of an artificial human limb or joint (eg artificial knee), or of a heart pacemaker might be considered as protectable by UK UDR? Are there any other examples of such products?

9.44   However, it is not enough for the purposes of this exclusion that the article in suit is simply intended to be placed in, around, or against another article. The excluded design features must be such as to 'enable' the article to be so placed:

■ *A Fulton Co Ltd v Grant Barnett & Co Ltd* [2001] RPC 16 (HC)

The rectangular umbrella decision (see previously para 9.32). The judge stressed that section 231(3)(b)(i) only provides that UK UDR cannot subsist in features of shape or configuration which *enable* the article to be so placed so that either article can perform their function. In that case, the particular features which gave the umbrella case its shape (the rectangular box-shape and the outward-facing seams) were not designed to enable it to perform the function of containing the umbrella: they were so designed to 'perform the function of looking attractive and promoting sales of the product, not to perform the function of enabling the case to be placed around the umbrella' (para 75).

9.45   By itself, the 'must fit' exclusion does not deprive designs of UK UDR protection altogether: only the design features which enable the article to be fitted to another article in order for either article to perform their function are unprotected as a result. For example:

■ *Baby Dan AS v Brevi Srl and Another* [1999] FSR 377 (HC)

The child safety barriers case (see previously para 9.31). The barriers were made up of component parts. It was argued that this meant that there was no UK UDR protection as all such parts had to fit together to create the barrier as whole. This argument was rejected. It was held that the 'must fit' exception did not exclude the various parts of the barrier relied upon, in its embodiment not as a number of parts but as one single larger article, that is, as a barrier itself. Hence, the design of parts of the barrier, such as the cam housing and the spindle retainer, were protected.

9.46   The most significant more recent case on this exclusion is *Dyson v Qualtex*, concerning spare or 'pattern' parts for Dyson vacuum cleaners.

---

[47] [1997] RPC 289 per Laddie J at 424.
[48] *Action Storage Systems Ltd v G-Force Europe.com Ltd* [2017] FSR 18 (IPEC), para 68, followed in *Cantel Medical (UK) Ltd v Arc Medical Design Ltd* [2018] EWHC 345 (Pat), paras 224–226.

■ *Dyson Ltd v Qualtex (UK) Ltd* [2005] RPC 19 (Mann J); aff'd [2006] RPC 31 (CA)

While the parties agreed that large numbers of the disputed parts were affected by the 'must fit' exception—such as the stop on the main wand handle of the cleaner which interacted with the stop on the release catch and aspects of the cable winder and tools[49]—at first instance the judge ruled that many others were not: for example, airholes in the top of the head of the device's stair tool. On appeal, various points of principle emerged. First, a clearance (ie empty space) which arises as a result of the design of the two articles is capable, in principle, of forming excluded subject matter: the two articles in question do not have to touch in order for there to be a relevant interface. However, this clearance must be intended to *enable* one or other of the articles to work, not just to avoid *interfering* with the functioning of that article.[50] The exclusion will apply to features which make an article function more effectively or safely.[51] It also does not matter in what order the articles concerned are designed.[52]

Exercise

Consider in the light of the foregoing (1) the view of Robert Englehart QC in *Parker v Tidball* [1997] FSR 680 that a leather carrying case for a mobile phone is caught by the 'must fit' exception; and (2) the contrasting view of Park J in *A Fulton Co Ltd v Grant Barnett & Co Ltd* [2001] RPC 16 that an umbrella case, designed to fit around an umbrella, is not. Which view is, in your opinion, correct as a matter of the interpretation of section 213(3)(b)(i) of the CDPA 1988? Can you reconcile these cases?

Key points on the 'must fit' exception

- The 'must fit' exception applies only to the interconnecting parts of the relevant article.

- The relevant design features must be intended to enable the relevant article to be connected to or placed in, around, or against another article so that either article can perform its function.

- The fact that the connection or placement may be effected in different ways does not prevent the relevant features of any one particular design which achieves this connection or placement being subject to the 'must fit' exception.

'Must match'

9.47   This exclusion has been described as the 'aesthetic counterpart' to the 'must fit' exclusion.[53] When the CDPA 1988 was passing through Parliament in the House of Lords, it was commented:[54]

> The must match exception is intended to prevent monopolies arising in the first place, and to preserve the benefits of competition. Although design right is only a right to prevent copying, it is quite clear that in circumstances where a competitor has no choice but to copy if he is to produce a part which will match, then if there were no must match exception he would be completely shut out of the market. This is not a question of abuse but of basic policy. And I have to say that this Government does not wish to create monopolies in this way in any sector of industry . . . And we should be quite clear about this: the absence of a must match exception would enable competition in certain kinds of product to be totally frozen out. In our view that is not the way that the markets should operate.

---

[49] The full and lengthy list can be found in a schedule to Mann J's judgment.

[50] *Dyson Ltd v Qualtex (UK) Ltd* [2006] RPC 31 (CA), paras 36 and 38.

[51] ibid, paras 40–44.   [52] ibid, para 46.

[53] M Howe, *Russell-Clarke and Howe on Industrial Designs* (9th edn, 2016), para 4-029.

[54] Parliamentary Debates, 29 March 1988, HL, col 699.

Question

Is there an equivalent of the UK UDR 'must match' exception in the law of registered designs (see Chapter 8)?

9.48   The 'must match' exclusion is not a blanket exclusion of all accessory or spare parts. To be excluded, the relevant design features of the article in suit must be 'dependent' on the appearance of the larger article of which the article in dispute is intended to form part. However, there is no definition of what 'dependent' means or what degree of dependency is required for the exclusion to bite. As Mann J pointed out in *Dyson Ltd v Qualtex (UK) Ltd*:[55]

> most consumer goods are likely to have been produced from a designer's pen (or CAD package). If made up of more than one part (which, again, most will have been) then each of those parts is likely to have been designed with the others in mind, and to fit in.

It was argued that 'the design of each will be dependent on the appearance of the whole because that is how the designer will have intended it' (para 60). This analysis would, however, have the effect of exempting most external aspects of a product's design from UK UDR, a conclusion Mann J found unacceptably wide. Instead he took from the earlier case law, dealing with the equivalent provision in the then UK registered design law, a test of design dependency which made the 'must match' exception bite only where changing the appearance of the article for which UK UDR was claimed would make the appearance of the overall article 'radically different'.[56] In assessing this, the saleability of the replacement article would be useful evidence or a cross-check, since consumers would probably not buy something which radically changed the appearance of the overall product. Applying this test, on the facts Mann J held that the design features of the Dyson vacuum cleaner handle were not caught by the 'must match' exclusion, because they could be changed without radically affecting the appearance of the vacuum cleaner, and there was no evidence to show that consumers required this utilitarian household product to retain its overall appearance.[57] The test and its application to the facts were essentially approved in the Court of Appeal. Describing the notion of 'dependency' as an 'elusive concept', Jacob LJ said:[58]

> 'Dependency' must be viewed practically. In some cases the answer is obvious—the paradigm example being body parts of cars. In others it may be necessary to examine the position more carefully. But unless the spare parts dealer can show that as a practical matter there is a real need to copy a feature of shape or configuration because of some design consideration of the whole article, he is not within the exclusion. It is not enough to assert that the public 'prefers' an exact copy . . . The more there is design freedom the less is there room for the exclusion. In the end it is a question of degree—the sort of thing where a judge is called upon to make a value judgment.

Jacob LJ held that, if as a practical matter there was design freedom, then there was no dependency (para 63).

 Question

What is meant by the 'dependency' test for a 'must match' design?

---

[55] [2005] RPC 19, para 60.   [56] ibid, paras 63–64.

[57] ibid, para 80. However, Mann J had accepted the status of Dyson machines as 'design icons' (para 71). This may implicitly justify the view that the designers had earned the reward of UK UDR, of which they should not be deprived by giving the exceptions too wide scope.

[58] *Dyson Ltd v Qualtex (UK) Ltd* [2006] RPC 31, para 64.

9.49   The exception does not apply to 'families' of items such as dinner services and crockery sets. The requirement that, for this exclusion to apply, the replacement article should be an 'integral part' of the other article whose appearance it is to match prevents this result. Take the example of a cup and saucer in a tea set: while the two items are undoubtedly meant to 'match', neither forms an 'integral part' of the other. See also:

■ *Mark Wilkinson Furniture Ltd v Woodcraft Designs (Radcliffe) Ltd* [1998] FSR 63 (HC)

The kitchen furniture case (see para 9.33). It was held that the 'must match' exclusion did not apply to the plaintiff's kitchen units because the complete fitted kitchen was a series of matching articles, none of which formed 'an integral part of' the others.

 Discussion point   For answer guidance visit **www.oup.com/uk/brown5e**.

How do the UK UDR 'must fit/must match' exceptions differ to the law applying to registered designs (see Chapter 8)?

Key points on the 'must match' exception

- The 'must match' exception catches designs of articles which are subordinate in aesthetic terms to the overall design of another article.

- However, the requirement of dependency upon the appearance of another article of which the article in question is to be an integral part restricts the scope of the exception; whether there is such a 'dependency' will be a value judgment turning on the extent to which there is design freedom or a different design would radically alter the appearance of the overall article.

Original and not 'commonplace'

9.50   Designs must be 'original' to attract UK UDR: CDPA 1988, s 213(1). Section 213(4) states that a design is not 'original' for UK UDR purposes if it was 'commonplace in the design field in question' at the time of its creation.

Case law shows that a two-step approach should be taken to UK UDR originality, asking:

(1)   whether the design is original in the copyright sense; and

(2)   whether or not the design is commonplace in the design field in question.

9.51   Until recently, the requirement that a design be original in the copyright sense had been a relatively straightforward question of whether the design was independently produced as a result of the designer's own skill and labour, and not copied from the work of another.[59] This followed old UK case law on copyright originality. However, Court of Justice case law on the concept of 'originality' has now impacted on UK copyright law.[60] This raises the question of whether the copyright-based element of the test for UK UDR originality has also changed. This question has yet to be clearly resolved. In *Whitby Specialist Vehicles*, the court proceeded on the assumption that the requirement of originality must now be interpreted in line with Court of Justice case law on originality in copyright, in essence requiring creativity on the part of the

---

[59] On the copyright concept of originality, see paras 3.19–3.28.   [60] See paras 3.25–3.28.

designer.[61] In a later case, however, Hacon J suggested that the Court of Justice copyright case law could have no direct bearing on UK UDR.[62] The issue was discussed further, but not decided, in *Action Storage*.[63] It remains to be seen how future cases treat this issue, particularly cases in which the UK UDR design in dispute is a largely or even purely functional one. Clarification of the position at appellate level would be helpful.

9.52 The second part of the test for originality—that is, that the design is not commonplace—has been further developed in UK case law which is, on any view, *not* affected by these European copyright law developments:

■ *Ocular Sciences Ltd v Aspect Vision Care Ltd* [1997] RPC 289 (Laddie J)

The contact lenses case (see para 9.23). The defendants argued that the lens designs were commonplace; the plaintiffs' response was that the combinations of dimensions for which UK UDR was claimed had not been used before and were not commonplace. Laddie J held that:

> Any design which is trite, trivial, common-or-garden, hackneyed or of the type which would excite no particular attention in those in the relevant art is likely to be commonplace. This does not mean that a design made up of features which, individually, are commonplace is necessarily itself commonplace. A new and exciting design can be produced from the most trite of ingredients. But to secure protection, the combination itself must not be commonplace (at 429–430).

On the facts, Laddie J accepted expert evidence that there were no features to distinguish the plaintiff's designs from other lens designs available on the market. The plaintiff's designs were commonplace.

■ *Farmers Build Ltd v Carier Bulk Materials Handling Ltd* [1999] RPC 461 (CA)

The case concerned competing slurry separators. The plaintiffs' slurry separator was in part based on the designs of two earlier separators, and internally the machinery was based around 'hoppers' which the respondents argued had long been in use for agricultural machinery. Counsel for the defendant submitted that all of the parts relied upon in the action and their combination as a whole were commonplace. However, it was held by the Court of Appeal that neither the parts nor the whole could be described as commonplace, even though they might involve basic articles and simple engineering principles. The requirement that a design not be commonplace was not equivalent to a requirement of 'novelty'. Having reviewed the authorities and legislative background and considered UK UDR in the round, Mummery LJ explained that the assessment of 'commonplace-ness' should be as follows (at 482–483). First, the court should compare the design of the article in which design right is claimed with the design of other articles in the same field, including the alleged infringing article, as at the time of the creation of the design in suit. Secondly, it should assess originality bearing in mind that, taking into account the functional aspect of design compared to pure works of art, one design may be very similar to, or even identical with, another design but not have been copied. To assess whether the design is commonplace, the court needs to ascertain how similar that design is to the design of similar articles in the same field of design. This is a comparative exercise which must be conducted objectively and in the light of the evidence, including evidence from experts in the relevant field on the similarities and differences, and their significance. The closer the similarity of the designs to each other, the more likely it is that the designs are commonplace, especially if there is no causal link (such as copying) which would account for the similarity. If a number of designers working independently of one another in the same field produce very similar designs, this may indicate that there is only one way of designing that article. On the other hand, if there are aspects of the design which are not to be found in any other design in the field, the court would be entitled to conclude that the design in question was not commonplace. A commonplace *article* can have an un-commonplace shape or configuration.[64]

---

[61] *Whitby Specialist Vehicles Limited v Yorkshire Specialist Vehicles Limited and Others* [2014] EWHC 4242 (Pat), para 43.

[62] *Raft Limited v Freestyle of Newhaven Limited and Others* [2016] EWHC 1711 (IPEC), para 9.

[63] *Action Storage Systems Ltd v G-Force Europe.com Ltd* [2017] FSR 18 (IPEC), paras 19–22.

[64] For a later illustration of this, see *A Fulton Co Ltd v Grant Barnett & Co Ltd* [2001] RPC 16, para 54 (umbrella cases are commonplace articles, but the rectangular shapes in suit were not a commonplace design for such articles).

Discussion point   For answer guidance visit **www.oup.com/uk/brown5e**.
What is the difference between 'original' and 'not commonplace'?

9.53   The UK UDR requirement that a design be original and not commonplace in its design field looks like a halfway house between the copyright requirement of originality and the registered design standards of 'novelty' and 'individual character'. The differences with the registered design standards was stressed in *A Fulton Co Ltd v Grant Barnett & Co Ltd*,[65] where the court observed:

> A design should not be denied design right protection merely because the defendant, in researching what is often referred to as the 'prior art', discovers an obscure article which is fairly similar to the design in which design right is claimed. That would not be enough to make the claimant's design commonplace (para 52).

9.54   The assessment of whether a design is original in the UK UDR sense will relate to those aspects of the design which are left once the application of any relevant exclusions from protection has been determined. There are some further sub-questions which arise in relation to the 'commonplace' test at section 213(4) of the CDPA 1988:

(1) The design field question: what is the 'design field' against which the design claiming UK UDR should be assessed?

9.55   In *Scholes Windows Ltd v Magnet Ltd*,[66] a case concerning historically influenced window frame designs made in unplasticated PVC, it was held at first instance that the design field was window frames generally, including timber sash frames as well as uPVC frames. This was upheld by the Court of Appeal. Design was defined in relation to shape and configuration, not in relation to materials or the nature/purpose of the article in question, and the design field should therefore be also defined in relation to shape or configuration. In considering the design field, the court had to take account of what designs were in the field at the time of the creation of the design in question, including old designs such as Victorian window frames, which were still in use and could be seen by designers and interested parties in many houses. There was no reason not to include old designs if they could fairly and reasonably still be regarded as in the design field at the relevant time. In *Lambretta Clothing Co Ltd v Teddy Smith (UK) Ltd*,[67] it was held that 'a reasonably broad approach' to the design field was called for (para 45). What mattered was the sort of designs with which 'a notional designer of the article concerned would be familiar' (para 45). In this case, the design of well-known actual sportswear (whether strictly so-called or not) would be part of the background in the mind of a designer wishing to give a garment a sporty image.

(2) The territorial question: what is the geographical extent of the relevant design field?

9.56   There has been some uncertainty in the case law as to whether the relevant design field was limited to designs available in the UK or more widely.[68] Going forward, that uncertainty has now been resolved by an amendment introduced in the Intellectual Property Act 2014 which explicitly fixes the assessment of 'commonplace-ness' by reference to all qualifying countries. As amended, section 231(4) CDPA 1988 now reads in full:

> A design is not 'original' for the purposes of this Part if it is commonplace in a qualifying country in the design field in question at the time of its creation; and 'qualifying country' has the meaning given in section 217(3) (CDPA, s213(4)).

[65]   [2001] RPC 16.   [66]   [2002] FSR 10 (CA).   [67]   [2005] RPC 6 (CA).

[68]   For example, contrast *A Fulton Co Ltd v Totes Isotoner (UK) Ltd* [2003] RPC 27 (Fysh QC, aff'd without comment on this issue [2004] RPC 16), where it was held that the design field was limited to the UK, and *Dyson Ltd v Qualtex (UK) Ltd* [2003] RPC 27, where the design field was held not to be limited to designs marketed in the UK. See also *Guild v Eskandar Ltd* [2001] FSR 38 (Rimer J, setting a global test in a case concerning ladies' luxury fashion, not addressed on subsequent appeal); and *Spraymiser Ltd & Snell v Wrightway Marketing Ltd* [2000] ECDR 349 (in which the court made its comparison with a US design).

This amendment is, however, not retrospective: so, for designs which pre-date the effective date of the amended definition the old (and somewhat confused) case law will still apply.[69]

(3) The 'whose eye' question: in assessing the similarity of the design in question to other designs in the field, through whose eye is the court looking—the designer's or the customer's?

9.57 In *Farmers Build Ltd v Carier Bulk Materials Handling Ltd*,[70] Mummery LJ said that the comparative exercise must be conducted objectively, with the benefit of expert evidence in the field but, in the end, the assessment was one of fact and degree for the court. In *Lambretta Clothing Co Ltd v Teddy Smith (UK) Ltd*,[71] as noted previously the Court of Appeal said that what mattered was the sort of designs with which *a notional designer* of the article concerned would be familiar. However, the Court of Appeal took a slightly different approach in *Scholes Windows Ltd v Magnet Ltd*, approving the approach of the first instance judge in which he had made his comparison by considering the similarities and differences in the designs from the point of view of a person to whom it was ultimately intended that the design should appeal, rather than from the point of view of an expert in window design of window horns. Mummery LJ commented:[72]

> I would reject the submission made on behalf of Scholes that the comparisons should be made from the point of view of the designer who is expert in the design field in question. Expert evidence is admissible to assist the court in the perception and appreciation of the differences and similarities in the designs compared. But it is not necessary to be an expert in the design field in question either to appreciate the similarities and differences between the designs compared or to form an opinion whether the design in which design right is claimed is 'commonplace'. At the end of the day it is for the court and not for the experts, whether they be parties or witnesses called by the parties, to determine objectively on all the evidence whether the design is commonplace.

This approach—focusing on the perception of the person to whom the design is intended to appeal—was recently endorsed in *Albert Packaging v Nampak*, a case involving the design for a sandwich carton.[73]

Key points on what constitutes an 'original' design for UK UDR purposes

- To be 'original', a design must possess originality in the copyright sense. It remains to be seen how developments in European copyright law will impact on how the UK courts approach this aspect of UK UDR originality.

- In addition, the design must also be 'not commonplace' in the 'design field in question'.

- It is the 'commonplace-ness' of the design, not the article, which is to be tested.

Duration

Length of protection

9.58 According to section 216(1)(a) of the CDPA 1988, UK UDR lasts for 15 years from the end of the calendar year in which the design was first recorded in a design document, or in which an article was made to the design, whichever of these occurs first. According to sections 216(1)(b) and (2) of the CDPA 1988, however, the duration of UK UDR is restricted if, within five years of the end of that calendar year, articles made to the design are made available for sale or hire anywhere in the world by or with the licence of the design right owner. The right will then expire ten years from the end of the

---

[69] See *Action Storage Systems Ltd v G-Force Europe.com Ltd* (IPEC) [2017] FSR 18, para 38.
[70] [1999] RPC 461 (CA).   [71] [2005] RPC 6, para 45.   [72] *Scholes Windows Ltd v Magnet Ltd* [2002] FSR 10 (CA), paras 48–49.
[73] *Albert Packaging Ltd v Nampak Cartons & Healthcare Ltd* [2011] FSR 32, para 31.

calendar year in which that event occurred. Accordingly, the 15-year period is a maximum which will be reduced by commercial exploitation of the design during the first five years of its existence.

9.59   UK UDR is significantly shorter than both registered design right's maximum period (25 years) and copyright (lifetime of the author plus 70 years). This reflects a key policy decision, that UK UDR should be a lesser right in general than others available in this field. Further, the term for which there is an *exclusive* right may be shortened by licences of right available during the last five years of the UK UDR term (see para 9.61). The clear policy is to encourage design registration where that is possible.

Figure 9.1 Duration of UK UDR

```
                                               15 years
Design document/article - - - - - - - - - - - - - - - - - - - - - - - - - - - - - - - - - - - - - - - - - - - - - - - - - - - - EXPIRY
     made to design

          OR - - - - - - - -  <5yrs  - - - - - - -  Article lawfully  - - - - - - -  +10yrs  - - - - - - - - - - -  EXPIRY
                                                     made available
                                                     for sale or hire
```

  Question

What is the maximum period of UK UDR protection?

Commencement

9.60   Three events are of importance with regard to starting time periods running:

(1)   recording the design in a design document;

(2)   making an article to the design;

(3)   lawfully making an article made to the design available for sale or hire.

(1) or (2), whichever is the earlier, starts the 15-year period, while (3), if within five years of the earlier of (1) or (2), starts the ten-year period.

■ *Dyson Ltd v Qualtex (UK) Ltd* [2005] RPC 19 (Mann J); [2006] RPC 31 (CA)

The question arose as to whether taking orders for machines which had not yet been made constituted 'making available for sale'. Mann J noted that: 'One could make a logical case for saying that in the context of the Act commercial exploitation starts when articles are offered for sale, whether manufactured or not; and one could make a case for saying that it starts when articles are offered having been made, or when they are first made after an offer' (para 307). He held, however, that the natural meaning of the statutory words 'made available for sale' connoted something that was actually in existence, and that merely taking orders was not 'making available'. Prototypes or samples were not available for sale. On appeal, this approach was approved by Jacob LJ (paras 115–119).

■ *Ifejika v Ifejika* [2012] FSR 6 (Patents County Court)

The court rejected an argument that sales had to be on a sufficient scale to satisfy the reasonable demands of the public for the purposes of section 216(1)(b) of the CDPA 1988. It was held that there was no basis for implying into section 216(1)(b) any requirement that sales had to be on a certain scale. Any making available for sale, on any scale, is relevant for section 216(1)(b) to apply.[74]

---

[74]   [2012] FSR 6, para 129.

Figure 9.2 Duration of UK UDR with licences of right during last five years

Licences of right during last five years

9.61   A further limit on the duration of design right is to be found in section 237 of the CDPA 1988, which provides for licences of right to be obtainable during the last five years of the UK UDR term. In effect, this means that the design right owner can have an exclusive claim to the design for as little as only five years after his initial exploitation of it. Figure 9.1 illustrating duration needs to be adjusted as shown in Figure 9.2 to take account of this.

The short term is clearly designed to foster the competitive environment. It contrasts sharply with the potential length of the protection arising through design registration and therefore encourages the use of that system.

> **?** **Question**
>
> How do licences of right promote competition?

9.62   A licence of right is one which the licensee is entitled as of right to have from the owner of the UK UDR in question, but for which negotiation about terms and conditions (including royalties) is permissible. If, however, the parties cannot agree, according to section 237(2) of the CDPA 1988 the terms will be settled by the Comptroller of Patents, Designs and Trade Marks.

9.63   An example of proceedings before the Comptroller in a licence of right case is as follows:

■ *NIC Instruments Ltd's Licence of Right (Design Right) Application* [2005] RPC 1 (Patent Office)

N had been infringing A's UK UDRs in bomb-disposal kits and, having ceased to do so, sought a licence of right (in order to limit the damages, it would have to pay in respect of the infringements—see para 9.64). The parties having failed to agree terms, the matter was referred to the Comptroller. It was agreed that the Comptroller should approach the matter on the basis of what willing parties would have agreed. This was not the same as an assessment of damages that would be payable for infringement. It was held that willing parties do not negotiate by way of demands but by taking account not only of their own but also of the other side's interests, so that the agreement gives fair benefits on each side, achieving a halfway house or compromise. In the absence of comparable licences, the approach would be through splitting of the profits available to the licensee. A 50:50 split would not be appropriate outside the pharmaceuticals field (in which research and development costs greatly exceeded manufacturing ones); in the field of bomb-disposal kits, where research and development (R&D) costs were unlikely to be high, the parties would have chosen a 25:75 split, with 75 per cent going to the licensee. The Comptroller also held that he would not include terms (1) prohibiting sub-licensing (no jurisdiction to do so); (2) requiring N to mark the goods as those of A (evidence that disadvantageous in the market); (3) providing a warranty that the UK UDR existed, was owned by A, and would expire on 31 December 2005 (inappropriate when the licence was being determined by the Comptroller rather than parties); or (4) providing for termination on breach (because the licensee could immediately demand a new licence). The full text of the licence imposed appears at the end of the report of the case.[75]

9.64   The availability of licences of right has one other important aspect under section 239 of the CDPA 1988. When a right owner raises proceedings for infringement of a design in respect of which a licence of right is available under the statute, the defendant may undertake to take a licence of right at any time before a final order is made in the proceedings. This may be done without any admission of liability, and has three important effects in relation to the remedies which the court may grant:

- no injunction or interdict may be granted against the defendant (in other words, he may carry on with his hitherto infringing activities);

- no order for delivery up of infringing articles or of the means of making infringing articles may be made against the defendant; and

- the amount recoverable against the defendant by way of damages or on an account of profits shall not exceed double the amount payable by him as licensee if such a licence (ie a licence of right) on those terms had been granted before the earliest infringement.

9.65   This provision does not apply to infringements committed before licences of right were available; so, the situation may arise where a defendant was infringing UK UDR before and after the date on which licences of right became potentially available (ie five years before the right would have anyway expired). All relevant remedies would apply to the pre-licence availability infringements; but they would be severely restricted for the post-licence availability ones.

9.66   The potential significance of this capacity to cut down the remedies available to the right owner is well shown by the following case:

■ *Ultraframe (UK) Ltd v Eurocell Building Plastics Ltd* [2005] RPC 36 (CA)

The case concerned findings of infringement of UK UDR in kits of parts for conservatories, after which judgment the defendant offered to take a licence of right, thereby limiting the damages payable in accordance with section 239 of the CDPA 1988. The UK UDR had expired as the proceedings continued, and the claimant argued that a licence of right was no longer available. It was held that a licence of right could be obtained to restrict damages liability for infringement even after the UK UDR had expired. The licence under section 239 was a licence not of the UK UDR as such, but for the infringements that had been committed, and there was nothing in the section meaning that the undertaking had to be given within any particular period as long as there were proceedings for infringement.

 Discussion point   For answer guidance visit **www.oup.com/uk/brown5e.**

In the light of the two decisions just described, what would your advice be to a party sued for in-fringement of a UK UDR who wished to dispute the existence of the right, its scope in relation to his or her product, and that there had been infringement; and therefore to fight the action in all respects and continue his or her trading activities?

---

[75] For commentary, see J Reed, 'Royalties for design right "licences of right"' [2005] EIPR 298–301.

Rights in UK UDR

Ownership

9.67 According to section 214 of the CDPA 1988, the 'designer' of a design is the person who creates the design or, if the design is computer-generated, the person by whom the arrangements necessary for the creation of the design are undertaken (CDPA, s 214(1) and (2)). This latter scenario should be distinguished from that where a human designer uses the computer as a tool towards the creation of the design, when it will not be computer-generated within the meaning of the Act and the usual rules as to ownership, employment, and commissions will apply.

9.68 The rules on first ownership of UK UDR have recently been amended by the Intellectual Property Act 2014 in order to bring into line the rules on design ownership for all forms of design protection in the UK (see further also Chapter 8). By section 215, the default position is that the designer is the first owner of the UK UDR in a design. After the amendments effected by the 2014 Act there are two circumstances in which the designer is not the owner:

(1) where a design is created by an *employee in the course of his employment*;

(2) where a design qualifies for design right protection by virtue of section 220 CDPA 1988 (qualification by reference to first marketing of articles made to the design).

In the first case, UK UDR belongs to the employer.[76] In the second case, the person by whom the articles in question are marketed is the first owner of UK UDR.[77]

■ *Intercase Ltd v Time Computers Ltd* [2004] ECDR 8 (Patten J)

B was director, controlling shareholder, and employee of MW Ltd, a furniture manufacturing company. The company supplied worktops to a college. B designed a product called the I-Desk to deal with problems encountered with other desk styles. An issue in the case was whether B had carried out his design work in the course of his employment with MW Ltd. It was held that the test to be applied was whether the work done fell within the employee's duties, not simply whether it was done during normal office hours or with the benefit of materials provided at the employer's expense, although these matters could be evidence of the work having been done in the course of employment.

9.69 Under the old ownership rules, pre-dating the amendments made by the 2014 Act, the commissioner of a design was the first owner of any UK UDR in the commissioned design. Although this is no longer the case for all designs created after the commencement of the 2014 Act, this rule will still apply to designs created on commission before that date.

■ *Bruhn Newtech Ltd v Datanetex Ltd and Another* [2012] EWPCC 17 (Patents County Court, currently unreported)

This dispute concerned rights in a product designed and made for the claimant by the defendant. The claimant argued that it owned any UK UDR in the design because the design had been commissioned from the defendant. However, a distinction was drawn between a contract commissioning a design and a contract for the supply of goods. The fact that some of the goods to be supplied had to be designed by the supplier did not make the contract a commission for UK UDR purposes. For there to be a commission for UK UDR purposes, there had to be some fact or matter from which to infer that designs, not just goods, were being ordered and that the supplier was not to retain the freedom to reuse the design devised by him.

---

[76] CDPA 1988, s 215(3).   [77] CDPA 1988, s 215(4).

Question

Who is the first owner of UK UDR?

Infringement

9.70   The exclusive right in UK UDR is to *reproduce the design for commercial purposes*:

(1) by making articles to the design;

(2) by making a design document recording the design for the purpose of enabling such articles to be made (CDPA 1988, s 226(1)).

UK UDR is infringed by doing either (1) or (2) or by authorising another to do so without the licence of the right holder.[78] It thus draws on two copyright concepts: reproduction (see paras 4.24ff) and authorisation (see paras 4.70ff). The requirement of a causal link of copying means that UK UDR, unlike the rights conferred by a patent or a registered design, is *not a full monopoly right in the design* in question. This is a limitation of UK UDR by comparison with the protection conferred by design registration. Again, therefore, the policy of encouraging registration of designs is apparent.

 Question

What is the difference between the nature of the exclusive right under a registered design and under UK UDR?

9.71   It is important to note that UK UDR is *a commercial right*, protecting only against copying for commercial purposes. The expression 'commercial purposes' is defined at section 263(3) of the CDPA 1988.

> **Key points about infringement of UK UDR**
>
> • Infringement is *reproduction* by making an article to the design, or by making design documents for the purpose of enabling such articles to be made.
> • The right is therefore *not a full monopoly right*, unlike registered design right.
> • The infringing act must be *for commercial purposes*.

9.72   The exclusive rights just described are said to give rise to 'primary' infringement of UK UDR. There are also 'secondary' infringements, like those in copyright (paras 4.80ff), committed by importing or possessing for commercial purposes or dealing in the course of a business in an article which is, and which the defendant knows or has reason to believe is, an infringing article.[79] An infringing article is one the making of which infringed UK UDR or, in the case of an imported article, would have infringed UK UDR had it been made in the UK.[80] The key distinction between primary and secondary infringements, as in copyright, is that the latter depends on knowledge where the former depends on copying, regardless of whether or not the copyist knew or had reason to know that this was infringement.

---

[78] CDPA 1988, s 226(3).   [79] CDPA 1988, s 227.   [80] CDPA 1988, s 228.

Reproduction by making articles to the design

9.73 Reproduction means copying the design, directly or indirectly, so as to produce articles 'exactly or substantially to that design'.[81] The infringing articles do not need to be the same type of articles as those of the UK UDR claimant.[82] An aspect of the copyright approach to 'reproduction' which has been used in UK UDR cases is the inference of copying based on sufficient similarity between the claimant's design and the allegedly infringing article and opportunity for the alleged copier to have access to the design. This should, however, be treated with care, as the following case illustrates:

■ *Virgin Atlantic Airways Ltd v Premium Aircraft Interiors Group Ltd* [2009] ECDR 11 (Lewison J)

V alleged that UK UDR in various aspects of the design of a business-class aircraft seat had been copied.[83] Lewison J found 'helpful' the approach of Lord Millett in the copyright case, *Designers Guild Ltd v Russell Williams* (see para 4.28) to the drawing of inferences in relation to copying: similarities had to be sufficiently close, numerous, or extensive as to be more likely the result of copying than coincidence. However, it was also necessary to bear in mind the 'warnings' of Mummery LJ in the *Farmers Build* case, where he had cautioned:[84]

> Substantial similarity of design might well give rise to a suspicion and an allegation of copying in cases where substantial similarity was often not the result of copying but an inevitable consequence of the functional nature of the design . . . Copying may be inferred from proof of access to the protected work, coupled with substantial similarity. This may lead to unfounded infringement claims in the case of functional works, which are usually bound to be substantially similar to one another . . . [The court] must not forget that, in the field of designs of functional articles, one design may be very similar to, or even identical with, another design and yet not be a copy: it may be an original and independent shape and configuration coincidentally the same or similar.

On the facts, in *Virgin Atlantic* the UK UDR claims were rejected, the claimant failing to show copying of its designs.

9.74 Infringement of UK UDR is significantly different from infringement of copyright in another respect as well: whereas copyright is infringed by reproduction of any substantial part of a work in any material form,[85] UK UDR is infringed by making articles 'exactly or substantially to the design':

■ *L Woolley Jewellers Ltd v A and A Jewellery Ltd* [2003] FSR 15 (CA)

The product in question here was a pendant on a chain worn around the neck, with obsolete and imitation coins inserted in the pendant and held in place by 'lugs'; these could also be formed within a bezel (a captive ring with lugs placed over the circumference of the insert). The area around the insert contained an outline of three hearts into which the bail (through which a chain could be attached) had been inserted, while the central portion of the bail itself had been cut out in a heart shape. The first instance judge had expressed the view that the 'substantial part' test in copyright was relevant to infringement of the UK UDR in the design. It was held that this was the wrong approach. There was a difference between an inquiry whether the item copied formed a substantial part of a copyright work and an inquiry (the correct approach for UK UDR) whether the *whole* design containing the copied element is substantially the same design as the design enjoying UK UDR protection.

---

[81] CDPA 1988, s 226(2), (4).
[82] *Electronic Techniques (Anglia) Ltd v Critchley Components Ltd* [1997] FSR 401 at 418.
[83] UK UDR was not considered when this case later reached the Court of Appeal on patent questions: see [2010] RPC 8.
[84] *Farmers Build Ltd v Carier Bulk Materials Handling Ltd* [1999] RPC 461 at 481–82.
[85] CDPA 1988, ss 16(3)(a) and 17(2); see paras 4.13ff.

Question

Explain the difference between reproduction of any substantial part of a work (copyright), and making articles exactly or substantially to a design (UK UDR).

9.75   Questions arise about how to approach determining when an article has been made 'exactly or substantially' to a design. Where the design in which UK UDR is claimed is only 'part' of an article, the comparison must be with the corresponding 'part' of the alleged infringement, not of the two articles as a whole.[86] Through whose eyes do we judge this? The *Klucznik* case on pig fenders was the first to discuss how to approach these matters; it continues to be referred to in later cases such as *Virgin Atlantic* (see para 9.73).[87]

■ *C & H Engineering Ltd v F Klucznik and Sons Ltd* [1992] FSR 421 (Aldous J)

The allegedly infringing pig fender had a rounded tube or roll bar on top but it differed from the first fender in having flaring sides which enabled it to be stacked with other fenders. The claim of infringement failed. Although there was substantial similarity in respect of the roll bars, the overall designs of the fenders were different. Aldous J said (at 428):

> Whether or not the alleged infringing article is made substantially to the plaintiff's design must be an objective test to be decided through the eyes of the person to whom the design is directed. Pig fenders are purchased by pig farmers and I have no doubt that they purchase them taking into account price and design. In the present case, the plaintiff's alleged infringing pig fenders do not have exactly the same design as shown in the defendant's design document. Thus it is necessary to compare the plaintiff's pig fenders with the defendant's design drawing and, looking at the differences and similarities through the eyes of a person such as a pig farmer, decide whether the design of the plaintiff's pig fender is substantially the same as the design shown in the drawing.

Question

How may it be determined that an allegedly infringing article has been made to a design?

9.76   Subsequent cases have also assessed the question of whether the alleged infringement is substantially to the design through the eyes of customers, as the persons 'to whom the design is directed'.[88] Problems inherent in such an anthropomorphic test may begin to emerge, however, in those cases where the key features of the design and the offending article are too fine to be picked up by anyone's unaided eye, as for example with contact lenses.[89]

---

[86] *Dyson Ltd v Qualtex (UK) Ltd* [2006] RPC 31 (CA), para 113.   [87] [2009] ECDR 11, para 32.

[88] See, eg, *Mark Wilkinson Furniture Ltd v Woodcraft Designs (Radcliffe) Ltd* [1998] FSR 63 at 74–75 (a person interested in purchasing a fitted kitchen); *A Fulton Co Ltd v Grant Barnett & Co Ltd* [2001] RPC 16 at para 89 (members of the buying public).

[89] *Ocular Sciences Ltd v Aspect Vision Care Ltd* [1997] RPC 289 (Laddie J), at 424:

> The fact that the defendants' lenses also cannot be distinguished from the plaintiffs' on mere visual inspection does not prove that they are sufficiently close for the purposes of infringement. When a plaintiff relies on the most detailed and specific dimensions to support his claim to the existence of design right, he can only succeed on infringement if the defendants' designs are extremely close in design.

> **Key points on reproduction by making articles to the design**
>
> - Infringing reproduction may be direct or indirect and relate to articles made exactly or substantially to the design.
>
> - The correct approach to the question of whether an article has been reproduced 'substantially' to the design in which UK UDR is claimed is to ask whether the design containing the copied element is substantially the same as the design enjoying UK UDR (remembering that UK UDR may subsist in parts of articles only), not the copyright test of whether the element copied formed a substantial part of the original work.
>
> - Similarity is tested through the eyes of the person to whom the design is directed.

Reproduction of the design by making a design document for the purpose of enabling articles to be made to the design

9.77   Section 226(1)(b) of the CDPA 1988 makes it an infringement of UK UDR to reproduce the design for commercial purposes by making a design document for the purpose of enabling articles to be made to the design. There are some important differences compared to section 226(1)(a) discussed previously in paras 9.73–9.76:

■ *Società Esplosivi Industriali SpA v Ordnance Technologies (UK) Ltd* [2008] RPC 12 (Lindsay J)

This case arose from what was at first a joint venture between the parties to design multiple warhead systems. After the joint venture broke down, the claimant sued for infringement of UK UDR in certain warhead designs under section 226(1)(b). The judge held that, whereas infringement under section 226(1)(a) of the CDPA 1988 was enlarged by section 226(2) to cover both articles made exactly and substantially to the design in suit, section 226(2) did not apply to infringement under section 226(1)(b).[90] Section 226(1)(b) also raised questions of intention in relation to the words 'for the purpose of' making articles to the design. The judge held that this required proof that, at the material time, the infringer made the infringing record of the design with the purpose that articles should thereby be made. There was no infringement where the record of the design created by the defender had not gone beyond design study and evaluation, to manufacture or an intention to manufacture working from that record. The use of a protected document as a starting point for the making of further design documents which were variations upon the protected original, even where that making had been in the course of a commercial purpose, did not in itself constitute an infringement.[91]

Exceptions to exclusive rights

9.78   Until recently, there were no exceptions to UK UDR like those for registered designs (private and non-commercial use, experimental purposes, citation, and teaching—see previously para 8.123). However, the Intellectual Property Act 2014 has now introduced a new set of exceptions at sections 244A and 244B CDPA 1988. This could perhaps have been done more neatly (it is, for example, questionable whether UK UDR needs

---

[90]   It has been suggested that this interpretation is not supported by a closer reading of the wording of s 226 when properly analysed and that, as a matter of policy, it is 'verging on the irrational': M Howe, *Russell-Clarke and Howe on Industrial Designs* (9th edn, 2016), para 4-101.

[91]   See further the note on this case by S Vousden, '*Società Esplosivi Industriali SpA*: on confidences, copying designs, and company directors' [2008] EIPR 332–36. See also S Yavorsky, 'Negotiating an IP minefield: infringing design documents' (2008) 3(6) JIPLP 361–63.

a defence for private and non-commercial acts given that infringement must be commercial in any event—contrast sections 226(1) and 224A(a) CDPA 1988), but essentially the new exceptions mirror the exceptions to registered design infringement. It remains to be seen whether the UK courts will adopt any of the more controversial aspects of the now developing Court of Justice case law on registered design exceptions (see para 8.126 in particular). UK UDR's exclusivity is also quite significantly limited by the availability of licences of right five years after the first marketing of the article to which the design was applied (see paras 9.61–9.66).

Interaction with copyright

9.79   We looked in Chapter 8 at the interaction between registered designs and other IP rights, including copyright. As was noted there and in the introductory sections of this chapter (see paras 9.8–9.12), there are important provisions in the CDPA 1988 which were enacted to curtail the availability of copyright claims in the UK in relation to certain designs. Alongside the creation of UK UDR, these provisions were the second key part of the move in the CDPA 1988 to remove, or at least substantially cut down, the role of copyright in relation to industrial designs. However, as we shall see, there has been some reform in this area. In this section, we look at these provisions of the CDPA 1988 in more detail.

9.80   Copyright may arise in relation to a design in various ways. An article may itself qualify for copyright protection if, for example, it constitutes a sculpture or a work of artistic craftsmanship. A design may also begin life as a sketch, a drawing, or a more worked-up design blueprint. All such drawings may fall within the scope of copyright subject matter, typically as an artistic work. Artistic copyright can subsist in such drawings, no matter how functional or simple the content recorded there, as long as there is sufficient originality. Copyright can be infringed by the making of products to the design, because the copyright in the drawings as a two-dimensional artistic work could be infringed by a three-dimensional reproduction. Because copyright prevents indirect as well as direct copying, there can be infringement of the drawings as the underlying artistic work even where they are not seen and the copyist simply copies an article made to the design recorded in the artistic work. The problems caused by this were discussed previously (see paras 9.8–9.12) However, although this is the basic position, by sections 51 and 52 of the CDPA 1988, the intention was that the scope for enforcement of the copyright in certain designs should be severely cut back, with the aim of ensuring that, for the most part, copyright was to become a marginal form of protection in the industrial design field. Section 51 of the CDPA 1988 (see paras 9.81–9.88) remains in force; however, section 52 (see paras 9.89–9.93) has been repealed.

Restricting copyright

Section 51 of the CDPA 1988

9.81   Section 51(1) of the CDPA 1988 provides that it is *not* infringement of any copyright in a design document or model recording or embodying a design for anything other than an artistic work or a typeface to make an article to the design or to copy an article made to the design. A design document for these purposes is defined as:[92]

> any record of a design, whether in the form of a drawing, a written description, a photograph, data stored in a computer or otherwise.

For the purposes of section 51, as recently amended by the Intellectual Property Act 2014 consistent with the amendments to section 213(2) of the CDPA (see paras 9.23–9.26), 'design' is defined as:[93]

> the design of the shape or configuration (whether internal or external) of the whole or part of an article, other than surface decoration.

---

[92] CDPA 1988, s 51(3).   [93] CDPA 1988, s 51(3).

—that is, albeit slightly differently worded to incorporate in section 51(3) the exclusion of surface decoration, the kind of design that is protected by UK UDR.

9.82   It is important to grasp that section 51 recognises copyright in design documents (where it exists). But the usefulness of this copyright is carefully restricted because section 51 provides a defence to a copyright infringement claim based on the design document. If the design is for anything other than an artistic work or typeface, section 51 provides that it is not infringement of copyright to make an article to the design or to copy an article made to the design.

9.83   As should be apparent from this, in terms of whether the section 51 defence is available the key question is what, as a matter of copyright law, the design in question is *for*. If the design is for anything *other than* an artistic work or typeface, the effect of section 51 is that the unauthorised making of three-dimensional articles by copying either directly or indirectly from a design document cannot constitute copyright infringement. If, however, there is a design document *for an artistic work*—for example, a sketch recording the design for a sculpture or for a work of artistic craftsmanship—or for a typeface, then under section 51 there is no defence and it is possible to enforce the copyright in the design document.

9.84   It will therefore be vital to distinguish when a drawing or model is the design of an artistic work and when it is not. Only in the latter case will protection in copyright be unavailable. The most crucial things to keep in mind in approaching the question are:

- which three-dimensional works attract copyright (eg works of artistic craftsmanship and sculptures); and

- the distinction between shape and configuration on the one hand (which falls within the definition of 'design' for the purposes of s 51) and surface decoration on the other (which does not).

9.85   The operation of section 51 is well illustrated by the *Lucasfilm* case:

■ *Lucasfilm Ltd v Ainsworth* [2009] FSR 2 (Mann J); [2010] FSR 10 (CA); [2011] 3 WLR 487 (SC)

This case was concerned with the designs for Imperial stormtrooper helmets and armour featured in the film *Star Wars*. A had made the helmets and armour used during filming, from initial storyboard sketches and a clay model prepared for L. These were design documents and a model recording a design. The key question was therefore whether, as design documents, they were *for* items (the helmets and armour) which were, or were not, in themselves copyright artistic works. Mann J summarised his conclusions as follows:[94]

> [Section 51] is therefore capable of barring a copyright claim in relation to the design document if it is for 'anything other than an artistic work'. If the items were not artistic works, the section works in Mr Ainsworth's favour and prevents his acts being infringements. The designs could only be for artistic works in this case if they were for a sculpture or a work of artistic craftsmanship. I have held that they were not artistic works in either of the two candidate senses. Therefore the designs were for something other than an artistic work and s.51 operates in Mr Ainsworth's favour to prevent his copying of the work being an infringement of copyright.

The first instance decision was upheld on appeal to the Court of Appeal and Supreme Court, both higher courts upholding the first instance judge's characterisation of the helmets and armour as not constituting copyright artistic works of sculpture and, as a consequence, applying section 51 of the CDPA 1988 to exclude a copyright claim (see also para 3.62).

[94]   [2009] FSR 2, para 141.

Discussion point   For answer guidance visit **www.oup.com/uk/brown5e**.

Why do designs for artistic works retain full copyright?

9.86   Section 51 is not without its difficulties, however:

■ *Lambretta Clothing Co Ltd v Teddy Smith (UK) Ltd* [2005] RPC 6 (CA)

This is the track top case (for the facts see para 9.32). The shape of the top was not protected in UK UDR because it was not original. The key issue for section 51 purposes related to the colourways of the top. Although there was no claim in UK UDR because the colourways were excluded from UK UDR protection, there was a design document drawn by a director of the plaintiffs. So, the defendants' top might have been treated as copied (indirectly) from this design document and therefore as an indirect infringement of copyright in the design document. It was held, however, that section 51 barred any claim to artistic copyright infringement. For the majority, it was not possible to divorce the colourways from the shape of the top—as noted by Jacob LJ: 'Neither physically nor conceptually can they exist apart from the shapes of the parts of the article . . . If artistic copyright were to be enforced here, it would be enforced in respect of [the] whole design drawing. But that is not allowed by s 51' (para 39). It is notable, however, that Mance LJ dissented, commenting as follows:

> in order 'to make an article to the design' or 'to copy an article made to the design' embodied in a drawing, it is, because of the definition in s 51(3), still necessary to conclude that the article was made, or was a copy of an article made, to the design, meaning 'the design [as embodied in the drawing] of any aspect of the shape or configuration . . . of the whole or part of an article, *other than surface decoration*'. Only if it was, does s 51 prevent there being any copyright infringement (para 80; emphasis added).

Therefore, Mance LJ argued, since the surface decoration was not part of the 'design' as defined by the CDPA 1988, the limitation of copyright under section 51 did not apply.

■ *Flashing Badge Co Ltd v Groves* [2007] FSR 36 (HC)

This case was about design drawings for flashing novelty badges with messages such as '40 Today', 'Let's Party', and 'Happy Birthday' presented on them in a stylised way along with images such as balloons and cakes with candles. The outline shape of each of the badges followed the outline of the relevant artistic designs. The question was whether section 51 of the CDPA 1988 applied to prevent the claimant's action for copyright infringement against an importer of virtually identical badges from China. Granting summary judgment for copyright infringement, Rimer J held that each drawing was a design document incorporating (1) a design for an artistic work and (2) a design for something other than an artistic work, in this case an article in the nature of a badge in the same outline shape as the artistic work. Section 51 had no relevance to (1) because they were designs for artistic works. Section 51 applied only to (2), which was not an artistic work. It followed that section 51 applied, if at all, only to a copyright claim in the shape or configuration of the badge minus the surface decoration. Section 51 provided no defence in respect of an infringement of copyright in the graphic design which provided the surface decoration of the badges. Distinguishing *Lambretta*, Rimer J described *Lambretta* as a case which 'appears to have turned on its special facts'. He concluded:[95]

> It is true that the design of the shape of the badge follows the outline of the design for the artistic work on the face of each badge. But the latter design is in the nature of a graphic design which is in no sense something

---

[95]   See further the note on this case by E Derclaye, '*Flashing Badge Co Ltd v Groves*: a step forward in the clarification of the copyright/design interface' [2008] EIPR 251–54.

which (unlike the *Lambretta* colourways) can only exist as part of the shape of the badge. It is a design which can be applied to any other substrate and which, if so applied, would enjoy copyright protection for the infringement of which s 51 would afford no defence (para 22).

9.87 Overall, if section 51 operates to exclude a claim in copyright, the only claim available in terms of the scheme of the CDPA 1988 is under UK UDR, if at all. However, it may well be that there is no valid or subsisting UK UDR claim (as was, eg, the case in *Lucasfilm*). The claimant may also not actually plead a UK UDR case. This does not matter—there is no requirement that UK UDR be available as an alternative to copyright. If there is no UK UDR claim and section 51 operates to exclude a copyright claim, there will be no infringement of rights at all under the CDPA 1988, whether in copyright or in UK UDR.

9.88 If section 51 operates so as to retain a claim in copyright, it is possible that there may be parallel claims in copyright and UK UDR. For example, there may be a design document for an item which is a work of artistic craftsmanship for copyright purposes and which also has an 'original' shape and configuration such as to entitle it to protection in UK UDR. In these circumstances, the scheme of the CDPA 1988 is to force the claimant to rely on his copyright claim only. Section 236 of the CDPA 1988 provides that:

> Where copyright subsists in a work which consists of or includes a design in which design right subsists, it is not an infringement of design right in the design to do anything which is an infringement of copyright in that work.

This concludes the move, in the CDPA 1988, to separate the artistic from the industrial in terms of design and copyright laws.

Key points on section 51 of the CDPA 1988

- The section restricts when copyright in a design document or model can be enforced.
- The key issue is whether the design is for an item which qualifies for protection as a copyright artistic work (eg as a work of artistic craftsmanship or sculpture) or is for a typeface.
- If the design document is for an artistic work or a typeface, the copyright claim will survive. If not, making an article to the design recorded in the design document does not infringe copyright.

Section 52 of the CDPA 1988

9.89 Separately from section 51 of the CDPA 1988, the Act also introduced a further provision, to be found at section 52, limiting the extent to which copyright could play a role in relation to commercially exploited designs.

9.90 Section 52 of the CDPA 1988 dealt with artistic works which, although not excluded from enforceability under section 51, were subsequently exploited by being made into articles by an industrial process and marketed (exposed for sale or hire) in the UK or elsewhere.[96] Section 52 provided that, at the end of the period of 25 years (a term derived from the Berne Convention provisions on works of applied art—see para 8.5) from the end of the calendar year in which such articles were first marketed, the work could be copied by making articles of any description, or doing anything for the purpose of making articles of any description, without infringing copyright in the work.

---

[96] 'Making by an industrial process' was defined by the Copyright (Industrial Process and Excluded Articles) (No 2) Order 1989 (SI 1989/1070) as, in broad terms, the making of 50 or more articles.

■ *Lucasfilm Ltd v Ainsworth* [2009] FSR 2 (Mann J); [2010] FSR 10 (CA); [2011] 3 WLR 487 (SC)

The defence at section 52 of the CDPA 1988 was pleaded in addition, and as an alternative to, the section 51 defence. The artistic works covered by section 52 in this case were L's preliminary drawings. Mann J stated that the purpose of section 52 was to 'shorten the copyright period applicable to some copyright items which are reproduced industrially and then sold, to a period of 25 years from the date when they were first marketed' (para 144). It was held that the designs of the Stormtrooper helmet and armour had been reproduced industrially for more than 25 years, for example as toy models of Stormtroopers. The section 52 defence therefore succeeded, in addition and as an alternative to the defence under section 51. It was held that it did not matter whether the relevant articles were made in the UK or elsewhere. The decision was affirmed by the Court of Appeal. Section 52 was not substantively addressed by the Supreme Court, which disposed of the appeal on other grounds.

9.91   Section 52(4) of the CDPA 1988 empowered the Secretary of State to make orders excluding from the operation of section 52 articles of a primarily literary or artistic character. Examples are the production of books and the exploitation of a painting or a photograph by the manufacture of posters, books and posters both being commercial products which retain primarily literary or artistic character. In these cases, full artistic copyright was retained.[97]

9.92   While not affecting the subsistence of copyright in an affected work, the objective of section 52 was to restrict the duration of protection for that work to a period paralleling the maximum period for a registered design (see para 8.128). As noted in para 9.80, however, section 52 has now been repealed. This repeal was initiated by the UK IPO in response to the ruling of the Court of Justice in *Flos SpA v Semeraro Casa e Famiglia SpA* (see previously para 8.132),[98] in particular the finding by the Court of Justice that Article 17 of the Designs Directive does not leave member states free to determine the term of protection in copyright for designs. The concern was that section 52 constituted an impermissible restriction on copyright term in this context. However, the move to repeal section 52 was criticised and it has been argued that repeal was not necessary, with concerns having been expressed about the correctness of *Flos* and, more widely, about the implications of *Flos* in terms of a potential return to 'industrial copyright' in designs (the difficulties engendered by 'industrial copyright' were discussed from a UK historical perspective at paras 9.8–9.12).[99]

9.93   The mechanics of the repeal of section 52 have also proved contentious. After consultation, the UK government initially decided to set a five-year transitional period, with the repeal of section 52 to come into effect in 2020. However, this was challenged by judicial review for being too long, in response to which the UK government expedited the repeal date to July 2016. The repeal of section 52 affects a wide range of market sectors, with businesses having relied on section 52 to permit them to market products ranging from character merchandising to furniture and fashion design. With section 52 repealed, relevant works, including works for which section 52 had previously been engaged, are protected against copying for the much longer copyright term of life of the author plus 70 years. This is likely to have a significant impact on businesses which had hitherto relied on section 52 to allow them to market products. Businesses were given a transition period to late January 2017 to sell off or destroy existing stocks. How the repeal of section 52 will affect competition in the affected sectors and consumers going forward remains to be seen.

[97] Copyright (Industrial Process and Excluded Articles) (No 2) Order 1989 (SI 1989/1070).
[98] Case C-168/09, 27 January 2011 [2011] ECDR 8.
[99] See L Bently, 'The return of industrial copyright?' [2012] EIPR 654–72.

> ## Key points on section 52 of the CDPA 1988
>
> - Section 52 CDPA 1988 provided that, if an artistic work was exploited commercially within the meaning of section 52, the right to rely on copyright to prevent copying by making articles of any description was lost 25 years after first marketing of articles based on the work.
> - However, section 52 has now been repealed; the impact of this in the marketplace is yet to be seen.

Community UDR

About this topic

9.94   Now we turn to the second major form of unregistered design protection, Community UDR.[100] Community UDR is the unregistered form of Community design protection. Recital 16 to the Community Design Regulation emphasises the utility of Community UDR to sectors where designs have a short market life and where there is no need for the longer duration of registered protection and the burdens of the filing system are a disadvantage. Community UDR also has an important role to play where a putative registrant is relying on the grace period discussed previously (paras 8.75–8.76) while he decides whether or not to file. Community UDR follows much of the same scheme of protection as Community registered designs, although with some important points of difference. The existence of the Community UDR is expressly without prejudice to national laws relating to unregistered designs (such as UK UDR) or to trade marks or other distinctive signs, patents and utility models, typefaces, civil liability (ie tort or delict), and unfair competition (passing off in the UK).[101] A design protected by Community UDR may also be protected by copyright under the national laws of the member states.[102] As with registered designs, the provisions of the CDPA 1988 could apply in the UK to restrict the ways in which any coexisting copyright in the design could be infringed.

> ## Key point on Community UDR
>
> - Community UDR is the unregistered form of Community design protection. It is very different from UK UDR and follows much of the same scheme of protection as the Community registered design.

9.95   Like the registered form of Community design protection, Community UDR will be affected by Brexit. After Brexit, because the UK will no longer be a member of the EU, the UK will no longer fall within the territorial scope of Community UDR protection. The draft Withdrawal Agreement which has been negotiated between the UK and EU contains specific provision to deal with this at Article 57.[103] It provides as follows:

> The holder of a right in relation to an unregistered Community design which arose before the end of the transition period in accordance with Regulation (EC) No 6/2002 shall in relation to that unregistered Community design *ipso iure* become the holder of an enforceable intellectual property right in the United Kingdom, under the law of the United Kingdom, that affords the same level of protection as that provided for in Regulation (EC) No

---

[100]   See generally VM Saez, 'The unregistered Community design' [2002] EIPR 588–90.

[101]   CDR, Art 96(1); see para 8.130.   [102]   CDR, Art 96(2); see para 8.131.

[103]   See https://assets.publishing.service.gov.uk/government/uploads/system/uploads/attachment_data/file/756374/14_November_Draft_Agreement_on_the_Withdrawal_of_the_United_Kingdom_of_Great_Britain_and_Northern_Ireland_from_the_European_Union.pdf.

6/2002. The term of protection of that right under the law of the United Kingdom shall be at least equal to the remaining period of protection of the corresponding unregistered Community design under Article 11(1) of that Regulation.

In other words, the UK will be obliged to create its own equivalent to Community UDR protection, to provide for continuity of protection in the UK for the remainder of the period of subsistence of all then-existing rights in Community UDR. In the event of a 'no-deal' Brexit, the UK has indicated that it will also take this step.[104] The UK Government 'no-deal' notice adds:

> In addition to this, the UK will create a new unregistered design right in UK law which mirrors the characteristics of the unregistered Community design. This means that designs which are disclosed after the UK exits the EU will also be protected in the UK under the current terms of the unregistered Community design. This new right will be known as the supplementary unregistered design right.

The detail of this proposed new right remains to be fleshed out.

Community UDR and Brexit

When the UK leaves the EU, the UK will no longer fall within the territorial scope of Community UDR. Reflecting this, according to the current draft of the EU–UK Withdrawal Agreement, the UK will be obliged to create equivalent rights in UK law to continue to protect in the UK all then-subsisting rights in Community UDR.

If there is a 'no-deal' Brexit, the UK Government has indicated that it will take similar steps. The UK Government has also signalled its intention to create a new UK unregistered design right, to be called the 'supplementary unregistered design right', in terms the same as Community UDR protection.

Question

What are the major distinctions between UK UDR and Community UDR?

Designs to which Community UDR applies

9.96   The designs to which Community UDR applies and the core concepts in terms of validity and infringement are defined in the same way as for Community registered designs. Thus, the discussions of the following key points in connection with Community registered designs apply as much to Community unregistered designs as to Community registered designs:

- *Design* as the *appearance* of the whole of part of a *product* (see paras 8.23–8.33).
- Possession of *novelty* and *individual character* (see paras 8.41–8.78), the date at which this is assessed for Community UDR being the date upon which the design was first made available to the public (CDR, Arts 5(1)(a) and 6(1)(a)).
- Exclusion of *designs solely dictated by the technical function* of the product and on other grounds (see paras 8.79–8.90).
- *Complex products* (see paras 8.91–8.97).
- *Must match* or *repair* defence (see paras 8.104–8.105).
- Invalidity, scope of protection, and defences (see paras 8.110–8.127).

---

[104] UK Government, 'Trade marks and designs if there's no Brexit deal', 24 September 2018, www.gov.uk/government/publications/trade-marks-and-designs-if-theres-no-brexit-deal/trade-marks-and-designs-if-theres-no-brexit-deal.

9.97 Notice that all this necessarily implies that *Community UDR cannot apply to any design which is incapable of registration under the Community registered design system*. This is an important contrast with UK UDR, which may protect designs not capable of registration. There may be unregistered designs which enjoy UK UDR in the UK but which will not have Community UDR. The best example would be a product whose design was dictated solely by function such as to be excluded from protection under the Community Design Regulation. Insofar as it was not caught by the UK UDR 'must fit' or any of the other exceptions to UK UDR protection, then that design would be protected in the UK by UK UDR, but not by Community UDR.

 Question

Explain why Community UDR cannot apply to a design incapable of registration as a Community registered design.

Commencement and duration of Community UDR

9.98 Unlike for Community registered designs, there is no need for the design to be registered for Community UDR to arise. Instead, according to Article 11(1) of the Community Design Regulation, Community UDR arises when the design is first made available to the public within the Community. This can be by way of publication, exhibition, use in trade, or otherwise (CDR, Art 11(2)). Article 11(2) of the Community Design Regulation also provides that a design is deemed to be been disclosed if there has been publication, exhibition, use in trade, or otherwise in such a way that, in the normal course of business, these events could reasonably have become known to the circles specialised in the sector concerned, operating within the Community. However, this does not arise if the making available occurred under explicit or implicit conditions of confidentiality (CDR, Art 11(2)).

9.99 In *Gautzsch Großhandel*, the Court of Justice was asked whether a design could be considered to have been made available to the public within the Community in a way which could reasonably have become known to the circles specialised in the sector concerned for the purpose of Article 11 CDR if disclosed only to traders (rather than, say, designers or manufacturers). The Court of Justice held that traders could not, in principle, be excluded from the 'circles specialised in the sector concerned' and that this could amount to a relevant disclosure on the facts, which were for the national court to determine.[105]

9.100 There has been some doubt over whether, when read together, the net effect of Article 11(1) and 11(2) of the Regulation requires the first 'making available to the public' of the design for which Community unregistered design right is claimed to take place geographically within the territory of the Community. For example, could making a design available to the public overseas trigger the subsistence of Community unregistered design right if that event could reasonably have become known to the circles specialised in the sector concerned operating within the Community? A further provision, Article 110a(5) CDR, has been inserted into the Regulation to address this, stating that a design which has not been made public within the territory of the Community shall not enjoy protection as an unregistered Community design. Although the issue has not come before the General Court or the Court of Justice, the German Supreme Court in *Gebäckpresse*[106] has confirmed that, for Community unregistered design right to arise, first disclosure of the design must take place within the territory of the Community. A first disclosure outside the Community not only does not give rise to Community unregistered design right, but may also be novelty-destroying with regard to any subsequent attempt to claim design protection.[107]

---

[105] Case C-479/12 *H Gautzsch Großhandel GmbH & Co KG v Münchener Boulevard Möbel Joseph Duna GmbH* [2014] ECDR 14, paras 24–30.
[106] I ZR 126/06, [2009] GRUR 79.
[107] See further A Gartner, 'Bundesgerichtshof (Pastry Press) (I ZR 126/06): the disclosure of designs outside the European Community—the Federal Supreme Court's "*Gebäckpresse*" decision and its implications' [2010] EIPR 181–83.

9.101   Article 82(2) CDR provides:

> In proceedings in respect of an infringement action or an action for threatened infringement of an unregistered Community design, the Community design court shall treat the Community design as valid if the right holder produces proof that the conditions laid down in Article 11 have been met and indicates what constitutes the individual character of his Community design. However, the defendant may contest its validity by way of a plea or with a counterclaim for a declaration of invalidity.

Given this provision, it will be important for design owners relying on Community UDR to keep evidence of their first marking of the relevant design. Beyond this, Article 85(2) only requires the design right holder to indicate the features of his design which he claims give the design individual character. As confirmed by the Court of Justice in *Karen Millen*, in any challenge to validity the burden of proof of lack of individual character remains on the party challenging the design.[108]

9.102   Disclosure having occurred, the Community UDR then lasts for *three years* from the date on which the design was first made available to the public. This duration is significantly shorter than both UK UDR, even at its shortest, and Community registered design protection, which lasts for up to 25 years. This short duration aligns with the intention that Community UDR be relied upon primarily to protect designs with a short shelf-life. The best example of an industrial sector with short market life products is the clothing fashion industry, where designs are turned over on a seasonal basis, for which registration would probably not be economical.

Rights conferred

Ownership

9.103   So far as appropriate, the same rules about ownership apply as in the Community registered design (see previously para 8.106). If an unregistered Community design is disclosed or claimed by a person not entitled to it, the entitled person may claim to be recognised as the legitimate holder of the design. Such a claim will become barred three years after the disclosure, unless the party making the disclosure was in bad faith.[109]

Exclusive right

9.104   Like a Community registered design, Community UDR confers on its holder the *exclusive right to use the design and to prevent any third party not having his consent from using it*, the scope of protection conferred including any design which does not produce a different overall impression on the informed user.

9.105   However, unlike the Community registered design, which confers a full monopoly right so that the right is available even against a party who is unaware of the existence of the prior design, Community UDR only confers the right to prevent use of the design if the contested use results from *copying* the protected design (CDR, Art 19(2)). The contested use will not be deemed to result from copying if it results from an independent work of creation by a designer who may be reasonably thought not to be familiar with the design made available to the public by the Community UDR right holder (CDR, Art 19(2)). The justification for this difference in treatment between Community registered designs and Community UDR is that a party proposing to put a design into the marketplace can check the register for any similar

---

[108] Case C-345/13 *Karen Millen Fashions Ltd v Dunnes Stores* (Court of Justice) [2014] Bus LR 756, para 47.
[109] CDR, Art 15(1), (3).

prior registered designs, but cannot do so for unregistered ones. Fairness requires that such a person be liable only if that person knows, or ought reasonably to know, of that prior unregistered design and right. The policy is summarised thus in recital 21 to the Community Design Regulation:

> The exclusive nature of the right conferred by the Community registered design is consistent with its greater legal certainty. It is appropriate that the unregistered Community design should, however, constitute a right only to prevent copying. Protection could not therefore extend to design products which are the result of a design arrived at independently by a second designer.

Key points about Community UDR

- Most of the core concepts and substantive legal provisions are the same as for the Community registered design.
- The term of Community UDR is only three years. It is aimed at the protection of designs on their way to being registered, or with a short market life.
- The right protects only against contested uses which result from copying of the design in which Community UDR is claimed.

Discussion point   For answer guidance visit www.oup.com/uk/brown5e.

- What is the purpose of Community UDR?
- To what products will the Community UDR typically apply?
- How do the main features of Community UDR (protected designs, duration, rights, defences) compare, contrast, and interact with registered design protection?
- Likewise, how does Community UDR contrast with the UK UDR?
- Why was UK UDR kept in force, despite the introduction of Community UDR?

Further reading

Books

General

M Howe, *Russell-Clarke and Howe on Industrial Designs* (9th edn, 2016)

History and policy

HL MacQueen, *Copyright, Competition and Industrial Design* (2nd edn, 1995)

Articles

UK UDR

S Ashby and C Smith, 'Unregistered design law: the good, the bad, and the ugly' (2018) 13(4) JIPLP 315–24

A Coulthard and L Bently, 'From the commonplace to the interface: five cases on unregistered design right' [1997] EIPR 401–11

E Derclaye, 'The British unregistered design right: will it survive its new community counterpart to influence future European case law?' (2003–04) 10 Columbia J European Law 265

E Derclaye, '*Flashing Badge Co Ltd v Groves*; a step forward in the clarification of the copyright/design interface' [2008] EIPR 251–54

S Hird and M Peeters, 'UK protection for recombinant DNA—exploring the options' [1991] EIPR 334–39

D Meale and V Leitch, 'Aspects of UK unregistered design right: guidance from *Neptune v Devol*' (2018) 13(3) JIPLP 175–76

A Michaels, 'The end of the road for "pattern spare" parts? *Dyson Ltd v Qualtex (UK) Ltd*' [2006] EIPR 396–98

W Pang and R Burstall, 'Sculpting an effective design protection system' (2012) 7(6) JIPLP 430–36

J Reed, 'Royalties for design right "licences of right"' [2005] EIPR 298–301

J Reynolds and P Brownlow, 'Increased legal protection for schematic designs in the United Kingdom' [1994] EIPR 398–400

J Sykes, 'Designs: the unregistered design right: interpretation and practical application of the must match exemption' (2006) 1(7) JIPLP 442–46

S Vousden, '*Società Esplosivi Industriali SpA*: on confidences, copying designs and company directors' [2008] EIPR 332–36

D Wilkinson 'Case closed: functional designs protected by design right' [2007] EIPR 118–22

S Yavorsky, 'Negotiating an IP minefield: infringing design documents' (2008) 3(6) JIPLP 361–63

Interaction with copyright

L Bently, 'The return of industrial copyright?' [2012] EIPR 654–72

Community UDR

E Derclaye, 'CUDR and CRDR post-Brexit from a UK and EU perspective—will all unregistered design rights become history?' (2018) 13(4) JIPLP 325–31

A Gartner, 'Bundesgerichtshof (Pastry Press) (I ZR 126/06): the disclosure of designs outside the European Community—the Federal Supreme Court's "*Gebäckpresse*" decision and its implications' [2010] EIPR 181–83

C-H Massa and A Strowel, 'Community design: Cinderella revamped' [2003] EIPR 68–78

VM Saez, 'The unregistered Community design' [2002] EIPR 588–90

A Tischner, 'The role of unregistered rights—a European perspective on design protection' (2018) 13(4) JIPLP 303–14

Part IV

Patents

Introduction

This Part of the book explores the law of patents over three chapters. Chapter 10 considers the nature of and rationales for patents, and the application process in the context of the various patent regimes that operate at the national, European, and international levels. We will examine current developments within these regimes against the background of the justifications that are commonly advanced for patent protection. Chapter 11 then explores patentability, what is required in order to obtain a patent. Crucial to this exercise is a discussion of exceptions to patentability, with two key instances being biotechnological inventions and software patents. We use these examples to explore how well patent law adapts to new technological advances and challenges and we consider whether reforms to patent regimes are required. Chapter 12 deals with claim construction, what activities constitute patent infringement, defences for alleged infringers, and patent revocation, that is, the claim that a patent is somehow invalid and should be struck down.

Sources of the law: key websites

- Patents Act 1977, as amended to July 2018
  www.ipo.gov.uk/patentsact1977.pdf

- The patents related sections of the Copyright, Designs and Patents Act 1988, as amended to 1 July 2015
  https://assets.publishing.service.gov.uk/government/uploads/system/uploads/attachment_data/file/439324/CDP_Act_1988_Parts_5_and_6.pdf

- European Patent Convention 2000
  www.epo.org/law-practice/legal-texts/html/epc/2010/e/index.html

- TRIPS Agreement 1994 as amended 2017
  www.wto.org/english/docs_e/legal_e/31bis_trips_01_e.htm

- Paris Convention for the Protection of Industrial Property 1883, as amended
  www.wipo.int/treaties/en/ip/paris/trtdocs_wo020.html

- Patent Cooperation Treaty 1970, as amended
  www.wipo.int/pct/en/texts/articles/atoc.htm

- Patent Law Treaty 2000
  www.wipo.int/treaties/en/ip/plt/trtdocs_wo038.html

- Decisions of the courts in the various jurisdictions of the UK, for which see BAILII
  www.bailii.org

- WIPO Standing Committee on the Law of Patents
  www.wipo.int/scp/en

10

Patent regimes and the application process

Introduction

Scope and overview of chapter

10.1   This chapter examines the architecture and procedures of contemporary patent systems as they currently operate in the UK, within the European patent system, and through international agreements, instruments, and procedures. This chapter also reviews changes over time and areas of particular debate and possible future evolution. All patent regimes operate through a registration process, meaning that patent protection is only granted after rigorous consideration of the criteria for patentability as applied to each putative invention. For present purposes, a valid patent normally lasts for 20 years and provides the patent holder (the patentee) with 'absolute' monopoly over their invention—although note the consideration in Chapter 1 regarding whether or not a true monopoly is conferred. Patents confer the strongest of all monopolies available in intellectual property (IP) law, and it makes patent protection one of the most sought after of Intellectual Property Rights (IPRs).

10.2
> ### Learning objectives
>
> By the end of this chapter you should be able to describe and explain:
> - the various justifications offered for the existence of patent regimes;
> - the nature of the various patent regimes, as well as their similarities and differences;
> - the current challenges for patent law, particularly regarding international development, and options for reform;
> - the processes and procedures for obtaining patent protection.

10.3   Unlike copyright, patent protection does not come into existence with the creation of the relevant subject matter, but rather must be granted by an intellectual property office after an application and examination process. These processes will be described, including the issue of who is entitled to apply for, and receive, a patent. So, the chapter looks like this:

- Patent regimes: past and present (10.4–10.13)
- Rationales of patent protection (10.14–10.22)
- The European dimension (10.23–10.36)
- The international dimension (10.37–10.73)

- Further reform: patent regimes in the future (10.74–10.77)
- Patent procedures (10.78–10.113)

Patent regimes: past and present

Early history

10.4   The essential features of the modern patent system can be seen in the earliest origins of that system which began, in Europe at least, as a form of state or monarch grace and favour. Monopolies over trade practices or production were initially used as a reward for loyalty or as a form of privilege, done through the grant of *letters patent* (an 'open letter') as proof that the privilege—the monopoly—had been bestowed. The first recorded patent in England was for a method of making stained glass given to John of Utynam by King Henry VI in 1449.[1] From the very beginning, however, there has been an expectation of reciprocity as between the granter of the monopoly—be it monarch or state—and the grantee. Thus, the monopoly holder would be expected to undertake certain obligations to their monarch, or, as typified by the Venetian Republic, the grantee would undertake to disclose the elements of their new 'craft' in return for the privilege of a market monopoly of ten years. Venice was the first state to establish a patent system, done by decree in 1474, in an attempt to attract traders to introduce products and processes not known in Venice at that time. This encouraged innovation in the Republic while avoiding conflict with the powerful guilds that held considerable sway over the markets.[2] Other states followed suit, each using the device of monopoly as the incentive to inventors to enter the social contract with the state. But the terms of this social contract have been in dispute since the earliest of times, and the courts have always been willing to strike a monopoly down if the balance of interests has not been appropriately struck. Thus, in *Darcy v Allin*[3] a monopoly from Queen Elizabeth I over trade in playing cards was overturned, partly on the basis that there was no discernible advantage to the public of allowing such a state of affairs to continue. Parliament, too, has shown antipathy towards monopolies since early times, especially those which were, in effect, at the unfettered discretion of the Crown. This culminated in the 1624 Statute of Monopolies which had the general aim of preventing Crown monopolies. Section 6, however, stated:

> Provided also (and be it declared and enacted) that any declaration before mentioned shall not extend to any letters patent and grants of privilege for the term of fourteen years or under, hereafter to be made, of the sole working or making of any manner of new manufacture within this realm, to the true and first inventor and inventors of such manufactures which others at the time of making such letters patent and grants shall not use, so as also they be not contrary to the law or mischievous to the state, by raising prices of commodities at home, or hurt of trade, or generally inconvenient.

10.5   This provides an exception to the rule, and then stipulates an exception to the exception. The exception to the rule that Crown monopolies should not be granted is the proviso that the 'true and first inventor' of 'any manner of new manufacture' could receive a 14-year-long privilege over their invention, but the exception to this is that this monopoly should not be abusive or abused in ways contrary to law, state interests, trade and economic interests, or indeed, if it were 'generally inconvenient'.

 Discussion point   For answer guidance visit **www.oup.com/uk/brown5e.**

Why do you think that a period of 14 years was chosen, as opposed to 13 or 15, or some other figure?

---

[1]   *Gowers Review of Intellectual Property* (HM Treasury, 2006) (hereafter 'Gowers Review'), para 1.13.
[2]   See CM Belfanti, 'Guilds, patents and the circulation of technical knowledge: northern Italy during the early modern age' (2004) 45 Technology and Culture 569.
[3]   (1602) 77 ER 1131.

10.6   We see, then, elements in the early history of patents which we can still recognise in our modern system. These are:

- the patent system as a mechanism to encourage innovation;
- the notion of social contract between state and patentee, with corresponding obligations on both sides;
- the centrality of monopoly to the regulation of that contract;
- the desire for a balance of interests as between society and the patentee;
- the idea that the monopoly should rightly go to the inventor of the new creation.

10.7   Other matters have changed. The law in the UK no longer talks of 'manner of new manufacture'.[4] We thus have to look elsewhere for some guidance on what constitutes an invention.[5] Patents are now granted for a maximum of 20 years, although 'in the UK typically fewer than 50 per cent of patents are renewed beyond the tenth year'.[6] The search for a just balance is, however, a constant.

10.8   It is important to note that the grant of patents remained discretionary under the Statute of Monopolies of 1624. It was not until the 19th century that procedural form and a degree of certainty of process was introduced to the British patent system. The Patent Office was not established until 1852,[7] and it did not begin thorough examination of patent applications, in the sense of a proper scrutiny of the existing art, until 1905.[8] Prior to this it was sufficient merely to lodge a specification—a description of the invention—with the Patent Office to obtain protection.[9] Reforms brought about by the Patents, Designs and Trade Marks Act 1883 introduced a more robust procedure for examining applications, but even then it was largely a matter of checking for deficiencies in the formalities of an application and for insufficiency in the description of the invention itself.[10]

10.9   There were certain adverse social consequences of such lax procedures. It meant, for example, that patents of dubious or no worth could be obtained relatively easily and then waved over competitors as a threat; it also generated considerable uncertainty as to where the boundaries of legitimate trading lay. Movements in various European countries took up against the patent system around this time,[11] and the Dutch actually abolished their system in the period 1869 to 1912. In the UK, many trade organisations railed against patents in the 18th and 19th centuries, and bodies such as the Royal Society of Arts lobbied governments against the worst excesses of patent monopolies.[12] Indeed, the Society created an alternative scheme to the patent system in an attempt to achieve the same social ends but without the restrictions that monopolies can bring. The Society offered cash *premiums* for innovations in certain areas, and published *Lists* advertising these widely. The Lists set questions or problems requiring resolution, thereby providing a partly directed policy of innovation for British society. Importantly, from 1765, no person was to be considered as a candidate for a premium if they had previously obtained a patent for the invention for which the premium was offered. The premium acted as an incentive to innovators to disclose their inventions early and to allow others to build on their expertise. No monopoly over the invention was given.

---

[4] The laws in the United States, Canada, Australia, and New Zealand still refer to this concept in some form or another, displaying their colonial roots.

[5] The UK law changed with the passing of the Patents Act 1977, which brought the UK into line with the European Patent Convention 1973.

[6] See I Hargreaves, *Digital Opportunity: A Review of Intellectual Property and Growth* (2011) ('the Hargreaves Review', para 6.9, 53. For a worldwide perspective, see World Intellectual Property Organization (WIPO), *World Intellectual Property Indicators* (2014).

[7] Patent Law Amendment Act 1852. Initially there existed Commissioners who were replaced by the Office itself in 1883. The Office is currently located in Newport, Gwent but its original home was in Southampton Buildings, London, where it shared space with the Secretaries of Bankrupts and Lunatics!

[8] As a result of the Patents Act 1902.   [9] This system was introduced by the Patent Law Amendment Act 1852.

[10] Interestingly, this reflects many utility models systems which exist elsewhere in Europe, see paras 10.75ff.

[11] Various countries have gone without patent systems at one time or another, see HC Wegner, *Patent Harmonisation* (1993) at 17, and E Schiff, *Industrialization without National Patents: The Netherlands, 1869–1912, Switzerland, 1850–1907* (1971).

[12] Royal Society for the Encouragement of Arts, Manufactures and Commerce: www.thersa.org. The Society itself points out that in many ways the broad aim of the Society is not entirely dissimilar to that of the patent system.

Discussion point For answer guidance visit **www.oup.com/uk/brown5e**.

What are the advantages of the premium system compared to the patent system? Equally, can you think of any disadvantages?

10.10 The premium system did not survive, but the Royal Society of Arts continues its struggle against inappropriate monopolies. A contemporary example of this is the Adelphi Charter.[13] This instrument was drawn up by a distinguished group of interested individuals and parties concerned about the ever-expanding nature of IPRs and the possible consequences for the public domain of their aggressive enforcement. The Charter calls on governments and other bodies to adopt new strategies for thinking about, and protecting, intellectual property and the public interest. It consists of nine statements of principle which could be taken to guide intellectual property policy in the future in ways that might result in the striking of a different balance of interests to that which exists today. Three of the principles give a flavour of the tone of the document:

(1) Laws regulating intellectual property must serve as means of achieving creative, social and economic ends and not as ends in themselves ...

(3) The public interest requires a balance between the public domain and private rights. It also requires a balance between the free competition that is essential for economic vitality and the monopoly rights granted by intellectual property laws ..., and ...

(9) There must be an automatic presumption against creating new areas of intellectual property protection, extending existing privileges or extending the duration of rights.

10.11 The establishment of a patent registration system was a move to create a gate-keeping device. Such a system provides a relatively clear indication of thresholds that have to be met in order for patent protection to be granted; that is, that the invention must be new, involve an inventive step, and be capable of industrial application. It also serves to ensure that the obligation of the applicant to disclose the invention in a way that furthers the public interest is fully discharged.[14] Moreover, and just as importantly, it is a mechanism for weeding out innovations that have been deemed not to be inventions, such as discoveries, or which are to be excluded on a number of policy grounds, for example that they offend against common decency or morality. We should be very clear, therefore, that the process of examining a patent application is not some technical box-ticking exercise. Indeed, the examination of a patent application involves the assessment of a plethora of policy considerations which are designed to reflect the policy objectives of the patent system itself. How well this is achieved is another question.

Internationalisation of patent protection

10.12 We have already seen in the context of copyright and designs that IPRs started their life as creatures of national territorial effect only, meaning that protection was only afforded to innovators in their own country. The same was true, and remains true, of patents. But patents have always had an international dimension. From earliest times, part of the reason for granting a monopoly to a national was for fear that foreigners might otherwise dominate a domestic market. By the same token, as we have seen, the Venetian Republic used its own system of encouraging innovation to attract those from outside the Republic to bring new crafts and methods of manufacture to the city. Indeed, the prospect of international trade has been inherently bound up with the development of patent protection over the years. This was particularly

---

[13] Royal Society of Arts at www.eurim.org.uk/activities/ipr/0510rsacharter.pdf.

[14] This was one of the major criticisms of the system during the pre-registration period, see generally on this period B Sherman and L Bently, *The Making of Modern Intellectual Property Law* (1999), 101–10.

acute in the 19th century with the advent of the Industrial Revolution and at a time when various European patent systems were developing along similar lines and cross-jurisdictional influence was common. The vagaries of international trade meant that there was a growing urgency to ensure that IP was recognised and mutually protected across national boundaries for the benefit of all. Thus, just as we had the emergence of the Berne Convention in respect of copyright in 1886 (see Chapter 4), so too the international community (or much of it) foresaw an unmet need for an instrument to protect other forms of intellectual property, specifically patents, but far more broadly and crudely, *industrial property*.[15] In this way the Paris Convention of 1883 was born,[16] obliging signatory states to provide appropriate protection for the range of interests subsumed under the rubric of 'Industrial Property', being 'patents, utility models, industrial designs, trade marks, service marks, trade names, indications of source or appellations of origin, and the repression of unfair competition'.[17] This Convention says nothing specific about the substantive elements of patent law for its signatory countries—beyond the obligation to provide protection—but it did bring about various important reforms.

The *main features* of the Paris Convention perform, in numerous ways, similar functions as the Berne Convention does for copyright. In other ways, the Paris Convention distinguishes industrial property as a class apart from copyright and its related rights. Thus:

- The principle of *national treatment* was established in the Paris Convention, ensuring that each signatory state will afford the same rights to foreigners of other signatory states as to its own nationals (Art 2). Nationals of non-contracting states are also entitled to national treatment under the Convention if they are domiciled in a contracting state or if they have a 'real and effective industrial or commercial establishment' in a contracting state (Art 3).

- An applicant enjoys a *12-month right of priority from the date of first filing of a patent in a signatory country* (Art 4). This means that no subsequent filing of related applications in other countries within this period will be invalidated by the earlier filing, nor will any publication or use of the invention affect patentability. It also means that the novelty of all such applications will be tested by reference to the period before the first filing. We discuss the significance of this in paras 11.10ff.

- *National patents remain independent of each other*, therefore the granting of a patent in one contracting state does not oblige the other contracting states to grant a patent; a patent cannot be refused, annulled, or terminated in any contracting state on the ground that it has been refused or annulled or has terminated in any other contracting state (Art 4*bis*).

- *The focus is on the inventor* who has the right to be named as such in the patent (Art 4*ter*). The primary right holder, in the first instance, is the inventor. While this may be varied by contract or by the existence of an employer/employee relationship, such modifications to the general rule are left to domestic laws.

10.13   The Paris Convention remains of central significance in the protection of patents, and it is allied to the more recent Trade-Related Aspects of Intellectual Property Rights (TRIPS) Agreement 1994, see paras 10.45–10.48, in that a signatory state to the latter instrument must also comply with the core provisions of the Paris Convention, notably Articles 1–12 and 19.[18]

---

[15] Paris Convention for the Protection of Industrial Property (1883), revised at Brussels on 14 December 1900, at Washington on 2 June 1911, at The Hague on 6 November 1925, at London on 2 June 1934, at Lisbon on 31 October 1958, and at Stockholm on 14 July 1967, and as amended on 28 September 1979.

[16] There are currently 177 contracting parties to the Convention (October 2018).   [17] Paris Convention, Art 1(2).

[18] Agreement on Trade-Related Aspects of Intellectual Property Rights (1994), Art 2.

> **Key points on the early history**
>
> - Contemporary patent law began as a system of grace and favour, but a central feature from early on has been the idea of the patent as a form of 'social contract' with obligations on both sides.
>
> - In return for patent protection, then, a patentee must make the invention public.
>
> - The monopolistic effects of patents have always been viewed with suspicion, and attempts to minimise these include limiting the duration of a patent (currently to 20 years in most cases).
>
> - In the 19th century, and throughout the 20th century, the process of internationalisation of patent law has gathered pace, making it today one of the most harmonised areas of law, at least in terms of substantive law.

Rationales of patent protection

10.14   There is no single rationale for the patent system—indeed, some claim that it makes little sense at all. But its 400-year-long history speaks to the fact that it must be achieving some useful purpose(s), and a 2012 World Intellectual Property Organization (WIPO) report on patenting activity worldwide reveals that 2011 was the first year in which patent filings exceeded an annual rate of two million and that in the same year China overtook the United States as the largest patent office in the world.[19] Internationalisation of patent filing had grown in 2017; 253,500 were filed using the international system, an increase of 4.5 per cent on 2016. 56,624 were filed from the United States and 48,882 from China. This, in turn, is linked to a marked rise in the use of the international application mechanism as a conduit to foreign markets.[20] Patents are, it would seem, a big success worldwide.

10.15   There has, however, always been a need to justify the patent system. Its existence is not self-evidently in the public good and its approach of offering a market monopoly is not manifestly the best means to strike a balance of potentially competing interests. The interests at stake include those of inventors, their competitors, consumers, researchers, and the state itself. As we have seen, a patent is often described as a form of social contract between the patentee and the state, whereby the award of a patent monopoly is given in return for public disclosure of the invention. This reveals an irony in the way that the patent system operates: an exclusionary private property right is given in return for public dissemination of the details of the invention. Why so?

10.16   Various rationales for patents have been advanced over the years, and it is probably the case that each has held sway at one time or another in the development of patent law policy. The idea of the patent as a *reward* for inventive activity is difficult to sustain, however, because the need for a reward does not require that a monopoly be given. Rewards can take many forms, such as prizes or one-off payments, without any risk of adverse effects on the market.[21] Rather, the most commonly advanced rationale for the social contract approach is the *incentive* function that it is thought to represent. This is the view that the prospect of what is often termed a monopoly is so attractive that it will encourage innovation and that it represents the best means to secure adequate returns for intellectual endeavour; moreover, the public disclosure requirement acts as a further spur to others to invent around a particular invention and to receive their own protection. This rationale rests, however, on certain assumptions. For example, it assumes that the value of innovative activity outweighs increased costs to consumers, and that any monopolies granted will not be used to block,

---

[19] WIPO, *World Intellectual Property Indicators* (2012), 6, www.wipo.int/edocs/pubdocs/en/intproperty/941/wipo_pub_941_2012.pdf.

[20] This was established by the Patent Cooperation Treaty (PCT) 1970 (see paras 10.39–10.40). International applications through the PCT saw an 11 per cent growth in 2011 and the fastest since 2005; see WIPO, *World Intellectual Property Indicators* (n 19). See also G Scellato et al, 'Study on the Quality of the Patent System in Europe' (2011) https://ris.utwente.nl/ws/portalfiles/portal/5146011/PDF_study_on_the_quality_of_the_patent_system_en.pdf. For 2017 figures, see www.wipo.int/publications/en/details.jsp?id=4234.

[21] EC Hettinger, 'Justifying Intellectual Property' (1989) 18 Philosophy and Public Affairs 31–52.

rather than encourage, development in a particular field.[22] It also presupposes that citizens will be in a position to pay higher costs and that the necessary infrastructures are in place to support further innovation. Neither of these last two assumptions stands for many developing countries, calling into question the rationale and value of the patent system to those countries. A World Bank publication has indicated that patent rights over high-technology products are of most value in large, middle-income, developing countries where imitation of an invention is most likely, while export decisions to poorer countries often do not depend on the existence of IPRs in those countries, since the threat of imitation is lower because of lack of infrastructure.[23] In the UK, political priority has been accorded to IP. The Intellectual Property Act 2014 provides for the Secretary of State to report to Parliament on their view of how IP legislation has contributed to innovation and economic growth.[24] This led, for example, to the 2016 'Promoting Innovation and Growth' report, in which the then Minister of State for Energy and Intellectual Property stated that the Government 'recognises the importance of IP, expressed through our manifesto commitments to make the UK the best place to patent, innovate and grow a business'.[25] The UK IPO also commissions valuable research on patents, including on the patenting landscape across particular technologies.[26] It should be borne in mind, however, that patents are only one part of a wider landscape of encouraging innovation. For example, initiatives based in tax[27] and the activities of the UK government's agency Innovate UK (including in respect of funding and competitions) are also highly relevant.[28]

10.17   The UK has also seen recognition, notably in the Hargreaves report, of problems which can arise from patents, notably patent thickets when there are many patents in a particular area and numerous licences may be required to actually manufacture products. The report called for a focus in patent fee structures regarding innovation and growth goals, and for consideration to be given to 'encourag[ing] patentees to assess more carefully the value of maintaining lower value patents, so reducing the density of patent thickets'.[29] The UK IPO produced a 2011 report[30] showing the full complexity of the problem and how the motivations for and effects of patent practices vary significantly between sectors. It considered that solutions will come from looking both at 'technology type' and 'stage of development'.[31] In 2013, a report prepared for the UK IPO concluded, after a focus on empirical analysis, that there was a reluctance to enter areas where there are patent thickets.[32] Revised fee structures could only address the issue of the existence or possible existence of patent rights: for those who have them, can afford them, and can afford to use them as a threat, the advantages of creating thickets remain. And fee changes will do nothing to address the litigation threat culture that largely drives the uncertainties that are at the heart of the problem.

---

[22] A survey funded by the European Commission found that about one-third of European patents are not used for any commercial or industrial purposes, and that one-half of these are used as 'blocking' patents, ie to prevent competitors from using the protected technology, see European Commission, 'Study on Evaluating the Knowledge Economy: What are Patents Actually Worth? The Value of Patents for Today's Economy and Society', Final Report, 23 July 2006, 10. See also I Troy and R Werle, *Uncertainty and the Market for Patents* (2008). This issue is also the focus of *The Economist* (August 2015).

[23] C Fink and CA Primo Braga, 'How stronger protection of intellectual property rights affects international trade flows' in C Fink and KE Maskus (eds), *Intellectual Property and Development: Lessons from Recent Economic Research* (2005). See also World Bank, *Global Economic Prospects 2008: Technology Diffusion in the Developing World* (2008).

[24] Intellectual Property Act 2014, s 21.

[25] See https://assets.publishing.service.gov.uk/government/uploads/system/uploads/attachment_data/file/552791/innovation-and-growth-report-sept-15-16.pdf, p2.

[26] See UK IPO, 'Eight Great Technologies' (2014) https://assets.publishing.service.gov.uk/government/uploads/system/uploads/attachment_data/file/360986/Eight_Great_Technologies.pdf.

[27] See Corporation Tax Patent Box Guidance Note, www.gov.uk/guidance/corporation-tax-the-patent-box. This led to disagreements with Germany and agreement as to a new approach was reached in late 2014: www.gov.uk/government/uploads/system/uploads/attachment_data/file/373135/GERMANY_UK_STATEMENT.pdf.

[28] See the website at www.gov.uk/government/organisations/innovate-uk.

[29] Hargreaves Review, Recommendation 6, 63.

[30] HM Government, Government Response to the Hargreaves Review of Intellectual Property and Growth (2011), 8.

[31] IPO, *Patent Thickets* (2011).

[32] B Hall et al, 'A study of patent thickets' (2013) at www.gov.uk/government/publications/a-study-of-patent-thickets.

10.18   The *public disclosure* requirement in patent law should not be underestimated. It is an essential feature of the arrangement between the patentee and the state, and a patent can be struck down on grounds of *insufficiency* if adequate disclosure is not made in a patent application.[33] Adequate disclosure requires that the essential features of the invention are made public and that the means to make or reproduce the invention are revealed in a way that would enable a person skilled in the particular field ('the art') to do so.[34] The European Patent Office (EPO) claims that its searchable patent databases now provide the most efficient, detailed, and up-to-date source of information in over 50 technical fields. The stringent disclosure requirements mean that 70 per cent of information contained in patents is not available anywhere else.[35] This can, of course, be a disincentive to apply for a patent, leading to innovators choosing rather to rely on trade secret protection, discussed in Chapter 17.

10.19   From a more positive perspective, it has been argued that patents perform a *signalling* function, that is, indicating the innovative and productive capacity of the patent holder and signalling that they may be a sound investment for the future.[36] Patent portfolios are certainly a key consideration for venture capitalists.[37]

10.20   *Human rights discourse* has become more prevalent in recent years both in support of, and against, the existence and exercise of IPRs. On the one hand, it is important to note that the 1948 Universal Declaration of Human Rights provides that 'Everyone has the right to the protection of the moral and material interests resulting from any scientific, literary or artistic production of which he is the author',[38] suggesting that individual creators have a human rights claim to IP. On the other hand, the UN Sub-Commission on Human Rights has pointed to the potential inherent conflict which IPRs can generate *face-à-face* other economic, social, or cultural rights, considering there to be an actual conflict as a result of how states had implemented TRIPS, and rights other than IP should trump in any case of conflict.[39] But not everyone sees these two regimes as in inherent conflict.[40] Few rights, even human rights, are absolute. Limitations can be placed on the exercise of rights in an attempt either to protect the rights and freedoms of others or to achieve an overall equitable balance of interests. In contemporary policy terms, it is clear that *balance* is the watchword of the day. The language of human rights might help us to frame the discussion, but it is unlikely to provide any universal solution.[41]

10.21   Human rights perspectives have not only had the effect of opening up dialogue about the nature of IPRs, but they have also led to a greater appreciation of relationships between the intellectual property world and other social realms. An example of this is the potential *regulation* function of the patent system. Just as the grant of a patent might encourage innovation, so it might follow that the denial of a patent might dissuade certain forms of innovation. In this sense, the patent system could be seen as a means to regulate or control undesirable inventions. Alternatively, undesirable uses of the power which a patent provides might also be regulated through the patent system, for example through greater use of compulsory licences

---

[33] Patents Act 1977, ss 14(3) and 72(1)—see further paras 12.72–12.86.

[34] See generally *Kirin-Amgen v Hoechst Marion Roussel (No 2)* [2005] RPC 9. See further discussion in paras 12.65ff.

[35] See the Espacenet database at http://worldwide.espacenet.com and EPO, *Global Patent Data Coverage* (2011).

[36] Commission on Intellectual Property Rights, Innovation and Public Health, *Public Health, Innovation and Intellectual Property Rights* (2006), 21, www.who.int/intellectualproperty/documents/thereport/ENPublicHealthReport.pdf.

[37] See, eg, consideration by WIPO at www.wipo.int/sme/en/documents/venture_capital_investments_fulltext.html. See also David A McGrory 'A Private Institutional Investment Perspective' in Abbe EL Brown (ed), *Environmental Technologies, Intellectual Property and Climate Change: Accessing, Obtaining and Protecting* (2013).

[38] UN General Assembly Resolution 217A(III), UN Doc A/810, at 71, Art 27(2).

[39] See, eg, UN High Commissioner for Human Rights, Sub-Commission on Human Rights, Intellectual Property Rights and Human Rights, Resolution 2000/7, 17 August 2000, via www.aaas.org/sites/default/files/SRHRL/PDF/IHRDArticle15/E-CN_4-SUB_2-RES-2000-7_Eng.pdf. This is an area of ongoing activity; see the appointment of UN Special Rapporteurs and the preparation of reports, notably in 2012 A/HRC/20/26 and in 2015 A/70/279.

[40] See HL MacQueen, 'Towards utopia or irreconcilable tensions? Thoughts on intellectual property, human rights and competition law' (2005) 2(4) SCRIPTed 452–66 and L Helfer, 'Human rights and intellectual property: conflict or co-existence?' (2003) 5 Minnesota Intellectual Property Review 47.

[41] PK Yu, 'Reconceptualizing intellectual property interests in a human rights framework' (2007) University of California Davis Law Rev 1039–149.

or more generous interpretations of patent defences. Little work has been done to date on the interface between patent and regulation regimes,[42] but a few cautious comments can be offered here. First, the denial of a patent in no way prohibits innovation, it merely removes an incentive. Plenty of innovative behaviour carries on without the potential of a patent, and there is no guarantee that the denial of protection will have the desired dissuasive effect. The *efficiency* of this alleged regulatory function is therefore open to question. Secondly, the assessment of which inventions are undesirable is a complex matter, involving ethical and moral considerations which may be beyond the competence of a patent office examiner. Moreover, given the nature of the patent system in requiring secrecy about an invention prior to applying for a patent, there will have been little or no opportunity for broader social debate about an invention, thereby raising questions about the *legitimacy* of quasi-regulatory decisions about the value, or otherwise, of a particular invention. Notwithstanding, there has been increased reliance on the exclusions provisions in patent law in recent years, especially in the field of biotechnological inventions,[43] implying that the rationale of the patent system may, once again, be changing.[44]

10.22   It matters very much which of these rationales is promoted over any other in the development and implementation of patent policy. A public interest mandate will require evidence that the dual aims of dissemination of knowledge and increased innovation can be achieved before there is any strengthening of IP rights, or indeed, the introduction of new rights. A focus on the individual inventor's claims would, however, promote new and more robust forms of protection.

 Exercise

Consider which of these, or other, rationales are operating as you read more about the different regimes and features of patent law. Are we always striking the right balance? And read this report from the UK IPO (2018): 'When do firms not use patents and trademarks to protect valuable innovations?' https://assets.publishing.service.gov.uk/government/uploads/system/uploads/attachment_data/file/744844/SIPU.pdf. What impact does this have on your view of the relevance of the rationales?

The European dimension

10.23   Easily the most far-reaching reforms of the 20th century for UK patent law came in the period of 'Europeanisation', which produced the European Patent Convention (EPC, 1973, as amended) after long negotiations throughout the 1960s. The Patents Act 1977 incorporated these reforms into domestic law,[45] and in doing so swept away many of the vestiges of the uniquely British regime that had gone before.[46] We have already seen, for example, that the law no longer requires proof of 'a manner of manufacture', although the reforming measures did not provide us with a replacement definition of an invention. It is now assumed that if an applicant clears the hurdles of patentability then it has produced an 'invention'.[47]

---

[42] See GT Laurie, 'Patents, patients and consent: exploring the interface between regulation and innovation regimes' in H Somsen (ed), *The Regulatory Challenge of Biotechnology* (2007).

[43] Gowers Review, para 2.30 reported that 4,382 out of the 23,688 known human genes had been patented.

[44] cf the collective reply of German patent attorneys to the European Commission's survey on IP policy, n 22, wherein they opined (at 10) that 'there is no reason for a political debate on principles concerning patent protection in view of ethical behaviour, protection of the environment, health protection, or freedom of information'.

[45] Relevant laws in the 20th century were the Patents Acts of 1902 and 1949. European laws had, nonetheless, been approximating over the years and in many respects patent laws were very similar.

[46] Consider the early 20th-century proposals for a 'British Empire patent', see C Wadlow, 'The British Empire patent 1901–1923: the "global patent" that never was' [2006] IPQ 311.

[47] cf the discussion on the need for an 'invention' in *Biogen v Medeva* [1997] RPC 1, especially per Lord Mustill at 31, where the door was not firmly closed on the issue but neither their Lordships nor counsel could think of a pertinent example.

10.35   Whatever happens in the EU, the issue of language remains an important and difficult issue. Within the EPC system it has been dealt with by the provisions of the *London Agreement* from 2000.[79]

This Agreement allows signatory parties that share an official language with the EPO to waive, wholly or partially, the translation requirement under the EPC (Art 65) that a patent be filed in their national language. Countries that do not share a language with the EPO can also waive this requirement, as long as the patent has been granted in an official EPO language. The Agreement came into force in May 2008 when France ratified the Agreement. This Agreement can reduce the costs of patenting in Europe up to 45 per cent when the countries designated by the patentee have signed up to the Agreement. The approximate cost of the translation of an average length patent into one other language lies around €1,100. This results in €5,500 for five translations, which is the average number of foreign states for which protection is sought and around €40,000 for the translations which you would need to obtain patent coverage in all 38 EPC countries under the current regime.

10.36   We can sum up the European scene as follows:

European Patent Organisation
- European Patent Convention (2000)
- 38 signatory countries
- European Patent Office—grants 'European' patents for designated countries—enforced domestically
- No appeal body from signatory states
- Opposition proceedings to object to patent grant on specified grounds

European Union
- Programme of harmonising measures
- 28 members
- Unitary Patent Package pending—this will create one right enforceable throughout the Union with a single dispute settlement body   the Unitary Patent Court
- Referral possible from Unitary Patent Court to the Court of Justice in same way as from national courts

The international dimension

10.37   WIPO and the World Trade Organization (WTO) are each responsible for administering important treaties on patent protection at the international level. These perform a harmonising or approximating function for both formal and substantive aspects of patent law.

WIPO: streamlining patents

10.38   Two instruments are currently administered by WIPO which considerably facilitates the process of applying for a patent.

10.39   The *Patent Cooperation Treaty* (1970, as amended) (PCT) is another product of fervent patent reform emerging from the 1960s, this time at the initiative of the United States.[80] The Treaty is designed to facilitate the process when an applicant is applying for patents simultaneously in numerous jurisdictions worldwide.[81] It is *not* a granting procedure and merely provides a conduit whereby a single application can be processed and searched by a qualified international body before being sent to national or regional intellectual property offices for full consideration. Anyone who is a national or resident of a contracting

---

[79] European Patent Organisation, Agreement dated 17 October 2000 on the application of Art 65, EPC (London Agreement) (2001) 12 OJEPO 549. An informative guide has been produced by the EPO at www.epo.org/law-practice/legal-texts/london-agreement.html.

[80] You can read the current text of the PCT at www.wipo.int/pct/en/texts/articles/atoc.htm.

[81] Full details are available at www.wipo.int/pct/en.

[82] There were 152 contracting states to the PCT as of October 2018. See www.wipo.int/treaties/en/ShowResults.jsp?lang= en&treaty_id=6.

state[82] can file a single international patent application, either in his national office, or at the EPO if the state is also a signatory to the EPC, or at the International Bureau of WIPO in Geneva.[83] This single application is then subject to an 'international search' from which an international research report is prepared. This contains details of published documents that might cause problems for an invention in terms of its patentability; that is, because they may demonstrate that the invention is not 'new' (see paras 11.8ff). It is also possible for applicants to request an international preliminary examination which results in a non-binding written opinion on patentability.[84] If an applicant does not withdraw their application at this point, the report becomes a public document,[85] although the written opinion does not.

10.40   The application is then sent for consideration to national or regional offices as designated by the applicant.[86] While the results of the international search do not guarantee that an invention will be 'novel' for all purposes in the designated countries, it does provide the applicant with 'reasonable probability' of receiving patent protection, according to WIPO. Moreover, the procedure not only greatly limits costs, but it can also speed up the process for obtaining patent protection, especially in countries which do not have adequate search facilities. Applicants also have time within the PCT process—up to 18 months—to amend their application before proceeding to designated foreign offices, and, indeed, to decide whether to proceed at all, weighing up the various considerations such as appointing local patent agents, preparing translations, and paying national fees. It is also claimed that this process furthers the public interest in that the systematic publication of international reports—carried out by approved authorities[87]—means that third parties are better placed to assess the patentability of any given invention and to assess the state of the art at any given time. The importance of the quality of searches is crucial to the success and efficiency of any patent system.[88] The success of the PCT is demonstrated by the fact that it had received one million applications from around the world by the end of 2004 and exceeded two million by the end of 2011.[89]

10.41   WIPO established the *Standing Committee on the Law of Patents* in 1998 with a remit to take debate and international patent reform forward into the 21st century. The Committee's membership is broad, including all members of WIPO itself as well as non-members, and various intergovernmental and non-governmental agencies. It aims to contribute both to formal and substantive reforms of patent law, and in this regard has had two core projects:

- Patent Law Treaty (2000). This treaty harmonises patent procedures and formalities for filing, obtaining, and maintaining patent protection. It entered into force on 28 April 2005 and had been ratified by 40 contracting parties as of October 2018. This includes the UK, where it entered into force on 22 March 2006, which resulted in some changes to domestic law.[90]

- Substantive Patent Law Treaty (2001–present). This draft treaty aimed to harmonise the substantive elements of patent law, such as novelty, inventive step/non-obviousness, and industrial applicability/

---

[83] See further WIPO, *History of the PCT Regulations (June 19, 1970–July 1, 2014)*, www.wipo.int/pct/en/texts/pdf/pct_regulations_history.pdf.

[84] PCT, Ch II.   [85] This is published by the International Bureau.

[86] An application through PCT automatically constitutes an election of all contracting states in the first instance, but in reality, applicants are selective about the countries they wish to target. See Rule 53.7 of the Regulations under the PCT (1 July 2018), www.wipo.int/export/sites/www/pct/en/texts/pdf/pct_regs.pdf.

[87] International searches are carried out by approved International Searching Authorities (PCT, Art 16) and there also exist International Preliminary Examination Authorities (PCT, Art 32). Regulations under the PCT impose minimum requirements on authorities appointed by the PCT Union (Rule 36 and Rule 63).

[88] This point was made very clearly by industry and patent attorneys alike in the 2006 public consultation on the future of the patent system in Europe carried out by the European Commission (n 22).

[89] WIPO, *PCT Yearly Review: The International Patent System* (2012), 10.

[90] The UK passed the Regulatory Reform (Patents) Order 2004 to make the necessary changes to domestic law.

utility, interpretation of claims, and disclosure,[91] with a view to streamlining application documentation, greater legal certainty on an international level, and, as always, a reduction in costs. Proposals that its scope be extended[92] met with challenge from Brazil[93] on behalf of the Group of Friends of Development.[94] These recalled that WIPO has undertaken to develop a proposal to establish a development agenda for the organisation and requested that the continuation of the negotiations of the Treaty be on the basis of the draft treaty as a whole, including all these elements and also questions of provisions on the transfer of technology, anti-competitive practices, and the safeguarding of public interest flexibilities to ensure that appropriate balance is brought to the content of the instrument. Work on this treaty stalled in 2006.

10.42   The *Patent Law Treaty* (2000), as indicated, mandates a maximum number of formal requirements that can be imposed on patent applications, although individual contracting parties can be more generous if they wish.[95] Important features that have been harmonised include the standardisation of requirements to obtain a filing date: (1) an indication that the elements received by the Office are intended to be an application for a patent for an invention; (2) indications that would allow the Office to identify or to contact the applicant (or both); (3) a part which appears to be a description of the invention (this part can be filed in any language or could even merely be a drawing).[96]

10.43   Signatories include the United States, the European Patent Organisation, and Japan. Other countries representing the remaining members of the top five patent offices of the world[97]—China, South Korea—will doubtless follow suit. The effect of the Patent Law Treaty therefore will be near-global harmonisation of procedures for obtaining patent protection.

10.44   At the time of writing in 2018, the next meeting (December 2018) will explore exceptions and limitations, co-operation between national offices, patents and health—particularly regarding databases, confidentiality of communication with advisers, and technology transfer.[98]

WTO: the TRIPS Agreement (1994)

10.45   We have discussed the nature of the TRIPS Agreement in Chapter 1 and elsewhere in the book, thus far.[99] You will recall that the TRIPS Agreement was concluded in 1994 as part of the Uruguay Round of the General Agreement on Tariffs and Trade (GATT). It is administered by the WTO and parties to the Agreement are subject to the WTO's dispute settlement system.[100] This entails the possible imposition of

---

[91]   See www.wipo.int/patent-law/en/draft_splt.htm. This variation in terminology reflects current different approaches to the criteria for patentability around the globe. Thus, while European patent law talks of 'inventive step' and 'industrial applicability', US law employs the terms 'non-obviousness' and 'utility'. This is not merely a question of semantics because the terms are interpreted quite differently, meaning that access to patent protection is variable (it is generally far easier in the United States). Note, that in TRIPS, Art 27(1)—which requires 'patents shall be available for any inventions, whether products or processes, in all fields of technology, provided that they are new, involve an inventive step and are capable of industrial application'—there is a caveat which provides: 'For the purposes of this Art, the terms "inventive step" and "capable of industrial application" may be deemed by a Member to be synonymous with the terms "non-obvious" and "useful" respectively.'

[92]   WIPO, Standing Committee on the Law of Patents, Eleventh Session, Geneva, 1 and 2 June 2005 (SCP/11/3), www.wipo.int/edocs/mdocs/scp/en/scp_11/scp_11_3.pdf.

[93]   WIPO, Standing Committee on the Law of Patents, Statement Received from Brazil, Eleventh Session, Geneva, 1 and 2 June 2005 (SCP/11/4), www.wipo.int/edocs/mdocs/scp/en/scp_11/scp_11_4.pdf.

[94]   The Group of Friends of Development consists of Argentina, Brazil, Bolivia, Cuba, Dominican Republic, Ecuador, Egypt, Iran, Kenya, Peru, Sierra Leone, South Africa, Tanzania, and Venezuela.

[95]   Patent Law Treaty, Art 2. The exception to this relates to Art 5 and mandatory requirements about obtaining a filing date.

[96]   Patent Law Treaty, Art 5(1), (2).

[97]   These five offices account for a large majority share of all patent applications. See WIPO, *World Intellectual Property Indicators* (n 19), 5.

[98]   www.wipo.int/patent-law/en/scp.htm and SCP/21/1 Prov.

[99]   See generally, D Matthews, *Globalising Intellectual Property Rights: The TRIPS Agreement* (2002).

[100]   See here for an account of the Dispute Settlement System: www.wto.org/english/thewto_e/whatis_e/tif_e/disp1_e.htm.

trade sanctions for non-compliance. The linking of obligations to protect intellectual property with the attractiveness of trade privileges available under GATT was a stroke of genius by those parties frustrated by the fact that many countries had not signed up to previous international instruments such as the Paris and Berne Conventions and were openly infringing intellectual property on an unprecedented scale. Many of these countries were, however, also developing countries desperate for increased trade to improve their economic circumstances. Few could resist the trade attractions of the Uruguay Round, and TRIPS was the bitter pill they had to swallow.

10.46   The implications for patent law from TRIPS are, first and foremost, that the agreement represents the first international measure to harmonise substantive patent provisions. Article 27(1) of TRIPS provides:

> Subject to the provisions of paragraphs 2 and 3, patents shall be available for any inventions, whether products or processes, in all fields of technology, provided that they are new, involve an inventive step and are capable of industrial application.

10.47   There are two points to note about this. First, it makes clear that there are three common criteria for patentability and, secondly, signatory states are obliged to make protection available for *any* inventions in *all* technological fields. This has required significant changes to law in numerous states which previously did not have a robust patent system or specifically excluded certain types of invention from protection, such as pharmaceuticals.[101]

10.48   TRIPS permits, but does not require, exclusions from patentability, providing in Article 27(2) and (3) that:

> 2. Members may exclude from patentability inventions, the prevention within their territory of the commercial exploitation of which is necessary to protect *ordre public* or morality, including to protect human, animal or plant life or health or to avoid serious prejudice to the environment, provided that such exclusion is not made merely because the exploitation is prohibited by their law.
> 3. Members may also exclude from patentability: (a) diagnostic, therapeutic and surgical methods for the treatment of humans or animals; (b) plants and animals other than micro-organisms, and essentially biological processes for the production of plants or animals other than non-biological and micro-biological processes. However, Members shall provide for the protection of plant varieties either by patents or by an effective *sui generis* system or by any combination thereof.

Note the judicious use of the term 'may' here. These are not mandatory exclusions and were, in fact, included largely at the behest of European states and the EU, which already have such provisions in their patent law (see para 11.87). There are no such exclusions in the United States, although a high number of countries have some form of morality exclusion in their law.

Patents and international development

10.49   Many discussions regarding TRIPS and its possible reform have been directly bound up with the morality of the Agreement itself. The current round of negotiations is part of the *Doha Development Agenda*, and dates back to the Fourth Ministerial Conference in Doha, Qatar in November 2001, with halting progress ever since. This resulted, inter alia, in the Doha Declaration, which serves as the template and mandate for further negotiations in a number of subjects central to improved international trade, one of which is the protection of IPRs. This stressed once more the importance of balance in achieving this protection, stating in Article 17 that the implementation and interpretation give to TRIPS must be in a manner 'supportive of public health, by promoting both access to existing medicines and research and development into new medicines'. Further articulation of this came in a separate instrument—the Declaration on the TRIPS Agreement and Public Health[102]—which stresses the need to recognise that the WTO and TRIPS are part of the wider global, social public health crisis affecting developing and least developed countries (LDCs), most particularly in terms of securing access to affordable medicines to treat conditions such as HIV/AIDS, malaria, and tuberculosis.

---

[101]   China and India are obvious examples.
[102]   14 November 2001: www.wto.org/english/thewto_e/minist_e/min01_e/mindecl_trips_e.htm.

10.50   All of this was prompted by an attempt by South Africa to address its own chronic public health problems through changes to patent law. The South African Medicines and Medical Devices Regulatory Authority Act 1998 allowed the Ministry of Health to 'determine that the rights with regard to any medicine under a patent granted in the Republic shall not extend to acts in respect of such medicine which has been put onto the market by the owner of the medicine, or with his or her consent' (Art 15C).[103] Inter alia, this would give the South African state the power to manufacture patented pharmaceuticals under compulsory licence and/or import cheaper generic drugs from abroad. The reaction by the pharmaceutical industry and the United States was immediate, with the latter imposing economic sanctions through the removal of preferential tariff treatments (making imports from the United States economically unviable). Pharma, for its part, filed a law suit against the law. The Act never saw the light of day. Yet the resulting public and activist outrage led to changes in approach and awareness in respect of IP and its wider impact.

10.51   The WTO Public Health Declaration introduced in para 10.49[104] agrees that TRIPS does not and should not prevent members from taking measures to protect public health, and that WTO members have the right to use, 'to the full', the flexible provisions found in the Agreement itself to support the right to public health and promote access to medicines for all. What are these flexible provisions? They are articulated in Article 5 of this Declaration and include the right of each member to grant compulsory licences on the grounds that they consider appropriate, and the freedom of each member to determine its own regime of exhaustion of rights. In other words, the same mechanisms as deployed by South Africa are available under TRIPS. There are, however, certain restrictions, most notably that the compulsory licence provisions in the 1994 Agreement are solely concerned with producing drugs for a domestic market. This causes an immediate problem for countries which do not have domestic manufacturing capacity, and means, potentially, that the LDCs, which may also experience the most severe public health crises, are the ones most disadvantaged under the law. They are, indeed, doubly disadvantaged because it would also mean that another country could not rely on the provisions to come to their aid since an *export* of drugs made under compulsory licence would be a violation of TRIPS. By the same token, a solution is not immediately apparent from the perspective of developed countries, which have a concern that too liberal an approach to compulsory licensing may result in their own markets being flooded. The Declaration instructed the TRIPS Council to pursue a solution[105] which was eventually reached in August 2003.[106]

10.52   The solution is effectively a form of waiver over the obligations of members under Article 31(f) of TRIPS.[107] This provides that any compulsory licensing system should be 'authorized predominantly for the supply of the domestic market of the Member authorizing such use'. The Council Decision allows an exporting member to waive these obligations when exporting to an 'eligible importing member', being any LDC member, and any other member that has made a notification to the Council for TRIPS of its intention to use the system as an importer.[108] The waiver operates to the extent *necessary* for the purposes of production of a pharmaceutical product(s) and its export. Further conditions include notification of specific needs

---

[103] This is effectively a use of the 'exhaustion principle' which we discuss further in Chapter 19.

[104] Declaration on the TRIPS Agreement and Public Health, 20 November 2001, Doc No WT/MIN(01)/DEC/2.

[105] Para 6 provides:

We recognize that WTO members with insufficient or no manufacturing capacities in the pharmaceutical sector could face difficulties in making effective use of compulsory licensing under the TRIPS Agreement. We instruct the Council for TRIPS to find an expeditious solution to this problem and to report to the General Council before the end of 2002.

[106] General Council Decision of 30 August 2003 on the Implementation of Paragraph 6 of the Doha Declaration on the TRIPS Agreement and Public Health: WT/L/540 and Corr.1, 1 September 2003.

[107] There are, in fact, three waivers: (1) exporting countries are not bound by the provisions of Art 31(f); (2) importing countries are not bound to pay reasonable remuneration to the patent holder (this is borne by the exporter); and (3) exporting restrictions are waived for developing and least developed countries which are members of a regional trade agreement, when at least half of the members are classed as least developed countries when the export decision is made.

[108] Paragraph 2. It is possible to notify that the system will only be used in a limited way, eg only in the case of a national emergency or other circumstances of extreme urgency or in cases of public non-commercial use. Indeed, some countries and trading blocs have notified that they will not be using the system as an importer to protect domestic markets. These include the United States, the UK, and many other European states.

for drugs and the tailoring of licence terms accordingly, labelling requirements to set these products apart from others in the market, and a public disclosure requirement, via the internet, informing of quantities and distinguishing features to be exported. The TRIPS Council plays a key role in the operation of this system: it is charged with receiving and administering all notifications and with producing an annual report on the system as a whole. This has, however, only been used once by Canada and Rwanda.[109]

10.53   Indeed, a 2006 Oxfam report claimed that little had changed in the first five years after the adoption of the Doha Declaration[110] and, indeed, little has changed since. This is partly because the provisions and protections of TRIPS can be circumvented in bilateral or regional agreements between countries when there is an imbalance of bargaining power and weaker states agree to so-called TRIPS-plus obligations discussed in Chapter 1—tying them further into IP protection—in return for economic or trade benefits. The United States relies heavily on such an approach. Oxfam has also called on poorer states to resist these moves and recommends that G8 countries provide the necessary technical, political, and economic support to allow poorer states to enact TRIPS safeguards.[111]

10.54   Work nonetheless continued at the WTO[112] and in 2017, TRIPS was amended. Any member country can now manufacture and export pharmaceutical products under compulsory licence for public health reasons. Changes will be required in domestic laws, and steps have been taken at EU level.[113] The Amendment was designed to reflect the terms of the original waiver as closely as possible because there are strong political reasons not to re-open the issues. But the amendment process still went slowly—it took 12 years for the necessary two-thirds of the WTO membership to accept the amendment. Other countries have until December 2019 to accept the amendment and until then will operate under the waiver.[114]

10.55   The Amendment[115] creates Article 31bis. This reiterates the core principle that it is lawful to produce pharmaceutical products under compulsory licence for export to countries lacking production capacity. A new annex goes on to specify further matters such as an obligation on an importing member to take 'reasonable measures' within their means to prevent re-exportation, and a duty on all members to ensure that effective legal means are in place to prevent the import of goods made under the scheme which have been unlawfully diverted to their market.[116] The annex specifies the terms for using the system and includes definitions, obligations of notification to TRIPS Council, and an ongoing duty of the Council to carry out annual reviews. Finally, an appendix to the annex lays out criteria to assess whether a country lacks manufacturing capacity such that it can rely upon the Amendment.

10.56   It should be further noted that an additional outcome of these ongoing negotiations is that LDCs have now until 2033 to provide patent protection for pharmaceuticals,[117] and the deadline for other IPRs was extended in 2013 to 2021.[118]

---

[109] See WTO dedicated webpage of notifications: www.wto.org/english/tratop_e/trips_e/public_health_e.htm.

[110] Oxfam International, *Patents v Patients: Five Years After the Doha Declaration* (2006), http://policy-practice.oxfam.org.uk/publications/patents-versus-patients-five-years-after-the-doha-declaration-114562.

[111] The White Paper, *Eliminating World Poverty: Making Globalisation Work for the Poor* pointed to the need for intellectual property regimes to work better for poor people. See http://webarchive.nationalarchives.gov.uk/+/http:/www.dfid.gov.uk/Documents/publications/whitepaper2000.pdf.

[112] The Sixth Ministerial Conference which took place in Hong Kong in December 2005 reaffirmed the importance of the 2003 Council Decision and endorsed the work of the Council on an Amendment of the TRIPS Agreement, Draft Ministerial Declaration, 18 December 2005, WT/MIN(05)/W/3/Rev 2.

[113] Regulation (EC) No 816/2006 of the European Parliament and of the Council of 17 May 2006 on compulsory licensing of patents relating to the manufacture of pharmaceutical products for export to countries with public health problems (2006) OJ EU, 9 June 2006, L157/1.

[114] See www.wto.org/english/tratop_e/trips_e/amendment_e.htm.

[115] General Council, Doc No WT/L/641, 8 December 2005, Amendment of the TRIPS Agreement, Decision of 6 December 2005.

[116] Other provisions include the prohibition on a patent holder receiving 'reasonable remuneration' from both an exporting and an importing state, the release of developing country members from Art 31(f) obligations when involved in a regional agreement with countries facing the same public health crisis, and the retention of existing TRIPS flexibilities.

[117] WTO TRIPS Council IP/C/73, 6 November 2015.

[118] WTO IP/C/64, 12 June 2013, extending deadline in Art 66(1) of TRIPS.

Discussion point   For answer guidance visit **www.oup.com/uk/brown5e**.

How much flexibility do the words 'to the extent necessary' in Article 31*bis* provide for those who would rely on this provision, or indeed, who would object to others relying on this provision?

10.57   Critics assessing the success of the Doha Declaration in 2006 have argued that it is largely a failure and indeed that the Doha Round should be brought to an end. It is suggested that the requirements of the system such as notification of specific type and quantity of drugs, labelling requirements, or the need to negotiate directly with the patent holder are too onerous;[119] that it is essentially a protectionist system—in that it allows countries to act as exporters while blocking access to their own markets—and thereby undermines the economies of scale for developing countries with manufacturing capacity but no access to high-income markets. That said, it is acknowledged that the problem is not simply with the WTO or its Agreements. The TRIPS Plus agreements often mean that developing countries are willing to give up reliance on the TRIPS provisions for other economic advantages, such as reduced trade barriers. A 2006 World Bank report on the economics of HIV/AIDS treatment in Thailand suggested that such concessions come at significant cost:[120] reliance on the compulsory licensing scheme could reduce the costs of second-line therapy by 90 per cent, cutting the Thai government future budgetary obligations by US$3.2 billion to 2025 and reducing by half the costs of life-years saved under its National Access to Antiretroviral Program for People Living with HIV/AIDS. Thailand issued a compulsory licence to manufacture a generic version of the HIV/AIDS drug Efavirenz in November 2006,[121] which has since been followed by several more compulsory licences for a number of different drugs.[122]

10.58   Other hurdles for developing countries and LDCs are that they are often ill-equipped to amend national laws to take full advantage of TRIPS flexibilities, and international bodies, such as UN agencies or the World Health Organization (WHO), are often under-resourced to provide the necessary technical support.

10.59   This said, the WHO has taken a strong interest in IP and public health—possibly as a direct result of the Doha Declaration and the outrage which followed the South African events—and established a Commission on Intellectual Property Rights, Innovation and Public Health (CIPIH) in 2004.[123] The CIPIH 2006 report[124] called for a holistic approach to crises in public health: 'The market alone, and the incentives that propel it, such as patent protection, cannot by themselves address the health needs of developing countries.'[125] Furthermore, the CIPIH report questioned whether current regimes of intellectual property protection have led to innovation or better access to medicines, particularly because market mechanisms and incentives do not lead to research and development that is directed towards the needs of developing countries. The CIPIH issued 60 recommendations, key among which was the call for a Global Plan to examine the challenges at each of the stages of discovery, development, and delivery of pharmaceuticals and other health products needed to secure public health. The WHO responded swiftly and the World Health Assembly adopted Resolution WHA 59.24 in May 2006 calling on the Director General to establish an Intergovernmental Working Group (IGWG) to draw up a strategy with contributions from member

---

[119]   Médecins Sans Frontières, Campaign for Access to Essential Medicines (1999–present) www.msfaccess.org/.

[120]   The World Bank, *The Economics of Effective AIDS Treatment: Evaluating Policy Options for Thailand* (2006), xxxl–xl, www.worldbank.org/.

[121]   D Schuettler, 'Activists hail Thai move to make generic AIDS drug' (2006) Reuters UK, 30 November, www.reuters.com/article/healthNews/idUSBKK5661020061130.

[122]   F Rozanski, *Developing Countries and Pharmaceutical Intellectual Property Rights: Myths and Reality* (2007) and CM Correa (ed), *A Guide to Pharmaceutical Patents* (2008), vols 1 and 2.

[123]   WHO Resolution (WHA 56.27, 2003), http://apps.who.int/gb/archive/pdf_files/WHA56/ea56r27.pdf.

[124]   CIPIH, *Public Health, Innovation and Intellectual Property Rights* (WHO, 2006), www.who.int/intellectualproperty/documents/thereport/ENPublicHealthReport.pdf?ua=1.

[125]   ibid, 17.

states and the global community.[126] The IGWG presented its Global Strategy and plan of action to the World Health Assembly at its Sixty-First Meeting in 2008, which adopted the plan by resolution WHA 61.21.[127] This notes that technological innovation should be supported by IP, that IP rights do not and should not prevent measures to protected public health, and that IP's incentives do not alone deliver new product needs when the paying market is small or uncertain. The plan's elements are promotion of research and development (R&D), capacity building, technology transfer, using the flexibilities of TRIPS, incentive schemes, improved delivery and access, sustainable funding, and monitoring and reporting. Activity is ongoing: the WHO has a work programme, 'Public health, innovation, intellectual property and trade' and in April 2012, the WHO's Consultative Expert Working Group on R&D: Financing and Coordination recommended that governments start new negotiations over a global R&D convention.[128] There is also collaboration with other institutions, for example in February 2018, a symposium exploring health and innovative technologies was attended by WHO, WTO, and WIPO on Trade and Public Health.

Evolutionary law and policy: WHO

10.60   This ambitious WHO strategy to develop a Global Plan for addressing crises in public health, and also its involvement in collaboration demonstrates well that although patents may be a part of the problem, they can also only be a part of the solution. Multi-level strategies will be required and part of the challenge is to understand how the operation of the world's patent systems interacts with other systems of regulation, health promotion, development, environmental protection, and even notions of justice. This approach embraces the interconnectedness of these systems and seeks solutions through those connections.

10.61   Intellectual property also contributes to other international development issues. The TRIPS Agreement itself required review of Article 27(3)(b) regarding the patentability of plants and animals other than micro-organisms, and of essentially biological processes for the production of plants or animals other than non-biological and microbiological processes.[129] This review began four years after the Agreement came into force (1999) and is ongoing.[130] The permissibility of plant and animal patents remains in dispute with lobbying arguing, on the one hand, that these are necessary to promote innovation and aid technology transfer and, on the other, that patenting causes problems of access, especially for farmers in gaining access to seed, that excessively broad patents can lead to the misappropriation of genetic material, and that this in turn may lead to breaches of state responsibilities under the UN Convention on Biological Diversity (CBD; see para 10.66).

Article 27(3)(b) debate

10.62   Solutions include: (1) removal of the provisions; (2) retention of the provisions with clarification as to definitions; and (3) a complete ban on plant and animal patenting. Such polar opposite views have given rise to concern that the Review remains inconclusive, and the TRIPS Council moved to find common ground for agreement with a view to producing a Council Decision, but this has yielded no results so far.

---

[126]   A Special Issue of the Bulletin of the World Health Organization (vol 84(5), May 2006, 337–424) is dedicated to the topic: www.who.int/bulletin/volumes/84/5/en/index.html.

[127]   For details, see WHA Resolution 61.21, www.wpro.who.int/health_research/wha61_21_global_strategy_poa_health_innovation_may2008.pdf.

[128]   WHO Consultative Expert Working Group on Research and Development (CEWG): Financing and Coordination, 'Research and development to meet health needs in developing countries: strengthening global financing and coordination' (2012), UK Government, 'Changes to copyright law in the event of no deal' (26 October 2018).

[129]   Note, however, that TRIPS, Art 27(3)(b) obliges its members to provide effective protection for plant varieties either under patent law or in some *sui generis* form (or a combination thereof). See generally, LR Helfer, *Intellectual Property Rights in Plant Varieties: International Legal Regimes and Policy Options for National Governments* (FAO 2004), and for the European perspective, M Llewelyn and M Adcock, *European Plant Intellectual Property* (2006) and G Wurtenberger et al, *European Community Plant Variety Protection* (2006).

[130]   TRIPS Council, Review of the Provisions of Art 27(3)(b), Paper IP/C/W/369/Rev 1, revised 9 March 2006, see further for a current overview of the related issues: www.wto.org/english/tratop_e/trips_e/art27_3b_background_e.htm.

10.63 There is agreement regarding (1) acceptance of every member state's right to adopt appropriate regimes to protect plant varieties by an effective *sui generis* system; (2) that the TRIPS Agreement and the CBD should be implemented in a mutually supportive and consistent manner; (3) that the TRIPS Agreement, being a minimum standards agreement, does not prevent members from protecting traditional knowledge; (4) the importance of documentation of genetic resources and traditional knowledge in helping better patent examination.[131]

10.64 Outstanding issues include: (1) the proposal to eliminate patent availability for all life forms (including micro-organisms), the need to clarify the terms in Article 27(3)(b);[132] (2) the protection of traditional knowledge;[133] and (3) consideration of ways to make the TRIPS Agreement and the CBD mutually supportive.[134] There have also been proposals to consider the provisions of Article 27(2) (that inventions can be excluded from patentability if prevention of commercial exploitation is necessary to protect *ordre public* and morality).

IP and international development beyond Doha?

10.65 The Doha Declaration itself further extended the remit of the TRIPS Council to consider the interconnectedness of TRIPS to other regimes.[135] Paragraph 19 requires the Council to consider the relationship between TRIPS and the CBD, as well as the challenges of protecting traditional knowledge and folklore, with which it can have strong links.

10.66 The CBD (see paras 10.61–10.64 above) was one of the outputs of the Earth Summit in Rio de Janeiro in 1992. World leaders agreed on a strategy for sustainable development. The CBD is a central element of that strategy, with three principal objectives:

(1) the conservation of biological diversity;

(2) the sustainable use of its components; and

(3) the fair and equitable sharing of the benefits arising out of the utilisation of genetic resources.

10.67 There are concerns in some quarters that the provisions of the CBD and TRIPS are fundamentally incompatible. The two main arguments are, first, the TRIPS Agreement actually requires that certain genetic material—such as micro-organisms—be patentable under Article 27(3)(b), as we have seen. This therefore allows private parties to gain private property rights over material which is guaranteed by the CBD to be the exclusive sovereign domain of signatory countries.[136] Secondly, TRIPS allows patent and other IPRs over genetic material without providing that certain core provisions of the CBD—such as the need for prior informed consent and benefit sharing—are complied with.[137] The CBD's Nagoya Protocol on Access to Genetic Resources and Fair and Equitable Sharing of Benefits of 2010 introduces a second level of relationship. This notes that IP and royalties can be one way of sharing benefit which arises from use of resources, but in its Annex it also confirms that there are many other sources of benefit sharing.[138]

---

[131] African Group, IP/C/W/404, 2; Zimbabwe, IP/C/M/36/Add 1, para 201. [132] Zimbabwe, IP/C/M/37/Add 1, para 197.

[133] African Group, IP/C/W/404, 4. [134] ibid, 5.

[135] See L Laxman and AH Ansari, 'The interface between TRIPS and CBD: efforts towards harmonisation' (2012) 11(2) J Int Trade Law & Policy, 108–32.

[136] See, eg, African Group: IP/C/W/404, IP/C/W/206, IP/C/W/163, IP/C/M/40, paras 76–79; Kenya: IP/C/M/47 para 68, IP/C/M/36/Add 1, para 233, IP/C/M/28, para 144.

[137] See, eg, African Group: IP/C/W/404, IP/C/W/206, IP/C/W/163; Brazil: IP/C/W/228, IP/C/M/48, para 37, IP/C/M/29, paras 146 and 148, IP/C/M/28, para 135, IP/C/M/27, para 122; Brazil et al: IP/C/W/429/Rev 1, IP/C/W/356.

[138] Regulation 511/2014 was passed by the EU implementing the Nagoya Protocol and this has also been criticised by the patent profession in the UK as imposing significant restrictions on innovation because of the new access procedures to be followed by CIPA: 'The Nagoya Protocol: new laws that may damage public health and UK science' CIPAJ 2015, 44(6), 23–24.

10.68   The potential for conflict between the CBD and TRIPS, although disputed in other quarters,[139] has set the agenda for the TRIPS Council discussion in this field of reform. Opinion has largely divided along economic lines, with developing countries arguing that TRIPS should be amended to bring the two treaties into line. Within this there are two camps: those that argue that TRIPS should exclude genetic patents altogether (this view is mostly advanced by the African Group),[140] and those who argue that there is insufficient provision in TRIPS to achieve an appropriate balance between the objectives of the two treaties, for example requirements of consent, disclosure of the origin of genetic material, and benefit sharing. Strong proponents of this view are Brazil and India. Options range from:

- do nothing to amend the treaties, but implement in a mutually supportive manner;
- implement in a mutually supportive manner and seek further evidence of the extent to which conflict arises in practice and might require changes to the patent system;
- accept that there is no inherent conflict but seek ways to ensure or enhance the mutual supportiveness of both Agreements (with or without amendment to TRIPS);
- accept that there is inherent conflict and amend TRIPS accordingly.

Details of minutes of TRIPS Council are at https://docs.wto.org/dol2fe/Pages/FE_Search/FE_S_S006. aspx?Query=(%20@Symbol=%20ip/c/m/*)&Language=ENGLISH&Context=FomerScriptedSearch& languageUIChanged=true#.

10.69   In another example of institution collaboration—or possible fragmentation of issues—there has been discussion on these themes at WIPO. The Conference of the Parties of the CBD invited WIPO to carry out a technical study on disclosure requirements in patent applications,[141] and this led to ongoing activity.[142] Notably, the WIPO Intergovernmental Committee on Intellectual Property and Genetic Resources, Traditional Knowledge and Folklore (IGC) reached sufficient consensus in February 2012 to produce a negotiating text for submission to the WIPO General Assembly in the same year.[143] The WIPO General Assembly then agreed 'to continue intensive negotiations and engagement in good faith, with appropriate representation, towards concluding the text(s) of an international legal instrument(s) which will ensure effective protection of genetic resources, traditional knowledge and traditional cultural expressions'. The United States and three other nations opposed this move. The United States in particular favours national action, whereby it would be left to individual states to use national legislation and contractual arrangements to impose obligations of disclosure or benefit sharing as they see fit.[144]

10.70   Disputes endure over a requirement of disclosure of genetic origin or traditional knowledge in patent applications when the invention is 'directly based' on genetic resources. A 2012 draft of a WIPO Consolidated Document on IP and Genetic Resources contained possible but virtually diametrically opposed options: (1) countries shall provide in legislation a mandatory disclosure requirement; or (2) may provide in their national patent legislation a mandatory disclosure requirement, or (3) patent disclosure requirements shall not include a mandatory disclosure relating to genetic resources . . . unless such disclosure is material to the patentability criteria of novelty, inventive step, or enablement (discussed in Chapter 11).[145] Discussions continued at WIPO, and in 2014 a new consolidated document and draft

[139] See the summary of discussion on these issues in IP/C/W/369/Rev 1 and IP/C/W/370/Rev 1.

[140] The African Group is an alliance of all African states.

[141] See resulting report at www.wipo.int/edocs/pubdocs/en/tk/786/wipo_pub_786.pdf (2004).

[142] See generally www.wipo.int/tk/en/genetic and Disclosure Requirements table (2017), www.wipo.int/export/sites/www/tk/en/documents/pdf/genetic_resources_disclosure.pdf.

[143] WIPO/GRTKF/IC/19/7.   [144] United States, IP/C/W/257.

[145] www.wipo.int/edocs/mdocs/tk/en/wipo_grtkf_ic_23/wipo_grtkf_ic_23_4.pdf Annex p11 Article 3.

articles (as agreement could not be reached) were prepared for the General Assembly.[146] Much text remains in square brackets and alternative wordings are often provided. Key issues included the recording of traditional knowledge in a database, and the making of this available to patent examiners. No agreements were reached in 2014; however, in 2015 the General Assembly agreed the mandate and work programme of the IGC for 2016/17. A primary focus was common understanding of core issues such as the definition of misappropriation, beneficiaries, what subject matter is entitled to protection, and the relationship with the public domain.[147] The IGC mandate was affirmed in 2017, with a focus on narrowing gaps and reaching understanding on core issues.[148] It will be interesting to see how this develops.

10.71 These CBD and WIPO activities should also be viewed in the context of activity at the WTO. A group of eight developing countries (including Brazil, China, and India) put forward to amend TRIPS itself with a new Article 29*bis* on disclosure of origin of biological resources. This proposal has been co-sponsored by several other countries since it was first drafted in May 2006.[149] The proposal states:[150]

Proposed Article 29*bis* TRIPS

Disclosure of origin of biological resources and/or associated traditional knowledge

1. For the purposes of establishing a mutually supportive relationship between this Agreement and the Convention on Biological Diversity, in implementing their obligations, Members shall have regard to the objectives and principles of this Agreement and the objectives of the Convention on Biological Diversity.
2. Where the subject matter of a patent application concerns, *is derived from or developed with biological resources and/or associated traditional knowledge*, Members *shall require applicants to disclose the country providing the resources and/or associated traditional knowledge*, from whom in the providing country they were obtained, and, as known after *reasonable inquiry*, the country of origin. Members shall also require that applicants provide information including evidence of compliance with the applicable legal requirements in the providing country *for prior informed consent for access and fair and equitable benefit-sharing* arising from the commercial or other utilization of such resources and/or associated traditional knowledge . . .

[. . .]

5. Members shall put in place effective enforcement procedures so as to ensure compliance with the obligations set out in paragraphs 2 and 3 of this Article. In particular, *Members shall ensure that administrative and/or judicial authorities have the authority to prevent the further processing of an application or the grant of a patent and to revoke*, subject to the provisions of Article 32 of this Agreement, *or render unenforceable a patent when the applicant has, knowingly or with reasonable grounds to know, failed to comply with the obligations in paragraphs 2 and 3 of this Article or provided false or fraudulent information.*

---

[146] See Intergovernmental Committee on Intellectual Property and Genetic Resources, Traditional Knowledge and Folklore, Consolidated Document relating to intellectual property and genetic resources, Twenty-Eighth Session, 7–9 July 2014, WIPO/GRTKF/IC/28/4, www.wipo.int/edocs/mdocs/tk/en/wipo_grtkf_ic_28/wipo_grtkf_ic_28_4.pdf.

[147] See www.wipo.int/export/sites/www/tk/en/igc/pdf/igc_mandate_1617.pdf.

[148] See www.wipo.int/tk/en/igc/.

[149] Amongst others by South Africa, for a full list of countries see WTO IP/C/W/474 Adds 1–9.

[150] WT/GC/W/564, 31 May 2006 (emphasis added).

Exercise

Critically assess this proposal in the light of the other options offered by other countries or alliances. The highlighted passages are likely to be most controversial. In particular, what do you think of the proposal to link non-disclosure to revocation or unenforceability of the patent? See also IP/C/W/491, TN/C/W/49 and Adds, and TN/C/W/59.

10.72   The broader political question, is that of the legitimacy to initiate change in these areas. Certainly, it is only for the WTO to seek to amend TRIPS, but broader issues are at stake such as relationships with the CBD and the protection of traditional knowledge.

10.73   While WIPO probably has more technical expertise in the field, it has been argued that the WTO mandate in the Doha Declaration has a specific development remit, making it the better body to take matters forward.[151] Either way, WTO only has authority over the TRIPS Agreement, while reforms to formal aspects of patent law—such as the creation of a genetic origin disclosure requirement—will require changes to WIPO instruments such as the PCT or the Patent Law Treaty (see paras 10.39–10.40).

Further reform: patent regimes in the future

10.74   WIPO has been involved[152] in delivery of the Sustainable Development Goals,[153] which include health, zero hunger, clean water, energy, climate action, educational opportunities, and sustainable economic growth. A particular evolving issue is the relationship between IP and climate change. At a practical level, WIPO has set up WIPO Green to facilitate technology transfer and collaboration.[154] Yet there have been arguments, reflecting views seen in relation to health and possible justifications for patents, that patents impose a barrier to effective technology transfer and use of technology to respond to the challenges of climate change; conversely, there is the view that without patents, valuable technologies (such as improved wind turbines or smart meters to assist in efficient energy use) would not be developed.[155] These issues are being explored, to no firm conclusion, at the TRIPS Council.[156] A further contribution comes from the climate change space. The United Nations Framework Convention on Climate Change, and its Kyoto Protocol and Paris Agreement[157] accord importance to technology and its transfer and impose obligations on states. Yet they do not engage directly with the fact that IP will be owned by private entities who may not wish to transfer it. Valuable work is ongoing through the Technology Mechanism to encourage development and transfer of technology and information.[158] The prospect of patents posing a fundamental challenge to this may be a remote possibility—or may be an imminent challenge. You may find these interesting areas to monitor.

[151]   See, eg, Brazil: IP/C/M/49, para 155, IP/C/M/42, para 101, IP/C/M/36/Add 1, para 199.

[152]   See, eg, www.wipo.int/meetings/en/doc_details.jsp?doc_id=331416.

[153]   See www.ip-watch.org/2017/05/19/wipo-sdgs-differing-views-committee-ip-development/.

[154]   www.wipo.int/wipogreen/en.

[155]   For consideration and reference to wider sources, see AEL Brown (ed), *Environmental Technologies, Intellectual Property and Climate Change: Accessing, Obtaining and Protecting* (2013) and AEL Brown, 'Intellectual Property and Climate Change' in R Dreyfuss and J Pila (eds), *The Oxford Handbook of Intellectual Property Law: V. The Political Economy of Intellectual Property* (2017) .

[156]   See WTO webpage www.wto.org/english/tratop_e/trips_e/cchange_e.htm.

[157]   For agreements and details of activity, see https://unfccc.int. Note in particular UNFCCC Art 4(3) and (5), Kyoto Protocol Art 3(14) and 10(c) and Paris Agreement Arts 6(8) and 10.

[158]   http://unfccc.int/ttclear/support/technology-mechanism.html.

Evidence and policy making

Exercise

1. The UK IPO published a five-year strategy 2015–2020, 'Making life better by supporting UK creativity and innovation', https://assets.publishing.service.gov.uk/government/uploads/system/uploads/attachment_data/file/528791/Corporate_5_Year_Strategy.pdf.

   Key goals are promoting UK growth through IP policy; delivering high-quality rights; and educating and enabling business to understand, manage, and protect their IP. Do you agree with these goals?

2. One key recommendation of the Hargreaves Review (see para 1.35) was a move to evidence-based policy making, rather than mere rhetoric. Evidence should be clear, verifiable, and peer review should be possible; see www.gov.uk/government/uploads/system/uploads/attachment_data/file/32563/ipreview-finalreport.pdf and see also consideration in these UK IPO blog posts: https://ipo.blog.gov.uk/2013/09/02/good-evidence-for-policy-building-partnerships; https://ipo.blog.gov.uk/2014/04/11/upcoming-research-whats-next; https://ipo.blog.gov.uk/2014/11/05/supporting-innovation-and-growth. Consider the extent to which this is likely to work and the challenges which might be encountered. You might find it useful to return to this question throughout your study of patents and other IPRs.

Do we need new innovation-related IP rights?

10.75 The Gowers Review of Intellectual Property of 2006[159] considered whether new rights are required to meet the needs of new and emerging technologies. The patent system has been put to the test in recent decades with the advent of biotechnologies and information technologies, including software and electronic business methods, as we see in Chapter 11. But it has also been argued that patent law sets the threshold too high for protection, necessitating a system of 'petty patents' or 'utility models' which can protect less inventive, but no less valuable, innovations. A utility model can be seen as a form of patent-like protection but which usually does not last as long (six–ten years) and which is subject to far less stringent criteria, especially concerning the equivalent notion of inventive step, which will not require as high a level of inventiveness as we find in patent law. Utility model protection is variable around the Union, with some countries such as the UK having no such protection. A proposal to approximate laws around the Union concerning utility models was proposed after a Green Paper from 1995.[160] The proposal[161] was not well received, and even after amendment[162] and a consultation exercise the majority of respondents (75 per cent) was against the introduction of a new scheme.[163] Arguments included a lack of clarity or agreement on the qualifying criteria, and a concern that the scheme would not help small-to-medium-sized enterprises, as promised, but would rather open an avenue for big business to corner yet another area of the market. Moreover, it was felt that while utility model protection might be helpful for those operating in a local market, it could not be justified at the supranational level.[164] After a long gap, in 2013 a study was carried out into the economic impact of utility model legislation in the EU. This found little evidence of impact of use of utility models systems, and a diversity of views in respect of the introduction of an EU utility model.[165]

---

[159] https://assets.publishing.service.gov.uk/government/uploads/system/uploads/attachment_data/file/228849/0118404830.pdf.

[160] Commission Green Paper of 19 July 1995 on the Protection of Utility Models in the Single Market, COM(1995) 370 final.

[161] Proposal for a European Parliament and Council Directive approximating the legal arrangements for the protection of inventions by utility model, COM(1997) 691 final and Amended proposal, 12 July 1999, COM(1999) 309 final/2.

[162] European Commission, 'Summary report of replies to the questionnaire on the impact of the Community utility model with a view to updating the Green Paper on protection by the utility model in the internal market', SEC(2001) 1307.

[163] WIPO explains utility models at www.wipo.int/sme/en/ip_business/utility_models/utility_models.htm.

[164] See http://ec.europa.eu/growth/industry/intellectual-property/patents/utility-models/index_en.htm.

[165] Via http://bookshop.europa.eu/en/study-on-the-economic-impact-of-the-utility-model-legislation-in-selected-member-states-pbE T0415184/?CatalogCategoryID=C5gKABstvcoAAAEjZJEY4e5L.

10.76   Length of protection and costs are also a factor—many new technologies may have a short shelf life, thus obviating the need for protection over 20 years, while high registration, translation, and enforcement costs mean that many small-to-medium-sized enterprises are effectively excluded from the patent system. The Hargreaves Review in 2011 noted, for example, that fewer than 50 per cent of patents are renewed beyond their tenth year;[166] the Gowers Review rejected in 2006 any special case for utility model patents, software patents, biotechnology and genetic patents, and business methods patents.[167] In fact, it is claimed to be a strength of the IP system that it has not responded with the creation of new rights for new developments, which would mean added complexity and increased cost.

10.77   Economics play a large part in this. Not only are there significant costs in setting up and administering new rights, but there is precious little evidence that their establishment would improve the economic situation,[168] or that they are necessary to encourage innovation.[169] Indeed, there is evidence from the United States that business method patents and gene patents can have an anti-competitive effect which de-incentivises rather than encourages innovation.[170] The UK and EPO take a harder line on these kinds of patents than the United States and the Gowers Review recommendation was that this should remain the position unless good economic cause can be shown to justify change. The point has been 'noted' by the UK IPO.

Discussion point   For answer guidance visit **www.oup.com/uk/brown5e**.

What other costs would be involved with the introduction of new IPRs? How might these new rights impact on existing rights?

Exercise

Visit the UK IPO website to check which changes have, or have not, been initiated or implemented by the time you read this chapter, and what new ones have been introduced. Are you convinced by the reasons given? And, are they based in evidence? See: www.ipo.gov.uk.

Patent procedures

The patenting procedure

10.78   We have already seen that there are various routes to obtaining patent registration, either via national (UK IPO), European (EPO), or international (PCT) avenues. It is recognised that while international harmonisation of patent systems has been significantly slower than in other areas of IP law, there is much that can still be achieved through closer cooperation between countries and their respective intellectual property offices. In the UK IPO five-year strategy 2015–2020, 'Making life better by supporting UK creativity and innovation', a key outcome is that IP systems are simpler to use and less costly at national and international level. It is important to appreciate, however, that different countries may use patent laws in different ways depending on their particular needs. Gowers recommended the following:

- UK IPO should work more closely with African patent offices to help them to take full advantage of flexibilities within the TRIPS Agreement.

---

[166] Hargreaves Review, para 6.19.   [167] Gowers Review, para 4.113.
[168] 'There seems to be no correlation between the existence of a utility model patent and innovation': ibid, para 4.112.
[169] The example is given of the US software industry, which 'grew exponentially without pure software patents', ibid, para 4.114.
[170] ibid, paras 4.118–4.121.

- UK IPO should encourage international reconsideration of time limits for compliance with TRIPS for least developed countries.

- UK government should encourage WTO members to ratify the Amendment to Article 31*bis* on access to medicines (paras 10.55–10.57).

- UK government and UK IPO should pursue work-sharing agreements with other IPOs, for example to avoid duplication of searches of the prior art.

Hargreaves commended the lead that the UK has taken on collaborating with at least six other countries to reduce duplication of effort worldwide and attempt to speed up granting. Examples include the Patent Prosecution Highway, Vancouver Group Mutual Exploitation and Utilisation Implementation Project, and work with the US Patent and Trademark Office to tackle backlogs. The Intellectual Property Act 2014 later enabled greater sharing of information with overseas patent offices.[171] The net outcome is, however, always the same—patents are granted with territorial effect only in the countries for which protection was sought, and this can be a very costly process if multiple filing is contemplated.

10.79   There is therefore a lot of strategic and economic thinking required in developing a patent strategy, including an assessment of one's actual and potential markets, a weighing up of the costs of patenting against possible returns, a judgement on whether it is worth seeking protection in a country where imitation is unlikely, and a sense of future behaviour of competitors. Time is also against the prospective patentee. Any delay in registering an invention increases the likelihood that a rival might release their own version of the invention, thereby thwarting any chances of future protection; by the same token, seeking protection at too early a stage in the development of an invention can seriously limit the scope of monopoly obtained—the inventor is only entitled to protection for what they have actually contributed to the sum total of human knowledge (known as 'the state of the art', see further paras 11.10–11.13).

10.80   The starting point to understanding the scope and content of a patent monopoly is the patent application itself. In this section we describe the patent application process for the UK, although this largely reflects the processes of the EPO and the PCT. If the UK is designated in a European patent application the resulting patent is treated entirely as if it were a UK patent.[172] We also consider the constituent elements of a UK patent application.

10.81   The critical event in the process of any patent application is the obtaining of its priority date. Normally, this is the date when the application is filed with the UK IPO,[173] but crucially it can be up to 12 months earlier if a patent has been filed in another WTO country and the later application is 'supported by matter' contained in the earlier application.[174] The importance of the priority date cannot be underestimated because it is the date from which the novelty of an invention will be tested. Only if the invention was publicly available *prior* to the priority date is there a problem. It is therefore perfectly acceptable to disclose the invention after obtaining the priority date; indeed, it is common practice to begin marketing at this point or after publication of the application (see paras 10.108ff). You may have seen the term *patent pending* attached to various products. This refers to products marketed in the time period between the priority date and the grant of the patent and it puts rivals on notice of the patent application.

10.82   It is also possible to make an 'early filing' on provision of a few key pieces of information to the UK IPO, being a written indication that a patent is sought, the identification of the person applying for

[171] Intellectual Property Act 2014, s 18.   [172] Patents Act 1977, ss 77–78; Patent Rules, Part 5; EPC 2000, Art 64.

[173] Patents Act 1977, s 5(1), as amended.

[174] Patents Act 1977, s 5(2), as amended. The Comptroller also has a discretion to allow an unintentional late filing: Patents Act 1977, s 5(2A)–(2C), as amended. This has its roots in the Paris Convention.

the patent, a description of the invention, or a reference to an earlier relevant application.[175] This mechanism is far short of a full application, but allows the prospective applicant up to 12 months to ponder the patent strategy and to decide whether a full application is merited. It also serves to secure an early priority date.

10.83   For the full application, the Patents Act 1977 lays down stringent criteria as to its form and content. Section 14(2) of the Act provides that every application must contain:

- a *request* for the grant of a patent;

- an *abstract* which gives technical information about the invention and the field to which it contributes; it also serves to facilitate future searches but does not form part of the state of the art;[176]

- a *specification* which is the part of the application that contains (1) a description of the invention; (2) the claim or claims as to what has been invented and what a monopoly is sought for; and (3) any drawings referred to in the description or claims.

10.84   The inventor must sufficiently disclose the invention in the specification to allow effective examination of its suitability for a patent. The criterion is that 'the specification shall disclose the invention in a manner which is clear enough and complete enough for the invention to be performed by a person skilled in the art'.[177] If this has not happened but a patent is nonetheless granted, it can be a ground for subsequent revocation of the patent for *insufficiency*.[178] We consider this in Chapter 12 (paras 12.74–12.86). As a result of all these requirements, the average page length of a European patent is 22 pages.

10.85   An invention is described in words and pictures and, in the case of inventions involving living organisms, by a deposit of samples under the Budapest Treaty 1977.[179] Note, however, that there is no obligation to describe the fastest, most efficient, or most economical way to perform the invention. Such knowledge—'know-how'—invariably remains out of the public domain and provides the patentee with additional commercial advantage in the exploitation of their invention.

 Exercise

The best way to make sense of these arcane terms and to understand patent applications is to read them for yourself.[180] Various patent databases exist. One of the most comprehensive is Espacenet, which is maintained by the EPO: http://worldwide.espacenet.com.

10.86   Figure 10.2 shows an example of a patented invention from the United States for Animal Ear Protectors with the Patent Number US4233942.[181] Go to the Espacenet website and do a Quick Search for this patent using the Patent Number.

The first thing you will see is this picture and the *Abstract* of the patent which sums up the invention thus:

This invention provides a device for protecting the ears of animals, especially long-haired dogs, from becoming soiled by the animal's food while the animal is eating. The device provides a generally tubular shaped member for containing and protecting each ear of the animal, and a member to position the tubular member and animal ears away from the mouth and food of the animal while it is eating.

[175] Patents Act 1977, s 15(1).   [176] Patents Act 1977, s 14(7), as amended.   [177] Patents Act 1977, s 14(3), as amended.
[178] Patents Act 1977, s 72(1)(c).   [179] www.wipo.int/treaties/en/registration/budapest.
[180] Note, procedures and processes in the EPO and through the PCT do not use the term 'specification' but, simply, 'patent application'.
[181] Also published as GB2040663(A) and FR2448289(A1).

Figure 10.2 Patent application for Animal Ear Protectors

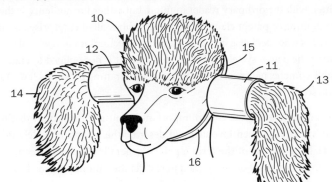

Now go to the *Description* section of the patent, where we find more detail about the invention. Note, in particular, two features: (1) the applicant has described 'the prior art', that is, the existing state of knowledge before this invention; (2) the applicant describes how this invention solves a previously unsolved problem, viz, protecting the ears of long-eared animals when they eat or drink. In other words, the applicant is explaining how this device is *new* and *inventive*. We return to the specifics of the law on these points in Chapter 11. A final point to note about the description is that it must support the claims, otherwise the patent may be denied or invalidated in due course.[182]

10.87   The *Claims* are arguably the most important part of a patent. Claims serve at least two vital functions. First, they describe in technical detail the essence of the invention; secondly, they establish the limits of the monopoly that a successful applicant will eventually enjoy. You can only legitimately claim for actual technical contribution to human knowledge—to the state of the art—and any claims which exceed the boundaries of your contribution can be struck out. Overly broad claims can be a problem when a new technology emerges and patent examiners are unfamiliar with the science and so unsure about what, precisely, has been added to the state of the art.[183] Section 14(5) of the Patents Act 1977 states that:

> The claim or claims shall—(a) define the matter for which the applicant seeks protection; (b) be clear and concise; (c) be supported by the description; and (d) relate to one invention or to a group of inventions which are so linked as to form a single inventive concept.

10.88   Our invention for Animal Ear Protectors only has one claim. Here it is:

> 1. A device for protecting animal ears comprising: a pair of generally tubular protectors each of which is formed of a sheet of self-biasing material which in their free state tend to form themselves into said generally tubular protectors; each of said protectors being longitudinally openable to allow easy insertion of one of said animal ears; and positioning means for flexibly joining one end of one protector in spaced apart relationship with one end of the other protector and for securing said device to the head of said animal such that the longitudinal axis of each protector and a portion of each ear of said animal, are held generally horizontally and approximately perpendicularly to the head of said animal whereby the ends of said animal ears are separated by a distance greater than the width of the head of said animal.

10.89   There are numerous points to observe about this passage. First, consider the use of language. It may strike you as a rather convoluted way of describing two tubes placed over a dog's ears. But the purpose of claims

---

[182] Patents Act 1977, ss 14(5)(c) and 72(1)(c).

[183] This description straddles two 'traditional' approaches to claim drafting: the 'central claiming system' whereby the objective is to define the kernel of the invention and the scope of protection flows from the precise contribution to the state of the art. This is still largely the approach in Continental Europe. It is to be contrasted with the 'peripheral claiming system', where the task is to demarcate the boundaries of the monopoly that is being claimed. This reflects more the position in the UK and the United States.

is to describe the specific *technical* contribution that this particular invention makes to the state of the art. Indeed, it is not written with the ordinary reader in mind, but rather the audience is the person skilled in the relevant art. The drafting of patent claims is in fact a highly skilled enterprise, usually undertaken by patent agents or attorneys who specialise in particular fields of technology and who also provide advice and guidance on navigating the patent system.[184] While an applicant is not obliged to engage the services of a patent agent, the highly complex nature of the application and drafting processes indicate that it is strongly in their interests to do so.

10.90   The *precision* of the language in claims is also important because it must both distinguish the present invention from what has already been invented and describe the invention widely to secure as broad a monopoly as possible. Note the use of the term 'a pair of generally tubular protectors'—why 'generally'? Well, it may be because the applicant does not want to restrict their monopoly solely to 'tubular' protectors because then it would be easy to invent around their contribution, for example by producing square protectors. This is an issue of *interpretation* of claims and the approach of the courts to this is a matter of considerable importance, especially in infringement proceedings, which we examine in Chapter 12.

10.91   Most patent applications have numerous claims. The general approach is to begin with the first claim as the broadest and to claim narrower features of the invention and/or to pick out particular features of the invention in subsequent claims. In this way, if some claims are struck out, for example for being too broad, the applicant might still have a chance of receiving some, albeit narrower, protection through the remaining claims.

10.92   Let's consider another example. Do an Espacenet search for an invention relating to an insert for a cat lavatory (EP1720404).[185] Here are the first few claims:

1. An insert (1) which can be placed in a lower part (5) of a cat lavatory and is replaceable, characterised in that the blank of the insert (1) is substantially rectangular, the corners (7) of the insert (1) being sloped.
2. The insert as claimed in Claim 1, characterised in that the insert is a pouch (6).
3. The insert as claimed in either of Claims 1 or 2, characterised in that the blank of the insert (1) is substantially rectangular or square.

 Question

What is *inventive* about this insert compared to all the other available cat litter accessories? How would you find out?

Drafting of claims

10.93   The way in which a claim is drafted is of considerable importance for the scope of protection eventually received. The previous claims in respect of the cat litter insert rely on the term 'characterised in' to distinguish particular features of this invention from others already part of the state of the art. This is typical of the European approach. Various categories of claims exist and are used around the world. The UK has a fairly liberal approach to claim drafting and there is no prescription in law as to how claims should be drawn up.[186] In contrast, the EPO has strict guidelines about drafting[187] and does not permit all kinds of claims, as we

---

[184]   See, eg, the Chartered Institute of Patent Attorneys, which was established in 1882: www.cipa.org.uk.

[185]   Note that this was filed in German. The English claims are found in WO2005094567, a member of the same patent family, and related by priority. For more details, see http://worldwide.espacenet.com/publicationDetails/inpadocPatentFamily?CC=EP&NR=1720404A1&KC=A1&FT=D&ND=3&date=20061115&DB=EPODOC&locale=en_EP.

[186]   *Kirin-Amgen v Transkaryotic Therapies* [2003] RPC 3 (CA) per Aldous LJ at paras 29–31.

[187]   Guidelines for Examination in the European Patent Office, Part F, November 2017, www.epo.org/law-practice/legal-texts/guidelines.html (EPO Guidelines) and Implementing Regulations to Part III of the Convention, last amended October 2014, rule 43, www.epo.org/law-practice/legal-texts/html/epc/2013/e/rpiii.html (Implementing Regulations).

shall see later (at paras 10.96–10.100). Moreover, the EPC Guidelines impose a fee if an application has more than 15 claims,[188] and the number of claims cannot be indefinite because 'the number of the claims shall be reasonable in consideration of the nature of the invention claimed'.[189]

10.94 It is commonly said that an invention can be a *product* or a *process*. This is reflected in the categories of claims that are most commonly used—product or process claims—and it is important to distinguish between the two because the legal effects of a patentee's monopoly can be affected by the choice of claim category.[190] A *product claim* is often characterised by a claim to a device, substance, embodiment, or compound, that is, to the physical entity making up the invention. A monopoly over the product itself is a strong one because it prevents all uses of the product by a competitor and it does not matter if the product was made by independent, non-rivalrous means. A *process claim* is as its name suggests—a claim to a means of producing something. Such claims are often characterised by language such as a method, use, or system, for example a 'system for storing information'. A simple process claim is additionally useful because it extends protection to the products directly obtained by the process itself.[191]

10.95 *Product-by-process claims* are to be distinguished from the last example. These are product claims where the product is described by reference to its process of manufacture rather than by its own characteristics. For example, 'the product obtained by the process described in claim 1'. This distinguishes your invention from other similar products already on the market. Your monopoly will only extend to products made by your particular process, and may not therefore interfere with other products made by different means. Product-by-process claims are also helpful when it is difficult or impossible to describe your product by reference to its own characteristics, for example if you have invented a useful compound but you do not yet know its structure or composition.

10.96 Despite these benefits, product-by-process claims are frowned on by the EPO; however, they have generally been acceptable in the UK. The EPO will only allow such claims when it is not possible to describe the product by any other means and when the product is patentable in its own right.[192] A product is not rendered novel merely by the fact that it is produced by means of a new process.[193] In 2005, the House of Lords ruled that 'it is important that the United Kingdom should apply the same law as the EPO'.[194] Views vary, however, on whether this has actually led to a change in practice and this issue is discussed in Chapter 12.

10.97 In terms of drafting claims generally, we may know what a product does—that is, how its functions—without yet knowing its essential *technical features*—that is, how it is structured or constituted. Normally, it is the description of these technical features which is required for a successful patent application.[195] *Functional claims* can be acceptable 'provided that a skilled person would have no difficulty in providing some means of performing this function without exercising inventive skill',[196] and notably when the claimed features of the invention 'cannot otherwise be defined more precisely without restricting the scope of the claim'.[197]

Exercise

Can you think of any other advantage to drafting claims in terms of an invention's function rather than its technical features?

---

[188] Implementing Regulations, rule 45.   [189] Implementing Regulations, rule 43(5).

[190] See the comments by the EPO in T378/86 *MOOG/Change of category* [1988] OJEPO 386.   [191] EPC 2000, Art 64(2).

[192] EPO Guidelines, Part F-IV-9, para 4.12 and T150/82 *IFF/Claim categories* [1984] OJEPO 309, paras 10–11.

[193] EPO Guidelines, Part F-IV-9, para 4.12 and T150/82 *IFF/Claim categories* [1984] OJEPO 309, paras 10–11.

[194] *Kirin-Amgen Inc and Others v Hoechst Marion Roussel Ltd and Others* [2005] 1 All ER 667, [2005] RPC 9.

[195] EPO Guidelines, Part F-II-7, para 4.5, and Implementing Regulations, rule 43(1).   [196] EPC Guidelines, Part F-IV-1, para 2.1.

[197] T694/92 *MYCOGEN/Modifying plant cells* [1998] EPOR 114, para 4.

10.98   Article 82 of the EPC provides that a 'European patent application shall relate to one invention only or to a group of inventions so linked as to form a single general inventive concept'.[198] It is not unusual, however, especially in the pharmaceutical and biotechnology industries, for one patent application to concern many different, yet related, embodiments of a single inventive concept. Examples include thousands of different variations on a particular chemical compound or related elements of a gene sequence. In such circumstances, patent agents will invoke *representative claims* which allow specific examples to be given of the invention's particular features which are held out to be present across the range of products claimed. It would be impractical and self-defeating for the patent system to require more specific details or separate patent applications for each and every product.

10.99   Similarly, the *Markush claim* is frequently used in the chemical industry, where vast numbers of related entities can be claimed together. The distinguishing feature is that this type of claim allows 'alternatives' to be claimed as functional equivalents; that is, various permutations of different entities will produce the same inventive result and so are claimed to fall within the monopoly. This is acceptable as long as the alternatives are of a similar nature and can fairly be substituted for one another.[199] These *Markush* claims contain symbols to refer to the sub-groups. This type of claim is named after the first inventor successfully to use it.[200]

10.100   *Swiss-type claims* were developed to get around problems of non-patentability of second or subsequent uses of existing compounds for medical treatment.[201] Consider, for example, that you find out that athlete's foot cream is also good for curing acne: can you patent the product in these terms or for this second use? You cannot patent the product because it is already known and therefore not *new*. Medical use is also already known, and so what is new is the *method* of treatment, but there is a further problem because historically methods of treatment of the human or animal body have been excluded from patentability.[202] The EPO Enlarged Board of Appeal addressed this issue by following a practice first adopted by the Swiss Federal Intellectual Property Office and held that claims could be formulated in a certain way to be permissible.[203] That formulation is a claim to '*use of substance X in the manufacture of a medicament for the treatment of condition Y*'. The claim, then, is to the method of manufacture, not to the method of treatment. Because of the origin of the formulation, this became known as a Swiss-type claim. This legal fiction was addressed by reforms introduced by EPC 2000.[204] It is now no longer necessary to adopt Swiss-type claims because:[205]

> In the case of an invention consisting of a substance or composition for a specific use in any such method, the fact that the substance or composition forms part of the state of the art shall not prevent the invention from being taken to be new if that specific use does not form part of the state of the art.

This now allows a simple claim of 'substance X for use in treatment of disease Y'.

10.101   Finally, we can consider the role of *omnibus claims*. These claims rely on references to the description of the invention in respect of their technical features and are commonly used in the UK. An example is 'A process in accordance with claim 1 substantially as described in the foregoing Example I [from the specification]'. In the EPO, omnibus claims are not allowed except where 'absolutely necessary'.[206] This could be, for example, when the invention has features which can only be expressed by means of drawings or graphs defining a particular shape.

10.102   *Disclaimers* can be used to define an invention in a way that avoids problems of patentability such as non-novelty,[207] for example by expressly excluding certain features of the invention because these are already

[198] See also Implementing Regulations, rule 44, which requires a 'technical relationship' among all claimed inventions involving the same or corresponding special technical features.

[199] EPO Guidelines, Part F-V-4, para 5.   [200] Eugene Markush, US patent 1,506,316, granted on 26 August 1924.

[201] See Patents Act 1977, s 4A(3) for first medical use.   [202] See Patents Act 1977, s 4A(1).

[203] G5/83 *EISAI/Second Medical Indication* [1985] OJEPO 64.   [204] EPC 2000, Arts 53(c) and 54(4).

[205] Patents Act 1977, s 4A(4), as amended and EPC, Art 54(5).

[206] Implementing Regulations, rules 43(6). See also T0150/82 *IFF/Claim categories* [1984] OJEPO 309.

[207] See EPO Guidelines, Part H-V-6, para 3.5.

part of the state of the art.[208] But what happens if you want to disclaim features of your patent after it has been granted? This was considered by the Enlarged Board of Appeal in two cases[209] which held that post-grant disclaimers are possible in limited circumstances; namely, (1) to restore novelty by delimiting a claim against the state of the art; (2) to restore novelty by delimiting a claim against an accidental anticipation; and (3) to disclaim subject matter that is non-technical and so, non-patentable.

From preparation to application

10.103   Once you have completed your patent application form you can submit it to the UK IPO for examination.[210] The day-to-day business and the formal procedures of the UK IPO are governed by the Patents Rules 2007, as amended.[211]

10.104   The stages in the process are:

(1) Submission of patent specification (description of invention as minimum) and application form and *request for grant of a patent* form (£60 if paid at this stage, £75 if paid at stage 3).

(2) Receipt issued from UK IPO with application number and confirmation of *priority date.*[212]

(3) *Request for national online search* and filing of appropriate fee (£150 within 12 months). Add claims and abstract if not present.

(4) *Preliminary examination* to ensure formal requirements of the application are met and search of the 'prior art' to determine if invention is new and inventive. A search report will be prepared and sent to the applicant highlighting any materials that may pose problems for patentability as well as other technical materials showing what has been done in the field (£100).[213]

(5) *Publication of the patent* (18 months after the priority date).[214]

(6) *Substantive examination online*—a thorough consideration of the application by a skilled patent examiner to determine if it meets the requirements for patentability (£100).[215]

(7) Substantive examination report issued and period for amendment, if required. This will be to increase the prospects of approval, but regard must always be had to the patentability requirements.

(8) If all criteria are met, the patent is *granted, the application is published in its final form, and the patent certificate is sent to the patentee.*[216]

10.105   In total, it costs around £400–25 in official fees to apply for a UK patent. Professional patent attorney fees will be substantially more.

Who can apply for a patent?

10.106   Anyone can apply for a patent.[217] They do not need to be the inventor, although if this is the case they must have some entitlement in law to apply, for example through contractual arrangement, and the basis for this must be made clear at the time of application.[218] The inventor is entitled to be named both in the application

---

[208] T4/80 *BAYER/Disclaimer* [1982] OJEPO 149.

[209] See G01/03 *PPG INDUSTRIES/Disclaimer* [2004] OJEPO 413 and G02/03 *GENETIC SYSTEMS CORP/Synthetic antigens* [2004] OJEPO 448.

[210] Guidance on applying for a patent is available from the UK IPO; see www.patent.gov.uk/p-apply.pdf, and for a full set of forms and charges see www.gov.uk/government/publications/patent-forms-and-fees/patent-forms-and-fees.

[211] SI 2007/3291, as amended. See https://assets.publishing.service.gov.uk/government/uploads/system/uploads/attachment_data/file/694249/Patents-Rules-2007-06042018.pdf (consolidated 6 April 2018).

[212] Patents Act 1977, s 15.   [213] Patents Act 1977, ss 15A and 17.   [214] Patents Act 1977, s 16(1) and Patents Rules, r 26.

[215] Patents Act 1977, s 18.   [216] Patents Act 1977, s 18.   [217] Patents Act 1977, s 7(1).   [218] Patents Act 1977, s 7(2).

and the patent.[219] It will be assumed that the applicant is entitled to apply until the contrary is proven.[220] Matters of dispute over entitlement to the patent are referred to the Comptroller in the first instance.[221] At the EPO, revisions have been adopted in an attempt to streamline processes for gaining and maintaining a patent. There are some important changes: (1) applicants can file in any language and do not need to submit an EPO official language translation until later in the process (Art 14(2)); (2) applicants may request 'further processing' of their application if they fail to comply with time limits (Art 121(1)); (3) the EPO will move to a system of search and examination of an application by the same examiner when previously these have been separate systems. This was designed to improve the efficiency of the Office.

10.107   The UK, Europe, and almost all other countries of the world apply the so-called *first-to-file* approach to patent entitlement, that is, that priority of claim depends solely on who is first to submit a complete application to the patent office. The United States, in contrast, had a *first-to-invent* procedure which requires a far more nuanced examination of the processes leading up to a patent application and a need to determine at what point an 'invention' occurred. The best claim is that of an inventor who first conceived of the invention and then reduced it to practice and filed a patent application. Provided that they can prove this process, then they will have a stronger claim than someone who was first to file but cannot establish prior invention. But this often proved to be a difficult and costly process. After lengthy and considerable debate, the America Invents Act was passed by Congress in September 2011 and came into effect on 16 March 2013. Section 3 of the new Act now introduces a form of first-to-file into the United States, albeit that early disclosures such as presentations, demonstrations, or postings on company websites about an invention can serve a 'territory marking' function. Thus, while the United States has moved substantially to the position already followed by the rest of the world, it remains to be seen whether the transition will be total or expeditious.

 Discussion point   For answer guidance visit **www.oup.com/uk/brown5e**.

What are the pros and cons of first-to-invent as opposed to first-to-file?

10.108   An application for a patent may be withdrawn at any time before the patent is granted and any withdrawal of such an application may not be revoked.[222] The earlier date of the publication of the patent application is also important for at least two reasons. First, at this time all correspondence and details of the invention are released into the public domain destroying the last vestiges of secrecy—and this remains the position even if the patent is not granted. Secondly, this is the date from which the patentee can sue for infringement, after the patent is actually granted.[223] After the application has been published, any person (possibly a competitor or an activist?) may make observations to the comptroller and this can have an impact on substantive decisions.[224] The initial protection for the invention is for four years. Thereafter, the patent must be renewed annually on the payment of increasing fees up to a maximum of 20 years.[225]

10.109   A standard UK patent usually takes between two to three years to grant, but in some areas and in some other offices it is longer. For example, the EPO can take up to ten years to grant a patent. An accelerated examination and search is now available from the UK IPO. This involves collapsing both processes and paying both fees together. This means that a patent can be granted within a few months of publication. These have been particular initiatives in respect of green technology applications.[226]

---

[219] Patents Act 1977, s 13.   [220] Patents Act 1977, s 7(4).

[221] Patents Act 1977, s 8. Post-grant disputes are handled under s 37. See IPO, 'Patents: Deciding Disputes', at www.gov.uk/government/uploads/system/uploads/attachment_data/file/354747/Patents_Deciding_Disputes_Rebrand_2014.pdf and www.gov.uk/guidance/patent-disputes-resolution-hearings.

[222] See Patents Act 1977, s 14(9).   [223] Patents Act 1977, s 69.   [224] Patents Act 1977, s 21.

[225] This 20-year period is calculated from the filing date, see ibid, s 25(1).

[226] See, eg, www.gov.uk/government/publications/patents-fast-grant.

Post-grant amendments

10.110   Sections 27(1) and 75(1) of the Patents Act 1977, as amended, provide the Comptroller and the courts with discretion to allow the amendment of a patent once it has been granted; the former section deals with circumstances when the request is from the proprietor themselves, and the latter with cases when the validity of the patent is in dispute, for example in infringement or revocation proceedings, even if it is not an issue in the particular circumstances.[227] In exercising their discretion, the Comptroller and the courts must also now have regard to relevant principles in the EPC, for example Regulations made under the Convention or EPO Guidelines or rulings from the EPO Boards of Appeal or Opposition Division. This is to ensure closer approximation and consistency of approach in signatory countries.[228] The UK IPO offers a service whereby requests for amendments are made publicly available and those who may oppose them are given notice of the application to amend.[229] You cannot apply to amend your patent in favour of more subject matter or a broader monopoly.[230] Amendments can only maintain, or more usually restrict, the scope of protection originally received. Co-owners must act jointly if they wish to amend or revoke their patent.[231]

10.111   At the EPO, EPC 2000 reforms[232] mean that a proprietor, or consenting co-proprietors, can apply to amend or revoke a patent in *any* proceedings in which validity can be an issue. Further, a proprietor can request revocation or limitation of their patent before the EPO after the opposition period,[233] with any such amendments to effect in all countries for which the European patent was designated.[234] This, in effect, creates a centralised amendment system. There is also a limited form of appeals proceedings, when any party adversely affected by the decision of the Board of Appeal may file a petition for review by the Enlarged Board of Appeal. This procedure can only be used if there is a fundamental procedural defect in Board of Appeal proceedings or if a criminal act may have had an impact on the Board's decision.[235]

 Discussion point   For answer guidance visit **www.oup.com/uk/brown5e.**

What sorts of factors do you think would influence the Comptroller or court one way or another in exercising its discretion to amend a patent?

10.112   The application process can be a lengthy, costly, and uncertain process. In the UK IPO the Patent Opinions Service established in 2005 offers an avenue for parties in dispute over the validity or infringement of a UK or European patent to make representations and receive a non-binding ruling from a patent examiner. After a series of consultations, the impact of opinions changed with the Intellectual Property Act 2014;[236] if an opinion is issued that the requirements for patenting are not met, then the comptroller may revoke the patent, subject to opportunities for review, appeal, observation, and amendment.[237]

10.113   In Chapter 11 we consider the criteria for patentability and the exclusions.

---

[227] Such circumstances are outlined in the Patents Act 1977, s 74.
[228] Patents Act 1977, s 75(5), as inserted by the Patents Act 2004, s 2(5).
[229] See www.gov.uk/guidance/requests-to-amend-a-patent-after-grant.   [230] Patents Act 1977, s 76(2), (3).
[231] Patents Act 1977, s 36(3)(a), as amended by the Patents Act 2004, s 9.   [232] Article 138(3).
[233] Article 105a.   [234] Article 105b(3).   [235] Article 112a.
[236] Regarding binding opinions in respect of registered designs; see now also Intellectual Property Act 2014, s 28A.
[237] Intellectual Property Act 2014, s 16. See also UK IPO, 'Opinions: resolving patent disputes' www.gov.uk/guidance/opinions-resolving-patent-disputes.

Further reading

Books

GB Dinwoodie and Rochelle C Dreyfuss, *Neofederalist Vision of TRIPS: The Resilience of the International Intellectual Property Regime* (2012)

PW Grubb and PL Thomsen, *Patents for Chemicals, Pharmaceuticals and Biotechnology: Fundamentals of Global Law, Practice and Strategy* (6th edn, 2016)

D Matthews, *Globalising Intellectual Property Rights: The TRIPS Agreement* (2002)

Luke McDonagh, *European Patent Litigation in the Shadow of the Unified Patent Court* (2016)

HVJ Moir, *Patent Policy and Innovation: Do Legal Rules Deliver Effective Economic Outcomes?* (2013)

E Morgera, M Buck, and E Tsioumani, *The 2010 Nagoya Protocol on Access and Benefit Sharing in Perspective. Implications for International Law and Implementation Challenges* (2013)

MP Pugatch (ed), *The Intellectual Property Debate: Perspective from Law, Economics and Political Economy* (2006)

T Takenaka, *Patent Law and Theory: A Handbook of Contemporary Research* (2009)

Reports

Commission on Intellectual Property Rights, Innovation and Public Health, *Public Health, Innovation and Intellectual Property Rights* (2006)

European Commission, *Pharmaceutical Sector Inquiry Report* (2009)

Gowers Review of Intellectual Property (HM Treasury, 2006)

I Hargreaves, *Digital Opportunity: A Review of Intellectual Property and Growth* (2011)

Articles

AF Christie, 'Non-overlapping rights: a patent misconception' (2010) 32(2) EIPR 58

E Derclaye, 'Patent law's role in the protection of the environment: reassessing patent law and its justifications in the 21st century' (2009) 40(3) IIC 249

MA Gandia Sellens, 'The viability of the unitary patent package after the UK's ratification of the Agreement on a Unified Patent Court' (2018) 49(2) IIC 136–52

AM Imam, 'How does patent protection help developing countries?' (2006) 37(3) IIC 245

J Pila, 'The European patent: an old and vexing problem' (2013) 62(4) ICLQ 917 62(4)

J Straus and N-S Klunker, 'Harmonisation of international patent law?' (2007) 38 IIC 907, and the reply from C Health (2008) 39 IIC 210

Patentability

Introduction

Scope and overview of chapter

11.1 This chapter is about what is required in order to obtain a patent. The first section deals with the issue of patentability and explores the criteria which are applied by an intellectual property office in examining a patent application. These are *novelty, inventive step*, and *industrial applicability*. Equally important, however, are the exclusions from patentability, which will then be considered.

11.2 Patent law protects inventions, but interestingly there is no legal definition of *invention*.[1] Rather, the eligibility of a new product or process for patent protection is considered in a two-step process. The patent examiner will consider what is *not* an invention under the law, or at least, what will not be entitled to patent protection. Well-established lists of exclusions from patentability exist in most legal systems and it is essential to understand both what is on such lists and why certain subject matter is excluded. The reasons are many and varied, as we shall see. It is in these exclusions that many cultural and jurisdictional differences lie in the application of patent law. The examiner will also test an invention against the positive criteria for patentability, which are *novelty* (does the invention already exist and is it in the public domain?); *inventive step* (is the invention sufficiently innovative to represent a significant move forward in the field?); and *industrial applicability* (can the invention be made or used in any kind of industry?). These criteria operate as threshold devices to determine whether a particular invention makes a sufficient contribution to human knowledge and experience to merit the award of a monopoly. Article 27(1) of the Trade-Related Aspects of Intellectual Property Rights (TRIPS) Agreement ensures that all countries are agreed that these are the relevant criteria for patentability.[2] But it is in the interpretation given to these criteria by national courts where differences emerge, and we will focus on the courts of the UK jurisdictions in this regard.

11.3 The UK Patents Act 1977 and the European Patent Convention 2000 set out the key provisions for patenting. This chapter also explores the EU Biotechnology Directive. This, and its drivers, warrant some special attention throughout this chapter. The rationale behind the Biotechnology Directive[3] was elegantly simple. Europe was lagging behind other economic areas, in particular the United States, and unevenness of approach towards biotechnological inventions throughout the member states was at odds with the Commission's plans for completion of the internal market. The aim of the Directive is equally

---

[1] But see the Patents Act 1977, s 125(1).
[2] TRIPS, Art 27(1): 'Subject to the provisions of paragraphs 2 and 3, patents shall be available for any inventions, whether products or processes, in all fields of technology, provided that they are new, involve an inventive step and are capable of industrial application.'
[3] A full copy of the text of the Directive is available at http://eur-lex.europa.eu/LexUriServ/LexUriServ.do?uri=OJ:L:1998:213:0013:0021:EN:PDF.

straightforward: to harmonise the law throughout all member states, making it clear that biotechnological inventions are patentable, subject to certain narrowly defined exceptions and limitations.

11.4   Biotechnology concerns the application of scientific techniques to living organisms with a view to manipulation of these organisms. There is a complex debate about the propriety of granting patents over genetic and biological materials. First, how can property rights be granted over genes or partial gene sequences which, after all, seem to be no more than mere discoveries? Secondly, how appropriate is it to grant exclusive rights over the building blocks of life or, indeed, life itself in the form of genetically engineered organisms? Finally, if this is to happen, what is the optimal policy to ensure that research is not hindered by the grant of these patents and that individual human (and competing commercial) interests are also respected? Many patents have been granted, and the UK IPO guidance has been issued.[4]

11.5

> ### Learning objectives
>
> By the end of this chapter you should be able to describe and explain:
>
> - the meaning and operation of the criteria for patentability;
> - the exclusions from patentability and their underlying rationales, with particular reference to software and biotechnology-related innovation.

11.6   Once granted, a patent confers on the patentee a range of rights and the monopoly (or perhaps more accurately power conferred) is arguably the strongest within intellectual property law. But as with all intellectual property rights, limits can be placed on that power such as Crown use or compulsory licences, which are discussed in Chapter 12. Moreover, what can be given can also be taken away, and patents are vulnerable throughout their life to a claim for revocation; that is, that the patent should be struck from the patent register because it was erroneously granted. This is also discussed in Chapter 12. So, the rest of the chapter looks like this:

- Protectable subject matter (11.7–11.84)
- Excluded subject matter (11.85–11.194)
- Exceptions to patentability (11.195–11.239)

Protectable subject matter

11.7   Section 1(1) of the Patents Act 1977 states:

A patent may be granted only for an invention in respect of which the following conditions are satisfied, that is to say—
(a) the invention is new;
(b) it involves an inventive step;
(c) it is capable of industrial application;
(d) the grant of a patent for it is not excluded by subsections (2) and (3) below . . .

---

[4] See generally UK IPO, 'Examination Guidelines for Patent Applications relating to Biotechnological Inventions in the Intellectual Property Office' (2013), as amended, available at https://assets.publishing.service.gov.uk/government/uploads/system/uploads/attachment_data/file/512614/Guidelines-for-Patent-Applications-Biotech.pdf.

We will consider here what we might call the 'positive criteria' for patentability. Each of these criteria sets a threshold hurdle that the prospective patentee must clear in order to secure a patent. The rationale for each criterion is different, but collectively they serve to ensure that only previously unavailable, highly innovative, and useful inventions receive patent protection.

Novelty

11.8   The policies underpinning the novelty requirement are to prevent the disutility of re-inventing the wheel, to ensure that matter which is already in the public domain is not brought (once again) under private control, and to protect parties who have been happily using a product or process publicly from being stopped from doing so on the grant of a patent over the same or substantially the same product or process.

11.9   There are certain key questions that we must ask in order to know whether an invention will be new. These are:

(1)   What constitutes the public domain for these purposes?

(2)   How much information about an invention must have been in the public domain before this becomes a problem for patent purposes?

11.10   Novelty is covered by section 2 of the Patents Act 1977, as amended, and the equivalent provisions are found in Articles 54 and 55 of the European Patent Convention (EPC) 2000. Section 2(1) of the 1977 Act provides that 'An invention shall be taken to be new if it does not form part of the state of the art.' The state of the art is the public domain for patent purposes. Section 2(2) provides that:

> The state of the art in the case of an invention shall be taken to comprise all matter (whether a product, a process, information about either, or anything else) which has at any time before the priority date of that invention been made available to the public (whether in the United Kingdom or elsewhere) by written or oral description, by use or in any other way.

11.11   This is clearly an extremely wide definition which is global in scope and which covers any manner by which information about an invention might be disclosed. Something becomes part of the state of the art on the day that it is made available to the public, and this does not even require that members of the public have actual sight of the information, merely that they can have access to the information, either freely or on payment of a fee.[5] An obscure article may, therefore, be published in a journal that no one ever reads but it would still be part of the state of the art. Moreover, this publication can be anywhere in the world and in any language. Note too, by implication, it does not matter *who* makes a public disclosure, and this includes the prospective patentee themselves. This is why it is so important to keep information about an invention out of the public domain until you have secured a *priority date*. You should recall from Chapter 10 that the priority date is normally the filing date of the patent application with an intellectual property office, unless an earlier filing has taken place in another office within the previous 12 months, in which case that date becomes the priority date.[6] Novelty is only tested by reference to the state of the art *prior* to the priority date.

11.12   The state of the art is forever expanding—we can only add to it; information, once added, always remains a part of it. It is dangerous to pass information to third parties without stipulating a confidentiality clause, ideally by contract; even communication to one individual can be enough to make information public.[7] Allowing the public an opportunity to examine the details of an invention in circumstances where a skilled person would become aware of the core technical features of the invention would amount to public

---

[5]   See further the EPO Enlarged Board of Appeal in G1/92 *Availability to the Public* [1993] EPOR 241.
[6]   See para 10.81.
[7]   *Bristol-Myers Co's Application* [1969] RPC 146. In T482/89 *TELEMECHANIQUE/Single sale* [1992] OJEPO 646 a single sale was enough to anticipate.

disclosure.[8] It is even possible for something to become part of the state of the art if it is merely seen in public if a skilled person[9] on seeing it would be able to discern its core features with sufficient detail to reproduce the invention.[10] Equally, 'publicly available' is a relative term. The details of an invention must not only be physically accessible but also sufficiently intellectually intelligible by the skilled person using their common general knowledge. Thus Floyd J held in *H Lundbeck A/S v Norpharma SpA*[11] that 'matter may be contained in a document but so submerged in it as not to be available'. Finally, and for the purposes of testing novelty only, it is important to note that the state of the art includes the content of any patent applications designating the UK[12] published on or after the priority date of the invention in question.[13] Article 54(3) EPC 2000 makes the contents of European patent applications relevant to the state of the art.

11.13   If an invention already exists in the state of the art then we say that a subsequent patent application or invention is *anticipated*.

■ *Pall Corporation v Commercial Hydraulics (Bedford) Ltd* [1990] FSR 329

The patent in suit concerned 'hydrophilic microporous membranes' for filters. The membranes were capable of being wetted through in less than one second, yet when heated to a temperature just below the softening temperature the membrane reverted to a hydrophobic material. An action of infringement was brought by the plaintiff, which was met with a counterclaim of revocation on the ground of lack of novelty. It was alleged that the plaintiff had anticipated their own invention by prior use. The plaintiff had given sight of the claimed product to a potential customer. No details of the nature or construction of the membranes were disclosed to the customer or the other suppliers represented at the test, and the nature of the membrane could not have been ascertained simply by sight of the membrane. The plaintiff also sent samples to other potential customers but these were sent under conditions of confidence and the customers knew that the membranes were experimental and secret. It was held that (1) the use of the membranes in the comparison test did not place the invention in the state of the art because the use was not a sale or supply in the course of trading, nor did it make the samples available to the public; and (2) the sending of samples to potential customers in confidence did not amount to anticipation because this did not make the samples available to the public. The obligation of confidence ensured that the relevant information was kept in the private, as opposed to the public, domain.

11.14   The law of confidence can be an extremely important tool in the protection of information surrounding the development of an invention in the period prior to application and the award of a priority date. Unlike the United States which provides for 'grace periods'—the period of one year prior to filing is exempt from consideration for the purposes of testing novelty—Europe will consider everything made available to the public up to the priority date. Compare this decision with *Monsanto Co (Brignac's) Application*[14] in which a process patent was sought concerning the production of nylon having finely divided carbon black uniformly dispersed therein. Thirty or forty copies of a *Technical Information Bulletin* containing details of pigmentation of synthetic fibres (including nylon) were given to salesmen of the company developing the

---

[8]   *Milliken Denmark AS v Walk Off Mats Ltd and Another* [1996] FSR 292 (hire of mats to the public would allow an expert to discover its novel qualities and perform the invention).

[9]   See *Folding Attic Stairs Ltd v Loft Stairs Co Ltd* [2009] FSR 24.

[10]   See *Lux Traffic Controls Ltd v Pile Signals Ltd and Faronwise Ltd* [1993] RPC 107; cf *Kavanagh Balloons Pty Ltd v Cameron Balloons Ltd* [2004] RPC 5.

[11]   [2011] EWHC 907 (Pat).

[12]   It is important to remember that this can therefore cover applications via the UK IPO, the EPO, and/or the Patent Cooperation Treaty (PCT). In this last regard, the application must not only have been published under the PCT (Art 21) but it must also have entered the national phase for UK patents or the regional phase for European (UK) patents, ie that the necessary translation has been carried out and the appropriate fee paid: see Patents Act 1977, ss 79, 89, 89A, and 89B. The abstract of any patent application does not form part of the state of the art for these or any other purposes: Patents Act 1977, s 14(7) .

[13]   Patents Act 1977, s 2(3), as amended. Note, this does not apply to the test for inventive step, see Patents Act 1977, s 3, discussed at para 11.45.

[14]   [1971] RPC 153.

process. Opposition to the grant of the patent on the ground of lack of novelty was successful because the salesmen were considered by the court to be members of the public and in the absence of a fetter on them this amounted to prior publication. No evidence was led that the brochures had in fact been distributed to customers, but this was not considered to be necessary in order for anticipation to have taken place.

11.15   There are strict rules about which kinds of document can anticipate an invention and in which circumstances. Many of these were established many years ago and remain relevant today.

■ *General Tire and Rubber Co v Firestone Tyre and Rubber Co* [1972] RPC 457

This was a decision by the Court of Appeal. The plaintiffs claimed infringement of their patent for oil-extended rubber by the defendants, who counterclaimed for revocation of the patent, inter alia, on grounds of novelty. It was alleged that the patent had been anticipated by certain documents published prior to the priority date of 20 November 1970. The patent in suit was for a process for making a compound suitable for tyre treads by mixing synthetic rubber with oil and carbon black (a mixture referred to as 'oil-extended rubber') and for the product thus made. The earlier publications relied upon by the defendants were:

(1)   a Viennese patent dated 17 May 1943 for 'Semperit (a)' (compound with carbon black for tyres);

(2)   a Viennese patent dated 15 January 1945 for 'Semperit (c)' (extended synthetic rubber);

(3)   an English patent dated 2 August 1944 for 'Wilmington' (oil and latex invention);

(4)   two articles published in August 1947 and March 1950 in 'Rubber Age' (experiments using oil and carbon black to soften rubber).

It was held that:

- Alleged anticipatory matter must be interpreted at the date of its publication and without regard to subsequent events.[15]

- The alleged anticipatory material must be interpreted by a reader skilled in the relevant art at the relevant date (see bullet above). If the art is one having a highly developed technology, the notional skilled reader to whom the document is addressed can be a team, whose combined skills would normally be employed in that art in interpreting and carrying into effect instructions such as those contained in the document to be construed.

- Alleged anticipatory materials must be considered separately; it is not permissible to combine earlier unconnected publications to show anticipation[16] (compare with the concept of 'mosaicing' discussed later in terms of inventive step, para 11.49).

- If, in light of the previous points, the alleged anticipatory material contains a clear description of, or clear instructions to do or make something which would infringe the prospective patentee's patent if granted, the patent in suit will have been shown to lack the necessary novelty.[17]

- By corollary, if the prior publication contains a direction which is capable of being carried out in a manner which would infringe the patentee's claim, but would be at least as likely to be carried out in a way which would not do so, the patent in suit will not have been anticipated (although it might fail on grounds of obviousness, see paras 11.52ff).

---

[15]   The EPO authority on this is Case T/396/89 *UNION CARBIDE/High tear strength polymers* [1992] EPOR 312.

[16]   *British Ore Concentration Syndicate Ltd v Mineral Separation Ltd* (1909) 26 RPC 124.

[17]   Endorsed by the House of Lords in *Synthon v SmithKline Beecham* [2006] RPC 10 at paras 21–25. The prior art need not disclose exactly the same invention in all its facets (see *Glaverbel SA v British Coal Corporation* [1995] RPC 255), but it must normally disclose all of the technical features of the claim which is under scrutiny.

- 'A signpost, however clear, upon the road to the patentee's invention will not suffice. The prior inventor must be clearly shown to have planted his flag at the precise destination before the patentee.'[18]

- Given this, the *General Tire and Rubber* patent had not been anticipated by the prior publications. None of the publications planted a flag at the spot of GTR's invention. They were concerned essentially with different aims and different means of realising those aims.

11.16 The test to be applied is the 'notional skilled reader', and we might see this as a similar policy device to that used in tort/delict, viz, the 'reasonable person'.

11.17 The need to plant a flag in the exact spot claimed by the patent in suit means that prior publications or prior uses of matter which incidentally disclose a future invention might not anticipate the invention. In fact, the House of Lords has considered what is required for anticipation and has confirmed that this comprises two elements: (1) prior disclosure; and (2) enablement.

■ *Synthon BV v SmithKline Beecham plc* [2006] RPC 10

The dispute related to a salt of Paroxetine which is used to treat depression. Although one salt form of the compound had been marketed for some time, both parties to the dispute discovered, more or less simultaneously, another salt form which was far more suitable for pharmaceutical use (PMS). Both applied for patent protection within a few months of each other. Synthon's application referred to a group of salts of which one was PMS. Before this was published, however, SmithKline claimed priority on its own application and was successful in receiving a patent for a particular form of crystalline PMS. Synthon brought proceedings claiming that the invention had been anticipated by their own patent application on the basis of section 2(3) of the Patents Act 1977. It was held that there had been anticipation and this required the proof of two matters: first, that the Synthon application disclosed the invention which had been patented (prior disclosure); and, secondly, that an ordinary skilled man would be able to perform the disclosed invention if he attempted to do so by using the disclosed matter and common general knowledge (enablement).

11.18 This is a refinement on the approach to date.[19] The court stressed that these are two separate, albeit related, matters. As we have seen previously, a *prior disclosure* must be construed as it would have been understood by a skilled person at the date of the disclosure and not with the benefit of hindsight. Moreover, in order to anticipate, a prior disclosure must disclose subject matter such that, if performed by the skilled person, it would *necessarily* infringe the patent.[20] The prior disclosure must firmly plant the flag on the patentee's invention: 'the infringement must not merely be a possible or even likely consequence of performing the invention disclosed by the prior disclosure; it must be necessarily entailed. If there is more than one possible consequence, one cannot say that performing the disclosed invention will infringe.'[21] But note: the prior disclosure need not be expressed in the same form or by reference to the same parameters as the invention. Indeed, people do not even need to *know* what they are making[22]—the question is whether the relevant essential features of the invention are in the public domain.[23]

---

[18] See too *Koninklijke Philips Electronics NV v Princo Digital Disc GmbH; Koninklijke Philips Electronics NV v Chin-Shou Kuo* [2003] EWHC 1598 (Ch).

[19] Followed in eg *Wagner International AG v Earlex Ltd* [2012] EWHC 984 (Pat); *Hospira UK Ltd v Cubist Pharmaceuticals LLC* [2016] EWHC 1285 (Pat).

[20] See *Boegli-Gravures SA v Darsail-ASP Ltd* [2009] EWHC 2690 (Pat).

[21] *Synthon BV v SmithKline Beecham plc* [2006] RPC 10, para 11.17, per Lord Hoffmann at para 23.

[22] Case T303/86 (*CPC Int*) [1989] 2 EPOR 95 (a process for the manufacture of flavour concentrates was anticipated because it could not be distinguished from known cooking and frying processes which, albeit incidentally, produced versions of the said flavour concentrates. It was irrelevant that the chefs in question had no idea that this was so).

[23] *Merrell Dow Pharmaceuticals Inc and Another v HN Norton & Co Ltd and Others* [1996] RPC 76.

11.19 *Enablement* requires that the ordinary skilled person must be able to perform the invention from the information disclosed.[24] This is closely allied with the concept of sufficiency, which we discuss in Chapter 12 (paras 12.74ff). In *Synthon*, Lord Hoffmann said that he accepted that enablement meant the same thing in that case as it means for sufficiency, but he also remarked that this might not always be so because the perspective of the skilled person can change. For example, when considering sufficiency, the skilled person is attempting to reproduce the invention, while in a test for novelty the prior art may have disclosed the invention but not specifically identified it—the task of the skilled person is therefore different. In similar fashion, the role of the skilled person changes depending on whether we are discussing prior disclosure or enablement. With the former, the role is to understand what is meant by the prior disclosure, while with enablement the concern is whether the skilled person can 'work' the invention. It is important, therefore, to see the two concepts as distinct.

Exercise

Can you envisage any circumstances where there would be prior disclosure but no enablement? Could the converse hold true?

11.20 The House of Lords had ruled on novelty on a number of occasions prior to this decision. Various elements of those decisions remain valid.

■ *Asahi Kasei Kogyo KK's Application* [1991] RPC 485

The patent claimed by Asahi Kasei Kogyo KK was for a human protein (human tissue necrosis factor) produced by genetic engineering and useful in the treatment of tumours. The application was rejected by the Patent Office on the ground of lack of novelty under section 2(3) of the Patents Act 1977 because of information contained in another pending patent application filed by Dainippon. Although this second application had a filing date later than the application in suit, it claimed priority from an earlier application, which disclosed and claimed the protein but did not disclose any method of preparing it. The appeal went all the way to the House of Lords.

Key dates:

- Asahi Kasei Kogyo KK filed in UK on 4 April 1985 (priority claimed United States, 6 April 1984);
- Dainippon filed European patent on 26 February 1985 (priority claimed Japan, 6 March 1984).

It was held that matter comprised in the state of the art for the purposes of sections 2(2) *and* 2(3) had to be the subject of an *enabling disclosure*; that is, there must be enough information available to allow the skilled person to reproduce the invention. This is now refined in the light of the two-part test in *Synthon*. The point remains, however, that an invention is not made available to the public merely by a published statement of its existence, unless the method of 'working' the invention is so obvious as to require no explanation. There was no anticipation because the Dainippon application did not disclose the means to make the protein.

11.21 The interpretation given to section 2(3) can lead, albeit in rare circumstances, to double patenting. Imagine the following scenario:

6 March 1984	6 April 1984	26 February 1985	4 April 1985
Japan	United States	Europe	UK
Not enabling	Priority claimed	Protein claim	Protein claim

---

[24] Note, Synthon made a mistake in describing PMS in its application, but this was not a problem because it was held that the notional skilled person would nonetheless produce SmithKline's invention if he set out to make it using Synthon's instructions. The approach in *Synthon* was followed in *Jushi Group Co Ltd v OCV Intellectual Capital LLC* [2018] EWCA Civ 1416.

If the UK application is not anticipated by the European application because the former can claim priority from the US application, and if the Japanese application is not an enabling disclosure, then the UK patent can be granted. However, because the European patent claims priority from the Japanese patent, the state of the art in respect of the European patent will be tested prior to 6 March 1984, and will thereby exclude the contents of the US patent application. In this way it is also possible for the European patent to be granted. The House of Lords recognised this possibility in *Asahi* but considered that it would occur only rarely.[25]

■ Merrell Dow Pharmaceuticals Inc and Another v HN Norton and Co Ltd and Others [1996] RPC 76

Merrell Dow obtained a patent in 1972 for terfenadine, an antihistamine drug. When the patent expired in 1992 other companies (including Norton) began to manufacture and sell the drug. Merrell Dow had carried out extensive research into antihistamines in the intervening period and discovered that, once ingested, terfenadine was rapidly metabolised by the human liver and a by-product was produced: an acid metabolite. It was further discovered that this acid metabolite was almost exclusively responsible for the antihistamine effects of terfenadine. Merrell Dow sought and received a patent over the acid metabolite in 1980. When after 1992 other companies began to produce terfenadine, Merrell Dow brought infringement proceedings against them in respect of the production of the acid metabolite inherent in the use of terfenadine. The defendants counterclaimed that the 1980 patent had been anticipated by the use of terfenadine in clinical trials and by the specification of the appellant's earlier patent which had published information on the chemical composition of terfenadine and its antihistamine effect. The appeal was taken to the House of Lords.[26]

It was held that:

- The appeal be dismissed. In essence, the revocation claim was based on two arguments: anticipation by use and anticipation by disclosure. Regarding the former, it was held that use only makes an invention part of the state of the art if the use itself makes information about the details of the invention available to the public. Mere use is not enough. Thus,[27] secret use of a product or process prior to a patent application cannot be part of the state of the art. The ingestion of the drug by those taking part in trials did not *in se* reveal any information to the public about the existence of the acid metabolite.

- The question of anticipation by disclosure, which concerned the specification in the 1972 patent over terfenadine and its uses, revealed information which led to the production of the acid metabolite. Merrell Dow had argued that they could not anticipate that which they did not know to exist—the chemical composition of the acid metabolite. However, one can know the same thing under many different descriptions. Section 2(2) does not confine the state of the art to the chemical composition of products. It is the invention which must be known. The terfenadine patent describes a chemical and its effects on the body, one such effect being the antihistamine effect (which was caused by the acid metabolite). Lord Hoffmann stated that 'an invention is part of the state of the art if the information which has been disclosed enables the public to know the product under a description sufficient to work the invention'. He concluded: 'if the recipe which inevitably produces the substance is part of the state of the art, so is the substance as made by the recipe'. Indeed, this was supported by the EPO in T303/86 *CPC/Flavour Concentrates*,[28] in which the EPO's Technical Board refused an application to patent flavour concentrates on the ground that recipes in existing cookbooks, although not containing any references to flavour concentrates, nevertheless had the effect of making them.

---

[25] For a discussion of the issues on double patenting, see *Synthon BV v SmithKline Beecham plc* [2003] RPC 607 and in the Court of Appeal at [2003] RPC 114. See also E Nettleton et al, 'EPO decisions: double patenting' (2009) 38(4) CIPAJ 268.

[26] Given the extensive range of patenting in the chemical field and the particularities that can arise, the UK IPO has produced specific guidance; see IPO, Examination Guidelines for Patent Applications Relating to Chemical Inventions in the Intellectual Property Office (2014, 2017), www.gov.uk/government/publications/examining-patent-applications-relating-to-chemical-inventions.

[27] Unlike the law prior to 1977 (Patents Act 1949).   [28] [1989] 2 EPOR 95.

11.22   On one view this decision is consistent with those discussed earlier, such as *General Tire and Rubber Co,* which held that if alleged anticipatory material contains a clear description of, *or clear instructions to do or make,* something which would infringe the disputed patent (if valid), the disputed patent will have been shown to lack the necessary novelty.

11.23   The House of Lords' reservations on anticipation by use have since been distinguished, however, by Pumfrey J in *Halliburton Energy Services Inc v Smith International (North Sea) Ltd.*[29] It was stated that 'the law has always been that clear and unmistakable directions to do or make something within the claim will, if they form part of the state of the art, anticipate the claim'. The fact that *Merrell Dow* concerned a chemical produced inside the human body and so not analysable/available, was thought to make a difference. In the instant case the invention was a mechanical drill bit which could serve as a 'dumb' anticipation by conveying sufficient information to enable it to be dumbly reproduced.[30] Notwithstanding, it remains the case that a prior use must give clear and precise directions to reproduce an invention before it will amount to anticipation.[31]

11.24   Disclosure in the age of the internet has been addressed by the EPO. It has confirmed that the mere sending of an email containing details of an invention is not necessarily disclosure as such, assuming of course that this was not done on a confidential basis.[32] Furthermore, the use of specific URLs to host information puts it in a rather grey area between public and private: if the URL is so straightforward to guess, then this tends towards the public domain; if it is complex, then information found at its site can be as good as private data. The EPO has offered the following non-exhaustive test to consider the issues.[33]

> Where all the conditions set out in the following test are met, it can be safely concluded that a document stored on the World Wide Web was made available to the public:
> (i)   If, before the filing or priority date of the patent or patent application, a document stored on the World Wide Web and accessible via a specific URL, could be found with the help of a public web search engine by using one or more keywords all related to the essence of the content of that document and
> (ii) remained accessible at that URL for a period of time long enough for a member of the public, i.e. someone under no obligation to keep the content of the document secret, to have direct and unambiguous access to the document, then the document was made available to the public in the sense of Article 54(2) EPC.

11.25   The greater availability of information online and the growth of collaborative and community approaches to research (as well as challenges to the legitimacy and robustness of patents), led to the development of the peer-to-patent initiative. This enabled those other than patent examiners to contribute to what is considered as part of the state of the art in respect of an application. Pilots were held in the United States and then elsewhere, including in the UK.[34] These gave rise to changes in office practice in the United States and in the UK to an online observations button for comments to be added more readily.

Discussion point   For answer guidance visit **www.oup.com/uk/brown5e.**

To complete fully the novelty tests, notably those in *General Tire* and in *Synthon* there is the question of the scope of the invention. This is explored in more depth in Chapter 12 from the infringement perspective. Be aware, however, that approaching this exercise from just a question of novelty (or indeed obviousness) or infringement can be risky. A wide interpretation of the claim may catch an infringer; but this could lead to a finding of anticipation when viewed against the prior art. Such a situation has been termed the horns of a dilemma. Can you find the case where this term came from? And can you devise a scenario involving such horns?

---

[29] [2006] RPC 2; aff'd [2006] EWCA Civ 1715.   [30] See also *Evans Medical Ltd's Patent* [1998] RPC 517.
[31] *Quantel Ltd v Spaceward Microsystems Ltd* [1990] RPC 83.
[32] See Case T2/09 *PHILIPS/Public availability of an email transmitted via the internet* [2012] EPOR 41.
[33] Case T153/96 *PHILIPS/Public availaibility of documents on the World Wide Web* [2012] EPOR 40.   [34] See www.peertopatent.org.

The complex relationship between the protection conferred by a patent and its construction to assess validity faces uncertainty in the light of the decision of the Supreme Court in *Eli Lilly v Actavis* in 2017.[35] These two approaches have traditionally been considered in the same way, looking, as seen in paras 12.57–12.66 to what is covered by a literal and also purposive approach to the patent.[36] In *Eli Lilly v Actavis* the Supreme Court took a new approach to establishing the scope of the power conferred regarding the place of purposive construction and equivalents. The Supreme Court also stated that there was a difference between the extent of the protection conferred by a claim and interpreting a claim.[37] The Supreme Court decision is considered in depth in paras 12.67–12.70 regarding infringement. It is also important to note the decision here as it raises the prospect of (1) different approaches being taken to the two parts of infringement/validity dilemma; or (2) the new approach developed by the Supreme Court to the scope of patents, with regard to equivalents, also applying say to novelty instead of the established purposive approach.

Subsequently Arnold J in *Generics v Yeda Research*[38] rejected the proposal that equivalents should be relevant to novelty.[39] Arnold J considered that the Supreme Court could not have been removing purposiveness from interpretation of patents, given that a patent describes an invention to establish a legal monopoly.[40] The Supreme Court had been considering infringement and not novelty; and Arnold J considered that another decision of the Supreme Court would be needed to bring about a new approach to novelty.[41] It remains to be seen how this will develop. A splitting of approaches to construction regarding validity and infringement would be a significant change in patent law.[42]

Novelty at the margins

11.26   There are two sets of circumstances where claims to products have required a specialised approach in order to secure protection. The perspectives of the UK and the EPO have not always been in symmetry, although the process of approximation continues These are the cases of (1) product-by-process claims; and (2) selection patents.

Product-by-process claims

11.27   The UK has traditionally allowed this kind of claim whereby a product could be claimed by reference to its process of manufacture rather than by its own technical features. The claim might read, for example, 'the product obtained by the process described in claim 1'. Although this would give a more restricted right through the necessary link of the product and process, it could prove useful if someone manufactured products outside the country using a patented process and then imported the products—infringement proceedings could still be brought. Moreover, such a formulation is important when it is difficult to define the product by its own characteristics, for example if you cannot discern its structure. The EPO, however, has always taken a restricted view of such claims. It will only allow them when it is not possible to describe

[35] *Actavis v Eli Lilly* [2017] UKSC 48.

[36] See also *Generics (UK) Ltd (t/a Mylan) v Yeda Research and Development Company Ltd* [2017] EWHC 2629 (Pat), para 159.

[37] *Actavis v Eli Lilly* [2017] UKSC 48, paras 33.

[38] *Generics (UK) Ltd (t/a Mylan) v Yeda Research and Development Company Ltd* [2017[EWHC 2629 (Pat), see paras 134–135 regarding changes in approach to construction.

[39] *Generics (UK) Ltd (t/a Mylan) v Yeda Research and Development Company Ltd* [2017[EWHC 2629 (Pat), paras 161–167. Validity was also absent when the Court of Appeal considered *Eli Lilly v Actavis* in *Icescape Limited v Ice-World International* [2018] EWCA Civ 2219 (see discussion in paras 12.67–12.70).

[40] *Generics (UK) Ltd (t/a Mylan) v Yeda Research and Development Company Ltd* [2017] EWHC 2629 (Pat), para 138.

[41] ibid, para 161. Validity was also absent when the Court of Appeal considered *Eli Lilly v Actavis* in *Icescape Limited v Ice-World International* [2018] EWCA Civ 2219 (see discussion in para 12.70).

[42] See discussion in J Strath and R Jacob, 'Actavis v Lilly: the madness begins' (2018) 13(3) JIPLP 169–71 and S Moore et al, 'The High Court considers the doctrine of equivalents in the context of patent infringement and novelty' (2018) 40(3) EIPR 205–6.

the product other than in terms of a process of manufacture *and* when the product is patentable in its own right (ie novelty is not derived from the novelty of the process).[43]

11.28   The House of Lords considered this in *Kirin-Amgen Inc and Others v Hoechst Marion Roussel Ltd* regarding a European patent for the production of erythropoietin (confusingly, 'EPO') by genetic engineering (recombinant DNA technology). The core novelty question was: what counted as a new product given that EPO had already been purified from urine by others? The court noted that the UK was the only signatory state to the EPC to accept product-by-process claims,[44] that it is important that the UK should apply the same law as the EPO and the other member states when deciding what counts as new for the purposes of the EPC, and that on the facts the product in itself was not new compared to the state of the art. The House of Lords held that the correct interpretation of the law is that found in Article 64(2) EPC: 'If the subject-matter of the European patent is a process, the protection conferred by the patent shall extend to the products directly obtained by such process.'[45] The UK IPO has confirmed that it will now take the view that 'a claim to a product obtained or produced by a process is anticipated by any prior disclosure of that particular product per se, regardless of its method of production'.[46] Further, in *Hospira v Genentech*,[47] Birss J considered that from UK and EPO authorities on product-by-process claims, to be novel a product is to be obtained by all attributes of the process and has to have some novel attribute conferred on it by the process, as compared to the existing product.

Selection patents

11.29   We have established that mere mention of the existence of a substance is not fatal in terms of novelty— the prior art must plant a flag at the specific spot of an invention, for example by describing not only a substance's existence, but perhaps also its structure, its function, its special qualities, and the means to make it.[48] This is very useful in the chemical and biotechnological industries, where many thousands of substances or compounds or groups thereof may be known to exist, but where their particular properties are yet to be discovered and put to use. The refining or particularising of knowledge from the general to the specific can be achieved through *selection patents*. These concern the selection of entities from a wider known class or group and an attempt to patent them for particular qualities such as improved performance or novel use. Selection patents can be obtained provided there is no anticipation as defined earlier.

11.30   For example, in *Beecham Group's (Amoxcycillin) Application*,[49] Beecham held a patent for a wide class of penicillins from which it identified nine as being particularly effective and for which a further patent was sought. The case concerned one type from the group of nine which, it had been established, was especially amenable to absorption in the blood. The question arose as to whether the mention of the penicillin in the previous patent amounted to anticipation. The Court of Appeal held that it did not because the mention in the previous patent of the penicillin did not disclose any details regarding the efficacy of the drug in humans (it concerned only mice). Similarly, in *EI Du Pont de Nemours (Witsiepe's) Application*[50] the House

[43]   Guidelines for Examination in the European Patent Office (November 2018) http://documents.epo.org/projects/babylon/eponet.ns-f/0/2A358516CE34385CC125833700498332/$File/guidelines_for_examination_2018_hyperlinked_en.pdf (EPO Guidelines), Part F-IV, para 4.12, and T150/82 *IFF/Claim categories* [1984] OJEPO 309, paras 10–11. Remember, however, that Art 64(2) EPC states that the protection given by a claim for a process extends to the product of that process. This provides some residual comfort to patentees. The same provision is found in the Patents Act 1977, s 60(1)(c).

[44]   See also Case T150/82 *International Flavors & Fragrances Inc* [1984] OJEPO 309.

[45]   *Kirin Amgen Inc and Others v Transkaryotic Therapies Inc and Others (No 2) (aka Kirin-Amgen Inc v Hoechst and Others)* [2005] 1 All ER 667; [2005] RPC 9.

[46]   See UK IPO, 'Examining Guidelines for Patent Applications Relating to Biotechnological Inventions in the Intellectual Property Office (2013) (n 5), para 14.

[47]   *Hospira UK Ltd v Genentech Inc* [2014] EWHC 3857 (Pat).

[48]   Arguments that an existing product or process is tantamount to an 'equivalent' are better dealt with as questions of obviousness rather than novelty, since it is unlikely to be the case that all essential features have been revealed.

[49]   [1980] RPC 261.   [50]   [1982] FSR 303 (HL).

of Lords allowed a selection patent on a copolymer, despite prior art which had suggested that copolymers of this type could be produced with a number of variants from what had already been invented in the field. Crucially, there was no evidence that these variants had been tried, let alone that they revealed the particular properties possessed by the invention in the instant patent. The mere raising of a possibility does not defeat novelty.

11.31   The general rule which is accepted in the UK, and maybe in the EPO,[51] is that compounds are novel provided that no members of the sub-group are *specifically* described in the prior publication, even if they have been described in general terms.[52] If this has happened, then even the discovery of a new property will not be enough to establish novelty. The later patent must state the precise advantage of the selected invention over the prior art, otherwise 'it is merely an arbitrary selection among things already disclosed, and will lack novelty'.[53] Moreover, the Court of Appeal has confirmed that giving clear and unmistakable directions to use the *common general knowledge* to produce a specific material is no answer to a challenge of novelty.[54]

Biotechological inventions

11.32   These inventions deserve some special reflections regarding novelty. It might be objected that a biotechnological invention cannot be patented because it is not new in the strict sense required by patent law, because it can already be found in the natural world. You will remember, however, that novelty requires that the invention be available to the public before the priority date of the patent application. The key word here is *available*. It is not enough to anticipate an invention simply to know that a product exists in nature if it cannot also be accessed by human beings. At the very least, there must be evidence both of its availability and the means to reproduce it. Thus, in *Asahi Kasei Kogyo KK's Application*[55] (see para 11.20) the mere mention of the existence of human tissue necrosis factor in an earlier patent application in Japan was not enough to defeat the instant patent over a genetically engineered version of the protein which had been developed to assist in treating tumours.

 Question

Does this imply that the product must already have been produced before it will anticipate a later patent? Is it enough merely to provide instructions on how to produce it?

11.33   Another technique that has been used to avoid problems of novelty is to claim the artificially manufactured version of the product. Higher life forms (eukaryotics) contain segments of DNA in their genetic make-up that do not code for proteins. These segments are called *introns*. Lower life forms (prokaryotics), such as bacteria, do not contain introns.[56] Genetic engineering techniques can remove these introns, leaving only the 'purified' form of the DNA, which is known as copy or complementary DNA (cDNA). cDNA does not exist in nature and so it is argued that a claim to cDNA products is not a claim to a naturally occurring

[51]   See Case T658/91 *SANOFI/Enantiomer* [1996] EPOR 24, but compare with T198/84 *HOECHST/Thio-chloroformates* [1985] OJEPO 209 and Case T1042/92 *PFIZER/Penem* [1995] EPOR 207.

[52]   See also *Dr Reddy's Laboratories (UK) Ltd v Eli Lilly and Co* [2010] RPC 9.

[53]   *Ranbaxy (UK) Ltd and Another v Warner-Lambert Co* [2005] EWHC 2142 (Pat) per Pumfrey J at para 64.

[54]   See *Ranbaxy (UK) Ltd and Another v Warner-Lambert Co* [2007] RPC 4 at para 41, quoting the court of first instance in this regard. The prior art here was an earlier co-pending application which explicitly pointed the way towards the invention under challenge and merely required the application of the common general knowledge to carry it out.

[55]   *Asahi Kasei Kogyo KK's Application* [1991] RPC 485.

[56]   This information is important to bear in mind when you read *Biogen v Medeva* [1997] RPC 1.

entity.[57] You should note, however, that cDNA sequences perform exactly the same function as the natural version of the same sequences.

11.34 The European Directive on the protection of biotechnological inventions confirms that patents are available for:[58]

> An element isolated from the human body or otherwise produced by means of a technical process, including the sequence or partial sequence of a gene, even if the structure of that element is identical to that of a natural element.

11.35 However, it also reiterates that patents are not available for 'the human body or its parts in their natural state or for the simple discovery of one of its elements'.[59] The equivalent provisions were incorporated into UK law by the Patents Regulations 2000.[60] The EPO Guidelines for Examination confirm that '[i]n principle, biotechnological inventions are patentable under the EPC',[61] while also incorporating the qualifications outlined previously.

11.36 Nonetheless, a patent based on a naturally occurring entity is always open to the claim that the entity has already been extracted from its natural environment and utilised by humans. This kind of challenge has been successful in two high-profile cases. The Mexican government and other parties secured the revocation of a patent over corn plants with improved oil composition in 2004 on the ground that the patent lacked *novelty*; that is, that maize having the characteristics described in the patent was already known and available in Mexico.[62] A similar challenge saw the defeat of the Neem Tree Oil patent in 2000 for lack of novelty based on evidence from India.[63]

Question

Sometimes, free availability of the innovation is precisely what is sought and patents are seen to stand in the way of this. Consider the realm of health care, where the public health benefits of greater access to medicines, therapies, diagnostic tools, or even research tools are generally considered a public good. If the true aim is to ensure free access, then why not publish results of work on, say, the SARS virus (for details see https://medbroadcast.com/condition/getcondition/sars) and thereby put the knowledge in the public domain? This would effectively nix any future patents. Is there any advantage to be gained for the research community by obtaining a patent and then licensing it on liberal and generous terms, beyond, of course, a possible financial benefit for the patentee?

What can be excluded from the state of the art?

11.37 The starting premise in testing novelty is that everything which is available to the public *as a matter of fact* is counted as part of the state of the art. This can be varied only in a few narrow circumstances and the onus is on the applicant to satisfy the intellectual property office or court that the exceptions should apply. These are detailed in section 2(4) of the Patents Act 1977, which provides that (1) disclosures about the invention which are made in breach of confidence[64] or unlawfully; and (2) disclosures made by the inventor at a recognised international exhibition can be excluded from the state of the art provided that the patent is

---

[57] *HOWARD FLOREY/Relaxin* [1995] EPOR 541.

[58] Directive 98/44/EC of the European Parliament and of the Council of 6 July 1998 on the legal protection of biotechnological inventions (hereafter 'Biotechnology Directive'), Art 5(2).

[59] Biotechnology Directive, Art 5(1).

[60] Patents Regulations 2000 (SI 2000/2037), incorporating Sch A2 into the Patents Act 1977.

[61] EPO Guidelines, Part G-II, para 5.2.

[62] European Patent 0744888.   [63] European Patent 0436257.   [64] See *Threeways Pressings Ltd's Application* [2012] RPC 129.

applied for within six months of the disclosure in question. The relevant date for calculation purposes is the *filing date*. The applicant must prove on the balance of probabilities that there was a breach of confidence or unlawful act leading to disclosure, or in the case of exhibition, they must provide a statement on applying for the patent that this invention has been exhibited and provide a certificate from the exhibit organisers confirming the details of this within the next four months.[65] Only exhibitions which come under the terms of the Convention on International Exhibitions (1928, as amended 1951) can count, and this is unlikely to include regular industry trade fairs. The six-month window will be helpful to an inventor who is the victim of a breach of confidence only if the invention is at a sufficient stage of development to make it worthwhile applying for a patent. At best, it may mean that a more restrictive monopoly will be granted; at worst, it might preclude patent protection altogether if the invention is only in the idea or concept phase.

Question

What must an international exhibition do to qualify under the 1928 provisions?

Exceptions to exceptions: the case of 'medical use' patents

11.38   It has been a long-standing general principle of novelty in the UK that a known substance cannot be claimed for a new use, even if that use has never previously been described, unless the substance requires some form of transformation to make it suitable for that use. For example, a public announcement system cannot be claimed for use in attracting dogs if all that happens is that high-pitched whistle sounds are played through the system. But if the system must be technically modified to broadcast high-frequency signals inaudible to human ears, then it may be patentable in respect of that use. Thus, in *IG Farbenindustrie AG's Patents* it was stated: 'no man can have a patent merely for ascertaining the properties of a known substance'.[66] The strategy in such a case is then not to attempt to claim the *product* but to claim a new *method* of using a known material.

11.39   The EPO takes a different approach. The EBA has held in two decisions[67] that a claim to a new use of a known product is possible, as long as the claim identifies the use as a technical effect and it was previously unknown to the public. The new technical effect can be the mere uncovering of a new use for the substance. For example, in G2/88 *MOBIL OIL III/Friction Reducing Additive*[68] a product originally developed as a lubricant to prevent rust was found also to have qualities to reduce friction and a patent was allowed in this respect.[69] The advice from the UK IPO, however, is that this approach should not be followed. This is consistent with *Tate & Lyle Technology v Roquette Freres* when a use of maltotritol for a previously unsuspected effect was found to have been anticipated by prior art, even though the industry had not actually known what it was doing.[70]

11.40   But the UK recognises an exception to its general rule and this is in the realm of substances or compositions for treatment of the human or animal body.[71] We have already seen that *method* patents in this field are exceptions to patentability, but also noted that this does not apply to compounds or substances *used* in those methods. This point is specifically addressed in section 4A(3) of the Patents Act 1977. This states that

---

[65] See Patents Rules 2007 (as amended), r 5.   [66] (1930) 47 RPC 289 at 322.

[67] Case G2/88 *MOBIL OIL III/Friction Reducing Additive* [1990] OJEPO 93 and G6/88 *BAYER/Plant Growth Regulating Agent* [1990] OJEPO 114.

[68] [1990] OJEPO 93.

[69] *MOBIL* was applied in *BOARD OF REGENTS, UNIVERSITY OF TEXAS/Cancer Patent* (T1780/12) 2014 EPOR 28, when the Technical Board of Appeal rejected arguments of double patenting, as a different invention was claimed in the two patents, pursuant to 'Swiss-style' claims.

[70] [2010] FSR 1 and see UK Manual of Patent Practice (February 2016 as amended), para 2.14.

[71] Note this does not extend to apparatus (see para 11.239).

in relation to a method of treatment of the human or animal body by surgery or therapy, or a method of diagnosis practised on the human or animal body:

> in the case of an invention consisting of a substance or composition for use in any such method, the fact that the substance or composition forms part of the state of the art shall not prevent the invention from being taken to be new if the use of the substance or composition in any such method does not form part of the state of the art.

11.41   We observed previously that usually the way around the 'no new use' rule is to claim a method of new use; but this could not apply in the case of methods for therapy, surgery, or diagnosis because these are already specifically excluded from protection. Section 4A(3) therefore offers a way out of the problem: it operates as an exception to an exception.

Discussion point   For answer guidance visit **www.oup.com/uk/brown5e**

Look back at the definitions of the 'therapy' and 'surgery' in the previous section on method exclusions and in particular consider what we said about cosmetic methods of treatment. Are they 'therapeutic'? How does this affect the application of section 4A(3)? What about cosmetic surgery?

First and second medical use

11.42   A strict application of novelty from within the UK tradition should still impose limits on which medical uses can be claimed for a known substance. In particular, it would seem clear from section 4A(3) that only the first medical use can be claimed. Once a substance is deployed for a medical use this becomes part of the state of the art for any future additional medical uses and destroys novelty as a result.[72] Thus in *Bayer AG (Meyer's) Application*[73] a claim to 'Compound X for use in combating medical condition Y' was refused because compound X was already known as a therapy. But the influence from Europe is strong and the courts in the UK jurisdictions are not always able to resist it.

11.43   Developments over the years now mean that in some circumstances a second medical use *can* be claimed. This (further) exception was created by the EBA in G05/83 *EISAI/Second Medical Indication* in which it held that limitations to patentability should be construed narrowly—a common mantra[74]—and that legislative purpose did not overtly preclude second and subsequent uses and therefore they should be allowed. The Enlarged Board of Appeal (EBA) qualified this slightly, however, and required that such second or subsequent use claims should take a particular form following the practice of the Swiss Federal Intellectual Property Office. Because of this, they had been known as 'Swiss-type' claims (see para 10.100). The form is normally: '*use of substance X in the manufacture of a medicament for the treatment of condition Y*'. The focus, then, is to the method of manufacture of a new application of a known substance. This may be seen as one sophistic step too far. Nonetheless, the possibility of claiming second and subsequent medical uses has now been directly embraced by the EPO, and EPC 2000 removed the need to use Swiss-type claims.[75]

11.44   This reform is now found in section 4A(4) of the Patents Act 1977, as amended by section 1 of the Patents Act 2004. This puts to bed any residual doubts that second medical use claims were valid in the UK.[76] In

---

[72] Note, there must be actual evidence of prior therapeutic *use* of the substance to destroy novelty for later medical applications; it is not enough that a possible medical use has been discussed: see UK Manual of Patent Practice (February 2016 as amended), para 4A.25.

[73] [1984] RPC 11.   [74] Although see Case G1/07, n403, para 3.1.

[75] See EPC 2000, Art 54(5): 'Paragraphs 2 and 3 shall also not exclude the patentability of any substance or composition referred to in paragraph 4 for any specific use in a method referred to in Article 53(c), provided that such use is not comprised in the state of the art.'

[76] Previously they had only been grudgingly accepted; see *Wyeth's Application* [1985] RPC 545 and *Bristol-Myers Squibb v Baker Norton Pharmaceuticals* [2001] RPC 1, in which the court refused to rule on the correctness of *Easai* but did indicate that there were 'strong reasons' to maintain the view expressed by the judges in *Wyeth*, which followed *Easai* despite reservations.

Actavis UK Ltd v Merck[77] the Court of Appeal held that a valid second medical use claim can be made for a new and inventive dosage regime, despite the fact that the substance in question had been used in the prior art to treat the same condition at a different dosage. In this case there was such a low expectation of a successful treatment by applying this dosage that it was a novel idea and the claim was granted.[78] In Case G02/08 *ABBOTT RESPIRATORY/Dosage regime*[79] the EBA opined that there is no reason to consider dosage regimes differently to acceptable second medical uses. More far-reachingly, however, in determining what counts as an acceptable second medical use, the EBA held that EPC 2000 (Art 54(5)) now permits the patenting of a further specific use of a known medicament *even for the same disease* as long as it is claimed in a method of therapy,[80] and that Swiss-type claims should no longer be used.[81]

> ### Exercise
>
> Consider the implications of these decisions allowing the patenting of dosage regimes. Is there a risk that this will lead to the extension of patent protection? Consider the scenario where, through usage of a patented medicine, it becomes clear which dosage regime is most effective in the treatment of the disease and the dosage regime becomes patentable in its own right.

> ### Key points on novelty
>
> - This is a global test: material published before the priority date anywhere in the world can anticipate so that the invention is not new.
>
> - If material is in the public domain that is enough for it to be part of the prior art and able to anticipate so that the invention is not new.
>
> - Each individual piece of prior art must be considered separately.
>
> - Material can anticipate if it meets the tests set out in *General Tire* and *Synthon* regarding interpretation by the notional reader, and has a clear and enabling description of the invention.
>
> - There many additional complexities around disclosure by use, medical uses, and product by process claims.
>
> - Biotechnological inventions are novel (and not discoveries) if the claim is for a purified entity isolated from its natural environment. Mere knowledge of a naturally occurring product is not enough to anticipate; prior availability of the claimed invention must be shown.

Inventive step

11.45   The policies underlying the inventive step requirement involve the need to show merit by reaching a sufficiently high level of inventive activity to justify the award of the power of the patent. Also, an inventive step must demonstrate some advantage over what has gone before for the benefit of society; a departure

---

[77]   *Actavis UK Ltd v Merck* [2008] EWCA Civ 444.

[78]   Note too in the EPO it has been stated in Case T1758/07 *HANKKIJA-MAATALOUS/Food additive* [2011] EPOR 2 that second and subsequent medical indications can be protected by directing claims to a process for preparing the medicament—characterised by the use of the substance or composition—rather than direct use claims.

[79]   Case G2/08 *Dosage Regime/ABBOTT RESPIRATORY* [2010] EPOR 26.

[80]   See J Cockbain and Sigrid, 'Is the Enlarged Board of Appeal of the European Patent Office authorised to extend the bounds of the patentable? The G5/83 *Second Medical Indication/EISAI* and G2/08 *Dosage Regime/ABBOTT RESPIRATORY* cases' (2011) 42(3) IIC 257–71.

[81]   Now followed in the UK; see IPO, Practice Notice (Patents Act 1977: Second medical use claims) [2010] Bus LR 1242, now in UK Manual of Patent Practice (February 2016 as amended), para 4A.26–27.31.

from the prior art which has no advantages, or which represents a disadvantage, should be denied protection for lack of inventive step.[82] Finally, and as a parallel with the rationale behind novelty, the public should not be prevented from doing things which are simply obvious extensions or developments of what they were already doing.[83]

11.46 Inventive step is also referred to as non-obviousness—indeed, US law uses this term.[84] Inventive step is defined in section 3 of the Patents Act 1977, as amended, and the equivalent provisions are found in Article 56 EPC 2000. Section 3 provides:

> An invention shall be taken to involve an inventive step if it is not obvious to a person skilled in the art, having regard to any matter which forms part of the state of the art by virtue only of section 2(2) above (and disregarding section 2(3) above).

11.47 This raises three questions:

(1) What is the state of the art for the purposes of testing inventive step?

(2) What traits or qualities does the person skilled in the art possess?

(3) How do we know when something is 'obvious' to the person skilled in the art?

State of the art

11.48 The starting point for assessing the state of the art for inventive step purposes is the same as that we use for testing novelty, namely the definition in section 2(2) of the Patents Act 1977—so it includes virtually the sum total of human knowledge that is available to the public anywhere in the world. It does not include, however, the content of any patent applications designating the UK and filed before the priority date of the current application under scrutiny (s 2(3)).

 Question

Why are patent applications excluded from inventive step but not from novelty?

11.49 We saw that in order to defeat novelty a single piece of prior art must directly plant the flag on the applicant's invention and it is not possible to combine different pieces of prior art in order to say that something is not new.[85] This combining process is called *mosaicing*. In contrast, this is perfectly permissible when testing inventive step as long as this is something that the person skilled in the particular art would have done. This is an important limit. The activities of the person skilled in the art clearly vary from technology to technology, and this explains why the criterion of inventive step is something of a moveable feast. The subtle relationship between inventive step and novelty was explained by Lord Hoffmann in *Synthon*: [i]f performance of an invention disclosed by the prior art would not infringe the patent but the prior art would make it obvious to a skilled person how he might make adaptations which resulted in an infringing invention, then the patent may be invalid for lack of an inventive step but not for lack of novelty.'[86]

11.50 A feature of the state of the art which is not necessarily field-specific is *common knowledge*.[87] The courts will often assume that certain features, practices, or possibilities are so manifestly self-evident that they

---

[82] Case T119/82 OJEPO 5/84.   [83] *Windsurfing International Inc v Tabur Marine (GB)* [1985] RPC 59 at 77.

[84] 35 USC, para 103.

[85] See too EPO Guidelines, Part G-VII, para 4: 'it is fair to construe any published document in the light of subsequent knowledge and to have regard to all the knowledge generally available to the person skilled in the art the day before the filing or priority date valid for the claimed invention'.

[86] *Synthon BV v SmithKline plc* [2006] RPC 10 at para 25.

[87] For a rare instance of an appeal court overturning a trial judge's assessment of common knowledge, see *Apimed Medical Honey Ltd v Brightwake Ltd* [2012] EWCA Civ 5.

do not need to be spelled out in detail but can be assumed to be part of the skilled person's experience. This applies both to general common knowledge and to field-specific common knowledge.[88] In *MedImmune Ltd v Novartis Pharmaceuticals UK Ltd*[89] the Court of Appeal found that even if a concept had not been used, it could still be part of the common general knowledge—although factually this will be unlikely.

11.51   While it is theoretically the case that the entire sum of publicly available information is at the fingertips of the skilled person, the intellectual property office or court will ask what was the particular skilled person in the field under scrutiny likely to come across and consider together.[90] The more obscure the connections necessary across different fields, and the more documents that have to be mosaiced to come up with the invention, the more likely it is that the invention will be found to have an inventive step. Relevant factors include (1) the age of the documents; (2) the role of references in linking one document to others; (3) the proximity of fields from which the prior art comes; (4) the amount of effort or analysis required of the skilled person in identifying the relevant features in the prior art; and (5) the ubiquity of some documents in the field such that they form part of the common knowledge.[91]

11.52   The question of whether it is appropriate to look across and between technical fields is largely answered by the nature of the problem to be solved and whether the relevant skilled person would be expected to look for parallels in related fields where, perhaps, similar problems are encountered.[92] Similarly, it is also possible to consider that the skilled person might call upon the expertise of others in related fields in attempting to solve their problem. Indeed, the person skilled in the art might, in fact, be a team of different specialists and this should include those relevant to the field(s) of the invention.[93]

■ *Conor Medsystems Inc v Angiotech Pharmaceuticals Inc and Another* [2008] RPC 28

This case involved a challenge on the grounds of obviousness to a patent relating to a device used in coronary surgery called a *stent*. This is implanted into diseased arteries to keep them from collapsing. The problem facing the skilled person was how to develop stents that did not cause restenosis (closure of the artery channel)—a pre-existing problem for 33–50 per cent of patients treated with existing techniques. Here it was held that the person skilled in the art and trying to solve the pre-existing problem would be a team which would include, inter alia, an interventional cardiologist and someone familiar with drugs for treating cancer. All of the experts would bring their own knowledge to the problem. In the instant case where the invention involved coating the stent with taxol (an anti-angiogenic), it was held by the Court of Appeal to be obvious that the skilled person would consider taxol to be worth testing to see what its properties were. However, the House of Lords ruled that the prior art merely mentioned taxol as one of an undifferentiated (and large) number of drugs which could be tried and this was insufficient to make it obvious that taxol would prevent restenosis. The correct question to ask was whether it was obvious to use a taxol-coated stent to prevent restenosis. The patentee had disclosed a plausible invention which, if it worked, could be patentable as long as the solution itself was not obvious. It is the technical solution which must be tested for obviousness, not the question of whether it was obvious to try taxol (among many other compounds).

---

[88] On the relevance of (even highly-technical) sector standards as forming part of the common knowledge, see *Nokia v Ipcom* [2009] EWHC 3482 (Pat); confirmed on appeal [2011] EWCA Civ 6.

[89] [2012] EWCA Civ 1234.

[90] But even publication of material a few days before the priority date can be fatal in terms of inventive step; see *Merck Sharp & Dohme Corp v Teva UK Ltd* [2011] EWCA Civ 382.

[91] A good step-by-step illustration of what the skilled person might know and mosaic is found in *Ivax Pharmaceuticals UK Ltd v Akzo Nobel NV; Arrow Generics Ltd v Akzo Nobel NV* [2007] RPC 3.

[92] Case T176/84 *MOBIUS/Neighbouring Field* [1986] OJEPO 50.

[93] *Schlumberger Holdings Ltd v Electromagnetic Geoservices AS* [2009] RPC 19.

> **Question**
>
> Could this variability in the application of the inventive step test lead to unfairness in terms of the standards to which different technologies might be held? Consider in the light of the decision in *Hospira v Genentech* [2016] EWCA Civ 1185—the key issue is the scientific evidence, rather than a willingness to try because of the prospect of commercial reward.

The qualities of the person skilled in the art

11.53   The idea of the person skilled in the art is a device used by intellectual property offices and courts to assess the merits of any given innovation. We are concerned with the notional expert; the courts will hear evidence in each case on what that expert might be expected to know. They are an ordinary member of their field who is aware of everything in the state of the art.[94] They are, however, unimaginative and with no inventive capacity. Thus, Lord Reid stated in *Technograph v Mills & Rockley*: '[i]n dealing with obviousness, unlike novelty, it is permissible to make a "mosaic" out of the relevant documents, but it must be a mosaic which can be put together by an unimaginative man with no inventive capacity'.[95] The range of qualities of this person was helpfully summarised for us by Jacob LJ in *Rockwater v Technip France SA and Another*:[96]

> the person would be, first and foremost, 'a nerd'. Beyond the traits we have just discovered, they are forgetful, in that they will not join the dots between different pieces of prior art unless it is obvious to do so, and unconnected matter will drift from their memory as they moves through the literature. They can, however, have the prejudices of their field, which may be long-standing assumptions that a particular avenue of research will be fruitless. Those who prove otherwise have, therefore, a good chance of clearing the inventive step hurdle. Similarly, those who identify a problem for the first time and provide a means to overcome it should have few difficulties.[97]

> For example, in *Dyson Appliances Ltd v Hoover*[98] the issue of prejudice was raised and held to be relevant in determining what the skilled person would consider obvious to do. The advent of the bagless vacuum cleaner was an innovation that came out of the blue—no one had even perceived a problem with conventional machines.

11.54   The skilled person is not expected to pursue avenues that they would regard as futile.[99] As the EPO Guidelines put it: 'The term "obvious" means that which does not go beyond the normal progress of technology but merely follows plainly or logically from the prior art; i.e. something which does not involve the exercise of any skill or ability beyond that to be expected of the person skilled in the art.'[100] Timing is also vitally important. We ask the skilled person to consider what was obvious at the time of the priority date and it is crucial to guard against the vagaries of ex post facto analysis—many things may appear obvious with hindsight.[101] It is not appropriate to define the class of expert so broadly that the specific knowledge and prejudices of those most closely involved in the actual field with which the patent is concerned do not form part of the prejudices and attributes of the skilled person.[102]

11.55   Evidence on what the skilled person would know or do is taken from relevant experts at first instance. Appeal courts do not have an opportunity to re-hear evidence and should not overrule a trial judge's

---

[94] See, eg, *WL Gore & Associates GmbH v Geox SpA* [2008] EWHC 2311 (Pat), in which the person skilled in the art was held to be a person or team with a practical interest in the functional aspects of shoe design.

[95] [1972] RPC 346 at 355.   [96] [2004] EWCA Civ 381; [2004] RPC 46, paras 6–10, quote para 7.

[97] See, eg, *El-Tawil v Comptroller General of Patents* [2012] EWHC 185 (Ch).   [98] [2001] RPC 26.

[99] *Hallen Co v Barbantia (UK) Ltd* [1991] RPC 195.   [100] EPO Guidelines, Part G-VII, para 4.

[101] *Ferag AG v Muller Martini Ltd* [2007] EWCA Civ 15.

[102] *Mayne Pharma Ltd and Another v Debiopharm SA and Another* [2006] EWHC 1123 (Pat).

findings of fact unless there are very good reasons to do so. The position was summed up by Lord Hoffmann in *Biogen v Medeva*:[103]

> The need for appellate caution in reversing the judge's evaluation of the facts is based upon much more solid grounds than professional courtesy. It is because specific findings of fact, even by the most meticulous judge, are inherently an incomplete statement of the impression which was made upon him by the primary evidence. His expressed findings are always surrounded by a penumbra of imprecision as to emphasis, relative weight, minor qualification and nuance (as Renan said, la vérité est dans une nuance), of which time and language do not permit exact expression, but which may play an important part in the judge's overall evaluation . . . Where the application of a legal standard such as negligence or obviousness involves no question of principle but is simply a matter of degree, an appellate court should be very cautious in differing from the judge's evaluation.

The test for obviousness

11.56   The criterion of 'inventive step' can be thought of as a misnomer. It is not inventive for someone to take the next logical, obvious *step* in the development of any given field of technology; rather, what is required is a *leap* forward in ways that would not be obvious to others working in the field. It is an objective test. The classic approach to this question was laid down in:

■ *Windsurfing International Inc v Tabur Marine (GB) Ltd* [1985] RPC 59 (CA)

The patent in suit claimed a wind-propelled apparatus for use on water with a sail attached to a surfboard and two arcuate booms attached to the sail—imagine an ordinary windsurf board. In an action for infringement of the patent, the defendants counterclaimed that the patent was invalid both on grounds of novelty and obviousness. The novelty issue arose from prior use of a similar device by a third party and obviousness was argued both in relation to this prior use and/or in view of a printed publication which appeared before the priority date of the patent. The publication was an article entitled 'Sailboarding—Exciting New Water Sport', which described the basic concept as that of the patent except that the sail was square-rigged. The prior use was allegedly ten years prior to the patent application by a 12-year-old boy who had built a sailboard and used it on public waterways on summer weekends over two consecutive seasons. This sailboard differed from that claimed only in that the booms were straight and not arcuate. It was held that the patent was invalid both on grounds of novelty and obviousness. As regards novelty it did not matter that prior use was by a private individual and in a non-commercial setting. Of relevance was the extent of the public nature of the use which, in the case, was considerable, even though in relative terms the public use was of short duration. Obviousness is to be tested by asking what would have been obvious to a person skilled in the particular art at the time of the priority date of the patent.

11.57   *MedImmune Ltd v Novartis Pharmaceuticals UK Ltd*[104] stressed the importance, when identifying the inventive concept, of the claim made by the patentee. The challenges of the construction of this are explored in chapter 12. The *Windsurfing* test was reformulated by the Court of Appeal in 2007 in *Pozzoli SPA v BDMO SA*.[105] The following should be taken as an accurate reflection of the current approach and *Windsurfing* and *Pozzoli* should be read together.

> #### The *Windsurfing/Pozzoli* approach
>
> (1) (a) Identify the notional 'person skilled in the art'.
> (1) (b) Identify the relevant common general knowledge of that person.
> (2) Identify the inventive concept of the claim in question or if that cannot readily be done, construe it.
> (3) Identify what, if any, differences exist between the matter cited as forming part of the 'state of the art' and the inventive concept of the claim or the claim as construed.[106]

---

[103] [1997] RPC 1 at 45.   [104] [2012] EWCA Civ 1234.
[105] [2007] FSR 37. An explanation of this reformulation can be found at paras 15 and 16.
[106] The UK Manual of Patent Practice (February 2016 as amended) offers the following helpful instruction:

In determining whether an invention is obvious in the light of a given document combined with common general knowledge, other documents, or instances of prior use, there are two major considerations: (i) whether the skilled person could reasonably be expected to find the document in conducting a diligent search for material relevant to the problem in hand … and (ii) whether, if he had found the document, he would have given it serious consideration (para 3.75.1).

(4) Viewed without any knowledge of the alleged invention as claimed, do those differences constitute steps which would have been obvious to the person skilled in the art or do they require any degree of invention?

 Question

Before reading on, ask yourself—what is the inventive concept involved with a windsurf board? Is it the sail, the boom, the board or something else?

11.58   The inventive concept in *Windsurfing* was the 'free-sail': a sail attached to an unstayed spar on one side which is connected to the board by a universal joint, that is, a joint having three axes of rotation. This allows the sail to be manipulated to power and control the board without the need for a rudder or other means. The inventive concept described in the publication was essentially that contained in the patent. The essential difference between the two was the shape of the sail: square in the publication, triangular in the patent. This, however, made no practical difference in the determination of obviousness. The prior use by the young boy was of a device essentially the same as the vehicle described in the patent in suit save that the booms were straight and not arcuate. It would have been obvious to anyone skilled in the art in 1958 on witnessing the boy's board that an improvement would be to replace the straight booms with arcuate booms. Indeed, the straight booms formed such a shape when the board was put to water.

11.59   The importance of the *Windsurfing/Pozzoli* structured approach[107] is to get the court in the right frame of mind to test obviousness and to avoid the trap of applying hindsight.[108] Here is an old but valuable illustration of the importance of defining 'inventive concept'.

■ *Parks-Cramer Co v GW Thornton and Sons Ltd* [1966] RPC 407 (CA)

This was an appeal to the Court of Appeal concerning a patent for a device used to clean the floor around textile machines of 'fly' (or lint) by the automatic and repeated passage of an overhead vacuum cleaner having vacuum tubes extending almost to the floor. An action for infringement was brought which was met with a counterclaim alleging invalidity on ground of obviousness. Inter alia, it was alleged that the invention was obvious because of general knowledge of the problem about the collection of fly or lint in textile factories and the existence of certain patents previously granted which were aimed at alleviating the problem. Such patents included (1) overhead devices which blew the fly onto the floor for collection; and (2) suction devices aimed at the parts of the machine where most fly accumulated. None of these machines sought to deal with the problem of accumulation of fly upon the floor of the factory generally or in particular with the accumulation of fly in the aisles. Finally, (3) a number of devices were developed in an attempt to clean factory floors of fly and some were patented. They operated on the principle of directing air currents across the floor in one direction so as to blow the fly towards fixed collecting points where the fly was removed by suction into ducts or collecting chambers. None of these devices proved satisfactory in practice. On the basis of these points, it was argued by the defendants that the extension of the basic ideas disclosed by these devices and patents to using a vacuum device to clean factory floors of fly was obvious.

It was held that:

• The patent was valid. The inventive concept contained in the plaintiff's patent was this: if you pass a suction nozzle closely adjacent to the floor repeatedly at regular intervals over a fixed path along the aisles between and at the ends of rows of machines the suction will remove the fly from *the whole of the floor* and *not merely* that part of the floor which is in the relatively narrow direct track of the suction nozzle.

---

[107]   Though the modified test of *Pozzoli* is now mainly used, the *Windsurfing* approach is still valid and used occasionally, eg in *Handi-Craft Co v B Free World Ltd* [2007] EWHC 10 (Ch).
[108]   *Wheatley v Drillsafe Ltd* [2001] RPC 7.

- It was not obvious that by passing such a machine over the floor in such a manner that the whole of the floor would be cleaned and not just a narrow tract.

- The problem which the plaintiff sought to solve had been a problem since the early 1950s. Many individuals and companies had sought to solve it but no one had been successful. It had occurred to no one that the solution lay in passing a suction tube repeatedly over a narrow track in the aisles.

- The evidence shows that the plaintiff's machine was an immediate commercial success and although this could be attributable to many other factors, this point fortified the view that it was not obvious to solve the problem in the way in which the plaintiff did.

11.60 It would appear that the inventors themselves did not even appreciate the efficacy of their invention in cleaning the whole of the floor rather than a narrow tract. Yet, not only did this not affect the validity of the patent, it aided the court in determining that the invention was not obvious: the plaintiff was very experienced in the field of cleaning devices for use in textile mills.[109]

11.61 The House of Lords in 2004 in *Sabaf SpA v MFI Furniture Centres Ltd and Others* noted that before we consider whether an invention is obvious, we must first decide what the invention is or whether it is merely a collocation, that is, the juxtaposition of devices or inventions which do not make up a unified whole. It was held that two features in respect of gas burners for kitchen cookers were a mere collocation, being a means to draw air in above the burner and a way of controlling flow under the burner which did not interact with each other—there were therefore two inventions, neither of which differed significantly from the prior art in line with the *Windsurfing* structure.[110] The example offered by the EPO on this point is microprocessors. which are interconnected individual transistors and interact to do something over and above the sum of the individual transistors.[111]

11.62 Against this backdrop, the Court of Appeal in *Conor* best summed up the position:[112]

> In the end the question is simply 'was the invention obvious?' This involves taking into account a number of factors, for instance the attributes and common general knowledge of the skilled man, the difference between what is claimed and the prior art, whether there is a motive provided or hinted by the prior art and so on. Some factors are more important than others. Sometimes commercial success can demonstrate that an idea was a good one. In others 'obvious to try' may come into the assessment. But such a formula cannot itself necessarily provide the answer. Of particular importance is of course the nature of the invention itself.[113]

11.63 Commercial success or its unlikelihood can be a *faux ami*.[114] Numerous factors can play a role in the success of an invention in the market and many of them may have nothing to do with inventiveness. One should be cautious, especially when dealing with the commercial success of a product subject to anterior patent protection, as there is a clear reason why no one else has ever launched a similar product.[115] Further, the court in *Hospira v Genentech*[116] (see para 11.28) considered that it was not necessary that the skilled person 'would' have reached the conclusion without an inventive step; it was enough that they 'could' have done—although because of a variety of options such as whether it was worthwhile commercialising, they may have chosen not to do so.

---

[109] For an interesting application to children's buggies, see *Phil & Ted's Most Excellent Buggy Co Ltd v TFK Trends for Kids GmbH* [2014] EWCA Civ 469; for games players, see *Koninklijke Philips Electronics N.V. v Nintendo of Europe GmbH* [2014] EWHC 1959 (Pat); and for the speed of wind turbines, see *Wobben v Siemens* [2017] EWCA Civ 5.

[110] [2004] UKHL 45; [2005] RPC 10.   [111] EPO Guidelines, Part G-VII, para 7.

[112] *Conor Medsystems Inc v Angiotech Inc and Another* [2007] EWCA Civ 5, para 45.

[113] For an example of challenges for the trial in applying the evidence before them, see decision of the Court of Appeal in *Teva UK Ltd v Leo Pharma A/S* [2015] EWCA Civ 779.

[114] But neither is it altogether irrelevant: *Dyson Appliances Ltd v Hoover Ltd* [2002] RPC 22: 'commercial realities cannot necessarily be divorced from the kinds of practical outcome which might occur to the skilled addressee as worthwhile'.

[115] *Dr Reddy's Laboratories (UK) Ltd v Eli Lilly and Co* [2008] EWHC 2345 (Pat), para 187.

[116] *Hospira v Genentech* [2016] EWCA Civ 780.

Discussion point   For answer guidance visit **www.oup.com/uk/brown5e.**

How many different factors can you think of that might influence market success?

11.64   The key question in deciding whether commercial success is a relevant factor in determining inventive step lies in being able to identify *why* there was commercial success and to assess whether this was because of inventiveness. In *Haberman v Jackel*[117] the invention was very simple and concerned the product known as the 'AnyWayUp Cup'—a cup especially designed to help babies to make the transition from suckling to proper feeding (UK Patent 2266045—why not try to find this on Espacenet?).

11.65   The inventiveness was said to lie in the fact that the cup sealed between sips and so avoided drips. Rival companies had similar devices which worked through various mechanisms. It was argued that Haberman had not produced anything outside the normal workshop modifications which had long been available to those in the art. It was a simple solution to a known problem using known and readily available expedients.

11.66   Laddie J laid out a list of factors that might have a bearing on a determination of obviousness:[118]

Inventive step: some of the considerations

(1) What was the problem which the patented development addressed?

(2) How long had that problem existed?

(3) How significant was the problem seen to be?

(4) How widely known was the problem and how many were likely to be seeking a solution?

(5) What prior art would have been likely to be known to all or most of those who would have been expected to be involved in finding a solution?

(6) What other solutions were put forward in the period leading up to the publication of the patentee's development?

(7) To what extent were there factors which would have held back the exploitation of the solution even if it was technically obvious?

(8) How well has the patentee's development been received?

(9) To what extent can it be shown that the whole or much of the commercial success is due to the technical merits of the development, that is, because it solves the problem?

This is not an exhaustive list but it is a helpful guide, which may point either towards or away from inventiveness.[119]

 Exercise

Consider each of these factors and the ways in which they might influence a determination of obviousness.

11.67   In the end Ms Haberman kept her patent. She took a step forward that many others in the field could have taken during the long period during which the problem was known but did not. Nor did the simplicity of the invention defeat inventiveness; indeed, rather the opposite—if it was so straightforward, then why had it not been done before? Moreover, evidence to the court suggested strongly that the tremendous commercial success of the cup was due primarily to its technical quality and contribution to the state of the art—it did not leak.

---

[117] [1999] FSR 683.

[118] As stated in *Generics (UK) Ltd and Others v H Lundbeck A/S* [2009] UKHL 12, in the end the question of obviousness must be considered on the facts of each single case.

[119] Building on in particular *Generics (UK) Ltd and Others v H Lundbeck A/S* [2009] UKHL 12, the court must attach weight to any particular factor in taking into account all the relevant circumstances.

11.68   Meeting an unmet need may be evidence of inventiveness, but it is not inventive merely to take advantage of an upturn in economic circumstances which create a market not previously existing (eg by making certain materials affordable when previously they were not). Similarly, it is not because it has taken a lot of time and expense to bring a product to market that this could in any sense imply inventiveness.[120]

Obvious to try

11.69   We have mentioned previously the idea of 'obvious to try', which is often offered as a gloss on the obviousness test.[121] The House of Lords confirmed in *Conor Medsystems Inc v Angiotech Pharmaceuticals Inc*[122] that an invention can only be obvious if there is an expectation of success and noted that the expectation of success must be assessed in the light of the purpose for which the invention is intended; that is, the solution to the technical problem that it is intended to fix. Furthermore, when evaluating the reasonable expectation of success, one must consider without hindsight the attractiveness of the route at the time, taking into account all the surrounding circumstances.[123] Lord Hoffmann's views on the question of 'obvious to try without any expectation of success' are worth noting: 'This oxymoronic concept has, so far as I know, no precedent in the law of patents.'[124]

The EPO approach

11.70   The EPO adopts a problem-and-solution approach. It asks what is the pre-existing technical problem and is it solved by a technical solution? The approach in the EPO and in the UK are much the same at this broad level. But the EPO has developed a three-point test which differs somewhat from the UK. Non-obviousness is determined by:

   (1)   determining the 'closest prior art';

   (2)   establishing the 'objective technical problem' to be solved; and

   (3)   considering whether or not the claimed invention, starting from the closest prior art and the objective technical problem, would have been obvious to the skilled person.[125]

11.71   The closest prior art often restricts the search to the same technical field as the invention and looks for the most promising point from which an obvious development towards the invention might be made. This is to be assessed on the day before the filing or priority date of the invention.[126] The objective technical problem is formulated by comparing the prior art with the distinguishing features of the invention. Occasionally, this formulation may be at odds with how the applicant has framed the problem in the patent application. This requires a reformulation of the problem in the application since the technical formulation is supposed to be the objective assessment of the problem to be solved. The technical problem can be interpreted broadly and may only cover an alternative means to produce the same or similar effects in the state of the art.

11.72   This test differs most significantly from the UK in its starting point of seeking (only) the closest prior art. As Pumfrey J said at first instance in *Ranbaxy*:[127]

> [I]ts concentration on the closest prior art, which must stem from a belief that if an invention is not obvious in the light of the closest prior art it cannot be obvious in the light of anything further away. This runs the risk of offending against the principle that a skilled man must be permitted to do that which is obvious in the light of each individual item of prior art seen in the light of the common general knowledge.

[120]   *Teva v Gentili* [2003] EWHC 5 (Pat); [2003] EWCA Civ 1545.
[121]   Its origins are found in *Johns-Manville Corporation's Patent* [1967] RPC 479.
[122]   *Conor Medsystems Inc v Angiotech Pharmaceuticals Inc* [2008] RPC 28. See also *Saint-Gobain PAM SA v Fusion Provida Ltd and Another* [2005] EWCA Civ 177.
[123]   See A Carter, '*Conor Medsystems Inc v Angiotech Pharmaceuticals Inc and Others*: House of Lords judgment clarifying the assessment of "inventive step"' (2008) 30(10) EIPR 429. See also *Generics (UK) Ltd v Daiichi Pharmaceutical Co Ltd* [2009] EWCA Civ 646.
[124]   See also *Omnipharm Ltd v Merial* [2011] EWHC 3393 (Pat), para 92, involving spot-on flea treatments; CA appeal at [2013] EWCA Civ 2—obvious to try is not an independent ground of obviousness.
[125]   EPO Guidelines, Part G-VII, para 5.   [126]   EPO Guidelines, Part G-VII, para 5.1.   [127]   [2005] EWHC 2142 (Pat), para 69.

That said, Pumfrey J did not in the end consider that there are differences of principle at stake as between the jurisdictions.[128]

Exercise

Compare the UK approach to three other means of testing inventiveness:

(1) Would the person skilled in the art, having regard to any item(s) of prior art or common general knowledge, have arrived at the claimed invention (which is the European approach)?

(2) Would any item(s) of prior art or common general knowledge have motivated a person skilled in the art to reach the claimed invention (which is the Japanese approach)?

(3) Would any item(s) of prior art or common general knowledge have motivated, with a reasonable expectation of success, a person skilled in the art to reach the claimed invention (which is the US approach)?

Which of these is a softer or harder option? What are the advantages and disadvantages of the UK maintaining its current approach?

11.73 Biotechology inventions again raise their own issues for obviousness. In *Genentech Inc's Patent*[129] the Court of Appeal considered the validity of Genentech's patent for human tissue plasminogen activator (t-PA), a protein occurring naturally in the human body that assists in the dissolution of blood clots. Genentech was able to produce sufficient quantities of t-PA in a sufficiently pure form to market as a therapeutic agent through the application of standard recombinant DNA techniques. At least five other teams embarked on similar work at considerable expense and with a degree of uncertainty of success. Genentech was the first to succeed in establishing t-PA's genetic sequence and sought a patent for products that included t-PA produced by genetic engineering techniques and processes used in its production. Revocation of the patent was sought, inter alia, for lack of inventive step. It was held that:

- The patent was invalid for lack of inventive step. It was obvious to a person skilled in the art to set out to produce human t-PA by recombinant DNA technology. All steps taken by Genentech in establishing the composition of the relevant sequences and applying that knowledge to produce t-PA were applications of known technology towards a known end without any original step.

- The fact that at least five other teams embarked towards the same goal using the same techniques was a sign of obviousness. Being the first to succeed was not enough; but if no one else had set out to produce the invention this might be evidence that it was not obvious.

- Laborious and costly effort did not necessarily involve an inventive step, even if it amounted to more than the exercise of proficiency.

11.74 In coming to this decision the Court of Appeal opined that the skilled person in such a hi-tech industry must possess a degree of ingenuity and inventiveness, for otherwise they would not be part of the industry at all. Moreover, inventiveness could be assessed by reference to a research team where this is the standard

---

[128] See also Jacob LJ in *Actavis UK Ltd v Novartis AG* [2010] EWCA Civ 82 and *Teva UK Ltd v AstraZeneca AB* [2012] EWHC 655 (Pat). For an evaluation of the parallel and largely consistent fates of Apple's European Patent in national enforcement action, see IPKat, 'Apple's European slide-to-unlock patent declared invalid in Germany', 6 September 2015, http://ipkitten.blogspot.co.uk/2015/09/apples-european-slide-to-unlock-patent.html.

[129] [1989] RPC 147 (CA).

working practice in a particular area.[130] It has been observed that this decision seems to set a higher standard of test of obviousness for hi-tech industries such as the biotechnology industry.[131] This could mean that problems which are encountered on the route to the end goal are more likely to be seen as everyday run-of-the-mill hiccups for the hi-tech skilled person and that their resolution is less likely to exhibit inventiveness. Invention is the norm in an industry such as biotechnology and as the law stands it is eminently sensible that the concept of the skilled person, used to test obviousness, should assume the traits of those working in the field in question.[132] Overly zealous application of this view might, however, lead to a paradox in practice, namely, that those who make significant advances in the name of benefiting humanity and who spend considerable sums in the process, are less likely to be rewarded by the grant of a patent in recognition of their endeavour.

11.75   This, of course, depends entirely on the attitude and approach of the courts to interpreting these criteria. At the time of the *Genentech* decision there were concerns that a different standard was being laid down for the biotechnology industry and this was fuelled by the suggestion in that case that an additional requirement existed for patents involving biological material to show that there was an 'invention' over and above the basic criteria of patentability.[133] But there is no real evidence of the biotechnology industry suffering discriminatory treatment subsequent to *Genentech* and Lord Hoffmann was unconvinced by the additional criterion in delivering the House of Lords' ruling in *Biogen v Medeva*.[134] Although he did not rule out the possibility that in the future it might be possible for a novel creation to satisfy all statutory criteria and yet not be properly describable as an 'invention', he noted that neither the draftsmen of the EPC, nor those who drew up the 1977 Act, nor indeed counsel for the defendants, could offer a single example of such a creation. For the time being, then, to satisfy the standard criteria on patentability *is* to produce an invention.

11.76   The Nuffield Council on Bioethics has called for more stringent assessments of the criteria of patentability and most notably that of inventive step.[135] The Council conjectures that many patents have been granted for so-called inventions that do not meet these rigorous requirements. Moreover, it notes that the US and European interpretations of this criterion differ slightly but to a sufficient degree to make a real difference to a prospective patentee's chances of success. Thus, while in Europe we consider the need for 'inventive step', that is, that there must be evidence of non-obvious inventiveness on the part of the inventor, the US interpretation focuses on 'non-obviousness' so that as long as the particularities of the result were not obvious to an expert, then the criterion is satisfied—for example, that the precise sequence of bases that would appear in a recombinant DNA molecule would not be obvious to an expert. This latter is a lower threshold and consequently means that genetically engineered products remain, potentially at least, more easily patentable in the United States than in Europe. By the same token, it has been established in the EPO[136] and the UK IPO[137] that it is obvious to claim a specific recombinant DNA sequence if all of the techniques necessary to produce it are known. Equally, now that many genomes have been sequenced and large-scale use of bioinformatics to find homologous sequences or polypeptides is common, the use of data mining to uncover 'new' genes or sequences will not normally be sufficient to demonstrate inventive step.[138] The corollary is that the use of non-obvious techniques, perhaps involving bioinformatics tools, can overcome this objection.

---

[130] [1989] RPC 147 (CA) at 278. Also *Schlumberger Holdings Ltd v Electromagnetic Geoservices AS* [2009] RPC 19.

[131] See too Case T39/93 *POLYMER POWDERS/Allied Colloids* [1997] OJEPO 134 at 149.

[132] For some guidance on relevant characteristics in the biotechnology field of the knowledge of persons skilled in the art, see Case T455/91 *GENETECH ET AL/Expression in yeast* [1995] OJEPO 684.

[133] ibid, 263.   [134] *Biogen v Medeva* [1997] RPC 1.

[135] Nuffield Council on Bioethics, *The Ethics of Patenting DNA* (2002).

[136] Case T886/91 *BIOGEN INC/Hepatitis B virus* [1999] EPOR 361.

[137] *Collaborative Research's Patent* BL O/86/94.

[138] UK IPO, 'Examining patent applications for biotechnological inventions' (2016), para 34.

> **Key points on inventive step**
>
> - At the heart of this is the non-inventive person skilled in the art at the priority date, and their common general knowledge.
>
> - Assessment of inventive step can include mosaicing of pieces of prior art—if this mosaicing would have been done by the non-inventive person skilled in the art.
>
> - Follow the *Windsurfing/Pozzoli* tests to identify if there was the necessary intellectual leap so that there is an inventive step.
>
> - For biotechnological inventions, using traditional genetic engineering techniques to isolate material or bioinformatics to conduct data mining is unlikely to be inventive.

Industrial applicability

11.77 This final criterion for patentability ensures that we maintain the industrial or technical nature of inventions. The relevant section of the Patents Act 1977, as amended, is section 4(1), with the equivalent provisions being found in Article 57 EPC 2000. Section 4(1) states:

> an invention shall be taken to be capable of industrial application if it can be made or used in any kind of industry, including agriculture.

We have already covered the other provisions in sections 4 and 4A (paras 11.44ff) when we discussed methods of treatment of the human and animal body and use claims. The concept of 'industry' is construed very widely and does not necessarily involve a for-profit purpose.[139] Note that the test is whether something can be *made* or used in industry, so widening the scope further, and the requirement is only that the invention is *capable* of use in industry or agriculture; no actual evidence of effective use is required.

11.78 Something can be held to lack industrial applicability if its essential nature is aesthetic, artistic, or intellectual. There is, therefore, some overlap with the kinds of considerations we saw earlier in respect of section 1(2) of the Patents Act 1977. The two tests are, however, distinct. An example of something being denied protection was a method of initiating introductions between people in *John Lahiri Khan's Application*, which was also rejected under section 1(2) as a method of doing business.[140]

11.79 Beyond this, there is little else to say about this provision. It does not cause problems in the vast majority of cases. One area which has required refinement, however, is in respect of biotechnological inventions because of the need to show the *function* of any new gene sequences or fragments unearthed during scientific research.

11.80 The Biotechnology Directive states that full or partial gene sequences with no known function will not be patentable,[141] and this has been confirmed by the European Court of Justice (ECJ).[142] It has also been endorsed by the UK IPO[143] and the EPO, which has ruled that mere speculative function for a genetically engineered gene sequence cannot lead to the conclusion that it is capable of industrial application.[144] Indeed, the EPO Guidelines now provide that 'the industrial application of a sequence or a partial sequence

---

[139] *Chiron Corp v Murex Diagnostics Ltd and Others* [1996] RPC 535 at 607.

[140] UK IPO *Manual of Patent Practice* (February 2016 as amended), para 4.03 (BL O/356/06).

[141] Biotechnology Directive, Art 5(3) read in conjunction with recitals 23 and 24. See too Patents Act 1977, Sch A2, para 6.

[142] Case C-377/98 *Kingdom of the Netherlands v Council of the European Union and the European Parliament* [2002] FSR 36 at para 74 of the judgment. Also see the preliminary ruling of the Court of Justice in Case C-428/08 *Monsanto Technology LLC v Cefetra BV* [2012] 3 CMLR 7, [2011] All ER (EC) 209, [2011] FSR 6, confirming that a DNA sequence is unpatentable in European law if it fails to perform the function described for it in the patent application, even where it had previously performed that function (or could do so again, if extracted).

[143] UK IPO, 'Examining applications for biotechnological inventions', paras 59–65 and see *Aeomica Inc* BL O/286/05 31.

[144] *Icos Decision* [2002] OJEPO 293, http://archive.epo.org/epo/pubs/oj002/06_02/06_2932.pdf.

of a gene must be disclosed in the patent application. A mere nucleic acid sequence without indication of a function is not a patentable invention.'[145]

11.81   The issue of biotechnology and industrial applicability was considered for the first time in 2011 by the Supreme Court in the UK in *Eli Lily & Co v Human Genome Sciences*.[146] This case concerned a patent for a polynucleotide sequence which Eli Lily sought to revoke on the ground that, amongst other things, the specification failed to disclose an invention capable of industrial application. The argument was that the prediction of the uses of the sequence were purely speculative. Article 57 EPC states clearly that an invention is only patentable if it is 'susceptible of industrial application'. Any invention which does not comply with this should be revoked (see also section 72(1) of the Patents Act 1977). The Supreme Court confirmed that English courts ought to follow any principles of law clearly laid down by the Technical Boards of Appeal of the EPO (paras 96–102).[147] This, however, does not preclude divergence on matters of fact based on the evidence presented to each judicial body (as happened in this case).

11.82   Central to the question of industrial application for claims to gene sequences or proteins is adequate description of their function. A patent will not be given if it is not possible to disclose how the sequence or protein can be used. Merely describing existence and structure is not enough. The Supreme Court's view was that the law should be taken as that laid down in the jurisprudence of the Technical Board of Appeal in the EPO, albeit that this did not preclude a UK-specific different outcome (para 91). The question for the Supreme Court was whether the first instance judge had followed the principles laid down in the EPO jurisprudence. If he had, it was not the Supreme Court's place to displace his ruling (unless the conclusion was not one that could reasonably have been reached).

11.83   The Supreme Court was not satisfied that the EPO principles had indeed been followed. It concluded that the appeal should succeed on the point that the claimed invention met the requirements of Article 57 EPC, viz that it displayed industrial applicability in the sense that a 'plausible' or 'reasonably credible' claimed use, or even an 'educated guess' as to function can suffice (paras 106–111).[148] This is a heavily policy-driven decision, with the Supreme Court stating: 'Just as it would be undesirable to let someone have a monopoly over a particular biological molecule too early, because it risks closing down competition, so it would be wrong to set the hurdle for patentability too high' (para 130).

11.84   In the United States, the equivalent criterion requires *utility*, an issue which has caused some controversy in the context of biotech patents over the years. Various attempts were made in the early 1990s to patent Expressed Sequence Tags (ESTs), being partial gene fragments with no known utility. The rationale, however, was that these might point the way to complete gene sequences and so may help to stake a claim to the full sequences once these were found. The US Patent and Trademark Office (USPTO) rejected such claims, and most notably those of the National Institutes of Health, for lack of utility: the function of the invention could not be sufficiently described. Since then, the USPTO has revised its guidelines on utility (2017).[149] An invention now must show a 'specific and substantial and credible utility', but it should be noted that 'credible' here includes a theoretical credible use; that is, it is not necessary to show that the invention actually works in order to obtain a patent. There is therefore no specific prohibition on the patenting of ESTs, or indeed, other gene variations such as Single Nucleotide Polymorphisms (SNPs),[150] as long as the criteria for patentability are met.

---

[145]   EPO Guidelines, Part G-III, para 4.

[146]   [2011] UKSC 51; [2012] 1 All ER 1154; [2012] RPC 6.

[147]   For a good illustration of EPO approaches, see Case T898/05 *ZYMOGENETICS/Hematopoietic Cytokine Receptor* [2007] EPOR 2.

[148]   For comment, see T Minssen and D Nilsson, 'The industrial application requirement for biotech inventions in light of recent EPO & UK case law: a plausible approach or a mere "hunting license"?' (2012) 34(1) EIPR 689. Equally, the plausibility of a claim about the scope of a prediction in claims does not require proof that the invention works in every case; see *Regeneron Pharmaceuticals Inc v Genentech Inc Bayer Pharma AG v Genentech Inc* [2013] EWCA Civ 93. See also A Odell-West, 'Has the Commodore Steered the Fleet onto the Rocks?' (2013) 4 IPQ 279.

[149]   www.uspto.gov/web/offices/pac/mpep/documents/2100_2107.htm#sect2107.

[150]   SNPs, as their name suggests, are sequences of identical DNA that vary from the norm in only a single base pair. Despite these extremely minor differences, SNPs can be used as markers for particular genes and may play a key role in understanding the genetic basis for individual patient response to medicines.

Exercise

You might like to consider the different approaches adopted in, again, the United States, Europe, and Japan in these comparative studies of biotechnology patent practices: www.trilateral.net/projects/biotechnology.html.

Key points on industrial application

- To be patentable, the invention needs to be capable of industrial application.
- This requirement is met if the invention is made or can be used in any kind of industry.
- This is mainly a challenge regarding biotechnological innovation: a function of the innovation needs to be disclosed, but it would suffice if there is a plausible or reasonably credible promise of a function.

Excluded subject matter

11.85 Even if an invention meets the requirements discussed in the first section of this chapter, it may still not be patentable. The base for this is Article 52(2) EPC 2000, which came into force in December 2007,[151] and equivalent provisions in section 1(2) of the UK Patents Act 1977:[152]

(2) The following in particular shall not be regarded as inventions within the meaning of paragraph 1:
 (a) discoveries, scientific theories and mathematical methods;
 (b) aesthetic creations;
 (c) schemes, rules and methods for performing mental acts, playing games or doing business, and programs for computers;
 (d) presentations of information.
(3) Paragraph 2 shall exclude the patentability of the subject-matter or activities referred to therein only to the extent to which a European patent application or European patent relates to such subject matter or activities *as such* (emphasis added).

11.86 If an innovation is caught by these exclusions, then it is not an invention from the patent law perspective. This means that it is not subject to the obligations placed on countries, by TRIPS, to have patents for inventions in all fields of technology. A key point lies in the two little words '*as such*'. The interpretation of these words by intellectual property offices and courts around Europe has had a profound impact on the scope of the exclusions from patentable inventions. The trend has been towards a narrowing interpretation of the provisions resulting in a corresponding expansion in the scope of patentable inventions in a number of controversial areas.

11.87 It is also important to note Article 53 EPC[153] and the UK equivalent provisions in section 1(3) and (4) and section 4A of, and Schedule A2 to, the 1977 Act. Schedule A2 deals with biotechnological inventions the subject of the European Directive[154] and which we explore in more depth in paras 11.195–11.209.[155]

---

[151] See the 16th edition of the EPC here for the current collection of Convention and all related instruments: www.epo.org/law-practice/legal-texts/epc.html.
[152] As amended by the Patents Act 2004.
[153] Note the text of Art 53(a) has been brought into line with TRIPS, Art 27(2), which reads: 'Members may exclude from patentability inventions, the prevention within their territory of the commercial exploitation of which is necessary to protect *ordre public* or morality.' EPC 1973 talked of '*publication* or exploitation' as being offensive to morality or *ordre public*. 'Publication' was deleted.
[154] Biotechnology Directive.
[155] The UK implemented the provisions of the Directive in the Patents Regulations 2000, which amended the Patents Act 1977 Patents Regulations 2000 (SI 2000/2037).

Article 53

Exceptions to patentability
European patents shall not be granted in respect of:

(a) inventions the commercial exploitation of which would be contrary to 'ordre public' or morality; such exploitation shall not be deemed to be so contrary merely because it is prohibited by law or regulation in some or all of the Contracting States;

(b) plant or animal varieties or essentially biological processes for the production of plants or animals; this provision shall not apply to microbiological processes or the products thereof;

(c) methods for treatment of the human or animal body by surgery or therapy and diagnostic methods practised on the human or animal body; this provision shall not apply to products, in particular substances or compositions, for use in any of these methods.

 Question

What is the basis for excluding the respective categories of subject matter in Article 52 as opposed to Article 53? How are they different?

11.88   As Pumfrey J stated in *Shopalotto.com's Application*:[156] '[a] moment's thought will show that it is not possible to provide an exhaustive definition of "invention". The Convention does not attempt to interpret the word but provides a list of things which are excluded, whether or not they would be regarded as inventions.'[157]

■ *Aerotel Ltd v Telco Holdings Ltd and Others* [2006] EWCA Civ 1371; [2007] RPC 7

This case involved two appeals which raised issues about the interpretation of Article 52 and the approach of the British courts to considering excluded subject matter. The *Aerotel* appeal concerned a system and a method of making a telephone call from any available telephone station using a prepaid code. An action for infringement was met with a counterclaim for revocation on the grounds that the invention was merely a method of doing business. Macrossan's invention related to an automated method of producing the necessary documents to incorporate a company.[158] This had been rejected by the Patent Office as unpatentable and the High Court agreed, holding that it was as a method of performing a mental act by a computer.[159] The Court of Appeal similarly rejected Macrossan's appeal as a method of doing business and a claim to a computer program as such. Aerotel won, however, because the primary claim was to a new device, while their second claim was to the use of the new device, and therefore not only to a method of doing business *as such*. In handing down this ruling, the Court of Appeal sought to provide a 'definitive statement' on how the UK should approach the interpretation of Article 52.

11.89   The court began by distinguishing the class of excluded matter under Article 52 from the matter mentioned in Article 53. Article 52 deals with things that are not considered to be inventions, while Article 53 is concerned with exceptions to patentability. The importance of the distinction lies in the fact that exceptions should be construed narrowly,[160] but the same does not apply to non-inventions.[161] The correct approach

[156] [2005] EWHC 2416 (Pat); [2006] RPC 293 at para 6.

[157] There was discussion in *Biogen v Medeva* [1997] RPC 1 of the need to prove an 'invention' over and above the established criteria for patentability; while this was not entirely ruled out no example could be given of where this would be required. See further J Pila, *The Requirement for an Invention in Patent Law* (2010).

[158] You can read Macrossan's claims at http://v3.espacenet.com/textclam?DB=EPODOC&IDX=GB2388937&F=8&QPN= GB2388937.

[159] [2006] EWHC 705 (Ch).

[160] See, eg, Case T19/90 *HARVARD/Oncomouse* [1990] OJEPO 376 and Case T356/93 *PLANT GENETIC SYSTEMS/Glutamine Synthetase Inhibitors* [1995] EPOR 357. Compare discussion at paras 11.199ff.

[161] *Aerotel v Telco Holdings Ltd and Others* [2006] EWCA Civ 1371, para 12.

towards exclusions is to attempt to identify the underlying policy for each exclusion and to give effect to it through interpretation. The court could, however, find no single principle or rationale that unifies all of the examples in Article 52; each must be considered on its own terms.[162] Moreover, the courts have confirmed it to be an exercise in judgement and not something that can be reduced easily to systematic analysis.[163]

11.90   The Court of Appeal has indicated that the underlying rationales may be different depending on the example in question. Moreover, we find no real help from the *travaux préparatoires* of the EPC to assist us in understanding these exclusions.[164] We are left, then, to consider the existing case law on each example to appreciate the reasons for its exclusion from patent protection, and some additional help is provided by the EPC Guidelines for Examination.

11.91   The EPO Guidelines provide, for example, that the list of things which are not regarded as inventions includes items which are either too abstract (eg a discovery or scientific method) and/or which are non-technical (eg aesthetic creations). An invention can be in any field of technology but it must be concrete and have technical character.[165] Let us consider each of the categories of exclusion in turn.[166]

Discoveries, scientific theories, and mathematical methods

11.92   This category is thought to contain items which are too abstract or indistinct to be the proper subject of patent protection. Also, numerous examples of natural products have accordingly been the subject of patents. These range from sequences or partial sequences of DNA, protein molecules and recombinant DNA molecules used as research tools, to purified forms of bacteria, vitamins, and viruses. How can this be? An interesting issue is discoveries. Anton van Leeuwenhoek of Holland (1632–1723) is credited as being the father of microscopy. His invention of new methods to grind and polish lenses led him to be the first person to see and describe bacteria. Clearly, he did not invent those bacteria but merely discovered them using an invention. Conversely, discoveries often lead to inventions. For example, Sir Alexander Fleming (1881–1955) was working in 1928 on colonies of the bacterium *Staphylococcus aureus*, which can be dangerous to humans, when a batch accidentally became contaminated by a mould that killed off the bacterium. This was penicillin—the first antibiotic—and further work by Fleming and others led to production of penicillin in large, high-quality doses. A patent was eventually granted in 1948 for a method of mass production of penicillin.[167]

Exercise

Fleming did not attempt to patent penicillin itself, but would he have been successful if he had tried? On this issue and in general, you may also find it helpful to look back to the sections discussing novelty, discovery, and biotechnology (see paras 11.32–11.36). Do you think that the absence of a patent on the product contributed to the fact that it took 20 years to go from discovery to mass production?

---

[162] For the impact on UK IPO granting practice, see Practice Notice (PO: Patents Act 1977: Patentable Subject Matter) (No 1) [2007] RPC 8 and Practice Notice (PO: Patents Act 1977: Patentable Subject Matter) (No 2) [2008] RPC 15. But for comment on a different approach in the EPO, see N Gardner and P England, 'European Union: patents—exclusion from patentability' (2008) 30(1) EIPR N5–6.

[163] See *Really Virtual Co Ltd v UK Intellectual Property Office* [2012] EWHC 1086 (Ch).

[164] J Pila, 'Art 52(2) of the Convention on the Grant of European Patents: what did the framers intend? A study of the *travaux préparatoires*' (2005) 36 IIC 755 and ED Ventose, 'In the footsteps of the framers of the European Patent Convention: examining the *travaux préparatoires*' (2009) 31(7) EIPR 353.

[165] Guidelines for Examination in the European Patent Office, Part G-II, para 1.

[166] It was noted in *Protecting Kids the World Over (PKTWO) Ltd, Re* [2011] EWHC 2720 (Pat); Ch D (Patents Ct) that *Aerotel* is also a helpful approach when dealing with inventions that have multiple possible exclusions, para 36.

[167] W Kingston, 'Antibiotics, invention and innovation' (2000) 29(6) Research Policy 679–710.

11.93   One of the problems that has been thrown up for the biotechnology industry has been the objection that attempts to patent biotechnological products is nothing more than an attempt to patent a living thing; that is, something already pre-existing in nature and so merely a discovery. Where, then, do we draw a line between a discovery and an invention? The answer is in the concept of *technical effect*, which we have considered previously.

11.94   It is argued that it is not an invention to uncover a pre-existing and naturally occurring entity.[168] However, the terms 'discovery' and 'invention' have particular technical legal meanings in patent law which reflect fundamental policy objectives, including the encouragement of innovation and the reward of endeavour. As seen in para 11.92, one way to think about an invention is that it is a technical solution to a pre-existing and as yet unresolved technical problem. While discoveries and inventions both contribute new knowledge to the sum total of human understanding, an invention does so through the *application* of that knowledge, for example by making something available that was previously beyond our reach. Thus, the mere discovery of the base pair sequence of a gene cannot be the subject of a patent, but locating a previously unknown gene, determining its function, and making it accessible for further exploitation is an example of a technical solution to the pre-existing problem of the inaccessibility of the genetic product.

11.95   If human intervention can bring about a specific technical effect or application of discovery, then the embodiment of that technical effect or application can be the subject of a patent. Consider the EPO Guidelines:[169]

> If a new property of a known material or article is found out, that is mere discovery and unpatentable because discovery as such has no technical effect and is therefore not an invention within the meaning of Article 52(1). If, however, that property is put to practical use, then this constitutes an invention which may be patentable. For example, the discovery that a particular known material is able to withstand mechanical shock would not be patentable, but a railway sleeper made from that material could well be patentable. To find a previously unrecognised substance occurring in nature is also mere discovery and therefore unpatentable. However, if a substance found in nature can be shown to produce a technical effect, it may be patentable. An example of such a case is that of a substance occurring in nature which is found to have an antibiotic effect. In addition, if a micro-organism is discovered to exist in nature and to produce an antibiotic, the micro-organism itself may also be patentable as one aspect of the invention. Similarly, a gene which is discovered to exist in nature may be patentable if a technical effect is revealed, eg its use in making a certain polypeptide or in gene therapy.

11.96   This means that an invention that happens to involve biological or genetic material can be patentable even though the material also exists in nature, provided that the invention makes a technical contribution to the state of the art. This can be achieved by removing it from its natural environment and by characterising the contribution by the isolation of the substance and its new-found availability. Similarly, merely to find a naturally occurring substance is a pure discovery; but if you are able to put it to some tangible use, for example as an antibiotic, then it may be patentable in respect of this particular technical effect. An invention requires some evidence of human ingenuity in realising a particular use for a discovery[170] or in making it available to the public in a form which previously it was not. An example of this last point is the case of *HOWARD FLOREY/Relaxin* before the Opposition Division of the EPO.[171] The patent in suit concerned a naturally occurring protein produced by women during childbirth to ease the passage of the child. Howard Florey had isolated and determined the chemical structure of the substance and was then able to produce it in a form which made it a marketable product, but the objection was that this remained a discovery. The Opposition Division, however, ruled otherwise, holding that a newly isolated

---

[168]   For arguments of this kind, see Genewatch UK at www.genewatch.org.

[169]   EPO Guidelines, Part G-II, para 3.1.

[170]   The Court of Appeal in *Genentech Inc's Patent* [1989] RPC 147 confirmed that a claim to the practical application of a discovery did not relate to the discovery as such.

[171]   Case T741/91 *HOWARD FLOREY/Relaxin* [1995] EPOR 541.

and characterised substance was not a mere discovery, but rather an industrially applicable technical solution to a pre-existing technical problem. A further relevant point in respect of a claim in the patent to the gene sequence itself was the fact that the form of the sequence claimed by the patentee was 'purer' than that found in nature and so sufficiently distinct to be patentable. These concepts are now embodied in the Biotechnology Directive, which provides that 'An element isolated from the human body or otherwise produced by means of a technical process, including the sequence or partial sequence of a gene, may constitute a patentable invention, even if the structure of that element is identical to that of a natural element.'[172] Note, in particular, that such a patent would *not* give a patentee any claim over naturally occurring elements *within* the human body.

All of this was confirmed by the House of Lords in *Kirin-Amgen v* Hoechst *Marion Roussel*,[173] which summed up the position thus:

(1) to find a new substance or micro-organism in nature is a discovery and not an invention;

(2) but if it is necessary to isolate and extract the substance—as will almost always be the case—then the relevant process, as well as the material obtained by this process, could both be patentable;

(3) furthermore, if the material had no previously recognised existence, and can be adequately identified without reference to the process by which it is obtained, then it may be patentable per se.

11.97 The US Supreme Court has addressed their 'product of nature' doctrine—being a version of the discovery exclusion—in two high-profile cases. In 2012, in *Mayo v Prometheus*,[174] albeit not a biotech case as such, a patent on a method of drug delivery was held to be non-patentable as an example of natural law: 'the claims inform a relevant audience about certain laws of nature; any additional steps consist of well-understood, routine, conventional activity already engaged in by the scientific community; and those steps, when viewed as a whole, add nothing significant beyond the sum of their parts taken separately. For these reasons we believe that the steps are not sufficient to transform unpatentable natural correlations into patentable applications of those regularities' (judgment, at 11). A few days later, the Court sent back a challenge over gene patents held by *Myriad* in respect of the BRCA 1 and 2 breast cancer gene, to the district court to reconsider in the light of the *Mayo* decision. The gene patents were upheld again and the case on patentability of genes bounced back to the Supreme Court to decide the matter once and for all.

11.98 This 2013 *Myriad v Association of Molecular Pathology* decision proved both controversial and disappointing. The Supreme Court found that genes which had been isolated from the body could not be patented; but they could be patented if they were created synthetically.[175] This decision did not engage with *Mayo* and the question of natural laws. The practical meaning of this for patients and for scientists, and more fundamental questions, such as the extent to which genes should be able to be patented, remain unclear.[176] The validity of an Australian patent in respect of BRCA 1 was also challenged, this time by an individual activist in *D'Arcy v Myriad Genetics*.[177] In 2015, the High Court (the final court of appeal) found that this patent was also invalid. This was based, however, on the different legal test for an invention in Australia—that it is not a method of manufacture. The High Court found that the essence of the invention was information which was in the gene sequences. It did not matter whether or not there had been artificial creation.

---

[172] Article 5(2) of the Biotechnology Directive.

[173] [2005] RPC 9. The case is also known as *Kirin-Amgen Inc v Transkaryotic Therapies Inc (No 2)*; see para 11.28.

[174] 132 S Ct 1289 (2012).   [175] 569 US 576 (2013).

[176] Useful commentary is in D Burk, 'The Curious Incident of the Supreme Court in Myriad Genetics' (2014) 90 Notre Dame Law Review 505–542;. See also R H Stern 'Association for Molecular Pathology v Myriad Genetics: sieving the gene pool (Case Comment)' (2013) 35(11) EIPR 685–90.

[177] See [2015] HCA 35 earlier decisions and pleadings, www.hcourt.gov.au/cases/case_s28-2015.

Discussion point   For answer guidance visit **www.oup.com/uk/brown5e**.

The European Parliament felt it necessary to issue a Resolution in October 2001 calling on the EPO to reconsider the grant of patents to Myriad Genetics over the BRCA1 and BRCA2 ('breast cancer') genes (4 October 2001, B5–0633, 0641, 0651, and 0663/2001), www.europarl. europa.eu/sides/getDoc.do?pubRef=-//EP//TEXT+TA+P5-TA-2001-0523+0+DOC+XML+V0// EN&language=HU. In 2002, the Nuffield Council on Bioethics pointed out that because of the breadth of the patents as they were originally granted, 'there are currently no other methods of diagnosing the presence of the breast cancer susceptibility gene BRCA1 that can be used without infringing the patents'.[178] As the Nuffield Council itself has asked: is it in the public interest that there is only one diagnostic test available for a particular disease? Will patents such as those that assert rights over BRCA1 inhibit further research, even in the context of other diseases? Or does the prospect of a strong reward act as a stronger incentive to innovate? Reflect on the Nuffield Council's proposals. You may find this of interest: K Liddell et al, 'Patents as incentives for translational and evaluative research: the case of genetic tests and their improved clinical performance' [2008] 3 IPQ 286.

11.99   Patentees have also argued that the invention as claimed does not exist naturally in this particular form. For example, in the *Icos Decision*[179] the EPO held that the production of a purified and isolated nucleic acid having a sequence that does not exist in nature, is not a discovery.[180] Moreover, the power conferred by a patent over such an invention can be considerable. Often the breadth of an exclusive right over natural product inventions can make it very difficult to invent around, and this can have adverse consequences for further and future research in any number of fields requiring access to the material.

11.100   We see, then, that it is possible through human endeavour to take something from an excluded category such as discovery and make it an invention, and so patentable. The same is true with respect to the other two exclusions in this category when we go from the abstract to the tangible. Thus, while a scientific theory about a fifth dimension is just an example of an abstract concept and unpatentable, the application of that theory to produce a device that could dematerialise and re-materialise objects through space would be patentable, as would any related processes.[181] Similarly, a mathematical method in itself is purely intellectual and intangible (eg a shortcut method of long division), but a device which deploys this method may itself be patentable if the subject matter has a technical character—consider encrypting/ decrypting or signing electronic communications.[182] The distinction was considered by the EPO Technical Board of Appeal in *VICOM/Computer-related invention*,[183] which related to an invention involving a mathematical method applied to data which resulted in an enhanced digital image on a computer. The core question was which aspects of this invention were patentable and where should the line be drawn between a mathematical method *as such* and an invention which was an application of such a method? The Board defined 'mathematical method' as something which is carried out on numbers and which produces a result in numerical form, that is, it remains in an abstract form. On this interpretation the Board rejected claims to a means of filtering data digitally on a conventional computer as they involved

---

[178] Nuffield Council on Bioethics, *The Ethics of Patenting DNA* (2002), para 5.4.
[179] *Icos Decision* [2002] OJEPO 293, http://archive.epo.org/epo/pubs/oj002/06_02/06_2932.pdf.
[180] It should be noted, however, that this patent failed on other grounds, including lack of inventive step and lack of industrial applicability.
[181] See applied to semiconductivity in EPO Guidelines, Part G-II, para 3.2.
[182] EPO Guidelines, Part G-II, para 3.3, which also has other examples.
[183] Case T208/84 [1987] OJEPO 14.

processes indistinguishable from a mathematical method. Conversely, the Board upheld claims to the method of using the mathematical method to process images because the output of the method was a real-world technical effect on the quality of the images. An area likely to receive lots of attention in this field is artificial intelligence and machine learning, and the 2018 EPO Guidelines address this.[184]

Aesthetic creations

11.101   Examples of aesthetic creations which are excluded include literary, dramatic, musical, and artistic works.[185] This should sound familiar as the realm of protection offered primarily by copyright. We have seen in Chapter 1 how the international history of intellectual property protection has always drawn a division between industrial property on the one hand (Paris Convention 1883) and copyright and its related rights (Berne Convention 1886) on the other. The principal reason why aesthetic creations are excluded is because they are not technical in nature and do not, normally, represent a technical contribution to our experiences. Their contribution lies elsewhere and their appreciation is usually entirely subjective. This is not to say that inventions cannot have aesthetic features, merely that those features cannot form the basis of patent protection if their sole contribution is in the realm of aesthetics. If, however, an aesthetic feature produces a *de facto* technical effect, then it may be patentable. The classic example that is cited in this regard is *ITS Rubber Ltd's Application*,[186] in which the main claim simply read:

> 1. A squash ball having a surface of a blue colour.

What possible difference could colour make to the functioning of a squash ball? Well, the claim was upheld on evidence that the particular colour chosen improved visibility of the ball during play. The contribution was therefore not merely aesthetic.[187] Note too that technical means which produce an aesthetic effect can be patentable even if the aesthetic effect itself cannot. For example, a machine may be set to produce a beautiful wood carving (not patentable in itself) but the new machine or the technical process used to program may be patentable. As always, the intellectual property office will be concerned not with the form of a claim but with the question of whether the essential nature of the invention is solely aesthetic or contains technical features.

 Discussion point   For answer guidance visit **www.oup.com/uk/brown5e**.

The *ITS Rubber Ltd* case was decided under the 1949 Act. Do you think it would face any additional problems under the current legislation?

Schemes, rules, and methods for performing mental acts, playing games, or doing business, and programs for computers

11.102   Schemes, rules, and methods for performing mental acts, playing games (which would include video games and virtual worlds), or doing business are similarly excluded in the first instance because of their abstract or intellectual character.[188] Much discussion in recent years has circled around the role of software and computers in this regard and this is considered in depth below (paras 11.114–11.186).

---

[184] EPO Guidelines, Part G-II, para 3.3.1 (including references to cases). See also para 3.3.2 regarding simulation, design, or modelling.
[185] See the Patents Act 1977, s 1(2)(b).   [186] [1979] RPC 318.   [187] EPO Guidelines, Part G-II, para 3.4.
[188] EPO Guidelines, Part G-II, para 3.5.1-3.

Mental acts

11.103   Examples of methods of performing mental acts include schemes for doing arithmetic, learning to read, or speaking a new language. Similarly, a claim which merely lays out the steps for decision-making or the performance of a particular task will be rejected.

■ *Halliburton Energy Services v Smith International (North Sea) Ltd* [2006] RPC 2

This dispute before the Patent Court related to two patents concerning various features of drill bits for drilling in rock. In particular, two claims related to 'a method of designing a roller cone bit' comprising steps which involve calculating measurements and making adjustments to parameters to achieve optimal effectiveness of the bit. Pumfrey J held that these claims were 'directed purely to the intellectual content of the design process and the criteria according to which decisions on the way to a design are made'. Accordingly, as framed, these were merely claims to a method for performing a mental act and would be excluded or require redrafting to take them outside the excluded category.[189]

■ *Fujitsu Ltd's Application* [1997] RPC 608

Applicants applied for a UK patent claiming priority from an earlier Japanese application in respect of an invention for a 'Method and Apparatus for creating synthetic crystal structure images'. The apparatus was a conventional computer programmed to allow an operator to select parameters, such as atoms or lattice vectors, to create pictorial representations of how the combined chosen structures would look. A Principal Examiner rejected the application, however, stating that it related both to a method for performing a mental act and to a program for a computer. The Court of Appeal similarly rejected the appeal, stating that it is a question of fact whether a claim to an invention is to anything more than disqualified matter. It was relevant for the court that a significant amount of (human) input from an operator was required in order to carry out the task. Methods of solving a problem or providing advice remain examples of excluded methods of performing a mental act, even if performed by a computer.[190]

11.104   The position on the relationship between mental acts and computer programs remained unclear, with *obiter* comment by the Court of Appeal in *Aerotel/Macrossan*,[191] a 2008 Practice Notice[192] following the judgment of the Court of Appeal in *Symbian Ltd's Application*.[193] *Halliburton Energy Services Inc's Applications* then held that the mental acts exclusion must be interpreted narrowly; that is, to involve human mental means.[194] This means that any claims to implement an invention with a computer will not fall foul of this particular exclusion, albeit that it might still be excluded as a computer program as such (see further paras 11.114ff). A UK IPO Practice Notice of 2011 followed suit.[195]

11.105   The EPO similarly tends to draw a distinction between mental acts which human beings can perform and automated acts which go beyond human capacity, for example in terms of the alacrity or difficulty of the task.[196] Thus, method claims were allowed in *IBM/Editable document form*[197] for a method for maintaining

---

[189] Note, the objection here was to the form of the claims, not to the substance of the invention which could have industrial utility, see Pumfrey J at para 218. Note also that part of this case was appealed to the Court of Appeal for lack of sufficiency and we discuss this at para 12.84.

[190] See also *Gale's Application*, para 11.125.

[191] '[W]e are doubtful as to whether the exclusion extends to electronic means of doing what could otherwise have been done mentally', per Jacob LJ, *Aerotel*, para 62.

[192] UK IPO, Practice Notice: Patents Act 1977: Patentability of Computer Programs (2008), [2009] Bus LR 625

[193] [2008] EWCA Civ 1066.   [194] [2011] EWHC 2508 (Pat), [2012] RPC 129.

[195] Practice Notice (Patents Act 1977: Patentability of mental acts), Intellectual Property Office, 17 October 2011, [2012] Bus LR 1264.

[196] See *Research in Motion UK Ltd v Inpro Licensing SARL* [2006] RPC 20 at para 186 where Pumfrey J found technical effect in 'computers running faster and transmitting information more efficiently . . .' On appeal: [2007] EWCA Civ 51 (although the point here made at first instance was not contested).

[197] Case T110/90 [1995] EPOR 185.

formats of documents transferred between word processors. In other cases, however, text manipulation inventions have been denied protection for lack of technical contribution.[198] For example, the Technical Board of Appeal in *IBM/Document abstracting and retrieval*[199] rejected a computer system for creating and storing abstracts obtained from archives, inter alia, because the claims merely described an automated means of performing a task which could be carried out manually. It was not enough that the task was performed by technical means—that is, through a computer; the invention itself must make a technical contribution beyond that which can be done by humans.

Question

Is a method of performing a mental act still excluded if it is performed by a computer rather than a human being? Consider the 2018 EPO Guidelines, Part G-II, para 3.5.1.

Playing games

11.106 The rules on patentability of games were shaken up by the decision in *Shopalotto.com Ltd's Application*.[200] Strangely, the position had remained unchanged since an Official Ruling in 1926,[201] despite the sweeping changes brought in by the Patents Acts of 1949 and 1977, not to mention innumerable revisions in the meantime.

■ *Shopalotto.com Ltd's Application* [2006] RPC 7

This was an appeal against a decision of the Deputy Director of the Patent Office that computer apparatus configured to provide a lottery playable via the internet was unpatentable under section 1(2) of the Patents Act 1977. The appellant argued that he should benefit from the Official Ruling on board games handed down in 1926 and based on interpretation of the definition of an invention contained in section 93 of the Patents and Designs Acts 1907 and 1919. This was to the effect that board games are eligible for a patent if they involve apparatus for playing a game which includes one or more playing pieces and a marked board together with instructions on how the game is played. The appellant argued that this should be applied by analogy to his online game. Pumfrey J made the powerful point that the 1926 Ruling cannot serve as a guide to the 1977 Act in the light of the EPC (1973). The patentability of games should be assessed in the same manner as all other potential excluded categories, and a claim which falls wholly into an established category should be excluded. Moreover, in the instant case the claimed invention was, in effect, to a general-purpose computer providing a web server, which makes no original contribution to the art.

11.107 The UK IPO then issued a Practice Notice on patentability of games.[202] This follows the judgment in *Shopalotto*.[203]

Methods of doing business

11.108 Innovative ways of tackling everyday business problems are not normally patentable. This issue attracts a lot of attention in the context of the internet, where fears have arisen that patent thickets relating to e-commerce practices might considerably restrict the commercial viability and attractiveness of cyberspace as a place to do business. British Telecom claimed at the turn of the century that it had been granted a US patent over hyperlinking technology more than 20 years previously (US Pat No 4,873,662); it sought,

---

[198] Case T38/86 *IBM/Text clarity processing* [1990] EPOR 606.   [199] Case T22/85 [1990] EPOR 98.

[200] [2006] RPC 7.   [201] Official Ruling 1926(A); (1926) 43 RPC Appendix, p i.

[202] *Practice Notice 'Patents Act 1977: Patentability of games'* [2006] RPC 8. See also UK IPO Manual of Patent Practice (July 2015), para 1.32.

[203] See too *IGT's Applications* [2007] EWHC 1341 (Ch).

and failed, to enforce rights against some US internet service providers. But perhaps the most famous internet-related business method patent involves Amazon.com, which devised a method for managing online orders and called it the 'One-Click' system (US Pat No 5,960,411). The method allows the customer to enter their personal and credit card details only once with the company and thereafter the customer can order products simply by clicking on the item on screen, whereupon Amazon can access the necessary billing information directly from the customer's account. Beyond customer convenience, the commercial advantage is that this effectively does away with the potential disincentive faced by customers who have to re-enter data for each purchase. Amazon was granted a patent on this business method in September 1999, but this was challenged by Barnes and Noble. In February 2001 the US Court of Appeals for the Federal Circuit in Washington DC lifted a preliminary injunction that had barred Barnesandnoble.com from using the one-click technology. The matter was finally settled out of court in 2002 and the patent remains in the United States. It was rejected by the EPO in 2011, but on the basis of lack of inventive step.[204] Other examples of applications for patents include new methods of bar-coding banking materials to improve customer services,[205] display mechanisms on buses to let customers know if they are picking up or dropping off,[206] coding mechanisms to protect customers' identity,[207] a scheme to allow prisoners to trade sentence time for corporal punishment,[208] and a method to facilitate introductions between people wearing mutually recognisable artefacts, such as rings.[209] Note how under the last two examples, 'business' enjoys a wide interpretation in law and does not necessarily have to imply commercial interests.

11.109   The essential mantra remains the same in all cases, however: does the invention solve a technical problem rather than merely tackle a business problem?

11.110   It was previously thought that the exclusion of a method of doing business referred to the conduct of an entire business endeavour,[210] but this has been rejected by the Court of Appeal in *Aerotel/Macrossan*, where it was held that there is no reason for such a narrow interpretation and that business methods should not be restricted to abstract matters or completed transactions. Double-entry bookkeeping is neither abstract nor an output of a business transaction, but it remains a method of doing business.[211] On this basis, then, the court rejected Macrossan's claim for an automatic method of providing the necessary documents to incorporate a company because this method was for the essence of the business itself; that is, to provide advice and documentation.

11.111   As we have seen elsewhere, the mere automation of a process or operation does not change its essential character. Thus, in *Merrill Lynch's Application*,[212] a known computer system was programmed in known computer language to provide a data-processing-based system for implementing an automated trading market for securities. The Court of Appeal held that if there was any contribution to human knowledge it was in the production of a trading system; that is, a method of doing business. Moreover, the fact that this may be an improvement on previous systems is irrelevant: 'the prohibition in section 1(2)(c) is generic; qualitative considerations do not enter into the matter'.

11.112   Methods of doing business which solve technical problems can be patentable. This was confirmed by the EPO in *PENSION BENEFIT SYSTEMS/Controlling pension benefits systems*,[213] which related to a computer system that performed a number of pension-related tasks, including calculations, speculation, and the control of the benefit system to ensure periodic payments to subscribers. Despite rejecting this particular

---

[204] T1244/07 *1-Click/ AMAZON*, 21 January 2011.   [205] *Good News Pty Ltd's Application* (Patent Office Hearing Officer: BL O/124/84).

[206] *Crawford v Jones* [2005] EWHC 2417 (Pat).   [207] *Peter Williams' Application* (IPO Hearing Officer: BL O/038/07).

[208] *Melia's Application* (Patent Office Hearing Officer: BL O/153/92).

[209] *John Lahiri Khan's Application* (Patent Office Hearing Officer: BL O/356/06).

[210] *Macrossan's Patent Application* [2006] EWHC 705 (Ch).

[211] *Aerotel Ltd v Telco Holdings Ltd and Others* [2006] EWCA Civ 1371, paras 69–70, citing the French and German texts of the EPC in support of this interpretation.

[212] [1988] RPC 1.   [213] [2002] EPOR 52.

appeal for want of technical character, the Technical Board of Appeal confirmed that a method claim that relates to a method of doing business can be patentable as long as it is technical, and that apparatus claims, even if they are programmed to function in a business environment, cannot be excluded because Article 52 EPC does not mention apparatus. A caveat to add to this is that it is dangerous to attempt to dress up a business method claim as an apparatus claim because the task of the patent offices and the courts is to examine the substance, not the form of the claim. Moreover, an attempt to get around a technical problem by modifying a essential-rather than by solving the problem by technical means—is insufficient to bring technical character to an invention.[214]

11.113   Many business method claims are linked to computer-implemented inventions, as the previous example demonstrates,[215] and they are considered further below in this context (see para 11.114ff). For now, it is interesting to note that many business arrangements implemented over the internet have been refused protection. These include:

- a method for offering personalised financial products;[216]
- a method of creating and distributing advertising material;[217]
- a system to allow a client to monitor progress made on a building site;[218]
- a system for ordering food.[219]

It seems clear that merely providing a service or assistance over the internet will not be enough on its own to merit patent protection, but each innovation must be considered on its own merit to determine whether it displays the necessary *technical effect*. The mere possibility of this, however, is not enough, and there needs to be a specific focus on the technical progress.[220]

Programs related to computers

11.114   The next paragraphs explore 'software-related invention' in the context of Article 52(2) EPC and section 1(2) 1977 Patent Act. We use this term to describe inventions that employ software to perform their function and where the inventive contribution is embodied within the software itself. We avoid the term 'computer program related-inventions' to prevent confusion with the exclusion of computer programs as such in Article 52(3). We consider it unhelpful to employ the expression 'computer-implemented inventions', which has been deployed by the European Commission in its attempts at reform, because this does not cover all of the inventions discussed herein. The term 'software-related invention' should, therefore, be taken to encompass both (1) inventions that are described solely in terms of the software (eg the program(s) that it contains); and (2) inventions that claim products or processes whose functionality depends on software (eg computers or methods for performing certain functions or tasks).

11.115   Prospective patentees of software-related inventions have faced a double offensive from Article 52(2). Computer programs have been objected to because they embody one or more of the pre-existing exclusions; for example it is sometimes argued that a program represents no more than an automated means to perform a mental act.[221] However, computer programs are also the subject of a specific prohibition and can be objected to in their own right without the need to rely on other exclusions. Why is this so?

---

[214] See Case T258/03 *HITACHI/Auction method* [2004] 12 OJEPO 575.
[215] The Court of Appeal confirmed in *Symbian Ltd's Application* [2009] RPC 1 that a business method implemented on a 'conventional computer system' would be excluded as a pure business method.
[216] *Accucard's Application* (BL O/145/03).   [217] *Adgistics Ltd's Application* (BLO/297/04).
[218] *Ashizawa's Application* (BL O/201/03).   [219] *Fujitsu's Application* (BL O/121/04).
[220] EPO Guidelines, Part G-II, para 3.5.3.
[221] See, eg, *Merrill Lynch's Application* [1989] RPC 561; *Gale's Application* 1991] RPC 305; *Fujitsu's Application* [1997] RPC 608; and more recently, *Aerotel Ltd v Telco Holdings Ltd* [2006] EWCA Civ 1371 and *Symbian Ltd v Comptroller General of Patents, Designs and Trademarks* [2009] RPC 1. These cases were discussed in paras 11.125–11.133.

Why are computer programs excluded from patentability?

11.116   The drafting of the EPC 1973 was a long and arduous process lasting throughout the 1960s and into the early 1970s. Much of this time was taken up debating the need for, and the terms of, the exclusions from patentability. When the final version of the EPC was adopted in 1973 the specific prohibition on patenting computer programs had found its way into the instrument, but its inclusion was by no means a given.[222] Indeed, computer programs received no mention whatsoever in the outcome of the first round of negotiations. Opinion was greatly divided when the matter was eventually debated in the second round, with the UK showing most antipathy towards software-related inventions, calling them 'merely the mathematical application of a logical series of steps in a process which was no different from a mathematical method [already] excluded'.[223] Moreover, there was concern about including a specific prohibition against computer programs lest genuinely inventive developments related to software also be excluded. Nonetheless, the provision found its way into law. The point to note, however, is the degree of ambivalence that has surrounded this particular exclusion from the start. We therefore began the modern European era of patentability with a tension over the patent protection of computer programs and a genuine desire to strike a balance between the exclusion such as it is and the imperative to protect well-deserving inventions irrespective of whether they are in some way connected to software. It is the resolution of this tension and the striking of this balance that has preoccupied the EPO (and others) ever since.

11.117   It should not be thought that because Article 52(2) EPC seems to take a double swipe at patent applications relating to software that such patents are rarely granted. Indeed, the European Commission confirmed in 2002 that over 20,000 so-called computer-implemented inventions had been granted by the EPO alone;[224] many thousands more have been awarded by national offices.[225] By corollary, around this time commentators indicated that only around 100 software-related inventions have experienced any problems before the EPO.[226] This gives rise to the obvious question: how was and is the exclusion being interpreted? In order to understand the answer to this question, it is first important to understand some essential features of computer software.

Computer software: the functions

11.118   The World Intellectual Property Organization (WIPO) defined a computer program in 1978 as: 'a set of instructions capable, when in a machine-readable medium, of causing a machine having information-processing capabilities to indicate, perform or achieve a particular function, task or result'.[227] This definition remains broadly accurate today, in that software is essentially a means of processing information in order to control the functioning of a computer, other device, or a technical process. And, to the extent that there is a functional output from the operation of software, this technical end result may be the subject matter of a successful patent application.[228] Although the claimed invention in such cases would not normally be

---

[222]   It has even been suggested that its inclusion was a mistake; see G Kolle, 'The patentable invention in the European Patent Convention' (1974) 5 IIC 140–56.

[223]   Taken from the report of discussions in October 1971. See too S Davis, 'Computer program claims: the final frontier for software inventions' [1998] 20 EIPR 429.

[224]   European Commission, Proposal for a Directive of the European Parliament and of the Council on the patentability of computer-implemented inventions, COM(2002) 92 final, 20 February 2002, 2.

[225]   The overall figure from around Europe was estimated to exceed 30,000, in 2002; see 'Proposal for a Directive on the patentability of computer-implemented inventions—frequently asked questions' MEMO 02/32.

[226]   L Cohen, 'The patenting of software' [1999] 12 EIPR 607. For an excellent account of European software patenting law and practice, see K Beresford, *Patenting Software under the European Patent Convention* (2nd rev edn, 2009) .

[227]   See WIPO Model Provisions on the Protection of Computer Software, Geneva 1978, s 1(i).

[228]   See, eg, *Raytheon Co v Comptroller General of Patents, Designs and Trade Marks* [2007] EWHC 1230 (Pat). Here the court considered that where a claimed technical contribution exists independently of whether it is implemented by a computer, in the sense that it embodies a technical process lying outside the computer, the contribution will not be a computer program as such and can therefore be the subject of a patent application. This will be so even if the only practical way of implementing the invention will be on a computer.

the program per se, the value of the invention will nonetheless be inherently bound up with the role of the software. This highlights the central role that software plays in technological development across a wide range of fields and it should lead us to question the desirability of attempting to separate patentable and non-patentable elements of an invention. Indeed, the EPO has repeatedly stressed the need to consider inventions 'as a whole' when assessing their patentability.[229] Nonetheless, from the patentee's perspective, it is in their interests to seek protection for as many separate elements of the invention as possible, giving rise to a multiplicity of rights to control, each of which can be exploited and defended against a variety of competitors. Thus, while it may be reassuring that the inclusion of a software element in an invention will not necessarily be a bar to the patentability of that invention, the prudent patentee will also seek protection for the software element itself. We present no comment at this stage on the broader acceptability of this strategy but instead offer it as one of the reasons why there has been a sustained push from the software industry to extend protection in the realm of computer programs. Indeed, the Hargreaves Review in 2011 found a significant rise in patent applications in this section in recent years, especially compared to other sectors including biotech. And yet, it was not at all clear from the evidence base that the increase also represented a corresponding rise in innovation in the area. Rather, it gave rise to a concern about patent thickets as we discussed in paras 10.17–10.19 and the recommendation from Hargreaves is that Europe should continue to resist business method patents (a significant subset of software-related patenting).[230]

11.119   A number of analogies have been used over the years to describe software, some more helpful than others. The most obvious and ubiquitous parallel that is made is between the computer code[231] and 'literary works', as these are understood in copyright law. We have already explained the rudimentary operations of computers and the software used to run them in Chapters 2 and 3, where we discuss copyright protection of computer programs. But the protection that is afforded to computer code by copyright is simply in the expression of that code and does not extend to the functionality of the software; that is, to the effects that the software has when run on a computer, or to the underlying ideas and principles of the software. Yet, this is often where the true value of the software lies. It is this functionality which is the proper subject of patent protection.

 Question

What other differences can you think of between the protection afforded to software by copyright and that which might arise under patent law?

11.120   Further analogies about computer software being simply an automated means to perform mental acts vastly oversimplify the capabilities and complexities of contemporary software and probably have very little bearing on current practice, although this continues to be a problem where it has become enshrined in law. Moreover, there is no escaping the fact that the means by which software employs algorithms to perform its tasks—that is, through the application of a set of prescribed logical procedures to solve a particular

---

[229] See, in particular, Case T208/84 *VICOM/Computer-related invention* [1987] EPOR 74 and Case T26/86 *KOCH AND STERZEL/X-ray apparatus* [1988] EPOR 72.

[230] I Hargreaves, *Digital Opportunity: A Review of Intellectual Property and Growth* (2011), www.gov.uk/government/publications/digital-opportunity-review-of-intellectual-property-and-growth, paras 6.21–6.26.

[231] Computer code can take a variety of forms including 'source code', ie the alphanumerical code input to the computer by the programmer using an established language, and 'object code', ie the binary code read by the computer to control its functioning. Source code cannot be read by the computer and must first be converted to binary code by the computer's compiler. Both codes are potentially protectable by copyright by virtue of the inclusion of 'computer program' in the definition of 'literary work' in the Copyright, Designs and Patents Act 1988, s 3(1). While 'computer program' is not defined by the 1988 Act, TRIPS, Art 10(1) confirms that 'Computer programs, whether in source or object code, shall be protected as literary works under the Berne Convention (1971).' Moreover, Council Directive 91/250/EEC of 14 May 1991 on the legal protection of computer programs and the codified version of Directive 2009/24/EC simply states in the preamble that 'the term "computer program" shall include program in any form'.

problem—is in essence the deployment of mathematical formulae towards a particular end result. As we know, mathematical formulae cannot be patented, but confusion has arisen because of a general failure to distinguish pure formulae, on the one hand from the application of those formulae to produce a technical outcome, on the other. It is the same distinction that must be drawn between computer software in itself and the effects that its operation brings about.

11.121   A common concern also underpins these examples, namely, the desire to exclude mere abstracts from protection, inter alia, because these are difficult to define, impossible to police, and result in excessively broad monopolies. It has been argued that a computer program falls into this category, for where is the tangible embodiment of a computer program that consists of nothing more than a series of instructions? To the extent that these might be expressed in a written form, the program has a tangible expression which is protected by copyright. But beyond this, what *is* a computer program? This, however, simply reinforces the need to be clear about the difference between the abstract idea underlying the program and the products or processes that it influences. As Beresford has said, 'the wisest course is … to direct software claims clearly to a physical product or apparatus or a physical process'.[232]

11.122   Self-evidently, the primary effect of computer software is to make a computer work and it does this by controlling the processing of data within the computer's internal circuits. But, as the EPO Guidelines for Examination make clear, 'such normal physical effects are not in themselves sufficient to lend a computer program technical character'.[233] Rather, 'if a computer program is capable of bringing about, when running on a computer, a *further technical effect* going beyond these normal physical effects, it is not excluded from patentability'.[234]

11.123   The architecture of software is a central feature of its protectability. In the realm of copyright, it has been confirmed that the originality requirement can be found in the overall structure and layout of the software, thereby extending the protection to non-literal aspects of the work.[235] Software architecture can have a significant impact on the speed and efficiency of a program and novel architectures can result in considerable improvements in the operability of the software and the functions that it performs. To this extent, these technical features of the software may provide a means to bring about a technical effect susceptible to patent protection.

11.124   A final point to note about the central features of computer programs is that while software can only operate in the appropriate hardware, it can be stored separately in a variety of mediums such as CDs or USB sticks and it can be sent and received over the internet or by attachment to email. In other words, software can be bought, sold, and transferred free of any hardware apparatus. This can have important implications in terms of scope of protection and infringement proceedings as we shall see (para 11.174 regarding developments in the United States).

Software-related inventions and UK case law

11.125   The approach in the UK historically has been to ask if the invention makes a 'technical contribution' to the state of the art—that is, to the sum total of human knowledge—and if so, it will be patentable as long as the contribution is not solely in the realm of excluded matter.[236] A technical contribution is one which produces a *technical effect*, and in most cases this means a real-world change in the state, operation, or function

---

[232]   Beresford, *Patenting Software under the European Patent Convention* (2nd edn, 2006).

[233]   EPO Guidelines, Part G-II, para 3.6, citing Case T1173/97 *IBM/Computer Programs* [2000] EPOR 219 and Case G003/08 *Programs for Computers*.

[234]   EPO Guidelines, Part G-II, para 3.6. See eg Case T130/11 *MICROSOFT/On-demand property system* [2016] EPOR 28.

[235]   *Cantor Fitzgerald International v Tradition (UK) Ltd* [1999] Masons CLR 157; [2000] RPC 95 and *Nova Productions Ltd v Mazooma Games Ltd* [2007] RPC 25 (CA).

[236]   See *Merrill Lynch's Application* [1988] RPC 1, and also *Gale's Application* [1991] RPC 305 and *Fujitsu's Application* [1996] RPC 511; see paras 11.125–11.133.

of something tangible.[237] The problem is that the term *technical contribution* suffers from an 'inherent vagueness',[238] and its utility and limits were probably best summed up in this way:[239]

> If you look at the case law on the subject, both here and in Munich, you will find many references to 'technical contribution', 'technical result', and so on, being touchstones by which these cases are decided. The use of the word 'technical' as a short-hand expression in order to identify patentable subject-matter is often convenient. But it should be remembered that it was not used by the framers of the Patents Act 1977 or the European Patent Convention when they wanted to tell us what is or is not an 'invention'. In any case the word 'technical' is not a solution. It is merely a restatement of the problem in different and more imprecise language. I am not claiming that it is wrong to decide cases with reference to the word 'technical'. It happens all the time. What I am saying is that it is not a panacea. It is a useful servant but a dangerous master.

11.126   In fact, the need to find a *technical* contribution may have been downgraded by the Court of Appeal in *Aerotel*. The court reviewed all of the existing UK and European Patent Office (EPO) rulings and opined that its ruling would be the 'definitive statement' on patentable subject matter. While confirming the authority of existing precedents,[240] the court set about 'reformulating' the test under Articles 52(2) and (3) to be applied into a four-step approach, and considered that there was no suggestion that section 1(2) had a different meaning. The steps are:

(1) Properly construe the claim.

(2) Identify the actual contribution.

(3) Ask whether it falls solely within the excluded subject matter.

(4) Check whether the actual or alleged contribution is actually technical in nature.

The fourth criterion is merely a final check which should be deployed only when the application has passed the first three criteria.[241] The presence or absence of a technical effect is therefore only a subsidiary matter which speaks to patentability rather than exclusion.[242] A UK IPO Practice Note was published on the issue of patentable subject matter.[243] This approach was followed in various cases including *Astron Clinica Ltd and Others v The Comptroller General of Patents*, where it was confirmed that the first three steps should answer whether the invention is excluded, with the fourth step being a final check (although a necessary one in the light of *Merrill Lynch*).[244] *Astron Clinica*[245] concerned computer program carrier claims which were not directly considered in the *Aerotel* case but thought to be excluded by its approach. Kitchin J held that where claims to a method performed by running a suitably programmed computer or to a computer programmed to carry out the method were allowable, a claim to the program itself should also be allowable *provided that* the computer program implements a patentable invention. This resulted in a further Practice Notice[246] in which the UK IPO confirmed that where a claim to a computer program is drafted to reflect the features of the invention which would ensure the patentability of the method which the program is intended to carry out when it is run, examiners would no longer object to claims to a computer program or a program on a carrier; and pointed out that the decision restored the UK to its position prior to *Aerotel* with respect to claims to programs themselves.

11.127   The *Aerotel* test was reconsidered by the Court of Appeal in *Symbian Ltd.*[247] Here the court confirmed that the *Aerotel* test is intended to be, in substance, the same test that prior UK case law applied; the fundamental question to be answered remains whether there is a *technical contribution*. It considered that it might be

---

[237] In this respect the UK broadly followed the EPO; see Case T208/84 *VICOM/Computer-related Inventions* [1987] EPOR 74, but see further paras 11.145–11.149.

[238] See *Aerotel Ltd v Telco Holdings Ltd and Others* [2006] EWCA Civ 1371, para 124.   [239] ibid.

[240] ibid.   [241] ibid, paras 46–47.

[242] See the ruling of the Hearing Officer in *John Lahiri Khan's Application* (BL O/356/06).

[243] *Practice Note (Patents Act 1977: Patentable Subject Matter)* [2007] Bus LR 672.

[244] *Astron Clinica Ltd and Others v The Comptroller General of Patents* [2008] EWHC 85 (Pat), para 45.

[245] ibid.   [246] *Practice Notice (Patents Act 1977: Patentable subject matter) (No 2)* [2008] Bus LR 978.

[247] *Symbian Ltd v Comptroller General of Patents, Designs and Trademarks* [2008] EWCA Civ 1066.

necessary to fuse the third and the fourth steps into a single step as it is not as important *when* the technical contribution is identified as it is to consider whether the invention makes a relevant technical contribution to the art.[248] The patent in *Symbian* was upheld as more than a claim to a computer program 'as such' because the application disclosed a real-world effect of making a computer work better. The technical problem concerned the working of electronic libraries and how to ensure they continue to work effectively when changes are made to the library data. The invention in suit effectively provided a solution to this problem.

11.128   The net result of the *Symbian* ruling is that a program is patentable even if it solves a problem with the running of a computer or with programming itself, including making it run faster or more reliably. It does not follow, however, that the mere presence of computer hardware is sufficient to render a computer program patentable. This case is helpful in providing further insight into when a 'technical contribution' is more than solely a computer program.[249] It also suggested that fusing the third and fourth steps of the *Aerotel* test would help towards reconciling UK and EPO jurisprudence. The UK IPO thereafter issued a further Practice Notice in December 2008.[250] This Notice confirms that the four-step test is the correct test for determining whether an invention falls under excluded subject matter. It further notes that when considering whether the contribution is more than solely a computer program, one must consider what the program does as a matter of practical reality. If it results in a computer running faster or more reliably, it may be considered to provide a technical contribution even if the invention solely addresses a problem in the programming.[251] It is not sufficient merely to include claims to computer hardware to avoid the exclusion, and a claim to a computer program can be allowable 'if the claim reflects the features of the invention which would ensure the patentability of the method which the program is intended to carry out when it is run'. *Symbian* also confirms that other excluded material (eg business methods) cannot be rendered patentable merely by being implemented on a conventional computer system (para 27).[252] The UK Practice Notice confirms a point of divergence with the EPO;[253] however, in *HTC Europe v Apple*[254] the Court of Appeal stated that whether one followed the *Aerotel* approach or that taken by the EPO (there in *Duns Licensing*, see para 11.166), one should end up at the same destination.

11.129   It is useful to view the *Symbian* ruling, and in particular *Aerotel*, in a comparative and historical context. The Court of Appeal acknowledged the importance of decisions from the Boards of Appeal of the EPO and that they have 'great persuasive authority' for the UK courts.[255] Notwithstanding, it did not follow the available rulings because it considered that the EPO jurisprudence is currently unstable.[256] The court also looked beyond Europe to the United States and noted the contrasting approach to patentability where 'everything under the sun that is made by man' is patentable.[257] While this may overstate the position somewhat, it is clear that the US policy is to ensure that the categories of patentable invention are given wide scope.[258]

11.130   In *Aerotel* the court stated specifically that the approach for the future is not a departure from what has gone before, but merely a reformulation of the approach established in a trio of cases: *Merrill Lynch's Application*,[259]

---

[248] *Symbian Ltd's Application* [2008] EWCA Civ 1066; [2009] RPC 1 at para 58.

[249] As had been noted previously by Pumfrey J in *Bloomberg LLP and Cappellini's Applications* [2007] EWHC 476 (Pat), not all 'technical effects' are relevant for the fourth step of the *Aerotel/Macrossan* test. The relevant technical effect has to be one that is more than the expected effect from the mere loading of a program on to a computer.

[250] *Practice Notice (Patents Act 1977: Patentability of computer programs)* [2009] Bus LR 625.

[251] *Practice Notice (PO: Patents Act 1977: Patentability of computer programs)* [2009] Bus LR 625, para 5.

[252] M Kenrick, 'Software patentability—where are we, and where might we be going?' (2008) 37(7) CIPAJ 378.

[253] See *Dell Products LP's Application* (BL 0/321/10).   [254] (2013) RPC 30, EWCA Civ 451, paras 35–41.

[255] See *Merrell Dow v Norton* [1996] RPC 76, per Lord Hoffmann at 82. See also *Eli Lilly & Co v Human Genome Sciences Inc* [2010] EWCA Civ 33.

[256] *Aerotel Ltd v Telco Holdings Ltd and Others* [2006] EWCA Civ 1371, paras 29–30. But see Case T154/04, *DUNS LICENSING ASSOCIATES/Estimating Sales Activity*, OJ 2/2008, 46.

[257] *Aerotel Ltd v Telco Holdings Ltd and Others* [2006] EWCA Ci 1371, paras 13–15. The quote was famously stated by the US Supreme Court in *Diamond v Chakrabarty* 447 US 303, 100 S Ct 2204 (1980) in respect of the patentability of a man-made, oil-eating bacterium.

[258] Confirmed by the Congress Committee Reports when patents laws were being re-codified in 1952: S Rep No 1979, 82nd Cong, 2nd Sess, 5 (1952); HR Rep No 1923, 82nd Cong, 2nd Sess, 6 (1952).

[259] [1989] RPC 561.

Gale's Application,[260] and *Fujitsu's Application*.[261] The ruling in *Merrill Lynch* endorsed an EPO ruling in *Vicom* regarding a method and apparatus claim for digitally processing and manipulating images in the design field, to the extent that the mention of excluded matter within a claim is not fatal to its validity as long as the invention, when considered as a whole, makes a technical contribution to the art. In *Gale's Application*[262] the court rejected an attempt to link the program (for calculating a square root) to a piece of technical apparatus (a ROM chip) because the sole contribution nonetheless lay in automated instructions to perform a function that could otherwise be done by means of a mental act; that is, in an excluded category. Finally, in *Fujitsu's Application*[263] the claim was to a method and apparatus for modelling a synthetic crystal structure when designing inorganic materials for applications in chemistry and physics. The user would select key parameters and the computer would display the resulting novel structure. The Court of Appeal read *Vicom* not to mean that claims to the digital processing of real images are always allowable, but rather that the technical contribution in that case lay in the way the enhanced image was produced. This was by means of the program technically and precisely controlling the quality of the image—a matter which was beyond human intervention. In *Fujitsu*, the user provided all necessary information to produce the final image of the combined structure. The program merely supplied a means to reproduce the image automatically and faster; a process that would in the past have been represented in substantially the same fashion by a physical model. This was insufficient to demonstrate technical contribution within the terms of UK and European patent law.

11.131   *Aerotel* purports not to disturb these rules.[264] Further, the House of Lords refused a request by McCrossan to appeal the case, meaning that *Aerotel* now forms the basis of the UK approach towards patentable subject matter. An early post-*Aerotel* example concerned the rejection of Sony's data structure for communicating metadata (*Sony UK Ltd* BL O/010/07). The contribution as outlined in the claims was found in the data structure whose function was to form part of the instructions in a computer network for interrogation, retrieval, and communication of metadata. As such, it was excluded as a computer program. The fourth question was not asked, begging the question why it has been retained at all.[265] Tantalisingly, however, the Hearing Office suggested that the data structure could be seen to embody a technical effect if described differently (as an apparatus), but this was not so in the claims in question. Such a remark may be worrying if it suggests that problems of exclusion can be avoided by simple alternative claim drafting.

11.132   Subsequent decisions in the UK context include:

- *Halliburton Energy Services Inc's Applications*,[266] in which it was held that the mental acts exclusion in patent law must be interpreted narrowly; that is, to involve human mental activity. This means that any claims to implement an invention with a computer will not fall foul of this particular exclusion, albeit it might still be excluded as a computer program as such. A UK IPO Practice Notice has again been issued.[267]

- *Protecting Kids the World Over (PKTWO) Ltd's Patent Application*[268] involved an electronic monitoring system to alert parents by email or text if their child has been exposed to inappropriate electronic communications. This was patentable because, following the *AT&T* signposts,[269] it was helpful to consider the task performed by the program and ask whether it produced a novel real-world effect. An alarm in the physical world alerting the user to activity on the computer met this criterion: 'The invention solved a technical problem lying outside the computer, namely how to improve on the inappropriate communication alarm generation provided by the prior art' (paras 32–35).

---

[260] [1991] RPC 305.   [261] [1997] RPC 608.   [262] [1991] RPC 305.   [263] [1997] RPC 608.

[264] Although the court doubted whether a method for performing a mental act executed by computer would be excluded: *Aerotel Ltd v Telco Holdings Ltd and Others* [2006] EWCA Civ 1371, para 62.

[265] The fourth step has in other cases been applied regardless of a failure to meet the third step; see, eg, *Bloomberg LLP and Cappellini's Applications* [2007] EWHC 476 (Pat). For more information see para 11.126.

[266] [2011] EWHC 2508 (Pat), [2012] RPC 129.

[267] *Practice Notice (Patents Act 1977: Patentability of mental acts)*, Intellectual Property Office, 17 October 2011 [2012] Bus LR 1264.

[268] [2011] EWHC 2720 (Pat); [2012] RPC 13.   [269] *AT&T Corp Excel Communications Inc*, 172 F 3rd 1352 (Fed Cir, 1999).

- *HTC Europe Co Ltd v Apple Inc, Apple Inc v HTC Corp*[270] related to various patents owned by Apple regarding their mobile touch-screen devices. A patent involved computer devices with inputs which were capable of responding to more than one touch at the same time. Claim 1 and 2 of the patent described a method for handling touch events on a multi-touch device. This was unpatentable as a computer program as such. In contrast, other patents relating to other features which were not excluded on this ground because they produced sufficient technical effect, viz, the slide-to-unlock feature and the zoom-image feature, both solved a real-world problem with effect beyond the software itself.

11.133　How far, then, is there a divergence between the approaches in the UK (before and after *Aerotel* and *Symbian*) and that of the EPO? It is interesting to note that the decision of the Court of Appeal in *HTC Europe v Apple*[271] considered that its solution would be reached whether one followed the *Aerotel* approach (see para 11.88), or that taken by the EPO in *Duns Licensing* (see para 11.166). In the section that follows consider for yourself whether the court decisions discussed so far are moving the UK further away from, rather than towards, the EPO position.

Software-related inventions and the development of EPO jurisprudence

11.134　We are about to embark on an account of the evolution of thinking in the EPO towards software-related inventions—the uncertainty of which was noted in *Aerotel* (see para 11.88). To make sense of this process you need to be aware of certain key features of the EPO's approach to patentability: a patentee must show that they have an invention with *technical character* in the sense that it produces a *technical effect*. Where does this focus come from?

> **Exercise**
>
> Examine Articles 52–57 EPC and the EPO Guidelines for Substantive Examination, Part G-II, and the EPC Implementing Regulations, rules 27 and 29 (all available on the EPO website).[272] Where does the need for technical character and technical effect arise in European patent law?

11.135　The need to demonstrate *technical character* and *technical effect* permeates all of the jurisprudence of the EPO. While it is not stated explicitly in the criteria for patentability in Articles 54–57 EPC, *technical effect* is used to test inventive step: has the invention made a *technical contribution* to the art? Moreover, while neither the term *technical character* nor *technical effect* appears in Article 52 EPC regarding exclusions from patentability, the need to demonstrate *technical character* has become the single most important factor in restricting the scope of these exclusions.[273] Nowhere is this more true than in the context of computer programs. Indeed, the current position can be summed up as follows:

> **Summary of EPO position**
>
> As long as a software-related invention is of a technical character (in the sense of producing a technical effect) it will be eligible for patent protection. It does not matter that the essence of the invention falls into an excluded category; that is, that the technical character is found in a computer program.

270 [2012] EWHC 1789 (Pat).
271 [2013] RPC 30 (the first instance decision is discussed in bullet 3 in para 11.132).
272 Implementing Regulations as of 13 December 2017, www.epo.org/law-practice/legal-texts/html/epc/2016/e/ma2.html.
273 Confirmed as a valid approach in Case T931/95 *PENSION BENEFIT SYSTEM/Controlling pension benefits systems* [2002] EPOR 52 and see too Case T1227/05 *INFINEON TECHNOLOGIES/Circuit Simulation I* [2010] EPOR 9; Case T1784/06 *COMPTEL/Classification method* [2013] EPOR 9.

Thus, we have the most recent version of the EPO Guidelines (2018) stating (G-II, 3.6):

> Computer programs are excluded from patentability under Art 52(2)(c) and (3) if claimed as such. However, following the generally applicable criteria for Art 52(2) and (3) (G-II, 2) the exclusion does not apply to computer programs having a technical character. In order to have a technical character, and thus not be excluded from patentability, a computer program must produce a 'further technical effect' when run on a computer. A 'further technical effect' is a technical effect going beyond the 'normal' physical interactions between the program (software) and the computer (hardware) on which it is run. The normal physical effects of the execution of a program, e.g. the circulation of electrical currents in the computer, are not in themselves sufficient to confer technical character to a computer program.

What is the relationship between technical character and further technical effect?

11.136 Technical character is demonstrated by bringing about a further technical effect; that is, changes in the workings of apparatus, products, or processes achieved by technical means. Relevant technical effects include:

(1) the control of an industrial process;

(2) the control of the internal functions of a computer itself or its interfaces;

(3) determining emissions by an X-Ray device;

(4) implementing security measures for protecting boot integrity; or

(5) countermeasures against power analysis attacks.[274]

These are mere examples and the clear message to patent attorneys who must draft claims for software-related inventions is to focus their attention on the possible technical effects which can be brought about by the computer program, for it is in these that protection will be secured.[275]

11.137 The net effect of this position is that the seemingly absolutist prohibition on the patenting of computer programs *as such* is illusory. It is no longer a matter of interpreting the provisions of Article 52 EPC (albeit narrowly), for the emphasis has shifted from considering what is *not* patentable to considering what *is* patentable, the primary requirement being that the putative invention displays technical character.[276] Of course, this does not preclude the need to show that the invention is new, involves an inventive step, and is capable of industrial application in the normal way; but it does leave us to question what, if anything, remains of the exclusion of computer programs from European patent law. This also differs from the *Aerotel* four-step test; and reflecting this, the Technical Board of Appeal has stated that *Aerotel* is 'irreconcilable with the European Patent Convention'.[277]

Exercise

Before reading any further, consider whether there is any need to retain an exclusion of computer programs in Article 52 EPC. You might like to consider the discussions about possible removal of the provision at the Diplomatic Conference to revise the EPC in 2000: http://documents.epo.org/projects/babylon/eponet.nsf/0/a3d02eeebea84306c12572ae00500cdc/$file/conference_proceedings_en.pdf.

---

[274] EPO Guidelines, Part G-II, paras 3.6 and 3.6.1.

[275] Although see the comments in T1543/06 *Gameaccount* quoted in *AT&T Knowledge Ventures LP's Patent Application* [2009] FSR] 19:

The Board is of the firm belief, that it cannot have been the legislator's purpose and intent on the one hand to exclude computer programs from patent protection, while on the other hand awarding protection to a technical implementation thereof, where the only identifiable contribution of the claimed technical implementation to the state of the art is the excluded subject-matter itself. The Board believes Article 52(2) EPC is intended as substantive in nature, rather than able to be easily circumvented.

This led the Board to conclude:' the mere technical implementation of excluded subject-matter *per se* cannot form the basis for inventive step. The Board concludes that inventive step can be based only on the particular manner of implementation.'

[276] After Case T931/95 *PENSION BENEFIT SYSTEMS/Controlling pension benefits systems* [2002] EPOR 52 and Case T641/00 *COMVIK/Two identities* [2004] EPOR 10; followed in Case T588/05 *WEST DIRECT/Computer assisted telemarketing* [2010] EPOR 12.

[277] See para 11.167.

How have we arrived at this position?

11.138   Reflecting the discussion at UK level (see paras 11.125ff) we can plot the course of EPO thinking on software-related inventions in roughly three stages. A brief assessment of this is useful to understanding and to wonder what what might happen next. Here, these stages will be explored chronologically. First was the period from the establishment of the EPO in 1978 until 1985 when the Examination Guidelines were changed in respect of computer programs. Secondly came the post-1985 period, which is characterised by an increasingly liberal attitude towards these inventions when considerably fewer restraints applied, with some notable exceptions. Thirdly came the modern era, which began in 1998/99 with the two important rulings in Case T935/97 *IBM/Computer Programs*[278] and Case T1173/97 *IBM/Computer Programs*.[279] This era ushered in the effective demise of the computer program exclusion.

Stage 1: 1978–1985

11.139   We need not dwell on the national positions that prevailed prior to signing of the EPC in 1973 and the establishment of the EPO in 1978, although suffice to say that patents had been granted for software-related inventions in a variety of countries.[280] But this was set to change somewhat by virtue of the exclusion of computer programs in the EPC and the requirement of signatory states to bring their laws into line with the Convention. All eyes looked to the EPO for an indication of how patenting practice in this new era would take shape—although as has been seen, in the UK the approaches were not always followed. The point remains, however, that while national intellectual property offices and courts are not bound by the rulings of the EPO, they do consider them to be highly persuasive, and for reasons that we have already examined it is preferable to keep discrepancies to an absolute minimum.

11.140   The original version of the EPO Guidelines had this to say about computer programs:[281]

> If the contribution to the known art resides solely in the computer program then the subject matter is not patentable in whatever manner it may be presented in the claims.

Here the focus is firmly on the fact that the computer program is an example of an excluded category of invention and that if the essence of the claims in an application is to a computer program, then those claims should be rejected, no matter the invention's actual technical contribution, function, or effect.[282]

11.141   Interestingly, there is precious little evidence of an antipathetic attitude from the Examining Division of the EPO towards inventions involving computer programs during this period, and the Board of Appeal did not even hear, let alone reject, any relevant appeal during this time. Nonetheless, after consultation on the Guidelines, during which time the EPO came under considerable pressure to amend the provisions, the text was changed in 1985, with the claim to be focussed on as a whole. It is possible that much of this pressure was brought to bear because of the widespread perception that the restriction on patenting was more stringent than was borne out by practice.

11.142   We see here a crucial shift in emphasis away from reasons to exclude protection towards reasons to extend protection to a claimed invention. The framework has thereby been established to allow the EPO more latitude in its interpretation of Article 52, a task to which it took with considerable gusto.

Stage 2: 1985–1998/99

11.143   The direction of EPO jurisprudence during this period was set by the first decision of the Board of Appeal to consider the exclusion of computer programs, Case T208/84 *VICOM/Computer-related invention*,[283]

---

[278] [1999] EPOR 301.   [279] [2000] EPOR 219.

[280] See, eg, in the UK, *Slee and Harris's Applications* [1966] RPC 194; [1966] FSR 51 and *Burroughs Corporation (Perkins') Application* [1974] RPC 147; [1973] FSR 439.

[281] [1978] OJEPO 1.

[282] Paragraph 3.6. Note, previous editions of the Guidelines also included the following statement: 'A computer program claimed by itself or as a record on a carrier, is not patentable irrespective of its content.' This has now been removed. Why?

[283] [1987] EPOR 74.

mentioned above from its impact in the UK in para 11.100. This remained the most influential decision throughout this period and it continues to be a milestone of considerable significance. The case involved an appeal against the rejection by the Examining Division of claims related to (1) a method of digitally processing images with a view to enhancing their features, for example the clarity of the image; and (2) specifically designed apparatus to carry out this method. It was a particular feature of the claimed invention that all of this could be done considerably faster and more efficiently than was possible in conventional computers of the time. The inventors acknowledged, however, that the invention itself could be implemented using a suitably programmed conventional computer. The Examining Board rejected the application on the grounds that it was for a mathematical method and/or a computer program as such.

11.144   The Board of Appeal disagreed on both counts holding:

- As regards the *method* of image processing:
  (i)   methods of processing images, including simulated images, are susceptible of industrial application under Article 57 EPC—that is, they are sufficiently technical to be the proper subject of patent law;
  (ii) if the claim in question is directed towards a *technical process* which is carried out on a *physical entity*—here, an image (albeit one stored as an electric signal)—and that process brings about changes in that entity—here, the manipulation of the image to enhance or alter certain features—then this is a *technical effect* sufficient for the purposes of patent law;
  (iii) while it is true that such a process can be described in mathematical terms, for example the operation of a mathematical algorithm on data, the effect of this operation is not merely to produce more abstract data but rather to produce a real change in a real image and therefore there is an effect beyond the simple execution of the mathematical method;
  (iv) it is irrelevant that the idea underlying the invention resides in a mathematical method as long as the process that is claimed goes beyond the mere mathematical method *as such*;
  (v)   it is also irrelevant that the technical means used to bring about the technical effect is by way of a computer program, since the claim is to the process carried out under the control of the program and not to the program *as such*.
- As regards the *apparatus* containing the software for processing the images, it was held that:[284]

claims which can be considered as being directed to a computer set up to operate in accordance with a specified program (whether by means of hardware or software) *for controlling or carrying out a technical process* cannot be regarded as relating to a computer program as such . . . .

11.145   It is interesting and important to note that the need for specificity of claim was emphasised in *Vicom*. Thus, it was stated that:[285]

a 'method for digitally filtering data' remains an abstract notion not distinguished from a mathematical method so long as it is not specified what physical entity is represented by the data and forms the subject of the technical process . . . .

This was an important qualification because the original claims before the Examining Division did not specify image manipulation and spoke only of a method of 'digitally filtering . . . data', which was a broad and unacceptable claim given the nature of the invention in question.

Discussion point   For answer guidance visit **www.oup.com/uk/brown5e**.

Does the previous comment about the exclusion of a method for digitally filtering data mean that such a claim could never succeed? Can you envisage examples where such a claim might be important to a prospective patentee? How might such a claim be successfully framed?

---

[284] [1987] EPOR 74 at 80 (para 15 of judgment).   [285] ibid, at 90 (para 7 of judgment).

11.146   The net result from *Vicom* was that process *and* product claims involving both mathematical methods and computer programs became clearly patentable under the EPC. The essential lesson should be self-evident: the drafting of the claims should be to the process or product itself, emphasising the technical features used to bring about the technical effect and ensuring that any mention of a computer program (or mathematical method) is as a means to achieve the technical result, not an end in itself. In particular:

- *process claims* are to a method of achieving a technical result by means of a computer program operating on appropriate hardware;

- *product claims* are to a computer, or similar device, incorporating a computer program.

Note: in both cases there is the need to link the software to hardware via the claims. This becomes important when we come to consider the third stage of EPO jurisprudence.

Successful examples that followed *Vicom* include:

(1)   a method claim for processes of regulating error messages within a computer system, Case T115/85 *IBM/Computer-related invention*;[286]

(2)   a method claim for maintaining formats of documents transferred between word processors, Case T110/90 *IBM/Editable document form*;[287]

(3)   an apparatus claim for an X-ray device controlled by a computer to monitor tube voltages to ensures optimal exposure while protecting against overload, Case T26/86 *KOCH AND STERZEL/ X-ray apparatus*;[288]

(4)   method and apparatus claims for a system for providing product-specific data in a service station for recognition and editing of design and function states, Case T1242/04 *MAN/Provision of product specific data*.[289]

Exercise

Consider each of these judgments and identify the all-important technical effect.

11.147   It is interesting to note that in virtually all of these cases (and many more successful appeals to the Board of Appeal) the appellants amended their initial (rejected) claims after communication with the Board; indeed, this also happened in *Vicom*. Not only does this help to account for the high number of successful appeals to the Board of Appeal, but it also re-emphasises the crucial point that careful drafting of claims is key.

Discussion point   For answer guidance visit **www.oup.com/uk/brown5e**.

Does it follow that skilful drafting can avoid Article 52 problems for any kind of method, device, or software-related invention? Consider also the approach to drafting provided in the EPO Guidelines (2018) in F-II, para 4.12 and in F-IV, para 3.9.

11.148   In each of the previous examples the role of the computer program was as a *technical means* to realise the *technical effect* that was central to the invention. One might think as a result of these rulings that as long as a computer program is not claimed directly, sufficient protection can be gained for any software-related invention. The reality has not been quite so straightforward and a number of hurdles have remained.

---

[286] [1990] EPOR 107.   [287] [1995] EPOR 185.   [288] [1988] EPOR 72.   [289] [2007] EPOR 45.

11.149 It has been confirmed many times that a computer program on appropriate hardware can provide the necessary *technical means* in this equation, as each of the previous cases demonstrates.[290] But problems remain as to what amounts to a *technical contribution* and, indeed, what is a *technical problem*. Two topics demonstrated the concerns in this period. These are (1) software-related inventions in the field of textual processing; and (2) business method patents.

Software-related inventions and textual processing

11.150 The EPO Board of Appeal has held on a number of occasions that claims directed at processes or devices to assist the user in the processing or manipulation of text or language do not demonstrate a *technical* contribution to the art, but rather a contribution in non-technical areas such as aesthetic creations, methods of performing mental acts, or mere presentations of information. Put another way, the EPO has found that if the sole contribution is in an excluded category, protection will be denied. Thus, for example, in Case T22/85 *IBM/Document abstracting and retrieval*[291] the Board of Appeal rejected a claim relating to a system for creating and storing abstracts from archived documents by means of a key word search because:[292]

(1) the claims simply outlined an excluded category, namely, schemes, rules, and methods for performing mental acts; in particular, it was considered that the claim merely described an automated means of key word search and abstract creation that could be carried out manually in essentially the same fashion;

(2) it was insufficient merely to show that technical means, that is, a computer program running on hardware, had been used to bring about the result because the contribution itself was non-technical; and

(3) 'the true problem to be solved was that of establishing a set of rules for document abstracting and retrieval on the basis of textual properties of the documents to be handled *which problem cannot be qualified as technical*' (emphasis added).

11.151 We need not see these cases, or others like them,[293] as a necessary departure from the general trend laid down in *Vicom*. Indeed, the position is well summed up in Case T121/85 *IBM/Spell Checker*,[294] which involved an automatic spell-checking and correction system that was denied protection by the Board of Appeal. The central passage deserves quotation in full:

Such spelling is basically not of a technical but of a linguistic nature. A correctly spelled word represents an abstract linguistic information and a correct spelling relates therefore to the correctness of an information and not to any physical entity. A wrong spelling can be detected by performing mental acts with no technical means involved.

This does not necessarily mean that a system automatically performing, instead of a human being, the same spelling checking act is excluded from patentability. Rather, this will depend on whether the manner in which it is automated, involves features which make a contribution in a field outside the range of matters excluded from patentability under Art. 52(2) in connection with Art. 52(3) EPC.

11.152 Note, once again, the stress on the need to show technicality. Has this become an overriding consideration? Consider, too, the reference to 'physical entity', which we also see appearing in *Vicom*. The indication seems to be that to bring about a change in a physical entity takes the claim more readily into the technical field, and 'physical entity' has been defined broadly to include non-tangible entities such as computer images[295] and television signals.[296]

---

[290] See, in particular, Case T26/86 *KOCH AND STERZEL/X-ray apparatus* [1988] EPOR 72.

[291] [1990] EPOR 98.   [292] ibid, at 105.

[293] Other failed appeals include Case T52/85 *IBM/Semantically related expressions* [1989] EPOR 454 (automated editing functions to list semantically connected expressions are linguistic, not technical in character); Case T65/86 *IBM/Text processing* [1990] EPOR 181 (automated means to correct contextual errors in a document involved no technical steps that a human being would not also perform in the same task); Case T1177/97 *SYSTRAN/Translating natural languages* [2005] EPOR 13 (the use of a 'longest word-stem match' system to assist in computer translation was based on linguistic considerations and did not solve a technical problem); and Case T1086/07 *XEROX/Document summaries* [2012] EPOR 21 (system of indicators to solve the problem of indicating on a summary document where the summarised portions came from in the original document was merely presentation of information).

[294] Unreported.

[295] Case T208/84 *Vicom Computer-related Invention* [1987] OJEPO 14 (for subsequent approaches, see also Case T643/00 *CANON/Searching image data* [2007] EPOR 1).

[296] Case T163/85 *BBC/Colour television signal* [1990] EPOR 599.

Business method patents

11.153   Much furore has surrounded the prospect of business method patents. The EPO position was initially laid out in Case T769/92 *SOHEI/General purpose management system*,[297] which concerned apparatus and method claims for a novel user interface allowing the input of management data across a broad spectrum of activities, including financial, inventory, personnel, and construction management. The advantage of the system was that it allowed the user to input all of these data via one interface and for them to be processed automatically towards a variety of different ends via one medium. Previously different systems had to be learned for different spheres of management. The Examining Division rejected the application as (1) mere presentation of information; (2) a method of doing business; and (3) a computer program as such. In keeping with established case law, however, the Board of Appeal upheld the claims (albeit after amendment) on the following grounds:

- The program on the computer was merely the technical means to implement the invention and was not claimed as such; what was required was technical character and technical effect; similarly, this would not be an example of the mere presentation of information if technical character was present.

- The 'user-friendly' interface allowing multiple inputs of data and the structured execution of the method for automatically processing those data on the system provided sufficient technical character.

- The subject matter was not excluded if it involved, or implied, at least one aspect or component, which was not excluded from patentability.

- No objection could be raised that the claims related only to 'doing business' because the subject matter of the claims—which could be generalised across a range of possible uses and were not necessarily restricted merely to business ends—could not be said to be merely abstract and non-technical.

11.154   Beyond reiterating the rule in *Vicom*, this EPO decision makes it clear that it is not problematic to an application to include aspects of business management in claims—that is, non-technical features—as long as the claims cannot be taken as solely directed to those ends and, of course, further technical effect is also represented.

11.155   Similarly, in Case T1002/92 *PETTERSSON/Queuing system*[298] an application was allowed for a system of managing queues of people in business establishments by allocating turn-numbers and displaying free service points automatically. The Board of Appeal confirmed that the central claim was to technical apparatus that solved the technical problem of efficient queue management without the need for human input and by means of the interaction of various cooperating technical components. It was stressed that just because one practical application of such a system was in the service of customers of a 'business equipment' did not mean that the claimed subject matter was a method of doing business *as such*. Moreover, while the Board accepted that one element of the claim probably was tantamount to a method of doing business—this being the means of 'deciding which particular turn-number is to be served at the particular free service point' (because it could equally be achieved by means of human intervention involving essentially the same steps)—the claim was to be viewed as a whole and a mix of technical and non-technical elements would not necessarily be excluded from patentability as long as the technical character resides in the technical elements, as was the case in the present application.

11.156   To the extent that the problem to be solved is solely a way of automating business practices, this is non-technical in character and will remain unpatentable in Europe. This was held to be the case in Case T931/95 *PENSION BENEFIT SYSTEMS/Controlling pension benefits systems*,[299] in which the Technical Board rejected an appeal for lack of technical character. In doing so, it confirmed a number of crucial points:

- a *technical* invention does not lose its technical character simply because it is used for a non-technical purpose (eg a method of doing business);

---

[297] [1996] EPOR 253.   [298] ibid, 1.   [299] [2002] EPOR 52.

- a method claim, as long as it is *technical*, may relate to a method of doing business and still be patentable;

- an apparatus claim, even if the apparatus is programmed for use in fields such as business or economy, cannot be an example of excluded subject matter since such products (ie apparatus) are not mentioned in Article 52(2) EPC.

11.157 The appeal failed for the method claims because the claimed invention only described steps in a process for controlling a pension benefit scheme which were for administrative, actuarial, or financial purposes; typically non-technical purposes. It was not enough to point to data processing and computer means employed to execute these purposes, since there was no corresponding disclosure of a technical problem requiring a solution, nor of a solution that represented a technical effect.

11.158 Looking forward beyond this period, subsequent examples of unsuccessful business method applications include:

- claims to a method for running 'what if' scenarios in business databases for the purposes of business planning and information modelling (lack of technical character and the reference to their use in databases was not enough)—Case T1149/06 *IBM/Database back-solving*;[300]

- a system to gauge potential reduction of environmental impact of products (in essence, a management tool to decide between investment strategies and as such lacked sufficient technical character)—Case T1147/05 *RICOH/Environmental impact information*.[301]

Stage 3: 1998/99–present

11.159 We have seen that software patenting practice in the EPO had undergone a gradual evolution towards more liberal interpretations of the EPC. The *IBM* decisions in 1998 and 1999 decisions which are now discussed forced further radical change by addressing two outstanding issues, namely, (1) the continuing exclusion of direct claims to the computer program, as opposed to claims to a method or apparatus run by a program; and (2) the continuing prohibition on claims to the program on a transferable medium such as a disk, as opposed to the software on some form of hardware such as a computer or similar device.

11.160 The fact that computer programs could not be claimed directly was a clear indication that the exclusion in Article 52(2) still held some sway, even if it could be drafted around in many circumstances. In *Vicom*, for instance, the Board of Appeal expressly stated that the computer program itself was not patentable.[302] But this had given rise to a number of objections from the software industry. For example, it was frequently pointed out that the hardware was often an irrelevancy in the inventiveness of the claimed entity, which usually lay in the computer program itself. Moreover, these limitations had potentially serious adverse consequences for the scope of protection afforded. Effective infringement remedies could be denied to patentees with software-related patents in at least two circumstances: (1) a method claim will normally only be infringed directly by someone who runs the program, leaving a lacuna in terms of restricting suppliers of programs; (2) relatedly, if the claim is to the software in tandem with the hardware, and suppliers are to be challenged, they must supply both elements—that is, the computer with the software loaded on it. This leaves the problem of pursuing competitors who merely supply the program itself. The problem becomes all the more acute when one considers that today programs can be transferred, uploaded, and downloaded across the internet without any need for a medium at all.[303]

---

[300] [2010] EPOR 3.   [301] [2008] EPOR 34.

[302] [1987] EPOR 74 at 81 (para 18 of the judgment). Note, however, that Davis has suggested that despite this the practical effect was to allow the patenting of programs in their own right: S Davis, 'Computer program claims' [1998] EIPR 429.

[303] See *Menashe Business Mercantile Ltd v William Hill Organisation Ltd* [2003] 1 All ER 279 (where the supply of CDs to individuals in the UK to enable them to communicate with a host computer outside the UK and thereby to engage in an interactive casino gaming system was held to be an infringement of a patent over the said system held by the claimants. This was an example of 'supply of means relating to an essential element of the invention' under the Patents Act 1977, s 60(2) because the CD allowed UK residents to use the claimed system within the UK even though the host computer was in another country). See Chapter 12 for further comment.

The *IBM/Computer program* cases

11.161   The EPO Technical Board of Appeal set out to remedy these perceived anomalies in the *IBM/Computer program* cases. Case T935/97 *IBM/Computer programs*[304] and Case T1173/97 *IBM/Computer programs*[305] essentially embody the same ruling, delivered by the same members of an appropriately constituted Board of Appeal some seven months apart. The respective applications included (1) claims to a 'computer program product' embodying a means to alter the display of information in a text window on a computer when that window was partially obscured by a second window to ensure the information remained visible to the user (T935/97); and (2) a 'computer program product' comprising a method for resource recovery in the event of system failure (T1173/97).
It was found that:[306]

> a patent may be granted not only in the case of an invention where a piece of software manages, by means of a computer, an industrial process or the working of a piece of machinery, but in every case where a program for a computer is the only means, or one of the necessary means, of obtaining a technical effect . . . where, for instance, a technical effect of that kind is achieved by the internal functioning of a computer itself under the influence of the said program' . . . In other words, on condition that they are able to produce a technical effect . . ., all computer programs must be considered as inventions within the meaning of Article 52(1) EPC, and may be the subject-matter of a patent if the other requirements provided for by the EPC are satisfied.

11.162   The full implications of the EPO's preoccupation with technical character are revealed in these decisions. In both rulings, the Board made the following statement:[307]

> The exclusion from patentability of programs for computers as such . . . may be construed to mean that such programs are considered to be mere abstract creations, lacking in technical character . . . This means that programs for computers must be considered as patentable inventions when they have technical character.

At first sight this relatively innocuous comment might seem to add nothing to the established case law. But it moves the law forward quite considerably in at least two respects. First, it speaks of 'computer programs' themselves being patentable. Secondly, given that we are dealing here with the exclusions from patentability, and considering that technical character must be shown in all cases when assessing the criteria of novelty, inventive step, and industrial applicability, where does this leave the exclusion of computer programs *as such* in EPO patent law? Does it not, in fact, reduce the exclusion simply to a need to satisfy the criteria for patentability and thereby collapses the distinction between excluded and patentable software-related inventions altogether? Although the Board does state that a 'computer program as such' would be one which is a non-technical program, such a program, like any non-technical invention, would fail the patentability criteria anyway.

11.163   The Board also held in the *IBM/Computer program cases*:

- In recognition of the fact that a computer program cannot bring about a technical effect until it is run on a computer, it is sufficient to demonstrate that a computer program has the *potential* to bring about a 'further technical effect', thereby confirming the acceptance of claims to computer programs in themselves.

- The Board drew a parallel between computer hardware and a medium on which the program is stored, for example a disk, as being merely 'the material object on which the physical changes carried out by running the computer take place'.[308] Thus, not only does this remove the need to link software and hardware in claims but, arguably, it also frees computer programs claims from any tangible medium at all.[309]

---

[304] [1999] EPOR 301.   [305] [2000] EPOR 219.   [306] Case T935/97 *IBM/Computer programs* [1999] EPOR 301 at 310.

[307] ibid, at 309; Case T1173/97 *IBM/Computer programs* [2000] EPOR 219 at 226.

[308] See, eg, Case T935/97 *IBM/Computer programs* [1999] EPOR 301 at 312.

[309] For the possible implications of this, especially on the internet, see R Hart, 'Computer program-related patents' [1999] CLSR 188. See also D Attridge, 'Challenging claims! Patenting computer programs in Europe and the USA' [2001] 1 IPQ 22.

- The Board sought to apply logic in defence of its rulings bringing the law to this point. It referred to the *Vicom* decision, wherein it was stated that 'it would seem illogical to grant protection for a technical process controlled by a suitably programmed computer but not for the computer itself when set up to execute the control'—that is, to allow the method claim but not the related apparatus claim, and by analogy the present Board found it 'illogical to grant a patent for both a method and the apparatus adapted for carrying out the same method, but not for the computer program product, which comprises all the features enabling the implementation of the method and which, when loaded in a computer, is indeed able to carry out that method'.[310]

 Question

Even if this is accepted as a matter of logic, to what extent should policy be dictated by logic? What other considerations are at play here? Can 'illogical' policies ever be defended?

11.164   Two potential hurdles to establishing this precedent did not deter the Board of Appeal. These were the 1985 EPO Guidelines on Examination which, as we have seen, expressly prohibited program claims on non-hardware media,[311] and existing case law from the EPO itself which had stressed, inter alia, that: 'exclusion under Article 52(2)(c) and (3) EPC applies to all computer programs, independently of their contents, that is independently of what the program can do or perform when loaded into an appropriate computer'. In other words, the exclusion from patentability of computer programs *as such* was a much more literal and direct interpretation of this term, and the presence or otherwise of technical character was irrelevant.[312] How, then, could the Board reconcile its policy shift with established practice? In fact, it could not do so and preferred to point out that a Board of Appeal is bound neither by the EPO Guidelines[313] nor by previous decisions of the Boards. The instant Technical Board then found it easier to depart from the Guidelines rather than previous decisions; it expressly distinguished prior case law to the extent that it excluded all computer programs as such and irrespective of their content.[314] A possible problem does, however, remain in the realm of claims relating to computer programming itself, which has been held to be akin to the performance of a mental act and so unpatentable.[315] This aspect of the prior case law was not overruled in the present cases, although there is evidence in other decisions that programming that brings about the all-important technical effect can be protected.[316] One can, however, struggle too hard to make sense of legal decisions in the mistaken belief that logic and reason are always the order of the day. The general trend is nonetheless clearly towards patentability. As is considered in para 11.135, the EPO Guidelines have been revised to conform to these and subsequent rulings.[317]

Post-*IBM/Computer Program* approaches

11.165   The *IBM* cases served as the nail in the coffin of consistency for the EPO. As noted, Boards of Appeal are not bound by each other's decisions, which in itself can lead to considerable uncertainty. There were two other cases which warrant attention. The Technical Board of Appeal modified the *Pension Benefit Systems*

---

[310] See Case T935/97 *IBM/Computer programs* [1999] EPOR 301 at 313.

[311] Part C–IV, para 2.3.

[312] Cases include Case T26/86 *KOCH AND STERZEL/X-ray apparatus* [1988] EPOR 72; Case T110/90 *IBM/Editable document form* [1995] EPOR 185; Case T164/96 *Bosch, Bosch/Electronic computer components* [1995] EPOR 585, and the unreported ruling in Case T204/93 *ATT/System for generating software source code*.

[313] Article 23(3) EPC.

[314] Case T935/97 *IBM/Computer programs* [1999] EPOR 301 at 315. See too Case T1173/97 *IBM/Editable document form* [1995] EPOR 185 at 233, distinguishing the earlier Case T204/93 *ATT/System for generating software source code*.

[315] Case T204/93 *ATT/System for Generating software source code*.

[316] *Bosch/Electronic computer components* [1995] EPOR 585.

[317] See n 51, G-II para 3.6.

(see para 11.156) in *Hitachi* (T258/03), holding that it is not a display of technical character to circumvent a technical problem by modifying a business method as opposed to finding some truly technical means to resolve the problem.[318]

11.166   In Case T154/04 *DUNS LICENSING ASSOCIATES/Estimating sales activity*[319] it was accepted that claims can contain both technical and non-technical features and this will not necessarily be fatal to the eligibility of the invention for protection. However, non-technical features will be ignored if they do not contribute to the resolution of the technical problem; indeed, there must be such a *technical* problem in the first place—this is defined as a problem which an expert in the field might be asked to solve. There was no technical problem in the instant case—it concerned merely a means to gather information about sales activities in various outlets and then to apply statistical methods to estimate future sales. This was quintessential business research and using a computer to generate the result did not make it *technical*. This has since been translated into the EPO Guidelines thus: '[t]he mere possibility of using technical means is not sufficient to avoid exclusion.'[320]

11.167   This widening of approach set the scene for complete divergence in the years to come. The English Court of Appeal in *Aerotel* declined to attempt to follow EPO jurisprudence as it was 'mutually contradictory'[321] (see also para 11.88). In considering three post-*IBM* cases, the court in *Aerotel* concluded that there were, in fact, numerous approaches advocated by the Board of Appeal:

> ### Three versions of the EPO 'any hardware' approach
>
> (1) Where a claim is to a method which consists of an excluded category, it is excluded by Article 52(2) even if hardware is used to carry out the method. But a claim to the apparatus itself, being 'concrete' is not so excluded. The apparatus claim is nonetheless bad for obviousness because the notional skilled man must be taken to know about the improved, excluded, method.
>
> This is the *Pension Benefits* approach (see paras 11.112 and 11.156).[322]
>
> (2) A claim to hardware necessarily is not caught by Article 52(2). A claim to a method of using that hardware is likewise not excluded, even if that method as such is excluded matter. Either type of claim is nonetheless bad for obviousness for the same reason as in the previous point.
>
> This is *Hitachi* (see para 11.165),[323] expressly disagreeing with *Pensions Benefits* about method claims.
>
> (3) Simply ask whether there is a claim to something 'concrete', for example an apparatus. If yes, Article 52(2) does not apply. Then examine for patentability on conventional grounds—do not treat the notional skilled man as knowing about any improved excluded method. This is the approach taken in another case, *MICROSOFT/Data Transfer*.[324]

---

[318] There was reference in the decision to Case T1173/97 *IBM/Computer programs* [1999] EPOR 219. Looking forward, the Technical Board of Appeal applied *Hitachi* in T424/03 *MICROSOFT/Data transfer* [2006] EPOR 40 and held that 'a computer system including a memory (clipboard) is a technical means and consequently the claimed method has technical character in accordance with established case law'.

[319] [2007] EPOR 38, referring to Case T1173/97 *IBM/Computer programs* [2000] EPOR 219 and to Case T 258/03 *HITACHI/Auction Method* [2004] 12 OJEPO 575.

[320] EPO Guidelines Part G-II, para 3.3. See also Case T1575/07 *ACCENTURE/Managing maintenance* [2012] EPOR 36.

[321] *Aerotel Ltd v Telco Holdings Ltd and Others* [2006] EWCA Civ 1371, para 25. Note also decision of the Court of Appeal in *Lantana Ltd v Comptroller General of Patents, Designs and Trade Marks* [2014] EWCA Civ 1463 para 52 that EPO boards took a different approach to English courts and could only be a limited assistance to the Court of Appeal in determining whether the approach of the English judge is flawed.

[322] Case T931/95 *PENSION BENEFIT SYSTEMS/Controlling pension benefit systems* [2001] OJEPO 441; [2002] EPOR 52.

[323] Case T258/03 *HITACHI/Auction method* [2004] 12 OJEPO 575; [2004] EPOR 55.

[324] Case T424/03 *MICROSOFT/Clipboard formats*, 23 February 2006, www.epo.org/law-practice/case-law-appeals/recent/t030424eu1.html.

11.168 The *Aerotel* court's contribution to the EPO debate, beyond refusing to follow any of these as noted in para 11.129[325] was to formulate questions for the Enlarged Board of Appeal to consider, in the hope that this could lead to the approaches being considered together.[326] A national court has no authority, however, to refer such questions (although the President of the EPO does). But it was the sincere wish of the English Court of Appeal that the EBA consider these matters with a view to establishing, at last, some clarity and certainty for European patent law with respect to software.[327] This eventually happened in October 2008, when the President of the EPO referred questions to the EBA—these were, however, different from the ones posed by the Court of Appeal—and the clarity sought was not provided. The final ruling appears as G3/08 *Programs for Computers*.[328]

G03/08 *Programs for Computers* (Enlarged Board of Appeal, 2010): Questions for the EPO Enlarged Board of Appeal

(1) Can a computer program only be excluded as a computer program as such if it is explicitly claimed as a computer program?

(2a) Can a claim in the area of computer programs avoid exclusion under Article 52(2)(c) and (3) merely by explicitly mentioning the use of a computer or a computer-readable data storage medium?

(2b) If question 2a is answered in the negative, is a further technical effect necessary to avoid exclusion, said effect going beyond those effects inherent in the use of a computer or data storage medium to respectively execute or store a computer program?

(3a) Must a claimed feature cause a technical effect on a physical entity in the real world in order to contribute to the technical character of the claim?

(3b) If question 3a is answered in the positive, is it sufficient that the physical entity be an unspecified computer?

(3c) If question 3a is answered in the negative, can features contribute to the technical character of the claim if the only effects to which they contribute are independent of any particular hardware that may be used?

(4a) Does the activity of programming a computer necessarily involve technical considerations?

(4b) If question 4a is answered in the positive, do all features resulting from programming thus contribute to the technical character of a claim?

(4c) If question 4a is answered in the negative, can features resulting from programming contribute to the technical character of a claim only when they contribute to a further technical effect when the program is executed?[329]

G3/08 decision

(1) In exercising their right of referral, a President of the EPO is entitled to make full use of the discretion granted by Article 112(1)(b) EPC, even if their appreciation of the need for a referral has changed after a relatively short time.

(2) Different decisions by a single Technical Board of Appeal in differing compositions may be the basis of an admissible referral by the President of the EPO of a point of law to the Enlarged Board of Appeal pursuant to Article 112(1)(b) EPC.

(3) As the wording of Article 112(1)(b) EPC is not clear with respect to the meaning of 'different/abweichende/divergent' decisions, the provision has to be interpreted in the light of its object and purpose according to Article 31 of the Vienna Convention on the Law of Treaties. The purpose of the referral right under Article 112(1)(b) EPC is to establish uniformity of law within the European patent

[325] It further noted that the Supreme Court of Germany (Bundesgerichtshof) has also refused to follow *Hitachi*, n 165, para 29.

[326] [2006] EWCA Civ 1371, paras 75–76.

[327] Note, the Technical Board of Appeal in *DUNS LICENSNG AUTHORITIES/Estimating sales activity* [2007] EPOR 38 (para 12.117), stated that *Aerotel* was 'irreconcilable with the European Patent Convention', para 43.

[328] [2010] EPOR 36.

[329] For comment and criticism of the questions and, indeed, the entire approach to 'software patents', see RB Bakels, 'Software patentability: what are the right questions?' (2009) 31(10) EIPR 514.

system. Having regard to this purpose of the presidential right to refer legal questions to the Enlarged Board of Appeal, the notion 'different decisions' has to be understood restrictively in the sense of 'conflicting decisions'.

(4) The notion of legal development is an additional factor which must be carefully considered when interpreting the notion of 'different decision' in Article 112(1)(b) EPC. Development of the law is an essential aspect of its application, whatever method of interpretation is applied, and is therefore inherent in all judicial activity. Consequently, legal development as such cannot on its own form the basis for a referral, only because case law in new legal and/or technical fields does not always develop in linear fashion, and earlier approaches may be abandoned or modified.

(5) Legal rulings are characterised not by their verdicts, but by their grounds. The Enlarged Board of Appeal may thus take *obiter dicta* into account in examining whether two decisions satisfy the requirements of Article 112(1)(b) EPC.

(6) Case T 424/03 Microsoft does deviate from a view expressed in T 1173/97 IBM, concerning whether a claim to a program on a computer-readable medium necessarily avoids exclusion from patentability under Article 52(2) EPC. However, this is a legitimate development of the case law and there is no divergence which would make the referral of this point to the Enlarged Board of Appeal by the President admissible.

(7) The Enlarged Board of Appeal cannot identify any other inconsistencies between the grounds of the decisions which the referral by the President alleges are divergent. The referral is therefore inadmissible under Article 112(1)(b) EPC.

11.169 The Enlarged Board of Appeal in effect, refused to recognise the problem. The EPO is less concerned with excluded matter as long as technical character can be found. Indeed, the advice to EPO examiners is now to move beyond a consideration of technical character and to proceed directly to consider questions of novelty and inventive step. The rationale is that in assessing inventive step the examiner must establish which technical problem has been solved by the invention. If no technical problem can be found, then the implication is that no technical character is present.[330] Debate continues. Notably, in 2018 the EPO Guidelines explored when the invention is realised in a distributed computing environment (F-IV, para 3.9).

> ### Key points on software-related innovation
>
> - Patents are currently available for the following:
>   - a product which carries out its function by means of a computer program;
>   - a method which is executed by means of a computer program;
>   - a computer program itself (whether or not claimed together with a product, process, or carrier medium).
> - This is provided that:
>   - in all cases the claimed invention demonstrates that it has technical character in the sense of being capable of producing a technical effect in the real world;
>   - for a computer program, it is sufficient to demonstrate that it has the potential to produce a technical effect when run on an appropriate medium or, arguably, is somehow otherwise associated with a piece of hardware, but this must be more than merely speculative.

---

[330] See, eg, Case T1244/07 *AMAZON/1-Click* [2011] EPOR 39 and Case T 1784/06 *COMPTEL/Classification method* [2013] EPOR 9. For commentary on decisions T1769/10 *IGT* and T1051/07 *SK Telecom* that 'appear out of step with earlier EPO case law on the patentability of computer-implemented inventions and other "mixed" inventions containing interacting technical and non-technical features', see IPKat (24 June 2012) at http://ipkitten.blogspot.co.uk/2012/06/on-threshold-of-dream-patents-and.html.

Discussion point 1 For answer guidance visit www.oup.com/uk/brown5e.

The breadth of the law now means that it is no longer necessary to claim the software and the hardware, but is it ever expedient to do so? Might there be any advantages in doing so?

Discussion point 2

In Case T22/85 *IBM/Document abstracting and retrieving* it was stated *per curiam* that: 'It cannot have been intended by the Contracting States that express exclusions from patentability could be circumvented simply by the manner in which the invention is expressed in the claim.'[331] To what extent does this remain true in the light of recent case law and the latest version of the 2018 EPO Guidelines?

11.170　Building on this, it is useful to explore business methods patents in more depth. We saw that business method patents generally receive short shrift in Europe. How does this compare with the position in the United States? Signature Financial Group Inc had different outcomes on each side of the Atlantic when it tried to patent its data-processing system for managing financial services and portfolio returns across a variety of funds. In the EPO, the application was rejected by the Examining Division for lack of technical character. This EPO application was in respect of essentially the same invention as the United States application, which led to the landmark dispute *State Street Bank and Trust Co v Signature Financial Group*.[332] That patent was held to be valid, in a decision that revolutionised business method patenting in the United States and set in motion a furore surrounding the practice worldwide.

11.171　In *State Street* the US Court of Appeals for the Federal Circuit upheld the claims to this data-processing system and put an end to speculation that a business method exception applies in the United States. Indeed, it is generally acknowledged that *State Street*[333] went further in establishing the precedent that 'pure' business methods are patentable; that is, methods which are not dependent on software. While our remit does not extend to an analysis of US law where the statutory provisions and considerations are different, the disparity of approach towards the *State Street* invention—and in particular the need in Europe to establish technical character beyond the standard criteria—indicates that prospective patentees face more hurdles in this area in Europe compared to the experience across the Atlantic.

11.172　Some comments on *State Street* are of assistance in our present discussion. There are no statutory exclusions in US law,[334] and common law exclusions which have grown up over the years—for example in the realm of mathematical algorithms, formulae, or calculations[335]—have been interpreted in an increasingly narrower fashion.[336] Thus, while the *State Street* invention had been rejected by the lower court because it was an 'algorithm', the Court of Appeal held that the system was a 'machine' in the proper sense of statutory subject matter, and that:[337]

> every step-by-step process, be it electronic or chemical or mechanical, involves an algorithm in the broad sense of the term . . . [and] since §101 expressly includes processes as a category of invention which may be patentable . . . it follows that it is no ground for holding a claim is directed to non-statutory subject matter to say it includes or is directed to an algorithm. This is why the proscription against patenting has been limited to *mathematical* algorithms (emphasis added).

The court went on to stress that the emphasis in patent examination should be on the essential characteristics of the subject matter and, most notably, whether it displays 'practical utility' in the sense of producing a

---

[331] See n 296, 104–05.　[332] 149 F 3d 1368 (Fed Cir, 1998).

[333] In tandem with *AT&T Corp v Excel Communications Inc*, 172 F 3rd 1352 (Fed Cir, 1999).

[334] 35 USC, para 101.　[335] *Gottschalk v Benson* 409 US 63 (1972).　[336] See *In re Alappat* 33 F 3d 1526 (Fed Cir, 1994).

[337] *State Street Bank and Trust Co v Signature Financial Group* at 1375.

'useful, concrete and tangible result'. This renders an invention statutory subject matter, 'even if the useful result is expressed in numbers, such as price, profit, percentage, cost or loss'.[338]

11.173   The approach of *State Street* was reviewed in *In re Bilski*,[339] regarding a method of hedging risk in the field of commodities trading. The Court of Appeals found that this lacked patentable subject matter. Rather than applying the 'useful, concrete and tangible result' approach which had been used in *State Street*, the court considered that the sole test for determining patentability of a process was the 'transformation-machine test': that is, it must be shown that the invention transforms the nature of an article into a different state or thing, or that it is somehow connected to apparatus or a machine. In the instant case it was not possible to satisfy such a test and this led to the denial of patent protection. Given this uncertainty, the United States Supreme Court heard the case in 2010 as *Bilski v Kappos*.[340] The Supreme Court affirmed the judgment of the Court of Appeals, but revised various aspects of its decision, most particularly clarifying its own previous jurisprudence: 'This Court's precedents establish that the machine-or-transformation test is a useful and important clue, an investigative tool, for determining whether some claimed inventions are processes under § 101. The machine-or-transformation test is not the *sole* test for deciding whether an invention is a patent-eligible "process"' (emphasis added). The majority held that the invention in suit was unpatentable as an 'abstract idea' in the instant case. Going forward, however, there remains dispute in the United States about what, precisely, constitutes such an abstraction. Further, given that decision in respect of abstract idea, the court did not go on to consider what constitutes a patentable process; and business method patent disputes continue and patents continue to be granted.[341]

11.174   In 2014, the United States Supreme Court again considered business method patents, regarding a scheme for mitigating settlement risk, in *Alice Corporation v CLS Bank International*.[342] The Supreme Court focused on the fact that the claims were for implementation of an abstract idea, and not patentable. In so doing, as well as referring to *Bilski*, the court referred to some biotechnology patent decisions (*Myriad* and also *Mayo*) considered at para 11.97–11.98, *Alice* has been criticised for a narrow approach to the issues before it, and lacking depth and engagement with key questions of what should be patentable.[343]

 Question

(Reminder: *Pension Benefits Systems* and *State Street* were both denied protection in Europe yet were successful in the United States.)

How approximate is the US need for 'practical utility' to the European requirement of 'technical contribution'? What impact does the continued existence of an express exclusion for methods of doing business have on European patent law and is it desirable that it should remain? How far is the US concern with an 'abstract idea' similar to the European limitation of 'as such'?

Should business method patents be treated differently?

11.175   It has been seen that business method patents have proved controversial. In the following, we recite some of the arguments that have been mounted against them.

---

[338] ibid, at 1375.   [339] 545 F 3rd 943, 88 USPQ 2nd 1385 (Fed Cir, 2008).
[340] 130 S Ct 3218 (2010).
[341] cf *Ultramercial v Hulu* 657 F 3d 1323 (Fed Cir, 2011) and *Dealertrack v Huber*, No 2009-1566, 2009-1588 (Fed Cir, 20 January 2012).
[342] 572 US 208.
[343] See, eg, LL Ouellette, 'Patentable subject matter and non-patent innovation incentives' (2015) 5 UC Irvine Law Rev 1115, SSRN: http://ssrn.com/abstract=2499204.

(1) In what sense can a method of doing business be seen as an example of *industrial* property? That is, how can the protection of such a method achieve the original aims of the patent system which is to encourage *technological* innovation and development?

(2) What is a 'business method'? How can this be defined with sufficient precision to delimit clearly the scope of the power conferred by a patent? The problem is not just one of definition because indistinct and potentially broad claims necessarily impact on the scope of the power granted, calling its entire validity into question.

(3) A single business method could have applications across a very broad range of fields, thereby potentially leading to an excessively broad patent which might hinder rather than encourage innovation. Moreover, unlike other technical fields such as the biotechnology or pharmaceutical industries, the respective outlays in research and development costs are minimal for business methods and so the reward is disproportionate to the inventive effort. Yet the economic impact of such patents could be just as great or greater than other fields of technology.

(4) Many of the ways of doing business that form the subject of these patents have been around for a long time; a method of doing business does not become inventive simply because it is carried out on using computers or via the internet.

(5) The prior art relating to business methods is difficult, if not impossible, to discern. This is partly because those employing effective methods kept them secret in the absence of other means of protection. It is also because of the infinite varieties of business methods that are being employed daily. If there is less evidence to reject applications this could result in an increase in patents, leading to a plethora of potentially dubious rights. To complicate matters, patent examiners are not necessarily qualified in this field, and this too might lead to questionable and undeserving patents.

(6) To open up the categories of patentable subject matter will necessarily result in a restriction of material in the public domain.

(7) It can be very easy to infringe a business method patent, leaving competitors uncertain about permissible acts and extremely vulnerable to infringement actions.

(8) Large corporations will be the ones to benefit as they are best placed to obtain and defend such patents. Small and medium-sized enterprises will lose out as a result and this will leave the relevant technical field to be ruled by technology oligarchies, none of which is in the ultimate interests of the consumer.

(9) There is simply no need for these patents because the fields where they are sought, for example the internet, have progressed exceptionally well to date without patent protection and there is no requirement for further incentive.

(10) 'Those who favour some form of patentability for business methods have not provided the necessary evidence that it would be likely to increase innovation. Unless and until that evidence is available, ways of doing business should remain unpatentable.' (UK Patent Office Consultation 2001)

 ### Exercise

Evaluate the arguments just listed regarding business method patents along the following lines:

(1) Which are about satisfying the essential criteria of patent law?

(2) Which are practical, legal, and/or economic arguments?

(3) Which are objections that only relate to (pure) business method patents; that is, they cannot be applied to other areas such as biotechnology, software, or indeed more traditional manufacturing inventions?

Comparative approaches

11.176 The next sections explore in more depth the approaches taken in the United States and in the EPO at the intellectual property office and also set out the position in Japan.

The US Patent and Trademark Office

11.177   The following is an extract from the 2016 Preliminary Examination Instructions:[344]

(1) *Alice Corp* establishes that the same analysis should be used for all types of judicial exceptions, whereas prior USPTO guidance applied a different analysis to claims with abstract ideas (*Bilski* guidance in *Manual of Patent Examining Procedure* (MEP) 2106 (II)(B)) than to claims with laws of nature (*Mayo* guidance in MPEP 2106.01). (2) *Alice Corp* also establishes that the same analysis should be used for all categories of claims (eg product and process claims), whereas prior guidance applied a different analysis to product claims involving abstract ideas (relying on tangibility in MPEP 2106(II)(A)) than to process claims (*Bilski* guidance). (3) Despite these changes, the basic inquiries to determine subject matter eligibility remain the same as explained in MPEP 2106(I). First determine whether the claim is directed to one of the four statutory categories of invention, i.e. process, machine, manufacture, or composition of matter. Next, if the claim does fall within one of the statutory categories, determine whether the claim is directed to a judicial exception (ie law of nature, natural phenomenon, and abstract idea) using Part 1 of the two-part analysis detailed below, and, if so, determine whether the claim is a patent-eligible application of an exception using part 2.

Japanese Patent Office

11.178   2015 Guidelines provide that:[345]

if a matter necessary to define an invention . . . involves any means contrary to a law of nature . . . the claimed invention is not considered to be a statutory invention . . . when acclaimed inventions is considered as any of (i) to (v) below, the claimed invention is not deemed to utilize a law of nature, and thus, is not considered as a statutory 'invention' . . . (i) Any laws other than a law of nature (e.g. economic laws), (ii) Arbitrary arrangements (e.g. a rule for playing a game as such), (iii) Mathematical formulae, (iv) Mental activities of humans, or (v) Those utilizing only (i) to (iv) (e.g. methods for doing business as such). Even if a part of matters specifying the invention stated in a claim utilizes a law of nature, when it is judged that the claimed invention as a whole does not utilize a law of nature, the claimed invention is deemed as not utilizing a law of nature . . . On the contrary, even if a part of matters specifying the invention stated in a claim does not utilize a law of nature, when it is judged that the claimed invention as a whole utilizes a law of nature, the claimed invention is deemed as utilizing a law of nature. The characteristic of the technology is to be taken into account in judging whether a claimed invention as a whole utilizes a law of nature . . . For inventions relating to a method for doing business, playing a game, or calculating a mathematical formula, since there are cases in which the claimed invention a part of which utilizes an article, apparatus, device, system, computer software etc., is judged as not utilizing a law of nature when considered as a whole, whether they are 'creation of a technical idea utilizing a law of nature' shall be carefully examined. On the other hand there is possibility for an invention to be considered as a 'creation of a technical idea utilizing a law of nature' where the invention is made having an intention of utilizing computer software such as software used in doing business, in playing a game or in calculating mathematical formula as a whole, even though the invention is made related to a method for doing business, playing a game, or calculating a mathematical formula.

The outcome in Japan is that if appropriately drafted claims that clearly define when viewed as a whole are a technical idea utilizing the law of nature, then software-related means of carrying out business practices will be considered as patentable subject matter.

European Patent Office

11.179   EPO Guidelines provide that:[346]

Computer programs are excluded from patentability, . . . if claimed as such. However, following the generally applicable criteria the exclusion does not apply to computer programs having a technical character . . . In order to have a technical character, and thus not be excluded from patentability, a computer program must

---

[344] www.uspto.gov/web/offices/pac/mpep/s2106.html in view of the Supreme Court Decision in *Alice Corporation Pty Ltd v CLS Bank International* see para 11.174.

[345] See JPO Examination Guidelines for Patent and Utility Model in Japan (2015) 2.1.3–4; 2.2 Examination Guidelines for Patent and Utility Model in Japan (2015), www.jpo.go.jp/tetuzuki_e/t_tokkyo_e/files_guidelines_e/all_e.pdf; compare JPO Examination Guidelines for Patent and Utility Model in Japan (2009), Part II: Requirements for Patentability, Chapter 1: Industrially Applicable Inventions, section 1.1, www.jpo.go.jp/tetuzuki_e/t_tokkyo_e/Guidelines/2_1.pdf, which made much less reference to computer software.

[346] EPO Guidelines, Part G-II, para 3.6 and see also examples of further technical effects, information modelling, and data retrieval in 3.6.1-3.

produce a 'further technical effect' when run on a computer. A 'further technical effect' is a technical effect going beyond the 'normal' physical interactions between the program (software) and the computer (hardware) on which it is run. The normal physical effects of the execution of a program, e.g. the circulation of electrical currents in the computer, are not in themselves sufficient to confer technical character to a computer program . . . Examples of further technical effects which confer technical character to a computer program are the control of a technical process or of the internal functioning of the computer itself or its interfaces . . . The presence of a further technical effect is assessed without reference to the prior art. It follows that the mere fact that a computer program serving a non-technical purpose requires less computing time than a prior-art program serving the same non-technical purpose, does not on its own establish the presence of a further technical effect . . . Likewise, comparing a computer program with how a human being would perform the same task is not a suitable basis for assessing if the computer program has a technical character . . . A computer program cannot derive a technical character from the mere fact that it has been designed such that it can be automatically performed by a computer. 'Further technical considerations' going beyond merely finding a computer algorithm to perform a task are needed. They have to be reflected in claimed features that cause a further technical effect. If a claim is directed to a computer program which does not have a technical character, it is objected to under Art 52(2)(c) and (3). If it passes the test for having technical character, the examiner then proceeds to the questions of novelty and inventive step . . . 'Computer-implemented invention' is an expression intended to cover claims which involve computers, computer networks or other programmable apparatus wherein at least one feature is realised by means of a computer program . . . A computer program and a corresponding computer implemented method are distinct from each other. The former refers to a sequence of computer-executable instructions specifying a method while the latter refers to a method being actually performed on a computer . . . Claims directed to a computer-implemented method, a computer-readable storage medium or a device cannot be objected to under Art 52(2) and (3) as any method involving the use of technical means (e.g. a computer) and any technical means itself (e.g. a computer or a computer-readable storage medium) have technical character and thus represent inventions in the sense of Art 52(1).

European Union reform

11.180 The inexorable shift in patent practice over the years has led to numerous claims that the law is now unclear and uncertain. This challenge attracted the attention of the European Commission, particularly when it sees any such criticism of intellectual property law to be a legitimate basis for bringing yet another area within its ever-widening harmonisation programme. The Commission identified so-called 'computer-implemented inventions' as a priority issue following its consultation and Green Paper on the Community Patent and Patent System in Europe from 1997[347] and then the Commission released its proposal for a Directive on the patentability of computer-implemented inventions in 2002.[348] The European Commission cited the UK experience, and in particular *Merrill Lynch*, as a reason to harmonise the law in this area, suggesting that 'a computer program-related invention that amounts to, for example, a method of doing business . . . is considered unpatentable even if a technical contribution (in the terms defined in the Directive) can be found'.[349] This instrument was defeated in the European Parliament in July 2005. It is illuminating to consider its core provisions to understand what objectors were so concerned about. It is also a very salutary lesson for intellectual property law and policymakers: the defeat of the Computer-implemented Inventions Directive was a direct result of heavy lobbying and may indicate a real shift of power in the policy and political arena.

11.181 The Commission tried to hold a single line: this was an attempt to maintain the status quo while providing clarity on the legal position in Europe. There was, however, one notable exception. The proposal began with the premise that 'computer-implemented inventions' should be treated like any other field of technology[350] and that these should be patentable as long as they demonstrate 'technical contribution', which was defined

---

[347] Promoting Innovation through Patents: Green Paper on the Community Patent and the Patent System in Europe, COM(1997) 314 final, 24 June 1997.

[348] COM(2002) 92 final, 20 February 2002.

[349] Commission Proposal on the patentability of computer-implemented inventions, COM(2002) 92 final, 20 February 2002, 10.

[350] ibid, Art 3.

as 'a contribution to the state of the art in a technical field which is not obvious to a person skilled in the art'.[351] The focus, then, was on the criteria for patentability, and the Commission was at pains to point out that it did not seek any amendment to these criteria; the requirement of technical contribution was simply an elaboration on the criterion of inventive step. The proposal made it incumbent on patent examiners to consider the invention as a whole and to accept the presence of both technical and non-technical features in an application as long as the technical contribution was found in the technical aspects of the invention.[352] To this extent, the proposal follows the current EPO jurisprudence and also reflects the recent changes of approach in the UK (see paras 11.125ff).

11.182   While the focus, then, would be on member states' equivalent provisions to Article 56 EPC (criteria for patentability), there was, in fact, a general conflation between the exclusion of subject matter and these criteria throughout the instrument. An important result of a shift in focus from exclusions to inventive step, however, is to remove the possibility of applications being rejected *ab initio*. An examiner will consider the exclusions before the criteria of novelty, inventive step, and industrial applicability. If it is thought that an exclusion is contained in the application it will be rejected before there is any substantive consideration, including, importantly, a search of the prior art. This shift in emphasis would, therefore, operate in the applicants' favour.

11.183   The proposal departed from EPO practice in one important respect in that it sought to clarify that protection should only be provided for a 'computer-implemented invention'. This was defined as:[353]

> any invention the performance of which involves the use of a computer, computer network or other programmable apparatus and having one or more prima facie novel features which are realised wholly or partly by means of a computer program or computer programs.

11.184   In other words, a claim to an invention under the proposal, be it to a product (a computer or other apparatus) or a process (a method) must be linked to a computer. This would have been a return to the position under *Vicom* and a clear retrenchment from the rulings in the *IBM* decisions and subsequent case law. The concern is that the effect of the current EPO jurisprudence might be to prevent 'reverse engineering' of elements of programs and other activities considered legitimate within the industry and important to its development.

11.185   This seemingly cautious approach was lambasted by the European Economic and Social Committee, which called upon the Commission to rethink the proposal entirely anew.[354] The Committee dismissed as 'legal casuistry' the attempt to distinguish between protection of software itself and computer-implemented inventions and warned that the proposal would nonetheless 'open the way to the future patentability of the entire software field'. The Committee went on to challenge the economic case for patents in this field and to warn of the potentially adverse impact that patenting practice might have for our knowledge-based society, and in particular the internet and the free circulation of free/open-source software. It called for a far more cautious approach still, which it wished to be based on more empirical evidence of the economic and employment consequences of various proposals, including leaving matters to the vagaries of the market.

11.186   This internal institutional wrangle over the proposal reflects broader, deeper divides about the issue of software patenting, which have been seen in this chapter. These are most evident in the European Parliament, where the Directive was roundly defeated by an overwhelming majority of 648:14. Open-source and free software groups were particularly active in the lobbying process, arguing that the promised economic benefits were far from proven and that such a law would, rather, have a stifling and restricting effect on

---

[351] ibid, Art 2(b).   [352] ibid, Art 4(3).   [353] ibid, Art 2(a).

[354] Opinion of the Economic and Social Committee on the 'Proposal for a Directive of the European Parliament and of the Council on the patentability of computer-implemented inventions', OJ C61/154, 14 March 2003.

innovation and development. The triumph of these groups, and to an extent the triumph of the Parliament over the Commission, has led to broader questions being asked about the operation of the democratic process within the EU. Who would have thought that intellectual property could be so political?

Discussion point   For answer guidance visit www.oup.com/uk/brown5e.

What is the underlying rationale for excluding computer programs in Europe, especially when they are patentable in most other legal systems? Does the role of copyright in software protection make a difference? Can this approach be sustained? You may find it useful to reflect on the fact that the *Gowers Review of Intellectual Property* (HM Treasury, 2006), para 4.114,[355] recommended that the UK should maintain its policy of not extending patent rights beyond their current limits. The Review found mixed evidence of the success of 'pure' software patents, particularly from the United States, where the evidence actually seems to indicate that the software industry grew exponentially in the *absence* of patent protection. Other evidence suggests that where protection is available it is used negatively to restrict competitors rather than positively to encourage further innovation.

Presentations of information

11.187   The concern of this exclusion is the *content* of information. No claim will be sustained if it relates solely to the expression of information or the conveyance of meaning or decisions on where and how to display information.[356] Patent law is not in the business of giving protection to pretty pictures, TV images, radio signals, books, sounds, diagrams, codes, or symbols which derive their value from the meaning they convey to human beings. Thus, in *Townsend's Patent Application*[357] the problem to be solved was the thorny issue of how to ensure fair distribution of the treats found behind the doors on an advent calendar and to prevent the early-riser in the family from scoffing the lot! Mr Townsend's solution was to put markings on the doors to indicate the turn of each user to open a door. He argued that this was not a presentation of information because the correct interpretation of the exclusion only covered *expression* of information and not *provision* of information; that is, it was restricted to *how* information is conveyed and not *what* is conveyed. It is the difference between the advent calendar being designed in the shape of a sleigh (how) and stating, 'three more days to Christmas' (what). Laddie J disagreed and held that the exclusion covers both instances of presenting information on an ordinary interpretation of the provision. The calendar was refused protection.

11.188   This means that any method or means of conveying information which is characterised only by the content of the information will be excluded. It does not matter that some physical device or apparatus is used to convey the information or that such a device or apparatus can be moved around.

■ *Crawford v Jones* [2005] EWHC 2417 (Pat)

The application related to a display system for buses to indicate to passengers whether the bus was in picking-up or setting-down only mode. The claims were to Boarding and Exit Bus Indicators, being visual or audible apparatus. Notwithstanding, the application was refused, inter alia, as solely a method of presentation of information. The only advance in the art was the nature of the information displayed on the front of the bus, but this was not of a technical nature.

---

[355] https://assets.publishing.service.gov.uk/government/uploads/system/uploads/attachment_data/file/228849/0118404830.pdf.
[356] *Autonomy Corp Ltd v Comptroller General of Patents, Trade Marks and Designs* [2008] EWHC 146 (Pat).
[357] [2004] EWHC 482 (Pat).

11.189   The implication of a decision like *Crawford* is that if a presentation of information *is* of a technical nature then it might be patentable, and this is indeed true. As we now know, solving a pre-existing problem by technical means is the way to make a technical contribution. In *Cooper's Application*[358] the problem was how to fold a newspaper without hindering reading, and the successful invention was to arrange the layout of text to allow this. Similarly, in *Fishburn's Application*[359] the particular arrangement of text on a ticket meant that information was not lost when the ticket was torn, and the patent was upheld. In *Gemstar-TV Guide International v Virgin Media Ltd*[360] the dispute related to three patents relating to electronic versions of programme guides that help consumers to navigate the ever-increasing range of viewing options available. Two of the patents were revoked as involving merely presentation of information. As was said: 'The purpose of the invention is to achieve the display of information in a user-friendly way by user-friendly means' (para 45). And as Mann J confirmed: 'what achieves patentability is some real world technical achievement outside the information itself'.

11.190   These questions came into play again in *HTC Europe Co Ltd v Apple Inc*[361] involving a dispute over four patents related to mobile phone technologies. Of interest for present purposes was the feature of one of the inventions which is familiar to any user of hand-held devices: the 'sweep to unlock screen' image. It was argued that this was a mere presentation of information because it simply told the user how their gesture was progressing. This was rejected by Floyd J, who held that the particular invention did not fall foul of this particular exception: 'There is a sense in which the invention provides a technical effect outside the computer, namely an improved switch. Moreover, this is a real world effect which is not limited to the presentation of information.'[362] Although this was an obvious (and therefore unpatentable) feature to produce in today's world, the invention was not caught by the particular exclusion of a simple presentation of information.[363]

11.191   The EPO Guidelines make it clear that if the presentation of information has new technical features, then there could be patentable subject matter in the information carrier, or in the process or apparatus for presenting the information, or even in the manner of presentation itself.[364] Examples include a kit comprising a product which also has instructions, and displaying several images side by side in low resolution and allowing selection and display at higher resolution. Put differently, an invention can function by presenting information and still be patentable as long as the sum and substance of that invention is not only found in the presentation of the information.

11.192   The general European approach is laid out in the decision of the Technical Board of Appeal in *KONINKLIJKE PHILIPS ELECTRONICS/Picture retrieval system*.[365] The invention related to a system of picture storage and retrieval and included a claim to a record carrier which provided recorded picture data to any part of the system and consisted of a picture access data structure which controlled the operation of the retrieval device. The data structure was the novel part of the invention but the claim to its record carrier was refused as a means of presenting information. The Technical Board of Appeal upheld the appeal against this, however, and found that the data structure provided the necessary technical nature to the invention. Moreover, it sought to draw a distinction between two types of information: cognitive data and functional data.[366] The invention was patentable because the record carrier was concerned with functional data and the operation of a system which produced a new technical effect. It is to be contrasted with *XEROX/Document summaries*,[367] where the claimed invention related to a summary of indicators in a summary document that

[358] 19 RPC 53.   [359] 57 RPC 245.   [360] [2009] EWHC 3068 (Ch), aff'd [2011] EWCA Civ 302.
[361] [2012] EWHC 1789 (Pat).   [362] [2012] EWHC 1789 (Pat), para 236.
[363] This approach was supported when the Court of Appeal heard the case; see [2013] EWCA Civ 451 2013 RPC 30, paras 35–41, 50 et seq, see para 11.38.
[364] EPO Guidelines, Part G-II, para 3.7.   [365] Case T1194/97 [2000] OJEPO 525; [2001] EPOR 25.
[366] It relied on Case T163/85 *BBC/Colour television signal* [1990] OJEPO 379.
[367] Case T1086/07 [2012] EPOR 21.

indicated where the section originated in the complete document. This was held to be mere presentation of information resulting from the processing of summarising and which had no connection with the technical means to produce it.

 Exercise

The *PHILIPS/Picture Retrieval* decision also contains an explanation of the rationale for this particular exclusion. Look this up and then consider it against all the other possible rationales for the exclusions in Article 52 EPC.

Key points on exclusions under Article 52

- It is essential to read the provisions of the law carefully. If we look back at Article 52(2), it states: 'The following in *particular* shall not be regarded as inventions'[368] and Article 52(3) states: 'The provisions of paragraph 2 shall exclude patentability of the subject-matter or activities referred to in that provision only to the extent to which a European patent application or European patent relates to such subject-matter or activities *as such*'.

- This means that the list of exclusions is *non-exhaustive*, and indeed in the UK the Secretary of State has the power to expand it (Patents Act 1977, s 1(5)).

- The '*as such*' qualification is extremely important. It means that only claims which fall squarely within a category of excluded matter will be struck down. Inventions which straddle patentable and non-patentable matter can survive if the technical features meet the other criteria for patentability.

11.193   There is one example of the courts excluding matter from protection for something which is not in Article 52 EPC/section 1(2) of the Patents Act 1977. In *Lux Traffic Controls Ltd v Pike Signals Ltd and Faronwise Ltd*[369] the invention related to apparatus to control traffic through a system that detected non-motion in vehicles and responded by holding the traffic lights to allow drivers more time. Although the court allowed the apparatus claims, Aldous J had this to say (at 138):

> s.1(2) of the Act comprises a non-exhaustive catalogue of matters or things which are not patentable. Although not specifically mentioned, I believe a method of controlling traffic as such is not patentable, whether or not it can be said to be a scheme for doing business. The field expressly excluded by the section concerns mere ideas not normally thought to be the proper subject for patents which are concerned with manufacturing.

11.194   This may do no more than express the common rationale underpinning many of the exclusions that abstracts, such as ideas, are not a suitable case for patenting. By the same token, it demonstrates that the categories of exclusions are not closed and policy in the future may expand the list of non-inventions. Legislative changes would, however, require to be initiated by the Secretary of State and laid before both Houses of Parliament for approval.

---

[368] The equivalent provision in the Patents Act 1977, s 1(2), states: 'It is hereby declared that the following (*among other things*) are not inventions.'
[369] [1993] RPC 107.

Exceptions to patentability

11.195   Let us turn now in more depth to the exceptions to patentability contained in Article 53 EPC 2000 and reproduced in section 1(3) and (4) and Schedule A2 of the Patents Act 1977, building in turn on the EU Biotechnology Directive and its place in both systems. For ease, the text of Article 53 is again set out below (see para 11.87).

Article 53

European patents shall not be granted in respect of:

(a) inventions the commercial exploitation of which would be contrary to 'ordre public' or morality; such exploitation shall not be deemed to be so contrary merely because it is prohibited by law or regulation in some or all of the Contracting States;

(b) plant or animal varieties or essentially biological processes for the production of plants or animals; this provision shall not apply to microbiological processes or the products thereof;

(c) methods for treatment of the human or animal body by surgery or therapy and diagnostic methods practised on the human or animal body; this provision shall not apply to products, in particular substances or compositions, for use in any of these methods.

Morality and *ordre public*: EPO roots

11.196   It has sometimes been claimed that morality has nothing to do with patent law, but this is clearly nonsense.[370] The decision whether or not to grant a patent is not some mechanistic process which merely involves a checklist of technical details. Rather, it entails many nuanced considerations and value judgements on whether the numerous criteria for patentability have been met. The entire IP system is based on fundamental notions of merit and justice concerning the appropriateness or otherwise of granting exclusive rights. This is what the morality provision in patent law is about.[371] Further, Europe has long contemplated a role for moral concerns in the decision-making process about the grant of a patent.[372]

11.197   The morality provisions in TRIPS appear largely at the insistence of European states and as a reflection of their history, but the morality provisions in European patent law mostly lay dormant until the advent of contemporary biotechnology patenting, whereupon they were aggressively invoked by parties harbouring a plethora of doubts about biotechnology, of which patenting practices are merely a small part. The debacle has largely been played out on the European stage in the Opposition Division of the EPO and also in the institutions of the EU. There is a lot of confusion about the role and remit of the morality provision, which has been fuelled by the advent of biotechnology patents.[373] Indeed, the provision had rarely been invoked before the arrival of this technology but now we have a rich literature on the topic, a series of EPO rulings, a harmonising EU Biotechnology Directive, and disputes as to how this should be applied.

 Exercise

Before reading any further, consider what is meant by 'inventions the commercial exploitation of which would be contrary to . . . morality'. How do we know when something is immoral? Note: it is the commercial exploitation of the invention which must be immoral, not necessarily the invention itself. Why is this so? What difference does this make?

---

[370]   We will not name the guilty; they know who they are.

[371]   For a good analysis, see L Bently and B Sherman, 'The ethics of patenting: towards a transgenic patent system' (1995) 3 Med LR 275; O Mills, *Biotechnological Inventions: Moral Restraints and Patent Law* (2016).

[372]   Strasbourg Convention 1963. For commentary, see O Mills, *Biotechnological Inventions: Moral Restraints and Patent Law* (2005).

[373]   Y Min, 'Morality: an equivocal area in the patent system' (2012) 34(4) EIPR 261–65.

11.198 EPC 2000 revised the text of Article 53 to bring it into line with Article 27(2) of TRIPS.[374] Previously, the provisions concerned 'inventions the publication or exploitation of which would be contrary to *ordre public* or morality'. Now the concern is with the commercial exploitation of the invention. It is arguable that much of the confusion which has surrounded the interpretation of these provisions has stemmed from a lack of clarity about the purpose of the law as well as its limits. The purpose of the law has been stated in the EPO Guidelines to be: 'to deny protection to inventions likely to induce riot or public disorder, or to lead to criminal or other generally offensive behaviour'.[375] But the denial of a patent cannot prevent the use of an invention; it may, at best, act as a disincentive to producing it. Moreover, it is not possible to deny a patent merely because exploitation is prohibited by law.[376] Nonetheless, various groups have seized on the morality provision in an attempt to strike down patents in certain controversial areas such as animal testing, stem cell technologies, or environmental impact. The strong suspicion is that the real objection is to the science not to the patent per se. If so, this use of the morality provision is largely futile.[377] The revised version of Article 53 better reflects the true limit of the patent system, which is to grant a commercial monopoly. It is entirely correct, therefore, that we may have concerns about the appropriateness of *commercial* exploitation.[378] So far there have been few cases looking at the interpretation of this revised article. However, morality jurisprudence with regards to biotechnological inventions is developing rapidly.

11.199 The inherently subjective nature of morality and the increasing presumption in favour of patentability have led the patent-granting institutions of Europe to interpret the morality provisions of patent law very narrowly.

■ *HARVARD/Oncomouse* [1991] EPOR 525

The EPO allowed a patent on a transgenic animal that had been bred as a research tool for cancer studies despite objections that it was immoral to patent life, especially when that life was created simply to suffer. The Examining Division held[379]—on a strictly utilitarian analysis—that the potential benefit to mankind outweighed the suffering of these animals, and as such was no bar to patent protection. Moreover, the specific wording of the claim related to 'non-human mammals' and this was deemed to be much wider than 'animal varieties' and therefore was not expressly excluded by Article 53(b). It was stated that 'An "animal variety" or "race animal" is a sub-unit of a species and therefore of even lower ranking than a species. Accordingly, the subject-matter of the claims to animals *per se* is considered not to be covered by . . . Article 53(b).'

11.200 Opposition proceedings were immediately instituted against the decision and these remained unresolved for a decade, during which time the patent remained in force. A resolution was eventually found in 2001 and the patent stood, but its scope was restricted to 'transgenic rodents containing an additional cancer gene' rather than 'any non-human transgenic mammal';[380] it was further restricted

---

[374] TRIPS, Art 27:

Members may exclude from patentability inventions, the prevention within their territory of the commercial exploitation of which is necessary to protect *ordre public* or morality, including to protect human, animal or plant life or health or to avoid serious prejudice to the environment, provided that such exclusion is not made merely because the exploitation is prohibited by their law.

[375] EPO Guidelines, Part G-II, para 4.1.

[376] See the Patents Act 1977, s 1(4) and EPC 2000, Art 53(a).

[377] This is not to deny that there may be perfectly legitimate concerns about the commercialisation of technologies.

[378] Although note that the EPO Guidelines state: 'The EPO has not been vested with the task of taking into account the economic effects of the grant of patents in specific areas of technology and of restricting the field of patentable subject-matter accordingly', G-II, para 4.1.3, and see too G1/98 NOVARTIS II/*Transgenic plant* [2000] OJEPO 111, reasons 3.9.

[379] The Examining Division originally declined to consider the morality of the grant as outside its competence ([1990] EPOR 4) but was subsequently directed to do so by the Technical Board of Appeal ([1990] EPOR 501).

[380] By way of contrast, the Supreme Court of Canada revoked the Harvard patent over Oncomouse itself (but not the process to manufacture it) in December 2002, claiming that, 'A higher life form is not patentable because it is not a "manufacture" or "composition of matter"': see *Harvard College v Canada (Commissioner of Patents)* [2002] SCJ No 77. This ruling cannot now be changed except by express legislation.

in 2004 to cover merely 'transgenic mice'.[381] The trend towards allowing patenting was continued in *LELAND STANFORD/Modified animal*,[382] where the patent for an immuno-compromised chimera mouse was upheld and the EPO ruled that the controversial nature of the technology did not, in and of itself, act as a bar to patenting.

11.201   The provisions of Article 53 were reined in further in *PLANT GENETIC SYSTEMS/Glutamine Synthetase Inhibitors*.[383] Here the EPO held that it was only prepared to entertain challenges on grounds of morality if actual evidence of harm to society could be demonstrated. The case concerned the patentability of crops that had been genetically modified to be resistant to herbicides, and the concern was a threat to the environment if such hybrids were released. Extending its ruling from *Oncomouse*, however, the Technical Board of Appeal sought verifiable data that the environment was at risk from the invention *before* it would apply the *Oncomouse* balancing test.[384] No evidence could be produced and the patent was granted, despite other findings that a high degree of moral opprobrium towards such inventions existed among sectors of the European population. The Board opined that survey evidence and opinion polls indicating distaste for patents over genetically modified organisms were insufficient evidence by which to judge the overall European moral tone.

11.202   In *HOWARD FLOREY/H2 Relaxin*[385] (see also para 11.96 regarding discovery) the EPO affirmed that the morality provision should only be applied to prevent the grant of patents that would universally be regarded as outrageous. The patent in suit related to a genetically engineered human protein, H2 relaxin, which women produce during childbirth to soften the pelvis. The patent had been challenged on a number of grounds: (1) that the grant of the patent would be tantamount to slavery of women because it involved the 'dismemberment of women and the sale of their parts'; (2) that it was offensive to human dignity to use pregnant women for profit; and (3) because DNA was life itself, patenting of human DNA was intrinsically immoral.[386] The Office rejected each of these claims. DNA, it said, is not life but merely a means to carry chemical information. Moreover, the taking and modification of samples was in no way an approximation to slavery. This was particularly not so when the donors had given their free and informed consent. This, in itself, was considered enough to accord respect to human dignity. Interestingly, however, it is not clear what the women consented to, and in particular whether they were ever told of the prospect of patents being granted over material derived from them and the consequent economic potential.[387]

11.203   An example of the restrictive approach to the interpretation of the morality clause is found in *MICHIGAN STATE UNIVERSITY/Euthanasia compositions*.[388] Numerous parties objected to the patent for both product and use claims in respect of a composition for administering humane euthanasia in lower animals. Various objections were lodged, ranging from the concern that 'lower animal' could encompass 'human', that the product might be used more broadly in society, and that it was an affront to the human right to life under Article 2 of the European Convention on Human Rights. All arguments were rejected and the position confirmed that exceptions should be interpreted narrowly. In particular, objections should concern the *publication or exploitation* of the invention (interpreting EPC 1973, Art 53(a)). Many arguments, for example whether the development of the composition itself was immoral or, indeed, the act of granting it a patent is immoral, therefore simply fell outside the remit of the Board. It was held that the claims were perfectly clear and unambiguous in their application to lower mammal life forms, and not humans. Moreover, the practice of humane euthanasia in animals was widely practised and accepted and so in conformity with societal notions of morality and *ordre public*.

[381] Case T315/03 *HARVARD/Transgenic animal* [2005] EPOR 31.   [382] [2002] EPOR 2.
[383] *PLANT GENETIC SYSTEMS/Glutamine synthetase inhibitors* [1995] EPOR 357.   [384] ibid at 373.
[385] *HOWARD FLOREY/Relaxin* [1995] EPOR 541.   [386] ibid.
[387] See G Laurie, 'Patents, patients and consent: exploring the interface between regulation and innovation regimes' in H Somsen (ed), *The Regulatory Challenge of Biotechnology* (2007), Ch 11.
[388] Available on the EPO website at www.epo.org/law-practice/case-law-appeals/recent/t010866eu1.html.

11.204   This all culminates in the current EPO Guidelines which provide that:[389]

> A fair test to apply is to consider whether it is probable that the public in general would regard the invention as so abhorrent that the grant of patent rights would be inconceivable. If it is clear that this is the case, objection should be raised under Article 53(a); otherwise not. The mere possibility of abuse of an invention is not sufficient to deny patent protection pursuant to Art. 53(a) EPC if the invention can also be exploited in a way which does not and would not infringe 'ordre public' and morality.

Morality, *ordre public*, and stem cell research: EU developments

11.205   First, some background (see also para 11.4 regarding biotechnology). The scientific breakthrough of isolating human embryonic stem cells holds great therapeutic promise in a number of areas, including spinal cord injuries, Parkinson's disease, stroke, and transplantation therapy[390] and also challenges on morality grounds. The Biotechnology Directive was originally proposed in 1988, but suffered a very difficult passage and was vetoed by the European Parliament in 1995. While it was eventually adopted in 1998 and contains morality provisions that broadly reflect the jurisprudence of the EPO discussed in paras 11.196ff, there was no time to incorporate any mention of human embryonic stem cell technologies. The resulting controversy has beleaguered the Directive ever since and has brought about a sea change in attitude in the EPO.

11.206   The problem of the inherent subjectivity as to what constitutes immoral conduct was tackled by the EU legislature in the Biotechnology Directive by listing four examples of inventions that should automatically be excluded. These are: (1) processes for cloning human beings; (2) processes for modifying the germ line genetic identity of human beings; (3) uses of human embryos for industrial or commercial purposes; and (4) processes for modifying the genetic identity of animals which are likely to cause them suffering without any substantial medical benefit to man or animal, and also animals resulting from such processes.[391] The CJEU has confirmed that Article 6(2) leaves no discretion to member states with regard to the unpatentability of the processes and uses which it sets out because the very purpose of the provision is to give definition as to exclusions.[392]

11.207   These provisions have now also been incorporated into the Implementing Regulations of the EPC as rule 28 (formerly 23d) to ensure consistency of approach as between the Union's member states and the EPO.[393] It is very debatable whether this has resulted in any more clarity. A key debacle concerned the patentability of human embryonic stem cell inventions which involve the destruction of human embryos for their production.

11.208   Article 6 embodies the morality provisions of the Directive. It states:

1.   Inventions shall be considered unpatentable where their commercial exploitation would be contrary to ordre public or morality; however, exploitation shall not be deemed to be so contrary merely because it is prohibited by law or regulation.

2.   On the basis of paragraph 1, the following, in particular, shall be considered unpatentable:

    (a) processes for cloning human beings;

    (b) processes for modifying the germ line genetic identity of human beings;

    (c) uses of human embryos for industrial or commercial purposes;

    (d) processes for modifying the genetic identity of animals which are likely to cause them suffering without any substantial medical benefit to man or animal, and also animals resulting from such processes.

---

[389] EPO Guidelines, Part G-II, para 4.1.

[390] JA Thomson et al, 'Embryonic stem cell lines derived from human blastocysts' (1998) 282 Science 1145.

[391] Biotechnology Directive, Art 6(2). See also Sch A2 to the Patents Act 1977, as amended.

[392] C-456/03 *Commission v Italy* [2005] ECR I-5335, at points 78–79.

[393] EPC Implementing Regulations, www.epo.org/law-practice/legal-texts/html/epc/2013/e/ma2.html.

11.209   So while morality per se is left undefined, specific examples have now been included as part of a non-exhaustive list.[394] The last one (d) is a modification of the test laid down in *HARVARD/Oncomouse*, albeit in a more rigorous fashion, requiring substantial *medical* benefit to outweigh potential suffering to the animal. It remains, nonetheless, a crude felicific calculus and a questionable measure of morality from the philosophical perspective. Note too, that the prohibition is now restricted to the immorality of the 'commercial exploitation' of the invention, and no longer refers to its 'publication' as was the case in Article 53 EPC 1973. This re-emphasises the fact that the moral dubiety of the patent grant should properly be focused on the way in which the monopoly is exploited.

Question

Why were these particular examples chosen? Have any important matters been left out? Is this an appropriate measure of 'morality' for the purposes of patent law? Should the morality provision remain in European patent law?

Human embryonic stem cell inventions

11.210   Although Article 6 excludes uses of human embryos from patenting, it says nothing about cells or cell lines derived from embryos.[395] Nor is it clear whether the prohibition on processes for cloning human beings relates only to reproductive cloning techniques or extends to cloning to produce stem cells for therapeutic purposes.[396] Human embryo research is ethically problematic for a number of reasons, all of which centre upon the moral status of this organism. A particular concern surrounding embryonic stem cell technologies for many years was that we needed both to use and destroy a human embryo to produce valuable embryonic stem cell cultures. The prospect of then patenting those cultures or other products derived from embryonic stem cells is all the more problematic for many groups. There have been significant developments in relation to the product of human embryonic stem cell lines without the destruction of embryos,[397] and this could end the ethical debate surrounding stem cell inventions. It remains to be seen if other methods will be scientifically equivalent to or better than embryonic stem cells.[398] Thus the debate is far from over.

Exercise

The EPO has granted patents in respect of stem cell technologies which claim not to destroy embryos. Can you find these patents using the Espacenet facility?[399]

---

[394]   The exclusions from patentability in the UK regulations state: 'the following are not patentable', while the Directive makes it clear that the exclusions are mere examples of exclusions. Is the UK in breach of its obligations?

[395]   Article 5(1) of the Directive provides: 'The human body, at the various stages of its formation and development, and the simple discovery of one of its elements, including the sequence or partial sequence of a gene, cannot constitute patentable inventions.'

[396]   Stem cells are relatively undifferentiated cells of the same lineage (family type) that retain the ability to divide and cycle throughout postnatal life to provide cells that can become specialised and take the place of those that die or are lost.

[397]   See, eg, iPS (Induced Pluripotent Stem cells). which are produced from reprogrammed adult somatic cells, argued by many to avoid the ethical dilemmas; see SA Brockman-Lee, 'Embryonic stem cells in science and medicine: an invitation for dialogue' (2007) 4 Gender Medicine 288 and LM Solomon and SA Brockman-Lee, 'Embryonic stem cells in science and medicine, part II: law, ethics, and the continuing need for dialogue' (2008) 5 Gender Medicine 3; cf JC Watt and NR Kobayashi, 'The bioethics of human pluripotent stem cells: will induced pluripotent stem cells end the debate?' (2010) Open Stem Cell J 18. See I Murnaghan, 'Creating Embryonic Stem Cells without Embryonic Destruction', 12 September 2015, www.explorestemcells.co.uk/creating-embryonic-stem-cells-embryo-destruction.html.

[398]   See, eg, M Leslie, 'Reprogramme stem cells work as well as those from embryos', AAAS Science, 26 October 2015, http://news.science-mag.org/biology/2015/10/reprogrammed-stem-cells-work-well-those-embryos.

[399]   See, eg, Case T1156/09 (*Osteoblast-Neuronal cell transdifferentiation/KANEKA*) of 21 June 2012: www.epo.org/law-practice/case-law-appeals/recent/t091156eu1.html; Case T1199/08 (*Selected sperm/XY*) of 3 May 2012: www.epo.org/law-practice/case-law-appeals/recent/t081199eu1.html; Case T2464/10 (*Anticoagulant protein/IMPERIAL*) of 25 May 2012: www.epo.org/law-practice/case-law-appeals/recent/t102464eu1.html; Case T0811/11 (*Differentiated progenitor cells/ADVANCED CELL TECHNOLOGY*) of 11 July 2011: www.epo.org/law-practice/case-law-appeals/recent/t110811eu1.html.

11.211   The European Group on Ethics in Science and New Technologies (EGE) reported that by 2002 over 2,000 patent applications had been lodged around the world involving both human and non-human stem cells, a quarter of which related to embryonic stem cells. Over a third of all stem cell applications had been granted, as had a quarter of those related to embryonic stem cells.[400] The EGE urged a cautious approach and recommended 'excluding the patentability of the process of creation of a human embryo by cloning for stem cells'.[401] It also stated that unmodified stem cells with no use should not be patentable, and this is in keeping with the functional approach towards biotechnological patents already outlined in paras 11.79ff.

11.212   The EGE Opinion was, however, rejected *in toto* by the Opposition Division (OD) of the EPO when it heard the so-called 'Edinburgh Patent' case only a few months later. The patent in suit related to *animal* transgenic stem cells but numerous groups raised opposition proceedings to the grant of the patent, inter alia, on the grounds that 'animal' includes 'human' in the scientific taxonomy. In amending the patent to exclude mention of human or animal embryonic stem cells, the OD interpreted the Article 53(a) EPC morality clause and the EPO equivalent guidelines to Article 6 of the Biotechnology Directive very broadly and in a manner which was completely at odds with the existing EPO case law. The OD noted that the provisions could be interpreted in two ways: *narrowly*, to mean that only commercial uses of human embryos *as such* are excluded from patentability, or *broadly*, to mean that human embryonic stem cells—which as we have noted can only be obtained by destroying an embryo—are also not patentable. The OD preferred the latter approach, arguing that since embryos *as such* are already protected by Rule 23(e) (equivalent of Art 5(1) of the EC Directive), a similar interpretation of Rule 23(d)(c) (equivalent of Art 6(2)(c) of the EC Directive) would be redundant, and this could not have been the intention of the legislator.[402]

11.213   This approach was then followed in the Examining Division of the EPO, most notably in respect of the application of the Wisconsin Alumni Research Foundation (WARF) which was responsible for developing the first techniques to isolate human embryonic stem cells in 1998. The application was for European patents in respect of 'primate embryonic stem cells', or more particularly, embryonic stem cell cultures (that is, stem cell *products*), but the application also disclosed the means to make such products, as one would expect. Thus, the application disclosed a method for preparing embryonic stem cells from primate blastocysts. It was accepted, but not demonstrated in the application, that this method was also enabling of the production of human embryonic stem cells. Moreover, the sole method of production of the stem cell cultures that was described involved the use, and destruction, of embryos. The Examining Division held that all of the claims which could be extended to human embryonic stem cells were invalid on grounds of immorality. It did so on the basis of an extremely literal and broad interpretation of Rule 23(d)(c): 'European patents are not to be granted in respect of . . . inventions which concern . . . uses of human embryos for industrial or commercial purposes.' In sum, the Division held that: 'The use of an embryo as starting material for the generation of a product of industrial application is considered equal to industrial use of this embryo.' The rationale here is that the claimed cultures are inseparable from the means to make them. It is, therefore, in a literal sense, necessary to 'use' embryos to create the claimed invention. The message from this ruling is that the moral concern goes far beyond patenting itself and extends to general instrumentalisation. It implies that mere involvement—use—of embryos in the research and development of an invention is sufficient to bar the patentability of that invention.[403]

11.214   The matter was referred to the EBA in November 2005 with four key questions:

---

[400] EGE, *Ethical Aspects of Patenting Inventions Involving Human Stem Cells*, Opinion No 16, 17 May 2002, para 1.16.

[401] ibid, para 2.5.   [402] See G Laurie, 'Patenting stem cells of human origin' [2004] EIPR 59.

[403] Rejection of a presumption in favour of narrow interpretation of exclusions was expressed by the Enlarged Board of Appeal in Case G1/07 *MED-PHYSICS/Treatment by surgery* (C1/07) [2010] EPOR 25. For English judicial angst about not giving the exclusions too wide an interpretation, see *Research in Motion UK Ltd v Inpro Licensing SARL* [2006] EWHC 70 (Pat), [2006] RPC 20, affirmed by the Court of Appeal: [2007] EWCA Civ 51.

Embryonic stem cell patents: questions for the EPO Enlarged Board of Appeal

(1) Does Rule 23d(c) EPC apply to an application filed before the entry into force of the rule?

(2) If the answer to question 1 is yes, does Rule 23d(c) EPC forbid the patenting of claims directed to products (here: human embryonic stem cell cultures) which—as described in the application—at the filing date could be prepared exclusively by a method which necessarily involved the destruction of the human embryos from which the said products are derived, if the said method is not part of the claims?

(3) If the answer to question 1 or 2 is no, does Article 53(a) EPC forbid patenting such claims?

(4) In the context of questions 2 and 3, is it of relevance that after the filing date the same products could be obtained without having to recur to a method necessarily involving the destruction of human embryos (here: eg derivation from available human embryonic cell lines)?

 Question

Before reading any further, consider how would you answer questions 2–4? By reference to what moral matters would you justify your responses?

11.215   There is a fear in some quarters that confusion surrounding the morality provisions results in a stifling of stem cell research around Europe. It is important to consider too the extent to which the patent system should purport to perform a regulatory function in respect of science. That is the legitimate role of state governments and it may be a role that is usurped by an unelected administrative body that is able to pass judgement on the morality of new technologies. This is particularly problematic when one considers the example of the UK, which invests millions of pounds a year in support of stem cell research. Is it acceptable that these efforts might be thwarted by the EPO?

11.216   The EBA delivered its decision in *WARF/Embryonic Stem Cell Patents* in November 2008. This stated that European patent law forbids the patenting of claims directed to products which, at the filing date of the application, could be prepared exclusively by a method which necessarily involved the destruction of the human embryo from which the products are derived; and this is so *even if* the method is not part of the claims.[404] Moreover, if after the filing date a method is discovered which allows the same products to be obtained without having recourse to a method which necessarily involves the destruction of human embryos, this will not 'fix' an application. There was a further issue of whether additional questions on this matter should be referred to the ECJ as it touched on the wording of the Biotechnology Directive, but it was ruled that there were no grounds for such a referral. As for the other questions referred to the EBA, since the answer to the second question was yes, the third question concerning the interpretation of Article 53 was not considered and remains open to debate. The EBA did state, however, that:[405]

> it is important to point out that it is not the fact of the patenting itself that is considered to be against *ordre public* or morality, but it is the performing of the invention, which includes a step (the use involving its destruction of a human embryo) that has to be considered to contravene those concepts (para 41).

---

[404] Decision G2/06 *WARF/Stem cells* [2009] EPOR 15.

[405] For commentary, see generally A Plomer and P Torremans (eds), *Embryonic Stem Cell Patents: European Law and Ethics* (2009); P Treichel, 'G2/06 and the verdict of immorality' (2009) 40(4) IIC 450; and M Rowlandson, '*WARF/Stem cells* (G2/06): the *ordre public* and morality exception and its impact on the patentability of human embryonic stem cells' (2010) 32(2) EIPR 67.

11.217 This issue was also considered at the ECJ. *Brüstle v Greenpeace* was a dispute as to the patentability of isolated and purified neural precursor cells, processes for their production from embryonic stem cells, and their use for treatment of neural defects. Greenpeace sought revocation of a German patent for its alleged contravention of the domestic patent law embodying Article 6(1) and (2) of the Biotechnology Directive, which—as we have seen—states that patents may not be granted for inventions whose commercial exploitation would be contrary to *ordre public* or morality, and that, in particular, patents may not be granted for uses of human embryos for industrial or commercial purposes.

11.218 In November 2009, the Bundesgerichtshof (German Supreme Court) sent three questions to the ECJ. The ECJ was asked to consider for the first time whether human embryonic stem cell inventions are properly described as an 'embryo' for the purposes of patent law. On this question, the ECJ fully recognised that a 'degree of sensitivity' was merited in the light of the diverse attitudes around Europe. Most surprisingly, however, it denied that it was being asked a moral question, preferring instead to characterise the issue as a matter of legal interpretation. As a term of art in EU law not referencing any domestic law, the ECJ was duty bound to provide an independent and uniform interpretation throughout Europe. It defined 'embryo' as:

(1) any human ovum after fertilisation;
(2) any non-fertilised human ovum into which the cell nucleus from a mature human cell has been transplanted; and
(3) any non-fertilised human ovum whose division and further development have been stimulated by parthenogenesis.

Although these latter entities have not been fertilised, it reasoned, they are nonetheless capable of commencing development into a human being and so, according to the ECJ, must be excluded from patentability.[406] The self-evident breadth of this conceptualisation—apparently arrived at in a morality-free zone—has been roundly criticised for its failure to take into account the underpinning value and diverse approaches to human dignity around the continent.[407] This is in contrast to the Advocate General, who did engage with these points.[408]

11.219 On a second question—whether embryos used in research represent their 'industrial and commercial uses'—the ECJ answered in the affirmative. Indeed, once again a broad exclusionary approach was adopted:[409]

> The fact that destruction [of the human embryo] may occur at a stage long before the implementation of the invention, as in the case of the production of embryonic stem cells from a lineage of stem cells the mere production of which implied the destruction of human embryos is, in that regard, irrelevant.

11.220 The next stage was a referral to the CJEU from an English court in *International Stem Cell v Comptroller General,* regarding the extent to which there could be no patent if the embryo could not develop into a human being. The CJEU held[410] that an unfertilised ovum, whose division and development is stimulated by parthenogenesis, was not an embryo within Article 6(2)(c) if it was not inherently capable of developing into a human being. It was therefore not excluded from patenting. The UK IPO issued guidance in 2015 which takes into account both *Brüstle* and *International Stem Cell.*[411] It will again be interesting to see how matters develop for both funding and patenting.

---

[406] [2011] ECR I-9821.

[407] See, eg, S Harmon, G Laurie, and A Courtney, 'Dignity, plurality and patentability: the unfinished story of *Brüstle v Greenpeace* (Case Comment)' EL Rev 2013 38(1) 92–106.

[408] [2011] ECR I-9821 AG28, 44–46, 75–90.

[409] ibid, para 49. See also EPO in Case T2221/10 *TECHNION/Culturing stem cells* [2014] EPOR 23.

[410] Case C-343/13 *International Stem Cell v Comptroller General* [2015] 2 CMLR 26.

[411] See www.gov.uk/government/publications/inventions-involving-human-embryonic-stem-cells-25-march-2015.

Exercise

Consider the wider implications of these decisions to exclude or permit patent protection in respect of inventions developed using embryonic stem cells against the backdrop of scientific developments. What are the social, ethical, scientific, and economic issues at stake? In particular, where does this leave a country like the UK which actively encourages embryonic stem cell research? Do these rulings have any impact on the incentive to research in Europe?

Discussion point   For answer guidance visit **www.oup.com/uk/brown5e.**

Do you consider that inventions involving the destruction of human embryos should be prohibited by the morality provisions? On what basis do you justify your response?

Exercise

Which factors do you think should be weighed in the balance in considering the morality of patents and inventions?

Exercise

The new frontier? Consider the possible challenges that might be created for the patent system by the advent of synthetic biology. See http://synthethics.eu/index.html; European Group on Ethics in Science and New Technologies to the European Commission (EGE), *Opinion 25: Ethics of Synthetic Biology* (2009), www.coe.int/t/dg3/healthbioethic/cometh/ege/20091118%20 finalSB%20_2_%20MP.pdf; and for information on filings in this field, see contributions to Nature Biotech Special Edition 'Focus on Synthetic Biology' (2009) 27(12) Nature Biotech 1127. What lessons might be learned from experiences with biotechnology patents to date? Consider also the work of Group of Experts to monitor and advise on biotechnology and patenting in Europe, as was required by the Biotechnology Directive itself http://ec.europa.eu/transparency/regexpert/ index.cfm?do=groupDetail.groupDetail&groupID=2973, and the European Group on Ethics in Science and New Technologies, which advises on Commission policy https://ec.europa.eu/ info/research-and-innovation/strategy/support-policy-making/scientific-support-eu-policies/ european-group-ethics-science-and-new-technologies-ege_en.

Plant and animal varieties

11.221   In *PLANT GENETIC SYSTEMS/Glutamine Synthetase Inhibitors* the claims to the plant itself were revoked under Article 53(b). It was held that because the genetically altered plant could reproduce and pass on its resistance in a relatively stable manner, it qualified as a 'plant variety' and as such should be excluded from patentability. The argument that the plant was a product produced by a microbiological process was rejected because the insertion of the resistant gene was but one small part of the general process of replicating the plant.[412]

---

[412]   The EBA refused to hold that *Oncomouse* and *PGS* were in any way inconsistent in *Inadmissible referral* [1996] EPOR 505.

11.222 The permissibility of patenting genetically engineered plants was later considered by the EBA. It held in *NOVARTIS*[413] that only claims to 'plant varieties' in themselves are excluded from patent protection. This extends to genetically engineered plant varieties. It does not, however, rule out the possibility that 'plant-related products', including plants themselves, can receive patent protection. For present purposes, then, suffice it to note that the practical outcome of these plant cases is that as long as the patentee does not specifically claim a *variety* in his patent application, then a genetically engineered or otherwise 'invented' plant will not face successful challenge on the basis of Article 53.[414] But even with this, and while 'microbiological processes or the products thereof' are patentable, this is not carte blanche to claim that genetically engineered processes or products always qualify, since the overarching limitation will be to assess the substance of the claims to ensure that a plant variety is not claimed. Once again, however, this is not problematic, since it directs patent attorneys to pay particular attention to the way in which claims are drafted. Whether it leads to sophistic distinctions is another matter.

Essentially biological processes

11.223 'Essentially biological processes' in themselves are excluded from patentability in the EPC. In *Novartis*, the EBA seemed to endorse the provisions of the Biotechnology Directive, which had been adopted by that time. Article 2(2) states: 'A process for the production of plants or animals is essentially biological if it consists *entirely* of natural phenomena such as crossing or selection' (emphasis added). Products (as in plants and animals) which result from these processes are not expressly excluded.[415] This has been considered in a line of cases at the EPO.

> ### EPO Essentially biological process cases
>
> #### G2/07 and G1/08 *Essentially biological processes* [2011] EPOR 27
>
> The essential question here—referred to the EBA for clarification—was whether the selection and crossing of plants by human intervention escaped the prohibition on patentability as contained in Article 53(b).
> The EBA held that what had to be examined was the essence of the invention in question, taking into account the nature and overall contribution of human intervention and the extent of its impact on the results achieved. This had to be more than mere trivial interference and not be something that could occur naturally. Moreover, the significance of the intervention would be tested against traditional breeders' processes and must go beyond these. Furthermore, if the processes of manipulation introduced or significantly modified a trait in the genome of the biological subject matter that went beyond merely the result of mixing of the genes through sexual crossing, then this took the activity outside the scope of the exclusion.[416]
>
> #### *Essentially Biological Patent Processes* G2/12 *(Tomatoes)* and G2/13 *(Broccoli)* [2015] EPOR 28
>
> In 2015, the EBA ruled that the exclusions for essentially biological processes for the production of plants do not cover a product claim to the plant itself (provided it is not otherwise prohibited as a plant variety).[417] The European Commission then issued a Notice concluding that it was not the intention of the Biotechnology Directive for plants and animals resulting from essentially biological processes to be patentable.[418] It will be interesting to note how this develops, particularly if a case is referred to the Court of Justice.

---

[413] Case G1/98 *NOVARTIS II/Transgenic plant* [2000] EPOR 303.

[414] Confirmed in Case T775/08 *MONSANTO/Glyphosate tolerant alfalfa* [2011] EPOR 28.

[415] See also Case T19/90 *HARVARD/Onco-mouse* [1990] OJEPO 376 [1990] EPOR 501, para 4.9.2.

[416] Case T775/08 *MONSANTO/Glyphosate tolerant alfalfa* [2011] EPOR 28.

[417] For earlier decisions, see Case T1242/06 *STATE OF ISRAEL/Tomatoes II* [2012] EPOR 42 and see Case T 83/05 *Plant BioScience/Broccoli* [2013] EPOR 39 and SJR Bostyn, 'Resolving the conundrum of the patentability of plants produced by an essentially biological process: squaring the circle' (2013) 35(7) EIPR 383–96.

[418] European Commission on certain articles of Directive 98/44 on the legal protection of biological inventions reference C/2016/6997, https://eur-lex.europa.eu/legal-content/EN/TXT/?uri=CELEX%3A52016XC1108%2801%29.

11.224   Article 3(1) of the Biotechnology Directive provides that inventions which are new, which involve an inventive step, and which are susceptible of industrial application shall be patentable 'even if they concern a product consisting of or containing biological material or a process by means of which biological material is produced, processed or used'. Moreover, Article 3(2) states that 'Biological material which is isolated from its natural environment or produced by means of a technical process may be the subject of an invention even if it previously occurred in nature.'

11.225   This is a direct endorsement of the policy direction that had been rigorously pursued by the EPO.[419] Indeed, the relevant provisions of the EPC were brought into line with the key Articles of the Biotechnology Directive by a Decision of the Administrative Council of the European Patent Organisation of 16 June 1999.[420] This was necessary to avoid confusion and disharmony because the Directive clearly only applies to the 28 member states of the EU, while the signatories to the EPC include these states and, currently, 11 others.[421] The policy in action can still, however, be problematic. The challenges of drafting claims are considered in the 2018 EPO Guidelines regarding the need for limitations to the technically produced product.[422]

Methods of treatment of the human or animal body

11.226   EPC 2000 moved this provision from Article 52(4) under EPC 1973 to Article 53(c). Previously, methods of treatment were excluded from protection because they were considered not capable of industrial application, and now they are specifically excluded as exceptions to patentability.[423] This make no difference in practice but is thought to be more in keeping with the underlying reasons for such an exclusion, namely, to ensure that patents do not unduly interfere with matters of public health,[424] rather than to maintain a fiction about industrial applicability. The deep irony about this provision, however, is that it has always been accompanied by a rider that *substances* or *compositions* for use in a method of treatment or diagnosis are patentable.[425] The challenge was summed up by the Court of Appeal in *Bristol-Myers Squibb v Baker Norton Pharmaceuticals*:[426]

> [Section 4(2)—excluding methods of treatment] has the limited purpose of ensuring that the actual use, by practitioners, of methods of medical treatment when treating patients should not be the subject of restraint or restriction by patent monopolies. The difficulty is to decide whether the restraint concerns a method of treatment as opposed to that which is available for treatment.

 Question

Why do you think that methods of treatment are unpatentable but substances or compositions are patentable? Is that not somewhat inconsistent since they are both concerned with public health?

11.227   We have to establish the parameters of this provision in order to make sense of it. Note, for example, that it does not exclude *all* methods of treating the human or animal body, only those related to 'therapy' and 'surgery'. Similarly, it is only diagnostic methods which are 'practised on' the human body that are excluded. We must explore the case law to understand more.[427]

---

[419]   For example, the essence of the rulings in *Oncomouse* and *Plant Genetic Systems* is essentially reproduced in Art 4.
[420]   http://archive.epo.org/epo/pubs/oj99/7_99/7_4379.pdf.
[421]   There are 38 signatory states to the EPC (as at November 2018).
[422]   EPO Guidelines, Part F-IV, 4.12 and Part G-II, 5.2, 5.4.1 (also applying to plant and animal claims).
[423]   See the Patents Act 1977, s 4(2), which was amended by the Patents Act 2004, s 1, and now Patents Act 1977, s 4A(1).
[424]   See Case G05/83 *EISAI/Second medical use* [1985] OJEPO 64.
[425]   See now the Patents Act 1977, s 4A(2) and Art 53(c) EPC 2000.   [426]   [2001] RPC 1.
[427]   Because the concern of this provision is interventions designed to maintain life or improve health, it does not extend to methods that bring about death, nor does it affect the patentability of methods carried out on the dead body; see Case T182/90 *SHELL/Blood flow* [1994] OJEPO 641.

Therapy

11.228   Therapy concerns the medical treatment of disease, including cure and prevention.[428] The approach is the same whether we are considering animal or human bodies. The 'medical' or 'veterinary' nature of the treatment is an important determinant in deciding whether a claim falls foul of the provision. This is because the provision is designed so as not to hinder professionals in their job, therefore if the method can be performed by someone who does not have the specialised professional skills, it is more likely to imply that the method is patentable.[429] By the same token, if a procedure requires oversight from a professional, such as laser modification of a lenticule implanted on the cornea, then the invention will normally fall within the exclusion.[430] Irrespective of who performs it, the method must be for some therapeutic purpose; non-therapeutic purposes are patentable. Thus, in *Schering's Application*[431] it was held that contraception is not a therapy because pregnancy is not an illness. The inclusion of some therapeutic element in a contraceptive method would, however, invoke the exclusion.[432] This was confirmed by the EPO Technical Board of Appeal in 2012 in *BAYER SCHERING PHARMA AG/Composition for contraception*.[433] While reiterating that contraceptive use is not therapeutic because pregnancy is not an illness, the Board stressed that the inherent features of the principal claim to reduce common side effects of contraceptive use through reduce-dose hormones *was* therapeutic. The patent failed as a result. The matter has to be decided 'exclusively on the basis of the actions carried out during such use and the effect is obtained'. The circumstances of use are relevant. So, methods of termination of pregnancy,[434] inducing labour, and *in vitro* fertility treatment are all considered unpatentable because all must be carried out under medical supervision. Treatments to kill parasites or head lice have been found to be 'therapy'.[435]

11.229   What happens if a part of you is taken away for treatment and returned? This was considered in *Schultz's Application* before the UK Patent Office which concerned extracorporeal blood dialysis and filtration methods.[436] It was held that this method was unpatentable because there was no need for the treatment to be carried out on the body itself to be excluded. That particular qualification relates only to diagnostic methods (see para 11.235) Note, however, that the exclusion applies on the proviso that the human material is returned to the same human body.

11.230   *Enhancement* of the human or animal body, for example through cosmetic treatments for humans or treatment of stock animal to improve meat or milk yields, is generally not thought of as 'therapy'. Thus, hair and nail treatments are patentable.[437] But sometimes a method can have both cosmetic and therapeutic benefits. If the two cannot be separated out, then the method is, once again, unpatentable. For example, in *L'ORÉAL/Protection against UV*[438] the method of skin protection against the effects of ageing (cosmetic) also had a physiological and beneficial effect on the skin (therapeutic) and so was held to be unpatentable.[439] In contrast, in *ROUSSEL-UCLAF/Thenoyl peroxide*[440] it was possible to distinguish a method of cleansing the skin of comedones (blackheads) as personal hygiene (patentable) from a use of the method as a treatment for acne (unpatentable).

---

[428]   *Unilever (Davis's) Application* [1983] RPC 219.

[429]   Case T245/87 *SIEMENS/Flow measurement* (1989) OJEPO 171.

[430]   Case T24/91 *THOMSON/Cornea* [1995] OJEPO 512.

[431]   [1971] RPC 337. The equivalent in the EPO is Case T74/93 *BRITISH TECHNOLOGY/Contraceptive method* [1995] OJEPO 712.

[432]   Case T820/92 *GENERAL HOSPITAL/Contraceptive method* [1995] OJEPO 113.

[433]   [2012] EPOR 23.   [434]   *Upjohn (Kirkton's) Application* [1976] RPC 324.

[435]   See Case T116/85 *WELLCOME/Pigs I* [1989] OJEPO 13; cf *Stafford-Miller's Application* [1984] FSR 258 decided under the 1949 Act.

[436]   BL O/174/84, discussed in the Examination Guidelines for Patent Applications relating to Medical Inventions in the UK Intellectual Property Office, October 2016, www.gov.uk/government/publications/examining-patent-applications-for-medical-inventions/examination-guidelines-for-patent-applications-relating-to-medical-inventions-in-the-intellectual-property-office, para 41.

[437]   See *Joos v Commissioner of Patents* [1973] RPC 79.

[438]   Case T1077/93 *L'ORÉAL/Protection against UV* [1997] OJEPO 546.

[439]   The same issue of inseparability of therapeutic and non-therapeutic applies for methods to remove plaque from teeth: Case T290/86 *ICI/Cleaning plaque* [1992] OJEPO 414.

[440]   Case T36/83 [1986] OJEPO 295. Similarly, see Case T144/85 *DU PONT/Appetite suppressant* [1986] OJEPO 30.

Exercise

How would you categorise the use of skin patches to assist people in giving up smoking? Is this a therapy? Is smoking an illness? What about diet pills which can be used both by people who are morbidly obese and those who want to lose weight for aesthetic reasons?

Surgery

11.231   It must be remembered that 'surgery' in this context is a technical term of art used in patent law. It has been held to involve any non-insignificant[441] intervention on the body by operation or manipulation in an attempt to maintain the life or health of the human or animal body.[442] Unlike the previous category of therapy, the law does not draw a distinction between therapeutic and non-therapeutic interventions; it is concerned only to know if the method of intervention is surgical in nature. Thus, cosmetic surgery techniques are generally excluded as well as curative surgery (but see paras 11.233). Moreover, 'surgery' has enjoyed a wide definition in the sense that it has not been restricted to methods that involve a direct invasion of the body; hence the term 'manipulation' covers non-invasive techniques such as re-setting of broken bones or repositioning. Once again, however, the need for technical skill and expertise in the performance of the method is a significant factor in establishing whether the exclusion applies. Thus in *Occidental Petroleum's Application*[443] it was stated that the involvement of a surgeon necessarily meant that the procedure was surgical in nature; by the same token, it does not follow that the absence of a surgeon means that a method is not surgical if it still requires a degree of skill in its execution, for example by a nurse.[444]

Question

Do you think that the work of tattoo or piercing artists would count as 'surgery' under the law?

11.232   The status of cosmetic interventions and the surgical exclusion is complex. In *GENERAL HOSPITAL/Hair removal method*[445] the invention concerned a method of hair removal from the skin by optical radiation. The Technical Board of Appeal after consulting the *travaux préparatoires* of the EPC, held that 'the intention of the legislator was that only those treatments by therapy or surgery are excluded from patentability which are suitable for or potentially suitable for maintaining or restoring the health, the physical integrity, and the physical well being of a human being or an animal and to prevent diseases'.[446]

Discussion point   For answer guidance visit www.oup.com/uk/brown5e.

What would the position be in respect of breast augmentation surgery or correction of the shape of the nose? Are these always and necessarily 'cosmetic'?

---

[441] The use of needles for the extraction of blood or administration of medicines is considered 'insignificant' for these purposes; see Case T182/90 [1994] OJEPO 641.

[442] Case T35/99 *GEORGETOWN UNIVERSITY/Pericardial access* [2000] OJEPO 447.

[443] BL O/35/84, see UK IPO *Manual of Patent Practice*, para 4A.09.

[444] Citing *Allen's Application* (BL O/59/92) (method of inserting markers in body for NMR and CT scans).

[445] Case T383/03 [2005] OJEPO 159.

[446] ibid, 4 of judgment. See further Case T9/04 *KONINKLIJKE PHILIPS ELECTRONICS NV/Medical diagnostic imaging* [2007] EPOR 10, point 6 of the Reasons.

11.233 In G 01/07 *MEDI-PHYSICS/Treatment by surgery*, however, the EBA found that purpose was irrelevant. The relevant procedure involved a method of obtaining images of patients requiring that a contrast agent be injected into the heart. Did this invasive element prove fatal to the entire claim, even though it was in no way treatment or curative in its own right? The EBA departed from existing case law in holding that the technical definition which has grown up over the years is too broad. A new concept of 'surgery' in patent law was therefore required. The EBA stopped short of providing a definition, but it did point to key elements that should be weighed in the balance at first instance. Thus the exclusion should operate to strike down claims (1) over the kinds of interventions for which the medical profession is specifically trained; (2) over physical interventions on the body which require professional medical skills; and (3) over methods which involve health risks, even when carried out with requisite medical professional care and expertise. Other factors that might be of relevance include the degree of complexity involved and the degrees of intervention or risk involved, but none is determinative and each case will have to be judged on its facts.[447]

 Exercise

What are the implications of this ruling from the EPO? It seems both broad and narrow at the same time—broad because it upholds a wide role for the exclusion of *any* method if it involves surgery, but also narrow in that it now purports to restrict what counts as 'surgery'. Can you think of examples of interventions that might fall on either side of the line?

11.234 Are there any further limitations to this exclusion? Well one further and important point dealt with by the EBA in *MED-PHYSICS/Treatment by surgery* was the role of disclaimers. The question is this: if you run the risk of falling foul of the surgery exclusion because one element of your procedure counts as 'surgery', is it possible simply to disclaim or exclude this as part of your claim for protection? The EBA confirmed that there is nothing to prevent you attempting to do so, but it will be a question of fact whether the resulting disclosure is sufficient as a matter of law. The EPC (Art 84) requires that patent claims must be clear and disclose all of the essential features of the invention needed to reproduce it. It will be a matter for first instance bodies to determine in each case whether this is so. A final point to note is that none of this affects claims to what are known as 'purely technical methods', that is, method claims about the operation of a device used in health care as opposed to claims to health-related methods which themselves involve treatment, surgery, or diagnostic methods.[448] Let us now turn to consider the last of these.

Diagnostic methods practised on the body

11.235 There has been some confusion and dispute over the years about the precise meaning of the exclusion of diagnostic methods,[449] and this has now been considered by the EBA in an attempt to bring clarity to the subject.

---

[447] [2011] 3 OJEPO 134. See also UK IPO *Manual of Patent Practice* (February 2016, as amended), para 4A.11.1.

[448] Case T9/04 *KONINKLIJKE PHILIPS ELECTRONICS NV/Medical diagnostic imaging* [2007] EPOR 10 is an example of this. If, however, there is a functional link to the effects of the device on the body, this will be excluded. Once again, this will fall to be considered on the technical circumstances of each case. See also *BAYER SCHERING PHARMA AG/Composition for contraception* [2012] EPOR 23.

[449] Compare, eg, Case T385/86 *BRUKER/Non-invasive measurement* [1988] EPOR 357 and Case T964/99 *CYGNUS/Device and method for sampling substances* [2002] OJEPO 4.

■ **G01/04** *CYGNUS/Diagnostic methods*

This case involved a referral on a point of law from the President of the EPO to the EBA.[450] In summary, the essential question was whether 'diagnostic methods practised on the human or animal body' excluded only those claims to methods containing *all* of the procedural steps necessary to a medical diagnosis—for example, the examination phase *and* the data collection phase *and* the comparison phase *and* the discovery of deviation phase *and* the deductive clinical decision phase—or whether the exclusion applied if any *one* of these steps could be used for diagnostic purposes or related to diagnosis. It was held that:[451]

> The method steps to be carried out prior to making a diagnosis as an intellectual exercise . . . are related to examination, data gathering and comparison . . . If only one of the preceding steps which are constitutive for making such a diagnosis is lacking, there is no diagnostic method, but at best a method of data acquisition or data processing that can be used in a diagnostic method . . . .

11.236   In other words, only claims which encompass all of the steps required to come up with a definitive diagnosis are excluded from protection. It means that methods which may represent interim steps in a differential diagnosis and which may be a value in diagnosis will be patentable in themselves as long as they do not lead directly to a diagnosis. Examples include the taking of a sample, methods of internal imaging (eg X-rays or MRI scanning), and methods for measuring temperature. This is a particularly narrow interpretation of the exclusion provisions, but one which the EBA felt able to adopt on the basis that it is a 'matter of principle' that European patents should be granted for inventions that meet the requirements of Article 52(1).

11.237   This does not mean that a claim must laboriously lay out all steps in a process; rather, it must adequately describe the invention for which protection is claimed,[452] and if the method *in fact* allows a diagnosis to be made it will be excluded.

11.238   The exclusion is also subject to the proviso that the method is practised *on the human or animal body*. The EBA has decided that this means that the patient or animal must be present to perform the step in question. Furthermore, to be excluded *all* of the technical steps in the method must be performed on the body, but this does not include the final step of joining the dots and actually deciding on a diagnosis because this is a purely intellectual exercise and therefore not technical.[453]

 Exercise

Is it possible to reconcile the decisions of the Enlarged Boards of Appeal in G01/04 (diagnostic methods) and G01/07 (treatment by surgery)? (Hint: read G01/07 for the EBA's own take on the issues.) Do these kinds of decisions point to the need for a single body of appeal as we discuss in Chapter 10 in respect of the unified patent court?

11.239   Finally, what about implements or other apparatus that are used for the purposes of therapy, surgery, or diagnosis—are these affected by the exclusion? Well, the exclusion relates to *method claims* and not *product claims*, and so normally medical devices should be as patentable as non-medical devices. But an invention which is characterised by its use—for example, 'in surgery'—will not be granted protection. For instance, in *TELETRONICS/Cardiac pacing*[454] the principal claim was to a method of operating a pacer in accordance with the required cardiac output while a person is exercising, and the Technical Board of Appeal held that

---

[450] [2006] EPOR 15.   [451] ibid, para 6.2.2.   [452] Patents Act 1977, s 14(5)(a).
[453] See further Case T1197/02 *AUSTRALIAN NATIONAL UNIVERSITY/Detection of glaucoma* [2007] EPOR 9.
[454] Case T82/93 [1996] OJEPO 274.

this was, in essence, a claim involving a step that was a method of treatment. This was enough to defeat the patent and amendment at the opposition stage was not permissible. The lesson lies in careful drafting of claims in the first place. As we discuss in para 11.70, claims to 'purely technical methods' about the operation of a device should succeed.

 Patent legislation and Brexit

Most of UK patent legislation comes from changes made at national policy level and in the light of obligations under the EPC, and reflects obligations imposed by TRIPS. All this will not be changed by Brexit. Biotechnology is at the moment framed in the light of the Directive and CJEU decisions have a key role. Brexit would change this; however, given the agreed link between the EPO and the Directive, in this area the decisions of the CJEU in the UK will continue to be of some direct impact.

Further reading

Books

D Castle (ed), *The Role of Intellectual Property Rights in Biotechnology Innovation* (2009)

P England, *Intellectual Property in the Life Sciences: A Global Guide to Rights and Their Applications* (2011)

D Koepsell, *Who Owns You? Science, Innovation and the Gene Patent Wars* (2015)

A Plomer and P Torremans (eds), *Embryonic Stem Cell Patents: European Law and Ethics* (2009)

AK Rai and ER Latty (eds), *Intellectual Property and Biotechnology* (2011)

M Rimmer, *Intellectual Property and Biotechnology: Biological Inventions* (2008)

H Somsen (ed), *The Regulatory Challenge of Biotechnology* (2007)

GA Stobbs (ed), *Software Patents Worldwide* (2009)

Reports

Department of Trade and Industry and the Intellectual Property Institute, *Patents for Genetic Sequences: the Competitiveness of Current UK Law and Practices* (2004)

EPO, *Patents and the Fourth Industrial Revolution—The Inventions Behind Digital Transformation* (2017)

Articles

RJ Aerts, 'The unitary patent and the Biotechnology Directive: is uniform protection of biotechnological inventions ensured?' (2014) 36(9) EIPR 584–67

D Booton, 'Patents for diagnostic tools: an economic analysis' (2013) 3 IPQ 187

S Bostyn, 'How biological is essentially biological? The referrals to the Enlarged Board of Appeal G2/07 and G1/08' (2009) 31(11) EIPR 549

S Burke, 'Justifications for patents as applied to human–animal chimeras' (2012) 34(4) EIPR 237

RS Crespi, 'The human embryo and patent law: a major challenge ahead' [2006] EIPR 569

S Gaisser et al, 'The phantom menace of gene patents' (2009) 458(7237) Nature 407

SHE Harmon, G Laurie, and A Courtney, 'Dignity, plurality and patentability: the unfinished story of *Brüstle v Greenpeace*' (2013) 38(1) EL Rev 92

CM Holman, 'Trends in human gene patent litigation' (2008) 322(5899) Science 198

A Huttermann and U Storz, 'A comparison between biotech and software related patents' (2009) 31(12) EIPR 589

K Liddell et al, 'Patents as incentives for translational and evaluative research: the case of genetic tests and their improved clinical performance' [2008] 3 IPQ 286

MA Majumder et al, 'Ethical challenges of patenting "nature": legal and economic accounts of altered nature as property' in BA Lustig et al (eds), *Altering Nature: Concepts of 'Nature' and 'The Natural' in Biotechnology Debates* (2008)

McMahon, 'An institutional examination of the implications of the unitary patent package for the morality provisions: a fragmented future too far?' (Legislative Comment) (2017) 48(1) IIC 42–70

T Minssen and D Nilsson, 'The industrial application requirement for biotech inventions in light of recent EPO and UK case law: a plausible approach or a mere "hunting licence"?' (2012) 34(10) EIPR 689

K Moon, 'The nature of computer programs: Tangible? Goods? Personal property? Intellectual property?' (2008) 31(8) EIPR 396

R Onslow, 'Software patents—a new approach' (2012) 34(1) EIPR 710

J. Pila, 'Art 52(2) of the Convention on the Grant of European Patents: what did the framers intend? A study of the *travaux préparatoires*' (2005) 36 IIC 755

KE Rodriguez and N Groenendjik, 'High-quality patents for emerging science and technology through external actors' (2012) 34(4) EIPR 221

M Rowlandson, '*WARF/Stem cells* (G2/06): the *ordre public* and morality exception and its impact on the patentability of human embryonic stem cells' (2010) 32(2) EIPR 67

RM Schwartz and T Minssen, 'Life after Myriad: the uncertain future of patenting biomedical innovation and personalised medicine in an international context' (2015) 3 IPQ 189

A Sims, 'The case against patenting methods of medical treatment' [2007] 29(2) EIPR 43

Springer Briefs in Biotech Patents, available at http://link.springer.com/bookseries/10239

S Thambisetty, 'The learning needs of the patent system and emerging technologies: a focus on synthetic biology' (2014) 1 IPQ 13

P Treichel, 'G2/06 and the verdict of immorality' (2009) 40(4) IIC 450

G van Overwalle, 'The implementation of the Biotechnology Directive in Belgium and its after-effects. The introduction of a new research exemption and a compulsory licence for public health' (2006) IIC 889

G van Overvalle, 'Exclusive ownership versus open commons: the case of gene patents' (2013) 4(2) WIPOJ 139–56

M Varju and J Sandor, 'Patenting stem cells in Europe: the challenge of multiplicity in European Union law' (2012) 49(3) CML Rev 1007

M Yan, 'Morality—an equivocal area in the patent system' (2012) 34(4) EIPR 261

The power of a patent

Introduction

Scope and overview of chapter

12.1 This chapter concerns the rights that a patentee enjoys and who can be a patentee, the circumstances in which infringement actions might be sought, the defences that are available, the prospect of revocation, and some points on exploitation. For an explanation of the application of the rules on free movement of goods and of EU competition law on exploitation practices, see Chapters 19 and 20.

12.2
Learning objectives

By the end of this chapter you should be able to describe and explain:

- the range of rights conferred by the grant of a patent, ownership, and the limits of the rights conferred;
- the circumstances in which infringement proceedings can be brought and the common counterclaim of revocation;
- the available defences to an action for patent infringement;
- exploitation of patents.

12.3 Once granted, a patent confers on the patentee a range of rights, and the power is arguably the strongest within intellectual property law. But as with all intellectual property rights, limits can be placed on the power, such as Crown use or compulsory licences. Moreover, what can be given can also be taken away, and patents are vulnerable throughout their life to claim for revocation; that is, that the patent should be struck from the patent register because it was erroneously granted. Infringement proceedings are often met with a counterclaim for revocation. It is therefore necessary to consider infringement and revocation together. The chapter then examines the available defences to an action for patent infringement and concludes with a different perspective, by exploring exploitation. So, the chapter looks like this:

- Patent rights and their limits (12.4–12.34)
- Infringement proceedings (12.35–12.71)
- Revocation (12.72–12.86)
- Defences (12.87–12.99)
- Exploitation (12.100–12.109)

Patent rights and their limits

12.4   So, you have applied for your patent, your invention has not been excluded on one or more policy grounds, and you have satisfied a patent examiner that your invention is new, inventive, and of a technical nature. What now?

12.5   Your patent[1] is a right to exclude everyone from the market, even the so-called innocent infringer, for a period up to a maximum of 20 years. It is a form of *personal property* in much the same way as any other thing you own. Thus, it can be sold, assigned, licensed, mortgaged, or otherwise transferred to other parties.[2] A patent is an asset over which securities can be granted and so against which capital can be raised. This is explored in more depth in paras 12.100ff.

12.6   A patent will be granted initially for four years but can be extended annually for a maximum of 20 years. Supplementary Protection Certificates (SPCs) are available in the case of pharmaceutical inventions and agrochemicals inventions. These permit an extension of the term for a further five years to compensate for the stringent regulatory approval mechanisms which these inventions are often subject to before being given access to the market,[3] and have been the subject of some case law.[4] The European Parliament and Council adopted a Regulation on medicines for paediatric use which includes a further six-month extension to an SPC as an incentive to produce in the area in 2006.[5] The UK Intellectual Property Office (IPO) has issued guidance on all SPCs.[6]

12.7   Even within the term of the patent, there are limits on the power to exclude. The core unifying feature of the various limits is our old friend, the public interest. At the most general level and as with other intellectual property rights (IPRs), the European principle of free movement of goods and competition law can impose limits on the way patents are exploited. We discuss these in Chapters 19 and 20, respectively.

12.8   There are also limits within patent law. If we accept that the whole ethos behind the patent system is to encourage inventions that become available to the public, then this end is thwarted if someone seeks and receives patent protection but then does not exploit the invention and keeps the technical details out of the public domain. For these reasons there are *compulsory licences* under sections 48 et seq and 53 of the Patents Act 1977. There was discussion of compulsory licensing, from an international and developing country perspective, regarding access to medicines in chapter 10 at paras 10.51–10.59. Broadly, a common criterion is that a compulsory licence cannot be sought until three years after the grant of the patent to give the patentee a fair chance to exploit the invention himself. A compulsory licence can be sought by a third party if a patent holder refuses to grant licences for use on reasonable terms and when the patentee is not exploiting the invention. They are included because it is considered to be in the public interest for an invention protected by a patent to be worked. This reflects the quid pro quo justification of patents.

---

[1]   This applies to patent applications as well.

[2]   Patents Act 1977, s 30 for England, Wales, and Northern Ireland and s 31 for Scotland, where a patent is 'incorporeal moveable property'. Assignations or grants of security are subject to the provisions of the Requirements of Writing (Scotland) Act 1995.

[3]   Regulation (EC) No 469/2009 of the European Parliament and of the Council of 6 May 2009 concerning the supplementary protection certificate for medicinal products (Codified version) (1) 2009 OJ L 152 16 June 2009 and Regulation (EC) No 1610/96 of the European Parliament and of the Council, created a Supplementary Protection Certificate for plant protection products, and entered into force on 8 February 1997. Note also section 128B and Schedule 4A Patents Act 1977 as amended.

[4]   Disputes over SPCs arise in terms of the 'product' they are certified to cover and whether the invention and the product to be authorised are one and the same; see *Takeda Chemical Industries Ltd's SPC Applications (No 3)* [2004] RPC 3. See also *Neurim Pharmaceuticals v The Comptroller General of Patents* [2011] EWCA Civ 228, *Actavis Group PTC EHF v Sanofi Chancery Division* [2012] EWHC 2545 (Pat), and *Actavis Group PTC EHF v Boehringer Ingelheim Pharma GmbH* [2013] EWHC 2927 (Pat), making a reference to the *CJEU and Eli Lilly v Human Genome Sciences* (C-493/12) [2014] RPC 21, considering the need for an active pharmaceutical ingredient to be specified in a patent for an SPC to be available.

[5]   Regulation (EC) No 1901/2006 of the European Parliament and of the Council of 12 December 2006 on medicinal products for paediatric use and amending Regulation (EEC) No 1768/92, Directive 2001/20/EC, Directive 2001/83/EC, and Regulation (EC) No 726/2004. The amendments are incorporated in Regulation (EC) No 469/2009.

[6]   UK IPO, *Supplementary Protection Certificates* (2014), www.gov.uk/guidance/supplementary-protection-certificates.

12.9   UK law was amended in 1999 to take account of the measures to be found in the Agreement on Trade-Related Aspects of Intellectual Property Rights (TRIPS) concerning compulsory licences.[7] The UK Patents Act 1977[8] now contains two different procedures for the grant of compulsory licences. One of these is for World Trade Organization (WTO) proprietors, and the other for non-WTO proprietors. A WTO proprietor is a person who is a national of, or domiciled in a country which is a member of the WTO, or who has a real and effective industrial or commercial establishment in a WTO country.[9] There are fewer occasions on which a compulsory licence will be granted in respect of a WTO proprietor as compared with a non-WTO proprietor.

12.10   For example, those grounds on which a compulsory licence will be granted in respect of a WTO proprietor include circumstances where:

- the demand for a patented product in the UK is not being met on reasonable terms;[10]
- the owner's failure to license a patent on reasonable terms has a blocking effect on future improvements;[11]
- the failure to license a patent on reasonable terms unfairly prejudices the establishment or development of commercial or industrial activities in the UK;[12]
- as a consequence of terms in the licence the manufacture, use, or disposal of materials in the UK not protected by the patent or the development of industrial activities in the UK is unfairly prejudiced.[13]

12.11   A compulsory licence will be granted in respect of a non-WTO proprietor in circumstances where:[14]

- the patented invention is capable of being commercially worked in the UK but is not being so worked, or not worked to the fullest extent as is reasonably practicable;[15]
- the patented invention is a product and the demand in the UK is not being met on reasonable terms, or is being met by way of importation from a country that is not a member state of the WTO.[16]

12.12   Few applications are made for compulsory licences. The *Gowers Review of Intellectual Property* recommended, for example, that model licence templates be established to facilitate agreements on mutually beneficial terms and obviate the need for difficult and protracted negotiation on a case-by-case basis or, indeed, the need to revert to compulsory licences at all.[17] Some commentators do not, however, see lack of applications as indicating that the provisions are not working. Rather, the fact that the measures are present in the law may serve as a necessary backdrop against which patent owners license third parties in circumstances where they might otherwise be tempted to refuse.[18] The Organisation for Economic Co-Operation and Development (OECD) has also argued that there should be an increase role for compulsory licences regarding biotechnology and genetic engineering, although this is not popular with industry. This may sometimes, be enough to force a patentee's hand to negotiation with potential licensees.[19]

Question

Do you think that the propositions regarding the effectiveness of compulsory licensing are correct? Justify your response.

---

[7] Patents and Trade Marks (WTO) Regulations 1999 (SI 1999/1899).   [8] Patents Act 1977, s 48.
[9] Patents Act 1977, s 48(5)(a), (b).   [10] Patents Act 1977, s 48A(1)(a).   [11] Patents Act 1977, s 48A(1)(b)(i).
[12] Patents Act 1977, s 48A(1)(b)(ii).   [13] Patents Act 1977, s 48A(1)(c).   [14] Patents Act 1977, s 48B.
[15] Patents Act 1977, s 48B(a).   [16] Patents Act 1977, s 48B(b).
[17] *Gowers Review of Intellectual Property* (HM Treasury 2006) (Gowers Review), paras 5.48–5.49.
[18] Note also the Patents and Plant Variety Rights (Compulsory Licensing) Regulations 2002 (SI 2002/247).
[19] See, eg, Report from the Commission to the European Parliament and the Council, Development and Implications of Patent Law in the Field of Biotechnology and Genetic Engineering, COM(2002) 545 final, 7 October 2002, para 4.1.3; European Group on Ethics in Science and New Technologies, 'Ethical aspects of patenting inventions involving human stem cells' Opinion No 16 (17 May 2002), para 2.9; and the House of Commons Science and Technology Committee, *Human Genetics: The Science and the Consequences*, Third Report (6 July 1995), paras 212–214.

12.13   'Crown use' is a further limitation to a patent right.[20] This can happen when any government department or someone authorised by a government department (in writing) considers that it is in the services of the Crown to use and exploit an invention. Any act which would normally be considered an infringement is not so considered in these circumstances. 'Services of the Crown' includes supply of anything for foreign defence purposes, production or supply of specified drugs or medicines, and such purposes relating to the production or use of atomic energy or research into matter connected therewith as the Secretary of State thinks necessary or expedient.[21] Compensation is payable, however, to the patentee or exclusive licensee on the basis of the loss of profit of the contract that might have arisen for provision of the invention.[22] The Crown or its agents do not need to apply to the Comptroller to take action, but any disputes will be resolved by the courts.[23]

Ownership and compensation

Ownership

12.14   We saw in Chapter 10 that anyone is at liberty to apply for a patent,[24] but who is entitled to be named as the inventor? It is important to know the answer to this because a patent is granted primarily to the inventor or joint inventors,[25] or to someone entitled to the invention by law or agreement, or ultimately a successor of either of these two categories.[26] It is the status of inventor and co-inventor that interests us here. The inventor is entitled to be named in the patent application and resulting patent even if they are not the applicant.[27] Section 7(3) of the 1977 Act states that: 'In this Act "inventor" in relation to an invention means the actual deviser of the invention and "joint inventor" shall be construed accordingly.' The test to determine inventorship is twofold: (1) what is the inventive concept; and (2) who devised that concept?[28]

12.15   You will recall from previous sections that the inventive concept is the kernel of the invention—it is the essential technical heart of the new innovation and its inventor must do more than simply proffer an initial prompt or a mere idea about where to start. That said, it is not necessary to be the one to reduce the invention to practice. If you contribute an idea that consists of the essential elements of a claim—for example, a proposal on the solution and the means to arrive at it—then this would qualify as inventorship.[29]

■ *IDA Ltd and Others v University of Southampton and Others* [2006] RPC 21

This was a dispute about who invented a cockroach trap. The existing art was provided by Professor Howse of Southampton University and involved a trap which worked by luring the insect into a box with bait, whereupon its feet would become contaminated with electrostatic talcum powder. This caused the insect to slip onto fly paper and die. A member of IDA, specialists in magnetic powders, read about the invention and wondered if it would work with magnetic powder—an advantage because it would not lose its 'stickiness'. He shared his idea with Mr Metcalfe in a telephone conversation and the patent in dispute was one subsequently lodged by Mr Metcalfe in which he claimed: 'a composition comprising particles containing or consisting of at least one magnetic material'. It was held: 'This was the sole key to the information in the patent. That key was provided solely by Mr Metcalfe. Putting it another way, insofar as there is anything inventive in the patent, it was provided only by him.' It did not matter that the inventive concept was an idea because the idea provided the entire technical solution (forever-sticky magnetic powder) to the technical problem (the ongoing effectiveness of a cockroach trap).

---

[20] Patents Act 1977, ss 55–58.   [21] Patents Act 1977, s 56(2).   [22] Patents Act 1977, s 57A.
[23] Patents Act 1977, s 58.   [24] Patents Act 1977, s 7(1).   [25] Patents Act 1977, s 7(2)(a).
[26] Patents Act 1977, s 7(2)(b), (c).   [27] Patents Act 1977, s 13.
[28] *Henry Brothers (Magherafelt) Ltd v The Ministry of Defence and the Northern Ireland Office* [1999] RPC 442.
[29] *Stanelco Fibre Optics Ltd's Applications* [2005] RPC 15.

12.16   In a dispute over entitlement to a patent, the question is simply who has an entitlement to claim to be an inventor; each claimant must establish why they have a claim to a proprietary interest in the instant patent and/or why the patentee is not entitled to it if the challenger is seeking to be named as sole inventor.[30]

Co-owners

12.17   Inventions are frequently made up by a combination of multiple features, and if different people have contributed different features towards a unitary invention then each person is considered as a co-inventor.[31]

■ *Staeng Ltd's Patent* [1996] RPC 183

The invention in question had been devised in an incremental fashion by two employees of two separate companies—one providing an initial design, the other providing an idea for improvement. It was held that this was an example of joint invention. The inventive concept lay in the use of a coiled spring to hold a cable to an adaptor—the idea of such a device came from the employee seeking to be named as sole inventor. However, the problem was solved by the other inventor, who also had expertise in the area, unlike the first employee who, it was found, would not have come up with the solution but for the role of the second employee.

12.18   Disputes such as these are resolved primarily on the basis of the evidence which the court is willing to accept. Reliable evidence of what was said, or agreed, or done, is of crucial importance. The most prudent thing to do is to begin a collaborative relationship with a written contract which addresses issues of ownership from the beginning.

12.19   The rights of co-inventors are dealt with by section 36 of the Patents Act 1977, as amended. The guiding principle is that each owner is entitled to an equal, undivided share of the property;[32] an equal share in benefits from the patent; and has an independent right to exploit the invention without the need to consult or involve co-owners.[33] This does not extend, however, to the granting of licences, assignations/ assignments, or mortgages. This requires the consent of all co-owners.[34] Reforms from the European Patent Convention (EPC) 2000 allow owners to apply to amend or revoke their own patent after grant, but in the case of co-owners this must be with the consent of all owners.[35] It is possible, however, to vary some of these rights by agreement, for example that one of the co-owners can grant licences unilaterally. Moreover, the Comptroller has the discretion to vary these provisions if it is thought that to do so would result in a fairer balance of interests.[36] Any disputes over who might have a valid proprietary interest in a patent are similarly determined by the Comptroller in the first instance.[37] This discretion survived a human rights challenge when it was argued before the Court of Appeal in *Derek Hughes v Neil Paxman* that the discretion could not be legitimately exercised to require a co-owner to grant a licence.[38] The court disagreed, pointing out that it could not be the case that the legislator intended the exploitation of patents to be frustrated by deadlock situations. Moreover, there was no breach of human rights as long as the Comptroller acted rationally, fairly, and proportionately in the light of all of the circumstances. The scope of the discretionary power was not so wide as to be arbitrary.[39]

[30]   See *Yeda Research and Development Co Ltd v Rhone-Poulenc Rorer International Holdings Inc and Others* [2008] RPC 1 on seeking to be substituted as the sole inventor.

[31]   It is not enough for one party merely to follow the instructions of another; see *Stanelco Fibre Optics Ltd v Biopress Technology Ltd* [2005] RPC 319.

[32]   Patents Act 1977, s 36(1).   [33]   Patents Act 1977, s 36(2).

[34]   Patents Act 1977, s 36(3)(b). In Scotland this also extends to the granting of a security. See also paras 12.101.

[35]   Patents Act 1977, s 36(3)(a), as amended by Patents Act 2004, s 9.   [36]   Patents Act 1977, s 37(1).

[37]   Patents Act 1977, s 37(1), and Part 7 of the Patents Rules 2007 (as amended) on proceedings heard before the Comptroller. Section 38 of the 1977 Act deals with the transfer of patents and section 8 of the 1977 Act deals with the resolution of questions about entitlement to the patent which arise *before* grant.

[38]   [2006] EWCA Civ 818.

[39]   On the complexities of pursuing ownership in an international context and the associated international private law challenges, see *Innovia Films Ltd v Frito-Lay North America, Inc* [2012] EWHC 790 (Pat).

The employer/employee relationship

12.20   The Patents Act 1977, s 39 says:

(1) Notwithstanding anything in any rule of law, an invention made by an employee shall, as between him and his employer, be taken to belong to his employer for the purposes of this Act and all other purposes if—

  (a) it was made in the course of the normal duties of the employee or in the course of duties falling outside his normal duties, but specifically assigned to him, and the circumstances in either case were such that an invention might reasonably be expected to result from the carrying out of his duties; or

  (b) the invention was made in the course of the duties of the employee and, at the time of making the invention, because of the nature of his duties and the particular responsibilities arising from the nature of his duties he had a special obligation to further the interests of the employer's undertaking.

(2) Any other invention made by an employee shall, as between him and his employer, be taken for those purposes to belong to the employee.

Let's explore the elements of this provision. First, the default position is that inventions created by an employee belong to the employee and this cannot be varied by contract—such a term would be unenforceable.[40] Moreover, no one else who works with an employer, such as a consultant, need worry about their inventions (although this might give rise to problem of co-ownership, see para 12.17). It is important to know, therefore, when someone is an *employee*. This is determined on standard labour/employment law principles[41] and the distinction is made between a contract of service (employee) and a contract of services (consultant or commissioned work).[42] Only in the specific circumstances outlined previously can an employer lay claim to an employee's invention. 'Invention' in this case does not simply mean a patentable invention (that is, one that meets the patentability criteria in this chapter), but it extends to any invention in a broad sense made by an employee and satisfying the criteria laid out earlier in section 39. So, a claim may be made to an invention even if a patent will not, and could not, be sought.

12.21   The provisions apply when an employee has invented something *either* in the course of their normal duties *or* when specific duties are assigned to them and in *both* cases the nature of those duties is such that an invention is the likely result.[43] Moreover, in other contexts when an employee has a *special obligation* to further their employer's interests, then resulting inventions may also be claimed. This class of employee usually includes managers or directors with overarching responsibilities which necessarily encompass inventive activity within a business. The Court of Appeal in *Liffe Administration & Management v Pinkava*[44] ruled on the meaning of 'normal duties' under section 39(1) of the Patents Act 1977 and dismissed an employee's claim to an invention relating to an electronic trading system that he had devised while employed by Liffe. The ruling emphasised that the test under section 39(1)(a) is an objective one and that duties are not only established and set in the terms of the original contract, but may evolve over time as the job changes. It was also stated that the expectations an employer might have that an invention will result from an employee's normal duties should be directly linked to the person and the skills they possess; the reasonableness of the expectation should be judged accordingly. If a person is hired to innovate, it would normally follow that the provisions of section 39(1) would be satisfied.

---

[40] See *Electrolux v Hudson* [1977] RPC 312. See too Patents Act 1977, s 42(2), which makes unenforceable any attempt to derogate from the rights of the employee in respect of his own inventions, and *UK Manual of Patent Practice* (February 2016 as amended), paras 42.03–42.04.

[41] On the nature of the duty of fidelity between employee and employer, see *Helmet Integrated Systems Ltd v Tunnard and Others* [2007] FSR 16.

[42] In the design case of *Ultraframe UK Ltd v Fielding* [2004] RPC 24 (see also para 9.66) it was said that a contract of service is typified by (1) circumstances where the servant has agreed that, in consideration of a wage or other remuneration, he or she would provide their own work and skill in the performance of some service for their master; (2) he or she agreed, expressly or implicitly, that in the performance of that service, they would be subject to the other's control in a sufficient degree to make the other master; and (3) the provisions of the contract were consistent with it being a contract of service. Control is key.

[43] An early decision is *Harris' Patent* [1985] RPC 19, which considered the pre-1977 Act position where this area was governed by the common law.

[44] [2007] RPC 30.

■ *Greater Glasgow Health Board's Application* [1996] RPC 207

A Registrar employed by the health board in the Tennent Research Institute invented an optical spacing device for use with an indirect ophthalmoscope. He conceived this idea while at home and not during his professional duties. His job description stated that his duties were clinical in nature: he had a duty to serve in the out-patient department, and this included casualty, ophthalmic, and general care of in-patients and ophthalmic surgery. His job description also included a number of other functions, which were not described as duties, and which included undergraduate and postgraduate teaching. He was also 'expected to avail himself of the facilities provided' for basic and clinical research. This having been said, his Head of Department did not consider that he was employed to carry out research. The health board argued that because of the very nature of his working environment in a research institute, he was expected to use his experiences of treating patients to produce novel forms of treatment and prevention. The patent was taken in the name of the board and the dispute arose when Dr Montgomery argued that he should be named as sole inventor. It was held that Dr Montgomery should be named as such. It was fallacious to expect that a person with clinical duties and responsibilities towards patients should necessarily be required by his contract to devise novel ways of diagnosing and treating patients. The fact that he was employed within a research institute was not, of itself, determinative of the issue. The focus must be on the terms of the employment contract as they stood, and these clearly revealed that his duties were clinical in nature and not innovative.

12.22   Another relevant factor in this case was that the creation of the invention had nothing to do with the carrying out of his duties. Dr Montgomery was a junior member of staff who spent nearly all of his time treating patients. He made the invention in his own time, he was not working to treat any particular patient or class of patients; indeed, he was concerned with the problem of eye examination generally—the invention could not be reasonably expected to result from his duties.

12.23   The importance of evidence in these cases is illustrated by *Liffe Administration and Management v Pinkava and Another*, which was also discussed in para 12.21. Evidence to the court at first instance[45] showed that the inventions developed by the employee were not part of his normal duties as a product manager employed in the marketing and product management department, but that they did arise directly from a project he was assigned to work on to develop an exchange tradable contract, and this was evidenced by the nature of the initial discussions and subsequent focus of the project. The employee tried to argue that the inventions were ones unlikely to arise from the discharge of his duties, inter alia, because the employer had no history of invention. This was held not to be necessary for section 39(1) to apply, as the employer (any employer?) had a clear interest in new developments and products. It was also relevant from the evidence that the employee was known as an 'ideas man' in the firm and the expectation was that he would be creative in the discharge of his duties. This was confirmed by the Court of Appeal in dismissing the appeal.[46]

Key point on employee invention

- It is not sufficient merely to produce an invention which would assist an employer in tackling the problems which they face in the course of their business or profession. This is an example of an *indirect* invention which, at best, builds on the general experience and stock of knowledge of the individual inventor, *qua* an individual and not *qua* employee. Rather, an invention which is to fall to an employer must result from the workings of an employee *qua* inventor, in other words, when the job of work *directly* requires them to invent or their duties *directly* lead them to invent; all as a *direct* consequence of doing their job of work.

---

[45]   [2006] EWHC 595 (Pat).
[46]   See also *Cinpres Gas Injection Ltd v Melea Ltd* [2008] RPC 17.

12.24   Consider now *Staeng Ltd's Patent* (para 12.17). The circumstances of this dispute involved, inter alia, the question of whether an employee of company H, which was soon to be taken over by company S, could be named as the sole inventor of an invention which was not part of the business of his employer. The invention in suit related to a means of securing an electrical cable sheathing to the body portion of a 'connector backshell adaptor'. Company H was not in the business of backshell adaptors, but rather was concerned with developing products for the cable industry. All technology relating to backshell adaptors had to be bought in from company S. The employee argued that it was not reasonable to imply that an individual's obligations included the making of an invention if that invention was not within the business of the employer. The employer argued that its broader business interests included backshell adaptors and, indeed, it had marketed S's adaptors as though they were its own. The employee's duties involved innovation and the seeking out of novel uses for existing products. It was held that the invention belonged to the employer. The employee had made the invention in the course of his normal duties and the circumstances were such that the invention might reasonably be expected to result from the carrying on of his duties. The intimate connection between the products produced by the employer and the invention meant that the invention was within the broad field of the employer's business. Furthermore, the position of the employee as a senior executive with knowledge and insight into the business's future interests, viz, the merger, meant he had a *special obligation* under section 39(1).

12.25   Factors which might make a difference in these cases therefore include:

- Where was the invention produced (work or home)?
- Was the invention produced during working hours?
- What is the standing of the employee within the employer's hierarchy?
- What are the specific contractual duties and which other duties can reasonably be inferred?
- What role has the employee actually assumed in the discharge of their duties?

 Question

Do you think it is relevant if materials from the workplace are used to create the invention?

12.26   We can easily imagine a situation where an employer might be entitled to an employee's invention, but that the employee's claim to the invention is partial because they have invented the product or process jointly with someone else who is not an employee. In such cases what should the employer do?

12.27   These questions were addressed by the Scottish Court of Session in *Goddin and Rennie's Application*.[47] In this case the patent concerned covers for circular tanks, in particular fish tanks. While the original design was conceived by G in respect of his salmon-rearing business, the design was improved by R, who was commissioned to make the net covers. Initially both contributors were named on the patent application, but a dispute arose and G brought a claim that the patent application should proceed solely in the name of his company, W. The arguments were: first, R's contribution was merely ancillary to the inventive principle, which had been discovered by G. Secondly, even if that were not the case, the contract of services contained an implied term that W was entitled to the exclusive benefit of what R devised in the course of his work. The court held that G was entitled to the patent in his name alone. R's contract was clearly to produce an improved design, but the contract would not make business sense unless it contained an implied term that any improved design was the property of W. This having been said, certain features of the frame for the nets

---

[47]   [1996] RPC 141.

had been suggested by R prior to, and separately from, the contract and as such he was entitled to the benefit of the features introduced by them. As a consequence, while G was entitled to the patent, R was entitled to an irrevocable exclusive licence, with power to sub-license in respect of the features which he had added.

12.28   This ruling in respect of the IP of the commissioned person, and the authorities on which it is based,[48] reflects some of the approaches we have seen in copyright law where there has been recognition of *equitable interests* in respect of commissioned work (see para 3.11). While the starting point is that a commissioned person retains the IPR of that which a person creates, it is also true that it is illogical to enter a contract with someone to create a new entity if there is no underlying assumption that the entity will come within the control of the commissioner. It makes sound sense to read an implied clause into the contract in these circumstances. Note, however, that the law does not specifically recognise equitable interests in the context. The practical approach is that the commissioned person should include an *express* term that any IPRs are to be retained if that is their intention. In practice, of course, it is unlikely that any such term will be accepted. More likely to survive is a term which specifically states that the invention is to be regarded as having been created jointly with licensing or other rights specified accordingly.

Compensation of employees for certain inventions

12.29   Sections 40 and 41 of the Patents Act 1977 provide for a compensation scheme for employees when the provisions of section 39 apply or when they have transferred their patent rights to their employer and the benefit in return is inadequate.[49] These provisions have been reformed over the years to widen the circumstances in which compensation might be paid. Thus section 40(1) now provides:

> Where it appears to the court or the comptroller on an application made by an employee within the prescribed period that—
>
> (a) the employee has made an invention belonging to the employer for which a patent has been granted,
> (b) having regard among other things to the size and nature of the employer's undertaking, the invention or the patent for it (or the combination of both) is of outstanding benefit to the employer, and
> (c) by reason of those facts it is just that the employee should be awarded compensation to be paid by the employer,
>
> the court or the comptroller may award him such compensation of an amount determined under section 41 below.

12.30   Note: compensation can be triggered when the patent *or* the invention *or* both prove to be of outstanding benefit to the employer. Previously, the scheme could only be invoked when the *patent* was of outstanding benefit. Not only was this more difficult to prove, but it necessitated that a patent was granted. As we have seen, even non-patentable inventions can be claimed by employers and even those which are patentable might sometimes be better protected by other means, for example trade secrets (see Chapter 17). This anomaly has now been rectified. Notwithstanding, a serious hurdle still faces the employee because the qualifying threshold remains the same: there must be an *outstanding benefit* to the employer. How do we know when this has happened?

■ *British Steel plc's Patent* [1992] RPC 117

In this case the employer contended that the benefit derived from the employee's invention of a new valve, for use in steel-making, should not be linked to the patented product itself but rather to the extensive development work expended on it by the employer after the application had been filed. This work had been carried out to remove what the Comptroller's hearing called 'major technical obstacles [which] stood in

---

[48] *Bogrich & Shape Machines Ltd's Application*, 4 November 1994, unreported.
[49] S Wolk, 'Remuneration of employee inventors—is there a common European ground? A comparison of national laws on compensation of inventors in Germany, France, Spain, Sweden and the United Kingdom' (2011) 42(3) IIC 272–298.

the way of the deployment of the rotary valve'. Thus, the employer had to incur considerable development costs before any tangible benefit accrued. This argument was, however, rejected by the hearing officer. The employee's claim was refused, however, because benefits had not (yet) flowed to the employer from the grant of the patent. Thus, a real benefit must be shown and not merely the promise of benefit.

12.31   Is this 'just'? Were it otherwise, the paradox would arise whereby the more an employee invention departs from traditional technology the less likely it would ever be that they would receive compensation because of the necessary development costs which would be incurred by the employer.

12.32   Benefit from a patent is readily provable if the employer is in receipt of royalty payments from licensees. If, however, the employer chooses to exploit the invention himself, it becomes harder to prove.

 Discussion point   For answer guidance visit **www.oup.com/uk/brown5e**.

How many reasons can you think of for an increased order book?

■ *GEC's Patent* [1992] RPC 107

The employer obtained a patent for a cockpit display unit which had been invented by their employee for use in military aircraft. The US Air Force placed substantial orders. Unfortunately, contracts could not be fulfilled because units had to be redesigned and tested. Further contracts were placed for non-patented equipment worth $75 million each. In 1986 the employer signed a main contract to supply redesigned equipment based on the patented invention. This contract was worth $72 million. The employee argued that the early sums of $75 million should be regarded as benefits deriving from the possession of a patent over the invention. It was argued that such contracts would not have been agreed but for the initial order based on the patent. It was held that the evidential burden falls on the shoulders of the employee. He was unable to discharge this given the overall size of the firm involved; in relative terms, the figures in question were not 'outstanding'.

■ *Kelly and Another v GE Healthcare Ltd* [2009] RPC 12

This case is the first to award compensation to employees under section 40 of the 1977 Act. Two inventors sought a share of the profits under section 40 as compensation for the invention of a compound used in radioactive imaging which they developed while employed as research scientists. In deciding whether the patents were of 'outstanding benefit' to the company, the court took all circumstances into consideration, including the size and nature of the employer's undertaking, and came to the conclusion that the benefits of the invention went far beyond anything that could normally be expected to arise from the sort of work the employees had undertaken. The benefit was not limited to profits from sales as the resulting patents also protected the business against generic competition and were highly influential in achieving corporate deals. The patents had recently expired, which allowed the court to quantify more exactly the benefit those patents had brought to the employer. Courts had shown themselves unwilling in previous cases to speculate on future benefits that patents might bring, but as that was unnecessary here, this could not bar the award of compensation.[50]

---

[50] See A Odell West, '*Kelly v GE Healthcare Ltd*: employee innovation in health care—deciphering ownership and the alchemy of "outstanding benefit"' (2010) 32(9) EIPR 449 and C Howell, 'Extra compensation for inventive employees: is our system equitable, unbiased and motivating?' [2011] 4 IPQ 371.

> ### What is an 'outstanding benefit'?
>
> (1) Benefit in question must exist at time of employee's application (future possible benefits affect quantum of compensation only).
> (2) 'Outstanding' is much more than 'substantial' and 'valuable'.
> (3) 'Outstanding' must be assessed in the light of all facts and circumstances. Thus, compensation is more likely from a smaller firm than a larger firm. Paradoxically, this is likely to mean that smaller firms will be liable to pay compensation which only larger firms can truly afford.

12.33   The scheme also applies when an employee retains an entitlement to their invention but has assigned it or granted an exclusive licence to their employer and when the benefit under the contract is 'inadequate' and it is 'just' that the employee should be awarded compensation.[51] In cases where the employer has further assigned the rights to another, the Court of Appeal has ruled that the basis of any compensation to be paid is to be calculated on the details of the actual assignee and its actual attributes; that is, there is to be no notional auction of the value of the patent because this could artificially and vastly inflate its potential worth well beyond what an assignee could ever afford.[52]

Question

How would you assess what was 'inadequate' and 'just' in these circumstances? Could you get access to your employer's accounts to see what income had been generated?

12.34   Section 41 of the 1977 Act deals with the amount of compensation to be awarded.[53] This must obviously be decided on a case-by-case basis. The guiding parameters include the following: (1) the aim is to confer a *fair share* of the benefit of the invention and/or the patent; (2) *benefit* includes money and money's worth from exploitation of the invention and/or patent; (3) it is assessed by reference to the following, among other things; (4) nature of the employee's duties and any benefits from the invention; (5) the effort and skill he has displayed; (6) the efforts and skill of others in developing the invention; (7) the effort and skill of the employer in bringing the invention to fruition and market.

Infringement proceedings

12.35   It is all very well to have a range of sophisticated patent rights but these are worthless in the absence of a robust enforcement system. We consider broader issues of enforcement in Chapter 21; here we concentrate on enforcement of patents through infringement proceedings. We have already established that patents are creatures of territorial effect only, and so infringement proceedings in the UK can only be brought with respect to activities within its shores. It is also trite to note that the law is only concerned with acts done during the life of the patent. Infringement proceedings can be brought for any conduct from the date the patent application is published to the end of the patent's term.[54] Those who can bring infringement proceedings include the proprietor of the patent, co-proprietors,[55] and exclusive licensees.[56]

---

[51]   Patents Act 1977, s 40(2)(d).

[52]   See *Shanks v Unilever plc* [2011] RPC 12. For comment, J Pila, '"Sewing the fly buttons on the statute": employee inventions and the employment context' (2012) 32(2) OJLS 265.

[53]   Amended by the Patents Act 2004, s 10(3).

[54]   Albeit that the right cannot be enforced until the patent is actually granted, see the Patents Act 1977, s 69.

[55]   Each co-proprietor can do any act independently with respect to the invention which would otherwise be an infringement: Patents Act 1977, s 66, and each can bring independent infringement proceedings without the consent of the others subject to the proviso that co-owners are made parties to the proceedings, s 66(2).

[56]   An exclusive licensee has the same right as the proprietor to bring infringement actions; see Patents Act 1977, s 67(1).

12.36   The first thing to note when you read the cases is that an action for infringement is often met with a counterclaim that the patent is invalid and should be revoked. We therefore deal with revocation in the next section at para 12.72. This possibility means that a patent is at risk throughout its term. It is a strategic question whether it is worth bringing infringement proceedings when this might result in the complete extinguishing of your property right in the long run.

12.37   If proceedings are brought, it ends up being an extremely costly business. The Gowers Review estimated, for example, that a firm challenging a patent can expect to pay £750,000 for a simple case, and if one loses, the costs of the other side could bring the total to over £1.5 million.[57]

12.38   This section is divided into two parts. In the first part we consider the grounds for infringement actions and the types of conduct which qualify. In the second part we consider how the courts approach the interpretation of patent claims because it is in this interpretation that we discover the fine lines between legitimate and illegitimate conduct with respect to patented inventions.

 Exercise

Have a look at *Warner Lambert v Generics (UK) t/a Mylan* [2018] UKSC 56 and the list of those involved at the start, and para 121. Reflect on what this suggests for the importance of patents and infringement, now and as you work through the chapter.

What counts as patent infringement?

12.39   Article 64(3) EPC 2000 makes it clear that infringement proceedings are to be dealt with by national law. In the UK, the principal infringing acts are laid out in section 60(1) and 60(2) of the Patents Act 1977.

> 60(1) Subject to the provision of this section, a person infringes a patent for an invention if, but only if, while the patent is in force, he does any of the following things in the United Kingdom in relation to the invention without the consent of the proprietor of the patent, that is to say—
>
> > (a) where the invention is a product, he makes, disposes of, offers to dispose of, uses or imports the product or keeps it whether for disposal or otherwise;
> > (b) where the invention is a process, he uses the process or he offers it for use in the United Kingdom when he knows, or it is obvious to a reasonable person in the circumstances, that its use there without the consent of the proprietor would be an infringement of the patent;
> > (c) where the invention is a process, he disposes of, offers to dispose of, uses or imports any product obtained directly by means of that process.

12.40   So, as we can see, it is important to know what kind of invention we are dealing with because what counts as infringement depends on this and, sometimes, on the knowledge of the alleged infringer. Note, however, that in the context of a product there is no knowledge requirement. This means that even the so-called innocent infringer can be liable if they carry out any of the acts detailed in section 60(1)(a), which deals with product inventions or in section 60(1)(c), which deals with process inventions which result in a product. It is irrelevant whether the infringer knew of the patent or of the lack of owner consent. This is referred to as 'absolute' liability.[58] Mental issues can arise, however, in respect of this form of direct infringement of what is still often termed a Swiss claim (see para 11.43) as this scheme 'was not framed with such purpose-limited process claims in mind'.[59]

---

[57] Gowers Review, para 3.21. For a global overview from 2010, see WIPO, 'IP litigation costs' www.wipo.int/export/sites/www/wipo_magazine/en/pdf/2010/wipo_pub_121_2010_01.pdf.

[58] *Merrell Dow v Norton* [1996] RPC 76 per Lord Hoffmann at 92.

[59] *Warner Lambert v Generics (UK) t/a Mylan* [2018] UKSC 56, paras 63, 187.

12.41   In *Warner Lambert v Actavis Group (t/a NHS England)*,[60] Warner Lambert had a patent for the use of pregalbin for treating pain or neuropathic pain, and they marketed a product for use for several purposes, including treatment of pain. Under prescription rules, pharmacists could deliver a bioequivalent product if pregalbin is named, in the prescription. The Court of Appeal held that the 'for' in the patent meant that there must be a mental element in assessing infringement. The 'for', in this context, could not mean 'suitable for'. Further, an argument for a subjective test on the part of the manufacturer of the bioequivalent was rejected; the manufacturer must know or reasonably foresee the intentional use of it by the end user for the relief of pain.[61] In another dispute relating to pregalbin in the Supreme Court, there were some differing views, although there was an awareness that their remarks were *obiter* and of their possible impact on different cases.

12.42   Lord Mance said:[62]

> [i]t may be going too far in favour of generic manufacturers to suggest as an absolute rule that a generic product, prepared, presented and put on the market, must always be viewed in isolation by reference only to its own packaging and instructions, and without regard to the realities or of the market for which it is prepared and into which it is being released.

Two judges found that intention was irrelevant, and the sole issue is whether the product as it emerges from the manufacturing process, including any information accompanying it, is suitable for the uses which is the subject of the patent; one judge considered that it depended on the objective appearance and characteristics of the product as prepared, presented, and put on the market; however, in rare cases the context may make it obvious that this should not be taken at face value and it may be that the generic manufacturer should positively exclude use for the purpose the subject of the patent; and two judges considered that the question was whether the alleged infringer subjectively intended to target the market which was the subject of the patent.[63]

 Question

Can we justify such a draconian approach to liability in most cases, and such an uncertain one regarding so called Swiss claims?

12.43   Let us now consider each of the infringing behaviours within section 60 in turn.

Making the invention

12.44   It is clearly an infringement to make copies of someone else's existing invention (deliberately or otherwise subject to the 'Swiss'-related point noted in para 12.40), but what is the position if you buy the original item under patent and then modify it or repair it? This question was considered by the House of Lords in *United Wire Ltd v Screen Repair Services (Scotland) Ltd*,[64] which involved mesh screen assemblies used in sifting and filtering machines. The defendants tried to enter the market by selling reconditioned versions of the plaintiffs' screens which had been stripped down and had new mesh applied. They then tried to argue that this was mere 'repair' and not 'making' and so outside the scope of section 60(1). It was held that while 'genuine repair' is a legitimate activity, this conduct went far beyond and was equivalent to reproducing an infringing assembly. The concepts of 'repair' and 'making' are entirely distinct in patent law, with the latter involving some form of manufacture. The right to repair is not an implied licence, but rather the residual right left over once the parameters of patent protection have been demarcated by the operation of section 60. In the instant case, the disassembly of the product was so extreme that it effectively ceased to exist and its reconstitution with new elements was in effect a new infringing manufacture.

---

[60] [2015] EWCA Civ 556.   [61] ibid, paras 113–128.
[62] *Warner Lambert v Generics (UK) t/a Mylan* [2018] UKSC 56, para 217.
[63] ibid, para 15(3), 67–86, 137–74, 197–218.   [64] [2001] RPC 24.

12.45   The Supreme Court clarified this area in *Schutz (UK) Ltd v Werit UK Ltd.*[65] The case involved a dispute over alleged infringement of a patent on large container devices for transportation of goods that included a strong frame capable of supporting rough treatment and considerable weight, into which were inserted 'bottles'—being plastic containers that were protected by the frame but which necessarily had to be changed with relative frequency because of damage or contamination. The question was whether the provision of replacement bottles by companies not holding the patent was an infringement. The judge at first instance had proposed a 'whole inventive concept' test whereby he suggested that in considering infringement under this heading the court must 'ask whether, when the part in question is removed, what is left embodies the whole of the inventive concept of the claim'. This was rejected by the Court of Appeal, but the Supreme Court upheld the finding of non-infringement. The Supreme Court confirmed that the meaning of 'making' necessarily is context specific, and that any approach adopted by the courts involves ordinary understandable meaning and requires a careful weighing of factors. In the instant case it was relevant to ask whether the bottle was 'such a subsidiary part of the patented article that its replacement did not involve "making" a new article'. On balance, it was held that it was, being a free-standing and replaceable component that had no connection to the inventive concept as described in the patent claims. It did no substantial work to the essential features of the claimed invention.

Disposing of, offering to dispose of, or using the invention

12.46   Manifestly it is not an infringement of a patent for someone who has bought an example of an invention to sell it on as a piece of personal property—this is another example of the residual rights that the purchaser enjoys; moreover, attempts by a patent proprietor to prevent the sale and circulation of goods that they have placed on the market themselves will be faced with challenges under European Union law because the principle of exhaustion of rights will apply, as will the principle of free movement of goods (see Chapter 19). Rather, this provision concerns the commercialisation of infringing copies of an invention, and must include, at least, selling.[66]

Importing the invention

12.47   Here we are concerned with the activities of someone who imports an invention in the course of their trade, for example with a view to selling them on. A mere carrier or someone who arranges the importation on behalf of the owner of the goods is not considered to be a direct infringer because they have no legal or beneficial interest in those goods.[67] This is true even if this person has sold the goods to the now owner outside the UK.[68] It is possible for two or more parties involved in the importation business to be jointly liable as joint tortfeasors, but this requires a common design or concerted action on all parts. The mere supplying of goods outside the jurisdiction for sale within the jurisdiction is not constitutive of joint tortfeasorship. Nor is it illegal to pass on information to domestic regulatory authorities on behalf of another party who has an intention to receive approval to sell versions of the invention on the domestic market. This does not make the third party complicit in the seller's commercial venture.[69] In keeping with the fragmented territorial nature of patent protection, the European Court of Justice ruled that it is not possible to bring patent infringement proceedings in one state against a group of allegedly infringing parties in various different states, *even if* those parties belong to the same corporate group and *even if* they have been acting in an identical or similar manner with respect to infringing activity.[70]

---

[65]   [2013] UKSC 16; [2013] 2 All ER 177.
[66]   *Kalman and Another v PCL Packaging (UK) Ltd and Another* [1982] FSR 406.
[67]   *Sabaf SpA v MFI Furniture Centres Ltd* [2004] UKHL 45.
[68]   Compare the trade mark case of *Waterford Wedgwood plc v David Nagli Ltd* [1998] FSR 92, in which the seller imported the goods into the UK while still retaining ownership rights. This constituted infringement.
[69]   *Generics (UK) Ltd v H Lundbeck A/S* [2006] EWCA Civ 1261; aff'd [2009] UKHL 12.
[70]   Case C-539/03 *Roche Nederland BV and Others v Primus and Another* [2006] All ER (D) 186 (Jul), OJ C 224 of 16.09.2006, 1.

Keeping the invention

12.48   Once again, we are concerned here with acts done in the course of trade; acting as a mere custodian of goods does not amount to 'keeping' within the terms of the Act which has been interpreted to mean 'keeping in stock' with a view to furthering business ends. In *McDonald and Another v Graham*[71] the invention in question was promotional 'Z cards', which were designed to fold out to show publicity material and to fold back down to the size of a credit card. Despite instructions to destroy any remaining copies in his possession, a business associate of the patentee was found to have a stock on his business premises. His argument that these were for private or experimental use did not hold on the evidence. Rather, he was 'keeping them in stock for the purposes of his business in order to make use of them as and when it would be beneficial to him to do so'. In contrast there was no finding of 'keeping' in *Smith, Kline and French Labs Ltd v Harbottle*[72] when a quantity of the drug Cimetidine was shipped through Heathrow on its way to Nigeria and held in a British Airways' bonded warehouse under the custodianship of Harbottle. It was held that this was not an example of 'keeping' under the statutory provision. The *Oxford English Dictionary* reveals 26 nuanced meanings of this word and the correct approach for the court was to identify the mischief to be avoided and interpret the term accordingly. If the mere holding of material in a warehouse was intended to be caught by this law it would have been expressed in far stronger terms.[73]

12.49   Section 60(1)(c) (discussed in para 12.40 in relation to the mental element) confirms that a patent over a process gives control over any products derived from that process. This can be a useful tool if, say, the process is performed outside the jurisdiction but the end products are imported into the UK—infringement proceedings could still be brought. The caveat, however, is found in the specific wording of the subsection when it talks of 'any product obtained *directly* by means of that process'.

■ *Pioneer Electronics Capital Inc v Warner Music Manufacturing Europe GmbH* [1997] RPC 757

This case involved a patented process for manufacturing CDs. The rival company's imported versions of the product certainly seemed to involve the process, but had they been 'directly' obtained? It was held that the question fell to be decided by reference to Article 64(2) EPC, the terminology of which had its origin in German law. The German authorities were consistent in their approach, taking 'directly' (*unmittelbar*) to refer to the product with which the process ended. It was not correct to say that the finished disc was an identical copy of the master. The allegedly infringing devices in the instant case differed in material ways from the patented process, notably for having gone through three further stages of production. A new and different product emerged from each stage. Could this still be 'directly obtained'? The Court of Appeal used the expression 'without intermediary', implying, perhaps, that the result should be immediate and precluding any possibility of further processing. But the Patent Court has considered the issue in 2005 and raised the possibility from German jurisprudence that it is not the number of intermediary stages which is important, but the question of whether they are material to the identity of the product—only if it emerges with the same identity as the invention will there be infringement.[74]

Indirect infringement

12.50   These are all so far examples of *direct* infringement which involve direct dealings with the invention itself. Section 60(2) deals with indirect or contributory infringement. It states:

> a person . . . also infringes a patent for an invention if, while the patent is in force and without the consent of the proprietor, he supplies or offers to supply in the United Kingdom a person . . . with any of the means relating

---

[71]   [1994] RPC 407.   [72]   [1980] RPC 363.

[73]   This is also a more accurate reflection of the sense in which the term is employed in the Community Patent Convention, Art 29(a), and the two instruments should be read in tandem where possible.

[74]   *Halliburton Energy Services Inc v Smith International and Others* [2005] EWHC 1623 (Pat).

to an essential element of the invention, for putting the invention into effect when he knows, or it is obvious to a reasonable person in the circumstances, that those means are suitable for putting, and are intended to put, the invention into effect in the United Kingdom.

12.51   The important issues are well illustrated in the case of *Menashe Business Mercantile Ltd and Another v William Hill Organisation Ltd*,[75] which also tells us something about what is meant by infringement occurring in the UK. The case involved an online gaming system linked to a central computer in the Caribbean. Customers were sent software on CDs which allowed their home computers to communicate with the host computer. The patentees owned an interactive gaming system with a host computer that operated in a similar fashion to that of the defendants, but could this system be infringed when the defendants' computer was offshore? Moreover, could the supply of CDs to British customers amount to supply of the means for putting the invention into effect? It was held that the alleged infringers' host computer was 'used' in the UK by customers in a very real sense and it did not matter that it was physically located abroad. The key issue was whether persons in the UK had been supplied with the means of implementing the invention, and this was so through the supply of the CDs which allowed access to the host computer and so to the entire online gaming system. The supply of the CDs in the UK would be taken as intended to put the invention into effect and the patent was infringed.

12.52   The classic example of contributory infringement is the supply of kits for an invention which are assembled at a later date. Clearly, if you provide all of the necessary elements of an invention you are supplying the 'essential element' of the invention. But section 60(3) provides that if you merely provide 'staple commercial products' which someone else takes and puts together into an infringing device or apparatus, you may not be liable for infringement, for example if you merely provide the nuts and bolts and electrical circuits. For contributory infringement your level of knowledge, or indeed intention to be complicit, are relevant factors in whether infringement proceedings could be brought or would succeed.[76] The relevant intention is that of the end user and not the supplier, as such.[77] Notwithstanding, a 'reasonable person' approach to what is known and likely to be understood is adopted by the courts to infer the necessary contributory infringement. Thus, in *KCI Licensing Inc and Others v Smith & Nephew plc and Others*[78] a supplier of a canister for use in patented wound treatment that involved 'clamp means' to prevent the escape of liquid was held to have infringed the patent, even though no clamps were supplied or any suggestion made about use of the canister by the supplier. This was so because it was obvious to a person in the hospital environment how the canister would be used and the necessary clamps were easily available.[79]

 Question

What counts as 'staple commercial products'?

12.53   In *Warner Lambert v Actavis* discussed in para 12.41, the Court of Appeal commented that an invention may be put into effect if pregalbin is manufactured by one person who supplies it to another, who then intentionally uses it. This, together with the knowledge requirement, could lead to indirect infringement. The Court of Appeal allowed the claim to proceed to trial and considered that this could be consistent with decisions in the Netherlands and Germany.[80] The (different) Supreme Court pregalbin decision (*Warner Lambert v Generics (t/a Mylan)*[81] supported the approach taken in *Menashe* (see para 12.51). There was

[75] [2003] 1 All ER 279; [2003] 1 WLR 1462.   [76] Patents Act 1977, s 60(2) and (3).

[77] *Grimme v Scott* [2010] EWCA 1110, followed in *Actavis UK Ltd v Eli Lilly* [2015] EWCA Civ 555.   [78] [2010] EWCA Civ 1260.

[79] For a discussion of the principles relevant to an assessment of damages in indirect infringements, see *Fabio Perini SpA v LPC Group plc* [2012] EWHC 911 (Ch).

[80] *Warner Lambert v Actavis Group (t/a NHS England* [2015] EWCA Civ 556, paras 136–138. Note also Supreme Court *Warner Lambert* pregalbin decision (see para 12.41), when the court was willing to take a different approach.   [81] [2018] UKSC 56 (see para 12.84).

disagreement, in *obiter* remarks, as to whether both upstream and downstream activity could infringe and whether the protection in the purpose limited patents would be narrower than for other patents.[82]

> **Key points on infringing acts**
>
> • There must be a infringing act within the list in the Patents Act.
>
> • The focus is on the activity—intention and knowledge are, in the main, irrelevant. Remember them for contributory infringement.
>
> • There are battles regarding the interpretation of all acts which can constitute infringement and there are particular complexities regarding repairs, kits, and purpose-limited patents.

Interpretation of patent claims

12.54   Even if there is a relevant act, in the UK, during the term of the patent, the question of whether there is infringement is far from straightforward. There might be a 'direct hit', a 100 per cent copy (knowingly or otherwise). But a rival may have produced their own version of an invention aimed at the same technical problem which solves it in similar technical ways, perhaps with similar features—but is not identical. How do we know if these differences—often termed variants—can still infringe a patent? This brings us to the complex question of *interpretation and construction of patent claims*. We have already considered the importance of careful drafting of claims in Chapter 10, and we have made the point that it is imperative to choose the language of claims carefully because this will delineate the nature, breadth, scope of any power granted, and validity as against prior art and the common general knowledge. We now turn to consider the rules that apply when these claims have to be interpreted.

> **Exercise**
>
> Before embarking on this, look back to Chapter 11 to the discussion point after para 11.25. Refresh your memory on the horns of the dilemma (between infringement and validity), and see how your scenario would fare in the evolving tests about to be set out.

12.55   It is probably in the realm of interpretation and construction that EPC 1973 brought most changes to the law in the UK. Article 69(1) EPC 1973 provided that 'The extent of the protection conferred by a European patent or a European patent application shall be determined by the terms of the claims', and the drawings and description shall also be used to interpret the claims. This remains unchanged in EPC 2000 and its UK equivalent is found in section 125 of the Patents Act 1977. Article 69 has, however, been accompanied by a Protocol on Interpretation of Article 69 because a variety of approaches were used around Europe at the time the EPC was drafted. The Protocol is designed to provide guidance to national courts on how to tackle interpretation in a uniform fashion that is in keeping with the spirit of the Convention. That spirit is grounded in the Continental legal tradition, which favours a *purposive approach* to interpretation; that is, one that seeks to give effect to the underlying reasons for the particular legal provision.

12.56   This posed a challenge for the UK, which had a very different tradition and was inclined to adopt a *literal approach* to claim interpretation; that is, to ask what is the literal meaning of the words used. What we have seen, then, in the past quarter-century or so, is a shift of perspective among the judiciary in the UK jurisdictions in an attempt to accommodate a more purposive stance.[83] It is a matter of ongoing discussion

---

[82]   ibid, paras 88, 135, 187.
[83]   For an example of purposive interpretation in action, see, eg, *Convatec Ltd v Smith & Nephew Healthcare Ltd* [2011] EWHC 2039 (Pat), [2012] RPC 9.

as to how well they have fared. This process actually began before Article 69 and its Protocol came about, as we see at paras 12.57.ff, but for the sake of completeness here are the principal provisions of the Protocol as embodied in EPC 2000.

Protocol on Interpretation of Article 69 EPC—Article 1

Article 69 should not be interpreted as meaning that the extent of the protection conferred by a European patent is to be understood as that defined by the strict, literal meaning of the wording used in the claims, the description and drawings being employed only for the purpose of resolving an ambiguity found in the claims.

Nor should it be taken to mean that the claims serve only as a guideline and that the actual protection conferred may extend to what, from a consideration of the description and drawings by a person skilled in the art, the patent proprietor has contemplated.

On the contrary, it is to be interpreted as defining a position between these extremes which combines a fair protection for the patent proprietor with a reasonable degree of legal certainty for third parties.

12.57   This clearly eschews a literal approach (which is thought to be too narrow), but equally it does not give carte blanche to discover a patentee's true purpose or intentions (which is thought to be too broad). The expectation is that a middle course should be steered; one which seeks both certainty and fairness of outcome. It is by no means an easy task and helps to explain why patent interpretation is a complex business. It is important that we begin by laying out the parameters of Article 69 and its Protocol because, as Lord Hoffmann indicated in *Kirin-Amgen v Hoechst Marion Roussel Ltd*,[84] these embody the only compulsory question in claim interpretation, namely, 'What would the person skilled in the art have understood the patentee to have used the language of the claim to mean?' Everything else—that is, any approaches that have been developed over the years (see paras 12.60ff) are mere guidance towards an answer to this question. This is still the case. As will be seen, there have been several landmark cases in this area, as the directions of courts have changed. A valuable starting point remains a seminal House of Lords' ruling which sets out, both factually and legally, the issues which pervade patent construction and interpretation.

■ *Catnic Components Ltd v Hill and Smith* Ltd [1982] RPC 183 (HL)

Catnic were the proprietors of a patent in respect of steel lintels of considerable commercial success. The defendants decided to enter the field and to copy Catnic's lintels. Catnic served a writ on the defendants for patent infringement and as a result the latter changed the design of their lintels by slanting the rear support member at 6°–8° from the vertical, compared to that of the plaintiffs which was perpendicular to the base (see Figures 12.1 and 12.2). Claim 1 of the patent required that the rear support member 'extend vertically'. The question therefore arose as to whether the new lintels made by the defendants infringed the patent of the plaintiffs. This would not be so on a literal interpretation of the words used.

It was held that:

- The patent had been infringed. A literal interpretation of the wording of claims in a patent is not the correct approach to adopt when interpreting claims unless this is clearly the intention of the patentee. The English tradition of applying a 'pith-and-marrow' perspective was no longer appropriate.[85] A purposive rather than literal approach to interpretation is appropriate.

- The effect of the angulation of the rear support member was negligible as regards the load-bearing capacity of the lintel. At an angle of 6° the reduction is only 0.6 per cent. At 8° the reduction is 1.2 per cent. In other words, this had no material effect on how the lintel worked.

---

[84] [2005] RPC 9.
[85] The 'pith-and-marrow' approach was invented by Lord Cairns in *Clark v Adie* (1877) 2 App Cas 315 at 320 and involved a rather vague approach of stripping the invention down by the removal of 'immaterial' or 'non-essential' features or integers to deter what, if anything, the infringer had taken.

- The question to be asked in each case is as follows: would persons with practical knowledge and experience of the kind of work in which the invention is intended to be used understand that strict compliance with the particular descriptive word or phrase appearing in the claim was intended by the patentee to be an essential requirement of the invention so that *any* variant would fall outside the monopoly claimed, even though it could have no material effect upon the way the invention worked?

- The question is to be answered in the negative only when it would be apparent to any reader skilled in the art that a particular descriptive word or phrase used in a claim cannot have been intended by a patentee, who was also skilled in the art, to exclude minor variations which, to the knowledge of both them and the readers to whom the patent is addressed, could have no material effect upon the way in which the invention worked.

- In this case no plausible reason was advanced why any rational patentee should want to place so narrow a limitation on his invention. To do so would render their monopoly worthless for all practical purposes.[86]

Figure 12.1 Claimant's lintel

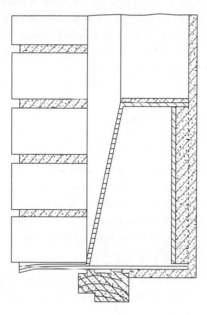

Figure 12.2 Defendant's lintel

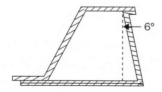

---

[86]   cf *Verathon Medical (Canada) Ltd v Aircraft Medical Ltd* [2011] CSOH 19.

12.58   The decision has had a considerable role to play in changing the way in which patents function and influencing how patents are seen, even though, as will be seen, there have been many subsequent leading cases. It was no longer possible (as it was pre-*Catnic*) to make minor changes in a product or process in an attempt to evade the terms of the monopoly. Improvements in efficiency or speed of operation will not necessarily lead to a patentable invention, and they will infringe an existing patent if the essential idea embodied in the patent remains unchanged. By the same token, it does not follow that a purposive approach is necessarily more generous to the patentee. It is contingent on what the skilled person would consider the purpose to be, and this may be fairly narrow in scope.[87]

12.59   *Catnic* was a movement towards bringing the UK into line with the approaches of the EPO and other European Continental patent courts, which apply a purposive interpretation to patents as a matter of course.[88] This does not, however, mean that we had achieved consistency across Europe—although courts are ever anxious to argue that this has been done.[89]

12.60   The case which illustrates this all too well, and which put an important gloss on the *Catnic* decision, is *Improver Corporation v Remington Consumer Products Ltd*.[90] Again, although case law has moved on, this case still provides valuable context for the interpretation and construction debate. Litigation was conducted on the same matter in both England and Germany. The dispute concerned an electronic hair-removing device for women called the 'Epilady'. The device functioned through the use of a high-speed, rotating, arc-shaped spring which plucked hair from the skin. The alleged infringing device—the 'Smooth & Silky'—performed the same function by the use of a high-speed, rotating, arc-shaped synthetic rubber rod into which were cut slits which captured the hairs. In England, the court applied *Catnic*. It came to the conclusion that the patent had not been infringed: although the variant made no material difference to the way in which the invention worked, and that to adopt the rubber rod was obvious to a person skilled in the art, the fact that the words of the relevant patent claim referred specifically to a 'helical spring' and made no mention of any other mechanism for working the invention meant that the interpretation of the term 'helical spring' could not be stretched to include a rubber rod. In the equivalent German decision, the court came to the opposite conclusion. This is a classic example of the problems which can arise in patent interpretation and of the challenges of enforcing patents in parallel actions. The German court was satisfied that the patent was infringed because of the lack of material difference and the obviousness of replacing the spring with a rubber rod. It saw no reason to dwell on the actual words of the patent.

12.61   This is the issue of *equivalents* to a patented invention. That is, although they may differ in appearance, form, or even certain technical features, there can be infringement if they amount, in essence, to the embodiment of the same inventive concept and the modifications do not bring about a material change in the way the variant works. Note, however, that while it is acceptable in the UK to talk of these variants as 'equivalents', this is not to be confused with the idea of a *doctrine of equivalents*, which embodies a particular test for infringement, and is often used as a shorthand to refer to the approach in the United States.[91] The concern with the US doctrine of equivalents is that it has been interpreted to extend protection to things beyond the boundaries of the claims which perform substantially the same function in substantially the same way

[87] As to what and how much the skilled reader can be expected to know about the law and practice of the patent system, see *Virgin Atlantic Airways Ltd v Premium Aircraft Interiors UK Ltd* [2009] EWCA Civ 1062.

[88] The same purposive approach is employed in Scotland; see *Trunature Ltd v Scotnet (1974) Ltd and Others* [2006] CSOH 114.

[89] For example, the House of Lords in *Kirin-Amgen Inc v Hoechst Marion Roussel Ltd* [2005] RPC 9 took the view that the purposive approach in *Catnic* is 'precisely in accordance with the Protocol', para 48. See further P England, 'Towards a single pan-European standard—common concepts in UK and continental European patent law: Part 1: scope of patent protection and inventive concept' (2010) 32(5) EIPR 195.

[90] [1990] FSR 181.

[91] As Lord Hoffmann said in *Kirin-Amgen Inc v Hoechst Marion Roussel Ltd* [2005] RPC 9, para 37: 'it is frankly acknowledged that it allows the patentee to extend his monopoly beyond the claims'. See *Graver Tank & Manufacturing Co Inc v Linde Air Products Co* 339 US 605 at 607 (1950). See also J Brinkhof, 'Is there a European doctrine of equivalence?' (2002) 33 IIC 911.

to obtain the same result.[92] This is precisely what *Catnic* set out to avoid—it is the claims which delimit the scope of the power conferred by the patent, nothing more, and it is bad policy to allow this to extend beyond the scope of claims as these have been drafted. Indeed, the courts of the UK jurisdictions have been generally very wary of discussion of equivalents. Hoffmann J's Improver Questions[93] can be depicted as shown in Figure 12.3.

Figure 12.3 The Improver Questions

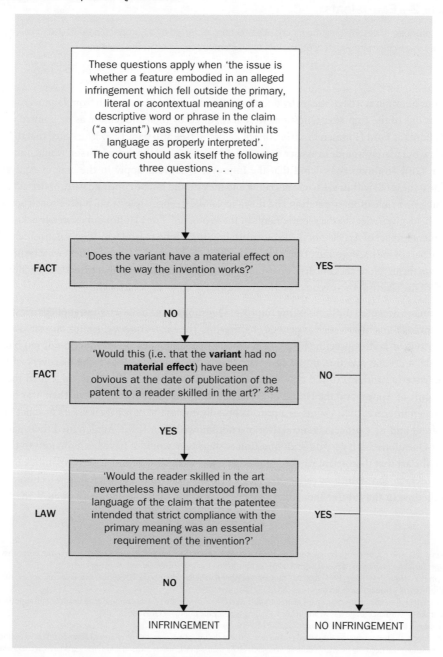

[92] *Festo Corp v Shoketsu Kinzoku Kogyo Kabushiki Co Ltd* 535 US 722 (2002)—US Supreme Court upholding existing approach.
[93] Also known as the Protocol Questions: *Wheatley v Drillsafe Ltd* [2001] RPC 133 at 142.

12.62 Under the Improver Questions, then, the important issue was to consider the language of the claims as these are drafted in the specification.[94]

12.63 The next twist came when EPC 2000 added a new Article 2 to the Protocol on Interpretation of Article 69 thus:

> ## Article 2—Equivalents
> For the purpose of determining the extent of protection conferred by a European patent, due account shall be taken of any element which is equivalent to an element specified in the claims.

12.64 The obvious question is what is meant by 'due account' and did the UK approach from *Improver* conform?[95] The limitations of the Improver Questions were recognised by their progenitor, as he pointed out in the House of Lords as Lord Hoffman in *Kirin-Amgen v Hoechst* (see also para 12.57): he stated that they are not a rule of law, but merely a guide to assist a court in determining what the skilled person would understand.[96] Moreover, Lord Hoffman considered that the Improver Questions apply in the case of equivalents to determine if these fall within the scope of claims, and they should not be confused with, or detract from, the overarching principle of interpretation laid down in *Catnic* the principle of purposive construction. This, the court held, gives effect to the requirements of the Protocol.[97] Lord Hoffmann expressly acknowledged the imminent impact of Article 2 of the Protocol, stating 'there is no reason why [equivalence] cannot be an important part of the background of facts known to the skilled man which would affect what he understood the claims to mean'. Note: the concern is to avoid any concept of equivalence that extends protection beyond the limits of the claims;[98] there is no objection to the idea of equivalence as such.

12.65 Lord Hoffmann accepted the limits of the Improver Questions most notably when applied to fast-moving, high-technology inventions such as genetic engineering. The *Kirin-Amgen* dispute concerned artificially made versions of erythropoietin (EPO)—a hormone that stimulates the production of red blood cells in the body. A crucial question in the case was what is the invention? Was it the discovery of the EPO gene sequence (a product) or the new means to make it (a process)? The trial judge held the former, but the Court of Appeal and the House of Lords opted for the latter. The problem, then, was how could Kirin-Amgen interpret their claims to a process broadly enough to cover their rival's product produced by a different and new process (gene activation) not known when Kirin-Amgen filed their patent? The Improver Questions ask a very difficult question at stage two: would it have been obvious to the person skilled in the art that the variant worked in the same way as the invention? Unless we imbue this person with considerable foresight, how can we expect them to envisage how a completely new technology would work sometime in the future? Indeed, it may not be obvious that it would work at all.[99] The Improver

---

[94] Contrast this with *Kastner v Rizla and Another* [1995] RPC 585. where the Court of Appeal seemed to take the purposive approach several stages further, with interpretation at a general level of abstraction leading to a conclusion of infringement.

[95] Note, in *PLG Research v Ardon* [1995] RPC 287 the Court of Appeal doubted whether the UK approach was in conformity with interpretation of the Protocol in other European countries, especially Germany.

[96] See *Warheit and Another v Olympia Tools Ltd and Another* [2002] EWCA Civ 1161 for an example of an unsuccessful appeal which tried to argue that the first instance judge was wrong in law for failing to apply the Improver Questions.

[97] *Kirin-Amgen Inc v Hoechst Marion Roussel Ltd* [2005] RPC 9, para 48.

[98] The essence of the test is whether the skilled person can perform the invention over the entire area of claimed invention without undue burden and without the need for inventive skill; see *Novartis AG v Johnson & Johnson Medical Ltd* [2010] EWCA Civ 1039 and *Sandvik Intellectual Property AB v Kennametal UK Ltd* [2011] EWHC 3311 (Pat), [2012] RPC 23.

[99] Lord Hoffmann suggested in passing that a better way to ask the second question would be to follow the German approach and ask if the variant solves the problem underlying the invention by means which have the same technical effect, *Kirin-Amgen Inc v Hoechst Marion Roussel Ltd* [2005] RPC 9, para 75. This is certainly in keeping with the underlying rationale of patent protection in Europe.

Questions did not help in such cases,[100] and instead Lord Hoffmann fell back on the general principle: 'The question is always what the person skilled in the art would have understood the patentee to be using the language of the claim to mean.' On this basis, the court held that the skilled person would not have understood the claims to be sufficiently general to encompass the future technology of gene activation. Note: this is not to say that the skilled person cannot foresee future developments; it is to state that the claims must be able to encompass new developments within their original terms. Conversely, if the claims do cover the new innovation, then an action for infringement will still succeed even if the new variant is inventive in its own right.

12.66   Doubts of this kind about the limits of the Improver Questions had already been raised in other cases by the Court of Appeal.[101] The Improver Questions could be helpful, however, when inventions and modifications deal with figures, measurements, and angles, as in *Catnic*, because these are measurable differences. In *Smith and Nephew v ConvaTec Technologies*[102] the Court of Appeal applied the *Kirin-Amgen* approach in respect of numerical range in claims (1–25), finding that such claims should be treated the same as any other claims. As for other cases, the House of Lords had this to say in *Kirin-Amgen*:[103]

> No doubt there will be patent lawyers who are dismayed at the notion that the Protocol questions do not provide an answer in every case. They may feel cast adrift on a sea of interpretative uncertainty. But that is the fate of all who have to understand what people mean by using language.

The distinct impression conveyed by the House of Lords at this point was that the UK approach at this time was that it conformed to Article 2 of the Protocol.

12.67   Against this backdrop, a new approach was taken when the Supreme Court reconsidered patents, interpretation, and construction in *Actavis v Eli Lilly*[104] in 2017. This involved use of pemetrexed disodium, with vitamin B12, to make a medicament for treatment of cancer. A key issue was whether 'pemetrexed disodium' covered any forms of pemetrexed (a chemical known to have therapeutic effects on cancerous tumours) which were soluable, or only this specific chemical compound. Lord Neuberger, with whom the other judges agreed, considered that as a matter of ordinary language, it was clear that the claim only covered 'pemetrexed disodium'.[105] In deciding this, the court considered that Article 2 of the Protocol and its approach to equivalents means the court can look away from the literal meaning of a claim in all cases—not only when the claim was ambiguous; the issue was how far the court could look.[106] Further, the court found that there was a difference between interpreting a claim and the extent of the protection conferred by it—the potential impact of this from the perspective of validity was noted after para 11.25.[107]

12.68   When considering approaches to what is covered by claims and variants, the Supreme Court reviewed the decisions in *Catnic, Improver*, and *Kirin-Amgen*, decisions from Germany, France, Italy, Spain, and the Netherlands, and Article 2 of the Protocol.[108] The Supreme Court noted that some guiding principles were necessary as had been sought to be provided in these cases.[109] The Supreme Court stated clearly that it was departing from *Catnic*[110] and in *Kirin-Amgen* (which it noted had followed *Improver*, which had built on *Catnic*...).[111] A new test was then developed.[112] This test is now summarised.

---

[100]   In fact, they lead to the unusual outcome that the answer to Q1 might be 'no' (leading to an inference of infringement) but because the technology is new and non-obvious, the answer to Q2 might also be 'no' (which implies no infringement). This was the case in *Kirin-Amgen* and also in *Union Carbide v BP Chemicals Ltd* [1999] RPC 409.

[101]   In particular, see *Wheatley v Drillsafe Ltd* [2001] RPC 133 and *Pharmacia Corp v Merck and Co* [2002] RPC 775.

[102]   [2015] EWCA Civ 607.   [103]   *Kirin-Amgen Inc v Hoechst Marion Roussel Ltd* [2005] RPC 9, para 71.

[104]   *Actavis v Eli Lilly* [2017] UKSC 48.   [105]   ibid, para 30.   [106]   ibid, para 33.

[107]   ibid, para 33.   [108]   ibid, paras 35–52.   [109]   ibid, para 53.

[110]   ibid, para 54.   [111]   ibid, para 54.   [112]   ibid, paras 33, 54–56, 58, 59–66.

The variant is to be viewed through the eyes of the notional addressee of the patent. There are two key questions. These have previously been conflated and the court considered that 'so long as [the second set of questions] are treated as one of interpretation, it will lead to wrong results' (para 56 of decision).

Q1. Does the variant infringe as matter of normal interpretation? Assessing this is a question of interpretation (para 54 of decision). For example, does vertical cover something not at 90 degrees—a similar issue to that seen in *Catnic*? Here, something which is not pemetrexed disodium cannot be covered applying normal interpretation. This is bringing into patent law more conventional principles of interpretation of any legal document.

Q2. If the variant does not infringe as a matter of normal interpretation, does the variant infringe because it varies from the invention in immaterial way(s). Assessing this will require looking to facts and evidence, as it cannot be addressed by normal interpretation (para 54 of decision). For example, is a slotted rubber rod within the term 'helical metal spring'—as in *Improver* (see para 12.60)? To determine this, a patent-specific approach, reformulating *Improver*, is developed—although this remains as guidelines, not strict rules. This is considered consistent with the approaches of German, Italian, and Dutch courts (para 62 of decision).

- To answer Q2:
  - 2A—even if not within the literal meaning of the claim, does the variant achieve substantially the same result in substantially the same way as the inventive concept revealed by the patent?
  - 2B—would the person skilled in the art reading the patent at the priority date, knowing that the variant achieved substantially same result as the invention, see it as obvious that the variant did so in substantially the same way as the invention?
  - 2C—would such a person have concluded that the patentee nonetheless intended that strict compliance with the literal meaning of claim was an essential requirement of the invention?
- For infringement (if there is no literal infringement), we need to answer 'yes' to 2A, 'yes' to 2B and 'no' to 2C.

12.69   Lord Neuberger also held that courts could have some regard to the patent file history (eg the negotiations with the UK IPO regarding novelty) in limited cases. His Lordship referred to this being useful when an issue was unclear and the file could unambiguously resolve the point, or if it would be contrary to the public interest for the file to be ignored—say it was stated in the file that a variant was not said to be covered, and it is now being argued that it is.[113]

12.70   This new Supreme Court test of *Eli Lilly v Actavis* was considered by the Court of Appeal in *Icescape Limited v Ice-World International,* in a dispute regarding a system for cooling mobile ice rinks.[114] The Court of Appeal noted that the approach in *Eli Lilly v Actavis* was 'markedly different from that which the courts in this country have adopted since *Catnic*' and that this was clearly deliberate given the points made by Lord Neuberger regarding conflation of two issues.[115] Lord Kitchin, sitting in the Court of Appeal, went on to consider the interpretation issue. His Lordship noted that patents (being unilateral documents, setting out power claimed) are different from contracts, and that questions of purposive interpretation would still arise in the first question and be the subject of 2A.[116] Regarding the reformulated questions (which Lord Kitchin termed by the Actavis Questions) in 2A–C, Lord Kitchin considered that this introduced to the UK the question of equivalence (which is, of course, referred to in the Protocol),[117] and that he must have regard to the 'patent's inventive core'.[118] It will be interesting to see how this issue develops. At the time of writing, there is concern from the profession about uncertainty and of new risk for competitor's products which

---

[113] ibid, paras 87 and 88.
[114] *Icescape Limited v Ice-World International* [2018] EWCA Civ 2219.   [115] ibid, para 59.   [116] ibid, paras 59 and 70.
[117] ibid, para 60.   [118] ibid, para 72.

were carefully designed around the then understanding of patent construction. Future editions of this book are likely to have more and more charts setting out tests which courts move on from but which - like *Catnic*, *Improver*, and *Kirin Amgen* - cannot be entirely ignored.

Declaration or declarator of non-infringement

12.71   The issues discussed so far can also arise in the context of an order of non-infringement. It is possible to apply under section 71 of the Patents Act 1977 to the Comptroller or the courts for a declaration (or declarator in Scotland) of non-infringement in respect of either past or future acts done with or to a patented invention. The procedure requires the person seeking the order first to apply to the proprietor in writing for a written acknowledgement of the declaration or declarator claimed;[119] the proprietor should also be furnished with the full particulars of the acts in question at this time.[120] Only if this acknowledgement is refused or simply not given can the applicant then seek a formal declaration or declarator from the Comptroller in the first instance. The tests for infringement in such cases are those outlined earlier.[121] Note that while it is possible to put the validity of the patent in issue in such proceedings, a finding of invalidity does not, in itself, result in revocation of the patent. For that we have to turn to our next section, which deals with this particular procedure.

Key points on interpretation and non-infringement

- Is the alleged infringing product or process the same as that covered by the patent or close enough to be covered by the patent as properly interpreted and construed? This is assessed by applying the test in the EPC Protocol with guidance (at present) from the Actavis Questions.

- There can be a declaration of non infringement.

Revocation

12.72   We have seen in the previous sections how an action for infringement is often met with a counterclaim for revocation. This is dealt with by section 72(1) of the Patents Act 1977, as amended, with the equivalent provisions appearing as Article 138 EPC 2000. The fact that a revocation procedure exists stands in testament to the fact that the patent granting system is not infallible. Patents may be granted when it is not a patentable invention (one of the exclusions or exceptions should have applied, or a lack of novelty, inventive step, or industrial application (paras 11.8–11.84),[122] they may be granted to someone who is not entitled to the patent (para 10.106ff.), the patent application does not sufficiently disclose the invention to allow it to be performed by the skilled person (and thereby discharge the public disclosure obligation), the patent confers too broad a power to control compared to what the invention actually contributes to the state of the art[123] (para 10.16ff and 10.84ff), or patents have been extended through amendment beyond the boundaries which should have been allowed (paras 10.110ff).

---

[119]   On the requirements, see *Mallory Metallurgical Products Ltd v Black Sivalls and Bryson Incorporated* [1977] RPC 321.

[120]   An incomplete written description can be saved by accompanying drawings: *MMD Design & Consultancy Ltd's Patent* [1989] RPC 131.

[121]   For an example of an application, see *Actavis UK Ltd v Eli Lilly & Co* [2015] EWCA Civ 555 considered at n 364 which also considers the extent to which declarations could be made in respect of other countries. More generally, see *UK Manual of Patent Practice* (February 2016 as amended), para 71.02.

[122]   Patents Act 2004 amended the Patents Act 1977 to make it clear that it is possible to revoke a patent on the grounds that it does not comply with the provisions of new section 4A (methods of treatment and diagnosis on the human or animal body; see paras 11.87ff).

[123]   See in particular, *Biogen Inc v Medeva plc* [1997] RPC 1 per Lord Hoffmann at 53–54.

12.73   Two particular points must be considered in the context of revocation. First, as noted at para 10.27, an EP patent might be found to be valid in one court action in a UK jurisdiction, and then subsequently be amended at the EPO, including in respect of some of the claims which were relevant to the first action. Is the first finding of validity *res judicata*, and as a result the requirement to pay damages in respect of it must remain? Interests of certainty might suggest that it should be.[124] The Supreme Court clarified the position in *Virgin Atlantic v Premium Airways*;[125] however, finding that fairness and commercial certainty meant that regard must be had to subsequent findings of invalidity. Secondly, a key issue in discussions regarding the Unified Patent Court (also discussed in para 10.30ff) was the possibility of infringement and validity being considered separately (as has been the case traditionally, eg in Germany) rather than in a defence and counterclaim as in the UK jurisdictions. The Unified Patent Court Agreement (UPCA) provides[126] for different scenarios, depending on where the action is raised (central, local, or regional division), the views of the local and regional division, and of the parties, but it will still be possible for infringement and validity to be heard together. It will be interesting to note how this develops.

12.74   There is one substantive matter which warrants further discussion. This is the question of *insufficiency*; that is, the challenge that the patent application does not sufficiently disclose the invention to allow it to be performed by the skilled person.[127] Article 83 EPC 2000 (and the Patents Act 1977, s 14) require that: 'The [European] patent application shall disclose the invention in a manner sufficiently clear and complete for it to be carried out by a person skilled in the art.'

12.75   The rationale of this provision was explained in *Visx Inc v Nidek Co Ltd*:[128]

> The thinking behind this provision is that, as part of the quid pro quo of the monopoly granted by a patent, the patentee should give proper public disclosure of the invention: this enables the public to work the invention at the expiry of the monopoly period. The provision also exists to allow the court to revoke a patent if satisfied that the monopoly claimed by it is wider than its contribution to the art.

12.76   Questions of insufficiency have long been a part of UK patent law and the Court of Appeal has confirmed that the pre-1977 approach remains valid and equally applicable today.[129] That said, there have been few hard-and-fast rules to emerge from the courts and there has always been a desire to maintain a balance of interests between the patentee and the public and to guard against setting too high a standard for disclosure simply because the matter is inherently complex.[130]

12.77   The issue is a question of fact, dependent on the nature of the invention and the particular knowledge and skills of the notional expert.[131] These factors should be ringing bells—you have come across them before. Can you remember in which section? Well, the House of Lords drew the parallel between the requirements of sufficiency and the requirements of enabling disclosure used to test novelty (para 11.17) in *Synthon BV v SmithKline Beecham*.[132] After discussing some of the historical cases,[133] Lord Hoffmann stated the following:[134]

> In the present case the Court of Appeal was reluctant to say that the test of enablement of a prior disclosure for the purpose of anticipation was the same as the test of enablement of the patent itself for the purpose of sufficiency. But I can think of no reason why there should be any difference and the Technical Board of Appeal has more than once held that the tests are the same: see *ICI/Pyridine Herbicides* [1986] 5 EPOR 232, para 2; *COLLABORATIVE/Preprorennin* [1990] EPOR 361, para 15. In my opinion, therefore, the authorities on section

---

[124]   *Coflexip SA v Stolt Offshore* [2004] EWCA Civ 213.   [125]   [2014] AC 160.   [126]   Article 33.3. See also paras 10.30ff.
[127]   *Regeneron Pharmaceuticals Inc v Genentech Inc* [2012] EWHC 657 (Pat), unsuccessful appeal in [2013] EWCA Civ 93—assertion that invention would work across the scope of the claim has to be plausible or credible.
[128]   *Visx Inc v Nidek Co Ltd and Others (No 2)* [1999] FSR 405.
[129]   *Mentor Corporation v Hollister Inc* [1993] RPC 7.
[130]   See *Halliburton Energy Services Inc v Smith International (North Sea) Ltd and Others* [2005] EWHC 1623 (Pat) at paras 129–139, endorsed by the Court of Appeal at [2006] EWCA Civ 1715.
[131]   The specification must enable the invention at the date of filing; see *Biogen v Medeva* [1997] RPC 1.   [132]   [2005] UKHL 59.
[133]   See, eg, *Valensi v British Radio Corporation* [1973] RPC 337; *Mentor Corporation v Hollister Incorporated* [1993] RPC 7; and *Biogen Inc v Medeva plc* [1997] RPC 1.
[134]   *Kirin-Amgen Inc v Hoechst Marion Roussel Ltd* [2005] RPC 9, para 27.

72(1)(c) are equally applicable to enablement for the purposes of sections 2(2) and (3). There may however be differences in the application of this test to the facts; for example, because in the case of sufficiency the skilled person is attempting to perform a claimed invention and has that goal in mind, whereas in the case of prior art the subject-matter may have disclosed the invention but not identified it as such. But no such question arises in this case, in which the application plainly identified crystalline PMS as an embodiment of the invention.

We must, therefore, consider the authorities discussed previously as part of the novelty criterion when considering what amounts to sufficiency of disclosure.

Exercise

Look back at the section on novelty (paras 11.8ff) to familiarise yourself with the relevant case law. Consider, in particular, which of the cases had an issue of insufficiency in tandem with one of novelty.

12.78   If the specification effectively claims too much for the invention, as was the case in the key case of *Biogen v Medeva*, then the application or patent will be invalid for insufficiency.[135] It is a frequent problem with new and emerging technologies that early patents are granted broadly by IPOs before the offices and the courts get to grips with the true nature of the technology. *Biogen* was an early attempt to keep the UK on a narrow path. In this case the patentee was the first to isolate the genetic sequence coding for EPO but it was held that the invention was a new process for isolating EPO, not the product as such. The claims, however, sought to cover new processes *and* EPO products which could be achieved without reliance on the patented invention, including those which could not have been contemplated when the patent was initially filed. Thus, the invention as disclosed did not allow the skilled person to work this range of inventions and was invalid for insufficiency.

12.79   Similarly, in *Biogen*, all that could be described (at best) was an invention for a molecule produced by crude genetic engineering techniques which exhibited antigen specificity for core and surface hepatitis B antigens in host cells. Yet, what was claimed was an invention which covered *all* molecules displaying HBV antigen specificity produced by *any* technique using *any* host. In holding that the monopoly claimed was too broad and observing that the patent would be invalid for insufficiency, Lord Hoffmann focused on the extent to which the invention made a technical contribution to the state of the art. The technical contribution made was a way of working with HBV to produce recombinant molecules which had antigen specificity *in the absence* of knowledge about the make-up of the genetic sequence. It was confirmed that monopolies will be awarded for inventions *only* to the extent that the inventions contribute to the state of the art. In particular, if there are available ways of achieving the same result without relying on the invention (and therefore without relying on its contribution to the state of the art) then those ways fall outside the monopoly which can legitimately be claimed by the patentee of the invention in question. Here, once the sequences of the HBV genes were known, it was easily possible to produce HBV antigens without using the patentee's technique at all. In sum, what is disclosed must enable the invention to be worked *to the full extent* of the protection claimed; that is, if your invention embodies a principle which is capable of general application across a wide range of products, then it is permissible to claim all such products. Furthermore, Lord Hoffmann confirmed that in such cases it is not necessary for the patentee to prove that their principle applies in all cases—one example is sufficient to amount to an enabling disclosure. However, if the patentee claims different products or processes in the same application, each must be described by a separate enabling disclosure. Moreover, if no unifying principle links the claimed inventions together, then all that can be claimed is that which can be described.[136] However, if the patentee claims different products or processes in the same application, each must be described by a separate enabling disclosure.

---

[135]   On the fuzzy edges of claims and the impact on arguments about insufficiency, see *Generics (UK) Ltd (t/a Mylan) v Yeda Research & Development Co Ltd* [2012] EWHC 1848 (Pat).

[136]   See also application of this approach in *Human Genome Science Inc v Eli Lilly & Co* [2012] EWCA Civ 1185.

Exercise

The facts and law of *Biogen* might lead you to think that you need to have advanced scientific knowledge to be a patent lawyer. Is this the case? Reflect on this idea and return to it at the end of your studies.

12.80   In *Kirin-Amgen v Hoechst* the House of Lords invalidated the core claims of a patent over genetically engineered EPO—a protein found in minute levels in the body which regulates the production of red blood cells—in large part because of the unsustainability of the breadth of the claims made by the patentee.[137] The patentees claimed, in essence, *any* way of making EPO by recombinant DNA technology and the resultant forms of EPO, but their patent specification did not disclose an invention which was capable of furnishing the person skilled in the particular art with sufficient information to realise such a broad range of possibilities. Lord Hoffmann confirmed that it is possible to claim that an invention discloses 'a principle capable of general application' and accordingly to have a monopoly over the entire class of products which flow from the application of that principle, but this case was not such an example.[138] Rather, Lord Hoffmann laid down a three-point test to determine sufficiency, that is, whether the claims are sustained by the actual contribution that the invention makes to human knowledge. This is:

- What exactly is the invention?
- What does the application claim to enable the skilled man to do?
- Does the specification actually enable him to do it?

This may seem trite, but the first question is of crucial importance. The patentees sought to have the court believe that they had invented a product, a form of EPO, but their Lordships took a different view, holding that they had, in fact, invented a way of making EPO; that is, a process. Moreover, the process that was revealed was not one which taught a skilled expert *any* way of making EPO by recombinant DNA technology, nor did it reveal a way of making EPO in such general terms as to cover the process used by the defendants. A further point made by the court concerns the role of the skilled expert in interpreting the language used by the applicant in drafting their claims: 'what would a person skilled in the art have understood the patentee to have used the language of the claim to mean?' In other words, the courts will use the notional expert as a device to limit ex post facto interpretations by a patentee in an attempt to broaden the scope of his monopoly. This is particularly pertinent when new technologies emerge and the patentee attempts to argue that they are also caught by their patent.[139]

12.81   In *Generics (UK) Limited and Others v H Lundbeck A/S*[140] the validity of a patent over a novel product, the effective agent in the antidepressant drug Citalopram, was upheld and the impact of the precedent in *Biogen* was clarified.[141] The product in question was Escitalopram, an enantiomer, whose separation and isolation was a non-trivial matter. The patentees claimed the product and associated processes and difficulties arose because the inventiveness of the product was claimed solely by reference to the means used to make it. As well as challenges on the grounds of novelty and inventive step, the core concern was that if this product claim stood, it would provide a monopoly over the substance itself, irrespective of how it might be made, but when the patentees had only disclosed one method of production. Was this an overly broad monopoly? Had there been sufficient disclosure?

---

[137]   *Kirin Amgen Inc and Others v Hoechst and Others* [2005] 1 All ER 667; [2005] RPC 9.
[138]   For an example of this, see Case T 0292/85 *GENENTECH/Polypeptide expression* [1989] OJEPO 275 discussed by Lord Hoffmann at paras 112–113.
[139]   See M Fisher, 'Extracting the price of a patent: enablement and written description' [2012] 4 IPQ 262.
[140]   [2009] UKHL 12.
[141]   P Watterson, 'Appeal court reluctance: complex evidence, obviousness and related matters' (2012) 7(5) JIPLP 358.

12.82   The House of Lords held unanimously that the patent was valid. At first instance the trial judge had revoked the patent, relying on *Biogen*, and on the ground that: 'The first person to find a way of achieving an obviously desirable goal is not permitted to monopolise every other way of doing so.' But the House of Lords distinguished *Biogen* not as dealing with a product claim, but rather as being concerned with an unusual product/process hybrid claim whose breadth was clearly too wide. In contrast, the court in *Generics* found the product invention to be both novel and involving inventive step because the means used to produce it was in no way obvious to a person skilled in the art. Accordingly, and as a product in itself, it was entirely in keeping with UK and EPO jurisprudence[142] that a product patent should provide a monopoly irrespective of the means to make it. Reiterating the point that a monopoly should only extend as far as the 'technical contribution' made by the teaching of the patent, the House of Lords found that the respondent's contribution was 'to make available, for the first time, a product which had previously been unavailable, namely the isolated (+)-enantiomer of citalopram. On that basis, it would appear to follow that the respondent was entitled to claim the enantiomer.'[143]

12.83   It can be seen, then, that it can matter very much how an invention is described and interpreted by the courts in giving effect to patent law. Lord Neuberger ventured the following further distinction between product claims and process (or process-type) claims:[144]

> When considering the validity of a simple product claim . . . [as in *Generics*] . . . it may be that concentrating on the identification of the inventive step rather than the technical contribution can lead to error. 'Inventive step' suggests how something has been done, and, in the case of a product claim at any rate, one is primarily concerned with what has been allegedly invented, not how it has been done. On the other hand where the claim is for a process or (as in *Biogen*) includes a process, the issue of how the alleged invention has been achieved seems to be more in point.

The careful policing of the boundaries of the tests for patentability is now a clear policy objective, advocated in many quarters.

12.84   The Court of Appeal considered insufficiency in *Halliburton Energy Services Inc v Smith International (North Sea) Ltd and Others*.[145] It confirmed that a patent for rotary cone drill bits was invalid for insufficiency because it required too much work from the skilled person to reproduce the various features of the invention. This involved claims both to the design and use of simulation systems in respect of the drill bits, and required enormously lengthy and complex calculations from the notional expert to reproduce the invention. The court held that if the patent involved an unreasonable amount of work in the light of all of the relevant circumstances, then it would be regarded as not containing an enabling disclosure.[146] Significant regard was had to EPO case law when the Supreme Court considered sufficiency regarding claims for a specified medical use of a known pharmaceutical compound in *Warner Lambert v Generics* in 2018 regarding pregalbin.[147]

■ *Warner Lambert v Generics UK (t/a Mylan)* [2018] UKSC 56

Claim 1 referred to 'treating pain', claim 2 referred to 'inflammatory pain', and claim 3 referred to 'neuropathic pain'.[148] The Supreme Court held that claims 1 and 3 are invalid as the disclosure covers only inflammatory pain.[149] The court referred to the 'patent bargain' and the need for disclosure[150] and commented that 'without

---

[142]   Case T409/91 *EXXON/Fuel Oils* [1994] OJEPO 653, para 3.3.

[143]   Per Lord Neuberger at para 83.   [144]   Per Lord Neuberger at para 101.

[145]   [2006] EWCA Civ 1715 (see para 12.76).

[146]   The EPO uses a test of 'undue effort', which is also relevant for these purposes; see Case T923/92 *GENENTECH/Human tPA* [1996] EPOR 275. See also *Generics (UK) Ltd (t/a Mylan) v Yeda Research & Development Co Ltd* [2013] EWCA Civ 925.

[147]   *Warner Lambert v Generics (UK) t/a Mylan* [2018] UKSC 56. Note *Warner Lambert v Generics (UK)* CA [2016] EWCA Civ 1006, which had been followed in *Actavis Group v ICOS Corp* [2017] EWCA Civ 1671.

[148]   *Warner Lambert v Generics (UK) t/a Mylan* [2018] UKSC 56, para 5.

[149]   ibid, para 15(2), 48–54. See paras 55–60 noting different approaches taken in other European national courts and considering that a different English approach was warranted.

[150]   ibid, para 17.

some disclosure of how or why the known product can be expected to work in the new application, it would be possible to patent the manufacture of known compounds for the purpose of treating every conceivable relevant condition without having invented anything at all'.[151] This raises the issue of plausibility and whether this should be positive or negative.[152]

Lord Sumption stated that 'plausibility is not a term of art, and its content is inevitably influenced by the legal context'[153] and that:[154]

- the proposition that a product is efficacious for treatment of a given condition must be plausible (and if it has different pathologies then the assertion must be plausible in relation to all of them);
- a proposition is not made so by a bare assertion or disclosure of a mere possibility;
- a claim may be plausible by a specification showing a reason why it was worth trying and there must be something to cause the skilled person to think there was a reasonable prospect that the assertion was true, based on direct impact on the disease, either through data or reasoning, and that all of this must be taught by the patent when read in light of the common general knowledge.

Lord Hodge argued:[155]

- it was not necessary for the patent to disclose evidence of plausibility and plausibility could be refined by established tests and subsequent data;
- if the patent makes the claimed effect plausible, then it is for the objector to provide a base for their doubt.

Lord Mance agreed with Lord Hodge, considering that there should be no need to disclose a reason for the assertion to be true.[156]

12.85   It is possible to apply to amend claims in response to a challenge of revocation,[157] and this will be considered at the discretion of the court.[158] These amendments cannot attempt, however, to add matter to the existing patent.[159]

12.86   A final point: Article 105a EPC 2000 provides that a proprietor of a patent can apply for revocation of their own instrument through a centralised procedure with effect throughout all countries for which the patent was granted. Can you find the equivalent provision in the Patents Act 1977?

Key points on revocation

- A patent can be granted and can be taken away.
- Raising an infringement action is risky as it is likely to lead to a validity challenge on the basis of (once again) novelty, obviousness, and industrial application.
- Sufficiency is a central issue.
- Amendment can save patents.

---

[151] ibid, para 20.   [152] ibid, see paras 23–35 for a comprehensive review of UK and EPO case law.   [153] ibid, para 37.
[154] ibid, in particular paras 37 and 39.   [155] ibid, paras 180–181.   [156] ibid, paras 195–196.
[157] See para 10.121ff.   [158] *Hsiung's Patent* [1992] RPC 497.
[159] *LG Philips Co Ltd v Tatung (UK) Ltd and Others* [2006] EWCA Civ 1774. For further amendment issues, see *Ratiopharm GmbH v Napp Pharmaceutical Holdings Ltd* [2009] RPC 18.

Defences

12.87   Section 60(5) of the Patents Act 1977 provides a list of nine acts which would be infringing but for this statutory protection, shall not be so. Some of these are slightly obscure and you can read them for yourself. We are going to concentrate on the four main defences:

(1)   acts done privately and which are not commercial;

(2)   acts done for experimental purposes;

(3)   farmers' privileges;

(4)   activities relevant to regulatory approval of generics.

Private and non-commercial acts

12.88   This defence requires that the use of a patented invention is only for private purposes *and* non-commercial ends. 'Private' means for one's own use, and it is the opposite to 'public'; it is not a synonym for 'secret' in these circumstances.[160] The rationale is probably that such acts are of minimal or no threat to a patentee. You will recall that in *McDonald v Graham*[161] the invention concerned promotional 'Z cards', copies of which were kept by a former business partner, who then passed unlicensed copies on to a design team to consider how he might design his own version. The infringement action was in relation to 'keeping' an infringing product and this was upheld on the evidence, which showed clearly that the defendant was keeping the product in stock for the purposes of his business. There was, therefore, no need for the Court of Appeal to consider the defences specifically, although it did hold that the trial judge was entitled to find on the evidence that a sufficient case was made out of use by the defendant for non-private and commercial purposes. Cases involving disputes over whether there is indeed commercial or non-commercial use would similarly turn on the evidence put to the court, and an important part of that evidence is the subjective intentions of the alleged infringer.[162]

Experimental purposes

12.89   In contrast to section 60(5)(a), discussed in para 12.88 there is no mention of the need for experimental purposes to be non-commercial, therefore it seemed possible that experimental acts can be carried out which may ultimately lead to a commercial benefit. This issue was controversial. The defence was discussed by the Court of Appeal in *Monsanto Co v Stauffer Chemical Co and Another*,[163] where it was decided that the word 'experiment' is an ordinary word and not a term of art of patent law; that is, it takes an ordinary meaning and not any specialised meaning for the purposes of the defence. The Court of Appeal also drew a distinction between experiments carried out to discover a new thing, or to test a hypothesis, or even to test the parameters of an invention under new conditions, with other acts which would not fall within the defence, such as trials performed to demonstrate to a third party that a product works or work done to gather information to satisfy a third party (eg a customer or a safety regulatory body) of the workings of a product or process. In *Smith Kline & French Laboratories Ltd v Evans Medical Ltd*[164] the argument was rejected that a patentee impliedly consents to experiments to test the validity of their patent; moreover, for the defence to succeed the acts in question must be done for purposes directly related to the subject matter of the patent as defined in the claims.[165] Thus, you could not use someone's reagent invention in a

---

[160]   Compare, then, the argument that 'prior use' is also an available defence; that is, that one was using the invention before it was subject to a patent. It should be self-evident to you at this stage that such a claim could only succeed if that prior use had been in secret and out of the public domain; otherwise, a patent would be invalid for lack of novelty.

[161]   [1994] RCP 407 (see para 12.48).   [162]   *Smith Kline & French Labs v Evans Medical* [1989] FSR 513.

[163]   [1985] RPC 515.   [164]   [1989] FSR 513.

[165]   Applied in *Meter-Tech LLC v British Gas Trading* [2016] EWHC 2278 (Pat) regarding pre-payment utility metering system.

trial-and-error fashion to find out if a third party's chemical invention worked efficiently. Here the direct experimentation would only be with the chemical invention. In *Auchincloss v Agricultural & Veterinary Supplies Ltd*[166] it was not a defence to make and experiment with a composition designed to destroy viruses and other micro-organisms for the purposes of obtaining regulatory approval. It is possible for the defence to apply if the experiment has a commercial purpose as long as it also has the experimental purpose.[167]

12.90   Note, however, that even if an experimental use defence applies, this would not necessarily extend to someone who supplies the means to carry out the experiment (which would otherwise be an infringing act) and they might be liable for contributory infringement.[168]

12.91   There is considerable diversity of approaches to experimental defences around the world, including within Europe. Two examples illustrate the point.

12.92   The German Supreme Court has held that the equivalent provisions in German law 'in principle exempts all experimental acts as long as they serve to gain information and thus to carry out scientific research into the subject-matter of the invention' and that this even extends to research into 'possible new uses hitherto unknown',[169] and this is true *even if* there is an associated commercial purpose to the experimentation.[170] The English Patents Court has accepted this general approach but modified it slightly by suggesting that the assessment of whether 'experimental use' exists 'should involve the consideration whether the immediate purpose of the transaction in question is to generate revenue'.[171] The position in Europe more widely remains patchy, with a research exemption operating across a number of European jurisdictions but in a disharmonious fashion.[172]

12.93   In stark contrast, the position in the United States was drastically clarified in *Madey v Duke University*,[173] by the US Court of Appeals for the Federal Circuit, which all but reduced the effectiveness of the defence to nothing. It now only applies for 'amusement, to satisfy idle curiosity, or for strictly philosophical inquiry'; it is not available in respect of *any* activity which is 'in furtherance of the alleged infringer's legitimate business'. And in the particular circumstances of the case, this was held to extend to a university whose very 'business' is research. The presence or absence of profit motive is irrelevant and so the defence is equally unavailable to not-for-profit organisations. This is clearly a draconian measure that is open to serious question as to how it furthers the public interest. It has required, in turn, further initiatives to protect research and product development. For example, the US Supreme Court ruled in *Merck KGaA v Integra LifeSciences Ltd*[174] that there is an immunity from infringement proceedings in respect of preclinical research and experimentation which is 'reasonably related' to obtaining necessary information for regulatory approval before the US Food and Drug Administration. This, then, continues to exclude fundamental or other research not carried out with the intention of seeking future drug approval. It also remains unclear whether the use of research tools to develop therapeutic agents is covered.

12.94   So what should happen in the UK? The Gowers Review pointed to a paper by the Department of Trade and Industry and the Intellectual Property Institute which argues that the research exemption is unclear, not widely used, and in need for reform.[175] Evidence from the United States indicates that one in six projects is stopped or never started because of IPRs. In an attempt to avoid this for the UK, the Gowers recommendation

---

[166] [1997] RPC 649, and on appeal [1999] RPC 397.   [167] *Meter-Tech LLC v British Gas Trading* [2016] EWHC 2278 (Pat).

[168] See *Monsanto v Stauffer* [1985] RPC 515 (see para 12.50 on contributory infringement).

[169] *Klinische Versuche (Clinical Trials) I* [1997] RPC 623.   [170] *Klinische Versuche (Clinical Trials) II* [1998] RPC 423.

[171] *Corevalve Inc v Edwards Lifesciences* [2009] FSR 8, para 77.

[172] See generally G van Overwalle (ed), *Gene Patents and Public Health* (2007).

[173] 307 F3rd 1351 at 1362 (Fed Cir, 2002); petition to the Supreme Court denied 27 June 2003 (No 02-1007).

[174] 545 US 193 (2005), interpreting 35 USC §271(e)(1)—The Drug Price Competition and Patent Term Restoration Act 1984 (also known as the Hatch-Waxman Act).

[175] Gowers Review, paras 4.5–4.1,2; Department of Trade and Industry and the Intellectual Property Institute, *Patents for Genetic Sequences: The Competitiveness of Current UK Law and Practices* (2004).

is to clarify the experimental purposes defence to facilitate experimentation, innovation, and education. The proposed model is taken from Switzerland, which promotes the pursuit of knowledge about the object of an invention, exempts only non-commercial purposes, and specifically allows the use of the invention for teaching purposes. The UK IPO launched a consultation in 2008 on the research exception, in which the majority of respondents indicated that clarification of the scope of the exception would be useful, especially when the judiciary would assist in providing guidance in order to give it legal weight. But there was no clear evidence to suggest that the current research exception hinders research in the UK.[176]

Exercise

Look at the Gowers Review and the provisions of Swiss law. Critically assess this proposal to follow the Swiss model, considering the arguments that might be put from all sides on whether this is appropriate for the UK.

Farmers' privileges

12.95   New defences were introduced to the Patents Act 1977 as a result of negotiations on the Biotechnology Directive, which we discuss in Chapter 11. These are designed to ensure that farmers using traditional harvesting and livestock reproduction techniques are not hindered in their work by the existence and exercise of IPRs relating to biological material. There are two particular defences.

12.96   Section 60(5)(g) concerns propagating material for plants, including material that may be the subject of a patent, which has been sold to a farmer by the patent owner for use in agriculture. The defence provides that the farmer may use the material for further propagation of the material on their own land without infringing any patent. This is not a catch-all provision, however; section 60(6A) of the Act provides that the defence is only available in respect of certain varieties of material, and these are detailed in paragraph 2 of Schedule A1 to the Act. Common harvest like wheat, oats, and potatoes are covered. Moreover, if use is authorised under the Act, the farmer must still pay the patent owner 'equitable remuneration' for that use, although this cannot be more than what the farmer would pay to buy more material from the owner. 'Small farmers' are exempt from this payment, being, in the case of exempted varieties, a farmer who grows plants on an area not larger than necessary to produce 92 tonnes of material.[177]

12.97   Section 60(5)(h) provides a similar scheme for farmers who breed livestock or otherwise deal in reproductive material. The law does not restrict which animal varieties can be the subject of the exemption. The main prohibition, however, is that the farmer cannot sell on any animal or material derived from their 'use' as part of a 'commercial reproductive activity'.[178]

Clinical trials and generic product development

12.98   Section 60(5)(i) is concerned with the conduct of clinical trials for the approval of therapeutic products based on patented inventions. It was introduced into domestic law as a result of two Directives concerning, respectively, veterinary[179] and human[180] medicinal products. These are often known as 'Bolar' exemptions,

---

[176] UK IPO, 'Patent Research Exception Consultation: Summary of Responses' (2008), https://webarchive.nationalarchives.gov.uk/20140603152124/http://www.ipo.gov.uk/response-patresearch.pdf.

[177] Council Regulation (EC) No 2100/94 of 27 July 1994 on Community plant variety rights, Art 14(3), third indent.

[178] Patents Act 1977, s 60(6B). Regarding equitable remuneration, see decision of *Saatgut- Treuhandverwaltungs v Vogel* (C-242/14) Court of Justice.

[179] Article 13(6) of Directive 2001/82/EC on veterinary medicinal products.

[180] Article 10(5) of Directive 2001/83/EC on medicinal products for human use, amended by the Directive 2004/27, Art 10(6).

based on establishment arrangements in the United States. These exemptions operate when generic drugs manufacturers are seeking regulatory approval for their products. They provide protection for acts done on generic medicines to demonstrate that they are bio-equivalent to a patented product; the point is, from the perspective of the generic manufacturer, it can rely on the patentee's prior regulatory approval if bio-equivalence can be shown. The problem is that while, clearly, generics can be produced once a patent expires, manufacturers do not want to have to wait until this time before carrying out trials and seeking regulatory approval. A Bolar exemption therefore works to allow this activity *before* a patent expires with a view to facilitating a wider market in generics *after* it expires. This is the European equivalent to the US Supreme Court ruling in *Merck* (para 12.93).

12.99   A 2012 consultation by the UK IPO acknowledges further the problems and has sought views on how the UK should proceed.[181] From the 2012 Response it appears that the vast majority of responses agreed with a change in the law, leading to amendments from 2014.[182] This exempts from infringement anything done for the purpose of a medicinal product assessment (for humans or animals) as it will be regarded as done for experimental purposes in respect of the subject matter of the invention. This would cover activities required to secure regulatory approval to market innovative drugs, and also activities necessary for public authorities to provide health care or give information to them about the carrying out of health care. This could include data to support assessment by the National Institute for Health and Clinical Excellence (NICE).

> **Key points on defences**
>
> - There is a list of defences in the Patents Act.
> - New defences are introduced from time to time.
> - There are battles regarding the interpretation of all defences, with experimental purposes and pursuing regulatory goals having attracted attention over the years.

> **Exercise**
>
> Having reached the end of this part of the chapter, consider how many ways a person faced with an action for patent infringement can respond—seeking a defence is only one option. What are the relative merits of any particular strategy? Are defences an easy answer to deeper problems with the patent system?

Exploitation

12.100   Legislation provides that patents are a form of personal property, and in Scotland incorporal moveable property.[183] So as well as using the patent to restrict the activity of others, patent owners may wish to share the patent (licence), or sell it to others (assign). This may be for a variety of reasons: from enabling quicker meeting of societal needs to enabling some financial reward to be gained from the innovation while choosing to focus on other activities, to enabling others to make a necessary contribution to bring related products to market—for example, someone else might have a relevant factory or distribution network which the patent owner does not have.

---

[181]   UK IPO, 'The Research and Bolar Exceptions: A Informal Consultation on Patent Infringement in Pharmaceutical Clinical and Field Trials' (2012), https://webarchive.nationalarchives.gov.uk/20140603125121/http://www.ipo.gov.uk/response-2011-bolar.pdf.

[182]   The 2014 Legislative Reform Order amended the Patents Act 2014 No. 1997, including Section 60(6)(D)–(G). See explanatory document at www.legislation.gov.uk/uksi/2014/1997/pdfs/uksiod_20141997_en.pdf. See also L Cohen and L Peirson, 'The UK research and "Bolar" exceptions: broadening the scope for innovation' 2013 8(11) JIPLP 837–45.

[183]   Patents Act 1977, ss 30(1) and 31(1)(2).

12.101   Patent legislation includes specific rules on assignments and licensing, including measures on compulsory licensing and licences of right.[184] Some transfers of rights must be in writing and signed by or on behalf of the transferor,[185] otherwise all such transactions are void. This applies to assignments (assignations in Scotland), mortgages, and transfers on death.[186] Licences do not need to be in writing and do not involve any transfer of property.[187] An assignment/assignation or an exclusive licence can give the right to bring infringement proceedings[188] or disputes over Crown use.[189] An exclusive licensee can bring independent infringement proceedings without the need to refer to the owner.[190] This section discusses these issues in more depth, some specific and topical examples of exploitation practices, and controls on those practices primarily within the domains of patents, and will highlight a number of contemporary exploitation issues focusing on the policy and regulatory issues that arise.

Assignment/assignation

12.102   The owner of a patent may choose to assign that right to a third party. An assignment (known as assignation in Scotland) is the transfer of ownership of a patent from one party to another.[191] When a patent is assigned, the assignee stands in the shoes of the assignor and can deal with the right as they wish. For UK patents owned by more than one party, each co-owner can only assign their share if the others consent to the assignment.[192]

12.103   An assignment of a patent does not require to be registered to be effective. However, assignments can be registered at the UK IPO.[193] Registration gives the registrant priority against anyone who has an earlier unregistered right in the patent as long as the registrant had no notice of the earlier right;[194] as with trade marks, the costs of pursuing acts of infringement prior to registration of the assignment are withheld from assignees who do not register within six months.[195]

12.104   Assignments, assignations, and other transfers of rights can be entered in the Register of Patents with the effect that this will give priority over someone who claims an earlier transaction if (1) the earlier transaction was not registered; and (2) the person claiming under the later transaction was unaware of the earlier transaction.[196] Moreover, assignees who register within six months of the transfer can then claim damages or an account of profits for infringements of the patent prior to the transaction.[197]

> ### Key point on assignment/assignation
>
> - There are rules relating to assignment/assignation for patents, and different rules exist for other IPRs. Care must be taken to ensure the correct rules are followed.

[184] Patent Act 1977, ss 30(3) and (4)(b), 31(3)–37, 46–47, 48–50.

[185] It is no longer necessary for all parties to sign as of 1 January 2005, see Regulatory Reform (Patents) Order 2004 (SI 2004/2357).

[186] For a Scottish perspective on assignations and loss of rights to sue, see *Buchanan v Alba Diagnostics Ltd* [2004] RPC 34. For comment, see RG Anderson, '*Buchanan v Alba Diagnostics*: accretion of title and assignation of future patents' (2005) 9(3) Edinburgh LR 457.

[187] For discussion see *Allen & Hanburys Ltd v Generics (UK) Ltd and Gist-Brocades NV and Others and the Comptroller General of Patents* [1986] RPC 203 per Lord Diplock.

[188] Patents Act 1977, s 30(7).   [189] Patents Act 1977, s 58.   [190] Patents Act 1977, s 67.

[191] The word 'assignment' can, in context, also refer to the actual legal document effecting this transfer: *Siemens Schweiz AG v Thorn Security Ltd* [2008] EWCA Civ 1161; [2009] Bus LR D67, para 88.

[192] Patents Act 1977, s 36(3).

[193] See UK IPO, 'Change or update your patent', www.gov.uk/change-or-update-your-patent and section 32 *UK IPO Manual of Patent Practice* (February 2016, as amended).

[194] Patents Act 1977, s 33.

[195] Patents Act 1977, s 68. In *Schutz (UK) Ltd v Werit UK Ltd* [2013] RPC 16, the Supreme Court clarified that section 68 of the Patents Act 1977 only prohibits recovery of costs in respect of infringements committed prior to registration of the relevant assignment; where infringement spans the period before and after registration, there will be an apportionment of costs and the portion attributed to post-registration infringement will be recoverable.

[196] Patents Act 1977, s 33(1).   [197] Patents Act 1977, s 68.

Question

What would happen if you have applied for registration but this has not taken place when someone comes forward with an earlier claim?

Licensing

12.105   Licensing is a central feature of the exploitation of intellectual property rights. There can be an exclusive licence, when the licensee is the only person able to do the relevant acts (including raising infringement proceedings),[198] excluding even the patent owner; or there can be a non-exclusive licence, in respect of particular activities and alongside the patent owner. Like most IPRs, patents are principally exploited through licences and sub-licences and, normally, sub-licences can be further assigned and mortgaged.[199] Patents, applications, licences, and sub-licences can vest in personal representatives on death in the same way as any other piece of personal property. The registration points in para 12.104 also apply to exclusive licensees.[200]

12.106   Patents tend to be exploited in a unitary fashion where the licensee is given the right to exploit the bundle of rights in different countries and the number of patents which can relate to a product. As this mode of exploitation makes the relationship between the patent owner and the licensee easier to manage, collecting societies (discussed in related to copyright in para 6.42ff and 20.83ff) do not exist in this area. Rather, the terms of the bargain will be the subject of negotiation between the parties. Key issues are likely to be the activities which are the subject of the licence and the manner of payment (say, a guaranteed one-off payment or say 5 per cent of future profit—what suits will depend on the market and the parties). Also, it has long been realised that the terms of a licence may have anti-competitive impacts, and so competition law regulates certain clauses that may be found in exploitation agreements. Chapter 20 contains a discussion of the application of the Technology Transfer Block Exemption Regulation to, inter alia, patent agreements.

12.107   As well as entering specific one-to-one contracts for exploitation of a patent, a patentee has a mechanism at their disposal known as *licences as of right*.[201] The patentee requests that an entry be made in the Register that licences are available as of right and this allows any party who wishes to take a licence on terms they are willing to accept through agreement or by intervention from the Comptroller.[202] A licensee of right can request that the patentee bring infringement proceedings to protect the invention and if nothing is done within two months can bring infringement proceedings themselves.[203] A subsequent application can be made to have the patent removed from the Register in this respect, although at that stage the request can be opposed by any interested parties.[204] The UK IPO maintains an open standards web database containing all patents issued under licence of right.[205]

---

[198]   ibid, s 30(7) and for Scotland s 31(7).

[199]   Patents Act 1977, s 30(4)(a), subject to s 36(3), which deals with the need for consent of co-owners.

[200]   Patents Act 1977, s 67, 68.

[201]   Patents Act 1977, s 46.

[202]   See the *UK IPO Manual of Patent Practice* (February 20016 as amended), paras 46.01–46.79 for details on the scheme.

[203]   Patents Act 1977, s 46(4).   [204]   Patents Act 1977, s 47.

[205]   This was following a recommendation in Gowers Review, para 5.50. See UK IPO, 'Patents Endorsed Licence of Right and Patents Not in Force', www.ipo.gov.uk/p-dl-licenceofright.htm.

Exercise

The UK IPO has produced guidance on licensing intellectual property, including licences of right, www.gov.uk/guidance/licensing-intellectual-property. This includes a checklist and a skeleton licence. Have a look at this and think about what might be the three most important things to pick up. What factors influence your answer?

12.108   The discussion of biotechnology patents in Chapter 11 raised concerns as to the power of the patent owner and of the importance of sharing. Concern has been expressed, in both the public and private sectors, as to the impact of granting patents over DNA sequences, and the consequent effect that might have for researchers, firms, and clinical users on legal access to genetic inventions. These arose because of concerns about how some genetic inventions, especially those used in genetic testing, had been exploited to the detriment of patients, principally because aggressive licensing practices had inhibited access to genetic tests.[206]

12.109   In 2006 the OECD published guidelines for the licensing of genetic inventions used in health care systems.[207] There is also a 2006 OECD Recommendation, laying out principles and best practices for achieving 'a balance between the delivery of new products and services, healthcare needs, and economic returns'.[208] The general spirit of the instrument is to foster openness, sharing, cooperation, and further innovation through responsible licensing practices. An OECD Recommendation is by no means legally binding, but it does represent the views and political will of 34 of the most economically influential global democracies.[209]

Exercise

Critically assess the provisions of the OECD Recommendation, https://one.oecd.org/document/C(2005)149/REV1/en/pdf and consider how its provisions might be implemented in practice. You might find it useful to reflect on your answer to the previous exercise in the light of this.

Key points on patent licensing

- There are different kinds of licence and many commercial decisions to be made as to terms.

- Concerns over exploitation of patents in the health care domain have resulted in the promulgation of a series of Guidelines designed to facilitate licensing.

---

[206] See B Williams-Jones, 'History of a gene patent: tracing the development and application of commercial BRCA testing' (2002) 10 Health Law J 123–46 and C Beauchamp, 'Patenting nature: a problem of history' (2012) Stanford Technology Law Rev, http://ssrn.com/abstract=2152105.

[207] See OECD, *Guidelines for the Licensing of Genetic Inventions* (2006), www.oecd.org/sti/emerging-tech/36198812.pdf. See also Human Genetics Commission, 'Intellectual Property and DNA Diagnostics' (October 2010), www.gov.uk/government/news/human-genetics-commission-s-report-on-dna-diagnostics. This built on an OECD workshop in 2002; see commentary at ELDIS, 'Genetic inventions, intellectual property rights and licensing practices', www.eldis.org/document/A12146.

[208] OECD, *Recommendation on the Licensing of Genetic Inventions* (2006), Council of the OECD, 23 February 2006, (2005)149/Rev1.

[209] The OECD includes the United States and the UK, but not China or India; cf KS Jayaraman, 'Is India's "patent factory" squandering funds?' (2006) 442 Nature 120.

>   **Patent legislation and Brexit**
>
> - Patent law in the UK derives from the EPC, which is outside the EU. The EU becomes relevant with the notable exception of the Biotechnology Directive - relevant here to farmers' rights.
>
> - EU law also has some relevance regarding Supplementary Protection Certificates and the references in the legislation regarding defences (directly and indirectly) to EU legislation regarding clinical data and regulatory trials (all of which are mentioned in the draft withdrawal agreement—Article 60).
>
> - Brexit may have a significant impact on the Unified Patent Court arrangements.

Further reading

Books

C Birss et al, *Terrell on the Law of Patents* (18th edn, 2016)

CIPA, *Guide to the Patents Acts* (9th edn, 2016)

C Heath (eds), *Patent Enforcement Worldwide* (2015)

J Pila, *The Requirement for an Invention in Patent Law* (2010)

Reports

R Sagar and A Nagarsheth, *Ownership of Employee Inventions and Remuneration: A Comparative Overview* (2006)

Articles

O Brand, 'The dawn of compulsory patent licensing' [2007] 2 IPQ 216

A Feros, 'Extending the Bolar exception to innovators?' (2013) 8(3) JIPLP 187

M Fisher, 'A case-study in literalism? Dissecting the English approach to patent claim construction in light of *Occlutech v AGA Medical*' [2011] 3 IPQ 283

G Grant and D Gibbons, 'Inventive concept—is it a good idea?' [2005] EIPR 170

C Howell, 'Extra compensation for inventive employees: is our system equitable, unbiased and motivating?' [2011] 4 IPQ 371

N Jadeja, H Smith-Willis, and H Hurdle, 'Case back into the sea of uncertainty–a doctrine of equivilants in UK law? The Supreme Court ruling in Actavis v Eli Lilly' (2018) 13(7) JIPLP 564

C Lawson, 'The breeders' exemption under UPOV 1991, the Convention on Biological Diversity and its Nagoya Protocol' (2015) 10(7) JIPLP 526

A Odell West, '*Kelly v GE Healthcare Ltd*: employee innovation in health care—deciphering ownership and the alchemy of "outstanding benefit"' (2010) 32(9) EIPR 449

T Shah, J Raeburn, and H Sheraton, 'Actavis v Eli Lilly: English Supreme Court shakes up approach to patent infringement by equivalents' [2017] EIPR 78

ED Ventose, '"Farming" out an exception for animals to the method of medical treatment exclusion under the European Patent Convention' (2008) 30(12) EIPR 509

C Von Drathen, 'Patent scope in English and German law under the European Patent Convention 1973 and 2000' (2008) 39(4) IIC 384

A Von Hellfeld, 'Patent infringement in Europe: the British and the German approaches to claim construction or purposive construction versus equivalency' (2008) 30(9) EIPR 364

P Widera, 'Has pemetrexed revived the doctrine of equivalents?' (2018) 13(3) JIPLP 238

Part V

Registered trade marks

Introduction

This Part of the book explains and discusses the law of registered trade marks within their international, European, and domestic setting. Chapter 13 explains the regulatory framework for the protection of registered trade marks, highlighting the international treaties and European Regulations and Directives which shape trade mark law within the domestic arena. It also introduces the theoretical underpinnings and justifications for registered trade mark protection, and the contemporary debates—often heated—which continue on this issue. Chapter 14 considers the definition of a registrable trade mark, 'absolute' grounds for refusal or invalidation of a registered trade mark, and the rules on revocation of a registered mark. Chapter 15 examines the 'relative' grounds for refusal or invalidation of a registered trade mark, infringement, and defences.

Trade marks are ubiquitous. In modern society, the consumer is surrounded daily by trade marks that are designed to distinguish the goods and services provided by one trader from those of another. As we see in Chapter 14, the breadth and range of the different types of mark which can be registered has expanded enormously, from traditional forms of trade mark such as words and logos through to a wide range of so-called 'non-traditional marks' such as 3D product shapes, colours, sounds, holograms, motion marks, and more.

Trade marks are, at their core, designed to indicate the origin of the goods and services. But, as will be seen in the following discussion, it is argued by many that trade marks also play other roles, including that of a quality indicator, a means of advertising, and a vehicle for investment in brand image. The extent to which registered trade mark law recognises these other functions as worthy of protection directly impacts on the scope of protection afforded to registered trade marks. It remains a topic of hot debate as to whether registered trade mark protection should extend beyond 'classic' infringement cases such as counterfeiting and confusing use of marks by competitors to protect against 'free riding' or uses of a mark which, although not confusing, could damage the reputation of the trade mark. As we see in Chapter 15, as scope of the registered trade mark monopoly expands, registered trade mark law increasingly brings into play concerns around free competition and freedom of expression.

What is at stake in these debates is of enormous value to businesses. According to the Forbes 2018 Ranking of the World's Most Valuable Brands, in 2018 Apple was valued at $182.8 billion, Google at $132.1 billion, Microsoft at $104.9 billion, Facebook at $94.8 billion, and Amazon at $70.9 billion. When such sums are at issue, trade mark owners and competitors are willing to litigate to ensure that they can obtain even the smallest competitive advantage over their rivals. Reflecting this, registered trade mark law has seen more preliminary references to the Court of Justice than any other area of intellectual property law. As we shall see, registered trade mark law has also recently been the subject of an extensive reform exercise by the European Union. We will consider the implications of this throughout the registered trade mark chapters. We will also consider the implications of Brexit, which may be particularly pronounced in the trade mark context.

Sources of the law: key websites

- UK Intellectual Property Office ('UK IPO'), for which see
  www.gov.uk/topic/intellectual-property/trade-marks

- EU Intellectual Property Office ('EUIPO') (formerly the 'Office for Harmonisation in the Internal Market' or 'OHIM'), for which see
  https://euipo.europa.eu/ohimportal/en/trade-marks

- Paris Convention for the Protection of Industrial Property, for which see the World Intellectual Property Organization (WIPO) website
  www.wipo.int/treaties/en/text.jsp?file_id=288514

- Madrid Agreement and Protocol, for which see the WIPO website
  www.wipo.int/madrid/en/legal_texts

Trade marks 1: key features, theoretical underpinnings, and the national, EU, and international regimes

Introduction

Scope and overview of chapter

13.1   The purpose of this chapter is threefold. First, it will outline the key features of how registered trade marks work and how they compare to other forms of intellectual property right. Second, it will explain the theoretical underpinnings and justifications for registered trade mark protection. As will become clear from this analysis, the rationale for registered trade mark protection is far from settled. Third, this chapter will introduce the legal regime for the protection of registered trade marks from a national, European Union (EU), and international perspective. Through a series of treaties, certain minimum international standards for the protection of registered trade marks have been established. Registered trade mark law has been subject to an intensive exercise of harmonisation within the EU, culminating most recently in an extensive trade mark reform package adopted in 2015. From a UK perspective, however, the future of registered trade mark law is likely to be significantly impacted by Brexit. This chapter considers the implications of Brexit for registered trade mark law, insofar as it is possible to say what those implications will be at the time of writing.

13.2   **Learning objectives**

By the end of this chapter you should be able to describe and explain:

- the key features of registered trade mark protection;
- the theoretical underpinnings and justifications for registered trade marks;
- the major international, European, and national (UK) instruments concerning trade marks;
- the potential implications of Brexit, insofar as known at the time of writing.

13.3   The rest of this chapter looks like this:

- Registered trade marks—key features (13.4–13.7)
- Registered trade marks—theoretical underpinnings (13.8–13.13)
- The regulatory framework, including Brexit (13.14–13.51)

Registered trade marks—key features

13.4   There are a number of key points of difference between registered trade marks and the other intellectual property rights discussed in this book. The length of the monopoly conferred by a trade mark registration is the first of these. Patents give a monopoly for a limited period of time of 20 years.[1] Copyright is typically protected for up to 70 years after the death of the author.[2] Registered designs give a monopoly of up to 25 years.[3] Trade marks, in contrast, can give a monopoly which lasts indefinitely. Registration of a trade mark in the UK lasts for ten years from the date of filing.[4] However, a trade mark owner can renew a registration indefinitely for successive 10-year periods with the result that, if renewed in this way, registration may be perpetual.[5] Bass plc registered the red triangle logo shown in Figure 13.1 on 1 January 1876.

Figure 13.1 Bass logo

It was the first mark to be registered in the UK trade mark register and is still registered.

13.5   The nature of the registered trade mark monopoly is also very different to other intellectual property (IP) rights. Trade marks have to be registered in respect of specified goods and services for which the mark is, or will be, used. All goods and services are classified according to their nature into one of 45 different classes based on the Nice Agreement Concerning the International Classification of Goods and Services, an international agreement administered by the World Intellectual Property Organization (WIPO).

Web link

You can find a copy of the Nice classification at www.wipo.int/classifications/nice/en/classifications.html.

Question

Which Nice classes cover the following goods/services: legal advice, spades, wine, tractors, paper?

Registration of a mark does not give the trader a monopoly in the mark *per se* or in the goods or services in connection with which the mark is registered. Instead, the registration protects the relationship between the mark and those goods or services for which it is registered. As a result, multiple unconnected traders

---

[1] For a discussion on patents, see Chapter 12.   [2] For a discussion on copyright and duration of protection, see Chapter 3.
[3] For a discussion on registered designs, see Chapter 8.   [4] Trade Marks Act (TMA) 1994, s 42(1),   [5] TMA 1994, s 43.

may use the same sign as a registered marks in relation to different goods or services without necessarily conflicting with each other. For example, in the UK, the mark POLO is used and registered in respect of confectionery, clothing, and cars.

13.6 Because a trade mark registration can be kept on the register indefinitely, unlike a patent, design, or copyright work, a registered mark will not fall into the public domain after a specified time. To provide a counterbalance for this, there are important rules requiring the trade mark owner to put a registered mark to 'genuine use'. These rules are, in effect, the *quid pro quo* for perpetual protection. The use requirement seeks to balance the interests of the trade mark proprietor and competitors. Marks which are not put to 'genuine use' are open to challenge (revocation), thereby freeing them for competing traders to use. This deters trade mark owners from stockpiling registered marks without using them, putting competitors at a competitive disadvantage.

13.7 Although registered trade marks occupy their own particular place within the intellectual property family, there is potential for overlap between trade marks and other rights. This can create very particular tensions because of the potentially perpetual nature of the trade mark monopoly. For example, if it were possible to obtain a registered trade mark for the shape of a product which was linked to the way the product worked, it might be possible—through that trade mark registration—indefinitely to exclude competitors from adopting the same or similar shapes and, thereby, the same or similar technical functionality in their own products. Monopoly protection over aspects of technical functionality could in effect be obtained without the need to meet the very demanding threshold requirements of patent law. Trade mark law could also be used to perpetuate protection beyond the much shorter period of patent protection. These are regarded as highly undesirable outcomes from a policy perspective and, as we shall see further in Chapter 14, registered trade mark law contains certain specific grounds for objection to registration designed to regulate these concerns.

Discussion point   For answer guidance visit **www.oup.com/uk/brown5e**.

Can you summarise the key features of registered trade mark protection, and compare those features to the other principal IP rights?

Registered trade marks—theoretical underpinnings

13.8 In the relationship between the trade mark owner and consumer, trade marks perform a vital function of indicating the *origin* of the goods or services being sold. In other words, as trade mark lawyers often put it, the trade mark functions as a *badge of origin*. This function is at the heart of the existence of trade marks. The Court of Justice has recognised this since its earliest case law on trade marks, identifying the origin-denoting function of a trade mark as its 'essential function':[6]

> the essential function of the trade mark . . . is to guarantee the identity of the origin of the trade marked product to the consumer or ultimate user.

As the Court has also said:[7]

> With regard to trade mark rights, it should be observed that such rights constitute an essential element of the system of undistorted competition which the Treaty aims to establish and maintain. In such a system enterprises must be able to gain customers by the quality of their products or services, which can be done only by virtue of the existence of distinctive signs permitting identification of those products and services. For a trade mark to be able to play this part, it must constitute a guarantee that all the products bearing it have been manufactured under the supervision of a single enterprise to which responsibility for their quality may be attributed.

[6] Case C-3/78 *Centrafarm v American Home Products* [1979] FSR 189, para 12.
[7] Case C-10/89 *Cnl-Sucal NV SA v HAG GF AG* [1991] FSR 99, para 13.

13.9   As we shall see in Chapter 14, the ability of a mark to act as an indicator of the origin of goods or services in line with its 'essential function' is a key criterion for registrability. Preventing damage to the origin function of a mark—for example, damage which might be caused by the use of a confusingly similar sign by a competitor—is also at the heart of the infringement regime discussed at Chapter 15. This ties in with the law-and-economics theoretical justification for trade mark rights. This school of thinking argues that trade marks are beneficial to the smooth functioning of the marketplace because they help consumers locate the product or service which they wish to purchase and thereby reduce consumer 'search costs'—that is, the costs in terms of time and effort that would otherwise be required to identify the particular product desired if there were no distinguishing marks to help in this process.[8] This very commerce-driven rationale stands in contrast with the justifications for the protection of patents, copyright, and designs, each of which seeks to encourage creativity and/or innovation and to reward the creator. Although some commentators have proposed other rationales for registered trade mark protection,[9] according to the dominant economic perspective there is no such reward for creativeness in the rationales underpinning registered trade mark protection: the theoretical underpinnings are generally regarded as far more market-focused.

13.10 The importance attached to the 'essential function', and the role it plays for consumers, ties into a further important function of a trade mark, which is to indicate to the consumer the *quality* of the particular goods or services sold in connection with a particular mark:[10]

> the relevance of the trade mark's function as a guarantee of origin lies . . . in the fact that the trade mark conveys to the consumer certain perceptions as to the quality of the marked goods. The consumer is not interested in the commercial origin of goods out of idle curiosity; his interest is based on the assumption that goods of the same origin will be of the same quality.

As Advocate General Jacobs further put it:[11]

> Without trade mark protection there would be little incentive for manufacturers to develop new products or to maintain the quality of existing ones. Trade marks are able to achieve that effect because they act as a guarantee, to the consumer, that all goods bearing a particular mark have been produced by, or under the control of, the same manufacturer and are therefore likely to be of similar quality. The guarantee of quality offered by a trade mark is not of course absolute, for the manufacturer is at liberty to vary the quality; however, he does so at his own risk and he—not his competitors—will suffer the consequences if he allows the quality to decline. Thus, although trade marks do not provide any form of *legal* guarantee of quality . . . they do in economic terms provide such a guarantee, which is acted upon daily by consumers.

The quality of the goods or services concerned may be high-end or it may be more basic: the key is that, when consumers see a familiar registered trade mark, they expect to get the *same* quality as they experienced in previous purchases or that they have come to anticipate from advertising.

13.11 It is argued that trade marks also perform a range of further functions. Another such function of a trade mark might be said to be that of *advertising* the goods or services sold by the trader in connection with the mark. Many traders invest not only time and effort, but also substantial sums in bringing a particular mark to the attention of the public. For many the hope will be that eventually such is the recognition of the mark on the consumer market it is then the mark that will sell the product:[12]

---

[8] There is a rich literature examining the economic case for trade mark protection. For only a small selection see, eg, WM Landes and RA Posner, *The Economic Structure of Intellectual Property Law* (2003); WM Landes and RA Posner, 'Trade mark law: an economic perspective' (1987) J Law and Economics 268; NS Economides, 'The economics of trade marks' (1988) 78 TMR 523; RW Holzhauer, 'Jenever and jumping wild cats' in R Towse (ed), *III The Economics of Intellectual Property* (2002), 418; IPL Png and D Reitman, 'Why are some products branded and others not?' in R Towse (ed), *III The Economics of Intellectual Property* (2002), 207; SL Carter, 'The trouble with trademark' in R Towse (ed), *III The Economics of Intellectual Property* (2002), 373.

[9] See, eg, B Beebe, 'The Semiotic Analysis of Trademark Law' (2004) 51 UCLA L Rev 621; J Fromer, 'The Role of Creativity in Trademark Law' (2011) 86 Notre Dame Law Rev 1885.

[10] Case C-10/89 *SA Cnl-Sucal NV v Hag GF AG* [1991] FSR 99, Advocate General Jacobs at 129–30.

[11] ibid, Advocate General Jacobs at 109–10.

[12] *Souza Cruz SA v Hollywood SAS*, OHIM Third Board of Appeal Case R283/1999–3 [2002] ETMR 64, para 67.

the trade mark is not only a sign affixed to a product to indicate its business origin, but is also a vehicle for communicating a message to the public, and itself represents financial value. This message is incorporated into the trade mark through use, essentially for advertising purposes, which enables the trade mark to assume the message itself, whether informatively or symbolically. The message may refer to the product's qualities, or indeed to intangible values such as luxury, lifestyle, exclusivity, adventure, youth etc.

13.12 A trade mark might also be seen as an *investment*. Much time and money is spent on building consumer awareness of a particular mark and association with brand image:[13]

> The fact remains that a mark also acts as a means of conveying other messages concerning, inter alia, the qualities or particular characteristics of the goods or services which it covers or the images and feelings which it conveys, such as luxury, lifestyle, exclusivity, adventure, youth. To that effect the mark has an inherent economic value which is independent of and separate from that of the goods or services for which it is registered. The messages in question which are conveyed inter alia by a mark with a reputation or which are associated with it confer on that mark a significant value which deserves protection, particularly because, in most cases, the reputation of a mark is the result of considerable effort and investment on the part of its proprietor.

13.13 These further functions of a trade mark are sometimes referred to as the 'communication functions' of a trade mark. One of the most important debates in registered trade mark law has been—and remains—how far these further functions should be recognised and protected separately from the 'essential function' of indicating origin. One argument against this is that these further functions of the mark only ever come into play if the mark is already working as a badge of origin. On this view, the priority of registered trade mark law should be to focus on infringements which impair the mark's ability to function as a badge of origin—for example, infringements which cause a likelihood of confusion among consumers. The quality, advertising, and investment functions are considered by many as merely subsets of the basic function of indicating the origin of the goods and services:[14]

> It is also argued that trade marks have other functions, which might be termed 'communication', investment, or advertising functions. Those functions are said to arise from the fact that the investment in the promotion of a product is built around the mark. It is accordingly reasoned that those functions are values which deserve protection as such, even when there is no abuse arising from misrepresentations about either origin or quality. However, those functions seem to me to be merely derivatives of the origin function; there would be little purpose in advertising a mark if it were not for the function of that mark as an indicator of origin, distinguishing the trade mark owner's goods from those of his competitors.

On the other hand, others argue that the further functions of a trade mark should be protected in their own right by registered trade mark law:[15]

> It seems to me to be simplistic reductionism to limit the function of the trade mark to an indication of trade origin . . . Experience teaches that, in most cases, the user is unaware of who produces the goods he consumes. The trade mark acquires a life of its own, making a statement, as I have suggested, about quality, reputation and even, in certain cases, a way of seeing life.
>
> The messages it sends out are, moreover, autonomous. A distinctive sign can indicate at the same time trade origin, the reputation of its proprietor and the quality of the goods it represents, but there is nothing to prevent the consumer, unaware of who manufactures the goods or provides the services which bear the trade mark, from acquiring them because he perceives the mark as an emblem of prestige or a guarantee of quality. When I regard the current functioning of the market and the behaviour of the average consumer, I see no reason whatever not to protect those other functions of the trade mark and to safeguard only the function of indicating the trade origin of the goods and services.

[13] Case T-93/06 *Mülhens GmbH & Co KG v OHIM* [2008] ETMR 69, para 26.
[14] Case C-337/95 *Parfums Christian Dior and Parfums Christina Dior BV v Evora BV* [1997] ETMR 323, Advocate General Jacobs, para 42.
[15] Case C-206/01 *Arsenal Football Club plc v Reed* [2002] ETMR 82, Advocate General Ruiz-Jarabo Colomer, paras 46–47.

As we shall see in Chapter 15, the (highly disputed) further functions of a trade mark have become increasingly protected in the law of registered trade mark infringement. This has come about both as a result of certain provisions in the EU trade marks regime (particularly the extended protection against infringements for 'marks with a reputation') and, separately, as a result of further (highly controversial) case law development by the Court of Justice. The further functions of a mark play a particular role if it is decided that the scope of the protection conferred by the mark should go beyond the prevention of consumer confusion to extend into protecting a mark against non-confusing 'free-riding' or reputationally damaging infringements. The effect of infringement on the consumer, and thereby on the mark's ability to perform its essential function of indicating origin, is no longer relevant. Rather, the focus turns to the value of the mark *per se*. As we shall see, there remains considerable—and heated—debate over whether it is properly the job of registered trade mark law to protect marks in these sorts of circumstances. From a law-and-economics perspective, there is seen to be a risk that rewarding trade mark owners through registered trade mark law for their investment and advertising in lifestyle and similarly aspirational messages risks leaving consumers vulnerable to making irrational product purchasing decisions, selecting one product over another not because of their respective objective qualities but because of the sway which one particular trade mark owner's advertising may have. This in turn may cause consumers to pay more for goods than the products are really worth, with consequent impacts on the efficient functioning of the market. These debates over the proper scope of registered trade mark protection seem likely to continue, both in the EU and in the UK post-Brexit.

 Exercise

Revisit this discussion of trade mark theory once you have finished the chapters on trade marks in this book. In the light of everything you have studied, what is your view on the proper focus of registered trade mark protection?

 Exercise

Go into a supermarket and browse the goods on the shelves. Look at the trade marks on those products. What impressions do you get? Imagine then a supermarket full of products between which there is no differentiation. The shape of the goods and their packaging are alike. How do you make your choices?

Key points on registered trade mark law's theoretical underpinnings

- It is widely agreed that the 'essential function' of a trade mark is to function as a badge of origin; that is, to indicate the origin of the goods or services for which it is registered. This is very important to the requirements for registrability discussed further in Chapter 14. Preventing damage to the origin function of a registered mark—for example, through use of a confusingly similar sign by a competitor—is also at the heart of the infringement regime discussed at Chapter 15.

- There are, however, on-going debates as to whether (and, if so, how far) trade mark law should also recognise various further functions of trade marks, including their ability to act as an indication of quality, a means of advertising, and a vehicle for investment. These are sometimes referred to as the 'extended' or 'communication' functions of a mark. As we will see further in Chapter 15, this is a particular issue in terms of the scope of protection to be afforded to registered trade marks against infringement.

Note: collective and certification marks

In the discussion above, we have been considering the theoretical underpinnings of the classic form of registered trade mark protection. It is this form of trade mark protection that is our focus in this textbook.

It is worth being aware, however, that there are certain further forms of trade mark protection which have quite different rationales. These are called 'certification' and 'collective' trade marks.

Broadly speaking, 'certification' marks are intended to guarantee that the goods or services to which they are applied possess certain specific defined characteristics. The owner of a 'certification mark'—typically, some form of trade association—does not use the mark itself, but authorises others to use the mark where their goods or services are certified as having the relevant defined characteristics.

'Collective' marks are intended to show that the relevant goods or services emanate from a member of a particular trade association. They work, in essence, as a guarantee of membership of that trade association.

As will be evident from this brief explanation, both 'certification' and 'collective' marks are quite different to classic registered trade marks which are, as we have discussed, focused first and foremost on performing the task of distinguishing the goods and services of one undertaking from those of all other undertakings. 'Certification' and 'collective' marks are, in practical terms, of more niche interest than the classic form of registered trade mark protection discussed in this textbook. They are both now protected at the UK level under the TMA 1994 (as amended) (see sections 49–50 and Schedules 1 and 2) and at the pan-EU level under the EUTMR 2017 (see Articles 74–93). We will not discuss 'certification' or 'collective' marks further in this textbook, but the UK IPO has published useful guidance (www.gov.uk/government/publications/collective-and-certification-trade-marks), as has the EUIPO (https://euipo.europa.eu/ohimportal/en/certification-and-collective-marks). See also J Belson, *Certification and Collective Marks: Law and Practice* (Edward Elgar 2017), and M Repas and T Kerestes, 'The certification mark as a new EU-wide industrial property right' (2018) 49(3) IIC 299–317.

The regulatory framework

13.14   The purpose of this section is to discuss the regulatory framework in depth to provide a foundation for discussion in the ensuing chapters on substantive trade mark law. In particular, it is to enable the reader to appreciate how domestic law and procedure are shaped by both EU and international requirements. Harmonisation has played an enormous role in shaping trade mark law at the UK and EU levels; that harmonisation is in a new phase of further development as a result of an EU trade mark reform package instituted in 2015, which we will discuss further below. The UK is presently updating its domestic registered trade mark law to reflect the requirements of the 2015 reform package. However, the position is likely to be significantly impacted thereafter by Brexit. The likely impact of Brexit, insofar as it can be known at the time of writing, is outlined further below.

Key measures at the national (UK), EU, and international level

National (UK)

Trade Marks Act 1994

This implements the Trade Mark Directive and obligations from international treaties. Extensive amendments implementing the requirements of the EU's 2015 reform package are, at the time of writing, due to enter into force in January 2019.

European

EU Trade Mark Regulation 2017

Governs the supranational EU trade mark (formerly the 'Community trade mark')

Trade Marks Directive 2015

Latest version of Directive harmonising the law on registered trade marks in EU member states

International

Administered by the World Trade Organisation (WTO):

TRIPS Agreement

Substantive minimum standards

Makes reference to Paris

National treatment

Most favoured nation clause

Administered by WIPO:

Paris Convention

Substantive minimum standards

National treatment

Madrid Agreement

Streamlined application process

Central attack

Madrid Protocol

Streamlined application process

Conversion to national applications

Trade Mark Law Treaty

Procedural rules

Singapore Treaty

Procedural rules

Nice Classification

The current regulatory framework: domestic (UK) and European

13.15   Registered trade mark law was the EU's first foray into the harmonisation of IP rights. The first version of the Trade Marks Directive (First Council Directive 89/104/EEC) was enacted in December 1988. Member states were required to amend their national registered trade mark laws to bring them in line with the Directive. For many member states, this represented a ground-breaking new registered trade mark law regime, broadening significantly both what could be registered as a trade mark and the scope of protection against infringement. Alongside the Directive, the EU was also working on creating its first ever new unitary IP right, the 'Community trade mark'. The first version of the Community Trade Mark Regulation (Regulation 40/94/EC) was enacted in December 1993. Updated versions of both the Directive and the Regulation were issued in 2008–2009 (Directive 2008/95/EC and Regulation 207/2009/EC), although without any significant substantive changes for present purposes.

13.16   Across these versions of the Directive and the Regulation, the provisions dealing with the definition of a registrable trade mark, grounds for refusal, invalidation, revocation and infringement, and defences were very similar, if not identical. This is because the rules on these matters were intended to be the same at both the national level (for national trade mark registrations) and EU level (for Community trade marks, as they were then called), albeit that the geographical extent of the right differed between the two systems. Common concepts and legal provisions were to be interpreted the same way. As noted by the Advocate General in *SA Société LTJ Diffusion v SA Sadas*[16] in relation to the parallel provisions of the Directive and Regulation:[17]

> [W]hen the Community legislature takes care to express itself in that manner—as it clearly did in the field of trade marks—the presumption is very strong indeed that the two measures are intended to be interpreted in the same way. The fact that they will be applied in different legal and factual circumstances does not detract from that presumption.

As we shall see, case law dealing with the Directive and the Regulation is effectively interchangeable where dealing with common concepts and rules. For both national and EU-level trade mark rights, the Court of Justice is the final arbiter in matters of interpretation of the EU regime. There have been a very great many preliminary references to the Court of Justice—well over one hundred—on the Directive and Regulation.

---

[16]   Case C-291/00 *SA Société LTJ Diffusion v SA Sadas*, Advocate General's opinion reported at [2002] ETMR 40.

[17]   ibid, AG opinion, para 25.

Discussion point   For answer guidance visit **www.oup.com/uk/brown5e.**

The area of registered trade marks has attracted more case law at European level than any other intellectual property right. Why do you think this is so?

13.17   More recently, the EU embarked on a major review of registered trade mark law, looking at the state of harmonisation of national laws and at the functioning of the Community trade mark system. A very substantial study was produced by the Max Planck Institute in 2011, which made a number of recommendations for reform.[18] Thereafter, the European Commission put forward proposals and amendments to both the Directive and Regulation, which were pursued through the EU's legislative processes. This resulted in:

- a new and substantially revised Trade Marks Directive (EU) 2015/2436 (the 'TMD 2015'). Member states were required to update their national registered trade mark laws to align with the TMD 2015 by January 2019; and

- a new and substantially revised European Union Trade Mark Regulation (EU) 2017/1001 (the 'EUTMR 2017'). The name of the 'Community trade mark' has been changed to the 'European Union trade mark' (or, as we shall call it, the 'EU trade mark' for short). The EU initially passed an amending regulation (Regulation 2015/2424) which required to be read in conjunction with the old version of the Regulation. However, this was difficult to follow and the EUTMR 2017 now represents a complete and consolidated codified version of the changes made. The EUTMR 2017 has applied since 1 October 2017.

Throughout the trade mark chapters of this book, we will refer in the first instance to the provisions of the new TMD 2015 and EUTMR 2017, referring back to the older versions as required. Many of the key cases will refer to the older versions of the Directive and Regulation and there have been some changes to Article numbering, particularly in the TMD 2015.

UK registered trade marks

13.18   The current legislation in the UK governing registered trade marks is contained in the Trade Marks Act 1994 ('TMA 1994'). The TMA 1994 was introduced to implement First Council Directive 89/104/EEC. The TMA 1994 repealed the earlier UK legislation relating to registered trade marks which had been contained in the Trade Marks Act 1938. The TMA 1994 Act governs UK national registered trade marks.

13.19   At the time of writing, the TMA 1994 is in the process of being updated to reflect the updated requirements of the TMD 2015. Amendments to the TMA 1994 will be brought into effect by The Trade Mark Regulations 2018 (SI 2018/825), which will come into force on 14 January 2019. This date falls well before the UK's Brexit 'exit date' of 29 March 2019, so the amended version of the TMA 1994 will come into force whatever ultimately happens in relation to the UK's withdrawal from the EU. Throughout the registered trade marks chapters of this book, we will refer to the TMA 1944 as due to be amended by SI 2018/825.

Web link

The IPO has a website at www.gov.uk/government/organisations/intellectual-property-office. It has a section that is devoted entirely to trade marks, giving both general information on trade marks and access to a database containing details of registered marks, pending applications for registration, and information on applications which have been refused.

---

[18]   Max Planck Institute for Intellectual Property and Competition Law, *Study on the Overall Functioning of the European Trade Mark System* (February 2011).

Exercise

To familiarise yourself with the site and in particular the trade mark database, go to the UK IPO site and carry out a number of searches in the trade mark register. Can you find the Bass logo mentioned previously?

Place of application and procedure: UK

13.20   A UK registered trade mark has effect within the territory of the UK.[19] To apply for a UK registered trade mark, an application is made to the UK Intellectual Property Office ('UK IPO') which has its main office in Newport, Wales. Application forms can be found on the UK IPO website. The application must include a request for registration, the name and address of the applicant, a statement of the goods or services in relation to which it is sought to register the mark, and a representation of the trade mark.[20] The applicant must also include a statement that the trade mark is being used by the applicant or with his consent in relation to the goods and services applied for or that the applicant has a bona fide intention to use it.[21] The date of filing is the date on which all the relevant information is given to the Registrar.[22] The filing date is the one on which matters of priority under the Paris Convention may be settled.[23] The filing fee is currently £200 (or £170, if filed in outline) for one class of goods or services and £50 for every additional class.

13.21   Since 2007, the practice at the UK IPO has been that a trade mark examiner will examine the application on absolute grounds to see if it is registrable. The trade mark examiner will examine the application to see whether the mark applied for falls within the definition of a registrable mark and meets the criteria for registration set out in section 3 TMA 1994 (as amended) (as to which, see further Chapter 14). Previously UK trade mark applications were also examined on relative grounds, which meant that the trade mark examiner tried to assess conflict with earlier marks to see if the mark should be refused registration. This was changed in light of the fact that the EUIPO only undertakes examination on absolute grounds for EU trade marks. This disparity had resulted in an anomalous situation in which it was proving easier to register a mark as an EU trade mark than it was as a UK trade mark registration. Now, the trade mark examiner will still search their records for earlier rights, but will merely bring those rights to the attention of the applicant to allow the applicant to decide whether to proceed with the application. It is up to the owner of any earlier conflicting right to oppose the application on relative grounds. Once the application has been accepted it is published in the Trade Marks Journal.[24]

Web link

You can access the Trade Marks Journal online at the UK IPO website at www.gov.uk/check-trade-marks-journal.

After publication, there is a two-month period during which third parties can oppose the application (extendable to three months, if the opponent files a notice of intention to oppose). If the parties do not settle their disagreement on the application, there may be a hearing before determination of registrability by the Registrar.

---

[19]   TMA 1994 (as amended), s 108: England and Wales, Scotland, Northern Ireland, and Isle of Man.
[20]   TMA 1994 (as amended), s 32(2).   [21]   TMA 1994 (as amended), s 32(3).   [22]   TMA 1994 (as amended), s 33(1).
[23]   TMA 1994 (as amended), s 35.   [24]   TMA 1994 (as amended), s 38.

13.22   An appeal lies from a decision of the Registrar either to an 'Appointed Person' or to the court.[25] If an appeal is made to an Appointed Person, the Appointed Person may refer the matter to the court if it appears that a matter of general legal importance is involved, or if the Registrar requests referral, or if such a request is made by any party to the proceedings.[26] If the Appointed Person hears the appeal, his decision is final.[27] If there is no opposition (or if any opposition proceedings are resolved through negotiation), the trade mark will be registered[28] and the registration published in the Trade Marks Journal. The period of protection is backdated to the date of filing of the application.[29] The filing date is also the date from which the rights of the owner are enforceable against third parties (although no enforcement action may be taken until such time as the trade mark is registered)[30] as well as the date from which the 10-year term of the trade mark registration is calculated for renewal purposes. The date of grant of the registration remains relevant should the registered mark face a revocation challenge on grounds of non-use (see further Chapter 14).

13.23   The UK IPO website contains a 'Manual of Trade Marks Practice' giving full details of the application procedure, other formal and administrative steps in the registration process, and extensive guidance on how the UK IPO will apply substantive trade mark law to the filings and cases before it. The UK IPO also regularly issues Practice Amendment Notices, which give details of changes in procedures amending existing practices as case law develops.

13.24   A UK registered trade mark is an item of personal property (in Scotland, incorporeal movable property).[31] In terms of formalities, an assignment of a UK registered mark need only be signed by the assignor.[32] An assignment of a UK registered trade mark can be partial in respect of only some of the goods or services covered by the trade mark registration, and can also be limited geographically or in manner of use.[33] If a transaction concerning a UK trade mark is not registered, it will be ineffective as against a person acquiring a conflicting interest in or under the mark who does not know of the transaction.[34] An assignee who does not register within six months of the transaction cannot recover costs in respect of pursuing acts of infringement that occur prior to registration of the transaction.[35]

EU trade marks

13.25   Not only is it possible to obtain a trade mark covering the UK but, as explained in para 13.15, since 1994 it has been open to traders to register a trade mark at the pan-EU level, that registration being effective throughout the territory of member states of the EU. When first established by Council Regulation 40/94/EC, this was called the 'Community trade mark'. The name has now changed to the 'European Union trade mark' (or 'EU trade mark' for short). EU trade marks are granted and administered by the European Union Intellectual Property Office ('EUIPO', formerly called the Office for Harmonisation in the Internal Market or 'OHIM' for short).

Web link

The database containing applications for and information on EU trade marks can be found at the EUIPO website at https://euipo.europa.eu/ohimportal/en.

---

[25] TMA 1994 (as amended), s 76(2).   [26] TMA 1994 (as amended), s 76(3).   [27] TMA 1994 (as amended), s 76(4).
[28] TMA 1994 (as amended), s 40.   [29] TMA 1994 (as amended), s 40(3).   [30] TMA 1994 (as amended), s 9(3).
[31] TMA 1994 (as amended), s 22.   [32] TMA 1994 (as amended), s 24(3).   [33] TMA 1994 (as amended), s 24(2).
[34] TMA 1994 (as amended), s 25(3).   [35] TMA 1994 (as amended), s 25(4).

Exercise

Familiarise yourself with the EUIPO website by searching the trade mark database. Note that the website also contains much useful information concerning decisions made in relation to EU trade marks. Look under 'eSearch Case Law' and you will see that you can access decisions of the Boards of Appeal, of the General Court (formerly the Court of First Instance), and of the Court of Justice (formerly the ECJ). The website also includes details of current EUIPO practice and links to the relevant legal texts.

The main features of the EU trade mark system

13.26   By contrast with a national trade mark, an EU trade mark is effective throughout the member states of the EU. Article 1(2) EUTMR 2017 provides:

> An EU trade mark shall have a unitary character. It shall have equal effect throughout the Union: it shall not be registered, transferred or surrendered or be the subject of a decision revoking the rights of the proprietor or declaring it invalid, nor shall its use be prohibited, save in respect of the whole Union.

The EU trade mark was the first example of a supranational EU IP right (and is, in broad terms, the model upon which the Community registered design is based). Prior to the introduction of the EU trade mark, a trader who wished to have a trade mark registration in multiple member states of the EU would have had to apply separately to each trade mark office in each member state. With the EU trade mark, only one application needs to be made to the EUIPO and the resulting EU trade mark registration is effective in all member states.

13.27   It was stated in para 13.26 that an EU trade mark has effect throughout all the member states within the EU. However, there are circumstances in which that will not be the case, called by some the 'Emmental cheese' provisions because a 'hole' may subsist in the unitary character of the EU trade mark.[36] These 'holes' arise because Articles 137 and 138 EUTMR 2017 (formerly Articles 110 and 111 CTMR 2009) preserve the right to invoke an earlier right law to prevent the use of a later EU trade mark in one or more member states. Annand and Norman give a number of examples of how these provisions may work in practice. Two of these are as follows:[37]

> A is the owner of a trade mark registered in France. A can oppose or apply to cancel a later conflicting CTM. Alternatively [and this is where the 'Emmental cheese' provisions arise] A can object to the use of the CTM in France by bringing an infringement action under French law before a French court.

> B is the owner of an unregistered trade mark in the United Kingdom. B can oppose or apply to cancel a later conflicting CTM. Alternatively B can bring an action in passing-off before a United Kingdom court to prevent use in the United Kingdom.

Because the owner of the earlier conflicting right chooses not to oppose the *registration* of the EU trade mark, nor to apply for its cancellation, but instead to challenge the *use* of the EU trade mark within the member state in question, the EU trade mark remains technically valid and effective throughout all member states. However, in practice it cannot be used in the member state (or states) where the earlier right subsists, because the owner of the earlier right in that jurisdiction may be able to sue. Thus, the EU trade mark is like a piece of cheese with a hole (or holes) in it.[38]

---

[36] RE Annand and HE Norman, *Blackstone's Guide to the Community Trade Mark* (1998), 128.   [37] ibid, note 88.

[38] There are also certain circumstances in which an injunction for infringement of an EU trade mark may not cover the whole of the EU: see further Chapter 21.

Place of application and procedure

13.28 EU trade marks are applied for at the EUIPO, formerly called the 'Office for Harmonisation in the Internal Market' or 'OHIM' for short). The EUIPO maintains the EU trade mark register. Any natural or legal person may be the proprietor of an EU trade mark.[39] An EU trade mark applicant is not required to have a commercial establishment in the EU. Examiners at the EUIPO make decisions relating to the conditions of filing of an EU trade mark,[40] absolute grounds for refusal,[41] oppositions,[42] and decisions to revoke or declare an EU trade mark invalid.[43] An EU trade mark will not be examined on relative grounds, although there are provisions for the generation of search reports identifying potentially problematic earlier rights.[44] An appeal lies from any one of these decisions to the EUIPO Boards of Appeal and, thereafter, the General Court.[45] A further right of appeal lies from the General Court to the Court of Justice.

13.29 If an application for an EU trade mark has been examined and accepted, it is published.[46] During a period of three months thereafter, third parties may make observations arguing that the mark should not have been granted on absolute grounds or oppose the application on relative grounds.[47] If the application is rejected it may be converted to national applications retaining the original filing date[48] (but not in those member states to which the ground of refusal relates). Where there is no opposition the mark will be registered.[49] The 10-year period of registration runs from the filing date.[50]

13.30 The effects of an EU trade mark (including the grounds of infringement) are governed by the EUTMR 2017. Beyond this (eg in terms of procedure), enforcement of an EU trade mark is left to national law.[51] Each member state has designated first and second instance national courts—called 'EU trade mark courts'—to deal with litigation concerning EU trade marks. In the UK, the main first instance EU trade mark courts are the High Courts of England and Wales and of Northern Ireland, and the Court of Session in Scotland.[52]

13.31 Article 19(1) EUTMR 2017 provides that:

> an EU trade mark as an object of property shall be dealt with in its entirety, and for the whole area of the Union, as a national trade mark registered in the Member State in which, according to the Register:
>
> (a) the proprietor has his seat or his domicile on the relevant date;
> (b) where point (a) does not apply, the proprietor has an establishment on the relevant date

failing which as a national trade mark registered in the member state where the EUIPO is based (i.e. Spain). An assignment of an EU trade mark must be in writing and signed by or on behalf of all of the parties to the transaction.[53]

Assignment of an EU trade mark can be partial in respect of only some of the goods or services covered by the trade mark registration.[54] Otherwise, however, an EU trade mark must be dealt with 'in its entirety, and for the whole area of the Union'.[55] For as long as any transfer has not been entered on the EU trade mark register, the assignee may not invoke the rights arising from registration of the EU trade mark.[56]

Discussion point   For answer guidance visit **www.oup.com/uk/brown5e.**

Why might a trader want to have a single trade mark registration effective throughout the EU? Consider the advantages and disadvantages of EU trade mark protection.

---

[39] European Union Trade Mark Regulation (EUTMR) 2017, Art 5.   [40] EUTMR 2017, Art 41.   [41] EUTMR 2017, Art 42.
[42] EUTMR 2017, Art 47.   [43] EUTMR 2017, Arts 63–64.
[44] EUTMR 2017, Art 43. An applicant may request a search report from the EU IPO (Art 43(1)) and/or other national offices (Arts 43(2)–(3)). Owners of earlier EU trade marks identified in the EU search report will be notified of publication of the application (Art 43(7)).
[45] EUTMR 2017, Arts 66–72.   [46] EUTMR 2017, Art 44.   [47] EUTMR 2017, Arts 45–46.   [48] EUTMR 2017, Art 139.
[49] EUTMR 2017, Art 51.   [50] EUTMR 2017, Art 52.   [51] EUTMR 2017, Arts 17 and 129(2).
[52] Community Trade Mark Regulations 2006 (SI 2006/1027).   [53] EUTMR 2017, Art 20(3).   [54] EUTMR 2017, Art 20(1).
[55] EUTMR 2017, Art 19(1).   [56] EUTMR 2017, Art 19(11).

The advantages of the EU trade mark over a portfolio of national marks

13.32   Procedural simplification:

- Applying for an EU trade mark greatly simplifies the procedure for trade mark owners. Only one application need be made in one language and one set of fees paid, resulting in a single right effective throughout the EU.

- Having a single EU trade mark makes it much easier for trade mark owners to manage their portfolio of registered trade marks (eg for monitoring and paying renewals).

13.33   Seniority:

- An additional advantage of the EU trade mark is the system of 'seniority'. (This is not to be confused with the system of 'priority' under the Paris Convention—see paragraph 13.42 below.) The EU trade mark 'seniority' rules allows the owner of an EU trade mark to claim the seniority of an earlier national registration for the same mark, registered for the same goods and services, in any member state when applying for an EU trade mark.[57] The effect of a successful claim of seniority is that the trade mark proprietor can let the earlier national registration lapse, while at the same time have the same rights as if the national trade mark had continued to be registered. The purpose of the seniority rules is to permit trade mark owners to centralise ownership of trade marks in member states in a single mark (the EU trade mark) without jeopardising the rights accrued under individual national trade marks, many of which will have been long-standing well before the creation of the pan-EU trade mark.

13.34   Enforcement benefits:

- In certain circumstances, an EU trade mark court hearing an infringement dispute will have jurisdiction in respect of acts of infringement committed or threatened in any member state of the EU.[58] In effect, this empowers EU trade mark courts to grant remedies (such as injunctions or damages) which cover the whole of the EU.[59] Raising proceedings for infringement of an EU trade mark before an EU trade mark court in this way is therefore a highly efficient and effective way of dealing with cross-border and multi-state infringements.

13.35   Single market benefits:

- Having trade marks registered in different member states by the same trader can cause problems for the internal market. Where a trade mark owner chooses different trade marks for different member states, it has the potential effect of partitioning the single market along territorial boundaries (see further Chapter 19). A trade mark owner could maintain national registrations for the same mark in several member states with a view to keeping out parallel imports placed on the market by the trade mark owner or with his consent in another member state of the Union.

 Question

Why might a trader not want an EU trade mark but prefer instead to maintain national registrations?

---

[57] EUTMR 2017, Arts 39–40.   [58] EUTMR 2017, Art 126(1).   [59] See further the discussion in Chapter 21.

Brexit—what are the implications for registered trade mark law?

13.36 Having looked at the current position on UK and EU trade mark protection, we need to turn to consider the implications of Brexit. The most significant impact of Brexit for registered trade mark law will be that, when Brexit takes effect, the UK will no longer be covered by the EU trade mark. This will affect the territorial reach of all EU trade marks. It will impact upon all EU trade mark owners, wherever they are based: any trade mark owner who was relying upon an EU trade mark to give him registered trade mark protection in the UK will no longer have rights in the UK.

13.37 This is obviously a potentially very serious concern for trade mark owners from around the world. There are therefore provisions dealing with this issue in the draft Withdrawal Agreement which has been negotiated between the EU and UK. This Withdrawal Agreement is intended to govern the UK's withdrawal from the EU after a 'transition period' during which the future trading relationship between the parties can be negotiated. The most recent version of the Withdrawal Agreement at the time of writing (issued 14 November 2018) provides at draft Article 54:[60]

> The holder of any of the following intellectual property rights which have been registered or granted before the end of the transition period shall, without any re-examination, become the holder of a comparable registered and enforceable intellectual property right in the United Kingdom under the law of the United Kingdom.

It adds specifically in relation to EU trade marks:

> the holder of a European Union trade mark registered in accordance with Regulation (EU) 2017/1001 of the European Parliament and of the Council shall become the holder of a trade mark in the United Kingdom, consisting of the same sign, for the same goods or services (draft Article 54(1)(a)).

Among other details, draft Article 54(4) provides that a new UK right created pursuant to the Withdrawal Agreement shall inherit the same renewal date as the corresponding EU trade mark from which it has, in effect, been cloned. Draft Article 54(5)(a) requires that the new UK right be deemed to have the same date of filing or priority as the corresponding EU trade mark. By draft Article 55(1), the registration and grant of the new UK right will be carried out free of charge by relevant entities in the UK, using the data available from the EU trade mark register. By draft Article 59(1), the holders of pending applications for EU trade marks will have a nine-month window post-Brexit to refile in the UK claiming the same filing, priority, and seniority dates as for the original EU trade mark application.

13.38 At the time of writing, it remains to be seen whether the draft Withdrawal Agreement will be formally concluded between the EU and UK in this form, or at all. In the event of a 'no-deal' Brexit (that is, if the UK exits the EU without concluding any form of Withdrawal Agreement or other agreement on a transition period), the UK has indicated its intention to carry out, of its own accord, a broadly similar exercise.[61]

13.39 Separately from the arrangements for EU trade marks, there are also broader questions about the direction which UK registered trade mark law will take post-Brexit. As explained in Chapter 1, although after Brexit preliminary references to the Court of Justice of the European Union (CJEU) will no longer be possible from the UK courts to the Court of Justice, according to the European Union (Withdrawal) Act 2018 existing decisions of the CJEU will have the same status as decisions of the UK Supreme Court. According to section 6(2) of the European Union (Withdrawal) Act 2018, the UK courts may also 'have regard to anything done on or after exit day by the European Court, another EU entity or the EU so far as it is relevant to any matter before the court or tribunal'. It would therefore be possible for UK courts to decide to treat

---

[60] See: https://assets.publishing.service.gov.uk/government/uploads/system/uploads/attachment_data/file/756374/14_November_Draft_Agreement_on_the_Withdrawal_of_the_United_Kingdom_of_Great_Britain_and_Northern_Ireland_from_the_European_Union.pdf.

[61] UK Government, 'Trade marks and designs if there's no Brexit deal', 24 September 2018, www.gov.uk/government/publications/trade-marks-and-designs-if-theres-no-brexit-deal/trade-marks-and-designs-if-theres-no-brexit-deal.

future CJEU trade mark decisions as persuasive in their own interpretation of the TMA 1994 (as amended). It will also necessitate an appeal to the UK Supreme Court to reverse principles derived from existing CJEU trade mark jurisprudence. That said, it seems almost inevitable that, on some matters, the UK courts and the CJEU will at some point begin to diverge in their preferred approach.

 Registered trade marks and Brexit

When the UK leaves the EU, the UK will no longer fall within the territorial scope of the EU trade mark.

According to the current draft of the EU–UK Withdrawal Agreement, EU trade mark registrations existing at the end of the withdrawal transition period will, in effect, be cloned onto the UK trade mark register in order to provide continuity of protection in the UK. This will be free for all EU trade mark owners. The cloned UK right will inherit the same filing, priority, and renewal dates as the EU trade mark from which it is derived. The owners of pending EU trade mark applications will have a time-limited (nine-month) window after Brexit to make a parallel UK filing claiming the same filing, priority, and seniority dates as the original EU trade mark application.

In the event of a 'no-deal' Brexit, the UK has indicated its intentions to carry out a broadly similar exercise of its own accord. Either way, however, how UK courts approach the future interpretation of the TMA 1994 (as amended) remains to be seen.

The regulatory framework: international

13.40   Finally, let us turn to the international regulatory framework. Both the World Intellectual Property Organisation (WIPO) and the World Trade Organization (WTO) administer international treaties pertaining to trade marks.

WIPO: Paris Convention for the Protection of Industrial Property 1883 (Paris Convention)

13.41   The Paris Convention is one of the oldest international intellectual property treaties, dealing not only with registered trade marks but also, inter alia, unregistered marks, patents, and registered designs. It has 177 signatories, including the UK.[62] The basis of the Paris Convention is that of national treatment.[63] This means that contracting states are required to treat nationals (whether companies or individuals) of foreign contracting states as they would their own nationals. Thus, nationals of states which have signed the Convention must be able to register trade marks in the UK register and have the benefit of the law relating to those marks applied in the same way that it does to UK nationals.[64]

13.42   The Paris Convention does not provide for any central mechanism for filing trade marks. However, very importantly (in terms of trade mark filing strategy, in particular) the Paris Convention does provides for a system of *priority*.[65] This means that a trade mark owner who has filed an application to register a mark in one contracting state has a period of time (Article 4C: six months) during which he or she may file another application for the same mark in other contracting states, the effective date in terms of assessing the validity of those later filings being backdated to the filing date of the first application. In this way, the later filings can gain priority over any other trade marks filed by unconnected third parties in the period between the trade mark owner's first and later filings. This may be particularly useful for businesses which are looking to

---

[62] As of November 2018.   [63] Paris Convention, Art 2.

[64] National treatment extends also to companies and individuals who are not nationals of a contracting state, but who are domiciled or have a real and effective industrial or commercial establishment in the territory of one of the countries of the Union: ibid, Art 3.

[65] ibid, Art 4.

protect trade marks in a number of different countries in anticipation of a global roll-out of a new brand: it allows them to make one single filing first—thereby keeping their costs down—and to assess thereafter in the six-month priority window to proceed with the chosen trade mark globally or if (for example) too many objections are raised, to change to another brand.

13.43   Another important provision in the Paris Convention deals with unregistered marks[66] (rather than registered marks). This imposes an obligation on contracting states to protect well-known marks *even* where they have not been registered. The purpose is to protect those proprietors of well-known marks who have not commenced using their marks in a particular signatory state from activities of third parties who might attempt a pre-emptive registration. The Court of First Instance (now the General Court) considered some of the requirements in *El Corte Inglés v OHIM*—and referred to Article 2 of the Joint Recommendation concerning the provisions on the protection of well-known trade marks adopted by the Assembly of the Paris Union and the General Assembly of WIPO:[67]

> In determining whether a mark is a well-known mark within the meaning of the Paris Convention, the competent authority can take into account any circumstances from which it may be inferred that the mark is well known, including: the degree of knowledge or recognition of the mark in the relevant sector of the public; the duration, extent and geographical area of any use of the mark; the duration, extent and geographical area of any promotion of the mark, including advertising or publicity and the presentation, at fairs or exhibitions, of the goods and/or services to which the mark applies; the duration and geographical area of any registrations, and/or any applications for registration, of the mark, to the extent to which they reflect use or recognition of the mark; the record of successful enforcement of rights in the mark, in particular, the extent to which the mark has been recognised as well known by competent authorities; the value associated with the mark.

13.44   The Paris Convention also requires Convention countries to prevent the use and registration of 'armorial bearings, flags and other State emblems' of the countries of the Convention,[68] and to provide effective protection against unfair competition.[69]

Exercise

Read the Paris Convention. Clarify in your own mind how the system of priority works.

WIPO: The Madrid Agreement and Protocol

13.45   The Madrid Agreement for the International Registration of Marks (1891) and the Madrid Protocol of 1989 are both administered by WIPO. The Madrid Agreement and Protocol provide a mechanism for securing what are known as 'international' trade mark registrations. This is a bit of a misnomer: there is no single registration with international effect, as such. The Madrid system permits a single application to be made to apply for registered trade mark protection in many countries. In effect, what results is a bundle of separate trade mark rights in the various designated jurisdictions. The Madrid System does not create any kind of single unitary supranational international trade mark right, although the resulting national rights do remain linked, and certain administrative tasks such as transfers and renewals continue to be handled centrally via WIPO, rather than at each national office.

- **Madrid Agreement**: the applicant must first obtain a registration in their home state, which must be a party to the Agreement (which the UK is not). Only then may an application be made to WIPO for a corresponding international registration via their national office. Providing the application complies

---

[66]   ibid, Art 6*bis*.   [67]   Case T-420/03 *El Corte Inglés SA v OHIM* [2008] ETMR 71, para 80.
[68]   Paris Convention, Art 6*ter*.   [69]   ibid, Art 10*bis*.

with certain formalities, it is registered as an international mark. This is notified to all contracting states designated in the international application. Each designated state is then responsible for dealing with their own designation of the international registration as if it were a national application filed directly in that country. Whether the designation qualifies for protection or it is in conflict with relevant earlier rights is determined according to the domestic substantive trade mark law of that contracting party.

- **Madrid Protocol**: the UK is a party to the Madrid Protocol 1989. An application for registration of a mark must be made in one of the countries which have signed up to the Madrid Protocol[70] and be based on a pre-existing registration *or* application filed in that office. As with an International application filed under the Agreement, once the 'home' office has satisfied itself that the application conforms with the existing application or registration, it is forwarded to WIPO for examination for compliance with the formal requirements of the Protocol. When satisfied, the mark is registered as an international mark, and details are passed to those countries designated in the application. Again, each designation is then dealt with in each of the designated countries as if it had been made directly to that national office.[71] The EU acceded to the Madrid Protocol in 2004. As a result, an EU trade mark application or registration can be used as the basic mark for an international application and the EU can be designated in an international application via the Madrid Protocol.

One of the problems with the Madrid Agreement, and why the Madrid Agreement has attracted relatively few signatories, is because of the provision on what is known as '*central attack*'.[72] The international registration remains dependent on the home registration for a period of five years. During this time, if the home registration ceases to have effect (perhaps through non-renewal, a declaration of invalidity, or revocation for non-use), then the international registration is lost, including all national protection derived therefrom in the various designated signatory states. The position under the Madrid Protocol is less harsh. Although the five-year dependency remains, under the Madrid Protocol if the home application or registration is refused or invalidated in whole or in part, the dependent rights are not lost. Instead, the holder has the option to 'transform' some or all of the international rights into equivalent national or regional (eg EU trade mark) applications or registrations,[73] which become independent of the original international registration.

Exercise

Draw a diagram highlighting the various registration routes that can be taken by a trader who wishes to have a registered trade mark effective in the UK.

WIPO: The Trade Mark Law Treaty

13.46   The Trade Mark Law Treaty (TLT) was signed in Geneva on 28 October 1994. The TLT aims to streamline registration procedures. Its scope is quite limited: Article 2 TLT provides that its provisions apply to marks consisting of 'visible signs'. The TLT does not apply to hologram marks, non-visible signs, or collective, certification, or guarantee marks. The TLT goes on to make provisions for the form and content of the application (Art 3), the filing date (Art 5), and other procedural formalities such as changing a name and address (Art 10) and correcting mistakes (Art 12).

The Treaty had 54 contracting states as of November 2018.

[70] Madrid Protocol, Art 2(1).   [71] Madrid Protocol, Art 4.   [72] Madrid Agreement, Art 6.
[73] Madrid Protocol, Art *9quinquies.*

WIPO: Singapore Treaty on the Law of Trademarks

13.47   The purpose of the Singapore Treaty on the Law of Trademarks 2006 is to update the TLT. Not long after the adoption of the TLT it became apparent that it needed to be revised, largely as a result of the 'dot.com' revolution, the introduction of email, and internet-based communications. For instance, the TLT contains provisions obliging states to accept communications in paper form. The Singapore Treaty is also broader in scope than the TLT, which only covered visible marks. The Singapore Treaty encompasses any mark that a contracting party may offer. So, for example, if a contracting party protects sound marks, the provisions of the Singapore Treaty apply, but if a contracting party does not allow for sound marks, that party has no obligation to provide for them.

13.48   The Singapore Treaty is separate from the TLT. Article 27 of the Singapore Treaty governs the relationship between the two and provides that, between parties that are signatories to both Treaties, the Singapore Treaty will govern. Unlike the TLT, the Singapore Treaty creates an 'Assembly of the Contracting Parties', which, among other powers, allows for modification of the treaty regulations and model forms used under the Treaty. The goal of this Assembly is to help to keep the Singapore Treaty up to date.

13.49   The Treaty was finalised in March 2006. It came into force in March 2009 and, as at November 2018, there were 47 contracting states.

WIPO: Nice Agreement concerning the International Classification of Goods and Services for the Purposes of the Registration of Marks

13.50   Note the comments on the Nice Agreement, a classification Treaty, in paragraph 13.05.

WTO: Agreement on Trade-Related Aspects of Intellectual Property Rights including Trade in Counterfeited Goods (TRIPS)

13.51   The TRIPS Agreement resulted from the Uruguay Round of the General Agreement on Tariffs and Trade (GATT) discussions held under the auspices of the WTO. The Agreement, which is administered by the WTO, was passed in 1994. There are a number of points to note:[74]

- TRIPS does not provide either for its own mechanism for registration of marks, or for a mark to be registered in more than one territory (cf the EU trade mark). TRIPS does provide for certain minimum standards in relation to trade marks (and other intellectual property rights) which must be incorporated into national laws of contracting states. For instance, contracting states must apply the Paris Convention standards relating to trade marks;[75] TRIPS also adopts a broad definition of a sign which is capable of being registered as a trade mark; requires trade mark registration to extend to marks for services;[76] and defines the rights conferred by a registered mark.[77]

- As with other international conventions, the principle of national treatment is incorporated into the TRIPS Agreement.[78]

- Unlike other international conventions and treaties, TRIPS includes a most favoured nation clause.[79] This broadly means that if any contracting state gives to any other contracting state preferential treatment, then that concession must also be given to all other contracting states.

- If a state fails to adhere to its obligations under any of the agreements administered by WIPO, then another state may bring a reference to the International Court of Justice. No such intellectual property reference has been made. By contrast, under TRIPS, failure by a state to adhere to its obligations may lead to GATT dispute settlement procedure and ultimately to sanctions withdrawing GATT privileges to that state.

---

[74] See also the discussion in Chapter 1.   [75] TRIPS, Art 2(1).   [76] TRIPS, Art 15.   [77] TRIPS, Art 16(1).
[78] TRIPS, Art 2.   [79] TRIPS, Art 3.

Exercise

Read the TRIPS Agreement provisions on registered trade marks and, in relation to trade marks, list five key points of similarity and/or difference between the provisions found in that agreement as compared with the EUTMR 2017 and the UK TMA 1994.

Key points on the regulatory framework

- Domestic (UK) law is contained in the TMA 1994 and is shaped by European and international obligations. The TMA 1994 is currently being amended to reflect updates in the most recent version of the Trade Marks Directive (EU) 2015/2436. Those amendments will take effect in January 2019.

- The EUTMR 2017 governs the EU trade mark, a supranational pan-EU trade mark right effective throughout the territories of the member states of the EU.

- WIPO administers the Madrid Agreement and Protocol, which provide for a streamlined international registration process for trade marks across different countries.

- The Paris Convention (WIPO) and TRIPS (WTO) both contain substantive minimum obligations regarding trade marks.

- The Trade Mark Law Treaty and the Singapore Treaty contain obligations relating to procedural matters for the registration of trade marks

Further reading

Books

L Bently, J Davis, and J Ginsburg, *Trade Marks and Brands: An Interdisciplinary Critique* (2011)

GB Dinwoodie and MD Janis (eds), *Trademark Law and Theory: A Handbook of Contemporary Research* (2008)

A Griffiths, *An Economic Perspective on Trade Mark Law* (2011)

N Pires de Carvalho, *The TRIPS Regime of Trademarks and Designs* (2006)

J Roberts, *International Trade Mark Classification: A Guide to the Nice Agreement* (3rd edn, 2007)

Studies

Max Planck Institute for Intellectual Property and Competition Law, *Study on the Overall Functioning of the European Trade Mark System* (February 2011), https://publications.europa.eu/en/publication-detail/-/publication/5f878564-9b8d-4624-ba68-72531215967e.

Chapters

WR Cornish, 'Intellectual property: omnipresent, distracting, irrelevant?' in *Clarendon Law Lectures* (2004), 73–110

Articles

G Dinwoodie, 'Architecture of the international intellectual property system' (2002) 77 Chicago-Kent Law Rev 993

G Dinwoodie, 'Trademarks and territory: detaching trademark law from the nation-state' (2004) 41 Houston Law Rev 885

R Ghafele, 'Trade mark owners' perspectives on the Madrid System: practical experiences and theoretical underpinnings' (2007) 2(3) JIPLP 160–69

N Isaacs, 'Should the United Kingdom adopt a European system for the registration of trade marks?' [2006] EIPR 71–73

L Jaeschke, 'The quest for a superior registration system for registered trade marks in the UK and EU: an analysis of the current registration system in the UK, the CTM registration system and coming changes' [2008] EIPR 25

L Loughlan, 'Trade marks: arguments in a continuing contest' [2005] 3 IPQ 294–308

G Lunney, 'Trademark monopolies' (1999) 48 Emory Law Journal 367

SM Maniatis, Trade mark rights—a justification based on property [2002] 2 IPQ 123–71

SM Maniatis and AK Sanders, 'A consumer trade mark protection based on origin and quality' [1993] EIPR 406–15

F Schechter, 'The rational basis of trade mark protection' (1927) 40 Harv LR 813

S Schnell, 'The Community trade mark: unitary EU right—EU-wide injunction?' (2011) 33(4) EIPR 210–26

A von Muhlendahl, 'Community trade mark riddles: territoriality and unitary character' [2008] EIPR 6

J Weberndorfer, 'The integration of the Office for Harmonization in the Internal Market into the Madrid system: a first field report' [2008] EIPR 216

Trade marks 2: definition of a registrable trade mark, absolute grounds for refusal and invalidation, and revocation

Introduction

Scope and overview of chapter

14.1 As a result of the European Union (EU) trade marks regime, the types of signs that can be registered as trade marks have expanded. Whereas in the past registration at the national level was often traditionally limited to words, logos, and similar signs, such is the breadth of the EU regime that all manner of two- and three-dimensional marks and other visual and non-visual indicia may now fall within the definition of a registrable trade mark. Many questions have been considered by the Court of Justice, on preliminary references from national courts or appeals from the General Court, concerning the definition of what constitutes a registrable trade mark and the grounds upon which trade mark registrations should be refused or invalidated. The reasoning of the Court of Justice in these matters has been particularly influenced by purposive and public interest considerations.

14.2 The purpose of this chapter is to examine the definition of a registrable trade mark and the rules governing the drafting of the specification of goods and services which forms part of every trade mark registration, to discuss the absolute grounds for refusal and invalidation of a trade mark registration, and to consider the law dealing with revocation of a registered mark. As we shall see, a number of important changes have been brought about by the EU's 2015 trade mark reform package mentioned in Chapter 13. As discussed in Chapter 13, as far as UK law is concerned, the approach adopted in this chapter will be to refer to the Trade Marks Act (TMA) 1994 as amended by SI 2018/825: those changes are, at the time of writing, due to enter into force in January 2019. This chapter will also use Trade Marks Directive 2015/2436 ('TMD 2015') and EU Trade Mark Regulation 2017/1001 ('EUTMR 2017') as its primary reference points in terms of EU-level legislation, referring back to older versions of the Directive and Regulation as appropriate. Care should be taken to note that there are some changes of Article numbering in TMD 2015 compared to older versions of the Directive in particular.

14.3 Proceeding on this basis, the definition of a registrable trade mark is to be found at section 1 TMA 1994 (as amended), Article 3 TMD 2015, and Article 4 EUTMR 2017. The grounds on which an application for registration of a trade mark can be refused are set out in sections 3 and 5 TMA 1994 (as amended), Articles 4–5 TMD 2015, and Articles 7–8 EUTMR 2017. The grounds for refusal of an application divide into *absolute* and *relative* grounds. *Absolute* grounds for refusal are essentially concerned with the characteristics and qualities of the mark applied for itself; *relative* grounds look to whether there are conflicts with relevant earlier rights. Our focus in this chapter is on *absolute* grounds for refusal. In registered trade mark law, the *relative* grounds for refusal of an application mirror the grounds for infringement of a registered mark; we will therefore look at relative grounds alongside infringement in Chapter 15.

14.4   Absolute grounds for refusal of a trade mark application apply to applications when they are filed and examined. However, a trade mark registration may also be *invalidated* after grant. The grounds for invalidation of a registered mark are essentially a mirror of the absolute and relative grounds for refusal— revisiting, in essence, the question of whether the mark should ever have been registered in the first place. The consequence of a mark being found invalid is that the registration is deemed never to have been made.[1] The grounds for invalidation are set out at section 47 TMA 1994 (as amended), Articles 4–5 TMD 2015, and Articles 59–60 EUTMR 2017. As far as *absolute* grounds are concerned, section 47(1) TMA 1994 says:[2]

> The registration of a trade mark may be declared invalid on the ground that the trade mark was registered in breach of section 3 or any of the provisions referred to in that section (absolute grounds for refusal).

With this in mind, subject to some relatively minor points of difference which we will highlight as required, as we work our way through the absolute grounds of refusal discussed in this chapter it is important to remember that the same principles will apply to invalidation of an already-registered mark. In contrast to invalidation, the rules on *revocation* of a trade mark registration are concerned with changes in circumstances which have arisen in the time period since the registration was granted—for example, whether the registered mark has been put to 'genuine use' or whether it has become misleading or generic. Revocation of a registered trade mark is governed by section 46 TMA 1994, Articles 16 and 19–20 TMD 2015, and Articles 18 and 58 EUTMR 2017. The effect of revocation is that the rights of the trade mark owner are deemed to cease as from the date of the application for revocation or, if the grounds existed at an earlier date, that date.[3] We will consider revocation at the end of this chapter.

14.5   **Learning objectives**

By the end of this chapter you should be able to describe and explain:

- the definition of a registrable trade mark;
- the rules which have developed around the drafting of the trade mark specification;
- the absolute grounds for refusing or invalidating a trade mark registration and when a mark may overcome these by proof that it has become distinctive through use; and
- the rules governing revocation of registered trade marks.

14.6   The rest of this chapter looks like this:

- The definition of a registrable trade mark (14.7–14.22)
- The specification of goods and services (14.23–14.28)
- Non-distinctive, descriptive, and customary marks (14.29–14.58)
- Distinctiveness through use (acquired distinctiveness) (14.59–14.72)

---

[1] Section 47(6) TMA 1994 (as amended). This does not affect transactions which are past and closed.

[2] See also Art 4 TMD 2015 (the absolute grounds listed there relating both to refusal of an application and invalidation); and Art 59 EUTMR 2017 (identifying the grounds for invalidation of an EU trade mark as breach of Art 7 EUTMR 2017 and bad faith).

[3] Section 46(6) TMA 1994 (as amended).

- Exclusion from registration of certain shapes and signs consisting of 'other characteristics' (14.73–14.86)
- Public policy and morality (14.87–14.90)
- Deceptive marks (14.91–14.92)
- Marks prohibited by law, protected emblems, and geographical indications (14.93–14.94)
- Bad faith (14.95–14.101)
- Revocation (14.102–14.115)

The definition of a registrable trade mark

Section 1(1) TMA 1994 (as amended); Article 3 TMD 2015 (formerly Art 2 TMD 2008); Article 4 EUTMR (formerly Art 4 CTMR 2009)

14.7   Section 1(1) TMA 1994 (as amended) defines a registrable trade mark as follows:[4]

(1) In this Act "trade mark" means any sign which is capable –

(a) of being represented in the register in a manner which enables the registrar and other competent authorities and the public to determine the clear and precise subject matter of the protection afforded to the proprietor, and

(b) of distinguishing goods or services of one undertaking from those of other undertakings.

A trade mark may, in particular, consist of words (including personal names), designs, letters, numerals, colours, sounds or the shape of goods or their packaging.

This definition has been significantly revised as part of the 2015 reform package. The most significant change is in relation to representation of the mark on the trade mark register. Before the 2015 reforms, the definition of a registrable mark required the sign applied for to be 'capable of being represented graphically'. In the early years of the EU trade mark regime, this generated a number of Court of Justice cases elaborating on this requirement for graphic representation. Indirectly, this became a testing ground on how far the then new EU regime was prepared to protect so-called 'non-conventional' trade marks. The changes adopted in 2015 reflect a push for even greater flexibility and openness in what may be registered as a trade mark, alongside a recognition that (particularly since trade mark registers are now most commonly consulted online) a range of different formats can be used accurately to represent a mark over and above simple graphic representation.

14.8   According to the new definition, there are three criteria which must be met for a mark to be registrable:

- the mark must be a 'sign';
- it must be capable of being represented in an acceptable manner on the register; and
- it must be capable of distinguishing goods or services of one undertaking from those of another.

However, the third criterion noted above (that the mark be capable of distinguishing) is subsumed into the absolute grounds for refusal discussed further at para 14.29ff. In early case law there was some discussion as to whether this language imposed a separate and independent requirement of distinctiveness: in other words, whether there was a category of marks which inherently could not distinguish between goods and

---

[4] See also Art 3 TMD 2015 (formerly Art 2 TMD 2008) and Art 4 EUTMR (formerly Art 4 CTMR 2009). Note that the definition in the TMD 2015 and EUTMR 2017 is worded slightly differently to the definition in the TMA 1994 (as amended): take care to quote accurately if quoting from the Directive or Regulation.

services for the purposes of this definition, irrespective of whether or not the further and detailed absolute grounds for refusal set out later in the EU trade mark regime applied. This was put to the Court of Justice in *Koninklijke Philips Electronics NV v Remington Consumer Products Ltd.*[5] The Court held that there was no separate or independent distinctiveness requirement, saying:[6]

> there is no class of marks having a distinctive character by their nature or by the use made of them which is not capable of distinguishing goods or services within the meaning of Article 2 of the Directive.

In *West (t/a Eastenders) v Fuller Smith & Turner* the Court of Appeal said that the effect of the judgment in *Philips v Remington* was that:[7]

> the second half of the definition of 'trade mark' in s.1(1) of the Act . . . must be viewed as imposing no distinctiveness requirement separate from that imposed by Articles 3(1)(b), (c) and (d) and 3(3). Thus, there is no requirement that the mark be both 'capable of distinguishing' and 'not devoid of any distinctive character'.

14.9   There are therefore only two issues for us to concentrate on in this section of the chapter, in terms of the definition of a potentially registrable trade mark: what may be considered as a 'sign'; and what is required in terms of appropriate representation on the register. As we shall see, these two requirements are, in their way, each concerned with requiring specificity from the trade mark applicant, avoiding uncertainty as to what has been registered and avoiding over-reach in the scope of the trade mark monopoly.

What may be considered a potentially registrable 'sign'?

14.10   None of the TMA 1994 (as amended), TMD 2015, or EUTMR 2017 define what is meant by a 'sign'. The list of examples in section 1(1) TMA 1994 (as amended) is not exhaustive. Many different types of sign are accepted for registration as trade marks.

- Simple word marks that have been registered include 'ROLLS-ROYCE' and 'TESCO'. Phrases which have been registered as trade marks include 'A Mars a day helps you work, rest and play'.[8] Many words are registered in combination with or as part of a device or a graphic such as that shown in Figure 14.1.[9]

Figure 14.1 Rolls-Royce logo registration

---

[5] Case C-299/99 *Koninklijke Philips Electronics NV v Remington Consumer Products Ltd* [2002] ETMR 81.

[6] ibid, para 39 (referring to the old Article numbering of the Directive: this corresponds to what is now Art 3 TMD 2015).

[7] *West (t/a Eastenders) v Fuller Smith & Turner Plc* [2003] FSR 44, para 35. The distinctiveness requirements referred to in this quotation at Arts 3(1)(b), (c), and (d) and 3(3) of the then version of the Directive can now be found at Arts 4(1)(b), (c), and (d) and 4(4) TMD 2015.

[8] UK Trade Mark No 1438989, class 30, proprietor: Mars Chocolate (UK) Limited.

[9] EU Trade Mark No 23069, classes 7 and 12, proprietor: Rolls-Royce plc.

- The shape of the packaging of goods has been registered, as in Figure 14.2,[10]

Figure 14.2 Coca-Cola bottle registration

as has the shape of goods such as the Mini, shown in Figure 14.3.[11]

- Colours, such as that described in Figure 14.4.[12]
- Sounds have been registered, such as the McDonald's jingle shown in Figure 14.5.[13]

Figure 14.3 BMW Mini registration

Figure 14.4 Purple colour registration

PURPLE as a colour applied overall to
and subsisting in the goods, the
colour purple being definable within
chromacity coordinate parameters,
according to the CIELAB system, of
L between 0 and 90, a between +5
and + 100, and b between –5 and –100.

---

[10] UK Trade Mark No 2000546, class 32, proprietor: The Coca-Cola Company.
[11] UK Trade Mark No 2002390, classes 6, 12, 16, and 28, proprietor: Bayerische Motoren Werke Aktiengesellschaft.
[12] UK Trade Mark No 2009633, class 3, proprietor: Chemisphere UK Ltd.
[13] EU Trade Mark No 3903101, class 43, proprietor: McDonald's International Property Company, Ltd.

Figure 14.5 McDonald's jingle registration

14.11   However, the requirement for a 'sign' does have some limiting effect. Its purpose has been identified by the Court of Justice as being to prevent the abuse of trade mark law to obtain an unfair competitive advantage.[14] The judgment of the European Court of Justice (ECJ) in *Dyson Ltd v Registrar of Trade Marks*[15] demonstrates that not everything applied for will successfully pass this threshold requirement. In this case, Dyson sought to register a UK trade mark relating to its bagless cyclonic vacuum cleaners. The focus was on the transparent collecting bin which formed part of those vacuum cleaners. The application contained representations showing two versions of the cleaner, one upright and one cylinder model. The two representations are shown at Figure 14.6.

The representations were accompanied by the text: 'The mark consists of a transparent bin or collection chamber forming part of the external surface of a vacuum cleaner as shown in the representation.'

Figure 14.6 Dyson trade mark representations

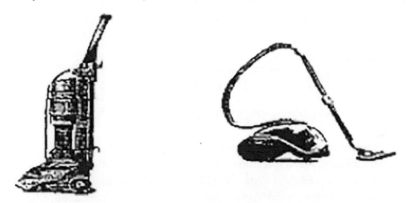

The application was turned down on various absolute grounds and, on appeal to the English High Court, questions on acquired distinctiveness were referred to the ECJ. However, rather than answering the questions referred, the ECJ found it necessary to answer the prior question (which it raised of its own motion) whether the mark applied for actually even constituted a 'sign' within the meaning of the TMD. It was common ground between the parties that the subject matter of the application was not a particular type of transparent collecting bin, but rather 'in a general and abstract manner, all the conceivable shapes of such a collecting bin'.[16] The representations which Dyson had filed were intended as only examples. The ECJ highlighted that what had been applied for was, as a result, capable of 'a multitude of different appearances'. The subject matter of the application was therefore not specific or something which was capable of being perceived visually.[17] The ECJ highlighted concerns over the anti-competitive impacts of letting such subject matter be registered:[18]

> Given the exclusivity inherent in trade mark right, the holder of a trade mark relating to such a non-specific subject matter would obtain an unfair competitive advantage . . . since it would be entitled to prevent its

---

[14] Case C-49/02, *Heidelberger Bauchemie GmbH* [2004] ETMR 99, para 24.
[15] Case C-321/03 *Dyson Ltd v Registrar of Trade Marks* [2007] ETMR 34.   [16] ibid, para 35.   [17] ibid, paras 36 and 37.
[18] ibid, para 38.

competitors from marketing vacuum cleaners having any kind of transparent collecting bin on their external surface, irrespective of its shape.

The subject matter of the application was a 'mere property of the product' and did not constitute a 'sign' within the meaning of what was then Article 2 of the Directive and is now Article 4 TMD 2015.[19]

14.12   Thus there will be some subject matter that is unregistrable because it does not constitute a 'sign' within the meaning of the legislation. Quite where the boundaries lie has developed on a case-by-case basis. The Court of Justice has confirmed that 'pure colour marks' (that is, marks consisting purely of a colour *per se*, without any specific spatial delimitation) may be capable of constituting a 'sign' when used in relation to goods or services: whether this is so is to be assessed in each case against the context of how the colour or colour combination is used.[20] The same also applies to colour combinations.[21] More recently, the Court of Justice has also confirmed that the design of the layout of a retail store can constitute a 'sign'. In *Apple Inc v Deutsches Patent- und Markenamt*, Apple applied for the mark shown in Figure 14.7 below. The ECJ accepted that this could constitute a 'sign', even in the absence of any indication in the trade mark filing of the actual size or proportions of the retail store that it depicted.[22]

Figure 14.7 Apple store layout

14.13   Other cases do, however, illustrate that the requirement for a 'sign' may have significant bite, particularly where there is (perhaps mistaken) imprecision in the filing of the application or attempted over-reach in what is claimed. In *Société des Produits Nestlé SA v Cadbury UK Ltd*, the English Court of Appeal rejected as not constituting a 'sign' a trade mark application by Cadbury.[23] The mark applied for was described in the application as: 'The colour purple (Pantone 2685C), as shown on the form of application, applied to the whole visible surface, or being the predominant colour applied to the whole visible surface, of the packaging of the goods'. The reference to this colour as the 'predominant' colour of the packaging was problematic. As noted by Sir John Mummery, the use of this word 'opens the door to a multitude of different visual forms'.[24] There was, as a result, 'wrapped up in the verbal description of the mark an unknown number of signs'.[25] In *JW Spear & Sons Ltd, Mattel Inc and Mattel UK Ltd v Zynga Inc*,[26] the English Court of Appeal upheld the invalidation of a trade mark registration intended to represent a blank Scrabble tile. The representations of the mark are shown at Figure 14.8 and were accompanied by this description: 'The mark consists of a three-dimensional ivory-coloured tile on the top surface of which is shown a letter of the Roman alphabet and a numeral in the range 1 to 10.' It was held that this did not constitute a 'sign' because of the numerous different 'permutations, presentations and combinations' of these features which were possible.[27]

---

[19] ibid, para 39.   [20] Case C-104/01, *Libertel Groep BV v Benelux-Merkenbureau* [2003] ETMR 63, para 27.
[21] Case C-49/02, *Heidelberger Bauchemie GmbH* [2004] ETMR 99, paras 24 and 42.
[22] Case C-421/13 *Apple Inc v Deutsches Patent- und Markenamt* [2014] ETMR 48, para 19.
[23] *Société des Produits Nestlé SA v Cadbury UK Ltd* [2014] ETMR 3.   [24] ibid, para 50.   [25] ibid, para 55.
[26] *JW Spear & Sons Ltd, Mattel Inc and Mattel UK Ltd v Zynga Inc* [2014] ETMR 5.   [27] ibid, para 32.

Figure 14.8 JW Spear & Sons Scrabble tile representations

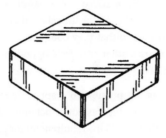

Representation on the register

14.14   As noted in para 14.7, the requirements governing representation on the trade mark register have been amended in the TMA 1994 (as amended), TMD 2015, and EUTMR 2017 by the 2015 reform package. There is no longer a requirement that a mark must be 'capable of being represented graphically'. However, for the reasons explained further below, a good understanding of the case law on graphic representation is still needed to assist in interpreting the new law.

14.15   The first case before the Court of Justice to consider the requirement of graphic representation was *Sieckmann v Deutsches Patent- und Markenamt*.[28] This concerned an application to register an odour (sometimes called an 'olfactory' mark). The applicant had submitted an odour sample in a container, which he described as 'balsamically fruity with a slight hint of cinnamon' and a written description giving the chemical formula of the relevant substance (C_6H_5–CH = $CHCOOCH_3$).

 Question

When you read the description 'balsamically fruity with a slight hint of cinnamon', does a particular smell come to mind? Can you be sure exactly how the applicant's odour actually smelled?

---

[28]   Case C-273/00 *Ralf Sieckmann v Deutsches Patent- und Markenamt* [2003] ETMR 37.

At the time, the list of examples of potentially registrable marks given in the definition at what was then Article 2 of the Directive included only various different sorts of visually perceptible marks. The first question before the Court was whether the then requirement of graphic representation meant that the definition of what constituted a registrable mark only covered signs which were capable of being perceived visually. If not limited in this way, the next question was how the applicant's smell mark could be graphically represented. The Court held that a registrable trade mark could consist of a sign which in itself may not be capable of being perceived visually, provided that it could be represented graphically. That graphic representation had to enable the sign to be represented visually, for example through images, lines, or characters, so that it could be precisely identified. The representation had to be:[29]

- clear;
- precise;
- self-contained;
- easily accessible;
- intelligible;
- durable; and
- objective.

These criteria have subsequently become known as the 'Sieckmann seven'. The ECJ emphasised the role of the requirement of graphic representation in the 'sound administration' of the trade mark registration system.[30] This requirement was intended to define the mark so that it was possible to determine the precise subject of trade mark protection. This was essential both for the relevant authorities and the public, particularly other economic operators: the authorities so that they could carry out examination of applications and maintain a 'precise' register of trade marks; other economic operators so that they could check and know what competitors claimed as their rights.[31]

14.16   In *Sieckmann*, the ECJ held that it was not possible to graphically represent an odour by means of the chemical formula of the relevant substance: this was not sufficiently intelligible, clear, or precise, nor did it actually represent the odour itself. Neither would the requirement for graphic representation be satisfied by a written description (not clear, precise, or objective) or by the provision of an odour sample (not durable or, in any event, a form of graphic representation). Attempts to register 'taste marks' have faced similar difficulties.[32]

 Question

Think back to the discussion in Chapter 13 about the 'essential function' of trade marks as indicators of the origin of goods and services. With this in mind, what is your view on whether smells and tastes operate as trade marks? Can you think of any examples of smells or tastes which are relied upon by consumers as an indication of origin?

14.17   Other forms of non-conventional mark could more easily be represented graphically in accordance with the *Sieckmann* criteria. In *Shield Mark BV v Joost Kist*,[33] the ECJ considered various sound marks relating to the opening of Beethoven's *Für Elise* and (separately) the sound of a cockcrow. These were represented in different ways, including (for the *Für Elise* marks) using a musical stave and the written sequence of notes 'E, D#, E, D#, E, B, D, C, A' and (for the cockcrow marks) the onomatopoeia 'Kukelekuuuuu' (the Dutch equivalent to the English 'cock-a-doodle-do') and the written description 'a cockcrow'. The Court ruled

---

[29] ibid, para 55.   [30] ibid, para 47.   [31] ibid, paras 47–51.

[32] See, eg, *Eli Lilly and Company's Application* (OHIM Second Board of Appeal, Case R 120/2001-2) [2004] ETMR 4, concerning an attempt to register the 'taste of artificial strawberry flavour' in respect of pharmaceutical products.

[33] Case C-283/01 *Shield Mark BV v Joost Kist HODN Memex* [2004] ETMR 33.

that the *Sieckmann* criteria were not met in this case by textual written description, onomatopoeia, or by merely stating the sequence of musical notes. However, the *Sieckmann* criteria were satisfied if a sound mark was represented in full musical notation (by a stave divided into bars with a clef, musical notes, rests, and so on), as this would give a 'faithful representation' of the sequence of sounds forming the melody for which registration was sought.[34] For an example of a sound mark represented in this way, see the jingle shown earlier at Figure 14.5.

14.18   It was also possible to represent a pure colour mark in accordance with the *Sieckmann* criteria. In *Libertel Groep BV v Benelux-Merkenbureau*,[35] Libertel applied to register the colour orange as a trade mark for telecommunications goods and services. The application contained an orange-coloured rectangle together with the word 'orange'. When this was turned down by the Benelux Trade Mark Office, Libertel appealed and the Dutch Supreme Court remitted the matter to the ECJ. The ECJ held that the *Sieckmann* criteria could not be satisfied by reproducing on paper a sample of the colour in question: this did not satisfy the requirement of durability. A verbal description might also not be adequate. However, a colour sample together with a designation of the colour using an internationally recognised identification code (such as the Pantone system) would be sufficient.

14.19   Since *Libertel*, a number of 'pure colour' marks have been registered as EU trade marks: for example, a deep cranberry colour registered by Deutsche Telekom for, inter alia, merchandising and finance activities;[36] and lilac by Kraft Foods in class 30 for chocolates and chocolate products.[37] It was, however, harder to register abstract combinations of colours. In *Heidelberger Bauchemie GmbH*,[38] the applicant sought to register a two-colour combination of blue and yellow for a range of building products. The applicant submitted a rectangular colour sample, the upper half of which was blue and the lower half of which was yellow. It also included a written description with colour codes and the explanation: 'The trade mark applied for consists of the applicant's corporate colours which are used in every conceivable form, in particular on packaging and labels.' Aside from the question of whether this constituted a 'sign' (see above para 14.12), the Court held that a graphic representation of combination of two or more colours, designated in the abstract and without contours, needed to be 'systematically arranged by associating the colours concerned in a predetermined and uniform way'.[39] The 'mere juxtaposition' of colours without shape or contours, or reference to use of those colours in 'every conceivable form' was not sufficiently precise.

14.20   This case demonstrates that, in practical terms, registering an abstract colour combination may be hard to achieve for a corporate livery the precise appearance of which will differ from one product to another when applied to different goods. More recent examples of similar failed attempts to register colour combinations can be found, at the EU level, in *Red Bull GmbH v EUIPO* and, in the UK, in *Glaxo v Sandoz*:

■ **Joined Cases T-101/15 and T-102/15 *Red Bull GmbH v EUIPO* (General Court) [2018] ETMR 11**

This case concerned two applications by Red Bull to register a combination of two colours, blue and silver. Both applications were accompanied by a colour sample, showing the colours one above the other. In the first application, the colour sample was accompanied by the written description: 'Protection is claimed for the colours blue (RAL 5002) and silver (RAL 9006). The ratio of the colours is approximately 50%–50%.' In the second application, the colour sample was accompanied by the written description: 'The two colours will be applied in equal proportion and juxtaposed to each other.' The applications were refused by the EUIPO Cancellation Division and Board of Appeal. On appeal to the General Court, those refusals were upheld. Citing *Heidelberger Bauchemie*, the General Court held that the written descriptions did not provide additional precision on what the systematic arrangement of the two colours was said to be. The

---

[34] ibid, para 62.   [35] Case C-104/01 *Libertel Groep BV v Benelux-Merkenbureau* [2003] ETMR 63.
[36] EU Trade Mark No 004636676.   [37] EU Trade Mark No 000031336.
[38] Case C-49/02 *Heidelberger Bauchemie GmbH* [2004] ETMR 99.   [39] ibid, para 33.

only information that was provided was that each colour would occupy one half of the total space occupied by both: the written descriptions did not stipulate the relevant spatial positions of the two colours (eg side by side, or one above the other). The colours were not associated in a predetermined or uniform way, and it was possible that there would be several different combinations of the two colours.

■ *Glaxo Wellcome UK Ltd (t/a Allen & Hanburys), Glaxo Group Ltd v Sandoz Ltd* [2017] ETMR 27 (Court of Appeal)

This dispute concerned the validity of an EU trade mark registered in respect of asthma inhalers. The registration contained the representation of the mark shown at Figure 14.9.

Figure 14.9 Glaxo trade mark representation

This was accompanied by the description: 'The trade mark consists of the colour dark purple (Pantone code 2587C) applied to a significant proportion of an inhaler, and the colour light purple (Pantone code 2567C) applied to the remainder of the inhaler.' The Court of Appeal upheld the lower court's conclusion that the mark was invalid. The written description referred to 'an inhaler', not just the specific inhaler shape shown in the representation. It was, however, hard to understand how the arrangement of colours shown in the representation would appear if applied to a differently shaped inhaler. Kitchin LJ commented: 'I believe that the public, including economic operators, looking at the certificate of the Trade Mark on the register, would be left in a position of complete uncertainty as to what the protected sign actually is.' [40] The application lacked the necessary clarity, intelligibility, precision, specificity, or accessibility and permitted numerous different combinations of the dark and light purple colours.

? **Question**

How likely do you think it is that a trade mark applicant can adequately represent an abstract colour combination, such as a corporate livery applied to different products, following these cases?

14.21   As noted above, as a result of the 2015 reform package, the requirement of graphic representation has been removed from the definition of a registrable trade mark. This reflected findings in the Max Planck Study mentioned in Chapter 13 that the graphic representation requirement was regarded as outdated and that there should be a more liberal practice regarding non-traditional marks, albeit subject still to

---

[40] *Glaxo Wellcome UK Ltd (t/a Allen & Hanburys), Glaxo Group Ltd v Sandoz Ltd* [2017] ETMR 27, para 80.

adequate provision for legal certainty.[41] Across the TMA 1994 (as amended), TMD 2015, and EUTMR 2017 the requirement is now that the relevant sign must be capable of being 'represented on the register in a manner which enables the competent authorities and the public to determine the clear and precise subject matter of the protection afforded to its proprietor' (Art 3(b) TMD 2015).[42] The recitals to the TMD 2015 add important further detail:[43]

> In order to fulfil the objectives of the registration system for trade marks, namely to ensure legal certainty and sound administration, it is also essential to require that the sign is capable of being represented in a manner which is clear, precise, self-contained, easily accessible, intelligible, durable, and objective. A sign should therefore be permitted to be represented in any appropriate form using generally available technology, and thus not necessarily by graphic means, as long as the representation offers satisfactory guarantees to that effect.

14.22   As we can see, the guidance in the recitals to the TMD 2015 open up the possibility of using any form of 'generally available technology' to represent a mark. The EUIPO has indicated that it will accept a wide range of digital file formats, including MP3 files (for sound marks) and MP4 video files (for motion marks, holograms, and multimedia marks—the latter being a new category of mark which the EUIPO will now accept, as a result of the reform package). However, as the stipulations on clarity, precision, and so on which appear in the recitals to the TMD 2015 and EUTMR 2017 also make clear, the 'Sieckmann seven' criteria will also remain relevant going forward.

Key points on the definition of a registrable trade mark

- The subject matter applied for must constitute a 'sign'. This requires the subject matter to be specific: something which is capable of taking on a multitude of different appearances will not be registrable.

- As a result of the 2015 reform package, the requirement of 'graphic representation' has been abolished. However, the mark must still be capable of being represented on the register in a way which enables the competent authorities and the public to determine the 'clear and precise' subject matter of the protection afforded by registration.

- Many trade marks will still satisfy these requirements by use of graphical representations. However, new and different formats for representing a mark, such as MP3 sound files or MP4 video files, can now also be used. However, the recitals to the TMD 2015 and EUTMR 2017 still require that, in order to be registrable, a sign should be clear, precise, self-contained, easily accessible, intelligible, durable; and objective. As a result, earlier case law from the Court of Justice (*Sieckmann* and later cases) is likely to remain relevant going forward.

 Discussion point   For answer guidance visit **www.oup.com/uk/brown5e**.

How much of a difference do you think that the changes introduced by the 2015 reform package will really make in practice? How many marks not considered capable of graphic representation will now be capable of adequate representation on the register?

---

[41] Max Planck Institute for Intellectual Property and Competition Law, 'Study on the Overall Functioning of the European Trade Mark System', February 2011, https://publications.europa.eu/en/publication-detail/-/publication/5f878564-9b8d-4624-ba68-72531215967e, 66.

[42] The definition of a registrable trade mark now also explicitly includes the non-visual example of sounds.

[43] Recital 13 TMD 2015; see also Recital 10 EUTMR 2017.

The specification of goods and services

14.23   When considering many of the key aspects of registered trade mark law (including assessment of distinctiveness and infringement), the representation of the mark is not considered in isolation but in relation to the goods or services claimed in the trade mark filing. It is therefore appropriate at this point of the chapter to consider the Court of Justice case law that has developed around the drafting of the specification of goods and services which forms a vital part of every trade mark application. This case law has led to the introduction of new provisions in the TMD 2015 and EUTMR 2017 as part of the EU's reform package.

14.24   An early issue related to the registrability of 'retail services'. Although it is now well settled that retail services can form the subject matter of an application, this was originally controversial—the argument being that retail marks do not actually operate as an indicator of origin for the goods being sold. However, the point was resolved by the preliminary reference to the ECJ in *Praktiker Bau*, in which the ECJ confirmed the registrability of retail services.[44] The Court saw no reason under the Directive or general principles of Community law why services relating to the retail of goods should be precluded from registration, noting that retail services included activities such as the selection of the range of goods offered for sale and other services aimed at inducing consumers to buy from that trader rather than a competitor. Retail services could be referred to using wording in the specification such as 'bringing together of a variety of goods, enabling customers to conveniently view and purchase those goods', together with specification of the types of goods concerned.[45] The Court of Justice has subsequently also confirmed that it is possible to register a mark for the retail of services.[46] However, it remained controversial as to whether mark could be registered for retail services in relation to retail of the applicant's own goods. Did this, for example, really involve the sort of selection of product range said to constitute part of the activities that make retail services registrable? The issue was addressed by the Court in the *Apple Store* preliminary reference, the CJEU ruling that retail services could be registered where they went beyond simply those services which were integral to offering for sale the retailer's own goods: the ECJ gave the sample of product demonstration seminars provided in-store by Apple.[47]

14.25   Since then, the major issue which has arisen in relation to trade mark specifications has been in relation to the use of Nice classification 'class headings' for the text of the applicant's specification. As we saw in Chapter 13, the Nice classification systems allocates goods and services into one of 45 different classes. The heading for each class summarises the general type of goods or services falling within that class. For example, the class heading for Class 8 reads: 'Hand tools and implements, hand-operated; cutlery; side arms, except firearms; razors'. There has, for many years, been a practice in some EU member states of trade mark applicants using the Nice class heading as their trade mark specification. There have been two longstanding, but opposing, views on what goods and services are actually claimed when the class heading terminology is adopted. On one view, stating the Nice class heading meant that all goods or services within that class were thereby claimed. The opposing view was that the goods and services claimed were limited strictly literally to those referred to in the text of the class heading. Whichever approach was preferred would produce a very different understanding of what goods and services were covered within the specification, with significant implications both in relation to infringement (the grounds for which differ depending on whether the infringer's goods can be said to be identical, similar, or dissimilar to those in the trade

---

[44]   Case C-418/02 *Praktiker Bau- und Heimwerkermärkte AG* [2005] ETMR 88.

[45]   ibid, paras 49–50. In C-501/15P *EUIPO v Cactus SA* [2018] ETMR 4, the CJEU confirmed that this ruling did not apply retrospectively to marks registered before the date of the *Praktiker Bau* judgment: marks registered before then which did not claim retail services in accordance with the Court's directions could not be said implicitly to include them.

[46]   Case C-420/13 *Netto Marken-Discount AG & Co KG v Deutsches Patent- und Markenamt* [2014] ETMR 52, applying similar rules as in *Praktiker Bau*.

[47]   Case C-421/13 *Apple Inc v Deutsches Patent- und Markenamt* [2014] ETMR 18, paras 25–26.

mark owner's specification) and in relation to other matters such as the assessment of distinctiveness or descriptiveness, or revocation for non-use. With different registries and courts taking different approaches, uncertainty threatened the objective of the EU regime that registered trade marks should enjoy the same protection in all member states.

14.26 The issue came before the CJEU in the *IP TRANSLATOR* case.[48] The Chartered Institute of Patent Attorneys applied for registration in the UK of the mark IP TRANSLATOR for services in class 41, using the class heading for Nice class 41 ('education; providing of training; entertainment; sporting and cultural activities') as the specification of services. The UK IPO took the view that this covered all services in class 41 and rejected the application for non-distinctiveness and descriptiveness in relation to 'translation services' (which fall within class 41), even though those services were not mentioned in the specification as filed. The decision was appealed and questions referred to the Court of Justice on the use of Nice class headings. The Court responded by stressing that the specification of goods and services needs to be sufficiently clear and precise to enable the competent authorities and economic operators, on that basis alone, to determine the extent of protection sought.[49] While some Nice class headings might be sufficiently precise, others might not: use of class headings was not precluded, but whether the requirements of clarity and precision were met was to be assessed on a case-by-case basis.[50] An applicant had in any event to specify whether the application was to cover all of the goods and services in the class or only some, and if so, which.[51]

14.27 The *IP TRANSLATOR* ruling provoked consternation among trade mark owners and practitioners. Many trade mark registrations had been filed using class headings in the belief that they thereby covered all of the goods and services in the class. The Court of Justice's decision seemed to put the scope of those registrations in doubt. However, since the *IP TRANSLATOR* judgment, the position has become clearer in a number of respects. First, in an appeal from the General Court, the CJEU confirmed that the *IP TRANSLATOR* judgment did not have retrospective effect on marks that had already been registered before that date.[52] The EU legislators have now also acted on the issue in the 2015 reform package. For EU trade marks, the relevant provisions can now be found at Article 33 EUTMR 2017. Articles 33(2) and (3) EUTMR 2017 repeat the requirements of sufficient clarity and precision from *IP TRANSLATOR* and the Court of Justice's finding that Nice class headings can be used provided that they comply with those requirements. However, Article 33(5) EUTMR 2017 now goes further, formally adopting the approach that use of class headings shall *not* be taken to cover all goods or services within the class. Instead, the language of the specification will be construed literally:

> The use of general terms, including the general indications of the class headings of the Nice Classification, shall be interpreted as including all the goods or services clearly covered by the literal meaning of the indication or term. The use of such terms or indications shall not be interpreted as comprising a claim to goods or services which cannot be so understood.

Corresponding provisions for national marks can be found at Articles 39(2), (3), and (5) TMD 2015 and have been introduced, for the UK, into the secondary legislation governing the filing of trade mark applications.[53] To assist the owners of already-registered marks which had used class headings in the specification with the intention to capture a broader range of goods or services, transitional provisions were also introduced. By Article 33(8) EUTMR 2017, proprietors of EU trade marks registered before 22 June 2012 which used class headings in the specification were given until 24 September 2016 to declare that their intention had been to claim goods or services going beyond those listed in the literal wording of the class heading and to specify those further goods. Failure to have made such a declaration results in the specification being deemed to

---

[48] Case C-307/10 *Chartered Institute of Patent Attorneys v Registrar of Trade Marks* [2012] ETMR 42. [49] ibid, paras 46–49.
[50] ibid, paras 54–56. [51] ibid, para 61.
[52] Case C-577/14 P *Brandconcern BV v EUIPO, Scooters India Ltd* (16 February 2017, currently unreported).
[53] Rule 8, paras 2(b), (2A), and (2B), Trade Mark Rules 2008, as amended by SI 2015/825.

extend only to the goods or services clearly covered by the literal meaning of the indications included in the class heading.

14.28   In the meantime, there is one further ongoing point of uncertainty. In *Sky Plc v Skykick UK Ltd*,[54] the question arose as to whether a lack of clarity in the whole or part of a specification could result in the registration being declared invalid. The judge at first instance, Arnold J, concluded that the point was not *acte clair* and has referred the following question to the CJEU:

> Can an EU trade mark or a national trade mark registered in a Member State be declared wholly or partially invalid on the ground that some or all of the terms in the specification of goods and services are lacking in sufficient clarity and precision to enable the competent authorities and third parties to determine on the basis of those terms alone the extent of the protection conferred by the trade mark?

It remains to be seen how this issue will be resolved. On the one hand, the grounds for invalidation set out in the TMD 2015 are, on their face, exhaustive. On the other hand, the 2015 reforms do not stipulate what the consequences of failure to meet the requirement of clarity and precision should be if an application is erroneously accepted by the relevant registry. The CJEU has also been asked to opine specifically on whether a term such as 'computer software'—which may cover an enormous range of different goods—is sufficiently clear and precise.

Key points on the specification of goods and services

- A mark can be registered for retail services in relation to retail of both goods and services. There is also some scope to register a mark for retail services in relation to sale of the trade mark owner's own goods.

- Use of Nice classification 'class headings' is now regulated by the TMA 1994 (as amended), TMD 2015, and EUTMR 2017 as a result of the 2015 reform package. Nice class headings can be used in the specification provided that they are sufficiently clear and precise to enable the competent authorities and public, on that basis alone, to determine the extent of protection sought. Specifications framed in general terms, including through the use of Nice class headings, will be read literally: they will not be taken to include any goods or services which do not fall within a literal reading of the terms used.

Non-distinctive, descriptive, and customary marks

Sections 3(1)(b), (c) and (d) TMA 1994 (as amended); Articles 4(1)(b), (c) and (d) TMD 2015 (formerly Arts 3(1)(b), (c) and (d) TMD 2008); Articles 7(1)(b), (c) and (d) EUTMR 2017 (formerly Arts 7(1)(b), (c) and (d) CTMR 2009)

14.29   The absolute grounds for refusal of a trade mark application are set out at section 3 TMA 1994 (as amended), Article 4 TMD 2015, and Article 7 EUTMR 2017. The ground for refusal at section 3(1)(a) TMD 1994 (as amended) refers to 'signs which do not satisfy the requirements of section 1(1)' and is tied to the definition of what constitutes a registrable trade mark, in particular the requirements for a 'sign' and for adequate representation on the register (above at paras 14.7–14.22).[55] Beyond this, the three grounds for refusal at sections 3(1)(b)–(d) TMA 1994 (as amended) constitute the most important absolute grounds of objection

---

[54] *Sky Plc v Skykick UK Ltd* [2018] ETMR 23, paras 154–174; see also the supplementary decision at [2018] EWHC 943 (Ch). At the time of writing, the case is pending as Case C-371/18.

[55] See also Art 4(1)(a) TMD 2015 and Art 7(1)(a) EUTMR 2017. See also para 14.8 above in relation to the decision in *Philips v Remington* on this point.

to a trade mark application. They may come into play in a wide variety of cases. Under these provisions, the following may not be registered:

- trade marks which are devoid of any distinctive character (TMA 1994 (as amended), s 3(1)(b); Art 4(1)(b) TMD 2015; Art 7(1)(b) EUTMR 2017) (non-distinctive marks);

- trade marks which consist exclusively of signs or indications which may serve, in trade, to designate the kind, quality, quantity, intended purpose, value, geographical origin, or the time of production of the goods or of rendering of the service, or other characteristics of the goods or service (TMA 1994 (as amended), s 3(1)(c); Art 4(1)(c) TMD 2015; Art 7(1)(c) EUTMR 2017) (descriptive marks);

- trade marks which consist exclusively of signs or indications which have become customary in the current language or in the bona fide and established practices of the trade (TMA 1994 (as amended), s 3(1)(d); Art 4(1)(d) TMD 2015; Art 7(1)(d) EUTMR 2017) (customary marks).

Each of these sections yields to the proviso (discussed in detail at paras 14.59–14.72 below) that, even though a mark may fail these tests, if it can be shown that the mark has acquired a distinctive character as a result of the *use* that has been made of it, then the mark may be registrable. So, if a mark is not inherently distinctive (distinctive by nature), if it is used and it can be shown through that use to have become distinctive (distinctive by nurture) within the relevant time period, then it will be capable of registration.

14.30   These provisions are central to trade mark law in delineating what can and what cannot be registered as a mark. They have, unsurprisingly, generated a good deal of case law, both in the context of refusal of pending applications and invalidation of already-registered marks.[56] The more relaxed the legal standards on what marks may be registered, the fewer marks may remain in the 'public domain' for competing traders to use. This is particularly so where a mark may be one that competitors may wish, legitimately, to use in the course of their own trade, such as a descriptive or allusive term or one which is generally used to describe the characteristics of the relevant goods. There is also an important policy decision to be made as to how far the interests of competitors should be taken into account 'up front' at this stage by refusing trade mark applications, or should be left to be dealt with on a case-by-case basis by allowing marks to be registered and tackling competitor interests through the defences to infringement. On this issue, the ECJ rejected early on the argument that competitor interests were adequately protected via the defences to infringement. Instead, the Court of Justice emphasised that there should be 'stringent and full' examination of trade mark applications 'in order to prevent trade marks from being improperly registered'.[57]

Question

When considering what signs should be excluded from registration, when and how do you think that the respective interests of the trade mark owner, the competitor, and the consumer should be balanced? Explain and justify your response.

14.31   The Court of Justice has stressed that each of the absolute grounds for refusal is *independent* of the others and requires separate examination.[58] Nonetheless it is also accepted in the case law that objections may

---

[56] Remembering that grounds for invalidation effectively mirror grounds for refusal: see in particular s 47(1) TMA 1994 (as amended), Art 4 TMD 2015, and Art 59(1)(a) EUTMR 2017.

[57] Case C-104/01 *Libertel Groep BV v Benelux Merkenbureau* [2003] ETMR 63, para 59. See also Joined Cases C-108/97 and 109/97, *Windsurfing Chiemsee Produktions- und Vertriebs GmbH v Boots- und Segelzubehör Walter Huber and Another* [2000] Ch 523, para 28.

[58] Joined Cases C-53/01, C-54/01, and C-55/01 *Linde AG, Winward Industries Inc, Rado Uhren AG* [2003] ETMR 78, para 67; Case C-329/02 *SAT.1 Satellitenfernsehen GmbH v OHIM* [2005] ETMR 20, para 25; Case C-64/02 P *OHIM v Erpo Möbelwerk* [2005] ETMR 58, para 39; and many subsequent CJEU decisions.

overlap.[59] Importantly, the Court of Justice has repeatedly stressed that the absolute grounds for refusal must be interpreted in the light of the general interest underlying each of them.[60]

Distinctiveness

Section 3(1)(b) TMD 1994 (as amended); Article 4(1)(b) TMD 2015; Article 7(1)(b) EUTMR 2017

14.32   Much of the case law deals with trade marks challenged for being devoid of distinctive character. The paramount consideration here is the need to ensure that the mark applied for functions as an indication of origin—in other words, that it is capable of distinguishing the goods and services of one trader from those of another. As the ECJ said in *SAT.1*, the public interest underlying the distinctiveness requirement is 'manifestly, indissociable from the essential function of a trade mark'.[61]

14.33   In *Libertel*,[62] the pure colour mark case discussed at para 14.18, the ECJ also considered 'colour depletion' concerns as part of the underlying rationale for the distinctiveness requirement. It said:[63]

> the fact that the number of colours actually available is limited means that a small number of trade mark registrations for certain services or goods could exhaust the entire range of colours available. Such an extensive monopoly would be incompatible with a system of undistorted competition, in particular because it could have the effect of creating an unjustified competitive advantage for a single trader.

There was therefore 'a public interest in not unduly restricting the availability of colours for the other operators who offer for sale goods or services of the same type as those in respect of which registration is sought'.[64] However, the ECJ has subsequently rejected attempts to bring a broader 'availability' public interest into the ambit of the distinctiveness test.[65] Such considerations are relevant to the requirement of descriptiveness (to be found at s 3(1)(c) TMD 1994 (as amended), Art 4(1)(c) TMD 2015, and Art 7(1)(c) EUTMR 2017), but not the requirement of distinctiveness. In case law since *Libertel*, the focus of the Court's distinctiveness rulings has remained very much on the mark's ability to perform the essential function of indicating origin as the key public interest consideration.

14.34   For a mark to be considered distinctive, it 'must serve to identify the product in respect of which registration is applied for as originating from a particular undertaking, and thus to distinguish that product from products of other undertakings'.[66] Distinctiveness must be assessed by reference to the goods and services applied for.[67] In assessing distinctiveness, the perception of the average consumer of those goods or services is central.[68]

14.35   The Court of Justice has repeatedly insisted that the test of distinctiveness is the same for all types of mark.[69] However, this finding has been somewhat contradicted by certain quasi-factual principles which the Court has also developed. According to the Court, it may be harder in practice to establish the distinctiveness of marks consisting of, say, the shape of goods compared to more traditional forms of mark such as words or a logo.[70] The Court has stressed that the average consumer is not in the habit of making assumptions about

---

[59] Case C-363/99 *Koninklijke KPN Nederland NV v Benelux-Merkenbureau* [2004] ETMR 57, para 85; Case C-90/11 *Strigl v Deutsches Patent- und Markenamt* (unreported), para 20; Case C-517/99 *Merz & Krell GmbH & Co* [2002] ETMR 21, para 35; Case C-265/00 *Campina Melkunie BV v Benelux-Merkenbureau* [2004] ETMR 58, para 18.

[60] Case C-299/99 *Koninklijke Philips Electronics NV v Remington Consumer Products Ltd* [2002] ETMR 81, para 77.

[61] Case C-329/02 *SAT.1 Satellitenfernsehen GmbH v OHIM* [2005] ETMR 20, para 27.

[62] Case C-104/01 *Libertel Groep BV v Benelux-Merkenbureau* [2003] ETMR 63.   [63] ibid, para 54.   [64] ibid, para 55.

[65] Case C-329/02 *SAT.1 Satellitenfernsehen GmbH v OHIM* [2005] ETMR 20, para 36.

[66] Joined Cases C-53/01, C-54/01, and C-55/01 *Linde AG, Winward Industries Inc, Rado Uhren AG* [2003] ETMR 78, para 40.

[67] ibid, para 41.   [68] ibid, para 41 (see further the discussion on the 'average consumer' in Chapter 15).

[69] Case C-299/99 *Koninklijke Philips Electronics NV v Remington Consumer Products Ltd* [2002] ETMR 81, para 48; Joined Cases C-53/01, C-54/01, and C-55/01 *Linde AG, Winward Industries Inc, Rado Uhren AG* [2003] ETMR 78, paras 42–49; Case C-404/02 *Nichols Plc v Registrar of Trade Marks* [2005] ETMR 21, para 24.

[70] Joined Cases C-53/01, C-54/01, and C-55/01 *Linde AG, Winward Industries Inc, Rado Uhren AG* [2003] ETMR 78, para 48.

the origin of products on the basis of features such as the shape of the goods, their colour, or the shape of their packaging.[71] As a result, although the requirement of distinctiveness is in theory the same for all categories of mark, in practice it may be harder to meet for many so-called non-conventional marks.

 Discussion point   For answer guidance visit **www.oup.com/uk/brown5e**.

What is your view on the Court of Justice's assumptions about the consumer perception of different categories of mark? Do you think that it is right to say that consumers do not understand aspects of product presentation, such as shape or colours, as indicators of trade origin? Do you think that consumer perception may have evolved at all since the Court of Justice's first decisions on this issue?

Descriptiveness

Section 3(1)(c) TMD 1994 (as amended); Article 4(1)(c) TMD 2015; Article 7(1)(c) EUTMR 2017

14.36   The policy underlying the descriptiveness objection is that marks falling within its scope should be freely available for use by all. According to the Court of Justice, the old Article 3(1)(c) TMD 2008 (the provision that is now Art 4(1)(c) TMD 2015):[72]

> pursues an aim which is in the public interest, namely that descriptive signs or indications relating to the characteristics of goods or services in respect of which registration is applied for may be freely used by all . . . Article 3(1)(c) therefore prevents such signs and indications from being reserved to one undertaking alone because they have been registered as trade marks.

14.37   To be refused for descriptiveness or to invalidate an existing registration on this ground,[73] there is no need to show that the mark is currently being used descriptively by other traders: it will be unregistrable if it is capable of being so used.[74] It is irrelevant whether there are other, more usual ways of designating the same characteristics of the relevant goods or services: there is no requirement that, to be refused, a mark must be the only way of designating such characteristics.[75] The references to kind, quality, quantity, intended purpose, value, geographical origin, or the time of production of the goods or of rendering of the service do not constitute an exhaustive list of relevant 'characteristics'. The reference to 'characteristics' highlights that signs which are descriptive under Article 4(1)(c) TMD 2015 and Article 7(1)(c) EUTMR 2017 are those which designate a property of the goods or services for which registration is sought.[76] That does not have to be an important property or attribute of the relevant goods or services: a mark may be objectionable for descriptiveness whether the characteristic described is essential or merely ancillary.[77] The descriptiveness objection is not confined to word marks: as the ECJ has noted, there is nothing in principle which prevents this objection applying to 'a wide variety' of marks including, for example, shapes.[78] It is possible that a mark which is descriptive of some goods or services and thus unregistrable would be registrable in connection with other goods or services for which it is distinctive.[79]

[71] Case C-104/01 *Libertel Groep BV v Benelux-Merkenbureau* [2003] ETMR 63, para 65; Joined Cases C-53/01, C-54/01, and C-55/01 *Linde AG, Winward Industries Inc, Rado Uhren AG* [2003] ETMR 78, para 48; Case C-218/01 *Henkel KGaA v Deutsches Patent- und Markenamt* [2005] ETMR 45, para 52; Case C-173/04 P *Deutsche SiSi-Werke v OHIM* [2006] ETMR 41, para 28.

[72] Joined Cases C-108/97 and C-109/97 *Windsurfing Chiemsee Produktions- und Vertriebs GmbH v Boots- und Segelzubehör Walter Huber and Another* [2000] Ch 523, para 25.

[73] See s 47(1) TMA 1994; Art 4(1)(c) TMD 2015; and Art 59(1)(a) EUTMR 2017.

[74] Joined Cases C-108/97 and C-109/97 *Windsurfing Chiemsee Produktions- und Vertriebs GmbH v Boots- und Segelzubehör Walter Huber and Another* [2000] Ch 523, para 30.

[75] Case C-363/99 *Koninklijke KPN Nederland NV v Benelux-Merkenbureau* [2004] ETMR 57, para 57.

[76] Case C-51/10 P *Agencja Wydawnicza Technopol sp z oo v OHIM* [2011] ETMR 34, paras 49–50.

[77] Case C-363/99 *Koninklijke KPN Nederland NV v Benelux-Merkenbureau* [2004] ETMR 57, para 102.

[78] Joined Cases C-53/01, C-54/01, and C-55/01 *Linde AG, Winward Industries Inc, Rado Uhren AG* [2003] ETMR 78, para 69.

[79] Case C-363/99 *Koninklijke KPN Nederland NV v Benelux-Merkenbureau* [2004] ETMR 57, para 113.

Customary signs

Section 3(1)(d) TMD 1994 (as amended); Article 4(1)(d) TMD 2015; Article 7(1)(d) EUTMR 2017

14.38   This ground of refusal excludes from registration marks which have become customary in current language or trade practices. In essence, this is directed at marks which may at one time have been distinctive, but which have become generic by the time the trade mark application is filed. According to the Court of Justice, the purpose of this objection is to prevent registration of signs or indications which are not capable of distinguishing the goods or services of one undertaking from those of others.[80]

14.39   For this objection to bite, the mark must have become customary in the current language or in the bona fide and established practices of the trade to designate the goods or services in respect of which registration is sought.[81] In *Alcon v OHIM*, the Court of Justice heard an appeal relating to an invalidity dispute over the mark 'BSS' which had been registered for ophthalmic pharmaceutical preparation and sterile solutions for ophthalmic surgery.[82] The validity of the registration was challenged as being contrary to what is now Article 7(1)(d) EUTMR 2017, on the basis that 'BSS' was the common acronym for 'buffered salt solution' or 'buffered saline solution'. Whether this was the case was assessed from the perspective of ophthalmologists and ophthalmic surgeons practising in the EU. However, by analogy with further Court of Justice case law on revocation, the perspective of members of the relevant 'trade' may not always be the only relevant perspective: in some cases the perception of the final consumer may also be relevant.[83] The objection is not confined to marks which are descriptive of the properties or characteristics of the goods or services.[84] It may, for example, apply to advertising slogans or other indications of quality or incitements to purchase the relevant goods or services, if customary in current language or the relevant practices of the trade.[85]

Different categories of mark

14.40   Having considered the key principles governing the requirement of distinctiveness and the grounds of refusal for descriptiveness and customary signs, it is instructive to look at how various different categories of trade mark have fared in terms of these key absolute objections to registration. In this section, we will run through various categories of trade mark in turn. There have been a very great many decisions from national courts, the EU Intellectual Property Office (EUIPO), General Court, and Court of Justice, so the focus here is on a selection of the key cases.

Colours

14.41   In *Libertel*, the ECJ considered whether a pure colour mark could be considered to have distinctiveness. Noting that the perception of the relevant public was not necessarily the same in relation to a sign consisting of a colour *per se* as it would be in the case of a word or figurative mark, the Court held that distinctiveness for a pure colour mark was 'inconceivable save in exceptional circumstances' in the absence of prior use.[86] However, a pure colour mark could be registrable on proof of acquired distinctiveness (see further para 14.59ff).

[80] Case C-517/99 *Merz & Krell GmbH & Co* [2002] ETMR 21, paras 28 and 37.   [81] ibid, para 31.
[82] Case C-192/03 P *Alcon Inc v Office for Harmonisation in the Internal Market (Trade Marks and Designs) (OHIM)* [2005] ETMR 69.
[83] Case C-409/12 *Backaldrin Österreich The Kornspitz Co GmbH v Pfahnl Backmittel GmbH* [2014] ETMR 30.
[84] Case C-517/99 *Merz & Krell GmbH & Co* [2002] ETMR 21, paras 35–36. The Court emphasised that descriptiveness is the key criterion under what is now Art 7(1)(c) EUTMR but not Art 7(1)(d) EUTMR.   [85] ibid, paras 39–40.
[86] Case C-104/01 *Libertel Groep BV v Benelux-Merkenbureau* [2003] ETMR 63, para 66.

Three-dimensional marks

14.42 The ECJ emphasised in *Henkel KGaA v OHIM*[87] that, in principle, three-dimensional shape marks are registrable.[88] The key question is how far the mark must be removed from the shape normally used in the trade in order to be considered distinctive. In *Henkel*, the preliminary reference concerned two applications to register the three-dimensional shapes of dishwasher detergent tablets featuring different coloured layers. The Court reasoned that, the more closely a shape mark resembled the shape most likely to be taken by the product in question, the more likely it was to be devoid of distinctive character.[89] In the Court's view, only a shape mark which 'departs significantly from the norm or customs of the sector and thereby fulfils its essential function of indicating origin, is not devoid of any distinctive character'.[90]

14.43 The upshot is that only relatively unusual shapes are likely to be capable of demonstrating inherent distinctiveness. However, in English case law questions have also persisted as to whether satisfying the requirement that a shape depart significantly from the norm or customs of the sector is, on its own, sufficient to demonstrate inherent distinctiveness, or whether something more is required. The issue arises from the Court of Justice's statement that a shape mark is registrable if it:[91]

> departs significantly from the norm or customs of the sector and *thereby fulfils* its essential function of indicating origin (emphasis added).

14.44 This issue was considered most recently by the English Court of Appeal in *London Taxi Corp Ltd v Frazer-Nash Research Ltd*.[92] The dispute concerned alleged infringement of a Community (now 'EU') trade mark and a UK trade mark registration belonging to the London Taxi Corporation (LTC) both for the shape of the London taxi cab. Images from LTC's EU trade mark registration are at Figure 14.10.

Figure 14.10 LTC EU trade mark registration

[87] Joined Cases C-456/01 P and C-457/01 P *Henkel KGaA v OHIM* [2005] ETMR 44.   [88] ibid, paras 30 and 31.
[89] ibid, para 39.
[90] ibid, para 39. See also Joined Cases C-473/01 P and C-474/01 P, *Proctor & Gamble Co v OHIM* [2004] ETMR 89 (another dishwasher tablet case); Case C-218/01 *Henkel KGaA v Deutsches Patent- und Markenamt* [2005] ETMR 45, para 49 (dealing with the shape of packaging); Case C-136/02 *Mag Instrument v OHIM* [2005] ETMR 46 (an application to register the shape of a torch); and many other subsequent shape-mark cases.
[91] Joined Cases C-456/01 P and C-457/01 P *Henkel KGaA v OHIM* [2005] ETMR 44, para 39.
[92] *London Taxi Corp Ltd (t/a London Taxi Co) v Frazer-Nash Research Ltd* [2018] ETMR 7.

It was counterclaimed that the two registrations were invalid for lack of inherent distinctiveness. At first instance, the judge held that the requirement of a significant departure from the norm or customs of the sector was a necessary, but not in itself a sufficient, condition for registration. It also had to be shown that, like for all other marks, the marks in dispute were perceived by the average consumer as identifying the origin of the goods.[93] However, it was argued for LTC that, in light of further case law, it was clear that a significant departure from the norm was both a necessary *and* a sufficient condition for inherent distinctiveness.[94] At the Court of Appeal, Floyd LJ (giving the leading judgment) noted that there was 'much force' in these submissions. In his view, however, the matter was not *acte clair* and had it been determinative of the case, a preliminary reference to the CJEU would have been needed.[95] In any event, on the facts the Court of Appeal agreed with the trial judge and held that there was no significant departure from the norm. Assessing this was a three-step test: first, determining what constitutes the relevant sector; secondly, identifying the common norms and customs of that sector (if any); and finally, deciding whether the mark applied for departs significantly from those norms and customs.[96] In this case, existing shapes of not only licensed black cabs but also of private hire vehicles were relevant, which could in effect be any model of saloon car. The Court of Appeal concluded that—whether considered individually or as a whole—the features of the London taxi cab shape shown in LTC's registrations were simply minor variants on the norms and customs of the car sector as a whole.[97]

14.45   Distinctiveness is not the only potential challenge for shape marks; the descriptiveness objection at Article 4(1)(c) TMD 2015 and Article 7(1)(c) EUTMR may also apply. An early preliminary reference concerned the shape of a bottle used to hold liquid wool detergent.[98] Noting that some goods (such as liquids) did not possess an intrinsic shape and had to be packaged in order to be marketed, the packaging 'impos[ed] its shape on the goods'.[99] In such cases, for the purposes of trade mark examination, the shape of the packaging had to be assimilated to the shape of the product. The ECJ held that a trade mark which consisted of a 3D shape assimilated to the shape of the relevant goods could, in appropriate cases, serve to designate characteristics of the goods so packaged.[100]

'Position' marks

14.46   Practice has developed at the EUIPO to accept marks said to consist of 'the specific way in which the mark is placed or affixed on the goods'—so-called 'position marks'.[101] In effect, a 'position mark' consists of the placement of a particular element or feature on a particular part of a product. Position marks may also be recognised in other jurisdictions, albeit not always as a specific category of mark in their own right. An example of a registered EU position mark is at Figure 14.11.

This mark, which was accepted by the EUIPO as inherently distinctive, has the accompanying written description:

> Red stripe placed longitudinally along an item of footwear partly covering the rear area of the sole and partly the rear area of the item of footwear. Any moulding seen on the sole or on the rear part of the item of footwear and/or production characteristics are not part of the trade mark.

14.47   Position marks are an area of evolving practice. However, it may be difficult to satisfy the basic requirement of inherent distinctiveness. In *X Technology Swiss GmbH v OHIM*, the General Court rejected as inherently

---

[93] [2016] EWHC 52 (Ch), paras 165–172. See also the earlier decision in *Bongrain SA's Trade Mark Application* [2005] RPC 14, per Jacob LJ at para 25 ('As a matter of principle I do not accept that just because a shape is unusual for the kind of goods concerned, the public will automatically take it as denoting trade origin, as being the badge of the maker').

[94] Referring to Case T-629/14 *Jaguar Land Rover Ltd v OHIM* [2016] ETMR 12.

[95] *London Taxi Corp Ltd (t/a London Taxi Co) v Frazer-Nash Research Ltd* [2018] ETMR 7, para 42.   [96] ibid, para 45.

[97] ibid, paras 46–49.   [98] Case C 218/01 *Henkel KGaA v Deutsches Patent- und Markenamt* [2005] ETMR 45.

[99] ibid, para 33.   [100] ibid, para 42.   [101] European Union Trade Mark Implementing Regulation (EU) 2018/626, Art 3(3)(d).

Figure 14.11 EU trade mark no 001027747 belonging to Prada SA

non-distinctive a mark consisting of the orange colour of the toe end of a sock (see Figure 14.12).[102] Applying the same case law test as developed for shape marks, in the General Court's view, there was no significant divergence from the norms or customs of the hosiery sector; the mark applied for would be perceived by the relevant public only as a decorative element, rather than as having trade mark significance. More recently, the General Court has also rejected position marks applied for by Steiff, the famous German maker of teddy

Figure 14.12 X Technology Swiss GmbH 'position mark'

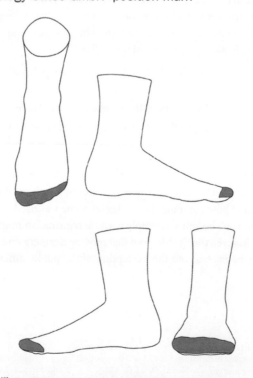

---

[102] Case T-547/08 *X Technology Swiss GmbH v OHIM* (unreported).

bears.[103] The marks applied for included an elongated rectangular fabric label attached fixed to the ear of soft toy via a metal button (see Figure 14.13). The General Court concluded that the marks were not sufficiently different from the norms of the toy industry and any differences between the marks applied for and what was customary in the sector were insufficient to confer distinctiveness.

Figure 14.13 Steiff 'position mark'

Sounds

14.48   In *Globo Comunicação e Participações S/A v EUIPO*,[104] the General Court considered the inherent distinctiveness of a sound mark, graphically represented in musical notation and described by the applicant as 'a sound which resembles a telephone ringtone' and 'a particular electronic ringing sound evoking sonar equipment, which consists of the repetition of two notes'. The applicant had applied to register this in relation to a range of goods and services, including television broadcasting services in class 38. The General Court accepted that, in some economic sectors such as broadcasting, it was common for the consumer to identify a product or service in that sector by a sound element such as a jingle. However, a sound needed to have 'a certain resonance' which would enable the consumer to perceive and regard it as a trade mark.[105] A 'banal combination of notes' or one which was characterised by 'excessive simplicity'—such as, in this case, the simple repetition of two identical notes—would not suffice.[106]

Personal names

14.49   Personal names are regularly used by traders in the course of trade. There may, however, be a challenge in showing that a name is inherently distinctive. *Nichols Plc v Registrar of Trade Marks*[107] concerned an application to register the surname 'Nichols' for vending machines and other goods. Stressing that no distinction is to be drawn between assessing the distinctiveness of names and other categories of marks, the Court rejected the imposition of stricter specific assessment criteria such as looking at the number of persons with the name (the UK IPO's then practice was to look at telephone directories to determine how common a surname was) or at how commonly the relevant name was used in the trade.[108] Neither could an application to register a name be refused simply because registration might give to the first comer a competitive advantage.[109] However, the ECJ stressed that proving distinctiveness for names might be more problematic than for other marks because the perception of the public differs as between categories of marks.[110]

---

[103] See Cases T-433/12 and T-434/12 *Margarete Steiff GmbH v OHIM* (unreported).
[104] Case T-408/15 *Globo Comunicação e Participações S/A v EUIPO* (unreported).   [105] ibid, para 45.   [106] ibid, paras 46 and 51.
[107] Case C-404/02 *Nichols plc v Registrar of Trade Marks* [2005] ETMR 21.   [108] ibid, paras 24–26.   [109] ibid, para 31.
[110] ibid, para 28.

Combinations of words

14.50 Much case law has revolved around the question as to whether and in what circumstances combinations of words can be registered where one or both words might be taken to indicate the kind, quality, quantity, or intended purpose of the goods or services, or the combination as a whole is allusive of these matters. In *Baby Dry*[111] the ECJ said that the descriptiveness objection at what is now Article 7(1)(c) EUTMR 2017 only related to marks which served 'in normal usage', from a consumer's point of view, to designate the the goods or services applied for, either directly or by reference to one of their essential characteristics.[112] According to the Court:[113]

> any perceptible difference between the combination of words submitted for registration and the terms used in common parlance of the relevant class of consumers to designate the goods or services or their essential characteristics is apt to confer distinctive character on the word combination enabling it to be registered as a trade mark.

The case concerned an application to register the mark 'BABY-DRY' for diapers in classes 16 and 25. The Court concluded that, while 'unquestionably' alluding to the function of the goods, the mark 'BABY-DRY' consisted of a 'syntactically unusual juxtaposition' of words which was not a familiar expression in English; it was a 'lexical invention' which was registrable.[114]

14.51 There was considerable disquiet at the generosity which this decision displayed in favour of registrability, with concerns that the Court had failed to appreciate the strength of the monopoly the first comer would obtain over descriptive marks as a result of the legal test which it had formulated. However, not long afterwards, the ECJ started to tighten the parameters of what would be acceptable in this sort of case. In *Wrigley v OHIM*[115] the ECJ re-emphasised the public interest underpinning the descriptiveness objection at Article 7(1)(c). It was not necessary for a mark to be objectionable for the mark actually to be in use at the relevant time in a way which was descriptive of the goods or services applied for. It was sufficient that the mark could be used for such purposes. The mark should therefore be refused registration 'if at least one of its possible meanings designates a characteristic of the goods or services concerned'.[116] This time, the ECJ rejected the mark in suit ('DOUBLEMINT') as unregistrable.

14.52 Where a neologism (ie a new word) is created, that may not necessarily be registrable if it does not differ sufficiently from the sum of its parts.

■ Case C-265/00 *Campina Melkunie BV v Benelux-Merkenbureau* [2004] ECR I-1699; [2005] 2 CMLR 9

This case concerned an application to register the word 'BIOMILD' for various foodstuffs, including milk products. The application was rejected on the basis that it conveyed solely that the products were biological and mild. In giving judgment, the ECJ first stated that, as a general rule, 'the mere combination of elements, each of which is descriptive of characteristics of the goods or services in respect of which registration is sought, itself remains descriptive of those characteristics within the meaning of Article 3(1)(c) of the Directive even if the combination creates a neologism'.[117] Simply bringing those elements together could only result in a mark which was descriptive. However, if there was a perceptible difference between the neologism and 'the mere sum of its parts'—enough to create an impression 'which is sufficiently far removed from that produced by the mere combination of meanings lent by the elements of which it is composed'—then the mark may be registrable.[118]

---

[111] Case C-383/99 P *Procter & Gamble Company v OHIM ('BABY-DRY')* [2002] ETMR 3.   [112] ibid, para 39.   [113] ibid, para 40.
[114] ibid, paras 43–44.   [115] Case C-191/01 P *OHIM v WM Wrigley JR Company* [2004] ETMR 9.
[116] ibid, paras 31–32.
[117] Case C-265/00 *Campina Melkunie BV v Benelux-Merkenbureau* [2005] 2 CMLR 9, para 39. See also Case C-363/99 *Koninklijke KPN Nederland NV v Benelux-Merkenbureau* [2004] ETMR 57 and Case C-273/05 *OHIM v Celltech R&D Ltd* [2007] ETMR 52.
[118] Case C-265/00 *Campina Melkunie BV v Benelux-Merkenbureau* [2005] 2 CMLR 9, para 41.

Slogans

14.53   The ECJ has confirmed that slogans may be registrable. In *Erpo Möbelwerk* the Court rejected the imposition of stricter criteria for assessing the distinctiveness of slogans.[119] However, the caveat that the relevant public might not perceive a slogan as an indicator of origin applied. The case law was developed further in *Audi AG v OHIM*.[120] Audi sought to register the slogan 'Vorsprung durch Technik' ('Progress through technology') as an EU trade mark for goods in a wide range of classes. On appeal, the CJEU reiterated that 'it is inappropriate to apply to slogans criteria which are stricter than those applicable to other types of sign';[121] however, the relevant public's perception was not necessarily the same for slogans as for other marks and it could be more difficult to prove distinctive character.[122] Imaginativeness was not a requirement.[123] All marks that are slogans or other incitements to purchase the relevant goods convey, to a greater or lesser extent, an objective message: however, that fact alone does not make them devoid of distinctive character. A slogan can express even a simple objective message and yet still also be capable of indicating the commercial origin of the relevant goods or services to the consumer. This is particularly the case if the slogan is 'not merely an ordinary advertising message' but has 'a certain originality or resonance'.[124]

Symbols

14.54   It can be difficult to demonstrate inherent distinctiveness, particularly for marks consisting of a single symbol. There is no requirement for a specific level of linguistic or artistic creativity or imaginativeness on the part of the trade mark proprietor; what is required is an assessment of whether the mark at issue is capable of distinguishing the goods and services applied for, viewed by reference to the perception of the relevant public in the usual way.[125] In relation to an application for the Greek alpha symbol 'α' in class 33, however, while the CJEU noted that the distinctiveness test was the same as for any other mark it also observed (as it has done for other categories of mark) that, for the purposes of applying that test, the relevant public's perception is not necessarily the same and it could prove more difficult to establish distinctiveness in relation to certain categories of mark.[126]

Numerals

14.55   Numerals too can be registered as trade marks. In *Agencja Wydawnicza Technopol sp z oo v OHIM* the applicant sought to register the mark '1000' for brochures and periodicals in class 16.[127] Before the CJEU, the arguments focused on what is now Article 7(1)(c) EUTMR 2017. The Court emphasised that the fact that the mark was composed exclusively of numerals was not, in itself, a bar to registration.[128] The CJEU stressed that the word 'characteristic' 'highlights the fact that the signs referred to in Article 7(1)(c) . . . are merely those which serve to designate a property, easily recognisable by the relevant class of persons, of the goods or the services in respect of which registration is sought'.[129] A sign can only be refused registration if it is reasonable to believe that it will actually be recognised by the relevant class of persons as a description of one of those characteristics.[130] Where the general public might believe that the sign '1000' as applied to a publication which could, for example, contain a collection of 1,000 crossword puzzles, then it was appropriate to refuse registration.

In contrast, where a number has no such signification, the objection will not apply. *WHG (International) Ltd, WHG Trading Ltd and William Hill Plc v 32Red Plc*[131] concerned, *inter alia*, the validity of a UK trade

---

[119]   Case C-64/02 P *OHIM v Erpo Möbelwerk GmbH* [2005] ETMR 58 (concerning the slogan 'Das Prinzip der Bequemlichkeit'—'The Principle of Comfort').

[120]   Case C-398/08 P *Audi AG v OHIM* [2010] ETMR 18.   [121]   ibid, para 36.   [122]   ibid, para 37.   [123]   ibid, para 39.

[124]   ibid, paras 56–57. For a further example of case involving a disputed slogan, see Case C-311/11 P *Smart Technologies ULC v OHIM* [2012] ETMR 49 ('WIR MACHEN DAS BESONDERE EINFACH'—'We make special things simple').

[125]   Case C-265/09 P *OHIM v BORCO-Marken-Import Matthiesen* [2011] ETMR 4, paras 31–32 and 38.

[126]   ibid, para 33.   [127]   Case C-51/10 P *Agencja Wydawnicza Technopol sp z oo v OHIM* [2011] ETMR 34.

[128]   ibid, para 29.   [129]   ibid, para 50.   [130]   ibid, para 50.

[131]   *WHG (International) Ltd, WHG Trading Ltd and William Hill Plc v 32Red Plc* [2012] ETMR 14.

mark registration for the number 32 registered in respect of, among other things, online casino services, including roulette. The Court of Appeal noted:[132]

> At the end of the day, the point is a very short one. In *Technopol* . . ., 1000 was capable of describing a feature of the goods in respect of which registration was sought, such as the number of pages or works or the number of crossword puzzles in periodicals. The bare number 32 is not descriptive of any characteristic of the services provided by the respondent. It is merely an allusion to an aspect of the game which the punter will play if he or she uses the respondent's services. The number does not in any way characterise the respondent's services in the sense of describing what will be supplied.

Geographical place names

14.56   In *Windsurfing Chiemsee*, the ECJ made various comments on the registrability of geographical place names under what is now Article 7(1)(c) EUTMR 2017. In addition to the general public interest underlying this objection, it is in the public interest that signs which may designate the geographic origin of the goods applied for remain available because they may be an indication of the quality or other characteristics of the goods, and may influence consumer tastes by associating the goods with a place which gives rise to a favourable response.[133] Registration will be refused both where the place name designates a specific geographical location which is already famous or known for the relevant goods and which is associated by consumers or traders with the category of goods concerned, and where, even if not so known at the time, it is reasonable to assume that such an association may be established in future.[134] Factors to consider include the degree of familiarity among relevant persons with the place name, the characteristics of the place designated by that name, and the category of goods concerned.[135] However, registration of a place name is not precluded if the place name is such that consumers or traders are unlikely to believe that the category of goods concerned originates there.[136] In applying these rules the CFI found that the name 'Cloppenburg' (the name of a town in Lower Saxony in Germany) was registrable in connection with retail services.[137] In contrast, an application to register the 'CANARY WHARF' as a UK trade mark for various goods and services, including real estate investment and related services, was refused.[138] The sign applied for was the name of a general business district and the services for which registration was sought were 'precisely the kind of services one would expect to be offered by or to businesses in that district'.[139]

Foreign words

14.57   An interesting issue arose in *Matratzen Concord AG v Hukla Germany SA*,[140] concerning the trade mark 'Matratzen', registered in Spain by Hukla in respect of furniture including beds and similar goods. 'Matratzen' means mattresses in German. Matratzen Concord sought to have the registration invalidated on the grounds that it was descriptive of the nature, quality, characteristics, or geographic origin of the products or services that it purported to distinguish. The question referred to the ECJ was whether a mark could be registered in one member state if it was descriptive in the language of another member state. The ECJ observed that there was nothing specifically in what was then Article 3 TMD (now Art 4 TMD 2015) on this point. It was necessary to assess the perception of the relevant parties, in trade and among average consumers: because of linguistic, cultural, social, and economic differences between

---

[132] ibid, para 64.
[133] Cases C-108/97 and 109/97, *Windsurfing Chiemsee Produktions- und Vertriebs GmbH v Boots- und Segelzubehör Walter Huber and Another* [2000] Ch 523, para 26.
[134] ibid, paras 29–31.   [135] ibid, para 32.   [136] ibid, para 33.
[137] Case T-379/03 *Peek & Cloppenburg KG v OHIM* [2006] ETMR 33. The relevant public was at most only moderately familiar with this place name and there was nothing to suggest a link with the category of services applied for.
[138] *Canary Wharf Group Plc v Comptroller General of Patents, Designs and Trade Marks* [2015] FSR 34.   [139] ibid, paras 25 and 29.
[140] Case C-421/04 *Matratzen Concord AG v Hukla Germany SA* [2006] ETMR 48.

member states, a trade mark which is devoid of distinctive character or descriptive of the relevant goods or services in one member state may not be so in another member state.[141] The determining factor for registrability would be how the term would be understood by the relevant parties in the state where registration was sought. Articles 4(1)(b) and (c) TMD 2015 and corresponding provisions in the TMA 1994 (as amended) and EUTMR 2017 do not preclude the registration, as a national trade mark, of a term borrowed from the language of another member state in which it is devoid of distinctive character or descriptive:[142]

> unless the relevant parties in the Member State in which registration is sought are capable of identifying the meaning of the term.

14.58   There was a move by the European Commission to change this rule in the 2015 reform package, aiming to reverse the *Matrazten* decision and to make national marks unregistrable in any EU member state if descriptive in the language of any other EU member state. However, this met with opposition during the legislative process and did not make it into the TMD 2015. In the meantime, for an EU trade mark, distinctiveness and descriptiveness must be assessed with reference to all languages of the EU. Descriptiveness in one language will be enough to make a mark inherently unregistrable. The decision of the General Court in the *Caffè Nero* case is a good example.[143] The applicant sought to register the word mark CAFFÈ NERO for goods in class 30, including coffee, and retail services related to coffee in class 35. The application was refused for descriptiveness under Article 7(1)(c) on the basis that *'caffè nero' was* the Italian for 'black coffee'. However, it may be possible to overcome this sort of objection by proof of acquired distinctiveness. In *Phonebook of the World v OHIM*, it was found that 'PAGINE GIALLE', Italian for 'yellow pages', was a validly registered mark. It was descriptive of telephone directories and related services in Italy, but it had become distinctive through use there, while in the rest of the EU the expression was not understood by the average consumer.[144]

Key points on distinctiveness, descriptiveness, and customary marks

- Non-distinctive, descriptive, and customary marks are all excluded from registration unless it can be shown that they have become distinctive through use.

- For a mark to be inherently distinctive, the mark must function as an indicator of origin for the goods or services applied for. This is assessed through the eyes of the average consumer. The test of distinctiveness is the same for all types of marks, but for some categories of mark (such as shapes or colours) inherent distinctiveness may be difficult to demonstrate in light of the Court of Justice's assumption that consumers tend not to perceive such signs as indicators of origin.

- Marks will be refused for descriptiveness both where the mark is currently in descriptive use by other traders and also if it may be liable to be so used in the future. There is no requirement that the mark be the only way of designating the characteristics of the goods or services.

- Marks will also be refused if they have become customary in current language or trade practices. The perception of end users of the relevant goods or services may also be relevant. This objection can also apply to slogans or other incitements to purchase.

---

[141]   ibid, paras 24–25.   [142]   ibid, para 26.   [143]   Case T-29/16 *Caffè Nero Group Ltd v EUIPO* (unreported).
[144]   Case T-589/11 *Phonebook of the World v OHIM* [2013] ETMR 15.

Distinctiveness through use (acquired distinctiveness)

Proviso to section 3(1) TMA 1994 (as amended); Articles 4(4) and (5) TMD 2015 (formerly Art 3(3) TMD 2008); Article 7(3) EUTMR 2017 (formerly Art 7(3) CTMR 2009)

14.59 As was indicated earlier (para 14.29), section 3(1) TMA 1994 (as amended) provides that each of the absolute grounds of refusal at sections 3(1)(b)–(d) is subject to the proviso that a sign which is inherently unregistrable may become distinctive through use.[145] This is not an independent right to have a trade mark registered, but a 'major exception' to the grounds for refusal listed in section 3(1)(b)–(d).[146] The rationale is that, although there are public policy reasons for excluding from registration marks which lack inherent distinctiveness or which are descriptive or customary, they are overridden if consumers have in fact come to understand the mark in question as an indicator of origin.

14.60 Proving acquired distinctiveness means proving that the mark has, as a matter of fact, come to serve as an indicator of the origin of the relevant goods and services. In *Philips v Remington*, the ECJ emphasised that:[147]

> the identification, by the relevant class of persons, of the product as originating from a given undertaking *must be as a result of the use of the mark as a trade mark* and thus as a result of the nature and effect of it, which make it capable of distinguishing the product concerned from those of other undertakings.

14.61 Useful guidance on what evidence is required to show that a mark has become distinctive through use was given by the ECJ in *Windsurfing Chiemsee*. The Court said that there must be an overall assessment of the evidence that the mark has come to identify the goods and services as originating from a particular undertaking. The following factors could be taken into account:

- the market share held by the mark;
- how intensive, geographically widespread, and long-standing use of the mark has been;
- the amount invested by the trade mark applicant in promoting the mark;
- the proportion of the relevant class of persons who, because of the mark, identify the relevant goods as originating from a particular undertaking;
- statements from chambers of commerce and industry or other trade and professional associations.[148]

Survey evidence may also be used, although the ECJ rejected the argument that such surveys need to reach a specific predetermined percentage level of recognition of the mark in question.[149] Acquired distinctiveness will be proved if the evidence shows that the 'relevant class of persons, or at least a significant proportion thereof, identifies goods as originating from a particular undertaking because of the trade mark'.[150] This will be very much fact- and evidence-based in each case.

14.62 For pending applications, in the UK and for EU trade marks it is necessary to show that the mark in question has acquired distinctiveness *before* the date upon which the application for registration was filed.[151] In

---

[145] See also Arts 4(4) and (5) TMD 2015 and Art 7(3) EUTMR 2017.

[146] Cases C-108/97 and 109/97, *Windsurfing Chiemsee Produktions- und Vertriebs GmbH v Boots- und Segelzubehör Walter Huber and Another* [2000] Ch 523, para 45.

[147] Case C-299/99 *Koninklijke Philips Electronics NV v Remington Consumer Products Ltd* [2002] ETMR 81, para 64.

[148] Cases C-108/97 and 109/97, *Windsurfing Chiemsee Produktions- und Vertriebs GmbH v Boots- und Segelzubehör Walter Huber and Another* [2000] Ch 523, para 51.

[149] ibid, paras 52–53. See also Joined Cases C-217/13 and 218/13, *Oberbank AG, Banco Santander SA and Santander Consumer Bank AG v Deutscher Sparkassen- und Giroverband eV* [2014] ETMR 56, paras 33–49.

[150] Cases C-108/97 and 109/97, *Windsurfing Chiemsee Produktions- und Vertriebs GmbH v Boots- und Segelzubehör Walter Huber and Another* [2000] Ch 523, para 52.

[151] Proviso to s 3(1) TMA 1994 (as amended); Art 7(3) EUTMR 2017. See also Case C-542/07 P *Imagination Technologies Ltd v OHIM* [2010] ETMR 19, para 42. The TMD 2015 gives member states the option to allow an application to proceed to registration where distinctiveness is shown to have been acquired after the date of filing but before the date of registration: Art 4(5) TMD 2015.

invalidation disputes, a mark can be shown to be validly registered if it has acquired distinctiveness after the date of registration.[152]

Secondary marks

14.63   Proof of acquired distinctiveness can be particularly difficult for so-called 'secondary marks'; that is, marks such as slogans, product shapes, or colours which are not, in themselves, the primary branding used by the trade mark owner. The difficulty is that secondary marks are rarely used by the trade mark owner on their own. Instead, they will tend to be accompanied by more readily recognised indicators of origin such as the main product name, trade mark owner's 'house mark', or a logo. As a result, it may be harder to show that a secondary mark is, in its own right, understood by consumers as an indicator of the origin of the goods.

14.64   The Court of Justice has confirmed that it is, at least in theory, possible for a secondary mark to become distinctive through its use as part of, or in conjunction with, another registered mark. In *Société des Produits Nestlé SA v Mars UK Ltd,*[153] Nestlé applied for registration of the words 'HAVE A BREAK' for goods in class 30. The mark was held to be devoid of inherent distinctiveness and so the case turned on whether 'HAVE A BREAK' could be shown to have acquired distinctiveness through use. The difficulty was that those words were used as part of the slogan 'Have a break . . . Have a Kit Kat', which was itself separately registered, along with the 'Kit Kat' mark. One view might be that there was no use of the words 'HAVE A BREAK' as an independent trade mark. However, while noting that, as held in *Philips*, acquired distinctiveness must result from use of the relevant mark 'as a trade mark', the Court of Justice concluded that the mark applied for need not necessarily have been used independently.[154] There was no such restriction in the TMD.[155] The expression 'use of the mark as a trade mark' in this context referred solely to use of the mark for the purposes of the identification, by the relevant class of persons, of the product as originating from a given undertaking.[156] Such identification (and thus acquisition of distinctive character) could result from use of the mark applied for as component part of another registered trade mark or in conjunction with another, separate registered trade mark. The Court held:[157]

> In both cases it is sufficient that, in consequence of such use, the relevant class of persons actually perceive the product or service, designated exclusively by the mark applied for, as originating from a given undertaking.

There may be limits as to how far a trade mark applicant can take this sort of argument, however: in *Coca-Cola Co v OHIM*, the applicant failed to convince the General Court that evidence of use and recognition of its famous fluted bottle shape (itself registered as a trade mark) could support a claim to acquired distinctiveness for a later-filed application for a more abstract version of the Coca-Cola bottle shape, this time with no fluting.[158]

14.65   Even if the 'HAVE A BREAK' case makes it clear that a mark does not have to have been used on its own to be in a position to prove acquired distinctiveness, issues still arise (in terms of English case law, at least) around what is required in terms of proof of the necessary consumer reaction. On the one hand, a strict view might demand that acquired distinctiveness can only be shown if a consumer actually relies on the shape in question to recognise the origin of the relevant goods. Alternatively, a more generous test would be to ask simply whether the consumer associates the shape with the trade mark owner or one of its brands.

14.66   In another case involving Nestlé, *Société des Produits Nestlé SA v Cadbury UK Ltd,*[159] questions on this issue were referred to the Court of Justice for a preliminary ruling. This case concerned Nestlé's ability to register the shape of the Kit Kat bar as a trade mark. The shape is shown in Figure 14.14.

---

[152]   Proviso to s 47(1) TMA 1994 (as amended); Art 4(4) TMD 2015; Art 59(2) EUTMR 2017.
[153]   Case C-353/03 *Société des Produits Nestlé SA v Mars UK Ltd* [2005] ETMR 96.   [154]   ibid, para 27.
[155]   ibid, para 28.   [156]   ibid, para 29.   [157]   ibid, para 30.
[158]   Case T-411/14 *Coca-Cola Co v Office for Harmonisation in the Internal Market (Trade Marks and Designs) (OHIM)* [2016] ETMR 25. *Nestlé* was distinguished. In the *Coca-Cola* case, the later-filed mark was not clearly distinguishable from the earlier fluted-shape mark: the later mark was absorbed into the earlier mark such that their silhouettes overlapped.
[159]   Case C-215/14 *Société des Produits Nestlé SA v Cadbury UK Ltd* [2015] ETMR 50.

Figure 14.14 Registering the shape of a Kit Kat bar

In the English High Court, Arnold J agreed with the hearing officer's conclusion that there was no evidence that Nestlé's marketing resulted in the relevant public *relying* on the shape of the product alone to identify its trade origin.[160] He also opined that it was 'inherently unlikely' that the public used the shape to confirm the authenticity of the four-fingered 'Kit Kat' bar, and noted instead that each of the Kit Kat fingers was imprinted with the trade mark KIT KAT, indicating that consumers did not rely on the product shape but on the trade mark 'Kit Kat'.[161] However, the judge concluded that the circumstances in which a secondary trade mark such as the Kit Kat shape could acquire distinctive character remained unclear and referred the following question to the Court of Justice:

> In order to establish that a trade mark has acquired distinctive character following the use that had been made of it within the meaning of Article 3(3) of Directive 2008/95 . . ., is it sufficient for the applicant for registration to prove that at the relevant date a significant proportion of the relevant class of persons recognise the mark and associate it with the applicant's goods in the sense that, if they were to be asked who marketed goods bearing that mark, they would identify the applicant; or must the applicant prove that a significant proportion of the relevant class of persons rely upon the mark (as opposed to any other trade marks which may also be present) as indicating the origin of the goods?

The CJEU reframed the question referred, posing the issue as a choice between (on the one hand) an interpretation whereby the relevant class of persons must perceive the goods or services designated exclusively by the mark, as opposed to any other mark which might also be present, as originating from a particular company or (on the other hand) whether it would be sufficient to prove that a significant proportion of the relevant class of persons recognised that mark and associated it with the applicant's goods.[162] Addressing this question, the Court ruled that:[163]

> regardless of whether [the use of the mark in question] is as part of another registered trade mark or in conjunction with such a mark, the trade mark applicant must prove that the relevant class of persons perceive the goods or services designated exclusively by the mark applied for, as opposed to any other mark which might also be present, as originating from a particular company.

The Court of Justice thus placed emphasis on consumer perception as a key factor, a test which differs from consumer reliance.

14.67   When the case returned to the English High Court, Arnold J expressed concern that the CJEU had re-written the question which he had referred and had thereby not answered it, failing in particular to deal with the 'reliance' issue. The case was appealed and the legal position has thereby been finessed by the Court of Appeal, which has arguably in effect re-introduced a requirement of reliance. Emphasising that a shape

---

[160] *Société des Produits Nestlé SA v Cadbury UK Ltd* [2014] ETMR 17, para 50.   [161] ibid, para 51.
[162] Case C-215/14 *Société des Produits Nestlé SA v Cadbury UK Ltd* [2015] ETMR 50, para 58.
[163] *Nestlé v Cadbury* (CJEU), para 67.

could become very well known by being sold on a very large scale and by reference to a highly distinctive brand, Kitchen LJ explained that nonetheless:[164]

> That does not necessarily mean that the public have come to perceive the shape as a badge of origin such that they would rely upon it alone to identify the product as coming from a particular source. They might simply regard the shape as a characteristic of products of that kind or they might find it brings to mind the product and brand name with which they have become familiar. These kinds of recognition and association do not amount to distinctiveness for trade mark purposes, as the CJEU has now confirmed in its decision in this case.

Kitchen LJ recognised that the CJEU had not referred to the concept of 'reliance' in its judgment. However, in his view:[165]

> Perception by consumers that goods or services designated by the mark originate from a particular undertaking means they can rely upon the mark in making or confirming their transactional decisions. In this context, reliance is a behavioural consequence of perception.

It was therefore considered legitimate to consider whether consumers would rely upon the sign applied for, used on its own, as denoting the origin of the goods or services.[166] On the facts, acquired distinctiveness was not shown. A particular challenge for Nestlé was that, because of the product wrapper, the shape of the goods was not visible at or before the point of sale. There was also little evidence that Nestlé had actually used the shape as a trade mark, as required in case law since *Philips*: there was, for example, no evidence that the shape applied for had featured in Nestlé's promotional or advertising material. Nestlé had submitted in evidence a survey in which respondents were shown a picture of the shape applied for and asked various questions; the results showed that at least half of the respondents thought that the picture shown to them was a 'Kit Kat'. However, this was taken as evidencing at best that just a significant proportion of the relevant public recognised the shape and associated it with Kit Kat, not that they 'perceived' it as an indicator of origin in the sense noted above. It was (somewhat harshly) also queried whether the survey responses could in any event have indicated that respondents just recognised the shape as 'a product which looked like a Kit Kat', rather than specifically the Nestlé product.[167] The Court found it relevant that other manufacturers sold similarly shaped chocolate bars.

14.68   The *London Taxi Corp* case also further demonstrates the challenges facing the trade mark owner in proving acquired distinctiveness for marks such as shapes.[168] Whether the LTC shape marks had acquired distinctive character was a matter of dispute. The Court of Appeal approached this issue applying its own test as formulated in the *Nestlé* appeal. It was not sufficient to show that a significant proportion of the relevant class of persons recognised and associated the mark with the trade mark owner's goods—it had to be shown that consumers perceived that the goods designated by the mark originated with a particular undertaking and no other.[169] LTC did not succeed in demonstrating this. Floyd LJ emphasised that, in addition to the usual assumption that consumers do not expect shapes to be indicators of origin, in this case passengers hiring a black cab (who could be included as relevant 'consumers') would be more focused on the provider of the taxi service than the manufacturer of the taxi itself. It would be 'hard to interest them, far less educate them, in the topic of whether the shape of the taxi is an indication of a unique trade source'.[170] Whether the shape of the taxi had acquired trade mark significance also had to be distinguished from any more generalised understanding that taxis of that shape were licensed London cabs.[171] It was therefore particularly important for LTC to adduce evidence showing that consumers had come to understand that there was only one manufacturer of taxis of the relevant shape; however, no sufficient such evidence had been provided.[172]

---

[164] *Société des Produits Nestlé SA v Cadbury UK Ltd* [2017] ETMR 31, para 78.   [165] ibid, para 82.   [166] ibid, para 84.

[167] ibid, para 89. Contrast Case T-112/13 *Mondelez UK Holdings & Services Ltd v EUIPO* [2017] ETMR 13, a set of parallel proceedings before the General Court concerning Nestlé's parallel EU trade mark. In those proceedings, the shape was held to have acquired a distinctive character in some EU member states including the UK, although was refused registration because acquired distinctiveness had not been demonstrated throughout the whole of the EU (see further para 14.71).

[168] *London Taxi Corp Ltd (t/a London Taxi Co) v Frazer-Nash Research Ltd* [2018] ETMR 7.   [169] ibid, para 53.

[170] ibid, para 66.   [171] ibid, para 66.   [172] ibid, para 67.

Geographical extent

14.69   The question arises as to the geographical extent of the territory for which acquired distinctiveness must be shown. This is a particular issue for EU trade marks. Article 7(2) EUTMR 2017 provides that a trade mark is not to be registered 'notwithstanding that the grounds of non-registrability obtain in only part of the Union'. This reflects the unitary character of EU trade marks: an EU trade mark must have distinctive character, whether inherent or acquired, across the whole of the EU. For an EU trade mark, it is therefore necessary to show that a mark has acquired distinctiveness in all of those member states where it would be regarded as non-distinctive.[173]

14.70   For an inherently non-distinctive word mark, this is likely to be related to the question of where the relevant language or languages are spoken. For example, *Ford Motor Company v OHIM*[174] concerned an application to register the word 'OPTIONS' for insurance and similar financial services. It was shown that the word had acquired distinctiveness in various countries, including the UK, but not in France. The applicant did not prove distinctiveness of the word 'OPTIONS' in the French language and the objection to registration was upheld. As HHJ Hacon put it in *Sofa Workshop Limited v Sofaworks Ltd*:[175]

> the proprietor of a word mark must establish acquired distinctiveness in all Member States in which the average consumer is liable to recognise its descriptive character. How many Member States will depend not only on how widely the language of the mark is spoken, but also on the mark itself. The specific issue is how that particular mark is likely to be interpreted in each Member State.

14.71   Proof of acquired distinctiveness will be particularly burdensome for a mark which has been found to be inherently non-distinctive across the whole territory of the EU. This is likely to be the case for many non-conventional marks such as colours or shapes. Where a mark is inherently non-distinctive across the whole EU, acquired distinctiveness must be proved across the whole EU. The Court of Justice had ruled that it would be unreasonable to require proof of the acquisition of distinctiveness for each individual member state.[176] However, it has recently revisited this issue in *Mondelez*, the invalidation proceedings on Nestlé's EU trade mark registration for the 'Kit Kat' shape which have been running in parallel to the English litigation noted in para 14.67.[177] In those parallel proceedings, the General Court had rejected Nestlé's appeal on proof of acquired distinctiveness, ruling that there had been no assessment of whether there was acquired distinctiveness in Belgium, Ireland, Greece, and Portugal. On appeal to the CJEU, the CJEU reiterated that, to be registered, a mark such as Nestlé's 'Kit Kat' shape mark which was inherently non-distinctive across the EU, must be shown to have acquired distinctiveness under what is now Article 7(3) EUTMR 2017 across the whole of the territory of the EU. However, the means of proving such acquired distinctiveness might relate to several member states at the same time. This could arise, for example if several member states were grouped together in the same distribution network and were treated, particularly for marketing purposes, as a single market. The relevant evidence might also relate to more than one member state at a time if there was a sufficient geographic, cultural, or linguistic proximity between member states such that the public in one state has knowledge of the products or services present on the market in the other. Overall, however, the evidence submitted in support of a claim to acquired distinctiveness had to be capable of establishing that distinctive character had been acquired throughout the member states of the EU.[178] Nestlé's appeal was dismissed. Mondelez is a salutary reminder that the threshold is clearly demanding (and expensive) for those seeking to prove distinctiveness through use for the purposes of registration of an EU trade mark.

---

[173]   Case C-25/05 P *August Storck KG v OHIM* (unreported), para 83.
[174]   Case T-91/99 *Ford Motor Company v OHIM* [2000] ETMR 554.
[175]   *Sofa Workshop Limited v Sofaworks Ltd* [2015] ETMR 37, para 66.
[176]   Case C-98/11 P *Chocoladefabriken Lindt & Sprungli AG v OHIM* [2012] 5 WLUK 756, para 62.
[177]   Case C-84/17 P *Société des Produits Nestlé SA v Mondelez UK Holdings & Services Ltd (formerly Cadbury Holdings Ltd)* [2018] ETMR 38.
[178]   ibid, paras 79-83.

14.72   The geographical extent of acquired distinctiveness differs for a national trade mark and was considered in *Bovemij Verzekeringen NV v Benelux-Merkenbureau*.[179] The question was whether the sign 'EUROPOLIS' had acquired a distinctive character in the Benelux territory for services including insurance and financial affairs. In the instant case, the Dutch word 'polis' referred to an insurance contract and so the grounds for refusal existed only in that part of Benelux where Dutch was spoken. The Court stressed that registration of a trade mark at the national level could only be allowed if it was proven that the trade mark had acquired distinctive character through use throughout the territory of the relevant member state or, in the case of Benelux, throughout the part of the territory of Benelux in which there existed a ground for refusal.[180]

> **Key points on acquired distinctiveness**
>
> - A mark which lacks inherent distinctiveness or is descriptive or customary may become distinctive through use. To overcome these objections by proof of acquired distinctiveness, it must be shown that the mark has come to be understood, as a matter of fact, as an indicator of the origin of the trade mark owner's goods or services.
>
> - To overcome objections raised against a trade mark application, acquired distinctiveness must be shown to exist as at the date of filing. To overcome invalidity objections, distinctiveness acquired after registration will also be relevant.
>
> - For an EU trade mark it is necessary to show that a mark has acquired distinctiveness throughout all parts of the EU where the relevant objection applies. For word marks, this may be linked to the language(s) in which the relevant word is non-distinctive, descriptive, or customary. For other marks (particularly marks such as shapes and colours), the trade mark owner may need to prove distinctiveness throughout the whole of the EU.
>
> - For a national mark, it is necessary to show that it has become distinctive through use throughout the territory of the member state.
>
> - A mark may be shown to have acquired distinctiveness both where it is used independently by the trade mark owner and where it is used as part of, or in conjunction with, another mark. Some disagreement persists as to whether it is sufficient to show that consumers perceive such a 'secondary mark' to be an indicator of origin or must actually be shown to rely upon it in their purchasing decisions.

Exclusion from registration of certain shapes and signs consisting of 'other characteristics'

Section 3(2) TMA 1994 (as amended); Article 4(1)(e) TMD 2015 (formerly Art 3(1)(e) TMD 2008); Article 7(1)(e) EUTMR 2017 (formerly Art 7(1)(e) CTMR)

14.73   Another important set of absolute grounds for refusal or invalidation is at section 3(2) TMA 1994 (as amended). Before the amendments effected by SI 2018/825 to implement the 2015 reform package, this section provided that a sign would not be registered as a trade mark if it consisted exclusively of:

- the shape which results from the nature of the goods themselves;

---

[179]   Case C-108/05 *Bovemij Verzekeringen NV v Benelux-Merkenbureau* [2007] ETMR 29.   [180]   ibid, para 23.

- the shape of the goods which is necessary to attain a technical result; or

- the shape which gives substantial value to the goods.

As a result of the 2015 reform package, these exclusions have now been extended to cover not only shapes but also signs consisting exclusively of other 'characteristics' which offend against any of the three limbs of section 3(2). The new section 3(2) TMA 1994 now reads as follows (with the new text shown in emphasis:[181]

> A sign shall not be registered as a trade mark if it consists exclusively of –
>
> (a) the shape *or another characteristic* which results from the nature of the goods themselves,
>
> (b) the shape *or another characteristic* of the goods which is necessary to attain a technical result, or
>
> (c) the shape *or another characteristic* which gives substantial value to the goods.

In this section of the chapter, we will consider the case law that has developed under the old formulation of these grounds for refusal and the implications of the extension of these objections from 'shapes' to 'other characteristics' of a sign.

14.74   The general public interest underpinning the three grounds for refusal at section 3(2) TMA 1994 has been said by the Court of Justice to be 'to prevent trade mark protection from granting its proprietor a monopoly on technical solutions or functional characteristics of a product which a user is likely to seek in the products of competitors'.[182] To allow such registrations would 'form an obstacle preventing competitors from freely offering for sale products incorporating such technical solutions or functional characteristics in competition with the proprietor of the trade mark'.[183] In early case law, the ECJ described the section 3(2) TMA 1994 objections as a 'preliminary obstacle' to registration.[184] Critically, it is not possible for a sign which is refused under section 3(2) TMA 1994 to be registered by proving acquired distinctiveness: the proviso at section 3(1) TMA 1994 does not apply. Even if the mark in question has, in fact, become distinctive, if one of the grounds of refusal at section 3(2) TMA 1994 is engaged the mark cannot be validly registered.[185] In this instance, consumer interests are secondary insofar as the risk of confusion is concerned: even if consumers perceive the sign as an indicator of origin of the relevant goods (and may, therefore, be confused if others also use the sign), the anti-competitive implications of allowing the objectionable sign to be registered and related interests in favour of consumer choice are considered to outweigh these considerations.

14.75   The three limbs of section 3(2) TMA 1994 are not mutually exclusive but must each be applied independently.[186] This was confirmed in *Société des Produits Nestlé SA v Cadbury UK Ltd*.[187] Nestlé had sought registration of the three-dimensional sign representing the shape of a four-fingered chocolate bar as a trade mark in respect of, inter alia, chocolate bars, biscuits, pastries, and cakes in the UK—shown in Figure 14.11 earlier. Various objections under section 3(2) TMA 1994 were considered. The CJEU

---

[181] See also Art 4(1)(e) TMD 2015 and Art 7(1)(e) EUTMR 2017. In a currently pending case, Case C-21/18 *Textilis Ltd v Svenskt Tenn Aktiebolag*, the Court of Justice has been asked to clarify whether the broadening of the scope of the exclusion is retroactive, such that it can be used to invalidate an EU trade mark for a 'characteristic' other than shape registered before the new provision took effect.

[182] Case C-299/99 *Koninklijke Philips Electronics NV v Remington Consumer Products Ltd* [2002] ETMR 81, para 78. Given that the third of the three exclusions at what are now Art 4(1)(e) TMD 2015 and Art 7(1)(e) EUTMR 2017 has in particular long been thought to relate to aesthetic or decorative features of shape, there has been some criticism of the weight placed in these pronouncements by the ECJ on technical functionality as the concern underlying all three of these objections: see in particular A Quaedvlieg, 'Shapes with a technical function: an ever-expanding exclusion? (2016) 17 ERA Forum 101–17.

[183] Case C-299/99 *Koninklijke Philips Electronics NV v Remington Consumer Products Ltd* [2002] ETMR 81, para 78.

[184] ibid, para 76.

[185] See, eg, Case C-48/09 P *Lego Juris A/S v OHIM* [2010] ETMR 63, para 47. See also Case C-371/06 *Benetton Group SpA v G-Star International BV* [2008] ETMR 5.

[186] Case C-205/13 *Hauck GmbH & Co KG v Stokke A/S* [2014] ETMR 60, paras 37–43.

[187] Case C-215/14 *Société des Produits Nestlé SA v Cadbury UK Ltd* [2015] ETMR 50.

confirmed that an application could only be refused if any one ground was fully applicable to the sign at issue.[188] An application could not be refused if the grounds of objection were each only partially established.

'Shape' and 'other characteristics'

14.76   As noted above, in their pre-2015 form the exclusions at section 3(2) TMA 1994 were applicable only to marks consisting exclusively of a 'shape'. In *Henkel KGaA v Deutsches Patent- und Markenamt*,[189] the ECJ confirmed that packaging of goods may constitute the shape of the goods within the meaning of what is now Article 4(1)(e) TMD 2015, where the packaging must be assimilated to the shape of the goods (eg packaging for liquids). The CJEU has also confirmed that a two-dimensional sign representing the shape of a product could be considered a 'shape'. In *Yoshida v OHIM*[190] the CJEU reviewed whether the shape-mark objections were applicable to what the trade mark applicant claimed was merely a two-dimensional figurative mark. That mark contained rows of black dots and resembled a knife handle, as shown in Figure 14.15.

Figure 14.15 The figurative marks (*Yoshida v OHIM*)

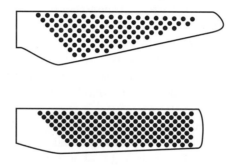

The General Court had ruled that what is now Article 7(1)(e) EUTMR 2017 applied not only to three-dimensional marks but also to two-dimensional marks where all of the essential characteristics of the sign performed a technical function.[191] This finding was approved by the Court of Justice. The CJEU also confirmed that it is permissible to look to all relevant material when assessing the essential characteristics of the sign. This could include material extraneous to the graphic representation and any description contained in the filing for the mark in question. In this case, that meant that it was possible to look to the trade mark applicant's actual product to understand the nature and function of the black dots shown on the knife blade. Those dots had been identified by the Board of Appeal as concave dents intended to achieve a 'non-skid' effect.[192]

14.77   More recently, the CJEU has taken a much more literal approach to the question of whether a given sign constitutes a 'shape'. In *Louboutin*, the CJEU had to consider the applicability of what is now Article 4(1)(e) TMD 2015 to a Benelux mark registered by Christian Louboutin in relation to high-heeled shoes in class 25.[193] The Louboutin mark is shown in Figure 14.16.

[188] ibid, paras 46–48 in particular.
[189] Case C-218/01 *Henkel KGaA v Deutsches Patent- und Markenamt* [2005] ETMR 45 para 37.
[190] Joined Cases C-337/12 P to 340/12 P *Pi-Design AG and Others v Yoshida and OHIM* [2014] ETMR 32.
[191] ibid, para 51.   [192] ibid, para 18.
[193] Case C-163/16 *Christian Louboutin v Van Haren Schoenen BV* [2018] ETMR 31.

Figure 14.16 Louboutin mark

In the application, the mark was described as follows: 'The mark consists of the colour red (Pantone 18-1663TP) applied to the sole of a shoe as shown (the contour of the shoe is not part of the trade mark but is intended to show the positioning of the mark).' In the context of infringement proceedings, the question arose as to whether the Louboutin mark was a 'shape' such that the 'substantial value' exclusion at what is now Article 4(1)(e)(iii) TMD 2015 would apply. The question was referred to the Court of Justice. The CJEU responded that:[194]

> in the context of trade mark law, the concept of 'shape' is usually understood as a set of lines or contours that outline the product concerned.

A colour per se, without an outline, could not constitute a shape.[195] In any event, in light of the explicit wording in the description of the mark, the Court concluded that Louboutin's registration did not relate to a specific shape of sole for high-heeled shoes.[196]

14.78   Given the extension to 'other characteristics' effected by the 2015 reform package, the implications of this more literal approach to 'shape' may be limited. The TMD 2015 and EUTMR 2017 do not stipulate what 'other characteristics' of a sign may be relevant under the expanded rules. The Max Planck Institute 2011 Study referred to the broadly equivalent US rules on functionality, which cover not only shapes but also types of sign such as colours and sounds. The Study considered, for example, that the sound of a motorbike might result from the technical properties of its engine and could thus be said to result from the nature of the goods.[197] Similarly, a colour might be necessary to achieve a technical result (eg enhanced visibility) or might give substantial value to goods (eg if it conveys particular messages about the goods). It remains to be seen how the revised objections are applied in practice.

Which consists 'exclusively'

14.79   All three objections at section 3(2) TMA 1994 only apply if the contested sign consists 'exclusively' of the relevant objectionable shape (or, after the 2015 reform package, 'other characteristic'). What is meant by 'consisting exclusively' of the relevant subject matter was considered by the CJEU in the context of what

---

[194] ibid, para 21.   [195] ibid, para 22.

[196] ibid, para 25. The 'main element' of the sign was the colour claimed by reference to the Pantone colour code; the mark could therefore also not be regarded as consisting 'exclusively' of a shape: para 26.

[197] Max Planck Institute for Intellectual Property and Competition Law, 'Study on the Overall Functioning of the European Trade Mark System' (February 2011), 72.

is now Article 4(1)(e)(ii) TMD 2015 in *Lego Juris A/S v OHIM*.[198] The Court held that a sign 'consists exclusively' of the shape of goods necessary to achieve a technical result:[199]

> when all the essential characteristics of the shape before a technical function, the presence of non-essential characteristics with no technical function being irrelevant in that context.

The presence of 'one or more minor arbitrary elements' in a three-dimensional sign would not affect the conclusion that the sign 'consisted exclusively' of a shape necessary to obtain a technical result. In contrast, a shape with a 'major non-functional element' would not fall within the ground of refusal.[200] The same principles also apply to testing whether a sign 'consists exclusively' of objectionable subject matter for the other indents at Article 4(1)(e) TMD 2015 and Article 7(1)(e) EUTMR 2017.[201]

Nature of the goods themselves (s 3(2)(a) TMA 1994 (as amended); Art 4(1)(e)(i) TMD 2015; Art 7(1)(e)(i) EUTMR 2017)

14.80   Section 3(2)(a) TMA 1994 provides that a sign shall not be registered where it consists exclusively of a shape (or, after the 2015 reform package, 'other characteristic') that results 'from the nature of the goods themselves'. What is meant by this reference to a shape 'resulting from the nature of the goods themselves' has provoked considerable uncertainty.

The prevailing view was that this ground of objection was narrow, applying where there was no other possible shape for the goods in question.[202] There was, however, also a concern that this narrow interpretation would render the exclusion effectively meaningless. It took a long time for a case on interpretation of this provision to come before the CJEU. In *Hauck GmbH & Co KG v Stokke A/S*,[203] however, the Court of Justice was finally asked to provide clarification on what is now Article 4(1)(e)(i) TMD 2015 by the Dutch Hoge Raad. The case concerned registration of the shape of the 'Tripp-Trapp' children's chair. One of the questions before the Court of Justice was whether the objection at Article 4(1)(e)(i) applied only to a shape which was 'indispensable to the function of the product in question', or whether it also applied to a sign consisting exclusively of a shape with 'one or more characteristics which are essential to the function of that product and which consumers may be looking for in the products of competitors'.[204] The CJEU rejected the first of these two possible interpretations, noting that this would narrow the scope of the ground for refusal only to 'regulated' products (whose shape was prescribed by legal standards) or 'natural' products (for which there was no substitute).[205] This was not consistent with the underlying objectives of this ground for refusal. Instead, the Court concluded that the ground for refusal now at Article 4(1)(e)(i) TMD 2015 extends to 'shapes with essential characteristics which are inherent to the generic function or functions of [the] goods'.[206] Article 4(1)(e)(i) applies to a 'sign which consists exclusively of the shape of a product with one or more essential characteristics which are inherent to the generic function or functions of that product and which consumers may be looking for in the products of competitors'.[207]

The design of the Tripp-Trapp Chair is as shown in Figure 14.17.

---

[198] Case C-48/09 P *Lego Juris A/S v OHIM* [2010] ETMR 63.   [199] ibid, para 51.   [200] ibid, para 52.

[201] See, eg, Case C- 205/13 *Hauck GmbH & Co KG v Stokke A/S* [2014] ETMR 60, para 21.

[202] See, eg, the Court of Appeal in *Philips Electronics NV v Remington Consumer Products Ltd* [1999] ETMR 816:

> Subsection 2(a) has to be construed in the context of subsections (b) and (c). It is intended to exclude from registration basic shapes that should be available for use by the public at large. It is difficult to envisage such shapes, except those that are produced in nature such as bananas [per Aldous LJ at 829].

[203] Case C- 205/13 *Hauck GmbH & Co KG v Stokke A/S* [2014] ETMR 60.   [204] ibid, para 15.   [205] ibid, para 24.

[206] ibid, para 25.   [207] ibid, para 27.

Figure 14.17 Design of the Tripp-Trapp Chair

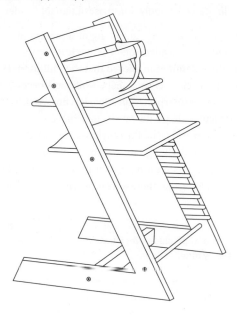

The reference by the Court to 'generic function' is unclear. In *Hauck* the Court of Justice suggested that the characteristics of generic function are those that consumers would look for in the products of competitors and which were designed to perform an identical or similar function.[208] The concern is that allowing one trader to monopolise such characteristics would make it difficult for competitors to give their products a shape which is suited to the use for which their products are intended.[209] However, concerns have been expressed that this aspect of the decision in *Hauck* creates an unclear overlap with the technical exclusion at indent (ii) of Article 4(1)(e) TMD 2015 and Article 7(1)(e) EUTMR.[210] The CJEU has also not explained what approach should be taken to deciding what constitutes the 'goods themselves' for these purposes.

Necessary to achieve a technical result (s 3(2)(b) TMA 1994 (as amended); Art 4(1)(e)(ii) TMD 2015; Art 7(1)(e)(ii) EUTMR 2017)

14.81   Section 3(2)(b) TMA 1994 (as amended) provides that a sign shall not be registered where it consists exclusively of a shape (or, post-2015, 'other characteristic') that is 'necessary to obtain a technical result'. The ECJ elaborated on the underlying public interests in *Koninklijke Philips Electronics NV v Remington Consumer Products Ltd*.[211] The Court explained that what is now Article 4(1)(e)(ii) TMD 2015 is intended to:[212]

> preclude the registration of shapes whose essential characteristics perform a technical function, with the result that the exclusivity inherent in the trade mark right would limit the possibility of competitors supplying a product incorporating such a function or at least limit their freedom of choice in regard to the technical solution they wish to adopt in order to incorporate such a function in their product.

A shape whose essential characteristics perform a technical function and were chosen to fulfil that function should be freely used by all.[213] Article 4(1)(e)(ii) also reflects the aim of not allowing the use of trade mark registration to acquire or perpetuate exclusive rights relating to technical solutions,[214] the thinking being

---

[208] ibid, para 26.   [209] ibid, para 26.

[210] See, eg, A Kur, 'Too common, too splendid, or "just right"? Trade mark protection for product shapes in the light of CJEU case law', Max Planck Institute for Innovation and Competition Research Paper No 14-17.

[211] Case C-299/99 *Koninklijke Philips Electronics NV v Remington Consumer Products Ltd* [2002] ETMR 81.

[212] ibid, para 79.   [213] ibid, para 80.   [214] ibid, para 82.

that it would be wrong for the indefinite protection achievable through trade mark registration to be used to perpetuate the strictly time-limited monopoly otherwise obtainable under patent law in particular.

14.82   In *Philips*, Philips had registered a trade mark consisting of a picture of a three-headed rotary electric shaver. Remington also marketed three-headed rotary shavers. Philips accused Remington of infringing their registered trade mark. In turn, Remington alleged that the Philips mark was invalid on a number of grounds, including that it consisted exclusively of a shape which was necessary to obtain a technical result. The case was referred to the ECJ on the interpretation of what is now Article 4(1)(e)(ii) TMD 2015. The key question was what makes a particular shape 'necessary' to achieve a technical result. Philips argued that this meant that the shape in question had to be the only possible shape for that function, but Remington opposed this.[215] After outlining the underlying rationale of what is now Article 4(1)(e)(ii) TMD 2015 as noted above, the ECJ held that there was nothing in that provision that allowed the conclusion that the objection could be overcome by showing that there were other shapes that could achieve the same technical result.[216] The Court held:[217]

> Where the essential functional characteristics of the shape of a product are attributable solely to the technical result, Article 3(1)(e), second indent, precludes registration of a sign consisting of that shape, even if that technical result can be achieved by other shapes.

14.83   The interpretation of this ground of objection was developed further by the CJEU in *Lego Juris A/S v OHIM*.[218] The CJEU noted that what is now Article 7(1)(e)(ii) EUTMR 2017 reflected a 'balancing' of considerations intended to 'help establish a healthy and fair system of competition'.[219] On the one hand, Article 7(1)(e)(ii) meant that traders could not 'use trade mark law to perpetuate, indefinitely, exclusive rights relating to technical solutions'.[220] On the other hand, by limiting the ground of refusal to signs which consist 'exclusively' of the shape of goods which is 'necessary' to obtain a technical result:[221]

> the legislature duly took into account that any shape of goods is, to a certain extent, functional and that it would therefore be inappropriate to refuse to register a shape of goods as a trade mark solely on the ground that it has functional characteristics. By the terms 'exclusively' and 'necessary', that provision ensures that solely shapes of goods which only incorporate a technical solution, and whose registration as a trade mark would therefore actually impede the use of that technical solution by other undertakings, are not to be registered.

The CJEU reiterated that the fact that the same technical result may be achieved by other shapes is irrelevant.[222] The key requirement is that all of the sign's essential characteristics perform the technical function of the goods at issue.[223] The essential characteristics of the sign are its most important elements, the identification of which must be carried out on a case-by-case basis. There is no systematic hierarchy between the types of elements of which a sign may consist. An assessment of a sign's essential characteristics can look directly at the sign's overall impression or first examine in turn each of its elements: it can accordingly be carried out by a simple visual analysis or be based on a detailed examination.[224]

14.84   It has subsequently been further confirmed that what is now Article 3(1)(e)(ii) TMD 2015 applies only to the manner in which the relevant goods function and not in respect of the manner in which the goods were manufactured.[225] The CJEU has also spoken further, in the *Simba Toys* case, on the assessment of technical functionality.[226] The case concerned the registration as a trade mark of the 'Rubik's Cube', the three-dimensional puzzle that is thought to be the best-selling toy of all time. Seven Towns Limited (STL) was the owner of various intellectual property rights related to the 'Rubik's Cube'. This included, amongst

---

[215] For discussion of similar issues in registered design law, see Chapter 8.
[216] Case C-299/99 *Koninklijke Philips Electronics NV v Remington Consumer Products Ltd* [2002] ETMR 81, para 81.
[217] ibid, para 83.   [218] Case C-48/09 P *Lego Juris A/S v OHIM* [2010] ETMR 63.
[219] ibid, para 44.   [220] ibid, para 45.   [221] ibid, para 48.   [222] ibid, paras 53–62.   [223] ibid, para 72.
[224] ibid, paras 69–71.   [225] Case C-215/14 *Société des Produits Nestlé SA v Cadbury UK Ltd* [2015] ETMR 50, paras 52–57.
[226] Case C-30/15 P *Simba Toys GmbH & Co. KG v EUIPO, Seven Towns Ltd (intervener at first instance)* [2017] ETMR 6.

other things, an EU trade mark registration for the sign shown in Figure 14.18 which was registered for 'three-dimensional puzzles' in Class 28 in 1999.

Figure 14.18 The Rubik's Cube application

The validity of the shape as a trade mark was challenged by Simba Toys. For the purposes of what is now Article 4(1)(e)(ii) TMD 2015, the essential characteristics of the registered sign were taken to consist of its cube shape and the grid structure on each surface of the cube. The General Court had rejected Simba Toys' arguments relating to the rotating capability of the toy, on the basis that those arguments were based on knowledge of the rotating capability of the vertical and horizontal lattices of the 'Rubik's Cube' and that that capability in any event resulted not from the shape shown in the registration but from an invisible internal mechanism. The General Court had taken the view that inferring the existence of an internal rotating mechanism from the graphic representations of that mark was not consistent with the requirement that any inference must be drawn with sufficient certainty and as objectively as possible from the shape as graphically represented. However, the CJEU disagreed. It reiterated that, as it had held in *Lego*, when examining the functional characteristics of a sign account may be taken of relevant material which is extraneous, and in addition to, the graphic representation shown in the registration and any description of the mark filed as part of the application.

Substantial value (s 3(2)(c) TMA 1994 (as amended); Article 4(1)(e)(iii) TMD 2015; Article 7(1)(e)(iii) EUTMR 2017)

14.85   Finally, section 3(2)(c) TMA 1994 provides that a shape (or, after the 2015 reform package, 'other characteristic') which gives 'substantial value' to the goods will not be registrable. This objection was understood to be inspired by provisions of pre-harmonisation Benelux law, but its interpretation and application were unclear. It was thought to be directed to aesthetically valuable shapes (wholly decorative or ornamental) and to be intended to create a demarcation between copyright or design protection on the one hand and trade mark protection on the other. However, it was by no means clear that this demarcation was necessary or that this exclusion (unlike, say, the exclusion for technical functionality) was really aimed at solving any genuine competitiveness concerns. There was a sense that this exclusion also created a form of 'Catch 22' situation for distinctive shapes—as the Max Planck Institute put it in its 2011 Study:[227]

---

[227] Max Planck Institute for Intellectual Property and Competition Law, 'Study on the Overall Functioning of the European Trade Mark System' (February 2011), 73.

Worse, it might present a dilemma for particularly ambitious designs: as indicated above, (only) products which are significantly different from existing forms may, under the standards established in ECJ jurisprudence, qualify as being inherently distinctive—however, if that makes them also particularly attractive for consumers, they may . . . for the same reason by barred from protection forever.

The General Court's decision in *Bang and Olufsen v OHIM*[228] seemed to illustrate the trade mark owner's dilemma: in this case, the General Court noted that the design of speakers would be an important element in the choice made by the consumer:[229]

Indeed, the shape for which registration was sought reveals a very specific design and the applicant itself admits, at para. 92 of the application in particular, that that design is an essential element of its branding and increases the appeal of the product at issue, that is to say, its value.

Protection was denied (see Figure 14.19). Reflecting the concerns noted above, the Max Planck Institute Study of 2011 recommended abolishing this ground of objection, but this was not taken up in the 2015 reform package.

Figure 14.19 Bang & Olufsen loud speaker

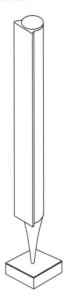

14.86   The leading case on what is now Article 4(1)(e)(iii) TMD is now *Hauck GmbH & Co KG v Stokke A/S*, the Tripp-Trapp chair case.[230] The referring court in that case was unsure how to apply what is now Article 4(1)(e)(iii) given that, while the shape of the Tripp-Trapp chair gave it significant aesthetic value, it also had other characteristics—such as safety, comfort and reliability—which gave it essential functional value. The CJEU stressed the underlying aim of Article 4(1)(e)(iii) as being to prevent trade mark protection being used to extend indefinitely the life of other IP rights which are subject to more limited time periods.[231] In the Court's view, a 'shape which gives substantial value to the goods' could not be limited only to shapes with only artistic or ornamental value as there would be a risk that shapes with both essential functional characteristics and significant aesthetic value would not be caught.[232] Article 4(1)(e)(iii) could apply to a sign which consisted exclusively of the shape of a product 'with several characteristics each of which may give that product substantial value'.[233] The assessment could take into account the nature of the category of goods concerned, the artistic value of the shape in question, its dissimilarity from other shapes in

[228] Case T-508/08 *Bang and Olufsen v OHIM* [2012] ETMR 10.   [229] ibid, para 74.
[230] Case C- 205/13 *Hauck GmbH & Co KG v Stokke A/S* [2014] ETMR 60.   [231] ibid, para 31.   [232] ibid, para 32.
[233] ibid, para 36.

common use on the market concerned, any substantial price difference in relation to similar products, and any evidence of a promotion strategy focused on accentuating the aesthetic characteristics of the product in question.[234] There remains considerable uncertainty over where *Hauck* leaves the interpretation and application of Article 4(1)(e)(iii) TMD 2015/Article (1)(e)(iii) EUTMR 2017, with concern that—again— there is now also undue overlap with the technical functionality exclusion at indent (ii).[235] In the *London Taxi Corp* case, the Court of Appeal considered there to remain points of uncertainty over the application of what is now Article 4(1)(e)(iii) TMD 2015 and indicated that it would have referred further questions to the CJEU had that been necessary to dispose of the dispute.[236]

Discussion point   For answer guidance visit **www.oup.com/uk/brown5e**.

To what sort of 'other characteristics' do you think the objections at section 3(2) TMA 1994 (as amended) are likely to be applied? How do you think this expansion of the scope of the exclusion may shape the direction of future case law under each of the three limbs of section 3(2) TMA (as amended)?

Key points on the exclusion from registration of certain shapes and 'other characteristics' of a sign

- Pursuant to section 3(2) TMA 1994 (as amended) (see also Arts 4(1)(e) TMD 2015 and Art 7(1)(e) EUTMR 2017) a sign may not be registered if it consists exclusively of a 'shape' or 'other characteristic' which results from the nature of the goods themselves, is necessary to achieve a technical result, or adds substantial value to the goods.

- These objections are motivated by an intention to avoid anti-competitive trade mark monopolies, albeit that this rationale has been articulated most clearly in relation to technical functionality.

  - If any of the objections apply, the sign will not be registrable: it is not possible to overcome these objections by proof of acquired distinctiveness.

  - Before the 2015 reform package, these objections applied only to signs which consisted exclusively of an objectionable 'shape'; it remains to be seen how the extension of these objections to signs consisting exclusively of objectionable 'other characteristics' will operate in practice.

Public policy and morality

Section 3(3)(a) TMA 1994 (as amended); Article 4(1)(f) TMD 2015; Article 7(1)(f) EUTMR 2017

14.87   Public policy and morality and public deception also have a role to play in preventing certain trade marks from being registered.

Under section 3(3) TMA 1994 a mark will not be registered if it is 'contrary to public policy or to accepted principles of morality' (see also Art 4(1)(f) TMD 2015 and Art 7(1)(f) EUTMR 2017). These are two

---

[234]   ibid, para 35.

[235]   See, eg, A Kur, 'Too common, too splendid, or "just right"? Trade mark protection for product shapes in the light of CJEU case law', Max Planck Institute for Innovation and Competition Research Paper No 14-17 and A Quaedvlieg, 'Shapes with a technical function: an ever-expanding exclusion? (2016) 17 ERA Forum 101–17.

[236]   *London Taxi Corp Ltd (t/a London Taxi Co) v Frazer-Nash Research Ltd* [2018] ETMR 7, paras 70–76.

separate but potentially overlapping grounds for objection. The EUIPO has identified as the rationale for these exclusions that the actions of 'the Office should not positively assist people who wish to further their business aims by means of trade marks that offend against certain basis values of civilised society'.[237] The EUIPO sees no conflict between the bar on immoral marks and protected rights to free speech—the prohibition on registering immoral marks does not impede the freedom of expression of the trade mark owner to go ahead and use the mark:[238]

> The application of Article 7(1)(f) EUTMR is not limited by the principle of freedom of expression . . . since the refusal to register only means that the sign is not granted protection under trade mark law and does not stop the sign from being used—even in business.

14.88   What is contrary to public policy[239] or accepted principles of morality may change over time. For instance, the word 'Hallelujah'[240] was refused registration for women's clothing under the 1938 Act on the ground that it was offensive. Also considered offensive, in 1947, was the proposed use of 'Oomphies' for footwear.[241] Both would be likely to be immediately acceptable under the 1994 Act. Certain words do, however, still offend against morality. In 2001, an application to register the words 'Tiny Penis' in connection with articles of clothing was turned down on the grounds that it offended against current principles of morality.[242] The word sign FCUK was not, on the other hand, considered offensive and the mark was allowed to be registered as a trade mark.[243]

14.89   In *Basic Trademark SA's Trade Mark Application*,[244] concerning an appeal against a refusal to register the word 'JESUS' on the basis that to do so would be contrary to public policy, it was stressed that any objection on the grounds of public policy must relate to the intrinsic qualities of the mark and not to the personal qualities of the applicant for registration.[245] The objection also cannot be based upon the nature of the goods or services claimed.[246] Further, mere offence to the public, such as that the public would consider the mark distasteful, is not enough: 'it is only in cases where it is plain that an accepted principle of morality is being offended against that registration should be denied'.[247] It is necessary to find the dividing line between distaste and outrage—where the latter is likely to undermine current religious, family, or social values amongst an identifiable section of the public.[248] Words which contain profane language will not be registrable[249] nor will signs that glorify terrorism.[250] In *Pooja Sweets & Savouries Ltd's Trade Mark Application*,[251] the Appointed Person allowed the registration of the word 'pooja',[252] a religious Hindu ritual, in the marks in relation to some certain foodstuff, noting that this would not cause serious offence to reasonable people of normal levels of sensitivity and tolerance, including those who were themselves observant Hindus. CURVE, on the other hand, was refused registration as an EU trade mark on the ground that the word was the plural

[237]   EUIPO *Guidelines for Examination of EU Trade Marks* Part B, s 4, Ch 7, 3.   [238]   ibid.

[239]   The expression 'public policy' referred to matters of the kind covered by the French legal term 'ordre public'. *Philips Electronics NV v Remington Consumer Products Ltd* [1998] RPC 283.

[240]   *Hallelujah Trade Mark* [1976] RPC 605.

[241]   This was overturned on application to the court, and the name registered: *La Marquise's Footwear Application* (1947) 64 RPC 27. Apparently 'Oomphies' was derived from 'Oomph', denoting sex appeal, and had achieved significance, meaning those qualities in connection with a film actress with whom the word had originated.

[242]   *Ghazilian's Trade Mark Application* [2002] ETMR 57.

[243]   *French Connection Ltd's Trade Mark Application (No 81862)* [2007] ETMR 8.   [244]   [2005] RPC 25.

[245]   ibid; see also Case T-140/02 *Sportwetten GmbH Gera v OHIM & Intertops Sportwetten GmbH* [2006] ETMR 15. *French Connection Ltd's Trade Mark Application (No 81862)* [2007] ETMR 8.

[246]   Case T-140/02 *Sportwetten GmbH Gera v OHIM & Intertops Sportwetten GmbH* [2006] ETMR 15: an application to challenge the validity of an EU trade mark for bookmaking and other services relating to gambling was dismissed because the objection was based upon the nature of the services claimed and not the nature of the mark.

[247]   *Ghazilian's Trade Mark Application* [2002] ETMR 57, para 21.

[248]   See also *CDW Graphic Design Ltd's Trade Mark Application* [2003] RPC 30, where the trade mark registry refused an application to register the domain name http://www.standupifyouhatemanu.com/ as a trade mark on public policy grounds. It was enough to show that the normal and fair use of such a trade mark would be likely to lead to criminal or offensive behaviour.

[249]   Case R 111/2002-4 (Dick & Fanny).   [250]   Case R 176/2004-2 (Bin Laden).

[251]   *Pooja Sweets Ltd v Pooja Sweets & Savouries Ltd* [2015] 2 WLUK 243.

[252]   Pooja, spelled phonetically as *puja* in English, is a prayer ceremony performed by Hindus to host, honour, and worship one or more deities, or to spiritually celebrate an event.

of the Romanian word 'curvă', which translates to *prostitute* or *whore* in English, and would be viewed by the relevant Romanian speaking public as an insulting and obscene statement.[253] The standard to be applied is that of the reasonable person with normal levels of sensitivity and tolerance.[254]

14.90   The ECJ has recognised that the concept of public policy varies from country to country and that a restrictive measure based on public policy may be based on a value not shared by all member states.[255] The public, however, is not limited to the public targeted by the mark. The relevant public is rather the public at large who could be confronted with the sign in their daily life.[256] The Court of Justice will consider the provisions again in a pending appeal from the General Court concerning an attempt to register the title of a successful film as a trade mark.[257] The General Court upheld the earlier decisions to refuse registration of *Fack Ju Göhte* on the grounds that the mark was offensive to the German-speaking public, especially when combined with a reference to a highly regarded author (Goethe). The General Court rejected arguments that the mark would be seen as pithy and humorous, and that the objection that the public would be shocked by the mark was undermined by the popularity of the film, which had been seen by millions of people since the date of its release.

  Question

How should morality for the purposes of trade mark law and freedom of expression under Article 10 of the Convention for the Protection of Human Rights and Fundamental Freedom be balanced? Read LP Ramsey, 'A free speech right to trademark protection' (2016) 106 Trademark Rep 797. Do you agree with the EUIPO's position that refusal to register a mark based upon morality or public policy grounds has no impact upon freedom of speech?

  Exercise

Find out what marks have been refused registration as EU trade marks on the grounds that to do so would be contrary to public policy or to accepted principles of morality. How are the different views of morality in member states dealt with? How should they be dealt with?

Read Case T-232/10 *Couture Tech Ltd v OHIM* [2012] ETMR 5 which concerned this logo:

Figure 14.20 Case T-232/10 *Couture Tech Ltd v OHIM* [2012] ETMR 5

Why was the sign refused registration?

---

[253] Case T-266/13 *Brainlab AG v OHIM*.   [254] Case R 176/2004-2.   [255] Case C-36/02 *Omega Spielhallen GmbH*.
[256] Case T-52/13 *Efag Trade Mark Company GmbH v OHIM*, paras 16–19; 39–40.
[257] Pending Case C-240/18 P, appealed from Case T-69/17 *Constantin Film Production GmbH v EUIPO* (unreported).

Discussion point   For answer guidance visit **www.oup.com/uk/brown5e**.

Do you think that the case law discussed here adequately covers all of the public policy considerations that might arise in relation to trade mark registration? Do you think that there is any role for
this ground of objection in relation to the appropriation of public domain cultural creations? Read
the article M Senftleben, '*Vigeland* and the status of cultural concerns in trade mark law—the EFTA
Court develops more effective tools for preservation of the public domain' (2017) 48 IIC 683–720,
which discusses a decision of the EFTA Court in relation to an attempt to register works by Gustav
Vigeland, an eminent Norwegian sculptor, as trade marks. Do you think that EU courts should take a
similar approach to cultural works the EFTA Court took in the *Vigeland* case?

Deceptive marks

14.91   A mark may be considered to be deceptive under section 3(3)(b) TMA 1994 (as amended) if it is 'of such a
nature as to deceive the public (for instance, as to the nature, quality or geographical origin of the goods or
service)' (see also Art 4(1)(g) TMD 2015 and Art 7(1)(g) EUTMR 2017).

14.92   The concept of deceptiveness was considered by the Court of Justice in *Elizabeth Florence Emanuel v
Continental Shelf 128 Ltd*.[258] The case concerned a trade mark registration for the name 'Elizabeth Emanuel',
which had been filed by the designer of that name in the 1990s. Ownership of the trade mark had been
assigned, along with all corresponding goodwill, when the designer sold her business and the designer had
ceased to be involved with the activities of the new owners. Some time later, she sought to revoke the trade
mark registration on the basis that it had become deceptive. The Court held that the public interest which
justified the ground of objection at what is now Article 4(1)(g) TMD 2015 was one of consumer protection,
reflecting a risk of confusion in the mind of the average consumer, 'especially where the person to whose
name the mark corresponds originally personified the goods bearing that mark'.[259] However, Article 4(1)
(g) presupposed:[260]

> the existence of actual deceit or a sufficiently serious risk that the consumer will be deceived.

In the present case, even if a consumer was influenced into purchasing a garment because of the name by
imagining that the relevant individual was involved in the design, the 'characteristics and the qualities of
that garment remain guaranteed by the undertaking which owns the trade mark'.[261] Consequently, the
name was not in and of itself of a nature to deceive the public as to the nature, quality, or geographical
origin of the product it designated. If there was an intention by the owner of the trade mark to make
the consumer believe Ms Emanuel was the designer, that could be fraudulent behaviour and would be
a matter for the national court, but would not be deception for the purposes of what is now Article 4(1)
(g) TMD 2015.[262]

Question

Can you think of any sign which might be refused registration on the ground that it might be
deceptive?

---

[258] Case C-259/04 *Elizabeth Florence Emanuel v Continental Shelf 128 Ltd* [2006] ETMR 56.   [259] ibid, para 46.
[260] ibid, para 47.   [261] ibid, para 48.   [262] ibid, para 50.

Marks prohibited by law, protected emblems, and geographical indications

Sections 3(4), (4A)–(4D) and (5) TMA 1994 (as amended); Articles 4(1)(h)–(l) TMD 2015; Articles 7(1)(h)–(m) EUTMR 2017

14.93   Further absolute grounds of refusal are to be found in sections 3(4) and (5) TMA 1994. Section 3(4) prohibits registration of marks to the extent that their use would be prohibited in the UK by any enactment or rule of law or by any provision of EU law (other than relating to trade marks—see the clarifying amendment inserted at section 3(4) TMA 1994 by SI 2018/825). Section 3(5) relates to specially protected emblems. These would include, for example, the Union Jack, and any sign that would lead to indication of a connection with the Royal Family. The Paris Convention requires Convention countries to prohibit the registration of 'armorial bearings, flags and emblems' of the countries of the Union.[263] The ECJ has confirmed that there is broad protection for state emblems.[264]

14.94   Implementing the 2015 reform package, new sections 3(4A)–(4D) have been inserted into the TMA 1994 by SI 2018/825. These prohibit the registration of marks contrary to relevant instruments protecting protected designations of origin ('PDOs'), geographical indications ('GIs'), traditional terms for wine and plant variety rights.[265]

Bad faith

Section 3(6) TMA 1994 (as amended); Article 4(2) TMD 2015; Article 59(1)(b) EUTMR 2017

14.95   Section 3(6) TMA 1994 (as amended) provides that a trade mark shall not be registered if or to the extent that the application is made in bad faith. This is also a ground for invalidation in UK law pursuant to section 47(1) TMA 1994. Under Article 4(2) TMD 2015, bad faith is now a mandatory ground for invalidation across member states and an optional ground for refusal of a pending application. For an EU trade mark, bad faith is a ground for invalidation only (see Article 59(1)(b) EUTMR 2017).

14.96   There is no definition of bad faith in the TMA 1994 (as amended), TMD 2015, or EUTMR 2017. In *Gromax Plasticulture Ltd v Don & Low Nonwovens Ltd*[266] Lindsay J said this of bad faith:[267]

> I shall not attempt to define bad faith in this context. Plainly it includes dishonesty and, as I would hold, includes also some dealings which fall short of the standards of acceptable commercial behaviour observed by reasonable and experienced men in the particular area being examined. Parliament has wisely not attempted to explain in detail what is or is not bad faith in this context: how far a dealing must so fall-short in order to amount to bad faith is a matter best left to be adjudged not by some paraphrase by the courts (which leads to the danger of the courts then construing not the Act but the paraphrase) but by reference to the words of the Act and upon a regard to all material surrounding circumstances.

14.97   Cases concerning bad faith applications have occurred where there has been an attempt to register a mark for which the applicant knows there is a competing claim,[268] where the applicant is an employee,[269] where

---

[263] Paris Convention, Art 6*ter*.

[264] Joined Cases C-202/08 P and C-208/08 P *American Clothing Associates SA v OHIM* [2010] ETMR 3.

[265] There are now also relative objections relating to geographical indications, as to which see further Chapter 15.

[266] [1999] RPC 367 at 379.

[267] Approved of by the Court of Appeal in *Harrison v Teton Valley Trading Co Ltd* [2005] FSR 10. See also *Maslyukov v Diageo Distilling Ltd and Another* [2010] EWHC 443 (Ch), para 36.

[268] See, eg, *Harrison v Teton Valley Trading Co Ltd* [2005] FSR 10.   [269] *Casson's Trade Mark* (1910) 27 RPC 65.

there is an agreement to the contrary,[270] where the applicant is aware of the existence of a well-known company name the same as the sign,[271] or where an application is made to register a trade mark based on an older trade mark in which there is residual goodwill.[272] The relevant date for assessing whether an application to register a trade mark was made in bad faith is the application date.[273] When considering issues of bad faith, a person is presumed to act in good faith unless the contrary is proved.[274]

14.98   *Harrison v Teton Valley*[275] concerned the name 'China White'. The proprietors of a nightclub 'Chinawhite' had traded under the name for a number of years. As part of their business activity they discussed developing a cocktail with their bar manager—to be called China White. The bar manager informed Harrison of these developments and he proceeded to apply for registration of the name. The Court of Appeal considered that the application had been made in bad faith. The test is a combined one of dishonesty and acceptable commercial behaviour observed by reasonable and experienced persons in the commercial area under consideration:[276]

> dishonesty requires knowledge by the defendant that what he was doing would be regarded as dishonest by honest people, although he should not escape a finding of dishonesty because he sets his own standards of honesty and does not regard as dishonest what he knows would offend the normally accepted standards of honest conduct.

In *Harrison* the court found that on the facts of the case—that the applicant knew of the nightclub, and that a drink, China White, was sold at the club—the application was in bad faith.

14.99   By contrast, in *Hotel Cipriani SRL v Cipriani (Grosvenor Street) Ltd*[277] the Court of Appeal upheld the finding of the lower court that it was not bad faith on the part of one party who registered a mark when they knew that a third party used the same mark for similar goods and services elsewhere in the EU, a key difference being that the applicant had used that mark for many years and it was one in which they had a reputation (Cipriani).

14.100   In *Cipriani* the Court of Appeal followed the judgment of the ECJ in *Chocoladefabriken Lindt & Sprüngli AG v Franz Hauswirth GmbH*.[278] The CJEU had been asked to determine a question concerning the registration as an EU trade mark of a chocolate bunny (Figure 14.21) and the challenge to the registration by other producers of chocolate bunnies (Figure 14.22). In determining bad faith, the Court of Justice said that the factors to be taken into account were, in particular:

- the fact that the applicant knows or must know that a third party is using, in at least one member state, an identical or similar sign for an identical or similar product capable of being confused with the sign for which registration is sought;

- the applicant's intention to prevent that third party from continuing to use such a sign; and

- the degree of legal protection enjoyed by the third party's sign and by the sign for which registration is sought.

14.101   Most recently, questions on bad faith have arisen again in relation to the breadth of the specification of goods and services claimed by trade mark owners. Although the TMA 1994 (as amended) requires an applicant to declare on filing that they have a bona fide intention to use the mark for the goods or services claimed (and failure to do so is deemed to amount to bad faith under s 3(6)) the extent to which this is compatible with harmonised EU trade mark law has remained unclear as there is no corresponding requirement in the TMD or EUTMR.[279] In the *Sky Plc v Skykick UK Ltd* case (see also para 14.28 above),[280] the High Court

---

[270] *Mary Wilson Enterprises Inc's Trade Mark Application* [2003] EMLR 14.   [271] Case T-321/10 *SA PAR Srl v OHIM*.
[272] *Jules Rimet Cup Ltd v Football Association* [2007] EWHC 2376 (Ch); Case T-327/12 *Simca Europe Ltd v OHIM*, paras 62–67.
[273] Case C-529/07 *Chocoladenfabriken Lindt & Sprüngli AG v Franz Hauswirth GmbH* [2009] ETMR 56, para 35; *Red Bull GmbH v Sun Mark Ltd* [2013] ETMR 53, para 131.
[274] *Red Bull GmbH v Sun Mark Ltd* [2013] ETMR 53, para 133.   [275] *Harrison v Teton Valley* [2005] FSR 10.
[276] ibid, para 25, quoting from *Twinsectra Ltd v Yardley* [2002] 2 AC 164, para 36.   [277] [2008] EWHC 3032 (Ch).
[278] Case C-529/07 *Chocoladefabriken Lindt & Sprüngli AG v Franz Hauswirth GmbH* [2009] ETMR 56.
[279] See, eg, *Knoll AG's Trade Mark* [2003] RPC 10; *LABORATOIRE DE LA MER Trade Marks* [2002] FSR 51, para 19; *Ferrero SpA's Trade Marks* [2004] RPC 29.
[280] *Sky Plc v Skykick UK Ltd* [2018] ETMR 23; [2018] EWHC 943 (Ch). As noted at para 14.28 above, at the time of writing, the case is pending before the Court of Justice as Case C-371/18.

has sought clarification from the Court of Justice as to whether, under EU trade mark law, it can constitute bad faith to apply to register a trade mark without any intention to use it in relation to the specified goods or services. In this infringement dispute, Skykick challenged the validity of various registrations for the mark SKY belonging to the entertainment and communications company based upon the sheer breadth of coverage of goods and services in the relevant trade mark specifications. Although some items in the specification could be explained, for example, as covering avenues of potential future use, registration in respect of other items (eg 'fuel additives' and 'whips') could not be explained on that basis. The trial judge concluded that 'the specifications include goods and services in respect of which Sky had no reasonable commercial rationale for seeking registration'.[281]

Key points on the exclusion of registering a trade mark based on public policy and morality, deceptive marks, and applications in bad faith

- Objections on the grounds of public policy must relate to the intrinsic qualities of the mark and not to the personal qualities of the applicant or the nature of the goods or services applied for.

- Mere offence to the public, such as that the public would consider the mark distasteful, is not enough.

- The standard to be applied is that of the reasonable person with normal levels of sensitivity and tolerance; for a mark to be considered deceptive there needs to be evidence of actual deceit or a sufficiently serious risk that the consumer will be deceived.

- An application made in bad faith will be refused considering both dishonesty and acceptable commercial behaviour observed by reasonable and experienced persons in the commercial area under consideration.

Figure 14.21 Lindt bunny

---

[281] *Sky Plc v Skykick UK Ltd* [2018] ETMR 23; [2018] EWHC 943 (Ch), para 250.

Figure 14.22 Franz Hauswirth bunny

Revocation

Non-use

Sections 46(1)(a)–(b), (2) and (3) TMA 1994 (as amended); Articles 16 and 19 TMD 2015; Articles 19 and 58 EUTMR 2017

14.102   A registered trade mark must be put to genuine use in the territory in which it is registered (for a national registered mark, the relevant member state; for an EU trade mark, 'in the Union'). If a registered trade mark has not been put to genuine use within five years following the date of completion of the registration procedure, or if such use of the trade mark has been suspended for an uninterrupted period of five years, the registration may be revoked unless there are 'proper reasons' for non-use.[282] The mark may not be revoked if genuine use is commenced or resumed after the expiry of the five-year period but before the application for revocation.[283] There are also provisions in the TMA 1994 (as amended), TMD 2015, and EUTMR 2017 requiring proof of 'genuine use' for marks relied upon in opposition and infringement proceedings.[284]

---

[282] TMA 1994 (as amended), s 46(1)(a) and (b); Arts 16(1) and 19(1) TMD 2015; Arts 18(1) and 58(1)(a) EUTMR 2017. The 'date of the completion of the registration procedure' must be determined in each member state in accordance with the procedural rules on registration in force in that state: Case C-246/05 *Armin Häupl v Lidl Stiftung & Co KG* [2007] ETMR 61.

[283] TMA 1994 (as amended), s 46(3); Art 19(2) TMD 2015. If that commencement or resumption of use occurs within three months before the making of the application for revocation, it shall be disregarded unless preparations for the commencement or resumption of use began before the trade mark proprietor became aware that the application for revocation might be made: TMA 1994 (as amended), s 46(3); Art 19(3) TMD 2015; Art 58(1)(a) EUTMR 2017. The aim of this is to make it impossible for a trade mark owner to start or restart use of his mark simply for the purposes of defeating a revocation action which he may become aware of shortly before it is commenced.

[284] Section 11A TMA 1994 (as amended); Arts 17 and 44 TMD 2015; Art 127(3) EUTMR 2017.

14.103   The recitals of the Trade Marks Directive give an indication as to why a trade mark will be revoked if it is not used:[285]

> Trade marks fulfil their purpose of distinguishing goods or services and allowing consumers to make informed choices only when they are actually used on the market. A requirement of use is . . . necessary in order to reduce the total number of trade marks registered and protected in the Union and, consequently, the number of conflicts which arise between them. It is therefore essential to require that registered trade marks must actually be used in connection with the goods or services for which they are registered or, if not used in that connection within five years of the date of the completion of the registration procedure, be liable to be revoked.

This objective reflects the basic principle that registered trade marks should be used, and if not used then a registration will be vulnerable to challenge.

Traders are thus discouraged from stockpiling registered trade marks, thus keeping them from competitors.

14.104   The leading authority on what constitutes 'genuine use' is the decision of the ECJ in *Ansul BV v Ajax Brandbeveiliging BV*.[286] The court held that 'genuine use' denoted 'use that is not merely token, serving solely to preserve the rights conferred by the mark' but instead use must be consistent with the essential function of a trade mark, which use is 'consistent with the essential function of a trade mark' to guarantee the origin of relevant goods or services to the consumer or end user.[287] 'Genuine use' requires use of the mark, either by the trade mark proprietor or with his consent, in relation to goods on the market or about to be marketed where preparations to secure customers are underway through such activities as advertising campaigns.[288] Purely internal use by the relevant undertaking is insufficient.[289] As the Court put it:[290]

> The protection the mark confers and the consequences of registering it in terms of enforceability vis-à-vis third parties cannot continue to operate if the mark loses its commercial raison d'être, which is to create or preserve an outlet for the goods or services that bear the sign of which it is composed, as distinct from the goods or services of other undertakings.

In assessing genuine use, regard is to be had to 'all the facts and circumstances relevant to establishing whether the commercial exploitation of the mark is real', looking in particular at whether the use in question is 'viewed as warranted in the economic sector concerned to maintain or create a share in the market for the goods or services protected by the mark'.[291] This assessment may include looking at matters such as the nature of the goods or services in issue, the characteristics of the market concerned and the scale and frequency of use of the mark. The Court stressed, however, that use of the mark does not always have to be quantitatively significant for it to be deemed genuine: the position will depend on the characteristics of the goods or service concerned on the relevant market.[292]

14.105   The Court of Justice has continued to stress that use which is not quantitatively significant may be sufficient to constitute 'genuine use' in appropriate circumstances. The issue arose in a case concerning the registered mark 'Laboratoire de la Mer'. In this case the use comprised the sale of £800 worth of cosmetics containing seaweed to a firm in Banff, Scotland. There were five deliveries between 1996 and 1997, with the items packed in containers bearing the mark with recommended retail prices of between £5 and £30. The goods were apparently to be sold by sub-agents, but there was no evidence that any of the goods ever reached consumers. A reference was made to the ECJ asking, inter alia, for interpretation of the requirement of genuine use.[293] The Court repeated the points made in *Ansul*, emphasising that there were no abstract de minimis quantitative thresholds for determining 'genuine use' and that this depended on a case-by-case

---

[285]   Recital 31 TMD 2015.
[286]   Case C-40/01 *Ansul BV v Ajax Brandbeveiliging BV* [2003] ETMR 85.
[287]   ibid, para 36. See also C-234/06 P *Il Ponte Finanziaria SpA v OHIM* [2008] ETMR 13, para 72.
[288]   Case C-40/01 *Ansul BV v Ajax Brandbeveiliging BV* [2003] ETMR 85, para 37.   [289]   ibid, para 37.
[290]   ibid, para 37.   [291]   ibid, para 38.   [292]   ibid, para 39.
[293]   Case C-259/02 *La Mer Technology Inc v Laboratoires Goëmar SA* [2004] ETMR 47.

assessment which was for the national court to carry out.[294] The Court stressed that even 'minimal use' could be sufficient to qualify as genuine, if justified in the sector concerned for the purpose of preserving or creating market share for the goods or services protected by the mark.[295] The case was re-heard by the High Court and then appealed to the Court of Appeal.[296] The Court of Appeal considered that the owner of the mark in the UK wanted to create an outlet that was sufficient to qualify as genuine use. The Court of Appeal came to the view that there was nothing which indicated that the consumer or end-user market was the only relevant market for determining whether use of a mark is genuine. In the instant case there were arm's-length sales to a third party, who imported the goods. The fact that the use was on the import market and was modest did not prevent that from being genuine use.

14.106   Some uses of a mark will not be sufficient to constitute 'genuine use'. It will not be enough to use a mark on free gifts handed out as a reward for purchasing other goods: such free items are not distributed with the aim of penetrating the market for such goods.[297] It is, however, possible for a not-for-profit organisation to put a mark to genuine use where it uses the mark to identify and promote the goods or services for which it is registered to the general public.[298] In a more recent dispute involving an EU trade mark which should, perhaps, have been registered instead as a collective trade mark (see Chapter 13), the CJEU has confirmed that affixing a mark to goods solely as a label of quality (rather than origin) would not constitute 'genuine use' under what is now Article 18 EUTMR 2017.[299]

14.107   For revocation purposes, relevant 'use' of the mark includes use of the trade mark 'in a form . . . differing in elements which do not alter the distinctive character of the mark in the form in which it was registered'.[300] The purpose of this provision is to allow the trade mark owner, in commercial exploitation of the mark, to make minor variations to the mark which adapt it better to the trade mark owner's marketing and promotion requirements while without altering its distinctive character.[301] The variant form of the mark can itself also be a registered mark.[302] There may be 'genuine use' of a mark where the mark has been used independently and also where it has been used as a part of or in conjunction with another mark.[303] In *Specsavers v Asda*, an issue arose over whether there had been genuine use of a wordless logo mark belonging to Specsavers (see Figure 14.23).[304] The logo had only been used with the name 'Specsavers' superimposed over it (see Figure 14.24), both 'Specsavers' and the combined word/logo being separately also registered as trade marks.

Figure 14.23 Specsavers wordless logo mark

[294]   ibid, paras 22 and 25 in particular.
[295]   Case C-259/02 *La Mer Technology Inc v Laboratoires Goëmar SA* [2004] ETMR 47, para 21.
[296]   *Laboratoires Goëmar SA v La Mer Technology Inc* [2005] ETMR 114.
[297]   Case C-495/07 *Silberquelle GmbH v Maselli-Strickmode GmbH* [2009] ETMR 28.
[298]   Case C-442/07 *Verein Radetzky-Orden v Bundesvereinigung Kameradschaft Feldmarschall Radetzky* [2009] ETMR 14.
[299]   Case C-689/15 *WF Gözze Frottierweberei GmbH v Verein Bremer Baumwollbörse* [2017] Bus LR 1795. The trade mark owner was an association representing undertakings operating in the cotton textiles sector and licensed the disputed mark to its affiliates as a mark of product quality.
[300]   TMA 1994 (as amended), s 46(2); Art 16(5)(a) TMD 2015; Art 18(1)(a) EUTMR 2017.
[301]   Case C-553/11 *Rintisch v Eder* [2013] ETMR 5.
[302]   ibid. This is now reflected in the revised wording of s 46(2) TMA 1994, as amended by SI 2018/825.
[303]   Case C-12/12 *Colloseum Holding AG v Levi Strauss & Co* [2013] ETMR 34. Levi Strauss was the holder of a position mark which consisted of 'a rectangular red label, made of textile, sewn into and protruding from the upper part of the left-hand seam of the rear pocket of trousers, shorts or skirts'. The issue was whether this mark had been put to genuine use since, in use, the tab always carried the house mark LEVI'S.
[304]   Case C-252/12 *Specsavers International Healthcare Ltd v Asda Stores Ltd* [2013] ETMR 46.

Figure 14.24 Specsavers registered mark with 'Specsavers' superimposed

The CJEU held that this was use of the wordless logo mark in a different form to that which had been registered, but the differences did not alter its distinctive character. There was therefore 'genuine use' pursuant to what is now Article 18(1)(a) EUTMR 2017.

14.108   The geographical extent of use required to constitute 'genuine use' is a particular issue for EU trade marks. The issue was considered in *Leno Merken BV v Hagelkruis Beheer BV*.[305] The Court was asked to determine what constituted genuine use 'in the Community' (now 'Union') for the purposes of what is now Article 18 EUTMR 2017 and, in particular, whether use in one member state would be enough to satisfy that requirement. The mark in dispute, 'ONEL', had been used in the Netherlands but no proof of use was provided for any other member state.

The Court of Justice did not answer the questions referred particularly clearly. The Court indicated that territorial borders should be disregarded when deciding if there had been genuine use of a trade mark 'in the Community'.[306] If 'genuine use' was to be assessed by reference to the territories of member states, that would frustrate the objectives of the EU trade mark system as an EU-wide unitary right.[307] The Court noted that 'there is admittedly some justification for thinking that a Community trade mark should—because it enjoys more extensive territorial protection than a national trade mark—be used in a larger area than the territory of a single Member State'.[308] However, in certain circumstances if the market for the goods or services for which an EU trade mark was been registered was in fact restricted to the territory of a single member state, it could not be ruled out that use in a single member state could be sufficient to constitute 'genuine use' of an EU trade mark.[309] As 'genuine use' had to be assessed on a case-by-case basis it was not possible to stipulate an abstract minimum geographic scope of use.[310] It was for the national court to assess the position in light of all relevant facts and circumstances.[311]

In *The Sofa Workshop Ltd v Sofaworks Ltd*[312] HHJ Hacon sitting in IPEC summarised the Court of Justice's case law thus:

(1) [T]he question of whether there has been 'genuine use in the Community' is not to be approached from the perspective of whether there has been use of the mark in more than one, two or any other particular number of member states. Territorial borders are to be disregarded;

(2) [A] Community trade mark is put to genuine use in the Community where it is used in accordance with its essential function, which is to guarantee the identity of the origin of the goods or services for which it is registered, and used for the purpose of maintaining or creating market share within the European Community for the goods or services covered by the mark;

(3) [W]hether the mark has been so used will depend on all relevant facts and circumstances, including the characteristics of the market concerned, the nature of the relevant goods and services, the territorial extent and scale of use, and the frequency and regularity of use;

---

[305] Case C-149/11 *Leno Merken BV v Hagelkruis Beheer BV* [2013] ETMR 16.   [306] ibid, para 57.   [307] ibid, para 42.
[308] ibid, para 50.   [309] ibid, para 50.   [310] ibid, para 55.
[311] ibid, para 58.   [312] *The Sofa Workshop Ltd v Sofaworks Ltd* [2015] ETMR 37.

> (4) [P]urely in relation to the territorial extent of use, genuine use in the Community will in general require use in more than one member state; and
>
> (5) [A]n exception to that general requirement arises where the market for the relevant goods or services is restricted to the territory of a single member state.

14.109   Revocation will not occur on the grounds of non-use if there are 'proper reasons for non-use'.[313] 'Non-use' here refers to both a situation where there has been no use at all of the mark and where its use has been only limited, such as to fail to qualify as 'genuine use'.[314] A question as to whether there would be 'proper reasons' where there was delayed implementation of the corporate strategy being pursued by the trade mark proprietor for reasons outside his control was referred to the ECJ in *Armin Häupl v Lidl Stiftung & Co KG*.[315] The disputed mark was registered in various territories, including Austria, for ready-meals. However, Lidl had been delayed in opening supermarkets in Austria by 'bureaucratic obstacles' and thus had not sold the goods in Austria within the requisite five-year period. The Court expressed concern that the objectives of the scheme of revocation for non-use would be undermined if too broad a scope was given to the concept of 'proper reasons', for example to encompass any obstacle arising independently of the will of the trade mark owner.[316] In order to be taken into account, any obstacles had to have a direct relationship with the trade mark. The obstacle did not have to make use of the mark impossible: there would also be 'proper reasons' where use of the mark was unreasonable—for example, if the only way to use the mark was to sell the trade mark owner's goods in competitor outlets.[317] These difficulties had to 'arise independently of the will of' the proprietor of the mark and it was for the national court to assess whether it would have been unreasonable for the proprietor to change his business strategy in order to get around the difficulty.[318] It thus seems that the hurdle may be high to show non-use is reasonable.

Liable to mislead

14.110   Revocation can also take place if, after the date upon which it was registered, in consequence of the use made of it by the proprietor or with his consent in relation to the goods or services for which it is registered, the mark is liable to mislead the public, particularly as to the nature, quality or geographical origin of those goods or services.[319] It will be recalled from the discussion in paragraphs 14.91–14.92 that a mark that is liable to mislead the public is precluded from registration. This section is the counterpart to the non-registrability of a mark in that if, after having successfully been registered, a mark becomes likely to mislead the public, then it can be revoked.

14.111   The case law discussed at paragraphs 14.91–14.92 above will be relevant here. In addition, interesting questions arise over the extent to which, if a trade mark has been licensed to another, the trade mark owner needs to maintain quality control over the goods or services produced under the mark in order to avoid the mark becoming vulnerable to revocation on this ground. The issue was referred to the ECJ by the House of Lords in *Scandecor Developments AB v Scandecor Marketing AB*,[320] but the case settled before judgment was given by the ECJ. The issue has, however, come before the CJEU again in *WF Gözze Frottierweberei GmbH v Verein Bremer Baumwollbörse*.[321] The Court reiterated its finding in *Emanuel* (see paragraph 14.92 above) that the risk of deception presupposes actual deceit or a sufficiently serious risk that consumers

---

[313] TMA 1994 (as amended), s 46(1)(a) and (b); Art 16(1) TMD 2015; Art 18(1) EUTMR 2017.

[314] Case C-252/15 P *Naazneen Investments Ltd v OHIM* [2016] ETMR 29, paras 77–78.

[315] Case C-246/05 *Armin Häupl v Lidl Stiftung & Co KG* [2007] ETMR 61.   [316] ibid, para 51.   [317] ibid, paras 52–53.

[318] ibid, para 54.   [319] TMA 1994 (as amended), s 46(1)(d); Art 20(b) TMD 2015; Art 58(1)(c) EUTMR 2017.

[320] [2001] ETMR 74 (HL).   [321] Case C-689/15 *WF Gözze Frottierweberei GmbH v Verein Bremer Baumwollbörse* [2017] Bus LR 1795.

will be deceived.[322] It is necessary to show that the trade mark as applied for *per se* creates such a risk.[323] The subsequent management of the mark and licences relating thereto are irrelevant.[324] A mark cannot be declared invalid for failure of the trade mark owner to carry out periodic quality controls over its licensees.[325]

Genericism

14.112   A registered trade mark may also be revoked if, after registration, in consequence of the acts or inactivity of the proprietor, it has become the common name in the trade for a product or service in respect of which it is registered.[326] The proprietor of a registered trade mark should therefore take care that the mark does not become generic. Although the legislation refers to a mark becoming the generic name 'in the trade', the ECJ has said that the relevant circles 'comprise principally consumers and end users'.[327] However, depending on the features of the mark for the relevant product, 'the influence of intermediaries on decisions to purchase, and thus their perception of the trade mark, must also be taken into consideration'.[328]

14.113   The genericism of the mark must be due to the action or inaction of the trade mark proprietor.[329] 'Inactivity' can include failing to take action against infringers, but is not limited to this: it includes any omission by which the trade mark proprietor 'shows that he is not sufficiently vigilant as regards the preservation of the distinctive character of his trade mark'.[330] The proprietor of a registered trade mark is thus well advised to take active steps in order to ensure that his mark does not become generic. Such measures may include, for example, emphasising the mark in comparison with surrounding text. *Backaldrin* also suggests that a trade mark owner should contact sellers of the trade mark owner's products to ensure that they in turn inform customers that the mark is registered.[331] As part of the 2015 reform package, a new section 99A has been inserted into the TMA 1994 (see also Art 12 TMD 2015 and Art 12 EUTMR 2017) which applies if the reproduction of a trade mark in a print or electronic 'dictionary, encyclopaedia or similar reference work' gives the impression that the mark constitutes the generic name of the goods or services for which the trade mark is registered. On a written request from the trade mark proprietor, the publisher must ensure that the reproduction of the mark is accompanied by an indication that it is a registered trade mark (s 99A(2) TMA 1994). This must be done without delay and, for printed works, no later than the next edition (s 99A(3) TMA 1994). Various remedies are available if the publisher does not act (s 99A(4) TMA 1994).

  Question

Can you think of any marks that have, in your view, become generic? How should a trade mark owner go about trying to prevent this? Consider the 'Don't say Velcro' campaign on YouTube: www.youtube.com/watch?v=rRi8LptvFZY&start_radio=1&list=RDrRi8LptvFZY&t=0. Do you think this is an effective way of tackling the issue?

---

[322] ibid, para 54.   [323] ibid, para 55.
[324] ibid, para 56.   [325] ibid, para 57.
[326] TMA 1994 (as amended), s 46(1)(c); Art 20(a) TMD 2015; Art 58(1)(b) EUTMR 2017.
[327] Case C-371/02 *Björnekulla Fruktindustrier AB v Procordia Food AB* [2004] ETMR 69, [2004] RPC 45, para 25. KORNSPITZ, known by bakeries as to be made with the trade mark holder's bread mix but perceived by the public as the common name for oblong-shaped bread rolls with a point at both ends, could be liable to revocation: Case C-409/12 *Backaldrin Österreich The Kornspitz Company GmbH v Pfahnl Backmittel GmbH* [2014] ETMR 30.
[328] Case C-371/02 *Björnekulla Fruktindustrier AB v Procordia Food AB* [2004] ETMR 69, [2004] RPC 45, para 25.
[329] Case C-409/12 *Backaldrin Österreich The Kornspitz Company GmbH v Pfahnl Backmittel GmbH* [2014] ETMR 30, para 32.
[330] ibid, para 34.   [331] ibid, para 34.

The extent of revocation

14.114   If a mark is to be revoked, then the question also arises as to the extent of that revocation. Section 46(5) TMA 1994 (as amended) provides that, where grounds for revocation exist in respect of only some of the goods or services for which the mark is registered, revocation shall relate to those goods or services only (see also Art 20 TMD 2015 and Art 58(2) EUTMR 2017). This becomes difficult, however, if the trade mark specification uses broad terminology (eg 'clothing', 'computer software', or 'alcoholic drinks') which may cover a multitude of different sub-categories of product in respect of only some of which the mark has been used. Must the mark be revoked altogether, or should the mark remain and only some of the goods or services in the specification be revoked by rewriting the specification? As the Court of Appeal has noted:[332]

> . . . there are here two competing considerations. On the one hand, a proprietor should not be able to monopolise the use of a trade mark in relation to a general category of goods or services simply because he has used it in relation to a few of them. A mark should remain registered only for those goods or services in relation to which it has been used. On the other hand, a proprietor cannot reasonably be expected to use his mark in relation to every possible variation of all of the goods or services covered by his registration.

The Court of Appeal has set out a four-step test which should be followed in such a case:[333]

> First, it is necessary to identify the goods or services in relation to which the mark has been used during the relevant period.

> Secondly, the goods or services for which the mark is registered must be considered. If the mark is registered for a category of goods or services which is sufficiently broad that it is possible to identify within it a number of subcategories capable of being viewed independently, use of the mark in relation to one or more of the subcategories will not constitute use of the mark in relation to all of the other subcategories.

> Thirdly, it is not possible for a proprietor to use the mark in relation to all possible variations of a product or service. So care must be taken to ensure this exercise does not result in the proprietor being stripped of protection for goods or services which, though not the same as those for which use has been proved, are not in essence different from them and cannot be distinguished from them other than in an arbitrary way.

> Fourthly, these issues are to be considered having regard to the perception of the average consumer and the purpose and intended use of the products or services in issue. Ultimately it is the task of the tribunal to arrive at a fair specification of goods or services having regard to the use which has been made of the mark.

In *Merck*, the question was whether the trade mark owner should retain its registration for 'pharmaceutical substances and preparations', when it had only used the relevant mark for pharmaceuticals for treatment of certain specific conditions. It was concluded that the contested specification of goods should be limited to the series of subcategories of products in relation to which the disputed mark had been used.

14.115   The CFI (now the General Court) considered this in *Mundipharma AG v OHIM*,[334] in which it looked at the categories and extent of use for the purposes of revocation. It said:[335]

> it is in practice impossible for the proprietor of a trade mark to prove that the mark has been used for all conceivable variations of the goods concerned by the registration. Consequently, the concept of 'part of the goods or services' cannot be taken to mean all the commercial variations of similar goods or services but merely goods or services which are sufficiently distinct to constitute coherent categories or sub-categories.

The desire is to be fair as between trade mark owner and competitor—to ensure that the proprietor is not stripped of protection with respect to all of the similar goods or services for which the trade mark has been used whilst ensuring space for the competitor in the market.[336]

---

[332] *Merck KGaA v Merck Sharp & Dohme Corp* [2018] ETMR 10, para 242.
[333] ibid, paras 245–248. See also *Maier v ASOS Plc* [2015] ETMR 26.
[334] Case T-256/04 [2007] ECR II-00449; see also Case T-126/03 *Reckitt Benckiser (Espana) SL v OHIM* [2005] ECR II-2861.
[335] Case T-256/04 *Mundipharma AG v OHIM* [2007] ECR II-00449, para 24.
[336] ibid, para 24.

> **Key points on revocation**
>
> - A registered trade mark must be put to genuine use: revocation may occur if it has not been put to genuine use within five years of registration.
>
> - Token use is not sufficient for genuine use.
>
> - Revocation will not occur if there are proper reasons for non-use.
>
> - Revocation can also occur where the use of a mark is liable to mislead the public as to the nature, quality, or geographical origin of the goods and services; if the use becomes misleading and if the mark becomes generic.

Further reading

Books

I Calboli and M Senftleben (eds) *The Protection of Non-Traditional Marks: Critical Perspectives* (Oxford University Press, 2018)

Studies

Max Planck Institute for Intellectual Property and Competition Law, 'Study on the Overall Functioning of the European Trade Mark System' (February 2011)

Articles

M Adams and A Scardamaglia, 'Non-traditional trade marks in Europe: an historical snapshot of applications and registrations' (2018) 40(10) EIPR 623–29

L Anamaet, 'The public domain is under pressure—why we should not rely on empirical data when assessing trade mark distinctiveness' (2016) 47(3) IIC 303–05

J Bergquist and D Curley, 'Shape trade marks and fast-moving consumer goods' [2008] EIPR 17

O Bray, 'Vorsprung for slogans in the courts: Audi's perseverance pays off' (2010) 5(6) JIPLP 400–02

B Clark, 'The chocolate menagerie: the General Court decides on bunny, reindeer and mouse shapes' (2011) 6(6) JIPLP 361–64

AG Chronopoulos, '*De jure* functionality of shapes driven by technical considerations in manufacturing methods' (2017) 3 IPQ 286–306

J Davis and A Durant, 'To protect or not to protect? The eligibility of commercially used short verbal texts for copyright and trade mark protection' [2011] 4 IPQ 345–70

NM Dawson, 'Bad faith in European trade mark law' [2011] 3 IPQ 229–58

G Engels and C Lehr, 'Sweets, cars and bottles—three-dimensional trade marks' (2017) 12(9) JIPLP 797–807

I Fhima, 'The public interest in European trade mark law' (2017) 4 IPQ 311–29

D Friedmann, 'EU opens door for sound marks: will scent marks follow?' (2015) 10(12) JIPLP 931–39

C Gielen, 'Substantial value rule: how it came into being and why it should be abolished' (2014) 36(3) EIPR 164–69

G Humphreys, 'Deceit and immorality in trade mark matters: does it pay to be bad?' (2007) 2(2) JIPLP 89–96

A Kur, 'Too common, too splendid, or "just right"? Trade mark protection for product shapes in the light of CJEU case law', Max Planck Institute for Innovation and Competition Research Paper No 14-17

C Lehr and G Engels, 'Taking a position' (2014) 9(7) JIPLP 607–14

M Lynch, 'Product configuration marks: the shape of things to come' (2017) 12(6) JIPLP 465–73

J Marshall, 'Colour trade marks: certainty, utility or impossibility' (2017) 12(10) JIPLP 860–66

JT Mirza, 'CJEU expands trade mark law to include the design of a store layout: Apple Inc v Deutsches Patent- und Markenamt (German Patent and Trade Mark Office)' (2014) 36(12) EIPR 813–17

A Muhlendahl, 'European trade mark law: registrable signs, service marks' (2014) 9(2) JIPLP 160–64

CH Perez, 'The possibility of IP protection for smell' (2014) 36(10) EIPR 665–74

A Quaedvlieg, 'Shapes with a technical function: an ever-expanding exclusion? (2016) 17 ERA Forum 101–17

M Senftleben, '*Vigeland* and the status of cultural concerns in trade mark law—the EFTA Court develops more effective tools for preservation of the public domain' (2017) 48 IIC 683–720

K Toft, 'JW Spear & Sons Ltd v Zynga Inc: is the latest Court of Appeal decision a game changer?' (2015) 26(7) Ent L R 242–46

V Torelli, 'A strong body of proof is essential in bad faith cases' (2015) 10(7) JIPLP 490–92

Trade marks 3: relative ground for refusal and invalidation, infringement, and defences

Introduction

Scope and overview of chapter

15.1 To appreciate the scope of the rights conferred by a registered trade mark, it is essential to understand the conditions under which a registered trade mark will be infringed by a third party and the circumstances in which the registered mark can be used to block a later-filed application. If a registered trade mark is infringed easily by third parties, the trade mark owner will have the benefit of a broad monopoly in the market. As with other areas of registered trade mark law there is a constant tension between the interests of the trade mark owner, those of competing traders, and the interests of the consumer.

15.2 Picking up on the discussion in Chapter 13 on the theoretical justifications for trade mark law, we see these tensions played out clearly in the case law on infringement and relative grounds for refusal discussed in this chapter. What exactly is registered trade mark law supposed to protect and what are the limits of the trade mark monopoly? The Court of Justice has dealt with numerous cases on infringement and relative grounds yet, as we shall see, the shape and direction of these aspects of registered trade mark law remain in flux. After cautious early post-harmonisation case law focused very much on protecting the origin function, the Court of Justice has more recently taken a far more expansive approach, conferring protection on the wider functions of trade marks as tools for advertising and investment in brand image that remain highly contested in theoretical terms. Contemporary issues generated by use of marks on the internet in fields such as keyword advertising have posed additional particular challenges. At the same time, the EU trade mark reform package has resulted in a number of relevant changes, particularly to the scope of trade mark defences—although not going as far as many had hoped to rein in the expansive trends in recent infringement case law.

15.3
> **Learning objectives**
>
> By the end of this chapter you should be able to describe and explain:
>
> - the principal relative grounds for refusal of a trade mark application;
> - the grounds upon which a trade mark will be infringed through unauthorised use by a third party; and
> - the scope of the principal defences in relation to an action for trade mark infringement.

15.4   In this chapter, we will start by looking at certain introductory points relating to the relative grounds for refusal of a trade mark and grounds of infringement. We will then look at some important preliminary general points on what constitutes 'use' of an allegedly infringing sign for the purposes of infringement. After that, we will look in turn at the three principal grounds for refusal of a trade mark and infringement: cases involving so-called 'double identity'; cases involving likelihood of confusion; and cases involving marks with a reputation. The provisions governing refusal of a trade mark on relative grounds mirror the provisions on infringement, so we will examine these together under each of these three headings. The chapter will finish with an examination of the principal defences to an action for trade mark infringement.

So, the rest of the chapter looks like this:

- Approaching the relative grounds for refusal and the grounds for infringement (15.5–15.9)
- 'Use' of a trade mark for the purposes of infringement (15.10–15.22)
- 'Double identity' cases (15.23–15.37)
- 'Likelihood of confusion' cases (15.38–15.58)
- Marks with a reputation (15.59–15.80)
- The principal defences to infringement (15.81–15.100).

Approaching the relative grounds for refusal and the grounds for infringement

15.5   Section 5 TMA 1994 (as amended), Article 5 of the Trade Mark Directive (TMD) 2015, and Article 8 of the EU Trade Mark Regulation (EUTMR) 2017 concern the *relative grounds* on which an application to register a trade mark might be refused if successful opposition is raised by the proprietor of an earlier mark or sign. These grounds thus look beyond the mark itself to other, earlier marks and other signs to ensure that an application does not conflict with pre-existing rights. By section 47 of the Trade Marks Act (TMA) 1994 (as amended), these relative grounds are also grounds for invalidation of a granted UK registration (see also Art 8 EUTMR 2017 in relation to EU trade marks). As we shall discuss in more detail, a mark may be refused or invalidated under sections 5(1)–(3) TMA 1994 (as amended) and Articles 8(1) and 8(5) EUTMR 2017 if:

- it is identical to an earlier trade mark and the goods or services for which registration is sought are identical to the goods or services for which the earlier trade mark is protected;[1]
- it is identical with or similar to the earlier trade mark and the application for registration is for similar or identical goods or services to those for which the earlier trade mark is protected, and there exists a likelihood of confusion on the part of the public which includes the likelihood of association with the earlier trade mark;[2]
- it is identical with or similar to an earlier trade mark, the earlier mark has a reputation, and the use of the later mark without due cause would take unfair advantage of, or be detrimental to, the distinctive character or the repute of the earlier mark.[3]

These three grounds of refusal and invalidation will be our focus in this chapter.

15.6   It will be noted that these three provisions all refer to 'earlier trade marks'. An earlier trade mark[4] includes an existing UK registered trade mark, an international trade mark (applied for under the Madrid system) designating the UK, or an EU trade mark. Applications for all of these will also count as 'earlier trade marks'. All need a date of application for registration earlier than that of the contested later filing, taking into account any priorities[5] or the seniority of an EU trade mark.[6]

---

[1] TMA 1994 (as amended), s 5(1); Art 8(1)(a) EUTMR 2017.   [2] TMA 1994 (as amended), s 5(2); Art 8(1)(b) EUTMR 2017.
[3] TMA 1994 (as amended), s 5(3); Art 8(5) EUTMR 2017.   [4] See generally TMA 1994 (as amended), s 6.
[5] TMA 1994 (as amended), s 6(1)(a).   [6] TMA 1994 (as amended), s 6(1)(b).

15.7   The remaining parts of section 5 TMA 1994 (as amended) seek to ensure that a sign will not be registered as a trade mark looking to other factors, notably whether the registration would infringe the intellectual property rights belonging to others—for instance, if the use of the mark would amount to passing off,[7] or would infringe another's copyright or design right.[8] These latter grounds of objection are particularly relevant to trade mark applications with figurative elements (such as logos) or for three-dimensional shapes or other aspects of product 'get-up'. As a result of the EU trade mark reform package, the relative objections to a trade mark application also now include prior rights in protected designations of origin and geographical indications.[9] The other relative grounds for refusal will not be considered further here: our focus will be on sections 5(1)–(3) TMA 1994 (as amended) and corresponding provisions of the EUTMR 2017. All the provisions of section 5 of the 1994 Act are subject to the proviso in section 5(5) which states that where the proprietor of an earlier trade mark consents to the registration of the later mark, then registration may proceed.[10]

15.8   The grounds on which a registered trade mark are infringed are to be found in sections 10(1)–(3) TMA 1994 (as amended), Article 10 TMD 2015, and Article 9 EUTMR 2017. Infringement proceedings may be commenced on or after the date on which the mark is entered on the register.[11] As the rights conferred by the 1994 Act are territorial, the proprietor may only sue in respect of infringements occurring in the UK, including the Isle of Man.[12] The rights conferred by the EU trade mark extend to all member states of the EU.

15.9   The grounds of infringement at sections 10(1)–(3) TMA 1994 (as amended), Article 10 TMD 2015, and Article 9 EUTMR 2017 mirror the relative grounds for refusal summarised at paragraph 15.5 above. They are to be interpreted in the same way and case law on these relative grounds and on infringement is therefore essentially interchangeable. The relative grounds for refusal and grounds of infringement will therefore be considered together in the rest of this chapter.

'Use' of a trade mark for the purposes of infringement

15.10   Before we turn to look in detail at the grounds of refusal and infringement at sections 5(1)–(3) and 10(1)–(3) TMA 1994 (as amended) and the corresponding provisions of the EUTMR 2017, we need to start by dealing with some important preliminary points about what constitutes 'use' of an allegedly infringing sign for the purposes of infringement.

Use 'in the course of trade'

15.11   As a first point, it is important to note that—as can be seen from the text of section 10 TMA 1994 (as amended) and Article 9 EUTMR 2017—in order to be actionable all allegedly infringing 'uses' of a sign must be 'in the course of trade'. In its seminal decision in *Arsenal v Reed*, the ECJ defined this as use which 'takes place in the context of commercial activity with a view to economic advantage and not as a private matter'.[13] This is rarely contentious in practice, although there may be occasional cases in which the issue arises: for example, in an application for an interim injunction the English High Court in *Unilever Plc v Griffin*[14] held that a Marmite jar appearing in the corner of a British National Party general election broadcast was purely political use and not use 'in the course of trade' such as to infringe Unilever's registrations for the word 'MARMITE' and for various versions of the Marmite label. The dividing line between acts conducted 'in the

---

[7] TMA 1994 (as amended), s 5(4)(a).   [8] TMA 1994 (as amended), s 5(4)(b).

[9] TMA 1994 (as amended), ss 5(4)(aa) and 5(4B); see also Art 5(3)(c) TMD 2015 and Art 8(6) EUTMR 2017.

[10] See also Art 5(5) TMD 2015.

[11] TMA 1994 (as amended), s 9(3)(a); Art 11(1) EUTMR 2017. The rights of the trade mark owner take effect from the date of the filing of the application for registration, so damages for infringement can be backdated: TMA 1994 (as amended), s 9(3). According to Art 11(2) EUTMR 2017, 'reasonable compensation' can be obtained for acts of infringement of an EU trade mark occurring between publication of the application and grant (see further Chapter 21).

[12] TMA 1994 (as amended), ss 9(1), 107, and 108.

[13] Case C-206/01 *Arsenal Football Club Plc v Matthew Reed* [2003] ETMR 19, para 40.   [14] [2010] FSR 33.

course of trade' and those which are private and non-commercial is most likely to be tested in the online environment, particularly for example where a private party is engaged in substantial activity on an auction site such as eBay. This has been considered by the Court of Justice of the European Union (CJEU): if, owing to their volume, their frequency, or other characteristics, the sales made on such a marketplace go beyond the realms of a private activity, the seller will be acting 'in the course of trade'.[15]

 Question

Thinking back to the discussion in Chapter 13 about the underlying theoretical rationale for registered trade mark protection, do you think it makes sense to limit infringement to activities which are 'in the course of trade'?

Infringing acts

15.12 A non-exhaustive list of examples of when a sign is 'used' for the purposes of section 10 can be found in section 10(4) of the TMA 1994 (as amended), Article 10(3) TMD 2015, and Article 9(3) EUTMR. This list has recently been expanded as part of the EU trade mark reform package.

Under the 1994 Act as amended, a sign is 'used' when a person:

- affixes it to goods or packaging;[16]

- offers to supply, stocks, or markets goods or services under the sign;[17]

- imports or exports goods under the sign;[18]

- uses the sign as a trade or company name, or as part of a trade or company name;[19]

- uses the sign on business paper and in advertising;[20] or

- uses the sign in comparative advertising in a manner contrary to the Business Protection from Misleading Marketing Regulations 2008.[21]

The references to use as a trade or company name and use in comparative advertising are both new to this list as a result of the EU trade mark reform package. Previously, although Court of Justice case law had established that use of a sign in comparative advertising could constitute infringement,[22] the case law on use of a sign in a trade or company name was rather less clear.[23] All of these acts are now firmly brought within the scope of infringement. As we shall see towards the end of this chapter in the discussion on defences, the inclusion of comparative advertising in this list of infringing 'uses' is counterbalanced to some degree by a new 'referential use' defence.

15.13 As a result of the EU trade mark reform package, a new section 10(3B) has also been inserted into the 1994 Act (as amended) in order to allow trade mark owners to take action against acts which are preparatory to trade mark infringement:

(3B) Where the risk exists that the packaging, labels, tags, security or authenticity features or devices, or any other means to which the trade mark is affixed could be used in relation to goods or services and that

---

[15] Case C-324/09 *L'Oréal SA and Others v eBay International AG and Others* [2011] ETMR 52, para 55.

[16] TMA 1994 (as amended), s 10(4)(a).   [17] TMA 1994 (as amended), s 10(4)(b).

[18] TMA 1994 (as amended), s 10(4)(c).   [19] TMA 1994 (as amended), s 10(4)(ca).

[20] TMA 1994 (as amended), s 10(4)(d).

[21] TMA 1994 (as amended), s 10(4)(e). Article 10(3)(f) TMD 2015 and Art 9(3)(f) EUTMR 2017 both refer to the corresponding EU-level legislation, Directive 2006/114/EC.

[22] Case C-533/06 *O2 Holdings Limited and O2 (UK) Limited v Hutchison 3G UK Limited* [2008] FTMR 55; Case C-487/07 *L'Oréal SA v Bellure NV* [2009] ETMR 55.

[23] Case C-23/01 *Robelco v Robeco Groep NV* [2003] ETMR 671; Case C-17/06 *Céline Sarl v Céline SA* [2007] ETMR 80.

use would constitute an infringement of the rights of the proprietor of the trade mark, a person infringes a registered trade mark if the person carries out in the course of trade any of the following acts—

(a) affixing a sign identical with, or similar to, the trade mark on packaging, labels, tags, security or authenticity features or devices, or any other means to which the mark may be affixed; or

(b) offering or placing on the market, or stocking for those purposes, or importing or exporting, packaging, labels, tags, security or authenticity features or devices, or any other means to which the mark is affixed.

As explained at Recital 26 TMD 2015 and Recital 20 EUTMR, trade mark owners are given the right to take action against these preparatory acts in order to allow them to combat counterfeiting more effectively. Trade mark owners have also been given a new right to take action against goods emanating from third countries which are in transit in the EU (not formally released into free circulation) where the packaging bears without authorisation a trade mark which is identical to the trade mark owner's registered mark 'or which cannot be distinguished in its essential aspects from that trade mark'.[24] This somewhat controversial measure is also intended to strengthen trade mark owners' position against counterfeiting.[25]

Use 'in relation to' goods and services

15.14   To infringe, a sign must be used 'in relation to' goods or services by the alleged infringer. It is, however, not inherently clear what this requires. Clearly, use of an allegedly infringing sign should be actionable where the sign is being used as a badge of origin in relation to the infringer's own goods—this is a classic scenario liable to give rise to consumer confusion. However, as originally enacted neither the Directive nor the Regulation said anything about whether it would be infringement for a third party to use a registered mark to refer to the trade mark owner's own goods or services—for example, in a comparative advertisement in which the third party compares the price or quality of its goods with those of the trade mark owner. This sort of use of a registered trade mark—accurately using the mark to refer to the trade mark owner's goods or services—is often referred to as 'referential' or 'nominative' use. The question of whether referential or nominative use should constitute infringement has been a recurring one throughout the history of the EU trade mark regime.[26]

15.15   The issue has often been framed in terms of the question of whether there must be use of the allegedly infringing sign 'as a trade mark' in order to infringe. However, the expression use 'as a trade mark' carries its own ambiguity. The expression is used by some to mean use to indicate the origin of the infringer's own goods. However, the expression is also used more widely to cover any use of the mark consistent with its origin function. Where the trade mark is used referentially to refer to the trade mark owner's goods or services, this is also a use of the mark which is in accordance with the origin function—in this case, correctly to identify the origin of the goods or services as the trade mark owner. The expression 'use as a trade mark' is therefore unhelpful in terms of clarifying matters.

15.16   The question of whether registered trade mark infringement should encompass 'referential' or 'nominative' use finds one manifestation in the question of what it means to say that infringing use must be 'in relation to' goods or services. The Court of Justice has held that there is use of a sign 'in relation to' goods or services where that use is 'for the purpose of distinguishing the goods or services in question as originating from a particular undertaking, that is to say, as a trade mark as such'.[27] It is clear from that the Court of Justice intended by this that use of a sign 'in relation to' goods and services encompasses referential use.[28]

[24] TMA 1994 (as amended), new s 10A; Art 10(4) TMD 2015; Article 9(4) EUTMR 2017.

[25] See further Recitals 21–25 TMD 2015 and M Senftleben, 'Wolf in sheep's clothing? Trade mark rights against goods in transit and the end of traditional territorial limits' (2016) 47(8) IIC 941–59.

[26] The issue mostly arises under s10(1) TMA 1994 (as amended) and corresponding provisions of the EUTMR, but has also arisen under s10(2) TMA 1994: Case C-533/06 *O2 Holdings Limited and O2 (UK) Limited v Hutchison 3G UK Limited* [2008] ETMR 55.

[27] Case C-63/97 *Bayerische Motorenwerke AG and Another v Ronald Karel Deenik* [1999] CMLR 1099, para 38; see also Case C-17/06 *Celine Sarl v Celine SA* [2007] ETMR 80, para 20.

[28] See also Case C-533/06 *O2 Holdings Limited and O2 (UK) Limited v Hutchison 3G UK Limited* [2008] ETMR 55, paras 35–36.

15.17   The expression use 'for the purpose of distinguishing the goods or services in question' is, perhaps, little better than other formulations in terms of clearly articulating what is at stake and what is required. However, the CJEU's case law is now codified in these terms in new Recital 18 TMD 2015, which states that infringement of a trade mark can only be established 'if there is a finding that the infringing mark or sign is used in the course of trade for the purposes of distinguishing goods or services'. [29] In any event, it is now unambiguously clear from the new examples of infringing 'use' in the TMD 2015 and EUTMR 2017 (discussed at paragraph 15.12 above) that referential use such as in comparative advertising is a form of potentially infringing 'use'. Case law on what constitutes 'distinguishing use' has also established that there will be a potentially infringing use 'in relation to' relevant goods or services where the infringer uses the sign in a way which establishes a link between the sign and the goods marketed or services provided by the infringer, even if the goods are not the infringer's own goods in the sense of having ownership of them.[30]

Use in the infringer's 'own commercial communication' and other cases allocating liability

15.18   Finally, we need to consider the further refinements on what constitutes infringing 'use' developed by the Court of Justice in the recent keyword advertising and subsequent cases. As these cases show, the CJEU has been seeking to develop further case law principles to allocate liability for registered trade mark infringement between, on the one hand, the entities most directly responsible for the relevant acts and, on the other, entities (such as online service providers) which—although technically involved—are not regarded as bearing the same culpability.

15.19   The issue was first considered in a series of joined cases concerning liability for registered trade mark infringement in relation to search engine keyword advertising. Every time a search engine is used to find something on the internet, the search engine not only returns results pertinent to the search terms entered by the user (so-called 'natural' results), but also displays small advertisements, called sponsored links, most commonly above or beside the natural search results. The display of those advertisements is by no means random. Rather, each advertisement is associated with certain keywords and is triggered every time the search term entered by the user matches one of the keywords. It is the advertisers who specify the keywords. The search engine receives revenue from the advertisers who pay to the search engine a specified amount each time an internet user clicks on a sponsored advertisement (pay-per-click). The ranking of the advertisements on the page depends on various factors, including other advertisers' bids.

15.20   The key issue from a trade mark infringement perspective is that search engines permit advertisers to 'buy' keywords that are the same as or similar to trade marks registered by third parties. So if a user searches online for 'Coca Cola', advertisements for a competitor drink might appear in the sponsored search results if the competitor has bid on 'Coca-Cola' as a keyword for their advertisement. This, it is argued by the trade mark owners, causes consumer confusion, trade mark dilution, and other harms. Search engines, on the other hand, argue that their business model would not function if they had to police their advertising customers' keyword purchases for potential infringements and that without revenue raised via keyword advertising, search engines would cease to exist. In any event, it is also argued, it is the advertisers who are responsible as it is they who choose the keyword, not the search engines.

---

[29] Contrast Art 10(6) TMD 2015, which carves out of the scope of harmonization effected by the Directive certain uses of signs 'other than . . . for the purposes of distinguishing goods or services'.

[30] Case C-62/08 *UDV North America Inc v Brandtraders NV* [2010] ETMR 25 (use of 'SMIRNOFF ICE' registered trade mark in invoices and business papers relating to a transaction for sale of a consignment of the 'Smirnoff Ice' product effected by Brandtraders on behalf of another vendor).

15.21   All of these issues came before the Court of Justice in *Google France*:

■ **Joined Cases C-236/08, C-237/08, and C-238/08** *Google France, Google Inc v Louis Vuitton Malletier SA and Others* **[2010] ETMR 30**

The CJEU considered which of the relevant parties involved in the sale and use of the contested Adwords— the advertisers or Google—'used' the registered trade marks for infringement purposes. The CJEU confirmed that, in choosing the contested keywords, the advertisers used the allegedly infringing signs.[31] However, it did not follow that the referencing service provider also used the sign:

> Although it is clear . . . that the referencing service provider operates 'in the course of trade' when it permits advertisers to select, as keywords, signs identical with trade marks, stores those signs and displays its clients' ads on the basis thereof, it does not follow, however, from those factors that that service provider itself 'uses' those signs within the terms of Article 5 of Directive 89/104 and Article 9 of Regulation No 40/94.
>
> In that regard, suffice it to note that the use, by a third party, of a sign identical with, or similar to, the proprietor's trade mark implies, at the very least, that the third party uses the sign in its own commercial communication. A referencing service provider allows its clients to use signs which are identical with, or similar to, trade marks, without itself using those signs.[32]

It made no difference that Google was paid by its advertising clients for the keyword service: according to the Court, 'the fact of creating the technical conditions necessary for the use of a sign and being paid for that service does not mean that the party offering the service itself uses the sign'.[33]

15.22   Although undoubtedly a pragmatic response to the challenges posed by keyword advertising, the *Google France* ruling met with some criticism. In *Google France*, the CJEU created a wholly new, case law-based test of its own devising ('own commercial communication') by way of gloss on the legislative text, drawing no support for its conclusions from either the the the Directive or the Regulation. It was also by no means clear what 'communication' the keyword advertisers were engaging in when purchasing their keywords, nor that Google's involvement in the process was strictly limited simply to making available the necessary 'technical conditions'.[34] Nonetheless, the CJEU reiterated its ruling in *L'Oréal v eBay*,[35] relying on the *Google France* test to draw a distinction between the different capacities in which an online marketplace provider such as eBay may 'use' a sign. Where an online marketplace provider itself purchases keywords to advertise on another search engine, such as Google, the auction site is acting as an advertiser and 'uses' the relevant sign for infringement purposes.[36] However, where the allegedly infringing signs are used in advertisements placed by third parties on the online marketplace, the online marketplace operator does not itself 'use' the signs.[37] In *Frisdranken Industrie Winters BV v Red Bull GmbH*[38] the CJEU applied similar principles to a 'real-world' scenario relating to the service of filling cans with carbonated beverages. The cans were supplied to the provider bearing various signs said to infringe Red Bull's trade marks. However, the CJEU held that a service provider which, under an order from and on the instructions of another person, merely filled cans already bearing the objectionable signs and which therefore merely executed a technical part of the production process of the final product (without, itself, having any interest in the appearance of the

---

[31] Joined Cases C-236/08, C-237-08, and C-238/08 *Google France, Google Inc v Louis Vuitton Malletier SA and Others* [2010] ETMR 30, para 51.

[32] ibid, paras 55–56.   [33] ibid, para 57.

[34] See, eg, T Bednarz, 'Keyword advertising before the French Supreme Court and beyond—calm at last after turbulent times for Google and its advertising clients?' (2011) 42(6) IIC 641–72; J Cornwell, 'Keywords, case law and the Court of Justice: the need for legislative intervention in modernising European trade mark law', (2013) 27(1/2) IRLCT 85–103.

[35] Case C-324/09 *L'Oréal SA and Others v eBay International AG and Others* [2011] ETMR 52.   [36] ibid, paras 84–85.

[37] ibid, paras 98–105.   [38] Case C-119/10 *Frisdranken Industrie Winters BV v Red Bull GmbH* [2012] ETMR 16.

cans) did not itself 'use' the allegedly infringing signs for infringement purposes.[39] Most recently in *Daimler v Együd*, the CJEU has confirmed that a party cannot be liable for allegedly infringing signs appearing in advertising on online search engines where that party had requested that the advertising be removed: this reflected the fact that only a party which has direct or indirect control of the act constituting the infringing 'use' is effectively able to stop that use if ordered to do so.[40]

  Question

What is your view on the 'own commercial communication' test developed by the CJEU in *Google France*? Do you think that this represents an effective or coherent way of dividing up responsibility for infringement in keyword advertising and other contexts?

Key points on infringing 'use'

- To infringe, use of a sign must be 'in the course of trade'. This requires that the use takes place in the context of commercial activity with a view to economic advantage and not as a private matter.

- Non-exhaustive examples of acts constituting 'use' of a sign can be found in the TMA 1994 (as amended), TMD 2015, and EUTMR 2017. As a result of the EU trade mark reform package, these now explicitly include use as a trade or company name and use in comparative advertising. Trade mark owners have also been given new rights to pursue certain preparatory acts and certain goods in transit.

- Use must be for the purpose of distinguishing goods or services, as defined further in Court of Justice case law.

- Use must be in the infringer's 'own commercial communication'. Online service providers such as search engines and auction sites do not 'use' an allegedly infringing sign merely by making available the technical conditions necessary for another party to effect such 'use'.

'Double identity' cases

Sections 5(1) and 10(1) TMA 1994 (as amended); Articles 5(1)(a) and 10(2)(a) TMD 2015 (formerly Arts 4(1)(a) and 5(1)(a) TMD 2008); Articles 8(1)(a) and 9(2)(a) EUTMR 2017 (formerly Arts 8(1)(a) and 9(1)(a) CTMR 2009)

15.23   The first of the relative grounds for refusal of a trade mark discussed in detail in this chapter is to be found at section 5(1) TMA 1994 (as amended). Section 5(1) provides that:

- a trade mark shall not be registered if it is identical with an earlier trade mark and the goods or services for which the trade mark is applied for are identical with the goods or services for which the earlier trade mark is protected.

---

[39] ibid, para 30.   [40] Case C-179/15 *Daimler AG v Együd Garage Gépjárműjavító és Értékesítő Kft* [2016] ETMR 27.

The corresponding provision on infringement at section 10(1) of the 1994 Act (as amended) provides that:

- a person infringes a registered trade mark if he uses in the course of trade a sign which is identical with the trade mark in relation to goods or services which are identical with those for which it is registered.

See also Articles 5(1)(a) and 10(2)(a) TMD 2015 and Articles 8(1)(a) and 9(1)(a) EUTMR 2017.

15.24 In its most classic form, section 10(1) TMA 1994 (as amended) is directed at counterfeiting and other similarly close forms of trade mark infringement. On its face, the simplicity of the provision befits this paradigm case of trade mark infringement in which consumer confusion seems, in effect, to be a given. However, as we shall see, section 10(1) TMA 1994 (as amended) and the corresponding provisions of the Directive and Regulation have in practice become far more complex and far-reaching than is apparent from the legislative text. This is as a result of important additional case law stipulations and developments emanating from the Court of Justice.

 Discussion point   For answer guidance visit www.oup.com/uk/brown5e.

The section refers to identical marks, and identical goods and services. What does 'identical' mean in this context?

Identity of marks

15.25 Important guidance on the identity of marks has been received from the Court of Justice.

■ **Case C-291/00 *LTJ Diffusion SA v Sadas Vertbaudet SA* [2003] ETMR 83**

LTJ was in the business of design, manufacture, and marketing of clothing. They had a registered mark, 'Arthur', in France in, inter alia, class 25 for clothing. Sadas, a mail order business marketing, inter alia, children's clothing, used and registered the mark 'Arthur et Félicie' in class 25. LTJ brought an action for infringement and to have the Sadas mark declared invalid. The ECJ was asked how the test of identity between registered mark and allegedly infringing sign was to be interpreted. In response, the Court said that it was to be interpreted strictly: 'The very definition of identity implies that the two elements compared should be the same in all respects.'[41] There would be identity between the sign and the trade mark 'where the former reproduces, without any modification or addition, all the elements constituting the latter'.[42]

However, the perception of identity between the sign and the trade mark must be assessed globally 'with respect to an average consumer who is deemed to be reasonably well informed, reasonably observant and circumspect'; the consumer may carry an imperfect picture of the marks with him and his attention is likely to vary as between categories of goods.[43] 'Insignificant differences' between the sign and the mark might go unnoticed by the average consumer.[44] Thus, a sign is 'identical' to a registered mark 'where it reproduces, without any modification or addition, all the elements constituting the trade mark or, viewed as a whole, it contains differences so significant that they may go unnoticed by an average consumer'.[45]

15.26 Whether a mark and later sign are identical will be a question of fact in every case. The question of identity has since been raised in the UK courts, for example in the following case.

[41] Case C-291/00 *LTJ Diffusion SA v Sadas Vertbaudet SA* [2003] ETMR 83, para 50.   [42] ibid, para 51.   [43] ibid, para 52.
[44] ibid, para 53.   [45] ibid, para 54.

■ *Reed Executive Plc and Another v Reed Business Information Ltd and Others* [2004] ETMR 56

The claimant had registered the trade mark 'Reed' for employment agency services. Reed Business Information set up the specialist job-related website, www.totaljobs.com. The website featured a logo containing the name 'Reed Business Information' and instructions to contact 'Reed Business Information' to advertise vacancies on the site. The question arose as to whether 'Reed Business Information' was identical or similar to the claimant's registered trade mark. Referring, inter alia, to *LTJ*, the Court of Appeal held that, since RBI had never used the word 'Reed' by itself but only in conjunction with other words or material, that use was not use of an identical mark.

15.27   Other courts have seen fit to ignore the use of extra words if they have no trade mark significance. So, in *Antoni Fields v Klaus Kobec Ltd*,[46] the addition of the word 'Limited' by the defendant to the registered mark 'Klaus Kobec' had no trade mark significance and could be ignored. Likewise, the addition of '.com' to the domain name klauskobec.com could be ignored: this domain name was also treated as identical to the registered mark. However, the domain names klauskobecfootball.com and klauskobecrugby.com were not identical to the registered mark.

Identity of goods and services

15.28   Whether the goods and services claimed in a later application or used by an infringer are identical to those covered by an earlier registered mark is a question of fact. It will be determined by reference to what is claimed in the specification of the registered mark and, in the infringement context, by what is actually being done by the alleged infringer.

■ *Avnet Inc v Isoact Ltd* [1998] FSR 16

Avnet had a registered mark 'Avnet' in class 35 for advertising and promotional services. Isoact, an internet service provider which offered customers in the aviation industry the opportunity to create their own webpages, including space to display advertisements, used the name 'Avnet'. When Avnet argued that its trade mark was infringed under section 10(1) of the 1994 Act, Isoact countered that its services were not identical to those covered by the registered mark. The court looked to 'the essence' of what the defendant actually did to see if those activities fell within the the specification of 'advertising and promotional services'. It was found that Isoact was not providing advertising and promotional services: unlike an advertising agent, all they did was provide space on the websites created for their customers for them to add their own advertising. Therefore, there was no identity between the respective services.

Damage to trade mark functions

15.29   Although in its paradigm form directed to counterfeiting and similarly close infringements, there is nothing in the text of section 10(1) TMA 1994 (as amended) and the corresponding provisions of the Directive and Regulation which limits their scope to this type of infringement. Quite the opposite, indeed: on its face, section 10(1) TMA 1994 is, and always has been, very broad in scope and thus quite capable of capturing other uses of registered trade marks—such as referential and nominative uses—which are arguably beneficial for consumers and for the functioning of the market. The Recitals to the Directive and Regulation are not particularly helpful in clarifying what was intended by the EU legislators. Recital 16 TMD 2015 provides:[47]

---

[46] [2006] EWHC 350 (Ch).   [47] See also Recital 11 EUTMR 2017.

The protection afforded by the registered trade mark, the function of which is in particular to guarantee the trade mark as an indicator of origin, should be absolute in the event of there being identity between the mark and the corresponding sign and the goods or services.

But what is meant by this reference to 'absolute' protection? Does it mean that protection should be genuinely absolute, in the sense that it should encompass all uses of an identical sign whether damaging to the trade mark owner or not? Or does it mean something else—perhaps, for example, simply that there is no requirement to prove likelihood of confusion under section 10(1), because section 10(1) is directed to the sort of case in which confusion can be assumed? The Court of Justice's response to these questions has been to read extra conditions into what are now Article 10(2)(a) TMD 2015 and Article 9(2)(a) EUTMR 2017 relating to the function of registered trade marks. Even in this, however, the Court of Justice's case law has not followed a consistent direction.

15.30   The ECJ's early case law had a confusing start. The ECJ decision in *BMW v Deenik* suggested that double identity protection would be truly 'absolute', encompassing even referential use of a mark (in this case, use of the mark 'BMW' to identify a business as a specialist in sale of second-hand BMW cars and their repair).[48] However, the ECJ's subsequent decision in *Hölterhoff v Freiesleben* suggested that what are now Article 10(2)(a) TMD 2015 and Article 9(2)(a) EUTMR 2017 would only be engaged if the allegedly infringing use was such as to damage 'the interests' which those provisions were intended to protect.[49] The case concerned the use by a professional jeweller of two registered trade marks ('SPIRIT SUN' and 'CONTEXT CUT') to describe, in commercial negotiations with another trade professional, the cut of certain precious stones. On the facts, it was held that this was a purely descriptive use, identifying the particular cut of the stones, and would not have been understood by the professional customer as an indicator of origin in relation to the stones supplied. The ECJ held that the interests protected by what is now Article 10(2)(a) TMD 2015 were not adversely affected in this case. However, perhaps unhelpfully, the ECJ did not explain what those 'interests' were.

15.31   In 2002, the Court of Justice considered the issues more thoroughly in the seminal case of *Arsenal v Reed*:

■ **Case C-206/01 *Arsenal Football Club Plc v Matthew Reed* [2003] ETMR 19**

Mr Reed sold souvenirs and memorabilia relating to the Arsenal FC football club which featured registered trade marks 'Arsenal' and 'Gunners', both registered by the club, and their logo, shown in Figure 15.1.

Arsenal argued that this infringed their registered trade marks. The English High Court's preferred view was that Mr Reed was not using the marks 'in a trade mark sense', but merely as a badge of allegiance to the club—and, so, there should be no infringement. However, the High Court accepted that it was unclear whether a registered mark could be infringed if it was being used in a way that did not signify trade origin. It referred the case to the ECJ. The ECJ noted (referring to the old Article numbering of the Directive):[50]

To answer the High Court's questions, it must be determined whether Art. 5(1)(a) of the Directive entitles the trade mark proprietor to prohibit any use by a third party in the course of trade of a sign identical to the trade mark for goods identical to those for which the mark is registered, or whether that right of prohibition presupposes the existence of a specific interest of the proprietor as trade mark proprietor, in that use of the sign in question by a third party must affect or be liable to affect one of the functions of the mark.

---

[48] Case C-63/97 *Bayerische Motorenwerke AG and Another v Ronald Karel Deenik* [1999] CMLR 1099.
[49] Case C-2/00 *Michael Hölterhoff v Ulrich Freiesleben* [2002] ETMR 79, para 16.
[50] Case C-206/01 *Arsenal Football Club Plc v Matthew Reed* [2003] ETMR 19, para 42.

The ECJ highlighted the importance of the 'essential function' of a trade mark 'to guarantee the identity of origin of the marked goods or services to the consumer or end user by enabling him, without any possibility of confusion, to distinguish the goods or services from others which have another origin'.[51] A registered trade mark 'must offer a guarantee that all the goods or services bearing it have been manufactured or supplied under the control of a single undertaking which is responsible for their quality'.[52] The Court reasoned from this that:[53]

> It follows that the exclusive right under Art. 5(1)(a) of the Directive was conferred in order to enable the trade mark proprietor to protect his specific interests as proprietor, that is, to ensure that the trade mark can fulfil its functions. *The exercise of that right must therefore be reserved to cases in which a third party's use of the sign affects or is liable to affect the functions of the trade mark, in particular its essential function of guaranteeing to consumers the origin of the goods* (emphasis added).

While certain 'purely descriptive uses' (such as in *Hölterhoff*) did not constitute infringement, the circumstances in the *Arsenal* case were different. In the Court's view, the presence of the 'Arsenal' mark on Mr Reed's goods was such as to 'create the impression that there is a material link in the course of trade between the goods concerned and the trade mark proprietor'.[54] Mr Reed's use of the 'Arsenal' mark was liable to jeopardise the guarantee of origin which was the essential function of the mark. There was therefore infringement.[55]

Figure 15.1 Arsenal Football Club logo

15.32   The matter returned to the ECJ in *Adam Opel AG v Autec AG*.[56] Opel had a trade mark registration for its logo, registered both for full-scale motor vehicles and for toys. Autec, a manufacturer of toy cars, affixed Opel's registered logo to their own toy cars. The Court reiterated its judgment in *Arsenal v Reed*, stating that the exclusive right under what is now Article 10(2)(a) TMD 2015:[57]

> was conferred in order to enable the trade mark proprietor to protect his specific interests as proprietor, that is, to ensure that the trade mark can fulfil its functions and that, therefore, the exercise of that right must be reserved to cases in which a third party's use of the sign affects or is liable to affect the functions of the trade mark, in particular its essential function of guaranteeing to consumers the origin of the goods.

This was a matter for the national court to determine by reference to what would be understood by the average consumer of the type of products in question.

---

[51] ibid, para 48.   [52] ibid, para 48.   [53] ibid, para 51.   [54] ibid, para 56.

[55] When the case was remitted back to the High Court, Laddie J took the view that the ECJ had exceeded its interpretative remit under the preliminary reference procedure and had made *ultra vires* findings of fact on the case: *Arsenal FC v Reed (No 2)* [2003] 1 All ER 137. Controversially, he found no infringement. Unsurprisingly, Arsenal successfully appealed: [2003] RPC 39. In *R v Johnstone* [2003] FSR 748 (HL), handed down shortly thereafter, the House of Lords held that infringement did require trade mark use (rather than the broader test of adverse effect on the origin function). This ruling must be doubted in light of the now firmly established Court of Justice case law discussed in the main body of the text.

[56] Case C-48/05 *Adam Opel AG v Autec AG* [2007] ETMR 33.   [57] ibid, para 21.

15.33   After *Arsenal* and *Adam Opel*, the focus of what are now Article 10(2)(a) TMD 2015 and Article 9(2)(a) EUTMR 2017 on damage to the essential function of the mark seemed settled in the case law. However, debate over whether the modern trade mark monopoly should extend further than this continued. In 2009, the Court of Justice returned to the issue again in *L'Oréal v Bellure*,[58] this time taking the case law in a bold new direction. In *L'Oréal v Bellure*, Bellure sold a various low-cost versions of imitations of L'Oréal's perfumes. There was nothing unlawful in this: there were no intellectual property (IP) rights in the UK preventing Bellure from marketing such 'smell-alike' fragrances. Bellure provided price comparison lists to retailers to show the price of their products relative to the corresponding L'Oréal fragrance. The price comparison lists used the names of L'Oréal's fragrances (such as 'Trésor', 'Miracle', and 'Anaïs-Anaïs'), which were registered as word marks, to identify the relevant L'Oréal products. It was accepted by all parties that the price comparison list was accurate and that Bellure's products did, indeed, smell the same as the L'Oréal fragrances. There was also no damage to the origin function of L'Oréal's marks. The question arose whether the use of L'Oréal's marks in these lists could nonetheless constitute infringement under what is now Article 10(2)(a) TMD 2015. The Court of Justice repeated its earlier rulings to the effect that infringement on this ground was reserved to cases in which the third party's use of the allegedly infringing sign affected or was liable to affect the functions of the mark. However, striking out in a new direction, the Court added new trade mark functions to the list of those said to be protected under this ground of infringement:[59]

> These functions include not only the essential function of the trade mark, which is to guarantee to consumers the origin of the goods or services, but also its other functions, in particular that of guaranteeing the quality of the goods or services in question and those of communication, investment or advertising.

15.34   In this judgment, the Court of Justice radically expanded the reach of infringement under what are now section 10(1) TMA 1994 (as amended), Article 10(2)(a) TMD 2015, and Article 9(2)(a) EUTMR 2017 from cases in which there is an adverse impact on the origin function of the registered mark to cases where there is no such harm, but there might be damage to the other more 'brand-oriented' functions of the mark such as its role in advertising or as a vehicle for investment. The decision triggered furious debate and disagreement across Europe. The extension of the law in this way and the opacity of the Court of Justice's pronouncement were strongly criticised by Jacob LJ when the case returned to the English Court of Appeal:[60]

> We are to consider whether the functions of communication, investment or advertising are liable to be affected, even though the use 'is not capable of jeopardizing the essential function of the mark which is to indicate the origin of the goods'. I am bound to say that I have real difficulty with these functions when divorced from the origin function. There is nothing in the legislation about them. Conceptually they are vague and ill-defined. Take for instance the advertising and investment functions. Trade mark owners of famous marks will have spent a lot of money creating them and need to continue to spend to maintain them. But all advertisements for rival products will impinge on the owner's efforts and affect the advertising and investment function of the brand in question. No-one would say such jostling for fame and image in the market should be stopped. Similarly all comparative advertising is likely to affect the value of the trade mark owner's investment.

Jacob LJ also expressed concern about the impact that the judgment seemed to have on freedom of information, consumer choice and, alongside that, freedom to trade:[61]

> The ECJ's decision in this case means that poor consumers are the losers. Only the poor would dream of buying the defendants' products. The real thing is beyond their wildest dreams. Yet they are denied their right to receive information which would give them a little bit of pleasure; the ability to buy a product for a euro or so which they know smells like a famous perfume.

---

[58] Case C-487/07 *L'Oréal SA v Bellure NV* [2009] ETMR 55.   [59] ibid, para 58.
[60] *L'Oréal SA v Bellure NV* [2010] RPC 23, para 30.   [61] ibid, paras 14–16.

Moreover there is no harm to the trade mark owner—other than possibly a 'harm' which, to be fair, L'Oréal has never asserted. That 'harm' would be letting the truth out—that it is possible to produce cheap perfumes which smell somewhat like a famous original. I can understand that a purveyor of a product sold at a very high price as an exclusive luxury item would not like the public to know that it can be imitated, albeit not to the same quality, cheaply—there is a bit of a message that the price of the real thing may be excessive and that the 'luxury image' may be a bit of a delusion. But an uncomfortable (from the point of view of the trade mark owner) truth is still the truth: it surely needs a strong reason to suppress it.

My second reason is more specific. It is about freedom to trade—indeed, potentially in other cases, to compete honestly. (This case is *a fortiori* for the parties' respective products are not in competition with each other.) If a trader cannot (when it is truly the case) say: 'my goods are the same as Brand X (a famous registered mark) but half the price', I think there is a real danger that important areas of trade will not be open to proper competition.

 Question

Read the ECJ judgment in Case C-487/07 *L'Oréal v Bellure* and that of the Court of Appeal in *L'Oréal SA v Bellure NV* [2010] RPC 23. What do you think of the arguments around consumer choice and competition made by the Court of Appeal? Where does the balance between fair and unfair competition lie?

15.35   *Bellure* generated particular concern that, although 'functions theory' had ostensibly started in *Arsenal* as a means of limiting the scope and reach of what are now Article 10(2)(a) TMD 2015 and Article 9(2)(a) EUTMR 2017, by radically expanding the range of protected functions 'functions theory' was no longer acting as a restraint on registered trade mark law but instead as a means of significantly enlarging the scope of protection. It was by no means clear that this was desirable, particularly since the EU legislators seemed already to have contemplated and provided for non-origin infringement in the more limited circumstances of what are now Article 10(2)(c) TMD 2015 and Article 9(2)(c) EUTMR 2017 (see further paras 15.59–15.80 below). That form of 'extended' protection is only available for marks with a reputation and is counterbalanced by the requirement of 'due cause'. There are no such limitations under Article 10(2)(a) TMD 2015 and Article 9(2)(a) EUTMR 2017, however—indeed, a double identity infringement case claiming damage to one of the new *Bellure* functions could be raised even without the registered mark having ever been used, let alone having acquired a reputation such as would qualify it for extended protection under Article 10(2)(c) TMD 2015 or Article 9(2)(c) EUTMR 2017.[62]

15.36   The opportunity to reconsider *Bellure* arose in the keywords cases, particularly in the *Google France* and *Interflora v Marks & Spencer* preliminary references.[63] Despite pressure to reverse its ruling in *Bellure* and to restrict double identity cases to where there is damage to the origin function only,[64] the CJEU persisted with the *Bellure* extended functions.[65] However, its consideration in these cases of some of the various individual functions listed in *Bellure* sends a more mixed message. In these subsequent cases, the Court appears on the one hand to have lowered the threshold for damage to the origin function; on the other, it seems to have tightened up when there will be damage to the advertising and investment functions, making it harder than was perhaps first thought for these wider functions to be engaged. It remains unclear quite how the extended *Bellure* functions are all to be defined and how, exactly, they are said to relate to each other.

---

[62] See further M Senftleben, 'Adapting EU trademark law to new technologies: back to basics?' in C Geiger (ed), *Constructing European Intellectual Property: Achievements and New Perspectives* (Edward Elgar 2013).

[63] Joined Cases C-236/08, C-237/08, and C-238/08 *Google France, Google Inc v Louis Vuitton Malletier SA and Others* [2010] ETMR 30; Case C-323/09 *Interflora Inc, Interflora British Unit v Marks & Spencer plc, Flowers Direct Online Ltd* [2012] ETMR 1.

[64] As the Advocate General put it in *Interflora*, 'it cannot be denied that the Court finds itself at a rather challenging situation as to the acceptability of its case law relating to Art. 5 of Directive 89/104 also in view of the criticism presented by numerous academic commentators and leading national trade mark judges': Case C-323/09 *Interflora Inc, Interflora British Unit v Marks & Spencer Plc, Flowers Direct Online Ltd* [2012] ETMR 1, para AG8.

[65] Joined Cases C-236/08, C-237/08, and C-238/08 *Google France, Google Inc v Louis Vuitton Malletier SA and Others* [2010] ETMR 30, para 77; Case C-323/09 *Interflora Inc, Interflora British Unit v Marks & Spencer Plc, Flowers Direct Online Ltd* [2012] ETMR 1, paras 36–40.

■ **Joined Cases C-236/08, C-237/08 and C-238/08** *Google France, Google Inc v Louis Vuitton Malletier SA and Others* **[2010] ETMR 30**

Having ascertained that the keyword advertisers were 'using' the allegedly infringing signs for infringement purposes (see para 15.21 above), the CJEU turned to the question of whether those uses were liable to have an adverse effect on the function of the various registered marks relied upon.

The Court started by considering whether the keywords had an adverse effect on the origin function of the registered marks. The CJEU stressed that the trade mark owner must be able to prohibit the display of third party keyword-triggered advertisements which internet users may erroneously perceive as emanating from the trade mark proprietor. There would be an adverse effect on the origin function if the third party's advertisement suggested an economic link between that third party and the proprietor of the trade mark. However, the Court also added:[66]

> In the case where the ad, while not suggesting the existence of an economic link, is vague to such an extent on the origin of the goods or services at issue that normally informed and reasonably attentive internet users are unable to determine, on the basis of the advertising link and the commercial message attached thereto, whether the advertiser is a third party vis-a-vis the proprietor of the trade mark or, on the contrary, economically linked to that proprietor, the conclusion must also be that there is an adverse effect on that function of the trade mark.

As has been noted in commentary, this shifts the onus of proof of infringement: instead of the onus being on the trade mark owner to demonstrate that the alleged infringement creates the impression of a material link in trade (as per *Arsenal*), the onus is now shifted to the infringer to demonstrate that his use of the contested sign is sufficiently clear.[67] The CJEU also considered whether the keywords were liable to damage the advertising function of the registered marks. However, perhaps surprisingly, it concluded that they did not. There would be infringement if the third party's keyword 'adversely affects the proprietor's use of its mark as a factor in sales promotion or as an instrument of commercial strategy'.[68] The Court accepted that the keywords had 'certain repercussions' for the trade mark proprietor's own advertising use of the mark, for example by forcing it to pay a higher price-per-click to the keyword referencing provider to ensure that its own advertisements appeared above those of other operators.[69] However, in the view of the Court that was not sufficient to show an adverse effect on the advertising function of the mark. The CJEU noted that the trade mark owner's own homepage would appear in the search engine's natural search results 'usually in one of the highest positions on that list'.[70] In the Court's view:[71]

> [t]hat display, which is, moreover, free of charge, means that the visibility to internet users of the goods or services of the proprietor of the trade mark is guaranteed, irrespective of whether or not that proprietor is successful in also securing the display, in one of the highest positions, of an ad under the heading 'sponsored links'.

There was therefore no harm to the advertising function.

---

[66] Joined Cases C-236/08, C-237/08, and C-238/08 *Google France, Google Inc v Louis Vuitton Malletier SA and Others* [2010] ETMR 30, para 90.

[67] See further, T Bednarz, 'Keyword advertising before the French Supreme Court and beyond—calm at last after turbulent times for Google and its advertising clients?' (2011) 42(6) IIC 641–72; R Arnold, 'The CJEU's Article 5(1)(a) jurisprudence: problems and solutions' (Feb 2012) Berichten industriele eigendom 58–63. The Court of Appeal in *Interflora* noted that the Court of Justice had articulated a new test under what is now Art 10(2)(a) TMD 2015 and Art 9(2)(a) EUTMR 2017: *Interflora Inc v Marks & Spencer plc* [2015] ETMR 5, para 132.

[68] Joined Cases C-236/08, C-237/08, and C-238/08 *Google France, Google Inc v Louis Vuitton Malletier SA and Others* [2010] ETMR 30, para 92.

[69] ibid, paras 93–94.   [70] ibid, para 97.

[71] ibid, para 97. See also Case C-278/08 *Die BergSpechte Outdoor Reisen und Alpinschule Edi Koblmüller GmbH v Günter Guni* [2010] ETMR 33, paras 29–37; Case C-558/08 *Portakabin Ltd and Portakabin BV v Primakabin BV* [2010] ETMR 52, paras 23–36.

■ **Case C-323/09** *Interflora Inc, Interflora British Unit vs Marks & Spencer Plc, Flowers Direct Online Ltd* [2012] ETMR 1

In this dispute, Marks & Spencer had purchased the keyword 'Interflora', a registered trade mark belonging to Interflora, on the Google search engine. The CJEU considered the impact of this on both the origin and advertising functions, in effect reiterating the points made in *Google France*.[72] With respect to the advertising function, the Court added:[73]

> the mere fact that the use, by a third party, of a sign identical with a trade mark in relation to goods or services identical with those for which that mark is registered obliges the proprietor of that mark to intensify its advertising in order to maintain or enhance its profile with consumers is not a sufficient basis, in every case, for concluding that the trade mark's advertising function is adversely affected. In that regard, although the trade mark is an essential element in the system of undistorted competition which European law seeks to establish . . ., its purpose is not, however, to protect its proprietor against practices inherent in competition.

The CJEU also considered the impact of the disputed keyword on the investment function of the registered mark. The Court identified the investment function as comprising the use of a trade mark 'to acquire or preserve a reputation capable of attracting consumers and retaining their loyalty'.[74] 'Substantial interference' with this would constitute an infringement.[75] However, the Court added:[76]

> it cannot be accepted that the proprietor of a trade mark may—in conditions of fair competition that respect the trade mark's function as an indication of origin—prevent a competitor from using a sign identical with that trade mark in relation to goods or services identical with those for which the mark is registered, if the only consequence of that use is to oblige the proprietor of that trade mark to adapt its efforts to acquire or preserve a reputation capable of attracting consumers and retaining their loyalty. Likewise, the fact that that use may prompt some consumers to switch from goods or services bearing that trade mark cannot be successfully relied on by the proprietor of the mark.

15.37   In the original proposals for the 2015 trade mark reform package, the European Commission proposed to undo the Court of Justice's case law in *Bellure* and subsequent judgments and to amend the TMD and EUTMR so as to stipulate that infringement under what are now Article 10(2)(a) TMD 2015 and Article 9(2)(a) EUTMR 2017 was to be limited to cases involving damage to the origin function only. However, this proposal triggered more intense debate.[77] It was ultimately knocked back during the course of the legislative process; in the end, no legislative changes were enacted and *Bellure* and subsequent cases continue to stand. It remains to be seen how the double identity case law will develop from here. It will take time for cases to consider all of the trade mark functions mentioned in *Bellure* (eg the 'communication' function has not been addressed by the Court of Justice yet) and to work out the appropriate balance of interests in both online and 'real-world' contexts.

 Discussion point   For answer guidance visit **www.oup.com/uk/brown5e**.

Can you discern a clear overall policy direction from the Court of Justice's decisions in *Bellure*, *Google France*, and *Interflora*? How do you think the case law should develop from here?

---

[72]   Case C-323/09 *Interflora Inc, Interflora British Unit v Marks & Spencer Plc, Flowers Direct Online Ltd* [2012] ETMR 1, paras 44–46 and 54–56.

[73]   ibid, para 57.   [74]   ibid, para 60.   [75]   ibid, para 62.

[76]   ibid, para 64.

[77]   See, eg, M Senftleben, 'Function theory and international exhaustion: why it is wise to confine the double identity rule in EU trade mark law to cases affecting the origin function' (2014) 36(8) EIPR 518–24; A Kur, 'Trade marks function, don't they? CJEU jurisprudence and unfair competition practices' (2014) 45(4) IIC 434–54.

> **Key points on 'double identity' cases**
>
> - Where goods/services and marks are identical (so-called 'double identity' cases) it is not necessary to show consumer confusion.
>
> - A sign will be considered identical to a registered mark where it reproduces, without any modification or addition, all the elements constituting the trade mark or, viewed as a whole, it contains differences so significant that they may go unnoticed by an average consumer.
>
> - When considering identity of services, the inquiry is as to what is actually done by the mark owner and applicant or alleged infringer.
>
> - For there to be 'double identity' infringement, it must also be shown that there is damage to one of the functions of the registered mark. Controversially, this includes not only the essential function of the trade mark as a guarantee of origin but also other functions, in particular the quality, communication, investment, and advertising functions.

'Likelihood of confusion' cases

Sections 5(2) and 10(2) TMA 1994 (as amended); Articles 5(1)(b) and 10(2)(b) TMD 2015 (formerly Arts 4(1)(b) and 5(1)(b) TMD 2008); Articles 8(1)(b) and 9(2)(b) EUTMR 2017 (formerly Arts 8(1)(b) and 9(1)(b) CTMR 2009)

15.38   The second relative ground for refusal of a trade mark considered in detail in this chapter can be found at section 5(2) TMA 1994 (as amended). Section 5(2) provides that a trade mark shall not be registered if because:

(a) it is identical with an earlier trade mark and is to be registered for goods or services similar to those for which the earlier trade mark is protected, or

(b) it is similar to an earlier trade mark and is to be registered for goods or services identical with or similar to those for which the earlier trade mark is protected,

there exists a likelihood of confusion on the part of the public, which includes the likelihood of association with the earlier trade mark.

Section 10(2) TMA 1994 (as amended) provides that a person infringes a registered trade mark if he uses in the course of trade a sign where because:

(a) the sign is identical with the trade mark and is used in relation to goods or services similar to those for which the trade mark is registered, or

(b) the sign is similar to the trade mark and is used in relation to goods or services identical with or similar to those for which the trade mark is registered,

there exists a likelihood of confusion on the part of the public, which includes the likelihood of association with the trade mark.

See also Articles 5(1)(b) and 10(2)(a) TMD 2015 and Articles 8(1)(b) and 9(2)(a) EUTMR 2017.

15.39   These sections will apply to the combinations of similar and identical marks or goods and services shown in Figure 15.2:

Figure 15.2 Similarity and confusion combinations

Mark	Goods/services
Identical	Similar
Similar	Identical
Similar	Similar

15.40   As can be seen, this relative ground of objection and ground of infringement is broader in scope than the 'double identity' rules we have been discussing so far. Instead of being limited to situations in which the objectionable sign and goods/services are identical to those registered, sections 5(2) and 10(2) TMA 1994 (as amended) extend to cover to situations in which the objectionable sign and/or goods/services are 'similar' to those registered. As a corollary of this broader scope, however, for there to be a valid objection to registrability or infringement it must be shown that there is a likelihood of confusion on the part of the public.

15.41   The breadth of the monopoly conferred on the trade mark under these grounds will depend what is taken to constitute 'similarity' between marks and goods and services, and how we assess 'likelihood of confusion'. One trader might have a logo of a black cat stretching itself, and register that in connection with slippers. A competing trader might then use a picture of a black cat stretching itself in connection with gloves. Are the goods similar? They are both items to be worn, but one is for use on the feet and the other for use on the hands. If the court finds them to be similar, then the owner of the first mark may be able to prevent competing traders from using the same (or a confusingly similar) logo in connection with a wide variety of goods and services. If on the other hand, the court finds the goods to be dissimilar, so the monopoly conferred by the trade mark is defined more narrowly. The same issues arise in relation to similarity of marks. To return to the previous example, if one trader has registered a logo of a black cat stretching in relation to slippers, would that prevent a competing trader from using a picture of a dog stretching in connection with slippers? Or a lion stretching itself in relation to slippers? If the cat, the dog, and the lion are found to be similar in trade mark terms, so the breadth of the monopoly granted to the first trader expands. The key is to decide how to determine similarity between the marks and the goods and services, and how to assess consumer confusion.

Exercise

Before you start reading through the rest of this chapter, consider the following scenario.[78]

- An application to the EU Intellectual Property Office (EUIPO) for the registration of the 'Skype' logo, for example, for audiovisual goods, peer-to-peer communications, electronic data transmission, and messaging services and computer services relating to software or to the creation and hosting of websites.

- An opposition based on the word mark 'Sky', for example, for audiovisual goods, telecommunication and computer services relating to software.

Imagine that you are the hearing officer faced with the application and opposition. How do you decide whether the 'Skype' sign is registrable? What factors do you take into account? Who do you have in mind when thinking about registrability? How do you compare the signs with the mark?
Revisit your answer when you have finished this chapter to see how many relevant factors you thought of.

---

[78] See, eg, Case T-423/12 *Skype Ultd v OHIM, Sky Plc* (General Court).

'Likelihood of association' and 'likelihood of confusion'

15.42 It will be seen that the wording of sections 5(2) and 10(2) TMA 1994 (as amended) and corresponding provisions of the TMD 2015 and EUTMR 2017 refer to 'likelihood of confusion . . . which includes a likelihood of association'. One of the earliest questions that arose on the interpretation of the EU trade mark regime was what is meant by this reference to 'likelihood of association'. 'Likelihood of association' seems to set a lower threshold standard for refusal or infringement than 'likelihood of confusion'. For example, you may *associate* 'Persil' and 'Ariel': both marks are used for soap powders in the marketplace. However, it is possible to associate 'Persil' and 'Ariel' in this way without *confusing* the two. If association as a test is sufficient for infringement, then the scope of protection conferred on registered marks is potentially very wide—spanning all sorts of competitor signs which might 'bring to mind' the registered mark without anyone actually being confused.

15.43 The reference to 'likelihood of association' in the EU trade mark regime has its origins in Benelux trade mark law and is exemplified by the old Benelux case *Monopoly v Anti-Monopoly*.[79] In this case, registration was refused for the mark 'Anti-Monopoly', not because the consumer would be *confused* as to the origin of the goods, but because a link would be made in the minds of the public with the trade mark 'Monopoly' due to their similarities. In other words, the consumer would *associate* the two marks—even though 'Anti-Monopoly' is quite clearly distinguished from 'Monopoly'. The circumstances in which the references to 'likelihood of association' were added to the Directive and Regulation during their drafting were somewhat opaque, but it was understood that this addition was intended as a drafting compromise to respond to concerns from the Benelux states that the then new Directive and Regulation might reduce the scope of protection conferred on registered marks compared to the pre-harmonisation Benelux position.

15.44 This was hotly contested in commentary and literature, but in any event the matter was definitively settled by the ECJ in one of its earliest trade mark cases, *Sabel BV v Puma AG*.[80] Puma had opposed an application by Sabel to register as a trade mark in Germany a logo of a 'leaping cat' together with the word 'Sabel', relying on two earlier German national trade mark registrations also for (slightly different) 'leaping cat' logos. The ECJ was asked about the meaning of the reference to 'likelihood of association' in the relevant provision of the Directive. In effect, the case turned on whether mere association of the 'semantic content' of the marks (ie the 'leaping cat' concept) was sufficient to give rise to a valid objection. However, the Court held that the mere association alone was not enough. In so doing, the Court emphasised that 'likelihood of confusion' is the key criterion:[81]

> In that connection, it is to be remembered that Article 4(1)(b) of the Directive is designed to apply only if, by reason of the identity or similarity both of the marks and of the goods or services which they designate, 'there exists a likelihood of confusion on the part of the public, which includes the likelihood of association with the earlier trade mark'. It follows from that wording that the concept of likelihood of association is not an alternative to that of likelihood of confusion, but serves to define it scope. The terms of the provision itself exclude its application where there is no likelihood of confusion on the part of the public.

15.45 This was subsequently re-confirmed in *Marca Mode CV v Adidas AG*.[82] It was therefore swiftly settled that 'likelihood of association' is at most a subset of 'likelihood of confusion', the latter being the key criterion. It is not sufficient for the purposes of sections 5(2) or 10(2) TMA 1994 (as amended), or the corresponding provisions of the TMD 2015 or EUTMR 2017, for a consumer to associate two marks: a likelihood of confusion must be shown. In *Canon v MGM*, the ECJ linked the concept of 'likelihood of confusion' explicitly to the 'essential function' of the mark. Emphasising that the essential function of the trade mark is

---

[79] *Edor Handelsonderneming BV v General Mills Fun Group*, Nederlands Jurisprudentie 1978, 83.
[80] Case C-251/95 *Sabel BV v Puma AG, Rudolf Dassler Sport* [1998] ETMR 1.
[81] ibid, para 18.
[82] Case C-425/98 *Marca Mode CV v Adidas AG and Adidas Benelux BV* [2000] ETMR 723.

to guarantee the identity of the origin of the marked product to the consumer or end user by enabling him, without any possibility of confusion, to distinguish the product or service from others which have another origin, the Court defined 'likelihood of confusion' as:[83]

> the risk that the public might believe that the goods or services in question come from the same undertaking or, as the case may be, from economically-linked undertakings.

Assessing likelihood of confusion

15.46   In *Sabel*, the ECJ went on to articulate various key principles which have governed how to approach the assessment of likelihood of confusion ever since. Referring to the Recitals of the Directive, the Court set out what has become known as the 'global appreciation' test for likelihood of confusion:[84]

> it is clear from the tenth recital in the preamble to the Directive that the appreciation of the likelihood of confusion 'depends on numerous elements and, in particular, on the recognition of the trade mark on the market, of the association which can be made with the used or registered sign, of the degree of similarity between the trade mark and the sign and between the goods or services identified'. The likelihood of confusion must therefore be appreciated globally, taking into account all factors relevant to the circumstances of the case.

The Court developed this further in *Canon v MGM*,[85] emphasising that there is a degree of interdependence between the different considerations:[86]

> A global assessment of the likelihood of confusion implies some interdependence between the relevant factors, and in particular a similarity between the trade marks and between these goods or services. Accordingly, a lesser degree of similarity between these goods or services may be offset by a greater degree of similarity between the marks, and vice versa.

15.47   In *Sabel*, the ECJ also set out the principle that:[87]

> the more distinctive the earlier mark, the greater will be the likelihood of confusion.

It has been suggested by some commentators that this assumption seems misplaced: the more well-known the registered mark, the more likely it is that consumers will be able to tell apart a similar sign—because they would not expect to see the well-known mark in any form other than the one to which they have become accustomed.[88] However, the Court of Justice's quasi-factual assumption that more distinctive marks are more easily infringed has become well established in the case law. Concern that a particular sign should be kept free for use by competitors is not a relevant consideration in assessing likelihood of confusion.[89]

Similarity between marks

15.48   For sections 5(2) or 10(2) TMA 1994 to be engaged, the registered mark and the contested later sign must be identical or similar. We have already addressed the Court of Justice case law on identical marks/signs (see paragraph 15.25 above). In *Sabel*, the ECJ also set out the key principles on how to assess similarity between marks. The Court referred to a:[90]

> global appreciation of the visual, aural or conceptual similarity of the marks in question, . . . based on the overall impression given by the marks, bearing in mind, in particular, their distinctive and dominant components.

---

[83] Case C-39/97 *Canon Kabushiki Kaisha v Metro-Goldwyn-Mayer Inc* [1999] ETMR 1, para 29. In Case C-278/08 *Die BergSpechte Outdoor Reisen und Alpinschule Edi Koblmüller GmbH v Günter Guni* [2010] ETMR 33, the Court of Justice appears to have merged the test for likelihood of confusion with the test for damage to the origin function of the mark in double identity cases (discussed at paragraph 15.36). It remains to be seen how far this ruling will be applied.

[84] Case C-251/95 *Sabel BV v Puma AG, Rudolf Dassler Sport* [1998] ETMR 1, para 22.

[85] Case C-39/97 *Canon Kabushiki Kaisha v Metro-Goldwyn-Mayer Inc* [1999] ETMR 1.   [86] ibid, para 17.

[87] Case C-251/95 *Sabel BV v Puma AG, Rudolf Dassler Sport* [1998] ETMR 1, para 24.

[88] Most recently, on the corresponding position in the United States, see B Beebe and SC Hempill, 'The Scope of Strong Marks: Should Trademark Law Protect the Strong More than the Weak?' NYU Law and Economics Research Paper No 18-04, https://ssrn.com/abstract–3073130.

[89] Case C-102/07 *Adidas AG v Marca Mode CV* [2008] ETMR 44.

[90] Case C-251/95 *Sabel BV v Puma AG, Rudolf Dassler Sport* [1998] ETMR 1, para 23.

15.49   The Court also stressed the importance of assessing this from the perspective of the 'average consumer':[91]

> The wording of Article 4(1)(b) of the Directive— ' . . . there exists a likelihood of confusion on the part of the public . . .'—shows that the perception of marks in the mind of the average consumer of the type of goods or services in question plays a decisive role in the global appreciation of the likelihood of confusion. The average consumer normally perceives a mark as a whole and does not proceed to analyse its various details.

The ECJ elaborated on this in *Lloyd Schuhfabrik*,[92] noting that:[93]

> the average consumer of the category of products concerned is deemed to be reasonably well-informed and reasonably observant and circumspect . . . However, account should be taken of the fact that the average consumer only rarely has the chance to make a direct comparison between the different marks but must place his trust in the imperfect picture of them that he has kept in his mind. It should also be borne in mind that the average consumer's level of attention is likely to vary according to the category of goods or services in question.

For instance, the consumer may give a higher level of attention when buying expensive items, such as cars, as compared with more everyday goods, such as food. That may reduce the likelihood of confusion between the marks at the moment when the consumer makes his choice.[94] There is, however, no principle that trade marks which are registered for goods of a particular value, technological advancement, or safety should enjoy greater protection. Perhaps surprisingly, the Court of Justice has also confirmed that how the registered mark has been used may be a relevant consideration in the comparison with the allegedly infringing sign: in *Specsavers v Asda*, the Court held that the colour or combination of colours in which the trade mark has been used affects how the average consumer perceives the mark and, therefore, is liable to increase the likelihood of confusion with a sign in a similar colour.[95]

15.50   Comparisons between marks will be very fact specific to each given case. Comparing word marks will often entail close consideration of their make-up in terms of the beginning, middle, and end elements, including overall spelling similarities and differences and how they will be pronounced. Conceptual and visual differences between two signs may counteract aural similarities between them, provided that at least one of those signs has, from the point of view of the relevant public, a clear and specific meaning, so that the public is capable of grasping it immediately.[96] There are no restrictions on which language(s) should be taken into account in assessing likelihood of confusion: the meaning and pronunciation of words in different languages must be taken into account in circumstances where the relevant public has a basic knowledge of the language in question.[97] The assessment of conceptual similarity of the marks should be judged by reference to the understanding of the relevant public. In *Red Bull GmbH v OHIM, Sun Mark Ltd*[98] the General Court evaluated the conceptual similarity between the marks BULLDOG and BULL. It noted that for the English-speaking part of the relevant public, it would be recognised that the signs referred to different animals. However, there was some degree of conceptual similarity:[99]

> both the bull, depicted by the earlier word marks, and the bulldog, described by the mark applied for, convey the image of animals from which a concentrated force emanates, a great muscular force often expressing itself aggressively towards their fellow creatures or human beings, especially when that power is on display in combat or at bullfights.

[91] ibid, para 23.
[92] Case C-342/97 *Lloyd Schuhfabrik Meyer & Co GmbH v Klijsen Handel BV* [1999] ETMR 690.   [93] ibid, para 26.
[94] Case C-361/04 *Ruiz-Picasso and Others v OHIM* [2006] ECR I-00643, para 40.
[95] Case C-252/12 *Specsavers International Healthcare Ltd and Others v Asda Stores Ltd* [2013] ETMR 46, para 37 in particular.
[96] Case C-361/04 *Ruiz-Picasso and Others v OHIM* [2006] ETMR 29.
[97] Case C-147/14 *Loutfi Management Propriété intellectuelle SARL v AMJ Meatproducts NV, Halalsupply NV* [2015] ETMR 35 (considering marks including both Latin and Arabic script).
[98] Case T-78/13 *Red Bull GmbH v OHIM, Sun Mark Ltd* [2015] ETMR 18.   [99] ibid, para 50.

A recent General Court case provides an interesting example of the assessment of similarity between two figurative marks:

■ Case T-398/16 *Starbucks Corp v EUIPO/Hasmik Nersesyan* [2018] ETMR 17

Ms Nersesyan filed an application to register the figurative mark shown at Figure 15.3 as an EU trade mark in respect of 'services for providing drinks' in class 43. Starbucks opposed the application on the basis of a large number of earlier EU trade marks, including the mark at Figure 15.4, claiming *inter alia* a likelihood of confusion.

Figure 15.3 Nersesyan application

Figure 15.4 Starbucks EU trade mark

The EUIPO Board of Appeal rejected the opposition. However, the General Court disagreed. The General Court highlighted three sets of visual similarities between the mark applied for and Starbucks' earlier EU trade marks. The signs, taken as a whole, were all characterised by the fact that they had the same general appearance. They comprised circular devices consisting of two parts: the figurative element in the centre (musical note and mermaid, respectively). That central element was surrounded by a broad band marked off, on the inside, by a white circle and, on the outside, by another white circle and border. The word elements in that band had the same placement. There was also commonality in the placement of the two white musical notes and two white stars appearing in that band. The similarity of general appearance was strengthened by the use of the same colours (black and white) and by use of the same font for the word elements 'STARBUCKS COFFEE' and 'COFFEE ROCKS'. The marks also contained the common word 'COFFEE'. Although there were a number of differences between the signs, the General Court concluded that they were similar and that there was a likelihood of confusion.

Discussion point   For answer guidance visit **www.oup.com/uk/brown5e**.

As well as aural and visual considerations, can you think of any other senses that might be used in assessing similarities between marks? Consider the debate in Chapter 14 as to whether taste and smell marks can be registered. Are there any implications for the assessment of similarity between marks arising from the removal of the requirement for graphic representation by the 2015 EU trade mark reform package?

Similarity between goods and services

15.51 In assessing similarity between goods and services, that they are registered in different classes of the Nice Agreement does not thereby make them dissimilar. The key case is *Canon v MGM*:

■ **Case C-39/97 *Canon Kabushiki Kaisha v Metro Goldwyn Mayer Inc* [1999] ETMR 1**

MGM had applied in Germany for registration of the word 'Cannon', to be used for, inter alia, video film cassettes. This was opposed by Canon on the basis that it infringed Canon's earlier word trade mark 'Canon', registered in Germany in respect of, inter alia, picture cameras and projectors, and television filming, transmission, and reproduction devices. The ECJ emphasised that, for the purposes of applying what is now Article 10(2)(a) TMD 2015, the goods or services in question must be similar or identical to those registered. On what may constitute similar goods or services, the Court said:[100]

> In assessing the similarity of the goods or services concerned, as the French and United Kingdom Governments and the Commission have pointed out, all the relevant factors relating to those goods or services themselves should be taken into account. Those factors include, inter alia, their nature, their end users and their method of use and whether they are in competition with each other or are complementary.

The Court held that in assessing the existence of a likelihood of confusion, a *lesser* degree of similarity between the products could be offset by a *greater* degree of similarity between the marks, or vice versa. The more distinctive the prior mark, either per se, or because of its market reputation, the greater the risk of confusion. Accordingly, the registration of a later trade mark application might have to be refused or infringement found despite a lesser degree of similarity between the products covered where the earlier mark, particularly its reputation, was highly distinctive.

15.52 The effect of this ruling is that the more distinctive the mark and the greater its reputation, the wider the protection conferred by the trade mark over progressively more dissimilar goods. The monopoly thus granted to the trade mark owner expands (in the sense that it covers a broader range of goods and services) depending on how distinctive the trade mark is considered to be. The judgment of the Court has been criticised on the ground that no matter the distinctiveness of the mark, some point must come at which the goods and services can no longer be regarded as similar, although the ECJ in *Canon* did emphasise that similarity of goods and services must be shown.[101]

 Question

What do you think of this approach linking the question of similarity of goods and services with the distinctiveness of the mark? Do you think that there is a threshold of similarity required in relation to either marks or goods? Should there be?

---

[100] Case C-39/97 *Canon Kabushiki Kaisha v Metro Goldwyn Mayer Inc* [1999] ETMR 1, para 23.

[101] ibid, para 22. The Court of Appeal doubted that there is a threshold of similarity required in relation to marks: *Esure v Direct Line Ltd* [2008] ETMR 77.

15.53   One of the elements to be taken into account in assessing similarity of goods is whether they are complementary.[102] Some guidance—albeit taking quite a strict approach—on what amounts to complementarity was given in *El Corte Inglés v OHIM*[103] concerning an application to register the word mark 'Piranha' in stylised form as an EU trade mark for clothing, footwear, and headgear in class 25, which was opposed by the owner of the Spanish word mark 'Piranha', registered in class 25 and also for leather goods in class 18. Considering whether there was complementarity between the clothing, footwear, and headgear goods applied for and class 18 leather goods, the Court of First Instance (CFI; now General Court) said:[104]

> goods are complementary if there is a close connection between them, in the sense that one is indispensable or important for the use of the other in such a way that customers may think that the responsibility for the production of those goods lies with the same undertaking . . . .

This narrow approach echoed the earlier case of *Mülhens GmbH & Co KG v OHIM*,[105] in which the CFI compared clothing and toiletries. Noting that 'in the fashion and body and facial care sectors, . . . goods whose nature, purpose and method of use are different, quite apart from being functionally complementary, may be aesthetically complementary in the eyes of the relevant public', the CFI added:[106]

> this aesthetically complementary nature must involve a genuine aesthetic necessity, in that one product is indispensable or important for the use of the other and consumers consider it ordinary and natural to use these products together . . . .

Time of assessment of likelihood of confusion

15.54   Where the distinctive character of a registered trade mark has been weakened as a result of the contested infringement, the relevant time for determination of likelihood of confusion is the time when the allegedly infringing sign began to be used rather than the time at which the matter comes to trial:

■ Case C-145/05 *Levi Strauss & Co v Casucci SpA* [2006] ETMR 71

Levi Strauss had registered its 'mouette' (seagull) stitching mark shown in Figure 15.5 in Benelux for clothes.

Figure 15.5 Levi Strauss trade mark

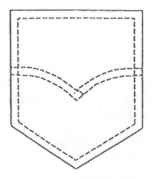

---

[102]   Case C-39/97 *Canon Kabushiki Kaisha v Metro Goldwyn Mayer Inc* [1999] ETMR 1, para 23.
[103]   Case T-443/05 *El Corte Inglés v OHIM* [2007] ETMR 81.   [104] ibid, para 48.
[105]   Case T-150/04 *Mülhens GmbH & Co KG v OHIM* (unreported).
[106]   ibid, paras 35–36.

Casucci sold jeans on the Benelux market with a sign as shown in Figure 15.6:

Figure 15.6 Casucci jeans

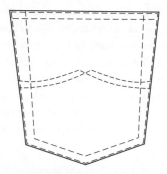

Levi Strauss sued for trade mark infringement. It lost at first instance and appealed to the Cour d'appel de Bruxelles, which in turn dismissed the appeal, saying that there was little difference between the two pocket designs and that Levi's sign could no longer be considered to be a highly distinctive mark since it was comprised of components the characteristics of which were by then common to the products owing to their widespread use. A question was referred to the ECJ asking at what point in time the national court should assess the distinctiveness of the registered mark for infringement purposes. The ECJ responded that the relevant time was when the sign which infringed the trade mark began to be used. If this assessment were pinned to a later point in time, the infringer might be able to take advantage of his own unlawful behaviour by alleging that the mark had become less well known, a development for which the infringer himself may have been responsible or to which he may have contributed. Where, at the time the infringing sign began to be used, the use of the sign constituted an infringement the national court could order that the sign no longer be used.

15.55 In *Interflora Inc v Marks & Spencer*,[107] the question arose as to whether the concept of 'initial interest' confusion has any place in EU trade mark law. Initial interest confusion is a US trade mark law-derived concept whereby there may be infringement if a consumer is initially confused as to the origin of goods and/or services, even though that confusion has been dispelled by the time a purchase is made. Despite the earlier case of *Och-Ziff Management Europe Ltd v Och Capital LLP*,[108] which embraced initial interest confusion, the Court of Appeal in *Interflora* was clear that this controversial doctrine is not a part of EU law. This concept was 'an unnecessary and potentially misleading gloss'[109] on the tests that the Court of Justice has articulated for infringement.

 Question

Interflora concerned initial interest confusion in the context of keyword advertising and the use of an identical mark/sign in connection with identical goods/services. Is there room for the concept of initial interest confusion in cases other than keyword advertising and/or where the infringement concerns similar marks and goods and services? What are the pros and cons of a doctrine of initial interest confusion?

---

[107] *Interflora Inc v Marks & Spencer Plc* [2015] ETMR 5.
[108] [2010] EWHC 2599.
[109] *Interflora Inc v Marks & Spencer Plc* [2015] ETMR 5, para 158.

Likelihood of confusion and composite marks

15.56   As will be seen from paragraphs 15.48–15.50 above, an assessment of the similarity between marks should be based on the overall impression created by the whole of the marks, looking in particular to their distinctive and dominant components. In relation to composite marks comprising several word elements it is possible, in some circumstances, for the overall impression to be dominated by one or more of those elements—for example, where the composite mark includes a well-known brand name alongside a less distinctive element. If a well-known brand name is added to an existing mark belonging to a third party, does the dominance and distinctiveness of the well-known element mean that there is no likelihood of confusion when the composite is compared to the earlier mark on its own? This poses a problem for the *Sabel* approach to likelihood of confusion: at least on the face of it, the addition of the well-known brand name removes the likelihood of confusion, thereby risking giving the owners of well-known marks free rein to 'swamp' existing third party marks.

15.57   This scenario was considered in *Medion AG v Thomson Multimedia Sales Germany & Austria GmbH*,[110] concerning the mark 'LIFE' registered in Germany by Medion for leisure electronic devices. Thomson marketed certain leisure electronic devices under the name 'THOMSON LIFE'. The question arose as to whether the addition of the element 'THOMSON' was sufficient to avoid a likelihood of confusion. The ECJ emphasised that assessing similarity between two marks means more than taking just one component of a composite trade mark and comparing it with another mark: the comparison had to be made by examining each of the marks in question as a whole. The overall impression conveyed to the relevant public by a composite trade mark may, in certain circumstances, be dominated by one or more of its components. However, it was also possible that, in a particular case, an earlier mark used by a third party in a composite sign could still have an independent distinctive role in the later composite sign, without necessarily constituting the dominant element of the later composite sign. Under those circumstances, the overall impression conveyed by the composite sign might lead the consumer to believe that the goods and services derive from economically linked undertakings. The Court pointed out that to conclude otherwise may well deprive the owner of an earlier mark of the exclusive rights conferred by the Directive where that earlier mark was a distinctive but not the dominant element of the later composite sign.[111] This may be the case where the owner of a widely known mark makes a composite sign using that mark and an earlier mark which is not itself widely known.[112] The *Medion* test has also been applied in the UK to the situation in which the common components of the two marks are similar, rather than identical, as was the case in *Medion*.[113]

 Question

Do you think that the ruling in *Medion* is consistent with the Court of Justice's general approach to assessing likelihood of confusion? How far does it qualify or amend the 'global appreciation' test?

Scope of protection for marks with a specific meaning

15.58   Although such cases are likely to be rare, if a mark is well known in a context other than that of indicating the origin of goods and services, this can make it easier for a consumer to differentiate between the two, and thus confusion is less likely to arise. This is particularly so where the original meaning of the mark overwhelms its distinctive capacity.

---

[110]   Case C-120/04 *Medion AG v Thomson Multimedia Sales Germany & Austria GmbH* [2006] ETMR 13.   [111]   ibid, para 33.
[112]   See recently also Case C-591/12 *Bimbo SA v OHIM* [2014] ETMR 41; Case C-20/14 *BGW Beratungs-Gesellschaft Wirtshuft mbH v Bodo Scholz* [2016] ETMR 1. The case law is discussed in J Blum and B Pollard, 'Bimbo and composite trade marks: a review of the European approach to assessing confusion' (2015) 37(1) EIPR 46–50 and P Davies, 'The case law of composite marks: what was Medion's right to LIFE?' (2015) 37(12) EIPR 803 07.
[113]   *Aveda Corp v Dabur India* [2013] EWHC 589 (Ch).

■ Case C-361/04 P *Ruiz-Picasso and Others v OHIM* [2006] ETMR 29

The Picasso estate had an EU trade mark for the word mark 'PICASSO', registered in respect of vehicles in class 12. Daimler Chrysler applied for registration of an EU trade mark for the word mark 'PICARO' also in respect of vehicles in class 12. Picasso opposed the application. The CFI upheld the decision of the Third Board of Appeal of the EUIPO to dismiss the opposition.

Picasso had relied on *Sabel* and *Canon*, arguing that trade marks which have a highly distinctive character, either per se or because of the reputation they possess on the market, enjoy broader protection than marks with a less distinctive character. The CFI, however, said that while the name 'Picasso' was well known as corresponding to the name of the famous painter Pablo Picasso, that connection was not capable of heightening the likelihood of confusion between the two marks in the instant case. On appeal to the ECJ, the Picasso estate argued that the CFI had paid insufficient heed to the distinctiveness of the mark Picasso—that it had only considered the name in relation to the artist and not in connection with the goods concerned. The Court, however, did not agree. The CFI had made a factual assessment that the word 'Picasso' had a clear and specific meaning for the public.[114]

> The reputation of the painter Pablo Picasso is such that it is not plausible to consider, in the absence of specific evidence to the contrary, that the sign PICASSO as a mark for motor vehicles may, in the perception of the average consumer, override the name of the painter so that that consumer, confronted with the sign PICASSO in the context of the goods concerned, will henceforth disregard the meaning of the sign as the name of the painter and perceive it principally as a mark, among other marks, of motor vehicles.

The ECJ upheld the CFI's ruling.

Key points on similarity and confusion

- The key principles for assessing likelihood of confusion have been brought together by and cited with approval most recently by the Court of Appeal in *Maier v ASOS*:[115]

  (a) the likelihood of confusion must be appreciated globally, taking account of all relevant factors;

  (b) the matter must be judged through the eyes of the average consumer of the goods or services in question, who is deemed to be reasonably well informed and reasonably circumspect and observant, but who rarely has the chance to make direct comparisons between marks and must instead rely upon the imperfect picture of them he has kept in his mind, and whose attention varies according to the category of goods or services in question;

  (c) the average consumer normally perceives a mark as a whole and does not proceed to analyse its various details;

  (d) the visual, aural and conceptual similarities of the marks must normally be assessed by reference to the overall impressions created by the marks bearing in mind their distinctive and dominant components, but it is only when all other components of a complex mark are negligible that it is permissible to make the comparison solely on the basis of the dominant elements;

  (e) nevertheless, the overall impression conveyed to the public by a composite trade mark may, in certain circumstances, be dominated by one or more of its components;

  (f) and beyond the usual case, where the overall impression created by a mark depends heavily on the dominant features of the mark, it is quite possible that in a particular case an element corresponding to an earlier trade mark may retain an independent distinctive role in a composite mark, without necessarily constituting a dominant element of that mark;

  (g) a lesser degree of similarity between the goods or services may be offset by a great degree of similarity between the marks, and vice versa;[116]

---

[114] Quoted by the ECJ at Case C-361/04 P *Ruiz-Picasso and Others v OHIM* [2006] ETMR 29, para 11.
[115] *Roger Maier, Assos of Switzerland SA v ASOS Plc, ASOS.com Ltd* [2015] ETMR 26, para 75.
[116] *32Red Plc v WHG (International) Ltd* [2012] EWCA Civ 19.

(h) there is a greater likelihood of confusion where the earlier mark has a highly distinctive character, either per se or because of the use that has been made of it;

(i) mere association, in the strict sense that the later mark brings the earlier mark to mind, is not sufficient;

(j) the reputation of a mark does not give grounds for presuming a likelihood of confusion simply because of a likelihood of association in the strict sense;

(k) if the association between the marks causes the public to wrongly believe that the respective goods [or services] come from the same or economically-linked undertakings, there is a likelihood of confusion.

Marks with a reputation

Sections 5(3) and 10(3) TMA 1994 (as amended); Articles 5(3)(a) and 10(2)(c) TMD 2015 (formerly Arts 4(3) and 5(2) TMD 2008); Articles 8(5) and 9(2)(c) EUTMR 2017 (formerly Arts 8(5) and 9(1)(c) CTMR 2009)

15.59   The third and final relative ground for refusal of a trade mark discussed in detail in this chapter can be found at section 5(3) TMA 1994 (as amended). Section 5(3) provides that a trade mark which is identical with or similar to an earlier trade mark shall not be registered if, or to the extent that:

> the earlier trade mark has a reputation in the United Kingdom (or, in the case of a European Union trade mark . . . , in the European Union) and the use of the later mark without due cause would take unfair advantage of, or be detrimental to, the distinctive character or the repute of the earlier trade mark.

Section 10(3) TMA 1994 (as amended) provides that a person infringes a registered trade mark if he uses in the course of trade, in relation to goods or services, a sign which is identical with or similar to the trade mark:

> where the trade mark has a reputation in the United Kingdom and the use of the sign, being without due cause, takes unfair advantage of, or is detrimental to, the distinctive character or the repute of the trade mark.

See also Articles 5(3)(a) and 10(2)(c) TMD 2015 and Articles 8(5) and 9(2)(c) EUTMR 2017.

15.60   According to Recital 10 TMD 2015, the purpose of these provisions is to provide 'extensive protection' to trade marks which have a reputation. These grounds of refusal and infringement were originally optional for member states to choose whether or not to implement them in their national laws. Most member states (including the UK) did enact them and they have now been made mandatory by the TMD 2015, as part of the EU trade mark reform package. When first enacted, the inclusion of these provisions in the Trade Marks Act 1994 marked a very significant departure from pre-harmonisation UK trade mark law. Sections 5(3) and 10(3) TMA 1994 are no longer underpinned by the classic 'anti-confusion' rationale for registered trade mark protection. Instead, sections 5(3) and 10(3) TMA 1994 mark a major move towards protecting the reputation associated with a registered trade mark and the investment made by the trade mark owner in promoting positive brand messages through the mark. The origins of this 'extended' form of trade mark protection are often traced to a seminal article by the American writer Frank Schechter and the subsequent enactment of 'anti-dilution' protection in US trade mark law.[117] At the European level, it is also traced to pre-harmonisation developments in German and other national laws.[118] The theoretical justification for this extended form of protection is, however, by no means settled

---

[117]   F Schechter, 'The rational basis of trademark protection' (1926–27) 40 Harv L Rev 813.

[118]   See, eg, I Simon Fhima, 'Exploring the roots of European dilution' (2012) 1 IPQ 25–38.

and there remains debate over whether the acts caught by these infringement provisions do, in fact, cause harm or are such as to merit infringement liability.[119]

 Question

Read F Schechter, 'The Rational Basis of Trademark Protection' (1926–27) 40 Harv L Rev 813. What is your view on whether 'extended' protection is justified for marks with a reputation? Come back to this question and revisit your answer after you have considered the detailed requirements and case law which has developed on these grounds of refusal and infringement. Do you think that this area of the law has a sound conceptual basis?

15.61   As originally enacted, these grounds of refusal and infringement applied only in respect of goods or services which were *not* similar to those for which the earlier trade mark was registered. This seemed counterintuitive: if the interests of the trade mark proprietor could be damaged by infringing use in relation to *dissimilar* goods or services, why not where the goods or services were the same or similar?

In early case law in *Davidoff & Cie SA v Gofkid*,[120] the ECJ addressed this, holding that these provisions applied not only when the contested goods or services were dissimilar but also where those goods or services were similar or identical to those for which the earlier mark was registered.

The Court noted that these provisions allowed stronger protection to be given to marks with a reputation than the protection conferred on other registered marks.[121] Although the legislative text referred (at the time) only to dissimilar goods and services, in the Court's view the overall scheme and objectives of the Directive required that marks with a reputation could not be left with less protection against uses for identical or similar goods than for dissimilar goods.[122] The Court re-affirmed this decision in *Adidas-Salomon AG and Adidas Benelux BV v Fitnessworld*.[123]

The wording of the 1994 Act was amended to bring it in line with the *Davidoff* decision not long after.[124] The relevant provisions of the TMD 2015 and EUTMR 2017 are now also explicitly stated to apply whether the contested goods or services are identical, similar, or dissimilar to those for which the earlier mark is registered.[125]

15.62   Returning to the provisions of the TMA 1994 (as amended), it will be seen that the requirements of sections 5(3) and 10(3) are that:

- the registered mark relied upon must have 'a reputation'; and
- the use of the later mark 'without due cause' would
  - take unfair advantage of; or
  - be detrimental to
- the distinctive character or the repute of the earlier trade mark.

The different types of harm, taking unfair advantage of distinctiveness or repute and causing detriment to distinctive character or repute, are alternative rather than cumulative conditions.[126]

---

[119] See, eg, G. Dinwoodie, 'Dilution as unfair competition: European echoes' in R Dreyfuss and J Ginsburg (eds), *Intellectual Property at the Edge: The Contested Contours of IP* (CUP 2014); I Simon Fhima, 'Dilution by blurring—a conceptual roadmap' (2010) 1 IPQ 44–87; M Senftleben, 'The trademark Tower of Babel—dilution concepts in international, US and EC trademark law' (2009) 40(1) IIC 45–77.

[120] Case C-292/00 *Davidoff & Cie SA and Zino Davidoff SA v Gofkid Ltd* [2003] ETMR 42.   [121] ibid, para 19.

[122] ibid, paras 23–25.

[123] Case C-408/01 *Adidas-Salomon AG, Adidas Benelux BV v Fitnessworld Trading Ltd* [2004] ETMR 10.

[124] Trade Marks (Proof of Use, etc.) Regulations 2004 (SI 2004/946).

[125] Arts 5(3)(a) and 10(2)(c) TMD 2015; Arts 8(5) and 9(2)(c) EUTMR 2017.

[126] Case C-252/07 *Intel Corporation Inc v CPM United Kingdom Ltd* [2009] ETMR 13, para 28.

'Reputation'

15.63   How well known does the registered mark have to be in order to have a 'reputation' for the purposes of these provisions? The ECJ considered this question in relation to national registered trade marks in *General Motors Corp v Yplon SA*.[127] The Court held that a mark had a 'reputation' if it was *known by a significant part of the public concerned by the product or services covered by that trade mark*.[128] Depending on the goods or services in question, the relevant public could consist of the public at large or a more specialised public, such as traders operating in a specific sector.[129] In assessing reputation, a national court should take into account all relevant facts, including the market share held by the trade mark, the intensity, geographical extent, and duration of its use, and the size of the investment made in promoting it.[130] It did not need to be shown that the mark had a reputation throughout the whole of the territory of the relevant member state: it was sufficient for it to have a reputation in a 'substantial part' of that territory.[131] Altogether, this case law sets perhaps a lower threshold for proof of reputation than might have been expected (certainly lower than the 'fame' requirement for anti-dilution protection in US law) and one which can be met even by proof of 'niche reputation' in a limited field.

15.64   In *Pago v Tirolmilch*, the CJEU considered how the requirement for a 'reputation' should apply to EU trade marks.[132] Under the EUTMR 2017, an EU trade mark is required to have a reputation 'in the Union' (formerly, 'Community').[133] The CJEU was asked whether it was sufficient for this purpose to have a reputation in one member state only. On the facts of the case referred, the mark had a reputation in Austria. The Court responded that reputation was required 'in a substantial part of the territory of the Community'.[134] Somewhat obliquely, the Court added 'in view of the facts of the main proceedings' the territory of the Member State in question (ie Austria) could be considered sufficient.[135]

15.65   This ruling been criticised for leaving the position uncertain. Setting the threshold requirement for reputation for EU trade marks in this way also leaves very much open the possibility that an EU trade mark may be said to have a reputation throughout the requisite part of the territory of the EU without actually being able to demonstrate such reputation in certain member states in which the EU trade mark may be enforced. On this issue, the Court of Justice has held that, if the owner of an EU trade mark can prove that his mark has a reputation in a substantial part of the Union, there will be no bar to opposing a later-filed application, even if the mark's reputation is not in the particular EU member state where that application was filed.[136] The Court has also held that, even if the earlier mark is not known to a sufficient part of the relevant public in that particular EU member state such as to be said to have a reputation there, 'it is conceivable that a commercially significant part of the latter may be familiar with it and make a connection between that mark and the later national mark'.[137]

Establishing a 'link'

15.66   Unlike sections 5(2) and 10(2) of the TMA 1994, under sections 5(3) and 10(3) TMA 1994 there is no requirement for a likelihood of confusion on the part of the public before registration is refused or infringement can occur.[138] A crucial point developed through Court of Justice case law, however, is that the

---

[127]   Case C-375/97 *General Motors Corporation v Yplon SA* [1999] ETMR 950.   [128]   ibid, para 26.   [129]   ibid, para 24.

[130]   ibid, para 28.

[131]   ibid, para 28. In the instant case, that might consist of a part of one of the countries (Benelux) comprising that territory: ibid, para 31. It is, however, not enough for a national mark to have a 'reputation' if it is only known in a city and surrounding area: Case C-328/06 *Nieto Nuno v Fraquet* [2008] ETMR 12.

[132]   Case C-301/07 *Pago International GmbH v Tirolmilch Registrierte Genossenschaft mbH* [2010] ETMR 5.

[133]   Articles 8(5) and 9(2)(c) EUTMR 2017.

[134]   Case C-301/07 *Pago International GmbH v Tirolmilch Registrierte Genossenschaft mbH* [2010] ETMR 5, para 30.   [135]   ibid, para 30.

[136]   Case C-125/14 *Iron & Smith kft v Unilever NV* [2015] ETMR 45, paras 15–25. The use of a mark in only two EU countries, the UK and Italy, was sufficient to prove that the relevant mark had a reputation in a substantial part of the EU, even though there was no evidence of reputation in Hungary where the dispute was proceeding.

[137]   ibid, para 30.

[138]   Case C-408/01 *Adidas-Salomon AG, Adidas Benelux BV v Fitnessworld Trading Ltd* [2004] ETMR 10, para 27. Some confusion arose in an early English case, *Baywatch Production Co Inc v Home Video Channel* [1997] FSR 22, where it was wrongly suggested that likelihood of confusion was an essential element for infringement of this subsection.

relevant section of the public must establish a *link* between the sign and the earlier mark with a reputation, albeit without being confused. As the Court put it in *Adidas v Fitnessworld*, referring to what was then Article 5(2) of the Directive:[139]

> The infringements referred to in Art 5(2) of the Directive, where they occur, are the consequence of a certain degree of similarity between the mark and the sign, by virtue of which the relevant section of the public makes a connection between the sign and the mark, that is to say, establishes a link between them even though it does not confuse them.

15.67 The existence of such a link is to be assessed globally, taking into account all relevant factors.[140] In the later case of *Intel*,[141] the ECJ spent some time elaborating on the assessment of this 'link' between mark and sign. The Court explained that, in the absence of such a link in the mind of the public, use of the later sign is not likely to take advantage of or be detrimental to the distinctive character or the repute of the earlier mark.[142] Addressing the issues in the context of a relative grounds objection (but in terms which apply equally to infringement cases), it said that the factors to be taken into account include:

- the degree of similarity between the conflicting marks. The more similar they are, the more likely it is that the later mark will bring the earlier mark with a reputation to the mind of the relevant public. But even if they are identical or very similar, that is not enough per se to establish a link;[143]

- the nature of the goods or services for which the conflicting marks are registered, including the degree of closeness or dissimilarity between those goods or services and the relevant section of the public. The marks may be registered for goods or services in respect of which the relevant publics do not overlap, in which case a link may not be established. Equally, if the goods or services are so dissimilar, the mark with a reputation may not be brought to mind;[144]

- the strength of the earlier mark's reputation. If it has a very strong reputation, that reputation may go well beyond the relevant public for the goods and services for which it is registered, such that a link will be established even where the relevant public for the later mark is wholly distinct;[145]

- the degree of the earlier mark's distinctive character, whether inherent or acquired through use. The stronger a mark, the more likely it is that the relevant public will call it to mind when confronted with a later identical or similar mark. If the mark is unique, the distinctive character will be stronger;[146]

- the existence of the likelihood of confusion on the part of the public. If confusion is established, then a link is necessarily established (although confusion is not, as noted in para 15.66, actually required).[147]

Overall, the fact that an average consumer would 'call the earlier mark to mind' is tantamount to the existence of a link.[148] Note, however, that the existence of a link by itself is not enough: one of the relevant harms (unfair advantage or detriment to distinctive character or repute) must be shown.[149]

15.68 In *Adidas v Fitnessworld*,[150] Adidas complained of the use by Fitnessworld of a motif consisting of two parallel stripes on clothing. It was argued that the two-stripe motif would be seen merely as an 'embellishment' of the relevant goods. The Court held that it was for the national court to decide, as a finding of fact, whether the relevant public would view the sign purely as an embellishment (and nothing further) or whether, notwithstanding that the sign might be viewed as an embellishment, the relevant 'link' with Adidas's registered three-stripe mark would also be established.[151] In the UK case *Whirlpool Corporation v Kenwood Ltd*,[152] Whirlpool tried to get Kenwood to change the design of its mixers shown in Figure 15.8 on the basis of its (Whirlpool's) EU trade mark shown in Figure 15.7.

[139] Case C-408/01 *Adidas-Salomon AG, Adidas Benelux BV v Fitnessworld Trading Ltd* [2004] ETMR 10, para 29.
[140] ibid, para 30.
[141] Case C-252/07 *Intel Corporation Inc v CPM United Kingdom Ltd* [2009] ETMR 13.   [142] ibid, para 31.
[143] ibid, paras 42 and 44–45.   [144] ibid, paras 42 and 46–49.   [145] ibid, paras 42 and 51–53.
[146] ibid, paras 42 and 54–56.   [147] ibid, paras 42 and 57–58.   [148] ibid, para 60.
[149] ibid, para 32.   [150] Case C-408/01 *Adidas-Salomon AG, Adidas Benelux BV v Fitnessworld Trading Ltd* [2004] ETMR 10.
[151] ibid, paras 39–40.
[152] *Whirlpool Corporation v Kenwood Ltd* [2008] EWHC 1930 (Ch), case aff'd on appeal [2009] EWCA Civ 753.

Figure 15.7 Whirlpool EU trade mark no 2174761

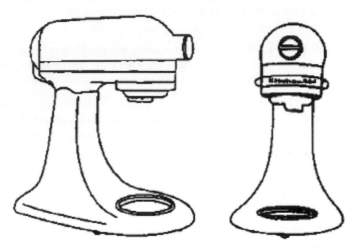

Figure 15.8 Kenwood kMix mixer

The High Court concluded that there was 'enough similarity between the bodywork of the kMix and that of the Artisan for each to remind people of the other whilst leaving them aware that the one they are looking at is not the one it reminds them of'.[153] However, the High Court concluded that there was no unfair advantage or relevant detriment caused.

The three types of relevant injury

15.69   If a trade mark owner can demonstrate the necessary reputation and 'link' between his mark and the later application or allegedly infringing sign, he must then demonstrate one of the types of injury stipulated in sections 5(3) and 10(3) TMA 1994. As noted in para 15.62, just one of these types of injury—taking unfair advantage, detriment to the reputation, or detriment to distinctive character—is needed.[154] The injury must be shown to exist or that there is 'a serious likelihood that such an injury will occur in the future'.[155] This must be assessed globally, taking into account all relevant circumstances.

Detriment to reputation: tarnishment

15.70   A mark can be *tarnished* where the use of the later sign is detrimental to its reputation. An example might be by using a phonetically similar word for a household cleaner as is registered for an expensive alcoholic beverage[156] or the same word as is registered for financial services for condoms.[157]

15.71   In *L'Oréal v Bellure*,[158] the ECJ said:[159]

> As regards detriment to the repute of the mark, also referred to as 'tarnishment' or 'degradation', such detriment is caused when the goods or services for which the identical or similar sign is used by the third party may be perceived by the public in such a way that the trade mark's power of attraction is reduced. The likelihood of such detriment may arise in particular from the fact that the goods or services offered by the third party possess a characteristic or a quality which is liable to have a negative impact on the image of the mark.

In the UK, Arnold J said in *Red Bull v Sun Mark*:[160]

> Detrimental effect occurs where the later mark is used for goods or services which provoke a reaction of annoyance or displeasure, whether through their intrinsic nature or because of the unpleasant mental association with the goods for which the earlier mark is reputed . . . It may also occur when the trade mark applied for is used in an unpleasant, obscene or degrading context, or in a context which is not inherently unpleasant but which process to be incompatible with the earlier mark's image.

The essence is that the mark with the reputation ceases to convey desirable messages to the public.

15.72   More recently a Spanish company's use of the name 'CRISTALINO' for its cava sparkling wine was held not to tarnish a champagne producer's UK and EU trade marks for 'CRISTAL' used for its premium brand champagne.[161] The judge in the High Court concluded that it would be a step forward in the law to say that tarnishment was found simply because use was in connection with cheaper goods.[162]

Detriment to distinctive character: blurring

15.73   Detriment to distinctive character was considered by the ECJ in *Intel*. The Court said:[163]

> As regards . . . detriment to the distinctive character of the earlier mark, also referred to as 'dilution', 'whittling away' or 'blurring', such detriment is caused when that mark's ability to identify the goods or services for which it is registered and used as coming from the proprietor of that mark is weakened, since use of the later mark

---

[153] ibid, para 80.   [154] Case C-252/07 *Intel Corporation Inc v CPM United Kingdom Ltd* [2009] ETMR 13, para 28.
[155] ibid, para 68.   [156] *Claeryn v Klarein* (1976) 7 IIC 420, Nederlandse Jurisprudentie 1975, 472.
[157] *CA Sheimer (M) Sdn Bhd's Trade Mark Application* [2000] RPC 484 (VISA for condoms and contraceptive devices).
[158] Case C-487/07 *L'Oréal SA v Bellure NV* [2009] ETMR 55.   [159] ibid, para 40.
[160] [2013] ETMR 53 para 93, quoting *Kerly's Law of Trade Marks and Trade Names* (15th edn) at paras 9–131.
[161] *Champagne Louis Roederer SA v J Garcia Carrion SA* [2015] ETMR 51.
[162] ibid, para 90. However, there was dilution and unfair advantage.
[163] Case C-252/07 *Intel Corporation Inc v CPM United Kingdom Ltd* [2009] ETMR 13, para 29.

leads to dispersion of the identity and hold upon the public mind of the earlier mark. That is notably the case when the earlier mark, which used to arouse immediate association with the goods or services for which it is registered, is no longer capable of doing so.

It is irrelevant whether the proprietor of the later mark does, or does not, gain any commercial benefit from the distinctive character of the earlier mark.[164] However, in *Intel* the ECJ has set a relatively stringent further requirement, stipulating that evidence is needed of a 'change in the economic behaviour of the average consumer of the goods or services for which the earlier mark was registered consequent on the use of the later mark, or a serious likelihood that such a change will occur in the future'.[165] The Court has stressed that this is an objective condition, which cannot be inferred solely from subjective elements such as consumer perception: the mere fact that consumers note the presence of the allegedly infringing sign is not sufficient.[166]

15.74   That said, the Court has also acknowledged that the trade mark proprietor is entitled to act before 'total loss of the trade mark's distinctive character' has taken place: he is entitled to act against all relevant uses which reduce the distinctiveness of the mark 'without . . . being required to wait for the end of the process of dilution'.[167] Causing detriment to distinctive character may include where the contested use of the mark contributes to turning it into a generic name.[168] In *Interflora v Marks & Spencer*, it was argued that the registration by Marks & Spencer of the 'Interflora' keyword caused detriment in this way. However, the CJEU did not agree that detriment to distinctive character by 'genericide' would necessarily always be the result of such action. Instead, the Court held:[169]

> when the use, as a keyword, of a sign corresponding to a trade mark with a reputation triggers the display of an advertisement which enables the reasonably well-informed and reasonably observant internet user to tell that the goods or services offered originate not from the proprietor of the trade mark but, on the contrary, from a competitor of that proprietor, the conclusion will have to be that the trade mark's distinctiveness has not been reduced by that use, the latter having merely served to draw the internet user's attention to the existence of an alternative product or service to that of the proprietor of the trade mark.

It was for the national court to assess what would be understood by the reasonably well-informed and reasonably observant internet user and to determine, on the basis of all the evidence, whether the keywords had such an impact on the market for flower-delivery services that the word 'Interflora' had come to designate, in the consumer's mind, any flower-delivery service.[170]

 Question

How easy do you think it would be to go about proving a change, or likely future change, in the economic behaviour of consumers as a result of trade mark dilution?

Unfair advantage

15.75   The 'unfair advantage' limb of sections 5(3) and 10(3) TMA 1994 is perhaps the most controversial of all of the forms of extended protection for marks with a reputation. It is notable that there is no equivalent provision in US anti-dilution laws. The leading case on 'unfair advantage' is the judgment of the Court of Justice in *L'Oréal v Bellure*.[171] This aspect of the dispute (separate to the price comparison lists discussed at paragraph 15.33 above) concerned various L'Oréal registered trade marks relating to the packaging and bottles of their perfumes (see, eg, Figure 15.9). Bellure's 'look-alike' packaging was said by the English High Court to 'wink at' the L'Oréal packaging (see, eg, Figure 15.10).[172]

---

[164] ibid, para 78.   [165] ibid, para 77.   [166] Case C-383/12 P *Environmental Manufacturing LLP v OHIM*, para 37.
[167] Case C-323/09 *Interflora Inc, Interflora British Unit v Marks & Spencer Plc, Flowers Direct Online Ltd* [2012] ETMR 1, para 77.
[168] ibid, para 79.   [169] ibid, para 81.   [170] ibid, paras 82–83.
[171] Case C-487/07 *L'Oréal SA v Bellure NV* [2009] ETMR 55.   [172] *L'Oréal SA v Bellure NV* [2007] ETMR 1.

Figure 15.9 Examples of L'Oréal registered marks

Figure 15.10 Examples of Bellure products

The questions referred to the Court of Justice included a question on the test for 'unfair advantage'. The Court summed up the notion of unfair advantage saying:[173]

> As regards the concept of 'taking unfair advantage of the distinctive character or the repute of the trade mark', also referred to as 'parasitism' or 'free-riding', that concept relates not to the detriment caused to the mark but to the advantage taken by the third party as a result of the use of the identical or similar sign. It covers, in particular, cases where, by reason of a transfer of the image of the mark or of the characteristics which it projects to the goods identified by the identical or similar sign, there is clear exploitation on the coat-tails of the mark with a reputation.

The Court also confirmed that the taking of unfair advantage is an actionable ground of infringement in its own right, not tied to detriment to the distinctive character or repute of the mark:[174]

> an advantage taken by a third party of the distinctive character or the repute of the mark may be unfair, even if the use of the identical or similar sign is not detrimental either to the distinctive character or to the repute of the mark or, more generally, to its proprietor.

[173] Case C-487/07 *L'Oréal SA v Bellure NV* [2009] ETMR 55, para 41.
[174] ibid, para 43. The Court of Justice also considered unfair advantage in the context of the price comparison lists: paras 66–80.

15.76   There is therefore no requirement for damage to the proprietor of the mark under this head. The focus is on the benefit to the free-rider, rather than on the detriment to the trade mark owner. The important factor in unfair advantage is the advantage gained by the unauthorised user of the sign.[175]

> The advantage arising from the use by a third party of a sign similar to a mark with a reputation is an advantage taken unfairly by that third party of the distinctive character or the repute of the mark where that party seeks by that use to ride on the coat-tails of the mark with a reputation in order to benefit from the power of attraction, the reputation, and the prestige of that mark and to exploit, without paying any financial compensation, the marketing effort expended by the proprietor of the mark in order to create and maintain the mark's image.

To determine whether the use of a sign takes unfair advantage of the distinctive character or repute of a mark, a global assessment must be undertaken which takes into account all factors relevant to the circumstances of the case including the strength of the mark's reputation, the degree of distinctive character of the mark, the similarity between the marks in issue, and the nature and degree of proximity between the goods or services.[176]

 Question

Describe in your own words what you understand to be meant by 'unfair advantage'. Why is this provision included in EU trade mark law? What does it mean for the scope of the monopoly conferred by a trade mark?

15.77   The CJEU's decision in *Bellure* was felt by many to be quite broad-brush, with little attempt to identify specifically what might make a third party competitor's advantage 'unfair'. However, the CJEU has since refined its approach in its more recent 'Adwords' case law in *Interflora v Marks & Spencer*, with greater emphasis on the issue of fairness and on the potential benefits for consumers in the marketplace which some third party conduct may bring about.

■ Case C-323/09 *Interflora Inc, Interflora British Unit v Marks & Spencer Plc, Flowers Direct Online Ltd* [2012] ETMR 1

In *Interflora*, in addition to the arguments under what is now Article 10(2)(a) TMD infringement was also claimed under what is now Article 10(2)(c) TMD 2015. The issue was whether Marks & Spencer's registration of the 'Interflora' keyword took unfair advantage for infringement purposes. The CJEU held that, when a competitor of the proprietor of a trade mark with a reputation selected that trade mark as a keyword in an internet referencing service, the purpose was to take advantage of the registered mark's distinctive character and repute. If internet users, having looked at the competitor's advertisement, purchased the product or service offered by the competitor instead of that of the proprietor of the trade mark to which their search originally related, then the competitor also derived a real advantage from the distinctive character and repute of the trade mark. Given that the advertiser did not, as a general rule, pay the trade mark proprietor any compensation in respect of that use, in the absence of 'due cause', such use could fall within the scope of what was then Article 9(1)(c) CTMR.[177]

The advantage obtained would be particularly likely to be regarded as unfair if the goods offered via the Adwords service were imitations of those sold under the registered trade mark.[178] However, this would not necessarily be the case where the goods were instead being offered simply as alternatives:[179]

---

[175] ibid, para 50.   [176] ibid, para 44.
[177] Case C-323/09 *Interflora Inc, Interflora British Unit v Marks & Spencer Plc, Flowers Direct Online Ltd* [2012] ETMR 1, paras 86–89.
[178] ibid, para 90.   [179] ibid, para 91.

where the advertisement displayed on the internet on the basis of a keyword corresponding to a trade mark with a reputation puts forward—without offering a mere imitation of the goods or services of the proprietor of that trade mark, without causing dilution or tarnishment and without, moreover, adversely affecting the functions of the trade mark concerned—an alternative to the goods or services of the proprietor of the trade mark with a reputation, it must be concluded that such use falls, as a rule, within the ambit of fair competition in the sector for the goods or services concerned and is thus not without 'due cause'.

This was for the national court to assess.

15.78 An example of a recent 'unfair advantage' decision can be found in *Future Enterprises Pte Ltd v EUIPO/ McDonald's*.[180] Future Enterprises applied to register the word mark 'MACCOFFEE' as an EU trade mark in relation to foodstuffs and drinks in classes 29, 30, and 32. This application was opposed by McDonald's on the basis of a large collection of earlier EU trade marks, including 'McDONALD's', 'McMUFFIN', 'McFLURRY', 'CHICKEN McNUGGETS', and 'McFEAST'. It was held that the mark applied for and these earlier marks differed visually, but had a certain degree of phonetic and conceptual similarity. The McDonald's marks constituted a 'family' of marks and the relevant public would establish a link between the mark applied for and that family of marks. The General Court upheld the EUIPO Board of Appeal's finding that it was highly likely that the mark applied for 'rode on the coat-tails' of the McDonald's marks.

'Due cause'

15.79 Finally, even if one of the relevant injuries can be shown, in order to successful make out a claim under sections 5(3) or 10(3) TMA 1994 the use of the allegedly infringing sign must be without *due cause*. Until recently, this criterion seemed somewhat overlooked in the CJEU's case law. The first case to address the requirement with any degree of substance was *Interflora v Marks & Spencer*. As noted in para 15.77, in this case the CJEU turned to the concept of 'due cause' in its discussion of 'unfair advantage', linking the notion of 'due cause' to the question of what was, or was not, 'fair competition' in the sector for the relevant goods or services concerned.[181]

15.80 The concept of 'due cause' has now been considered more fully by the CJEU in *Leidseplein Beheer BV v Red Bull GmbH*.[182] In this case, the CJEU has continued to take a relatively expansive approach to 'due cause', attributing to it an important role in moderating the overall impact of the extended protection conferred on marks with a reputation. Red Bull owned a Benelux trade mark registration for the word and figurative mark 'Red Bull Krating-Daeng', dating from July 1983. Before Red Bull had filed this mark, a Mr de Vries had been using the sign 'The Bulldog' for hotel, restaurant, and café services involving the sale of drinks. Mr de Vries subsequently registered various Benelux marks for 'The Bulldog', including a word and figurative mark 'The Bulldog Energy Drink', in respect of non-alcoholic drinks in class 32. Red Bull sued Mr de Vries for trade mark infringement. The Amsterdam Regional Court of Appeal found in favour of Red Bull, holding that the mark 'Red Bull Krating-Daeng' had a reputation in the Benelux and that Mr de Vries was taking advantage of that reputation in relation to energy drinks. The fact that Mr de Vries had previously used the mark 'The Bulldog' hotel, restaurant, and café services was not considered to constitute 'due cause' such as to avoid infringement. Mr de Vries appealed and the Netherlands Supreme Court referred to the CJEU the question of whether there could be 'due cause' where the allegedly infringing sign was already being used in good faith by the alleged infringer before the mark with the reputation relied upon against him had been filed. Red Bull argued that 'due cause' only covered objectively overriding reasons, but the CJEU disagreed. According to the Court:[183]

[180] Case T-518/13 *Future Enterprises Pte Ltd v European Union Intellectual Property Office (EUIPO)/McDonald's International Property Co Ltd* [2016] ETMR 41.
[181] Case C-323/09 *Interflora Inc, Interflora British Unit vs Marks & Spencer plc, Flowers Direct Online Ltd* [2012] ETMR 1, para 91.
[182] Case C-65/12 *Leidseplein Beheer BV, Hendrikus De Vries v Red Bull GmbH, Red Bull Nederland BV* [2014] ETMR 24.
[183] ibid, para 46.

the concept of 'due cause' is intended, not to resolve a conflict between a mark with a reputation and a similar sign which was being used before that trade mark was filed or to restrict the rights which the proprietor of that mark is recognised as having, but to strike a balance between the interests in question by taking account, in the specific context of Art 5(2) of Directive 89/104 and in the light of the enhanced protection enjoyed by that mark, of the interests of the third party using that sign. In so doing, the claim by a third party that there is due cause for using a sign which is similar to a mark with a reputation cannot lead to the recognition, for the benefit of that third party, of the rights connected with a registered mark, but rather obliges the proprietor of the mark with a reputation to tolerate the use of the similar sign.

It followed that 'due cause' may 'not only include objectively overriding reasons but may also relate to the subjective interests of a third party using a sign which is identical or similar to the mark with a reputation'.[184] In order to assess 'due cause', a national court should consider two factors: first, how long the allegedly infringing sign had been accepted by, and what its reputation was, with the relevant public; and second, the intention of the person using the allegedly infringing sign. As regards the latter, in order to determine whether the use of the allegedly infringing sign was in good faith, it was necessary to take account of the degree of proximity between goods covered by the registered mark and the goods and services for which the allegedly infringing sign has been used. It was also necessary to have regard to when the allegedly infringing sign was first used for a product identical to that for which that mark was registered, and when that mark acquired its reputation. Where the allegedly infringing sign had been in prior use in relation to services and goods which may be linked to the product covered by the registered mark, the use of the allegedly infringing sign in relation to that latter product could appear to be a natural extension of the range of services and goods for which that sign already enjoyed a certain reputation with the relevant public, rather than an attempt to take advantage of the reputation of the registered mark.[185]

> **Discussion point**   For answer guidance visit **www.oup.com/uk/brown5e**.
>
> In what other circumstances can you envisage the test of 'due cause' being used in the interests of fair competition? Do you think that the concept of 'due cause' is a satisfactory way of placing boundaries on the scope of the trade mark monopoly?

> ## Key points on trade marks with a reputation
>
> - These provisions extend to marks with a 'reputation' (defined in Court of Justice case law) and protect the extended functions of a mark. These provisions are engaged whether the allegedly infringing goods or services are the same as, similar to, or dissimilar to those covered by the reputated trade mark registration.
> - No consumer confusion is required.
> - The public must establish a link between the mark with the reputation and the application or allegedly infringing sign.
> - The trade mark owner must also show one of the relevant types of injury: unfair advantage or detriment to the distinctive character or repute of his mark.
> - The use of the later mark must also be without due cause.

---

[184] ibid, para 45.   [185] ibid, paras 53–58.

The principal defences to infringement

Sections 11 and 11A TMA 1994 (as amended); Articles 14 and 17 TMD 2015 (formerly Art 6 TMD 2008); Articles 14 and 127(3) EUTMR 2017 (formerly Art 12 CTMR 2009)

Question

When do you think a registered trade mark should be able to be lawfully used by an unconnected third party? Revisit your views once you have read this section.

15.81   Section 11 TMA 1994 (as amended) sets out the principal defences to registered trade mark infringement. The most important are in section 11(2), which has been amended to reflect changes introduced by the EU trade mark reform package. Section 11(2) TMA 1994 (as amended) provides that a registered trade mark is not infringed by:

(a)   the use by an individual of his own name or address;

(b)   the use of signs or indications which are not distinctive or which concern the kind, quality, quantity, intended purpose, value, geographical origin, the time of production of goods or of rendering of services, or other characteristics of goods or services; or

(c)   the use of the trade mark for the purpose of identifying or referring to goods or services as those of the proprietor of that trade mark, in particular where that use is necessary to indicate the intended purpose of a product or service (in particular, as accessories or spare parts).

All of this is subject to the proviso that the relevant use must be 'in accordance with honest practices in industrial or commercial matters'. See also Article 14 TMD 2015 and Article 14 EUTMR 2017.

15.82   Article 17 TMD 2015 has also introduced new defence to infringement where there is 'non-use' of the registered mark (see also Art 127(3) EUTMR 2017). This is intended to allow the alleged infringer to rely on no-use of the registered mark without having to pursue revocation. New section 11A(1) TMA 1994 (as amended) states that the trade mark owner is 'entitled to prohibit the use of a sign only to the extent that the registration of the trade mark is not liable to be revoked pursuant to section 46(1)(a) or (b) (revocation on basis of non-use) at the date the action for infringement is brought'.

The 'own name' defence

> **Note**
>
> The 2015 trade mark reform package restricts the 'own name' defence only to personal names and addresses of natural persons.

15.83   Before the changes brought about by the EU reform package, section 11(2)(a) TMA 1994 used to refer simply to 'the use by *a person* of his own name or address' (emphasis added). There was much debate as to whether this applied only to individuals (ie natural persons) or also to legal persons such as corporations. On one view, a legal person has a choice as to its name: so the justification for granting a defence to infringement seems rather less. However, Court of Justice case law had established that this defence was available both to individuals and in relation to company and trade names.[186] A key issue in relation to company and trade names was demonstrating compliance with the 'honest commercial practices' proviso.[187]

15.84   The changes effected by the EU reform package now restrict the availability of this defence to natural persons only. It will no longer be possible to rely on the 'own name' defence in respect of a corporate or trading name. The validity of the removal of this defence from corporate entities was challenged (in the context of the EUTMR 2017 in particular) in *Sky Plc v Skykick UK*.[188] The defendants argued that the removal of this defence from corporate entities was contrary to various provisions of the EU Charter of Fundamental Rights, including Article 16 (freedom to conduct business), Article 17 (right to property), Article 20 (equality before the law) and Article 21 (non-discrimination). The claimants countered that the revision effected in the 2015 reform package was simply intended to return the law to the position originally intended by the EU legislators, the intervening Court of Justice case law confirming the availability of the defence to legal persons having been wrong. Initially, Birss J concluded that both parties had an arguable position, but declined to make a pre-trial reference to the CJEU at that time.[189] After trial, it was concluded that the point was not determinative, since the defendants had not acted in accordance with the 'honest commercial practices' proviso. In any event, however, he did not accept that the removal of the defence was contrary to the EU Charter.[190]

Question

Do you support the changes made by the EU trade mark reform package to the availability of the 'own name' defence? Who is advantaged and who is disadvantaged by the changes?

The use of signs or indications which are not distinctive or which concern the characteristics of products

15.85   Before the EU trade mark reform package was implemented, Section 11(2)(b) of the 1994 Act simply referred to 'the use of indications concerning the kind, quality, quantity, intended purpose, value, geographical origin, the time of production of goods or of rendering of services, or other characteristics of goods or services'. This was designed to allow traders to use registered trade marks where they might wish to describe some of the characteristics of their own products or services.

15.86   The ECJ confirmed that, within the scope of section 11(2)(b), a relevant 'indication' must simply concern one of the characteristics set out there.[191] The ECJ also indicated that the use of a geographical indication could fall within the defence even where there was likelihood of aural confusion with a registered mark.

■ **Case C-100/02** *Gerolsteiner Brunnen GmbH & Co v Putsch GmbH* [2004] **RPC 39 (ECJ)**

This case concerned the registered trade mark 'GERRI', registered in relation to non-alcoholic beverages. The defendant marketed bottled drinks bearing the words 'KERRY SPRING' (containing mineral water from Kerry Spring). The owner of the 'GERRI' mark brought trade mark infringement proceedings. It was held that there was a likelihood of confusion between the marks and the case was referred to the ECJ on the question of whether this precluded reliance on the defence at what is now Article 14(1)(b) TMD 2015.

---

[186]   Case C-245/02 *Anheuser-Busch Inc v Budejovicky Budvar NP* [2005] ETMR 27, para 77; Case C-17/06 *Céline Sàrl v Céline SA* [2007] ETMR 80, para 31.

[187]   See most recently, eg, *Maier v Asos Plc* [2015] ETMR 26.

[188]   *Sky Plc v Skykick UK Ltd* [2017] ETMR 42 and [2018] ETMR 23.   [189]   See the case report at [2017] ETMR 42.

[190]   See the case report at [2018] ETMR 23, paras 323–355.

[191]   Case C-100/02 *Gerolsteiner Brunnen GmbH & Co v Putsch GmbH* [2004] ETMR 40, para 19.

The ECJ held that the only relevant test was whether or not the use of the words 'KERRY SPRING' was in accordance with honest practices in industrial or commercial matters: [192]

> The mere fact that there exists a likelihood of aural confusion between a word mark registered in one Member State and an indication of geographical origin from another Member State is therefore insufficient to conclude that the use of that indication in the course of trade is not in accordance with honest practices.

15.87   In *Adam Opel AG v Autec AG*[193] (the toy cars case, discussed at paragraph 15.32) questions were also referred to the ECJ concerning the defence at what is now Article 14(1)(b) TMD 2015. In particular the Court was asked whether affixing the Opel logo, as in the circumstances of the case, could fall within this defence.

The Court noted that, while what is now Article 14(1)(b) TMD 2015 was primarily intended to prevent the owner of a trade mark prohibiting competitors from using one or more descriptive terms forming part of the registered mark to indicate certain characteristics of their products, it was not limited to such a situation.[194] However, in the instant case, the defence did not apply: the affixing of a sign identical to a trade mark registered in respect of models of that make of vehicle in order to reproduce the vehicles was not an indication of the characteristics of the models but rather part of the faithful reproduction of the vehicle.[195]

15.88   In the UK, Henry Bell[196] was able to use the word 'Supreme' in connection with animal foods, as shown in Figure 15.11.

Figure 15.11 Supreme animal food

[192] ibid, para 25.   [193] Case C-48/05 [2007] ETMR 33.   [194] ibid, para 42.   [195] ibid, para 44.
[196] *Supreme Petfoods Ltd v Henry Bell & Co (Grantham) Ltd* [2015] ETMR 20.

This was despite the existence of the trade marks owned by Supreme Petfoods, as shown in Figure 15.12.

Figure 15.12 Supreme Petfoods trade marks

The court found that Bell's use of the sign 'Supreme' was in accordance with honest practices in industrial and commercial matters as the sign was being used as an indication of the quality of the feed.

15.89   The defence at section 11(2)(b) TMA 1994 (as amended) and corresponding provisions of the TMD 2015 and EUTMR 2017 now also cover signs and indications which are non-distinctive, whether or not they relate to relevant 'characteristics' of goods or services. Recital 27 TMD 2015 and Recital 21 EUTMR 2017 explain that the defences 'should further permit the use of descriptive or non-distinctive signs or indications in general'.

The use of the trade mark for the purpose of identifying or referring to goods or services as those of the proprietor of that trade mark, in particular where that use is necessary to indicate the intended purpose of a product or service (in particular, as accessories or spare parts)

15.90   Before the changes brought about by the EU reform package, section 11(2)(c) of the 1994 Act only covered use of an otherwise infringing sign 'necessary to indicate the intended purpose of a product or service (in particular, as accessories or spare parts)'. As noted by the Court of Justice, the objective of this provision was to:[197]

> enable providers of goods or services, which are supplementary to the goods or services offered by a trade mark proprietor, to use that mark in order to inform the public of the practical link between their goods or services and those of the proprietor of the mark.

[197]   Case C-558/08 *Portakabin Ltd v Primakabin BV* [2010] ETMR 52, para 64.

15.91   In *The Gillette Co v LA-Laboratories Ltd Oy*[198] the ECJ had the opportunity to consider the scope of this defence. It noted that the wording on intended purpose was not exhaustive and that the defence was therefore not limited to cases involving accessories or spare parts.[199] The defence also made no distinction between the possible intended purposes of the products.[200]

15.92   The Court of Justice also considered what it meant for use of an otherwise infringing sign to be 'necessary' to indicate intended purpose. In *BMW v Deenik*,[201] it was 'necessary' to use the 'BMW' mark to indicate that the defendant provided specialist BMW repair services, as this could not be communicated without using the registered mark.[202] In *Gillette*, the Court held that use of the otherwise infringing sign would be necessary where the trade mark was used to indicate the intended purpose of a product marketed by the defendant 'where such use in practice constitutes the only means of providing the public with comprehensible and complete information on that intended purpose in order to preserve the undistorted system of competition in the market for that product'.[203]

15.93   In assessing whether the defence is available, the whole circumstances of the case should be considered. If the use of the mark suggests that there is a connection between the third party and the trade mark owner, then the use is likely to be enjoined.

■ *Aktiebolaget Volvo v Heritage (Leicester) Ltd* [2000] FSR 253

Heritage had been an approved Volvo dealer, but that approval had been withdrawn. Heritage became a member of the Association of Independent Volvo Specialists, a group consisting of other motor dealers in the same situation. Heritage replaced a Volvo sign outside its premises with a new sign that read 'Independent Volvo Specialist', the word 'Volvo' being written in larger script than the other two. In addition, Heritage sent letters to customers that failed to indicate the true status of the relationship with Volvo. When challenged, Heritage argued that the use of the word 'Volvo' was necessary to describe the type of service being offered. The High Court found that while the use of the word Volvo was necessary to describe the service, such use had to be in accordance with honest commercial practices in which the *whole* circumstances of the use must be considered. Both the letters and the sign could be seen as deliberate attempts to cause confusion in the minds of its customers by indicating that a trading relationship still existed. The use was therefore *not* an honest use in the context of the motor trade.

15.94   Similarly in *Bayerische Motoren Werke AG v Deenik*,[204] the ECJ stressed that if the use of the mark makes customers believe that there is a commercial connection between that other party and the trade mark owner when in fact this does not exist, then such use would *not* be in accordance with honest commercial practices.

15.95   As a result of the EU's 2015 reform package, this defence has been significantly widened in scope. The principles articulated above will apply, but the defence will now cover all otherwise infringing uses which are for the purpose of 'identifying or referring to goods or services as those of the proprietor of that trade mark'. Recital 26 TMD 2015 and Recital 21 EUTMR 2017 explain that a trade mark proprietor:

> should not be entitled to prevent the fair and honest use of the mark for the purpose of identifying or referring to the goods or services as those of the proprietor.

Section 11(2)(c) TMA 1994 (as amended) and the corresponding provisions of the TMD 2015 and EUTMR 2017 have therefore beome a much broader defence for referential use. This will save from infringement uses of marks such as in comparative advertising.

---

[198]   Case C-228/03 *The Gillette Co v LA-Laboratories Ltd Oy* [2005] ETMR 76.
[199]   ibid, para 32.   [200]   ibid, para 38.
[201]   Case C-63/97 *Bayerische Motoren Werke AG v Deenik* [1999] ETMR 339.   [202]   ibid, para 60.
[203]   Case C-228/03 *The Gillette Co v LA-Laboratories Ltd Oy* [2005] ETMR 76, para 39.
[204]   Case C-63/97 *Bayerische Motoren Werke AG v Deenik* [1999] ETMR 339.

> **Question**
>
> What impact do you think there will be from the widening of this defence to cover referential uses of registered marks? How widely or narrowly do you think this amended defence is likely to be interpreted by the courts?

Honest practices

15.96   As noted at para 15.81, to benefit from the defences at section 11(2) TMA 1994 (as amended) (and Articles 14 TMD 2015 and EUTMR 2017) the defendant's use of the otherwise infringing sign must be 'in accordance with honest practices in industrial or commercial matters'. The ECJ has said that this proviso represents 'a duty to act fairly in relation to the legitimate interests of the trade mark owner'.[205]

15.97   In *The Gillette Co v LA-Laboratories Ltd Oy,*[206] the ECJ had the opportunity to consider what would meet the test of honest practices. Gillette had registered in Finland the trade marks 'Gillette' and 'Sensor' for, inter alia, razors and had marketed razors under this sign comprised of a handle and replaceable blades. LA-Laboratories also sold razors in Finland comprised of a handle and replaceable blades, but under the mark 'Parason Flexor'. This packaging bore a sticker stating: 'All Parason Flexor and Gillette Sensor handles are compatible with this blade.' Gillette objected to this affixing of its trade mark to the packaging. The ECJ confirmed that honest practices constitute a duty to act fairly in relation to the legitimate interests of the trade mark owner. As such, the use of a trade mark would not be in accordance with this test where:

- it is done in such a manner that it may give the impression that there is a commercial connection between the reseller and the trade mark proprietor;[207]

- where the use would affect the value of the trade mark by taking unfair advantage of its distinctive character or repute;[208]

- if the use discredits or denigrates that mark;[209]

- the third party presents its product as an imitation or replica of the product bearing the trade mark of which it is not the owner.[210]

It was for the national court to determine the otherwise infringing use was in accordance with honest practices, taking account of 'the overall presentation of the product marketed by the third party, particularly the circumstances in which the mark of which the third party is not the owner is displayed in that presentation, the circumstances in which a distinction is made between that mark and the mark or sign of the third party, and the effort made by that third party to ensure that consumers distinguish its products from those of which it is not the trade mark owner'.[211]

15.98   This approach to the 'honest commercial practices' proviso seems broadly unobjectionable. However, more recent case law concerning keyword advertising has complicated the position somewhat. In *Portakabin*, the CJEU emphasised that whether the proviso applied was to be assessed by taking account inter alia of:[212]

> the extent to which the use by the third party is understood by the relevant public, or at least by a significant section of that public, as establishing a link between the third party's goods and those of the trade mark proprietor or a person authorised to use the trade mark, and of the extent to which the third party ought to have been aware of that.

---

[205]   ibid, para 61; Case C-100/02 *Gerolsteiner Brunnen GmbH & Co v Putsch GmbH* [2004] ETMR 40, para 24; Case 228/03 *Gillette Co v LA-Laboratories Ltd Oy* [2005] ETMR 67, para 41.

[206]   Case C-228/03 *The Gillette Co v LA-Laboratories Ltd Oy* [2005] ETMR 67.   [207]   ibid, para 42.

[208]   ibid, para 43.   [209]   ibid, para 44.   [210]   ibid, para 45.   [211]   ibid, para 46.

[212]   Case C-558/08 *Portakabin Ltd v Primakabin BV* [2010] ETMR 52, para 67.

However, the Court also noted that there would be infringement of a registered mark under what are now Article 10(2)(a) or (b) TMD 2015 if the allegedly infringing use did not enable normally informed and reasonably attentive internet users, or enabled them only with difficulty to ascertain whether the goods or services referred to by the keyword-triggered ad originated from the trade mark proprietor or from a third party. In the event that this was established, the Court noted that:[213]

> it is unlikely that the advertiser can genuinely claim not to have been aware of the ambiguity thus caused by its ad. It is the advertiser itself, in the context of its professional strategy and with full knowledge of the economic sector in which it operates, which chose a keyword corresponding to another person's trade mark and which, alone or with the assistance of the referencing service provider, designed the ad and therefore decided how it should be presented.

If these conditions were made out, the Court held that the advertiser could not, in principle, claim to have acted in accordance with honest practices in industrial or commercial matters.[214] This seems highly problematic. Essentially, the Court appears to be saying that, if Article 10(2)(a) or (b) TMD 2015 are engaged, it is not possible for the infringer to demonstrate that his use of the relevant sign is in accordance with the honest practices provision. If this is the case, then the sphere of operation of the defences at section 11(2) TMA 1994 and Articles 14 TMD 2015 and EUTMR 2017 is effectively reduced to nil. The CJEU in *Portakabin* did mention that it was 'for the national court to carry out an overall assessment of all the relevant circumstances in order to determine whether there may be evidence to justify a contrary finding'.[215] However, this gives little practical assistance. It seems inherently unlikely that the EU legislators can have intended that the defences at Articles 14 TMD 2015 and EUTMR 2017 be effectively redundant and it is therefore to be hoped that the CJEU will have the opportunity to reconsider the position in due course.

Further considerations in relation to defences

15.99　There has been much discussion about whether the defences to trade mark infringement are adequate.[216] There is particular concern that there are no specific provisions in the TMD 2015 or EUTMR 2017 permitting artistic use or use of marks for criticism, comment, or parody. Some commentators have even suggested that there is a need for a broad 'fair use' defence.[217]

15.100　During the legislative passage of the TMD 2015 and EUTMR 2017, there were moves to further widen the defences to trade mark infringement. The European Parliament attempted specifically to include a parody defence. However, this could not be agreed and no such defence was formally enacted. However, Recital 27 TMD 2015 and Recital 21 EUTMR 2017 do contain the following statements:

> Use of a trade mark by third parties for the purpose of artistic expression should be considered as being fair as long as it is at the same time in accordance with honest practices in industrial and commercial matters. Furthermore, this Directive should be applied in a way that ensures full respect for fundamental rights and freedoms, and in particular the freedom of expression.

It is not clear, at present, how these Recitals will influence the future development of EU trade mark law going forward. On the face of the legislation, an otherwise infringing use will still need to fall within one of the specific grounds at section 11 TMA 1994 (as amended), Article 14 TMD 2015, and Article 14 EUTMR 2017 in order to be saved from infringement. Quite how these cover use 'for the purpose of artistic expression' is not self-evident. It is, however, possible that national courts may be able to bring artistic or parodic uses within, for example, the new broader 'referential use' defence and, in line of the Recitals, find them to be in accordance with honest practices.

---

[213] ibid, para 70.　　[214] ibid, para 71.　　[215] ibid, para 71.

[216] See, eg, M Senftleben et al, 'Recommendation on measures to safeguard freedom of expression and undistorted competition in EU trade mark law' [2015] EIPR 337.

[217] See, eg, LP Ramsay and J Schovsbo, 'Mechanisms for limiting trade mark rights to further competition and free speech' (2013) 44(6) IIC 671–700.

Exercise

For a case heard by the Supreme Court of Appeal in South Africa on matters of dilution, see *Laugh It Off Promotions CC v South African Breweries International (Finance) BV*[218] in which a parody by Laugh It Off Promotions on a T-shirt of Carling Black Label's trade mark was considered. In giving judgment, the Court weighed the right to freedom of speech (the parody of the trade mark) against the intellectual property rights in the mark and considered that placing the onus on the trade mark holder to adduce evidence to prove the likelihood of substantial economic harm as a result of this parody was an appropriate balance of these rights. The court found that harm to the mark had not been proven. Read and summarise the case, which you will find at www.saflii.org/za/cases/ZACC/2005/7.html (you will find images of the T-shirt and of the beer label in the text). Give your opinion of the balance the court found between freedom of expression and trade mark rights.

Key points on the principal defences to an action of infringement

- Each of the principal defences to infringement (own name; use of indications concerning quality, etc; use of a mark to indicate the intended purpose) is subject to the proviso that it must be in accordance with honest practices in industrial or commercial matters.

- These defences have been amended as part of the 2015 trade mark reform package. The 'own name' defence now only applies to natural persons. The defences for use of indications concerning characteristics of the goods or services now includes generally non-distinctive signs or indications as well. The defence for use of a mark to indicate intended purpose has now been widened to a general 'referential use' defence.

- Although it is not clear how they will be applied, the Recitals to the TMD 2015 and EUTMR 2017 also include provision on the use of marks for artistic expression and on fundamental rights and freedoms.

Further reading

Books

I Fhima, *Trade Mark Dilution in Europe and the United States* (2011)

I Fhima and D Gangee, *The Confusion Test in European Trade Mark Law* (2019)

J Phillips (ed), *Trade Marks at the Limit* (2006)

Book chapters

G Dinwoodie, 'Dilution as unfair competition: European echoes' in R Dreyfuss and J Ginsburg (eds), *Intellectual Property at the Edge: The Contested Contours of IP* (CUP 2014)

Articles

R Arnold, 'The CJEU's Article 5(1)(a) jurisprudence: problems and solutions' (Feb 2012) Berichten industriele eigendom 58–63

T Bednarz, 'Keyword advertising before the French Supreme Court and beyond—calm at last after turbulent times for Google and its advertising clients?' (2011) 42(6) IIC 641–72

A Blythe, 'Confusion online: does the test for trade mark confusion on the internet differ from that applied to infringement in other spheres?' (2014) 36(9) EIPR 563–68

---

[218] [2005] FSR 30 (Sup Ct, SA).

A Breitschaft, '*Intel, Adidas* & Co—is the jurisprudence of the European Court of Justice on dilution law in compliance with the underlying rationales and fit for the future?' [2009] EIPR 497

J Davis, 'Revisiting the average consumer: an uncertain presence in European trade mark law' (2015) 1 IPQ 15–30

I Fhima, 'How does "essential function" doctrine drive European trade mark law?' (2005) 36(4) IIC 401–20

I Fhima, 'Nominative use and honest practices in industrial and commercial matters—a very European history' [2007] 2 IPQ 117–47

I Fhima, 'Dilution by blurring—a conceptual roadmap' [2010] 1 IPQ 44–87

I Fhima, 'Exploring the roots of European dilution' [2012] 1 IPQ 25–38

I Fhima, 'Due cause' (2017) 12(11) JIPLP 897–905

I Fhima and C Denvir, 'An empirical analysis of the likelihood of confusion factors in European trade mark law' (2015) 46(3) IIC 310–39

A Griffiths, 'The trade mark monopoly: an analysis of the core zone of absolute protection under Art. 5(1)(a)' [2007] 3 IPQ 312349

A Griffiths, 'Trade mark monopolies in the digital age' (2017) 2 IPQ 123–51

S Harper and D Curley, 'Bubble confusion—the O2 decision' (2006) 28(9) EIPR 499–504

A Kur, 'Trade marks function, don't they? CJEU jurisprudence and unfair competition practices' (2014) 45(4) IIC 434–54

V McEvedy, 'Keywords and resales and other fair and referential uses' [2012] 3 IPQ 149–72

B Pollard and JJ Blum, 'Bimbo and composite trade marks: a review of the European approach to assessing confusion' (2015) 37(1) EIPR 46–50

M Rimmer, 'The black label: trade mark dilution, culture jamming and the no logo movement' (2008) 5(1) SCRIPTed 70, https://papers.ssrn.com/sol3/papers.cfm?abstract_id=868391

M Senftleben, 'The trademark Tower of Babel—dilution concepts in international, US and EC trademark law' (2009) 40(1) IIC 45–77

M Senftleben, 'Function theory and international exhaustion: why it is wise to confine the double identity rule in EU trade mark law to cases affecting the origin function' (2014) 36(8) EIPR 518–24

J Tarawneh, 'A new classification for trade functions' (2016) 4 IPQ 352–70

K Weatherall, 'The Consumer as the Empirical Measure of Trade Mark Law' (2017) 80(1) MLR 57–87

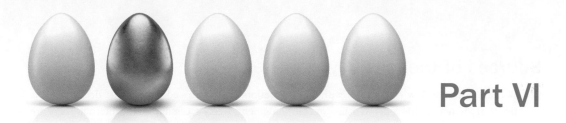

Part VI

Common law protection of intellectual property

Introduction

The various forms of intellectual property discussed in the previous chapters have all had their roots in statute. This Part of the book turns to consider the protection afforded to certain forms of intellectual property which have their base in common law: that is, the law developed in the decisions of the English and Scottish courts. There are two main forms of common law intellectual property (IP) protection: *passing off* and *breach of confidence*. It is important to emphasise that the common law IP rights each have their own independent character and scope. A further point is that English and Scots law in the two fields, while very similar, are not necessarily identical, and may still develop in slightly different ways. It must also be borne in mind that the rights have close relationships with other pieces of legislation, particularly regarding information regulation and human rights, as will be explored in this Part.

Chapter 16 on *passing off* explores the three elements which have classically been taken to amount to the legal wrong—goodwill, misrepresentation, and damage. The chapter then moves to consider extensions to this classical formulation of passing off, taking into account issues such as unfair competition.

Chapter 17 on *breach of confidence* examines the history and basic principles of the law of confidence, with reference to personal information, employment and post-employment scenarios, the relationship between trade secrets and innovation, a balance between the public interests in preserving confidence and in disclosure, and the impact of the Human Rights Act 1998.

These are followed by Chapter 18, which explores *control of information*. This discusses developments within the passing off and breach of confidence frameworks and in some cases beyond them, in particular as combined with human rights, and the consequences for the protection of personal privacy, and also the more commercial implications for the protection and exploitation of publicity and personality. This final section also looks to trade marks.

Sources of the law: key websites

- Because common law rights arise without registration, and are based upon court decisions, it is necessary to refer to the court websites for court judgments freely accessible on the internet. These are most conveniently gathered together on the British and Irish Legal Information website:
www.bailii.org

- Also important in respect of breach of confidence are decisions of the European Court of Human Rights, for which see the court website:
www.echr.coe.int/Pages/home.aspx?p=home

Reference will also be made to the following legislation and instruments:

- Human Rights Act 1998
www.legislation.gov.uk/ukpga/1998/42/contents

- Data Protection Act 2018
www.legislation.gov.uk/ukpga/2018/12/contents

- The European Convention on Human Rights 1950
www.hri.org/docs/ECHR50.html

- TRIPS
www.wto.org/english/tratop_e/trips_e/trips_e.htm

- Paris Convention for the Protection of Industrial Property
www.wipo.int/treaties/en/ip/paris/

Passing off

Introduction

Scope and overview of chapter

16.1   This chapter considers the action of passing off, a means by which one trader may prevent another from misleading customers by representing (or 'passing off') their goods or services as emanating from the claimant. Although conceptually this part of the law is linked to registered trade mark law by offering protection to unregistered trade marks which are nonetheless badges of identity in the marketplace, passing off is different in many important respects.

16.2
> ### Learning objectives
>
> By the end of this chapter you should be able to:
> - define and explain the scope of the action of passing off;
> - define and explain each of the principal elements of passing off, namely, goodwill, misrepresentation, and damage;
> - differentiate passing off from other, closely related aspects of intellectual property protection, such as registered trade marks;
> - understand and explain the role of passing off in the internet context;
> - discuss the relationship between passing off and concepts of unfair competition.

 Passing off and Brexit

The tort of passing off is a common law action and is therefore unlikely to be affected by the withdrawal of the United Kingdom from the European Union.

16.3   After an introductory discussion, the chapter analyses the leading judicial definitions of passing off, from which emerge the key elements of goodwill, misrepresentation, and damage. These elements are then taken in turn for more detailed discussion, and some specific issues are considered. The chapter concludes with discussion of key contemporary issues, in particular in relation to passing off and the internet, and unfair competition. So, the chapter looks like this:

- Overview of passing off (16.4–16.8)
- Definitions (16.9–16.12)
- Goodwill (16.13–16.34)
- Misrepresentation (16.35–16.56)
- Damage (16.57–16.60)
- Defences (16.61)
- The internet, passing off, and instruments of fraud (16.62–16.69)
- Unfair competition and passing off (16.70–16.73).

Overview of passing off

16.4   The action of 'passing off' is well established in the various jurisdictions of the UK, having first developed in English common law and then been received in the early 19th century in the Scottish courts.[1] Today there is little if any difference in the two jurisdictions on the subject. The usual question in passing off actions is whether, in marketing goods or services, one party has employed an identifying device or badge associated in the market with another party or parties. In its most typical form, the action concerns the use of words or names as trade marks:[2]

> The remedy which the law gives to a person who has used a particular name in trade is that he is entitled to prevent others from using the same name in such a way as is likely to mislead the public into thinking that the business or the goods so described is or are the business or goods of the claimant.

However, as long ago as 1842 Lord Langdale MR suggested that the action was of broader scope than merely the misleading use of names:[3]

> A man is not to sell his own goods under the pretence that they are the goods of another man; he cannot be permitted to practise such a deception, nor to use the means which contribute to that end. He cannot therefore be allowed to use names, marks, letters or other indicia, by which he may induce purchasers to believe, that the goods he is selling are the manufacture of another person.

In modern times, the action has been applied to stop a variety of forms of passing off, using not only names, but also a wide variety of other ways in which traders enable customers to identify their products and distinguish them from those of competitors. One way of thinking about passing off is as a form of protection for unregistered trade marks;[4] but the scope of protection offered by the common law extends beyond trade marks as such. This will be seen throughout this chapter, although it should also be borne in mind that passing off and trade marks are often part of the same action, and courts and parties in some cases have acknowledged that on their particular facts, success in a trade mark action would mean that there will also be passing off.[5]

---

[1] See on English law, C Wadlow, *The Law of Passing Off: Unfair Competition by Misrepresentation* (5th edn, 2016); H Carty, *An Analysis of the Economic Torts* (2nd edn, 2010), Ch 8; M Spence, 'Passing off and the misappropriation of valuable intangibles' (1996) 112 LQR 472. On the development of English law, see H Carty, 'The development of passing off in the twentieth century' and C Morcom, 'Leading cases in passing off' both in N Dawson and A Firth (eds), *Trade Marks Retrospective* (2000). For Scots law, see EM Clive, 'The action of passing off: its scope and basis' (1963) JR 117.

[2] *Meikle v Williamson* 1909 2 SLT 169 per Lord Skerrington at 172.

[3] *Perry v Truefitt* (1842) 6 Beav 66 at 73 (49 ER 749 at 752). Note that although Lord Langdale refers only to selling goods, it is clear that passing off also applies to the supply of services. There seems no reason why it should not also apply to the supply of incorporeals and of land and buildings.

[4] Trade Marks Act (TMA) 1994, s 2(2): 'No proceedings lie to prevent or recover damages for the infringement of an unregistered trade mark as such; but nothing in this Act affects the law relating to passing off.'

[5] See *Yell Ltd v Giboin, Zagg Ltd* [2011] EWPCC 009; *Schutz (UK) Ltd v Delta Containers Ltd* [2011] EWHC 1712 (Ch); cf *Westwood v Knight* [2011] EWPCC 8, paras 53–56 and 156; *Specsavers International Healthcare Ltd v Asda Stores Ltd* [2012] ETMR 17, para 9.

Basis of action: goodwill and misrepresentation

16.5   At one time, the right to prevent passing off was thought to arise because the claimant was assumed to have acquired, by exclusive appropriation, a right of property in a marketing device. However, it became unacceptable to suppose that there could be property rights in names or words, or that use alone could create such property rights. In England, the action came to be seen as based on two elements:

- the existence of trading *goodwill* or reputation, the desire of customers to buy from one trader rather than another, which was conceived of as a right of property of the first trader, especially as it had market value in the buying and selling of the business itself;
- the invasion of that right of property by means of a *misrepresentation*.

Marketing devices are an important element in goodwill because their use enables customers to identify the products of particular traders and to distinguish them from those of competitors. The association between device and trader means that use of the device by another trader may mislead the customer, who believes they are obtaining the goods and services of one trader while in fact receiving those of another. The typical injury in passing off is loss of custom to a competitor, while the wrong which leads to the injury is the false statement by the competitor. In Scotland, the action for passing off has been said to be 'based on the general right which everyone possesses not to have published about him or his goods, statements which are both untrue and prejudicial to his pecuniary interests'.[6]

 Question

What are the key concepts in passing off? Consider also the evolving debates on their underlying foundation; see H Carty, 'Passing off: frameworks of liability debated' [2012] IPQ 106. Revisit this issue again at the end of your study of this chapter.

16.6   As a result of its being rooted in the protection of goodwill, passing off is no longer confined to the case of one trader representing their goods as those of another. Wherever there is a misrepresentation damaging goodwill—for example, creating injurious associations in the public mind—there may be a claim for passing off. This is not to say that passing off has become a general law of unfair competition such as is found in various European jurisdictions.

Key points on general development of passing off

- Passing off starts with the idea that one person may not represent their goods or services as those of another and so gain business which should have gone to that other.
- In modern law, passing off is seen as protecting trading goodwill against misrepresentations in general, and this has been a basis for extending the scope of the action considerably.

---

[6]   EM Clive, 'The action of passing off: its scope and basis' (1963) JR 117, 134.

International background

16.7 Since passing off is a long-established common law matter, it has been less affected than other areas of intellectual property by international conventions. But it has been taken, alongside other matters such as consumer protection law, to satisfy the Paris Convention for the Protection of Industrial Property requirement for protection against unfair competition.

Paris Convention Article 10*bis*

(1) The countries of the Union are bound to assure nationals of such countries effective protection against unfair competition.

(2) Any act of competition contrary to honest practices in industrial or commercial matters constitutes an act of unfair competition.

(3) The following in particular shall be prohibited:

1. all acts of such nature as to create confusion by any means whatever with the establishment, the goods, or the industrial or commercial activities, of a competitor;

2. false allegations in the course of trade of such a nature as to discredit the establishment, the goods, or the industrial or commercial activities, of a competitor;

3. indications or allegations the use of which in the course of trade is liable to mislead the public as to the nature, the manufacturing process, the characteristics, the suitability for their purpose, or the quantity, of the goods.

In other countries, particularly in Europe, unfair competition is a civil wrong actionable at the hand of competitors, and is certainly wider in scope than passing off. But as passing off has developed and extended its scope, so questions have been raised as to whether it is itself moving in the direction of an unfair competition action or, indeed, as to whether an unfair competition action should be introduced by statute, to bring the UK closer to its European neighbours. This issue is discussed later in this chapter (paras 16.70ff).

16.8 The Paris Convention also requires the countries of the Union to protect 'well-known' marks from other member countries by refusing or cancelling registrations or, more importantly for passing off, prohibiting their use by way of reproduction, imitation, or translation, when liable to cause confusion.[7] This was implemented in the UK by section 56 of the Trade Marks Act (TMA) 1994, and has had an important effect on the law of passing off, to be discussed further below (para 16.16).

Definitions

16.9 A classical definition of passing off was given in the House of Lords by Lord Oliver in the 'Jif Lemon' case, *Reckitt & Coleman Products v Borden Inc*,[8] when he outlined what had to be shown for a party to succeed in a passing off action as follows:

> *First*, he must establish a *goodwill or reputation* attached to the goods or services which he supplies in the mind of the purchasing public by association with the identifying 'get-up' (whether it consists simply of a brand name or a trade description, or the individual features of labelling or packaging under which his particular goods are offered to the public, such that the get-up is recognised by the public as distinctive specifically of the plaintiff's goods or services. *Second*, he must demonstrate a *misrepresentation* (whether or not intentional) leading or likely to lead the public to believe that goods or services offered by him are the goods or services of the plaintiff. Whether the public is aware of the plaintiff's identity as the manufacturer or supplier of the goods and services is immaterial, as long as they are identified with a particular source which is in fact the plaintiff. For example, if the public is accustomed to rely upon a particular brand name in purchasing goods of a particular description, it matters not at all that there is little or no public awareness of the identity of the proprietor of the brand name.

---

[7] Paris Convention, Art 6*bis*.   [8] [1990] RPC 341, [1990] 1 WLR 491, [1990] 1 All ER 873.

Third, he must demonstrate that he suffers or, in a quia timet action, that he is likely to suffer *damage* by reason of the erroneous belief engendered by the defendant's misrepresentation that the source of the defendant's goods or services is the same as the source of those offered by the plaintiff (emphasis added).

This definition, with its trilogy of *goodwill, misrepresentation,* and *damage*, provides an excellent basic structure for an account of the typical case of passing off, where one trader simply sells goods or services in the guise of another trader's goods or services. Hence, it will be used to provide the principal headings in this chapter.

 Question

What does Lord Oliver add to our list of key passing off concepts (cf para 16.6)?

16.10   But as already mentioned, passing off has extended well beyond the typical case with which it began. While Lord Oliver's three elements remain at the heart of this extension, they require some further elaboration. That can be found in an earlier leading House of Lords case, *Erven Warnink v Townend*,[9] the 'Advocaat' case, still probably the most important decision on the extended version of passing off. Lords Diplock and Fraser gave the following definitions in their speeches.

Lord Diplock said (at 742):

[It is] possible to identify five characteristics which must be present in order to create a valid cause of action for passing off:
(1) a misrepresentation
(2) made by a trader in the course of trade,
(3) to prospective customers of his or ultimate consumers of goods or services supplied by him,
(4) which is calculated to injure the business or goodwill of another trader (in the sense that this is a reasonably foreseeable consequence), and
(5) which causes actual damage to a business or goodwill of the trader by whom the action is brought or (in a quia timet action) will probably do so.

Lord Fraser said (at 755–56):

It is essential for the plaintiff in a passing off action to show at least the following facts:
(1) That his business consists of, or includes, selling in England a class of goods to which the particular trade name applies;
(2) That the class of goods is clearly defined, and that in the minds of the public, or a section of the public, in England, the trade name distinguishes that class from other similar goods;
(3) That because of the reputation of the goods, there is goodwill attached to the name;
(4) That he, the plaintiff, as a member of the class of those who sell the goods, is the owner of goodwill in England which is of substantial value;
(5) That he has suffered, or is really likely to suffer, substantial damage to his property in the goodwill by reason of the defendant's selling goods which are falsely described by the trade name to which the goodwill is attached.

16.11   These two statements are not easily reconciled in all respects. Lord Fraser appears to confine passing off to the misuse of trade names in relation to goods, while Lord Diplock speaks simply of misrepresentations in the course of trade, without limiting the ways in which such misrepresentations may be made. It has long been clear, however, that services may be passed off as well as goods (see para 16.4) and that the form

_____

[9] [1979] AC 731, [1979] 3 WLR 68.

which the misrepresentation may take includes statements other than trade names. Lord Fraser's stress on activity and goodwill in England is also important but it is not thought that by this he meant to indicate that the law would be different in Scotland. In general it appears best to treat his remarks as directed entirely at the very special kind of case which he was then deciding, namely, one involving misuse of a trade name in which many traders, some from outside the UK, shared goodwill, and not as intended to restrict the scope of the action in other cases, or in Scotland. Lord Diplock's definition, on the other hand, comprehends not only such trade name cases but also all the other situations in which passing off has been held to have taken place.

 Exercise

What are the differences between (1) Lord Oliver's definition of passing off; and (2) those of Lords Diplock and Fraser; or between the definitions of Lords Diplock and Fraser? Does it matter and, if so, why? What do the definitions have in common? Consider this exercise now, and again when you have completed your study of this chapter.

Business context

16.12   The three definitions by Lords Oliver, Diplock, and Fraser have in common that passing off must take place in a business context. Although 'business context' has been widely interpreted in the courts to include, for example, charities,[10] in some cases an action has failed because the context has not been one of commercial activity. In *Kean v McGivan*[11] an action on behalf of a political party regarding the use of the initials 'SDP' failed because the plaintiff was not carrying on a business. Similarly, it may not be possible to prevent another person using the name of one's house.[12] Trade associations such as the Scotch Whisky Association can only sue in respect of their own trading activities as distinct from those of their members, although the members may sue together as individual organisations.[13]

 Discussion point   For answer guidance visit **www.oup.com/uk/brown5e**.

Can you conceive of circumstances in which use of the name of another person's house might be passing off? Is a political party any less in business than a charity? What about a school? Or a university?

Key points about the definition of passing off

There are three major elements to be established in a passing off action:

(1) goodwill;

(2) misrepresentation;

(3) damage.

This must all occur in a business context.

---

[10] See, eg, *British Diabetic Association v Diabetic Society Ltd* [1995] 4 All ER 812.
[11] [1982] FSR 119.
[12] *Day v Brownrigg* (1878) 10 Ch D 294.
[13] See *Consorzio Prosciutto di Parma v Marks & Spencer* [1991] RPC 351; *Chocosuisse Union des Fabricants Suisses de Chocolat v Cadbury* [1999] RPC 826.

Goodwill

Definition of goodwill

16.13 It is essential that the party claiming passing off should enjoy goodwill before any action can succeed.[14]

> Goodwill is 'the attractive force which brings in custom', or, 'whatever adds value to a business by reason of situation, name and reputation' (*IRC v Muller & Co's Margarine Ltd*).[15]

These definitions focus attention first on the existence of *customers* as the starting point for understanding the concept, and explain goodwill as that composite of *elements which leads to customers choosing to give their business to a particular trader, or to acquire that trader's product*. Reputation as such is not enough; customers must be attracted to the business as a result of a particular element or elements of a trader's activities. Court actions may involve several different sets of goodwill.[16] For there to be protectable goodwill in a device, it must be established that in the relevant market there is an association between it and a particular trader or class of traders. This association requires to be established by evidence. The trader's actual identity need not be known to the public, as long as the device is known to distinguish their product or services in the market.[17] The test for the existence of goodwill is less demanding than that of distinctiveness in relation to registered trade marks.[18] A modest amount of goodwill can suffice.[19]

Question

How may goodwill be defined?

16.14 In general the public's *association* of device with trader should *arise from use* of the device. The period of use need not have been long—three weeks was sufficient to justify the granting of an interlocutory injunction in one English case.[20] Publicity prior to the launch of a business may in exceptional circumstances create sufficient goodwill to permit the raising of an action of passing off.[21] Goodwill may survive the cessation of use if there is an intention appropriately manifested to return to business,[22] but if the goodwill is disposed of when the business is abandoned, then there can be no claim of subsequent passing off.[23] The purchaser of goodwill is entitled to protect it by actions of passing off, even against the former owner.[24] Goodwill may be lost over time where there is a cessation or significant reduction in activity and reputation.[25]

---

[14] See further H Carty, 'Passing off and the concept of goodwill' [1995] JBL 139.

[15] [1901] AC 217 per Lord Macnaghten at 223 and per Lord Lindley at 235.

[16] See also discussion in the fashion context in *Westwood v Knight* [2011] EWPCC 8, paras 152, 163, 176–177, 184–186, 202, and 205–207.

[17] *Birmingham Vinegar Brewery Co v Powell* [1897] AC 710; *Hoffmann-La Roche v DDSA* [1969] FSR 410.

[18] *Phones 4U Ltd v Phone4U.co.uk Internet Ltd* [2006] EWCA Civ 244, [2007] RPC 5. For the registered trade mark test of distinctiveness, see paras 14.59ff.

[19] *Lumos Skincare Ltd v Sweet Squared Ltd* [2012] EWPCC 22, paras 38–39.

[20] *Stannard v Reay* [1967] RPC 589.

[21] *BBC v Talbot* [1981] FSR 228; *My Kinda Bones v Dr Peppers Stove Co* [1984] FSR 289.

[22] *Norman Kark Publications Ltd v Odhams Press Ltd* [1962] 1 WLR 380; *Ad-Lib Club Ltd v Granville* [1972] RPC 673.

[23] *Star Industrial v Yap Kwee Kor* [1976] FSR 256 (PC).

[24] *Melrose Drover Ltd v Heddle* (1902) 4F 1120; see also *Cowan v Millar* (1895) 22R 833.

[25] *Alexander Fergusson & Co Ltd v Matthews McClay & Manson Ltd* 1989 SLT 795, but residual goodwill can remain, see *Westwood v Knight* [2011] EWPCC 8, para 216.

■ *Knight v Beyond Properties Pty Ltd* [2007] FSR 34

'Mythbusters' was the title of a series of primary school-age children's books published in the first half of the 1990s. From late 2003, 'Mythbusters' was used by others as the title for a 'dads and lads' TV series. The author of the book series sued the TV producers for passing off. The claim was dismissed. Although the title 'Mythbusters' was capable of generating exclusive goodwill, and the claimant had established a reputation in the UK sufficient to attract passing off protection between 1993 and 1996, it thereafter diminished so that it was no longer significant by 2003.

■ *Wise Property Care Ltd v White Thomson Preservation Ltd* [2008] CSIH 44

In 1976 W and T set up a company called WTP Ltd, carrying out business in property preservation services. In 1983 W and T went their separate ways, trading respectively as WTP (Northern) Ltd (WTPNL) and WTP (Southern) Ltd in different regions of Scotland. W was joined in WTPNL by his three sons, E, G1, and G2. In 2002 the sons left and set up a new company called White Preservation Ltd (WPL); E left this in 2004. In 2005 W retired and WTPNL was dissolved. In 2006 G1 and G2 sold the business and assets of WPL to Wise Property Care Ltd; Wise successfully ran the business until late 2007 as 'White Preservation, a division of Wise Property Care Ltd'. WPL's name was first changed to 'Gragav Ltd', then the company was dissolved. Wise separately set up a company called WPL but it never traded. In 2007 E set up a new company called WTP Ltd, adopting the business get-up of his father's former company and undertaking to honour its guarantees. The court accepted that in effect E was reviving a dormant business. Wise sued E's company for passing off. Interim interdict was granted on the balance of convenience. Wise had built up goodwill in the 'White Preservation' name; the companies were trading in the same business and region; consumers were confused, although local property professionals such as solicitors were not; and WTP Ltd was effectively a newcomer or interloper, the interests of which should be given less weight than those of the established business. Note that although the defender was a 'newcomer', it was in fact the only one of the two companies involved which had within its operation a member of the W family which had given its name to the business acquired by the pursuers.[26]

Goodwill and reputation: the problem of foreign goodwill

16.15   There are two problems:

(1)   the goodwill which a trader based here may enjoy abroad; and

(2)   that which a foreign trader may have in this country.

With regard to (1), a home trader may protect foreign goodwill by means of the action of passing off in relation to the act of export to the relevant overseas jurisdiction.[27] However, as concerns (2), English case law has established that there is no action for passing off where there is *reputation but no trading activity* in the UK.[28] The difficult situation is that of a well-known foreign trader whose distinctive indicia has been adopted by another party in the UK. The foreign plaintiff's passing off action will succeed only if they can show goodwill in the UK; merely being known there will not suffice. This does not necessarily mean having a place of business in England: goodwill could, for example, arise through sales of the foreign trader's goods within the jurisdiction. What is required to build up the requisite goodwill for an overseas services business—for example, a well-known hotel or restaurant—has, however, been less clear. Although one line of cases had indicated that there would be no goodwill within the jurisdiction unless bookings were made

---

[26]   For comment on this case, see CW Ng, 'A common law of passing-off? English and Scottish perspectives' (2009) 13 Edin LR 134.

[27]   See further, para 16.47.

[28]   *Anheuser-Busch Inc v Budejovicky Budvar* [1984] FSR 413; note Lord Fraser's speech in *Erwin Warnink v Townend* ('*Advocaat*') [1979] AC 731, with its reference to trade in England.

by UK-based customers through an office or agent located in the UK (the so-called 'direct bookings' test), there were signs that this approach was no longer regarded as appropriate.[29]

■ *Hotel Cipriani SRL v Cipriani (Grosvenor Street) Ltd* [2009] RPC 9, [2010] RPC 16

The Community trade mark 'Cipriani' was used for hotels in Venice, Lisbon, and Madeira by HC, members of the Orient Express Hotels Group. CGSL used the name on a sign for their restaurant in London. It was confirmed that the claimant had to own goodwill in the UK, rather than merely having a reputation in the UK. It was, however, sufficient to establish UK goodwill that the plaintiff's services were booked by customers in the UK. There was a significant volume of business placed with the plaintiff from the UK either by individuals or via travel agents or tour operators. Without formally deciding the issue, the Court of Appeal indicated that, in the modern context and with many businesses having webpages through which services or facilities could be booked directly online, the 'direct bookings' test may be 'increasingly outmoded' (para 124).

However, more recently the Supreme Court has reaffirmed a stricter approach based on the 'direct bookings' test:

■ *Starbucks (HK) Ltd v British Sky Broadcasting Group plc* (Supreme Court) [2015] ETMR 31

The claimant was the operator of an internet protocol television (IPTV) service in Hong Kong. The claimant's Hong Kong service operated under the brand name 'NOW TV'. The claimant objected to the defendant's launch of its own IPTV service called 'NOW TV' in the UK. The claimant's action for passing off before the English courts failed at first instance for want of protectable goodwill within the jurisdiction. The case also failed on appeal. The Supreme Court reaffirmed that mere reputation within the UK was not sufficient. What was required was actual customers within the jurisdiction. Even then, it was not sufficient that there were people within the jurisdiction who were customers of the claimant's service when they went abroad. The claimant needed to show that there were:

> people in this jurisdiction who, *by booking with, or purchasing from, an entity in this country*, obtained the right to receive the claimant's service abroad (para 52, emphasis added).

The requisite entity need not be a part or branch of the claimant and could be someone acting on the claimant's behalf.

16.16 While clearly established that mere reputation in the UK is insufficient, the insistence on the 'direct bookings' test is unfortunate given developments in cross-border e-commerce.[30] For some brands the consequences of this will be mitigated, however, by the enactment in section 56 TMA 1994 of the 'well-known mark' protection under the Paris Convention; under section 56, mere reputation is enough for the foreign trader to be able to protect its badge of identity in this country.[31]

England and Scotland

16.17 Since England and Scotland are independent legal systems, each is a foreign country in the other's legal system, and the problem of foreign goodwill thus takes on a particular character in this context.

---

[29] See also *Peter Waterman v CBS* [1993] EMLR 27 and *Jian Tools v Roderick Manhattan Group Ltd* [1995] FSR 924.

[30] See, in contrast, the recognition of international goodwill in the Australian case of *ConAgra v McCain Foods (Australia)* (1992) 23 IPR 193 (Fed Ct Aus).

[31] Note, however, *Microsoft Corporation's Applications* [1997–8] Information Technology Law Reports 361, in which 'Windows' was held not to be a well-known mark, at least in May 1991.

In *Flaxcell v Freedman*[32] a London trader using the name 'Dirty Dick's' was held entitled to interdict a Glasgow trader from trading as 'Dicky Dirts' as there was mail order business in Scotland for the London company. In *Pegasus Security Ltd v Gilbert*[33] an English company commencing business in Scotland obtained interim interdict against an existing Scottish business which had been using a similar name. In both cases it was established that the English trader had goodwill in Scotland despite not having an actual place of business there.

Regional or local goodwill

16.18   Just as goodwill may cross national boundaries, so it may not extend over the whole country but instead be confined to a particular locality. It is not clear whether protection in such cases is also confined to the locality in question, so that another trader may set up in another area using the same badges of identity as the first. In the leading English decision, the plaintiffs' operations were local in character but they were nonetheless granted an injunction covering the whole country.[34] There are other cases, however, where only restricted injunctions were obtained.[35]

The question of what constitutes an appropriate case is difficult, however. A business which can only offer services at a fixed location, such as a hotel, club, or restaurant, can nonetheless develop widespread goodwill as the result of passing custom, although its existence may be difficult to prove or disprove.

> ### Key points on goodwill
>
> - Goodwill is about bringing in customers, and in the law of passing off is to be distinguished from mere reputation.
> - Although commerce is increasingly international, it remains essential that a foreign trader must have actual goodwill, rather than mere reputation, in the UK to pursue an action for passing off.
> - Goodwill may also be regional or local in character.

Product goodwill: 'extended passing off'

16.19   The classical definitions of goodwill as the attractive force which brings in custom do not refer directly to what has been termed '*product goodwill*'; that is, *the reputation which a class of product has, as distinct from its manufacturer or seller*. Passing off nevertheless now protects goodwill of this kind, by finding that certain classes of products sold by reference to a particular name or identifier are associated with particular characteristics in the marketplace, which are the reason why they are purchased. This goodwill will be damaged if products without these characteristics can be marketed under the same name or identifier.[36] But the goodwill in such cases, unlike that protected by classical passing off, is not limited to one trader; instead it is shared by all who produce goods having the characteristics in question, and all have the right to claim passing off protection. Because the protection reaches further in this way, this is often known as '*extended passing off*'. It is to this form of passing off that the definitions of Lords Diplock and Fraser in the *Advocaat* case, quoted at para 16.10, are now typically applied.

---

[32] 1981 SLT (Notes) 131.   [33] 1989 GWD 26–1186.
[34] *Chelsea Man Menswear Ltd v Chelsea Girl Ltd* [1987] RPC 189.   [35] *Brestian v Try* [1958] RPC 161 (CA).
[36] See further S Naresh, 'Passing off, goodwill and false advertising: new wine in old bottles' (1986) 45 CJ 97.

Question

How does our previous definition of goodwill (para 16.13) now need to be revised?

Examples of product goodwill recognised by the courts in extended passing off actions include the following;

(1) Champagne

The region in which the Champagne vineyards are found is about 100 miles east of Paris around Rheims and Epernay, where there is a chalky, flinty soil and the climate is subject to extreme variations of heat and cold.

It appears that these factors give to the wine its particular qualities . . . [S]ince 1927 the Champagne Viticole district has been strictly limited by [French] law, and only certain vineyards are allowed in France to use the name 'champagne' . . . The wine is naturally sparkling wine made from grapes produced in the Champagne district by a process of double fermentation which requires a considerable amount of care . . . [I]n the UK . . . champagne is a wine specially associated with occasions of celebration so that (in addition to sales to persons who regularly buy wine), it is purchased on such occasions from time to time by many persons who are not in the habit of buying wine for consumption and are not educated in the nature or qualities of different kinds of wine.

(*Bollinger v Costa Brava Wine Co Ltd* [1961] 1 WLR 277 per Danckwerts J at 281–82)

(2) Scotch whisky

'Scotch whisky' as a description has obtained a particular standing . . . It may only be applied to a spirit distilled in Scotland from a mash of cereal grain saccharified by the diastase of malt. To such a spirit many individual brand names are applied but, irrespective of that, all producers satisfying the conditions applicable are entitled to describe their product as 'Scotch whisky' and to take action to protect the advantages conferred by such a right from improper use of that trade description.

(*John Walker & Sons v Douglas McGibbon* 1972 SLT 128 per Lord Avonside at 128)[37]

(3) Harris Tweed

Harris Tweed means a Tweed made from pure virgin wool produced in Scotland, spun, dyed and finished in the Outer Hebrides and handwoven by the Islanders at their own homes in the Islands of Lewis, Harris, Uist, Barra, and their several purtenances and all known as the Outer Hebrides.

(Harris Tweed Association 1934 definition of Harris Tweed, approved in *Argyllshire Weavers Ltd v A Macaulay Tweeds Ltd* 1965 SLT 21 per Lord Hunter at 33)

(4) Advocaat

The composition of Dutch advocaat (and therefore, in effect, of all the advocaat sold in England) is regulated by Dutch law and consists of hens' eggs, sugar flavouring and spirit. The spirit used is called in Dutch 'brandewijn'. Brandewijn is ethyl alcohol derived from grain or molasses. It is not the same as brandy which, at least in modern English usage, means a spirit derived from grapes.

(*Erven Warnink BV v J Townend & Sons (Hull) Ltd* [1979] AC 731 per Lord Fraser at 749)

(5) Swiss chocolate

The term 'Swiss chocolate' is the designation which has been used, save for very minor exceptions, only on chocolate made in Switzerland in accordance with Swiss food regulations. Subject to the restrictions

---

[37] Regarding 'pure malt', see Burness, 'Scottish Law December/January' IHL 2004, 116 (Dec/Jan), 87–88.

imposed by these regulations, those chocolates have been made to very different recipes. They taste different from each other and are no doubt of different qualities inter se. Notwithstanding these differences, together they have acquired a reputation for quality.

(*Chocosuisse Union des Fabricants Suisses de Chocolat v Cadbury Ltd* [1998] RPC 117 per Laddie J at 135; aff'd [1999] RPC 826)

(6) Vodka

Vodka has, on the judge's findings in this case, become known and recognised for its distinctive qualities as a particular kind of alcoholic drink. Why then, one asks, should it not be entitled to the same protection as champagne given that it satisfies the criteria which the House of Lords has laid down in *ADVOCAAT*?

(*Diageo North America Inc v Intercontinental Brands (UCB) Ltd* [2011] RPC 2 per Patten LJ at para 52; aff'g *Diageo North America Inc v Intercontinental Brands (UCB) Ltd* [2010] RPC 12)

(7) Greek yoghurt

FAGE's pleaded case was that all, or substantially all, of the yoghurt products sold in the UK since 1983 under or by reference to the phrase Greek yoghurt had complied with the following criteria: i. they were made in Greece; ii. they were made using a traditional Greek process whereby cows' milk is strained so as to remove the watery whey; iii. they contained no added sugar, sweeteners, non-milk thickeners or other additives . . . (para 19);

    I believe that the class of traders of whose products the phrase Greek yoghurt has become distinctive has been defined with reasonable precision. It comprises all those traders whose yoghurt is made in Greece according to the specification set out at [19] above (para 75)

(*FAGE UK Ltd v Chobani UK Ltd* [2014] ETMR 26 per Kitchin LJ (CA, affirming first instance decision)

In the *Chocosuisse* case, Laddie J pointed out that the protection of product goodwill was not available only to 'superior' products.[38] What mattered was the public's perception of a distinctive characteristic or characteristics to the product. This was upheld by the Court of Appeal in the *Diageo Vodka* case.

 Discussion point   For answer guidance visit **www.oup.com/uk/brown5e**.

Can you think of any other classes of product on the market in which the goodwill attaches to the product, whoever and no matter how many, manufacture it?

 Exercise

Consider the Parma Ham case (*Consorzio del Prosciutto di Parma v Marks & Spencer plc* [1991] RPC 351), in which a claim of passing off was rejected, and discuss whether in the light of the European Court of Justice (ECJ) decision, Case C-108/01 *Consorzio del Prosciutto di Parma v Asda Stores Ltd* [2003] ECR I-5121, Parma ham should now be held to enjoy product goodwill for the purposes of protection by actions of passing off in the UK. What about feta cheese (see Case C-465/02 *Germany v Commission of the European Communities* [2006] ETMR 16 (ECJ))?

---

[38] [1998] RPC 117 at 128–29.

abbreviations or combinations of letters and numbers are ever more important badges of identity, passing off can be used to protect such identifiers if they have become distinctive.
Examples of distinctive abbreviations, initials, and numerals:

- CA in *Society of Accountants in Edinburgh v Corporation of Accountants* (1893) 20R 750;
- BMA in *British Medical Association v Marsh* (1931) 48 RPC 565.

But not: FCUK in *French Connection v Sutton* [2000] ETMR 341.

16.30   What appears to be most important overall, therefore, is the creation or acquisition of distinctiveness in the marketplace of a word or combination of words (or letters and numerals). But the distinctiveness thus created or acquired can also be lost.[46] So a trader who invents a word for a product will have to be vigilant to prevent its use by other traders for similar products, since if this is not stopped the word will cease to be distinctive of the original product and become a *generic* term for all products of that particular kind. A well-known example is the word 'Linoleum' for a certain type of floor-covering, originally manufactured under a patent and using the name Linoleum by the patent holder alone. But once the patent had expired, other manufacturers moved into the market, also using the name Linoleum. The former patent holder's attempt to stop this was unsuccessful, on the grounds that the word had become a generic term for floor-covering of this type, and had ceased to be distinctive of the original manufacturer.[47]

 Question

Explain how an initially distinctive product name may become 'generic'. How can passing off actions help to prevent this?

16.31   On the other hand, in many extended passing off cases, initially descriptive words came once again also to indicate goods of a particular quality or set of characteristics in that context, so many traders making goods of that quality or with those characteristics could use the name without it necessarily losing its secondary and distinctive meaning.[48]

Key points about descriptive words and secondary meanings

- The use of ordinary words in the English language as part of a business identity can become associated with a particular trader in the marketplace, so that exclusive use can be claimed by way of the action for passing off. The words are then said to have acquired a 'secondary meaning'.

- Just as words can acquire a secondary meaning, so they can lose it if the trader fails to defend its exclusivity in the marketplace.

- Even invented words can become generic—that is, descriptive of all goods or services of a particular kind—if their exclusivity is not defended quickly enough.

---

[46]   *Burberry v Cording* (1909) 26 RPC 693.   [47]   *Linoleum Manufacturing Co v Nairn* (1878) 7 Ch D 834.
[48]   *Erven Warnink v Townend* [1979] AC 731.

Protectable devices: get-up

16.32   Get-up is '*the dress in which the goods are offered to the public*'.[49] If distinctive of the goods, a feature by which customers distinguish the product from those of competitors, it may be protected by an action of passing off. Get-up will usually be the packaging of the goods, either in whole or in part. Some examples are as follows.

(1)   The whole packaging such as:
- the Coca-Cola or the Haig 'Dimple' bottles in *Coca Cola v Barr* [1961] RPC 387; *John Haig & Co v Forth Blending Co* 1954 SC 35;
- the lemon-shaped container of lemon juice in *Reckitt & Colman Products v Borden Inc* [1990] 1 WLR 491.

(2)   Some feature of the packaging:

- colouring in *Hoffmann-La Roche v DDSA* [1969] FSR 410 (black and green colours of Librium capsules);
- stylised typeface of writing appearing on the goods in *Carrick Jewellery Ltd v Ortak* 1989 GWD 35–1624;
- the combination of some features of a vacuum cleaner, the name 'Henry', black bowler hat top, smiley face, and nose of hole for hose in *Numatic International Ltd v Qualtex UK Ltd* [2010] RPC 25.

However, the *shape of the product* itself generally *cannot* be a badge of identity and goodwill, although some part thereof may be. An example of a product shape denied protection was Cadbury's chocolate flake in *Cadbury Ltd v Ulmer GmbH* [1988] FSR 385. A more recent attempt—to protect the shape of kitchen measuring cups—also failed in *George East Housewares Ltd v Fackelmann GmbH & Co KG* [2017] ETMR 4 (IPEC). It remains possible but difficult to sustain an action in passing off based solely on the get-up of a product.[50]

 Exercise

Consider the distinction between 'get-up' and the shape of the product in the light of the cases where a container gives shape to an otherwise formless product, as in the drinks and lemon juice decisions. See the comments of Lord Oliver in *Reckitt & Colman Products v Borden Inc* [1990] 1 WLR 491 at 503, [1990] 1 All ER 873 at 884. Consider also that three-dimensional items, like the Coca-Cola bottle, could not be protected under the UK Trade Marks Act 1938, although they can be protected under the UK TMA 1994 (see para 14.10). How does this influence your view of the cases?

Key points about get-up

- Passing off will protect distinctive packaging, or distinctive aspects of the packaging, of goods.
- But the shape of the *product itself* cannot generally be a basis for a claim, although some distinctive part of the product may be.

---

[49]   *John Haig & Co v Forth Blending Co* 1954 SC 35 per Lord Hill Watson at 38.
[50]   See R Burbidge, 'Protecting product get-up via passing off: an IPEC update' (2017) 12 JIPLP 4.

16.33 Features of the way in which goods or services are offered to the public, other than packaging or shape, could be protected by the action of passing off: for example, the ambience or decor of a restaurant,[51] or the nature of 'back-up' services offered by authorised dealers in the goods of particular manufacturers,[52] or the conduct of business over the internet in a particular format and style.[53] The smell of a fine fragrance has been held not to form part of its goodwill protectable by passing off. In the Court of Appeal in that case, Jacob LJ said that a fragrance might be a source of goodwill, 'but that does not mean that anyone who seeks to emulate the fragrance is guilty of any wrong'.[54]

■ *easyJet v Dainty* [2002] FSR 6

In this case, the judge (at p 114) described how easyJet and the other 'easy-' businesses presented their image:

> I have talked already about the distinctive livery and logo or get-up which applies to the business and it can be described in words to those who are not familiar with it as portraying the following distinctive combination of features. First of all, the name 'easy' together with another word which alludes to the service in question being offered, so as to form one new word, such as the word 'easyJet' in the case of the airline, or 'easyRentacar' in the case of the third claimant. Secondly, the word 'easy' in this formulation is in lower case in the case of every one of the uses of the combination. Thirdly, in every combination the first letter of the second word is displayed as a capital letter so that easyJet has a capital J, easyEverything a capital E and easyRentacar a capital R. Fourthly, in every case the get-up is against a bright orange background with plain white lettering except on occasions where the colouring is reversed so that the background is white and the lettering is in the same distinctive orange colour, as has usually been associated with the product in question . . . [O]ne of the distinctive features is that business is either with, to do with, or conducted over the Internet so that the evidence suggests something of the order of 75, sometimes 81% of bookings on an individual day might be done and conducted over the Internet, . . . But it is a highly Internet organised business and this is a matter which also needs to be taken into account.

Key point on business image

- Passing off can protect the equivalent of 'get-up' for services, the image of a business.

Advertising themes and techniques

16.34 In *Cadbury Schweppes Pty Ltd v Pub Squash Co Pty Ltd*[55] Cadbury marketed their non-alcoholic soft drink 'Solo' in Australia showing dynamic young men quenching the thirst arising from their activities by drinking 'Solo'. Pub Squash began to market their rival soft drink product with a similar campaign. Cadbury's claim that this was passing off was rejected by the Privy Council because the original advertising campaign had not achieved exclusive goodwill for them. But Lord Scarman stated one effect of the *Advocaat* case as follows:[56]

> the tort is no longer anchored, as in its early nineteenth century formulation, to the name or trade mark of a product or business. It is wide enough to encompass other descriptive material, such as slogans or visual images, which radio, television or newspaper advertising campaigns can lead the market to associate with a plaintiff's product, provided always that such descriptive material has become part of the goodwill of the product. And the test is whether the product has derived from the advertising a distinctive character which the market recognises.

---

[51] See *My Kinda Town v Soll* [1983] RPC 407.   [52] *Sony v Saray* [1983] FSR 302.   [53] *easyJet v Dainty* [2002] FSR 111.
[54] *L'Oréal SA v Bellure NV* [2007] RPC 14 (Lewison J), [2008] RPC 9 (CA), para 127.
[55] [1981] 1 WLR 193 (PC).   [56] ibid, at 200.

> **Key point on advertising themes**
>
> • The *Pub Squash* case recognises the possibility of an advertising theme or slogan being part of the image of a business protectable by way of passing off.

Misrepresentation

16.35   Passing off provides a remedy for *misrepresentation*, appropriating, or otherwise diminishing the goodwill of another trader. A misrepresentation is a false statement of fact. In passing off, the false representation is that the goods or services in which the defendant trades are those of the claimant, or in some way have a business connection with the claimant, or have the particular qualities of the claimant's goods or services. It is comparatively easy to determine that this is what the defendant has done when using exactly the same device as the claimant in connection with an identical or similar product,[57] or even a similar name,[58] but even there it must be clear that the claimant's goodwill will be damaged.

■ *Mothercare UK Ltd v Penguin Books Ltd* **[1988] RPC 113 (CA)**

The claimant, a well-known retailer of goods for expectant mothers, babies, and young children, failed to establish that the use of the phrase 'Mother Care' in the title of a controversial book would lead the public to take the book as a publication of the retailer.

Yet even when the defendant has *copied* the claimant's badge of identity, passing off will not provide a remedy unless the latter's goodwill has been damaged.[59]

 Question

What is the typical misrepresentation in a passing off case?

16.36   Generally, the representation is of a more subtle kind than exact reproduction of a badge of identity, with either the nature of the defendant's statement, or the nature of the goods or services provided by the defendant, or the way in which the defendant conducts themselves in relation to the goods and services, or some combination of these things,[60] being different in some way from that of the claimant. The key factor is *the way in which the market reacts to the defendant's activities*. It must be shown that there has been, or that there is likely to be, *confusion about the existence of a trading link* between the defendant's product and the claimant as a result of what the defendant has done. In approaching this question, it is important to remember that the confused public need not be aware of the claimant's actual identity (see para 16.13). The simple existence of consumer confusion does not itself equate to misrepresentation.[61]

---

[57]   See, eg, *Kinnell v Ballantine* 1910 SC 246 ('Horseshoe' for boilers); *Carlsberg v Tennant Caledonian Breweries Ltd* [1972] RPC 847 ('Special Brew' for lager); *Thistle v Thistle Telecom Ltd* 2000 SLT 262 ('Thistle' in relation to telecoms hardware and services); *Future Publishing Ltd v Edge Interactive Media Inc* [2011] ETMR 50 ('Edge' in relation to computer games).

[58]   See *Woolley v Ultimate Products Ltd* [2012] EWHC 339 (Ch) regarding 'Henley' and 'Henleys', paras 37–41 and 42 regarding damage, aff'd on appeal *Woolley v Ultimate Products Ltd* [2012] EWCA Civ 1038. Similarly, see *Property Renaissance Ltd v Stanley Dock Hotel Ltd* [2017] RPC 12 regarding 'Titanic Spa' and 'Titanic Hotel Liverpool', paras 128–137.

[59]   See, eg, *County Sound plc v Ocean Sound plc* [1991] FSR 367; *Arsenal Football Club plc v Reed* [2001] RPC 922.

[60]   See, eg, *Specsavers International Healthcare Ltd v Asda Stores Ltd* [2011] FSR 1, paras 190–192.

[61]   *Comic Enterprises Ltd v Twentieth Century Fox Film Corp* [2016] ETMR 22, paras 157–158 (regarding the word 'glee').

■ *United Biscuits (UK) Ltd v Asda Stores Ltd* [1997] RPC 513

Asda began to market 'Puffin' biscuits to compete with United Biscuits' 'Penguin' biscuits. Asda were careful to design their packaging to avoid deception of customers, but at the same time sought to match, or challenge, or parody, the 'Penguin' style, using the image of the puffin and the name in black lettering alongside on the packaging, as well as similar colours and wrapping materials. See the report at 516 for colour images of the competing wrappers. It was held that there was passing off, in that customers might be led by the similarities of get-up to suppose that the two biscuits came from the same manufacturing source.

16.37 The courts have adopted an increasingly broad approach to what kinds of misrepresentation constitute passing off, although a narrower approach in a situation akin to 'Puffin/Penguin' was taken in *Mars UK Ltd v Burgess Group plc*. This involved advertisements for cat food, and greater regard was had to differences in colour and packaging.[62]

■ *Associated Newspapers plc v Insert Media Ltd* [1991] FSR 380

A business which inserted advertising material between the pages of national newspapers without the authority of the newspaper publishers was held to misrepresent that such authority had been obtained.

■ *British Sky Broadcasting Group plc v Sky Home Services Ltd* [2007] FSR 14 (Briggs J)

The claimant BSB provided extended warranty services under the name 'Sky Repair Protection Plan' in respect of satellite broadcast reception equipment on which its Sky satellite broadcasts were viewed. The defendant SHS also marketed and supplied extended warranty contracts using corporate names, including the word 'Sky' or confusingly similar words. It was held that there was passing off by way of implied misrepresentations, including failure of the SHS salesforce to correct the misapprehensions held by customers as to their links with BSB. BSB had held a *de facto* monopoly in their services and, in entering such a market, SHS had a duty to take care that their marketing methods did not convey the implicit message of a connection with the existing monopolist.

■ *National Guild of Restorers & Removers Ltd v Bee Moved Ltd* [2018] EWCA 1302 Civ

The claimant NGR, a trade association, was successful against BM, who included in an advertisement for removal services a moving checklist that included the phrase 'use a removal company who is a member of the National Guild of Removers and Storers'. The implication was that BM was a member of NGR and this was held to be passing off. BM was not liable for the use of the phrase 'Member of NGRS', which appeared briefly in an advertisement on a website that had been made by a third party: this was confirmed on appeal.

16.38 It is no longer the law that the misrepresentation should have been fraudulent. In England, once passing off was explained as a protection of property in goodwill, the importance of fraud waned as an element in the action, although it is still occasionally mentioned. Fraud was never important in Scotland. Intention to deceive may make proof of confusion and damage to goodwill easier, but intention not to deceive, as in the 'Puffin/Penguin' case (para 16.36), will not prevent a successful action of passing off if, nevertheless, customers are confused and the misrepresentation is shown to be deceptive.

16.39 This will, of course, very much depend on the facts of the case; the intention of the trader, even a decision to 'live dangerously' will not necessarily lead to a finding of passing off. Issues can arise in particular from different perspectives; for example, a decision by a marketing department to try to work alongside, while

---

[62] *Mars UK Ltd v Burgess Group plc* [2004] EWHC 1912 (Ch), in particular para 33.

still within the law, the product, service, or advertising campaign, say, of another or to bring another trader's product to mind without going so far as to cause confusion.[63]

■ *Moroccanoil Israel Ltd v Aldi Stores Ltd* [2014] EWHC 1686 (IPEC)

The claimant manufactured and sold a hair care product called 'Moroccanoil', containing argan oil. The claimant's product was sold in a brown bottle bearing a turquoise label with white and orange text, packaged in a turquoise box also bearing white and orange text. A supermarket chain, A, launched their own hair care product called 'Miracle Oil', also containing argan oil. A's product was sold in a brown bottle bearing a turquoise label with white, orange and black text, packaged in a turquoise box also bearing white, orange, and black text. The court rejected the argument that the name and get-up of A's product in combination constituted passing off. Although A's product might bring to mind the claimant's product that was not sufficient. This was not affected by evidence that A were intentionally 'living dangerously':

> I do not think there was anything unlawful in Aldi creating a product with get-up which brought the get-up of Moroccanoil to mind. I think Aldi intended to do so and succeeded, to the point that some of the public interested in hair oil thought that the similarities were cheeky and might infringe rights relating to design. That is not passing off. So living dangerously in that regard is not relevant (para 57).

The second issue is the use of descriptive words or geographical and personal names. With regard to the use of one's own name in relation to one's business, it is no longer (if it ever was) the law that there is a right to use one's own name which can be used to fend off a claim of passing off: 'a man is entitled to carry on his business in his own name so long as he does not do anything more than that to cause confusion with the business of another, and so long as he does it honestly'.[64]

Again, the claimant will have a remedy if the defendant's statement falsely suggests a trading connection between them, even if in other respects the defendant's statement is a true description of their goods or services.

Consider the following cases.

■ *Dunlop Pneumatic Tyre Co v Dunlop Motor Co* 1907 SC (HL) 15

The Court of Session and the House of Lords agreed that car dealers were entitled to use their surnames as a business name, even though it was already the company name of the tyre manufacturer claimants.

■ *Parker-Knoll Ltd v Knoll International Ltd* [1962] RPC 265 (HL)

Parker-Knoll, manufacturers of furniture, became so named after the English company Parker & Sons purchased a springing system for chairs invented by Wilhelm Knoll. Wilhelm's nephew, Hans Knoll, developed Knoll International as an international furniture business from the United States, and sought to enter the UK market. It was held that Knoll International could not enter the UK furniture market using the word 'Knoll', even though it was the personal name of their founder. A name may be used as a mark under which a person's goods are sold so that the name comes to mean goods sold by that person and not those of anyone else, even when that other has the same name.

---

[63] 'Living dangerously' can be particularly relevant here; see *Specsavers International Healthcare Ltd v Asda Stores Ltd* [2011] FSR 1, paras 190–192, para 193, and [2012] ETMR 17, paras 71 and 115–116 (although the appeal before it did not involve passing off), discussed in respect of passing off in *Fine & Country Ltd v Okotoks Ltd* [2012] EWHC 2230 (Ch), paras 177(9), (10), and 179.

[64] *Joseph Rodgers & Sons Ltd v WN Rodgers & Co* (1924) 41 RPC 277 per Romer J; approved in *Parker-Knoll Ltd v Knoll International Ltd* [1962] RPC 265 (HL), discussed in *Asprey & Garrard Ltd v Wra (Guns) Ltd and Asprey* [2002] ETMR 47, paras 41–45 and quoted in *Reed Executive plc v Reed Business Information Ltd* [2004] RPC 40 (CA) per Jacob LJ at para 109; see also *IN Newman Ltd v Richard T Adlem* [2006] FSR 16, paras 46–47.

BIBA Group v Biba Boutique [1980] RPC 143

An individual may not be free to use her nickname if that name is already associated in the public mind with an existing trader.

 John Haig & Co Ltd v John D D Haig Ltd 1957 SLT (Notes) 36

A man may be unable to give his name to his company if that name is already associated in the public mind with an existing trader in a relevant market. Here the new trader manufactured whisky liqueur chocolates, which was too close to the existing trader's whisky business.

 Question

To what extent may a trader use their own name in business?

Key points on misrepresentation

- The misrepresentation is a statement that the goods or services in which the defendant trades are those of, or have a business connection with, the claimant, or have the particular qualities of the claimant's goods or services.

- The misrepresentation must have damaged the claimant's goodwill by causing confusion in the marketplace for the goods or services.

- The misrepresentation need not have been fraudulent.

- Traders are not entitled to use descriptive terms or their personal names as those of their businesses if that would cause confusion with another's business.

Discussion point   For answer guidance visit **www.oup.com/uk/brown5e**.

Review the range of findings of misrepresentation in *Westwood v Knight* [2011] EWPCC 8, paras 157–158, 168, 190–191, 200, 202, 204, 212, and 220–221, and the findings regarding Knight's conduct, paras 222–226.

Is this what you would have expected given the cases discussed previously? Compare *Specsavers International Healthcare Ltd v Asda Stores Ltd* [2011] FSR 1, paras 190–192.

Confusion and misrepresentation

16.40   Confusion amongst the public as to the source of the goods or services, or as to their qualities in appropriate cases, is at the heart of passing off. The key factor is *the way in which the market reacts to the defendant's activities*. It must be shown that there has been, or that there is likely to be, *confusion about the existence of a trading link between the defendant's product and the claimant* as a result of what the defendant has done. It is not necessary that the whole of the public is confused, while it is not fatal to a claim that many members— even the majority[65]—of the public are not confused by the defendant's conduct. What matters is that there is,

---

[65]   See, eg, *Chocosuisse Union des Fabricants Suisses de Chocolat v Cadbury* [1998] RPC 117, [1999] RPC 826.

or there is likely to be, confusion amongst significant numbers of the public in the market where the parties operate.[66] Intention is again not required, but if there is a decision to 'live dangerously' this can form part of the analysis of the likely response of consumers.[67]

■ *Clark v Associated Newspapers* [1998] 1 All ER 959

The London Evening *Standard* carried a weekly parody of the diaries of Alan Clark, a well-known Conservative MP. The articles were entitled 'Alan Clark's Secret Political Diaries'.

Each article had a photograph of Clark and a byline indicating that it was in fact written by a journalist imagining how Clark would be recording events. It was held that this was passing off even though many readers would not be misled; but as an evening paper read by commuters on their homeward journeys, a substantial number would be confused, and that was enough. See also para 6.17 on moral rights and para 18.47 regarding personality aspects of this case.

■ *FAGE UK Ltd v Chobani UK Ltd* [2013] ETMR 28 (aff'd [2014] ETMR 26)

The defendants had introduced onto the UK market a product described as Greek yoghurt but manufactured in the United States. At first instance, the judge held that it was sufficient that a 'substantial proportion' of purchasers of UK Greek yoghurt (on the facts, probably in excess of 50 per cent of such purchasers) thought that 'Greek yoghurt' was made in Greece, even though that was only 'a modest proportion' of yoghurt eaters in the UK as a whole (para 133). That was sufficient also for there to be an actionable misrepresentation:

> if a sufficient goodwill is shown to be attached to the phrase Greek yoghurt among customers who believe that it is made in Greece, and that this matters to them, then the use of Greek yoghurt to describe yoghurt not made in Greece plainly involves a material misrepresentation. It is a misrepresentation to all those who think that Greek yoghurt is made in Greece. It is a material misrepresentation to those who think that, and consider that it matters to them (para 136).

It is permissible to lead evidence that members of the public have been confused. So, for example, in *Great North of Scotland Railway Co v Mann*,[68] which concerned the names of hotels, there was evidence that customers seeking one hotel had been taken to the other. In *Chill Foods (Scotland) Ltd v Cool Foods Ltd*[69] a letter from a supplier was used as evidence that there was confusion between the parties as a result of their similar trading names. In *Phones 4U Ltd v Phone4U.co.uk Internet Ltd*[70] emails from customers to the defendant's website showed that these people thought they were communicating with the claimant's business, even after visiting the website.

16.41   Where it is averred that the passing off consists of supplying one type of goods when another type has been asked for, the evidence gleaned from placing 'trap orders' may also be accepted by the courts. A systematic survey of the public may be used as evidence of the confusion caused by the defendant's activities,[71] but will often be subject to methodological challenge, since it is usually produced at the behest of one or other or the contending parties. Expert evidence may also be led to help the court to understand such matters as the nature of the marketplace and the attention which the typical customer gives to aspects of the appearance of a product in that marketplace.[72] Further, in *Arsenal Football Club plc v Reed*,[73] which concerned the sale of

---

[66] For an argument about the point in time at which confusion must take place in order to be legally actionable, see P O'Byrne and B Allgrove, 'Post-sale confusion' [2007] 2 JIPLP 315.

[67] *Fine & Country Ltd v Okotoks Ltd* [2012] EWHC 2230 (Ch), para 180.   [68] (1892) 19R 1035.

[69] 1977 SLT 38.   [70] [2007] RPC 5 (CA).

[71] See, eg, *Coca-Cola v Struthers* (1968) SLT 353; *Neutrogena Corporation v Golden Ltd* [1996] RPC 473; *Chocosuisse Union des Fabricants Suisses de Chocolat v Cadbury* [1999] RPC 826; *Numatic International Ltd v Qualtex UK Ltd* [2010] RPC 25 (see para 16.32); *Lumos Skincare Ltd v Sweet Squared Ltd* [2012] EWPCC 22, para 87(5), (6).

[72] See, eg, *Reckitt & Colman Products v Borden Inc* [1990] RPC 341, [1990] 1 WLR 491, [1990] 1 All ER 873 (see para 16.42); *Chocosuisse Union des Fabricants Suisses de Chocolat v Cadbury* [1999] RPC 826.

[73] [2001] RPC 46.

unlicensed merchandise bearing Arsenal insignia outside the club's ground, Laddie J suggested that the club could have set up a mock stall with the type of products sold only by the defendant and then interviewed customers to find out their motives and beliefs when purchasing Arsenal memorabilia. But the decision on whether or not there is confusion is ultimately for the judge.[74] In the *Arsenal* case, Laddie J was unwilling to infer confusion in the absence of evidence that it existed, because the defendant had been trading in the way complained of for 30 years, quite openly and extensively.[75]

Question

What level of public confusion must be shown for misrepresentation and a claim of passing off to be made out?

16.42   In many cases, the claimant will be seeking to prevent the defendant's activities, not on the basis that the public is already confused, but rather because of concern that the public is *likely* to be confused if the defendant's activities are allowed to continue unchecked. In testing the likelihood of confusion, two points must be borne in mind. One is the conditions in the market where the parties operate: 'Thirsty folk want beer, not explanations.'[76] Accordingly the differences between the devices of claimant and defendant, or any disclaimers which may be attached to the defendant's product, should only be given the degree of attention which the typical customer would use. However, it is not enough for there to be initial instance confusion if that confusion has been dispelled by the time of purchase:[77]

> If a customer makes an initial false assumption as to a trade connection between the claimant's and defendant's goods but that assumption is dispelled before any purchase is made and as a consequence the claimant suffers no damage, there is no passing off.

■ *Haig & Co v Forth Blending Co* 1954 SC 35

This case concerned the use of 'dimple'-shaped bottles for whisky. The defender's labelling was different from the pursuer's and the bottles were closed with corks rather than patent stoppers. There was little likelihood of confusion while the bottles remained unopened. But the whisky was sold in pubs, with the bottles open and a pourer attached to the top. With evidence that even barmen might confuse the rival products in the atmosphere of a pub, it was held that the defender's bottle was likely to cause confusion sufficient to amount to passing off.

■ *Reckitt & Coleman Products v Borden Inc* [1990] RPC 341, [1990] 1 WLR 491, [1990] 1 All ER 873

This case concerned the lemon-shaped containers of lemon juice sold typically in supermarkets. The shape, size, and colour of the containers were the same, but the neck-labels on the two products were different, and the word 'Jif' was embossed on the side of the plaintiffs' container. For colour photos of the competing 'lemons', see [1990] RPC at 343. There was evidence that members of the public picking up the defendants' lemon juice from open shelves in supermarkets would think that they were getting Jif lemon juice. The trial judge, Walton J, had said: 'One is typically dealing with a shopper in a supermarket, in something of a hurry,

---

[74]   See, eg, *Woolley v Ultimate Products Ltd* [2012] EWCA Civ 1038, paras 43 and 47.

[75]   Arsenal did not appeal against Laddie J's judgment on passing off. The case proceeded to other courts on issues about registered trade marks infringement: see further [2003] RPC 9 (ECJ), [2002] EWHC 2695 (Ch, Laddie J), [2003] RPC 39 (CA). But note the *obiter* comment of Aldous LJ in the Court of Appeal that he was unconvinced by Laddie J's rejection of the passing off claim ([2003] RPC 39, para 70).

[76]   *Montgomery v Thompson* [1891] AC 217 per Lord Macnaghten at 225.

[77]   *Moroccanoil Israel Ltd v Aldi Stores Ltd* [2014] EWHC 1686 (IPEC), para 25, emphasising that damage must also remain one of the elements of the tort.

accustomed to selecting between various brands when there is such a choice, but increasingly having to choose in relation to a wide range of items between the supermarket's "own brand" and one other brand, and no more' [1987] FSR 505 at 512. Lord Oliver said: 'The crucial point of reference for the shopper requiring Jif juice is the natural lemon-shape and size which had for many years, with only immaterial exceptions, been utilised solely by the respondents in the context of this particular trade' ([1990] 1 WLR 491 at 503).

16.43   The second point is, however, the consideration that if the defendant's activities would confuse or deceive only 'a very small, unobservant section of society',[78] then there is no passing off. The court must adopt the stance of the reasonable person in all the circumstances (personified in one Scottish case as 'the average citizen of Kilmarnock'[79]) and consider the likelihood of the person being confused. But it is important also to remember the diversity of customers in the marketplace, and that reasonableness is not some absolute objective standard in this context.[80]

■ *Taittinger SA v Allbev Ltd* [1993] FSR 641

This was a decision about passing off a carbonated, non-alcoholic soft drink as champagne by naming it 'Elderflower Champagne', selling it in outlets which also sold champagne, in bottles of the same shape, size, and colour as champagne, with labels and wired corks like those used for champagne. 'Elderflower Champagne' sold for £2.45 per bottle, while champagne was normally three or four times that amount at the time. It was held that there was passing off. The average person would not be deceived:

> But there is another section of the public. There is the simple unworldly man who has in mind a family celebration and knows that champagne is drunk for celebrations. He may know nothing of elderflower champagne as an old cottage drink. Seeing 'Elderflower' on a label with below the word 'Champagne' he may well suppose that he is seeing champagne. Since the simple man I have in mind will know little of champagne prices, he is likely to suppose that he has found champagne at a price of £2.45. I do not mean that I now refer to any majority part of the public or even to any very substantial section of the public, but to my mind there must be many members of the public who would suppose that the defendants' 'Elderflower' is champagne (per Sir Mervyn Davies at 654).

In the Court of Appeal, Peter Gibson LJ quoted this passage and added (at 667): 'It seems to me at least as likely that a not insignificant number of members of the public would think it had some association with champagne, if it was not actually champagne . . . [I]t is proper to take into account the ignorant and unwary.'

See also:

■ *Chocosuisse Union des Fabricants Suisses de Chocolat v Cadbury Ltd* [1998] RPC 117

This was a passing off action by manufacturers of Swiss chocolate against the UK company Cadbury, which was marketing a new chocolate product called 'Swiss Chalet'. It was held that there was sufficient confusion for passing off.

> I think it is clear that for many people, including some of those for whom the words Swiss chocolate mean a product of quality from Switzerland, the prominent use of the famous Cadbury name and get up will be enough to prevent them thinking that Swiss Chalet is a Swiss chocolate. Furthermore there are very many for whom the origin or connections of Swiss Chalet will be irrelevant . . . Many people, and particularly those who are more observant, would not be confused. For them the words "Swiss Chalet" will signify nothing but a pretty sounding name for a bar of chocolate . . . However, I have come to the conclusion that there are some who will be struck by the largest and most prominent word on the defendant's packaging, namely 'Swiss', and think it is a reference to an attribute of the product itself. I think it is likely that some will think that it is an indication that the product is Swiss chocolate . . . It is likely that the number who think that will be smaller than the number for whom there will be no confusion but, in my view, it is still likely to be a substantial number (per Laddie J at 143).

---

[78] *Newsweek Inc v BBC* [1979] RPC 441 per Lord Denning MR at 447.
[79] *Dunlop Pneumatic Tyre Co v Dunlop Motor Co* 1907 SC (HL) 15 per Lord James of Hereford at 17.
[80] See also discussion in *Fine & Country Ltd v Okotoks Ltd* [2012] EWHC 2230 (Ch), paras 75–82.

In the Court of Appeal, Chadwick LJ said that the conclusion, in the previous paragraph, of Laddie J on the evidence before him 'cannot be regarded as perverse' ([1999] RPC at 838) (see also para 16.19).

Key points on confusion

- The confusion required must involve significant numbers of the public in the market where the parties operate.

- Confusion may be shown by a variety of forms of evidence (eg surveys).

- Likelihood of confusion is also a basis for preventive action.

- The court must take account of conditions in the world where the goods or services are bought and sold—pubs, supermarkets, etc.

- The approach should not be from the perspective of the highly observant consumer; the less observant and unwary can be taken into account.

'Common field of activity'

16.44   It has sometimes been said that there can be no relevant confusion between the parties unless both are trading in a 'common field of activity'. The phrase was first used by Wynn Parry J in *McCulloch v May*,[81] to define what he thought was an essential element for a successful passing off action. He went on to hold that, because there was no common field of activity between the radio broadcaster plaintiff (known as Uncle Mac) and the cereal manufacturer defendant, it was not passing off for the latter to use the name of the former's radio character (Uncle Mac) in connection with his product Puffed Wheat. The concept has been applied in a number of subsequent English cases, notably those relating to character and personality merchandising, which is considered in more detail in Chapter 18.[82] But it has also been criticised.[83] Probably it is best explained in the words of Oliver J in *Lyngstad v Anabas*: 'not a term of art . . . a convenient shorthand term for indicating . . . the need for a real possibility of confusion'.[84] This seems to be the present approach of the English courts, and although passing off actions may fail on the factual basis that there has been no confusion between two different types of business, it is clear that a common field of activity between the parties is not an essential element in law.[85] It is not referred to as such in the classic definitions of passing off (see paras 16.9–16.12), and indeed appears to have been rejected by Lord Diplock in *Advocaat*.[86]

16.45   The cases which recognise the variety of types of damage which can be done to goodwill apart from deprivation of customers—for instance, association with activities tending to lower a trader's reputation—provide good examples of situations where there has been no common field of activity.[87]

■ *Lego System A/S v Lego M Lemelstrich Ltd* [1983] FSR 155

A passing off action was successfully brought by a toy manufacturer against the manufacturer of irrigation equipment, concerning the use of the name 'Lego'. Falconer J held that the Lego name was so well known that even on irrigation equipment it was bound to be associated with the plaintiffs, whose goodwill might

---

[81] [1947] 2 All ER 845. This case is also relevant in the context of character merchandising and passing off (see para 18.49).

[82] See *Wombles Ltd v Wombles Skips* [1975] FSR 488.

[83] See J Phillips and A Coleman, 'Passing off and the common field of activity' (1985) 101 LQR 242.   [84] [1977] FSR 62 at 67.

[85] See *Stringfellow v McCain Foods* [1984] FSR 413; *Miss World v James Street* [1981] FSR 309; *Mirage Studios v Counter-Feat Clothing* [1991] FSR 145.

[86] [1979] AC at 741–42.

[87] See *Dr Barnardo's Homes v Barnardo Amalgamated Industries* (1949) 66 RPC 103; *Annabels v Schock* [1972] RPC 838.

be damaged in respect of any move that they might make into the defendants' line of business. A distinction was drawn between the use of household names and other less well-known names and it was said that with regard to the former the absence of a common field of activity would probably be irrelevant.

16.46   The Scottish courts have not evolved any concept of 'common field of activity'. There have been cases where the fact that the parties were engaging in different types of business has led the court to hold that there was no passing off.[88] But this has clearly been on the basis that no confusion had been shown, rather than on the assumption that there was a substantive rule precluding the possibility of passing off.

> ### Key point on 'common field of activity'
> - It is not necessary that the parties to a passing off action be in the same field of business.

Deception in foreign markets

16.47   It is possible to sue any party in the UK who is involved as an exporter of the means of practising the deception in the foreign country, such as raw materials, distinctive shapes of bottles, and labels. This follows from *Johnston & Co v Orr-Ewing & Co*,[89] in which the House of Lords held that an exporting business might restrain another from passing off its goods as the plaintiff's in a foreign market. The wrong lay, not in the actual misrepresentation in the foreign market, but in export of the goods from England, enabling the misrepresentation and deception in the foreign market. This has since been applied in several Scottish and English cases concerning the use of the trade name 'Scotch Whisky' in overseas markets, in which it was held that producers of Scotch whisky were entitled to prevent the export of whisky to be used abroad in the production and sale of blended drinks under the name 'Scotch Whisky'.[90]

Can A supply goods which enable B to pass other goods off as C's?

16.48   Despite the case law noted previously on deception in foreign markets, it seems in general not to be passing off for a trader to supply another trader with the means enabling the latter to pass off other goods as those of a third trader. Examples of the situation might include the supply of labels, containers, or raw materials which the second trader requires to pass off their goods. Such supply may be a civil wrong in extreme circumstances, such as where the supplier knew of their customer's intentions or has actively participated in the customer's deceptive marketing; but there is no obligation to ensure that supplies are not used deceptively.[91]

Substitution selling as passing off

16.49   The simple case of passing off involves the defendant passing off their own goods and services as those of the claimant. This includes responding to a customer's order for particular goods of another trader by sending one's own, unless the customer is aware of what is done.[92] However, the law also provides a remedy

---

[88]   *Dunlop Pneumatic Tyre Co v Dunlop Motor Co* 1907 SC (HL) 15 (tyre manufacturer and motor dealer); *Scottish Union & National Insurance* 1909 SC 318 (marine insurance and fire and life insurance); *Scottish Milk Marketing Board v Drybroughs* 1985 SLT 253 (milk products and beer); *Pebble Beach Co v Lombard Brands Ltd* 2002 SLT 1312 (golf course and whisky marketing).

[89]   (1882) 7 App Cas 219.

[90]   *John Walker v Ost* [1970] RPC 489; *John Walker v Douglas McGibbon* 1972 SLT 128; *John Walker & Sons Ltd v Douglas Laing & Co Ltd* 1993 SLT 156 (decided 19 October 1976); *White Horse Distillers Ltd v Gregson Associates Ltd* [1984] RPC 61; *William Grant & Sons Ltd v Glen Catrine Bonded Warehouse Ltd* 1995 SLT 936; aff'd 2001 SC 901; 2001 SLT 1419.

[91]   *Paterson Zochonis Ltd v Merfarken Packaging Ltd* [1983] FSR 273.

[92]   *Purefoy Engineering Co Ltd v Sykes Boxall & Co Ltd* (1955) 72 RPC 89. Sending a catalogue or statement about the substitution with the goods comes too late; the customer should be told in advance.

where an intermediary between manufacturer or producer and the ultimate consumer, such as a retailer or publican, is responsible for presenting the goods or services as those of the claimant. It is passing off, for example, to sell beer as Bass when it is not.[93] The problem which a claimant may have to overcome here is the passage of their product name into the language as a generic term for that particular type of goods.[94]

> **Key point on substitution selling**
> • Supplying your own goods in response to an order of another's may be passing off.

Inverse passing off: A passes off B's goods as their own

16.50   English law has had some difficulty with the situation where the defendant, instead of representing their goods or services to be those of another, claims that goods and services in fact produced by another come from him. This may be inverse (or, reverse) passing off.

■ *Lucasfilm Ltd v Ainsworth* [2008] EWHC 1878 (Ch); [2009] FSR 2

For the facts of this case (the 'Star Wars' case), see also paras 3.62 and 3.71. It illustrates well the distinction between classic and inverse passing off. L relied on the goodwill and reputation generated by the film, asserting that this extended to the business of licensing toys, models, and other goods reproducing facets of the film, including the fictional characters in the film and their costumes. L's claim in passing off stemmed primarily from publicity on A's website, which stressed the authenticity of his products (see para 172):

> Andrew Ainsworth and Shepperton Design Studios created the original helmets and armour for the greatest sci-fi fantasy film of all time. Now, almost 30 years on and for the FIRST time ever, YOU can own an exclusive 1:1 collectible replica of the original movie helmets. **Made by the original prop-maker from the original moulds.** [The emboldening is in the original.] Produced and endorsed by Andrew Ainsworth at Shepperton Design Studios, these unique props offer collectors a rare opportunity of owning some of the most iconic designs of modern cinema. These unique collectibles are the ONLY helmets ever produced from the original moulds used to create the screen-used helmets . . . .

L argued that this would mislead members of the public into thinking that it had licensed or somehow approved the manufacture and sale of the helmets and armour. Furthermore, it was claimed that members of the public would be misled into thinking that A was the creator or designer of the helmets and body armour. Finally, L alleged that A's claims amounted to inverse passing off because he was passing off L's work as his own. It was held that A's website did not either expressly or impliedly suggest that A had the consent of L. References to authenticity were to the products' fidelity to the original designs. Despite A claiming incorrectly that he had been the original creator of the designs, this did not amount to misrepresentation about licensing. As there was no relevant misrepresentation, the claim in passing off failed. The inverse passing off claim also failed. A had not pretended that L's goods actually belonged to him, or that the goods he was selling were L's. His statement as to the origin of the goods was true. Though it was false to state that the creation of the original design was A's, this did not amount to a misappropriation of L's goodwill sufficient to satisfy the requirements of a claim of passing off as any misstatement made related only to A himself and not the goods he was selling. Note that this part of the case was not the subject of the appeals which are discussed at paras 9.85 and 9.90.

---

[93]   *Bass v Laidlaw* (1886) 13R 898; *Thomson v Robertson* (1888) 15R 880; *Thomson v Dailly* (1897) 24R 1173; *Bayer v Baird* (1898) 25R 1142; (1898) 6 SLT 98; *Bass v Laidlaw* (1908) 16 SLT 660.

[94]   See, eg, *Havana Cigar & Tobacco Factories Ltd v Oddenino* [1924] 1 Ch 179 ('Corona' describes shape and size of cigars generally).

■ *Bristol Conservatories v Conservatories Custom Built* [1989] RPC 455

The parties each supplied conservatories. CCB's salesmen showed photographs of BC's conservatories to potential customers, inducing them to think that they were CCB products. It was held at first instance that representing another's goods as your own was not passing off; but the decision was reversed in the Court of Appeal: there was passing off, but because CCB were representing that their own products were of the same quality as BC's (see para 16.51), rather than because the photographs showed CCB products.

There is Scottish authority that this kind of inverse passing off is actionable as such.[95]

Question

What is the difference between substitution selling (para 16.49) and 'inverse passing off'?
Is representing another's goods or services as yours passing off? See further on this H Carty, 'Inverse passing off: a suitable addition to passing off?' [1993] EIPR 370.

Passing off one quality of goods or services for another

16.51   The discussion thus far has been concerned with cases where there were misrepresentations as to the trading source of goods or services. Misrepresentations as to the quality of goods or services may also constitute passing off, even when the trading source is accurately represented.

■ *Spalding v Gamage* (1915) 32 RPC 273 (HL)

The plaintiffs manufactured and sold the 'Improved Sewn Orb' football. The defendants obtained a supply of the plaintiffs' rejected moulded balls, and sold them as 'Improved Sewn Orbs'. The House of Lords held that this was passing off.

16.52   A recurrent problem in this area of passing off concerns *parallel importing*, where goods are sold by the manufacturer under the same trade mark in several countries around the world, and then some sold in one country are imported to another for re-sale there, usually at a price lower than that at which they are sold ordinarily in the importing country. Where there is a difference in quality between the imported and the 'home' goods, the English courts have held that putting the imports on the market may be passing off.[96] But where the goods are of the same quality, then it is irrelevant that the imported goods were made by another company in the same group as the company raising the action in this country; no deception as to source or quality can be said to have occurred.[97] Claims for passing off have also been rejected when products have been re-boxed to comply with regulations for sale in another country, and sold only under a generic name; this was found to be an accurate name and there was no misrepresentation and also no evidence of confusion.[98]

16.53   It is also possible to pass off services as having qualities which they do not possess. Thus, it is passing off for a retailer to state that they are an authorised dealer in a particular product when they are not and are unable to offer the services which such a dealer should do.[99] The quality in question might be that of being connected to or under the control of the claimant, where that party enjoys a good reputation of some kind.

---

[95] *Henderson v Munro* (1905) 7 F 636 (interim interdict granted against the publication of a trade circular).
[96] *Wilkinson Sword v Cripps & Lee* [1982] FSR 16; *Colgate-Palmolive v Markwell Finance* [1989] RPC 497.
[97] *Revlon Inc v Cripps & Lee* [1980] FSR 85.
[98] *Boehringer Ingelheim KG v Swingward Ltd* [2004] 3 CMLR 3, paras 55–59 and see paras 20.29ff.
[99] *Sony v Saray* [1983] FSR 302.

Thus the British Legion, a charitable organisation for the benefit of First World War veterans, could prevent a local social club calling itself 'British Legion Club (Street)' when it had no connection with the Legion.[100] But the representation must be such as to suggest a connection in which the claimant has responsibility for or control over the quality of what the defendant offers. This can also apply to goods, as the following cases show.

■ *Harrods v Harrodian School* [1996] RPC 697

H, a well-known London department store, sued a school which was operating from a site known as 'The Harrodian Club' (because the store had once run a social club there for its employees under that name). The aim of the action was to stop the school calling itself 'The Harrodian School'. It was held that there was no passing off. Millett LJ said (at 713):

> It is not in my opinion sufficient to demonstrate that there must be a connection between the defendant and the plaintiff, if it is not a connection which would lead the public to suppose that the plaintiff has made himself responsible for the quality of the defendant's goods or services. A belief that the plaintiff has sponsored or given financial support to the defendant will not ordinarily give the public that impression.

■ *Arsenal Football Club plc v Reed* [2001] RPC 46

R had sold merchandise outside the Arsenal football club ground for about 30 years. The merchandise bore insignia associating it with the club, such as its name, nickname ('the Gunners'), its crest, and a logo of a cannon. From about 1987 the club began to license traders (but not R) to use these insignia on merchandise, which was then marketed as 'official' club merchandise. The club sued R in passing off to prevent his continued unlicensed operations. It was held by the High Court that there was no passing off. Use of the Arsenal insignia did not carry any message of trade origin. Some fans wanted to purchase only 'official' merchandise, but it did not follow that all Arsenal memorabilia would be taken by fans to have come from or be licensed by the club. There would have to be something more than the mere use of the insignia to make that statement, and here R actually made clear that his activities were unofficial.[101]

Celebrity endorsement cases are discussed further in Chapter 18.

Discussion point   For answer guidance visit **www.oup.com/uk/brown5e**.

Consider the previous cases in the light of *Irvine v Talksport* [2002] 2 All ER 414 after you have explored paras 18.47ff). Are they mutually consistent?

Key points on misrepresentations about the quality of one's goods or services

- Falsely representing one's goods or services as possessed of qualities associated in the market with another trader may amount to passing off.
- This can include cases where the representation (express or implied) is that the claimant exercises some form of quality control over the defendant's goods or services.

---

[100] *British Legion v British Legion Club (Street)* (1931) 63 RPC 555.

[101] Note, however, the *obiter* comment of Aldous LJ in the Court of Appeal that he was unconvinced by Laddie J's rejection of the passing off claim ([2003] RPC 39 at para 70), commented upon by S Middlemiss and S Warner, 'Is there still a hole in this bucket? Confusion and misrepresentation in passing off' (2006) 1 JIPLP 131 and C Wadlow, 'One more outing for *Arsenal*: a case of dilution or one for restitution?' (2006) 1 JIPLP 143. See further para 16.41.

Comparative advertising

16.54   It is generally legitimate for a manufacturer or retailer marketing goods or services to make comparisons of their product with others, or to draw attention to the compatibility of their product with that of another trader, for example as a replacement or an additional part. In no sense is the advertiser stating that their goods come from another trading source. Indeed, the whole purpose of comparative advertising in particular is to differentiate competing products in the public mind.

But if the comparison involves making specific and false claims of equivalent or greater quality for the advertised product, or false denigration of the quality of its rival, then the damage to the competitor's goodwill arising from the misrepresentation may be remedied through passing off.

■ *McDonald's Hamburgers Ltd v Burger King UK Ltd* [1986] FSR 45; aff'd on other points [1987] FSR 112

M sold hamburgers called 'Big Macs'. BK advertised their competing product (the 'Whopper'), using the slogan 'It's Not Just Big Mac'. Evidence showed that the public thought this meant that Big Macs were available at BK and that they could go to BK stores for them. It was held that, as the defendant's advertisement referring to the plaintiff's hamburgers had failed adequately to distinguish the two products from each other, there was passing off. The decision is not so much about false comparisons, however, as about the borderline between comparing products and representing that they come from the same trade source.

■ *Kimberly Clark v Fort Sterling* [1997] FSR 877

FS promoted their 'Nouvelle' toilet roll with the phrase, 'Softness guaranteed (or we'll exchange it for Andrex)'. It was held that this was passing off; there was a misrepresentation in that the statement would induce customers to think, wrongly, that Nouvelle was an Andrex brand.

Comparative advertising can also involve trade mark law, see paras 15.12ff.

Professional associations

16.55   Somewhat akin to the cases on misleading representations as to quality of goods and services are the decisions holding that misleading use of initials and letters which indicate membership of professional associations is passing off, for example BMA for the British Medical Association.[102] Thus, in Scotland members of the Corporation of Accountants Ltd and the Corporation itself were held not entitled to use the letters 'CA' and 'MCA' as an abbreviation of the qualification to be obtained from the Corporation, since the public associated them with the qualification of the members of the Society of Accountants in Edinburgh.[103]

 Exercise

Consider whether pre-sale misrepresentations can be remedied in passing off. See B Allgrove and P O'Byrne, 'Pre-sale misrepresentations in passing off: an idea whose time has come or unfair competition by the back door?' (2006) 1 JIPLP 413.

---

[102]   *British Medical Association v Marsh* (1931) 48 RPC 565.
[103]   *Society of Accountants in Edinburgh v Corporation of Accountants* (1893) 20R 750; *Corporation of Accountants v Society of Accountants in Edinburgh* (1903) 11 SLT 424.

> **Key points on misrepresentations as to quality**
>
> - While comparative advertising is generally legitimate, specific and false claims of equivalent or greater quality for one's own goods or services, or false denigration of a competitor's, can be passing off.
> - False use in business of initials and letters indicating a status or membership of a professional association is passing off.

Improper use of descriptive class designation: extended passing off

16.56 A very particular type of misrepresentation is found in the 'product goodwill' or 'extended passing off' cases, where what is protected is the goodwill attached to products of a particular kind rather than to a specific trader (see para 16.19). In such cases, the representation is that the product in question belongs to a particular class of goods, and arises through the use of a name for that class which is recognised by the public as identifying goods of that class and no others. The development of the law began in *Bollinger v Costa Brava Wine Co.*[104]

■ *Bollinger v Costa Brava Wine Co* [1961] 1 Ch 262

The producers of champagne sought and obtained an injunction to prevent the defendants from marketing a sparkling wine as 'Spanish Champagne'. The judge held that the word 'Champagne' could be used accurately only of sparkling wines produced in the Champagne district of France and that this was how it had come to be understood in the market. The inaccurate application of the name to a drink which lacked the necessary characteristics was therefore a misrepresentation which injured the goodwill of the genuine trader, and so constituted passing off.

Bollinger was approved and applied in a number of subsequent cases: for example, regarding the use of 'Sherry',[105] and 'Scotch whisky',[106] as well as further cases on 'Champagne'.[107] In *Argyllshire Weavers v Macaulay Tweeds*,[108] it was held that mill-spun tweed could not be marketed as Harris tweed. Full confirmation of *Bollinger*'s place in the law was finally given by the House of Lords in *Erven Warnink v Townend* (the *Advocaat* case):[109]

■ *Erven Warnink v Townend* [1979] AC 731

This case concerned the use of 'Advocaat' as a name for an alcoholic drink. An English firm was enjoined from marketing its product as 'Keeling's Old English Advocaat', since the drink was made up, not of brandewijn, egg yolks, and sugar, but rather of dried egg powder mixed with Cyprus sherry. It was also ruled that a name's lack of geographical connotations was immaterial to this form of misrepresentation; the action lay because the defendant's product was not made up of the correct ingredients, not because the correct ingredients came from a particular locality.

---

[104] [1961] 1 Ch 262.   [105] *Vine Products v Mackenzie* [1969] RPC 1.

[106] *John Walker & Sons v Henry Ost* [1970] 1 WLR 917; *John Walker v Douglas McGibbon* 1972 SLT 128; *Lang Brothers v Goldwell* 1980 SC 237.

[107] *Bulmer (HP) Ltd v Bollinger (J) SA* [1978] RPC 79; *Taittinger SA v Allbev Ltd* [1993] FSR 641.   [108] 1965 SLT 21.

[109] [1979] AC 731.

Since the *Advocaat* case, the most important decisions are *Taittinger SA v Allbev Ltd*[110] (the 'Elderflower Champagne' case), *Chocosuisse Union des Fabricants Suisses de Chocolat v Cadbury*[111] (regarding Swiss chocolate), *Diageo North America Inc v Intercontinental Brands (UCB) Ltd* (regarding vodka), and *FAGE v Chobani* (regarding Greek yoghurt).[112] In the 'Elderflower Champagne' case, where the eponymous product was sold at a very low price but in a get-up akin to that of real champagne, it was held that the misrepresentation was either that the drink was champagne or that it was in some way associated with the French champagne houses. In the *Diageo* case, the court found that applying 'Vodkat' 'plainly suggests that the product either is vodka or a version of vodka or contains or is made from vodka.'[113]

> **Key point on misrepresentation in extended passing off cases**
>
> - In such cases the representation is that the product in question belongs to a particular class of goods, and arises through the use of the name for that class when the disputed goods do not conform with the common characteristics of the class.

Damage

Damage to goodwill

16.57 The courts have recognised a variety of ways in which the goodwill of a trader may be damaged by the representations of another trader in connection with their goods and services. The most obvious form of damage is loss of custom, actual or potential, arising from confusion. Closely related to this is the attraction of custom by the defendant using the goodwill associated with the claimant. It may not be possible to show that the customer bought goods from the defendant which they would otherwise have bought from the claimant—for example, because the parties do not trade in the same field—but, nonetheless, an action of passing off will lie if the customer will associate the goods with the claimant to their potential detriment.[114] In *Knight v Beyond Properties Pty Ltd*,[115] the 'Mythbusters' case (for the facts see para 16.14), it was recognised that the claimant might have been able to claim for loss of opportunity to convert his books into a TV series had the evidence supported that as a real possibility (which it did not).

■ *Annabel's (Berkeley Square) Ltd v Shock* [1972] RPC 838

A was a well-known nightclub. S started an unconnected escort agency under the same name. It was held that there was passing off. Escort agencies did not have a good public image and, while S's agency was above reproach, it was inevitable that the two businesses would be associated in the public mind and that the nightclub's good reputation would be damaged, attracting to it the wrong kind of goodwill.

16.58 Damage to trading relationships with business customers, suppliers, distributors, and retailers, which have been recognised as part of goodwill, can also result from passing off activities, and so be a basis for action.[116] For an action to succeed, however, only one of the categories of damage which has been discussed must be established.[117]

---

[110] [1993] FSR 641. See para 16.43.   [111] [1998] RPC 117; aff'd [1999] RPC 826.

[112] [2010] RPC 12 and [2014] ETMR 26, respectively.

[113] *Diageo North America Inc v Intercontinental Brands (UCB) Ltd* [2010] RPC 12, para 167.

[114] See, eg, *Eastman Photographic Materials Ltd v Griffiths Cycle Corp* (1898) 15 RPC 105; *Walter v Ashton* [1902] 2 Ch 282; *Harrods Ltd v R Harrod Ltd* (1924) 41 RPC 74; *Dr Barnardos Homes v Barnardo Amalgamated Industries* (1949) 66 RPC 103; *Annabel's (Berkeley Square) Ltd v Schock* [1972] RPC 838; *Dash Ltd v Philip King Tailoring Ltd* 1988 GWD 7–304 (rev'd on other points 1989 SLT 39); *Phones 4U Ltd v Phone4u. co.uk Internet Ltd* [2007] RPC 5.

[115] [2007] FSR 34 (Ch).

[116] See, eg, *Chelsea Man Menswear Ltd v Chelsea Girl Ltd* [1987] RPC 189; *Highland Distilleries Co plc v Speymalt Whisky Distributors Ltd* 1985 SC 1; *Associated Newspapers plc v Insert Media Ltd* [1991] FSR 380.

[117] *Woolley v Ultimate Products Ltd* [2012] EWCA Civ 1038, para 48.

> **Key points on main forms of damage relevant to passing off**
>
> The main traditional forms of damage relevant to passing off are:
>
> - loss of custom, actual and potential;
> - attraction of custom by defendant using claimant's goodwill;
> - damage to claimant's reputation, and thence goodwill, through false associations;
> - damage to claimant's trading relations.

Dilution of a name

16.59   The defendant's activities may have the effect of diminishing goodwill by lessening the distinctive associations and reputation of the claimant's device ('dilution').[118] This has been especially important in the product goodwill cases (paras 16.19 and 16.56), where the action of passing off has been used to ensure that a name retains a particular meaning in the market and cannot be attached to any other product.[119] Here, again, it may well not be possible to show that the claimant has been deprived of custom, but the reputation of their product is endangered by the defendant's activities and so there can be a remedy. This kind of damage is often referred to as 'dilution'. The scope of dilution as a kind of damage has been the subject of controversy in the courts.[120]

■ *Taittinger SA v Allbev Ltd* [1993] FSR 641

This was the so-called 'Elderflower Champagne' case (see paras 16.43 and 16.56). In this case, only some of the public would be deceived by the defendant's use of the name 'Elderflower Champagne' that the product was champagne. But the judges of the Court of Appeal all thought that the damage extended beyond loss of custom to the blurring or erosion of the uniqueness attendant upon the word 'champagne'; to a gradual debasement or dilution not demonstrable in figures of lost sales, but diminishing the goodwill. The clearest statement was by Sir Thomas Bingham MR (at 678):

> Any product which is not Champagne but is allowed to describe itself as such must inevitably, in my view, erode the singularity and exclusiveness of the description Champagne and so cause the first plaintiffs damage of an insidious but serious kind . . . [A] reference to champagne imports nuances of quality and celebration, a sense of something privileged and special. But this is the reputation which the Champagne houses have built up over the years, and in which they have a property right. It is not in my view unfair to deny the defendants the opportunity to exploit, share or (in the vernacular) cash in on that reputation, which they have done nothing to establish. It would be very unfair to allow them to do so if the consequence was, as I am satisfied it would be, to debase and cheapen that very reputation.

But contrast Millett LJ in:

■ *Harrods Ltd v Harrodian School Ltd* [1996] RPC 697

An action by a London department store to prevent a school from trading as the 'Harrodian School' was unsuccessful (see para 16.53). On damage and the possibility of dilution of the Harrods name, Millett LJ said (at 716):

> To date the law has not sought to protect the value of the brand name as such, but the value of the goodwill which it generates; and it insists on proof of confusion to justify its intervention. But the erosion of the

---

[118] See, eg, *Rolls Royce v Dodd* [1981] FSR 517.

[119] See, above all, *Erven Warnink v Townend* [1979] AC 731; also *Macallan-Glenlivet plc v Speymalt Whisky Distributors Ltd* 1983 SLT 348; and *Highland Distilleries Co plc v Speymalt Whisky Distributors Ltd* 1985 SC 1.

[120] See further H Carty, 'Heads of damage in passing off' [1996] EIPR 487; A Murray, 'A distinct lack of goodwill' [1997] EIPR 345.

distinctiveness of a brand name which occurs by reason of its degeneration into common use as a generic term is not necessarily dependent on confusion at all . . . I have an intellectual difficulty in accepting the concept that the law insists upon the presence of both confusion and damage and yet recognises as sufficient a head of damage which does not depend upon confusion.

 Question

How far, if at all, does 'dilution' differ from the more traditional forms of damage recognised in passing off actions?

Does the concept of dilution blur the distinction between 'goodwill' and 'reputation' (para 16.13)?

Key points on dilution as a form of damage

- Dilution is a form of damage in which the defendant's activities in some way weaken or diminish the distinctive associations and reputation of the claimant's marketing device (typically a name), without necessarily depriving the claimant of customers.

- Dilution appears to be important in 'product goodwill' or 'extended passing off' cases, but has also been deployed in the case of false endorsement.

- Dilution is a controversial form of damage, since it seems to weaken the requirement of goodwill and lead passing off into the protection of reputation.

Damage need only be prospective

16.60   It is clear law that in general damage (of whatever kind) need not have been actually suffered before the action is brought. An injunction or an interdict can certainly be obtained because the likelihood of damage is reasonably anticipated. It has been said that there is a presumption of damage in cases where the defendant has sold goods as those of the claimant.[121] In cases of fraud, the burden of proving damage will be light.[122]

Defences

16.61   All the requirements of passing off as discussed so far in this chapter may be present, yet the party sued may have a defence. Some defences are of course implicit in the requirements of passing off which have been discussed; for example lack of goodwill, absence of confusion, that one is making honest use of one's own name. But there are some defences in passing off which arise even if all the other requirements of the claim are met. The scope of some of these is rather uncertain: for example, parody, as when it was held that there was no passing off by title in a film called 'Alternative Miss World' satirising a beauty competition.[123] But a defence of parody was of no avail in *Clark v Associated Newspapers Ltd*,[124] where the parodist had not done enough to prevent confusion as to the authorship of the work amongst readers; while in *Irvine v Talksport Ltd*[125] the suggestion that the manipulated picture of Irvine listening intently to a radio marked with Talksport insignia would be seen as a joke by its intended audience was rejected by the court. One of the most important defences in practice is *delay*—technically known as acquiescence, or taciturnity and

---

[121] See *Draper v Trist* (1939) 56 RPC 429.   [122] *Bulmer v Bollinger* [1978] RPC 79.
[123] *Miss World v James Street* [1981] FSR 309.   [124] [1998] RPC 261.   [125] [2003] EWCA Civ 423.

mora—on the part of the person raising the action of passing off: that is to say, despite knowing of the other party's activities, taking no steps to prevent them for a significant period of time. Thus, for example, in *Bulmer v Bollinger*[126] champagne houses were unable, after 18 years of use, to prevent cider being marketed as 'champagne perry'. In *Arsenal Football Club plc v Reed*,[127] the defendant traded openly outside the Arsenal ground for 30 years, and in such circumstances, especially when there was no evidence of actual confusion in the marketplace for the goods in question, the failure of the club's passing off action was unsurprising. An important discussion of the defence is in the following Scottish case, where it was rejected.

■ *William Grant & Sons Ltd v Glen Catrine Bonded Warehouse Ltd* 2001 SC 901

WG sought to prevent GC from using the name 'Grant's' in connection with the sale of gin, vodka, and other alcoholic drinks. WG had been selling whisky products under the name 'Grant's' since the 1920s, and gin and vodka since 1963. GC began using the name on gin in 1972 and on vodka in 1974. From 1986 GC's sales began to increase dramatically. GC believed they could use the name 'Grant's' as it had been the name of a company they acquired in 1972. GC defended WG's claim of passing off on the basis of acquiescence. The action was raised in 1992, although there had been communication between the parties since WG became aware of GC's activities in 1986. It was held that WG were not barred by acquiescence from a remedy for passing off. GC had exploited the name 'Grant's', not because they believed WG had consented, but because they believed they had a historical right to use the name. Further, acquiescence was being invoked to bar action in respect of future wrongs (ie continued passing off), but the evidence did not justify an inference that WG had consented irrevocably to GC passing their products off as WG's in the future. Knowledge was not the same as acquiescence. The court, although relying principally on Scottish authorities on personal bar (anglicé estoppel),[128] found support for its approach in the English design law case of *Farmers Build Ltd v Carier Bulk Materials Handling Ltd* [1999] RPC 461.

Question

What constitutes acquiescence or delay sufficient to prevent a party succeeding in a passing off action?

Key points on defences

- A defendant who can show that their activity went on for many years unchecked before the raising of the action has a good defence against an action of passing off.

- The technical names for this defence are *acquiescence, taciturnity, mora*, and *delay*.

- It follows that claimants should take prompt action when they learn of possible passing off.

The internet, passing off, and instruments of fraud

16.62   An important development in the use of passing off came in its use to control the phenomenon known as 'cyber-squatting'. This is an example of a commercial practice made possible by the internet. Domain names identifying and locating organisations on the internet are a crucial part of what is needed to do business there. In the 1990s, businesses were established which registered domain names comprising well-known

---

[126] [1971] FSR 405.   [127] [2001] RPC 922.
[128] On this aspect of the case, see E Reid, 'Acquiescence in the air' (2002) 4 JR 191.

trade marks and corporate and other names without the consent of the person owning the trade mark or goodwill in the name in question. These businesses then offered the domain names to the owners of the trade marks or goodwill, usually for very substantial sums, but typically did not themselves make much, if any, commercial use of the domain name on the internet. It was far from clear that this activity constituted infringement of any trade mark rights there might be in the name, although the phrase 'cyber-squatting' conveyed a sense that the businesses concerned had occupied the name without permission, and only because the real owners had left this particular part of their property vacant. So, the owners turned to the law of passing off as a way of evicting the 'squatters'. They gained their way in *British Telecommunications plc v One in a Million Ltd.*[129]

■ *British Telecommunications plc v One in a Million Ltd* [1999] 1 WLR 903 (CA)

OM were dealers in domain names who had registered the following names: ladbrokes.com; sainsbury. com; sainsburys.com; j-sainsbury.com; marksandspencer.com; cellnet.net; bt.org; virgin.org. Other dealers who were co-defendants in the case had registered marksandspencer.co.uk; britishtelecom.co.uk; britishtelecom.net, and britishtelecom.com. They were sued for passing off by Marks & Spencer plc, J Sainsbury plc, Virgin Enterprises Ltd, British Telecommunications plc, Telecom Cellular Radio Ltd, and Ladbrokes plc. The Court of Appeal held that there was passing off and that the plaintiffs were entitled to *quia timet* injunctions. Analysis of previous case law showed that an injunction could be granted against a defendant equipped with or intending to equip another with an instrument of fraud. A name which would, by reason of its similarity to the name of another, inherently lead to passing off, is such an instrument. The court could infer an intention to appropriate goodwill or enable others to do so, even if there was a possibility that such appropriation would not take place (the importance of this point being that there was little evidence that the 'cyber-squatters' intended actually to trade under the domain names or to sell the names to anyone other than the plaintiffs, although there were threats, express or implied, to do so contained in the communications between them and the owners).

16.63   The decision builds on earlier cases, mostly concerned with exporting material which would be used in the destination country to pass off goods as coming from a particular source in this country (para 16.47). In general, supply of the means by which another trader might pass off goods or services—for example, providing materials for bottling or labelling—is not passing off unless there is fraud or at any rate intention and knowledge on the part of the supplier (see para 16.48). The difficulty in the *One in a Million* case is that the domain names held by the cyber-squatters were of very little value in the hands of anyone other than the cyber-squatters and the companies whose names had been used. Had the cyber-squatters attempted themselves to trade under the domain names, or sold them to third parties so to trade, then there would have been passing off in the ordinary sense. So, it is difficult to see how cyber-squatting is really analogous to the earlier 'instruments of fraud' cases. The decision is also difficult to reconcile with the classic definitions of passing off by Lords Diplock, Fraser, and Oliver quoted at the outset of this chapter (see paras 16.9 and 16.10). The court clearly did not like the behaviour of the cyber-squatters, in particular the threatening way in which they advanced their offers to sell the domain names to the well-known companies; but in order to remedy that wrong, the law of passing off was probably extended further than ever before.

Question

What is cyber-squatting? Does this activity constitute passing off as usually understood?

---

[129]   [1999] 1 WLR 903 (CA).

16.64　The courts of both England and Scotland have, however, followed the *One in a Million* decision without much quibble.[130] In *easyJet v Dainty*,[131] the defendant registered the domain name 'easyRealestate.co.uk' and set up a website offering estate agency services; but he did no significant business through the site. He attempted to interest easyJet in his proposition, made use of 'easy-' style livery on the website, and ultimately attempted to sell his domain name to easyJet while threatening to sell to third parties. He was held liable for passing off, which was constituted in both its traditional form and in its 'instruments of deception' form. The judge ordered that the defendant's domain name be transferred to easyJet.[132] In *Phones 4U Ltd v Phone4U. co.uk Internet Ltd*,[133] the defendant commenced internet trading under the domain name as well as offering it for sale after learning of the claimant's existence and use of the trade name; the Court of Appeal thought this not materially different from the *One in a Million* case. In the more recent case of *Vertical Leisure Limited v Poleplus Limited*,[134] the defendant was a competitor of the claimant in the sale of pole exercise dance equipment (such as poles used by pole dancers). After registering six domain names incorporating the brand name for a new pole launched by the claimant, the defendant wrote to the claimant to offer the domain names for sale; the court held that *One in a Million* was clearly applicable and granted summary judgment on the claimant's passing off claim.[135]

16.65　*One in a Million* was distinguished, however, in *French Connection v Sutton*.[136] French Connection, a chain of fashion stores, began in 1997 to use the word FCUK in a widespread advertising campaign as well as registering it as a trade mark. Sutton, an internet consultant, registered 'FCUK.com' as a domain name, and set up a website at which he would advertise his consultancy. This was challenged by French Connection on the basis of the *One in a Million* case, and the evidence showed that Sutton had subsequently tried to sell his domain name to the company. However, Rattee J refused summary judgment, on the basis that FCUK was not a household name—or, indeed, the name of anything—in any way like the names involved in the *One in a Million* case; Sutton's website had offered services quite different from those of French Connection; and the registration of FCUK as a domain name had not been merely for the purpose of extracting money from French Connection but had rather been to draw the attention of internet users to Sutton's site:[137]

> According to the defendant's evidence, the letters FCUK together in that order was a well-known alternative used by people on the Internet as a means of circumventing various filters which were imposed by certain Internet Service Providers to prevent the use of the expletive FUCK in the material placed on the Internet. It is also the defendant's evidence that at the time he registered his domain name and, I think, still, FCUK is also known to a certain class of Internet users as indicating pornographic subject matter . . . [H]e thought that it might improve the level of custom for [his] business if he attracted to it unsuspecting persons interested in accessing a pornographic site.

16.66　In *Lifestyle Management Ltd v Frater*,[138] however, Frater used domain names which were very similar to those of the claimant. The court found, applying *One in a Million*, that this was 'deceptive use' of the name with 'acquired goodwill' to 'damage the owner of the name'.

16.67　Other attempts have been made to use the concept of the instrument of fraud to address new forms of conduct. In *L'Oréal SA v Bellure NV*,[139] the claimants complained of the defendants' importation, distribution, and sale of what were alleged to be copies—'smell-alikes'—of the former's perfumes, and argued that the

---

[130] For critical commentary, see C Thorne and S Bennett, 'Domain names—internet warehousing: has protection of well known names on the internet gone too far?' [1998] EIPR 468; C Colston, 'Passing off: the right solution to domain names?' [2000] LMCLQ 523; H Carty, 'Passing off and instruments of deception: the need for clarity' [2003] EIPR 188.

[131] [2002] FSR 6. See also *Easygroup IP Licensing Ltd v Sermbezis* [2003] All ER (D) 25 (car rental websites).

[132] See also *Yell Ltd v Giboin, Zagg Ltd* [2011] EWPCC 009, paras 185–189.

[133] [2007] RPC 5 (CA). See also *Tesco Stores Ltd v Elogicom Ltd* [2007] FSR 4 (Ch).

[134] [2014] EWHC 2077 (IPEC).

[135] Citing *Vertical Leisure* and *One in a Million*, the court in *Yoyo.Email Ltd v Royal Bank of Scotland Group plc* [2016] FSR 18 also came to the conclusion that domain name registration constituted passing off: para 16.

[136] [2000] ETMR 341.　　[137] ibid, at 345.　　[138] [2010] EWHC 3258 (TCC), para 11.

[139] [2007] RPC 14; aff'd on instruments of deception and the activities of third parties [2008] RPC 9 (CA), paras 128–132.

defendants' products were instruments of fraud and deception, making their activities passing off. The claim was, however, rejected by Lewison J: to be an instrument of deception the product had to be so inherently defective that its mere existence made it passing off waiting to happen. The names and packaging of the defendants' products did not fall into that category.

16.68   A further issue about passing off on the internet was raised in *Reed Executive plc v Reed Business Information Ltd* involving metatags.[140] RE, an employment agency which had been in business using the name 'Reed' since 1960, operated a website—reed.co.uk. RBI were publishers who had used the Reed name since 1983 and who in 1999 began to run a recruitment website called 'totaljobs.com'. There was visible use of the word 'Reed' on the site, and also invisible use, as the word 'Reed' had been used as a metatag in the creation of the site. Metatags are elements of the HTML language used to provide structured metadata about a webpage, that is, data about the material contained in the webpage. Metatags permit discovery of the website by search engines and also the generation of various forms of web advertising.[141] There was some evidence of confusion between the two websites in the *Reed* case, and RBI had made efforts by the date of trial to remove both visible and invisible uses of the word 'Reed'. Pumfrey J held that, while the visible uses of 'Reed' could constitute passing off, this was not so for the invisible metatags. The Court of Appeal held that there was no passing off at all, pointing to evidence that had been led about the results of searches under the phrase 'Reed jobs'. Jacob LJ said of this evidence:[142]

> In all cases where totaljobs was listed, it came below the Reed employment site in the search results (which, as is usual, included many other results, irrelevant to both sides). Obviously anyone looking for Reed Employment would find them rather than totaljobs. I am unable to see how there could be passing off. No one is likely to be misled—there is no misrepresentation. This is equally so whether the search engine itself rendered visible the metatag or not.

16.69   Questions also arise in the context of keyword advertising[143] on the internet as seen in *Victoria Plum Ltd v Victorian Plumbing Ltd*,[144] which concerned the sellers of bathroom products. Bidding for keywords can form the basis of a passing off action:[145]

> There is nothing in those advertisements to indicate the absence of a connection between the parties. Some users are likely to have clicked through to the Claimant's website, and their confusion is likely to have continued. The fact that many users may not be confused is not an answer. I consider that a substantial proportion of the relevant public are likely to have been misled into believing that the Claimant is, or is connected with, the First Defendant, and that this constituted a misrepresentation by the Claimant. In the circumstances I believe that there is a likelihood of damage.

 Question

Why do metatags and keywords create problems relevant to the law of passing off?
How do the cases discussed previously apply to passing off on the internet?

---

[140] [2003] RPC 12 (Pumfrey J); aff'd [2004] RPC 40 (CA).

[141] See further A Murray, 'The use of trade marks as meta tags: defining the boundaries' (2000) 8 IJLIT 263; A Blythe. 'Searching questions: issues surrounding trade mark use on the internet' (2013) 35 EIPR 9.

[142] [2004] RPC 40 (CA), para 147. For further comment see R Sumroy and C Badger, 'Infringing "use in the course of trade": trade mark use and the essential function of a trade mark' and S Maniatis, 'Trade mark use on the Internet' both in J Phillips and I Simon (eds), *Trade Mark Use* (2005).

[143] See para 15.18ff. The sale of Google AdWords is an example of search engine advertising on the internet.

[144] [2017] ETMR 8. The case concerned trade mark infringement with a counter-claim made for passing off.

[145] ibid, at 156.

Discussion point   For answer guidance visit **www.oup.com/uk/brown5e**.

What do you think will be the next internet issue in which passing off is used—for example, the use of hashtags? Do you see this as a natural progression, or an unwarranted expansion of the doctrine?

Unfair competition and passing off

16.70   As pointed out at the beginning of this chapter (para 16.7), passing off is as near as the laws of England and Scotland come to having a law of unfair competition such as is commonly found in the laws of other member states of the EU, and it is usually taken to satisfy the requirements of the Paris Convention in this regard. It has sometimes been suggested that the expansion of passing off from the simple case of representing one's goods as those of another and thereby damaging that other's goodwill, means that it would be better to speak now of unfair competition rather than passing off. A particularly strong instance of this development has been the growth of protection of product goodwill, with its ability to prevent dilution of a valuable reputation in trade in a certain class of goods. But other developments, such as the broadening concept of misrepresentation, the decreasing emphasis on confusion, and the recognition of 'dilution', are taking the law increasingly towards a basis in *misappropriation* of another's *reputation* (as distinct from goodwill), to enable one to reap profit and enrichment where another has sown the seed.[146] Laddie J has gone as far as to say that the 'underlying principle' of passing off is 'the maintenance of what is currently regarded as fair trading',[147] while Aldous LJ, unconvinced by Laddie J's rejection of the claim of passing off in the *Arsenal* case, suggested at the same time that the modern extensions of passing off meant that it was 'perhaps best referred to as unfair competition'.[148] If we consider again the prohibitions listed in Article 10*bis*(3) of the Paris Convention—

1. all acts of such nature as to create confusion by any means whatever with the establishment, the goods, or the industrial or commercial activities, of a competitor;
2. false allegations in the course of trade of such a nature as to discredit the establishment, the goods, or the industrial or commercial activities, of a competitor;
3. indications or allegations the use of which in the course of trade is liable to mislead the public as to the nature, the manufacturing process, the characteristics, the suitability for their purpose, or the quantity, of the goods

—then we can see that passing off is capable of dealing with all three. Indeed, passing off goes further in several respects. It would not be straightforward to say, for example, that the use of passing off to prevent false endorsement or cyber-squatting comes squarely within these prohibitions. In *L'Oréal SA v Bellure NV*[149] the Court of Appeal was invited to develop a tort of unfair competition, either because the present law was in derogation from the Paris Convention or as an evolution of the common law. The court held that there was no derogation from the Convention and vigorously rejected the argument that it could develop passing off to become a tort of unfair competition. Given that competition was not only lawful but also the mainspring of the economy, it was for Parliament rather than the judges to legislate for restraints upon competition. Jacob LJ was highly critical of the concept of misappropriation as the means of further developing the law, noting that there are 'real difficulties in formulating a clear and rational line between that which is fair and that which is not'.[150]

---

[146] A Kamperman Sanders, *Unjust Enrichment: The New Paradigm for Unfair Competition Law?* (1996).

[147] *Irvine v Talksport Ltd* [2002] 2 All ER 414, para 17.

[148] *Arsenal Football Club plc v Matthew Reed* [2003] RPC 39, para 70; commented upon by S Middlemiss and S Warner, 'Is there still a hole in this bucket? Confusion and misrepresentation in passing off' (2006) 1 JIPLP 131, and C Wadlow, 'One more outing for *Arsenal*: a case of dilution or one for restitution?' (2006) 1 JIPLP 143.

[149] [2008] RPC 9 (CA).

[150] ibid, para 140. See further L Harrold, 'The genie in the bottle: brand "free riding": what's permissible and what's not?' (2008) 3 JIPLP 511 and T Alkin, 'Should there be a tort of "unfair competition" in English law?' (2008) 3 JIPLP 48.

Exercise

Consider how each of the three prohibitions in the Paris Convention article on unfair competition is dealt with by the law of passing off.

16.71   There have been attempts to reform the law in this area. During the parliamentary passage of what is now the Trade Marks Act 1994, the following additional section was proposed, although ultimately the amendment was withdrawn:[151]

> After Clause 56, insert the following clause:
>
> **Unfair Competition**
>
> (1) Where any goods of the proprietor of a trade mark bearing the trade mark are associated in the course of trade with any label, packaging or container having an overall appearance of a distinctive character, it shall be an act of unfair competition, actionable as such, for any person in the course of trade to supply or offer to supply any such goods with or in any label, packaging or container which is similar in overall appearance, whether by reason of name, shape, colour, design or any combination thereof or otherwise, to the overall appearance of that of the proprietor's goods if the use of the label, packaging or container either—
>
>> (a) is likely to cause confusion, which includes a likelihood of association with the proprietor or the proprietor's goods; or
>>
>> (b) without due cause takes unfair advantage of, or is detrimental to, the distinctive character or repute of the appearance of the proprietor's goods or trade mark.

16.72   In March 2000 Lord McNally presented a Copyright and Trade Marks Bill before the House of Lords, which was again withdrawn, but which contained a clause which he described as follows:[152]

> Clause 3 seeks to tighten up the currently weak laws on competitive imitation. It is intended to prevent business from dressing up products so as to resemble competing goods, thereby taking unfair advantage of the original's reputation for quality and safety and investment in innovation and marketing. Such legislation is necessary because the imitation is designed deliberately to mislead consumers by stealing the identity and reputation of the rival product. When I was at the Retail Consortium I noted that it was not only the back-street trader who indulged in such copycat retailing. I believe that to steal a brand image is unfair to the initiator who over decades may have made an investment to win customer confidence in a particular product. At the moment, imitation is governed by passing-off law that dates from the 18th and 19th centuries. It is very vague and has proved ineffective in providing protection to rights owners. The required standard of proof under passing-off law is extreme and gives copycats immense freedom to copy designs in a way that misleads consumers. It is unrealistic to ask industry to fight legal actions and to lose just to prove a point. The lack of legal cases demonstrates the difficulty in bringing actions. I am proposing that courts are in the best position to decide what constitutes imitation. The Bill also gives the wronged party a chance to seek damages in cases where imitation is proven. The present laws, like so many others in this area, present a barrier to innovation by industry and consumers continue to be deceived.

Exercise

What difference, if any, would the amendment to the Trade Marks Bill have made to the law of passing off? Comment on Lord McNally's criticism of the law of passing off. Should there be a law of unfair competition to prevent imitative trading even if customers are not confused between the competing products?

---

[151] The amendment was tabled by Lord Reay: *Parliamentary Debates*, House of Lords, vol 552, 24 February 1994, cols 749–759.

[152] *Parliamentary Debates*, House of Lords, vol 610, 17 March 2000, cols 1888–1889. The whole debate on the Bill can be found at cols 1885–1906.

16.73 While the idea of replacing passing off with a more general law against unfair competition is attractive in some ways—in bringing the law in the UK into line with that of our fellow member states of the EU, in stopping the need to strain the basic concepts of passing off to meet new forms of unfair trading, and in enabling those who invest time, creativity, and labour in generating products and services attracting goodwill to gain appropriate rewards without quite so much risk of free-riding by less innovative or would-be competitors—there are countervailing arguments.[153] Perhaps the most potent is that, while a law of unfair competition would be justified ultimately as a protection of consumers, it would be administered through the courts and by way of litigation involving, not the consumer directly, but rather the suppliers competing for the consumer's custom. It is not immediately clear that this would be the most efficient or effective way of protecting the consumer from unfair trading practices. It has, in the meantime, been argued that the passing off cases should also be re-appraised in light of the Unfair Commercial Practices Directive 2005/29/EC.[154]

Further reading

Books

General

L Bently, B Sherman, D Gangjee, and P Johnson, *Intellectual Property Law* (5th edn, 2018), Chs 31–34

H Carty, *An Analysis of the Economic Torts* (2nd edn, 2010), Ch 11

D Llewelyn and T Aplin, *Cornish, Llewelyn and Aplin Intellectual Property: Patents, Copyright, Trade Marks and Allied Rights* (9th edn, 2019), Ch 17.1

C Ng, L Bently, and G D'Agostino, *The Common Law of Intellectual Property* (2010)

C Wadlow, *The Law of Passing Off: Unfair Competition by Misrepresentation* (5th edn, 2016)

Articles

General

H Carty, 'The common law and the quest for the IP effect' [2007] IPQ 237

M Spence, 'Passing off and the misappropriation of valuable intangibles' (1996) 112 LQR 472

Development of the law

EM Clive, 'The action of passing off: its scope and basis' 1963 JR 117 (Scots law)

Goodwill

H Carty, 'The dissipation of goodwill in the tort of passing off: an analysis' [2015] IPQ 177

J Davis, 'The continuing importance of local goodwill in passing off' (2015) 74 CLJ 419

S Naresh, 'Passing off, goodwill and false advertising: new wine in old bottles' (1986) 45 CLJ 97

CW Ng, 'Goodwill without borders' (2018) 134 LQR 285

Misrepresentation

A Blythe, 'Misrepresentation, confusion and the average consumer: to what extent are the tests for passing off and likelihood of confusion within trade mark law identical?' [2015] EIPR 484

J Griffiths, 'Misattribution and misrepresentation: the claim for reverse passing off as "paternity" right' [2006] IPQ 34

---

[153] See especially H Carty, *An Analysis of the Economic Torts* (2010), Chs 8, 11.
[154] P Johnson and J Gibson, 'The "new" tort of passing off' (2015) 131 LQR 476.

J Phillips and A Coleman, 'Passing off and
the common field of activity' (1985) 101
LQR 242

Passsing off and new challenges

J Davis, 'Passing off and joint liability: the rise and fall
of "instruments of deception"' [2011] EIPR 204

Unfair competition

R Arnold, 'English unfair competition law' (2013)
44 IIC 63

A Breitschaft, 'The future of the passing-off action
in the law against unfair competition—an
evaluation from a German perspective' [2010]
EIPR 427

J Davis, 'Why the United Kingdom should have
a law against misappropriation' (2010) 69(3)
CLJ 561

C Wadlow, 'Passing off at the crossroads again: a
review article for Hazel Carty, An Analysis of the
Economic Torts' [2011] EIPR 447

17

Breach of confidence

Introduction

Scope and overview of chapter

17.1 This chapter considers contemporary law and policy relating to the protection of confidential information. This has its own important place within the legal and innovation landscape, and is also intertwined with human rights and intellectual property (IP).[1] The chapter begins with an overview of confidential information, including its legal basis and international relevance. The chapter summarises some key cases to give examples of the issues which arise, and the approaches which are adopted by the courts. It then reviews the action for breach of confidence. This has a long history, which is traced through scenarios involving personal secrets, national security, employment, post-employment, and regulation. The complex relationship between breach of confidence and the Human Rights Act 1998 (HRA 1998), and the expansion of the action, is explored. The controversial impact of the action on the public domain and defences based on the public interest and freedom of expression is also considered.

17.2 After discussing the parties who may in fact be involved in the action, the chapter then discusses the evolving relationship between secrecy and innovation, and the impact of certain other forms of information control. The international perspective is also explored. Note that this chapter will not consider questions of remedy save in respect of springboard orders, nor will it discuss the grant of injunctions in the light of section 12 of the HRA 1998. These are considered in Chapter 21.[2] The HRA 1998 is considered in more detail from the personal information perspective in Chapter 18.

17.3

Learning objectives

By the end of this chapter you should be able to describe and explain:

- when information can be confidential, and information in respect of which there is a reasonable expectation of privacy, such as to be the subject of a breach of confidence action;
- when the courts will find that there is an obligation not to disclose information, or other basis for information not to be disclosed;
- who can complain about use of information, and against whom;

---

[1] Consider *Vestergaard Frandsen A/S v BestNet Europe Ltd* [2011] EWCA Civ 424, para 56 when the Court of Appeal considers, in the context of remedy, that a claim for misuse of technical trade secrets is a claim to enforce an IP right.

[2] See in particular paras 21.44ff and 21.55–56.

- industries and situations where breach of confidence questions arise frequently;
- defences to the action;
- the role of confidence and secrecy in innovation;
- the relationship between breach of confidence and IP in the commercial and adversarial contexts;
- other information-related legislation which can be relevant to confidential information and IP, including in the EU context; and
- the international perspective.

17.4   So, the rest of the chapter looks like this:

- Overview (17.5–17.14)
- Elements of action (17.15–17.58)
- Defences (17.59–17.70)
- Parties to action (17.71–17.73)
- Confidence and IP (17.74–17.77)
- Secrecy and innovation (17.78–17.82)
- IP and other information regulation (17.83–17.85)
- International perspectives and approaches (17.86–17.87)
- Conclusions and the future (17.88).

Overview

Basics

17.5   The action for breach of confidence prevents use and disclosure of confidential information. The traditional base requires an obligation of confidence. The obligation might arise under a contract, say of employment, or may be implied. The obligation could be implied from the circumstances of receipt of information (eg through eavesdropping, or finding documents marked 'confidential' in a dustbin), or from the relationship between the parties involved in disclosure of information (eg solicitor/client or wife/husband). However, not all confidential information will be protected in all circumstances; and not all information which people might wish to keep secret (say, a celebrity bad hair day captured in the street and then posted on a social networking site) will be considered to be confidential.

17.6   Breach of confidence was remoulded by the HRA 1998. The court used first the action, and secondly the obligations imposed by the HRA 1998 in respect of the right to a private life in Article 8 of the European Convention on Human Rights (ECHR), into an action for 'misuse of private information'. The first step of this action was that there was information in respect of which there is a reasonable expectation of privacy. This action provided new protection in the privacy field,[3] and is considered in Chapter 18. This approach also had an impact on breach of confidence. The action will now cover both traditional and remoulded approaches to breach of confidence.

---

[3]   *Campbell v MGN Ltd* [2004] 2 AC 457, [2004] UKHL 22, paras 11 and 14, although the House of Lords stressed then that there was still no overarching action for breach of privacy.

When will a claim succeed?

17.7   It is not always enough for a person complaining to establish the initial requirements. Other factors often need to be taken into account. For example, in employment cases there is a careful balance between protecting trade secrets of the employer (eg proposals for developing new products, marketing plans, customer lists, and source codes) after the employee has left, and the ability of the employee to move on and utilise their acquired skill and knowledge. There is also the long-established public interest defence, which has been important in national security cases, for instance. This defence requires a balancing of the countervailing public interests in, first, the continuing confidentiality of material and, secondly, the disclosure proposed.[4]

17.8   Freedom of expression has long formed part of the public interest defence. However, the HRA 1998 provided a different basis for freedom of expression to be considered. By relying on the protection set out in Article 10 ECHR for freedom of expression, courts have developed a more methodical approach. The question is: would the restriction on freedom of expression involved, by preventing publication of the information, be proportionate? This test is now used in respect of all aspects of breach of confidence. How far will or should the relationship between human rights and breach of confidence extend? Could human rights (eg to life under the ECHR) be relied upon by a company wishing access to details of a new secret (and unpatented) cancer drug or climate change technology?[5]

Confidence and IP

17.9   Protection of information by choosing to keep it secret (hence the frequent use of the term 'trade secrets') and relying on breach of confidence differs importantly from the protection conferred by IP rights. IP protects the expression of an idea, an invention as claimed, or a design. In contrast, breach of confidence protects the basic underlying information. Thus, use of information to create a valuable new product might be in breach of confidence, even if there is no infringement of IP, say because of differences between the 'old' and 'new' products. Likewise, removing customer lists and business plans (rather than copying them) might avoid copyright infringement—but their use in a new venture could be in breach of confidence.[6]

17.10   Further, by relying on trade secrets, rather than seeking patent protection it would be possible for an inventor to have permanent control[7] over the use of the technology—in the sense that the action does not have a time limit, unlike a patent. Breach of confidence has, however, its own restrictions. Keeping information secret would not prevent third-party reverse engineering attempts[8] or independent development—always assuming that the information can indeed be kept secret.

The international angle

17.11   Confidential information is covered by two international agreements:

- The Agreement on Trade-Related Aspects of Intellectual Property Rights (TRIPS), Article 39(1) and (2), which provide that undisclosed information shall be protected in particular situations (similar to those explored here); and Article 39(3), which provides that undisclosed data submitted for regulatory clearance shall be protected against unfair commercial use.

---

[4] See also reference to public interest in the context of an application for an interim injunction: *ABC v Telegraph Media Group Ltd* [2018] EWCA Civ 2329, where information was disclosed in breach of non-disclosure agreements.

[5] See, eg, discussions about the activities of Myriad in the United States in relation to cancer work; sources at www.bionews.org.uk/page_93851.

[6] For an example of a dispute concerning both copyright infringement and breach of confidence in a business context see, on appeal from the Court of Appeal of Jamaica, *Paymaster (Jamaica) Ltd v Grace Kennedy Remittance Services Ltd* [2017] UKPC 40.

[7] See Chapters 10–12.   [8] See para 4.22 regarding reverse engineering and copyright.

- Paris Convention, Article 10*bis*—which provides that there shall be protection from unfair competition, including by acts contrary to honest practices in industrial and commercial matters.

What is breach of confidence (legally)?

17.12   The legal nature of breach of confidence in the UK jurisdictions is unclear.[9] Also unclear is whether information may be considered a form of IP at all.[10] The UK Supreme Court considered this in 2012 in *Phillips v News Group Newspapers*,[11] in the context of the waiver of self-incrimination which applies to infringement of 'rights pertaining to any IP rights'.[12] When considering interception of mobile phone messages, the court found that for those purposes, all technical or commercial information which is confidential would be treated as IP—whether or not it would otherwise be so regarded. More widely, courts have found that confidential information is[13] (and also that it is not),[14] a form of property, and this is the subject of detailed academic debate.[15] Others argue that the breach of confidence action is based on contract, the English concept of equity[16] (which does not exist in Scotland), or something else again.[17] This debate is likely to continue.[18]

17.13   The EU Trade Secrets Directive[19] was adopted in 2016. A 'trade secret' is defined in Article 2(1) of the Directive and reproduces almost exactly the definition in Article 39(2) of TRIPS. The strength of protection offered under breach of confidence means that the UK already substantively protects trade secrets. It is thus only the enforcement, and certain other, elements of the Directive that have been transposed into UK law.[20]

 Breach of confidence and Brexit

The substance of breach of confidence as a common law action will not be affected by withdrawal. The regulations on enforcement and other matters implementing the EU Trade Secrets Directive are to become part of retained EU law.

---

[9]   See general consideration of the Scots position in *Laws of Scotland: Stair Memorial Encyclopaedia*, vol 18, Part II, paras 1451 et seq. See also T Aplin, L Bently, P Johnson, and S Malynicz, *Gurry on Breach of Confidence: The Protection of Confidential Information* (2nd edn, 2012), Ch 4.

[10]   *R v Licensing Authority, ex p Smith Kline & French Laboratories Ltd (No 1)* [1990] 1 AC 64 at 79–80, 88 ('*SKF*'). For an analysis of information as property, see T Aplin, 'Confidential Information as Property?' (2013) 24 King's Law Journal 2, 172–201.

[11]   [2012] UKSC 28.

[12]   Section 72(2)(a) and (5) Senior Courts Act 1981, and note equivalent provision in Law Reform (Miscellaneous Provisions) (Scotland) Act 1985, s 15(2)(a) and (5).

[13]   See Scottish cases *Brown's Trustees v Hay* (1898) 6 SLT 113; *EFH Technologies Ltd v Rytium Technology FZC* [2010] CSOH 143. In England see *Boardman v Phipps* [1967] 2 AC 46; *Roger Bullivant Ltd v Ellis* [1987] FSR 172, headnote para 2; *SBJ Stephenson v Mandy* [2000] FSR 286, headnote 2, 298.

[14]   *Force India Formula One Team Ltd v 1 Malaysia Racing Team Sdn Bhd* [2012] EWHC 616, paras 377–8 (Ch); *Fairstar Heavy Transport NV v Adkins* [2012] EWHC 2952 (TCC); [2013] EWCA Civ 886.

[15]   eg L Bently, 'Trade secrets: "intellectual property" but not "property?"' in HR Howe and J Griffiths, *Concepts of Property in Intellectual Property Law* (2013).

[16]   See consideration by the Court of Appeal in *Napier v Pressdram Ltd* [2009] EWCA Civ 443, paras 16–19; *Commissioner of Police of the Metropolis v Times Newspaper* [2011] EWHC 2705 (QB), para 106; *Società Esplosivi Industriali SpA v Ordnance Technologies (UK) Ltd (formerly SEI (UK) Ltd)* [2008] RPC 12, esp para 42.

[17]   See consideration in N Witzleb, 'Justifying gain-based remedies for invasions of privacy' (2009) 29(2) OJLS 325–63. A different Scots cause of action, the *actio in iniuriam*, has also been considered in respect of non-information privacy. See HL MacQueen, 'Searching for privacy in a mixed jurisdiction' (2006) 21 Tulane European & Civil Law Forum 73.

[18]   See also A Hudson, 'Equity, confidentiality and the nature of property' in HR Howe and J Griffiths, *Concepts of Property in Intellectual Property Law* (2013), and compare E Reid, 'Breach of confidence: translating the equitable wrong into Scots law' Jur Rev 2014 1, 1–13. For a wider analysis of differing rationales, see Aplin et al, *Gurry on Breach of Confidence: The Protection of Confidential Information* (2nd edn, 2012), Ch 3.

[19]   Directive (EU) 2016/943 of the European Parliament and of the Council of 8 June 2016 on the protection of undisclosed know-how and business information (trade secrets) against their unlawful acquisition, use and disclosure OJ L 157, 15 June 2016, 1–18 ('Trade Secrets Directive'). See, for a discussion of the draft text, T Aplin, 'A critical evaluation of the proposed EU Trade Secrets Directive' (2014) 4 IPQ 257–79 and G Grassie, 'Trade secrets: the new EU enforcement regime' (2014) 9(8) JIPLP 677–83.

[20]   See Explanatory Memorandum to the Trade Secrets (Enforcement, etc.) Regulations 2018 no 597. The regulations came into force on 9 June 2018.

17.14 Notwithstanding uncertainty in the development of the law of breach of confidence, a set of principles, considered in this chapter, has emerged. Most of these come from decisions of the English courts. However, there is also strong authority for the existence of a general obligation of confidence in Scots law, which is at least similar to that in England.[21] Further, the UK-wide impact of the HRA 1998 suggests that, at least at the outset of an action, the same principles should be considered in each jurisdiction. It also suggests that there may be some convergence between decisions.

How does it work in practice? Some important examples

■ *Coco v AN Clark Engineers Ltd* [1968] FSR 415, [1969] RPC 41

Coco designed a moped engine and then negotiated with Clark about its manufacture. These discussions broke down and Clark designed an engine very similar to Coco's. In proceedings for breach of confidence (copyright was not alleged), it was held that for an action in breach of confidence to succeed, there must be (1) a contract imposing an obligation of confidence or information received in circumstances where the reasonable person would think they were under an obligation of confidence; and (2) use of the information. The court was willing to find an obligation of confidence, but was not satisfied that there was use of confidential information. Undertakings regarding future use were provided.

■ *Roger Bullivant Ltd v Ellis* [1987] FSR 172 (CA)

An employee moved to a rival and took with him a copy set of index cards with customer details from his former employer. Some of the information in the cards was publicly available, and the employee would have remembered some of it anyway. However, as the cards had been taken, an injunction was granted preventing use of the information for a reasonable period.

■ *London Regional Transport v Mayor of London* [2003] EMLR 4 (CA)

This concerned proposed disclosure of a report critical of Private–Public Partnerships in respect of the London Underground. The Court of Appeal balanced the interests of non-disclosure of confidential and commercially sensitive information and the interests of the public in being informed as to serious problems with this method of funding. It carried out a careful balance, considering the pressing and recognised social need for restriction of any right; whether the proposed restriction was greater than necessary; and whether there were logical reasons for it. Ultimately, a proposed compromise with some information blanked out was found to be acceptable.

■ *HRH Prince of Wales v Associated Newspapers Ltd* [2008] Ch 57 (CA), [2007] 3 WLR 222

The Prince of Wales had kept personal diaries commenting on the handover of Hong Kong to China. The Court of Appeal found that given the HRA 1998, for breach of confidence there must be (1) confidential information and a relationship of confidence; (2) private information in respect of which there was reasonable expectation of privacy;[22] or (3) both. This must then be balanced against rights to freedom of expression.

---

[21] *Lord Advocate v Scotsman Publications Ltd* 1989 SLT 705 at 708 and 1988 SLT 490 ('*Scotsman*') at 503. See also *Laws of Scotland: Stair Memorial Encyclopaedia*, vol 18, Part II, paras 1451 et seq. Scottish courts have been reluctant, however, to accept that the position would necessarily always be so, given the evolving nature of the field: *Quilty v Windsor* 1999 SLT 346. at 347 and 355.

[22] Discussed in Chapter 18.

Exercise

Devise a scenario which you think might involve breach of confidence in the context of an innovation business. You might get some ideas from other exercises in this chapter.

The next section reviews in more detail the traditional action for breach of confidence.

Elements of action

17.15   A useful starting point continues to be the three-step test set out in *Coco v Clark* considered previously.[23] The test can be summarised as follows:

- information to be of a confidential nature;
- information to be communicated in circumstances of confidence such that the reasonable person in the position of the recipient would realise that the information was given to them in confidence;
- unauthorised use of the information—(possibly) to the detriment of the confider.

What type of information is protected?

17.16   Over the years, cases have dealt with all manner of information: from the highly personal about individuals, through sports, trade, business, and technical information, ideas for television shows, and political and historical information about government, and indeed DNA.[24] The essential question is whether the information is confidential. Whether this is so is, perhaps surprisingly, not always clear and cases can involve detailed analysis of the facts, which might seem to suggest little of interest in other cases.[25]

 Discussion point   For answer guidance visit **www.oup.com/uk/brown5e**.

Write down three types of information you think of as confidential. Review your answer after reading to the end of para 17.28.

Nature of information

17.17   Not all information can be confidential. From decided cases, it can be discerned that to qualify information need not be complex[26] or of commercial value,[27] although some form of creativity[28] would likely be required. Courts have been reluctant to protect mere 'tittle tattle';[29] but some personal information, such as private diaries and details of sexual activities, has been found confidential.[30] Although, as noted, claims are frequent in the employment context, not all details of workplace activities will be confidential.[31]

---

[23] The decision, treated as a landmark, built on existing authorities, particularly *Saltman Engineering Co Ltd v Campbell Engineering Co Ltd* (1948) 65 RPC 203—see *Coco v Clark* [1968] FSR 415 at 419.

[24] In contrast, regarding the lack of confidentiality of a community resource, see discussion in 'India: International Covenant on Economic, Social and Cultural Rights (1966) art. 11—*Emergent Genetics v Shailendra Shivan*' [2012] IIC 355.

[25] See, eg, *Force India Formula One Team Ltd v 1 Malaysia Racing Team Sdn Bhd* [2012] EWHC 616, paras 36–200 and *Jones v IOS (UK) Ltd (In Liquidation)* [2012] EWHC 348 (Ch).

[26] *Cranleigh Precision Engineering Ltd v Bryant* [1965] 1 WLR 1293 at 1310; *Coco v Clark* [1968] FSR 415, 420.

[27] *Nichrotherm Electrical Co Ltd v Percy* [1956] RPC 272; aff'd [1957] RPC 207. See Aplin et al, *Gurry on Breach of Confidence: The Protection of Confidential Information* (2nd edn, 2012), 162–63.

[28] *Coco v Clark* [1968] FSR 415, 419–20.

[29] ibid, 426; cf *Stephens v Avery* [1988] 2 WLR 1280, [1988] Ch 449 at 454, finding wholesale revelation of sexual activity not to be tittle-tattle.

[30] See *Cadell Davies v Stewart* (1804) Mor App Literary Property No 4, 1 June 1804 FC; *Argyll v Argyll* [1967] Ch 302; *Stephens v Avery* [1988] 2 WLR 1280, [1988] Ch 449; *Barrymore v News Group Newspapers Ltd* [1997] FSR 600; *Mosley v News Group Newspapers Ltd* [2008] EWHC 1777 (QB), [2008] EMLR 20, paras 5, 6, and 105–08.

[31] *Tillery Valley Foods v Channel Four Television Corporation* [2004] EWHC 1075 (Ch) (films of frozen meals for hospitals made by someone working undercover as an employee), para 11.

Already in the public domain?

17.18 The content of information in question (either in isolation or in a combination of sources)[32] or its value[33] likely must not be public knowledge. Yet, unlike with patents, absolute novelty is not required—the key is the level of accessibility of the information. Information may be publicly available but not so widely known that confidentiality is destroyed.[34] A claim in confidence has in the past survived publication of the information overseas.[35] However, this approach would now be difficult to sustain given increased global communication technologies.

17.19 Information might still be confidential if it is published to a finite group, say passengers on an aeroplane, or a small number of readers.[36] In *BBC v HarperCollins Publishers Ltd*[37] regarding the identity of an individual known as 'The Stig' in a television programme, the court held that even where 'information has been published, the nature of the publication or the places where the publication is available or the period for which the published information was available might lead a court to conclude that the information was not "so generally accessible" to have lost its confidential character'.[38] There, however, the information had become generally accessible (through 13 different publications), so it could no longer be considered as confidential.[39] When more than one person is involved in the subject matter of information (say, a sexual relationship) and only one wants to disclose it, the other might still claim the information to be confidential, and both attitudes will be relevant to the court.[40] Information shared with a friend in confidence, however, will be confidential to that friend.[41]

17.20 If information has been disclosed for limited, specified purposes, it will remain confidential in respect of other purposes. The Prince of Wales providing confidential access to his diaries, in the case summarised in para 17.14, to his authorised biographer did not mean that they were no longer confidential.[42] If information is disclosed as part of a project, then when the project is completed the information must still be treated as confidential, but it likely can still be used by those involved, depending on the original agreement.[43]

17.21 *Speed Seal Products v Paddington*[44] suggested that confidentiality was lost only if information was published with the consent of the person to whom an obligation of confidence was owed. This case drew heavily, however, from a decision which was more likely based on breach of fiduciary duty.[45] The House of Lords considered the issue in *Attorney General v Guardian Newspapers Ltd (No 2)* ('*Spycatcher*'),[46] regarding the proposed publication in a UK newspaper of the diaries of a former member of the security services, Peter Wright. These diaries had already been published abroad; however, the House of Lords indicated that it might have been prepared to grant an injunction against Wright (who was not a party). Yet, some Law Lords suggested that this would not have been based on breach of a continuing obligation of confidence.[47]

---

[32] *Coco v Clark* [1968] FSR 415, 420. *Saltman Engineering Co Ltd v Campbell Engineering Co Ltd* (1948) 65 RPC 203, 215.

[33] See on this issue generally, Aplin et al, *Gurry on Breach of Confidence: The Protection of Confidential Information* (2nd edn, 2012), 148–51.

[34] *R (on the application of Ingenious Media Holdings plc) v Revenue and Customs* [2017] EMLR 6, para 25. In *Imerman v Tchenguiz and Others* [2010] EWCA Civ 908 I stored confidential information on a server that was accessible to T, the controller of the server. The Court of Appeal held at para 79 that 'confidentiality is not dependent upon locks and keys or their electronic equivalents.' See also *Force India Formula One Team Ltd v 1 Malaysia Racing Team Sdn Bhd* [2012] EWHC 616, regarding relative confidentiality, paras 217–222, 259–264.

[35] *Franchi v Franchi* [1967] RPC 149 (publication of foreign patent).

[36] Aplin et al, *Gurry on Breach of Confidence: The Protection of Confidential Information* (2nd edn, 2012), 151–55. See also *Woodward v Hutchins* [1977] 1 WLR 760, [1977] 2 All ER 751, 764 (disgraceful conduct of popstars on aeroplane might have been confidential, if there had been slightly different facts). Compare *Lord Advocate v Scotsman Publications Ltd* 1989 SLT 705, which left open whether small number of copies distributed privately meant the work was not confidential.

[37] [2011] EMLR 6.   [38] ibid, para 53.   [39] ibid, paras 51ff.

[40] *A v B plc* [2002] EWCA 337; (2003) QB 195 (CA), paras 43(iii), 79–80.   [41] *McKennitt v Ash* [2006] EWCA Civ 1714, paras 29–32.

[42] *HRH Prince of Wales v Associated Newspapers Ltd (No 3)* [2008] Ch 57 (CA), [2007] 3 WLR 222, paras 21, 43.

[43] See *Torrington Manufacturing Co v Smith & Sons (England) Ltd* [1966] RPC 285; cf *Regina Glass Fibre Ltd v Werner Schuller* [1972] FSR 141.

[44] *Speed Seal Products Ltd v Paddington* [1985] 1 WLR 1327 at 1332–33.

[45] *Cranleigh Precision Engineering Ltd v Bryant* [1965] 1 WLR 1293, 93. *Speed Seal* was agreed with by *Lord Advocate v Scotsman Publications Ltd* 1989 SLT 705, at 491–94.

[46] [1988] 3 WLR 776 at 785–86, 789, 791, 795–96, 809, 817.

[47] Other possibilities considered were Crown copyright, profiting from own wrong and springboard. See ibid, 786, 796; compare 791, 809–12, 818. Regarding Crown copyright, see also para 3.111.

17.22   More generally, in a long-running dispute involving a mosquito net, Arnold J considered that there was no general principle that injunctions could be granted in relation to breach of confidence once information was in the public domain.[48]

17.23   The confidentiality of photographs has given rise to a lot of discussion. A photograph may be confidential—even if it has been published, has the same subject as a photograph proposed to be published, or was taken in public. The fact that one can take a photograph in public does not mean one can publish it, if the subject matter is clearly controlled. For example, photographs of the set for the album cover of the band Oasis were confidential, as there was a clear indication that photography was not permitted.[49]

17.24   In *Douglas v Hello!*,[50] a freelance photographer managed to attend the wedding of Michael Douglas and Catherine Zeta-Jones and take photographs to sell to *Hello!* magazine. The wedding party permitted no unofficial photography, and had an exclusive deal with *OK!* magazine. The Court of Appeal considered that special treatment was appropriate for photographs (as opposed to other information potentially in the public domain) because of the invasive nature of photographs, and impact of their re-publication.[51] The photographs disclosed private information, and the fact that there was a contract for publication of other photographs of the wedding did not change this.[52] Further, the House of Lords also found that the publisher, which had entered into a contract to publish the photographs, had the right to control the information in the photographs.[53]

17.25   Information disclosed in open court or read by the judge is not confidential.[54] However, confidentiality is retained if hearings are not in open court or are behind locked doors, with restricted access to information ('confidentiality clubs'), and excerpted judgments.[55] This can lead to practical problems; how can a case proceed properly without proper consideration of the information, regard to transparency, and also the need to respect information which remains confidential, as is frequently seen in technology cases?[56] It should also be borne in mind that, say in asylum and public law cases, fundamental questions of safety can arise from the disclosure of confidential information.[57]

Government information

17.26   Government information can be confidential, if the court is satisfied that the public interest in confidentiality exceeds the public interest in the information being available.[58] This is a special hurdle, given the importance

---

[48]   *Vestergaard Frandsen A/S v BestNet Europe Ltd* [2010] FSR 2 at first instance, notably paras 22, 68–76 (note that the appeal did not consider this point). Compare para 17.68 and *Northern Rock plc v The Financial Times Ltd* [2007] EWHC 2677 (QB), in particular paras 15, 19–20, 25; *Attorney-General v Blake* [2001] 1 AC 268 (HL); *Schering Chemicals Ltd v Falkman Ltd* [1982] QB 1, including an overview of earlier cases, see 36, 37, 39, 40 and per Lord Denning at 15–17, 21–22.

[49]   In *Creation Records Ltd v News Group Newspapers Ltd* [1997] EMLR 444, paras 461–464 and *Shelley Films Ltd v Rex Features Ltd* [1994] EMLR 134 at 148–49 it is unclear whether the basis for order preventing further publication was confidentiality or to prevent a springboard benefit—see paras 17.68ff.

[50]   *Douglas and Others v Hello! Ltd (No 3)* [2005] EWCA Civ 595, [2005] 3 WLR 881.

[51]   *Campbell v MGN Ltd* [2004] 2 AC 457, [2004] UKHL 22, paras 31, 73–75, *Douglas and Others v Hello! Ltd (No 3)* [2005] EWCA Civ 595, [2005] 3 WLR 881, headnote 1, and paras 85–88, 105–108 (referring paras 40–41, 77–80 to *Theakston v MGN Ltd* [2002] EMLR 22, when injunction had been granted regarding photos but not words, and also referring to *Von Hannover v Germany* (App No 59320100) [2004] EMLR 21; (2005) 40 EHRR 1, para 59). See further *Mosley v News Group Newspapers Ltd* [2008] EWHC 1777 (QB), [2008] EMLR 20, paras 16–23.

[52]   *Douglas and Others v Hello! Ltd (No 3)* [2005] EWCA Civ 595, [2005] 3 WLR 881, para 95.

[53]   And as such, to treat them as any other trade secret. The decision of the House of Lords is reported at *OBG Ltd v Allan* [2007] UKHL 21, [2002] 1 AC 1, see paras 117–122, 278, 307, 310, 325–329; cf 255–259, 298–300. For detailed consideration of different approaches taken by the House of Lords, see G Black, 'Douglas v Hello!—An OK! result' (2007) 4(2) SCRIPTed 161 and more detailed discussion in Chapter 18.

[54]   Including where only read by the judge in advance, and not referred to in court; *Smithkline Beecham Biologicals SA v Connaught Laboratories Inc (Disclosure of Documents)* [2000] FSR 1. See also *Crossley v Newsquest (Midlands South) Ltd* [2008] EWHC 3054 (QB).

[55]   See *EPI Environmental Technologies Inc v Symphony Plastic Technologies plc* [2006] EWCA Civ 3 for an example of a redacted judgment.

[56]   See *Samsung Electronics Co Ltd v Apple Retail UK Ltd* [2012] EWHC 2277 (Pat), and brief decision in *Omnipharm Ltd v Merial* [2011] EWHC 3064 (Pat). See also Aplin et al, *Gurry on Breach of Confidence: The Protection of Confidential Information* (2nd edn, 2012), 415–24.

[57]   *R v Secretary of State for Home Department, ex p S* [2012] EWHC 955 (Admin).

[58]   *Attorney General v Guardian Newspapers Ltd (No 2)* ('Spycatcher') [1988] 3WLR 776, 783, 785, 796, 807 and in Australia *Cth v Jonathan Fairfax & Sons Ltd* (1980) 147 CLR 39 and *Smith Kline & French Laboratories (Australia) v Secretary to the Department of Community Services and Health* [1990] FSR 617, paras 21–22, 29. See also Aplin et al, *Gurry on Breach of Confidence: The Protection of Confidential Information* (2nd edn, 2012), 189–93.

of government information being available to the public. This status of government information was established in the UK jurisdictions well before other information regimes, which are introduced below (paras 17.83ff), came into being.

> ### Key points on when information is confidential
>
> • Not all information can be confidential.
> • It is possible for information to be confidential if there has been limited sharing or some disclosure.
> • There is a special public interest test in respect of government information.

What *is* the information?

17.27 An important legal and practical question is whether, and how well, the information can be identified.[59] If it cannot be clearly identified and distinguished from other information, the court will be unable to determine if it is in fact confidential; also, any court order could not be set out with sufficient clarity.[60] This raises two different problems for the party complaining: the necessary detail might not be available (eg if information was communicated orally or developed in someone's head); and overspecification might in fact reveal more than had previously been known by the other side.[61]

> ### Key point on identifying the information
>
> • It is important to specify information, to enable liability to be determined and remedy to be properly framed.

>
>
> ### Exercise
>
> Split the following list into three groups: is this information confidential: YES, NO, MAYBE? Is further information required?
>
> • The formula for a new product which had been kept locked in a safe.
> • The formula for an industry-staple product, which was launched years ago and is easy to reverse engineer—but is locked in a safe.
> • Next year's exam papers.
> • Details of the proposed use of asylum seekers for unlicensed drug tests as a condition for their being permitted to remain in the UK.

---

[59] *Inline Logistics v UCI Logistics* [2002] RPC 32. For an example of a case where information was not identified with the necessary precision, see *FSS Travel & Leisure Systems v Johnson* [1999] FSR 505 (CA) at 513.

[60] Compare, however, the broad approach to framing of order preventing future disclosure in *Levin v Farmers Supply Association of Scotland* 1973 SLT (Notes) 43 at 44. Detail was considered important, however, in *Ocular Sciences Ltd v Aspect Vision Care (No 2)* [1997] RPC 289 at 359. This case is considered in respect of unregistered design rights at paras 9.42–9.43 and 9.52.

[61] The importance of detail in identifying the claim and evidence can be seen, eg, in *Force India Formula One Team Ltd v 1 Malaysia Racing Team Sdn Bhd* [2012] EWHC 616, paras 267ff, where lack of detail had some negative consequences.

Discussion point   For answer guidance visit **www.oup.com/uk/brown5e**.

Is posting on social media the equivalent of speaking to a friend on the phone? How well can established principles be adapted to new technology?

An obligation: circumstances of confidence

When will the obligation exist?

17.28   Continuing with the *Coco v Clark* three-part test, an obligation of confidence is required for breach of confidence. As noted in the *HRH Prince of Wales* summary in para 17.14, however, and as is considered further later, it is also possible for an action to be brought for breach of confidence if there is no such obligation.[62] The obligation of confidence can be based on contract, but it need not be.[63] *Coco v Clark* set out an objective test to be applied when there is no contract; would the reasonable person realise that the information was given in confidence: how would the circumstances of receipt of information impact upon the conscience of the reasonable person?[64] There have been cases questioning whether a subjective test might also be appropriate given the reference to 'conscience'. However, so far this has not proved significant in identifying obligations.[65]

17.29   Obligations have been identified in respect of information obtained after hacking into a password-protected website,[66] during a heart-felt confession from a friend,[67] or by using illegal means to listen to phone calls.[68]

Scope

17.30   Even if there is an obligation, its scope must be established in each case. For example, it might be acceptable to use, but not disclose, information[69] or to use information for a different, but related, purpose than that for which it was collected.[70] In 2001 in relation to disclosure of anonymised medical data by pharmacists to marketing companies, the Court of Appeal said the key question as to scope was the conscience of the reasonable pharmacist.[71]

Discussion point   For answer guidance visit **www.oup.com/uk/brown5e**.

Plans for the University of Edingow to take over the University of Glasburgh (which are being met with riots in the streets) are posted on a blog clearly described as 'Private to Members of the University of Edingow', but require no password. Ross, a student at Sydbourne, finds the information and sends it to Hamish at a newspaper. Was Ross under an obligation of confidence? If so, how wide was this obligation?

---

[62]   See also Aplin et al, *Gurry on Breach of Confidence: The Protection of Confidential Information* (2nd edn, 2012), Ch 7.

[63]   *Matalia v Warwickshire County Council* [2017] EWCA Civ 991 (obligation of confidence found in the context of the disclosure of information relating to an exam paper).

[64]   *Coco v AN Clark Engineers Ltd* [1968] FSR 415, 419–25; see also *Attorney General v Guardian Newspapers Ltd (No 2) ('Spycatcher')* [1988] 3 WLR 776, 805; and *Napier v Pressdram Ltd* [2009] EWCA Civ 443, para 42.

[65]   This was considered in *Carflow Products (UK) Ltd v Linwood Securities (Birmingham) Ltd* [1996] FSR 424 at 424, 429. See also *Commissioner of Police of the Metropolis v Times Newspaper* [2011] EWHC 2705 (QB), paras 107–121 and para 17.64, n 164.

[66]   Although merely encrypting information, without more, has been held not to create an obligation of confidence: *Mars UK Ltd v Teknowledge Ltd (No 1) The Times*, 23 June 1999 (Ch D). See J Watts, 'Copyright: reverse engineering and encryption' (1999) 21(9) EIPR N158.

[67]   Eg *Stephens v Avery* [1988] 2 WLR 1280, [1988] Ch 449, 451, 453, 456.

[68]   In *Francome v Mirror Group* [1984] 2 All ER 408. Compare *Malone v Commissioner of Police of the Metropolis (No 2)* [1979] Ch 344 (information obtained from official wire tap was not a breach of confidence). See also paras 17.60 and 17.62.

[69]   *Coco v Clark* [1968] FSR 415, 419 and 421. See Aplin et al, *Gurry on Breach of Confidence: The Protection of Confidential Information* (2nd edn, 2012), 664–73.

[70]   *In re the Baronetcy of Pringle of Stichill* 2016 SLT 723 (use of DNA evidence that had been collected for a different, but related, purpose allowed in dispute over a baronetcy in Scotland).

[71]   *R v Department of Health, ex p Source Informatics (No 1)* [2001] QB 424, para 31.

> ### Key points on bases of obligation of confidence
>
> - Obligation can arise under contract.
> - Obligation can arise from circumstances of receipt, assessed (likely) using an objective test.
> - The scope of an obligation is to be assessed in each case, using an objective test.

Duration

17.31   Provided the information in question remains confidential, the obligation is infinite. Contractually imposed obligations (if they are not otherwise objectionable) can continue after the contract term[72]—provided the information does remain confidential. This is one attraction for business of relying on confidential information, rather than, say, patents[73] in respect of vaccines or copyright[74] in respect of customer lists.

17.32   With government information, the obligation depends upon the public interest balance, and so the obligation may cease if this balance changes.[75] Different balances have been reached in respect of members of the security services[76] and government ministers.[77]

> ### Question
> Would you prefer to rely on patents or confidential information for your business?

> ### Key point on duration
> - There is no time limit, provided the information remains confidential.

17.33   Two categories merit further consideration: particular types of obligation (including, importantly, employment) and indirect recipients of information.

Special relationships

Employment

17.34   There is an obligation of confidence during a period of employment. If the contract is silent the court will imply an obligation, on the basis of good faith and fidelity. The nature of the obligation will vary;[78] however, courts have implied terms preventing injury to employers' interests.[79] Courts have found that this would cover disclosure of secret information to competitors[80] or to a trade union.[81] But note, too, that some additional protection is also granted to whistleblowers.[82]

---

[72]   *Lady Archer v Williams* [2003] EWHC 1670, [2003] EMLR 38, para 47. Regarding the likely limited impact of a breach of the contract, see *Rock Refrigeration Ltd v Jones* [1997] 1 All ER 1 (CA) and *Campbell v Frisbee* [2002] EWHC 328 (Ch); [2002] EWCA Civ 1374.

[73]   See paras 11.14 and S Nisar, 'Pre-filing disclosure of an invention is found to be in breach of an equitable obligation of confidence' (2012) 7(7) JIPLP 485–86.

[74]   See paras 3.37.   [75]   See para 17.24, *Douglas and Others v Hello! Ltd (No 3)* [2005] EWCA Civ 595, [2005] 3 WLR 881, para 104.

[76]   *Attorney General v Guardian Newspapers Ltd (No 2) ('Spycatcher')* [1988] 3 WLR 776, 782, 790–91, 794, 808; *Lord Advocate v Scotsman Publications Ltd* 1989 SLT 705, 709 (lifelong obligation of confidence).

[77]   *Attorney General v Jonathan Cape Ltd* [1976] QB 752 (diaries of Cabinet discussions can be published after a decent interval).

[78]   *Faccenda Chicken Ltd v Fowler* [1986] FSR 291 at 302.

[79]   Including work done outside office hours—see *Hivac Ltd v Royal Park Scientific Instruments Ltd* [1946] 1 Ch 169. See also Aplin et al, *Gurry on Breach of Confidence: The Protection of Confidential Information* (2nd edn, 2012), Ch 11.

[80]   *Printers & Finishers Ltd v Holloway* [1965] 1 WLR 1, and *Roger Bullivant Ltd v Ellis* [1987] FSR 172.

[81]   *Bents Brewery v Hogan* [1945] 2 All ER 570.   [82]   Under the Public Interest Disclosure Act 1998.

17.35   Regarding preparations for the period after employment, courts have implied terms preventing making or memorising lists of customers[83] (although there are difficulties of proof if the information was publicly available)[84] or soliciting customers to join a new venture.[85] Not all preliminary activity will necessarily be prohibited: it is a question of fact and degree.[86] Courts have also extended the same approach to uses of new technologies, for example, regarding use of the names from a LinkedIn account.[87] A statement that 'I did it at home, I know these people anyway and they think of me, not my (former) employer' is unlikely to work.

17.36   After the employment term has ended, courts will imply a further, more limited, obligation. According to the leading case, *Faccenda Chicken Ltd v Fowler*,[88] former employees must not use or disclose information which is a trade secret or which in all the circumstances is so confidential that it requires the same level of protection.

17.37   *Faccenda* suggests that a trade secret must not be the skill, know-how, and general knowledge of the employee.[89] Decided cases suggest that it will also depend upon:

- the nature of the employment (if an employee frequently works with confidential information, eg in a locked lab);[90]

- the nature of the information (possibilities include secret processes or designs,[91] and customer lists);[92]

- whether the employer impressed the confidentiality of the information on the employee (eg locked doors, training sessions, or whether information is openly available and discussed);[93]

- whether the information could be readily isolated from other information;[94]

- whether there would be real or significant harm if the information were disclosed.[95]

17.38   Given some uncertainties in applying these principles in practice, an employer could choose to be proactive and clarify information status in the contract; it might also include a clause preventing the employee from working in the same field, possibly in the same geographic area, for a period. These clauses, known as restrictive covenants, will not be implied into contracts. They are also scrutinised carefully by courts.[96] For example, the Supreme Court in *Vestergaard Frandsen A/S v BestNet Europe Ltd*[97] declined to imply a term

---

[83] *Robb v Green* [1895] 2 QB 315; *Faccenda Chicken Ltd v Fowler* [1986] FSR 291, 302; *Roger Bullivant Ltd v Ellis* [1987] FSR 172, 175–81; *JN Dairies Ltd v Johal Dairies Ltd* [2009] EWHC 1331 (Ch), *Intercity Telecom v Solanki* [2015] 2 Costs LR 315.

[84] See also *Roger Bullivant Ltd v Ellis* [1987] FSR 172, 183. Followed in *Bradford & Bingley plc v Holden* [2002] EWHC 2445, but compare *Universal Thermosensors v Hibben* [1992] 1 WLR 840 and *SBJ Stephenson v Mandy* [2000] FSR 286, 298. See also *Sectrack NV v Satamatics* [2007] EWHC 3003 (Comm).

[85] *Faccenda Chicken Ltd v Fowler* [1986] FSR 291, 302; *Roger Bullivant Ltd v Ellis* [1987] FSR 172.

[86] See also *ABK v Foxwell* [2002] EWHC 9, 2002 WL 499040; *Churchill Retired Living Ltd v Luard* [2012] EWHC 1479 (Ch), and the Law of Society of Scotland's Guidelines, 'Social Media—Advice and Information for the Legal Profession', www.lawscot.org.uk/members/rules-and-guidance/rules-and-guidance/section-e/division-b/advice-and-information/social-media-advice-and-information-for-the-legal-profession.

[87] *Hays Specialist Recruitment (Holdings) Ltd et al v Ions et al* [2008] EWHC 745 (Ch).

[88] [1986] FSR 291. Followed in Scotland in *Harben Pumps (Scotland) Ltd v Lafferty* 1989 SLT 752.

[89] *Faccenda Chicken Ltd v Fowler* [1986] FSR 291, 303, *FSS Travel & Leisure Systems v Johnson* [1999] FSR 505 (CA), 516 and see *Lansing Linde v Kerr* [1991] 1 All ER 418. *Faccenda*, 306 left open the question of whether it would be breach of confidence if the employee simply passed on or sold information, rather than used it themselves. See also *Crowson Fabrics Ltd v Rider* [2008] FSR 17.

[90] *Faccenda Chicken Ltd v Fowler* [1986] FSR 291, 304.

[91] ibid, 303–304; *Littlewoods Organisation Ltd v Harris* [1978] 1 All ER 1026, [1977] 1 WLR 1472.

[92] See also *AT Poeton (Gloucester Plating) Ltd v Horton* [2001] FSR 14.

[93] *Faccenda Chicken Ltd v Fowler* [1986] FSR 291, 305.

[94] ibid, 305. See also *FSS Travel & Leisure Systems v Johnson* [1999] FSR 505 (CA), 516.

[95] *Lansing Linde v Kerr* [1991] 1 All ER 418, [1991] 1 WLR 251 (CA), 270. Nominal damages only will be granted where a former employee made limited or no use of confidential information: *Marathon Asset Management v Seddon* [2017] FSR 36, para 157.

[96] This was stressed by the Court of Appeal in *Faccenda Chicken Ltd v Fowler* [1986] FSR 291, 304–05. Regarding garden leave as well as or instead of a restrictive covenant, see *GFI Group Inc v Eaglestone* [1994] FSR 535 (but compare *Provident Finance Group v Hayward* [1989] 3 All ER 298). In relation to England and Wales, the Fraud Act 2006, s 4 (fraud by abuse of position), may also have some impact: see consideration in B Allgrove and S Sellers, 'The Fraud Act 2006: is breach of confidence now a crime?' (2009) 4(4) JIPLP 278–82.

[97] [2013] UKSC 31.

into a contact of employment regarding trade secrets when a person does not know the trade secrets, and is not aware they are being misused. The Court stated: 'Although the protection of intellectual property is vital to the economic prosperity of the country, the law should not discourage former employees from benefitting society and advancing themselves by imposing unfair potential difficulties on their honest attempts to complete with their former employers.'[98]

17.39 *Faccenda* provides that a restrictive covenant will not be enforced unless the protection sought was reasonable and necessary to protect trade secrets or prevent abuse of personal influence over customers.[99] It is a difficult balance. Is an employer protecting legitimate business information which cannot be erased from memory, and might require a special protection for a time? Or is the employer placing an unreasonable restriction on the employee's ability to work elsewhere, exploiting their skill and know-how?[100] Laddie J was more succinct in *Polymasc Pharmaceuticals v Charles*:[101] is the clause 'too greedy'?[102]

17.40 It should also be borne in mind that in a case involving Formula 1 motor-racing technology, Arnold J was of the view that the same approach should be taken both to independent contractors and to employees.[103] Competition law concerns, considered in more detail in Chapter 20, can also be relevant here. In *Jones v Ricoh UK Ltd*[104] it was held that a very extensively drafted confidentiality agreement was in breach of Article 101 of the Treaty on the Functioning of the European Union (TFEU) and was void.[105]

Key points on employment relationship and beyond

- There is an obligation of confidence in the course of employment.
- After employment, there is an obligation not to disclose trade secrets or equivalent.
- Restrictive covenants are only enforced to the extent reasonable and necessary, balancing the interests of employer and employee.
- Problem areas are new product ideas, business plans, know-how sets and customer lists, social media connections, and accounts.

Exercise

Katie is headhunted to join Eversogood Ltd. Katie has been in charge of developing a new chocolate bar for FunFunFun Ltd. FunFunFun gave her no support, she worked on her own, and wrote nothing down. On joining Eversogood, Liz, her line manager, offered a team of researchers to work with Katie to develop a new chocolate bar. Being conscientious, Katie shared some ideas with her new team and, as some of them are overseas, they have started sharing ideas about this on Twitter, as it is so much quicker than the slow (but secure) corporate intranet. They then developed a much improved third-generation product. Discuss.

---

[98] ibid, para 44. [99] *Faccenda Chicken Ltd v Fowler* [1986] FSR 291, 303–04.

[100] *Lock International plc v Beswick* [1989] 1 WLR 1268; *Balston v Headline Filters Ltd (No 2)* [1990] FSR 385 (CA). See also *Hinton & Higgs (UK) Ltd v Murphy* 1989 SLT 450; *Roger Bullivant Ltd v Ellis* [1987] FSR 172; *Basic Solutions Ltd v Sands* [2008] EWHC 1388 (QB); *Wrn Ltd v Ayris* [2008] EWHC 1080 (QB), [2008] IRLR 889; *Mantis Surgical Ltd v Tregenza* [2007] EWHC 1545 (QB); and *Thomas v Farr plc and Hanover Park Commercial Ltd* [2007] EWCA Civ 118, [2007] ICR 932.

[101] [1999] FSR 711 at 719.

[102] See also Aplin et al, *Gurry on Breach of Confidence: The Protection of Confidential Information* (2nd edn, 2012), Ch 12. For an example of a court granting an injunction against a former employee for a 12-month notice period, see *Elsevier Ltd v Munro* [2014] EWHC 2468 (QB).

[103] *Force India Formula One Team Ltd v 1 Malaysia Racing Team Sdn Bhd* [2012] EWHC 616, paras 234, 235.

[104] [2010] EWHC 1743 (Ch). [105] ibid, paras 39–49.

Other special situations

17.41   Obligations of confidence exist where there is a particular relationship, as, for example, between professional adviser and client or doctor and patient.[106] Difficulties can arise when professionals move or firms merge—although it is clear that the obligations do continue.[107]

17.42   There are often specific restrictions on when information obtained on a particular statutory or regulatory basis can be used or passed to others. This could involve information obtained pursuant to, for example, the Police and Criminal Evidence Act 1984 or for regulatory product clearance.[108] The outcome in each case will depend on the proposed conduct, the wording of the legislation, and the function of the regulator.

17.43   There is an obligation of confidence in marriage and in stable relationships. The scope and, indeed, existence of this declines with the level of involvement,[109] and even within a marriage, one partner can still enjoy rights of privacy as against the other.[110]

Key points on special situations

- There is obligation of confidence within marriage or equivalent.
- There is obligation of confidence between professional adviser and client.

 Question

Does your best friend owe you an obligation of confidence? Consider in the light of *McKennitt v Ash* [2006] EWCA Civ 1714 (CA).

Indirect recipient

17.44   An employee might take information with them to a new employer, but may be unable to use the information without the colleagues and resources available with that new employer. Or a memory stick left in a laptop found on a bus might mean nothing to the 'finder', who then passes it to a friend in the IT industry. What is the position of these new recipients? This distinction can be important in practice—as the real concern of the original holder of the information might be what another business might do with it.

---

[106]   See Aplin et al, *Gurry on Breach of Confidence: The Protection of Confidential Information* (2nd edn, 2012), Ch 9 regarding particular relationships and responsibilities: consultants and contractors, licensing, bankers, ministers of religion, doctors and other health professionals, lawyers and other professionals, personal intimate relationships, and fidicuaries—although breach of that professional responsibility will not necessarily mean that there has been a breach of confidence: *May v Chartered Institute of Management Accountants* [2013] EWHC 1574 (Admin).

[107]   See *Surface Technology v Young* [2002] FSR 25.

[108]   Compare *R v Licensing Authority, ex p Smith Kline & French Laboratories Ltd (No 1)* [1990] 1 AC 64 at 79–80, 88, 70–78, 81–82, 84–85, 86–87, 89–90 and on the same facts *R v Licensing Authority, ex p Smith Kline & French Laboratories Ltd (No 1)* [1990] 1 AC 64. Regarding international perspectives more generally, see paras 17.86ff.

[109]   *Argyll v Argyll* [1967] Ch 302, 322, 329–30. Post-HRA 1998 authorities are also relevant here: *A v B plc* [2002] EWCA 337, paras 11(xi), 29, 43, 47; *McKennitt v Ash* [2006] EWCA Civ 1714 (CA), paras 29–30; *Theakston v MGN Ltd* [2002] EWHC 137, [2002] EMLR 22, paras 57–61, 74, 76; and *Mosley v News Group Newspapers Ltd* [2008] EWHC 1777 (QB), [2008] EMLR 20, paras 105–109. These are considered in more detail in paras 18.9ff.

[110]   *Imerman v Tchenguiz and Others* [2010] EWCA Civ 908, paras 54–71, 80–89.

17.45 The principles in *Coco v Clark* continue to apply here: would a reasonable person believe that the information was received subject to an obligation.[111] Third parties were considered in *Spycatcher*,[112] when the House of Lords suggested that there was an obligation of confidence not only in:

> those cases where a third party receives information from a person who is under a duty of confidence in respect of it, knowing that it has been disclosed by that person to him in breach of his duty of confidence, but also to include certain situations, beloved of law teachers—where an obviously confidential document is wafted by an electric fan out of a window into a crowded street, or where an obviously confidential document, such as a private diary, is dropped in a public place, and is then picked up by a passer-by.

17.46 The more intervening recipients there have been in respect of the information, the less likely it is that there will be an obligation:[113] say, a former employee tells a new colleague who later takes information to a third employer, or the finder on the bus passes it to a colleague with a plausible explanation. The key test for such recipients has been held to be dishonest conduct. Carelessness, stupidity, or naivety (eg believing the explanation without question) would not suffice.[114]

17.47 If there is no obligation, then, on that base, there can be no liability. However, if someone is subsequently told that information is confidential, there will be an obligation from that time.[115]

Key point on indirect recipients of confidential information

- Indirect recipients may be subject to obligations of confidence.

Exercise

Go back to Hamish, Ross, and Edingow (in the Discussion point following para 17.30). Is Hamish under an obligation of confidence? What about Hamish's editor? Draw a diagram setting out when there will be obligations of confidence, noting relevant factors.

Other bases for liability: the human rights impact

17.48 The Court of Appeal confirmed in *HRH Prince of Wales v Associated Newspapers Ltd*[116] summarised above in para 17.14 that even if there is no obligation of confidence on the bases discussed above, an action for breach of confidence can still be brought in respect of information for which there is a reasonable expectation of privacy pursuant to Article 8 ECHR. This second element (which can exist alongside an obligation) is considered in more detail in Chapter 18 in respect of personal information.[117] Courts have stressed, however, that the movement to human rights has not brought about a general action in respect of information.[118]

---

[111] In *Shelley Films Ltd v Rex Features Ltd* [1994] EMLR 134, the photographic agency was found to have knowledge of restrictions so was under an obligation not to publish, 149–51.

[112] *Attorney General v Guardian Newspapers Ltd (No 2) ('Spycatcher')* [1988] 3 WLR 776, 806.

[113] See Aplin et al, *Gurry on Breach of Confidence: The Protection of Confidential Information* (2nd edn, 2012), 263–65.

[114] *Thomas v Pearce* [2000] FSR 718 (CA) at 719, 721, which includes careful analysis of objective and subjective tests. See also *Carflow Products (UK) Ltd v Linwood Securities (Birmingham) Ltd* [1996] FSR 424.

[115] See, eg, *Surface Technology v Young* [2002] FSR 25. It is likely, given the equitable nature of the obligation, that even if someone pays for information, there will still be an obligation if there is the necessary knowledge: *Stephenson Jordan & Harrison Ltd v Macdonald & Evans* (1952) 69 RPC 10 at 16. See also *Burrows v Smith* [2010] EWHC 22 (Ch).

[116] [2008] Ch 57, [2007] 3 WLR 222, paras 64–65 per Lord Phillips. Note consideration of this case in respect of copyright at paras 5.33 and 5.38. See also *HRH Prince of Wales v Associated Newspapers Ltd* [2007] EWHC 1685 (Ch), which brought that matter finally to an end.

[117] See, eg, *Abbey v Gilligan* [2012] EWHC 3217 (QB) (emails in a business context regarding Sebastian Coe Ltd, against the backdrop of the award of the 2012 Olympics to London); the action was for breach of confidence, alternatively misuse of private information, para 20.

[118] *White v Withers LLP* [2008] EWHC 2821 (QB).

17.49   Human rights may also have introduced other linked bases for liability. The first possibility is that companies, as well as individuals, have their own rights to privacy under Article 8 ECHR.[119] The Court of Justice of the European Union (CJEU) considered this in *AbbVie v European Medicines Agency*[120] in respect of a decision by a regulator to provide third-party access to clinical study reports regarding the safety and efficacy of a product. It was argued that the reports involved commercial information which fell within Article 8 ECHR. The CJEU found that the existence of this right did not necessarily mean that the disclosure would cause serious and irreparable damage to them, nor that the information was commercially confidential, and this had not been established in this case.[121] However, the decision clearly supports the ability of companies to use this base of claim.[122] Support for a wider application of this can be taken from the Court of Appeal's decision regarding the extent to which confidential information of a company should be excluded from a public authority's statutory obligations in respect of audit—the court found that the obligation to disclose could be limited, perhaps by Article 8 ECHR.[123]

17.50   In that same case, the Court was more clearly of the view that the obligation could also be limited on the basis that confidential information was property within Protocol 1, Article 1 ECHR. It could therefore only be interfered with in some cases.[124] This provides, therefore, a human rights justification for the property base introduced at the start of this chapter. It will be interesting to see if these decisions lead to an increase in the number of claims by companies for breach of confidence which have human rights as their base.

Relevant conduct

What is required?

17.51   There must be some conduct for there to be a breach of confidence. The conduct can be of the old-fashioned kind, for example, giving a file to a competitor or a journalist (or, indeed, leaving it on the bus), or as was the case in *Kerry Ingredients (UK) Ltd v Bakkavor Group Ltd*,[125] a manufacturer using information given to them to manufacture a product in order to produce their own.

17.52   However, the nature of the breach is closely tied to the scope of the obligation; not all activities in relation to relevant information will constitute a breach. Thus, it can be breach of confidence to use or disclose information, including doing more with information than that to which the subject consented.[126] The disclosure of anonymised medical information by pharmacists to marketing companies was not a breach of their obligation of confidence. The interest of the subject was held to be in not being identified, rather than in the confidentiality of the underlying information.[127] Evidence is key—for example, the confidential idea of a TV show was found to have been disclosed, but the show which was alleged to have resulted was in fact found to have been developed independently.[128]

Detriment

17.53   It is unclear whether, for there to be breach of confidence, detriment must be suffered as a result of the disclosure. The requirement is suggested in *Coco v Clark*.[129] However, that case involved commercial secrets,

---

[119]   T Aplin, 'Commercial confidences after the Human Rights Act 1998' (2007) 10 EIPR 411, criticising the need for this.
[120]   *AbbVie v European Medicines Agency* (C-389/13 P(R)) [2014] 2 CMLR 21.
[121]   Case referred back to the General Court, which had quashed the decision of the regulator on the basis that the disclosure would irreparably damage AbbVie's business secrets and its right to an effective remedy.
[122]   Also Art 7 EU Charter of Fundamental Rights and Freedoms 2000, right to respect for private and family life.
[123]   *Veolia ES Nottinghamshire Ltd v Nottinghamshire CC* [2010] EWCA Civ 1214, esp para 141.
[124]   T Aplin, 'Confidential Information as Property?' (2013) 24 King's Law Journal 2. Regarding access to information more generally, see paras 17.83ff.
[125]   [2016] EWHC 2448 (Ch) (regarding production of flavoured cooking oils).
[126]   *Cornelius v De Taranto* (2001) 68 BMLR 62 involved overly wide disclosure of medical information in the circumstances.
[127]   *R v Department of Health, ex p Source Informatics (No 1)* [2001] QB 424, paras 34–35.
[128]   *Wade v British Sky Broadcasting Ltd* [2014] EWHC 634 (Ch), [2016] EWCA Civ 1214.   [129]   *Coco v Clark* [1968] FSR 415, 425.

where it is more likely that detriment would follow, so its consideration would seem uncontroversial. In other situations, say, disclosure to a new colleague who does not act on the information, there may be no detriment, and if the essence of the action is the obligation not to use, it would seem that 'loss' should not be required when there is use.[130] Discussions, in particular in *Spycatcher* (where it was noted that the necessary detriment could be a wider loss of morale of the security services), suggest that a broad approach may be taken by the courts.[131]

Intention

17.54   There is no requirement of intention. Thus, acts in good faith, unconscious use, and drawing on information obtained in long-forgotten circumstances, can still be in breach of confidence.[132]

Risk of use and disclosure

17.55   Breach of confidence is, as noted, a particular concern for solicitors[133] and accountants. Clients are often concerned if their former adviser moves firms. There have been a number of cases on confidentiality proposals, seeking orders that, for example, a partner does not go into the office for the duration of a particular matter, to remove the risk of use or disclosure of confidential information. If proposals for avoiding use or disclosure of such information are clear, robust, and avoid the possibility of interaction, the court will be likely to refuse orders.[134] The more ad hoc the arrangements, the more the potential for interaction,[135] the closer the nature of the transaction is to what had been done in the past, and if there is information which might be relevant when acting for a new client,[136] then the burden will shift. The second firm must establish there is no risk that there will be use; if not, it is likely that the court would make an order. Courts have considered these principles in cases involving in-house professional advisers but have concluded that the more general employment position, regarding movement of workers set out in *Faccenda* and the restrictive covenant cases, continues to apply.[137]

Regulatory powers

17.56   As noted, the scope of regulatory and statutory obligations in respect of information varies, as does what will constitute breach. Information obtained by the police under the Police and Criminal Evidence Act 1984 cannot be handed over to others without a subpoena.[138] Rather, it should be held for the purposes for which it is seized: investigation of crime.[139] Information can in some cases be passed to other bodies for

---

[130]   See consideration in *Laws of Scotland: Stair Memorial Encyclopaedia*, vol 18, Part II, para 1477.

[131]   *Attorney General v Guardian Newspapers Ltd (No 2) ('Spycatcher')* [1988] 3 WLR 776, 782, 785, 786, 800, 802, 806—the basis for the decision is unclear. The book had already been published. In *Lord Advocate v Scotsman Publications Ltd* 1989 SLT 705, 497, 500–01, 504–05 similar arguments of 'non-contents detriment' failed to prevent an injunction.

[132]   *Seager v Copydex Ltd (No 1)* [1967] FSR 211 at 212, 221, 224; *Terrapin Ltd v Builders Supply Co (Hayes) Ltd* [1967] RPC 375 at 390. Aplin et al, *Gurry on Breach of Confidence: The Protection of Confidential Information* (2nd edn, 2012), 673–76.

[133]   Including in respect of those who are not their clients. For consideration of this in relation to a firm of solicitors and its actions against alleged infringers of IP through downloading, see S Webb, 'The strictest confidence' (2011) 21(Jan) Sol 10–11.

[134]   *Koch Shipping v Richards Butler* [2002] EWCA Civ 1280.   [135]   *Young v Robson Rhodes* [1999] All ER 524.

[136]   *Prince Jefri Bolkiah v KPMG* [1999] 2 WLR 215, [1999] 2 AC 222 (HL) (arrangements criticised as ad hoc, and the court considered that a 'wait-and-see' approach or undertaking cannot suffice). See also *Marks & Spencer v Freshfields Bruckhaus Deringer* [2004] EWCA Civ 741; aff'g [2004] 1 WLR 2331 and *Winters v Mishcon de Reya* [2008] EWHC 2419 (Ch). As suggested in this case, regard should be paid in this context to other regulatory rules, eg of the Financial Services Authority (which has since been replaced by other bodies, including the Financial Conduct Authority); see also A Henderson, 'Confident about confidentiality? Civil claims for the misuse of price sensitive information' (2003) 24(4) Comp Law 116–18.

[137]   See decision of the Court of Appeal in *Caterpillar Logistics Services v Huesca de Crean* [2012] EWCA Civ 156; compare *Generics (UK) v Yeda Research and Development Co Ltd* [2012] EWCA 726, paras 28–40 and compare confidential Appendices para 42–89 and 97–107.

[138]   *Marcel v Commissioner of Police of the Metropolis* [1992] Ch 225, [1992] 2 WLR 50 (CA). The court considered that the original document owners should be told of the subpoena. In *Re Barlow Clowes Gilt Managers* [1992] Ch 208, [1992] 2 WLR 36, this was considered regarding information disclosed to liquidators and the scope for disclosure to directors of a company.

[139]   *Marcel v Commissioner of Police of the Metropolis* [1992] Ch 225, [1992] 2 WLR 50 (CA), 233–35. See also *Bunn v BBC* [1999] FSR 70 finding that a statement made to the police attracted confidentiality, as there was a strong public interest in encouraging full disclosure to the police.

public purposes; however, this should be done with care to avoid 'The dossier of private information . . . the badge of the totalitarian state'.[140] It has been found that information held under (a since repealed section of) the Banking Act 1987 cannot be passed on to any person—including as part of discovery and disclosure in civil litigation. The same information could be passed on, however, if it were also or later obtained through other means.[141]

17.57   Pharmaceutical companies (usually, but not necessarily, patent owners), supply confidential test data to medicines regulators to obtain regulatory clearance. It has been held that the regulator may use this data to assess whether clearance should also be granted to another company in respect of a generic product (usually for launch after the patent term). Courts considered that this use of information was consistent with the regulator's function in respect of public safety, and that requests for the data to be held as confidential could not be taken as preventing such use.[142] However, the court stressed that the regulator may not disclose the data to anyone else. It will be interesting to note whether the human rights base of argument explored in *AbbVie* (para 17.49) has an impact on this.

> ### Key points on conduct
>
> • What will constitute a breach is closely linked with the scope of the obligation.
>
> • The requirement of detriment is unlikely to be a stumbling block.
>
> • There is no element of intention.
>
> • Problems arise frequently for professional advisers and regulators.

17.58   Even the combination of confidential information and obligation/human rights base and use does not mean that an action will succeed. There are several defences. The most significant, particularly from the pre-HRA 1998 era, is that disclosure is in the public interest.[143]

Defences

Public interest defence

17.59   The roots of the public interest 'defence' lie in the concept of there being no confidence in iniquity[144] such that information about fraud, for example, could not be confidential. In the 1970s and 1980s, however, starting with *Fraser v Evans*,[145] this concept developed into broader defence of 'just cause for breaking confidence'. The House of Lords in *Spycatcher*[146] said:

> although the basis of the law's protection of confidence is that there is a public interest that confidences should be preserved and protected by the law, nevertheless that public interest may be outweighed by some

---

[140] *Marcel v Commissioner of Police of the Metropolis* [1992] Ch 225, [1992] 2 WLR 50 (CA), 235 et seq.

[141] *Price Waterhouse v BCCI (In Liquidation) (No 3)* [1997] 3 WLR 849, [1998] Ch 84 at 93–94, 97–99, 102–05, re the Banking Act 1987, s 82(1) (now repealed, on the disclosure of information by financial regulators see Financial Services and Markets Act 2000); regarding disclosure of confidential information for use in an Inquiry, see *O'Hara v The Belfast Health and Social Care Trust* [2012] NIQB 75.

[142] *R v Licensing Authority, ex p Smith Kline & French Laboratories Ltd (No 1)* [1990] 1 AC 64, 64–65, 68, 78–82, 84–85, 88–90. See also on the same facts *R v Licensing Authority, ex p Smith Kline & French Laboratories Ltd (No 1)* [1990] 1 AC 64.

[143] See consideration of the public interest in respect of copyright infringement at para 5.60ff.

[144] *Gartside v Outram* (1856) 26 LJ Ch 113 at 114; *Beloff v Pressdram* [1973] FSR 33; [1973] RPC 765 (this case is considered in respect of copyright at para 5.33).

[145] [1968] 3 WLR 1172, [1969] 1 QB 349 at 362. Followed in *Hubbard v Vosper* [1972] 2 WLR 389, [1972] 2 QB 84 (CA) (regarding publication of the confidential works of the Church of Scientology).

[146] *Attorney General v Guardian Newspapers Ltd (No 2) ('Spycatcher')* [1988] 3WLR 776, 807; also 785, 794–95, 798, 800–01, 812. See also *Lord Advocate v Scotsman Publications Ltd* 1989 SLT 705, 709, 710, 712–13.

countervailing public interest which favours disclosure . . . It is this limiting principle which may require a court to carry out a balancing operation, weighing against the public interest in maintaining the confidence against a countervailing public interest favouring disclosure.

17.60 The application of the public interest defence and balancing act has been criticised as open to 'idiosyncracy'.[147] The public interest defence was an important weapon for the free press, but its application was invariably controversial.[148] Further, disclosure in the public interest did not necessarily mean disclosure to the press. The police or a regulator would likely be deemed more appropriate by courts;[149] however, this would depend on the nature of the information and those involved.[150]

17.61 There are interesting examples of how a careful balance of interests has been carried out in the medical field. In 1988, identification of doctors being treated for AIDS was found not to be in the public interest, given the countervailing interest in encouraging seeking of treatment and in the confidentiality of medical records.[151] However, in 1989, the doctor–patient relationship was overridden by the public interest in public safety. A report on mental health regarding a person suffering from schizophrenia was sent ultimately to the Home Secretary and this was held not to be breach of confidence.[152]

17.62 Finally, the public interest defence might be available if public bodies are discharging their public function—for example, phone-tapping by the police.[153]

Key points on public interest defence

- This has developed from 'no confidence in iniquity' to a careful balance of important public interests in both confidence and disclosure.
- The identity and function of both parties may be important.

Freedom of expression and public interest defence

17.63 As in respect of the creation of a base of claim for breach of confidence, the HRA 1998 has had an impact on defences. This is on the basis of the right in Article 10 ECHR to freedom of expression. The second phase of the Court of Appeal's summary of the action in *HRH Prince of Wales v Associated Newspapers Ltd (No 3)* was that each of the bases of claim must then be balanced against Article 10.[154]

Article 10 ECHR

(1) Everyone has the right to freedom of expression. This right shall include freedom . . . to receive and impart information and ideas without interference by public authority and regardless of frontiers . . .

(2) The exercise of these freedoms, since it carries with it duties and responsibilities, may be subject to such formalities, conditions, restrictions or penalties as are prescribed by law and are necessary in a democratic society . . . for the protection of the reputation or rights of others, for preventing the disclosure of information received in confidence . . . .

---

[147] *R v Licensing Authority, ex p Smith Kline & French Laboratories Ltd (No 1)* [1990] 1 AC 64, 663.

[148] See Aplin et al, *Gurry on Breach of Confidence: The Protection of Confidential Information* (2nd edn, 2012), 683ff.

[149] *Initial Services Ltd v Putterill* [1968] 1 QB 396, 405; *Malone v Commissioner of Police of the Metropolis (No 2)* [1979] Ch 344, 376–78; *Francome v Mirror Group* [1984] 2 All ER 408, [1984] 1 WLR 892, 898. See also *Butler v Board of Trade* [1971] Ch 680 at 690 regarding the public interest in availability of information to authorities for use in criminal proceedings.

[150] *Lion Laboratories v Evans* [1985] QB 526.

[151] *X (HA) v Y* [1988] 2 All ER 648, 395–96. See also the decision of the ECtHR in *I v Finland* (2009) 48 EHRR 31.

[152] *W v Egdell* [1989] 2 WLR 689, [1989] 1 All ER 1089.

[153] *Malone v Commissioner of Police of the Metropolis (No 2)* [1979] Ch 344, 362, 367.

[154] *HRH Prince of Wales v Associated Newspapers Ltd (No 3)* [2008] Ch 57 (CA), [2007] 3 WLR 222, para 65 per Lord Phillips.

17.64   The Court of Appeal in *HRH Prince of Wales v Associated Newspapers Ltd (No 3)* had reviewed the public interest defence. It considered this defence to be more limited than that required by Article 10, and that there must rather be a balance on a proportionate basis.[155] This is supported by the earlier decision of the Court of Appeal in *London Regional Transport v Mayor of London*[156] in 2001, summarised in para 17.14. In *London Regional Transport*, the Court considered[157] that Article 10 was central to breach of confidence, provided a methodical approach based on proportionality,[158] and that it was more familiar to lawyers than the open flexibility of the pre-HRA public interest defence.[159] The key questions were: was there a pressing and recognised social need for the restriction on any right; was the proposed restriction greater than necessary; and were there logical reasons for it.[160]

17.65   Yet the terminology of the 'public interest' persists in post-HRA case law, including alongside references to Article 10.[161] It remains to be seen how this field develops. The Trade Secrets Directive provides that the action shall not apply in the case of legitimate freedom of expression and disclosure of public interest information to judicial, administrative, or public authorities.[162] There is also a limited public interest provision confined to revelations of 'misconduct, wrongdoing or illegal activity'.[163] But note also that the Trade Secrets Directive contemplates that rules for the protection of trade secrets ought to take into account public interests, including within that specific reference to public safety, health, and protection of the environment.[164]

> ### Key points on the impact of the HRA on defences to breach of confidence
>
> - Article 10 ECHR is an important part of an action for breach of confidence, irrespective of the starting point and type of information.
> - Article 10 is a wider counter to confidence than the pre-HRA public interest defence.
> - Article 10 will be assessed in a more methodical manner than the pre-HRA public interest defence.
> - But references to 'the public interest' continue to appear.

> ### Exercise 1
>
> Big Bad Oil Co funds research by Car Co to prove that green fuel could never work. Car Co finds that it would. An environmental charity uses surveillance devices to record discussions between Big Bad Oil Co and Car Co about this; the charity then gives the information to the UK government. The information cannot now be verified as records have been destroyed in a fire. Big Bad Oil want to sue the charity. Discuss.
>
> ### Exercise 2
>
> Article 10 ECHR has prevailed over confidentiality obligations in some cases. Could an argument based on the ECHR right to life and/or Article 10 lead to pharmaceutical companies being obliged to disclose new work, even if they choose not to patent it?

---

[155] ibid, paras 32, 54–60.   [156] [2001] EWCA Civ 1491.   [157] ibid, para 55.   [158] ibid, para 57.
[159] ibid, paras 29, 34–40, 57.
[160] ibid, paras 57–58. See examples in *Ashworth Hospital Authority v MGN Ltd* [2002] UKHL 29, paras 61–72; *Mersey Care NHS Trust v Ackroyd (No 2)* [2007] EWCA Civ 101, paras 9–39, 62–72, 76–82, 90 (concerning disclosure of identity of a source under the Contempt of Court Act 1981 regarding the medical records of a murderer); *Commissioner of Police of the Metropolis v Times Newspaper* [2011] EWHC 2705 (QB), paras 94–105.
[161] *Harrods Ltd v Times Newspaper Ltd* [2006] EWCA Civ 294, para 27; *Deloitte & Touche LLP v Dickson* [2005] EWHC 721 (Ch), paras 63–76; and *Tillery Valley Foods v Channel Four Television Corporation* [2004] EWHC 1075 (Ch), paras 8, 15–16, 18; *Abbey v Gilligan* [2012] EWHC 3217 (QB), paras 42–66, esp 48–50.
[162] Arts 1(2)(a), 5(a) Trade Secrets Directive.   [163] See Art 5(b), Trade Secrets Directive.   [164] Recital 21.

Unclean hands

17.66   If breach of confidence is based in equity, the complainant must, in accordance with standard principles, come with 'clean hands', having behaved properly themselves in respect of the relevant information. If not, the court may in its discretion refuse relief.[165]

Prior knowledge

17.67   A more apparently mundane defence is that the information received in confidence was already known.[166] It is difficult to distinguish between two sets of information and similar problems to those considered previously in the employment context that might arise here.[167]

Springboard

17.68   If someone subject to an obligation discloses or uses information in breach of this, and the information is then in the public domain,[168] are they free to use it? Special rules can apply, although they have not gone unchallenged.[169] These rules form the springboard doctrine: preventing (at least for a short period) persons who have breached confidence from getting a head start on others, and by avoiding doing preparatory work. This doctrine could apply to new theories and product designs, and also to lists of customer details. An early and still helpful summary of the doctrine is:[170]

> a person who has obtained information in confidence is not allowed to use it as a springboard for activities detrimental to the person who made the confidential communication, and springboard it remains even when all the features have been published or can be ascertained by actual inspection by any member of the public.

17.69   The controversial question is how long one must be subject to restraint when others can use the information freely. The aim is not to punish but to protect and to prevent unfair advantage;[171] and situations will vary, with courts reluctant to impose permanent restrictions.[172] A key question is how easily the information could have been obtained.[173] Much will depend, however, on the view of the court—sinister behaviour is never viewed kindly: 'having made deliberate and unlawful use of the plaintiff's property, he cannot complain if he finds that the eye of the law is unable to distinguish between those he could, if he chose, have contacted lawfully and those he could not'.[174]

Exercise

Back at Eversogood they are doing well in the market, building on Katie's good relationships with the supermarkets' area sales managers. They all went to university together and keep in touch through industry training courses. Just yesterday, however, Katie realised that she had left her FunFunFun contacts book in the bottom of her handbag. Eversogood's in-house legal counsel Graeme is concerned. Discuss.

---

[165] See *Stephenson Jordan & Harrison Ltd v Macdonald & Evans* (1952) 69 RPC 10, 196 and *Church of Scientology v Kaufman* [1973] RPC 627. Note that there is no doctrine of equity in Scotland, see para 17.12.

[166] See, eg, *Johnson v Heat and Air Systems Ltd* (1941) 58 RPC 229.

[167] See also *Laws of Scotland: Stair Memorial Encyclopaedia*, vol 18, Part II, para 1486.

[168] Note the debate considered in paras 17.18–17.20 as to whether the information does enter the public domain.

[169] See *Ocular Sciences Ltd v Aspect Vision Care (No 2)* [1997] RPC 289, 401 and *Vestergaard Frandsen A/S v BestNet Europe Ltd* [2013] UKSC 31, notably paras 67–93.

[170] *Terrapin Ltd v Builders Supply Co (Hayes) Ltd* [1960] RPC 128 at 130. See also Scottish case, *Levin v Farmers Supply Association of Scotland* 1973 SLT (Notes) 43 and Aplin et al, *Gurry on Breach of Confidence: The Protection of Confidential Information* (2nd edn, 2012), 643–53.

[171] *Roger Bullivant Ltd v Ellis* [1987] FSR 172, headnote paras 3, 183ff; and *UBS Wealth Management (UK) Ltd v Vestra Wealth LLP* [2008] EWHC 1974 (QB), [2008] IRLR 965.

[172] *Roger Bullivant Ltd v Ellis* [1987] FSR 172, 183–84, 186–87.

[173] See, eg, *Universal Thermosensors v Hibben* [1992] 1 WLR 840 which concerned a small market, and information could have been obtained from trade journals.

[174] See, eg, *Roger Bullivant Ltd v Ellis* [1987] FSR 172, 181; see also *Bradford & Bingley plc v Holden* [2002] EWHC 2445.

Parties to action

Who can raise an action?

17.70   Only the person to whom that obligation is owed,[175] or who has a reasonable expectation of privacy in respect of the information, can raise the action. If work generating information is carried out pursuant to a commission, the commissioner is owed the obligation.[176]

17.71   If protection of information, or information, is perceived as a property right as considered at the outset,[177] there might be scope for a wider basis of complaint.[178] This issue remains unclear. It is also discussed further in relation to *Douglas v Hello!* in Chapter 18.

Against whom

17.72   Consistent with the analysis so far, the action can be raised against the person in breach of an obligation of confidence (even if they were not aware of the obligation) or person who discloses information in respect of which there is a reasonable expectation of privacy. Persons inducing such conduct will also be liable, as will those engaging in it through a common design, and the Supreme Court has found that they must be aware of what they are doing and that there is dishonesty[179] rather than helping someone else in what is found to be a breach of confidence.[180] As cases move further away from the initial disclosure, care must be taken to focus on what has actually been done—arguments that 'they must have known' are unlikely to succeed.[181] If there is conduct in the course of employment, the employer could be vicariously liable.

17.73   The greater commercial threat may come from a subsequent employer who uses, or it is feared may use, the information. But unless they are under an obligation applying the tests set out there, they cannot be sued.

Key points on parties to action

- The person to whom obligation is owed or has a reasonable expectation of privacy in respect of the information can sue.

- The person in breach of obligation, discloser of information, and/or employer or person inducing conduct can be sued.

 Question

Once confidential information is disclosed, can a complaint be brought by anyone against anyone, anywhere, anytime? Would the answer be different if there was a patent?

---

[175] *Abbey v Gilligan* [2012] EWHC 3217 (QB); a person who had acted as agent for a company and another individual, not as a principal, did not have the benefit of an obligation of confidence and had no title to sue.

[176] *Fraser v Evans* [1968] 3 WLR 1172, [1969] 1 QB 349; *Apps v Weldite Products Ltd* [2001] FSR 39, para 102.

[177] See para 17.12.

[178] See also Aplin et al, *Gurry on Breach of Confidence: The Protection of Confidential Information* (2nd edn, 2012), 316–17.

[179] *Vestergaard Frandsen A/S v Bestnet Europe Ltd* [2013] UKSC 31.

[180] Compare *British Sky Broadcasting v Digital Satellite Warranty Cover* Ltd [2012] EWHC 2642 (Ch), which identified a relevant tacit agreement.

[181] *Force India Formula One Team Ltd v 1 Malaysia Racing Team Sdn Bhd* [2012] EWHC 616, paras 345–367.

Confidence and IP

Policy

17.74 The policy relationship between trade secrets, IP, and innovation is controversial and complex. The UK Intellectual Property Office (UK IPO) refers to use of trade secrets to protect innovation.[182] There is also an argument that if too many restrictions are placed on patents (eg compulsory licences,[183] defences,[184] intervention by competition law),[185] innovators wishing to control their work will choose not to patent,[186] and will instead rely on trade secrets.[187] This means that details of valuable innovation could be permanently outside the public domain—subject to the internal and external limits on trade secrets.[188]

> **Key point on policy**
>
> • Trade secrets and their treatment are an important part of the innovation debate.

Relative scope of protection

17.75 A change of jobs, or an inquiry[189] or demonstration[190] which come to nothing (and, of course, breakdowns in collaborations)[191] frequently lead to the development of a second set of products which are similar to existing ones. There may not be IP infringement, but there might still be breach of confidence—or vice versa—as different tests and principles are applied. But if both causes of action are available, it is quite legitimate for them to be pursued together.[192]

17.76 Examples of this are in *Creation Records* (regarding photo shoots for an album cover for the band Oasis) and *Shelley Films* (regarding a set for the film *Frankenstein*) both considered at para 3.71. In both cases it was clear that the event was private, and that there was to be no photography, even though it was possible to observe. Regarding *Frankenstein*, the court in *Shelley Films* considered it to be arguable that there was copyright in costumes, prostheses for an actor, and the set, and that there was a serious question in respect of breach of confidence.[193] In *Creation Records*, although there was no copyright in the assembled scene to be photographed,[194] the court held it to be an occasion of confidence.[195] Further, in a case involving wheelchair lifts,[196] there was a breach of confidence in respect of the initial idea, but no IP infringement because of the redesign which had taken place.

---

[182] See, eg, references to trade secrets in the UK Intellectual Property Office guidance on applying for a patent: www.gov.uk/guidance/before-you-apply-for-a-patent.

[183] See para 12.8ff.   [184] See paras 12.87ff.   [185] Considered in Chapter 20.

[186] See eg B Perens, 'Innovation goes public' (2008) 14(2) CTLR 36–40.

[187] See, eg, a study from the EU Intellectual Property Office on how firms use patents and trade secrets to protect their innovation: EUIPO, 'Protecting innovation through trade secrets and patents: Determinants for European Union firms' (2017), https://euipo.europa.eu/tunnel-web/secure/webdav/guest/document_library/observatory/documents/reports/Trade%20Secrets%20Report_en.pdf.

[188] See also Aplin et al, *Gurry on Breach of Confidence: The Protection of Confidential Information* (2nd edn, 2012), 77–88.

[189] In *Harrison v Project & Design Co (Red Car) (No 1) Ltd* [1978] FSR 81 an individual developed a chair lift and disclosed it to a company which they had visited. The company then did further work and patented its own product.

[190] In *Carflow Products (UK) Ltd v Linwood Securities (Birmingham) Ltd* [1996] FSR 424, 429, regarding a device for locking a steering wheel, no obligation was identified on the facts, and the court found one would be unusual in that industry.

[191] *Collag Corp v Merck & Co Inc* [2003] FSR 16; *Inline Logistics v UCI Logistics* [2002] RPC 32. Note if one collaborator leaves the others, that one person will have no right to control how remaining collaborators deal with the information, if the information was part of the relationship: *Murray v Yorkshire Fund Managers* [1998] 1 WLR 951 at 956, 957, 959–61.

[192] *HRH Prince of Wales v Associated Newspapers Ltd* [2006] EWHC 522 (Ch), para 183.; see also *British Sky Broadcasting Group plc v Digital Satellite Warranty Cover Ltd (In Liquidation)* [2012] FSR 14. Compare the fate of an action for breach of confidence after a patent entitlement dispute was struck out: *Markem Corp v Zipher Ltd* [2005] RPC 31, paras 111, 124, 126, 132.

[193] *Shelley Films Ltd v Rex Features Ltd* [1994] EMLR 134, 142–48.

[194] *Creation Records Ltd v News Group Newspapers Ltd* [1997] EMLR 444, 448.

[195] ibid, 452–54. See also *Banner v Endemol* [2017] EWHC 2600 regarding a gameshow format (the breach of confidence claim was barred).

[196] *Harrison v Project & Design Co (Red Car) (No 1) Ltd* [1978] FSR 81. See also *Seager v Copydex Ltd (No 1)* [1967] FSR 211, 225.

17.77   Breach of confidence can be helpful in respect of embryonic ideas—from books to products to research projects—to enable them to develop fully, such that copyright might become relevant.[197] There have been other cases involving television shows[198] and nightclubs. However, these 'ideas' can only be the subject of the action if the original information as communicated was developed, precise, original, and identifiable.[199] Secondly, the necessary obligation of confidence may be unlikely if there are discussions over dinner, in an industry where it is standard practice to share ideas openly without restriction,[200] or indeed where IP protection, rather than confidence, might be more reasonably expected.[201] As this covers a broad spectrum, the second element of breach of confidence might be problematic.

Key points on relative scope of protection

- There can be no IP infringement, yet breach of confidence, in respect of the same facts.
- Breach of confidence may protect ideas and early-stage innovation before it will be protected by IP rights such as patents.

Secrecy and innovation

Existing practice

17.78   The classic examples of the Coca-Cola formula and, in Scotland, the Irn Bru recipe, are often used as examples of how businesses can survive based on secrecy. As has been seen throughout this chapter, it is a real challenge for businesses actually to keep information secret. Court orders can be combined, payments made, but from a practical perspective, the damage is done. This means that few businesses follow the Barr's and Coca-Cola Company's route.

 Exercise

If you started a new business, would you rely on trade secrets rather than, for example, patents? Why/ why not? Do you think you would have given the same answer 20 years ago? What do you think your funders might say?

17.79   The position is, of course, rarely as clear-cut as this. As has been seen previously,[202] there are many situations in which breach of confidence can form part of a dispute alongside different IP rights. Innovators and their advisers may also choose to take a combined approach to IP and confidence. They may protect some by patents, some by database, some by copyright, and choose to keep secret the commercially valuable bits which make the whole thing work. The role of secrecy in innovation is well recognised from the policy perspective and this led to the Trade Secrets Directive (paras 17.13, 17.65). This proceeds from the premise that misappropriation of trade secrets has a negative impact on innovation and should be controlled.

---

[197] See Aplin et al, *Gurry on Breach of Confidence: The Protection of Confidential Information* (2nd edn, 2012), 172; also, *Prince Albert v Strange* (1849) H & T 1 protecting misuse of ideas in etchings.

[198] Consistent with early decisions protecting plots of plays—*Gilbert v Star Newspaper Company Ltd* (1894) 11 TLR 4.

[199] *De Maudsley v Palumbo* [1996] FSR 447, [1996] EMLR 460 at 467–70 (nightclub); *CMI Centers for Medical Innovation v Phytopharm plc* [1999] FSR 235 (vaccine); *Collag Corp v Merck* [2003] FSR 16 (pesticides); *Bailey v Graham* [2011] EWHC 2098 (Ch) (jerk sauce); *Wade v British Sky Broadcasting Ltd* [2014] EWHC 634 (Ch); [2016] EWCA Civ 1214 (idea for a TV show).

[200] *De Maudsley v Palumbo* [1996] FSR 447, [1996] EMLR 460, 464, 471 and *Carflow Products (UK) Ltd v Linwood Securities (Birmingham) Ltd* [1996] FSR 424. Compare *IBCOS Computer Ltd v Barclays Mercantile Highland Finance Ltd* [1994] FSR 275, 286 (obligation of confidentiality imposed in respect of source code, as usually regarded as confidential in industry).

[201] *Carflow Products (UK) Ltd v Linwood Securities (Birmingham) Ltd* [1996] FSR 424, 430.

[202] See paras 17.9ff and 17.74ff.

Know-how and confidentiality agreements

17.80   The Trade Secrets Directive refers to undisclosed know-how and commercial business information, defining trade secrets as follows:[203]

(a) it is secret in the sense that it is not, as a body or in the precise configuration and assembly of its components, generally known among or readily accessible to persons within the circles that normally deal with the kind of information in question;

(b) it has commercial value because it is secret;

(c) it has been subject to reasonable steps under the circumstances, by the person lawfully in control of the information, to keep it secret.

'Know-how' has a well-established place in innovation law already. Know-how agreements enable those pursuing a non-IP route to control the sharing and exploitation of their developments: subject, of course, to the essential problem noted previously that once information is disclosed, it is, generally, uncontrollable.[204] This is important because frequently innovators choose to share their confidential technology and expertise to make money, or must obtain or be permitted to use the IP of others so that they can make products with their own information.

17.81   Non-disclosure agreements are advisable,[205] although there is of course the question of how to identify the know-how, which is the subject of the agreements. This might lead to confidential attachments to agreements, named individuals who are to have access to particular information, and regimes for recording, storing, and destroying information.[206]

17.82   Competition issues might also arise in respect of know-how and collaboration agreements which could lead to them being found void.[207] Reliance on trade secrets (and so a failure to disclose requested information) could lead to arguments that this is an unlawful abuse of a dominant position.[208] These are considered in Chapter 20, in conjunction with competition implications for IP. As will be seen there, however, the European Commission in its investigation of Microsoft paid little regard to the fact that information sought to be disclosed was secret.[209] This is consistent with its broad approach to the case: the information should be disclosed, because of competition issues and the fact that it was the subject of IP or was secret did not matter. Recital 16 of the Trade Secrets Directive shows that competition remains a concern: 'In the interest of innovation and to foster competition, the provisions of this Directive should not create any exclusive right to know-how or information protected as trade secrets.' Reverse engineering and the independent discovery of know-how are specifically contemplated, but the former may be restricted by contract.[210]

Key points on commercial impact

- Confidential information can be the subject of research and development agreements.

- It is rare for businesses to rely wholly on confidentiality to protect their innovation—but they can.

---

[203] Article 2(1).   [204] See para 17.18ff on information in the public domain, for example.

[205] See draft agreements, available at www.gov.uk/government/publications/non-disclosure-agreements.

[206] Similar indeed to the arrangements in court actions: see para 17.27. Note generally Art 4(3)(b), Trade Secrets Directive (breach of a confidentiality agreement is unlawful).

[207] See paras 20.32ff regarding potentially relevant block exemptions.

[208] *EC Commission v Microsoft* at http://ec.europa.eu/competition/sectors/ICT/microsoft/index.html, 55, n 249 discussed at paras 20.56ff and consideration by the Court of First Instance: *Microsoft Corp v Commission of the European Communities* [2007] ECR II-3601, paras 273, 280, 285, 289, 667, 681, 689, 692–693 regarding the extent to which trade secrets should be treated in the same way as IP rights, and the consequences of this regarding possible intervention by competition.

[209] See paras 20.56–20.58.   [210] Recital 16 and Art 3(1)(a) ('independent discovery or creation' in the acquisition of a trade secret).

IP and other information regulation

17.83   Control and use of information lies at the heart of breach of confidence. Data protection and breach of confidence can be complementary, as can be seen from their consideration in many cases.[211] These questions are also addressed, from different perspectives, in evolving pieces of legislation relating to data protection,[212] freedom of information,[213] and state access to information for investigatory purposes.[214] Questions about the circumstances in which confidential business information will be disclosed are also raised, for example, in the context of EU competition investigations.[215] This is a controversial area, with questions of individual and collective faith in the state, and links between the state and companies at the heart of it.[216]

17.84   There is a complex relationship between freedom of information, confidentiality, and IP.[217] The first aims to require the disclosure of information, the others to control it in different ways.[218] Legislation has sought to balance these,[219] but there is inevitable uncertainty, which has once again led to litigation.[220] It is likely that this will become an increasingly important topic in the study of breach of confidence.

17.85   There has been particular activity in respect of environmental information. Much of this stems from the Aarhus Convention,[221] although this has a focus on disclosure by public authorities, thus not addressing private-sector information.[222] A wide variety of approaches can be seen in the case law, with the underlying legislation and the particular facts being key. The Court of Justice when considering obligations imposed by a regulation on the shipment of waste, found that these must be met even if this would involve the disclosure of trade secrets.[223] Yet regarding requests for information in respect of environment and pesticides, the Court of Justice considered that there must be a balance between the public interest in disclosure, and the private interest in non-disclosure must be carried out in each case.[224] In a case involving disclosure of information relating to the

---

[211] See, eg, *Secretary of State for the Home Department v TLU* [2018] EMLR 24; *Campbell, Re C's Application for Judicial Review* [2009] UKHL 15; and *Bluck v Information Commissioner* 2007 WL 4266111, [2008] WTLR 1; *Mosley v Google Inc* [2015] EWHC 59(QB). The Information Commissioner's Office provides guidance on data protection and other aspects of the regulation of information at https://ico.org.uk/for-organisations/guidance-index.

[212] See paras 18.27 and 18.28.

[213] Freedom of Information Act 2000; Freedom of Information (Scotland) Act 2002.

[214] Investigatory Powers Act 2016.

[215] See *Evonik Degussa GmbH v European Commission* [2017] 4 CMLR 28.

[216] Important decisions in this (wide) field include *Liberty v GCHQ* [2015] UKIPTrib 13_77-H_2, 2015 WL 3795703 (regarding whether UK authorities obtaining private communications from the United States authorities as part of PRISM was in breach of previous decisions of the tribunal and Art 8 ECHR); and *R (on application of Davis and Others) v Secretary of State for the Home Department* [2015] EWHC 2092 (Admin) (finding the, now repealed, Data Retention and Investigatory Powers Act 2014 to be in breach of EU law in respect of its protection of the fundamental right to a private life under EU law). See recently, eg, *R (on the application of National Council for Civil Liberties (Liberty)) v Secretary of State for the Home Department* [2018] EWHC 975 (Admin) (on part of the Investigatory Powers Act 2016, data retention, and incompatibility with fundamental rights).

[217] There is also a complex relationship between freedom of information and data protection legislation, *Common Services Agency v Scottish Information Commissioner* [2008] UKHL 47.

[218] Note also decision of the Court of Justice in *Google v Spain* [2014] 3 CMLR 50 regarding the so-called 'right to be forgotten'.

[219] See Freedom of Information Act 2000, ss 40 (personal information), 41 (confidential information), 43 (commercial interests), and 53 which provides some exemptions of need to comply with a notice; and Freedom of Information (Scotland) Act 2002, ss 33 (commercial interests), 36 (confidentiality), 38 (personal information), 53 (exemption from duty to comply). See also guidance from the Information Commissioner's Office, 'Intellectual property rights and disclosures under the Freedom of Information Act' (2012), https://ico.org.uk/media/for-organisations/documents/1150/intellectual_property_rights_and_disclosures_under_the_foia.pdf.

[220] Regarding 'commercial interests', see *Cabinet Office v Information Commissioner* (EA/2010/0031), September 2010 and *Visser v Information Commissioner* (EA2011/0188), 1 March 2012; regarding 'confidentiality', see *Moss v Information Commissioner* (EA/2011/0081), 28 February 2012; regarding scope of exemptions, see *R (on application of Evans) v Attorney General* [2015] UKSC 21 (regarding disclosure of letters of the Prince of Wales and Government departments).

[221] Convention on Access to Information, Public Participation in Decision-making and Access to Justice in Environmental Matters at www.unece.org/env/pp/treatytext.html and EU resulting legislation http://ec.europa.eu/environment/aarhus.

[222] See, eg, *Fish Legal v Information Commissioner* (C-279/12) [2014] 2 CMLR 36.

[223] Case C-1/11 *Interseroh Scrp and Metals Trading GmbH v Sonderabfall-Management-Gesellschaft Rheinland-Pfalz mbH*—preliminary reference from German court.

[224] Case C-266/09 *Stichting Natuur v College voor toelating van gewasbeschermingsmiddelen en biociden* regarding Council Directive 2003/4/EC.

location of mobile phone masts,[225] the Court of Justice ultimately found[226] that there must be a balance between the public interest in disclosure, and the public interest against disclosure. This second element could include a combination of relevant grounds listed, including 'intellectual property rights' and 'public security', and there need not be separate analyses. In the UK, the obligation to disclose environmental information under the Environmental Information Regulations 2004 has an exception which refers to IP.[227]

> **Key points on IP and other information regulation**
>
> • When working with or studying information, one cannot look merely to one doctrine.
>
> • One cannot assume that two regimes will operate in the same manner and without conflict.

 Exercise

Think back to the scenario you devised in the previous Exercise box regarding breach of confidence when starting a business. What other forms of regulation might be relevant? How could you find this out?

International perspectives and approaches

17.86 Courts in the UK jurisdictions have not considered TRIPS and the Paris Convention in any depth in respect of breach of confidence.[228] This is perhaps not surprising, given the strong (even if unclear) base of the breach of confidence action quite apart from these principles. Countries have taken a range of approaches to meeting the obligations set out in TRIPS and the Paris Convention.[229] It will be interesting to note how approaches change if more businesses choose to keep information secret, rather than embrace IP and its accompanying international regime.

17.87 Issues have arisen in respect of Article 39(3) of TRIPS and its requirement that undisclosed data submitted for regulatory clearance shall be protected against unfair commercial use. Attempts by Canada to reduce levels of exclusivity in respect of this data were found to be inconsistent with TRIPS,[230] and free trade agreements frequently require greater protection to be extended to regulatory data.[231]

 Discussion point   For answer guidance visit **www.oup.com/uk/brown5e**.

Do you think that the breach of confidence (with its human rights modifications) and the accompanying information legislation, result in the UK meeting its obligations under TRIPS and the Paris Convention? Devise a scenario in which the UK could be challenged at the World Trade Organization (WTO) Dispute Settlement Body in respect of Article 39.

[225] Case C-71/10 *Office of Communications v Information Commissioner* [2012] 1 CMLR 7, paras 27–28.

[226] ibid, paras 27–28.

[227] Regulation 12(5)(c) allows a public authority to refuse to disclose information where it would 'adversely affect' intellectual property rights. The exception for Scottish public authorities is found in reg 10(5)(c) Environmental Information (Scotland) Regulations 2004/520.

[228] See, eg, NP de Carvalho, *The TRIPS Regime of Antitrust and Undisclosed Information* (2008), Section 7; J de Werra, 'What legal framework for promoting the cross-border flow of intellectual assets (trade secrets and music)? A view from Europe towards Asia (China and Japan)' [2009] 1 IPQ 27–76.

[229] See report for the European Commission, 'Study on trade secrets and confidential business information in the internal market' at http://ec.europa.eu/DocsRoom/documents/27703, which led ultimately to the Directive.

[230] *Canada—Pharmaceutical Patents* WTO DS 114 at www.wto.org/english/tratop_e/dispu_e/cases_e/ds114_e.htm.

[231] For an overview, see L Brazell, 'The protection of pharmaceutical products and regulatory data: EU enlargement update' (2002) 24(3) EIPR 155–1161. See also para 17.11.

> **Key points on international perspectives**
>
> - Paris and TRIPS provide a relevant backdrop to breach of confidence.
> - The UK (probably) complies with them.
> - This area might become important in the future, particularly regarding regulatory data.

Conclusions and the future

17.88   Previous proposals for codification of the law of confidence[232] were not followed up. If codification should again be considered, the proposals need to be significantly reviewed given the HRA 1998's major impact on breach of confidence. The established dilemmas remain, however, such as ex-employees' skill and know-how, customer lists, the relationship with copyright, and the proper scope of defences. There will be an ongoing role for human rights and breach of confidence in considering control of information, and this will sit aside the other forms of information regulation which have been introduced. And as discussions continue regarding the shape of breach of confidence, it still has an important role as part of the innovation landscape.

Further reading

Books

T Aplin, L Bently, P Johnson, and S Malynicz, *Gurry on Breach of Confidence: The Protection of Confidential Information* (2nd edn, 2012)

L Edwards (ed), *Law, Policy and the Internet* (2018), Part II

Laws of Scotland: Stair Memorial Encyclopaedia vol 18, Part II, paras 1451 *et seq*

S McKay, *Blackstone's Guide to the Investigatory Powers Act 2016* (2018)

J Wadham, K Harris, and E Metcalfe, *Blackstone's Guide to the Freedom of Information Act* (5th edn, 2014)

Overviews of breach of confidence

L Bently, B Sherman, D Gangjee, and P Johnson, *Intellectual Property* (4th edn, 2014), Chs 44, 45, 46

D Llewelyn and T Aplin, *Cornish, Llewelyn and Aplin Intellectual Property: Patents, Copyright, Trade Marks and Allied Rights* (9th edn, Sweet & Maxwell 2019), Part 3

Articles and chapters

Privacy and human rights

T Aplin, 'Confidential Information as Property?' (2013) 24 King's Law Journal 2, 172–201

Legal status

L Bently, 'Trade secrets: 'intellectual property' but not 'property'?' in HR Howe and J Griffiths (eds), *Concepts of Property in Intellectual Property Law* (2013)

M Conaglen, 'Thinking about proprietary remedies for breach of confidence' [2008] 1 IPQ 82–109

J Glover, 'Is breach of confidence a fiduciary wrong? Preserving the reach of judge-made law' (2001) 21(4) Legal Studies 594–617

E Reid, 'Breach of confidence: translating the equitable wrong into Scots law' (2014) 1 Juridical Review 1

---

[232]   The Law Commission of Scotland, 'Report on Breach of Confidence' (Report 90, 1984); and, in England, the Law Commission (Report 110, 1981) (which also proposed an offence of misuse of trade secrets in 1997). See also 'Calcutt Report on Privacy and Related Matters' (Cmnd 1102, 1990).

Trade Secrets Directive

T Aplin, 'A critical evaluation of the proposed EU Trade Secrets Directive' (2014) IPQ 4, 257–79

R Niebel, L de Martinis, and B Clark, 'The EU Trade Secrets Directive: all change for trade secret protection in Europe?' (2018) 13 JIPLP 6, 445–57

SK Sandeen, 'Implementing the EU Trade Secret Directive: a view from the United States' (2017) 39 EIPR 1, 4–11

Commercial secrets

T Aplin, 'A right of privacy for corporations?' in P Torremans, *Intellectual Property and Human Rights. An Enhanced Edition of Copyright and Human Rights* (2008)

S Becthold and F Hoffler, 'An economic analysis of trade-secret protection in buyer–seller relationships' (2011) 27(1) JLE&O 137–58

M Bronckers and N McNelis, 'Is the EU obliged to improve the protection of trade secrets? An Inquiry into TRIPS, the European Convention on Human Rights and the EU Charter of Fundamental Rights' (2012) EIPR 673

H Carty, 'An analysis of the modern action for breach of commercial confidence: when is protection merited?' [2008] 4 IPQ 416–55

CDL Hunt, 'Rethinking surreptitious takings in the law of confidence' [2011] IPQ 66–85

S Gilotta, 'Disclosure in securities markets and the firm's need for confidentiality: theoretical framework and regulatory analysis' (2012) 13 EBOR 46 1, 45–88

N Searle, 'The criminalization of the theft of trade secrets: an analysis of the Economic Espionage Act' (2012) 2 IP Theory 2

A Taubman, 'Unfair competition and the financing of public-knowledge goods: the problem of test data protection' (2008) 3(9) JIPLP 591–606

J de Werra, 'How to protect trade secrets in high tech sports? An intellectual property analysis based on experiences at the America's Cup and in the Formula One Championship' [2010] EIPR 155

Trade secrets and innovation

T Aplin, 'Reverse engineering and commercial secrets' (2013) 66 CLP 341

N Wilkof, 'The econometrics of IP: the case of patents and innovation' (2014) 19 JIPLP 2014 2

Useful website

UK Information Commissioner's Office: www.ico.org.uk

18

Control of information, reputation, and intellectual property

Introduction

Scope and overview of chapter

18.1   This chapter considers the extent to which individuals should be able to prevent others referring to them and their activities and, conversely, to what extent individuals and companies should be able to commercialise and control a reputation which they have built. These topics are both legally important and of contemporary societal interest. They build upon the discussion of trade marks in Chapter 15, of passing off in Chapter 16, and of commercial information, human rights, and breach of confidence in Chapter 17.

18.2   These issues have been explored using practical labels such as privacy, merchandising, and endorsement, and more legal terms such as personality and publicity; yet the meaning of and distinction between these can be unclear.[1] Accordingly, this chapter focuses on the two essential elements of information and reputation. It will explore the different means by which the law enables businesses and individuals to commercialise and protect their reputation, and details of their personal activities. The chapter also explores justifications for this from the intellectual property (IP) perspective. It also briefly considers more recent developments in the law of data protection as a means of protecting individual privacy.

> ### Control of information and Brexit
>
> Passing off and misuse of private information, as common law actions, will remain after withdrawal. The Brexit implications arising in the context of data protection are outwith the scope of this chapter but it is important to note that the EU General Data Protection Regulation (GDPR) is intended to become part of retained EU law within the UK. In any event the Data Protection Act 2018 largely incorporates the requirements of the GDPR already.

---

[1] There is an extensive literature focusing on the protection of personality, eg H Carty, 'Passing off and the concept of goodwill' (1995) JBL 139–54; D Howarth, 'Privacy, confidentiality and the cult of celebrity' [2002] CLJ 264; H Carty, 'Advertising, publicity rights and English law' [2004] IPQ 209; T Frazer, 'Appropriation of personality—a new tort?' (1993) 99 LQR 281; P Jaffey, 'Merchandising and the law of trade marks' [1998] IPQ 240; G Scanlan, 'Personality, endorsement and everything' [2003] EIPR 563; G Davies, 'The cult of celebrity and trade mark: the next installment' (2004) 1(2) SCRIPTed 230; NR Whitty and R Zimmermann (eds), *Rights of Personality in Scots Law: A Comparative Perspective* (2009).

18.3   In summary, in the UK there is an action for misuse of private information, which arose from the combination of breach of confidence and the Human Rights Act 1998 (HRA 1998) introduced in Chapter 17. Trade marks can be obtained for a name, a signature, or the image (as in picture) of a person, if this has a distinctive character; but not if they are merely descriptive and 'image carriers'. Trade mark registrations can then be used to control merchandising. Passing off can prevent misrepresentation through merchandising practices, if the personality (be it real or fictional) has established goodwill; reputation is not enough. An important element in acceptance of this by courts has been the awareness of the public that official merchandising does occur. Passing off can also address false endorsement. If there is an agreement which relates to confidential information then the parties to that agreement can sue others if there is a breach of confidence. Otherwise, however, there is no right in respect of image (in the sense of reputation, rather than photograph), notwithstanding the plethora of image rights agreements involving, say, sporting celebrities. Gaps exist, therefore, in the protection conferred in respect of information and reputation. As discussed in Chapter 17 in relation to information regulation, Chapter 6 in respect of moral rights, and Chapter 15 in respect of trade marks with a reputation and dilution, some other avenues exist under the intellectual property umbrella, and additional avenues are referred to within this chapter. The result in the UK is still, however, an incomplete patchwork.

18.4   ### Learning objectives

By the end of this chapter you should be able to describe and explain:

- the evolving right to personal privacy and its base in human rights, particularly in respect of photographs;
- the obtaining and dealing with trade marks in respect of well-known personalities;
- the relationship between passing off and merchandising;
- the extent to which individuals and businesses can and do control the use of their image through endorsement and sponsorship;
- how rights to control image and information can be transferred.

 ### Exercise

Identify a situation which could involve at least two of the following issues: privacy, character merchandising, unauthorised endorsement, and use of image. Form your own views on how the law should apply to it. Review it after you have completed your work on this chapter.

18.5   So, the chapter looks like this:

- How it works in practice—some important examples (18.6)
- Personal privacy (18.7–18.28)
- Merchandising (18.29–18.51)
- Endorsement and sponsorship (18.52–18.58)
- Control of (public) image (18.59–18.61)
- Conclusions (18.62).

How it works in practice—some important examples

18.6   As will be seen from the summaries of the following cases, the points explored in this chapter are not new.

■ *Campbell v MGN Ltd* [2004] 2 AC 457 (HL)

This involved the newspaper publication of a photograph of supermodel Naomi Campbell in a public place, leaving a confidential Narcotics Anonymous meeting.[2] The House of Lords considered breach of confidence in conjunction with the obligations imposed on the court by the HRA 1998, and found that the action was in this context better named 'misuse of private information'. The House of Lords held that the photographs were private information. The right for this to be respected was then balanced against rights to freedom of expression, considering the nature of expression involved and of the information, and the extent to which C was a public figure. The House of Lords split 3:2[3] in favour of C. Significant weight was attached to her seeking medical treatment, and it was considered that restriction on freedom of expression in such circumstances was necessary and proportionate.

■ *Mirage Studios v Counter-Feat Clothing Co Ltd* [1991] FSR 145

The defendants applied the images of the Teenage Mutant Ninja Turtles, cartoon characters that are humanoid creatures with some of the features of turtles (notably half-shells), to their clothing products—without having a licence to do so from the creators of the characters. Browne-Wilkinson V-C held that this was passing off. A substantial section of the public knew that the reproduction of well-known characters on goods was generally licensed by the originators of the characters; the public would therefore assume that the goods so marketed had the approval of the originators for quality, and that the images used came from the originators rather than being copies. The public would therefore be misled by such unlicensed reproductions.

■ *Irvine v Talksport Ltd* [2002] EWHC 367 (Ch); [2003] EWCA Civ 423

A promotional brochure for T Ltd contained a manipulated image of the racing driver Eddie Irvine apparently listening to the radio station. I had no connection with the radio station. It was held that this was a representation of an endorsement of the radio station by I, and constituted passing off.

■ *Fenty v Arcadia* [2013] EWHC 2310 (Ch); [2015] EWCA Civ 3

A clothing store, Topshop, produced t-shirts bearing the image of the singer Rihanna. While the singer had entered into various sponsorship and merchandising agreements, she had no agreement with T for the production of the t-shirts. There was a misrepresentation that the t-shirt was endorsed by R. The court held that the use of the image constituted passing off. T's appeal was dismissed.

■ *OBG Ltd v Allan, Douglas v Hello! and Others* [2007] UKHL 21

The actors Michael Douglas and Catherine Zeta-Jones were married in New York and entered into an exclusive agreement with *OK!* magazine to publish the photographs of their wedding. *OK!* paid D and Z-J £1 million, and in return it was made clear to the many guests that cameras were not to be brought to the wedding; an obligation of confidence was imposed in respect of all photographs of the wedding. However, *Hello!* magazine obtained photographs from a freelance photographer who infiltrated the wedding. The House of Lords found that *OK!* (quite apart from D and Z-J) had an action against *Hello!* for breach of confidence.

---

[2] See also para 17.6, n 3.

[3] The House of Lords claimed to be united, however, on the questions of principle they considered. See *Campbell v MGN Ltd* [2004] 2 AC 457, para 36, per Lord Hoffmann.

Exercise

Can you identify common themes from the above cases?

Personal privacy

Before the Human Rights Act 1998

18.7 It is not a 21st-century phenomenon for individuals to wish to control references to their private life and activities.[4] Using the established doctrine of breach of confidence discussed in Chapter 17, on several occasions courts in England have found details of extramarital affairs, private artwork, sexual activities, or photographs to be confidential, and for there to be obligations of confidence.[5] In a 1903 Scottish case, *M'Cosh v Crow*,[6] the court found that a photographer was not entitled to display in his window photographs of children which had been taken with their consent. One of the judges, referring to English cases, argued that the relationship between the photographer and the customers was a confidential one. How widely can this extend? There is a continuum between private diaries kept under lock and key, details of sexually transmitted disease, an 'illegitimate' child of a campaigner for family values, a trip to the shop in old clothes by a minor celebrity, or a visit to the park of a stereotypical family of four.

18.8 In 1988 in *Spycatcher*,[7] discussed in Chapter 17, the House of Lords stated that 'the right to personal privacy is clearly one which the law should in this field seek to protect'.[8] This did not mean, however, that it did so protect. A 1990 report[9] recommended against the introduction of a statutory tort of infringement of privacy. But when a photographer gained unauthorised access to a hospital in the early 1990s and photographed a celebrity patient,[10] the law was found to have no means of response,[11] and there was no action for breach of privacy.[12]

Key points on the pre-Human Rights Act 1998 position

- Some private information was considered confidential for the purposes of breach of confidence.
- Obligations of confidence have been identified when there is no pre-existing relationship.
- But there was still a gap, and no legislation was proposed.

The HRA 1998, actions between persons, and opportunities for privacy

18.9 This section traces the significant impact of the HRA 1998 on breach of confidence, and the impact of the combination on the protection of personal privacy.[13] The HRA 1998 created possibilities for the use of human rights in combination with existing causes of action. Section 6 of the HRA 1998 prohibits a

---

[4] T Aplin, L Bently, P Johnson, and S Malynicz, *Gurry on Breach of Confidence: The Protection of Confidential Information* (2nd edn, 2012), 194–200.

[5] *Prince Albert v Strange* (1849) 1 H & T 1; *Argyll v Argyll* [1967] Ch 302; *Stephens v Avery* [1988] 2 WLR 1280, [1988] Ch 449; *X (HA) v Y* [1988] 2 All ER 648, [1988] RPC 379 (see also paras 17.18 and 17.44).

[6] (1903) 5 F 670.   [7] *Attorney General v Guardian Newspapers Ltd (No 2)* [1988] 3 WLR 776 ('*Spycatcher*').   [8] ibid, 782.

[9] Calcutt Report on Privacy and Related Matters (Cmnd 1102, 1990).   [10] *Kaye v Robertson* [1991] FSR 62.

[11] There was voluntary regulation of print media by the Press Complaints Commission, which closed in 2014 and was replaced by the Independent Press Standards Organisation, see www.ipso.co.uk.

[12] The limits of the action in respect of non-information matters are evident in the House of Lords' decision, *Wainwright v Home Office* [2003] UKHL 53 regarding strip searching of prison visitors. Regarding negative views of this by the ECtHR, see *Wainwright v United Kingdom* (App No 12350/04) (2007) 44 EHRR 40; *Peck v United Kingdom* (App No 44647/98) [2003] EMLR 15; (2003) 36 EHRR 41; and *Copland v United Kingdom* (App No 62617/00) (2007) 45 EHRR 37.

[13] Aplin et al, *Gurry on Breach of Confidence: The Protection of Confidential Information* (2nd edn, 2012), 200–22.

public authority (stated to include a court) from acting in a manner incompatible with Convention rights when, essentially, an alternative approach is available. Convention rights are defined to include Article 8 ECHR, the right to respect for private life, and its exceptions. This would seem to cover situations such as publication of photographs of private events. However, another Convention right is Article 10 ECHR, which was discussed in Chapter 17. This protects freedom of expression, with its own exceptions.[14] The combination of Articles 8 and 10 with the existing action for breach of confidence is a constant theme in the ongoing development of claims relating to information privacy.

> ## Web links
>
> Here are the links to the text of the ECHR in its entirety and to the HRA 1998:
>
> www.coe.int/en/web/conventions/full-list/-/conventions/treaty/005
> www.legislation.gov.uk/ukpga/1998/42/contents

Article 8 ECHR

(1) Everyone has the right to respect for his private and family life, his home and his correspondence.
(2) There shall be no interference by a public authority with the exercise of this right except such as is in accordance with the law and is necessary in a democratic society in the interests of national security, public safety or the economic well-being of the country, for the prevention of disorder or crime, for the protection of health or morals, or for the protection of the rights and freedoms of others.

Article 10 ECHR

(1) Everyone has the right to freedom of expression. This right shall include freedom . . . to receive and impart information and ideas without interference by public authority and regardless of frontiers . . .
(2) The exercise of these freedoms, since it carries with it duties and responsibilities, may be subject to such formalities, conditions, restrictions or penalties as are prescribed by law and are necessary in a democratic society . . . for the protection of the reputation or rights of others, for preventing the disclosure of information received in confidence . . . .

18.10   The ECHR is addressed to states, not individuals and companies.[15] Early concerns that this would therefore be of limited impact between private entities, were not realised. Articles 8 and 10 ECHR have had a central role in the privacy-related decisions between private entities; and as new social media make it easier for anyone to publish information about another, the opportunities this can provide will continue to be important.[16] Cases establishing the place of Articles 8 and 10 ECHR when courts consider breach of confidence are the decision of the Court of Appeal in *A v B plc* in 2002 (regarding publication of the extramarital activities of a footballer),[17] the House of Lords in *Campbell* in 2004 considered earlier,[18] and the Court of Appeal in *Douglas v Hello!* in 2005 regarding the claims of individuals in respect of their wedding photographs.[19] Further, the European Court of Human Rights (ECtHR) in

---

[14] In *Douglas and Others v Hello! Ltd (No 3)* [2005] 3 WLR 881 the Court of Appeal confirmed that the action for breach of confidence was also sufficiently precise to come within the prescribed by law restriction on free expression in Art 10, see paras 141–151.

[15] See, eg, G Phillipson, 'Transforming breach of confidence? Towards a common law right of privacy under the Human Rights Act' (2003) 66 MLR 726.

[16] *Applause Store Productions Ltd v Raphael* [2008] EWHC 1781 (QB).   [17] *A v B plc* [2003] QB 195.

[18] *Campbell v MGN Ltd* [2004] 2 AC 457, paras 17–18, 49, 50.

[19] *Douglas and Others v Hello! Ltd (No 3)* [2005] 3 WLR 881, paras 47–49. Article 8 ECHR was also considered by the Scottish Court of Session in *Martin v McGuiness* 2003 SLT 1424, regarding the conduct of a private investigator that was unlawful. The action, on the basis of the Scots claim of *actio iniuriarum* and Art 8 ECHR failed; there were *obiter* statements that maybe there should now be an action for privacy, but that this was not a live issue in the case.

Hannover (regarding photographs taken of Princess Caroline of Hannover, mainly in public places) in 2004 found that states might have positive obligations to introduce measures for exploration by individuals amongst themselves.[20]

Key point on HRA and individual actions

- National courts can use Articles 8 and 10 ECHR when considering actions for breach of confidence.

 Question

What are the limits on the Article 10 right to freedom of expression which might encourage privacy seekers?

Misuse of private information

18.11   So how did Articles 8 and 10 combine with breach of confidence and to what end? The key development came in 2004, when the House of Lords considered the question in *Campbell* which, despite the number of subsequent cases, still warrants detailed consideration.[21] Although different approaches were adopted by the Law Lords, key principles can be extracted for present purposes. There was still no overarching claim for invasion of privacy,[22] but they found that breach of confidence could and did deal with personal information.[23] Further, although they considered that, the necessary relationship of confidence (at the core of the action as discussed in Chapter 17), might be identified in personal information cases, it was 'awkward' to have to distinguish information from relationship.[24] Accordingly, in *Campbell* the House of Lords considered the action in this context would be better referred to as misuse of private information:[25] and the correct first question to be posed was whether the information was private. Information would be private if there was a reasonable expectation of privacy.[26] If there is a reasonable expectation of privacy, then Article 8 is engaged. The existence of the action was noted when the Court of Appeal confirmed, regarding a procedural formality, that misuse of private information was to be treated as a tort; moreover, breach of confidence and the misuse of private information are separate causes of action.[27] It is thus possible for uses of information to give rise to both breach of confidence and misuse of private information actions.[28]

 Discussion point   For answer guidance visit **www.oup.com/uk/brown5e**.

Lord Hoffmann in *Campbell* considered there to have been a 'shift in the centre of gravity' of breach of confidence regarding personal information, based not on extended duties of confidence and good faith but on autonomy and dignity.[29] Do you agree? Review your answer after you have considered the cases discussed in the following section.

---

[20] *Hannover v Germany* (App No 53920/00) (2005) 40 EHRR 1, paras 57 and 72. Considered also in *McKennitt v Ash* [2006] EWCA Civ 1714, paras 9–11 and *Reklos v Greece* [2009] EMLR 16, para 35.

[21] See also *A v B plc* [2003] QB 195, paras 4, 6, 9, 11(vi), (xi), (xii), and (xiii). The Court of Appeal did not, however, address ECHR authorities. The Court of Appeal in 2006 held *A v B plc* not to be binding on it in respect of how to conduct the balance in a case on similar facts: *McKennitt v Ash* [2006] EWCA Civ 1714, paras 60–63.

[22] Unlike the position in the United States: see *Campbell v MGN Ltd* [2004] 2 AC 457, para 11.

[23] ibid, paras 43–45, 47, 51, referring to *Prince Albert v Strange* (1849) 1 H & T 1, and *Attorney General v Guardian Newspapers Ltd (No 2)* [1988] 3 WLR 776 ('*Spycatcher*').

[24] *Campbell v MGN Ltd* [2004] 2 AC 457, paras 14, 49.   [25] ibid, para 14.   [26] ibid, paras 20–21.

[27] *Google v Vidal-Hall* [2015] EWCA Civ 311, para 21.   [28] See *Imerman v Tchenguiz and Others* [2010] EWCA Civ 908, paras 66–68.

[29] *Campbell v MGN Ltd* [2004] 2 AC 457, para 51.

The reasonable expectation of privacy

18.12   The House of Lords in *Campbell* considered that it would usually be obvious when there was a reasonable expectation of privacy.[30] Yet case law suggests that the 'reasonable expectation of privacy' will frequently give rise to uncertainty. The ECtHR in *Hannover* in 2004 considered that private life within Article 8 covered physical and psychological integrity; and that, even in public, public figures might engage in private acts in respect of particular zones of life.[31] The Court of Appeal in *Douglas v Hello!* in 2005 considered that the test must cover information personal to the person possessing it, which they do not intend to be shared with the general public; and that this might be clear from the nature or form of the information.[32]

18.13   This suggests clearly that the expectation can exist not only in respect of public figures engaging in private acts, but also those who are not public figures. It might seem less likely that the media would be interested in such persons—but the growth of social media means that boundaries between the private and the public become blurred (eg blogging has been found to be a public activity, and the identity of bloggers was not information in respect of which there is a reasonable expectation of privacy).[33] There is also the potential for all lives to come into the media spotlight without having sought it. The extent to which the existing court process can protect, for example, the privacy of the parents of murdered children effectively is one of the issues considered by the Leveson Inquiry,[34] which reported in 2012.[35]

18.14   An important decision regarding when there might be an expectation of privacy is that of the Court of Appeal in 2008 in *Murray*,[36] regarding the publication of a photograph of the son of JK Rowling, the author of the Harry Potter books. The photograph was taken, without consent, with a long-range lens when the child was being pushed along an Edinburgh street in his buggy. This is a photograph of an individual who is not a celebrity. The court at first instance[37] considered this to be an attempt by JK Rowling to exercise her own rights, and held that she could not have rights in respect of walking down the street. Yet the Court of Appeal considered that her son had his own rights, that he had a reasonable expectation of privacy,[38] and that these may, in some circumstances, be greater than those of his well-known mother. The Court of Appeal stressed that the reasonable expectation of privacy must always be assessed on the basis of the facts of each case and there could be no guarantees of privacy,[39] but that the following questions could be taken into account:[40]

> the attributes of the claimant, the nature of the activity in which the claimant was engaged, the place at which it was happening, the nature and purpose of the intrusion, the absence of consent and whether it was known or could be inferred, the effect on the claimant and the circumstances in which and the purposes for which the information came into the hands of the publisher.

[30] ibid, paras 21, 22, 92–94, 135 (and referring to the Australian case *Australian Broadcasting Corporation v Lenah Game Meats Pty Ltd* (2001) 208 CLR 199, para 42, considered at first instance, see paras 22, 93, 135, 166).

[31] *Hannover v Germany* (App No 53920/00) (2005) 40 EHRR 1, para 50. In England, see also *X v Persons Unknown* [2007] EMLR 10 and *Price v Powell* [2012] EWHC 3527 (QB).

[32] *Douglas and Others v Hello! Ltd (No 3)* [2005] 3 WLR 881, para 83.

[33] *The Author of a Blog v Times Newspapers Ltd* [2009] EWHC 1358 (QB) paras 2–11, 33.

[34] The Leveson Inquiry website has been archived: www.levesoninquiry.org.uk. For other discussion of the public interest and journalism, see *Mosley v News Group Newspapers Ltd* [2008] EWHC 1777 (QB), [2008] EMLR 20, paras 135–169; *Flood v Times Newspapers Ltd* [2009] EWHC 2375 (QB), [2010] EMLR 8.

[35] Part 2 of the Leveson Inquiry was cancelled in 2018: *Parliamentary Debates*, House of Commons, vol 789, 1 March 2018, col 810. A judicial review of the decision was unsuccessful: *R (on the application of Jefferies and Others) v Secretary of State for the Home Department, The Secretary of State for Digital, Culture, Media and Sport* [2018] EWHC 3239 (Admin). Note also previous UK consultations regarding the media and privacy; the UK government gave a negative response (Cm 5985, 2003) to the Fifth Report of the House of Commons Culture, Media and Sport Select Committee on Privacy and Media Intrusion (HC 458-1, 2003) and its recommendation of the introduction of a new privacy law against media intrusion. See, eg, Uncorrected Evidence 275, www.publications.parliament.uk/pa/cm200809/cmselect/cmcumeds/uc275-xv/uc27502.htm.

[36] *Murray v Express Newspapers plc* [2008] EWCA Civ 446; (2009) Ch 481.

[37] *Murray v Express Newspapers plc* [2007] EWHC 1908 (Ch), reviewed in paras 13 and 44 of *Murray v Express Newspapers plc* [2008] EWCA Civ 446; (2009) Ch 481.

[38] *Murray v Express Newspapers plc* [2008] EWCA Civ 446; (2009) Ch 481, para 12.   [39] ibid, paras 14–20, 27–37, 45, 55–58.

[40] ibid, para 36. Note the approach taken to an older child in *Spelman v Express Newspapers* [2012] EWHC 355 (QB), paras 35, 46, 53–56 although this decision focuses mainly on whether it is appropriate to grant an injunction.

It is interesting to note that in 2015, the Supreme Court found that there was no reasonable expectation of privacy in respect of photographs taken by CCTV of the alleged commission by a boy of a public order offence.[41]

18.15   In addition to information relating to children, another area which has received much attention is personal and sexual relationships. Cases suggest that the details of the existence of intimate relationships (as well as information obtained in the course of them) may be private, but this varies with the degree of stability;[42] details of sexual orientations, in circumstances where there was evidence that others knew of the position, has not been found to be information in respect of which there was a reasonable expectation of privacy.[43] Below is an example of a case concerning intimate relationships.

■ *PJS v News Group Newspapers Ltd* [2016] UKSC 26

PJS was the spouse of a celebrity with whom he had two children. The case concerned an interim injunction against the publication of information of sexual activities of PJS disclosed by one of his former sexual partners. The court at first instance refused to grant the injunction, but this was overturned by the Court of Appeal. However, following the publication of the information in media outlets in the United States, Canada, and Scotland and also on social media, the Court of Appeal discharged the injunction. PJS appealed. The Supreme Court acknowledged that a significant part of the population of England was aware of the identity of PJS and his spouse. However, the majority did not consider that the extent of the disclosure, especially in light of the distress that would be caused by further publication, was sufficient to lift the injunction.

18.16   Some other guidance can be extracted from English decisions (there are as yet no Scottish ones on point). Information will not be private if it is generally accessible (to be more flexibly applied than in respect of commercial information);[44] or if it relates to a criminal act (there is uncertainty here—drug taking might be private, but domestic violence or tax evasion would not be),[45] although Article 8 was engaged by the police taking photographs, and keeping them, of a person's participation at a demonstration.[46] The existence of an expectation in another jurisdiction (say California) can be considered but this will not necessarily mean that one would be found.[47] It is not necessary that a publisher knows or ought to know that there is a reasonable expectation of privacy—a marked but logical contrast to the position in respect of the obligation base for breach of confidence discussed in Chapter 17.[48]

> **Key points on reasonable expectation of privacy**
>
> - Expectation of privacy depends on the facts (but see *Murray*).
> - Even public figures can have an expectation of privacy.
> - It is less likely to apply to publicly available information.
> - It is more likely to apply to details of sexual relationships/long-standing relationships.

[41] In *JR38's Application for Judicial Review* [2015] UKSC 42.
[42] See, eg, *McKennitt v Ash* [2006] EWCA Civ 1714, paras 29–30 and see para 18.43; *Mosley v News Group Newspapers Ltd* [2008] EWHC 1777 (QB), [2008] EMLR 20, paras 24, 98–104; *Ferdinand v MGN Ltd* [2011] EWHC 2454 (QB), para 53, 54, 58; *CC v AB* [2006] EWHC 3083 (QB) (interests of spouses and children could be taken into account); *AAA v Associated Newspaper Ltd* [2013] EWCA Civ 554, paras 10–37 (disclosure of paternity); *B v D* [2014] EWHC 1442 (QB) (disclosure of sex worker and client relationship).
[43] *Trimingham v Associated Newspapers Ltd* [2012] EWHC 1296 (QB), paras 292–294, 305, 309–310, also 311–319 regarding photographs.
[44] *McKennitt v Ash* (1st instance) [2005] EWHC 3003, para 81. See also application of test in *McKennitt v Ash* [2006] EWCA Civ 1714, paras 21–23.
[45] *A v B* [2005] EWHC 1651, [2005] EMLR 36, para 32.
[46] Decision of the Court of Appeal, *Wood v Commissioner of Police of the Metropolis* [2009] EWCA Civ 414, paras 16–46, notably paras 45–46 (and regarding the breadth of what could be private).
[47] *Weller v Associated Newspapers Ltd* [2014] EWHC 1163 (QB), paras 45–46.   [48] See ibid, esp paras 129–136, 150–173.

Pictures and images

18.17 *Campbell, Murray,* and *Hannover,* amongst others, involve photographs. The impact of a photograph as a form of communicating information, rather than just using words, was discussed in Chapter 17 regarding the extent to which published photographs could still be confidential. The importance of photographs was also considered by the ECtHR in 2009 in *Reklos v Greece*,[49] regarding a photograph of the face of a newborn baby in a supposedly secure unit.[50] The ECtHR considered that the right to private life was, again, not 'susceptible to exhaustive definition',[51] but that it did cover rights to identity, personal development, and personality; and image was considered to be one of the key parts of personality.[52] This was confirmed in a further case before the ECtHR in 2012 involving Princess Caroline of Hannover.[53] The image is:[54]

> one of the chief attributes of . . . personality, as it reveals the person's unique characteristics and distinguishes the person from his or her peers. The right to the protection of one's image is thus one of the essential components of personal development. It mainly presupposes the individual's right to control the use of that image, including the right to refuse publication thereof.

Key point on image

- Publishing a photograph of someone raises special issues for privacy.

Exercise

Review the scenario you developed in the Exercise following para 18.4. Would there be a reasonable expectation of privacy?

Breach of confidence

18.18 It should be borne in mind that the action for misuse of private information has not replaced breach of confidence. This was stated clearly by the Court of Appeal in *HRH Prince of Wales v Associated Newspapers Ltd (No 3)* in 2006, discussed in Chapter 17. The Court of Appeal also dismissed arguments that there were now two actions for breach of confidence.[55] Rather, information would be either private, engaging Article 8, or confidential and subject to an obligation of confidence, or both; as relevant factors to assessing each overlapped,[56] as in *Campbell*[57] and as in *HRH Prince of Wales v Associated Newspapers Ltd (No 3)*.[58] These bases for non-disclosure of information were then to be balanced with Article 10 and its limits.

Impact of Article 10

18.19 The previous discussion could lead to an identification of information in respect of which there is a reasonable expectation of privacy, and so Article 8 is engaged and relevant. But this is, of course, not the end of the story. Article 8 must then be balanced with Article 10,[59] to establish whether the disclosure and

---

[49] [2009] EMLR 16.   [50] ibid, para 37.   [51] ibid, para 39.

[52] ibid, paras 40–43. For consideration of the parent/child relationship and its impact, see A Carter-Silk and C Cartwright-Hignett, 'A child's right to privacy: "out of a parent's hands"' (2009) 20(6) Ent LR 212–17.

[53] *Von Hannover v Germany* (App Nos 40660/08 and 60641/08) [2012] EMLR 16 (ECtHR, Grand Chamber).

[54] ibid. See also *Weller v Associated Newspapers Ltd* [2014] EWHC 1163 (QB), paras 64–79.

[55] [2008] Ch 57, [2007] 3 WLR 222, paras 64–65, referring to the New Zealand case *Hosking v Runting* [2004] NZCA 34.

[56] *HRH Prince of Wales v Associated Newspapers Ltd (No 3)* [2008] Ch 57, para 28.

[57] *Campbell v MGN Ltd* [2004] 2 AC 457, para 53.

[58] [2008] Ch 57, [2007] 3 WLR 222, paras 13, 14, 26, 28, 41, and 42. See also *McKennitt v Ash* [2006] EWCA Civ 1714, paras 15–18.

[59] *Campbell v MGN Ltd* [2004] 2 AC 457, paras 29, 85–86, 105, 167; *McKennitt v Ash* [2006] EWCA Civ 1714, paras 11, 46–47; and *Douglas and Others v Hello! Ltd (No 3)* [2005] 3 WLR 881, para 53.

publication is in fact misuse of private information. *Campbell* provides that the balance is to be rational, fair, and not arbitrary.[60] Each right is to be afforded equal weight at the outset,[61] and to be encroached upon no more than is necessary and proportionate.[62] The weight accorded to freedom of expression will vary with the facts. Some forms of expression deserve greater weight—political and educational speech receiving more than celebrity gossip.[63]

18.20   Carrying out this balance can be difficult. For example, the ECtHR in *Hannover* in 2004 indicated that the interests of the free press would prevail over Article 8 rights if publication contributed to debate in the general interest. There was a fundamental distinction between details of public figures in respect of their official functions, and details of their private lives; only in respect of the official functions should the press be a watchdog in the general interest.[64] A second set of cases was then raised by Princess Caroline of Hannover, involving a photograph of Princess Caroline and her husband walking down the street in St Moritz and photographs with her father Prince Rainier of Monaco, in the context of a discussion of his health. This reached the ECtHR again.[65] The ECtHR found that Germany's approach was not unreasonable; there is a margin of appreciation for states to take their own approaches to balancing Articles 8 and 10. There was a 'zone of interaction'[66] which, even if in public, might involve private life; freedom of expression extended to ideas that offend or shock; the press has an essential role in a democratic society; and that regard should be had to the nature of the report, the prior conduct of the person involved, the nature of publication, and circumstances of the photos.[67]

18.21   The *Hannover* decisions are important, as under the HRA 1998, courts are required to have regard to ECtHR decisions, and, for example, have looked to *Fressoz v France*[68] and the 2006 decision in *Editions Plon v France*.[69] English courts have also looked to Resolution 1165 of the Council of Europe (passed in the aftermath of the death of the Princess of Wales, regarding the relationship between Article 8 and Article 10 ECHR).[70] However, courts in the UK are not obliged to follow the ECtHR decisions,[71] and where there is a conflict between decisions of the House of Lords and the ECtHR, the House of Lords (and now the Supreme Court) must be followed.[72] The extent of enthusiasm of English courts referring to ECtHR decisions in their judgments suggests some scope for further synergy in development in this area at national level and at the ECtHR in this field.

18.22   Even with ECtHR guidance, the carrying out of this balance is difficult and hard to predict. The Court of Appeal has rejected an argument[73] that once a person reveals information about one zone in their life, they have a lower expectation of privacy in that zone,[74] and also that particular weight should be had to the

---

[60]   *Campbell v MGN Ltd* [2004] 2 AC 457, paras 115, 167. Regarding balancing in more extreme factual circumstances, see also *X (formerly known as Mary Bell v SO)* [2003] EWHC 1101 (QB); *S (A Child) (Identification: Restrictions on Publication)* [2004] UKHL 47; *Re Attorney General's Reference (No 3 of 1999)* [2009] UKHL 34.

[61]   *Campbell v MGN Ltd* [2004] 2 AC 457, para 55, *Hannover v Germany* (App No 53920/00) (2005) 40 EHRR 1, paras H9, H24, 11, 13, 18, 58–64, 69, 76–79.

[62]   *Campbell v MGN Ltd* [2004] 2 AC 457, paras 139–141, *McKennitt v Ash* [2006] EWCA Civ 1714, para 46. In *MGN Ltd v United Kingdom* (App No 39401/04) (2011) 29 BHRC 686 (ECtHR) the ECtHR found that there had been no breach of Art 10 by the finding of the House of Lords in *Campbell*, but found that Art 10 ECHR could be violated, if disproportionate success fees are imposed on the defendant, as this could put pressure on a defendant not to defend their case in court.

[63]   *Campbell v MGN Ltd* [2004] 2 AC 457, paras 148–149. See also *LNS v Persons Unknown* [2010] EMLR 16, paras 68–69.

[64]   *Hannover v Germany* (App No 53920/00) (2005) 40 EHRR 1, para H20, 63–65. Reference was made to Resolution 1165 (2005) 40 EHRR 1, at *Hannover*, para 67.

[65]   See *Von Hannover v Germany* (App Nos 40660/08 and 60641/08) [2012] EMLR 16 (ECtHR, Grand Chamber).

[66]   ibid, para 95.   [67]   ibid, paras 102–113.   [68]   (2001) 31 EHRR 2.

[69]   *Editions Plon* (2006) 42 EHRR 36, paras 49–53. For consideration of the Arts 8 and 10 balancing act, and the place of the public interest, see *AAA v Associated Newspaper Ltd* [2013 EWCA Civ 554, paras 38–45.

[70]   See *Campbell v MGN Ltd* [2004] 2 AC 457, paras 53, 107–110, 113–122, 140; *McKennitt v Ash* [2006] EWCA Civ 1714 pays particular regard to these decisions and the need to respect them, paras 37–42, 58–66; and *Mosley v News Group Newspapers Ltd* [2008] EWHC 1777 (QB), [2008] EMLR 20, paras 18, 21, 99–109.

[71]   HRA 1998, s 2.   [72]   *Murray v Express Newspapers plc* [2008] EWCA Civ 446; (2009) Ch 481, para 20.

[73]   Based on *A v B plc* [2003] QB 195.   [74]   *McKennitt v Ash* [2006] EWCA Civ 1714, 53–55.

Article 8 rights of children when balancing those rights.[75] Courts have considered it relevant if information is being disclosed to correct a 'false image' (used in this case in respect of a reputation, rather than a photograph) which has been created in respect of a person—say, regarding a supermodel's distaste for drugs,[76] or in respect of arguments that a footballer had now embraced family values.[77] This can lead a court down unexpected paths—the court was relieved not to need to decide whether or not the captain of the English men's football team needed to be a role model.[78] The court also rejected the argument[79] that conduct of one person in private must be unlawful, before another person should be permitted to criticise it in public on the basis of freedom of expression—'not all conduct that is socially harmful is unlawful'.[80]

18.23   The Court of Appeal in *HRH Prince of Wales v Associated Newspapers Ltd (No 3)* provided helpful guidance for the balancing act. The court should take into account whether in all the circumstances it was in the public interest that the obligation of confidence should be breached. Was a fetter on free expression necessary in a democratic society; was disclosure justifiable and proportionate in the light of obligations of confidence? Regard should be had to the nature of the information; the nature of the relationship (including whether there was a contract); and whether in all the circumstances it was legitimate for the information to be kept confidential or whether it was in the public interest for it to be made public.[81] If there was no contract, was a fetter on free expression necessary in a democratic society; and was disclosure proportionate?[82]

18.24   Like *London Regional Transport v Mayor of London* discussed in Chapter 17,[83] *HRH Prince of Wales* is another example of the ongoing importance of the term 'the public interest' in litigation in the HRA era.[84] As noted by the Court of Appeal in *McKennitt v Ash*, is it 'perhaps inevitable'[85] that these references to the public interest will continue, both in language and breadth of analysis? Yet the substance of the cases considered suggests that even if references to 'public interest' continue (and this is particularly likely in the context of remedies, as considered in Chapter 21, given references to it in s 12 of the HRA 1998), final outcomes will be reached on an ECtHR and Article 10-based approach[86] irrespective of the basis of claim or type of information.[87]

18.25   In a different context, the public interest was considered in *Ali v Channel 5*[88] regarding the filming of individuals being evicted from their home for a television programme. The claimants' Article 8 rights were found to be engaged and the restriction of the defendant's Article 10 rights was justified, with the court noting that the television programme focused on creating drama between the claimants and the landlord and not on issues of public interest.[89]

---

[75] *ETK v News Group Newspapers Ltd* [2011] EWCA Civ 439, paras 14ff, in particular para 19.

[76] *Campbell v MGN Ltd* [2004] 2 AC 457, see, eg, para 24.

[77] *Ferdinand v MGN Ltd* [2011] EWHC 2454 (QB), para 53, 54, 58, paras 64, 65, 66, 69.

[78] ibid, paras 87, 89–91.   [79] *LNS v Persons Unknown* [2010] EMLR 16.

[80] ibid, paras 99–104; see also *Ferdinand v MGN Ltd* [2011] EWHC 2454 (QB), paras 63, 64.

[81] *HRH Prince of Wales v Associated Newspapers Ltd (No 3)* [2008] Ch 57, paras 67–69 and see paras 30–31, 61–63, and 66–68 regarding CA.

[82] ibid, para 67 per Lord Phillips.

[83] See summary at para 17.14.

[84] See also *LNS v Persons Unknown* [2010] EMR 16, 62–63, 70 et seq and *Ferdinand v MGN Ltd* [2011] EWHC 2454 (QB), para 68.

[85] *McKennitt v Ash* [2006] EWCA Civ 1714, para 53.

[86] See also references in *Campbell v MGN Ltd* [2004] 2 AC 457, 56, 63, 85 (referring to *Spycatcher* then noting in para 86 change since HRA 1998, and also paras 106–110, 116 referring to ECtHR authorities and 142–143).

[87] *Douglas and Others v Hello! Ltd (No 3)* [2005] 3 WLR 881, paras 113–119. See also Aplin et al, *Gurry on Breach of Confidence: The Protection of Confidential Information* (2nd edn, 2012), 699–716 regarding defences. For details of damages payable after a finding of misuse of private information, see *Gulati v MGN Ltd* [2015] EWHC 1481 (Ch)—these should be compensatory, for distress and injury to feelings in the light of what events had taken place (there, phone hacking), and the impact on the values protected by privacy such as autonomy and dignity. The judgment in *Gulati v MGN* was upheld on appeal, subject to a 'small qualification' regarding the effect of repeated disclosures of information: [2017] QB 149, para 74.

[88] [2018] EMLR 17.

[89] ibid, para 210. See also on balancing Arts 8 and 10 in an application for an interim injunction: *XKF v BBC* [2018] EWHC 1560 (QB) ('doorstop' filming by a television crew of a police officer who had a spent criminal conviction). Criminal convictions are not necessarily private information but spent convictions may be, as in *NT1, NT2 v Google LLC v The Information Commissioner* [2018] EWHC 799 (QB).

Discussion point   For answer guidance visit www.oup.com/uk/brown5e.

A style magazine publishes pictures of a model leaving what is tipped to be the new fashionable beauty store. She is not happy as she has just signed a contract with a competitor. Discuss.

Key points on the impact of Article 10

- Article 8 and Article 10 start with equal weighting.
- The impact of Article 10 depends on facts and proportionality, but could look to:
  - the nature of the report;
  - the prior conduct of the person involved;
  - the nature of the publication;
  - the circumstances of the photos;
  - genuine debate or curiosity;
  - correction of false image;
  - an obligation of confidence;
  - public interest.

18.26   A further example of the balancing of Article 8 and Article 10 involved the publication of details of the participation of Max Mosley, the President of the Fédération Internationale de l'Automobile, the world motorsports body, in group consensual sexual activity of a sadomasochistic nature. The English court considered that there was a reasonable expectation of privacy in respect of participation in consensual sexual acts on private property.[90] In considering the Article 10 ECHR arguments, the court found that there was no public interest in publication.[91] Mosley then raised an action at the ECtHR claiming that UK law was in breach of Article 8 ECHR, since it does not provide for a legal duty for newspapers to contact a person before publishing private information related to that person. The ECtHR considered the chilling effect that could arise from this, doubts as to its effectiveness, and the wide margin of appreciation, and considered that Article 8 did not require pre-notification.[92]

Impact of data protection

18.27   Sensitive personal data under the Data Protection Act 1998, such as data relating to race, health, sexual orientation, and political and religious beliefs, has also been viewed as private for the purpose of identifying what information qualifies as private.[93] Data protection grounds were also raised, albeit unsuccessfully, in *Campbell*.[94] In Scotland, the Data Protection Act 1998 was deployed (unsuccessfully) in *Beyts v Trump International Gold Club Scotland Ltd*[95] in which a protester against a golf course development was

---

[90] Despite the subject matter, the court did not consider this to be a 'landmark' case: see *Mosley v News Group Newspapers Ltd* [2008] EWHC 1777 (QB), [2008] EMLR 20, para 234. But note K Hughes, 'Case comment. Horizontal privacy' (2009) 125 LQR 244–47.
[91] *Mosley v News Group Newspapers Ltd* [2008] EWHC 1777 (QB), [2008] EMLR 20, paras 24–25, 110–134, 170–171, 233.
[92] *Mosley v United Kingdom* (App No 48009/08) (2011) (53) EHRR 30, in particular para 132.
[93] *Green Corns Ltd v Claverly Group Ltd* [2005] EMLR 31, esp paras 62–64; *R (on the application of W) v Secretary of State for Health* [2015] EWCA Civ 1034.
[94] [2002] EWCA Civ 1373, paras 72–138.   [95] 2017 SLT (Sh Ct) 93.

photographed by golf course staff.[96] The Data Protection Act 1998 has now been largely superseded by the Data Protection Act 2018, which largely reflects the EU General Data Protection Regulation (GDPR).[97]

18.28   Data protection is also relevant in the employment context. *WM Morrison Supermarkets plc v Various Claimants*[98] concerned the criminal disclosure by a disgruntled employee of information about 99,998 employees including information such as their date of birth, gender, and bank account details. The employer was held to be vicariously liable for breach of confidence and misuse of private information.[99]

Key points on personal privacy

- There is no overarching claim of invasion of privacy.

- Breach of confidence covers personal information, although it is better termed misuse of private information.

- Key question (1): is there information in respect of which there is a reasonable expectation of privacy? If so, Article 8 is relevant.

- Key question (2): is it proportionate for disclosure of information to be prevented given Article 10 rights?

- A careful balance of Articles 8 and 10 is required—weight of Article 10 will vary with the type of expression, and the weight of Article 8 will vary with the context—public figures still have private lives.

- Decisions of the ECtHR and the Council of Europe Resolution are highly influential.

- Some aspect of personal privacy may be protected through other legislative means such as data protection law.

Merchandising

Introduction

18.29   This section moves from individuals wishing to keep information secret, to situations when companies or individuals wish to control the use which they and others can make of their commercial reputation and, colloquially, their brand. So, this discussion takes us back to trade marks and passing off. Merchandising can apply to real-world personalities—for example a well-known sportsperson—or entirely fictitious, for example cartoon or puppet characters in a television series such as *In the Night Garden*.

18.30   Merchandising might involve putting on the market a variety of products bearing the name or image of the person or character, or reproducing the image in either two- or three-dimensional form. This form of marketing is known as *spin off* or *character merchandising* when applied to fictional characters or entities, *personality merchandising* when the character is a real person. The boundary between character and personality merchandising may become blurred when, for example, the personality of an actor well known in a particular role is exploited in this sort of way.

---

[96] However, the pleadings focused narrowly on the failure of the defender to register as a data controller as opposed to a claim concerning privacy; see E Reid, 'Beyts v Trump International Gold Club Scotland Ltd: caught short on data protection and privacy' (2018) 21(3) Ed LR 411–17, 414.

[97] Regulation (EU) 2016/679 of the European Parliament and of the Council of 27 April 2016 on the protection of natural persons with regard to the processing of personal data and on the free movement of such data, and repealing Directive 95/46/EC. The GDPR, amongst other things, requires consent to be obtained for the processing of personal data.

[98] [2018] EWCA Civ 2339. Permission to appeal has been granted.

[99] ibid, paras 74–75, 79. That there was also a breach of s 4 Data Protection Act 1998 did not prevent the claimants making breach of confidence or misuse of information claims: para 60.

Question

What is merchandising? You may find the following helpful: HE Ruijsenaars, 'Legal aspects of merchandising: the AIPPI Resolution' [1996] 6 EIPR 330.

Trade marks

18.31   Starting with a fictional but actual example, a trade mark was obtained for the cartoon character 'Betty Boop'. In a merchandising dispute, challenges to its validity on grounds of distinctiveness failed, and the trade mark was found to be infringed. The court stated that it would have taken a different approach to validity if there has been sale of general film memorabilia from the 1930s.[100] The court also stressed that there is no free-standing right in England to control images, and that invented characters and real-life characters should be approached in the same way.

18.32   In real life, imagine that a fan of tennis player Serena Williams took a photograph of her as the fan was walking down the street, and applied that picture to the front of a T-shirt to be sold on market stalls. If a photograph of Williams had been registered as a trade mark in connection with articles of clothing, that fact might prevent any picture being applied to a T-shirt by another: one picture of Williams is likely to be similar to another.

Question

Read this last example again. What defence from registered trade mark law might the T-shirt vendor have in the given circumstances? You could have a look at paras 15.81ff.

Exercise

Choose the name of a well-known individual. Search both the UK Intellectual Property Office register and the European Union Intellectual Property Office register to see if you can find any registered trade marks consisting of or including that name.

18.33   Signatures of celebrities, both alive and dead, have been registered as trade marks in the UK. An example is Marilyn Monroe's signature, which was registered in class 3 in connection with cosmetics, soaps, shampoos, and foamable preparations for the bath.[101]

18.34   So a signature might be distinctive for the purposes of trade mark law[102] because of the script used and thus registerable. However, the registration of celebrity names as such has proved more problematic and has been called into question since the appeal in *Elvis Presley Enterprises Inc v Sid Shaw Elvisly Yours*.[103] This is a good example of the legal arguments and policy dilemmas which arise in this field.

---

[100]   *Hearst Holdings v AVELA Inc* [2014] EWHC 439 (Ch).

[101]   UK Trade Mark No 1308828, the estate of Marilyn Monroe (it has not been renewed).

[102]   In *Elvis Presley Enterprises Inc v Sid Shaw Elvisly Yours* [1999] RPC 567 the Court of Appeal found Elvis Presley's signature to be distinctive, but it was not registered because opposition based on a confusing similarity to an earlier mark used by a third-party merchandiser succeeded.

[103]   ibid; see also *Corsair Toiletries's Application* [1999] ETMR 1038 ('Jane Austen' for toiletries refused because it lacked distinctiveness). On the trade mark protection of personal names, see also para 14.49.

18.35   The Court of Appeal upheld the decision to overturn registrations of a variety of styles of the name 'Elvis Presley'. The court decided that a celebrity name was not registerable as a trade mark as it was not distinctive. The court appeared aware of the broad monopoly power that could be conferred on traders if celebrity names could be registered as trade marks. In the words of Simon Brown LJ:

> there should be no *a priori* assumption that only a celebrity or his successors may ever market (or licence the marketing of) his own character. Monopolies should not be so readily created.

18.36   The *Elvis Presley* case dealt with the law as it stood under the Trade Marks Act 1938 and it is not clear that the same result would have been achieved had the 1994 Act been in operation. Nonetheless, it has been followed in the decision by the trade mark registry to turn down the application to register the name 'Diana, Princess of Wales' as a trade mark.[104] In refusing the application, the registry emphasised that a name unique to a particular person did not of itself have distinctive character as a trade mark. The essential function of a trade mark was to guarantee that the items bearing it had originated under the control of a single undertaking responsible for their quality. Unless, therefore, such control could be shown, the use of a famous name to endorse a product was not a trade mark use. It would thus seem that the better known the personality, the less likely it is that a name will be registered as a trade mark because the name is not considered distinctive in the trade mark sense, as was seen in the 'Alex Ferguson' case.[105] But note the EU trade mark (EUTM) registration for 'Usain Bolt' (009787581)—does it depend on the nature of the underlying person and the means by which they have become known?

18.37   There are many examples, however, of the names of living and dead well-known personalities becoming distinctive and being registered as trade marks: Gucci, Dior, Versace, and Naomi Campbell[106] are all examples.

 Exercise

Have a look at the *Manual of Trade Marks Practice*.[107] What does it say about the registration of: famous names, badges of allegiance, names of deceased individuals or defunct groups, pictures of famous persons?

Key points on celebrities and trade marks

- The signature of a celebrity may be considered as sufficiently distinctive for registration as a trade mark.

- Where the name of a celebrity is seen as purely descriptive of the subject matter of goods, it will be unregisterable as a trade mark.

- Trade marks can be used to restrict use of fictional characters.

---

[104]   *Diana, Princess of Wales Trade Mark* [2001] ETMR 25. See also C Waelde, 'Commercialising the personality of the late Diana, Princess of Wales: censorship by the back door?' in N Dawson and A Firth (eds), *Perspectives on Intellectual Property: Trade Marks Retrospective* vol 7 (2000).

[105]   *In the matter of Application No 2323092B to register a trade mark in Class 16 by Sir Alexander Chapman Ferguson*, Trade Mark Decision O/26605. See also from Germany a decision in relation to a picture of Marlene Dietrich, discussed in F Traub, 'German courts reject trade mark application for portrait of Marlene Dietrich' [2009] Ent LR 111.

[106]   Numerous UK trade marks have been registered for these names and may be viewed by searching the UK trade mark register: www.gov.uk/search-for-trademark.

[107]   You can find the Manual on the UK Intellectual Property Office website at www.gov.uk/government/organisations/intellectual-property-office.

18.38   Even if registration can be obtained, case law suggests that the names of celebrities and other well-known people will have a more limited scope of protection than other trade marks. Consider the following:

■ **Case C-361/04 *Ruiz-Picasso v OHIM* [2006] ECR I-643**

An application was made by DaimlerChrysler to register 'Picaro' for vehicles. The estate of Picasso, owners of the Picasso trade mark for vehicles objected.

The European Court of Justice rejected the appeal and found that where the meaning of at least one of the two signs at issue is clear and specific so that it can be grasped immediately by the relevant public, the conceptual differences observed between those signs may counteract any visual and phonetic similarities between them.[108] When confronted with the word sign 'Picasso', the relevant public inevitably sees in it a reference to the painter and that, 'given the painter's renown with that public, that particularly rich conceptual reference is such as greatly to reduce the resonance with which, in this case, the sign is endowed as a mark, among others, of motor vehicles'.[109]

18.39   Thus it would appear that when the names of well-known people have been registered as trade marks, the better known the name the narrower the scope of protection will be granted as against similar marks, and the lower the distinguishing capacity of the mark in relation to the goods for which it is registered.[110]

> **Question**
>
> To what extent do you think the well-known status of a name will be able to displace any likelihood of confusion between the name and the use of the name as a mark?

18.40   Issues also arise with respect to future dealings with trade marks. *Elizabeth Florence Emanuel v Continental Shelf*[111] concerned the assignation, by Elizabeth Emanuel, a fashion designer, of the trade mark bearing her name along with a crest made up of two 'E's back to back. After ownership of the trade mark had then changed hands several times, Elizabeth Emanuel opposed a proposed amendment to the registered trade mark and applied for revocation of it on the ground that to let the mark stay on the register would be to deceive the public within the meaning of what is now Article 4(1)(g) of the Trade Mark Directive.[112]

18.41   It was argued that a significant proportion of the relevant public would believe that use of the trade mark indicated that the individual remained involved with the design or creation of the goods in relation to which the mark was used, and so using the name mark in a business in which the individual was not concerned would be deceptive. The Court did not accept this argument. The Court ruled that a trade mark which corresponds to the name of the designer and first manufacturer of the goods is not, for that reason, liable to revocation on the ground that that mark would mislead the public. This was particularly so where the goodwill associated with that mark has been assigned together with the business making the goods to which the mark relates.[113]

18.42   Although this might seem an odd result if the view is taken that a consumer might be confused that the named individual designer had not actually had a hand in designing the goods, it undoubtedly reflects what happens in commercial life.

---

[108] [2006] ECR I-643, para 20.   [109] Case C-361/04 *Ruiz-Picasso v OHIM* [2006] ECR I-643, para 15.46.
[110] See also Case C-16/06 P *Les Editions Albert René Sarl v OHIM* [2009] ETMR 21 and Case C-51/09 P *Barbara Becker v Harman International Industries* [2010] ETMR 53, regarding compound name and well-known surname.
[111] Case C-259/04 [2006] ECR I-3089.
[112] On trade marks likely to deceive, see paras 14.91ff and on the *Emanuel* case specifically, see para 14.92.
[113] Note that in contrast, according to the UK tax authorities, an unregistered trade mark does not exist as a separate asset and is not capable of assignment separate from the goodwill of the business in which it is used (see Capital Gains Manual, HMRC CG68210).

18.43   Consider, however, that in 2012 the Court of Justice considered an application for 'Elio Fiorucci'. The individual Elio Fiorucci, who had owned Fiorrucci SpA and had been very well known as a designer in the 1970s, objected, including with reference to protection of well-known names by Italian law. The Court of Justice found that the right to this name applied not only to use in a commercial context, but also to personality.[114]

Key points on well-known name trade marks

- The better known a name, the more likely it is that any confusion due to visual, aural, or conceptual similarities as between similar names may be displaced.

- An assignation of a trade mark consisting of the name of a well-known individual is not liable to be revoked purely on the ground that the individual no longer remains involved with the business carried on under the mark,

- But the well-known individual might be able to have an impact on future applications.

18.44   As well as the name of a well-known individual, one might (whether the celebrity or a third party) want to protect their image—in the sense of a picture, what the individual looks like. Early cases suggested that registration would be permissible on the ground that an image is distinctive. As was said in 1897:[115]

> it is difficult to suppose anything could be more distinctive than the portraiture of the man who was professing to be the manufacturer of that particular article.

18.45   However, the UK Intellectual Property Office refused to register images of the late Diana Princess of Wales as trade marks.[116] Applications were made to register 52 different images for a wide variety of goods and services. Unfortunately, the reasoning behind the refusal has not been made public, so one can only speculate as to what it might have been. In trade mark terms, the registry may have decided that the images were not distinctive. Diana was, after all, one of the most photographed people in the world for a number of years. Another ground for refusal might have been that there was no trade connection between the images and the goods and services in respect of which they were to be registered. Equally, there may have been a lack of any form of quality control over those products and services: an argument similar to that used to turn down the application to register her name as a trade mark.[117]

 Exercise

Have another look at the *Manual of Trade Marks Practice*. What does it say about the registration of pictures of famous persons?

18.46   It thus appears that neither the name (as opposed to the signature) nor the image of a well-known individual will be accepted in the UK for registration as a trade mark for certain goods unless the mark has acquired distinctiveness through use. For some goods the signs will be unregistrable. For those names and images

---

[114] *Edwin Co Ltd v Office for Harmonisation in the Internal Market (Trade Marks and Designs) (OHIM), Elio Fiorucci* [2011] ETMR 45, see paras 19, 20, 39, 65, 67.
[115] *Rowland v Mitchell* (1897) 14 RPC 37.
[116] 'Diana fund loses trademark battle' (1999) http://news.bbc.co.uk/1/hi/uk/272380.stm. It is understood that had the Fund decided to appeal the decision, then the reason for the initial refusal would have been publicly available. See also A Story, 'Owning Diana: from People's Princess to private property', at https://kar.kent.ac.uk/1894.
[117] See *Executrices of the Estate of Diana, Princess of Wales' Application* [2001] ETMR 25 (the name lacked distinctive character).

that are already registered it may be that in any dispute with a third party the scope of protection will be narrow or the registration vulnerable to being declared invalid as being merely descriptive of the goods for which it is registered. The more famous you are, the harder it might be to obtain a trade mark.

> **Key points on trade marks and the image of a celebrity**
>
> - The name and image of a celebrity can be registered as trade marks in certain circumstances.
> - For some goods, the signs will be unregisterable as they will not be considered as indicating origin.

Exercise

Should a well-known individual be able to protect elements of their personality as a registered trade mark? What justifications would you give? And what elements of their personality? If it were possible, what effect might this have on the availability of consumer goods in the marketplace?

Passing off

18.47 Passing off has been used when misrepresentations have been made in respect of authors, artists, or their work. It has been passing off for the author of any creative work to attach to it the name of another author, perhaps especially if that name is a *nom de plume*;[118] the author of a highly successful dramatic sketch was able to prevent a film being publicised as a version of his sketch;[119] and there may be passing off if the fanciful name of a musical band is used by another band.[120] When the *London Evening Standard* published a satire of the diaries of Alan Clark, an MP, this was found to be passing off; not enough had been done by the newspaper to remove the possibility of confusion in the mind of the typical reader.[121]

18.48 A greater variety of approaches has been taken in respect of merchandising. A court in Hong Kong held that an author may claim goodwill in a fictional character, and that a film producer who has a licence to use the story creating the character can also build up goodwill in it, which may be protected by a passing off action.[122] The 'Crocodile Dundee' cases in Australia[123] illustrate how the image of an actor and his character may coalesce. Paul Hogan played the character Crocodile Dundee in a series of films, which he also wrote. These cases involved the defendants' sale of goods making use of the 'Crocodile Dundee' name and image, and the Australian courts held that Hogan himself could bring an action for passing off.

18.49 Yet, save in the *Ninja Turtles*[124] case discussed previously, the English courts have been reluctant to recognise that the use of characters or personalities can be stopped by their originator, especially if they have not yet commenced trading operations using them. The argument is that goodwill, as distinct from reputation, is necessary before there can be a claim of passing off. Examples of unsuccessful claims include the following:

- Uncle Mac, children's radio character in *McCulloch v May* (1948) 65 RPC 58;
- Sherlock Holmes in *Conan Doyle v London Mystery Magazine Ltd* (1949) 66 RPC 312;

---

[118] *Marengo v Daily Sketch* (1948) 65 RPC 242 (HL). Note also the right to prevent false attribution in the Copyright, Designs and Patents Act 1988, s 84 (see para 6.17ff).
[119] *Samuelson v Producers Distributing Co* [1932] 1 Ch 201.
[120] *Hines v Winnick* [1947] 1 Ch 708 (Doctor Crock and his Crackpots); *Treadwell's Drifters Inc v RCL Ltd* 1996 SLT 1048 (The Drifters).
[121] *Clark v Associated Newspapers Ltd* [1998] 1 All ER 959.
[122] *Shaw Bros v Golden Harvest* [1972] RPC 559.
[123] *Hogan v Koala Dundee* (1988) 12 IPR 508; *Hogan v Pacific Dunlop* (1989) 12 IPR 225.
[124] *Mirage Studios v Counter-Feat Clothing Co Ltd* [1991] FSR 145, see para 18.6.

- Wombles of Wimbledon in *Wombles v Womble Skip* [1977] RPC 99;
- ABBA pop group in *Lyngstad v Anabas* [1977] FSR 62;
- Teletubbies in *BBC Worldwide v Pally Screen Printing* [1998] FSR 665.

18.50   Even where the character or personality is already being used under licence to market goods, English judges have found that the use of the image is not seen by the public as a representation of a connection with, or authorisation by, the originator of the character or individual in question. If there is a false claim of authorisation—for example, a claim that the merchandise is 'official'—then, but only then, may there be a misrepresentation.[125] This use of such wording can lead to some complex arguments and, indeed, can be a double-edged sword.[126] In 1997, the pop group 'The Spice Girls'[127] sought an application for an injunction to prevent an unauthorised trader selling 'Spice Girls' sticker collections. The court rejected arguments that the absence of the word 'unofficial' was sufficient to influence the public's perception of the origin of the goods.

18.51   Against this backdrop, the 2014 'Betty Boop' decision (see para 18.31) in respect of trade marks, is significant. The court found that the three established elements of goodwill, misrepresentation, and likelihood of damage were met; notably, the public was likely to think that the two sets of merchandise in question came from the same single source.[128]

> ### Key point on character and personality merchandising—passing off
>
> - Courts have been reluctant to allow the action for the unauthorised use of fictional characters and real persons in the marketing of products—evidence is key.

> ### Summary of key points on merchandising
>
> - Passing off can prevent some forms of merchandising.
> - Trade marks can provide the right to control the use of name, signature, and image (picture) in some cases.
> - The protection which exists stems from established principles—there is no dedicated comprehensive protection which applies to merchandising in its many forms.

Endorsement and sponsorship

Passing off and false endorsement

18.52   There is an important distinction between character and personality merchandising and endorsement, as Laddie J explained in the English decision *Irvine*, which was summarised previously:[129]

> When someone endorses a product or service he tells the relevant public that he approves of the product or service or is happy to be associated with it. In effect he adds his name as an encouragement to members of

---

[125] *Elvis Presley Trade Marks* [1997] RPC 543, 558 (Laddie J). This would also cover the Scottish case of *Wilkie v McCulloch* (1823) 2 S 413.
[126] See also *Arsenal Football Club plc v Reed* [2001] RPC 922 (Laddie J), where the defendant who made clear that his goods were *not* official Arsenal merchandise was found not to have engaged in passing off.
[127] *Halliwell v Panini*, unreported, 9 July 1997 (Ch D).
[128] *Hearst Holdings v AVELA Inc* [2014] EWHC 439 (Ch), paras 66–101, including consideration of previous case law.
[129] [2002] 2 All ER 414, [2002] FSR 60, para 9. See also *Fenty v Arcadia* [2015] EWCA Civ 3, para 36:

[C]haracter merchandising encompasses a range of activities which share the common feature that they involve the licensing of the names or likenesses of famous characters, whether real or fictional … Endorsement, on the other hand, describes one particular kind of relationship between the characters (or their creators) and the goods which bear their names or likenesses, and it implies authorisation and approval.

the relevant public to buy or use the service or product. Merchandising is rather different. It involves exploiting images, themes or articles which have become famous . . . It is not a necessary feature of merchandising that members of the public will think the products are in any sense endorsed [by the personalities or characters concerned].

18.53 The early view of the English courts was that, even if there was appropriation of goodwill by the false endorsement, the business being made by the defendant from its activities was not custom that would otherwise have gone to the person represented as making the endorsement.[130] English courts have looked in the past to defamation to address this type of scenario, for example when a champion amateur golfer was portrayed with a Fry's chocolate bar in an advertisement for that product, implying that he had been paid for an endorsement of the product, which was inconsistent with this amateur status.[131] By contrast, in the early Scottish decision of *Wilkie v McCulloch*,[132] a firm was stopped from representing that its ploughs were made under the inspection and authority of an individual who had developed a new kind of plough.

Exercise

How far does and should the law of passing off go in offering protection to aspects of individual personality against use by others constituting misrepresentation? What aspects of personality in addition to name, designation, and voice used in one's trade or profession might be covered? Is this the same as your approach in respect of trade marks?

18.54 A significant change in approach was taken in England by Laddie J in *Irvine*, which was approved by the Court of Appeal.[133] Eddie Irvine, the leading Formula 1 racing driver, was shown in a promotional brochure for Talksport Radio wearing his Ferrari racing gear and apparently listening intently to a radio marked with the Talksport insignia. This was, however, the result of manipulation of a photograph (lawfully acquired for reproduction by Talksport) which actually showed Irvine using a mobile telephone. It was held that this was passing off. Laddie J said (at para 39):

[I]t is common for famous people to exploit their names and images by way of endorsement. They do it not only in their own field of expertise but, depending on the extent of their fame or notoriety, wider afield also. It is common knowledge that for many sportsmen, for example, income received from endorsing a variety of products and services represent a very substantial part of their total income. The reason large sums are paid for endorsement is because, no matter how irrational it may seem to a lawyer, those in business have reason to believe that the lustre of a famous personality, if attached to their goods and services, will enhance the attractiveness of those goods or services to their target market. In this respect, the endorsee is taking the benefit of the attractive force which is the reputation or goodwill of the famous person.

18.55 The Court of Appeal applied *Irvine* when the retailer Topshop used an image of the well-known singer Rihanna on T-shirts, without her consent.[134]

The Court of Appeal found a relevant misrepresentation, through a false endorsement, although (once again) there is no right to protection of one's image. Here, although Rihanna had authorised the use of her name and image in other cases, it was for her, not the shop, to decide if this was to happen again; and the fact that she had had connections in the past made it more likely that consumers would think there was an endorsement this time.[135]

[130] *McCulloch v May* (1948) 65 RPC 58; *Elvis Presley Trade Marks* [1999] RPC 567 at 597 per Simon Brown LJ.
[131] *Tolley v Fry* [1931] AC 333.   [132] (1823) 2 S 413.
[133] [2002] EWHC 367 (Ch); [2003] EWCA Civ 423. See further M Learmouth, 'Eddie, are you OK? Product endorsement and passing off' [2002] IPQ 306.
[134] *Fenty v Arcadia* [2015] EWCA Civ 3.   [135] ibid, paras 19.

> **Key point on endorsement**
>
> - *Irvine* is authority that false endorsement is passing off because endorsement is established as a lucrative way in which personalities may exploit their fame.

 Discussion point   For answer guidance visit **www.oup.com/uk/brown5e**.

Do you agree that the endorsement of a well-known personality can be a source of goodwill? Does Article 8 ECHR require the protection of such goodwill? Whose goodwill—the trader whose products are endorsed or the personality doing the endorsing? And consider how your conclusions here relate to your views formed earlier regarding privacy.

Intellectual property and sponsorship agreements

18.56   As considered by Laddie J in *Irvine*, well-known personalities, characters, and businesses will frequently enter into agreements regarding the use of their name and image. Examples might be the sponsorship agreement entered into by various companies in respect of the Olympic Games; and, for example, the agreement between tennis player Andy Murray and Rado regarding a watch, which led to visible concern when he could not find the watch after winning the US Open in 2012.[136]

18.57   Yet, as seen previously in the discussion of passing off, endorsement, and trade marks,[137] the legal basis for this may be slim. As also noted in respect of passing off, the courts remain rather sceptical of the place of commercial reality and benefiting from one's profile. An important example comes from the decision in *LNS*,[138] which involved the publication in a newspaper of the fact of a sexual relationship involving the then English men's football captain with the partner of another member of the team. For present purposes, the court had concerns about the material put before it, and considered that the main priority of the footballer's business advisers was not privacy but the damage to commercialisation and sponsorship opportunities which could result.[139]

18.58   Whatever the attitude of the law, contracts involving image continue to exist, and give rise to their own disputes, such as *Proactive Sports Management v Rooney and Others*.[140] The agreement, which was entered into when footballer Wayne Rooney was very young, was ultimately found to be unenforceable as being in restraint of trade; but no issues arose as to whether or not there was such a thing as image rights.[141] The Court of Appeal then dismissed an appeal regarding restraint of trade.[142]

 Exercise

Look up *Proactive Sports Management v Rooney* [2010] EWHC 1807 (QB) (it is very long). Review the list of image rights extracted from the agreement, in paras 53 and 187 of the judgment, and details of brand development activities in paras 198 and 221–223. Reflect on this in the light of your work in this chapter so far.

---

[136] 'Tennis champ Andy Murray loses watch in moment of Victory' (2012), www.forbes.com/sites/paigereddinger/2012/09/11/tennis-champ-andy-murray-loses-watch-in-moment-of-victory.

[137] Para 18.31ff.   [138] *LNS v Persons Unknown* [2010] EMLR 16.   [139] ibid, paras 39, 49–52, 97 et seq, 127, 131.

[140] [2010] EWHC 1807 (QB).

[141] For an example of other disputes which can arise in relation to a sponsorship agreement, including the removal of a sponsor's name as part of a rebranding process and the extent to which this was a repudiatory breach, see *Force India Formula One Team Ltd v Etihad Airways PJSC* [2011] ETMR 10.

[142] *Proactive Sports Management v Rooney and Others* [2011] EWCA Civ 1444 and see para 93.

> **Key point on sponsorship**
>
> - Image rights lie at the heart of commercially valuable contracts.

Control of (public) image

18.59 The English courts took a different approach to the impact of agreements regarding confidentiality and the photographs. As discussed in Chapter 17 and previously, despite the size of their wedding, the Court of Appeal found that the wedding of Michael Douglas and Catherine Zeta-Jones was private, and that photographs of it were confidential. Douglas and Zeta-Jones succeeded in an action for both breach of confidence and misuse of private information when *Hello!* magazine published unauthorised photographs. The issue of present interest, also touched on in Chapter 17 (see para 17.24), is whether or not *OK!* could sue *Hello!*

18.60 The House of Lords[143] found that Douglas, Zeta-Jones, and *OK!* had entered into an agreement that each picture taken of the wedding would be a separate piece of information which *OK!* would have the exclusive right to publish—quite apart from the other pictures which had been published by *OK!*[144] So, *OK!* could sue *Hello!* Yet the focus must be on the trading, the contract,[145] and confidential information and the level of control held over it,[146] rather than reputation, image,[147] and the market value of the information.[148] There have been arguments that this risks turning information into a property right—which was also considered more generally in Chapter 17.[149] Conversely, there are both economic and dignity-based justifications for celebrities to be able to control their reputation and public image.[150]

> **Key points on agreements and control of information**
>
> - There can be agreements that information is confidential.
> - The parties to this can sue others if they publish it—this is not an image right.

18.61 Other countries have different approaches to control of public image and personality. In New York, legislation provides that one should not use the name, portrait, or picture of a living person without consent.[151] In California, one should not use the name, voice, signature, or photograph without prior consent.[152] Germany has a law on 'personality rights',[153] though freedom of expression can prevail over these (with more regard had to the personality rights of those under 18).[154] German copyright law requires that there must be consent to the publication of an image, but not if the publication involves an issue important to contemporary society.[155]

---

[143] *OBG Ltd v Allan, Douglas v Hello!* [2007] UKHL 21.

[144] ibid, per Lord Hoffmann at paras 122 and 123, although compare Lord Nicholls at paras 257–259.

[145] ibid, para 117 (Lord Hoffmann).　　[146] ibid, para 124; see also paras 118, 120.

[147] Although Lord Nicholls notes that the claim of Douglas and Zeta-Jones is based on images, ibid, paras 252–253.

[148] ibid, para 299 (Lord Walker).　　[149] ibid, para 300 (Lord Walker).

[150] See Aplin et al, *Gurry on Breach of Confidence: The Protection of Confidential Information* (2nd edn, 2012), 348–56, and G Black, *Publicity Rights and Image: Exploitation and Legal Control* (2011).

[151] New York Civil Rights Law, Art 5.　　[152] California Civil Code, s 3344.

[153] Arts 1(1), 2(1), and 5(1), (2) Grundgesetz (German Basic Law); see development prior to the 2012 *Hannover* decision, discussed at *Von Hannover v Germany* (App Nos 40660/08 and 60641/08) [2012] EMLR 16 (ECtHR, Grand Chamber), paras 41–45, 115–117, 123.

[154] See decision of the Federal Constitutional Court BVerG, 1 BvR 2499/09, 1 BvR 2503/09 (Jan 2012).

[155] Law in Copyright in Arts, ss 22 and 23.

Discussion point   For answer guidance visit www.oup.com/uk/brown5e.

Should there be an image right in the UK? If so, what would it look like? You might find the Guernsey legislation, an interesting mix of copyright and trade mark law, a useful starting point. Guernsey Image Rights (Bailiwick of Guernsey) Ordinance, 2012 and see also http://ipo.guernseyregistry.com/article/103037/What-are-Image-Rights.

Conclusions

18.62   The protection conferred in the UK in respect of control of information and reputation is very piecemeal. There is a right of privacy in respect of private information, and the decisions of the ECtHR will have a key role in developing this—save where a contrary approach has been taken since the HRA 1998 by the House of Lords, now the Supreme Court. The position is more controversial and less clear in respect of what can broadly be termed a personality right. Personality merchandising is a common feature of daily commercial life, and much money is made by individuals and organisations through these activities; but it does not thereby follow that the individual has an enforceable right in respect of their personality, at least from the perspective of the arguments in favour of intellectual property, which were discussed in Chapter 1. Granting a 'personality' or 'image' right would not necessarily add something more to the innovation/incentive/reward cycle.

Further reading

Books

H Beverley-Smith, A Ohly, and A Lucas-Schloetter, *Privacy, Property and Personality: Civil Law Perspectives on Commercial Appropriation* (2005)

N Moreham, M Warby, M Tugendhat, and I Christie (eds), *Tugendhat and Christie: The Law of Privacy and The Media* (3rd edn, 2016)

EC Reid, *Personality, Confidentiality and Privacy in Scots Law* (2010)

D Tan, *The Commercial Appropriation of Fame: A Cultural Analysis of the Right of Publicity and Passing Off* (2017)

Articles and chapters

General

G Black, 'Publicity and image rights in Scots law' (2010) 14(4) Edin LR 364–84

H Carty, 'The common law and the quest for the IP effect' [2007] IPQ 3, 237–66

F Hofmann, 'The right to publicity in German and English law' [2010] IPQ 3, 325–40

Privacy, human rights and the media

T Aplin, 'Filling the IP gap: Privacy and tabloidism' in M Richardson and S Ricketson (eds), *Research Handbook on Intellectual Property in Media and Entertainment* (2017)

T Aplin and J Bosland, 'The uncertain landscape of Article 8 of the ECHR: the protection of reputation as a fundamental human right?' in AT Kenyon (ed), *Comparative Privacy and Defamation Law* (2016)

E Barendt, 'Problems with the "reasonable expectation of privacy" test' (2016) 8 JML 2, 129–37

A Hurst, 'Data privacy and intermediary liability: striking a balance between privacy, reputation, innovation and freedom of expression' (2015) 26 Ent LR 6 187–95

R Moosavian, 'Stealing souls: Article 8 and photographic intrusion' (2018) 69(4) NILQ, 531–58

B Pillans, 'Private lives in St Moritz: Von Hannover v Germany (no 2)' (2012) Comms L 63

T Pinto, 'A private and confidential update—not for publication' (2007) 18(5) Ent LR 170–77

E Reid, 'Case comment. No sex please, we're European: Mosley v News Group Newspapers Ltd' [2009] Edin LR 116

M Richardson and G Dinwoodie, 'Publicity right, personality right, or just confusion?' in M Richardson and S Ricketson (eds), *Research Handbook on Intellectual Property in Media and Entertainment* (2017)

A Taubman, 'Is there a right of collective personality?' (2006) 28(9) EIPR 485–92

Personality and passing off

C Ng, 'The law of passing off—goodwill beyond goods' (2016) 47 IIC 7, 817–42

YH Lee, 'Putting a face to the game: the intellectual property implications of using celebrity likenesses in video games' (2018) 13(2) JIPLP 143–53

Part VII

Intellectual property, free movement of goods, and competition law in Europe

Introduction

This Part of the book has two chapters. The first chapter explains and discusses the interaction between free movement of goods and intellectual property rights. The second looks at the interaction between intellectual property rights and EU competition law.

There are four fundamental freedoms prescribed in EU law: freedom of movement of goods, persons, services, and capital. The goal is to establish the common market of the Union: there should not be any trade barriers or obstacles between member states. However, in the domain of intellectual property (IP), the exercise of IP rights can, and does, pose problems for the free movement of goods and thus the common market. Chapter 19 looks at the tensions between IP rights and the achievement of the common market. Intellectual property rights also confer a right to control on the holder, albeit one carefully crafted to provide a balance between innovation and other public interest goals. But sometimes the exercise of IP rights can confer on the holder an over-strong monopoly through which the right holder may occupy a position of strength which may in turn hamper competition in the marketplace; or owners of intellectual property rights may enter into agreements which may not, ultimately, be to the benefit of consumers. Chapter 20 discusses when EU competition law may be used to curb anti-competitive effects of the exercise of IP rights.

Sources of the law: key websites

- The treaties of the European Community (now Union)
  http://eur-lex.europa.eu/collection/eu-law/treaties.html

- Case law of the Court of Justice/ECJ and General Court/CFI
  www.curia.europa.eu

- For decisions of the courts in the various jurisdictions of the UK, see BAILII
  www.bailii.org

- For a list of the various notices issued by the Commission relating to competition rules, see
  http://ec.europa.eu/competition/antitrust/legislation/entente3_en.html

- Commission antitrust webpages
  https://ec.europa.eu/sport/policy/economic-dimension/antitrust-law_en

- The Technology Transfer Block Exemption Regulation (EU) No 316/2014 of 21 March 2014
  http://eur-lex.europa.eu/legal-content/EN/TXT/?uri=CELEX%3A32014R0316

Free movement of goods and intellectual property rights

Introduction

19.1 The purpose of this chapter is to discuss the European Union rules on the free movement of goods as they impact on intellectual property (IP) rights. There are four fundamental freedoms in EU law: the free movement of goods, persons, services, and capital. The achievement of these freedoms is prescribed as a means to establish the common market of the Community (now the Union): there should not be any trade barriers or obstacles between member states.

However, in the domain of intellectual property, the exercise of IP rights can, and does, pose problems for the free movement of goods, and thus the common market. How should the aim of establishing and maintaining a common market be reconciled with IP rights?

19.2 **Learning objectives**

By the end of this chapter you should be able to describe and explain:

- the tensions that underlie this area of the law;
- the rules permitting the free movement of IP-protected goods within the Community (extended to the European Economic Area or 'EEA');
- when a trade mark proprietor might have a legitimate interest to oppose the further circulation of goods otherwise in free circulation within the Community;
- the rules on international exhaustion of rights;
- the relation between IP rights and free movement of services;
- developments in exhaustion of rights and digital content.

Scope and overview of chapter

19.3 The first part of this chapter explains the tensions that arise between the aims of creating a common market and intellectual property (IP). The next part focuses on case law development, and in particular how the European Court of Justice (ECJ) as it was then sought to reconcile the tensions between IP rights and free movement principles. A particularly important aspect of this is the notion of consent by the IP owner to the placing of the protected goods on the market. While the IP owner will generally not be able to oppose the movement of protected goods once they have been placed on the market with their consent, there are circumstances in which the IP owner will have legitimate reasons to prevent further dealings. These are examined in the next part of the chapter. Discussion then moves to the concept of international exhaustion. Finally, the chapter considers free movement of services and developments in exhaustion of rights relating to digital content. Note that there have been changes to Article numbers within the key European treaties. When these are discussed, as indicated in the Preface, the present names (eg Art 34 TFEU) will be used, unless it is clearer to use the term in place at the time, when discussing arguments made in a case.

The rest of the chapter looks like this:

- Tensions between the aims of the common market and intellectual property (19.4–19.8)
- Free movement of goods: case law development (19.9–19.27)
- Legitimate reasons for using a trade mark to prevent further dealing (19.28–19.45)
- International exhaustion (19.46–19.61)
- Free movement of services (19.62–19.65)
- Exhaustion of rights and digital content (19.66–19.74)

Note that, although the relevant texts and some decisions refer to free movement within 'the Community', the rules set out in this chapter in fact apply across the EEA. References to 'the Community' should be read throughout with this in mind.[1]

Tensions between the aims of the common market and intellectual property

Treaty provisions

19.4 Article 34 of the Treaty on the Functioning of the European Union (TFEU) (ex Art 28 of the EC Treaty (EC)) prohibits restrictions that inhibit the free movement of goods throughout the Community, and thus the creation of a common market:

> Quantitative restrictions on imports and all measures having equivalent effect shall be prohibited between Member States.

The enforcement of an IP right within a given territory could be a 'measure having equivalent effect' to a quantitative restriction on imports. The prohibition on such measures is, however, subject to certain provisos to be found in Article 36 TFEU (ex Art 30 EC). These provisos include measures justified on the grounds of the protection of industrial and commercial property.

> The provisions of Articles 34 and 35 shall not preclude prohibitions or restrictions on imports, exports or goods in transit justified on grounds of public morality, public policy or public security; the protection of health and life of humans, animals or plants; the protection of national treasures possessing artistic, historic or archaeological value; or the protection of industrial and commercial property. Such prohibitions or restrictions shall not, however, constitute a means of arbitrary discrimination or a disguised restriction on trade between Member States.

---

[1] See Annex XVII of the EEA Agreement, www.efta.int/media/documents/legal-texts/eea/the-eea-agreement/Annexes%20to%20the%20 Agreement/annex17.pdf. The EEA is EU member states and Norway, Iceland, and Lichtenstein.

One of the difficulties the Court has faced in application of Article 34 (ex Art 28 EC) to the IP sphere is Article 345 TFEU (ex Art 295 EC):

> This Treaty shall in no way prejudice the rules in Member States governing the system of property ownership . . . .

The rules granting IP rights to those entitled is a system of property ownership. The task for the Court was thus to reconcile these provisions.

Competing interests

19.5   An IP right gives its owner a monopoly in the subject matter of the right for a defined period of time. IP rights are also mostly limited to a single territory. Thus, the owner of an IP right in one territory (eg a trade mark, patent, or copyright) could use that right to prevent goods bearing the same or a similar mark, an invention which would infringe the patent, or a work protected by copyright, from entering that territory from elsewhere. That is so even if the goods were produced by the same person in the other territory.

For example, if Company X has a registered trade mark in country A, and the same registered trade mark for the same goods in country B, the nature of the right conferred by the trade mark could enable Company X to prevent goods sold in country B from being imported by third parties into country A. Thus, the owner of the IP right could partition the market by enforcing the right in different territories.

This partitioning of the market could lead to price differentials between territories. In country A, Company X could sell the product for £10, but in country B it could sell it for £5. A parallel importer might realise that if the goods were bought in country B and imported into country A, the goods could be sold below the price normally charged in country A whilst still giving the parallel importer a profit. If Company X, as the IP right holder, were able to prevent the importation of the goods into country A, the parallel importer would not be able to do this. This could lead to consumers paying different prices for the same goods depending on where they were purchased.

19.6   The rules on free movement of goods, as they have been developed at European level, are designed to avoid this outcome whilst taking into account Article 345 TFEU (ex Art 295 EC). This has been achieved primarily by the ECJ looking behind the monopolistic nature of IPRs to the reason for their existence and their so-called 'specific subject matter'. The reason for the existence of IP rights is to obtain an economic return. Therefore, IP right holders are given the exclusive right to place the goods which are the subject of the IP right on the market within the Community for the first time; thereafter the right holder is unable to prevent further circulation of those goods throughout the Community. The right holder is said to have *exhausted* the rights associated with the IP right. However, it is important to note that the rights are only exhausted in relation to further movement of those particular individual goods placed on the market by the right holder or with their consent, and not in respect of the IP right more generally or the product type in a more abstract way.

19.7   Application of the rules on free movement of goods and their interface with IP takes place against a background containing diverse views—political, social, and economic—as well as differing national regulatory regimes designed to achieve domestic goals but which can conflict with European strategies.

- An IP owner will often argue that price differences between territories is an essential part of any business strategy. There are many reasons why the goods may be put onto the territories at different prices by the IP owner, not all of which are necessarily under the IP owner's control. In some circumstances, there may be no choice; for instance, in the case of pharmaceuticals the price may be set by the national regulatory authority. In other cases, consumers in one jurisdiction may be more willing to pay more for goods than in others: some freedom for the IP owner to cross-subsidise costs between jurisdictions may be seen as fundamental to economic survival. Other factors, such as labour and material costs, also have a bearing on the eventual price to be charged to the consumer.

- Parallel traders, on the other hand, may argue that the exhaustion rule actually benefits consumers. In a market with no barriers, prices will fall and so consumers pay less for the goods.

As between the IP owner and the parallel trader, the conflicts arise because of the profits that can be made from moving goods from one market (the cheaper market) to another (the more expensive market). Who should profit from the differential in prices? Should the IP owner be able to maintain the price differences? Or should the parallel trader be able to take advantage of them to their own financial benefit?

19.8   There are also relevant policy considerations at a member state level, particularly as regards protection of the European common internal market. Should the exhaustion rule only apply within the Community, or should a broad, international rule of exhaustion be favoured whereby goods can be brought into the Community by third parties from anywhere in the world? If consumer interests are at the forefront of thinking, then that might (but not necessarily) call for a rule of international exhaustion if the effect would be a reduction in prices. If, on the other hand, it is the interests of economic entities within the Community together with promoting investment within its boundaries that is of prime concern, then is it not preferable to maintain barriers at the external boundaries of the Community?

> **Key point on the goals of free movement of goods**
>
> - The rules on free movement of goods seek to reconcile the tensions between Articles 34, 36, and 345 TFEU (ex Arts 28, 36, and 295 EC).

Free movement of goods: case law development

19.9   At their most basic, the rules on exhaustion of rights provide that where goods which are the subject of IP rights are put on the market within the EEA by the right holder or with their consent, the right holder may not object to subsequent movement of those goods around the EEA. Right holders can, however, stop the import of goods into the EEA where those goods have been placed on the market outwith the EEA and are brought into the EEA without their consent.

19.10   This position has been reached through a series of cases starting as far back as the 1970s in which the ECJ developed rules which balance the interests of the IP holder with those of the creation of a common market.

Note that the numbering of the relevant Articles has also changed twice: Article 34 TFEU (ex Art 28, ex Art 30); Article 36 TFEU (ex Art 30, ex Art 36); and Article 345 TFEU (ex Art 295, ex Art 222). Again, the Article numbering which applies following the changes made by the Treaty of Lisbon will be used in this chapter, except where the discussion relates to historical events and/or where quotations from cases are used in the text.

19.11   The first case to consider the interaction between IPRs and the free movement of goods was *Deutsche Grammophon GmbH v Metro SB Grossmarkte GmbH & Co* (see Figure 19.1).[2] Deutsche Grammophon (DG) produced sound recordings. DG controlled retail prices in Germany and required an undertaking from its German retailers that they would only import goods from elsewhere with the agreement of DG, which would only be given if the goods were sold at the maintained price. DG exported sound recordings to a subsidiary in Paris. Those recordings were acquired in France and imported back into Germany, where Metro sold them below the price fixed by DG in Germany.

---

[2] [1971] CMLR 631.

Figure 19.1 *Deutsche Grammophon GmbH v Metro SB Grossmarkte GmbH & Co*

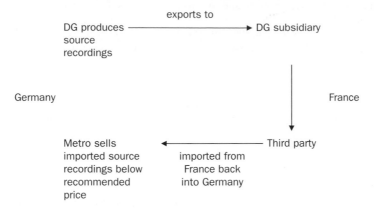

The effect of this was to undermine the system that DG had put into place to maintain retail prices in Germany. The case was referred to the ECJ. The Court ruled:[3]

> although the Treaty does not affect the existence of the industrial property rights conferred by the national legislation of a member-State, the exercise of these rights may come within the prohibitions of the Treaty. Although Article 36 permits prohibitions or restrictions on the free movement of goods that are justified for the protection of industrial and commercial property, it only allows such restrictions on the freedom of trade to the extent that they are justified for the protection of the rights that form the specific object of this property.

Here we see the ECJ making a distinction between the existence of an IP right, the exercise of that right, and the specific object or subject matter of the right.

19.12   In *Centrafarm v Sterling & Winthrop*[4] the ECJ addressed the parallel import of pharmaceuticals protected by patent and trade mark rights. Centrafarm, without the permission of Sterling, purchased the pharmaceuticals in the UK and Germany, where they had been marketed by Sterling or members of its corporate group, and imported them into the Netherlands where prices were higher. This was challenged by Sterling.

The ECJ said that derogations to the principle of free movement of goods were only permitted in respect of intellectual property to the extent that such derogations are justified for the protection of the rights which constitute the specific object of such property. As regards patents, the Court held that the specific subject matter is to reward the creative effort of the inventor. The inventor has the exclusive right to use an invention with a view to manufacturing industrial products and to put them into circulation for the first time either directly or by way of a grant of a licence to a third party, as well as to oppose infringements. As regards trade marks, the specific object of the right is to ensure to the holder the exclusive right to utilise the mark for the first putting into circulation of a product, and to protect him thus against competitors who would take advantage of the position and reputation of the mark by selling goods improperly bearing the mark. Any derogation from the principle of free movement of goods is not justified where the product, protected by the relevant rights, has been put onto the market by the right holder or with their consent.

In this case the ECJ identified the specific subject matter of intellectual property as being the economic reward that can be obtained from exploitation. However, once that reward has been obtained—through putting the goods on the market for the first time—the right to prevent further circulation is exhausted. The justification lies in the need to prevent the artificial partitioning of the market:[5]

> . . . if the patentee were able to prohibit the import of products covered by the patent which had been marketed in another member-State by him or with his consent he would be enabled to partition the national markets and thus to put into effect a restriction on trade between member-States without such restriction being necessary to ensure that he obtains the substance of the exclusive rights arising under parallel patents.

---

[3] ibid, para 11.   [4] [1974] ECR 1147.   [5] Case C-19/84 *Pharmon v Hoescht* [1985] ECR 2281, para 23.

Question

What have courts said to be the specific subject matter of different IP rights? For designs, look also at Case 144/81 *Keurkoop BV v Nancy Kean Gifts BV* [1983] FSR 381. How does this relate to the underlying justifications for IP discussed in Chapter 1?

19.13   The key requirement is that the goods must have been placed on the market by the right holder or with their consent. This principle has been codified in various EU IP instruments—Article 15 Trade Marks Directive 2015/2436/EU, Article 15 Community Trade Mark Regulation 2017/1001/EU, Article 15 Designs Directive 98/71/EC, Article 21 Community Design Regulation 6/2002/EC, and also the copyright provisions discussed at paras 20.67 and 20.68 later—although the underlying principles remain the same. For goods not placed directly on the market by the right holder, proof of consent becomes the central issue. Subsequent case law has helped to refine whether there is relevant consent in different scenarios. We also need a clear understanding of what constitutes 'placing goods on the market' for these purposes.

When are goods placed on the market?

19.14   For an IP right holder's rights to be exhausted, the relevant goods must have been put on the market within the EEA by or with the consent of the trade mark owner. What is meant by being 'put on the market' was considered by the ECJ in *Peak Holding AB v Axolin-Elinor AB*.[6] Certain goods were offered for sale in PPP's shops within the EU but were not sold to consumers. PPP sold these to a French company. The agreement contained a clause prohibiting the French company from selling more than 5 per cent of the goods in France. Of the remainder, the only European countries that could be supplied were Russia and Slovenia. None of the goods actually left the EEA. A large number of items were subsequently offered for sale in Sweden through Factory Outlet (FO). When sued for trade mark infringement, FO argued that PPP's rights had been exhausted by the sale to the French company and that the clause which prohibited resale in the EEA was of no effect.

The ECJ was asked:

- Had PPP put the goods on the market by importing them into the EU and offering them for sale in their shops?

If the answer was in the negative:

- Had the goods been put on the market and the rights exhausted when they were sold to the French company? If this was the case, what was the impact of the restriction on resale in Europe?

The ECJ confirmed that where goods are imported, or offered for sale in the proprietor's shops or in those of an associated company but without actually selling any of the goods, the rights in respect of those goods are not exhausted.[7] This is because at this stage the economic value of the mark in respect of the goods has not been realised. The ECJ went on to say that any transaction which transfers the right to dispose of the goods amounts to putting the goods on the market in the EEA regardless of any agreement prohibiting resale within the EEA. This is because the sale itself is enough to realise the economic value of the mark. Any third party acquiring the goods could not be sued for infringement of the trade mark.[8] It will be for the national court to apply the ruling of the ECJ to the facts of the case.

---

[6] Case C-16/03 [2004] ECR I-11313.   [7] ibid, paras 40–44.   [8] ibid, paras 54–56.

Question

Consider perfume and cosmetic testers (ie samples for in-store demonstration) and 'dramming' bottles (ie containers from which a small amount of product can be taken to give to consumers as a free sample). These are not intended for sale and are often marked 'Not for sale'. Are such testers 'placed on the market' for free movement purposes? Read Case C-324/09 *L'Oréal SA v eBay International AG* [2011] ETMR 52, at paras 68–73. Do you agree with the Court's reasoning on this issue? To what extent do you think it should be relevant whether the goods are given away for free?

Consent

Common origin and connected/unconnected undertakings

19.15   An early case on consent was *Van Zuylen Freres v Hag AC*.[9] The Hag trade mark was initially owned both in Germany and in Belgium by the same company. During the war, however, the Belgian mark was sequestrated and ownership passed to a third party. Some time later, the owner of the Hag mark in Germany wanted to import coffee bearing the mark into Belgium, where the mark was owned by the unconnected third party. The ECJ held that because the mark was originally held by one proprietor (ie had a common origin) in both jurisdictions, this entitled the German owner to market its goods in the Benelux countries.

19.16   There was much disquiet as a result of this case and at the importance attached by the Court to the historical common ownership of the mark in both countries, over and above the realities of now separate ownership of the mark and separate control and responsibility for the quality of goods sold under the mark in each country. The ECJ had a chance to revisit its judgment in 1990 in *SA CNL-Sucal NV v Hag GV*.[10] By this time CNL owned the Hag mark for its business in Belgium. CNL sought to import its products bearing the Hag mark into Germany. The ECJ, explicitly reversing its earlier judgment, said that CNL had no right to go into the German market. No consent had been given by the German proprietor of the trade mark.

19.17   This revised position was confirmed in *IHT Internationale Heiztechnik GmbH v Ideal Standard GmbH*.[11] The Ideal Standard trade mark was owned in Germany by a German subsidiary in the Ideal Standard group. In France, although originally owned within the same group, the mark had been assigned to a third party which had no legal or economic ties with the group. IHT then sought to import goods bearing the mark from France into Germany. The German company objected to goods bearing the mark being imported into Germany from France.

The ECJ confirmed that the German company could prevent parallel import of goods bearing the Ideal Standard mark originating in France into Germany. A trade mark is a guarantee of quality. There was no control by the German company or its group over the goods manufactured by the French assignee. The assignment of the mark in France had the effect of depriving the original proprietor of any form of quality control over the goods manufactured under the mark.

The ECJ confirmed that IP rights are exhausted, however, where goods are marketed by the right holder or by an economically linked undertaking: this principle, known as exhaustion of rights, applies where the owner of the trade mark in the importing state and the owner of the trade mark in the exporting state are the same, or where even if they are separate persons they are economically linked. A number of situations are covered: products put into circulation by the same undertaking, by a licensee, a parent company, a subsidiary of the same group, or by an exclusive distributor.[12]

⁹ [1974] ECR 731.   ¹⁰ [1990] ECR I-3711.   ¹¹ [1994] ECR I-2789.   ¹² ibid, para 34.

For trade marks, the decisive factor is whether the trade mark owner has the possibility of control over goods to which the mark is affixed to the country of exportation and the quality of goods that were placed on the market. If it did have such control, then it would be seen as having consented to the marketing. However, there would be no exhaustion of rights if there was no such control.[13]

The reality of ongoing activity can also be important. In a case involving Schweppes, after assignments the trade marks in one country were owned by a Schweppes company and in another by a Cocoa-Cola company. The court considered that as there had been a connection, and there was still activity and economic links creating the impression of a single global trade mark, the national trade mark owner could not oppose import.[14]

Differing levels of protection in different member states

19.18   Circumstances may arise in which there may be differing levels of protection for IP rights in member states, or protection may exist in one country but not in another.

19.19   The situation may arise, for example, where there is no IP protection in one jurisdiction such that third parties are free to manufacture and sell certain products there. However, that does not mean that those third parties are entitled to import those products into another member state where IP protection does subsist. In *EMI Electrola GmbH v Patricia Im-und Export*[15] the sound recording right in Cliff Richard's songs was extant under German law but had expired in Denmark. Patricia, an unconnected party, reproduced recordings of Cliff Richard songs in Denmark and attempted to import the sound recordings from Denmark into Germany. EMI in Germany was permitted to prevent this. The sound recordings made by Patricia had not been placed on the market by EMI or with its consent.

Question

This case led to the enactment of an EU Directive. Which one?[16]

19.20   The situation may also arise in which no IP protection exists in a member state but the owner has nonetheless proceeded with or consented to the marketing of his products there.

19.21   In *Merck & Co Inc v Stephar BV*,[17] Merck put drugs on the market in Italy, a country in which no patent protection for the drugs could be obtained at the relevant time. Merck did have a patent for the drugs in the Netherlands. Stephar purchased the drugs in Italy and sought to import them into the Netherlands. Merck invoked its patent rights in the Netherlands to prevent the importation. Merck acknowledged that it had consented to the marketing of the drugs in Italy, but argued that since no patent protection could be obtained there, it should not be seen as having exhausted its rights. The ECJ said that since consent had been given to the marketing of the drugs in Italy, Merck could not invoke its patent to prevent their importation into the Netherlands.[18]

19.22   This view was subsequently reaffirmed in *Merck & Co v Primecrown Ltd*.[19] Merck held patents in the UK for drugs which they also marketed in Spain and Portugal, where protection was not obtainable. The price of the drugs was

---

[13] See also consideration in *Flynn Pharma v Drugsrus Ltd* [2017] EWCA Civ 226, when goods were put on the market in a different member state with a different trade mark, without the consent of the trade mark owner, and then had the UK trade mark affixed for sale in the UK. The court dismissed an argument that enforcing a trade mark was a disguised restriction on trade within Art 36 TFEU.

[14] *Schweppes SA v Red Paralela* Case C-291/16 [2018] ETMR 13.   [15] [1989] ECR 79.

[16] See also *Warner Bros v Christiansen* [1988] ECR 2605 dealing with the rental of videos in Denmark which had been manufactured in the UK where no rental right subsisted.

[17] [1981] ECR 2063.

[18] Note that different arrangements applied when there were new member states in 2003, because of special arrangements in the Act of Accession, *Merck Canada v Sigma Pharmaceuticals Case* C539/13 [2015] RPC 30.

[19] [1996] ECR I-6285.

fixed by the respective governments. Merck argued that they had ethical obligations to place the drugs on the market in these countries to meet the requirements of the population. However, the ECJ did not find this argument sufficient to change the rule in *Merck v Stephar*. The Court pointed out that any anomalies that existed as between member states arising from differences in protection in the territories were disappearing with the harmonisation programme. The Court did note that if legal compulsion exists which requires marketing in a particular country, then the patent owner would not be deemed to have consented to the marketing. However, ethical considerations did not provide sufficient certainty to determine when an IP owner is deprived of the power to determine how to market a product.

 Question

What do you think of the argument deployed by Merck that it had ethical obligations to place the drugs on the territories in which no protection existed? Could ethical obligations ever give sufficient basis to enable an IP owner to argue successfully that there was no consent in relation to the marketing of a product?

Compulsory licensing

19.23   In contrast, where the right owner has been required to permit goods to come onto the market under a compulsory licence, those goods will not be seen as having been placed on the market by or with the consent of the IP owner. The IP owner will be able to prevent further movement of the goods:

■ Case C-19/84 *Pharmon v Hoescht* [1985] ECR 2281

Hoescht held a drug patent in the UK and the Netherlands. A compulsory licence was obtained in the UK by DDSA Pharmaceuticals Ltd to manufacture the drug in the UK, but subject to a prohibition on export. DDSA ignored the prohibition and sold the drug to Pharmon, which intended to market it in the Netherlands. Hoescht challenged this on the basis of its patent in the Netherlands. As Hoescht had not consented to the manufacture and marketing in the UK, there was no consent, and thus the sale of the drugs in the Netherlands could be prevented:[20]

> . . . where, as in this instance, the competent authorities of a Member State grant a third party a compulsory licence which allows him to carry out manufacturing and marketing operations which the patentee would normally have the power to prevent, the patentee cannot be deemed to have consented to the operation of the third party.

Marketing in breach of licence restrictions

19.24   A question also arises as to the interaction between licence terms and consent, specifically whether an IP right holder can be taken to have consented to first marketing by their licensee when the licensee places goods on the market in contravention of his licence terms:

■ Case C-59/08 *Copad SA v Christian Dior Couture SA* [2009] ECR I-34210

Christian Dior (Dior) entered into a trade mark licence agreement with Société industrielle lingerie (SIL) to manufacture and distribute luxury corsetry goods bearing the Christian Dior trade mark. In contravention of an express provision in the licence agreement, SIL sold goods bearing the Christina Dior trade mark to Copad, which operated discount stores and was outside Dior's selective distribution network. Dior sued SIL and Copad for trade mark infringement. The ECJ ruled that a:[21]

> licensee who puts goods bearing a trade mark on the market in disregard of a provision in a licence agreement does so without the consent of the proprietor of the trade mark where it is established that the provision in question is included in those listed in art. 8(2) of . . . [the Trade Marks] Directive.

---

[20] Case C-19/84 *Pharmon v Hoescht* [1985] ECR 2281, para 25.
[21] Case C-59/08 *Copad SA v Christian Dior Couture SA* [2009] ECR I-3421, para 51.

The list in Article 8(2), which the Court said was exhaustive, provides:

> The proprietor of a trade mark may invoke the rights conferred by that trade mark against a licensee who contravenes any provision in his licensing contract with regard to its duration, the form covered by the registration in which the trade mark may be used, the scope of the goods or services for which the licence is granted, the territory in which the trade mark may be affixed, or the quality of the goods manufactured or of the services provided by the licensee.

Thus, if a breach of contract falls within Article 8(2), the licensee will infringe the trade mark and consent will be considered to have been withdrawn. In this case, marketing to a discount chain was held to be in breach of the licence provisions relating to the 'quality of the goods' and thus negated consent.

Question

What do you think of the ECJ's ruling in *Dior v Copad*, particularly the finding that marketing to a discount chain was breach of a licence term relating to the 'quality of the goods'? What is the potential impact of this ruling in terms of the accessibility to consumers of parallel imported luxury goods?

Other consent scenarios

19.25 It has also been held by the ECJ that consent by the proprietor of a trade mark to marketing goods in the EEA by a third party who has no economic link may be implied where it can be inferred from facts and circumstances prior to, simultaneous with, or subsequent to the marketing where it can be unequivocally demonstrated that the proprietor has renounced his exclusive rights.[22] This is in line with the case law governing the inference of consent in cases involving the parallel importation of goods into the EEA from the rest of the world, discussed further at paras 19.47–19.53. The reader is referred to the discussion there for consideration of the standard required to demonstrate implied consent.

Key points on first marketing and consent

- Where goods which are the subject of IP rights are put on the market within the European Economic Area (EEA) by the right holder or with his consent, the right holder may not object to subsequent movement of those around the EEA.

- Consent is fundamental to free movement of goods. Consent will be inferred where goods are placed on the market within the EEA by an entity which is economically linked to the right holder. In contrast, there will be no relevant consent where goods are placed on the market under a compulsory licence or in breach of one of the trade mark licence terms referred to at Article 25(2) Trade Marks Directive. Such acts of marketing are outwith the right holder's control.

Parallel imports and the pharmaceutical industry: a further note

19.26 A number of the leading parallel imports cases have involved the pharmaceutical industry. Health care is a domain in which much governmental regulation exists in member states in relation to prices, packaging, and availability of drugs and many other aspects of the industry. The ECJ has long held that price differences

---

[22] Case C-324/08 *Makro Zelfbedieningsgroothandel ea v Diesel Spa* [2009] ECR I-10019.

as between member states resulting from governmental measures make no difference to the rules on exhaustion and the goal of attaining a common market.[23] But questions continue to be raised and referred to the ECJ in this area. One concerning the interaction between competition law and free movement of goods first arose in *Syfait v GSK*.[24] The Greek government requires that medicines sold in Greece are sold at the lowest price prevailing on the European market. GSK supplied wholesalers with drugs but found that many batches were being onward sold by parallel traders in other territories, where the price was higher. GSK decided to limit the supply of these products to the Greek wholesalers to the quantities needed to fulfil local need. The question arose as to whether it was an abuse of a dominant position (Art 82 EC [ex 86], post Lisbon Art 102 TFEU) for GSK to refuse to fill the wholesalers' orders where the intention was to limit parallel trade.[25]

In the event, the ECJ declined jurisdiction, as the questions had not been referred by a competent tribunal within the meaning of Article 234 of the EC Treaty (post-Lisbon Art 267 TFEU). The Advocate General Francis Jacob's Opinion is, however, of interest.

The Advocate General noted that an intention to restrain parallel trade would probably be a reason to condemn a refusal to supply, but that in certain circumstances it might be permitted. There were instances where parallel trade might result in inadequate supplies being available. Because parallel importers sourced products from the cheapest country, pharmaceutical companies might delay or stop the supply of drugs in countries where the price was lowest. The benefits of parallel trade would go to the wholesalers in the countries where prices were limited at the lowest level and not to the patients or to those paying for their treatment. It was thus the effect of the national law in fixing the price that would be paid for the drugs that segregated the market and not, in the instant case, the behaviour of GSK.

19.27   The same questions were referred to the Court by the Efetio Athinon in Joined Cases *Sot Lelos Kai Sia EE and Others v GlaxosmithKline Aeve Farmadeftikon Proionton (formerly Glaxowellcome Aeve)*[26] (see also para 20.54). The ECJ ruled that a dominant undertaking that refuses to meet ordinary orders from wholesalers in order to put a stop to parallel exports carried out by those wholesalers from one member state to another abuses its dominant position; it is for the national court to decide whether the orders are ordinary. A company could, however, counter, in a reasonable and proportionate manner, orders where the supplies were destined for the parallel market. So it is clear from this ruling that a company may act to limit orders where parallel markets are being supplied, the key difficulty being to determine what might be ordinary, and in the event that it is thought that an order does not fall within this category, the need to respond in a reasonable and proportionate manner.

Legitimate reasons for using a trade mark to prevent further dealing

19.28   A key question is as to when a trade mark proprietor may legitimately oppose the further dealing with goods placed on the market with their consent.

Article 15(2) of Trade Marks Directive 2015/2436/EU[27] provides:

> Paragraph 1 shall not apply where there exist legitimate reasons for the proprietor to oppose further commercialisation of the goods, especially where the condition of the goods is changed or impaired after they have been put on the market.

---

[23] Case C-15/74 *Centrafarm v Sterling* (1974) ECR 1147.
[24] *Synetairismos Farmakopoion Aitolias & Akarnanias (Syfait) and others v GlaxoSmithKline plc* [2005] ECR I-4609.
[25] For discussion on EU competition law under Art 101 TFEU (ex Art 81 EC), see Chapter 20.
[26] Joined Cases C-468/06 to C-478/06 [2008] ECR I-7139.
[27] Previous relevant provisions in 2008/95/EC consolidated version, previously First Council Directive 89/104/EEC.

This codifies earlier case law of the ECJ and the detailed principles of that case law still apply. A relevant scenario might be the removal of parallel imported product from its packaging, where the packaging set out information required by law (such as the identity of the manufacturer or list of ingredients) or the removal otherwise damages the product's image and the reputation of the relevant trade mark (see Case C-324/09 *L'Oréal SA v eBay International AG* [2011] ETMR 52 at paras 74–83, discussed para 19.14 previously). The issue of legitimate reasons to oppose further commercialisation has arisen in two further particular areas. The first concerns repackaging, most notably in the pharmaceutical industry, and the second concerns advertising where the IP is used by a third party in a promotional campaign.

The pharmaceutical industry, trade marks, and repackaging by parallel importers

19.29   The pharmaceutical industry is one of the main industries at the centre of cases on repackaged parallel imports. When drugs are imported from one member state into another, parallel importers often re-box or over-sticker the parallel imported product. The majority of the following cases deal with the pharmaceutical industry—although it should be noted that the rulings are not limited to that industry and will apply whenever the facts are relevant within other industry sectors.[28]

Some terminology on repackaging:

- *Re-boxing*: a parallel importer retains the original internal product packaging (eg a pill bottle or blister strip) but adds a new exterior carton.

- *Over-stickering*: a parallel importer retains the original internal and external packaging but adds additional labelling.

- *Co-branding*: the parallel importer adds its own brand name, logo, or house-style packaging design, for example including this on a new exterior carton.

- *De-branding*: a parallel importer removes the original trade mark from the product and does not replace it, for example using instead the generic name of the pharmaceutical product on a new external carton.

 Exercise

Have a look at the article by N Gross and L Harrold, 'Fighting for pharmaceutical profits: the decision of the ECJ in *Boehringer Ingelheim v Swingward*' [2002] EIPR 497 to get an idea of what the packages look like once some of these activities have occurred.

19.30   Parallel importers argue that such actions are necessary for the pharmaceutical products to be accepted in the member state of importation. Information about pharmaceutical products must be in the language of the member state in which they are going to be provided to consumers, so some intervention is going to be required for the goods to be marketable. National rules and consumer expectation may also require drugs to be purchased and presented in a particular way and in specified quantities. However, other than in de-branding cases, over-stickering and re-boxing invariably involve the affixing of the drug company's trade mark for the product back onto the imported product.

19.31   It will be recalled that the Trade Mark Directive provides that a trade mark owner can prevent a third party from using, in the course of trade, a sign which is identical or similar to the registered mark.[29] Use includes

---

[28] *Loendersloot (F) Internationale Expeditie v George Ballantine & Son Ltd* [1997] ECR I-6227.   [29] Trade Mark Directive 2015, Art 10.

fixing the sign to the goods or other packaging, importing the goods, and offering the goods for sale or putting them on the market.[30] Thus, pharmaceutical companies argue that, by over-stickering or re-boxing, parallel importers commit an infringement of their trade marks. As regards co-branding and de-branding, trade mark proprietors argue that the parallel importers are free-riding on the goodwill they have built up or, when the parallel importers use the generic name for a drug on the packaging, that this gives them an advantage when the patent expires.

19.32   There have been many cases brought before the ECJ dealing with repackaging. The key issue is whether reliance by the trade mark owner on their trade mark to oppose the marketing of the repackaged goods contributes to the artificial partitioning of the markets between member states. Key decisions include *Hoffmann-La Roche v Centrafarm*;[31] *Centrafarm v American Home Products*;[32] *Bristol-Myers Squibb v Paranova*;[33] and *Upjohn v Paranova*.[34] Why do you think there are so many cases?

From these cases it is apparent that a trade mark owner may legitimately oppose the further marketing of a pharmaceutical product where the importer has repackaged the product and reaffixed the trade mark unless the five so-called '*BMS* conditions' (named after the *Bristol-Myers Squibb v Paranova* case) are met:

- it is necessary to repackage the parallel imported product to achieve effective market access;
- the repackaging does not affect the original condition of the goods;
- the new packaging includes clear identification of who repackaged the product and the original manufacturer;
- the presentation of the repackaged product is not such as to be liable to damage the reputation of the trade mark and of its owner; and
- the parallel importer gives notice to the trade mark owner before the repackaged product is put on sale and, on demand, supplies him with a specimen of the repackaged product.

A parallel importer who repackages goods and re-applies the mark will need to satisfy these conditions if there is to be no infringement. Each condition has been developed further in case law.

Necessity to repackage

19.33   In *Bristol-Myers Squibb v Paranova*[35] the ECJ stressed that the power of the trade mark owner to oppose the marketing of repacked products should be limited only insofar as the repackaging is objectively necessary to market the product in the member state of importation.[36]

19.34   This was explored further in *Upjohn v Paranova*.[37] Paranova marketed an antibiotic under the name 'Dalacin C' in all member states except Denmark, Germany, and Spain. In these countries it used the name 'Dalacin', and in France it used 'Dalacine'. Paranova justified the differences by reference to the rules pertaining to registration of trade marks in the various countries. Upjohn bought goods in both Greece and France, repackaged them under the name Dalacin, and marketed them in Denmark. A reference was made to the ECJ asking when it was necessary to repackage the drugs.

The ECJ said that the test of necessity would be satisfied where:[38]

> the prohibition imposed on the importer against replacing the trade mark hinders effective access to the market of the importing Member State. That would be the case if the rules or practices in the importing Member States prevent the product in question from being marketed in that State under its trade mark in the exporting Member State. This is so where a rule for the protection of consumers prohibits the use, in the importing

---

[30] ibid, Art 10(3).   [31] Case C-102/77 [1978] ECR 1139.   [32] Case C-3/78 [1979] FSR 189.
[33] Joined Cases C-427/93, C-429/93 and C-436/93 [1996] ECR I-3457.   [34] Case C-379/97 [1999] ECR I-6927.
[35] Joined Cases C-427/93, C-429/93 and C-436/93 [1996] ECR I-3457.   [36] ibid, para 56.
[37] Case C-379/97 [1999] ECR I-6927.   [38] ibid, para 43.

Member State, of that trade mark used in the exporting Member State on the ground that it is liable to mislead consumers. In contrast, the condition of necessity will not be satisfied if replacement of the trade mark is explicable solely by the parallel importer's attempt to secure a commercial advantage.[39]

19.35   Thus where products purchased by the parallel importer cannot be placed on the market in the member state of importation in their original packaging by reason of national rules or practices relating to packaging, or where sickness insurance rules make reimbursement of medical expenses depend on a certain packaging, or where well-established medical prescription practices are based, inter alia, on standard sizes recommended by professional groups and sickness insurance institutions, repackaging would be necessary.[40] If the trade mark owner used a number of different pack sizes in the member state of importation, the fact that one of those pack sizes was also marketed in the member state of export would not be enough to demonstrate that repackaging is unnecessary: there would be partitioning of the market even if the importer were able to sell the parallel imported product in only part of the market in the member state of import.[41] It would not, however, be necessary where the parallel importer can reuse the original packaging for the purpose of marketing in the member state of importation by affixing labels to that packaging.[42]

19.36   The concept of necessity was revisited again in subsequent ECJ case law, particularly with reference to the issue of consumer resistance to over-stickered pharmaceutical products. The concern for parallel importers is that consumers will not accept over-stickered pharmaceuticals because they do not trust how the product appears. *Boehringer Ingelheim v Swingward Ltd*[43] concerned a variety of different methods of repackaging. The ECJ held that replacement packaging of drugs is objectively necessary if, without such repackaging, effective access to the market or to a substantial part of the market would be hindered as the result of strong resistance from a significant proportion of consumers to re-labelled drugs.[44]

When this ruling was applied by the High Court it was found that the respective trade marks had been infringed.[45] This resulted in an appeal to the Court of Appeal.[46] The Court of Appeal found that the High Court had been wrong to suggest that the ECJ had created an irrebuttable presumption that repackaging was prejudicial to the specific subject matter of the trade mark right. The Court of Appeal found that there was a strong resistance to the purchase of over-stickered drugs as it had a less neat and professional look than repackaging. Re-boxing was therefore necessary.

19.37   It is important to note from all of this that, in demonstrating the necessity to repackage, a parallel importer does not need to show that he will be barred from the whole of the relevant import market if he cannot repackage. It is sufficient that he will be hindered from achieving effective access to any substantial part of that market. This is illustrated by a recent further decision of the Court of Appeal:

■ *Speciality European Pharma Ltd v Doncaster Pharmaceuticals Group Ltd & Madus GmbH* (Court of Appeal) [2015] ETMR 19

The case concerned a pharmaceutical product which was marketed under various names and in different strengths in different jurisdictions ('Céris' in France, 'uriVesc' in Germany, and 'Regurin' in the UK). The product was sold in an ordinary 20mg tablet and a 60mg delayed-release tablet. The defendant initially imported the 20mg product from France and over-stickered with a label bearing the generic name of the drug. The defendant subsequently began affixing the name 'Regurin' to parallel imports of the 20mg product from France and the 60mg product from Germany. 'Regurin' was registered as a trade mark in the UK.

The key issue at trial was whether it was necessary for the defendant to rebrand the products as 'Regurin' to achieve effective market access in the UK. The first instance judge found that there was no such necessity.

---

[39] ibid, para 43.
[40] Joined Cases C-427/93, C-429/93, and C-436/93 *Bristol-Myers Squibb v Paranova* [1996] ECR 1-3457, paras 53 and 54.
[41] ibid, para 54.   [42] ibid, para 55.   [43] Case C-143/00 [2002] ECR I-3757.   [44] ibid, para 54.
[45] [2003] EWHC 2109 (Ch).   [46] [2004] ETMR 65, [2004] EWCA Civ 129.

This was reversed on appeal. In the UK, a pharmacist may dispense either a branded or unbranded product against a doctor's prescription which refers only to the active ingredient. However, if the prescription refers to the brand name for the product, a pharmacist is only permitted to dispense branded product. Furthermore, the UK regulator requires all delayed-release products to be marketed under a brand name, in order to ensure that it is possible to distinguish between different release formulations. For the 20mg product, the evidence demonstrated that only around 8.6 per cent of UK prescriptions identified 'Regurin' by brand; however, all prescriptions for the 60mg delayed-release product specified 'Regurin'. Although the proportion of prescriptions for the 20mg product which could only be met by dispensing branded product was relatively low, it was not insignificant. The Court of Appeal therefore concluded that, for both products, the defendant was hindered from reaching a substantial part of the market in which only 'Regurin'-branded product could be dispensed. The Court of Appeal also emphasised that, in determining whether it is necessary to re-brand and addressing what alternatives exist for the parallel importer, those alternatives must be realistic. It had been argued that the defendant could develop and publicise its own, new brand name for the parallel imported products, so that doctors could prescribe by reference to that new name, particularly for the 60mg product. This argument was rejected as unrealistic by the defendants, who argued that this would constitute a complete change of their business model and failed to take into account the inherently precarious nature of the defendant's supply line which could, for example, close off in the member state of export if the trade mark owner decided to restrict supply onto the market there to stop parallel imports. The Court of Appeal agreed that this was 'not a real world alternative'. It would, moreover, be 'verging on the irresponsible' to encourage a doctor to prescribe to a brand belonging to a parallel importer given the regular interruptions in supply which parallel importers experience in sourcing product on the marketplace.[47]

No effect on original condition of goods/information on repackager and manufacturer

19.38   In *BMS*, the ECJ confirmed that the 'original condition of the product' refers to the condition of the relevant pharmaceutical product inside its packaging. In determining whether there is any risk to the original condition of the product, account needs to be taken of the nature of the product and the method of repackaging. There is no relevant risk where the product is marketed in double packaging and the repackaging affects only the external packaging, leaving the inner packaging intact—for example, simply removing blister packs, flasks, ampoules, or inhalers from their original external packaging and putting them in new external packaging—or where the repackaging is carried out under the supervision of a public authority. It is not enough for trade mark owners to raise a hypothetical risk of error—there would have to be something demonstrably wrong with the new product as marketed by the parallel importer, such as incorrect patient information.[48] It should be noted that, in practice, in the UK the parallel distribution of pharmaceutical products is a regulated activity and that parallel importer's products and patient information leaflets are all subject to prior regulatory approval, so in practice this risk is highly unlikely. For this reason, this *BMS* condition has tended to have little (if any) practical significance.

19.39   The requirement to state clearly the identity of the manufacturer and parallel importer is similarly generally uncontentious in practice. This information must be 'printed in such a way as to be understood by a person with normal eyesight, exercising a normal degree of attentiveness'.[49]

Presentation of the repackaged product

19.40   In contrast, the *BMS* condition relating to the presentation of the repackaged product has proved very contentious indeed. In *Bristol-Myers Squibb v Paranova* the ECJ recognised that where repackaging was poor and untidy, the reputation of the mark might suffer. In practice, however, the parallel importer is

---

[47] *Speciality European* [2015] ETMR 19, paras 58–68 in particular.
[48] Joined Cases C-427/93, C-429/93, and C-436/93 *Bristol-Myers Squibb v Paranova* [1996] ECR I-3457, paras 58–66.   [49] ibid, para 71.

unlikely to want to market the imported product in such a way as it will also harm his own sales. These issues on product presentation are wider than this. Should the parallel importer be required to market the imported product in a box which matches that of the trade mark owner? Should parallel importers be required to use plain, unadorned packaging (such as plain white boxes)? Or could parallel importers be permitted to design their own box styles? For trade mark owners, there was a clear incentive to argue that parallel importers' packaging should take a form which would be commercially unattractive, to limit sales; for parallel importers, the key concern was to ensure that packaging could be attractively designed, so as to not put off consumers.

19.41   In *Glaxo Group v Dowelhurst*[50] Laddie J had suggested that repackaging was only to be tolerated to the extent that it could be shown to inflict the minimum possible damage on the mark. On appeal, a second reference was made to the ECJ in *Boehringer Ingelheim KG v Swingward Ltd*.[51] The ECJ took a different view. The Court held that the test of necessity of repackaging is directed only at the fact of repackaging and not to the manner or style in which a product is repackaged.[52] So, once it has been shown to be necessary to over-sticker or re-box, there is no further requirement that the particular style of over-stickering or re-boxing chosen also has to be necessary for the parallel importer to be able to market the product. An inappropriately repackaged product could damage the reputation of the mark not only if defective, of poor quality, or untidy but also where it detracted from the image of reliability and quality attaching to the product and the confidence it could inspire in the public.[53] De-branding, co-branding, over-stickering such as to obscure the trade mark, a failure to state that the trade mark belongs to the proprietor or where the name of the parallel importer is printed in capital letters, were in principle liable to damage the reputation of the trade mark. However, whether that was in fact the case was a question of fact for the national court.[54]

When the case returned to the English Court of Appeal, applying the judgment of the ECJ, Jacob LJ found that 'the defendants have complied with BMS condition 4 and in particular that their activities by way of re-boxing and re-labelling have not caused and will not cause damage to the reputation of the claimants' trade marks'.[55] This was despite the fact that the case included products which had been de-branded and products which had been co-branded with the parallel importers' own house-style boxing.

Exercise

Have a look at the examples of repackaging which were in dispute in the *Boehringer v Swingward* litigation by looking at the images contained in the first instance judgment at *Glaxo Group & Others v Dowelhurst Ltd (No 2)* [2000] FSR 529. Read the Court of Appeal's decision (reached many years later) on the issue of repackaging style at *Boehringer Ingelheim KG v Swingward Ltd* [2008] ETMR 36. Do you agree with the Court of Appeal that none of the parallel importers' repackaging styles were objectionable? Do you think that any of the repackaging styles gave rise to legitimate concerns for the trade mark owner?

Notice

19.42   Finally, to comply with the conditions, the parallel importer must give notice to the trade mark owner and supply samples of the packaging. The ECJ has said that it is for the parallel importer to give notice.[56] In *Boehringer v Swingward*[57] the ECJ said that on the evidence before it a period of 15 days would seem

---

[50] [2000] FSR 529.   [51] Case C-348/04 *Boehringer Ingelheim KG v Swingward Ltd* [2007] ETMR 71.
[52] See also Case C-276/05 *Wellcome Foundation v Paranova* [2008] ECR I-10479, in which the ECJ ruled that 'the condition of necessity is directed only at the fact of re-packaging the product inter alia by re-boxing it, and not the presentation of that new packaging'.
[53] Case C-348/04 *Boehringer Ingelheim KG v Swingward Ltd* [2007] ETMR 71, paras 41–44.   [54] ibid, paras 45–46.
[55] [2008] EWCA Civ 83, para 67.   [56] Case C-102/77 *Hoffmann-La Roche v Centrafarm* [1979] ECR 1139, para 12.
[57] Case C-143/00 [2002] ECR I-3759.

reasonable where the parallel importer chose to give notice by supplying a sample of the repackaged product. The Court did, however, say that the period was purely indicative and it was open to the parallel importer to allow a shorter time, and to the proprietor to ask for a longer time to react than that proffered by the parallel importer.[58] Where a parallel importer has not given prior notice, every importation of the product is in infringement until notice is given. The sanction should be proportionate and effective and may be treated in the same manner for those circumstances in which the goods were spurious.[59] It is for the national court to assess in the light of the circumstances whether the proprietor has had a reasonable time to react to the intended packaging.

Comment on the repackaging cases

19.43   The number of cases to come before the courts dealing with trade mark infringement, parallel imports, and repackaging appears to have prompted a sense of frustration amongst the judiciary. In the Court of Appeal in *Boehringer Ingelheim v Swingward Ltd*,[60] Jacob LJ highlighted the assumption made in the cases that the reaffixing of the trade mark to the goods, unless permitted by free circulation rules, infringes the registered trade mark. He pointed out that most people would not assume that a mark would be infringed simply by reaffixing the original trade mark to the goods or using a mark when marketing the goods. Such practices are a daily occurrence in commerce, where shopkeepers use signs to advertise goods which bear the trade mark of another and second-hand goods are sold by reference to the trade mark:[61]

> Sometimes I think the law may be losing a sense of reality in this area—we are, after all, only considering the use of the owner's trade mark for his goods in perfect condition. The pickle the law has got into would, I think, astonish the average consumer.

Jacob LJ suggested that the law of registered trade marks was being stretched to deal with conduct that would more happily sit under general unfair competition rules. Think back on your previous reflections— why is this happening?

Use of marks in advertising

19.44   As can be seen from the previous discussion, a concern of trade mark proprietors as goods are repackaged is for safeguarding the reputation of their marks. This also arises in the context of advertising. If a parallel importer wishes to re-sell the goods, then they would want to use the mark in advertising them. Where the re-seller makes those goods available to a different market, for instance where luxury goods are re-sold in supermarkets, then the trade mark owner may wish to control the way in which they are advertised over concern for the reputation of the mark. The question then arises as to whether the trade mark owner has a legitimate reason to do so: is safeguarding the reputation of the mark a legitimate reason for opposing certain styles of advertising?

19.45   Such an issue arose in *Parfums Christian Dior SA v Evora BV*.[62] Dior owned trade marks for, inter alia, perfumes sold to the luxury market. Evora owned a chain of chemist shops in which it sold Dior products which were parallel imports. Evora carried out a promotion, and in the literature it showed pictures of the packaging and of the bottles. Dior argued that such literature did not present the goods in the way that they wished: it did not conform to the prestige image Dior was keen to promote, so Dior brought an action for trade mark infringement.

The ECJ considered that the damage done to the reputation of a mark might be a legitimate reason to enable the proprietor to oppose further commercialisation.[63] However, a balance had to be struck between the

---

[58] ibid, para 57.   [59] Case C-348/04 *Boehringer Ingelheim KG v Swingward Ltd* [2007] ECR I-3391, para 64.
[60] [2004] ETMR 65, [2004] EWCA Civ 129.   [61] *Boehringer Ingelheim KG v Swingward Ltd* [2008] EWCA Civ 83, para 79.
[62] Case C-337/95 *Parfums Christian Dior SA v Evora BV* [1997] ECR I-6013.   [63] ibid, para 43.

legitimate interests of the trade mark owner from a re-seller using the mark in such a manner that might damage the mark, and the re-seller's legitimate interest in being able to re-sell the goods in question by using advertising methods which are customary in his sector of trade.[64] Where luxury goods were resold, the re-seller should try to prevent the advertising from affecting the value of the mark by detracting from the aura of luxury.

The ECJ did go on to note that where the re-seller used advertising methods common in the trade, even if those were not the methods the trade mark owner would have used, that was not a legitimate reason for the trade mark owner to oppose the use of the mark by the re-seller unless it could be established that the use would seriously damage the reputation of the mark. As an example, such damage could occur where the re-seller put the mark on an advertising leaflet in a context which would detract from the aura of luxury.[65]

> **Key points on legitimate reasons**
>
> • A trade mark owner may legitimately oppose further marketing of a product where the importer has repackaged the product and reaffixed the trade mark unless the so-called '*BMS* conditions' are met. The key requirement is that the repackaging must be necessary to achieve effective market access.
>
> • A trade mark owner may also oppose the use of a mark by an advertiser if the reputation of the mark is likely to be damaged.

International exhaustion: theory and related issues

19.46   It will be recalled that Article 15(1) of the Trade Mark Directive provides that a 'trade mark shall not entitle the proprietor to prohibit its use in relation to goods which have been put on the market in the Union under the trade mark by the proprietor or with the proprietor's consent' (and see also Art 7(1) of the previous Directive).

This would appear to limit the operation of the exhaustion doctrine to the the Union, as extended to the EEA. Is this then a minimum standard, or are member states free to apply a doctrine of international exhaustion?

> **Question**
>
> If one member state applied the doctrine of international exhaustion, what impact would this have on the movement of goods throughout the EEA where goods are imported from outwith the EEA and placed on the market in that member state?

19.47   The ECJ ruled on the question of international exhaustion in 1988.[66]

■ **Case C-355/96** *Silhouette International Schmied GmbH & Co KG v Hartlauer Handelsgesellschaft GmbH* **[1998] ECR I-4799**

Silhouette (S) manufactured designer spectacles under its trade mark, 'Silhouette'. It sold a number of outdated designs to a Bulgarian company on the condition that they would only be sold in Bulgaria (then not a member of the EU) and the former Soviet Union states. Hartlauer, an Austrian retailer, obtained some of these frames and sold them in their shops in Austria. S claimed that their trade mark had been infringed.

---

[64] ibid, para 44.   [65] ibid, para 46.

[66] Although note also early and clear consideration in Case C-51/75 *EMI Records Ltd v CBS United Kingdom Ltd* [1976] ECR 811.

The Court held that national rules which provided for exhaustion of rights in respect of goods which were put onto the market outwith the EC by the proprietor or with his consent, were contrary to Article 7(1). A member state had no discretion in this. The Court took the view that the Directive provided for full harmonisation of those rules which affect the functioning of the internal market.[67] Member states are thus not free to apply a regime of international exhaustion.[68]

19.48   The same position applies in relation to other IP rights—see again now Article 15 Community Trade Mark Regulation 2017/2001/EC, Article 15 Designs Directive 98/71/EC, Article 21 Community Design Regulation 6/2002/EC, and also the copyright provisions discussed at paras 19.67 and 19.68.

19.49   Parallel importers have sought to argue around the rule on international exhaustion by arguing on various bases that the mark owner had consented to the importation of goods into the EEA.

Consent and batches of goods

19.50   In *Sebago Inc and Ancienne Maison Dubois v GB Unic SA*[69] GB Unic imported shoes from El Salvador into Belgium bearing the 'Sebago' trade mark and sold them in retail outlets. GB Unic argued that whenever a trade mark owner consented to the placing of goods onto the market bearing a trade mark, then that consent extended to all goods of that type. The ECJ disagreed. Consent must relate to each individual item in respect of which exhaustion is pleaded. A trade mark owner does not place a whole stock of goods on the market through the act of selling one batch.

Implied consent

19.51   In a number of joined cases[70] concerning, inter alia, perfume and jeans, an argument arose over whether there was implied consent to marketing in the EEA from the trade mark owner.

■ Case C-414/99 *Zino Davidoff v A&G Imports* [2002] All ER (EC) 55

Zino Davidoff (ZD) wanted to prevent the import into England of goods bearing the marks 'Cool Water' and 'Davidoff Cool Water' which had been marketed with consent in Singapore. A&G argued that by marketing the goods in Singapore, ZD had given implied consent to their free circulation. The chain of distribution included a standard agreement in terms of which distributors undertook not to sell any products outside their assigned territories. However, no such term was imposed on distributors further down the chain. In the High Court, Laddie J held that interpretation of the contract under the applicable law (in this case English law) meant that consent could be implied. There was a rebuttable presumption that, in the absence of full and explicit restrictions being imposed on the purchaser at the time of purchase, the proprietor was treated as consenting to the goods being imported into and sold in the EEA.[71] When the case reached the ECJ, however, the Court took a very different view to Laddie J at first instance. The Court ruled that consent could be implied only where the facts and circumstances were such that the proprietor could be considered to have unequivocally demonstrated to have renounced his right to oppose the subsequent importation of those goods into the EEA.

---

[67] Case C-355/96 *Silhouette International Schmied GmbH & Co KG v Hartlauer Handelsgesellschaft GmbH* [1998] ECR I-4799, para 23.

[68] In an Advisory Opinion in Case E-9/07 *L'Oréal Norge AS v Per Aarskog AS and Others*, and reversing its earlier Advisory Opinion in Case E-2/97 *Mag Instrument Inc v California Trading Company Norway* [1997] EFTA Ct Rep 129, 2008 ETMR 60 the EFTA Court said that 'Article 7(1) of the Trade Mark Directive is to be interpreted to the effect that it precludes the unilateral introduction or maintenance of international exhaustion of rights conferred by a trade mark regardless of the origin of the goods in question.'

[69] Case C-173/98 [1999] ECR I-4103.

[70] Joined Cases C-414/99, C-415/99, and C-416/99 *Zino Davidoff SA v A&G Imports Ltd; Levi Strauss & Co Levi Strauss (UK) Ltd v Tesco Stores Ltd, Tesco plc; Levi Strauss & Co, Levi Strauss (UK) Ltd v Costco Wholesale UK Ltd* [2002] Ch 109, [2002] 2 WLR 321, [2002] All ER (EC) 55.

[71] At the same time *JOOP! GmbH and Zino Davidoff SA v M&S Toiletries Ltd* [1999] 2 CMLR 1056 was heard in the Scottish Court of Session—an almost identical case. Lord Kingarth noted that not only would the approach taken in the High Court mean that unless the trade mark owner blocked every avenue, they could be held as having consented to importation (an almost impossible task) but, in addition, making the issue of consent dependent on the law of contract would offend against the purpose of harmonisation in the Directive and lead to uncertainty in application. It was unclear whether the reference to presumed consent would be applied in the same way in Scotland as in England.

Consent could not be implied from:

- the failure of the proprietor to communicate to subsequent purchasers of the goods that they did not consent to their subsequent importation into the EEA;
- the fact that there was nothing on the goods to suggest that they were not to be imported into the EEA;
- the fact that the proprietor had transferred ownership without imposing any restrictions.

In addition, the Court said that it was irrelevant that the importer was unaware that the proprietor objected to their importation, or that authorised retailers had not imposed on their purchasers any contractual restrictions even if those retailers were aware of the proprietor's objection.

19.52   The Court of Appeal had the opportunity to consider when implied consent might arise in *Mastercigars Direct Ltd v Hunters & Frankau Ltd*.[72] This appeal concerned the importation into the UK of cigars from Cuba by Mastercigars. The Cuban company, Corporacion Habanos, had an exclusive UK distributor, Hunters & Frankau. It was claimed that a consignment of cigars infringed the trade mark in that no consent had been given to the placing of the goods on the market in the EEA. As no express consent had been given to the importation of the cigars, the key question was as to whether consent could be implied. In order to show implied consent, the factors had to demonstrate unequivocally that the trade mark proprietor had renounced any intention to enforce his rights. Unequivocal is not about the standard of proof; a proved act which is consistent with consent and consistent with its absence is not enough to draw the conclusion that goods had been marketed with the consent of the trade mark owner.[73]

The facts of the case—and in particular that when cigars were sold in Cuba they were sold by encouraging sales of up to $25,000, a level far too high for individual use, and that the purchaser was given appropriate customs documentation—showed that the sellers must have known that they would be used for onward resale in the end market. This was sufficient on the facts to demonstrate implied consent.

On who should give consent, the Court of Appeal said that it is insufficient for consent to be given by a licensee or connected company. What matters is the 'point of control' shown through actual knowledge and the actual practical control or right to exercise that control by the trade mark owner. In this case Corporacion Habanos exercised that control through the sale of cigars in retail outlets in Cuba.

19.53   In contrast, it has been found that consent cannot be inferred from the placing on the goods of the 'CE' symbol for regulatory approval in the EU, on goods put on the market outside the EEA.[74] For a long time, it was thought that proof of implied consent was in practice all but impossible. However, the Court of Appeal's ruling in *Mastercigars Direct* suggests that the standard set in the *Davidoff* case will not be insurmountable on the evidence, in the right case.[75]

 Question

Mastercigars gives an example of certain facts that will be taken to 'unequivocally demonstrate' that a trade mark proprietor had consented to importation of goods into the EEA. Can you think of other examples?

---

[72] *Corporacion Habanos SA v Mastercigars Direct Ltd* [2007] EWCA Civ 176, [2007] ETMR 44.   [73] ibid, para 19.
[74] *Roche Products Ltd v Kent Pharmaceuticals Ltd* [2006] EWCA Civ 1775.
[75] For other UK cases, see *Kabushiki Kaisha Sony Computer Entertainment Europe Ltd v Nuplayer Ltd* [2005] EWHC 1522 (Ch); *Sony Computer Entertainment Ltd v Electricbirdland Ltd* [2005] EWHC 2296 (Ch); *Hewlett-Packard Development Co LP v Expansys UK Ltd* [2005] EWHC 1495 (Ch); *KK Sony Computer Entertainment and Another v Pacific Game Technology (Holding) Ltd* [2006] EWHC 2509 (Pat); *Honda Motor Co Ltd v Neesam* [2008] EWHC 338 (Ch).

Consent and goods in transit

19.54   A question as to whether a trade mark proprietor had to consent to goods being brought into the EC for transit or customs storage arose in *Class International BV v Colgate-Palmolive Co and Others*.[76] The Beecham group owned the 'Aquafresh' Community trade mark for, inter alia, toothpastes. Class International, a parallel importer, brought into Rotterdam a container load of toothpaste products bearing the 'Aquafresh' trade mark, purchased from Kapex International, a South African undertaking. The Beecham group believed them to be counterfeit but a subsequent examination showed they were genuine goods. The ECJ said that the trade mark owner could not stop (ie consent was not needed) the goods being brought into the EC for the purposes of transit or customs storage. '"Importing" . . . requires introduction of those goods into the Community for the purposes of putting them on the market therein.'[77] Neither could the proprietor stop the goods from being offered for sale in a third country unless it was clear that they would subsequently be put on the market in the Community.[78] Conversely, however, if goods are brought into the Community under the suspensive customs procedure but are then released for free circulation within the Community, those goods will lose the protection of the customs system for goods in transit and will be treated as having been imported into the relevant member state. Where this has occurred without the trade mark owner's consent, infringement proceedings may be brought.[79]

19.55   A related question arose in *Montex Holdings Ltd v Diesel SpA*.[80] Here, Diesel objected to the transit through Germany of goods destined for Ireland bearing the Diesel mark. The goods had been assembled in Poland; there was no trade mark protection for the Diesel trade marks in Ireland. Referring to *Class International*, the ECJ held that a trade mark owner could only prohibit transit of goods through a member state in which the mark was protected and placed under the external transit procedure if the goods were subject to the act of a third party whilst in this procedure, which would necessarily entail their being put on the market in the member state of transit.[81] A theoretical risk that the goods could fail to reach their destination and that they would be marketed fraudulently in the state where trade mark protection existed, was insufficient to reach the conclusion that the transit infringed the rights of the trade mark proprietor.[82]

19.56   A further twist arose in *Nokia Corporation v Her Majesty's Commissioners of Revenue & Customs*.[83] In this case Her Majesty's Commissioners of Revenue & Customs (HMRC) refused to continue to detain a consignment of allegedly counterfeit mobile phones and accessories bearing the Nokia trade mark that HMRC had seized at Heathrow Airport and which were in transit from Hong Kong to Colombia. In order for there to be infringement of allegedly counterfeit goods under the Counterfeit Goods Regulation, the goods must in fact infringe someone's trade mark in the territory in question.[84] The court also said that the mere risk that the goods may be diverted into the internal market is not enough to constitute infringement. In coming to this conclusion, the court exposed a gap in the law which would prevent these allegedly counterfeit goods from being seized. The Court of Justice then found that the mere presence of goods under suspensive customs procedure did not mean that they were 'counterfeit goods'; there must be a proven intention to put them on the market in the EU. Examples of relevant factors were failure to state the destination of goods and failure to cooperate with the authorities.

[76] Case C-405/03 [2005] ECR I-8735.   [77] ibid, para 34.

[78] See also *Eli Lilly and Co and Another v 8PM Chemist Ltd* [2008] EWCA Civ 24. In Case C-115/02 *Administration des Douanes, Droits Indirects v Rioglass SA* [2003] ECR I-12705, the ECJ held that where goods lawfully manufactured in one member state are in transit in the Community with the destination being a non-member country, that does not involve any marketing of the goods in question.

[79] Case C-379/14 *TOP Logistics BV, Van Caem International BV v Bacardi & Company Ltd, Bacardi International Ltd* [2015] ETMR 43.

[80] Case C-281/05 [2006] ECR I-10881.   [81] Case C-281/05 *Montex Holdings Ltd v Diesel SpA* [2006] ECR I-10881, para 23.

[82] ibid, para 24.

[83] Joined Cases C-446/09 and C-495/09 *Nokia Corporation v Her Majesty's Commissioners of Revenue and Customs* [2012] ETMR 13.

[84] ibid, para 49.

Parallel importing and the burden of proof

19.57   The ECJ has said that the burden of proof lies on the person alleging consent to prove it, and not for the trade mark owner to prove its absence. This left parallel importers in something of a quandary. If a parallel importer had to prove consent to marketing within the EEA, then that may involve giving information on the distribution system through which the goods had been sourced. Once the trade mark owner had details of that source, then they could act to close it—thus leaving the parallel importer without supplies. The question over who should bear the burden of proof and at what stage in the proceedings has been the subject of further consideration.

> ■ **Case C-244/00 *Van Doren + Q GmbH v Lifestyle + Sportswear Handelsgesellschaft GmbH* [2003] ECR I-3051, [2003] 2 CMLR 6**
>
> Van Doren (VD) was the exclusive German distributor of goods bearing the 'Stussy' trade mark, owned by a Californian company. VD sued Lifestyle for selling goods bearing the trade mark in Germany. VD alleged that those goods were first put on the market in the United States. No consent had been given to their distribution in Germany. Lifestyle argued that the trade mark rights had been exhausted because the goods were sourced in the EEA, where they had been put on the market by the trade mark owner or with his consent. As German law provides that exhaustion operates as a defence to trade mark infringement, it was for the parallel importer to prove where the goods were sourced.
>
> The ECJ held that a rule of evidence that required a defendant relying on a plea of exhaustion to prove the conditions existed for the defence to be successful, was consistent with Community law. However, that rule might have to be qualified:
>
> - It was for the parallel importer to show that there would be a real risk of partitioning the markets if the burden of proof lay on them. This would be particularly so where the trade mark owner operated an exclusive distribution system.
>
> If they were successful, then:
>
> - it was for the trade mark owner to establish that the products were placed on the market outside the EEA by him or with his consent.
>
> If such evidence was forthcoming:
>
> - the burden shifted back to the parallel importer to prove the trade mark owner's consent to subsequent marketing of the products in the EEA.

19.58   Although this ruling provides some guidance, questions remain. For instance: what evidence would be required to show there is a real risk of market partitioning? Would it be enough to show that the trade mark owner operates an exclusive distribution system? Might price differences as between member states be sufficient? Suffice it to say that there will no doubt be more references to the ECJ before clarity is achieved.

19.59   A question over what a trader might have to do to show that reasonable steps had been taken to ascertain that goods had been placed on the market in the EU arose in the English High Court in *Sun Microsystems Inc v Amtec Computer Corporation Ltd*.[85] Amtec was sued by Sun for trade mark infringement in relation to servers that Amtec had purchased from a Danish intermediary. It transpired that the servers had not been put onto the market in the EEA by Sun or with Sun's consent. In seeking to discharge their burden of proof, Amtec argued that the Danish intermediary was known as a reputable European source of Sun products and that a term in the contract as between Amtec and the Danish intermediary had stipulated that the goods

---

[85] [2006] EWHC 62 (Ch), [2006] FSR 35.

should be of EU origin (which they were). Amtec also believed that the goods had originally been supplied by a distributor known to be an authorised seller of Sun products—thus adding to the belief that they had originally been put on the market with the authorisation of Sun. When the servers arrived, they were in boxes marked with the words 'Origin: United Kingdom' and the servers themselves had UK serial numbers. On investigation of the facts it transpired that the servers had not actually been put on the market in the EU by Sun or with their consent (they were destined for Israel) and Amtec accepted that they had infringed Sun's trade marks, but said that it had occurred innocently.

The court found that this was no defence to trade mark infringement saying:[86]

> There is no requirement of knowledge on the part of an infringing trader that he is infringing. To put that proposition another way, lack of knowledge is not a defence to infringement proceedings;
>
> It is not a defence for the trader to show that he took all reasonable steps open to him to establish that goods were put on the market by, or with the consent, of the trade mark proprietor.

The court did, however, limit the scope of the injunction, recognising that, without Sun's assistance, Amtec could do nothing to ensure that the goods it acquired had been placed on the market in the EEA with the consent of Sun.

Should there be a system of international exhaustion?

19.60   An issue that has troubled policymakers within the EU for many years is whether a system for international exhaustion should be introduced. The debate has focused on trade marks and was galvanised after the judgment of the ECJ in *Silhouette* in 1998 (para 19.47). In order to obtain a clearer picture of the economic aspects of a possible change to the exhaustion regime, the Commission commissioned a study in 1999 from the NERA Institute in London. The conclusions of that study were as follows.

- The short-term effects on consumer pricing of a change of exhaustion regime would vary from small (less than 2 per cent price reduction) for certain products to 'negligible' (0 per cent price reduction) for other products.

- The long-term effects of a change of exhaustion are more difficult to predict. It is, however, likely that the marginal, positive effect on consumer pricing in the long run will disappear.

- A change in the exhaustion regime may have an impact not only on pricing but, for example, also on product quality, product availability, after-sales services, and employment in Europe.

- Trade mark policy has only a marginal effect on parallel trade: other elements like distribution arrangements, transport costs, health and safety legislation and technical standards, and labelling differences may have a greater, and more direct, impact.

19.61   In May 2003 the issue was revisited, resulting in a Commission Working Paper, 'Possible abuses of trade mark rights within the EU in the context of Community exhaustion'.[87]

Set against the question as to whether the Community should move to a system of international exhaustion, the paper sought to identify whether there were any abuses of trade mark rights, to explain how they might have been addressed, and to identify deficiencies that may exist in the current legal provision.

Having examined selective distribution systems, abuse of a dominant position involving trade marks, and trade mark infringements, the conclusion of the report was that there was no evidence of deficiencies in the current legal provision relating to possible abuses of trade marks within the EU. It is still unlikely, several years on, that there will be any changes to the rules on Community-wide exhaustion in the near term. As a result, it is likely that the case law discussed previously, regarding the limits of Community-wide exhaustion, will continue to grow.

[86] ibid, para 21.   [87] SEC(2003) 575.

> ### Key points on international exhaustion
>
> - The exhaustion doctrine is limited to the EEA. Where goods have been placed on the market elsewhere in the world, consent to marketing in the EEA is required.
>
> - Consent relates to individual items put onto the market and not to goods of a particular type generally.
>
> - If there is no evidence of express consent to marketing in the Community, it is possible that consent may be implied. It must be shown, however, that the right holder has unequivocally renounced their right to oppose importation into the EEA. This threshold for implying consent is high.
>
> - The burden of proving consent lies on the parallel importer, but may shift between the parallel importer and the trade mark owner in certain limited circumstances.

Free movement of services

19.62   The doctrine of exhaustion, as discussed in para 19.60, applies to the right to control distribution. Within copyright it does not, however, apply to the right to rent, to perform, or to show a copy of a work in public. Here the specific subject matter of the right is to obtain a return from the exercise of the right, which includes performance of a work. In *Coditel v Cine Vog (No 1)*[88] the owner of the copyright in a film, 'Le Boucher', granted cinema and television rights in Belgium to Cine Vog for a period of seven years. During this period a German version of the film was transmitted by cable into Belgium by Coditel. Cine Vog sued Coditel for an infringement of their exclusive rights. The ECJ held that 'the right of a copyright owner and his assigns to require fees for any showing of a film is part of the essential function of copyright in this type of literary and artistic work'[89] and accepted that the copyright owner could place geographic restrictions on the exploitation of performing rights.

19.63   Similar questions were raised in respect of the rental right[90] and the sound recording right,[91] which received comparable rulings from the ECJ.

 Question

Explain why there is a distinction between the movement of goods around the Community and the movement of services. What policy goals underlie this distinction?

What Treaty provision deals with services?

19.64   As always, the law continues to evolve—most notably when challenged by new technologies. The law came under pressure with questions going to the heart of the interactions between copyright, free movement of goods and services, and competition law, discussed in Chapter 20,[92] in *Murphy v Media Protection Services*[93] joined with *FA Premier League v QC Leisure and Others*.[94] The new technology in question was decoders and the issue was the receipt of broadcasts of football matches via a decoder supplied by a supplier to the UK, where the broadcaster had the IP right to broadcast within a defined territory which did not include

---

[88] Case C-62/79 [1980] ECR 881.   [89] ibid, para 14.   [90] Case C-158/86 *Warner Bros v Christiansen* [1988] ECR 2605.

[91] Case C-402/85 *Basset v Sacem* [1987] ECR 1747.

[92] Media law is also relevant to the cases in that they involve the broadcasting of live football matches.

[93] Case C-429/08 [2008] EWHC 1666 (Admin).

[94] Case C-403/08, joined with Case C-429/08 in order of the President of the Court 3 December 2008, *Football Association Premier League Ltd v QC Leisure, Murphy v Media Protection Services Ltd* [2012] 1 CMLR 29.

the UK. Murphy purchased the decoder and used it to show the matches within licensed premises in the UK. The sale of the decoder in the third country was subject to the restriction that it could only be sold to a person who had an address in that country and was subject to an export ban as between the manufacturer and broadcaster. There was a criminal prosecution of the pub landlady (*Murphy*), and a civil *FA Premier League* action against the supplier of a decoder.[95] The key issue for this chapter is the decision of the Court of Justice regarding the UK copyright legislation and the free movement provisions in the Treaty, and the meaning of illicit device, in Directive 98/84/EC (the Conditional Access Directive), which provides that member states cannot restrict the free movement of conditional access devices.[96]

19.65   The Court of Justice held that member states were permitted under EU law to preclude the use of decoding devices from another member state only authorised for use in that other member state, those obtained using a false name, those put on the market only for private purposes, or those obtained in breach of contract.[97] These did not fall within the scope of the Conditional Access Directive. The question arose, however, whether such national legislation was in breach of free movement principles. Because the issues in suit were primarily focused on the right holders' satellite broadcasting services and the associated goods (the disputed decoders) were secondary to that, the Court held that the relevant national legislation had to be assessed from the perspective of free movement of services rather than free movement of goods. The UK legislation prohibiting use of the imported decoders was a restriction on freedom to provide services which could be permitted only if it was objectively justified. While the protection of IP could constitute one such justification, the broadcasters had already made a premium payment to the IP owner to secure territorial exclusivity.[98] This exceeded what was required to ensure appropriate remuneration to the right holders. The specific subject matter of IP was the right to exploit commercially IP, by granting licences in return for payment. This did not mean that the IP owner must get the highest possible remuneration, just what is reasonable in relation to the economic value of the service provided, given the actual or potential number of persons who enjoy or wish to enjoy the service. In the circumstances, the prohibition on using foreign decoding devices could not be justified in light of the objective of protecting IP rights.[99]

 Exercise

Do you agree with the ruling of the Court of Justice in *Murphy* that the specific subject matter of an IP right only requires the right holder to receive *reasonable* remuneration? How well does this sit with the early case law in which the concept of 'specific subject matter' was developed? How well does it sit with the underlying rationale for IP protection?

Exhaustion of rights and digital content

19.66   The Court of Justice in *Murphy* faced challenges reconciling free movement principles with evolution in the dissemination of audiovisual media. However, perhaps even greater challenges for the law of exhaustion of rights are posed by the internet and, in particular, the potential market for re-sale of digital content, such as downloaded software, films, music, video games, audiobooks, and e-books. Once purchased and downloaded, can digital content be 'resold' in the same way as physical items? In the United States, re-sales of iTunes files have been treated as falling outside the US rules on exhaustion and as therefore constituting an infringement.[100] In the EU, however, it is not clear that the issue will necessarily be decided the same way.

---

[95] Copyright, Designs and Patents Act 1988 (as amended), ss 297 and 298.

[96] 'Illicit device' is defined in Art 2(e): 'illicit device shall mean any equipment or software designed or adapted to give access to a protected service in an intelligible form without the authorisation of the service provider'.

[97] Joined Cases C-403/08 and C-429/08 *Football Association Premier League Ltd v QC Leisure, Murphy v Media Protection Services Ltd* [2012] 1 CMLR 29, paras 62–74.   [98] ibid, paras 93–95, 102–121; *Coditel* was distinguished.

[99] The ECJ also held that it could not be justified on the policy ground of encouraging live audiences at afternoon football games.

[100] *Capitol Records v ReDigi* (SDNY 30 March 2013).

19.67   The issue is most acute for copyright-protected works. The Directive on the harmonisation of certain aspects of copyright and related rights in the information society[101] (InfoSoc Directive) states at Article 4(2) that the distribution right provided for in that Article is subject to Community exhaustion. Article 4(2) does not itself distinguish between tangible or digital copies. However, the recitals to the InfoSoc Directive indicate that exhaustion under Article 4(2) should apply to tangible items only. Recital 28 of the Directive states:

> Copyright protection under this Directive includes the exclusive right to control distribution of the work incorporated in a tangible article. The first sale in the Community of the original of a work or copies thereof by the rightholder or with his consent exhausts the right to control resale of that object in the Community. This right should not be exhausted in respect of the original or of copies thereof sold by the rightholder or with his consent outside the Community.

Recital 29 adds:

> The question of exhaustion does not arise in the case of services and on-line services in particular. This also applies with regard to a material copy of a work or other subject-matter made by a user of such a service with the consent of the rightholder . . . Unlike CD-ROM or CD-I, where the intellectual property is incorporated in a material medium, namely an item of goods, every on-line service is in fact an act which should be subject to authorisation where the copyright or related right so provides.

Article 3(3) provides that there can be no exhaustion by any act of communication to the public or making available to the public of any right of communication or making available right arising under Article 3(1) or 3(2) InfoSoc Directive. Thus, under the InfoSoc Directive the act of uploading a work on to the internet does not exhaust the right, nor does the act of downloading. Permission is thus needed to download (a reproduction), print (a reproduction), or further distribute any copies of a work obtained from the internet.

19.68   Article 4(2) of the Software Directive 2009/24/EC also addresses exhaustion, stating:

> The first sale in the Community of a copy of a program by the rightholder or with his consent shall exhaust the distribution right within the Community of that copy, with the exception of the right to control further rental of the program or a copy thereof.

19.69   The issue of digital exhaustion came before the Court of Justice in the *UsedSoft* case. In *UsedSoft*, the Court found that there could be exhaustion of rights in relation to downloaded software. In reaching this conclusion, the Court had to navigate a way through the provisions of the InfoSoc Directive and the Software Directive:

■ **Case C-128/11** *UsedSoft GmbH v Oracle International Corp* **[2012] ECDR 19**

Oracle developed and marketed software. It distributed software via the internet, with customers downloading the software from Oracle's website. The download was governed by a licence agreement which gave the customer a perpetual, non-exclusive, non-transferable right to store a copy of the downloaded program on a server and to allow a certain number of users to access it. The disputed software could also be obtained in the form of a CD-ROM or DVD. UsedSoft marketed 'used' software licences acquired from Oracle customers for software which those customers had downloaded from the Oracle website and partial licences of such software where the customer only needed some of the permitted total users. Oracle sought to put a stop to this practice and the case was referred to the Court of Justice on the issue of whether Oracle's rights in the downloaded software had been exhausted by the transactions with Oracle's original customers.

The first question to be decided by the Court of Justice was whether the transaction between Oracle and its original customers constituted 'first sale . . . of a copy of a program' for the purposes of Article 4(2) of the Software Directive. Oracle argued that there was no act of sale, because there was no transfer of

---

[101] Directive 2001/29/EC of the European Parliament and of the Council of 22 May 2001 on the harmonisation of certain aspects of copyright and related rights in the information society. See also Case C-479/04 *Laserdisken ApS v Kulturministeriet* [2006] ECR I-8089, confirming that member states are precluded from retaining a domestic rule of international exhaustion.

ownership in the downloaded copy of the software. However, the Court disagreed. The concept of a 'sale' for these purposes required an autonomous and uniform European meaning. The Court regarded the downloading of a program and the conclusion of a user licence agreement as an indivisible whole, the download being pointless without a right to use the software. The making available by Oracle of a copy of its software and the conclusion of the user licence agreement were intended to make the copy usable by the customer permanently in return for payment of a fee. In such circumstances, there was a transfer of ownership in the downloaded copy of the software. The same conclusion would also be reached if the customer obtained their copy by CD-ROM or DVD. There was a 'sale' for the purposes of Article 4(2) Software Directive 2009/24.[102]

Oracle also argued that its rights could not be exhausted, since its making available of its software on its website constituted 'making available to the public' within the meaning of Article 3(1) InfoSoc Directive which, pursuant to Article 3(3) InfoSoc Directive, could not give rise to exhaustion. The Court disagreed that the InfoSoc Directive applied. Article 1(2)(a) InfoSoc Directive provided that the InfoSoc Directive did not affect, and was without prejudice to, the provisions of the Software Directive. The Software Directive was *lex specialis* in relation to the InfoSoc Directive, meaning that, whether or not Article 3(1) InfoSoc Directive might be engaged, it was overridden by Article 4(2) Software Directive 2009/24.[103] It was therefore only Article 4(2) of the Software Directive which was relevant.

Finally, it was argued that the exhaustion of rights provided for at Article 4(2) Software Directive only covered tangible copies of a work and not intangible copies downloaded from the internet. Again, the Court disagreed. The Court noted that Article 4(2) Software Directive itself drew no distinction between tangible and intangible copies. However, Article 1(2) Software Directive provided that protection under the Software Directive was to apply to 'the expression in any form of a computer program'. Noting also the recitals to the Software Directive, the Court concluded that it was clear that it was the intention of the EU legislature to treat tangible and intangible copies of computer programs in the same way. There could therefore be exhaustion of rights in downloaded software pursuant to Article 4(2) Software Directive 2009/24. From an economic point of view, the download of software over the internet and provision of a CD-ROM or DVD were functionally equivalent. To allow the owner of copyright in software which was downloaded over the internet the right to control further resale of the downloaded copy, thereby obtaining additional remuneration over and above that already obtained from the original transaction, would go beyond what was required to protect the specific subject matter of the relevant copyright.[104] It was not permitted to divide up and sell only part of a user licence for downloaded software if the original customer only needed a smaller number of users than that provided for in the licence agreement. However, where the licence as a whole was resold, provided the original customer made their copy of the software unusable at the time of resale, the person acquiring the downloaded copy from the original customer was a 'lawful acquirer' of the software and entitled to use it for its intended purpose.[105]

19.70   These sometimes rather convoluted findings by the Court of Justice have not been without criticism. The Court's views on what constitutes a 'sale' and on the functional equivalence between the provision of physical and digital software, together with the Court's decision to treat the online provision of software as a free movement of goods issue (rather than a free movement of services issue, as in *Murphy*) have, for example, all attracted comment. Looking forward, it is also not clear what the actual impact of *UsedSoft* will be: there has, for example, been speculation that software providers will simply adjust their business models to avoid entering into download transactions based on one-off payments in favour of an on-going periodic payment structure, which would be much harder to characterise as a one-off act of 'sale'.

---

[102] Case C-128/11 *UsedSoft GmbH v Oracle International Corp [2012] ECDR 19*, paras 38–48.

[103] ibid, paras 50–52 noting *obiter* also that the transfer of ownership for the purposes of Art 4(2) Directive 2009/24 would in any event convert an act constituting 'making available' into an act of distribution.

[104] ibid, paras 53–63.   [105] ibid, paras 73–88.

19.71 In the meantime, the principal question has been whether *UsedSoft* extends beyond 'pure' software to digital media files and other digital goods such as video games and e-books. Unlike 'pure' software, these other digital goods may be regarded as 'hybrid' products, in that they comprise both computer programs (giving the products their digital nature) and other copyright works (such as the literary text in an e-book, audiovisual works in video games, and so on). Should such 'hybrid' products be treated in the same way as computer programs following *UsedSoft*, or should they be treated differently?

19.72 There have been decisions of the Court of Justice on the InfoSoc and Software Directives which indicate that the most likely answer is that such 'hybrid' products will be treated differently to 'pure' software. The first such decision was in *Nintendo*, a reference concerning technical protection measures (TPMs) and the different TPM regimes under the InfoSoc and Software Directives. According to Advocate General Sharpston, the finding of the Court of Justice in *UsedSoft* that the Software Directive constituted *lex specialis* in relation to the InfoSoc Directive:[106]

> must be read as meaning that the provisions of Directive 2009/24 take precedence over those of Directive 2001/29, *but only where the protected material falls entirely within the scope of the former* [emphasis added].

The national court had found as a matter of fact that the videogames in suit did not consist merely of computer programs but were complex multimedia works comprising other works which were 'inextricable from the programs themselves'. Applying the rule articulated immediately above, because they were not solely composed of software but also consisted of other works as well, the video games fell outside the scope of the Software Directive and within the scope of the InfoSoc Directive. In comments directed to the issue of TPM protection but, it is submitted here, with potential parallels to the issue of exhaustion, AG Sharpston observed:[107]

> Where complex intellectual works comprising both computer programs and other material are concerned—and where the two cannot be separated—it seems to me that the greater, and not the lesser, protection should be accorded. If that were not so, right holders would not receive in respect of that other material the degree of protection to which they are entitled under Directive 2001/29.[108]

The Court of Justice agreed. The Court observed that videogames constitute complex matter comprising 'not only a computer program but also graphic and sound elements, which, although encrypted in computer language, have a unique creative value which cannot be reduced to that encryption'; insofar as the graphic and sound elements of the game were part of its originality, they fell, together with the entire work, within the scope of InfoSoc Directive.[109]

19.73 In *Art & Allposters International*, a case concerning the unauthorised use for printed canvasses by Allposters of images licensed for use to produce posters, the parties were in disagreement over whether exhaustion of the distribution right under Article 4(2) InfoSoc Directive was limited to the tangible object into which the copyright work or copies thereof were incorporated or whether it covered the 'intellectual creation' which was the subject of the copyright. The Court read Article 4(2) InfoSoc Directive as exhausting rights only in tangible objects.[110] Although digital exhaustion was not the subject matter of the *Allposters* preliminary reference, the Court's reasoning in *Allposters* indicates that the Court is unlikely to permit digital exhaustion under the InfoSoc Directive.[111] For all digital goods falling outwith the Software Directive, exhaustion would therefore not apply.

---

[106] Case C-355/12 *Nintendo Co Ltd, Nintendo of America Inc, Nintendo of Europe GmbH v PC Box Srl, 9Net Srl* [2013] ECDR 16, para AG34.
[107] ibid, para AG35.   [108] ibid, para AG35.   [109] ibid, para 23.
[110] *Art & Allposters International BV v Stichting Pictoright* (Case C-419/13) [2015] ECDR 8, paras 33–40.
[111] Note also that, in the context of VAT litigation, the Court has treated e-books as a form of electronically supplied service, rather than as a good, as discussed in E Rosati, 'Online copyright exhaustion in a post-Allposters world' (2015) 10 JIPLP 673.

19.74   The Court of Justice had an opportunity to explore digital exhaustion in the context of e-books, the rental and lending rights (Directive 2006/115 EC),[112] and Article 4(2) InfoSoc Directive in 2016, in *Vereniging Openbare Bibliotheken*.[113] The Court of Justice noted that the distribution right in Article 4(2) is distinct from the lending right, and found that member states in their legislation regarding lending, can require that the digital copy has been put on the market in the EU by the holder of the distribution right or with their consent, within the meaning of Article 4(2) of the InfoSoc Directive. This suggests an openness to digital exhaustion. The court did not, however, focus on the issue. Another reference has been made to the Court of Justice in the *TomKabinet* case, and the outcome is awaited.[114]

 Question

What are the legal and policy arguments for and against permitting exhaustion of rights in relation to digital products obtained over the internet? Do you agree with the *UsedSoft* decision and do you think it should apply to all digital goods?

Key point on free movement of services and digital goods

- Copyright gives to the owner the right to control distribution of a work incorporated in a tangible article. First sale in the Community exhausts that right within the Community. There is no exhaustion in respect of the rights to rent, show, or perform a work in public. For online distribution, the position is more complex: while there will be exhaustion of rights in relation to at least some downloaded software, there is uncertainty over the treatment of other downloaded digital goods.

 Free movement of goods and Brexit

EU law is at the heart of the intersection between free movement and IP, and Brexit is likely to have significant impact.

The draft UK Intellectual Property (Exhaustion of Rights) (EU Exit) Regulations to come into effect on Exit Day were released in November 2018. They provide that:

- any ability to bring an action relating to exhaustion of rights before this day will continue;
- UK legislation regarding Registered Designs, Copyright and Trade Marks is amended to cover goods put on the market in the UK or in the EEA, and refers to the 'UK–EEA area'.

Brexit could lead to calls for international exhaustion in the UK. The negotiated withdrawal agreement provides that the parties can establish their own regimes for exhaustion of rights.

---

[112] Directive 2006/115/EC of the European Parliament and of the Council of 12 December 2006 on rental right and lending right and on certain rights related to copyright in the field of intellectual property (codified version), https://eur-lex.europa.eu/legal-content/EN/ALL/?uri=CELEX%3A32006L0115, in particular Arts 1(1), 2(1)(b), and 6(1).

[113] Case C-174/15 *Vereniging Openbare Bibliotheken v Stichting Leenrecht* [2017] ECDR 3. See discussion in M Savič, 'The legality of resale of digital content after UsedSoft in subsequent German and CJEU case law' [2015] EIPR 414.

[114] Case C-263/18 *Nederlands Uitgeversverbond and Groep Algemene Uitgevers v Tom Kabinet Internet BV*.

Further reading

Book

C Stothers, *Parallel Trade in Europe: Intellectual Property, Competition and Regulatory Law* (2007)

Articles

I Avgoutis, 'Parallel imports and exhaustion of trade mark rights: should steps be taken towards an international exhaustion regime?' (2012) 34(2) EIPR 108–21

AEL Brown, 'Post-harmonised Europe: united, divided or unimportant' [2001] 3 IPQ 275–86

T Cottier, 'The exhaustion of intellectual property rights—a fresh look' (2008) 39 IIC 755

CB Graber, 'Tethered technologies, cloud strategies and the future of the first sale/exhaustion defence in copyright law' (2015) 5(4) QMJIP 389–408

K Maskus, 'The curious economics of parallel imports' (2010) 2(1) WIPO J 123–32

G Petursson and P Dyrberg, 'What is consent? A Note on Davidoff and Levi Strauss' (2002) 27(4) ELRev 464–71

T Rendas, 'Lex specialis(sima): videogames and technological protection measures in EU copyright law' [2015] EIPR 39

E Rosati, 'Online copyright exhaustion in a post-Allposters world' (2015) 10 JIPLP 673

M Savič, 'The legality of resale of digital content after UsedSoft in subsequent German and CJEU case law' [2015] EIPR 414

EU competition law and intellectual property

Introduction

20.1　It will have been apparent from reading previous chapters that there is an unending tension between those who would argue for expansion of intellectual property rights (IPRs) on the ground that such are needed to encourage creators, and those who seek to limit, and even to roll back, the parameters of the rights on the ground that over-strong rights can harm innovation. Wherever these boundaries lie, those parts within them give to the right holder exclusive rights to deal with the subject matter in the market.

20.2　It will be recalled that one of the underlying justifications for the grant of IPRs is that innovation will be encouraged. The monopoly granted by the IPRs has been carefully crafted to ensure that, despite the extent of the right, competition will thrive in the marketplace, ultimately for the benefit of consumers and users. But sometimes the exercise of IPRs can produce unexpected outcomes: perhaps an over-strong monopoly is acquired due to the popularity of a particular product protected by IPRs, and the right holder may then occupy a position of strength which may hamper competition in the marketplace; or owners of IPRs may enter into agreements which may not, ultimately, be to the benefit of consumers. Competition law, operated at national (UK) and European Union level, may then be used to regulate the behaviour of these entities in the marketplace.

Scope and overview of chapter

20.3　The purpose of this chapter, concentrating on EU competition law, is to provide an overview of some of the more common circumstances in which the Commission and the Court of Justice may intervene to regulate the exercise of IPRs by undertakings within the common market. The focus is on EU competition law as there is no international regime of competition rules. The Agreement on Trade-Related Aspects of Intellectual Property Rights (TRIPS) 1994 authorises members to provide for national competition rules within certain limits,[1] but does not oblige them to do so. Accordingly, competition law (called antitrust in the United States) emanates from regional and national rules which, in the UK, are now modelled on the EU provisions.

20.4　

> ### Learning objectives
>
> By the end of this chapter you should be able to describe and explain:
>
> - the tension between the application of competition law and the exercise of IPRs and how that relates to the underlying justifications for the grant of IPRs;
> - those circumstances in which competition law may be applied to moderate the exercise of IPRs in the relevant market;

---

[1] TRIPS Agreement, Arts 8(2), 31, and 40.

- clauses in intellectual property (IP) licensing agreements between undertakings that might be permissible in terms of EU competition law and those which are not;

- the conditions under which a refusal to supply products protected by an IP right might constitute an abuse of a dominant position by the right holder;

- the extent to which competition law can provide a defence to an infringement action;

- the impact of competition law on collective licensing.

20.5   The rest of the chapter looks like this:

- Theory of competition (20.6–20.10)

- Competition law and IP (20.11–20.19)

- Intellectual property and agreements between undertakings: Article 101 TFEU (20.20–20.41)

- Intellectual property and abuse of a dominant position: Article 102 TFEU (20.42–20.55)

- *Commission v Microsoft* (20.56–20.69)

- EU competition law in the UK courts: Eurodefences and limits on remedies (20.70–20.82)

- Collective licensing and EU competition law (20.83–20.92).

Theory of competition

20.6   Competition law seeks to regulate the behaviour of firms in the marketplace. In capitalist economies there is a belief that where there is competition between firms, this will ultimately be of benefit to consumers. This is because firms will:

- be unable to charge artificially high prices;

- continuously innovate to create new goods;

- make available those products necessary to meet consumer demand.

There is a theory that consumer welfare is maximised when there is *perfect competition*. In this model, available resources are *allocated efficiently*. This means that the consumer can buy the goods that they wish to buy, for the price they are prepared to pay, with this price not being above the marginal cost of production of the goods. Firms also work to *productive efficiency*. This means that the manufacturer makes goods for as low a cost as possible, while still making a profit. Such market conditions foster innovation or *dynamic efficiency,* in which the firm is constantly striving to create new, and better, products to meet consumer demand.

20.7   At the heart of this economic analysis of competition, which as will be seen, is important to competition law, lies the concept of *market power*. If any one firm (or number of firms acting in concert) has the ability to reduce output and raise prices without concern that competitors might enter the market and fill consumer demand at lower prices, then the firm is said to be able to exercise market power. A single firm which can act substantially independently of its competitors, and without regard to consumers, is said to be able to exercise monopoly power and to be a *monopolist*. Two or more firms which, consciously or subconsciously, act in furtherance of a common goal in pursuit of which they deviate from competitive behaviour are termed *oligopolists*. Firms which collude to alter the competitive structure of a market to their own advantage by, for example, fixing prices or limiting production, are said to form a *cartel*.

Question

Can you think of any flaws that might exist in this theory of perfect competition?

Can you think of any firm which you think is a monopolist through ownership and/or exercise of IPRs? Why have you thought of the particular firm? What factors have you considered important in your decision? Try and think of a second example from a different industry sector. Did you approach the exercise the same way? Revisit these questions once you have finished this chapter.

Workable competition

20.8   There are many flaws in the theory of perfect competition. Not only does it presuppose that decisions are made rationally by those decision-makers responsible for directing corporate strategy and behaviour in the marketplace, but it also assumes that consumers have perfect knowledge of market conditions and will also make rational decisions when it comes to purchases.

20.9   The deficiencies have led to the development of a theory of 'workable' or 'effective competition':[2]

> Effective competition connotes the idea that firms are subject to a reasonable degree of competitive constraint, from actual and potential competitors and from customers, and that the role of a competition authority is to be that such constraints are present on the market.[3]

The goal of EU and UK competition policy would appear to be predicated on this notion of effective competition[4] and is to maintain competition within the internal market.

Cartels and monopolies

20.10   In order to maintain a state of effective or workable competition, competition law is directed towards dealing with abuses that can occur to upset that state. These include:

- preventing agreements between firms that have the effect of restricting competition between them;
- checking behaviour by monopolists who might abuse their dominant position and prevent new competition emerging;
- ensuring that workable competition is maintained between oligopolists;
- monitoring mergers between independent firms the effect of which may be to concentrate the market and diminish competitive pressures.[5]

This chapter considers the first two of those as they relate to the exercise of IPRs and as regulated by Articles 101 and 102 Treaty on the Functioning of the European Union (TFEU) (ex Arts 81 and 82 EC). Note that the Article numbering which applies following the changes made by the Treaty of Lisbon will be used in this chapter except where the discussion relates to historical events and/or where quotations from cases are used in the text.

---

[2] R Whish and D Bailey, *Competition Law* (9th edn, 2018), 17–18.   [3] ibid, 18.

[4] See further discussion in D Llewelyn and T Aplin, *Cornish, Llewelyn and Aplin Intellectual Property: Patents, Copyright, Trade Marks and Allied Rights* (9th edn, 2019), paras 1-40–1-48.

[5] Whish and Bailey, *Competition Law* (n 2), 26 and more generally Chapter 1.

Competition law and IP

20.11   As IP laws confer on the owner exclusive rights, so the owner can prevent competition in relation to the subject matter of the right. However, there is a constant tension between the grant of those exclusive rights and the application of competition law. The aim is to find the balance between IPRs and competitive markets. On the interaction between IP and competition law, the Commission has stated:[6]

> The fact that intellectual property laws grant exclusive rights of exploitation does not imply that intellectual property rights are immune from competition law intervention. Articles 81 and 82 are in particular applicable to agreements whereby the holder licenses another undertaking to exploit his intellectual property rights. Nor does it imply that there is an inherent conflict between intellectual property rights and the Community competition rules. Indeed, both bodies of law share the same basic objective of promoting consumer welfare and an efficient allocation of resources. Innovation constitutes an essential and dynamic component of an open and competitive market economy. Intellectual property rights promote dynamic competition by encouraging undertakings to invest in developing new or improved products and processes. So does competition by putting pressure on undertakings to innovate. Therefore, both intellectual property rights and competition are necessary to promote innovation and ensure a competitive exploitation thereof.

 Exercise

Familiarise yourself with the terms of both Articles 101 and 102 TFEU. Consider the mischief they are aimed at and see if you can think of any examples where they might apply to the exercise of IPRs.

20.12   Some concepts are common in any discussion of competition law. The purpose of this section is to introduce some of these to assist the reader in understanding this chapter.

The relevant market

20.13   The term *market* is usually understood as the place where business is done between companies. As was discussed previously in paragraph 20.8, in a state of workable competition, firms will compete against each other in this market to the ultimate benefit of consumers. If a number of firms enter into an agreement which upsets competitive market conditions, or a monopolist is able to, and does, act independently of either competitors or consumers, then the market is said to be distorted.

20.14   But it is only behaviour on the *relevant market* that is taken into account when looking to the behaviour of these entities. This immediately leads to questions as to how the relevant market should be defined. For example, if there is an agreement between manufacturers to increase the retail price of wine, this would be unlikely to affect competition in the manufacture, distribution, and sale of all drinks, both alcoholic and non-alcoholic. A narrowing of this definition might look to alcoholic drinks. Narrowing it still further might concentrate on wines; or wines from a particular region. But taking a definition that is overly narrow can be equally problematic. For instance, raising the price of one brand of children's clothing might be considered an abuse if the market is defined as that particular brand.

■ **Case C-22/78** *Hugin Kassaregister AB and Hugin Cash Registers Ltd v Commission of the European Communities* **[1979] ECR 1869**

In this case the relevant market was defined very narrowly.[7] Hugin made cash register machines in London and had a 13 per cent share of the cash register market; Lipton, a small firm in South East England, serviced the registers. Hugin wanted to get into the servicing market and as part of that strategy it refused to supply

---

[6] Commission Notice, Guidelines on the application of Article 81 of the EC Treaty to technology transfer agreements, OJ 2004/C 101/02; the Commission also issued a Report on Competition Policy 2008, COM(2009) 374.

[7] Similar issues arose in Case T-30/89 *Hilti AG v Commission of the European Communities* [1991] ECR II-143.

spare parts to Liptons. In looking to the relevant market, both the Commission and the European Court of Justice (ECJ) found that it was in spare parts for the machines (although ultimately the Court found that there was no effect on interstate trade). Had the market been defined as that of the product (the cash register) *and* the spare parts, the outcome would have been different.

20.15 The Commission has published a Notice on Market Definition.[8] This sets out the factors that are taken into account in defining the relevant market. The Commission focuses on demand and supply product substitutability and potential competition. To determine the relevant market, it is necessary to investigate both the relevant product market and the relevant geographical market. The relevant product market includes those products which are regarded as interchangeable or substitutable by the consumer. This may be because of the characteristics of the products, the price, and intended use. The relevant geographical market refers to the area in which the businesses are involved in the supply and demand of products or services.

> ### Web link
>
> Read the Commission's Notice on Market Definition, which can be found at
> https://eur-lex.europa.eu/legal-content/EN/TXT/?uri=LEGISSUM%3AI26073.

Intra brand competition

20.16 Competition exists at different levels between businesses in the marketplace. A manufacturer may produce a particular product, for example soap powder. Wholesalers who purchase the soap powder from the manufacturer, and retailers who sell the soap powder to the consumer may then compete with each other in the downstream market. This is called *intra brand* competition—competition between distributors of the same brand. Here the goods are the same and therefore quality is an irrelevant factor. The price at which the product is sold, availability on the market, and the conditions under which it is sold may, however, be important. For example, the soap powder may be sold at a lower price in a discount supermarket as compared with a more upmarket store, but often without the amenities and services that the latter provides.

Inter brand competition

20.17 *Inter brand* competition is where competition exists between suppliers of competing products, for example two differently branded soap powders. Such competition is normally between different firms that have developed brands or labels for their products in order to distinguish them from other brands sold in the same market segment, although sometimes the same manufacturer may develop a number of differently branded products of the same kind. Ariel versus Persil is an example of inter brand competition. Consumers are interested in the quality and the price of the goods as well as, for many products, after-sales service.

Horizontal agreements

20.18 A horizontal agreement is one between two or more actual or potential competitors, operating at the same level of the production or distribution chain. Such an agreement may cover, for example, research and development, production, or purchasing. Horizontal agreements may restrict competition where they involve price fixing or market sharing, or where the market power resulting from the horizontal cooperation causes negative market effects with respect to prices, output, innovation, or the variety and quality of products, for example if those involved in an industry agree that one technology (a standard) is to be used

---

[8] Commission Notice on the definition of the relevant market for the purposes of Community competition law, OJ 1997/C 372.

for a particular purpose. On the other hand, horizontal cooperation can be a means to share risk, save costs, pool know-how, minimise inefficient duplication, increase consumer choice, and launch innovation more quickly. In particular for small and medium-sized enterprises, cooperation can be an important means by which to adapt to the changing marketplace.[9]

Vertical agreements

20.19   A vertical agreement is one entered into between two or more undertakings, each of which operates at a different level of the production or distribution chain. Vertical agreements tend to be less able to affect other parties and thus foreclose competition on the relevant market. However, where either party has a large market share in the relevant market, vertical agreements can affect third parties who supply the same or substitutable goods. An example would be an agreement between a distributor and a manufacturer which prevented other manufacturers from competing to sell goods to that distributor.[10]

Intellectual property and agreements between undertakings: Article 101 TFEU

20.20   Article 101 TFEU concerns agreements between undertakings which have the object or effect of preventing, restricting, or distorting competition within the common market, and which may affect trade between member states. The interpretation and application of this Article is central in determining the acceptable boundaries of agreements and the clauses they contain entered into between parties which relate to the exploitation of IP, through licensing, and also horizontal and vertical agreements.

Article 101 TFEU (ex Art 81 EC)

1. The following shall be prohibited as incompatible with the common market: all agreements between undertakings, decisions by associations of undertakings and concerted practices which may affect trade between Member States and which have as their object or effect the prevention, restriction or distortion of competition within the common market, and in particular those which:
   (a) directly or indirectly fix purchase or selling prices or any other trading conditions;
   (b) limit or control production, markets, technical development, or investment;
   (c) share markets or sources of supply;
   (d) apply dissimilar conditions to equivalent transactions with other trading parties, thereby placing them at a competitive disadvantage;
   (e) make the conclusion of contracts subject to acceptance by the other parties of supplementary obligations which, by their nature or according to commercial usage, have no connection with the subject of such contracts.
2. Any agreements or decisions prohibited pursuant to this Article shall be automatically void.
3. The provisions of paragraph 1 may, however, be declared inapplicable in the case of:
   – any agreement or category of agreements between undertakings;
   – any decision or category of decisions by associations of undertakings;
   – any concerted practice or category of concerted practices,
   which contributes to improving the production or distribution of goods or to promoting technical or economic progress, while allowing consumers a fair share of the resulting benefit, and which does not:
   (a) impose on the undertakings concerned restrictions which are not indispensable to the attainment of these objectives;
   (b) afford such undertakings the possibility of eliminating competition in respect of a substantial part of the products in question.

[9] For discussion of IP and competition issues relating to the development of technology standards, see M Lemley, 'Intellectual property rights and standard-setting organizations' (2002) 90 California Law Rev 1889. and P Treacy and S Lawrance, 'FRANDly fire: are industry standards doing more harm than good?' (2008) 3(1) JIPLP 22.

[10] See discussion in C-230/16 *Coty Germany v Parfumerie Akzente* [2018] 4 CMLR 9.

20.21   The Commission has said that, in the context of the single market programme, the objective of Article 101 TFEU (at that time Art 81 EC) is to protect competition on the market as a means of enhancing consumer welfare and of ensuring an efficient allocation of resources.[11] Article 101 provides that agreements within Article 101(1) are not only prohibited; they are also void, pursuant to Article 101(2) TFEU. However, Article 101(3) TFEU provides that the provisions of Article 101(1) TFEU may be declared inapplicable in specified circumstances—in other words, an agreement would not be in breach of Article 101(1) TFEU. This Article will be discussed from paragraph 20.29.

Article 101 TFEU and licensing agreements

20.22   A common way of exploiting intellectual property is through a licensing agreement. This might be when the holder of a patent does not have the financial resources to develop and exploit the patent, and so may enter into an agreement with a third party. Another example is when a singer may (at least in the past) need the help of a record company to record, market, and distribute recordings of performances, or of a collecting society to ingather sums due for the performance of that song in public. This can be brought about through a licence agreement. A licensee is permitted to do something that would otherwise be an infringement of another's rights. Such an agreement with one entity may well foreclose the IP owner from dealing with other parties, at least within the scope of the first arrangement, and thus be restrictive of competition as regards third parties. Equally, a licensing agreement may be pro-competitive. The owner will get a financial return while others can improve efficiency in terms of both manufacture and distribution of the products. The question then is as to when and where the prohibitions on anti-competitive conduct found in Article 101(1) TFEU might apply to licensing agreements concerning IP, such as to render an agreement void.

As will be seen from the text of Article 101 TFEU, an agreement is not within its scope unless:

- it has the object or effect of preventing, distorting, or restricting competition. Where an agreement has the object of preventing competition, for example through absolute territorial exclusivity, then there will be no need to examine the economic effect of the agreement in the market. Where it is not intended to foreclose competition, then the effect of the agreement in the market will have to be analysed. This can be a difficult exercise; see, for example, *GlaxoSmithKline Services Unlimited v Commission of the European Communities* [2009] ECR I-9291;

- it may affect trade between member states. Trade must be affected to an appreciable extent. The Commission has published a Notice on Agreements of Minor Importance which sets out the market share thresholds below which an agreement will be regarded as *de minimis*.[12] These are set at 10 per cent market share for agreements between competitors and at 15 per cent for agreements between non-competitors.

It should also be noted that any type of agreement between two or more entities might fall under Article 101 TFEU. An agreement does not have to be in writing and can extend to 'informal' understandings (concerted practices) between undertakings in the market, for instance an understanding not to enter the territory of another competitor.

Web link

For a series of model licensing agreements, see
www.gov.uk/government/publications/lambert-toolkit-model-research-collaboration-agreements.

---

[11] Guidelines on the application of Article 81(3) of the Treaty, 2004/C 101/08; see also https://eur-lex.europa.eu/legal-content/EN/TXT/?uri=LEGISSUM%3Al26114.

[12] Commission Notice on agreements of minor importance which do not appreciably restrict competition under Article 101(1) of the Treaty establishing the European Community (de minimis), OJ 2014/ C 291/1.

Exercise

The agreements referred to in the Web link have been prepared by the Lambert Committee, which was charged with developing model agreements for use where one of the parties to the agreement is an educational institution. Read through some of the agreements to familiarise yourself with the type of provisions to be found in these documents. In what ways do you think Article 101(1) TFEU might need to be considered? Revisit your answer when you have finished this section.

Case law, Article 101 TFEU, and IP agreements

20.23   In the early development of case law on the application of Article 81(1) EC to IP licences, the ECJ followed a fairly restrictive approach to what it considered may fall foul of the Treaty. This was a consequence of the pursuit of the goal of bringing about a free market between member states. This approach tended to be followed irrespective of broader economic benefits that may have been brought about through an agreement. In so doing, the ECJ developed a distinction between the *existence* and *exercise* of an IPR, which in turn led to a consideration of the *specific subject matter*. The existence/exercise dichotomy, which term was also discussed in paragraphs 19.11ff, can be seen in *Consten & Grundig v EEC Commission*.

■ **Case C-56/64** *Consten and Grundig v EEC Commission* **[1966] ECR 299**

A German manufacturer, Grundig, made electrical goods in Germany. Grundig entered into an agreement with Consten, a French distributor, whereby Consten would distribute Grundig's products in France under both 'Grundig' and 'Gint' trade marks. The intention was to grant Consten absolute territorial protection for the distribution of Grundig's products in France. Grundig sought to achieve this by:

- imposing certain terms on other wholesalers and distributors, including re-export bans and express terms prohibiting distribution of Grundig products in France; and

- entering into a licence agreement which authorised the exclusive use by Consten of Grundig's trade mark, Gint, in France, which would be assigned to Consten once the agreement came to an end.

The Commission condemned these agreements as a breach of what is now Article 101(1). Both parties sought annulment of the Commission decision.

The ECJ said:

- Article 101 (as it is now) applies to both horizontal and vertical agreements.

- An agreement between a manufacturer and distributor who are not in competition might have an adverse effect on competition between one of them and a third party. It is thus distortive of competition to make an agreement designed to insulate national markets.

Importantly for present purposes, the Court went on to say that the injunction contained *does not affect the grant* of those rights, but only *limits their exercise* to the extent necessary to give effect to the prohibition under what is now Article 101.

Points to note:

- The Court considered the licensing of the trade mark a material factor in the attempt to ensure for Consten absolute territorial exclusivity. This caused the agreement to fall foul of what is now Article 101. (Note, however, that the approach to territorial exclusivity has changed over time—see, eg, the *Nungesser/Maize Seeds* case discussed later at para 20.25.)

- The purpose of registration of the trade mark in France was to increase the protection against parallel imports into France of Grundig products. In other words, it was to give Consten its own means of repelling the parallel imports of genuine Grundig products from other member states.

20.24 In *Windsurfing International v Commission*,[13] the Commission and the ECJ used the concept of *specific subject matter* to determine the compatibility of what is now Article 101 TFEU with a patent licensing agreement.

■ Case C-193/83 *Windsurfing International v Commission* [1986] ECR 611

Windsurfing invented a rig for a sailboard. Patents were applied for in several countries, including Germany. Windsurfing entered into a number of agreements with licensees in Germany.

The provisions in the licence included:

- clauses tying patented goods to unpatented goods. The patent itself only covered the rig. The licence tied exploitation of the rig to exploitation of the sailboard. In other words, if a licensee wanted a licence to manufacture and sell the patented rig mechanism, they also had to manufacture and sell the sailboard;
- royalties to be calculated on the basis of sales of final assembled goods. This included both patented and unpatented products;
- a requirement to fix patent attribution and the logo to both patented and unpatented goods;
- a 'no-challenge' clause.

The Commission and then the ECJ found that a number of these clauses went beyond the *specific subject matter* of the patent. In other words, there was an attempt by the patentee to extend the patent monopoly.

The ECJ said:[14]

the clauses contained in the licensing agreements, in so far as they relate to parts of the sailboard not covered by the German patent or include the complete sailboard within their terms of reference, can therefore find no justification on grounds of the protection of an industrial property right.

 Question

What is a 'no-challenge' clause? Why might this be relevant to the interface between IP and competition?

 Exercise 1

Compare the emergence of the existence/exercise/specific subject matter doctrines used in the application of Article 101 TFEU to IP agreements with those developed in relation to the free movement of goods (see Chapter 19, in particular para 19.9ff).

Exercise 2

Consider ways in which you think agreements between undertakings dealing with IP might fall under the prohibitions in Article 101 TFEU. Might or should this extend to evolving forms of sharing, such as Creative Commons licences discussed at paragraph 6.52? Revisit this question at the end of your work in this chapter.

---

[13] Case C-193/83 [1986] ECR 611.   [14] ibid, point 36.

20.25   The Court of Justice and the ECJ have also used an economic-based approach (often termed a '*rule of reason*', particularly in the United States) in its application of Article 101 TFEU and its predecessors to IP agreements. Broadly this consists of an economic analysis of an agreement on the relevant market. If the agreement has pro-competitive effects which outweigh the anti-competitive effects, then it should not be prohibited by competition laws.[15]

This approach can be seen in *Nungesser v Commission*,[16] otherwise known as the *Maize Seed* case, in which the central question was whether an exclusive licence of plant breeders' rights infringed what is now Article 101(1).

■ Case C-258/78 *Nungesser v Commission* [1981] ECR 45

A French Institute developed varieties of maize seeds for which it held plant breeders' rights in French and German law. By a series of agreements, the German rights were partly licensed and partly assigned to a German undertaking. The French Institute agreed to ensure absolute territorial exclusivity for the production and sale of the seeds in Germany. It did so by pursuing the following strategy:

The French Institute agreed:

- not to license another undertaking in Germany to produce or sell the seeds;
- not itself to produce the seeds in Germany; and
- not itself to export seeds to Germany, and to obtain agreement from other licensees in other territories that they would not export seeds to Germany.

The Commission took a rigid view of what is now Article 101(1) and held that the grant of exclusive rights contravened its provisions. When the case was heard by the ECJ, the Court took a different approach. The ECJ sought to reconcile the objectives of free competition between member states and the wider competitive benefits of exclusive licences of IP rights. It did so by drawing a distinction between:

- '*open exclusive licences*' where exclusive rights are granted for one territory; and
- '*closed licences*' in terms of which steps are taken to ensure there is no competition from entities in other territories.

The ECJ said that open licences were acceptable. Some exclusivity may be essential to encourage a potential licensee to invest in a new product. Therefore, the agreement not to license another German undertaking and not to produce the seeds in Germany itself were acceptable. However, that part of the agreement by virtue of which the French Institute was to seek agreement from other licensees not to import into Germany, was void as it affected the position of third parties such as parallel importers.

20.26   Often, however, cases do not include detailed economic reasoning. Joined Cases *Murphy v Media Protection Services*[17] and *FA Premier League v QC Leisure and Others*[18] were criminal and civil actions, respectively, concerning the supply of decoders and receipt of broadcasts of football matches pursuant to an exclusive licence which prohibited the export of the decoders (see also para 20.77 and discussion in Chapters 3, 4, and 5). Was this in breach of Article 101? The court making the reference to the ECJ considered in detail the *Nungesser* arguments, economics, and issues arising from open and closed licensing.[19] In contrast, the Court

---

[15] For an in-depth discussion on the problems caused by segmentation of the internal market, see the European Commission's 'Online Commerce Roundtable Report on Opportunities and barriers to online retailing' at http://ec.europa.eu/competition/consultations/2009_online_commerce/roundtable_report_en.pdf.

[16] Case C-258/78 [1981] ECR 45.   [17] Case C-429/08 [2008] EWHC 1666 (Admin).

[18] Case C-403/08. Joined with Case 429/08 in order of the President of the Court, 3 December 2008.

[19] *Football Association Premier League Ltd v QC Leisure* [2008] EWHC 1411 (Ch), [2008] 3 CMLR 12, paras 336–368.

of Justice engaged in more limited discussion of economics and case law. It found that this exclusive licence provision regarding decoding devices was a restriction prohibited by Article 101.[20]

20.27 Yet, the economic balancing approach does seem to be pursued by the Commission:[21]

> The aim of the Community competition rules is to protect competition on the market as a means of enhancing consumer welfare and of ensuring an efficient allocation of resources. Agreements that restrict competition may at the same time have pro-competitive effects by way of efficiency gains. Efficiencies may create additional value by lowering the cost of producing an output, improving the quality of the product, or creating a new product. When the pro-competitive effects of an agreement outweigh its anti-competitive effects, the agreement is on balance pro-competitive and compatible with the objectives of the Community competition rules. The net effect of such agreements is to promote the very essence of the competitive process, namely to win customers by offering better products or better prices than those offered by rivals.

 Exercise

Can you see any drawbacks in the adoption of an economic rule of reason approach? How easy or difficult do you think it is for companies operating in the marketplace to carry out a detailed economic analysis of the effect of an agreement in the relevant market? Might this depend on the industry sector?

Article 101(2) TFEU

20.28 If an agreement falls within Article 101(1) TFEU, then it is void. A national court may determine if a particular clause is severable and those parts of the agreement not caught may continue.

Article 101(3) TFEU

20.29 Even if an agreement does fall under Article 101(1) TFEU, it may be exempted under Article 101(3). This Article exempts agreements which improve production or distribution of products, or which contribute to technical or economic progress. This is subject to the proviso that consumers must gain a share of the benefit. However, any restrictions should only be such as are indispensable and not eliminate competition in respect of a substantial part of the products in question.

20.30 A new procedural regime came into force on 1 May 2004 for the application of Article 81(3) EC (now Art 101(3) TFEU). Under the previous regime,[22] an application could be made to the Commission for exemption under this Article unless the agreement fell within one of the block exemption Regulations (discussed at paras 20.32ff). In 2004 a Regulation came into force under which Article 81(3) became directly applicable.[23] Under this, it is for businesses to self-assess whether an agreement falls under Article 101(1) TFEU. A ruling on the legality of an agreement will only be required if a dispute or complaint arises. At that point, national competition authorities and national courts will have concurrent jurisdiction with the Commission, including the right to rule on the legality of an agreement under Article 101(3) TFEU.

---

[20] Cases C-403/08 and C429/08 *Murphy v Media Protection Services Ltd, Football Association Premier League Ltd v QC Leisure* [2012] 1 CMLR 29, paras 134–146 and AG paras 243–251. See discussion in J Anderson, 'The curious case of the Portsmouth publican: challenging the territorial exclusivity of TV rights in European professional sport (Case Comment)' (2011) 11(3) International Sports Law Rev 53–60, in particular from 55.

[21] Commission Notice, Guidelines on the application of Article 81 of the EC Treaty to technology transfer agreements, OJ 2004/C 101/02, para 33; and see also Commission Regulation (EU) No 316/2014 of 21 March 2014 on the application of Article 101(3) of the Treaty on the Functioning of the European Union to categories of technology transfer agreements OJ 2014/L 93/17 recitals 4 and 5; see also the discussion at para 20.83 on collective licensing and Art 101 regarding *Re CISAC Agreement Case* [2013] 5 CMLR 15.

[22] Council Regulation No 17/62 of 6 February 1962.

[23] Council Regulation (EC) No 1/2003 of 16 December 2002 on the implementation of the rules on competition laid down in Articles 81 and 82 of the Treaty; for a 2009 report on Regulation 1/2003 and enforcement, see COM(2009) 206.

Question

What does direct applicability mean?

20.31   Alongside this new procedure the Commission issued a set of guidelines which set out the Commission's interpretation of the conditions for application of the exception contained in Article 101(3) TFEU, and to provide guidance on how the Commission will apply Article 101 TFEU in individual cases. In so doing the Commission indicated that it would weigh the pro- and anti-competitive effects of agreements between undertakings:[24]

> The assessment . . . consists of two parts. The first step is to assess whether an agreement between undertakings, which is capable of affecting trade between Member States, has an anti-competitive object or actual or potential anti competitive effects. The second step, which only becomes relevant when an agreement is found to be restrictive of competition, is to determine the pro-competitive benefits produced by that agreement and to assess whether these pro-competitive effects outweigh the anti-competitive effects.

Web links

The Commission has issued a raft of Notices and Communications resulting from their programme designed to update and modernise EU competition rules and procedures. These can all be found at http://ec.europa.eu/competition/antitrust/legislation/legislation.html, which also includes legislation regarding horizontal and vertical agreements. New issues continue to arise—for example, is an arbitration award which required royalties to be paid, even if a patent is then found, invalid in breach of Article 101, and what is the link between arbitration and competition? The Court of Justice considered this in *Genentech v Hoechst* (C-567/14), but more interesting is the opinion of the Advocate General, http://curia.europa.eu/juris/document/document.jsf?text=&docid=175146&pageIndex=0&doclang=EN&mode=req&dir=&occ=first&part=1&cid=191790. It will be interesting to see how this area develops.

Block exemption regulations

20.32   The Guidelines may not always, however, be the most important instruments to consider in relation to agreements. The Commission (acting on delegated authority from the EU Council of Ministers) may, pursuant to Article 101(3) TFEU, issue block exemptions relating to the licensing and sharing of IP. A block exemption specifies those conditions under which certain types of agreements are exempted from the prohibition laid down in Article 101(1) TFEU. When an agreement fulfils the conditions set out in a block exemption regulation, the agreement is automatically valid and so enforceable. Block exemption regulations exist in a number of sectors, including vertical agreements,[25] vertical restraints,[26] research and development (R&D) agreements,[27] technology transfer agreements,[28] and car distribution agreements[29] and have become a valuable tool for businesses.

The most important for current purposes is the Technology Transfer Block Exemption Regulation.

[24] Commission Notice, Guidelines on the application of Article 81(3) of the Treaty, OJ 2004/C 101/08, para 11.

[25] Commission Regulation (EU) No 330/2010 on the application of Article 101(3) of the Treaty on the Functioning of the European Union to categories of vertical agreements and concerted practices, OJ L102, 23 April 2010 and regarding specialisation agreements see Commission Regulation (EU) No 1218/2010 on the application of Article 101(3) of the Treaty on the Functioning of the European Union to certain categories of specialisation agreements OJ 2010/L 335/43.

[26] Commission Notice, Guidelines on Vertical Restraints, OJ 2010/C 130/01.

[27] Commission Regulation (EU) No 1217/2010 on the application of Article 101(3) of the Treaty on the Functioning of the European Union to certain categories of research and development agreements, OJ L 335, 18 December 2010.

[28] Commission Regulation (EU) No 316/2014 of 21 March 2014 on the application of Article 101(3) of the Treaty on the Functioning of the European Union to categories of technology transfer agreements, OJ 2014/L 93/17.

[29] Commission Regulation 461/2010 on the application of Article 101(3) of the Treaty on the Functioning of the European Union to categories of vertical agreements and concerted practices in the motor vehicle sector, OJ L129, 28 May 2010.

Technology Transfer Block Exemption Regulation

20.33   The initial IP block exemptions promulgated by the Commission dealt separately with the licensing of patents[30] and know-how.[31] These block exemptions were replaced in 1996 by one instrument, the Technology Transfer Block Exemption (TTBE),[32] covering technology transfer agreements generally. Following extensive consultation, the TTBE was replaced in 2004 by a revised Technology Transfer Block Exemption Regulation,[33] which was accompanied by its own very important set of guidelines[34] on the application of Article 101 TFEU to technology transfer agreements. These arrangements were always to expire in March 2014[35] and a new Block Exemption (TTBER)[36] and Technology Transfer Guidelines (TTBER Guidelines)[37] were introduced with effect from 1 May 2014. In contrast to the changes which came about in 2004, the broad approaches remain the same.

20.34   The TTBER is relevant to undertakings which enter into technology transfer agreements which deal with, inter alia, patents, know-how, software copyright, or a mixture of these IPRs.[38]

20.35   The TTBER distinguishes between licensing arrangements between competitors and non-competitors: the question is whether the agreement restricts actual or potential competition that would have existed without the agreement.[39] Competing undertakings may benefit from the exemptions only where the combined market share[40] of the parties does not exceed 20 per cent of either a relevant technology market or a relevant product market;[41] non-competing undertakings may benefit from the exemptions only where the market share of each party does not exceed 30 per cent of the relevant technology and product markets.[42] If parties have a market share in excess of that specified, then any contractual restrictions will be subject to analysis.

The Regulation works on the premise that any clauses which are not forbidden are exempt. Two classes of restrictions are set out and detail those clauses that would, or might (unless severable), cause the agreement to be non-exempt.

Hardcore restrictions

20.36   Hardcore restrictions[43] will, if included, mean that the agreement falls outwith the TTBER.[44] They vary depending on whether the agreement is one between competitors or non-competitors.

- Where the parties are competitors, then prohibited clauses include:

    (a) the restriction of a party's ability to determine its prices when selling products to third parties—for instance, by setting the exact price at which the products can be sold, or the range of prices with maximum rebates;

---

[30] Regulation 2349/84, OJ 1984 L219, amended by Regulation 151/93, OJ 1993 L21/8 and Regulation 2131/95, OJ 1995 L214/6.

[31] Regulation 556/89, OJ 1989 L61, amended by Regulation 151/93, OJ 1993 L21/8.

[32] Regulation 240/96, OJ 1996 L31/2.

[33] Commission Regulation (EC) No 772/2004 of 27 April 2004 on the application of Article 81(3) of the Treaty to categories of technology transfer agreements.

[34] Guidelines on the application of Article 81 of the EC Treaty to technology transfer agreements, 2004/C 101/02.

[35] See consultation process at http://ec.europa.eu/competition/consultations/2013_technology_transfer/index_en.html.

[36] Commission Notice, Guidelines on Vertical Restraints, OJ 2010/C 130/01.

[37] Guidelines on the application of Article 101 of the Treaty on the Functioning of the European Union to technology transfer agreements, OJ 2014/C L 89/3 (TTBER Guidelines).

[38] Commission Notice, Guidelines on Vertical Restraints, OJ 2010/C 130/01, Art 1(b). Note that the TTBE and the research and development and specialisation block exemptions are framed so that they do not apply to the same agreement.

[39] TTBER Guidelines (n 38), para 12.

[40] Market share is defined in terms of presence of the licensed technology on the relevant technology, or product and geographic market and includes the licensor's and all its current licensees' share of the market. TTBER, Art 1(j)–(m).

[41] Commission Notice, Guidelines on Vertical Restraints, OJ 2010/C 130/01, Art 3(1).   [42] ibid, Art 3(2).

[43] ibid, Art 4.   [44] ibid, Art 4(1), (2).

(b) the limitation of output, except limitations on the output of contract products imposed on the licensee in a non-reciprocal agreement or imposed on only one of the licensees in a reciprocal agreement;

(c) the allocation of markets or customers except:

 (i) the obligation on the licensor and/or the licensee, in a non-reciprocal agreement, not to produce with the licensed technology rights within the exclusive territory reserved to the other party, or to sell into the exclusive customer group reserved for the other party,

 (ii) the restriction, in a non-reciprocal agreement, of active sales by the licensee into the exclusive territory of another or to the licensor, provided the other was not a competing undertaking at the time of the conclusion of its own licence,

 (iii) the obligation on the licensee to produce the contract products only for its own use, provided that the licensee is not restricted in selling the product actively and passively as spare parts for its own products,

 (iv) the obligation on the licensee, in a non-reciprocal agreement, to produce the contract products only for a particular customer when a licence is granted to create an alternative source of supply for them,

(d) the restriction of the licensee's ability to exploit its own technology or the restriction of the ability of any of the parties to the agreement to carry out research and development, unless such latter restriction is indispensable to prevent the disclosure of the licensed know-how to third parties.

• Where the parties are not in competition then prohibited clauses include:

(a) the restriction of a party's ability to determine its prices when selling products to third parties, without prejudice to the possibility of imposing a maximum sale price or recommending a sale price, provided that it does not amount to a fixed or minimum sale price as a result of pressure from, or incentives offered by, any of the parties;

(b) the restriction of the territory into which, or of the customers to whom, the licensee may passively sell the contract products, except:

 (i) the restriction of passive sales into an exclusive territory or to an exclusive customer group reserved for the licensor,

 (ii) the obligation to produce the contract products only for its own use, provided that the licensee is not restricted in selling the contract products actively and passively as spare parts for its own products,

 (iii) the obligation to produce the contract products only for a particular customer, where the licence was granted in order to create an alternative source of supply for that customer,

 (iv) the restriction of sales to end users by a licensee operating at the wholesale level of trade,

 (v) the restriction of sales to unauthorised distributors by the members of a selective distribution system;

(c) the restriction of active or passive sales to end users by a licensee which is a member of a selective distribution system and which operates at the retail level, without prejudice to the possibility of prohibiting a member of the system from operating out of an unauthorised place of establishment.

 Exercise

Read the TTBER and the TTBER Guidelines. Explain why these particular clauses are considered to be restrictive of competition and thus prohibited in IP agreements. Note the rights which are covered by the TTBER.

Excluded restrictions

20.37   The TTBER also contains excluded restrictions.[45] These are clauses that do not fall under the TTBER and thus require individual assessment as to their pro- or anti-competitive effect. Their inclusion in an agreement does not prevent the TTBER applying to the rest of the agreement. Excluded restrictions include:

- obligations on the licensee to grant exclusive licences-back (or assignments-back) of improvements or new applications to the licensor or a third party;[46]

- no-challenge clauses—although the licensor can include a provision for termination of the exclusive licence in the event that a challenge to the validity of the intellectual property right is made;[47]

- obligations limiting the ability of the licensee to exploit its own technology;[48]

- restrictions on either party's R&D activities.[49]

 Question

What do you understand to be the differences between hardcore and excluded restrictions, and why does the treatment of the latter differ to the former?

20.38   The TTBER Guidelines state that analysis of the potential anti-competitive effect of an agreement should focus on the actual or potential competition that would have existed without the agreement. An example is given relating to inter-technology competition where two undertakings established in different member states cross-license competing technologies and undertake not to sell products in each other's home markets. Potential competition existing prior to the agreement is thus restricted. Equally, where a licensor places obligations on their licensees not to use competing technologies, the technology belonging to third parties would not be used. The result is that actual or potential competition that would have existed in the absence of the agreement is restricted.

20.39   On intra-technology competition, a licensor might restrict its licensees from competing with each other. Any potential competition that could have existed between the licensees is restricted. Examples of restrictions would include vertical price fixing and territorial or customer sales restrictions between licensees.[50]

Web link

The TTBER Guidelines contain useful wider guidance on the types of agreements that would be covered by the TTBER, and also on how agreements outside the TTBER should be evaluated. This can be important to agreements involving cross-licensing between several parties owning different sets of IP, which is relevant to the making and development of one product, as the TTBER applies only to agreements between two parties. The TTBER Guidelines also consider settlement agreements, including pay for delay (when a generic manufacturer acknowledges a patent which it has challenged, and refrains from selling their product for a period, in return for payment), no challenge clauses, licensing out of patents pool, and licensing when a patented technology has become essential to comply with a standard. The TTBER Guidelines can be found at http://eur-lex.europa.eu/legal-content/EN/ALL/?uri=uriserv:OJ.C_.2014.089.01.0003.01.ENG.

[45] ibid, Art 5.   [46] TTBER Guidelines (n 38), paras 129–130.   [47] ibid, paras 133–140.
[48] ibid, para 141.   [49] ibid, paras 142–143.
[50] ibid, Part 2.

Consequences of an agreement being in breach of Article 101(1) TFEU

20.40   If an agreement is in breach of Article 101(1) TFEU and does not benefit from the block exemption or come within Article 101(3), then:

- the agreement is automatically void and unenforceable;
- the Commission can impose a fine on the parties;[51]
- in the UK, directors of companies risk being disqualified under section 204 of the Enterprise Act 2002.

Exercise

Construct a decision tree showing the steps that need to be taken to ascertain whether clauses in an IP licensing agreement would fall within the parameters of the TTBER and explain the questions that would need to be asked at each step.

20.41   A number of concerns have been expressed over the application of the TTBER. These include the following:

- There is a need for parties (and their advisers) to assess their relevant market share to see if they can benefit from the block exemption.
- Agreements which are initially exempt can cease to be so if the market shares of the parties increase. This might occur if cutting-edge technology is involved.
- The regime will be implemented by national courts and competition authorities. This may lead to inconsistencies in approach.
- The Commission can withdraw the benefit of the block exemption if it considers that it offends Article 101(1) TFEU. This could lead to uncertainty for the parties.

Question

Can you think of any other difficulties that may be experienced with the application of the TTBER? What advantages do you think the TTBER provides?

Key points on intellectual property and agreements between undertakings: Article 101 TFEU

- Article 101 TFEU concerns agreements between undertakings which have the object or effect of preventing, restricting, or distorting competition within the common market, and which may affect trade between member states.
- The TTBER is relevant to undertakings which enter into technology transfer (licensing) agreements where those agreements deal with inter alia patents, know-how, software copyright, or a mixture of these IPRs.
- Where an agreement contains hardcore restrictions, it will fall outwith the TTBER.
- The pro- and anti-competitive effect of excluded restrictions need to be assessed on a case-by-case basis.

---

[51] See Guidelines on the method of setting fines imposed pursuant to Article 23(2)(a) of Regulation No 1/2003, 2006/ C 210/02.

Intellectual property and abuse of a dominant position: Article 102 TFEU

20.42   Article 102 TFEU concerns the prevention of abuse of market power by undertakings which occupy a dominant position within the common market.

> **Article 102 TFEU (ex Art 82 EC, Art 86 EEC)**
>
> Any abuse by one or more undertakings of a dominant position within the common market or in a substantial part of it shall be prohibited as incompatible with the common market insofar as it may affect trade between Member States.
>
> Such abuse may, in particular, consist in:
>
> (a) directly or indirectly imposing unfair purchase or selling prices or other unfair trading conditions;
>
> (b) limiting production, markets or technical development to the prejudice of consumers;
>
> (c) applying dissimilar conditions to equivalent transactions with other trading parties, thereby placing them at a competitive disadvantage;
>
> (d) making the conclusion of contracts subject to acceptance by the other parties of supplementary obligations which, by their nature or according to commercial usage, have no connection with the subject of such contracts.

20.43   All IPRs give some form of exclusive right to the owner. But it does not follow that the IP owner occupies a dominant position and is able to exert market power. Market power implies that a consumer will have no choice but to deal with the dominant entity—the monopolist: in other words, that there will be no substitutes for the product or services on offer by the monopolist. That is often not the case for the subject matter of IP. If the price of a painting by a favoured artist exceeds what most can afford, then another less well-known but more affordable artist may find favour; if the price of a patented remedy for a headache increases, then alternative therapies may have to be found; if the price of a well-advertised branded product exceeds reasonable expectations, then the consumer may look for other varieties. The extent to which other options cannot be found or will not find favour with a consumer may depend on, for example, technical advances or fashion.[52]

20.44   However, it is with the expansion of both the scope and subject matter of IPRs to cover, for example, new technological advances used by consumers in daily life, medicines essential to human health, and to compilations of information that cannot be obtained elsewhere that increasing attention is now being focused on the extent to which Article 102 TFEU may, in particular, be used to require the owner of an IP right to license its IP to a third party.

Dominant position

20.45   Article 102 TFEU refers to undertakings which occupy a dominant position. A dominant position relates to a position of economic strength enjoyed by an undertaking on the relevant market: the key test is that an entity must be able to hinder the maintenance of effective competition and be able to act to an appreciable extent independently of competitors and consumers, without loss of customers and/or competitor activity in response.[53] A dominant position in and of itself does not cause an entity to fall under the prohibition in Article 102 TFEU.[54] However, when that dominant position is *abused*, perhaps by foreclosing effective competition on the relevant market, then Article 102 TFEU may be brought into play.

20.46   Generally, abuse has been described as conduct by a dominant firm which seriously and unjustifiably distorts competition or causes it further to weaken.[55] This is an objective test, and may impose burdens on dominant undertakings not faced by others.

---

[52] D Llewelyn and T Aplin, *Cornish, Llewelyn and Aplin Intellectual Property: Patents, Copyright, Trade Marks and Allied Rights*, para 1-46ff.

[53] Case 27/76 *United Brands Co v Commission of the European Communities* [1978] ECR 207, para 65.

[54] Case C-78/70 *Deutsche Grammophon v Metro* [1971] ECR 487 and Case C-52/07 *Kanal 5 Ltd v Föreningen Svenska Tonsättares Internationella Musikbyrå (STIM) UPA* [2008] ECR I-9275, paras 21.26ff.

[55] See V Rose, D Bailey, C Bellamy, and G Child, *Bellamy and Child European Union Law of Competition* (7th edn, 2013), 785.

Case law

20.47 In the early cases, the ECJ made it clear that mere ownership of an IPR, and exercising it, for example to gain higher prices, would not necessarily involve a breach of what is now Article 102 TFEU.[56]

■ Case C-24/67 *Parke Davis v Probel* [1968] ECR 55

The ECJ considered whether the exercise of patent rights could be an abuse of a dominant position. Parke Davis, a US company, held a patent in the Netherlands for a certain chemical process. Probel delivered chloramphenicol to the Netherlands which had been sold freely in Italy. Parke Davis used its patent to complain.

The ECJ held:

- the existence of IPRs are not affected by Article 86;
- the exercise of rights cannot fall under Article 86 in the absence of abuse of a dominant position;
- a higher sale price does not necessarily constitute abuse.

The Court went on to say:[57]

> For this prohibition to apply it is thus necessary that three elements shall be present together: the existence of a dominant position, the abuse of this position and the possibility that trade between Member States may be affected thereby. Although a patent confers on its holder a special protection at national level, it does not follow that the exercise of the rights thus conferred implies the presence together of all three elements in question. It could only do so if the use of the patent were to degenerate into an abuse of the abovementioned protection.[58]

Thus, the mere exercise of IPRs does not constitute an abuse. However, the exercise of IPRs when used as an instrument of abuse, and where trade between member states may be affected, may be prevented under this Article.

Article 102 TFEU and the refusal to supply

20.48 One of the most interesting areas in which the interaction between Article 102 TFEU and the exercise of IPRs has occurred is in relation to the refusal to supply. When, if at all, can the owner of an IPR be required to supply a third party on the basis that a refusal to supply would amount to the abuse of a dominant position? After all, IPRs, by their nature, give to the owner exclusive rights. Could, or should, the application of competition law be used to limit the exercise of the right? Or should the IP owner have the absolute right, within the parameters of the monopoly, to decide not to license that right to a third party?

■ Case C-238/87 *Volvo v Veng* [1988] ECR 6211

A refusal to license was considered in *Volvo v Veng*. Volvo held the design right in the UK over front wings for cars. Veng imported panels into the UK from Italy and Denmark, where they had been manufactured without Volvo's consent. Volvo alleged infringement of its UK registered designs. Veng's defence was that Volvo's refusal to grant a licence was an abuse of a dominant position when Veng was willing to pay a reasonable royalty for a licence.

The question for this discussion that was put before the ECJ related to Volvo's refusal to grant a licence to others. Was this an abuse of a dominant position?

---

[56] Case C-24/67 *Parke Davis v Probel* [1968] ECR 55; see also Case C-78/70 *Deutsche Grammophon*, note 53.
[57] Case C-24/67 *Parke Davis v Probel* [1968] ECR 55, para 4.
[58] Case C-24/67 *Parke Davis v Probel* [1968] ECR 55, para 4.

The ECJ said:[59]

> It must also be emphasised that the right of the proprietor of a protected design to prevent third parties from manufacturing and selling or importing, without its consent, products incorporating the design constitutes the very subject-matter of his exclusive right. It follows that an obligation imposed upon the proprietor of a protected design to grant to third parties, even in return for a reasonable royalty, a licence for the supply of products incorporating the design would lead to the proprietor thereof being deprived of the substance of his exclusive right, and that a refusal to grant such a licence cannot in itself constitute an abuse of a dominant position.

So, a refusal in and of itself would not be an abuse of a dominant position, as a refusal to license others is part of the '*very subject-matter*' of an IP right. There has to be something more. The question is what more is needed? The ECJ went on to indicate those circumstances in which the exercise of an IP right may go beyond the subject matter of an IP right, and thus constitute an abuse of a dominant position:[60]

> the exercise by the proprietor of an exclusive right in a registered design in respect of car body panels may be prohibited by Article 86 if it involves, on the part of an undertaking holding a dominant position, certain abusive conduct such as the arbitrary refusal to supply spare parts to independent repairers, the fixing of prices for spare parts at an unfair level, or a decision no longer to produce spare parts for a particular model even though many cars of that model are still in circulation, provided that such conduct is liable to affect trade between Member States.

20.49   The examples given by the Court are interesting, and can be seen as related to the prohibitions laid down in Article 102 TFEU. So, for example, a decision no longer to produce spare parts for a particular model even though cars of that model were still in circulation would certainly prejudice consumers, and thus fall under Article 102(b) TFEU. Nevertheless, the mere refusal to license a third party (as opposed to an arbitrary refusal to supply spare parts to independent repairers) did not, at this stage, amount to an abuse of a dominant position.

 Question

Why might a refusal to license be a contentious issue both for the IP owner and for the third party seeking the licence?

20.50   Despite the position taken by the ECJ in *Volvo v Veng*, the question as to when and if a refusal to license a third party might amount to an abuse of a dominant position has come up in subsequent case law. In 1995, for the first time, the ECJ held that in *exceptional circumstances* a refusal to license might constitute an abuse of a dominant position. The case in which this arose was *RTE and ITP v Commission* ('*Magill*').

■ **Joined Cases C-241/91 P and C-242/91 P *RTE and ITP v Commission* (*Magill*) [1995] ECR I-743**

Television programmes were (and are) broadcast by different companies in the UK and Ireland, and only they held the details of the programmes to be broadcast each week. They disseminated weekly listings of their own output. Given the low level of originality in each jurisdiction the listings were protected by copyright. Magill, a Dublin company, put out a publication listing channels received in most Irish households. Almost immediately it was sued for copyright infringement. Magill complained to the Commission, which found the conduct of the Irish broadcasters to be an abuse of a dominant position. The Commission ordered them to supply all third parties with weekly listings in advance.

---

[59] *Volvo v Veng* [1988] ECR 6211, para 8.
[60] ibid, para 10. See also *CICRA v Renault* [1988] ECR 6039.

The ECJ upheld the decision of the Commission saying:

- mere ownership of an IP right cannot confer a dominant position;

- in the absence of harmonisation, the conditions for granting protection of IPRs is a matter for national rules;

- the exclusive right of reproduction is part of the author's right so that a refusal to grant a licence, even if it is the act of an undertaking holding a dominant position, cannot in itself constitute abuse of a dominant position;

- however, the exercise of an exclusive right by the proprietor may in *exceptional circumstances* involve abusive conduct.

The ECJ emphasised that the television companies were the only sources of the basic information on programme scheduling which is the indispensable raw material for compiling a weekly television guide. This meant that viewers who wished to obtain information on the available programmes had no choice but to buy the weekly guides from each TV company. The refusal of the companies to provide the basic information by relying on national copyright provisions thus prevented the appearance of a new product for which there was a consumer demand. Such a refusal constituted an abuse under Article 86 EC for which there was no justification.

The ECJ set out those *exceptional circumstances* in which a refusal to license may constitute an instrument of abuse. These are where there is:

- no actual or potential substitute for the product for which a licence is sought;

- demand for a product which is not provided by the rights owner;

- no objective justification for the refusal to license;

- interference in an adjacent/secondary market.

Discussion point   For answer **guidance** visit **www.oup.com/uk/brown5e.**

Can you think of any other examples in which these exceptional circumstances might apply to require the owner of an IP right to license that right to a third party?

20.51   *Magill* was considered by the Court of First Instance (CFI) in *Tierce Ladbroke v Commission*.[61] This involved the refusal to grant a copyright licence to enable the showing of films of horse races in betting shops. The CFI found that the refusal was acceptable as it did not concern a service which was essential for the exercise of the activity in question (betting). Neither did the refusal prevent the emergence of a new product.[62]

20.52   The matter was considered again by the ECJ in *IMS Health v NDC Health*:

■ **Case 418/01 *IMS Health v NDC Health* [2004] ECR I-5039**

IMS delivered sales data and other information on pharmaceutical services to pharmacies in Germany using a 'brick like' structure. This structure divided Germany into 1,860 areas, or 'bricks', corresponding to a particular geographical area. This structure, which had been developed by IMS with the assistance of its clients, was delivered free of charge to pharmacies and doctors' surgeries. It became the *de facto* standard for delivery of this type of pharmaceutical information. The structure was also protected by copyright. NDC developed its own structure derived from that of IMS. At the request of IMS the German court prohibited

---

[61] Case T-504/93 P *Tierce Ladbroke v Commission* [1997] ECR II-923.
[62] See also Case C-7/97 *Oscar Bronner GmbH & Co KG v Mediaprint* [1998] ECR I-7791.

NDC from using any structure derived from that belonging to IMS. However, the court also sought clarification from the ECJ as to whether a right holder's refusal to grant a licence constituted an abuse of a dominant position in circumstances where clients would reject any alternative competing pharmaceutical information unless they were delivered in the same way as the IMS product.

The ECJ, after referring to *Volvo AB v Veng*[63] and *Magill*,[64] reiterated that an exclusive right of reproduction forms part of an IP owner's rights. A refusal to grant a licence, even by a dominant undertaking, could not, of itself, constitute an abuse of Article 82 EC except in *exceptional circumstances*. The Court also repeated what it had said in earlier cases concerning the three cumulative criteria that must be met for a refusal to be regarded as abusive:

- the undertaking which requested the licence must intend to offer new products or services not offered by the owner of the copyright and for which there is a potential consumer demand—in other words, the refusal must prevent the emergence of a new product for which there is potential demand; it must not merely duplicate existing goods or services;

- the refusal cannot be objectively justified;

- the refusal must be such as to exclude competition on a *secondary market*. In this case it was for the national court to determine whether the brick structure constituted an *indispensable* factor in the downstream supply of regional pharmaceutical sales data. For the instant case the court said the test was whether the refusal reserved to IMS the market for the supply of pharmaceutical sales data in the member states by eliminating all competition in that market.

20.53   The judgment of the ECJ has led to considerable uncertainty in a number of areas. One question relates to what is meant by 'indispensable'. The ECJ said that determining whether a product was indispensable was a matter for the national court to determine, in the light of the evidence submitted to it. The national court must consider whether there are products or services which constitute alternative solutions. The ECJ gave some guidance as to the factors that may be taken into account in the instant case:[65]

> account must be taken of the fact that a high level of participation by the pharmaceutical laboratories in the improvement of the 1860 brick structure protected by copyright, on the supposition that it is proven, has created a dependency by users in regard to that structure, particularly at a technical level. In such circumstances, it is likely that those laboratories would have to make exceptional organisational and financial efforts in order to acquire the studies on regional sales of pharmaceutical products presented on the basis of a structure other than that protected by copyright. The supplier of that alternative structure might therefore be obliged to offer terms which are such as to rule out any economic viability of business on a scale comparable to that of the undertaking which controls the protected structure.

This begs the question as to whether the outcome would have been the same had the outside organisations not been involved in the creation of the brick structure but the product had still achieved significant market penetration due to the innovation of the right holder. While the creation of a new system (with or without the assistance of third parties) might be expensive, how expensive might it have to be before a compulsory licence might be granted? The ECJ referred to 'any economic viability'. But what may be economically viable for some third parties may not be economically viable for others. This, in turn, raises the question as to whether the test for economic viability depends on the entity seeking the licence.

Other questions also arise over what is meant by 'new products'. Certainly, the ECJ referred to new products as those not offered by the owner and for which there was a consumer demand, but also indicated that the party seeking the licence should not intend to limit itself essentially to duplicating the goods or services already offered on the secondary market.[66]

---

[63] See *Volvo v Veng* [1988] ECR 6211.   [64] See para 20.50.

[65] Case 418/01 *IMS Health v NDC Health* [2004] ECR-I-5039, see para 20.52.

[66] For further discussion on the 'new product' requirement, see H Meinberg, 'From *Magill* to *IMS Health*: the new product requirement and the diversity of intellectual property rights' [2006] EIPR 398.

20.54   The decision of the ECJ in *Sot. Lelos Kai*[67] challenged once again the interface between competition and IP law, with a particular focus on lack of objective justification. The case involves the pharmaceutical market and also concerns free movement of goods (see also para 19.27). The entry of the refusal to licence case law to fields outside information and spare parts caused fear in some quarters. Do you think the decision below strikes the right balance?

■ **Joined Cases C-468/06 to C-478/06 *Sot Lelos Kai Sia EE and Others v GlaxoSmithKline Aeve Farmadeftikon Proionton (formerly Glaxowellcome Aeve)* [2008] ECR I-7139**

In this case, the ECJ was faced with the following question:[68]

whether there is an abuse of a dominant position contrary to Art. 82 EC if a pharmaceutical company occupying such a position on the national market for certain medicinal products refuses to meet orders sent to it by wholesalers on account of the fact that those wholesalers are involved in parallel exports of those products to other Member States.

The ECJ looked into whether GSK had an objective justification for its refusal to supply medicinal products. The ECJ ruled that:[69]

even in Member States where the prices of medicines are subject to State regulation, parallel trade is liable to exert pressure on prices and, consequently, to create financial benefits not only for the social health insurance funds, but equally for the patients concerned, for whom the proportion of the price of medicines for which they are responsible will be lower.

The ECJ noted also that despite its dominant position, a pharmaceutical company may nevertheless take reasonable and proportional steps to protect its own commercial interests. The Court said that:[70]

Thus, although a pharmaceuticals company in a dominant position in a Member State where prices are relatively low cannot be allowed to cease to honour the ordinary orders of an existing customer for the sole reason that that customer, in addition to supplying the market in that Member State, exports part of the quantities ordered to other Member States with higher prices, it is none the less permissible for that company to counter in a reasonable and proportionate way the threat to its own commercial interests potentially posed by the activities of an undertaking which wishes to be supplied in the first Member State with significant quantities of products that are essentially destined for parallel export.

20.55   It should also be borne in mind that the ECJ in *IMS* stated that for there to be abuse, it was 'sufficient' for the three-step cumulative test discussed previously (see paras 20.52ff). This might not, therefore, be the only test. In the light of this, and also given its importance when considering the application of competition law in the technology sector, the litigation between the European Commission and Microsoft in *Commission v Microsoft* deserves special mention.

Commission v Microsoft

The case

20.56   Microsoft has been pursued by competition authorities regarding its power and the exercise of it.[71] In the EU, in 1998 Sun Microsystems lodged a complaint with the European Commission alleging that Microsoft had abused its dominant position in the desktop operating system market. Sun Microsystems argued that Microsoft's refusal to supply interface information to allow Sun Microsystem to create workgroup server operating systems that would interoperate with Microsoft's Windows desktop and server operating systems, amounted to an abuse of Microsoft's dominant position.

---

[67] Joined Cases C-468/06–C-478/06 [2008] ECR I-7139 [2008] ECR I-7139.   [68] ibid, para 28.
[69] ibid, para 56.   [70] ibid, para 71.
[71] Note also litigation in the United States, *US v Microsoft Corp* 231 F Supp 2d 144 (DCC 2002) concerned the bundling of Microsoft's Internet Explorer browser with its Windows desktop operating system. This led to a settlement in 2002.

Competitors and interoperability

20.57   By way of background, if a competitor in the market wishes to make a computer program that interoperates with an existing program, then it is essential for that competitor to obtain information with regard to the interface of the existing program. Thus, if a programmer wished to develop a spreadsheet program that would interoperate with Microsoft Word such that information could be passed between the two programs, then the programmer would need to know details of the interface to enable him to develop an interoperable program (see para 5.54). Sun Microsystems wanted to develop workgroup server operating systems that would interoperate with Microsoft's PC operating system. But Microsoft refused to supply the necessary information. In March 2004 (just before the decision of the ECJ in *IMS* was delivered) the Commission found that Microsoft had abused its market power by deliberately restricting interoperability between Windows PCs and non-Microsoft workgroup servers. The Commission imposed a fine of €497.2 million, and required certain undertakings from Microsoft concerning future behaviour.

20.58   When considering the case, the Commission stated that all circumstances should be taken into account, and that it was not limited by the *Magill* test.[72] In addition to the fine (imposed in part for this abuse and in part for the tying discussed in para 20.60), Microsoft was required to disclose complete and accurate information concerning the interface sufficient to allow those developing non-Microsoft workgroup servers to achieve full interoperability with Windows PCs and servers. This remedy was designed to allow competition to open up in the market for workgroup servers. Where the information is made available to parties in the European Economic Area (EEA), then Microsoft is entitled to reasonable remuneration. In addition, the information that is disclosed must be updated each time Microsoft places a new version of the relevant products on the market.

Bundling and customers

20.59   This Commission investigation was expanded in 2000 to consider the effects of the bundling of Microsoft's media player with its Windows 2000 PC operating system. The Commission decision also required Microsoft to offer PC manufacturers a version of the operating system without its media player. This gives the PC manufacturer the choice of whether to install Microsoft's media player onto the desktop, or that of another manufacturer. The decision thus lies first with the PC manufacturer, but through that the customer is able to decide which products to take. The Commission said Microsoft could offer a bundled version of its operating system with its media player, but was prohibited from using commercial, technological, or contractual terms (eg discounting) designed to make the unbundled version of Windows less attractive or which compromised its performance.

Review of the decision

20.60   Microsoft sought judicial review of the decision before the CFI.

■   Case T-201/04 *Microsoft Corp v Commission of European Communities* [2007] ECR II-3601

The CFI found that Microsoft had:

- refused to supply its competitors with 'interoperability information' or to permit them to use the information to develop products which competed with its own on the group server operating system market; and

- it had engaged in the tying of Windows Media Player with the Windows PC operating system affecting competition on the media player market.

---

[72] Commission Decision relating to a proceeding under Article 82 of the EC Treaty (Case COMP/C-3/37.792 *Microsoft*) March 2004, http://ec.europa.eu/competition/antitrust/cases/dec_docs/37792/37792_4177_1.pdf, para 558.

The refusal to supply the interoperability information

20.61   The CFI noted that while undertakings are, as a rule, free to choose business partners, in some circumstances a refusal to supply by a dominant undertaking can constitute an abuse of a dominant position unless it is objectively justified. For this, the CFI considered that it should apply the *IMS* test, which was by then available. The three preconditions were that:

- the refusal must relate to a product or service indispensable to the exercise of an activity on a neighbouring market;
- the refusal must be such as to exclude any effective competition on that market;
- the refusal must prevent the appearance of a new product for which there is demand.

The CFI found the Commission was correct in finding these conditions satisfied. The information protocols were indispensable for the development of a new product for which there was unmet consumer demand and without which there was a risk of elimination of viable competition. There was no objective justification for the refusal, even on the basis of intellectual property. The CFI agreed with the Commission's view that the points it had made regarding the need to balance innovation incentives was part of the objective justification. It was a not new test, as Microsoft had alleged.

20.62   In making this finding the CFI did, however, expand on the *IMS* criteria in two ways: first, that it considered that a 'risk' rather than a likelihood of elimination would suffice and that competition should be 'viable'; and, secondly, that the need for a new product was not the only relevant requirement but mentioned also technical development. What precisely is meant by these continues to be the subject of intense academic debate and will no doubt resurface in the courts in due course.

The tying (bundling) of Windows Media Player and Windows client PC operating system

20.63   The CFI upheld the part of the Commission decision relating to the bundling of Windows Media Player. The CFI agreed that Microsoft had a dominant position on the client PC operating systems market; that there was separate consumer demand for media players; that different companies were present in the market supplying the products; and that consumers continue to acquire competing media players separately. However, a consumer could not acquire the Windows operating system without simultaneously acquiring Windows Media Player. Through this there was a significant risk that competition would be weakened in such a way that an effective competitive structure could not be ensured in the near future. Microsoft had demonstrated no objective justification for this bundling. Consequently, the remedy imposed by the Commission was proportionate. Microsoft retained the right to continue to offer the version of Windows bundled with Windows Media Player and was required only to make it possible for consumers to obtain the operating system without that media player, a measure which does not mean any change in Microsoft's current technical practice other than the development of that version of Windows.

Exercise

Read in full the judgment of the ECJ in *IMS* and the decision of the CFI in the *Microsoft* case. What factors strike you in the discussions concerning secondary markets?

Do you think it correct that Microsoft be compelled to grant what is in effect a compulsory licence of its IP, and to what extent do you think this would be consistent with the compulsory licensing provisions in the Berne Convention and in TRIPS?

Essential facilities doctrine

20.64   Although the term 'essential facility' has not been used by the EU Courts, some have argued that the application of competition law to IP borrows heavily from the doctrine of essential facilities.[73] The concept of an essential facility developed in relation to physical infrastructure—for instance, a port or an electricity network—could be regarded as an essential facility. It is 'a facility or infrastructure which is necessary for reaching customers and/or enabling competitors to carry on their business'.[74] A facility is considered essential if it cannot be duplicated, or its duplication would be very difficult or expensive. If access to an essential facility is denied, this may be considered as an abuse of a dominant position, especially where it inhibits competition in a downstream market. Given that the ECJ has not explicitly embraced the terminology, it is difficult to know the extent to which it could be argued as applicable to IP cases, although *Magill* and *IMS* suggest that it is, albeit called by a different name.[75]

The proper boundaries between IP rights and the application of Article 102 TFEU

20.65   After the finding of the ECJ in *IMS, Sot Lelos Kai,* and *Microsoft,* there were concerns that an increasing number of cases likely to come before the Court of Justice (and national courts) concerning refusal to license IPRs. This has not in fact come about to the extent feared or hoped, with litigation rather focusing on standards and IP, as is considered in paragraph 20.66 and also paragraph 20.78. But at the heart of this is the same issue: where do the proper boundaries lie between compulsory licensing of an IPR and the grant and exercise of that right? As was stated at the outset of this chapter, the boundaries of IP have been expanding, drawing more and more subject matter within their scope, and thus within the exclusive domain of the right holder. Exploitation of IPRs also becomes increasingly complex, with the potential for tier upon tier of rights to be bound up in the ultimate delivery of a product or service to an end user. Ultimately, and as has been suggested in *Magill* and *IMS,* those rights can prove detrimental to the emergence of competition in secondary markets.

20.66   This is all the more so where one (or more) of those IPRs emerges as an industry 'standard', enabling the right holder to prevent the emergence of any form of competition in a secondary or related market; indeed, this may also be considered an essential facility, discussed in paragraph 20.64. Standards can arise formally through agreement, as noted in the discussion of horizontal agreements at paragraph 20.18, and through behaviour in the market, as was the case in *IMS*. IMS took the time and effort to liaise with customers to tailor a product that would meet their needs, which in turn meant that this structure became the accepted standard in the industry, thus potentially making it more likely that compulsory licensing will be ordered to allow others to compete in the secondary markets with IMS's own customers. A danger is that the overuse of competition law to require the licensing of IPRs might inhibit innovation.

20.67   At this point the tension between competition law and the exercise of IPRs becomes palpable. *Should* competition law be used in this way to define the exercise of IPRs? If a response to this question is 'no', then the further question arises as to the proper role of IP law: what is it that IP law is seeking to achieve, and does the law as it is currently constituted achieve those aims? *Sot Lelos Kai* illustrates that there are circumstances in which a company may take reasonable and proportional steps to protect its commercial interests, even where that might be construed as being an abuse of a dominant position, as long as it takes place within recognised parameters. As relations between business in the marketplace become ever more complex, the question becomes as to how many exceptions might need to be developed to the general rule or whether the shape of the general rule, and indeed the shape of the IP right, should be rethought.

---

[73] See, eg, Whish and Bailey, *Intellectual Property* (n 2), Ch 17; for discussion from the US perspective, see H Hovenkamp, MD Janis, and MA Lemley, 'Unilateral refusals to license' (2006) 2(1) JCL&E 1.

[74] See 'Glossary E' prepared by the European Commission DG Competition at http://ec.europa.eu/translation/spanish/documents/glossary_competition_archived_en.pdf; see the decision of the European Commission *in B & I Line plc v Sealink Harbours Ltd and Sealink Stena Ltd* [1992] 5 CMLR 255.

[75] Although note its place in Case C-7/97 *Oscar Bronner GmbH & Co KG v Mediaprint* [1998] ECR I-7791, AG paras 35–52, and see also the discussion by the High Court in *Attheraces v British Horseracing Board* [2005] EWHC 1553 (Ch), in which pre-race data were considered an essential facility.

20.68   The European Commission issued guidance in 2009 regarding its future enforcement priorities.[76] Echoing the discussion of the rule of reason at the start of this chapter, the guidance focuses on an economic approach, and also not only on protecting the consumer but on developing the market.[77] The guidance states that it will see refusal as a priority if the refusal relates to a product or service that is objectively necessary to be able to compete effectively on a downstream market, the refusal is likely to lead to the elimination of effective competition on the downstream market, and the refusal (in response to an actual request, although the refusal may be constructive, rather than actual) is likely to lead to consumer harm. The guidance refers to *Magill* and *IMS* and the need for a new product and technical development, but does also suggest a wider willingness to intervene.[78]

20.69   This approach would be consistent with more proactive steps which have been taken by the Commission in respect of other IP-related issues, looking outside the *IMS* test. Examples are the European Commission's inquiry into the pharmaceutical industry from 2008–09 regarding blocking or delaying generic competition.[79] This has led to montioring of 'pay-for-delay' patent settlement agreements, which arise when a generic competitor agrees not to enter the market and drops its challenge to validity of the patent, in return for a payment.[80] The Commission also investigated AstraZeneca regarding its conduct in respect of IP and marketing (legitimate in itself), which had an impact on regulatory procedures and market entry of generic drugs after IP had expired. This led to a finding of abuse, which was upheld by the Court of Justice.[81]

 Exercise

Review the underlying justifications for IP as found in Chapter 1. What do you think the position should be as regards compulsory licensing in cases such as *Magill*, *IMS*, and *Microsoft* and ongoing regulatory action from the Commission?

Key points on intellectual property and abuse of a dominant position: Article 102 TFEU

- Article 102 TFEU regulates the abuse of market power by undertakings which occupy a dominant position within the common market.

- In IP-related cases, questions relating to abuse of a dominant position have arisen in connection with a refusal to supply (license) a product protected by an IPR.

---

[76] 'Communication from the Commission—Guidance on the Commission's Enforcement Priorities in Applying Article 82 of the EC Treaty to Abusive Exclusionary Conduct by Dominant Undertakings' (24 February 2009), 2009 OJ C45/7.

[77] ibid, paras 5–8, 19–22; AC Witt, 'The Commission's guidance paper on abusive exclusionary conduct—more radical than it appears?' (2010) 35(2) EL Rev 214–35.

[78] 'Communication from the Commission—Guidance on the Commission's Enforcement Priorities in Applying Article 82 of the EC Treaty to Abusive Exclusionary Conduct by Dominant Undertakings' (24 February 2009), 2009 OJ C45/7, paras 75 et seq.

[79] http://ec.europa.eu/competition/sectors/pharmaceuticals/inquiry/communication_en.pdf.

[80] For details of report and ongoing activity in respect of the monitoring of patent settlements, see http://ec.europa.eu/competition/sectors/pharmaceuticals/inquiry. See also Press Release from 2014 regarding Servier at http://europa.eu/rapid/press-release_IP-14-799_en.htm; Case T-472/13 *H Lundbeck v European Commission* [2016] 5 CMLR 18; and consideration at UK national level, *Generics v Competition and Markets Authority* [2018] CAT 4.

[81] Commission Decision of 15 June 2005 relating to a proceeding under Article 82 of the EC Treaty and Article 54 of the EEA Agreement (Case COMP/A. 37.507/F3), http://ec.europa.eu/competition/antitrust/cases/dec_docs/37507/37507_193_6.pdf; Case T-321/05 *AstraZeneca AB v European Commission* [2010] ECR II-2805 and decision of Court of Justice C457/10 [0213] 4 CMLR 7. A similar approach was taken by an Italian regulator in respect of divisional patent applications, *Autorità Garante Delle Concorrenza e del Mercato v Pfizer Italia Srl* (Unreported) and commentary in C Stothers and MV Kerckhove, 'Is winter coming? The competition chill continues in Italian Antitrust Authority v Pfizer (Xalatan)' (2014) 36(11) EIPR 729–32. See also at UK level *Reckitt Benckiser Healthcare* CE/8931/08 OFT (2011) and early resolution agreement.

> • The boundaries of those 'exceptional circumstances' in which a compulsory licence will be granted are still being tested—there is a real risk of the more successful you are, the more you may be restricted.

EU competition law in the UK courts: Eurodefences and limits on remedies

20.70   The main distinction between the application of EU competition law and UK competition law is that there is no threshold requirement that trade between member states be affected for UK competition law to be relevant. In the UK, the Competition Act 1998, which came into force on 1 March 2000, is closely modelled on Articles 101 and 102 TFEU. Chapter I of the Act contains a prohibition on anti-competitive agreements, while Chapter II prohibits abuse of a dominant position in a market.

> **Web link**
>
> Information about the UK competition regime can be found at
> www.gov.uk/government/organisations/competition-and-markets-authority.

20.71   An important trend has been increasing use of competition law in the IP field, by infringement of European competition law being used as a defence in an action for infringement of IP belonging to another. This use of competition law as a shield is sometimes referred to as a 'Eurodefence'.[82]

20.72   Some cases clearly have no prospect of success and the defences are dismissed in summary judgment. This can be because there is no link at all between the alleged anti-competitive conduct (say, high pricing of unrelated technology or products) and the alleged infringement. This was particularly so in the first cases in which arguments were advanced.[83] Courts have stressed the need for a nexus between the alleged anti-competitive agreement and the proceedings in the context of an IP infringement action where defences based on breach of Community (now Union) law were raised. The identification of a nexus remains a key challenge; for instance, in *Sportswear Co v Ghattaura*[84] the court found that the necessary nexus[85] was absent.[86] Other cases have shown more openness to arguments and guidance as to what might be accepted.

20.73   One of these is *Intel Corporation v Via Technologies Inc and Others*[87] in which the application of both EU and UK competition law to patent licences was considered. At the heart of the case were questions concerning Intel's Pentium chip technology and Via's efforts to license the technology for their own products. Intel began two actions alleging that Via had infringed a number of Intel's patents. In defence Via raised matters concerning Intel's behaviour and what were then Articles 81 and 82 EC (and the corresponding provisions of the Competition Act 1998). Prior to remitting the case back to the High Court for trial, the Court of Appeal made some interesting observations on what was then Article 82.

---

[82] See, eg, *Intel Corporation v Via Technologies Inc and Others* [2002] EWCA Civ 1905, [2003] FSR 33, para 20.

[83] See, eg, *Philips Electronics NV v Ingman Ltd* [1998] 2 CMLR 839, [1999] FSR 112.   [84] [2006] FSR 11.

[85] ibid, paras 14–18. The court referred to *Sandvik Aktiebolag v KR Pfiffner (UK) Ltd* [2000] FSR 17 and *Intel Corporation v Via Technologies Inc and Others* [2002] EWCA Civ 1905, [2003] FSR 3.

[86] Another example where a Eurodefence was considered to have no prospect of success is *Microsoft Corporation v Ling and Others* [2006] EWHC 1619 (Ch).

[87] [2002] EWCA Civ 1905, [2002] All ER (D) 346, [2003] FSR 33.

20.74   The Court of Appeal said that for Article 82 to be infringed it was not necessary for an entity occupying a dominant position to entirely exclude a new product from the market. If this was otherwise, then a licence could be granted to a third party who never took any action in terms of the licence (in other words, just sat back and did not do what was permitted under the licence). The facts in the instant case might constitute 'exceptional circumstances' but would depend on the findings of fact made at the trial.[88] Further, if a term was included in a licence agreement that went beyond the terms necessary for the licensee to exploit the subject matter of the IPR, it would have to be justified on its own merits and not because of its inclusion in an IP licence.[89] Finally, Via might have a defence under Article 82 if Intel would only grant licences breaching Article 81 and that was part of abusive conduct by Intel. The Court of Appeal did not want to limit when there could be exceptional cases. As the facts as pleaded could give rise to an abuse, until evidence was heard on these facts it was not appropriate for a reference to be made to the ECJ.[90]

20.75   A second case in which a 'Eurodefence' was allowed to proceed to trial in the English courts is:

■   *Doncaster Pharmaceuticals Group Ltd v The Bolton Pharmaceutical Co Ltd* [2006] EWCA Civ 661, [2007] FSR 3

This case concerned the trade mark 'Kalten', pharmaceutical products, and the movement of these from Spain into the UK—parallel importing, as discussed in Chapter 19. The mark was originally held by AZ in both territories and under which it sold pharmaceutical products. In 2001 the mark was assigned to Teofarma, along with the product licence in Spain. In 2004 AZ assigned the UK mark to Bolton and entered into an agreement whereby the mark was to be used solely in connection with the marketing, promotion, sales, and distribution of the pharmaceutical product having certain contents and in accordance with the product specification. Doncaster had been engaged in buying the drugs in Spain, repackaging them under the 'Kalten' mark, and importing them into the UK. Bolton claimed trade mark infringement as against Doncaster. In response Doncaster argued that the rights had been exhausted by the placing of the drugs on the market in Spain. Bolton argued that this was not a case in which the rights had been exhausted. On the basis of *IHT Internationale Heiztechnik GmbH v Ideal Standard GmbH*[91] (discussed in para 19.17), they argued that there was no continuing economic linkage between Bolton, Teofarma, and AstraZeneca such that AZ could exercise any form of quality control over the products.

While at first instance summary judgment was granted, this was overturned by the Court of Appeal, which noted that this was not a case where there was a bare assignment of the mark but rather the assignment was accompanied by the product agreement and know-how licences. This had the effect of keeping a link with AZ which could give to AZ the possibility of control. This could result in Bolton being unable to enforce the mark as against Doncaster in the UK.

20.76   In future cases the actual facts, rather than the structure of agreements, will be key; it will be for the trial court to determine if there is a market sharing agreement supporting the assignation of the trade marks which would render the assignments void under Article 101 TFEU.[92] This openness was also seen in another parallel importing case, *Sun Microsystems v M-Tech* discussed in paragraph 19.59.[93] This involved the import to the UK from the United States of computer hardware disk drives against the backdrop of a large secondary market in the EEA. A network of agreements was argued to be in breach of Article 101. The

---

[88]   The court referred to Cases C-241/91 P and C-242/91 P *Radio Telefis Eireann v EC Commission (Magill)* [1995] All ER (EC) 416; Case 238/87 *Volvo (AB) v Erik Veng* [1988] ECR 6211; Case T-504/93 *Tierce Ladbroke SA v European Commission* [1997] ECR II-923; Case C-7/97 *Bronner (Oscar) GmbH & Co KG v Mediaprint Zeitings- und Zeitschriftenverlag GmbH & Co KG* [1998] ECR I-7791; and Case T-184/01R *IMS Health Inc v European Commission* [2001] ECR II-2349 considered at paras 20.50–20.53.

[89]   Case 193/83 *Windsurfing International Inc v European Commission* [1986] ECR 611 considered at para 20.24.

[90]   *Intel Corporation v Via Technologies Inc and Others* [2002] EWCA Civ 1905, [2003] FSR 33, paras 48–51.

[91]   Case C-9/93 [1994] ECR I-2789.

[92]   Case C-9/93 *IHT Internationale Heiztechnik GmbH v Ideal Standard GmbH* [1994] ECR I-2789, para 59.

[93]   *Sun Microsystems Inc v M-Tech Data Ltd* [2010] EWCA Civ 997, [2011] FSR 2.

Court of Appeal declined to limit the free movement and IP principles to those which had already been established, and found there to be an arguable connection between the competition and IP arguments. In 2012 the Supreme Court took a much narrower approach. It rejected arguments based on free movement and agreements, considered that the agreements delivered no nexus, and, as there was no arguable defence in EU law, declined to make a reference to the Court of Justice.[94]

20.77   Another significant case discussed at paragraph 20.26 is *FA Premier League Ltd v QC Leisure and Others*[95] which, along with *Murphy v Media Protection Services Ltd*,[96] concerns the importation and use of 'illicit' decoder cards. In *FA Premier League* the defendants raised a Eurodefence arguing that obligations imposed in the licence on foreign broadcasters to undertake to 'procure' that non-UK decoder cards were not authorised or enabled by the licensee or any sub-licensee or distributor, agent, or employee of such persons, which would have enabled anyone to view the foreign broadcaster's transmission outside the latter's territory, was incompatible with what was then Article 81 EC. The court said that this point could proceed to trial.[97] In *Murphy,* the criminal action, the national court had agreed that if Ms Murphy so wished she could put forward arguments of the impact of what were then Articles 28–30 and 49 EC and Article 81 EC on the grounds that 'the Respondent's case is effectively founded on an agreement or a network of agreements imposing restrictions unlawful and void under Art. 81 EC'.[98] On a joined reference made to the Court of Justice,[99] it found that the exclusive licence and the provisions regarding decoding devices were a restriction prohibited by what was by then Article 101 TFEU.[100] Following this, the national court in *FA Premier League* provided a declaration that the agreements were incompatible with Article 101 TFEU;[101] and Murphy's conviction was quashed.[102]

 Question

Should Eurodefences, and claims relating to the raising of an action, involve the same tests as those applying to the refusal to license cases?

20.78   Eurodefences have also been seen in respect of patents which are essential to formal standards (as discussed at para 20.65). In 2015, in disputes regarding mobile telephony, such defences were permitted to proceed to evidence.[103] The claim involved fair, reasonable, and non discriminatory (FRAND) licensing requirements, and whether injunctions could be sought when the relevant patent is an essential part of a formal standard, and the patent owner has declared that they will license the patent on a FRAND basis.

20.79   This draws on previous situations when patent ownership had not been disclosed when formal standards were being agreed, and/or the patent owner had the power to effectively hold an industry to ransom by claiming overly high royalties. This has led to Commission investigations,[104] to new practices within

---

[94] *Oracle America Inc (formerly Sun Microsystems Inc) v M-Tech Data Ltd* [2012] UKSC 27, [2012] 1 WLR 2026, paras 7–32 (in particular 30–32), 36.

[95] [2008] EWHC 44 (Ch).   [96] [2007] EWHC 3091 (Admin).   [97] [2008] EWHC 44 (Ch), paras 38–39, 57–59.

[98] *Murphy v Media Protection Services Ltd* [2007] EWHC 3091 (Admin), para 45, noting that these points had not been argued before the court. See also *Football Association Premier League Ltd and Others v LCD Publishing Ltd* [2007] EWHC 3171 (Ch), in which the court allowed LCD Publishing to furnish further and better particulars of a restraint of trade and competition defence to the terms of an agreement which prohibited pictures being published in magazines which were devoted to one football player or to one club.

[99] Regarding references to ECJ, see *Football Association Premier League Ltd v QC Leisure* [2008] 3 CMLR 12, paras 365–368.

[100] Joined Cases C-403/08 and C-429/08 *Murphy v Media Protection Services Ltd* [2012] 1 CMLR 29, paras 134–146.

[101] *Football Association Premier League Ltd v QC Leisure* [2012] 2 CMLR 16, paras 97–99.

[102] *Murphy v Media Protection Services Ltd* [2012] EWHC 466 (Admin), [2012] 3 CMLR 2, paras 8–10, see also para 12. Note that resistance remains to Eurodefences: see *Football Association Premier League Ltd v Luxton* [2016] EWCA Civ 109.

[103] *Samsung v Ericsson* [2016] EWCA Civ 489, reversing in part *Unwired Planet International v Huawei Technologies* [2015] EWHC 2097 (Pat) and *Unwired Planet International v Huawei Technologies* [2015] EWHC 1029 (Pat).

[104] See, eg, European Union Press Release, 'Antitrust: Commission accepts commitments from Rambus lowering memory chip royalty rates—Frequently Asked Questions' (9 December 2009), http://europa.eu/rapid/pressReleasesAction.do?reference=MEMO/09/544&format=HTML&aged=1&language=EN&guiLanguage=en.

standards bodies regarding disclosure and licensing,[105] and a Commission Communication from 2017 exploring accessibility of declarations, establishing essentiality, and what is meant by FRAND.[106]

20.80 A reference was made to the Court of Justice by a German court in *Huawei Technologies v ZTE Corp*[107] regarding whether a commitment to license the patent on a FRAND basis should remove the right to apply to the court for an injunction or interdict. In July 2015 the Court of Justice,[108] after considering established case law on IP and abuse of a dominant position, and also noting the human rights protection conferred on IP rights, considered that it was possible for there to be abuse by seeking an injunction in some cases. The key issue is, of course, when. The court indicated that:

- it would be an abuse if an injunction is sought without notice;
- if this notice leads to a willingness to take a licence, then a formal offer must be presented, specifying how the royalty is to be calculated; and
- the alleged infringer is to respond to this with reference to recognised practices and good faith and without delaying tactics.[109]

This test has been applied at national level.[110] Importantly, in *Unwired v Huawei*,[111] it is part of a long-running and complex set of related cases regarding standard essential patent for a formal telecoms standard, when declarations had been made regarding FRAND licences. The Court of Appeal considered that the Court of Justice had not set down mandatory prescriptive conditions, and that courts should look at the actual circumstances of the case.[112]

Exercise

Think in a bit more depth about what should come within FRAND. Reflect on this after you have read the following paragraphs and to set you up for the next exercise.

20.81 A deeper question of what FRAND can mean in a particular case was considered by, once again, the Court of Appeal in *Unwired v Huawei*.[113] The Court of Appeal set out some key practical detail: FRAND could involve a global licence,[114] and everyone need not always be offered the same licence, as long as the differences were not sufficient to give rise to distortion of competition.[115]

Exercise

Unwired v Huawei [2018] EWCA Civ 2344 engages in depth with the Commission SEP Communication discussed in paragraph 20.79. See in particular paragraph 266 of the Communication and the comment that:

Important features of the landscape are the need to ensure, on the one hand, that interoperable and safe technologies are widely disseminated through the use of standards and, on the other hand, that innovators are adequately rewarded for the investment that they have made and that they are encouraged to continue to invest in research and development and standardisation activities.

Do you think the FRAND test will be applied in the same way in decisions which start in an IP forum and in a competition forum? Think of any key differences in the approaches taken in the court's decision and in the Communication.

---

[105] See, eg, the ETSI webpage on IPR and links to IPR policy (Annex 6, revised 2018), www.etsi.org/WebSite/AboutETSI/IPRsInETSI/IPRsinETSI.aspx.

[106] COM(2017) 712 final.   [107] [2014] ECC 13 regarding a formal ETSI standard (n 9).   [108] C-170/13.

[109] Note that this proceeded in parallel with Commission investigations against Samsung which led to a settlement in 2014 (see http://europa.eu/rapid/press-release_IP-14-490_en.htm) and with a Commission's finding against Motorola in 2014 that there was abuse of a dominant position by Motorola seeking to enforce a patent against Apple in Germany when Motorola had committed to granting a FRAND licence and Apple had agreed to take a licence on terms to be set by the German court (see http://europa.eu/rapid/press-release_IP-14-489_en.htm).

[110] *Samsung v Ericsson* [2016] EWCA Civ 489 and see para 13 noting change to the ETSI policy (see para 20.79) as a result of this issue.

[111] *Unwired v Huawei* [2018] EWCA Civ 2344.   [112] ibid, paras 269–279.   [113] ibid, 2344.

[114] ibid, para 129.   [115] ibid, paras 208–209.

20.82   This all indicates that a Eurodefence can have an impact in a national action. It will be interesting to see how this field develops. Will competition law destroy the power to exclude conferred by IPRs or, as with the refusal to licence pursued in the competition regulatory framework, will the impact be more measured?

> **Key points on Eurodefences**
>
> - Competition law can provide a defence to an IP infringement action but there needs to be a nexus.
>
> - Declarations to license on a FRAND, the nature of any offer to license, and the seeking of an injunction/interdict can be relevant to determining whether there is an abuse.

Collective licensing and EU competition law

Overview of collecting societies

20.83   Exploiting works protected by copyright can cause practical problems for both the copyright owner and the prospective licensee. A copyright owner can find it difficult to keep track of third parties who wish to exploit those works in one form or another. Similarly, a licensee may wish to incorporate a large number of works protected by copyright into their repertoire, but have difficulty in tracing the copyright owners to obtain permission. For example, educational establishments and businesses often make copies of published literary works which do not fall under the fair dealing provisions in the copyright legislation[116] and broadcasters frequently use musical works which are protected by copyright. In order to facilitate the management of these rights, collecting societies were introduced (see para 6.44).[117] Through these, authors of works protected by copyright are able to assign or license their rights to the collecting societies (or the collecting society will act as agent on their behalf), which then manage the rights on behalf of their members. Thus, the authors are saved from having to spend a lot of time on administration, and those who wish to exploit the works have one place from which they can seek permission to use them.

20.84   Examples of collecting societies currently operating in the UK include the Copyright Licensing Agency (CLA) and the PRS for Music (formerly the Performing Rights Society (PRS) and the Mechanical Copyright Protection Society (MCPS)). Different societies operate in different ways. PRS for Music, which represents composers, authors, and publishers of music, has copyright assigned to it and administers licences and enforces copyright as the owner of the copyright. Royalties are distributed to the members in proportion to the use made of a particular work. In contrast, the MCPS was authorised by the composer, author, or publisher of a work to license the recording of the work on his behalf—there was no assignment of the copyright.

> **Web links**
>
> Have a look at the websites of the CLA: www.cla.co.uk, PRS for Music: www.prsformusic.com, and PPL: www.ppluk.com. Can you envisage any regulatory problems that might arise in their management and administration? Can you find any similar organisations in other jurisdictions?

20.85   Because collecting societies occupy a powerful role, both in relation to the authors of the works and in relation to users, some oversight of their activities has been found to be essential. If a collecting society manages a number of copyright works on behalf of their copyright owners, the collecting society may refuse to license the work to a particular individual or group, or it might seek to extract unreasonable royalties. This can raise competition issues.

---

[116] See Chapter 5.

[117] M Kretschmer, 'Access and Reward in the Information Society: Regulating the Collective Management of Copyright' (2007) at http://eprints.bournemouth.ac.uk/3695/1/CollSoc07.pdf.

Competition issues and collecting societies

20.86   Collecting societies are to be found in most jurisdictions and whereas, to date, they have tended to be largely concerned with activities within a particular territory,[118] they have operated between territories by means of reciprocal agreements. EU competition law has been applied to collecting societies by the ECJ/Court of Justice of the European Union (CJEU) and by the Commission. Three broad issues have been addressed: the relationship between collecting societies and users;[119] the relationship between collecting societies and their members (right holders);[120] and the reciprocal relationship between different collecting societies.[121] Developments will now be summarised.

- The ECJ has ruled that as a dominant undertaking, a collecting society cannot refuse—under Article 82 of the EC Treaty (EC) (now Art 102 of the Treaty on the Functioning of the European Union (TFEU))—to license a user in its own territory without a legitimate reason (for a discussion on Art 102 TFEU and a refusal to supply, see paras 20.48ff). Neither may collecting societies engage in collective action, the effect of which is to refuse to license the use of their repertoires to users in other territories, arguing that it would be impractical to set up a monitoring system in another territory.[122] The ECJ has also been vexed as to the differences in administrative costs of running a society and the level of royalties remitted to right holders as between societies located in different member states. It has been suggested that it may be the lack of competition in the market that leads to this result.[123]

- The Commission has said that a collecting society in a dominant position is not permitted to exclude members from other member states;[124] and that a requirement that an author assign all rights to a society, including online exploitation rights, amounts to an abuse of a dominant position in that it is the imposition of an unfair trading condition.[125] The ECJ has held[126] that mere application of a remuneration model on commercial broadcasters that is tied to the revenues of those television stations is not an abuse of a dominant position provided that the royalties are 'proportionate overall to the quality of musical works protected by copyright actually broadcast or likely to be broadcast'.[127] On the claim that it was an abuse of position to apply a different royalty calculation for commercial television stations and the public service broadcaster, STV, the ECJ ruled that the imposition of a different manner of computing the royalties could possibly be an abuse of a dominant position 'if it applies with respect to those companies dissimilar conditions to equivalent services and if it places them as a result at a competitive disadvantage, unless such a practice may be objectively justified'.[128]

---

[118] In Case C-425/07 P *AEPI Elliniki Etaireia pros Prostasian tis Pnevmatikis Idioktisias AE v Commission of the European Communities* [2009] 5 CMLR 2 the ECJ upheld a Commission Decision rejecting the complaint made by AEPI that Greece and the three main Greek collective management bodies (Erato, Apollon, and Grammo) were in breach of Arts 81 and 82 EC. In refusing the complaint, the Commission stated that: the alleged infringement is unlikely to seriously impede the proper functioning of the common market, given that all the parties involved are established in Greece and pursue their activities in that country alone. It is not foreseeable that that situation will change, that is to say, that the three ... bodies will start to pursue their activities in other countries in the near future ... The case does not, therefore, present the level of Community interest necessary for the Commission to open an investigation [para 11].

[119] Case 395/87 *Ministère Public v Tournier* [1989] ECR 2521.

[120] *Re GEMA No 1* [1971] CMLR D35; Case C-127/73 *BRT v SABAM* [1974] ECR 313.

[121] Case C-395/87 *Ministère Public v Tournier* [1989] ECR 2521; Cases C-110/88, 241/88, and 242/88 *Lucazeau v SACEM*, 13 July 1989 [1989] ECR 2811.

[122] Commission Notice, Guidelines on Vertical Restraints, OJ 2010/C 130/01.

[123] D Llewelyn and T Aplin, *Cornish, Llewelyn and Aplin Intellectual Property: Patents, Copyright, Trade Marks and Allied Rights*, 2.

[124] *GEMA I*, Decision of 20 June 1971, OJ L134/15; *GVL*, Decision of 29 October1981, OJ L370/49.

[125] *Banghalter et Homem Christo v Sacem* (Case COMP/C2/37.219), Decision of 6 August 2002.

[126] Case C-52/07 *Kanal 5 Ltd v Föreningen Svenska Tonsättares Internationella Musikbyrå (STIM) UPA* [2009] 5 CMLR 18.

[127] ibid, para 41.

[128] ibid, para 48. Followed by Case C-351-12 *Ochranný Svaz Autorský Pro Práva K Dílům Hudebním OS v Léčebné Lázně Mariánské Lázně AS* [2014] 4 CMLR 19, paras 87–8; Case C177/16 *Autortiesibu un Komunicesanas Konsultaciju Agentura/Latvijas Autoru Apvieniba v Konkurences Padome* [2017] 5 CMLR 19 (also considering details of pricing on different bases).

- In 1989 the ECJ concluded that reciprocal representation agreements as such do not fall under Article 81 EC (now Art 101 TFEU) provided they were not accompanied by concerted action or exclusivity.[129]

A particular issue is the music industry, as attempts are made to streamline the licensing processes which enable cross-border exploitation of music over many varied platforms, which will now be considered in more depth.

Cross-border exploitation of music and collecting societies

20.87   In 2001 the Commission investigated an agreement concerning simulcasting proposed by the International Federation of the Phonographic Industry (IFPI).[130] The IFPI brokered an agreement between a number of collecting societies from within Europe and beyond, each of which concerned the administration of the neighbouring rights of their record producer members for the purposes of broadcasting and public performance. This included the licensing of rights in sound recording of their members to users, determining tariffs, collecting and distributing royalties, and monitoring use.[131] As simulcasting involves the simultaneous transmission by radio and TV stations via the internet of sound recordings[132] across boundaries, the scope and the extent of the licences had to be rethought. A new multi-repertoire and multi-territorial licence was proposed and IFPI, on behalf of the collecting societies, sought an individual exemption under Article 81(3) EC. After imposing requirements to ensure competition between the collecting societies in respect of pricing,[133] and that there would be sufficient transparency in the relationship between the societies and their users by splitting the copyright and administrative fees,[134] the Commission granted an exemption under Article 81(3) EC until 31 December 2004.

20.88   This was followed in 2005 by consideration by the Commission of the terms of the 'Santiago Agreement' between the major European collecting societies in respect of music and the performing arts.[135] The agreement provided that each society could grant non-exclusive licences for the communication right from the repertoires of other societies, and the society responsible for granting the licence would be the one in the country in which the content provider had its economic seat (or which corresponded to the URL of the country of the website where the content provider is incorporated). The Commission believed that this arrangement would lead to an 'effective lock up of national territories'. After extensive consultations, the Commission issued a Notice[136] indicating that the parties had agreed inter alia to undertake for three years, 'not to be party to any agreement on licensing of public performance rights for online use with other copyright management societies containing an economic residency clause'.[137]

 Exercise

Do you think the concerns of the Commission in relation to the Santiago Agreement are valid? What sort of conditions might you want to see in an agreement between collecting societies to encourage competition?

---

[129] Case C-395/87 *Ministère Public v Tournier* [1989] ECR 2521; Cases C-110/88, 241/88, and 242/88 *Lucazeau v SACEM*, 13 July 1989 [1989] ECR 2811.

[130] Commission Decision of 8 October 2002 relating to a proceeding under Article 81 of the EC Treaty and Article 53 of the EEA Agreement (Case COMP/C2/38.014) (IFPI simulcasting), OJ C 231/18–C 231/21 (17 August 2001).

[131] ibid, para 9.   [132] ibid, para 2.   [133] ibid, para 120.   [134] ibid, para 121.

[135] See 38126 Santiago Agreement, http://ec.europa.eu/competition/elojade/isef/case_details.cfm?proc_code=1_38126; and V Dehin, 'The future of legal online music services in the European Union: a review of the EU Commission's recent initiatives in cross-border copyright management' (2010) 32(5) EIPR 220; I Brinker and T Holzmuller, 'Competition law and copyright—observations from the world of collecting societies' (2010) 11 EIPR 553.

[136] Notice published pursuant to Art 27(4) of Council Regulation (EC) No 1/2003 in Cases COMP/C2/39152—*BUMA* and COMP/C2/39151—*SABAM* (Santiago Agreement COMP/C2/38126) (2005/C 200/05).

[137] ibid, para 9.

20.89 A key decision then followed by the Commission, concerning argued anti-competitive practices of music collecting societies, including their existence and their having model agreements, in *Re CISAC Agreement*.[138] National collecting societies had made similar changes to the CISAC (International Confederation of Societies of Authors and Composers) model contract, such that authors are prevented from choosing or moving to another collecting society, and which restricted a collecting society from offering licences to commercial users outside their domestic territory. This resulted in segmentation of the market on a national basis, and commercial users wishing to offer a pan-European media service could not obtain a licence which covers several member states, but had to negotiate with each individual national collecting society. The Commission found that this network of agreements was the result of a concerted practice, in breach of Article 81 EC Treaty, and restricted the use of agreements regarding territory and membership.

20.90 In 2013 the General Court annulled part of the decision of Commission.[139] It considered that there was insufficient evidence of concerted practice coordination of agreements regarding territorial scope, and that the Commission did not render implausible explanations as to why the similar arrangements could not have resulted from parallel action by individual collecting societies. The Commission's decision regarding membership and territory remained.

EU policy change

20.91 Regulation of collecting societies within the EU is challenging because of the different directorates involved. These are DG GROW; DG Audiovisual, Media, Internet; DG Education, Youth, Sport and Culture; and DG Competition. The Commission has been actively considering the wider framework for the collective management of copyright and related rights over a number of years. The years from 2004 to 2014 saw Commission Communications, Studies, Recommendations, Reflection Documents, and a Green Paper.[140]

20.92 For the music industry this culminated in the Commission implementing a Directive on collective management and multi-territorial licensing.[141] The Directive has two key aims:

- to promote transparency and governance of collecting societies, including requirements on reporting and increased control by right holders over their activities
- to encourage multi-territorial and multi-repertoire licensing of authors' rights in the EU.[142]

In essence, the European Union wishes to consolidate the governance issues that have arisen in the series of court cases; and focus on one means of cross-border licensing—what is called a European passport. However, its intervention remains limited to the online management of musical works.[143] The situation is unchanged for other uses and other protected works.

---

[138] Case COMP/C2/38.698 Decision C (2008) 3435, [2009] 4 CMLR 12.

[139] *International Confederation of Societies of Authors and Composers (CISAC) v European Commission* (T-442/08) [2013] 5 CMLR 15.

[140] Communication from the Commission to the Council, the European Parliament, and the European Economic and Social Committee, *The Management of Copyright and Related Rights in the Internal Market*, COM/2004/0261 final; Study on a Community Initiative on the Cross-Border Collective Management of Copyright and an impact assessment on Reforming Cross-Border Collective Management of Copyright and Related Rights for Legitimate Online Music Services SEC(2005) 1254; Commission Recommendation of 18 October 2005 on collective cross-border management of copyright and related rights for legitimate online music services (2005/737/EC); European Parliament resolution on collective cross-border management of copyright and related rights for legitimate online music services, 15 September 2008; https://eur-lex.europa.eu/legal-content/EN/TXT/?uri=CELEX%3A52016DC0288 COM(2016) 0288 final; 2010 Communication 'A Digital Agenda for Europe' COM (2010) 245 final/2; Green Paper on the Online Distribution of Audiovisual Works in the European Union: Opportunities and Challenges towards a Digital Single Market COM (2011) 455.

[141] Directive 2014/26/EU of the European Parliament and of the Council of 26 February 2014 on collective management of copyright and related rights and multi-territorial licensing of rights in musical works for online use in the internal market.

[142] COM(2012) 372 final.   [143] Directive 2014/26/EU (n 143), Recital (12).

Exercise

Read the Directive 2014/26/EU (https://eur-lex.europa.eu/legal-content/EN/TXT/PDF/?uri=CELEX:32014L0026&from=EN), the Commission's Impact Assessment,[144] and the statement by Commissioner Barnier (Brussels, 4 February 2014). What do you think of the solutions adopted by the EU? Can you devise a system which would result in a multi-territorial and multi-repertoire system of licensing of content protected by copyright while respecting traditional forms of copyright ownership and exploitation and encouraging competition? Are there differences between music and other content that might warrant different treatment?

EU competition law and Brexit

The IP and competition interface will continue after Brexit although the elements of the new relationship are uncertain at the time of writing. For possible bases and content, see:

- Draft withdrawal agreement Annex 4, Part 5 notably Articles 16–18 (recognising the importance of competition and adapting Arts 101 and 102 TFEU), 21–24 (previous articles are to be interpreted using criteria arising from Arts 101 and 102, the UK is to have an independent authority and the UK and EU authorities are to cooperate on enforcement);

- Draft UK SI Competition (Amendment etc) (EU Exit) Regulations 2019 amending the UK Competition Act 1998 regarding block exemptions, removing references to Art 101 and Art 102, and providing for consistency in applying EU law before and after exit day if an EU law point arises.

In any event:

- If there is activity (say, a patent pool agreement) in the UK which has an impact in the EU, then Articles 101 and 102 will still be relevant.

- The Competition Act 1998 is very similar to Articles 101 and 102 TFEU, with the important difference that the 1998 Act focuses on trade in the UK rather than trade between member states. Activities which are purely within the UK can only be the subject of national law. However as seen, the effect on trade between member states is applied widely.

There will be an impact on the Eurodefence. The importance accorded to competition law draws from the special status of competition law within the TFEU. Without this, although the balance between IP and competition law will continue, the common theme of the treaty which drew the threads together will be absent. Further, if new issues arise regarding say injunctions and standards, courts in the UK jurisdictions will not be able to make a reference to the CJEU. There is the potential, therefore, for some future diversity between UK and EU approaches in the complex area. Might all these tests just discussed be untied?

EU law relating to multi-territorial licensing and collecting societies will not apply. UK Government Guidance of 24 September 2018 suggests that if there is 'no deal' UK collecting societies may wish to form new relationships with collecting societies in the EEA.

---

[144] Commission Staff Working Document, Impact Assessment. Accompanying the document Proposal for a Directive of the European Parliament and of the Council on collective management of copyright and related rights and multi-territorial licensing of rights in musical works for online uses in the internal market, document 52012SC0204.

Further reading

Books

S Anderman and H Schmidt, *EU Competition Law and Intellectual Property Rights. The Regulation of Innovation* (2nd edn, 2011)

S Bishop and M Walker, *The Economics of EC Competition Law: Concepts, Applications and Measurement* (3rd edn, 2010)

AEL Brown, *Intellectual Property, Human Right and Competition: Access to Essential Innovation and Technology* (2012)

V Rose, D Bailey, C Bellamy, and GD Child *Bellamy and Child, European Union Law of Competition* (2013 Pack, 7th edn, 2013)

E Rousseva, *Rethinking Exclusionary Abuses in EU Competition Law* (2010)

R Whish and D Bailey, *Competition Law* (9th edn, 2018), in particular Ch 19

Chapters

AEL Brown, 'Intellectual property: competition and the Internet' in L Edwards and C Waelde (eds), *Law and the Internet* (3rd edn, 2009)

Reports

European Commission, Fraunhofer Fokus, and Dialogic, 'Study on the interplay between standards and intellectual property rights (IPRs)' (2011), www.iplytics.com/download/docs/studies/ipr_study_final_report_en.pdf.

Articles

GS Ali, 'Collective monopolies: SIAE v Soundreef and the implementation of Directive 2014/26 in Italy' (2018) 40(2) EIPR 11

A Andreangeli, 'Interoperability as an "essential facility" in the Microsoft case—encouraging competition or stifling innovation' (2009) 34(4) EL Rev 584–611

A Andreangeli, 'Weathering the Murphy storm: domestic IP litigation and industrial consolidation as pragmatic responses to the Court of Justice's decision' (2016) 8(2) Journal of Media Law 173–97

V Angwenyi, 'Hold-up, hold-out and F/RAND: the quest for balance' (2017) 12(12) JIPLP 1012–23

D Bailey, 'Restrictions of competition by object under Article 101 TFEU' (2012) 49(2) CML Rev 559–99

B Batchelor, 'Application of the technology transfer block exemption to software licensing agreements' (2004) 10(7) CTLR 166–73

J Drexl, 'IMS Health and Trinko—antitrust placebo for consumers instead of sound economics in refusal-to-deal cases' (2004) 35(7) IIC 788

PA Geroski, 'Intellectual property rights, competition policy and innovation: is there a problem?' (2005) 2(4) SCRIPTed 422, www.law.ed.ac.uk/ahrc/script-ed/vol2-4/geroski.asp

AMP Gomez and MAE Arcila, 'Collective administration of online rights in musical works: analysing the economic efficiency of the Directive 2014/26/EU' 2014 7(3/4) International Journal of Intellectual Property Managment 103-119

D Howarth and K McMahon, '"Windows has performed an illegal operation": the Court of First Instance's judgment in the *Microsoft v Commission*' (2008) 29(2) ECLR 117–34

M Jakobs and F Hubener, 'SEP or no SEP? Open questions after Huawei/ZTE' (2016) ECLR 33

V Kathuria and J.C Lai, 'Royalty rates and non-disclosure agreements in SEP licensing: implications for competition law' (2018) 40(6) EIPR 357–67

B Ong, 'Anti-competitive refusals to grant copyright licences: reflections on the IMS saga' (2004) 26(11) EIPR 505–24

G Sidak, 'FRAND in India: The Delhi High Court's emerging jurisprudence on royalties for standard essential patents' (2015) 10(8) JIPLP 609–18

J Temple Lang, 'Defining legitimate competition: companies' duties to supply competitors and access to essential facilities' (1994) 18 FILJ 439

Part VIII

IP enforcement and remedies

Sources of the law: key websites

- The UK IPO website has a section devoted to IP crime and infringement.
  www.gov.uk/government/collections/ip-crime-and-enforcement-for-businesses-and-consumers

- The European Commission website has a section dealing with counterfeiting and piracy:
  https://ec.europa.eu/taxation_customs/business/customs-controls/counterfeit-piracy-other-ipr-violations_en

- and one devoted to enforcement at:
  https://ec.europa.eu/growth/industry/intellectual-property/enforcement_en

See also the website of the EUIPO Observatory:
  https://euipo.europa.eu/ohimportal/en/web/observatory/home?utm_content=bufferc159f&utm_medium=social&utm_source=twitter.com&utm_campaign=buffer

21

IP enforcement and remedies

Introduction

Scope and overview of chapter

21.1 It is of critical importance to an intellectual property (IP) right holder to be able to enforce his right and obtain a remedy if the right is infringed. To deal with the variety of IP infringements that can occur, a range of enforcement procedures and remedies have been developed which can be deployed in appropriate circumstances. These have their origins in international agreements (eg the Agreement on Trade-Related Aspects of Intellectual Property Rights (TRIPS)), EU legislation, and national law.

21.2 The majority of IP enforcement procedures are civil. IP rights are private rights and it is for the owner to take action where infringement occurs. Civil infringement claims require that a case be proved on the balance of probabilities. The remedies sought will depend on the circumstances of the case. For instance, an owner of copyright faced with an enterprise churning out pirated copies of a music CD is most likely to want the production of the unlawful CDs immediately halted and the copies destroyed. The right holder might also seek damages or account of profits, but whether such an enterprise would be in a position to pay might be questionable. By contrast, the owner of an infringed patent is likely to want to receive substantial damages for the wrong, as well as an order prohibiting such conduct in the future.

21.3 Separately from the available civil procedures and remedies, in response to the increased incidence of counterfeiting and piracy, a raft of criminal procedures have been introduced and developed over past years. In the areas of copyright, performers' rights, and trade marks, civil actions have for many years been boosted by criminal sanctions for those cases in which infringement is carried out on a commercial scale, such as the use of trade marks on counterfeit goods, or the production of pirated copies of CDs and DVDs. Criminal penalties have also more recently been introduced for design infringement. Criminal cases require proof beyond reasonable doubt, and may not carry the same remedies for the right holder as those available in civil disputes. Recognising that counterfeiting and piracy extend well beyond individual jurisdictions and to combat what some perceive to be organised crime, a number of measures updated over recent years now exist at European level to deal with infringers and infringing goods.

21.4   **Learning objectives**

The chapter will discuss enforcement procedures and remedies available to an intellectual property right holder in the event of infringement highlighting the tensions that arise and impact of EU initiatives in this area. It will also consider the UK rules which prohibit the making of 'unjustified threats' of infringement, which have recently been subject to a substantial legislative overhaul. By the end of this chapter you should be able to describe and explain:

- the UK rules which prohibit the making of 'unjustified threats' of infringement;

- the range of civil IP enforcement procedures and remedies available in the UK;

- recent developments in enforcement and remedies emanating from the EU and how these fit into the current UK framework;

- key provisions on criminal IP offences in the UK, cross-border EU legislation, and the provisions on enforcement to be found in TRIPS and their contribution to global intellectual property enforcement.

 IP enforcement remedies and Brexit

For much of what is covered in this chapter, Brexit will have little impact. The UK rules on 'unjustified threats' are a matter of domestic UK law, as are most rules relating to evidence, procedure and remedies in IP cases.

Where there are most likely to be issues post-Brexit is in relation to provisions of the EU's IP Enforcement Directive 2004/48/EC, which were not formally transposed into UK law. Some of these provisions—such as the rules relating to injunctions against intermediaries—have been given effect in the UK through case law, but what the status of this case law will be going forward after Brexit is not clear at this stage. It seems more likely that the courts will want to retain additional powers they have come to exercise as a result of the IP Enforcement Directive, but this will only become apparent in time. The application in the UK of the EU Regulation on customs enforcement of IP rights is also likely to be an area of change.

21.5   The rest of the chapter looks like this:

- Suspected infringements: unjustified threats (21.6–21.28)

- Remedies and recovery of evidence (21.29–21.83)

- Criminal enforcement (21.84–21.102)

- TRIPS and IP enforcement (21.103–21.113).

Suspected infringements: unjustified threats

21.6   Before we look at the formal process of enforcement, we must first consider the UK laws prohibiting the making of unjustified threats of infringement proceedings, an important aspect of pre-litigation conduct. If an IP owner suspects that there has been an infringement of an IP right it can be easy to issue threats alleging infringement. The IP right holder may be justifiably keen to have the infringing conduct stop as a matter of urgency. However, the issuing of threats alleging infringement can be damaging if the IP owner targets allegations of infringement at the alleged infringer's customers, rather than at the alleged infringer himself. Such customers are unlikely to want to engage with the substantive question of whether there is actually infringement, and may simply decide to stop stocking the relevant goods or using the relevant services. There is accordingly a risk of loss of custom for the alleged infringer, even a risk to the viability of his business as a whole, even if the allegations of infringement are wholly unfounded. Targeting customers in this way could be a strategic way for IP right holders to damage a competitors' business without ever taking on that competitor directly or having to prove the allegations of infringement.

21.7   To give some protection, for most IP rights (patents,[1] UK and Community trade marks,[2] UK registered designs,[3] UK unregistered design right,[4] and Community designs[5]—although notably not copyright, as discussed further at para 21.28, there is a statutory remedy for any person aggrieved by groundless threats of infringement proceedings. These rules are borne out of concern to prevent the tactical targeting of a business's customers as described above. They aim to make it permissible for the IP right holder to threaten proceedings against the person at the heart of an infringing sales network—for example, the person manufacturing or importing infringing goods. This sort of person is the primary actor in the chain of manufacture and distribution of infringing goods. On the other hand, the rules aim to prevent the sort of strategic targeting of customers described above. In the event of a successful claim by a person aggrieved for breach of the unjustified threats rules, they may be awarded a declaration that the threats are unjustifiable, an injunction against the continuation of the threats, and damages in respect of any loss sustained by reason of the threats.[6]

21.8   The UK rules on the making of unjustified threats have been very substantially overhauled as a result of the Intellectual Property (Unjustified Threats) Act 2017 ('the 2017 Act'). The 2017 Act makes extensive amendments to the threats provisions in the relevant IP legislation (the Patents Act 1977 (PA 1977), the Trade Marks Act 1994 (TMA 1994), the Registered Designs Act 1949 (RDA 1949) etc). This follows a process of consultation by the Law Commission which considered longstanding policy and legal problems with the statutory rules as they stood before the 2017 Act. In this section we start by briefly considering the old law and the problems which it generated, before turning to the current rules which are now embodied in the 2017 Act. The reforms introduced by the 2017 Act have effect from 1 October 2017. Even after these reforms, the legal rules remain complex and this remains an area fraught with legal risk and pitfalls for the IP right holder.

The unjustified threats rules before the 2017 Act

21.9   As explained in para 21.7, a key aim of the unjustified threats rules is to distinguish between, on the one hand, primary actors in the chain of manufacture and distribution of infringing goods and, on the other hand, secondary actors in that chain—such as the primary actor's customers. When we use the expressions 'primary' and 'secondary' in this way, we are not referring to the primary and secondary forms of infringement which may exist in relation to various IP rights (eg under the CDPA 1988). We are instead trying to draw a more general distinction between those classes of person who are most directly involved at the heart of an infringing network (to whom an IP right holder can—and should—be able to issue threats of infringement proceedings) and those who are involved further down the line (who could, if there were no regulation in this field, be targeted strategically as described in para 21.6).

---

[1] Patents Act 1977 (PA 1977), ss 70–70F (as amended).
[2] Trade Marks Act 1994 (TMA 1994), ss 21–21F (as amended); SI 2006/1027, reg 6 (as amended).
[3] Registered Designs Act 1949 (RDA 1949), ss 26–26F.
[4] Copyright, Designs and Patents Act 1988 (CDPA 1988), ss 253–253E (as amended).
[5] SI 2005/2339, regs 2–2F (as amended).
[6] PA 1977, s 70C(1); TMA 1994, s 21C(1); RDA 1949, s 26C(1); CDPA 1988, s 253C(1); SI 2005/2339, reg 2C(1).

21.10   A major problem with the unjustified threats rules as they existed prior to the 2017 Act was that they did not work well in terms of drawing this distinction. The old rules distinguish between primary and secondary actors by defining what was permitted in terms of the making of threats by reference to certain (tightly defined) acts of infringement rather than by reference to the different sorts of category of person who might be involved in infringing networks.

21.11   As a result, the rules were potentially over-generous in their protection of primary actors involved in infringement. The old rules in the pre-2017 version of the TMA 1994 illustrate the point. Under the old version of section 21(1) TMA 1994, it was not actionable to threaten a person with infringement pertaining to (a) the application of a mark to goods or packaging; (b) the importation of goods to which, or to the packaging of which, a mark had been applied; or (c) the supply of services under a mark. This was fine as far as it went—this rule made it permissible for the trade mark owner to threaten proceedings against the primary actor at the heart of an infringing sales network in relation to the specific acts identified at (a)–(c). However, the old version of section 21(1) TMA 1994 did *not* permit the making of threats against such a person which went beyond the specific acts listed there. So, for example, while it was safe to threaten infringement proceedings in relation to importation, it could be actionable if the threat of proceedings extended to the importer's advertising or sale of the infringing imported goods. This made it very hard in practice for trade mark owners to identify and communicate all of the matters of concern in pre-action correspondence. In practice, it was not possible for a trade mark owner to identify in a cease and desist letter all of the infringements of their registered trade mark which the primary actor was committing, or to ask them to undertake to stop all of those infringements, without risking an unjustified threats claim.

21.12   This position was seen as problematic on a number of fronts. For example, it conflicted with moves across England and Scotland to encourage potential litigants to engage in full and open pre-action correspondence to try to resolve disputes without recourse to the courts. Parties in England and Wales are, for example, required by the Civil Procedure Rules to engage in pre-action correspondence to avoid litigation. Under the old threats rules, however, communications about infringement might be framed as a threat, leaving no option for the right holder but to bring infringement proceedings and thereby defeating the objective of reducing avoidable litigation. The old unjustified threats rules were also regarded as generally too complex, and capable in turn of being exploited strategically by infringers who, instead of responding to substantively well-founded infringement claims, might be able to capitalise on a mistake in a cease and desist letter to counter with a claim for unjustified threats as a bargaining tool. The old rules also applied to professional legal advisers acting on behalf of an IP right holder, who could be sued (in their personal capacity and as a law firm) in relation to threats made on behalf of a client—for example, in a cease and desist letter issued in the name of the law firm. This created tensions in the professional relationship between adviser and client, with the potential that the adviser might even have to stop acting for his client if an unjustified threats claim was received because of the conflict of interest that would then arise between adviser and client.

21.13   Some limited reforms were made in 2004 to the threats rules in the PA 1977 to alleviate some of these difficulties in relation to threats of patent infringement proceedings. However, no changes to the legislation were made at that time for registered trade marks or designs. The overall issues of complexity and professional adviser liability also persisted. In 2014, the Law Commission commenced a consultation and proposed two alternative models of protection to replace the old rules. The first proposal had its roots in the 2004 reforms of patent law. The Law Commission proposed to extend those reforms to registered designs and trade marks so as to provide for a harmonised, and more useful, set of rules. The second proposal was to replace the entire threats regime with a new tort based on unfair competition. Although there was some support for the second option, overall consultees preferred the first proposal. In October 2015, the Law Commission reported on the results of the consultation and proposed draft reform legislation. That ultimately led to the 2017 Act.

Exercise

The October 2015 report of the Law Commission 'Patents, Trade Marks and Design Rights: Groundless Threats' (Law Com No 360) can be found at: www.lawcom.gov.uk/wp-content/uploads/2015/04/lc360_patents_unjustified_threats.pdf. When you have worked your way through this section of this chapter, come back to this report and read it. Which one of the two options for reforms proposed would you have chosen and why? How far do you think the reforms enacted will satisfactorily resolve the difficulties with the threats regime?

21.14   Having set the scene in terms of the background and policy issues, this section will now go on to look at the unjustified threats regime as it now stands as a result of the reforms enacted in the 2017 Act. Although major changes have been made, a lot of the pre-existing case law will remain highly relevant.

What is a 'threat'?

21.15   As a result of the 2017 Act, there is now a statutory definition of what constitutes an actionable 'threat'. This definition is the same across the rules for patents, trade marks, and designs, subject to minor differences to identify the relevant IP right. The new section 70(1) PA (taking the patent law version of the rules as an example) provides as follows:[7]

> A communication contains a 'threat of infringement proceedings' if a reasonable person in the position of a recipient would understand from the communication that—
>
> (a) a patent exists, and
> (b) a person intends to bring proceedings (whether in a court in the United Kingdom or elsewhere) against another person for infringement of the patent by—
>
>   (i) an act done in the United Kingdom, or
>   (ii) an act which, if done, would be done in the United Kingdom.

21.16   This statutory definition embodies pre-existing case law principles that a communication will constitute a 'threat' if it would be objectively perceived as such by the recipient. The difficulty is that 'threats' can be made in a number of ways. Often a 'threat' may be made in a letter, but the concept of a 'threat' is not limited, for example, to formal cease and desist correspondence. An actionable 'threat' could be made by email, or even orally. A communication also does not have to explicitly refer to infringement proceedings to be actionable as a 'threat': it is sufficient if it would be implicitly understood indicating that infringement proceedings might be commenced. It can be challenging to communicate a trade mark owner's position without issuing a communication which counts as a 'threat', as the following case shows:

■ *L'Oréal (UK) Ltd and Golden Ltd v Johnson & Johnson* [2000] ETMR 691

L'Oréal launched a range of shampoos for children called 'L'Oréal Kids'. They used the words 'No Tears' on the packaging. Johnson's owned registered trade marks for 'No More Tears' for baby shampoos. Solicitors for L'Oréal wrote to Johnson & Johnson seeking confirmation that no proceedings would be raised in the UK. Johnson replied that while they had not received instructions to commence infringement proceedings, they could offer no comfort as to future litigation. The letter included the following text:

> No decision has yet been made on whether to make a claim of trade mark infringement. You should, however, be aware that, at the same time as L'Oréal is commencing use of the mark, others in the UK market who

---

[7] See also TMA 1994, s 21(1); RDA 1949, s 26(1); CDPA 1988, s 253(1); and SI 2005/2339, reg 2(1).

had been using the mark . . . have now agreed to respect Johnson & Johnson's position and are stopping their use . . . Our clients do, after all, have six years in which they could commence proceedings . . . Bearing this in mind, we cannot give L'Oréal comfort at this stage and accordingly we must reserve all of Johnson & Johnson's rights.

Calling the letter a 'work of a master of Delphic utterances' the court found it to constitute a threat of legal proceedings on the basis that it would be understood as such by the ordinary recipient. The court stressed that:[8]

> the term 'threat' covers any intimation that would convey to a reasonable man that some person has trade mark rights and intends to enforce them against another. It matters not that the threat may be veiled or covert, conditional or future. Nor does it matter that the threat is made in response to an enquiry from the party threatened.

 Question

As an adviser to Johnson & Johnson, how would you have drafted the letter to L'Oréal in order to avoid liability?

21.17   The designs case *Quads 4 Kids v Campbell*[9] illustrates the less direct ways in which an actionable 'threat' may be made. eBay operates a policy whereby IP owners may notify eBay of alleged infringements of IP rights by way of filling in an online form—eBay's Verified Rights Owner (VeRo) programme. On receipt of a notice, eBay will remove the allegedly infringing items and then inform the seller. Campbell notified eBay in this way of the sale of quad bikes by Quads 4 Kids, which Campbell alleged infringed his Community design right. Campbell took no further proceedings with regard to infringement action against Quad 4 Kids once the goods had been removed from eBay. The court had to decide whether the submission of the online form could be regarded as a threat to bring infringement proceedings.

The court said that the test to apply was whether a reasonable person, in the position of the person allegedly threatened, would have understood that he might have been subject to infringement proceedings at some point in the future. The filling in of eBay's form did not necessarily mean that infringement proceedings were a possibility. However, the effect in this case was to enable Campbell to stop Quads 4 Kids from selling bikes by completing the form. The proper test was thus whether eBay would have understood that it could be subject to future infringement proceedings if it had not adopted the policy of removing any allegedly infringing items. As the answer to that was affirmative, the balance of convenience meant the injunction should be granted.

21.18   More recently, the Court reiterated in *Cassie Creations Ltd v Blackmore*:[10]

> in the real world a body like eBay is not in a position . . . to act as a judicial body, and in other areas of the law such as defamation and misuse of private information, the general position is that internet service providers and intermediaries tend to say that they are not in a position to get into the rights and wrongs of the matter; it has to be left between the various private parties who are arguing. That may lead them to continue to make material available, or to take steps to prevent or limit access to material, depending on the circumstances of any particular case; but where there is any significant risk that they will be exposed to substantive liability if they do not take steps with regard to dissemination after they have been put on notice of an alleged basis of claim, I consider that it is to be expected that they may choose to avoid the risk of liability by taking such steps.

---

[8]   *L'Oréal (UK) Ltd v Johnson & Johnson* [2000] ETMR 691, para 12.
[9]   [2006] EWHC 2482 (Ch).   [10]   [2014] EWHC 2941 (Ch), para 49.

Even though the dispute in *Cassie Creations* involved only a very small damages claim for the disputed threats, given the above the court held that it was not disproportionate or an abuse of process to pursue the threats action.

21.19 Both *Quads 4 Kids v Campbell* and *Cassie Creations* were only interim decisions. However, these cases do show that an IP right holder runs the risk of being taken to have issued a 'threat' by using the eBay VeRo programme or a similar form of notice-and-takedown. This issue was not explicitly addressed in the 2017 Act. Either way, the reforms enacted by the 2017 Act do make it explicit that group or mass communications can be actionable. For example, section 70(2) PA 1977 provides:[11]

> References . . . to a '*recipient*' include, in the case of a communication directed to the public or a section of the public, references to a person to whom the communication is directed.

21.20 Under the statutory provisions enacted by the 2017 Act, it is made explicit that actionable 'threats' are not limited to threats of proceedings in the UK courts. A communication may constitute an actionable 'threat' if it relates to court proceedings which may be brought in the UK or elsewhere. The key requirement is that the proceedings relate to 'an act done in the United Kingdom' or (in respect of future infringements) 'an act, which if done, would be done in the United Kingdom'.[12] This could be relevant in cases where an act committed in the UK may form the subject matter of proceedings in other jurisdictions—for example, where there is infringement of an EU trade mark or Community design across multiple jurisdictions or, in the future, a patent infringement subject to the jurisdiction of the Unified Patent Court. These statutory rules reverse pre-2017 case law which had held that, to be actionable, the threat needed to relate to infringement proceedings to be brought in the UK.[13] This is an important practice point which makes the UK threats rules an important consideration for right holders and their advisers globally.[14] However, pre-2017 case law indicates that a threat will not be actionable if made in the course of 'without prejudice' negotiations where there is an honest and genuine intention to try to settle the dispute.[15]

Who may bring an unjustified threats claim ('person aggrieved')?

21.21 Unjustified threats are actionable by any 'person aggrieved' by the threat.[16] This does not have to be the recipient of the threat—a party whose interests are indirectly adversely affected may also be able to sue. There is no need to demonstrate actual loss for someone to be 'a person aggrieved'; as the court has noted, demonstrating loss cannot be a prerequisite to the bringing of an unjustified threats action:[17]

> If it were, much of the practical value of the section would be destroyed . . . If a trader is trying to build a new business from scratch and at the very outset a competitor threatens his potential customers or partners with patent proceedings, the business may be destroyed or its growth seriously held back but, because the threats were made early, it may be impossible to prove any particular financial loss. It will all be too speculative. The threats provisions must be able to cater for that type of case.

All that is required is for the 'person aggrieved' to be able to show 'his commercial interests are or are likely to be adversely affected in a real as opposed to a fanciful or minimal way'.[18]

---

[11] See also TMA 1994, s 21(2); RDA 1949, s 26(2); CDPA 1988, s 253(2); and SI 2005/2339, reg 2(2). For an example under pre-2017 case law, see *Global Flood Defence Systems Ltd v Johann Van Den Noort Beheer BV* [2016] FSR 37 (concerning 'threats' in the form of notices posted on the right holder's website).

[12] See PA 1977, s 70(1)(b); TMA 1994, s 21(1)(b); RDA 1949, s 26(1)(b); CDPA 1988, s 253(1)(b); and SI 2005/2339, reg 2(1)(b).

[13] *Best Buy Co Inc v Worldwide Sales Corp Espana SL* [2011] FSR 30.

[14] See further J Fox, L Thompson, B Potts, and M Döring, 'UK threats: worldwide consequences?' (2018) 40(2) EIPR 74–84.

[15] *Unilever Plc v Procter & Gamble Co* [2000] FSR 344.

[16] See PA 1977, s 70A(1); TMA 1994, s 21A(1); RDA 1949, s 26A(1); CDPA 1988, s 253A(1); SI 2005/2339, reg 2A(1).

[17] *Brain v Ingledew Brown Bennison & Garrett (No 3)* [1997] FSR 511, 518–19.   [18] ibid, 520.

What threats will be actionable?

21.22   The new statutory provisions enacted by the 2017 Act aim to do away with the problems that used to arise under the old law. This is achieved through a two-step approach, based on the reform of patent law threats which was undertaken in 2004. First, the legislation identifies certain core acts of infringement—the acts which lie at the heart of any chain of infringing activities and which are committed by the primary actor(s) in that chain—in relation to which no threat is actionable. For patents, this can be found at section 70(2) PA 1977. Section 70(2) PA 1977 provides that:[19]

> A threat of infringement proceedings is not actionable if the infringement is alleged to consist of—
>
> (a) where the invention is a product, making a product for disposal or importing a product for disposal, or
> (b) where the invention is a process, using a process.

Second, the legislation (for patents, s 7(4) PA 1977) provides that threat will not be actionable in relation to other acts of infringement if that threat is made to a person who has done or intends to do one of the acts noted at (a) or (b) quoted above. The upshot of this is that it is possible, for example, to communicate to a person importing an infringing product that proceedings are threatened not only in relation to the act of importation, but also in relation to their other acts such as sale of the infringing imported product. However, threats of proceedings communicated to someone other than a primary actor—for example, an importer's customer—will not be saved by these rules. Such threats will be actionable and may give rise to infringement unless they fall within the class of 'permitted communications' discussed in para 21.24 or one of the relevant defences applies.

21.23   For comparison, for registered trade marks the equivalent provisions can be found at sections 21A(2), (4), and (5) TMA 1994. As the first step, section 21A(2) TMA 1994 provides that:[20]

> A threat of infringement proceedings is not actionable if the infringement is alleged to consist of—
>
> (a) applying, or causing another person to apply, a sign to goods or their packaging,
> (b) importing, for disposal, goods to which, or to the packaging of which, a sign has been applied, or
> (c) supplying services under a sign.

As the second step, sections 21A(4) and (5) TMA 1994 provide that a threat will not be actionable if that threat is made to a person who has done or intends to do one of the acts noted at (a)–(c) quoted above, where the threat relates to the doing of anything else in relation to the goods or their packaging or in relation to the relevant services. A similar approach is also taken to designs.[21] As can be seen, this means that the same general approach is now taken across all of the IP rights for which there are statutory threats rules. The result of these changes should be that an IP right holder should not be tied in the same sort of knots as previously in terms of only being able to refer to certain limited acts of infringement in correspondence with a primary actor involved in infringement. Instead, it should be possible for pre-action correspondence with a primary actor to be comprehensive in identifying the conduct to which the IP right holder objects.

21.24   In the new rules enacted by the 2017 Act, a threat of infringement proceedings which is not an express threat will also not be actionable if it is contained in a 'permitted communication'.[22] These new rules make it possible for an IP right holder to engage in certain communications with secondary actors in the infringement chain, which might otherwise be treated as implied threats of proceedings, without exposing themselves to unjustified threats liability. To be protected, a 'permitted communication' must be made for a 'permitted purpose'—giving notice that the relevant IP right exists, discovering whether or by whom it has been infringed by a relevant primary actor, giving notice of the IP right (where awareness is relevant to any

---

[19]   Section 70A(3) PA 1977 expands this to future acts.   [20]   Section 21A(3) TMA 1994 expands this to future acts.
[21]   See RDA 1949, ss 26A(2)–(4); CDPA 1988, s 253A(2)–(4); SI 2005/2339, reg 2A(2)–(4).
[22]   See PA 1977, s 70A(5); TMA 1994, s 21A(6); RDA 1949, s 26A(5); CDPA 1988, s 253A(5); SI 2005/2339, reg 2A(5).

proceedings which may be brought), or any other purpose identified by the court in the interests of justice.[23] All information relating to any implied threat in a 'permitted communication' must be necessary for the relevant permitted purpose and deal with information which the person making the communication reasonably believes is true.[24] 'Necessary' information in this context includes a statement that the relevant IP right exists and is in force or has been applied for, details in relation to the IP right which are in all material respects accurate and not misleading, and information enabling the identification of infringing products, processes, or services (as appropriate).[25]

Defences

21.25   It is a defence to any claim for unjustified threats for the right holder to show that the act(s) in relation to which proceedings were threatened constitute an infringement of the relevant IP right.[26] This will not help the IP right holder if his IP right is found to be invalid, however: an invalid IP right cannot be infringed. If the IP right holder shows that the relevant act(s) would have constituted infringement but his IP right is invalidated (eg on a counterclaim by the alleged infringer), he may be liable for unjustified threats. There is an important change here for patent owners compared to the pre-2017 rules. Before the 2017 Act, a patent owner who thought that he had a valid patent and had no reason to suspect otherwise would not be liable for unlawful threats if his patent turned out to be invalid. This was regarded as being of particular importance in the patent context, where invalidity may be triggered by obscure prior art of which the patent owner could legitimately be unaware. However, as a result of the 2017 Act this saving in relation to patents has now been removed.

21.26   There may also be a defence to an unjustified threats claim issued in circumstances where no primary actor can be located. The provisions enacted by the 2017 Act state that it is a defence to show that, despite having taken reasonable steps, the person who issued the threat has not identified the relevant primary actor and that, at the time of or before making the threat, had notified the recipient of the threat of the steps taken.[27] Similar provisions had previously been in place for patents, although the new rules introduced by the 2017 Act lessen the standard imposed on the IP right holder in terms of the attempts which he must make to try to locate the relevant primary actor(s).[28] It remains to be seen how far this assists IP right holders—much may turn on the interpretation of the phrase 'reasonable steps'.

Professional legal advisers

21.27   Acting on the concerns discussed in para 21.12, the 2017 Act introduces provisions which make it possible for professional legal advisers to issue threats on behalf of their client without themselves becoming liable.[29] This only applies to regulated lawyers, patent, or trade mark attorneys. Although not stated explicitly in the 2017 Act, it is understood that this provision is intended to benefit in-house solicitors as well as those in private practice. To benefit from this protection, in making the communication constituting the threat the advisor must be acting on the instructions of another person (ie his client) and that communication must identify the person upon whose instructions the adviser is acting.

---

[23] See PA 1977, s 70B(1)–(3); TMA 1994, ss 21B(1)–(3); RDA 1949, ss 26B(1)–(3); CDPA 1988, ss 253B(1)–(3); SI 2005/2339, reg 2B(1)–(3). 'Permitted purposes' do not include asking a person to cease their activities in relation to the relevant IP right, to deliver up or destroy products, or to give undertakings: PA 1977, s 70B(4); TMA 1994, s 21B(4); RDA 1949, s 26B(4); CDPA 1988, s 253B(4); SI 2005/2339, reg 2B(4).

[24] See PA 1977, s 70B(1); TMA 1994, s 21B(1); RDA 1949, s 26B(1); CDPA 1988, s 253B(1); SI 2005/2339, reg 2B(1).

[25] See PA 1977, s 70B(5); TMA 1994, s 21B(5); RDA 1949, s 26B(5); CDPA 1988, s 253B(5); SI 2005/2339, reg 2B(5).

[26] See PA 1977, s 70C(3); TMA 1994, s 21C(3); RDA 1949, s 26C(3); CDPA 1988, s 253C(3); SI 2005/2339, reg 2C(3).

[27] See PA 1977, s 70C(4); TMA 1994, s 21C(4); RDA 1949, s 26C(4); CDPA 1988, s 253C(4); SI 2005/2339, reg 2C(4).

[28] Under the old patent rules, the patent owner had to use his 'best endeavours' to locate the person who made or imported an infringing product or used an infringing process.

[29] See PA 1977, s 70D; TMA 1994, s 21D; RDA 1949, s 26D; CDPA 1988, s 253D; SI 2005/2339, reg 2D.

Other intellectual property rights

21.28   There are no unjustified threats provisions for other IP rights such as copyright, passing off, database right, and breach of confidence. It may, however, be possible to apply for a declaration of non-infringement and injunction restraining the making of allegations to the contrary:

■ *Point Solutions Ltd v Focus Business Solutions Ltd* [2006] FSR 31

This case concerned an application by Point for a declaration that its computer software did not infringe the copyright in the source code produced by Focus. Focus had not commenced a claim for copyright infringement, but Point alleged that Focus had alleged, both expressly and by implication, that Point's software infringed Focus's copyright through correspondence between the parties, and by statements to clients of Point. The court found that while Point had established that Focus had made the assertions, there was insufficient evidence to establish that Point had developed the software independently, no evidence that there was any impact on Point's business, and a concern that a grant of declaratory relief would foreclose a future claim for Focus. The declaration was thus refused. The judgment was affirmed on appeal.[30]

Exercise

Do you think there should be unjustified threats provisions in copyright law? If so, why? If not, why not?

Key points on unjustified threats

- Unjustified threats actions are available for UK and Community trade marks, patents, UK registered and unregistered design rights, and Community designs. The rules governing unjustified threats have been significantly overhauled by the Intellectual Property (Unjustified Threats) Act 2017, with the result that differences that existed between patents and other IP rights under the old law no longer apply.

- Under the provisions enacted by the 2017 Act, it is permissible to threaten court proceedings in relation to certain specific acts of infringement—in essence, acts committed by primary actors in the chain of manufacture and distribution of infringing goods. It is also permitted to issue certain other 'permitted communications'. There are defences to unjustified threats claims where the alleged infringer is shown to have infringed the relevant IP right and in relation to certain communications issued where the primary actor in the chain of infringement cannot be located. As a result of the 2017 reforms, professional legal advisers should now also be protected from liability in most circumstances.

---

[30]   *Point Solutions Ltd v Focus Business Solutions Ltd* [2007] EWCA Civ 14.

Remedies and recovery of evidence

The IP Enforcement Directive

21.29 In terms of civil procedures and remedies, the most significant developments in the UK and Europe in recent years have been brought about by Directive 2004/48/EC on the enforcement of intellectual property rights (the 'Enforcement Directive' or 'IPED').[31] The objective of the Enforcement Directive was to eliminate the disparities which existed across member states in the procedures and remedies available for enforcement of IP rights and to 'ensure a high, equivalent and homogeneous level of protection in the internal market' (Recitals 8–10). The Enforcement Directive was an ambitious intervention by the European Union (EU) and covers the full range of enforcement issues, from recovery of evidence and interim remedies to final remedies (such as injunctions and damages) and recovery of legal costs.

21.30 The Enforcement Directive is a *horizontal* harmonising instrument, meaning that it applies across the field of IP, rather than to any specific individual forms of IP right. The Directive does not itself define its exact scope, but Recital 13 and Article 2(1) indicate an intention to cover the full range of IP rights. Article 2(1) states that the Directive applies to 'any infringement of intellectual property rights as provided for by Community law and/or by the national law of the Member State concerned'. The Commission has also issued a statement indicating the intention to cover *at least* the following:[32]

- copyright;
- rights related to copyright;
- *sui generis* right of a database maker;
- rights of the creator of the topographies of a semiconductor product;
- trade mark rights;
- design rights;
- patent rights, including rights derived from supplementary protection certificates;
- geographical indications;
- utility model rights;
- plant variety rights;
- trade names, insofar as these are protected as exclusive property rights in the national law concerned.

This list does not include trade secrets, but the EU Trade Secrets Directive includes provisions similar to those in the IPED.[33]

21.31 The Enforcement Directive is a *minimum standards* harmonising instrument. This means that it permits national law rules which are more favourable to right holders to be preserved (Art 2(1) IPED). However, the Enforcement Directive also sets out some important general principles which are intended to govern measures, procedures, and remedies available for enforcement of IPRs. Article 3(1) IPED states that such measures, procedures, and remedies must be fair and equitable and must not be unnecessarily complicated or costly, or entail unreasonable time limits or unwarranted delays. Article 3(2) IPED states that all measures, procedures and remedies must also be 'effective, proportionate and dissuasive', must be applied in a manner which avoids creating barriers to legitimate trade, and must provide safeguards against abuse.[34]

---

[31] Directive 2004/48/EC of the European Parliament and of the Council of 29 April 2004 on the enforcement of intellectual property rights.

[32] Statement by the Commission concerning Article 2 of Directive 2004/48/EC of the European Parliament and of the Council on the enforcement of intellectual property rights (2005/295/EC) (13 April 2005).

[33] See Chapter III of Directive (EU) 2016/943 on the protection of undisclosed know-how and business information (trade secrets).

[34] See further M. Norrgård, 'The European principles of intellectual property enforcement: harmonisation through communication?' in A Ohly (ed), *Common Principles of European Intellectual Property Law* (2012); A Ohly, 'Three principles of European IP enforcement law: effectiveness, proportionality, dissuasiveness' in J Drexl et al (eds), *Technology and Competition: Contributions in Honour of Hanns Ullrich* (2009).

21.32   The Enforcement Directive will extend to proceedings related to infringement such as cross-border enforcement of a judgment or an action for costs for wrongful seizure of goods.[35] It will also apply in proceedings brought for recovery of information on infringing networks (see para 21.83 below) which are commenced against an infringer after the original infringement litigation has come to an end.[36] However, it does not apply to proceedings purely dealing with invalidation of IP rights or to disputes over 'fair compensation' under the InfoSoc Directive 2001/29/EC.[37]

21.33   In the UK, the IPED was implemented mainly by the Intellectual Property (Enforcement, etc) Regulations 2006 (SI 2006/1028). The detail of the Enforcement Directive takes inspiration from a variety of member states of the EU. Much—although notably not all—of what was required by the Enforcement Directive was already available in the UK, both in England and Scotland. However, as we will see throughout this part of this chapter, both the general principles and a number of specific measures found in the Enforcement Directive have nonetheless had a significant impact on UK law. We will consider the effect of the Enforcement Directive as appropriate as we work through the remainder of this chapter.

Preparing a case: obtaining and preserving evidence

21.34   As a first step, if an infringement of an IPR is suspected, it will be imperative for the owner to gather evidence of that infringement. In intellectual property cases it would be easy for a defendant to destroy much-needed evidence.

21.35   To counter this problem, case law in England and Wales developed a form of search order, authorising a search of the defendant's premises and to photograph, seize, or copy allegedly infringing material.[38]

21.36   Although this type of order can be of vital importance to a claimant to allow him to gain the evidence needed to prove a case, this is an invasive remedy, and so checks and balances exist to ensure such orders are granted only when appropriate and that their terms are not exceeded. There are three essential pre-requisites for the grant of a search order:[39]

- There must be a strong prima facie case.
- The damage, potential or actual, must be serious for the applicant.
- There must be clear evidence that the defendants have incriminating documents or things in their possession and a real possibility must exist that they may destroy the evidence.

Given that a search order is most often granted without the defendant appearing or being represented (to avoid tipping the defendant off), it is apparent that procedural safeguards are needed. These safeguards include: the need for the claimant to give a cross-undertaking in damages; time for the defendant to consider the order and seek independent legal advice; time for the defendant to seek a discharge of the order; the claimant's solicitor and an independent solicitor to accompany the search team; records to be kept of all material removed from the premises; and a date on which to report back to the court to facilitate claims for compensation to be made by the defendant.[40]

21.37   There are also provisions at Articles 6 and 7 of the Enforcement Directive relating to the obtaining and preservation of evidence. For infringements being conducted on a commercial scale, these extend to the

---

[35] Case C-406/09 *Real Chemie Nederland BV v Bayer Cropscience AG* (unreported); Case C-681/13 *Diageo Brands BV v Simiramida-04 EOOD* [2015] ETMR 47.

[36] Case C-427/15 *NEW WAVE CZ as v ALLTOYS spol s r o* [2017] ETMR 16.

[37] Case C-180/11 *Bericap Záródástechnikai bt v Magyar Szabadalmi Hivatal* (unreported); Case C-435/12 *ACI Adam BV and Others v Stichting de Thuiskopie and Another* [2014] ECDR 13.

[38] The rules for England and Wales can be found in Part 25 of the Civil Procedure Rules. In Scotland similar procedures exist under the Administration of Justice (Scotland) Act 1972, s 1.

[39] *Anton Piller KG v Manufacturing Process Ltd* [1976] Ch 55 (CA), Ormrod LJ.

[40] Civil Procedure Rules Practice Direction 25A.

provision of banking, financial, or commercial documents under the control of the opposing party, subject always to the protection of any confidential information contained therein.[41] The IPED includes similar procedural safeguards.

 Exercise

Give examples of those types of infringements of intellectual property infringement which you think would justify the grant of a search order.

21.38   An interesting further measure, found in copyright legislation, permits copyright owners to seize infringing copies of protected works from market stalls and car boot sales (a similar measure exists in relation to illicit recordings).[42] A copyright owner is not, however, allowed to seize infringing goods from premises where the infringer has a permanent place of business. If an infringing copy of a work is found for sale or hire and it is one that would entitle the copyright owner to apply for an order for delivery up, then he may detain the copies, or authorise others to do so on his behalf. Certain conditions are attached to the procedure.[43] These are that:

- a notice of the time and place of the proposed seizure must be given to a local police station;[44]
- nothing may be seized that is in the possession, custody, or control of a person operating from a permanent or regular place of business;
- no force may be used;[45]
- at the time when anything is seized a notice must be left in the prescribed terms at the place where the infringing copy is seized.[46]

21.39   In practical terms, a copyright owner may not have the courage to seize infringing copies of works from the stalls of market traders. In those circumstances he may feel it necessary to authorise another to do so on his behalf, such as trading standards officers or FACT, the Federation Against Copyright Theft.

Web links

Have a look at the FACT website at www.fact-uk.org.uk. Why was this organisation set up and who does it represent? Note also FAST (the Federation against Software Theft) at www.fast.org and the Alliance for Intellectual Property at www.allianceforip.co.uk. Can you find any other similar organisations?

Interim injunctions (England and Wales) and interim interdicts (Scotland)

21.40   In intellectual property disputes it is often of vital importance to the aggrieved party to have a case heard as quickly as possible with the aim of having the allegedly infringing acts halted before full trial. Thus, many civil intellectual property actions start with applications for interim injunctive relief (called an interim 'interdict' in Scotland). However, care needs to be taken in granting an interim injunction/interdict, as, if granted, in practical terms it can determine the outcome of the dispute if the case does not proceed to full trial. A defendant, prohibited from carrying out a particular act, may choose an alternative business strategy rather than wait for a number of years for a full hearing of the case. The effect of such an order may even be enough to close down a business if a line of business is prohibited and there are insufficient resources to defend the full action. For these reasons the courts have developed guidelines to be applied in cases where interim relief is sought.

---

[41]   IPED, Art 6(2) and Recital 14, defining what constitutes infringement 'on a commercial scale'.
[42]   CDPA 1988, ss 100 and 196.   [43] CDPA 1988, s 100.   [44] CDPA 1988, s 100(2).   [45] CDPA 1988, s 100(3).
[46]   CDPA 1988, s 100(4). Copyright and Rights in Performances (Notice of Seizure) Order 1989 (SI 1989/1006).

21.41 The leading case on interim injunctions in England and Wales is *American Cyanamid Co v Ethicon Ltd*.[47] The House of Lords enunciated a number of factors to be taken into account when deciding whether an interim injunction should be granted, the steps of which are represented in Figure 21.1.

Figure 21.1 *American Cyanamid Co v Ethicon Ltd*

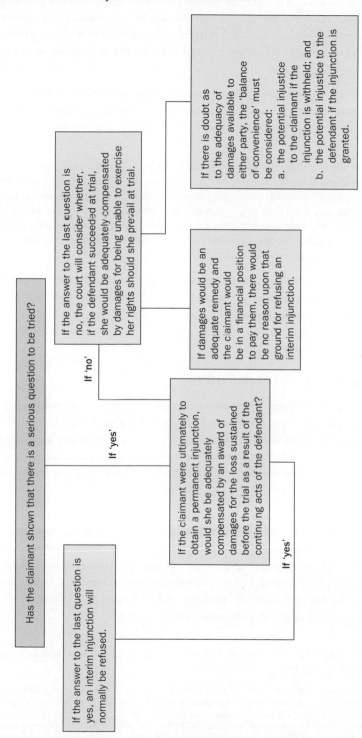

Has the claimant shown that there is a serious question to be tried?

If the answer to the last question is yes, an interim injunction will normally be refused.

If 'yes'

If the claimant were ultimately to obtain a permanent injunction, would she be adequately compensated by an award of damages for the loss sustained before the trial as a result of the continuing acts of the defendant?

If 'yes'

If damages would be an adequate remedy and the claimant would be in a financial position to pay them, there would be no reason upon that ground for refusing an interim injunction.

If 'no'

If the answer to the last question is no, the court will consider whether, if the defendant succeeded at trial, she would be adequately compensated by damages for being unable to exercise her rights should she prevail at trial.

If there is doubt as to the adequacy of damages available to either party, the 'balance of convenience' must be considered:

a. the potential injustice to the claimant if the injunction is withheld; and
b. the potential injustice to the defendant if the injunction is granted.

General comment:

The course to be taken is that which would involve the least risk of ultimate injustice, having regard to the actual and potential rights and liabilities of the parties on both sides.

[47] [1975] AC 396.

21.42   An interim injunction may be sought at any time, including before the action has been commenced. If it is very urgent, the application may even be heard and decided without notice to the defendant—although it would be normal for the case to be called again in court shortly thereafter for the defendant to argue his position if he wants the order lifted. In order to justify an interim injunction, a claimant must move quickly: if he delays after the circumstances said to justify the interim order have arisen, it will be difficult to show that there will be irrevocable damage to his interests which cannot be compensated in monetary terms. Seeking and obtaining an interim injunction is not risk-free: the claimant will be required to give a cross-undertaking in damages to compensate the alleged infringer if the interim order turns out to have been wrongly granted.

21.43   In Scotland, the procedure and approach are slightly different, although the same core considerations are relevant. The Scottish courts have tended to have more regard to the relative strength of the cases put forward by the parties at the interlocutory stage as one of the factors that go to make up the balance of convenience:[48]

> Whether the likelihood of success should be regarded as one of the elements of the balance of convenience or as a separate matter seems to me an academic question of no real importance, but my inclination is in favour of the former alternative. It seems to make good sense: if the pursuer or petitioner appears very likely to succeed at the end of the day, it will tend to be convenient to grant interim interdict and thus prevent the defender or respondent from infringing his rights, but if the defender or respondent appears very likely to succeed at the end of the day it will tend to be convenient to refuse interim interdict because an interim interdict would probably only delay the exercise of the defender's legal activities.

The procedure for obtaining an interim interdict in Scotland is different, although acting quickly remains important and there is also liability in damages for wrongful interdict. An important and useful procedural tool in Scotland is the 'caveat', a note which can be filed by any party with the Scottish courts which ensures that no interim interdict can be sought against that party without its nominated solicitors being put on notice and given the opportunity to attend court.

Freedom of expression, privacy, and interim relief

21.44   Of particular note in applications for interim relief are developments on the interaction between freedom of expression and privacy. Section 12(3) of the Human Rights Act 1998 provides that no relief should be granted that restrains publication prior to trial where such relief might affect the exercise of the right to freedom of expression as enshrined in the European Convention on Human Rights unless the applicant is *likely* to establish at trial that publication should not be allowed. Only if this test is met will the court go on to consider the *American Cyanamid* factors.

21.45   There has been much discussion as to the correct interpretation of the word 'likely' in this context. It was suggested in *Imutran Ltd v Uncaged Campaigns Ltd*[49] that it implies a higher test than that enunciated in *American Cyanamid*; that there should be a real prospect of success rather than success on a balance of probabilities. Subsequently, in *Cream Holdings Ltd v Banerjee*[50] the House of Lords confirmed that approach but left leeway for a court to do away with that higher standard where the circumstances make it necessary. The court emphasised that section 12(3) of the Human Rights Act 1998 made the 'likelihood of success' at trial an essential element in considering whether to make an interim order.[51]

---

[48] *NWL Ltd v Woods* [1979] 3 All ER 614 at 628. See also *Boehringer Ingelheim Pharma GmbH & Co KG v Munro Wholesale Medical Supplies Ltd* 2004 SC 468, [2004] ETMR 66; *Schuh Ltd v Shhh . . . Ltd* [2011] CSOH 123.

[49] [2002] FSR 2.   [50] [2004] UKHL 44, [2004] 3 WLR 918, para 20.

[51] *Miss World Ltd v Channel 4 Television Corporation* [2007] EWHC 982 (Pat). It was 'likely' for the purposes of HRA 1998, s 12(3) that the claimant would succeed in showing that the proposed broadcast of a programme called 'Mr Miss World' would infringe the registered trade mark 'Miss World' in terms of TMA 1994, s 10(1) and 10(2). In *Response Handling v BBC* [2007] CSOH 102 information on bank account details had been obtained in breach of confidence by an employee of the BBC, but the court was not satisfied that the pursuers were more likely than not to succeed at proof to restrain publication of the resultant television programme. See also *Boehringer Ingelheim Ltd v VetPlus Ltd* [2007] EWCA Civ 583 confirming that HRA 1998, s 12(3) also applied to trade mark infringement in comparative advertising cases.

21.46   The interaction between section 12(3) of the Human Rights Act 1998 and an application to have an interim injunction lifted was considered by the Court of Appeal in *Douglas v Hello!*.[52] The High Court initially granted an interim order restraining the publication by *Hello!* of a number of photographs taken at the wedding of Catherine Zeta-Jones and Michael Douglas, allegedly in breach of obligations of confidentiality and a 'right of privacy'.

The order was subsequently lifted by the Court of Appeal, which considered that preventing *Hello!* magazine from publishing the pictures before a full trial could, potentially, lead to incalculable damages, whereas the damage that *OK!* magazine might suffer was capable of calculation.[53]

However, this result was subsequently criticised in the next round of the case when it went to the Court of Appeal. Here the court thought there was no public interest (as opposed to public curiosity) grounds that justified lifting the interlocutory injunction.[54] Insufficient consideration had been given by the lower court to the likely level of damages which the Douglases would recover if an interlocutory injunction was refused and publication of the unauthorised photographs infringed their rights.[55]

On the question as to whether the Douglases would be *likely* to succeed at trial, the Court of Appeal took particular note of the reasoning in *Campbell v MGN*[56] in the House of Lords, and *von Hannover v Germany*[57] in the European Court of Human Rights, both of which were handed down after the interlocutory injunction in *Douglas v Hello!* had been lifted. The appeal court considered that the 'likelihood of success' threshold had been satisfied by the Douglases, who appeared to have 'a virtually unanswerable case for contending that publication of the unauthorised photographs would infringe their privacy'.[58] Only by granting an interlocutory injunction could the Douglases rights have been protected. By contrast, the financial interests of *Hello!* could have been satisfied by an undertaking by the Douglases to pay damages should they not be successful at trial.[59]

21.47   The courts are clearly alive to the tensions that arise at the stage of requesting interim relief in cases concerning both freedom of expression and privacy. After the comments on the harm done to the Douglases in allowing publication in *Hello!* courts may be more willing to grant interim relief where it is clear that there would be no satisfactory remedy should publication go ahead.[60]

Exercise

The case of *Douglas v Hello!* was a particularly challenging one for the courts to deal with. The substantive law on breach of confidence has been developing apace in recent years, making it difficult to decide when it might be appropriate to grant an interim order. Do you think that the Court of Appeal was correct in its assessment of where the balance between freedom of expression and confidentiality lay when considering the grant of an interim injunction? Would the same arguments apply in other IP cases—say, a case of copyright infringement involving reproduction of extracts from a diary, or a case of trade mark infringement involving comparative advertising?

---

[52]   [2001] 2 All ER 289, [2001] QB 967.
[53]   For the High Court decision on the merits, see [2003] EWHC 786 (Ch) and for the appeal *(No 3)* [2005] EWCA Civ 595.
[54]   *(No 3)* [2005] EWCA Civ 595, para 254.   [55]   ibid, para 255.
[56]   [2004] UKHL 22, [2004] 2 AC 457, [2004] 2 WLR 1232, [2004] 2 All ER 995.
[57]   *Von Hannover v Germany* (App No 59320/00) [2004] EMLR 21, (2005) 40 EHRR 16.
[58]   *(No 3)* [2005] EWCA Civ 595, para 253.   [59]   ibid, para 259.
[60]   Eg *Ms Elizabeth Jagger v John Darling and Others* [2005] EWHC 683 (Ch). Note also HRA 1998, s 12(4)(b), which provides:

The court must have particular regard to the importance of the Convention right to freedom of expression and, where the proceedings relate to material which the respondent claims, or which appears to the court, to be journalistic, literary or artistic material (or to conduct connected with such material), to (a) the extent to which (i) the material has, or is about to, become available to the public; or (ii) it is, or would be, in the public interest for the material to be published; (b) any relevant privacy code.

Guidance was given in interpreting this subsection by Woolf CJ in *A v B plc* [2002] EWCA Civ 337, para 11. In *Browne v Associated Newspapers Ltd* [2007] EWHC 202 (QB) various categories of information were reviewed in coming to the decision that, considering the factors under the Human Rights Act 1998 (HRA 1998), s 12(3) an injunction prohibiting the publication of information in the press would remain in force, but to a limited degree.

21.48   The years following the *Douglas* case witnessed an exponential increase in the number of applications for interim relief in privacy cases. Many of these concerned the private lives of celebrities.[61] In early 2011 public opinion was roused against these measures—termed by many 'gagging orders'. The concern was that the balance had been tipped too far against freedom of expression and too far in favour of the private lives of celebrities. In the face of high anxiety expressed in Parliament, by the press, and by leading politicians, the Master of the Rolls led a group to investigate the matter. In their report, it was noted that there was a difference between two types of injunctions being granted. One was a so-called 'super-injunction'. This is 'an interim injunction which restrains a person from: (i) publishing information which concerns the applicant and is said to be confidential or private; and (ii) publicising or informing others of the existence of the order and the proceedings'.[62] This type of injunction was granted only very rarely, and always for a fixed, and short, period of time.[63] The second type of injunction, an 'anonymised injunction' is 'an interim injunction which restrains a person from publishing information which concerns the applicant and is said to be confidential or private where the names of either or both of the parties to the proceedings are not stated'.[64] It is the latter type of injunction that was granted in the majority of the celebrity cases. Practice Guidance for the courts was issued as a result of the investigation which sets out clear guidelines for when such injunctions should be granted.[65]

Exercise

Read the Report of the Committee on Super-Injunctions: 'Super-Injunctions, Anonymised Injunctions and Open Justice'. What do you think of the conclusions and recommendations that they arrived at? Does this represent a fair balance between the various stakeholder interests?

21.49   There are, however, times when the information may be so widely available that court would feel the grant of an interim order to be inappropriate. In *Max Mosley v News Group Newspapers Ltd*[66] the High Court had to decide whether to grant an interim injunction prohibiting further publication of videos of Mosley engaged in sexual activity with prostitutes. While the court had little difficulty in deciding Mosley would prevail at trial, preventing further publication at the interim stage was judged to be unlikely to make any practical difference because it was so widely available it was, in essence, 'in the public domain'.[67] Allied to that was the argument that it would be inappropriate to restrain one organisation from publishing material when it was open to other media outlets, including competitors to publish the same information.[68] As a result, 'the granting of an order against this Respondent at the present juncture would merely be a futile gesture'.[69]

---

[61]   Cases included *ABC Ltd v Y* [2010] EWHC 3176 (Ch), [2011] 4 All ER 113; *Ambrosiadou v Coward* [2011] EWCA Civ 409, [2011] EMLR 21; *AMM v HXW* [2010] EWHC 2457 (QB); *ASG v GSA* [2009] EWCA Civ 1574; *Browne v Associated Newspapers Ltd* [2007] EWCA Civ 295, [2008] QB 103, [2007] EMLR20; *G v Wikimedia Foundation Inc* [2009] EWHC 3148 (QB), [2010] EMLR 14; *Goldsmith v BCD* [2011] EWHC 674 (QB), (2011) 108(14) LSG 20; *Gray v UVW* [2010] EWHC 2367 (QB); *JIH v News Group Newspapers Ltd* [2011] EWCA Civ 42, [2011] 2 All ER 324, [2011] EMLR 15.

[62]   Report of the Committee on Super-Injunctions: Super-Injunctions, Anonymised Injunctions and Open Justice, May 2011, iv.

[63]   *Ntuli v Donald* [2010] EWCA Civ 1276; *DFT v TFD* [2010] EWHC 2335 (QB). There had been two earlier cases which had raised concerns: *RJW & SJW v The Guardian Newspaper & Person or Persons Unknown* (Claim no HQ09) and *Terry v Persons Unknown* [2010] 1 FCR 659.

[64]   Report of the Committee on Super-Injunctions: Super-Injunctions, Anonymised Injunctions and Open Justice, May 2011, iv.

[65]   Practice Guidance: Interim Disclosure Orders, 1 August 2011 [2012] EMLR 5. Subsequent cases have included: *AMP v Persons Unknown* [2011] EWHC 3454 (TCC); *Spelman v Express Newspapers* [2012] EWHC 239 (QB); *KGM v News Group Newspapers* [2011] EWCA Civ 808; *Gray v News Group Newspapers Ltd* [2012] EWCA Civ 48; *Giggs v News Group Newspapers* [2012] EWHC 431 (QB); *Contostavlos v Mendahum* [2012] EWHC 850 (QB).

[66]   *Max Mosley v News Group Newspapers Ltd* [2008] EWHC 687 (QB).   [67]   ibid, para 33.

[68]   ibid, para 35; citing *Attorney-General v Times Newspapers Ltd* [2001] 1 WLR 885 at 895–96.

[69]   *Max Mosley v News Group Newspapers Ltd* [2008] EWHC 687 (QB), para 36. Mosley subsequently took his case to the European Court of Human Rights seeking a right to a pre-publication notification. He lost: *Mosley v United Kingdom* [2011] ECHR 774. On information being widely accessible and so refusing the grant of an interim injunction, see *BBC v HarperCollins Publishers Ltd* [2010] EWHC 2424 (Ch) (Stig).

Permanent injunctions/interdicts

21.50   After a finding of infringement, a permanent injunction or interdict may be granted to a claimant who proves his case at trial.[70] Article 11 IPED requires member states to ensure that courts may issue an injunction against an infringer aimed at prohibiting the continuation of the relevant infringement. Because of the UK courts' existing power to grant permanent injunctions or interdicts, it was not felt necessary to take any specific steps to transpose Article 11 into UK law. It would be wrong, however, to think that the Enforcement Directive has had no impact on the UK case law on the availability and grant of permanent injunctions.

21.51   The general obligations at Article 3 IPED have become particularly relevant. Although Article 3 IPED was never formally transposed into UK law, over the course of a series of cases the English courts have established that, in view of Article 3(2) IPED in particular, like all remedies for infringement, a permanent injunction must be proportionate.[71] In *HTC v Nokia*, Arnold J concluded:[72]

> In my view, the time has come to recognise that, in cases concerning infringements of intellectual property rights, the criteria to be applied when deciding whether or not to grant an injunction are those laid down by art. 3(2): efficacy, proportionality, dissuasiveness, the avoidance of creating barriers to legitimate trade and the provision of safeguards against abuse.

In appropriate cases, this means that the court must balance the various fundamental rights existing under EU law: for example, balancing the right of intellectual property at Article 17(2) of the EU Charter of Fundamental Rights against (if relevant) the right to freedom of expression, the right of the arts to be free from constraint, and other fundamental rights under the ECHR and EU Charter.[73] How far reference to proportionality will serve to limit the availability of permanent injunctions in practice remains to be seen, however. Technically, injunctions have always been a discretionary remedy and the court has always had the power to decline to grant an injunction where the infringement is trivial or technical, or unlikely to occur again.[74] In some cases, there may be no countervailing fundamental rights and thus no requirement to balance rights against each other.[75] The court may also take the view that an injunction can be both proportionate and at the same time still impose considerable burdens on the infringer. For example, in *Comic Enterprise*, after finding trade mark infringement the court proceeded to grant an injunction requiring the defendant, Twentieth Century Fox, to cease using the mark 'Glee' for its highly successful television series of that name and rejected the argument that this would not be fair or equitable. This was notwithstanding evidence submitted by the defendant that changing the name of the show would have a massive adverse impact, requiring huge marketing efforts to ensure that viewers were aware of the retitled series, associated it with the original series, and understood its relationship to the original programmes.[76]

21.52   For EU trade marks and Community designs, the national court's discretion on whether to grant an injunction is more limited. Article 130(a) EU Trade Mark Regulation 2017/1001 provides that if a national

---

[70]   See PA 1977, s 61(1)(a); CDPA 1988, s 96(2); TMA 1994, s 14(2); RDA 1949, s 24A(2).

[71]   *Virgin Atlantic v Premium Aircraft* [2010] FSR 15 at para 23; *Vestergaard Frandsen S/A and Others v Bestnet Europe Ltd and Others* [2011] EWCA Civ 424, para 56; *Interflora Inc v Marks & Spencer Plc (No 2)* (High Court) [2014] FSR 2, paras 16–17 and 20; *Thomas Pink Limited v Victoria's Secret UK Limited* (High Court) [2014] EWHC 3258 (Ch), para 11; *Interflora Inc v Marks & Spencer Plc (No 2)* (CA) [2015] ETMR 5, para 197.

[72]   *HTC Corporation v Nokia Corporation (No 2)* (HC) [2014] RPC 30, para 26, not considered on appeal. See, more recently, also *Merck KGaA v Merck Sharp & Dohme Corp and Others* [2017] EWCA Civ 1834.

[73]   *Comic Enterprise Ltd v Twentieth Century Fox Film Corp* (High Court) [2014] ETMR 51, paras 5–15; *HTC Corporation v Nokia Corporation (No 2)* (HC) [2014] RPC 30, para 27.

[74]   *Cantor Gaming Ltd v Gameaccount Global Ltd* [2008] FSR 4, para 112, indicating that this is unaffected by the IPED.

[75]   *HTC Corporation v Nokia Corporation (No 2)* (HC) [2014] RPC 30, para 28.

[76]   *Comic Enterprise Ltd v Twentieth Century Fox Film Corp* (High Court) [2014] ETMR 51 at paras 16–34, although the court did note that the injunction should allow the defendant to refer to the fact that its retitled show was previously known as 'Glee'.

court sitting as an EU trade mark court finds that the defendant has infringed or threatens to infringe an EU trade mark:[77]

> it shall, *unless there are special reasons for not doing so*, issue an order prohibiting the defendant from proceeding with the acts which infringed or would infringe the EU trade mark (emphasis added).

The interpretation of this provision was considered by the Court of Justice in *Nokia v Wärdell*.[78] In that case, although the defendant (an individual) had been found to have infringed the NOKIA trade mark, the national court had declined to issue an injunction because it was the defendant's first infringement and because the infringement was regarded as having resulted from carelessness. The Court of Justice responded that the expression 'special reasons' must be given a uniform interpretation. The objective was the uniform protection of the right conferred by the EU trade mark throughout the entire area of the EU. This provision did not permit a national court to make the grant of an injunction conditional on an obvious or 'not merely limited' risk of recurrence the infringing acts on the part of the defendant.

21.53 Turning back to think about all IP rights generally, the scope of the prohibition granted by a permanent injunction has also been the subject of some debate in light of the Enforcement Directive. In the UK, an injunction is conventionally worded in general terms prohibiting infringement of the relevant IP right but without specifying particular acts which are to be restrained. It has been argued that this broad, conventional form of injunction does not meet the requirement of proportionality as required by Article 3 IPED. This argument has, however, been rejected.[79]

21.54 It is, however, accepted that, while the conventional form of injunction will be appropriate in most cases, there will be times, in order to be fair to the defendant, that a more specific injunction may be ordered at the court's discretion.[80] Such injunctions have tended to be used in parallel imports cases where there may be a particular issue of proportionality given that the infringer is dealing in genuine goods and given that it may be difficult for the infringer himself conclusively to verify whether the goods have been placed on the market with consent. In such circumstances, a general injunction may operate as a barrier to legitimate trade.[81] For an example of a qualified injunction issued in such circumstances, see:

■ *Sun Microsystems Inc v Amtec Computer Systems Corp Ltd* [2006] FSR 35

This concerned the unlawful sale by Amtec of Sun computers which had not been put on the market in the European Economic Area (EEA) with the consent of Sun. Before selling computers in the EEA, Amtec had been to some lengths to ensure the goods they resold had been lawfully placed on the market. They used only a reputable supplier and included a term in their contract with that supplier stipulating that supplies should be of EU origin. The court accepted that a broad injunction, prohibiting Amtec dealing in Sun products, would have the practical effect of closing their legitimate business, a solution which would not be proportionate. Further, it was impossible for Amtec to know that the Sun products that it dealt with had been put on the market with consent unless Sun provided information on the products. Thus, a qualified injunction would be granted which would allow Amtec to deal in Sun products if:

- Amtec informed Sun by writing or by email of the serial numbers of products they were going to sell together with a description of the product indicating whether it was new or second-hand;

---

[77] See also Art 89(1) Community Design Regulation 6/2002/EC.   [78] Case C-316/05 *Nokia Corp v Wärdell* [2007] ETMR 20.

[79] *Interflora Inc v Marks & Spencer Plc (No 2)* (High Court) [2014] FSR 2, paras 20–22; *Enterprise Holdings Inc v Europcar Group UK Limited and Another* [2015] EWHC 300 (Ch), paras 1–3.

[80] *Specsavers International Healthcare Ltd v Asda Stores Ltd (No 2)* [2012] FSR 20, para 10; *Interflora Inc v Marks & Spencer Plc (No 2)* (High Court) [2014] FSR 2, para 23.

[81] *Interflora Inc v Marks & Spencer Plc (No 2)* (High Court) [2014] FSR 2, para 24.

- Sun had not responded within a defined period (between seven to 14 days) indicating that its records showed to its satisfaction that the product had not been put on the market in the EEA by it or with its consent; provided that

- Amtec did not know or believe that the product had not been put on the market in the EEA by, or with the consent of, Sun.

It is interesting to note that this type of limited injunction requires Sun and Amtec to work together to identify potentially infringing goods.

Exercise

Can you think of cases other than those dealing with parallel imports in which the scope of an injunction should be narrow? Do you think such limited injunctions are fair to both claimant and defendant?

21.55   In appropriate cases the courts may award a so-called 'springboard' injunction to restrain an infringer's activities for a period post-expiry of the relevant IP right. This might be appropriate, for example, in a case where an infringer managed to launch its own product onto the market immediately on the expiry of a patent by infringing the patent in the period immediately before patent expiry through the conducting of tests necessary to obtain marketing approvals. The infringer in such a case might be injuncted from marketing his product for the time period which it would have taken him to reach the market had he commenced tests only after the patent expired. Although it has been accepted that the concept of a 'springboard' injunction does not fit neatly within the IPED, it has been held that it would be consistent with the general principles at Article 3(2) IPED, particularly the requirements of effectiveness and dissuasiveness.[82]

21.56   It is also possible for a court to award damages in lieu of an injunction. In pre-IPED case law, this was possible in cases where the grant of a permanent interdict would be 'grossly disproportionate'. Article 12 IPED permits, although does not require, member states to provide for damages in lieu of an injunction. In recent case law it has been suggested that, in patent cases courts should be cautious of making an order for damages in lieu of injunction which would, in effect, be tantamount to a compulsory licence in circumstances where no compulsory licence would be available. The burden on the party seeking to show that the injunction would be disproportionate should be a heavy one, to a standard little different to the pre-IPED requirements.[83]

21.57   For IP rights protected under national law (patents, UK registered trade marks, UK registered designs, copyright, and so on), the territorial reach of an injunction will not extend beyond the UK. However, for EU-level IP rights (the EU trade mark and Community design) there are provisions which give national courts designated as an 'EU trade mark court' or 'Community design court' jurisdiction which extends to cover the whole of the EU. Those provisions can be found at Article 126 EU Trade Mark Regulation 2017/1001 and Article 83 Community Design Regulation 6/2002/EC. Whether a national court has this sort of pan-EU jurisdiction will depend on the basis upon which that court itself has jurisdiction over the dispute in hand, and will arise in particular if the court has jurisdiction because the defendant or claimant is domiciled in the relevant member state.[84] In such cases, these provisions in effect empower a national court to grant injunctions which cover the whole of the EU in terms of their territorial scope.

---

[82] *Smith & Nephew plc v Convatec Technologies Inc (No 2)* [2014] RPC 22, para 130.

[83] *HTC Corporation v Nokia Corporation (No 2)* (HC) [2014] RPC 30, para 32.

[84] And on various further grounds, see Arts 125(1)–(4) and 126 EUTMR 2017; and Arts 82(1)–(4) and 83 CDR 6/2002/EC. The national court will not have the power to grant a pan-EU injunction if its jurisdiction is based on the location of where the act of infringement was committed or threatened: Arts 125(5) and EUTMR 2017 and Arts 82(5) and 83 CDR 6/2002/EC.

21.58　Case law from the Court of Justice has, however, somewhat eroded the force of these provisions, at least as far as pan-EU injunctions for infringement of EU trade marks are concerned. In *DHL v Chronopost*, the Court of Justice noted that, in appropriate cases, the jurisdiction of a national court dealing with infringement of an EU trade mark may extend to the entire area of the EU.[85] Bearing in mind the unitary character of an EU trade mark and the objective of providing uniform protection for EU trade marks across all member states, an injunction issued by a national court in such a case should 'as a rule' extend to the entire area of the EU.[86] However, the territorial scope of an injunction could be restricted if the national court concluded that the acts of infringement were limited to a single member state or to only part of the territory of the EU; this could arise, for example, if use of the trade mark did not affect or was not liable to affect the functions of the registered trade mark in a given area, perhaps because of linguistic considerations.[87] Building on this, in *combit Software GmbH v Commit Business Solutions* the Court of Justice ruled that a national court should limit the territorial scope of an injunction if it found that the use of a similar sign to the registered mark did not create any likelihood of confusion in a given part of the EU (again, eg, for linguistic reasons) and, as a result, did not adversely affect the origin function of the registered mark in that part of the EU.[88] On the one hand, this approach seems to cut across the key principle of the unitary character of EU trade marks. On the other hand, some commentators have welcomed this approach as reflecting the realities of the differences in markets across different member states.[89] It remains to be seen whether similar case law might develop for Community designs, although the linguistic considerations which were clearly significant in the Court's reasoning in *DHL* and *combit* are less relevant when it comes to designs.

Delivery up

21.59　A court may order delivery up or destruction of infringing articles.[90] The purpose of such an order is to ensure that the infringing goods do not enter circulation. Article 10 IPED (not specifically implemented in the UK) also contains provision for the granting of 'corrective measures' including recall or removal from channels of commerce or destruction. It has been confirmed that an order for the destruction of infringing products under section 61(1)(b) PA 1977 is consistent with Article 10 IPED.[91]

Financial remedies

Damages

21.60　One possible form of financial remedy is an award of damages.[92] In UK law, in common with damages in other actions in tort and delict, the purpose of an award of damages is compensatory. Damages are intended to put the claimant back in the position he would have been had the infringement not occurred; they are not intended to be punitive. To be recoverable, the claimant's losses must have been foreseeable, caused by the infringement, and not excluded from recovery by public or social policy. In cases where a claimant has exploited his IP rights by manufacture and sale, among other heads of damage it is possible to claim lost profits from sales made by the infringer that would otherwise have come to the claimant. The claimant may also seek to recover lost profits on his own sales, for example if forced to drop his own price to compete with the infringer. It is also possible to claim a reasonable royalty on sales by the infringer which the claimant would not have made. The aim is to award a royalty in line with what would have been agreed between a

---

[85] Case C-235/09 *DHL Express France SAS v Chronopost SA* [2011] ETMR 33, para 38.　　[86] ibid, para 44.

[87] ibid, paras 46–48. On registered trade mark functions, see Chapter 15.

[88] Case C-223/15 *combit Software GmbH v Commit Business Solutions Ltd* [2016] Bus LR 1393.

[89] See, eg, A Kur, 'Case C-235/09, DHL Express France SAS v Chronopost SA' (2012), 49(2) CML Rev 753–66.

[90] See PA 1977, s 61(1)(b); CDPA 1988, ss 96(2), 99, and 195; TMA 1994, ss 14(2) and 16; Registered Designs Act 1949, s 24A(2) and 24C.

[91] *Merck Canada Inc v Sigma Pharmaceuticals Plc* (CA) [2013] RPC 35 at para 89.

[92] See PA 1977, s 61(1)(c); CDPA 1988, s 96(2); TMA 1994, s 14(2); RDA 1949, s 24A(2).

willing licensor and willing licensee, bearing in mind their respective bargaining positions, the information available to them, and the commercial context to the notional negotiation.[93]

21.61   In some instances (although notably not for registered trade mark infringement), it may not be possible to obtain an award of damages against an 'innocent infringer' who, at the time of the infringement, did not know, and had no reason to believe, that the relevant IP right subsisted.[94] The fact that an article is accompanied by the words 'registered' or 'patented' does not thereby mean that the defendant has knowledge. However, that does not apply if the number of the registration is included. The Intellectual Property Act 2014 has also amended section 62 PA 1977 to give patentees the alternative of marking their products with a web link leading to the relevant patent details. Generally, the courts have set a relatively high threshold for proof of 'innocence', expecting businesses to be aware of the possibility of IP protection and to carry out reasonably prudent checks. For example, in a recent UK unregistered design right (UDR) case, rejecting an argument that there had been innocent infringement, the judge commented:[95]

> I think the fallacy of the argument lies in the suggestion that in the normal course a defendant who comes across an article will have no reason to believe that design right subsists. In the context of an industrial article, that will generally not be the case. If the defendant picks up a stone from a beach, plainly a reasonable man in his position would have no reason to believe that design right subsists in its design. By contrast, he is likely to have good reason to suppose that design right subsists in an industrial article. He is deemed familiar with the law relating to UDRs, otherwise he could never reach any concluded view as to the subsistence of design right. Also, part of his reasonable make-up is the knowledge that industrial articles are commonly protected by UDRs. He is not an innocent abroad.

 Question

In what circumstances do you think that a person who infringes a right could successfully claim to be an 'innocent infringer'?

21.62   In most cases, if the infringement covers a period of time when the relevant IP right was pending as an application, it is possible to backdate the recovery of damages. For example, in UK patent law damages can be backdated to the date upon which the application for the patent was published.[96] In relation to EU trade marks, Article 11(2) EU Trade Mark Regulation 2017/1001 provides:

> *Reasonable compensation* may be claimed in respect of acts occurring after the date of publication of an EU trade mark application, where those acts would, after publication of the registration of the trade mark, be prohibited by virtue of that publication (emphasis added).

What is meant by this reference to 'reasonable compensation' was considered by the Court of Justice in *Nikolajeva v Multi Protect*.[97] Because acts of infringement caught by this provision would have taken place at a time when it was not certain that the trade mark would be registered, the Court of Justice took the view that 'reasonable compensation' in this context must be more limited than the damages which could be awarded to the proprietor of a trade mark for acts occurring after the date of registration. Thus, in the view of the Court, this provision only permits the recovery of the profits derived by the infringer from

---

[93] For the principal authorities on damages for IP infringement, see generally: *General Tire and Rubber Company v Firestone Tyre and Rubber Company Limited* [1976] RPC 197; *Gerber Garment Technology v Lectra Systems* (HC) [1995] RPC 383 and (CA) [1997] RPC 443; *Ultraframe (UK) Limited v Eurocell Building Plastics Limited and Another* [2006] EWHC 1344 (Pat).

[94] See PA 1977, s 62(1); CDPA 1988, ss 97(1) and 191J; RDA 1949, s 24B.

[95] *Kohler Mira Ltd v Bristan Group Ltd (No 2)* [2015] FSR 9, para 18.

[96] Section 69 PA 1977, although this is subject to a discretion on the part of the court to reduce the award if it would not have been reasonable for a third party to expect the patent to be granted in terms which covered the infringing act: PA 1977, s 69(3).

[97] Case C-280/15 *Nikolajeva v Multi Protect OU* [2016] ETMR 42.

use of the infringing sign during the relevant period; compensation for any wider harm which the trade mark owner may have suffered is excluded. This is, perhaps, a slightly curious outcome when one considers that the infringer's profits may, in some cases (particularly instances of counterfeiting) outstrip the losses incurred by the trade mark owner. Nonetheless, the Court of Justice appears to have taken the view that an account of profits is necessarily likely to be more limited than an award of damages. This may, at least in part, be attributed to the outstanding controversial points of interpretation on Article 13 of the Enforcement Directive, discussed at para 21.66ff below.

Additional damages

21.63   Additional damages may be awarded by a court in an action for infringement of copyright, rights in performances, and UK unregistered design right. The court is required to have regard to all the circumstances, and in particular to the flagrancy of the infringement and any benefit which may accrue to the defendant by reason of the infringement.[98] Flagrancy could include sales in breach of a court order.[99] Additional damages are in addition to an award of 'normal' damages and so a claimant can only elect for additional damages if normal damages are claimed.[100] This means that it is not possible to claim additional damages with an account of profits (for which para 21.65). Neither are additional damages available where ordinary damages are not granted, for instance in cases of innocent infringement.

21.64   The nature of the award of additional damages was considered at some length by Pumfrey J in the following case:

■ *Nottinghamshire Healthcare NHS Trust v News Group Newspapers Ltd* [2002] EWHC 409 (Ch)[101]

The case concerned the infringement of copyright in a photograph of a patient at Rampton Hospital published by the *Sun* newspaper. Copyright in the photograph belonged to the NHS Trust. While the measure of damages was to be calculated on the basis of infringement of copyright, the fact that the photograph was confidential, being part of a patient's medical records, does appear to have had a bearing on the decision. It was clear that the court wished to award additional damages taking into account the 'flagrancy of the infringement'.[102] But what did this phrase mean and what should the award of additional damages reflect? Should damages be exemplary in that an award would be intended both to compensate the claimant for the loss, and to teach the defendant that infringement does not pay? Or should they rather be aggravated, which would compensate the claimant for the loss, but would also take into account the injury to the claimant's feelings of pride and dignity, humiliation, distress, insult, or pain?[103] After much deliberation the court decided that an award of additional damages should not be punitive or exemplary in nature, pointing to the difficulties that would occur if this was not the case, particularly where an infringer was sued by successive claimants each seeking punishment for their respective interests. The example was given of a counterfeiter who had produced numerous CDs.[104] Pumphrey J did, however, consider that the section permitted an aggravation of an award of damages 'on a basis far wider than the factors admitted as aggravation at common law'.[105] In particular, it permitted an element of restitution. In the event £450 was awarded as the fee that would have been negotiated between a willing copyright owner and the newspaper and, having regard to the flagrancy and the need to do justice in the case, the total damages were set at £10,000.[106]

---

[98]   See CDPA 1988, ss 97(2), 191J(2), and 229(3).

[99]   See, eg, *Sony Computer Entertainment v Owen* [2002] EWHC 45 (Ch).

[100]   *Ravenscroft v Herbert* [1980] RPC 193; *Redrow Homes Ltd v Bett Brothers plc* [1999] 1 AC 197, [1998] 1 All ER 385, [1998] FSR 345.

[101]   See also *Experience Hendrix LLC v Times Newspapers Ltd* [2010] EWHC 1986 (Ch).

[102]   See CDPA 1988, s 97(2)(a).

[103]   *Nottinghamshire Healthcare NHS Trust v News Group Newspapers Ltd* [2002] EWHC 409 (Ch), para 33.

[104]   ibid, para 51.   [105]   ibid.   [106]   ibid, para 60.

In the words of the judge:[107]

> If this [sum of £10,000] exceeds the sum appropriate under section 97(2) having regard to the benefit to the Defendant, then no further infringements of this kind will take place. If further infringements consisting of the publishing of stolen photographs from medical records do take place, it will show the advantage to the newspaper still exceeds the award of damages.

However, there continues to be debate over the nature of an award of additional damages.[108] More recently, Lewison LJ in the Court of Appeal in *Phonographic Performance Limited v Andrew Ellis Trading as Bla Bar* rejected arguments that additional damages should be 'shoehorned into existing general legal taxonomy'; in his view, 'their legal character is sui generis'.[109] In his view (with which the other Lords Justice concurred) additional damages awarded in IP cases may be regarded as partly or even wholly punitive.[110] In Lewison LJ's view, the ability to award additional damages on this basis is unaffected by the IP Enforcement Directive, although he noted that a particularly excessive award of punitive damages might contravene the prohibition on abuse of rights at Article 3(2) IPED in light of recent Court of Justice case law.[111]

Account of profits

21.65   An alternative to a damages claim is a claim for an account of profits.[112] An account of profits is a discretionary equitable remedy. There is also continuing academic discussion about the exact nature of the remedy,[113] although one view is that it is based on the fiction that the infringer has carried out the infringing act on behalf of the right owner such that the owner is entitled to the profits made from the infringement and, by extension, the infringer is deprived of unfair or unjustified profits.[114] Once liability is established, the long-standing rule of UK law is that the IP owner can opt for either damages or an account of profits, but not both. An account of profits will look to the infringer's net profits, deducting any profits attributable to any non-infringing parts of the defendant's product.[115]

Article 13 of the Enforcement Directive

21.66   While the principles set out above governing damages and accounts of profits are long-standing in UK law, a number of as yet unresolved questions have been raised by Article 13 IPED. Article 13(1) IPED, which applies only to knowing infringement, provides as follows:

> Member States shall ensure that the competent judicial authorities, on application of the injured party, order the infringer who knowingly, or with reasonable grounds to know, engaged in an infringing activity, to pay the rightholder damages appropriate to the actual prejudice suffered by him/her as the result of the infringement.

---

[107] ibid. See also *PPL v Reader* [2005] EWHC 416 (Ch).

[108] See, eg, D Liu, 'Reforming additional damages in copyright law' (2017) 7 JBL 576–97; J Marshall, 'Aggravated or exemplary damages for copyright infringement?' (2017) 39(9) EIPR 565–73.

[109] *Phonographic Performance Limited v Andrew Ellis Trading as Bla Bla Bar* [2018] EWCA Civ 2812 (currently unreported), para 36.

[110] ibid, para 37.

[111] ibid, paras 39–42, considering the Court of Justice's decision in Case C-367/15 *Stowarzyszenie Olawska Telewizja Kablowa (OTK) v Stowarzyszenie Filmowcow Polskich (SFP)* [2017] ECDR 16 (see para 21.72 below).

[112] See PA 1977, s 61(1)(d); CDPA 1988, s 96(2); TMA 1994, s 14(2); RDA 1949, s 24A(2).

[113] See, eg, D Liu, 'Reflecting on an account of profits for infringement of intellectual property', (2017) 39(10) EIPR 623–38; J Marshall, 'Account of profit for infringement of intellectual property rights' (2018) 40(4) EIPR 260–69.

[114] *Bayer Cropscience KK v Charles River Laboratories Preclinical Services Edinburgh Ltd* [2010] CSOH 158.

[115] *Celanese International Corp v BP Chemicals Ltd* [1999] RPC 203.

When the judicial authorities set the damages:

(a) they shall take into account all appropriate aspects, such as the negative economic consequences, including lost profits, which the injured party has suffered, any unfair profits made by the infringer and, in appropriate cases, elements other than economic factors, such as the moral prejudice caused to the rightholder by the infringement; or

(b) as an alternative to (a), they may, in appropriate cases, set the damages as a lump sum on the basis of elements such as at least the amount of royalties or fees which would have been due if the infringer had requested authorisation to use the intellectual property right in question.

Recital 26 adds inter alia that the aim is 'not to introduce an obligation to provide for punitive damages, but to allow for compensation based on an objective criterion'.

21.67   Article 13(1) IPED poses a number of difficulties, perhaps most significantly the inclusion of 'unfair profits made by the infringer' in what is, at least on its face, a damages provision. As noted above, it has always been a long-established principle of UK law that a claimant must elect between damages or an account of profits, and cannot obtain both. In contrast, Article 13 IPED appears to some degree to merge the two concepts. There has also been considerable uncertainty over the meaning of the expression 'moral prejudice' (Art 13(1)(a)), the quantum of the 'lump sum' which can be awarded under Article 13(1)(b), and the extent to which damages under Article 13 can extend beyond the strictly compensatory.

21.68   At the time of implementation of the IPED into UK law, the government was unsure what the impact of Article 13 IPED should be taken to be. It therefore transposed Article 13 IPED effectively verbatim, leaving the task of interpreting the new law to the courts.[116] Scholarly commentary has suggested that Article 13 IPED marks a shift away from traditional tort law principles and awards of purely compensatory damages, making the long-standing UK approach (and, in particular, its requirement to elect between damages and an account of profits) potentially redundant.[117] However, the English courts have been resistant to arguments that Article 13 IPED affects the fundamental existing UK law principles on recovery of damages or on the award of an account. This resistance has been the subject of criticism, particularly when contrasted against the willingness of the English courts to give effect to 'new' European remedies such as injunctions against intermediaries (as discussed at paras 21.74ff below).[118]

21.69   Nonetheless, the English case law has shown little movement in favour of adjusting the traditional approaches to monetary remedies. In *Hollister v Medik*, the Court of Appeal reversed a first instance ruling which had reduced the amount payable on an account of profits by reference to the absence of loss to the right holder, stating:[119]

An assessment of the damage caused to the claimant forms no part of an account of the profits made by an infringer and the approach adopted by the judge constituted an illegitimate amalgamation of two quite different ways of assessing compensation.

---

[116] The Intellectual Property (Enforcement, etc.) Regulations 2006 (SI 1028/2013), reg 3. See also the accompanying Explanatory Memorandum, which comments:

Article 13(1) sets out a range of factors which must be taken into account in awarding damages. It includes a number of terms the meaning of which is unclear, for example 'actual prejudice' and 'moral prejudice'. It does not therefore seem appropriate to attempt to translate these terms into those of national law, and accordingly to ensure that the United Kingdom is in compliance with Article 13(1) the copy out approach has been adopted (para 3.1). (www.legislation.gov.uk/uksi/2006/1028/pdfs/uksiem_20061028_en.pdf).

[117] See, eg, J Fitzgerald and A Firth, 'Is Article 13 of the Enforcement Directive a redundancy notice for the account of profits remedy in the UK?' (2014) 9(9) JIPLP 737–41.

[118] J Cornwell, 'Injunctions and monetary remedies compared: the English judicial response to the IP Enforcement Directive' (2018) 40(8) EIPR 490–500.

[119] *Hollister Inc and Dansac A/S v Medik Ostomy Supplies Ltd* [2013] ETMR 10, para 71.

Although the Court of Appeal did accept that the scope of Article 13 was 'not entirely clear' and that the EU legislators could have used the term 'damages' in Article 13 in 'a broad sense to include both reimbursement of the right holder's lost profits and the return of profits made by the infringer',[120] subsequent case law has reiterated that there is no change to the basic UK law rule that a claimant cannot recover both damages and an account of profits.[121] Instead, the view has been taken that the reference to 'unfair profits' in Article 13(1)(a) IPED must mean something else. In *Henderson*, the first instance judged adopted the approach that 'unfair profits' would be recoverable in cases where the claimant would not receive adequate compensation if damages were assessed by reference to lost profits, moral prejudice and expenses (Art 13(1)(a) IPED), royalties (Art 13(1)(b) IPED), or account of profits. In such circumstances, there should be 'flexibility' to award a sum related to the profit the defendant made from his infringement:[122]

> This would arise, for example, if the defendant made no direct financial profit from the infringement—so an account of profits would be of little use—but his business expanded in volume and/or in reputation on the back of loss-leader infringements. For the claimant, aside from losing sales there would be a likelihood of further loss because of the expansion of a competing business. The expansion would not constitute a profit by the defendant in the usual direct sense, but it would be a contingent profit nonetheless and an unfair one.

It remains to be seen whether this approach will be upheld in future cases, particularly at the appellate level.

21.70 The UK courts have been prepared to entertain the argument that Article 13 acts as a new form of 'additional damages'. Thus, in *Henderson*, Article 13 IPED was held to have overtaken the UK additional damages rules. More recently, however, in *Absolute Lofts* Article 13 IPED and section 97(2) of the CDPA 1988 were held to coexist, the claimant being entitled to rely on whichever would provide the greater award.[123] *Absolute Lofts* suggests some greater degree of acceptance that Article 13(1) may not align with traditional English law damages rules, Hacon J commenting:[124]

> I think it would be a mistake to interpret the limitation on the award of damages in art. 13(1) —to the actual prejudice suffered by the rightholder—in the same way. To my mind it is a looser limitation than the English concept of strictly compensatory damages.

Interestingly, although Article 13 IPED was directed to an award 'appropriate to the actual prejudice suffered', it was held that this could include a restitutionary element based on the infringer's unfair profits (although always stopping short of awarding both damages and an account); the general requirement of deterrence at Article 3 IPED should also be taken into account in this context.[125] In the *Absolute Lofts* case, the 'actual prejudice' was that the claimant had not shared in the unfair profits made by the defendant from the infringement.[126] The court applied both section 97(2) of the CDPA 1988 and Article 13 IPED, coming to the conclusion that they would result in the award of the same sum.

21.71 *Absolute Lofts* also considered the 'lump sum' provision in Article 13(1)(b) IPED. It was accepted that the reference in Article 13(1)(b) to a lump sum 'such as at least' the sum due if the infringing acts had been licensed gives national courts 'express authority to go above what (using English terms) would have been

---

[120] ibid, para 60.

[121] *Henderson v All Around the World Recordings Limited* [2014] EWHC 3087 (IPEC), paras 72–77. See also *Absolute Lofts South West London Limited v Artisan Home Improvements Limited and Another* [2015] EWHC 2608 (IPEC), para 11.

[122] *Henderson v All Around the World Recordings Limited* [2014] EWHC 3087 (IPEC), paras 80–81. Endorsed in *Link UP Mitaka Limited trading as Thebigword v Language Empire Limited, Yasar Zaman* [2018] EWHC 2633 (IPEC).

[123] *Henderson v All Around the World Recordings Limited* [2014] EWHC 3087 (IPEC), para 97; *DKH Retail Ltd v H Young (Operations) Ltd* [2015] FSR 21, para 118; *Absolute Lofts South West London Limited v Artisan Home Improvements Limited and Another* [2015] EWHC 2608 (IPEC), paras 38–42.

[124] *Absolute Lofts South West London Limited v Artisan Home Improvements Limited and Another* [2015] EWHC 2608 (IPEC), para 53.

[125] ibid, paras 50–55.   [126] ibid, para 58.

negotiated between a willing licensor and willing licensee'.[127] A royalty-based award could be supplemented with the infringer's unfair profits or an award for moral prejudice: in Hacon J's view, given that the Enforcement Directive is a minimum-standards directive, 'as a matter of permissible national law there is apparently unfettered freedom' to exceed the normal hypothetical royalty.[128]

21.72   The ability to cumulate damages for moral prejudice under Article 13(1)(a) with a lump sum under Article 13(1)(b) has also been confirmed by the Court of Justice in *Liffers v Producciones Mandarina SL*.[129] Noting the use of the expression 'at least' in Article 13(1)(b) and observing the objective of the Enforcement Directive to ensure a high, equivalent and homogeneous level of IP protection, the Court of Justice held that determining an Article 13(1)(b) lump sum award on the basis of hypothetical royalties alone would only cover the 'material damage' suffered by the right holder; to be compensated in full for the 'actual prejudice suffered' in accordance with the opening words of Article 13 IPED, it had to be possible for the right holder also to claim compensation for any moral prejudice suffered.[130] In *Stowarzyszenie Olawska Telewizja Kablowa (OTK) v Stowarzyszenie Filmowcow Polskich (SFP)*, the Court of Justice has also confirmed that Article 13 does not preclude national legislation permitting a lump sum award of double the relevant hypothetical royalty.[131]

21.73   As can be seen, although there have not been many preliminary references to date, the Court of Justice's case law tends to favour a more, rather than, less generous approach to monetary awards under Article 13 IPED. Aside from this, the UK courts have also interpreted the concept of 'moral prejudice' at Article 13(1)(a). The Commission's Explanatory Memorandum issued during the course of the drafting of the Enforcement Directive indicated that 'moral prejudice' could arise from damage to brand image or reputation, but this approach has been rejected by the English courts.[132] In the UK, it has been held that 'moral prejudice' must relate to non-economic loss and that the expression 'moral prejudice' covers distress, injury to feelings, and humiliation; moral prejudice should only be recoverable, however, in cases where the claimant suffered little or no financial loss and would therefore be left with no, or disproportionately little, compensation if the loss was small but the moral prejudice significant.[133] It is not clear upon what basis these limitations on the recoverability of moral prejudice have been read into Article 13. Again, it remains to be seen how far this approach will be adopted in future cases or by the Court of Justice. Although not articulated by the Court of Justice in *Liffers* (above), it is implicit in the Court's judgment in that case that 'moral prejudice' is not a form of 'material damage'. However, the Court of Justice did not elaborate on what exactly the expression 'moral prejudice' should be taken to cover. Recent commentary has highlighted that moral damage is a 'notoriously nebulous concept': potentially relevant examples include the use of a copyright work belonging to a children's author in an adult entertainment context industry, or the use of scientific work to argue (erroneously) against the conclusions reached by its author.[134] If the Court of Justice were to interpret the concept of 'moral prejudice' in such a way as to capture either of these examples, this would be a significant departure from the current English case law approach.

---

[127] ibid, para 47.   [128] ibid, para 48.

[129] Case C-99/15 *Liffers v Producciones Mandarina SL* [2016] ECDR 22.

[130] ibid, paras 15–26 in particular.

[131] Case C-367/15 *Stowarzyszenie Olawska Telewizja Kablowa (OTK) v Stowarzyszenie Filmowcow Polskich (SFP)* [2017] ECDR 16. The Court of Justice did note that a double-royalty payment might so exceed the actual loss in some cases that it could be in breach of the prohibition on abuse of rights at Art 3(2) IPED, but otherwise hedged its position on whether the IPED does, or does not, prohibit punitive damages in national law: paras 28 and 29. There remains uncertainty as to how this issue will be resolved: see, eg, P Torremans, 'Compensation for intellectual property infringement: admissibility of punitive damages and compensation for moral prejudice' (2018) 40(12) EIPR 797–802.

[132] *Henderson v All Around the World Recordings Limited* [2014] EWHC 3087 (IPEC), paras 90–91.

[133] *Kohler Mira Ltd v Bristan Group Ltd (No 2)* [2015] FSR 9, para 60; *Henderson v All Around the World Recordings Limited* [2014] EWHC 3087 (IPEC), paras 84–94. Not awarded on the facts of the case: para 95.

[134] P Torremans, 'Compensation for intellectual property infringement: admissibility of punitive damages and compensation for moral prejudice' (2018) 40(12) EIPR 797–802.

Intermediary injunctions

21.74   One of the pressing issues to face courts in interpretation of the Enforcement Directive has been in relation to the grant of injunctions against intermediaries whose services are being used by another party to commit an infringement. The third sentence of Article 11 IPED states:

> Member States shall also ensure that rightholders are in a position to apply for an injunction against intermediaries whose services are used by a third party to infringe an intellectual property right, without prejudice to Article 8(3) of Directive 2001/29/EC.

21.75   Article 11 IPED sits alongside the previously enacted Article 8(3) InfoSoc Directive, which is in essentially the same terms but relates only to copyright.[135] In essence, Article 11 IPED extends the obligation to provide for injunctions against intermediaries from cases involving infringement of copyright and related rights, dealt with by Article 8(3) InfoSoc Directive, to all forms of IP infringement.[136] According to Recital 23 IPED, the conditions and procedures relating to intermediary injunctions are left to national laws.

21.76   An oddity in the UK is that, while the UK government felt that it was appropriate explicitly to transpose Article 8(2) InfoSoc Directive into UK law, creating the then new section 97A of the CDPA 1988, no steps were taken to transpose Article 11 IPED into UK law.[137] This triggered a series of judgments considering whether the English courts have the power to grant intermediary injunctions as required by Article 11 IPED pursuant to their inherent powers under section 37(1) of the Senior Courts Act 1981. The first case to consider this was *L'Oréal SA v eBay International AG*.[138] Arnold J concluded that Article 11 IPED provided a 'principled basis for the exercise of an existing jurisdiction in a new way'.[139] The point arose again, and was considered more fully at first instance and on appeal to the Court of Appeal in *Cartier v British Sky Broadcasting*.[140] In the Court of Appeal, Kitchin LJ concluded:[141]

> I believe that this court must now recognise pursuant to general equitable principles that this is one of those new categories of case in which the court may grant an injunction when it is satisfied that it is just and equitable to do so.

This has resolved the question of whether the English courts have the power to grant intermediary injunctions as required by Article 11. The *Cartier* case was appealed to the UK Supreme Court on the issue of who should bear the costs of implementing blocking orders (see paras 21.79ff below), but the question of jurisdiction was not further contested.

21.77   Who is an 'intermediary' for the purposes of Article 11 IPED? Unsurprisingly, most cases to date involving Article 8(3) or Article 11 have been directed to online service providers such as internet service providers (ISPs) and online market places. For an entity to be considered an 'intermediary' for these purposes, the entity must provide a service capable of being used by one or more other persons to infringe an intellectual property right; however, it is not necessary to show that there is any kind of 'specific relationship' between the relevant entity and the infringers.[142] It is important to remember that Article 11 IPED will also apply in a 'real-world' context too: in *Tommy Hilfiger Licensing v Delta Center*, for example, the Court of Justice held that the lessee of market premises, on which stalls and pitches for third party traders were provided could

---

[135]   Directive 2001/29, Art 8(3).

[136]   Article 9(1)(a) IPED also stipulates that interlocutory injunctions against intermediary must be available.

[137]   See, eg, *L'Oréal SA v eBay International AG* [2009] ETMR 53, paras 445–454; *Cartier International AG and Others v British Sky Broadcasting Ltd and Others* [2015] ETMR 1, paras 92 and 112–120. See also R Arnold, 'Website-blocking injunctions: the question of legislative basis' (2015) 37(10) EIPR 623–30.

[138]   *L'Oréal SA v eBay International AG* [2009] ETMR 53.

[139]   ibid at paras 444–464; see para 447 in particular.

[140]   *Cartier International AG and Others v British Sky Broadcasting Ltd and Others* [2015] ETMR 1 (Arnold J, High Court) and [2016] ETMR 43 (Court of Appeal). See also *Cartier International Ltd v British Telecommunications Ltd* [2016] ETMR 20, following Arnold J at first instance.

[141]   *Cartier International AG and Others v British Sky Broadcasting Ltd and Others* [2016] ETMR 43, para 65.

[142]   C-314/12 *UPC Telekabel Wien GmbH v Constantin Film Verleih GmbH* [2014] ECDR 12 at paras 32 and 35.

also be an 'intermediary' for these purposes.[143] In the online context, interesting questions remain as to whether the term 'intermediary' could be extended to other service providers such as payment processing service providers, search engines, or VPN operators.[144] In the 'real-world' context, relevant 'intermediaries' could include freight carriers and distributors.[145]

21.78   What can be required of an intermediary pursuant to Article 11 IPED? This question has been the subject of a number of references from different member states to the Court of Justice based on Article 8(3) and/or Article 11.[146] In response to a reference from the English High Court, in *L'Oréal v eBay* the Court held that under Article 11 IPED national courts should be able to require an online service provider, such as the operator of an online marketplace, to take measures not only to stop but also to prevent infringements of IPRs by users.[147] The measures ordered should be effective and dissuasive, although they could not go so far as to require active monitoring of all of the service provider's customers (which would be contrary to Art 15 E-Commerce Directive), should not create barriers to legitimate trade, and should be proportionate. Although ultimately a matter for the national court, the Court of Justice highlighted suspending infringers and making it easier to identify infringers as possible forms of order.[148] In contrast, in *Scarlet v SABAM* and *SABAM v Netlog*, the Court held that it would not be permissible to grant an injunction against an intermediary which was unlimited in time and which would require filtering systems to be installed to monitor all user information or communications for infringing content.[149] In the 'real-world' context, the Court of Justice held in *Tommy Hilfiger* that an intermediary could not be required to exercise 'general and permanent oversight over its customers'; however, the intermediary could be required to 'take measures which contribute to avoiding new infringements of the same nature by the same market-trader from taking place'.[150]

21.79   A particular form of intermediary injunction which has gained traction in recent case law is the so-called website 'blocking order'—that is, an order requiring ISPs to prohibit access to websites containing infringing material. In *UPC Telekabel Wien*,[151] the ECJ considered the permissibility of blocking orders. The Court explained that a balance between IP right holders' and users' fundamental rights is safeguarded so long as the blocking orders respect the following two conditions:[152]

(1) the measures taken do not unnecessarily deprive internet users of the possibility of lawfully accessing the information available; and

(2) the measures have the effect of preventing unauthorised access to the protected subject-matter or, at least, of making it difficult to achieve and of seriously discouraging the ISP's users from accessing the infringing subject matter.

21.80   Blocking orders have become common in the UK in relation to websites involved in copyright infringements and have recently even been granted to block live-streaming of content.[153] More recently, in *Cartier v BSkyB* the first blocking order outwith the copyright context under Article 11 IPED was granted in the UK, requiring ISPs to prevent access to websites selling counterfeit trade marked goods.[154] Arnold J held that, in terms of whether to grant the order, similar threshold conditions applied to intermediary injunctions ordered pursuant to Article 11 IPED as had been stipulated in section 97A CDPA 1988—in other words: the

---

[143] Case C-494/15 *Tommy Hilfiger Licensing LLC v Delta Center as* [2017] ETMR 5.

[144] M Husovec, *Injunctions Against Intermediaries in the European Union: Accountable But Not Liable?* (2017), 90.

[145] L Pechan and M Schneider, 'Carriers and trade mark infringements: should carriers care?' (2010) 5(5) JIPLP 350–57.

[146] For a full discussion, see M Husovec, *Injunctions Against Intermediaries in the European Union: Accountable But Not Liable?* (2017).

[147] Case C-323/09 *L'Oréal SA v eBay International AG* [2011] ETMR 52, paras 131–144.   [148] ibid, paras 141–142.

[149] Case C-70/10 *Scarlet Extended SA v Société Belge des Auteurs, Compositeurs et Editeurs SCRL (SABAM)* [2012] ECDR 4; Case C-360/10 *Belgische Vereniging van Auteurs, Componisten en Uitgevers CVBA (Sabam) v Netlog NV* [2012] 2 CMLR 18.

[150] Case C-494/15 *Tommy Hilfiger Licensing LLC v Delta Center as* [2017] ETMR 5, para 34.

[151] Case C-314/12 *UPC Telekabel Wien GmbH v Constantin Film Verleih GmbH* [2014] ECDR 12.   [152] ibid, para 63.

[153] See N Malovic, 'The evolution of copyright website blocking in the UK: live blocking orders' (2018) 40(12) EIPR 810–14, discussing case law involving the Football Association Premier League.

[154] *Cartier International AG and Others v British Sky Broadcasting Ltd and Others* [2015] ETMR 1 (High Court), [2016] ETMR 43 (Court of Appeal), and [2018] ETMR 32 (Supreme Court).

defendant must be a relevant service provider; users and/or the operator of the website to be blocked must infringe the claimant's IP rights; those users and/or operator must use the defendant's services to commit those infringements; and the defendant must have actual knowledge of this.[155] Arnold J also considered the application of the general principles at Article 3 IPED and a requirement to balance relevant fundamental rights.[156] In terms of the Article 3 IPED principle of 'effectiveness', Arnold J rejected the proposition that right holders had to demonstrate that the blocking order would be effective in reducing the overall levels of infringement of their IP rights; that said, the 'likely efficacy of the injunction in terms of preventing or impeding access to the target website' was an important factor and a blocking order was less likely to be proportionate if there was a large number of alternative websites which would be accessible to users.[157] In assessing the requirement of 'proportionality', the court had to consider whether there were alternative measures which were less onerous.[158] Further factors of particular importance included:

- the 'comparative importance' of the rights that are engaged and the justifications for interfering with those rights;
- the efficacy of the blocking measures sought, and in particular whether those measures would 'seriously discourage' the ISPs' subscribers from accessing the websites to be blocked;
- the costs associated with the blocking measures sought, and in particular the costs of implementing those measures;
- the dissuasiveness of the blocking measures sought; and
- the impact of those measures on lawful users of the internet.[159]

Arnold J granted the blocking orders sought, ruling that the ISPs should also bear the costs of putting the blocking orders into effect. His approach was upheld on appeal to the Court of Appeal. However, on appeal to the Supreme Court, the ruling on the costs of implementing the blocking orders was reversed. Highlighting that the blocking orders served the commercial interests of the right holders and that the ISPs themselves had committed no legal wrong, the Supreme Court held that the IP right holders should indemnify the ISPs for the costs incurred by them in putting the blocking orders into effect.[160]

 Exercise

Reflect on the provision for intermediary injunctions at Article 11 IPED. How do you think that the rules should be balanced to take into account all stakeholder interests?

Publicity orders

21.81   Article 15 IPED states:

Publication of judicial decisions

Member States shall ensure that, in legal proceedings instituted for infringement of an intellectual property right, the judicial authorities may order, at the request of the applicant and at the expense of the infringer, appropriate measures for the dissemination of the information concerning the decision, including displaying the decision and publishing it in full or in part. Member States may provide for other additional publicity measures which are appropriate to the particular circumstances, including prominent advertising.

---

[155] *Cartier International AG and Others v British Sky Broadcasting Ltd and Others* [2015] ETMR 1, paras 139–141; see also paras 142–157 considering the application of these rules to the facts of the case in hand.
[156] ibid, paras 158–191.   [157] ibid, paras 163–176.   [158] ibid, para 162.   [159] ibid, para 189.
[160] *Cartier International AG and Others v British Sky Broadcasting Ltd and Others* [2018] ETMR 31.

Recital 27 IPED explains that the purpose of such orders is to 'act as a supplementary deterrent to future infringers' and 'to contribute to the awareness of the public at large'.

21.82   Article 15 IPED only mentions granting publicity orders in cases in which there has been a finding of infringement. However, in *Samsung Electronics (UK) Ltd v Apple Inc,* the English courts have confirmed that publicity orders may also be available in cases where there has been a finding of non-infringement.[161] Apple had accused Samsung of infringing its registered Community design rights in its hand-held computers. Ultimately there was found to be no infringement. But, in the meantime, Apple had continued to make public statements suggesting that the Samsung products nonetheless infringed and had obtained orders against Samsung in Germany, which had been the subject of massive publicity in the press, in conflict with the non-infringement findings of the English High Court. The High Court ordered Apple to publicise a statement confirming the English judgment in various national newspapers and on its UK website for a period of six months,[162] initially reduced in the Court of Appeal to providing a link from the homepage to the notice for one month then, after Apple added additional and misleading text to the statement, reinstated as a notice on Apple's homepage for a further month.[163] Article 15 IPED was not specifically implemented into UK law because it was considered that the English courts already had the requisite powers pursuant to their general inherent jurisdiction under the Senior Courts Act 1981. This meant that the courts also had the inherent jurisdiction to publicity orders in cases involving a finding of non-infringement. Noting that no party should be automatically entitled to a publicity order in their favour, Sir Robin Jacob summarised the rationale underpinning the grant of orders in both infringement and non-infringement cases:[164]

> I am far from saying that publicity orders of this sort should be the norm. On the contrary I rather think the court should be satisfied that such an order is desirable before an order is made—otherwise disputes about publicity orders are apt to take on a life of their own as ancillary satellite disputes. They should normally only be made, in the case of a successful intellectual property owner where they serve one of the two purposes set out in art. 27 of the Enforcement Directive and in the case of a successful non-infringer where there is a real need to dispel commercial uncertainty in the marketplace (either with the non-infringer's customers or the public in general).

The Court of Appeal also stressed that it was important that the publicity order went no further than what was proportionate in the circumstances.[165] In recent cases, in setting the terms of publicity orders—particularly in deciding whether notices in the press are required over and above notices on the relevant parties' websites—the courts have been mindful of the extent to which the outcome of disputes have already generated sufficient press coverage to make further press advertising unnecessary.[166]

    Question

What do you think the proper scope of a publicity order should be? Justify your response.

Right of information

21.83   Finally, for infringements committed on a commercial scale, Article 8(1) of the Enforcement Directive requires that judicial authorities be given the power to order information to be disclosed as to the origin of the infringing goods and services and distribution mechanisms, and personal details of producers, distributors, suppliers, wholesalers, and retailers.[167] This requirement was specifically transposed into Scots law,[168] but was already available in the English courts.[169] Article 8 IPED has been the subject of a number

161   [2012] EWHC 2049 (Pat); aff'd on appeal [2013] FSR 9, [2013] FSR 10.
162   [2012] EWHC 2049 (Pat) at para 57.   163   [2013] FSR 9.   164   ibid, para 69.   165   ibid, para 85.
166   See, eg, *Cosmetic Warriors Limited, Lush Limited v Amazon EU SARL and Another* [2014] EWHC 1316 (Ch), paras 32–35; *Comic Enterprise Ltd v Twentieth Century Fox Film Corp* (High Court) [2014] ETMR 51, paras 52–53.
167   Enforcement Directive, Art 8 and Recital 14 (re 'commercial scale').
168   Intellectual Property (Enforcement, etc.) Regulations 2006/1028, reg 4(3).
169   *Norwich Pharmacal v Customs and Excise Commissioners* [1974] AC 133.

of references to the Court of Justice, looking at the balancing of this requirement of disclosure against other rights and interests, such as the protection of personal data and banking secrecy laws.[170] The Court of Justice has confirmed that an order under Article 8 IPED can be sought in separate proceedings after the original infringement litigation has come to an end: in the view of the court, it is 'not inconceivable' that an IP right holder may only become aware of the extent of the infringement of his rights only after the original proceedings have concluded.[171] The Court has stressed the importance of the Article 8 right of information—it is said to be:[172]

> a specific expression of the fundamental right to an effective remedy guaranteed in art. 47 of the Charter of Fundamental Rights of the European Union and thereby ensures the effective exercise of the fundamental right to property, which includes the intellectual property right protected in Art. 17(2) of the Charter . . . [The] right of information thus enables the holder of an intellectual property right to identify who is infringing that right and take the necessary steps, such as making an application for the provisional measures set out in Art. 9(1) and (2) or for damages as provided for in Art. 13 of Directive 2004/48, in order to protect that right. Without full knowledge of the extent of the infringement of his intellectual property right, the rightholder would not be in a position to determine or calculate precisely the damages he was entitled to by reason of the infringement.

The obligation to provide information is directed not only at the infringer of the relevant IP right but also at 'any other person' mentioned at Article 8(1)(a)–(d) IPED—that is, any person:

- found to be in possession of infringing goods on a commercial scale;
- found to be using infringing services on a commercial scale;
- found to be providing on a commercial scale services used in infringing activities; or
- indicated by the person above as being involved in the production, manufacture or distribution of the infringing goods or the provision of the infringing services.[173]

Exercise

Read the cases concerning the balancing of disclosure of information for infringements of IPRs committed on a commercial scale against countervailing interests. Do you think that the interests of the parties are being balanced fairly? What about wider policy considerations? Justify your response.

Key points on remedies

- Both interim and final injunctions (interdicts in Scotland) are available in IP infringement actions.
- Delivery up or destruction of infringing items are also available as remedies.
- According to established UK law, a claimant can elect between receiving damages to compensate for loss or an account of the infringer's profits. Damages may not be available against innocent infringers. Additional damages are available for copyright, rights in performances, and UK unregistered design right. It remains unclear what the impact of the Enforcement Directive will be on financial remedies going forward.
- Other forms of order are also available, including injunctions against intermediaries whose services are used by third parties to commit infringement, publicity orders, and orders for the disclosure of information on commercial networks.

---

[170] In particular, *Productores de Musica de Espana (Promusicae) v Telefonica de Espana SAU* (C-275/06) [2008] ECDR 10; *Coty Germany GmbH v Stadtsparkasse Magdeburg* (Case C-580/13) [2015] ETMR 39.

[171] Case C-427/15 *NEW WAVE CZ as v ALLTOYS spol s r o* [2017] ETMR 16, para 26 in particular.

[172] ibid, para 25.   [173] ibid, para 22.

Criminal enforcement

21.84   In the UK a number of criminal sanctions exist in the fields of copyright, performers' rights, trade mark infringement, and registered designs. The offences tend to relate to those circumstances where the infringer makes for sale, hire, or otherwise deals in the course of a business with infringing materials in the following circumstances, each of which is predicated on knowledge or reason to believe by the infringer. However, there are also some offences which are committed other than in the course of a business.

Copyright

21.85   The copyright criminal offences include:

- making for sale or hire, importing into the UK (other than for private and domestic use) or in the course of a business possessing with a view to committing an infringing act, selling or letting for hire, offering or exposing for sale or hire, exhibiting in public or distributing an article which is, and which the infringer knows or has reason to believe is, an infringing copy of a copyright work, or otherwise than in the course of a business distributing such an article to such an extent as to affect prejudicially the owner of the copyright;[174]

- making articles that are specifically designed or adapted for making infringing copies of copyright material or having such an article in one's possession, knowing or having reason to believe that it is to be used to make infringing copies;[175]

- in certain circumstances, communicating a work to the public.[176]

There are also further criminal offences including offences relating to unauthorised performances of a work in public and the unauthorised playing or showing in public of a sound recording or film;[177] unauthorised decoders;[178] and devices, products, or components which are primarily designed, produced, or adapted for the purpose of enabling or facilitating the circumvention of effective technological measures.[179]

 Exercise

What do you think of the inclusion of criminal sanctions being used against those who do not infringe in the course of a business, but do infringe to the extent that the interests of the owner are prejudicially affected? What do you think the test 'affect prejudicially' means? What do you think of the inclusion of criminal sanctions against those who distribute devices which could circumvent technological protection measures? Does it make any difference that copyright need not be infringed for the sanction to attach?

21.86   Offences can be committed not just by individuals but also by corporate entities. In *Thames Hudson Ltd v Design and Artists Copyright Society Ltd*[180] a criminal action[181] was brought against the directors of Thames Hudson Ltd by the Design and Artists Copyright Society (DACS). The matter concerned the publication and distribution of a book which contained an infringing copy of a painting. The case was allowed to

---

[174] CDPA 1988, s 107(1).   [175] CDPA 1988, s 107(2).   [176] CDPA 1988, s 107(2A).
[177] CDPA 1988, s 107(3).   [178] CDPA 1988, s 297A.   [179] CDPA 1988, s 296ZB.
[180] [1995] FSR 153.   [181] Pursuant to CDPA 1988, ss 107 and 110.

proceed at the same time as civil action was being taken. The criminal court suggested that the magistrate might, if the civil proceedings were found to be carried out with due diligence, use discretion to adjourn the final disposal of the criminal aspects of the case pending the decision in the Chancery Division.

Performers' rights

21.87   In relation to infringement of performers' rights, the following criminal sanctions exist:

- making for sale or hire, importing into the UK (other than for private and domestic use) or in the course of a business possessing with a view to committing a relevant infringing act, selling or letting for hire, offering or exposing for sale or hire or distributing a recording which is, and which the infringer knows or has reason to believe is, an illicit recording;[182]

- in certain cases where a performer's making available right is infringed;[183] and

- causing a recording of a performance made without sufficient consent to be shown or played in public, or communicated to the public, thereby infringing any performers' rights, if the infringer knows or has reason to believe that those rights are thereby infringed.[184]

Trade marks

21.88   Under the Trade Marks Act 1994 criminal sanctions are available inter alia where:

- a sign identical to, or likely to be mistaken for, a registered trade mark has been applied without the consent of the owner to goods, on packaging, or on labels;

- with view to gain or intent to cause loss to another.[185]

21.89   An interesting question concerning criminal liability fell to be decided by the House of Lords in *R v Johnstone*.[186] Johnstone had been making and disseminating CDs containing copies of bootleg recordings containing the name of the performer which had been registered as a trade mark. Johnstone was charged under section 92(1) TMA 1994 for falsely applying and using a trade mark. It was argued that, to be liable, civil infringement had first to be established which was not so in the instant case as the performers' names had not been used as indications of origin[187] but merely to identify the artists. The House of Lords found this argument to be correct: as a matter of principle if a name of an artist was used exclusively as an indication of the name of the performer in connection with the performance, this was merely descriptive and not an indication of the trade origin. Johnstone was therefore not guilty of this offence. A different defence was raised in *R v Boulter (Gary)*.[188] The applicant was charged with selling counterfeit and pirated music CDs bearing the logos of EMI and other recording companies. He raised the defence that the CDs that bore the trade marks were of such poor quality that no one would think that its trade origin was that of the trade mark owners. In other words, there would be no confusion. The Court of Appeal ruled that no confusion was needed to be guilty of the offence in section 92 because the issue was identity, and not similarity, of the marks. Regardless of how badly the marks were copied, they were identical to those registered to the recording companies, and used on identical goods. A counterfeiter could not avoid criminal liability by claiming that the goods are 'genuine fakes'.[189]

---

[182] CDPA 1988, s 198(1).   [183] CDPA 1988, s 198(1A).   [184] CDPA 1988, s 198(2).   [185] TMA 1994, s 92.

[186] [2003] UKHL 28, [2003] 3 All ER 884, [2003] 2 Cr App Rep 493, [2004] Crim LR 244. See also *R v Malik* [2011] EWCA Crim 1107.

[187] TMA 1994, s 11(2)(b).   [188] [2008] EWCA Crim 2375, [2009] ETMR 6.

[189] *R v Boulter*, para 9. For a discussion on whether a person charged with trade mark infringement believed on objectively reasonable grounds that the goods he was selling were genuine, see *Essex Trading Standards v Wallati Singh* [2009] EWHC 520 (Admin), 2009 WL 392234. In this case the High Court ruled that the respondent was not able to discharge the burden under TMA 1994, s 92(5).

Registered designs

21.90   The Intellectual Property Act 2014 introduced criminal penalties in relation to UK registered designs. It is, in particular, an offence if in the course of a business, a person intentionally copies a registered design so as to make a product exactly to that design, or with features that differ only in immaterial details from that design, knowing, or having reason to believe, that the design is a registered design.[190] It had originally been proposed that it should be sufficient for criminal infringement that the infringing product was made exactly or substantially to the design, but this was amended to the current, more stringent requirements (more akin to the 'novelty' test in registered design law rather than the wider civil infringement test of the same 'overall impression') during the legislative passage of the 2014 Act. It is a defence for the alleged infringer to show inter alia that he reasonably believed that the registration of the design was invalid or that he reasonably believed that he did not infringe.[191]

Counterfeiting and piracy

21.91   Counterfeiting and piracy have been the subject of a number of European initiatives to harmonise the rules as within member states of the EU. In particular, procedures relating to border control of the movement of goods infringing IPRs have been strengthened and sanctions available within member states bolstered.[192]

 Exercise

It can sometimes be very difficult to distinguish between a genuine article and a fake. Go to eBay and type in Mulberry handbag (or the name of any other designer goods you would like). Which are the genuine articles?

Have a look at the facts and figures published by the European Commission on the numbers of goods expected of infringing IPRs detained at borders. These can be found at http://ec.europa.eu/taxation_customs/customs/customs_controls/counterfeit_piracy/statistics/index_en.htm.

How many detentions were made in 2017? What types of goods were detained? What are the trends over time?

21.92   The current EU legislation dealing with this issue is Regulation 608/2013, concerning action to be taken by customs officials with respect to goods suspected of infringing certain IPRs and measures to be taken against goods found to infringe such rights.[193] It replaces a previous Regulation promulgated around a decade earlier,[194] which in turn replaced earlier versions of the Regulation dealing with the same subject matter.

21.93   The 2013 Regulation redefines the infringing goods covered. It refers to three classes of goods: 'counterfeit goods' (infringements of trade marks and geographical indications); 'pirated goods' (infringements of copyright and related rights, and designs); and 'goods suspected of infringing an intellectual property right' (covering other IP infringements and items such as circumvention devices and moulds for the manufacture of infringing items).

---

[190] RDA 1949, s 35ZA(1).   [191] RDA 1949, s 35ZA(4) and (5).
[192] Case C-132/07 *Beecham Group plc, SmithKline Beecham plc, Glaxo Group Ltd, Stafford-Miller Ltd, GlaxoSmithKline Consumer Healthcare NV and GlaxoSmithKline Consumer Healthcare BV v Andacon NV* for questions concerning powers of customs officers under Regulation (EC) No 1891/04 and Regulation (EC) No 1383/03.
[193] Regulation (EU) No 608/2013 of the European Parliament and of the Council of 12 June 2013 concerning customs enforcement of intellectual property rights.
[194] Council Regulation (EC) No 1383/2003 of 22 July 2003.

21.94   The purpose of the Regulation is to facilitate the seizure and destruction by customers and border authorities of infringing goods with the intention of preventing them from entering circulation in the EU. The Regulation sets out the procedure by which notice should be given to the relevant customs authorities and the action to be taken thereafter. In *Blomqvist*, the Court of Justice considered the application of the Regulation to goods purchased over the internet.[195] In that case, the infringing item (a fake Rolex watch) had been purchased over the internet from a Chinese website. There was an issue over whether there had ever been 'use in the course of trade' of the infringed trade mark within a member state. In a right-holder-friendly judgment, the Court of Justice held that the trade mark owner enjoys the requisite protection at the time when the infringing goods entered the territory of a member state merely by virtue of the acquisition of those goods; it was not necessary, prior to the sale, for the infringing goods to have been the subject of an offer for sale or advertising targeting consumers of that member state.

21.95   National governments have also been busy in developing responses to the increased incidence of counterfeiting and piracy. Trading standards officers also have some responsibility for the enforcement of legislation in this area.

> ### Web link
>
> If you look at the UK IPO website at www.gov.uk/government/collections/ip-crime-and-enforcement-for-businesses-and-consumers you will find various materials published by the UK IPO in relation to IP crime and enforcement.

21.96   A network of organisations, such as FAST, the British Software Alliance, and FACT, monitor markets and alert the relevant regulatory authorities to incidents of counterfeiting and piracy. Counterfeiting and piracy were subjects also discussed at the G8 meeting held at Gleneagles in Scotland in 2005. The ministers issued a document pledging to work together to draw up a plan to reduce the incidence of these activities over the coming years.[196] In 2006 the EU and the United States agreed to work together to develop approaches to defeat the rising tide of counterfeit and pirated goods coming from China and Russia, to be followed by Latin America and the Middle East.[197]

21.97   This heralded the start of negotiations for a proposed new international treaty designed to combat counterfeiting. In 2007 the European Commission stated that it intended to seek a mandate from member states to negotiate a new Anti Counterfeiting Trade Agreement (ACTA) with major trading partners, including the United States, Japan, Korea, Mexico, and New Zealand.[198] Three particular avenues would be pursued:

- building international cooperation leading to harmonised standards and better communication between authorities;

- establishing common enforcement practices to promote strong intellectual property protection in coordination with right holders and trading partners; and

- creating a strong modern legal framework which reflects the changing nature of intellectual property theft in the global economy, including the rise of easy-to-copy digital storage media and the increasing danger of health threats from counterfeit food and pharmaceutical drugs.

---

[195]   *Martin Blomqvist v Rolex SA, Manufacture Des Montres Rolex SA* (Case C-98/13) [2014] ECDR 10.
[196]   At Gleneagles in July 2005 the G8 statement 'Reducing IPR Piracy and Counterfeiting through more effective enforcement' was issued.
[197]   'US and EU Pledge to take action over fake Goods', *Financial Times*, 18 June 2006. See SABIP Report (Number EC001), 'IP Enforcement in the UK and Beyond: A Literature Review', 18 May 2009.
[198]   See IP/07/1573.

ACTA proved to be highly controversial[199] not only because of the view that it was negotiated in secret, but also because of the concern many held over the breadth of its provisions and effect on such rights as freedom of expression and privacy. In July 2012 the European Parliament voted to reject ACTA.[200]

> **Exercise**
>
> The definitions of counterfeiting and piracy have changed and would appear to have expanded in scope over the years. See how many different definitions you can find used in both European and UK instruments. What do you think of the use of the term 'piracy' in connection with individuals who download music files from the internet?

EU proposals on criminal enforcement

21.98   In June 2005 the Commission promulgated a proposal for a further Directive, this time aimed at criminal sanctions and remedies along with a proposal for a council Framework Decision to strengthen the criminal law framework to combat intellectual property offences.[201] This proposal, couched in language referring to obligations under TRIPS and Article 17(2) of the Charter of Fundamental Rights (which states that 'Intellectual property shall be protected') would extend criminal sanctions to all intentional infringements of an intellectual property right carried out on a commercial scale, as well as for attempting, aiding or abetting, and inciting such offences. The proposal for a Framework Decision set a threshold for criminal penalties of at least four years' imprisonment if the offence involved a criminal organisation or if it jeopardised public health and safety. The fine had to be at least €100,000–€300,000 for cases involving criminal organisations or posing a risk to public health and safety, although member states could apply tougher penalties.

21.99   The proposal was withdrawn after uncertainty as to the competence of the EC to legislate in the arena of criminal sanctions. That they did was (arguably) affirmed by the ECJ in *Commission v Council*,[202] where it was held that provisions of criminal law required for the effective implementation of Community law (in the instant case, criminal sanctions for environmental issues) fell under the EC Treaty.[203] The draft Directive was re-issued in amended form and adopted in April 2007 by the European Parliament. Concerns remained as to the scope of the measure and of the competence of the Commission to harmonise criminal sanctions.[204] The proposal was finally withdrawn by the Commission in 2010.[205]

21.100   While there may be sympathy for the fight against organised crime and its relationship to counterfeiting and piracy, a general anxiety is that, as it stood, the draft Directive could have extended far beyond this domain, most notably by reference to the rather vague standards of 'attempting, aiding, abetting and inciting' infringements. What was notable are the grounds on which the proposal had been justified. As with the original proposal, TRIPS was referred to. However, that Agreement only requires criminal sanctions to be applied in the area of wilful trademark counterfeiting or copyright piracy on a commercial scale.[206] This measure, by contrast, would have applied across the IP domains. Reference to the Charter of Fundamental

---

[199]   ACTA triggered a great deal of anxious blogging. Also, Electronic Frontier Foundation's opinion on ACTA at www.eff.org/issues/acta. See also 'Fact Sheet: Anti-Counterfeiting Trade Agreement', http://ec.europa.eu/trade/issues/sectoral/intell_property/fs231007_en.htm. But see M Blakeney, 'Trade mark survey: ACTA gives hope to trade mark owners' [2009] IPQ 1–6.

[200]   See www.bbc.co.uk/news/technology-18704192.   [201]   2005/0127(COD), 2005/0128(CNS).

[202]   Case C 176/03 *Commission v Council*.

[203]   For comment, see P Treacy and A Wray, 'IP crimes: the prospect for EU-wide criminal sanctions—a long road ahead?' [2006] EIPR 1.

[204]   See House of Lords European Union Committee 11th Report of Session 2006–07: The Criminal Law Competence of the EC, follow-up Report, 13 March 2007.

[205]   Withdrawal of obsolete commission proposals (2010/C 252/04) OJEU C 252/9.   [206]   TRIPS, Art 61.

Rights remained, cited as evidencing the obligation to protect intellectual property thus justifying the proposal: human rights standards have most often in the past been used as arguments for limiting the exercise of IPRs rather than providing a justification for tougher enforcement measures.

21.101   Had the proposal proceeded, the anxiety would have been as to whether the result would have represented a balance as between the legitimate concerns of right holders and those who fear for public health and the economy, whilst providing safeguards for non-commercial infringers and the general public interest.

> **Web link**
>
> The last amended draft Directive COM(2006) 168 final can be found at http://eur-lex.europa.eu/legal-content/EN/TXT/?uri=CELEX:52006PC0168. Read the draft. What do you think of the proposals and the basis on which they had been justified?

21.102   Although civil, criminal, and border procedures and remedies are independent, they are designed to work together in an integrated system. From border measures through to the receipt of an award of damages or a criminal prosecution, a right owner should be able to call upon appropriate procedures to vindicate a claim and receive a remedy for an infringement of a right.

Exercise 1

You are the owner of the copyright in a film. You have heard that DVDs featuring the film and copied without your consent or authorisation have been made in an East European country, not part of the EU. Some of these DVDs have been found in a market stall in Glasgow, others in retail shops in the Scottish Borders. You have heard that a further consignment is due to arrive at Rosyth within the next two weeks bound for a country outwith the EU. What do you do?

Exercise 2

You are the legal counsel for Legal and General. When on a trip to Myanmar you notice the T-shirts shown in Figure 21.2 for sale on a stall by the side of the road. What do you do?

Figure 21.2 Gegal & Leneral

TRIPS and IP enforcement

21.103   On enforcement matters, TRIPS is important for two reasons.

- TRIPS calls for effective enforcement measures to be available at the domestic level to allow action to be taken by intellectual property owners where rights are infringed. This includes the availability of certain remedies which should be considered a deterrent to further infringement.

- TRIPS provides a mechanism (through the World Trade Organization (WTO)) whereby disputes between member states may be settled. This is particularly so where one country alleges that another is not adhering to its obligations to incorporate the minimum standards of IP protection and enforcement mechanisms into domestic law as laid down in the Agreement.

Effective enforcement measures

21.104   TRIPS is the first international treaty in the IP sector to place obligations on member states relating to the enforcement of IPRs. Three areas of enforcement activity are laid down in the Agreement: civil and administrative procedures including remedies;[207] border measures;[208] and criminal procedures.[209]

21.105   Member states are to make available to right holders civil judicial procedures concerning the enforcement of any IPR including rules relating to representation,[210] evidence,[211] and the availability of injunctions and damages.[212] Border measures must be available to enable a right holder to prevent the importation of counterfeit trade mark and pirated copyright goods.[213] Criminal procedures and penalties must be applied in cases of wilful trademark counterfeiting or copyright piracy on a commercial scale.[214]

21.106   Four principles underlie each type of enforcement measure. These are that the action should be effective,[215] procedures should be fair and equitable,[216] decisions should be reasoned,[217] and there should be the opportunity to seek judicial review.[218] In addition, the measures should be applied in a manner that avoids creating barriers to legitimate trade and which provide safeguards against their abuse.[219]

21.107   The UK meets all the requirements imposed by TRIPS, and indeed some aspects of domestic enforcement procedures and remedies go beyond those to be found in that Agreement.

 Exercise

Look at TRIPS and compare the procedures laid down in that Agreement with the provisions in the EU Enforcement Directive. Which, if any, of those measures in the Directive go beyond what is required by TRIPS?

21.108   However, not all states which are members of TRIPS have been, or are, in compliance with the obligations to be found in that Agreement, including those on enforcement and remedies. This highlights the second, and important, aspect of TRIPS. If a member does not comply with its obligations, then a complaint may be taken to the Dispute Settlement Body (DSB) established by the WTO Agreement. Representatives of every

---

207 ibid, Part III, s 2.   208 ibid, Part III, s 4.   209 ibid, Part III, s 5.
210 ibid, Art 42.   211 ibid, Art 43.   212 ibid, Arts 44 and 45.
213 ibid, Art 51.   214 ibid, Art 61.   215 ibid, Art 41.
216 ibid, Art 41.2.   217 ibid, Art 41.3.   218 ibid, Art 41.4.   219 See generally ibid, Arts 41, 42, 43, 48.

WTO member sit on the DSB which was created to deal with disputes arising under the WTO Agreements. This it does in accordance with the provisions of the Dispute Settlement Understanding (DSU). Member states or trading groups recognised by the WTO may bring an action before a WTO Dispute Settlement Panel if they believe that another country or trading group has failed to meet its obligations under TRIPS. If a country or group is found not to have complied with TRIPS, trade sanctions can be imposed.[220] This mechanism has been used in a number of intellectual property cases, both where member states have not incorporated minimum standards on enforcement and remedies into their domestic law and in cases concerning alleged failures to implement the correct substantive level of intellectual property protection.

21.109   On enforcement and remedies, the United States has brought complaints against, inter alia, Denmark[221] and Sweden,[222] arguing that their domestic laws did not provide for provisional measures in civil proceedings as required by TRIPS. Both the actions settled when a mutually agreed solution was found. A case that went to a full panel hearing concerning the enforcement measures was taken by the United States against China alleging that China had not fulfilled a number of obligations in implementing the enforcement measures to be found in TRIPS into domestic law.[223] In a lengthy report, the Panel found that China failed to conform to its obligations in a limited number of ways concerning border measures and its failure to grant certain works protection by copyright.[224] The complexity of the dispute combined with the lack of clarity in the findings of the Panel has led commentators to conclude that the enforcement provisions lack the necessary precision and strength to cope with infringement on a global scale.[225]

21.110   Other complaints concerning the failure of member states' domestic substantive law to reflect obligations imposed by the Agreement have been heard by the full WTO Panel. The first in the copyright field was based on a complaint against the United States brought by the European Communities (EC) concerning section 110(5)(B) of the US Copyright Act.[226] This section exempts eating, drinking, and retail establishments of a certain size from liability for the public performance of music played from radio and television. It was alleged that this section was incompatible with obligations under both the Berne Convention and TRIPS.[227] In a lengthy decision the Panel analysed the compatibility of section 110(5)(B) with the three-step test to be found in both of those treaties.[228] On the first step of the test, the Panel found that section 110(5)(B) was not limited to certain special cases: it had been estimated that 70 per cent of eating establishments, 73 per cent of drinking establishments, and 45 per cent of retail establishments fell under the exemption. On the second part of the test the Panel found that section 110(5)(B) conflicted with a normal exploitation of a work. This was based on the principle that exempted uses may not compete with actual or potential means of economic exploitation: there would be a conflict between an exemption and normal exploitation if the exemption interfered with the ways in which a right holder would 'normally extract economic value' from a particular use of a work. On the third part of the test, the Panel found that the legitimate interests of the right holder were prejudiced, saying that prejudice becomes unreasonable when an exception causes, or has the potential to cause, an unreasonable loss of income to the authors; that actual and potential prejudice to the right holder should be taken into account; and that in analysing unreasonable prejudice the legitimate interests of copyright holders at large should be taken into account and not only the interests of right holders

---

[220] The WTO Agreement provides that 'Each Member shall ensure the conformity of its laws, regulations and administrative procedures with its obligations as provided in the annexed Agreements' (Art XVI:4).

[221] US DS83.   [222] US DS86.

[223] Panel Report, China—Measures Affecting the Protection and Enforcement of Intellectual Property Rights, WT/DS362/R (26 January 2009).

[224] For a list of the documents, see www.wto.org/english/tratop_e/dispu_e/cases_e/ds362_e.htm.

[225] KP Yu, 'The TRIPS Enforcement Dispute (September 13, 2010)' (2011) 89 Nebraska LR 1046–131; Drake University Law School Research Paper No 11–16, SSRN http://ssrn.com/abstract=1676558.

[226] As amended by the US Fairness in Music Licensing Act 1988.

[227] Article 11bis(1)(iii) and 11(1)(ii) of the Berne Convention concerning rights of public performance and communication to the public incorporated into TRIPS by virtue of Art 9(1) and with the three-step test in TRIPS, Art 13.

[228] For a discussion of the three-step test, see Chapter 5.

of the WTO member that initiated the complaint. In conclusion, the Panel Report found that section 110(5)(B) was indeed incompatible with obligations to be found in TRIPS and recommended that the DSB request the United States to amend its legislation.[229]

21.111   Patent disputes have also been heard by the Panel. The EU challenged various aspects of Canadian patent law, including the provision that would have meant that it was not an infringement of a patent to make a patented product during the life of the patent for the purpose of stockpiling it for sale after the patent expired. The Panel found this to be a violation of Canada's obligations under TRIPS, saying that manufacture for commercial sale is a commercial activity and that the character of that activity is not altered by mere delay of the commercial reward. Thus, and in practical terms, the enforcement of the right to exclude others from 'making' and 'using' a patented product during the patent term will necessarily give all patent owners a short period of extended exclusivity after the patent expires. Therefore, the stockpiling provision in the Canadian patent law was in breach of TRIPS and the Panel concluded that Canada should be required to amend its law to remove this provision.[230]

21.112   Many of the complaints settle prior to being heard by the Panel. For instance, a complaint was made by the United States against Ireland alleging that Irish legislation did not conform with, inter alia, obligations concerning rental rights for producers of phonograms.[231] The request for the establishment of the Panel was withdrawn after agreement was reached that Ireland would amend its copyright laws.

21.113   A different strategy concerning IPRs is being used by some states. Where a state had been found to be in violation of its obligations under TRIPS the Arbitrator may impose sanctions in an unrelated field. So when the United States was found in violation of its WTO obligations in respect of gambling and betting services, the Arbitrator found that Antigua may request authorisation from the DSB to suspend the obligations under the TRIPS Agreement in the areas of copyright and related rights; trade marks; industrial designs; patents and undisclosed information at a level not exceeding US$21 million annually.[232]

Web link

The WTO webpages can be difficult to navigate until you find your way around. Go to the home page and see if you can find information about disputes that have arisen concerning TRIPS. If in difficulty look at www.wto.org/english/tratop_e/dispu_e/dispu_agreements_index_e.htm?id=A26#selected_agreement.

In the list of headings you will find Intellectual Property (TRIPS). Go to these pages and browse though the documents. Revisit the pages at regular intervals to keep abreast of developments.

Exercise

Would you recommend establishing a procedure akin to that available for disputes arising under TRIPS to hear complaints made under other international treaties such as the Berne Convention? If so, why? If not, why not?

---

[229]   For the subsequent action, see R Owens, 'TRIPS and the Fairness in Music arbitration: the repercussions' [2003] EIPR 49. In an action against China DS362 the Panel found that China needed to amend certain of its laws relating to copyright and customs measures so as to conform with obligations under TRIPS.

[230]   WT/DS1114/13.   [231]   WT DS82/3, WT/DS115/3, IP/D/8/Add.1, IP/D/12/Add.1.

[232]   See WT/DS285/ARB. United States—Measures Affecting the Cross-Border Supply of Gambling and Betting Services. Recourse to Arbitration by the United States under Article 22.6 of the DSU. Decision by the Arbitrator. The holding has prompted a great deal of discussion. See, eg, I Wohl, 'The United States–Antigua Online Gambling Dispute', J Int Com Econ, Web version July 2009, www.usitc.gov/publications/332/journals/online_gambling_dispute.pdf. See also DS267 United States—Subsidies on Upland Cotton, in which Brazil may 'suspend' certain US IP rights.

Key points on TRIPS and IP enforcement

- TRIPS places obligations on member states to implement into their national laws certain minimum standards concerning remedies and sanctions for infringement of IPRs (as well as substantive provisions).

- TRIPS provides a mechanism (through the WTO) whereby disputes between member states as to their adherence or otherwise to obligations laid down in TRIPS may be raised and settled. TRIPS is the only international treaty to contain such an enforcement mechanism.

Further reading

Books

L Bently, J Davis, and J Ginsburg (eds), *Copyright and Piracy: An Interdisciplinary Critique* (2010)

M Husovec, *Injunctions Against Intermediaries in the European Union: Accountable But Not Liable?* (2017)

I Stamatoudi (ed), *Copyright Enforcement and the Internet* (2010)

O Vrins and M Scheider (eds), *Enforcement of Intellectual Property Rights through Border Measures—Law and Practice in the EU* (2006)

Articles

R Arnold, 'Website-blocking injunctions: the question of legislative basis' [2015] EIPR 623

L Blakeney and M Blakeney, 'Counterfeiting and piracy—removing the incentives through confiscation' [2008] EIPR 348

M Blakeney, 'International proposals for the criminal enforcement of intellectual property rights: international concern with counterfeiting and piracy' [2009] IPQ 1

E Bonadio, 'Remedies and sanctions for the infringement of intellectual property rights under EC law' (2008) 30(8) EIPR 320–27

J Cornwell, 'Injunctions and monetary remedies compared: the English judicial response to the IP Enforcement Directive' (2018) 40(8) EIPR 490–500.

I Davies and T Scourfield, 'Threats: is the current regime still justified?' (2007) 29(7) EIPR 259–65

P Davies, 'Costs of blocking injunctions' (2017) 4 IPQ 330–45

P England, 'Accessing damages for unjustified threats of patent infringement' (2014) 9 J Intellectual Property Law & Practice 951

J Fitzgerald and A Firth, 'Is Article 13 of the Enforcement Directive a redundancy notice for the account of profits remedy in the UK?' (2014) 9(9) JIPLP 737

J Fox, L Thompson, B Potts, and M Döring, 'UK threats: worldwide consequences?' (2018) 40(2) EIPR 74–84

N Fox, B Berghuis, I vom Feld, and L Orlando, 'Accounting for differences: damages and profits in European patent infringement' [2015] EIPR 566

B Godart, 'IP crime: the new face of organized crime—from IP theft to IP crime' (2010) 5(5) JIPLP 378

K Huniar, 'The Enforcement Directive—its effects on UK law' (2006) 28(2) EIPR 92–99

P Johnson, '"Damages" in European law and the traditional accounts of profit' (2013) 3(4) QMJIP 296

A Kur, 'Case C-235/09, DHL Express France SAS v Chronopost SA' (2012) 49(2) CML Rev 753–66

D Liu, 'Reflecting on an account of profits for infringement of intellectual property', (2017) 39(10) EIPR 623–38

D Liu, 'Reforming additional damages in copyright law' (2017) 7 JBL 576–97

V Lowe, 'The law of unintended consequences—a perspective on the draft Directive on criminal measures to enforce intellectual property rights' (2006) 163 Criminal Lawyer 3–5

N Malovic, 'The evolution of copyright website blocking in the UK: live blocking orders' (201) 40(12) EIPR 2018 810–14

J Marshall, 'Aggravated or exemplary damages for copyright infringement?' (2017) 39(9) EIPR 565–73

J Marshall, 'Account of profit for infringement of intellectual property rights' (2018) 40(4) EIPR 260–69

A Marsoof, 'The blocking injunction—a critical review of its implementation in the United Kingdom in the context of the European Union' [2015] IIC 632

L Pechan and M Schneider, 'Carriers and trade mark infringements: should carriers care?' (2010) 5(5) JIPLP 350

E Rosati, 'Intermediary IP injunctions in the EU and UK experiences: when less (harmonization) is more?' (2017) 12(4) JIPLP 338–50

P Sugden, 'How long is a piece of string? The meaning of "commercial scale" in copyright piracy' (2009) 31(4) EIPR 202–12

P Torremans, 'Compensation for intellectual property infringement: admissibility of punitive damages and compensation for moral prejudice' (2018) 40(12) EIPR 797–802

P Treacy and A Wray, 'IP crimes: the prospect for EU-wide criminal sanctions—a long road ahead?' (2006) 28(1) EIPR 1–4

G Urbanchuk, and J Tumbridge, 'Patent damages: the European landscape' (2008) 3(9) JIPLP 576

FG Wilman, 'A decade of private enforcement of intellectual property rights under IPR Enforcement Directive 2004/48: where do we stand (and where might we go)?' (2017) 42(4) EL Rev 509–31

Index